CORPORATE MANAGEMENT

(Text and Cases)

CORPORATE MANAGEMENT

(Text and Cases)

M.B. Shukla
M.Com., D.Phil
Professor, Dean and Director,
Institute of Management Studies,
Faculty of Commerce and Management Studies,
Mahatma Gandhi Kashi Vidyapith,
Varanasi.

Himalaya Publishing House
MUMBAI • NEW DELHI • NAGPUR • BENGALURU • HYDERABAD • CHENNAI • PUNE • LUCKNOW • AHMEDABAD • ERNAKULAM • BHUBANESWAR • INDORE • KOLKATA • GUWAHATI

First Edition : 2011

Published by : Mrs. Meena Pandey for **Himalaya Publishing House Pvt. Ltd.,**
"Ramdoot", Dr. Bhalerao Marg, Girgaon, **Mumbai - 400 004.**
Phone: 022-23860170/23863863, Fax: 022-23877178
E-mail: himpub@vsnl.com; Website: www.himpub.com

Branch Offices :

New Delhi : "Pooja Apartments", 4-B, Murari Lal Street, Ansari Road, Darya Ganj, New Delhi - 110 002. Phone: 011-23270392, 23278631; Fax: 011-23256286

Nagpur : Kundanlal Chandak Industrial Estate, Ghat Road, Nagpur - 440 018. Phone: 0712-2738731, 3296733; Telefax: 0712-2721215

Bengaluru : No. 16/1 (Old 12/1), 1st Floor, Next to Hotel Highlands, Madhava Nagar, Race Course Road, Bengaluru - 560 001. Phone: 080-32919385; Telefax: 080-22286611

Hyderabad : No. 3-4-184, Lingampally, Besides Raghavendra Swamy Matham, Kachiguda, Hyderabad - 500 027. Phone: 040-27560041, 27550139; Mobile: 09848130433

Chennai : No. 85/50, Bazullah Road, T. Nagar, Chennai - 600 017. Phone: 044-28144004/28144005

Pune : First Floor, "Laksha" Apartment, No. 527, Mehunpura, Shaniwarpeth (Near Prabhat Theatre), Pune - 411 030. Phone: 020-24496323/24496333

Lucknow : Jai Baba Bhavan, Church Road, Near Manas Complex and Dr. Awasthi Clinic, Aliganj, Lucknow - 226 024. Phone: 0522-2339329, 4068914; Mobile: 09305302158, 09415349385, 09389593752

Ahmedabad : 114, "SHAIL", 1st Floor, Opp. Madhu Sudan House, C.G. Road, Navrang Pura, Ahmedabad - 380 009. Phone: 079-26560126; Mobile: 09327324149, 09314679413

Ernakulam : 39/104 A, Lakshmi Apartment, Karikkamuri Cross Rd., Ernakulam, Cochin - 622011, Kerala. Phone: 0484-2378012, 2378016; Mobile: 09344199799

Bhubaneswar : 5 Station Square, Bhubaneswar - 751 001 (Odisha). Mobile: 09861046007

Indore : Kesardeep Avenue Extension, 73, Narayan Bagh, Flat No. 302, IIIrd Floor, Near Humpty Dumpty School, Narayan Bagh, Indore - 452 007 (M.P.). Mobile: 09301386468

Kolkata : 108/4, Beliaghata Main Road, Near ID Hospital, Opp. SBI Bank, Kolkata - 700 010, Phone: 033-32449649; Mobile: 09910440956

Guwahati : House No. 15, Behind Pragjyotish College, Near Sharma Printing Press, P.O. Bharalumukh, Guwahati - 781009 (Assam). Mobile: 09883055590, 09883055536

DTP by : Bright Computer Systems, Gayatri Nagar, Sitapur Road, Lucknow
Mobile : 9450614766, 9793630385

Printed at : A to Z Printers, New Delhi

PREFACE

In the present scenario, Indian corporate sector is being transformed in different dimensions. It is now treated as the vibrant sector of the Indian economy. Continuous economic reforms have ensured structural changes in corporate management practices. Nature, perception and expectations of stakeholders in Indian Corporate Sector are also changing. Change in corporate philosophy is also visible. Balancing act in corporate autonomy and accountability has forced the corporate houses to develop conducive internal environment for effective corporate governance. New cultural framework of public sector management started bearing fruits in the working of public enterprises and market capitalization of public enterprises improved tremendously.

Literature on this area is quite scanty, scattered and restricted to research studies and articles. No effort was made to develop a comprehensive text book on the subject. Professional managers and students need a book which can provide them conceptual clarity, updated information and critical analysis of the subject. The book is an attempt to fulfill all these requirements in a lucid manner. It is also intended to cover a wide coverage of the subject specially meant for corporate managers. Besides, efforts have also been made to incorporate latest policies, programmes and guidelines meant for Indian corporate sector enabling the book to be more meaningful for the corporate professionals.

In presentation of relevant material for the book, I have drawn heavily from the government reports, Public Enterprise Survey, SEB1 Reports and literature developed by the Institute of Company Secretaries of India, New Delhi for its students without which, it was impossible to prepare the book in present shape. So, I am personally indebted and thankful to all the government departments, organisations, agencies and the ICSI, New Delhi. I also acknowledge separately the Institute of Company Secretaries, New Delhi for its literature used in the preparation of the present text book. Critical comments and constructive suggestions for the improvement of this book are most welcome and will be highly appreciated.

A very special word of thanks to Ms. Swati my Ph.D. research scholar who has taken all pains in developing and providing base materials for the book. Without her help it was not possible for the present book to see the light of the day. I express my heartful gratitude to Sri.Niraj Pandey and Himalaya Publishing House for their constant encouragement and publishing the book in record time.

M.B.Shukla
Varanasi

CONTENTS

1 COMPANY MANAGEMENT

Corporate sector incorporates one of the most important form of business organization is called as company. A company form of business orgnisation is known as a Joint Stock Company. It is a voluntary association of persons who generally contribute capital to carry on a business, which is established by law and can be dissolved only by law. Persons who contribute capital become members of the company. This form of business has a legal existence separate from its members. This form of business organisations generally requires huge capital investment, which is contributed by its members. The total capital of a joint stock company is called share capital and it is divided into a number of units called shares. Thus, every member has some shares in the business depending upon the amount of capital contributed by him. Hence, members are also called shareholders. The companies in India are governed by the Indian Companies Act, 1956. The Act defines a company as an artificial person created by law, having a separate legal entity, with perpetual succession and a common seal.

A company being an artificial person cannot obviously manage the business itself. Actually, a company cannot act by itself. It has neither a mind nor a body of its own. It must act through some human agency. Hence, it has to depend on its shareholders for managing its affairs. But number of shareholders is quite large and normally they scattered all over the country. Therefore, the only practical option available to a company is that its large body of shareholders, who are the owners of the company, elect a suitable number of competent persons as directors for managing the affairs of the company. Thus, the persons by whom the business of the company is carried on are termed as directors. These directors need not necessarily be drawn from the ranks of the existing shareholders alone. Other experienced persons may also be appointed as directors subject to qualifying shares as per the requirement. The management of public limited companies is based on the principle of rule by majority. The will of the majority is supreme and it has been accepted as the guiding principle of company management in India, UK, US and many other countries. In terms of this rule, members pass resolution on various issues by either simple majority or by three-fourth majority. Once the resolution has been passed by the required majority, it is binding on all the members of the company, including those who voted against the motion. The institutions of the company are composed of two organs, the general body of shareholders and the board of directors. The board is the managerial body. It is the supreme executive authority to exercise control over the affairs of the company. It is constituted by the general body. Constituting the board means appointing directors.

For decades, the triple issues of ownership, control and management have been bugging corporates. Questions have been raised but no adequate answer has been found as to whether management can be segregated from the ownership, be it a professional or family management. Functionally, each of the three legs of corporate-ownership, management and control are interrelated and are in fact interdependent. Isolation of any one from the other can only lead to confusion. It is important to say that the management can only be a disciple of ownership. Control stems from ownership. Basically, ownership, control and management are the three dimensions of corporate management. Analysis of these dimensions is given below:

(*i*) **Ownership:** Ownership is a quintessence of the maximum (majority) number of shares held by a person or persons or other entities in combination, popularly called "promoters". Under the Indian model, each equity share commands a vote at any general meeting on all resolutions and proposals brought before it for consideration.

Resultantly, anyone who holds together with others or who can command sufficient voting strength at any general meeting would be able to pilot any proposal. The law, after gaining experience from the functioning of the corporates, prescribed key regulations to protect the interests of minority shareholders by laying down that certain transactions of far-reaching impact shall only have effect if approved by the shareholders by means of special resolution. This will require three-fourths majority votes of members present and voting against simple majority for an ordinary resolution. Summing up, it can be safely said that ownership (which includes persons acting in concert) is the fulcrum around which control and management revolve. However, strangely, there is no definition of it under any statute or regulation, including the SEBI Takeover Regulations, where emphasis on "control" without reference to ownership.

It is a cardinal rule of company law that prima facie, a majority of members of a company are entitled to exercise the powers of the company and generally to control its affairs. The resolution of a majority of shareholders passed at a duly convened and held general meeting upon any question with which the company is usually competent to deal is binding upon the minority and consequently upon the company.

Functioning of the company is governed by majority power for smooth running of the company. As per section 87 of the Indian Companies Act, 1956, every shareholder is entitled to vote in respect of such capital on every resolution placed before the meeting. The ordinary resolutions and special resolution are passed by simple majority $3/4^{th}$ majority respectively. Thus, whatever resolutions are passed by majority are binding on the minority also. But this is subjected to two important limitations-firstly, the powers of the majority of members, is subjected to the provisions of the company's memorandum and articles of associations; secondly, the resolution of majority must not be inconsistent with the provisions of any Act or constitute a fraud on minority depriving it of legitimate rights.

The company law provides for adequate protection for the minority shareholders when their rights are trampled by the majority. But the protection of the minority is not generally available when the majority does anything in the exercise of the powers for internal administration of the company. The court will not usually intervene at the instance of shareholders in matters of internal administration, and will not interfere with the management of its company by its directors so long as they are acting within the powers conferred on them under the articles of the company. In other words, the articles are the protective shield for the majority of shareholders who compose the Board of directors for carrying out their objects at the cost of minority of shareholders. The basic principle of non-interference with the internal management of company by the court is laid down in Foss v. Harbottle 67 E.R.189;(1843) 2 Hare 461. No action can be brought by a member against the directors in respect of a wrong alleged to be committed to a company. The company itself is the proper party of such an action.

The majority have a right to determine everything connected with the management of the company. Where a general meeting can confirm the action taken by the directors, the minority cannot be permitted to bring an action which might nullify the wishes of majority shareholders. However, the supremacy of the majority does not prevail in all situations, as over period of time, certain exceptions have developed. For instance under common law- ultra vires act, fraud on minority, wrongdoers in control, breach of duty etc. Also under Indian Companies Act, 1956, protection is affordable under section 106, section 397, 398, 234, 391 to 394 etc. Apart from these, scope for further exceptions is admitted where the rule of justice so requires.

The mandatory requirement of minimum 25 per cent public shareholding for continuous listing of companies will come into effect very soon. However, the new rules will not be applicable to government owned and infrastructure companies. Companies which have issued less than 25 per cent but have 10 per cent public holding and those companies with a market capitalization of over Rs. 1,000 crore or two crore of issued shares have also been exempted from the provision. These companies will have to ensure that a minimum of 10 per cent shares are held by the public. The group of persons holding control of voting power exercisable at the general meeting of a company are loosely called promoters, though, in fact, the person/persons who incorporated the company may be historical.

***(ii)* Control:** In the market for corporate control, managers or teams of managers compete for the rights to manage corporate resources. This market operates both within the firm and outside the firm. Transfers of control between management teams are accomplished either through internal control device typified by the board of directors or through external control mechanism including proxy contests and hostile takeovers. The control mechanism called upon at a particular instance depends on the ownership structure of the firm, the composition of the firm's board, the availability of outside bidders and dissidents, and so on. The incumbent management may opt to secure its position by increasing its voting power through creation of different classes of common stock or through changes of its financial policies involving debt and assets.

The SEBI Takeover code deals with the definition of control exhaustively and has revised the said definition from time to time backed by developmental behaviour. The present definition of the term control is contained in SEBI (Substantial Acquisition and Takeover) Regulation. Control includes the right to appoint directly or indirectly or by virtue of agreements or in any other manner majority of directors on the Board of the target company or to control management or policy decisions affecting the target company. However, in case there are two or more persons in control over the target company the cesser of any one of such persons from such control shall not be deemed to be a change in control of management nor shall any change in the nature and quantum of control amongst them constitute change in control of management provided this transfer is done in terms of Regulation 3 (1) (e). Also if consequent upon change in control of the target company in accordance with Regulation 3, the control acquired is equal to or less than the control exercised by person(s) prior to such acquisition of control, such control shall not be deemed to be a change in control. In a family-managed business, every member has to be accepted at face value, regardless of his ability, motivation and ambition. Each should enjoy the success of the business. Hindu undivided family has to be treated as a simple well-knit unit and the business should be carried on in the same spirit. Else, the dictum "United we stand, divided we fall" will come into operation.

***(iii)* Management:** The company is managed either by the board of directors or the managing director or a whole-time director or a manager as the case may be. Except for the directors named in the Articles of Association, all the directors, which include independent directors, are appointed by the shareholders at some point of time or the other. Directors among themselves elect a chairman to preside over a meeting or to hold the chairmanship for a specified period of time. The chairman of the board shall always preside at any general meeting. Normally, he has no executive powers. Appointment of managerial personnel and payment of remuneration is regulated under the Companies Act and the Listing Agreement.

The leading financial institutions may nominate directors on the board who are not liable to retire by rotation. Under Section 256 of the Companies Act, two-thirds of the total number of directors are persons whose office is liable for determination by retirement by rotation and one-third of such number retire at each annual general meeting and are eligible for reappointment. The person who commands the right to carry the proposal through at a general meeting proposes the appointment of a director and such incumbent gets elected.

Role of Promoters in Corporate Management

There is no legal definition of the term promoter. In the absence of any legal definition, most definitions of promoters are in terms of the functions that they usually perform. A promoter is one who performs the preliminary duties necessary to bring a company into existence. Before a company can be formed, there must be some persons who have an intention to form a company and who take the necessary steps to carry that intention into operation. Such persons are called 'promoters'. It is they who conceive the idea of forming the company and it is they, who take the necessary steps to incorporate it by registration, provide it with share and loan capital and acquire the business or property, which it is to manage.

The promotion of a company is a comprehensive term denoting the process by which a company is incorporated or bought into existence as a corporate body and floated or established financially as a going concern, by the issue of a prospectus. The person who assumes the primary responsibility of matters relating to promotion of a company is the promoter.

Promoters as per SEBI (Substantial Acquisition of Shares and Takeover) Regulations, 1997

"Promoters", unless otherwise provided elsewhere, means-

(*i*) any person who is directly or indirectly in control of the company,

(*ii*) any person named as promoter in any document of offer of securities to the public or existing shareholders or in the shareholding pattern disclosed by the company under the provisions of the Listing Agreement, whichever is later; or

(*iii*) any person named as person acting in concert with the promoter in any disclosure made in terms of the Listing Agreement with the stock exchange or any other regulations or guidelines made or issued by the Board under the Act, and includes,

(*a*) where the promoter is an individual:

(*i*) his spouse, parents, brothers, sisters or children;

(*ii*) any company in which twenty six percent (26%) or more of the equity share capital is held by him or by the persons mentioned in sub-clause (i) or any firm or Hindu undivided family in which he or she of the persons mentioned in sub-clause (i) is a partner or member;

(*iii*) any company in which a company specified in sub-clause (ii), holds more than fifty per cent (50%) of the equity share capital;

(*iv*) any firm in which the aggregate of his holding and the holdings of the persons mentioned in sub-clause (i) is more than fifty per cent (50%).

(*b*) where the promoter is a body corporate:

(*i*) a subsidiary or holding company of that body corporate;

(*ii*) any company in which the said body corporate holds twenty six per cent (26%) or more of the equity share capital;

(*iii*) any company which holds twenty six per cent (26%) or more of the equity share capital of the said body corporate;

(*iv*) any company in which persons acting in concert hold twenty six per cent (26%) or more of the equity share capital and those persons acting in concert also hold twenty six per cent (26%) or more of the equity share capital in such body corporate;

(*v*) any other body corporate under the same management as the said body corporate within meaning of sub-section (1B) of Section 370 of the Companies Act, 1956.

Until a company is formed, the promoters stands in a fiduciary capacity towards the company and its prospective shareholders. Hence, he must not make either directly or indirectly or through nominees etc., any profit out of his trust, unless the company after full disclosure of the facts consents. Such disclosure is ineffective if merely made to directors who are nominees of the promoters. Disclosure may be made either to an independent board or by means of a prospectus to the prospective shareholders. If the promoter makes a secret profit, the company can rescind the contract or compel him to account for it. Where all the members of a private company are cognizant of the facts, the rule would not apply.

A promoter is entitled to sell his own property to the company provided him make proper disclosure. This applies also to property which he acquires during the promotership and which he results to the company. If he fails to make disclosure, the company may either rescind the contract or compel the promoter to surrender the profit. A promoter has no right to demand any remuneration form the company for his promotional services in the absence of an express contract with the company. In the absence of such contract, he cannot even recover from the company payments he has made towards legal fees, stamp duties, registration fee or other expenses in connection with the formation of the company.

Indian Perspective of Corporate Management

Indian management scene has undergone a drastic change during the last four decades. Sole trading business, partnership firms, cooperative organizations and corporate entities are some of the major organizational structures by which we are conducting our businesses. But managers responsible for managing these businesses have also changed their orientation over the years. The methods of managing business enterprises in India are not quite the same even as were on the eve of the country's independence in 1947. While the overtone of management in India is still traditional, things have been changed to adopting professional management as a base for managing businesses especially corporate structured businesses. Earlier, central feature of the top management of big business in India was based on the proprietorship management. Ability to invest was associated with ability to manage. There was a remnant of medievalism when managerial talent was neither much needed nor much developed. "The joint stock principle was responsible for diffused ownership, but it would be better to say that it provides opportunities for diffusion as well as concentration; it all depends upon how the stock instrument is used."[1] In India, a minimum of two persons can form a private company and seven a public company, so that a single individual or family can virtually control or acquire the management of a company. But at the same time, by one can usually expect diffusion of unowned share-holding. Individuals and families can, again, control the management of a bloc of several big companies through a complex shareholding used in India not so much for diversification as for centralization of management control.

The 51 per cent share-holding represents a fair degree of concentrated ownership; and leaves out only 49 per cent of stock for diffused ownership. But if the concern is very profitable, even this diffusion may not take place.

"Diffusion is often practiced to unload worthless shares. The foundation for a closed group, oligarchic, or authoritarian management is thus laid in the case of most of the companies in India. From the first day of the laying of such a foundation, the company is managed in most cases as a personal property of controlling stockholders, and primarily in their interest."[2] Basically control and management of a corporate entity is a function of ownership. Level of control is determined by the level of ownership or shareholding pattern of the company. Quality of management system is also determined by the level of control which itself is governed by the effective shareholding. Earlier, diffusion of shareholdings was not broad based and concentrated ownership had given promoters or managing agency a centrally complete control to run the corporate entities as they wish. But in due course of time, regulatory framework has forced the promoters and other "party in concert" to ensure corporate democracy at least in the eyes of law.

Thus keeping the above facts in mind, we can study the Indian perspective of corporate management in two sub headings:

1. Traditional Management System
2. Modern Management System

1. Traditional Management System

Traditional Management System was totally governed by the centralized organizational structure. Authority was highly centralized to senior or top management. Actually, it was family governed management process. Commitment to top management was the basis for selection of managerial personnel. Recruitment of managerial cadre was restricted to only those persons who had the background of high standard families. Traditional Management System includes two traditional management practices (A) Managing Agency System and (B) Management system of subsidiaries of foreign companies.

A- Managing Agency System

A managing agent means any individual, firm or body corporate entitled to the management of substantially the whole of the affairs of a company by virtue of an agreement with the company or virtue of its memorandum or articles of association of the company. In India, this was a system of the management of big businesses by individuals or autonomous organizations who were engaged in the business of management. Whenever a company started, managing agent was associated with it. In other words, the promotion of companies was possible only when the managing agent prepared to provide financial, legal and entrepreneurial assistance to these companies. The birth of the company is the result of their pioneering efforts.

Without managing agent, a company cannot have a familiar personality before the general public and public cannot trusted upon the company. Managing agents were the persons who were responsible for developing a link between the company and its public shareholders. In this position, managing agents were expected to establish a direct communication between two. So it was necessary for the company to appoint and make provision in its prospectus for the appointment of managing agents. The general public and investors use to have faith and use to take more interest in a company with which a managing agent was associated. It was the goodwill of the Managing agency which tagged the brand image of the company.

Historical Perspective: This system was developed in India almost at the same time when the company form of organization was started becoming popular in India.

According to Vera Anstey "It was around 1833 when East India Company stopped trading activities in India, and consequent to this, managing agency system started gaining evolution. It is generally remarked that History, Geography, Economics had created such a condition in which this system was developed with its distinctive features."[3] Important features are as follows:

(*i*) **Historical factors:** It is historical fact that British came to India for the purpose of trading, export and import. Earlier they were generally engaged in trading activities alone but latter they were engaged in political activity also. Withdrawal of British merchants and joining of Indian traders had given a space for the development of managing agency system in India.

(*ii*) **Economic Factors:** It was thought by the British Merchants that the India has got great potentialities and abundant mining resources and in this way there was great scope for manufacturing industries. Thus, they tried to utilize surplus money with them for the development of certain industries there.

(*iii*) **Geographical factor:** Long distance between head offices in England and actual field of operation in India forced the British merchants to appoint managing agents. They had their agency houses for trading purposes but they were different in nature. Managing agents facilitated the British Merchants to do their businesses located at distant places.

(*iv*) **Non Availability of Capital Market:** Earlier in India, capital was very shy and capital market was not well developed. Banking facilities were also lacking as the foreign ruler was there and they did not encourage the establishment of banking facilities in India. They were simply interested to protect their interest of the manufacturing industries and in their own country. Managing agents were also engaged in ensuring funding facilities to companies of that time.

(*v*) **Lack of Entrepreneurship:** A lot of risk was created in Indian businesses due to non availability of capital and banking facilities. Entrepreneurship among the Indian businesses was also lacking at that time as majority of companies were engaged in trading activities. Actually managing agency system had given appropriates to some leading Indian traders to become first generation entrepreneurs.

Size and Structure of Managing Agency System

Managing agents were organized in various forms: sole tradership, partnership and joint stock companies. "Out of the 590 managing agents, 293 were in the form of sole traders and partnership and the rest 227 were private companies and 70 were in the form of public limited company. In 1954-55, when this system was free from existing restriction, only one company out of every six was managed by managing agents. In that year, there were 30,000 (29625 by exact) joint stock companies in India out of which 5,000 (5,055 to be exact) had the managing agent." [4]

But the managing agency system applied largely by bigger companies which is evidenced by the fact that out of the total capital of all the joint stock companies amounting to Rs. 9.7 billion, Rs. 4.6 billion fall under the control of managing agents. "All the managing agency firms were not of the same size and small managing agency firms predominated out of 3944 managing agents in India. In 1954-55, a large majority (3526) of companies were managed by only one company each. The percentage of these managing agents to the total number comes to 89.4 percent. Then there was the medium sized managing agents who manage 2 to 9 companies whose number was 401. They were 10.2 per cent of the total who managed 371 companies in all. The total capital of these 371 companies was Rs.1.1 billion. It amounted to 24.1 per cent of the paid up capital of all managed companies and to 11 per cent of the paid up capital of all the joint stock companies."[5] Overall position of big managing agents in India is indicated in exhibit-1:

Exhibit- 1
Big Managing Agents in India (1954-55)

Managing Agents	No. of Companies Managed	Managing Agent	No. of Companies Managed
1. Bird & Co.	40	10. Martin Burn	20
2. Andrewyale	39	11. H.V. Law	19
3. Mcleod	32	12. Shaw Wallace	14
4. Duncon Bros	28	13. Jorden Henderson	13
5. Birla Bros	27	14. Kilburn	12
6. Darnchand Thapar	26	15. Tata Industries	12
7. McMill & Bony	23	16. Willianson Nagar	11
8.. Octovious Steel	23	17. Begg Sulterland	10
9. Gilanders Arbuthot	22	**Total**	**371**

Functions of Managing Agents

Important functions of Managing agents were as follows:

1. **Promotion of Companies :** Managing agents were engaged in promotion process of companies which include preliminary investigations like the location, availability of factors of production, future development opportunities before the establishment of industrial unit. If the unit under consideration is new or risky project, managing agents extend these investigations to more years. Iron Steel, Hydroelectric, chemicals and

rubber industries were established after completing detailed thoroughly investigations in the field concerned. At the same time, they also use to bear all these risks about the promotion of the companies.

2. **Financing of the Company:** Managing agents also played significant role in providing sufficient capital to promoted companies. At that time, commercial banks also used to demand a guarantee from companies through these managing agents whenever some companies and borrowers approach a bank for loan purposes. These managing agents, with the help of banks, also provide foreign capital and exchange if needed for the import requirements of the company. They also provide funds for working capital, expansion and modernization purposes by purchasing a large number of shares and encourages their relatives and friends to purchase extra shares to facilitate the promoted companies for meeting their capital requirements.
3. **Management of Companies:** Managing agents were appointed to manage the affairs of companies. Generally, they use to manage more than one company at the same time. All the decision making activities were concentrated to these managing agents. These managing agents assisted by the team of qualified and experienced European managers who had built up a reputation in the field of management. This facility enables the companies to have a expertise management of their affairs.

Principle of Proprietorship

Proprietary management is the general rule which exists in India in the form of a single individual or family or a group holding the bulk of capital, either directly or through nominal shareholders. Most of these nominal shareholders were relatives or friends, who gives him or it the right to manage the company as he or it deems best without much fear of opposition or hindrance. This kind of proprietary management is, however, confined mostly to comparatively small or old-fashioned enterprises. It sometimes happens that the proprietor calls himself a firm of managing agents and figures legally as such, but this was more for reasons of prestige and to give an impression of bigness and has no real significance. The top management in this case does not have to encounter the problems typical of big corporate enterprises in the United States of America; and if there was no divorce between ownership and management, there was none between their interests.

Approximately 5,000 stock companies were managed in this way, but a large number of such companies had a fake managing agency arrangement, as stated above. Usually, the managing agents own an effective number of shares so as to retain their hold on the enterprise; and the results in the past have been rather unhappy. This type of management was associated in the minds of the people not merely with stereotyped management but also with an inhibition of natural business growth because management interests predominate and were selfishly served.

The power behind the scene were the proprietors, members of their family, or the nominees of the managing agents. Things were kept so finely poised that these persons can do practically what they like at the Board level. The situation was not so bad in all concerns but the picture should be more or less true in a great many companies. He is invariably either a member of the group himself or he works at the behest of a representative of the controlling group whose fiat runs through the entire organization and who even signs important contracts, may not be a director or even an employee of the company. The principle of proprietorship has been woven skillfully into the corporate fabric of India's business economy by shrewd capitalist financers.

Complete or substantial divorce between ownership and management is possible if the chief executive is a manager in Western countries, though it will be only a facade of separation if the chief executive does not have adequate authority delegated to him. A divorce between proprietorship and management results, whenever practiced, in a split between the ownership and management groups, and is a tendency on the part of management to pursue its self-interest in disregard of the shareholders well-being or company's prosperity. This has interfered with the natural evolutionary process of divorce; and the situation is likely to remain so for quite some time in the future. There are no traditions which can convince people that a management structure which has no financial stake in a company would still manage it in the best interests of shareholders. The problem is not merely on the adopting the Western structure of top management; it is basically on the building up traditions of loyal service, strengthening the ethical standards of professional managers, and cultivating a sense of pride in work well done. Traditions, national temper, cultural forces and business antecedents have a great deal of involvement in these equations.

Family ownership and management of big business is a very important feature of India's business world; and though not a typical management structure, it was fairly prevalent in the most influential section of big businesses. Family ownership and management was typified by such enterprises as Delhi Cloth Mills, Bombay Dyeing Mills, Birlas and Modi concerns. Here, again, the formal structure of managing agency may be adopted but may in fact be meaningless for the agency firm who belongs to the family. Managing agency concerns like those of Birlas, Tatas and Soorajmull Nagarmull seem to fall in this category.

Merits of Indian Managing System

At the level of operation management, the system of managing agents had been a peculiar feature of India's corporate world. Its merits were as follows:

(*i*) The promotion of companies was possible in India due to efforts made by the managing agents.

(*ii*) They were engaged in providing financial, legal and entrepreneurial assistance to promoted companies.

(*iii*) Managing agents had provided a familiar personality to the company so that company can be trusted upon by the public at large.

(*iv*) Managing agents played a crucial role in arranging managerial resources to companies promoted by them though most of these managers were drawn from the family, friends and relatives.

(*v*) Managing agents were also known to convert once tottering concerns into flourishing enterprises by dint of hard work and personal care and by pouring in finances sometimes borrowed on their personal security.

(*vi*) Managing agents were responsible for capital formation in the corporate sector and laid the foundation of the expansion programmes of old enterprises or established new ones.

Demerits of Managing Agency System in India: Demerits of managing agency system were as follows:

(*i*) They charge high cost of promotion from the promoted companies after their establishment.

(*ii*) They appoint themselves as their managing agents after the promotion and charge a high rate of remuneration from the company.

(*iii*) They had given more preference to those companies who were expected to produce only consumer goods as capital goods industries need more capital investment and have long gestation period.

(*iv*) Managing agents charge undesirable commission and fees when they guarantee the loan advances to the companies sanctioned by the bank. They also charge separate commission for arranging funds from their relatives and friends etc.

(*v*) They also control the powers in the management of the company by using all means of resources and create separate reserve funds by charging high remuneration of financial assistance extended by them.

(*vi*) They also entered in the speculative activities by using secret reserves created in promoted companies and manipulate the accounts with vested interests.

(*vii*) Decision making process of companies was concentrated to these managing agents. Companies were unable to follow an independent policy regarding the creation of reserves and funds, dividends declaration and provisions for depreciation etc.

(*viii*) They do not encourage Indian managers to join their promoted companies.

(*ix*) They prefer to follow the traditional management practices in managing their promoted companies.

Due to defective system of management and having monopolistic orientation, managing system was abolished from the Indian Corporate Management in 1970 by amending the Indian Companies Act, 1956.

B. Management Practices Followed By Subsidiaries of Foreign Companies

Another important dimension of traditional management practices was the management of subsidiaries of foreign companies in India. Management practices of these subsidiaries was quite similar to managing agency system in India. Prior to independence, large number of subsidiaries companies were working very well in the Indian industrial scene. Operational behaviour of parent companies except management culture was the same as of managing agency system in India. Head offices of these subsidiaries were situated in foreign countries such as U.S.A, U.K. etc. Operational management of these subsidiaries was totally governed by their head offices. Senior managers for Indian subsidiaries were generally recruited and trained in London and New York. A person who have proved himself as efficient at head office and loyal to owners of parent companies was sent out to India for management of these subsidiaries.

It is notable that all top management personnel were generally imported from the home offices. The second level of managers was also largely drawn from the foreigners. But at a later stage with pressure from the government and public, an increasing number of Indians found their positions in management of Indian subsidiaries. The third level of managers mostly drawn from the Indians but they had very low chance of promotion in these subsidiaries. If any one of the third level managers shows commitment, he was designated as a trainee for senior management programme and his training was arranged and provided at the head offices abroad. Some of these Indian managers of top management were given "home" leave to go to England, London and New York for vocational training and their traveling expenses were paid by these companies and they enjoyed the amenties as enjoyed by foreign senior managers.

Although, these firms brought with them newer and moderate method of technical and managerial know how but they have also considerably influenced by the political and social climate prevailing in India. These companies were also influenced with the activities being followed by the Indian Managing Agents. Liberal wages and salaries as well as other benefits like housing, medical facilities etc. were also provided by these subsidiaries as given by the managing agency system to its managerial personnel. At the same time, they also adopted unfair promotion practices and followed other discriminatory policies in appointment and promotional activities as of managing agency system. After independence, prevailing scenario was quite changed. Government adopted the policy of "Indianising" the management of these subsidiaries and later on it had nationalized some of them. Regulatory framework was so compelling that parent companies were forced to follow and implement the policies of the government. Some leading foreign oil companies such as Esso, Burmah Shell, Caltex and many other drug companies were also nationalized by the Government. Due to increasing interference of the government, some companies working as subsidiaries were sold out to Indian industrialists or government corporations. In some cases, parent companies had closed down their subsidiaries which were unable to work in changed environment.

Characteristics of Traditional Management System

Important features of traditional management system are as follows:

1. No Place for Professional Management : Prior to independence, Indian business and industries were run mostly on the traditional pattern. There was no systematic distribution of department according to the qualification, merit and experience of managers. "According to Census 1961, about 56 percent of managerial position in the private sector held by non-matriculates, 28 percent by matriculates, 2 percent diplomaholders and 14 percent by graduates. In technical managerial positions, 38 percent held by nonmatriculates. 36 percent by matriculates, 6 percent diplomaholders and 27 percent by graduates. It indicates that the 40 per cent of managerial positions in Indian industries held by the non-graduate persons. It is fact that it was not entirely because of non availability of university graduates or otherwise. The main reason was that enterprises or managing agents failed to create a conducive environment where professional managers can grow in proper perspective."[6] It was only during 1960's when significant improvement occurred in this direction.

2. Role for Managing Agent's Men: Important positions of the company were reserved for the members of the family, friends and relatives of the managing agents. The men with technical competence like engineers use to get some high posts but in most of the cases the need for such persons was very limited in business and industrial units of that time. Since cost of hiring of nongraduates or non technical personnel was quite low so they prefer the appointment of these persons on the job. It was expected that in due course of time they will get required training by experience for the job.

3. Family Recruitment and Placement: Only those persons were recruited as business executives who belong to rich and high standard families and educated in public school. Scientific rules and procedures for recruitment of managerial executives were also not in practice. In majority of cases, more emphasis was given on non academic qualities. Those who holding some professional degrees but not a members of rich family were unable to fit into the traditional pattern of management. These degree holders had more emphasis on theoretical study in their curriculum. They does not deal with applied problems in their academic study.

4. Non Challenging Job to Indian Business Executives: Executives in the business concerns were not very much satisfied with the job given to them as it was not so challenging in nature. In practice, they were given a routine job, which had no promotional opportunities in future. At the same time, they were assigned such a work which does not increase their skill for further promotion.

5. Business Environment was not Satisfactory: There was no place for modernity in traditional management practices. At that time India lacked free cities, cosmopolites centres which made trade respectable in Indian societies just as in societies of western countries. There was no management associations just as today to initiate the social responsibility of management towards public and increase the goodwill of managerial personnel in the minds of public at large. General perception of the public was that these managing agents create problems regarding availability of commodities, selling & distribution, buying of commodities and employment policies etc.

6. Divorce Between Talents and Business Profession: The traditional management does not provide enough intellectual challenges and opportunities for managerial leadership. It had diverted the best talents from business profession and industry to other professions. Uncertainty and insecurity of job discourage the talented persons to join as business executive in business and industry. Government services with less emoluments attracted these persons to a great extent. These person does not prefer to join business houses with more emoluments and perquisites. The apprehension was that their services will be terminated on minor conflicts and also on depressed market conditions and issues.

7. Lack of Scientific Management: Under the traditional management, no proper place was given to scientific management which is a requisite fundamental for modern management. Time and motion study was not in practice because traditional managers think it as a fruitless job and it leads to the wastage of time. These traditional managers were also not supposed to give proper attention on training facilities to their employees.

8. Decision Making Based on Hunches and Intuitions: Decisions to be taken by the traditional managers were based on their own thinking, hunches and intuitions. They do not take decisions on analysis and interpretation of past data and facts and figures. They think that this process is useless and costly. They misuse and misunderstood the meaning of planning in their management processes. They think that planning is only a guess about the future activity. There was no place for a scientific outlook in their decision making process, as it creates more risks in the businesses carried.

9. Inertia for Change: These traditional managers were not prepared and inclined to change their practices and adjust the organizational setup according to changing environment of Indian economy. They failed to develop scientific outlook towards a change. Their organizational set up and practices about dealing with problems were governed by traditional approach. Their views about modernity were not so uncourageous. They were not prepare to follow the modern management practices or professionalize their organizational structure. They were of the opinion that their traditional styles and practices are quite helpful and less costly in achieving their objectives or goals.

10. Non Enterprising: Traditional managers were not inclined to adopt and implement a risky project having long gestation period. They invest their money in only those industries which produce a high rate of return in a shortest possible time. They prefer to consumer goods industries rather than capital goods industries because consumer goods industries produce a better result in a lesser period.

2. Modern Management System

Managing is an important part of human activities. Human beings are supposed to form the social organizations for achieving the aims and objectives. As individuals, they could not accomplish their goals, so managing is necessary to ensure co-ordination of individual efforts. Group efforts are the mechanism to fulfill the social aspirations. Success of group efforts develops large but organized groups and consequently, the role of managers is required to be identifiable. Business organizations are promoted and managed to achieve their predetermined goals. "Therefore, managers of contemporary organizations ought to appreciate the important role they play in their respective organizations if they are to achieve set goals. Secondly, there is need to promote excellence among all persons in organizations especially among managers themselves."[7]

For the success of business organizations, we need four types of skills e.g. Technical skill, Human skill, Conceptual skill and Design skill. Technical skill deals with methods, processes and procedures. It also involves working with tools and specific techniques. Human skill is required for developing ability to work with people. It develops team work which is the direct result of cooperative efforts. It creates an environment in which people feel secure and free to express their opinions. Conceptual skill is the ability to see and analyze the macro dimension of the goal. It recognizes significant elements in a situation and to analyze the relationships among the elements. Design skill is the ability to solve problems in ways that will help the enterprise to achieve its goals. Managers are required to design a workable solution to the problem in the light of the realities they face.

Thus, the management is the process of designing and creating an environment for achieving organizational goals. In the process of management, managers carry out the functions of planning, organizing, staffing, leading and controlling. Managing is an essential activity at all organizational levels. Basic theme of the modern management is to create a surplus and to ensure productivity and quality in organizational activities. "Managing as practice is an art and organized knowledge about management is science. In this way, development of modern management involves the developments of concepts, principles and techniques. Business organization is an open system that operates within and interacts with the environment."[8] Modern management develops an environment where managers translate theory into reality to ensure productive use of resources at their disposal.

Basic difference between the traditional management system and modern management system is the approach by which these two systems are operating in the environment. Traditional management system is based on trial and error approach, hunches and intuitions, inertia for change etc. But modern management is governed by different factors like system approach, scientific approach, problem solving approach, behavioural approach, environmental adjustments etc. Modern management relies on the inputs from the external environment, transformation process, communication system, external factors, outputs and adjustment of the system as per the need of the various stakeholders. Professional management is synonyms of the modern management. Efforts have been made to study the different dimensions of corporate management practices in the present volume. Professional management is a process, based on decentralized authority, functional or hybrid departmentation a large core of skilled professionals, a technical support staff and little formalization. Professional management are supposed to operate more autonomously within the confines of their technical, standardized roles and they require effective coordination. These professional managers are responsible for achieving organizational goals and required to delegate a considerable amount of decision making authority and support with staff specialists.

Company Administration in India

Companies play very vital role in any economy. In our country, the Companies Act, 1956 primarily regulates the range of activities from formation to liquidation and winding up of companies. The Act prescribes regulatory framework for various aspects including organizational, financial and managerial aspects of companies. The winding up matters, presently are largely within jurisdiction of high courts. Regulations of the corporate governance, structure and obligation of companies towards their stakeholders, statutory disclosure obligations, powers of inspection, investigation and enforcement and company processes such as mergers/ amalgamations/ arrangements/ Reconstruction etc. constitute the main focus of the Act. In the functioning of corporate sector, along with freedom of operation of companies, protection of investors and shareholders are considered equally important. The Companies Act enables a statutory platform for essential Corporate Governance requirements essential for functioning of the companies with transparency and accountability recognizing and protecting the interests of various stakeholders. The main objects of the Act are summarized as under:-

(*a*) To enable the interests of the shareholders, to be protected through articulation of shareholders democracy;

(*b*) To safeguard the interest of other stakeholders such as creditors, financial institutional etc through appropriate disclosure;

(*c*) To provide a framework for regulation of processes of companies including mergers/ Amalgamation etc.; and

(*d*) To enable the Government with adequate powers of enforcement of the law in public interest and as per procedure prescribed by law so that the interest of all stakeholders may be protected from unscrupulous management.

Practice Questions

Objective Type Questions

1. Company is a
   (*a*) Voluntary association of persons
   (*b*) Mandatory association of persons
   (*c*) Public welfare association of persons
   (*d*) Profit making association of persons
2. Control is decided by:
   (*a*) Number of shareholders
   (*b*) Level of shareholding
   (*c*) Number of debenture holders

(*d*) Level of public float

3. Special resolution requires:

(*a*) Simple majority

(*b*) 3/4th majority

(*c*) 2/3rd majority

(*d*) None of these

4. Diffused ownership means:

(*a*) Promoters shareholding

(*b*) Shares controlled by party in concert

(*c*) Non promoters shareholding

(*d*) Shares held by Financial Institutions

5. East India Company stopped trading activities in India:

(*a*) 1836 (*b*) 1840

(*c*) 1834 (*d*) 1833

Ans: 1.(*a*), 2. (b), 3. (b), 4.(c), 5.(d)

Short Answer Questions

1. What is control?
2. What do you mean by public float?
3. What do you mean by shareholding?
4. What is executive management?
5. What are the demerits of Managing Agency System?
6. What is the present system Company Administration System in India?

Long Answer Questions

1. What is Company Management? Explain its different aspects?
2. Discuss the scope of company management. Also evaluate its components.
3. What do you mean by Managing Agency System? Examine its role in India's corporate development.
4. What is Traditional Management? How does modern management is superior to traditional management?
5. What do you mean by Promoter? Explain its functions.

References

1. Dr. Agarwala A.N. Emerging Dimensions of the Indian Management, Asia Publishing House, Bombay, 1970 p.46
2. Ibid.p.57
3. Chandrakant, L.S. Management Education and Training. D.B. Taraporewala & Sons, Bombay, 1973 p.28
4. Dr. Agarwala A.N. Emerging Dimensions of the Indian Management, op.cit p.64
5. Ibid.p66
6. Chandrakant L.S. Management Education and Training op.cit. p.42
7. Homans G.C. The Human Group Harcourt, Brace and World, New York, 1958, p.71
8. Fleet David. D. Vass and Peterson Tim O. Contemporary Management, it ought on Mifflin Company, 1994, 3rd edition, p.136

2 CORPORATE SECTOR IN INDIA

Corporate sector has been assigned a crucial role in the economic development of the country. Corporate sector constitutes important sectors like Mining, Manufacturing, Power, Service and Agriculture sectors etc. Large number of joint stock companies are working in different segments of economic activities. Even limited scale forming, seed arrangement, horticulture and floriculture etc have also been getting the direct support of joint stock companies. The Private, Public sector and joint sector are responsible for promotion of joint stock companies indicating growing support of private entrepreneurs, government and inter- company joint venture arrangements. The Government of India has already developed effective regulatory framework for the development of corporate sector in the country. Ministry of Corporate Affairs, SEBI and Competition Commission of India etc are leading institutions which are responsible for the development, monitoring and regulations of joint stock companies in India. Promotion of companies, and their regulation of companies, working, sickness, rehabilitation and liquidation are being managed by different specific institutions established for the purpose. Since 1991, efforts are being made to make these institutions more operational and effective for overall growth of corporate sector.

"Since Independence efforts have also been made to institutionalize the process of development and joint stock companies have already achieved this objectives to a large extent. Some of the companies are specially assigned to resource generation as well as its utilization. Development institutions have also been incorporated in the form of Joint Stock Companies."[1] These development institutions themselves have promoted large number of joint stock companies.

India's corporate sector has grown steadily over the past two decades in terms of number of registered companies and amount of paid up capital. "The corporate sector consists of closely held (private limited) and publicly held (public limited) companies, with about 8,00,000 registered companies at the end of 2008-09, about 40 percent of which are in the manufacturing sector. Private Limited Companies is the popular form of Joint Stock Companies in India as its promotion, working and regulation mechanism etc are quite easy. The study also shows that about 78 percent joint stock companies are working in the form of private limited companies. Besides, first generation entrepreneurs are also using private limited company form of organization to give a legal organizational framework to their businesses". Private limited companies comprise the majority of firms in the corporate sector, but account for less than one–third of total paid up capital. Government-owned enterprises (both public and private limited) are comparatively few in number but large in size, accounting for more than 25 percent of the paid up capital. ."[2]

However, post 1991 era, private sector companies are also doing well and outpacing the dominating position of public sector joint stock companies.

A Journey from Bombay Plan to Bombay Club

The Bombay Plan is the name commonly given to a World War II-era set of proposals for the development of the post-independence economy of India. The plan, published in 1944/1945 by seven leading Indian industrialists, proposed state intervention in the economic development of the nation after independence from the United Kingdom in 1947. Titled A Brief Memorandum Outlining a Plan of Economic Development For India, the signatories of the Plan were Jehangir Ratanji Dadabhoy Tata, Ghanshyam Das Birla, Ardeshir Dalal, Sir Sri Ram, Kasturibhai Lalbhai, Ardeshir Darabshaw Shroff and John Mathai. Thus, the signatories include important personalities of Indian Corporate Sector like G.D. Birla, who had wide interests in the textiles, jute and insurance; J.R.D. Tata, with interests in iron and steel and internal airlines; and Kasthuribai Lalbai, with interests in textiles and shipping. This is the well known "Bombay Plan". The Plan went through two editions: the first was published in January 1944. This first edition became "Part I" of the second edition, published in 2 volumes in 1945 under the editorship of Purushottamdas Thakurdas.

Although Jawaharlal Nehru, the first Prime Minister of India, did not officially accept the plan, "the Nehruvian era witnessed the implementation of the Bombay Plan; a substantially interventionist state and an economy with a sizeable public sector." Its perceived influence has given it iconic status, and "it is no exaggeration to say that the Bombay Plan has come to occupy something of a mythic position in Indian historiography. There is scarcely a study of post-war Indian economic history that does not point to it as an indicator of the developmental and nationalistic aspiration of the domestic capitalist class."

A key principle of the Bombay Plan was that the economy could not grow without government intervention and regulation. Under the assumption that the fledgling Indian industries would not be able to compete in a free-market economy, the Plan proposed that the future government should protect indigenous industries against foreign competition in local markets. Other salient points of the Bombay plan were an active role by government in deficit financing and planning equitable growth, a transition from an agrarian to an industrialized society, and—in the event that the private sector could not immediately do so—the establishment of critical industries as public sector enterprises while simultaneously ensuring a market for the output through planned purchases. Bombay plan provided an opportunity in two ways: Corporatisation of managing agency system and invitation to Government to play its interventionist role through promotion of corporate entities in the form of Joint Stock Companies. The material base of the optimistic note in the plan put forward by the Indian industrialists can now be summed up. Firstly, it is based upon an increased industrialization of India accentuated by the war. Secondly, on the weakened position of British capitalism. Finally, on the possibility of a deal with the American Capitalists. In fact, the fear of a revolution at home has forced them to seek the alliance of the American bourgeoisie.

The plan aims to provide a minimum standard of living in terms of food, clothing, housing, health and social services within a period of 15 year. To provide this, minimum with some extra money for the enjoyment of life and cultural activities, "the plan assumes that it is necessary to double the per capita income of the population. At the present rate of increase in the population, the total national income, has to be trebled in 15 years. To achieve this result, the Planners aim at increase of 135 per cent in agricultural production and 500 per cent in industrial production.

Although the Bombay Plan did not itself propose a socialist agenda, "virtually all" commentators acknowledge "that there is a direct line of continuity from the Bombay Plan of 1944-1945 to the First Five-Year Plan in 1950." An alternative line of reasoning is that the Bombay Plan was a reaction to the widespread social discontent of the 1940s (resulting from unprecedented industrial growth during wartime), and a product of the fear that the movement against colonial rule would become a movement against private property. Private entrepreneurs managing agents and traders had utilized this opportunity to convert their individual firms and partnership firms into Joint stock companies.

The Bombay Plan reaped criticism from all quarters on the following basis: (i) The far left criticized the capitalistic background of the Plan's authors or asserted that the plan did not go far enough. (ii) The far right foresaw it as a harbinger of a socialist society, and considered it a violation of the agreements of the United Nations "Bretton Woods Conference" (which Shroff had attended). (iii)Economists criticized the plan on technical grounds that (a) it did not take into account the fact that creating capital had an inflationary effect, and with that, (b) its authors had overestimated the capacity of the Indian economy to generate further capital. With rising prices, the purchasing power (for investments) would fall. The plan based upon an attractive schematism, ignores two vital questions. (i) It bases itself on the assumption of a continuation of capitalism internationally but fails to examine the relation of Indian economy with the international competition. In this sense, it is an attempt to create an economic autarchy. (ii) Secondly, it does not examine the most important problem in a prosperous development of Indian Capitalism – the agrarian revolution and the creation of a prosperous peasantry to provide the necessary internal market.

Of course, global capital is much more diffused and democratized now and Indian business men have easier access to capital than during those days. It is also interesting to note that leading business houses like Tata, Birla and Reliance have managed to diversify and expand their business in an indigenous framework. Form of Joint Stock Company has lent viable support on these business houses in their mission. They have accessed foreign technology but on their own terms, and without giving up their control over ownership of equity capital. The Reliance Group, for instance, has grown by leaps and bounds without any partnership with a foreign multinational. Thus, the Indian capitalist class still carries some of the nationalist approach of their pre-Independence predecessors. Indian entrepreneurs had enjoyed the supporting state intervention in business especially during regime of Late Pt. Nehru and Late Smt. Indira Gandhi. But at the same parlance, these entrepreneurs also supporting the new economic policies specially started in late 1980s. They have tremendously improved their competitive strengths with their foreign counterparts. Even they have started working as India's multinationals working in foreign countries. They have accumulated huge wealth with the help of public companies having huge market capitalization.

In 1992, the `Bombay Club' led a lobbying effort by domestic industrialists against removing trade barriers. It was a seductive argument. They said they are in favour of removing barriers to imports, but they first required `fair' competition with imports on a `level playing field'. Indian companies must get access to reliable and trustworthy electricity, high quality ports and airports, a sensible framework of labour law and a sound GST, a good financial system, etc. Only when all these things are done would Indian companies have a level playing field when competing against imports made by foreign companies. Only when these preconditions are met, it be fair to remove trade barriers. Thus, growing international competition and growing pace of globalization have forced the Indian Corpporates to be more competitive.

The Bombay Club that flourished in the 1990s wanted a level playing field for Indian industry. It argued that while the domestic industry faced several bottlenecks because of the existing policies and infrastructure problems, imports did not suffer from those handicaps. As a result, manufacturing companies in India had to face unfair competition from imports. "Cow boy approach" of foreign companies collaborating with domestic promoters in joint venture in India are not following the collaborative dharma. It was argued that several foreign companies failed to understand that spirit of partnership in a joint venture and used their Indian collaborator only as a matter of convenience because of policy imperatives, thanks to the limits imposed on foreign direct investment (FDI) in several sectors, and the lack of familiarity with the Indian market.

Of course the current capitalist class wants the State to play a minimalist role and protect its interests in a global context, such as in WTO. This may have been the case even in the 1940s, but for the circumstances, which had required a quick accumulation of capital to catch up with the rest of the world.

Even though the arguments of the Bombay Club were reasonable one, But its limitations were also as follows:

1. There are many inputs to production and every location in the world has a different set of price advantages. While a location in India fares badly on some inputs (such as electricity or roads) it fares well in others (such as the price of labour). Overall competitive advantage reflects the cost of all inputs. In India, some inputs like electricity are costlier, but other inputs such as labour are cheaper.
2. The exchange rate is a great equaliser. When a country removes trade barriers, imports get cheaper and the current account deficit tends to go up. But as long as the exchange rate is allowed to fluctuate, a currency depreciation results, which makes exports more competitive and imports costlier.
3. When India opened up, many firms died. Their death freed up capital and labour which went into other firms, often in other industries. So while India's opening up was a calamity for many individual firms and also some industries (e.g. computer hardware), it worked well for *India*, by rearranging the utilisation of labour and capital.
4. The Bombay Club, and old Indian economic policy makers, were pessimistic about what Indian firms are capable of. The events have belied this pessimism. When competitive pressure came upon Indian firms, they worked wonders on reshaping themselves, absorbing new technology, recruiting talent including foreigners, etc. The malleability of human behaviour exceeds the expectations of practical people.
5. Once the pressure of imports came on, political lobbying by Indian companies started pushing politicians on *reforms* -- e.g. cutting restrictions on foreign inputs such as coal or debt capital, building highways, breaking the grip of DOT over telecom, etc.

The "Bombay Plan" had become imperative because of the lack of adequate resources with the capitalist class to build India's economic infrastructure in quick time. JRD Tata has asserted this strategy was to be supported fully to "the extent they were essential for a rapid rise in the standard of living." Even GD Birla worked tirelessly towards this end and acted as the main conduit between leaders like Gandhi, Sardar Patel and the Indian industrialist. On behalf of the capitalist class, Birla did a great job of keeping the British authorities in good hum our while lending full support to the national movement. Thus, "The Bombay Plan" pitched for a largely State-led strategy of "creating basic industries in as short a time as possible."

Over the last 20 years, there has been a sea change in the economic policy landscape in India through effective implementation of economic reforms. Different segments of economic reforms are as follows :

(*a*) Financial Sector Reforms

(*b*) Banking Sector Reforms

(*c*) Tax Reforms

(*d*) Infrastructure Sector Reforms

(*e*) Public Sector Reforms

Thus, on the basis of above analysis we can say that India Inc. today is fired by a new spirit of entrepreneurship that is reflected in its growth in India and acquisitions aboard.

Growth of Indian Corporate Sector

The Indian corporate sector has two main components, namely, the government owned and privately owned companies. "The size of both the components, in terms of both numbers and capital, has grown fast, particularly since beginning of the 'seventies'. Government companies are mainly in the basic, heavy and capital intensive industries whereas the private sector is predominantly in industries which cater to the consumer markets directly. It is due to such a basic difference that while the government sector accounts for nearly two-thirds of the productive industrial capital, its share in the net value added is less than one-third.[1] And the opposite is true of the private sector. The differing nature of the activities undertaken by the two sectors is also reflected in the pattern of industrial activities of the two sectors. For instance, energy -- which is a pre-requisite for processes of economic development -- alone accounts for more than 44 per cent of the capital investment of the Central Government production enterprises; another 15 per cent investment is in steel, 11.4 per cent in chemicals, fertilizers and pharmaceuticals and nearly 8 per cent in minerals and metals."[3]

In 1956-57, the number of `public limited' private sector companies was 8,771 and in 1984-85 it stood at 26,813. The size of Paid up Capital PUC in this period increased from Rs. 696 crores to Rs. 14,569 crores.[5] The sector is marked by the existence of high degree of concentration, *i.e.* a small number of large sized companies enjoying a dominant place.

In 1980, the small sized companies, each with less than Rs. 5.0 lakhs PUC, accounted for nearly half of the public limited companies but had less than two per cent share of the PUC; on the other hand, less than six per cent of the large sized group, each with Rs. 1.0 crore and more of PUC accounted for nearly two-thirds of the gross PUC. The Companies with more than Rs. 50.00 lakhs each as PUC, are seen to account for a little less than four-fifths of the total PUC of the public limited companies of the private corporate sector. The highly skewed nature of the public limited companies is only too obvious.

During the period of 35 years from 1956-57 to 1990-91, number of companies increased from 29,357 to 2,24,452 a net increase of 195095 companies. Similarly, paid up capital also increased from Rs.1078 crore to 68111 crore during the same period. Thus, the number of companies and their paid up capital by more than 8 times and about 68 times respectively. Overall position"[4] regarding growth of Indian Corporate Sector is given in Exhibit-2.1.

Exhibit – 2.1
Growth of the Indian Corporate Sector
(1956-57-1990-91)

(PUC in Rs. Crores)

Year	Govt. Companies (Public & Private Limited)		Non- Govt. Companies				All Companies	
			Public Limited		Private Limited			
	No.	PUC	No.	PUC	No.	PUC	No.	PUC
(1)	(2)	(3)	(4)	(5)	(6)	(7)	(8)	(9)
1956-57	74	73	8771	696	20512	309	29357	1078

Contd....

1957-58	91	257	8255	756	19934	294	28280	1307
1958-59	104	429	7608	782	19691	305	27403	1516
1959-60	125	477	7151	814	19621	327	26897	1618
1960-61	142	547	6663	915	19344	356	26149	1819
1961-62	154	630	6399	1093	18422	296	24975	2019
1962-63	160	786	6404	1171	19058	300	25622	2257
1963-64	176	961	6474	1281	19282	361	25932	2603
1964-65	183	1115	6492	1329	19909	336	26584	2780
1965-66	214	1248	6410	1346	20386	355	27010	2949
1966-67	232	1392	6309	1402	20706	361	27247	3155
1967-68	241	1559	6497	1684	20606	430	27344	3674
1968-69	259	1715	6454	1712	21260	433	27973	3860
1969-70	282	1791	6436	1714	22242	447	28960	3979
1970-71	314	2064	6443	1775	23655	462	30412	4301
1971-72	352	2369	6703	2036	25212	536	32267	4941
1972-73	390	2998	6819	2176	27147	575	34356	5749
1973-74	450	4645	7071	2323	29964	663	37485	7631
1974-75	573	4966	7275	2484	32736	750	40584	8200
1975-76	651	6122	7593	2675	35162	822	43406	9619
1976-77	701	7175	7794	2808	37371	897	45866	10880
1977-78	745	8528	8028	3113	39521	957	48294	12598
1978-79	782	8315	8309	3240	42427	1020	51518	12575
1979-80	825	10070	8864	3445	46804	1091	56493	14606
1980-81	851	11443	9388	3550	52475	1152	62714	16145
1981-82	894	13309	10169	3716	61339	1245	74402	18270
1982-83	943	16535	11371	3839	70589	1347	82903	21721
1983-84	973	19511	12523	3996	80768	1455	94264	24962
1984-85	980	22447	14149	4260	92240	1578	107369	28285
1985-86	1020	27088	19837	7139	103522	2368	124379	36595
1986-87	1053	32873	21442	8435	118175	2660	140670	43968
1987-88	1104	37169	22507	9966	134713	2989	158324	50124
1988-89	1134	42572	23749	11773	155445	3358	180328	57704
1989-90	1160	47451	25217	13573	175751	3620	202128	64643
1990-91	1167	49424	26813	14569	196472	4117	224452	68111

Legal and Regulatory Framework for the Corporate Sector Prior to the 1991 Reforms."[5]

Prior to the 1991 reform, the main legislative acts before the launching of 1991 economic reforms governing Indian companies were the following:

(*i*) **The Companies Act of 1956** established the modern legal and regulatory framework for the corporate sector, giving power to the central government to monitor, regulate, and control the affairs of companies, including establishing the types and structure of companies and registration and reporting requirements.

(*ii*) **The Capital Issues (Control) Act, 1947** required any firm seeking to issue securities to obtain approval from the central government; this was done to ensure that the country's financial resources were channeled into areas that served the government's goals and priorities.

(*iii*) **The 1951 Industries Development and Regulation (IDR) Act** put in place a system of mandatory licenses, which acted to limit a firm's ability to expand capacity, change product mix, introduce new processes, and import machinery and equipment without obtaining various licenses from the central government.

(*iv*) **The Industrial Policy Resolution of 1956** reserved certain industries for the public sector, thus creating a large state-owned industrial and services sector.

(*v*) **The 1969 Monopolies and Restrictive Trade Practices Act** paved the way for widespread nationalization of Indian companies by establishing an asset-based classification of monopoly, but applying only to the private sector.

The government of India also had a number of policies aimed at directing the development of the corporate sector.

(*i*) Small-*scale industries* were specifically encouraged since 1967, and many product lines were reserved for the small-scale sector. This policy was put on a statutory footing by amending the IDR Act in 1984.

(*ii*) A policy of *import substitution* was implemented with high tariffs and a requirement of multiple import licenses, shielding domestic firms from foreign competition.

(*iii*) In order to foster industrialization, the government also set up three *development finance institutions*: the Industrial Development Bank of India (IDBI), the Industrial Finance Corporation of India (IFCI), and the Industrial Credit and Investment Corporation of India (ICICI), whose mission was to lend to industrial enterprises, often at below-market interest rates.

(*iv*) With *interest rates regulated* by the government, competition among financial institutions was very limited. Public financial institutions, which supplied the vast majority of loans to the public sector, had little incentive to monitor the lending activity (Khanna et al., 1999), which led to excess leveraging.

Exhibit-2.2

Number and Paid – up Capital of Joint Stock Companies at work in India

(Rs. in Crores)

As on 31st March		Public		Private		Total	
		Number	Paid-up Capital	Number	Paid-up Capital	Number	Paid-up Capital
	0	1	2	3	4	5	6
1971	---	6,690	2,091.5	23,632	1,422.2	30,322	4,513.7
1981	---	9,740	4,645.5	52,974	10,909.0	62,714	15,554.5
1991	---	27,358	38,567.8	1,97,094	36,230.1	2,24,452	74,797.9
1998	--	68,546	1,46,225.20	4,15,954	71423.41	4,84,500	2,17,648.61
1999	---	71,033	1,79,850.69	4,40,957	83,508.59	5,11,990	2,63,359.28
2000		73,862	2,20,348.39	4,68,572	98461.86	5,42,434	318810.25
2002	--	76,279	2,76,467.41	5,12,967	1,29,285.82	5,89,246	4,05,753.23
2003 (R)	--	76,523	3,20,629.21	5,35,632	1,36,429.50	61,21,55	4,57,058.71

Contd....

2004(P)	--	77,380	3,27,620.53	5,64,132	1,44,448.13	6,41,512	4,72,068.66
2005 (P)	--	78,410	3,44,228.13	5,81,372	1,53,811.17	6,59,782	4,98,039.30
2006(P)	--	79,076	3,72,703.40	6,18,934	1,61,439.78	6,98,010	5,34,143.18
2007(P)	--	80,741	3,98,194.33	6,68,136	1,70,172.56	7,48,907	5,68,366.89
2008(P)	--	81,378	4,10,816.71	6,80,843	1,79,813.65	7,62,221	5,90,630.36
2009 (P)	--	82,058	4,26,112.22	7,04,716	1,88,175.91	7,86,774	6,14,288.13

(R) Revised

(P) Provisional (Source: Department of Company Affairs Government of India.)

Financial Express: 8.6.2009)

During the last 40 years, the number of companies increased from 30322 in 1971 to 786774 in 2009. Thus, growth of number of joint stock companies comes to about 26 times. Paid up capital also increased tremendously during the same period. Overall position of number and paid up capital of joint stock companies at work in India is indicated in Exhibit 2.2.

The Exhibit-2.2 also shows that growth rate in number of private limited companies is quite high in comparison to growth rate available in number of public limited companies. Number of Private limited companies increased by about 30 times as against the growth of about 12 times in public limited companies. However growth in the size of paid up capital in private limited companies comes to 13 times which is quite lower than the growth available in paid up capital of public limited companies which is 22 times during 1971 to 2009.

Present Position of Indian Corporate Sector

7,86,774 companies limited by shares were at work in the country as on 31.03.2009. These comprised 7,85,183. Non-Government companies and 1,591 Government companies. Out of 7,86,774 companies limited by shares at work, 82,058 companies were public limited and 7,04,716 were private limited companies.

"84,848 companies limited by shares with authorized capital of Rs.53,220.94 crore were registered under the Companies Act, 1956 during the period from the 1st January, 2008 to 31st March, 2009. Out of these, 112 were Government companies with authorized capital of Rs. 4902.79 crore and 84,736 were Non-Government companies with authorized capital of Rs. 48318.15 crore." [6]

The Government companies limited by shares which were registered during the period from 1st January, 2008 to 31st March, 2009 comprised 72 public limited companies and 40 private limited companies with authorized capital of Rs. 4860.40 crore and Rs. 42.39 crore respectively. The Non-Government companies limited by shares which were registered during the period from 1st January, 2008 to 31st March, 2009 comprised 3,108 public limited companies and 81,628 private limited companies with authorized capital of Rs.18843.68 crore and Rs.29474.47 crore respectively.

During the period from 1st January, 2008 to 31st March, 2009 a total of 32,705 Non government companies limited by shares were reported to have gone into liquidation or to have been stuck off under section 560 (5) of the Companies Act, 1956.

Exhibit-2.3
Companies Limited by Shares at work as on 31st March, 2009
(State-wise Distribution)[7]

SI.No.	State/UT	Public. No.	Private No.	Total No.
1	2	3	4	5
1	Andhra Pradesh	6,378	51,946	58,324
2	Assam	680	4,795	5,475
3	Bihar	1,132	7,092	8,224
4	Chhattisgarh	318	2,962	3,280

Contd....

5	Gujarat	5,803	38,971	44,774
6	Haryana	975	7,670	8,645
7	Himachal Pradesh	333	2,147	2,480
8	J & K	235	2,029	2,264
9	Jharkhand	337	3,531	3,868
10	Karnataka	3,052	36,480	39,532
11	Kerala	1,563	15,519	17,082
12	Madhya Pradesh	1,292	10,257	11,549
13	Maharashtra	15,141	1,61,676	1,76,817
14	Manipur	39	141	180
15	Meghalaya	114	526	640
16	Mizoram	7	46	53
17	Nagaland	32	227	259
18	Orissa	798	6,849	7,647
19	Punjab	2,244	13,411	15,655
20	Rajasthan	1,826	22,469	24,295
21	Tamil Nadu	7,188	55,618	62,806
22	Tripura	21	109	130
23	Uttar Pradesh	4,732	22,210	26,942
24	Uttaranchal	281	1,706	1,987
25	West Bengal	9,916	82,698	92,614
26	A & N Islands	4	106	110
27	Arunachal Pradesh	22	257	279
28	Chandigarh	1,240	5,704	6,944
29	D & N Haveli	58	203	261
30	Daman & Diu	51	133	184
31	Delhi	15,880	1,41314	1,57,194
32	Goa	252	4,718	4,970
33	Lakshadweep	0	9	9
34	Pondicherry	114	1,187	1,301
	Total	**82,058**	**7,04,716**	**7,86,774**

2,546 foreign companies, as defined under Section 591 of the Companies Act, 1956 were in the country as on 31.12.2007. Another 380 foreign companies established their place of business in India 23 foreign companies have ceased to have their principal place of business in India during the period from 1st January, 2008 to 31st March, 2009. Thus, there were 2,903 foreign companies in India as on 31st March, 2009.

Policy Framework for Public Sector Joint Stock Companies

Keeping the changing business scenario in mind the Government of India had announced the adoption of a new approach towards the public sector on July, 1991. This was an important part of the new industrial policy. Silent features of new approach towards public enterprises given in the said Industrial Policy are as follows:

(i) Portfolio of public sector investments will be viewed with a view to focus the public sector on strategic, high-tech, and essential infrastructure. Whereas some reservation for the public sector is being retained there would be no bar for areas of exclusivity to be opened up to the private sector selectivity. Similarly, public sector will also be allowed entry in areas not reserved for it.

(ii) Public sector which are chronically sick and which are unlikely to be turned around will, for the formulation of revival/rehabilitation schemes, be referred to the Board for Industrial and Financial Reconstruction (BIFR), or other similar high level institutions created for the purpose. A social security mechanism will be created to protect the interests of workers likely to be affected by such rehabilitation packages.

(iii) In order to raise resources and encourage wider public participation, a new part of the government's share-holding in the public sector will be offered to mutual funds, financial institutions, general public and workers.

(iv) Boards of public sector companies would be made more professional and given greater powers.

(v) There will be a greater thrust on performance improvement through the Memorandum of Understanding (MoU) system through which management would be given greater autonomy and will be held accountable. Technical expertise on the part of the government would be upgraded to make the MoU negotiation and implementation more effective.

(vi) To facilitate fuller discussion on performance, the MoU signed between Government and the public enterprises would be placed in parliament. While focusing on major management issues, this would also help to place matters on day to day operations of public enterprises in their correct perspective.

The aggregate financial investment in PEs grew from Rs. 29 crore in 5 enterprises in 1951-52 to Rs. 4,55,409 crore in 242 enterprises in 2007-08. (Exhibit 1). Aggregate financial investment in CPSEs during 2007-08 increased by Rs.34933 crore, showing a 8.31% growth over 2006-07.

Exhibit 2.4
Growth in Investment

Particulars	Total Investment (Rs. in crore)	Enterprises (No.)
1	2	3
At the commencement of the 1st five year plan(1.4.1951)	29	5
At the commencement of the 2nd five year plan(1.4.1956)	81	21
At the commencement of the 3rd five year plan(1.4.1961)	948	47
At the end of 3rd five year plan (31.3.1966)	2410	73
At the commencement of the 4th five year plan(1.4.1969)	3897	84
At the commencement of the 5th five year plan(1.4.1974)	6237	122
At the end of 5th five year plan(31.3.1979)	15534	169
At the commencement of the 6th five year plan(1.4.1980)	18150	179
At the commencement of the 7th five year plan(1.4.1985)	42673	215
At the end of 7th five year plan(31.3.1990)	99329	244
At the commencement of the 8th five year plan (1.4.1992)	135445	246
At the end of 8th five year plan(31.3.1997)	213610	242
At the end of 9th five year plan(31.3.2002)	324614	240
At the end of 10th five year plan(31.3.2007)	420476	245
At the end of First year of Eleventh Five Year Plan (31.3.2008)	455409	242

Source: Public Enterprise Survey, 2008-09.

While the Central government continues to have the majority share (equity) holding in investment in terms of both equity and long term loans has been forthcoming from other parties as well, such as, the financial institutions, banks, private parties (both Indian and foreign), state governments and holding (parent) companies. The share of Central Government in total financial investment stood at 44.10 percent in 2002-03, it declined to 35.57 percent in 2007-08. The share of the financial institutions / banks (and 'other'), on the other hand, that was 35.44 percent in 2002-03 has gone up to 49.26 percent in 2007-08. In a way, this shows the greater confidence of Financial Institutions and banks in PEs. The share of foreign parties in total financial investment has also shown a decrease from 10.42 percent in 2002-03 to 7.59 percent in 2007-08.

Ministry of Corporate Affairs

Organisational Setup[8]

The ministry has a three tier organizational set-up for administration of the Indian Companies Act, 1956 namely, the Secretariat at New Delhi, the Regional Directors at Mumbai, Kolkata, Chennai and Noida (U.P.) and the Registrar of Companies in State and Union Territories and 20 offices of Registrars of Companies (ROCs) in State and Union Territories. 16 offices of the Official Liquidators who are attached to various High Courts functioning in the country are also under the overall administrative control of the Ministry.

(i) **Headquarters:** The set-up at the Headquarters include one secretary, one Additional secretary, two Joint Secretaries, one economic advisior, two directors of Inspection and Investigation and other officials providing expertise on legal, accounting, economic and statistical matters.

(ii) **Regional Directors:** The four Regional Directors are in-charge of the respective regions, each region comprising a number of State and Union Territories. They supervise the working of the offices of the Registrars of the Companies and the Official Liquidators working in their regions. They also maintain liaison between the respective State Governments and the Central Government in matters relating to the administration of the Companies Act, 1956. Certain powers of the Central Government under the Companies Act have been delegated to the Regional Directors. They have also been declared as Heads of Department. There is an Inspection Unit attached to the office of every Regional Director for carrying out the inspection of the books of accounts of companies under Section 209A of the Companies Act, 1956.

(iii) **Registrars of Companies:** Registrars of Companies (ROCs) appointed under section 609 of the Companies Act, 1956 covering various States and the Union Territories are vested to the primary duty of registering companies floated in the respective states. And the Union Territories and ensuring that such companies comply with statutory requirements under the Act. These offices function as registry of records, relating to the companies registered with them, which are available for inspection by members of the public on payment of the prescribed fee. The Central Government exercises administrative control over these offices through the respective Regional Directors.

(iv) **Official Liquidators:** The official liquidators are officers appointed by the Central Government under Section 448 of the Companies Act, 1956 and are attached to various jurisdictional High Courts. The official liquidators are under the administrative charge of the respective Regional Directors, who supervise their functioning on behalf of the Central Government. In the conduct of winding-up of affairs of the companies, however, Official Liquidators act under the directions and supervision of the High Courts. At the same time, the Central Government have the responsibility under Section 463 of the Companies Act, 1956 of exercising overall control over the Official Liquidators to ensure that they faithfully perform their duties and duly observe all the requirements imposed on them under the Act or the Rules there-under.

Subsidiary Organizations for Corporate Management

(i) **Company Law Board:** The Central Government constituted an independent Company Law Board, vide Notification No. 364 dated the 31st May, 1991. The Board is a quasi-judicial body which exercises some of the judicial and quasi–judicial powers which were earlier being exercised by the High Court or the Central Government. The Board is not subject to the control of the Central Government and has the powers to regulate its own procedures and act in its own discretion. The Board has its Principal Bench at New Delhi, an Additional Principal Bench for southern States at Chennai and four Regional Benches at Delhi, Mumbai, Kolkata and Chennai.

(*ii*) **The Monopolies and Restrictive Trade Practices Commission** : The Monopolies and Restrictive Trade Practices Commission (MRTPC), which is a quasi-judicial body, in an attached statutory office of the Ministry. The MRTP Commission established under Section 5 of the of the Monopolies and Restrictive Trade Practices Act, 1969, discharges functions as per the provisions of the Act. The main function of the MRTP Commission is to enquire into and take appropriate action in respect of unfair trade practices and restrictive trade practices. In regard to monopolistic trade practices, the Commission is empowered under Section 10 (b) to enquire into such practices (i) upon a reference made to it by the Central Government or (ii) upon its own knowledge or information and submit its findings to Central Government for further action.

The Act was amended from time to time during the last 38 years and major amendments took place in the years 1984 and 1991. The Government of India has now enacted the "The Competition Act, 2002" as amended to "The Competition (Amendment) Act, 2007 to replace the existing MRTP Act, 1969. As the said Act is yet to be notified, the provisions of the MRTP Act, 1969 are, still in vogue and this office continues to discharge its statutory functions and duties as prescribed under the Act.

(*iii*) **Director General of Investigation and Registration:** The Office of the Director General of Investigation & Registration was created in the year 1984 to perform certain statutory functions and duties under the MRTP Act, 1969 for the prohibition of monopolistic, restrictive and unfair trade practices so as to subserve its objective to protect the interests of the consumers in the country.

(*iv*) **Competition Commission of India:** The Competition Commission of India is presently engaged in following activities linked to competition advocacy and administrative measures relating to the operationalisation of the Companies Commission of India. The Competition Commission of India is also in the process of preparing various draft regulations required to be formulated under the Act through a consultative process. Recruiting professionals and support staff is one of the key areas identified by the Commission to enable it to effectively discharge its statutory functions.

(*v*) **Serious Fraud Investigation Office (SFIO):** The SFIO is a multi-disciplinary Investigating Agency, wherein experts from banking sector, capital market, company law, general law, forensic audit, taxation, information technology etc. work together to unravel a corporate fraud. At present, SFIO is carrying out investigation under provisions of the Companies Act from Sections 235 to 247. However, as approved by the cabinet, a separate legislation would be enacted for SFIO in second phase to provide adequate power and reach to this organization. For this purpose, the MCA has already set up Vepa Kamesam Committee to look into the need for enacting a separate legislation for SFIO and make suitable recommendation.

SFIO takes up investigations frauds characterized by (a) complexity, and having inter-departmental and multi-disciplinary ramifications, (b) Substantial involvement of public interest to be judged by size, either in terms of monetary misappropriation, or in terms of the persons affected; and (c) the possibility of investigations leading to, or contributing towards, a clear improvement in system, laws or procedures.

SFIO is headed by a Director as Head of Department. He is of the rank of joint Secretary to the Government of India. Below him, there are Additional Directors, Joint Directors, Sr. Assistant Directors and Assistant Directors, who form teams for investigation of a case. The Head Office of SFIO is at Delhi and there is one Branch Office in Mumbai.

Investment Climate and Indian Corporate Sector

A number of favorable factors have helped to improve the investment climate for the industry and to create considerable optimism on the manufacturing front. "India maintained an upward climb in the global competitiveness by initiating effective policies and programmes."[9] Corporate Sector in India has grown in terms sales volumes and profit volumes. Today Indian Corporates are trying to develop their subsidiaries in foreign countries. Some of the leading companies like Tata and Birla are trying to get the Indian multinational companies in other part of the world. However, Entry barriers adversely affect the investment climate of the state. One of the determinants of the investment climate for an industry is the ease with which the firms are able to enter into the business activities. Some of the step measures implemented by the Government have positively affecting the working and performance of Indian Join stock companies. These measures are as follows:

(*i*) **Dismantling of Industrial Licensing :** Industrial licensing had already been substantially dismantled and during the Tenth Five Year Plan period further measures were taken to pare it down. Drugs and pharmaceuticals including bio technology were delicensed in 2005. At the end of the Tenth Five Year Plan period only the following manufacturing activities needed industrial license:

(*i*) distillation and brewing of alcoholic drinks;

(*ii*) cigars and cigarettes of tobacco and manufactured tobacco substitutes;

(*iii*) electronic aerospace and defence equipment;

(*iv*) specified hazardous chemicals.

(*ii*) **Locational Freedom :** Entrepreneurs are free to select the location for setting up industry. Approval is required from the government for locating an industrial unit within 25 km of the periphery of cities having a population of more than one million according to the 1991 census, provided that is not within an industrial area designated before 24 July, 1991. However, these locational restrictions are not applicable for electronics, computer software, printing industries, and not applicable for electronics, computer software, printing industries, and other non-polluting industries that may be designated from time to time.

(*iii*) **Removal of Reserved Items :** Apart from the licensing restrictions, there are some restrictions arising from certain industries reserved for the public sector and for the small scale sector. Reservation for the public sector and for the small-scale sector. Reservation for the public sector is now very limited, covering only manufacturing involving certain substances relevant for atomic energy (as well as production of atomic energy and provision of railway transport). The list of items reserved for SSIs has been reduced to 114. Larger unit are allowed to manufactures items reserved for the small scale sector only if they undertake an export obligation of 50% of their industrial production.

(*iv*) **Liberalized FDI Policy :** The Foreign Direct Investment (FDI) policy was also successively liberalized during the tenth five year plan. Following a comprehensive review in 2006 it was further liberlised, particularly by allowing FDI under the automatic route for manufacture of industrial explosives and hazardous chemicals and making it easier for new investments by foreign investors who had entered into joint ventures with Indian partners earlier. At the end of the plan period, FDI upto 100% was permitted in all manufacturing activities except where the foreign investor had an existing joint venture/technical collaboration/trademark agreement in the same field of activity.

There are caps on the foreign equity in certain service sectors, viz., 20% on FM radio broadcasting; 26% on insurance, defence production, print and electronic media covering news and current affairs; 49% on air transport services, asset reconstruction companies, cable network, direct to home (DTH), hardware for unlinking, HUB, etc., 51% on single brand retailing of products; and 74% on atomic minerals, private sector banking, telecom services, and the establishment and operations of satellite. FDI is even prohibited in a few other services, viz., retail trading (except single brand product retailing), gambling and betting, lottery, and atomic energy. However, there is no foreign equity cap on any manufacturing activity other than in public sector undertakings (PSUs) for petroleum refining.

(*v*) **Exit Barriers :** Investment climate in the country is also affected by the exit barriers. Perhaps the most important exit barrier relates to Chapter V-B of the Industrial Disputes Act 1947 under which units with more than 100 employees cannot exit an unprofitable enterprise without the consent of the concerned State Government. This consent is often difficult and time consuming to obtain.

The other important exit barriers to the industries in India is the legal provision relating to insolvency, rehabilitation, liquidation, and winding up proceedings, which need to be simplified and be made time bound. The co-publication of the World Bank and the International Finance Corporation (2007) reports that resolving the insolvency cases takes upto 10 years in India against 2.4 years in China, 1.5 years in South Korea, and 3 years in the US. Similarly, the recovery rate of closing business is 13% in India compared to 82% in South Korea.

Policy framework for Public Shareholding in India

The Government of India is trying to increase the minimum public holding in all listed companies – whether government-and privately-owned –in last year's budget 2009-10."[10]

To do this, the government will have to amend the Securities Contract Regulation Rules. Ahead of this, the SEBI has already suggested to the finance ministry that the exercise to increase public shareholding should be phased instead of one time. At present, companies are subject to different public shareholding criteria depending on sector, ownership and share issue size.

For instance, telecom, IT and infrastructure companies and companies that issue a minimum 2 million shares and hold a public offer of at least Rs.100 crore are exempt from the 25% public shareholding requirement. These companies, however, have to ensure a minimum 10 percent non promoter holding during Initial Public Offers (IPOs). Stock exchanges, however have the discretion to exempt state owned corporations from this stipulation. Exempted companies and companies that have 20 million shares outstanding and a market cap above Rs.1,000 crore are required to maintain a minimum 10 percent public shareholding to remain listed. For all other companies, promoters are required to raise the public shareholding to 25% if it falls below that level after an IPO.

However, State owned firms, infrastructure companies and companies referred to Board of Industrial and Financial Reconstruction have been exempted from the continuous listing requirement as well. Sebi's suggestions for a phased increase in public shareholdings stems from representations by investment bankers who have argued that many companies may not need that much capital and that promoters may not want higher floating stocks because that would cap share price appreciation.

Exhibit-2.5
Top ten companies in which the public float is 25%

	Disinvestment	
	in %*	**Rs. crore#**
MMTC	24.33	41470.30
NMDC	23.38	44998.63
Power Fin Corpn.	14.78	4102.75
NTPC	14.50	24222.69
MRPL	13.57	1839.91
Natl. Aluminium	12.15	2865.97
Power Grid Corpn.	11.36	5115.93
SAIL	10.82	9188.45
Reliance Power	9.78	3320.38
Tech Mahnidra	7.97	916.07
Mundra Port	6.04	1550.68
Oracle Fin.Serv.	5.52	1036.39
Wipro	4.61	4435.97
IOCL	3.92	2983.76
DLF	3.64	1896.81
Tata Tele. Mah.	2.73	125.34
Tata Comm	1.15	99.59
Bharat Electron	0.86	135.77
Total		**150305.39**

*The extent to which total promoter holdings need to be reduced to ensure a minimum 25% of public holding

Total amount for disinvestment as per current market cap

At present, out of the top 100 companies listed on the Bombay Stock Exchange and the National Stock Exchange, 18 have a public holding of less than 25%. Ten of these are government-owned companies.

If all these companies were to follow a 25 percent public holding rule, they would collectively have to raise Rs.1,50,000 crore of money for the market at current market price. Given the government's huge disinvestment programme –some 30 state owned firms are scheduled for IPOs- it is unlikely to meet the 25 percent target even in the five year time frame. The practice of having a minimum public holding for listed companies is prevalent globally. Singapore and Hong Kong allow less than 25 percent public holding if the market cap is higher than a certain limit, whereas the UK follows a flat 25 percent norm.

Practice Questions

Objective Type Questions

1. Number of Leading industrialists were signatories of Bombay Plan:
   (*a*) 9 (*b*) 8
   (*c*) 7 (*d*) 6
2. Bombay Plan was based on
   (*a*) Neutral State (*b*) Participative State
   (*c*) Interventionist State (*d*) Cooperative State
3. Bombay Club was became active in:
   (*a*) 1998 (*b*) 1996
   (*c*) 1994 (*d*) 1992
4. Number of Foreign Companies working in India at the end of 2008-09 was
   (*a*) 2903 (*b*) 2803
   (*c*) 2703 (*d*) 2603
5. Minimum Public Float proposed for listing of Public Limited Companies
   (*a*) 10% (*b*) 15%
   (*c*) 20% (*d*) 25%

Ans: 1.(c), 2. (c), 3. (d), 4. (a), 5. (d)

Short Answer Questions

1. What is Bombay Plan?
2. What is Bombay Club?
3. What do you mean by Official Liquidation?
4. What are the functions of Company Law Board?
5. What are the functions that have been assigned to SIFO?

Long Answer Questions

1. "A Journey from Bombay Plan to Bombay Club shows that Indian entrepreneurs are quite active to change the environment in their favour". Do you agree with this statement? Give arguments in support of your answer.
2. Critically examine the present position of Corporate Sector in India.
3. Explain the features of organizational setup of Ministry of Corporate Affairs.
4. Discuss the functions of Competition Commission of India.
5. What do you mean by Investment Climate? How does it influence the working of Indian Corporate Sector?
6. What do you mean by Public Float? Examine its current guidelines.
7. Examine the role of Director General of Investigation and Registration in the working of Joint Stock Companies in India.

References

1. Business Line, Oct.14, 2008, p.7
2. Topalava Petia, Overview of The Indian Corporate Sector, IMF Working Paper WP/04/64, p.4
3. Goyal, S.K, Nature and Growth of the Indian Corporate Sector, Institute for Studies in Industrial Development, New Delhi, 1988, p.4
4. (i) Ministry of Industrial Development & Company Affairs, (Dept. of Company Affairs), Annual Report, 1986-87. (ii) Ministry of Law Justice & Company Affairs, Directory of Joint Stock Companies in India: 1980, Vol.1. Private and Public Limited Companies are grouped together in case of Government Companies.
5. Topalaya. Petia, Op.cit.P5
6. Annual Report 2008-09, Ministry of Corporate Affairs, Government of India, New Delhi, p.44
7. Ibid-p-6
8. Ibid.p.8
9. Eleventh Five Year Plan 2007-12, Volume III, Planning Commission of India, p.144-145
10. Business Standard. Feb. 15,2010, p.1

3 PROFESSIONAL MANAGEMENT

Management of a business enterprise is largely a function of environment in which enterprise is required to work. Family background of promoters, level of competition in the industry, regulatory framework of business, level of technical and business education in the country, ethos and values set for business are some of the determinants of management perspectives of business in the country. Earlier, Indian business scene was dominated by the traditional managers. Family members, relatives and friends of managing agency were the beneficiaries of managerial positions. To some extent, this system is still continuing in Indian business houses for the sake of promoter's own interest or grooming of next generation for the highest job. The wide growth of professional management as a career in the present form is entirely a post-war phenomenon. Before the Second World War, opportunities for Indian managers were quite limited and even not available in British owned commerce and industrial organizations. The Indian business houses generally reserved their important managerial positions for the family members of their promoters. The best Indian talents had no option except to join the administrative services of the government, law, medicine, pure research and teaching. Whatever prospects were available, they were limited to engineering students and that too in the Government public works department and ordnance factories. However, inadequate supply of engineering students from the limited number of engineering colleges at that time made the situation worst in these government departments. Business in India was not honoured in society by tradition. However, the foundation of organized business in the popular form of corporate entity in Indian context was laid down quite early. "On 31st December 1600, a Royal charter was granted to the company of Merchants of London trading into the Indies. The name was given to the company as the East India Company. The company began with 218 members and was governed by a Court of Directors although the directors were referred to rather confusingly as committee."[1]

It is important to note that the recruitment standards in business organizations were mostly based on non-academic qualities. Good academic performance of the candidate had no weight in their recruitment process. With the result, average Indian middle class youths having good academic degree but without good connectivity failed to get entry in these business organizations. It had created a renewed phase of frustration and bitter resentments among the middle class youths towards business. Degree and diploma holders were very badly handicapped in getting placement in industry and commerce. They were severely discriminated against in favour of the management trainees of the firms-raw graduates who had been trained in the practical operation of the firm, but knew nothing of the academic background of practical exposure in particular area.

It was not long before the wind of change began to blow in the Indian context. The industries started taking shape from the background of commerce oriented entities. It is universal fact that business is a risky phenomenon and it needs competent, skilled and trained management personnel to overcome the problem of risk. In the pre-independence scenario, due to short supply, engineers and accountants belonged to a class whose recruitment was by and large guided by considerations of qualifications and competence rather than of connections. Inspite of this supply demand mis-match "they were suffered for their specialization but generally confined to technical roles; very few made the grade to general management unless there were other incidental considerations similar to those which guided the selection of non-technical staff. With the emphasis on industry for national progress and the quickening of the pace of industrial growth in the country, and the expense and difficulty of getting good expatriates, the shortage of technical management staff became so acute that jobs began to be available to the increasing numbers of engineering graduated from simple middle class family circles, at salaries far higher than their parents had expected when they sent their sons to engineering colleges. The success of these men in their own spheres of management encouraged industries to look again at qualifications for entrance. In this, they were also influenced by the fact that managing agencies were still able to attract the limited output of the few public schools, Oxbridge returned candidates, and the sons of ICS officers. Candidates from this category usually sought jobs in a single purpose industrial organization only when a reputed managing agency failed to make available covenanted job."[2] Thus, it is quite true that older established trading houses had given more emphasis on connectivity in selection of candidates but they tried their level best to ensure a tradeoff between connectivity and competency of persons available for the job.

Emergence of Professional Management

"Industrialisation in India began with the first textile mills of Bombay and Ahmedabad. Their first technicians and even the women workers came from England, but gradually they were replaced by Indians. As the industry prospered, it developed further into chains of textile units, and later, in this century, it began to diversify in Bombay. The first example of diversification in India must have been that of Tatas, and much later, in the north that of Delhi Cloth Mills, whereas, the British and-the European companies got their managers from outside, the Indian companies always took them from their families. Professionalism in Indian Management began in the middle thirties when the British companies started to take in young Indian graduates from Oxford and Cambridge, well connected, as a concession to influence and growing aspirations.

In our Indian family companies there were very few truly professional managers. They took in technical people, but for general management they mostly relied upon their family members, brother, sons, nephews, cousins and distant relations, and, when they ran out of them, men of their caste and religion."[3]

The greatest revolution in the era of professional management in India started quite late specially in the mid 1950s when it became abundantly clear that industry had forged ahead and its systematic development was to be made only with competent manager having professional outlook. Change in technology demand for quality product and increasing risk perception etc forced the entrepreneurs to become more flexible towards professionals. At the same time, the wave of management education originating in Britain and America reached India due to favourable change in Indian business environment. Expatriates and Indians returning from Harvard or Henley had also started to join leading multinational companies working in India." This saw the growth of management associations in major cities and the laying of foundation of management education courses. Even in the established organizations of trade and commerce, the managing agencies, started to take active interest in management education and began to revise the values looked for in applications for managerial positions. The opening of this new channel of employment created tremendous impetus to seek jobs in industry. Families, which for generations had looked at law, medicine, teaching and government for careers, suddenly found their sons joining industry at salaries which did not quite fit it with the notation of clerks which was all they associated with employment in the private sector. There was a scramble from graduates- for admission as trainees."[4] Thus, there was a drastic change in the perception of society towards business which was expected to survive through professional managers.

It is a fact that business requires instinct and heredity but it also necessarily requires knowledge and intellect. Values responsible for success in business are entirely different from social values. So it is the job of education policy to open and enrich the mind of society about the importance of economic operations in nation's progress. It empowers the dynamic elements of society to look upon business and industry as a worthwhile area of pursuit for mental satisfaction.

An education system should also play its active role in motivating the vital factors of society to ensure for profitable use of resources. Keeping the emerging role of professional education in mind, the Government of India had taken initiative to establish Indian Institute of Management, Indian Institute of Technology and National Institute of Technology to produce professionals for the Indian Industry and Commerce. It is really a major contribution of the Government of India to make the country a truly modern India. The Government of India through its professional education policy provides a deeply embedded incentive to the children of working class people, farmers or clerks to succeed in business, as a professional manager. Now Indian middle class is the biggest supplier of talent to the different segments of economic and social development. It is also the biggest gainer of growing professionalism in Indian Commerce and Industry.

Nature of a Profession

The terms 'profession' and 'professional' are used in many different senses. Some of them are not relevant in the present context. The simple meaning of the word professional is a person who engages himself in sporting, artistic or some other leisurely activity for earning money rather than for merely enjoying it as a hobby. In this sense, it distinguishes a professional from an amateur. Similarly, in common parlance, the word profession is often used to denote a paid occupation, job or career. But the profession in the present environment is not to earn its livelihood. Profession has its own systems, approaches, processes and procedures for a set of objectives and behaviour. Profession has to integrate certain distinctive sociological and ethical attributes.

According to Professor A.M. Carr Sounders, 'a profession may be defined as an occupation, based upon specialized intellectual study and training, the purpose of which is to supply skilled service or advice to others for a definite fee or salary." Professional work is never viewed solely as a means to an end; it is the end itself. For the professional, his work becomes his life. The following are the main attributes of a profession: (a) body of systematized knowledge imparted to its members; (b) intellectual skills; (c) high degree of intellectual integrity; (d) a spirit of service and concern for social values; (e) regulated entry into the profession; (t) loyalty to institutions, which controls the admission, discipline and removal from the professional association on account of indiscipline or misconduct.

"Professionals" can be described as those who are fulfilling following criteria: (a) members of a profession possessed specialized knowledge or skill; (b) they hold themselves to higher ethical standards than other members of society; (c) they are self governing in the sense that they regulate entrance into the profession, monitor the performance of members, and expel those who violated their responsibilities; (d) they provide important benefits to society; and (e) they are accorded certain rights and privileges ordinarily denied to other occupational groups.

Attributes of a Profession

Attributes of a profession are as follows:[5]

1. Systematic body of theory : Every profession has a distinct body of organized theoretical knowledge and certain practical skills associated with it. Practical skill is nothing but it is an implementation process of theoretical knowledge. The practical skill flows out of the theory. Therefore, to have thoroughness in theoretical knowledge, one has first to learn the theory through adequate academic training. It constitutes two segments; theoretical training in conceptual framework of particular profession and practical training to test the conceptual knowledge attained during the process of theoretical training. It is the major difference between professional skills like those of surgeon and non-professional skills like that of brick laying. Here lies the role for Universities and Institutes who are required to certify their theoretical knowledge by issuing degrees, diplomas and certificates. Acquiring theoretical knowledge is intellectually more demanding than learning operational procedures and practical skills of a trade. The theory of rotating electricity machines is quite tough academic activity in comparison to learning process required for repair work of an electric motor. Due to this reason admission standards for entry into professional courses at the university/ institute level are made quite rigorous.

Theoretical knowledge of professional subjects is developed through academic study and research. Theoretical and practical development ensure advance professional knowledge among the persons who have got the admission in a particular profession. Change in thinking, perception, outlook is also the result of theoretical and practical training. Advancement in these areas creates newer areas of specialization and super-specialization, and it also requires higher levels of academic training. Professionals are required to continuously update their knowledge and skills to maintain their competence and effectiveness as per the change available in environment of a particular profession.

2. Professional authority: Professionals acquire a kind of authority through their specialized knowledge, skills and experience, continuous upgradation of knowledge, skills and exposure in the relevant field make the professional to exercise his authority in serving the cause of clients in a better way. Professional authority enables the professionals to provide effective solutions to the clients problems. Professionals are in a better position to easily analyse the causes and effects of a problem and they can establish relationship between the two. The clients have little knowledge as to what would be the best remedy for their problem. They cannot evaluate the implications and consequences of adopting different courses of actions, and have to be depend upon the professionals for necessary guidance and advice. Theoretical knowledge and training enable the professionals to evaluate the problem in proper context. Skill and experiences also help the professionals to solve the problem of clients in more methodological way. Thus, the client has to have trust and faith in the services being provided by the professionals. Actually trust and faith of clients create moral obligations on the part of professionals and it is their duty to help the clients. Duty bound professionals can win the confidence of their clients. If professionals are using their professional authority and trust to exploit the clients for personal gains, it means they are not following their ethical code and in that case they are following the worst kind of professional immorality.

3. Sanction of the community: Professionals are the part of the society. All professions are social constructs. Operation, growth, and importance of professions are guided by community sanction. It provides social acceptability to the professions. This sanction is given because the professions serve the society and satisfy some indispensable social needs. It also helps in realizing certain values which are cherished by the society. At present, due to societal approval, Central Government as well as State Governments have power to regulate the different kinds of professions in the country. Keeping social acceptability in mind, separate enactment is generally made by the government to provide necessary structure and framework for the operation of particular profession. Protection of different stakeholders by the profession is the ultimate objective of these enactments. Legal profession helps in ensuring justice to the society. Medical profession serves the society by relieving its suffering from diseases and by promoting good health. Engineering profession creates, develops and maintain infrastructure for material prosperity, conveniences and comforts of society at large. Service- motivation is a key element of the professional ethos and values. It is on this account that society treats these professionals with greater respect, accords a higher status, and ensures better payments in comparison to non- professionals. The community grants them considerable autonomy to regulate and manage their professions. In this process, professional bodies have a large say in deciding the entrance requirements and setting education standards. Some professional bodies like The Institute of Chartered Accountants of India, The Institute of Cost and Work Accountants of India, The Institute of Company Secretaries of India, The Medical Council of India and The Bar Council of India, issue certificate of practice without which one cannot practice. These certificates have legal validity. The community shows its sanction by conferring several powers and privileges to the professionals. One of them is protection of confidentiality of the communication between practitioners and their clients. It is treated as a privilleged communication and has legal protection. Another is the respect for professional judgement on technical matters affecting the life of the community. Public policies generally empower the professionals to play their regulatory role in their relevant field without fear and pressure.

4. Regulative code of ethics : Code of ethics regulates the professional behaviour. It is a set of rules mandatory for the professionals to follow in their actual practice. Sometimes, individual professional may lose sight of his professional ideas and values on account of personal gain, or of expediency. Professionals may also misuse their professional authority and privileges to the detriment of their clients, or of the society at large. Such unscrupulous acts of professionals lower the dignity and prestige of the profession concerned. Thus, all professions are required to evolve codes of ethics for regulating their member's professional practices and conducts. Formulation of codes of conducts in writing ensures an expected behaviour on the part of professionals. Underwritten conventions also guide the professionals in fulfilling their professional responsibilities. These code of conducts remind the members about their professional duties and obligations. The provisions of the codes also give guidelines for resolving situations of moral conflicts. With the help of codes, profession communicates its ethical concerns for society at large. It is in a form of commitment to the public and helps them to know the level and the quality of service they should expect from the professionals. The codes of conducts are expected to create a climate of trust between the profession and the general public. Existence of codes of professional ethics improves social esteem of the profession. Default in adherence of codes attracts social and legal action against the professionals.

5. The professional culture : Level of academic attainment, in-depth exposure in practice, level of adherence to code of conducts etc are some of the important factors which decide the nature of professional culture. Cohesiveness among the members is the most important testing criteria for a particular profession. Thus, every profession develops a special kind of group culture, which plays an important role in professional life. Professional culture shapes the image of the profession. One component of the professional culture is the value and importance of the profession. Professionals are required to provide valuable but specific service to the society, without which the quality of life would be adversely affected. They are supposed to have a sense of belonging to an honourable and dignified professional group. This sense of belonging, together with the sense of professional power, provides a strong cohesive force to the members of the profession. It serves a number of functions: (a) as a platform for sharing technical advances in the field; (b) for discussing matters of common interest to the profession; (c) for raising collective voice to influence the government policies, (d) for resolving intra-professional services, and (e) for formulating and enforcing code of professional ethics.

Determinants of Professional Management

Determinants of Professional management are as follows:

1. Level of Global integration : Global communication process ensures success of a business today. Now Political boundary is meaningless. The geographical distances of the world have been considerably shrunk and all commercial organizations are concerned with what happens elsewhere. One part of the globe is now ready to serve the purpose of other part of the world. Migration; cultural integration, level of skill development, competitiveness, merger and acquisition decide the level of competency of professional managers. So level of global integration affect the quality of professional management.

2. Emerging Role of Knowledge Workers : Acceptability of knowledge workers as a separate class is growing fastly. Growing pace for business and technical institutions have ensured an effective structure for professional courses in the country. At present, these institutions are the biggest suppliers of professionals. These professionals provide tools, techniques, process and procedures for effective operation of a business. Knowledge workers are an important ingredient of professional management.

3. Technology Upgradation : Advancement of technology provides a dynamic culture to the management. Integrated production behaviour, cost effectiveness and large scale production are the direct result of technology upgradation. It helps in formulating and understanding of implications, design, process, system and procedures of production and service behaviour of business organization. Larger the requirement of technological base, larger the need of professional managers in the business organizations. It also helps in application of professional management.

4. Change in Labour Behaviour : Growth and shift in labour force also determine the efficacy of professional management. Improvement in level of education, increase in support system for skill development and need to have a growth in career have change the whole structure of labour growth. Present labour force is guided by the need of achievement. There is need for motivation and support system to retain them. This can be done only by professional managers.

5. Level of Competitiveness : Competitiveness is the philosophy of global economy. Indian economy is now part of global economy. Competitiveness encourages the professional managers to manage the business organizations by ensuring cost effectiveness, core competency, and optimization in production and service behaviour. More and more companies are professionalizing their management to remain in their business for a long period.

Nature of Professional Management

"Nature of a particular discipline is generally defined in terms of scientific orientation and practical application. In this sense, "the management is defined as a science and its practice as a profession"[6]: So practice is the basic character of the professional management. Actually, theory develops analytical base for the management. It inculcates the scientific temper and ethos among the managers. Practice provides testing ground for the theoretical aspects of professional management. Managers are required to apply their theoretical knowledge in their functional behaviour.

"Professional in management today is one who has trained his mind in a manner that uses all available evidences and tools with a scientific outlook to narrow down the risks of decision making for the present and for the future, to sense the direction in which today's efforts must be made, to reap the benefits of tomorrow's development; to appreciate that today's nobody can make a success of his business in isolation either from public at large or from those whose livelihood depends on the business. The professional manager is not incidentally in business, he is there because he feels he has earned the right through a deliberate choice of career, through acquisition of knowledge and a training of mind which success in business will demand from one who has no stake in the capital."[7]

Thus, the professional manager is required to have theoretical knowledge and training in management and should also be inclined to have management as a career. He must know the difference between the risk bearing and risk taking phenomenon. Owners or shareholders are the risk bearers. Professional managers are the risk takers and ultimately they have to transfer this risk to the owners/shareholders. They do not have any interest in the capital and due to this reason they have to be neutral to the capital. "Professionals involvement comes from the pride and values of their profession and not from the ownership."[8] As a professional manager they are expected to serve the purpose of stake holders - shareholders, fellow managers, employees, society, government and other parties who have stake in the business. They must show their commitments to all and remain neutral to all. Professionals are required to serves the objectives of these stakeholders for which he has been appointed or hired. They are there to serve the purpose of a specific stakeholders but at the same time not at the cost of other stakeholders. Commitment and neutrality are the two important components of professional practice and these components are the backbone of codes of conduct generally prescribed for professionals.

Thus, a professional manager is one who has made his profession to manage resources in the interest of stakeholders. A separate body of knowledge is necessary to assist the management practitioner in achieving professional competence. That is called as professional management.

Definition of a Professional Manager

The task of identifying a professional manager was undertaken, for the first time, by the High Powered Expert Committee on simplification of the Companies Act, 1956 and the MRTP Act, 1969. This Committee was headed by Justice Rajendra Sachar. The Sachar Committee was appointed by the Government of India in June 1997. The Committee stated that some of the provisions of the Companies Act have proved to be ineffective to meet the present day needs of corporate management and administration. Hence, professionalisation of corporate management is the only alternative to achieve the objectives of a corporate entity.

Looking to the wide gap between the control and ownership on one hand and the management and ownership on the other, the Committee expressed the view that professionalisation of management is not a mere concept but, in fact, is an inevitable necessity for the wellbeing of the company itself. In suggesting a definition of "Professional Manager", the Committee in its Report observed that-[9] "A professional Manager is an individual who :

(*a*) belongs to the profession of law, accountancy, medicine, engineering or architecture; or

(*b*) is a member of a recognized professional body or institution, exercising supervisory jurisdiction over its members; or is a holder of a degree or diploma in management from any recognized institute of management or from any recognized university; or

(*c*) is a holder of a post- graduate degree from any recognized university (i) and possesses not less than five years experience in an executive capacity in a company, corporation or a body corporate or in the Government or (ii) posses minimum of ten years experience in an executive capacity in a company, corporation or a body corporate or in the Government."

In suggesting a definition of a professional manager, the Committee accorded equal weightage to qualification and experience. In doing so, the Committee observed. It has been pointed out to us that "professional approach to management is something which does not necessarily follow from the possession of certain professional qualifications, and that instances are not rare where such professional approach to management has been developed and applied by people not necessarily having professional qualification but having considerable experience in a particular field of corporate management. We are accordingly, suggesting definition of Professional Manager which takes into account the elements of specialized knowledge as well as specialized experience."[10] Survey also suggest that majority of chief executives of business enterprises did not have any formal professional degree but due to their long experience in their field made them successful managers in the corporate world.

Rationale of professional Management

Rationale of professional management are as follows :

1. Growing Space for Technology : Demand for professional managers arises due to growing integration of technology with business operations. The complexity of the technology accelerate the obsolescence rates in industries and it is imperative for the business to protect its future with the help of technological advances and innovations. Growing need of huge investment in technology and its products necessitated the appointment of professional managers in business organizations.

2. Growing Opportunities for Business : Proliferation of opportunities for business eroded the base of hereditary businessman's near monopoly in managerial appointments and opened the floodgates for knowledge workers to work as human relations specialist and the trained financial manager. Expansion and diversification strategies and need for core competency actually forced the business organizations to appoint professional managers. In present era, first generation entrepreneurs are also doing well and they have tested the benefits of appointing professional managers.

3. Need to Work as a Change Agent : During the last four to five decades the centuries old character of business has been changed. Decision making process, Compliance and reporting practices and other regulatory requirements have necessitated the appointment of professional managers in joint stock companies. Now they have to be consciously professional because they have no inherited instinct, which will be to their natural aid. Performance of managers largely depends on the success of environmental management. They are in the demand due to their ability to manage the prevailing environment in a better way. Secondly, being the product of a technological culture he able to integrate the applications of Science in evaluating options or looking at the crystal ball of the future.

4. Growing Demand for Environmental Training: There are large number of people who have the unnatural gift of possessing, qualities of judgements, but the demand and price for success are generally determined by the level of formal training in the environment in which managers are supposed to work and give the best possible results. The professionals are trained to systematically evaluate and assess the scope and limitations of every dimension of the problem. Science-based training tempered with a thorough knowledge help the managers to solve the problems in proper manner.

5. Intellectual Behaviour : Nature and scope of profession are always changing. But the basic theme of professional management is that it is governed by the human intellectual behaviour in business organization. Business performance is solely regulated by the manager's intellectual skills. So now each and every segment of business needs support of professional managers.

"The Ecclesiastical, the Medical and the Legal professions which are the traditional liberal professionals, cannot be the only profession for all the time and that with the change of time and expansion of spheres of human activity requiring specialization and expertise, more professions are bound to come up. But it order to qualify for being reckoned as liberal professional, a profession has to satisfy certain conditions, viz that the activity carried on by it must not be an activity of a commercial nature as a trade or business. The main asset of the professional man which he brings into the practice of his profession must be intellectual skill or manual skill controlled by intellectual behaviour. Apart from the skill, there should be a degree of intelligence and integrity and above all the professional man should be member of an organized profession for admission to which high academic or professional qualifications are required and the professional organization controls the admission to, the discipline in and removal from the profession on account of acts of indiscipline or misconduct. There must also be a code of professional ethics and in addition there must be a judicial remedy against exclusion from the profession on account of indiscipline or misconduct by the professional organizations II." The theoretical and practical skills helps the managers to shine their intellectual behaviour. Similarly, professional associations also help the professional system to work properly because they regulate the entry, training and development and discipline of professional managers. These professional associations are working as coordinating between the Government and Professionals and playing important role in the formulation of policies affecting the society at large.

Thus, in the present scenario professional management is the only way out to solve the problems of business organizations.

Requirements of Professional Manager

Following are the requirements of professional managers:

1. Formal Training in Profession : He should be innovative and must be able to enrich his professional skill with the help of science and technology. A manager should have formal training in his profession. A professional in management today is one who has trained his mind in a manner that uses available evidences and tools in a scientific manner. He must be able to narrow down the risks of decision making process. Decisions should not be based on hunches as in the case of traditional management. Decisions are to be taken on the basis of his professional knowledge, experience and experiments. If he is not professionally trained, he cannot take all these decisions and cannot understand the problems and intricacies of management which arise in - day-today activities of the business organizations.

2. Technological Background : He should be a product of modern technological culture: He should try to attain the knowledge of changes, innovations and inventions in his field of profession. It is the commitment of the professional manager to familiarize these changes and their implications with the public at large. At the same time, he should also be a computers savvy, as it is necessary tool of modern management. It is also a powerful tool to eliminate the various variables confronting professional managers in their decision- making process.

3. Sound Leadership Qualities : He must have sound leadership qualities to develop an effective organizational structure of the company. He should act as a leader of the team for achieving the desired goal of the organization. He should be effective in solving the organizational problems through his own knowledge, skill and experiences. He should be familiar with the techniques required in solving the various problems that arise in the organization such as labour strikes, lockout, labour unrest etc. Coordination and cooperation are the guiding principles of modern management techniques. Manager must always try to control the mutual conflicts of entire work force with the help of his leadership qualities.

4. Change agent : He should have environmental familiarity and unity. He should be able to adjust himself with changing environment. Professional qualification, conceptual clarity and skill enable the manager to use the process of environmental analysis in an effective way. Environmental analysis helps in strategy formulation. Discussion and mutual consultations with senior managers provide a clue to solve the immediate problems. It also encourages mutual cohesiveness in the organization. He should know that nobody can make or attain success without making necessary adjustments in the organization as per the requirement of environmental changes. As a professional manager, he should act as a change agent to incorporate required changes in policy and programmes of the organization so that he can reach to viable performance.

5. Societal Commitments : Business organizations are the product of society at large. So organizations are required to fulfill the expectations of society. This can be done only when managers understand the emotions of society. So he should be a product of social culture.

He should realize the, concept of culture of the society and implement it strictly in his decision making process. Behaviour of manager must be according to the needs of the society and he should also respect the value of society. Aspirations of consumers and labour are different but can be balanced by managers through his professional approach. He should not be guided solely by the principle of wealth creation in favour of shareholders but also by sharing of wealth with larger sections of society. Thus, he should give due attention to his social responsibility and fulfill the interests of different stakeholders.

6. Skill and Knowledge Based Orientation : Managers should be equipped with knowledge and skill. Professionals exercise power and authority but they also need to apply knowledge and skills as per the situational requirements. Professionals are required to observe the following criteria in their behaviour: (i) greater the power and authority exercised, greater is the need to observe professional code of conduct and ethics; (ii) greater is the need to be vigilant towards those who are affected by the exercise of power and authority; (iii) greater the aspirations of clients greater is the need to observe professional ethics and etiquette in dealing with the clients.

7. Professionalism in Decision Making : "Leadership is to be backed by Professional approach. Society should be professionally managed as it will provide professionally trained and matured political leadership. Professionalism gives those view-points that benefit of being backed by discipline and training; the two combined are likely to get the best decision. If in a family business, you have professional engineers, accountants and marketers, but all decision-making is centralized at top, with the head of the family, who has no professionalism but perhaps only experience and intuition, the decisions are not likely to be as good as that of a modern professional board."[12]

Management as a Profession in India

There is a growing controversy in India that whether management graduates opting for managerial career are professionals or they are just other graduates. Can a person who makes his managerial career be called professional? Meanwhile, the young graduates coming out from various universities, technological institutes and Institutes of management studies are assuming a professional status. In India, there is marked difference between traditional manager and the professional manager. "Typically, the traditional manager was either an owner or manager or in some way related with the owner - manager. The professional manager, on the other hand, occupies a managerial position mainly by virtue of his professional qualification, training, and ability. Owner - manager or his relatives do not have to be any less able than the professional manager. But the main difference between the two is the presence or absence of formal training in management."[13] He should be trained in the theory and practice of professional concerned. By now, there is a consensus on the following attributes which enable an occupation to be treated as profession.

1. Formal training in theory and its practices : This is the most critical requirement for a profession. Formal Training in theory enables the persons to have a thorough knowledge about the particular discipline. Similarly, it also provides exposure to the person about the working of a particular organization where he is working. Formal training in management has been known and conducted in the western countries, particularly in U.S.A for many decades but it started in India in a big way only five decades ago. Until that time, the managers were persons who belonged to the family of the owner-managers or who rose to top positions through on-the - job experience and hard work. Thus, the old generation of managers in India did not meet this requirement of professional status because they were lacking formal training in theory and its practices. Actually, it distinguishes them from the young mangers of today. But long experience and exposure in industries enable them to claim a professional status. Long experience and exposures also serve and help in the development of management theories.

2. Formal Membership of a Professional Association : Formal training in theory and practice in a particular profession enables the person to have a platform for his relationship with the profession. Membership of ill association ensures professional relationship among individual members. In words of Sounders Carr and Wilson, "Just as member of families in a primitive society do not form a state, so number of men though they perform similar functions do not make a profession if they remain in isolation. A profession can only be said to exist when there are fonds between the practitioners and these fonds can take up the shape of formal association."[14] While most of the trades or an occupation (which are today called professions) exists in ancient time, the major point that differentiates profession from the earlier occupations is the formal organization (in the shape of professional association) found in the modern profession.

The development of a profession therefore depends upon the existence of large body of experts held together by fonds. A Professional association helps its members in following way: (i) A formal professional organization protects the practitioners and their interest from the controls of the "lay public". At the same time, it also protects the public against the "menace of quacks" trying to pass for experts. (ii) A professional organization is an agency for the socialization of new entrants to the profession. (iii) It also helps its members in internalizing with standards of ethical behaviour. (iv) A formal organization can also expect from its members allegiance to its code of ethics. (v) A professional organization provides a framework and sanctions for the complex of obligations and responsibilities that its members have to undertake.

3. A code of ethics : Foundation of a professional life rests with the moral behaviour of members. Therefore, it is necessary that each profession should have a common code of ethical behaviour for its members. Formulation of code of ethics generally rests with the professional association concerned. Sometimes, code of ethics is already provisioned in the enactment by which specific profession is to regulated in the country. Professional association is also required to enforce its code of ethics through legal or semi-legal agencies. Effectiveness of professional association largely depends on the disciplined behaviour of its members. Regular meeting of the members, election, democratic behaviour, awareness programme, well defined code of conducts, monitoring and compliance etc are some of the important factors which creates effective environment for the implementation of code of conduct. Membership of a profession provides security and prestige to a person and at the sametime; it also makes certain demands from him such as conformity to the prescribed common code of behaviour.

Criteria for the Status of a Profession

Following criteria are helpful in providing status of a profession :

1. Availabilitv of Safety Net : A code of ethics provide a safety net to the clients. "The typical client who buys professional service is not in a position to judge its qualities for himself. Therefore, he must rely on the reputation of the individuals professionals as well as the standards of conduct maintained by the professional as a whole."[15] Code of ethics is generally mandatory in nature and members cannot, misuse their power and privileges in dealing with clients.

2. Professional Prestige : A particular profession is meant for service to society at large. Mission and vision of a profession are to be defined in terms of societal perspective. Members of a profession are just active human being to enlarge the scope of a profession. Contribution being made by the members actually bring appreciation and prestige for the profession itself. Conformity to ethical behaviour brings appreciation and prestige for the fellow members of a particular professional association. Non exploitation of clients (even when there is scope to do so) is considered an act of "self denial" which adds to the reputation and prestige of the entire profession.

The professionals which are at the top of the occupational hierarchy are known for their altruism. Actually members are required to follow the principle of "service before self."

3. Quality of Professional Service : The "gate keeper" role of practitioners also determines the status of a profession in the country. Generally, the client is unable to judge the quality of professional service for himself. He is entirely dependent on the service and intellectual skill of the professional experts. Thus, the Professionals are required to satisfy the expectations of their clients even at their personal losses or costs. "The physician is therefore seen as an "angel" who relieves pain, the lawyers guards the freedom and rights of the individual when they are threatened by the clergy. Man holds the key to open the gates of heaven and a teacher with his torch of knowledge illuminates the shady and dark corners of human ignorance."[16] Level of satisfaction of clients and status of a profession is directly related to each other.

4. Effective control of Professional body or Association : Formal organization of a profession exercises control over the entrance to professional schools as well as the training given to the candidates and the behaviour of individuals after they enter the profession. A profession that lacks such controls mechanism cannot be expected to have common standards of professional behaviour. The profession is expected to ensure its (commitment) to the principle of "service before self."

5. Level of Knowledge Enrichment Programme : A profession enjoys prestige through its professional organization that it has developed. Level of prestige is directly linked with the success of associations or relevant council in ensuring disciplined behaviour and knowledge enrichment programme among its members. Thus, the various organizations like All India Management Association. Institute of Chartered Accountants of India, Institute of Chartered Secretaries of India, Institute of Cost and Works Accountants of India, Medical Council of India, Bar Council of India, Institutions of Engineers etc. are regulating the behaviour of their members.

Keeping the above factors in mind, we can say that the management in India is a profession. The Young Managers coming out from professional and technical institutions and departments of engineering and technology and management studies of different universities may have a slight edge over their older counter parts with regards to their formal training. However, training alone does not bestow professional status to an occupational group. As long as these managers function in relative isolation and have not developed common fonds through a formal all India organization, there is no difference between them and other non professional groups.

Suggestive Framework

Following steps are required to be implemented to make the professional management in India more effective and viable:

1. National Ethos : The managers in business must be proud that they have been given opportunities to serve India in a vital sphere of industrial development. The manager is required to work as an instrument of corporate development. He should be equally proud of contribution to a national cause of economic development, which is the greatest priority in the country today.

2. Professional Approach : Managers must show a distinct professionalism in their behaviour. They should make efforts to improve the image of their organizations in the eye of public at large. They are supposed to ensure healthy nourishment to national life. Every organization has to do its best to create a favourable climate for its members without which economic development in a competitive economy is not possible.

3. Expert in the Field: Individual manager should act as a 'truly professional manager'. Public relations activities of the manager should be excellent in the sphere of management and he should command a fair vocabulary of modern managerial language. As a professional manager he has to play his regulatory, promotional and participative role in the organization where he is serving.

4. Accountable to Society : Managers are required to work for the society. They should be socially accountable for their behaviour. Now the concept of stockholders is changed to stakeholders. It is quite true that he has been appointed by the owners/shareholders in the organization and he has to maximize the wealth of shareholders. But at the same time, he is also required to serve the interest of different stakeholders who have their own stakes in the organization.

5. Practical Orientation : Managers needs conceptual and practical orientation. However, in practice, budding managers have to be to meet the resistance of cultural patterns and heritage. "They have to be made to realize that whatever they have learnt will be resisted in the application as being irrelevent; and yet the management concepts they have been taught are basic and unless they are applied no organization will propose."[17]

6. Dynamic Behaviour : Managers are required to breed professionalism in their organizations. They are the change agent and they should ensure implementation of necessary changes as per the symptoms available in the business environment. Professional managers provide dynamism to the working behaviour of an organization. "Our younger managers are changes agents and have to be trained not only how to introduce change but also how to meet the challenges that may be offered to change. Everybody wants change without a price. Management education has to teach change in all its aspects."[18]

7. Academic and Industry Coordination : Managers need to establish a dialogue between industry and the universities, the research institutions and other organizations which influence the minds of tomorrow's budding managers. Professional managers are required to implement the discoveries or innovations made by the universities laboratories. Fundamental discoveries or research achievements of universities and research organizations are to be tested and incorporated in the production system of industrial organizations. It will aid and accelerate the pace of economic development of the country.

8. Competitive Behaviour : The job of a managers is have to ensure effective utilization of resources at their command. Cost competitiveness enables the managers to make their organization viable and vibrant. In practice only viable organizations are successful in implementation of expansion and diversification strategies. The professional manager should not only be adequately equipped with the knowledge of the subject concerned but should also strive to search for and apply new knowledge in their functional behaviour.

Now, the orientation of professional management is shifted from 'responsibility to capital" to responsibility to stakeholders. Management is a distinct and leading group in industrial and commercial society. In the changed scenario, professionals have been assigned a crucial role in a dynamic environment.

PROFESSIONAL EDUCATION IN INDIA

Professional education plays a vital role in human resource development of the country by creating skilled manpower, enhancing industrial productivity and improving the quality of life. There are two important dimensions of professional management Technical education and specific professional education. Technical education covers courses and programmes in engineering, technology, management, architecture, town planning, pharmacy, applied arts & crafts, hotel management and catering technology. All India Council for Technical Education is the regulatory agency for these courses in the country. Specific professional education deals with medical, legal, Accounting etc. These professions are being regulated by different enactments.

The technical education system in the country can be broadly classified into three categories, viz. Central Government funded institutions, State Government/State-funded institutions & Self financed institutions. In 2008-09 there were 63 centrally funded institutions in the country. The 63 centrally funded institutes of technical & science education are as follows:[19]

Centrally Funded Institutions	Number of Institutions
Indian Institutes of Technology (IITs)	13
Indian Institutes of Management (IIMs)	7
Indian Institute of Science (IISc.)	1
Indian Institutes of Science Education & Research (IISERs)	5
National Institutes of Technology (NITs)	20
Indian Institutes of Information Technology (IIITs)	4
National Institutes of Technical Teachers Training and Research (NITTTRs)	4
Others	
Schools of Planning & Architecture (SPAs)	3
Indian School of Mine University (ISMU)	1
North-East Regional Institute of Science & Technology (NERIST)	1
National Institute of Industrial Engineering (NITIE)	1
National Institute of Foundry & Forge Technology (NIFFT)	1
Sant Longowal Institute of Engineering & Technology (SLIET)	1
Central Institute of Technology (CIT)	1
Total	**63**

There are four Boards of Apprenticeship Training (BOATs).

The Central Government is also implementing the following schemes, programmes :

(i) Technical Education Quality Improvement Programme (TEQIP) assisted by the World Bank.

(ii) National Programme for Earthquake Engineering Education (NPEEE).

(iii) Indian National Digital Library for Science & Technology (INDEST).

(iv) Technology Development Mission.

(v) NPTEL.

Promotion of R&D efforts, improvement in employability of trained graduates and postgraduates coming out of the technical institutes, are some of the areas where efforts are required. In 2008-09, several new measures were taken to implement the Government's vision of providing increased access with equity and excellence. The setting up of new Indian Institutes of Technology (IITs), Indian Institutes of Management (IIMs), Indian Institutes for Science Education & Research (IISERs), assisting the State Governments for the establishment of new polytechnics and the initiation of the process for setting up of Indian Institutes of Information Technology (IIITs) and National Institutes of Technology (NITs) are steps in this direction. The centrally funded technical institutions have also started implementing the OBCs reservation in admissions as envisaged under the Central Educational Institutions (Reservations in Admission) Act, 2006 from the year 2008-09.

National Level Councils

1. All India Council for Technical Education (AICTE). The All India Council for Technical Education (AICTE) was set up in 1945 and later on in 1987 given statutory status by an Act of Parliament. The AICTE has its headquarters in New Delhi and eight regional offices located at Kolkata, Chennai, Kanpur, Mumbai, Chandigarh, Bhopal, Bangalore and Hyderabad. The Council discharges its functions through a 21 member Executive Committee. In accordance with the functions assigned to it under Clause 10(k) of the AICTE Act, the Council grants approvals for starting new technical institutions and for introducing new courses or programmes in approved institutions. Approvals are accorded in consultation with respective state Governments and affiliating universities.

The Council is assisted by 10 Statutory Boards of Studies, namely, DG Studies in Engineering & Technology, PG Education and Research in Engineering & Technology, Management Studies, Vocational Education, Pharmaceutical Education, Architecture, Hotel Management and Catering Technology, Information Technology, Town and Country Planning and Technician Education. The AICTE grants approval for starting new technical institutions and for introduction of new courses. It also lays down norms and standards for such institutions. It also ensures quality development of technical education through accreditation of technical programmes. The AICTE also has a promotional role which it implements through schemes for promoting technical education for women, handicapped and weaker sections of the society, promoting innovations, faculty development & research giving grants to technical institutions etc. The technical institutions under the AICTE include post-graduate, under-graduate and diploma in the whole spectrum of technical education covering engineering/technology, pharmacy, architecture, hotel management and catering technology, management studies, computer applications and applied arts and crafts. The details of AICTE approved degree level and diploma level technical institutions for the academic year 2008-09 are summarized below:

Number of AICTE approved Technical Education Institutions and their Annual Intake.

(As on August 31, 2008)

S.No.	Programme	Degree		Diploma	
		NOI*	Intake	NOI*	Intake
1	Engineering & Technology	2368	841018	1659	471006
2	Architecture	106	4133	--	--
3	MCA	1137	81761	--	--
4	Pharmacy	1001	62307	575	32181
5	Applied Arts & Crafts	10	840	4	480

Contd....

6	MBA	1231	114641	--	--
7	PGDM	285	36418	--	--
8	Hotel Management	86	5847	86	4490
	Total	6244	1146965	2324	508157
	Grand Total	Institutions			8568
		Intake			1655122

NOI*-Number of Institutions

AICTE initiatives for overcoming imbalances in Technical Education : In order to overcome imbalances in technical education, the Council has taken up certain new initiatives as per details given below:

1. The Council has permitted second shift of polytechnic in an existing polytechnic institution and also a second shift of polytechnic in an existing engineering institution in order to ensure reducing of imbalance between engineering education and polytechnic education.
2. The Council has allowed second shift of engineering colleges in existing colleges only in those States where the number of seats available in engineering colleges per lakh of population is less than the all India average. It will reduce the regional imbalance of the number of seats in various States of the country.
3. The Council has taken a policy decision to allow establishment of new engineering institutions with at least three conventional branches as a mandatory requirement in the States where the number of seats available in engineering colleges per lakh of population are more than the all India average for a balanced growth of various streams of education in engineering & technology. In the states where the number of seats available in engineering colleges per lakh of population are less than the all India average, no such restriction is applicable.

The quality and scope of professional education in India has come a long way since the establishment of the first Indian Institute of Technology (IIT) in 1951 and the first Indian Institute of Management (IIM) in 1961. The continuous support by the government of India and India Inc. as well as the assiduous focus on the quality of education has since seen the IITs and IIMs become the country's premier institutes in the field of technical and management training. The age of liberalisation which began in the 90s brought in a number of multi-national companies (MNCs) eager to capitalise on the growing economy. This in turn gave further impetus to the development of institutes, especially business schools.

Shortcomings : Mushrooming growth of institutions imparting professional education in the country is not going to serve the purpose for which they have been created.

1. The AICTE recently reported that approximately 886 applications have been filed for starting engineering colleges and 1,084 applications for new management institutes in India. India now trains the largest number of MBAs with about 75,000 degrees handed out annually. The rapid growth and proliferation of B-schools across the nation has led to the emergence of institutes of dubious quality. The students are also facing the problem of employability.
2. An MBA degree by its very nature is the education given to people with work experience to further enhance their management skills. It is simply inconceivable that a student who has never spent a day in office before will be able to comprehend, analyse and resolve the issues and challenges of everyday management simply because he has successfully passed his exams and acquired his MBA. This is evident from the fact that 80 per cent of Common Aptitude Test (CAT) applicants are freshers or students in their penultimate year of graduation. This is precisely the reason why all the B-schools abroad compulsorily require two to five years of work experience as a pre-requisite to their admission process. In India, most B schools (including IIMs) admit approximately 50 per cent to 70 per cent freshers into their course every year.
3. The curriculum of B schools relies heavily on case studies based on corporate situations abroad. These case studies, albeit informative, do little to help students relate to them as the mindset and work culture in India is radically different from that of the West. The practices and policies followed by foreign corporations may be the best-fit in their respective situations; however they prove to be woefully inadequate or rather unrealistic when applied in the Indian scenario.

4. After the 60 years of independence we have failed to provide work-oriented education to our youth. The reality is it that 2.50 lakh youths go abroad to do studies every year. And with it India's 50.000 crore rupees are transferred to the economies of other countries and at the other end it is affecting the Indian economy adversely. People are spending this money to get work-oriented education and it is expected that by getting the professional education they will get work in those countries but in those countries the job opportunities are decreasing every year.
5. Professionals play an important role in their country's economic progress. But it is our misfortune that out school system is in a 'dilapidated and devastated' situation. Technical and work oriented education is just a dream. Professional education institutes are the base of every country's economic progress. But the gap between progressing and progressed countries cannot be filled in short term as for as the professional and technical education is concerned. Japan has 110 teachers for 1000 students for engineering, medical and other management courses. Germany has 76 teachers for 1000 students, America has 65, South Korea has 46 and China has 30. But in India there are only 3 teachers for the batch of 1000 students. That is why we are way behind to provide professional education to our students.
6. The education figures of some foreign counties will shock most of the Indians. In Canada 99 per cent students get technical education, in America 81 per cent, in France 50 per cent and in UK the percentage is 30. But in India, only 6 per cent students get technical education. To get itself into the row of progressed states India will have to increase this percentage from 6 per cent to 20 per cent. In present situation II per cent urban and 4 per cent rural students get higher education. And with these figures it looks impossible that India will be one among the progressed nations within some years. As the situation of our primary education is deteriorating every year same is happening with our higher education.

2. The Medical Council of India : The Medical Council of India was established in 1934 under the Indian Medical Council Act, 1933, with the main function of establishing uniform standards of higher qualifications in medicine and recognition of medical qualifications in India and abroad. The number of medical colleges had increased steadily during the years after Independence. It was felt that the provisions of Indian Medical Council Act were not adequate to meet with the challenges posed by the very fast development and the progress of medical education in the country. As a result, in 1956, the old Act was repealed and a new one was enacted. This was further modified in 1964, 1993 and 2001.

Objectives : The objectives of the Council are as follows.

1. Maintenance of uniform standards of medical education, both undergraduate and postgraduate.
2. Recommendation for recognition/de-recognition of medical qualifications of medical institutions of India or foreign countries.
3. Permanent registration/provisional registration of doctors with recognised medical qualifications.
4. Reciprocity with foreign countries in the matter of mutual recognition of medical qualifications.

Constitution of the Council : Under Section 3(1) of the Indian Medical Council Act, 1956, the Council consists of the following members, namely:

a. One member from each State other than a Union Territory to be nominated by the Central Government in consultation with the State Government concerned.

b. One member from each University, to be elected from amongst the members of the medical faculty of the University by members of the Senate of the University or in case the University has no senate, by members of the Court.

c. One member from each State in which a State Medical Register is maintained, to be elected from amongst themselves by persons enrolled on such Register who possess the medical qualifications included in the First and Second Schedule or in Part-II of the Third Schedule.

d. Seven members to be elected from amongst themselves be persons who possess the medical qualifications included in Part I of the Third Schedule.

e. Eight members to be nominated by the Central Govt.

The President and Vice-President of the Council shall be elected by the members of the Council from amongst themselves.

Functions: Important functions of the council are as follows:

1. Inspection/visitation with a view to maintain proper standard of medical education in India.
2. Permission to start new medical colleges, new Courses including P.G. or Higher Courses, increase of seats etc.
3. Recognition/de-recognition of
   a. Indian Qualifications
   b. Foreign qualifications
4. Indian Medical Register
   Maintenance of All India Medical Register of persons who hold any of the recognised medical qualification or for the time being registered with any of the State Medical Councils or Medical Council of India.
5. Registration
   a. Permanent registration
   b. Provisional registration
   c. Registration of Additional Qualification.
   d. Issue of Good Standing Certificates for doctors going abroad

3. Bar Council of India : The Bar Council of India constituted under the Advocates Act 1961 has several solemn duties to perform. Among others, it has to lay down the standards of professional conduct and etiquette and also standards of legal education. The State Bar Councils does enrolment of advocates and enforcement of discipline is part of the obligations of the State Bar Council and the Bar Council of India exercises appellate jurisdiction. The Bar Council of India is a body corporate having perpetual succession and a common seal, with power to acquire and hold property, both movable and immovable, and to contract, and may by the name by which it is known sue and be sued.

Functions of Bar Council of India: Under Section, 7(1) of the Advocates Act 1961 lays down the functions of the Bar Council of India, which are as follows:-

(*i*) to lay down standards of professional conduct and etiquette for advocates;
(*ii*) to lay down the procedure to be followed by its disciplinary committee and the disciplinary committee of each State Bar Council;
(*iii*) to safeguard the rights, privileges and interest of advocates;
(*iv*) to promote and support law reform;
(*v*) to deal with and dispose of any matter arising under this Act, which may be referred to it by a State Bar Council;
(*vi*) to exercise general supervision and control over State Bar Councils;
(*vii*) to promote legal education and to lay down standards of such education in consultation with the Universities in India imparting such education and the State Bar Councils;
(*viii*) to recognize Universities whose degree in law shall be a qualification for enrolment as an advocate and for that purpose to visit and inspect Universities or cause the State Bar Councils to visit and inspect Universities in accordance with such directions as it may given be in this behalf.
(*ix*) to manage and invest the funds of the Bar Council;
(*x*) to provide for the election of its members;
(*xi*) to perform all other functions conferred on it by or under this Act;
(*xii*) to do all other things necessary for discharging the aforesaid functions;

Composition of the Bar Council of India: The Bar Council of India consists of 18 Members. Out of the 18 Members, the Attorney General of India and the Solicitor General of India are Ex-officio Members. The other 16 Members represent the 16 State Bar Councils in the country. The Members are elected for a period of five years and the Bar Council of India elects its own Chairman and Vice-Chairman for a period of two years from among the Members of the Bar Council of India.

Statutory Committees of the Bar Council of India: The Bar Council of India has several committees out of which the Legal Education Committee and the Disciplinary Committees are Statutory Committees.

(*a*) **Legal Education Committee :** The Legal Education Committee consists of five Members of the Bar Council of India and five Members co-opted from outside and they represent Judiciary, Law Ministry, University Grants Commission and Academicians. This is a high powered committee which makes recommendations to the Bar Council of India on all matters pertaining to Legal Education in the country. The Legal Education Committee elects its own Chairman.

(*b*) **Disciplinary Committees :** One of the important functions of the Bar Council of India is to lay down standards of professional conduct and etiquette for Advocates under section 7(1)(b) (c) and (d) read with Section 49(1)(c) of the Advocates Act,1961. For this purpose u/s 35 of the Act complaints against Advocates for professional and other misconduct are received by the State Bar Councils. The Bar Council of India constitutes the Disciplinary Committees. Every Committee consists of three Members, out of which two Members are from the Bar Council of India and the third Member is co-opted from outside to enquire into the professional and other misconduct of advocates on the rolls of various State Bar Councils in the country. Under section 35(3) of the Act the Disciplinary Committees of the Bar Councils can reprimand the Advocate, suspend or remove the name from the roll of Advocates. The Disciplinary Committee of the Bar Councils have same powers as are vested in the Civil Court under Code of Civil Procedure,1908 in respect of summoning the witnesses and recording the evidence and appointment of Commissions. Under section 37 of the Act the appeal lies before the Bar Council of India against the order of the Disciplinary Committee of the State Bar Councils.

If the case is not disposed of within the statutory period of one year from the date of the receipt of the complaint or the date of initiation of the proceedings at the instance of State Bar Council, the same is transferred to the Bar Council of India under section 36B(I) of the Act. The Disciplinary Committees of the Bar Council of India continue the original case from the stage at which it was so left by the State Bar Council. The Disciplinary Committees of the Bar Council of India discharge the work of an appellate authority as well as exercise original jurisdiction.

4. Accounting And Audit Profession

4.1. Institute of Chartered Accountant of India

The Institute of Chartered Accountants of India (ICAI) is a statutory body established under the -Chartered Accountants Act, 1949 (Act No. XXXVIII of 1949) for the regulation of the profession of Chartered Accountants in India. During its nearly six decades of existence, ICAI has achieved recognition as a premier accounting body not only in the country but also globally, for its contribution in the fields of education, professional development, maintenance of high accounting, auditing and ethical standards. ICAI now is the second largest accounting body in the whole world. Established by an Act of Indian Parliament "The Chartered Accountants Act, 1949". The Indian Accountancy Profession will be the Valued Trustee of World Class Financial competencies, Good Governance and Competitiveness was set up in 1949 under the Chartered Accountants Act, 1949 even before adoption of Constitution of India in 1950. Since then Profession has grown leaps and bounds in terms of Membership and Student base.

Profession in India

1. 1,50,000 Members spread throughout the country and in different parts of the world
2. Sizeable studentship base
3. Increase in percentage of members joining industry
4. Chartered Accountants are rendering services in every walk of economic life - Politics, Judiciary, Government, Agriculture, Corporate, NGOs.
5. Profession is dominated by small firms
6. Increasing trends towards consolidation
7. Government of India looks at ICAI as partner in Nation Building
8. Technical Standards based on International Standards
9. Focus on Capacity Building in the emerging context

Size of firms

1. Vast majority SMPs with SME clients
2. Cost and time vis-a-vis detailed requirements of Standards

3. We do not believe in separate auditing Standards for audit of SMEs
4. alternative between "audit" and "review" likely to create confusion, not much value
5. addition seen w.r.t clients as well as costs and risks involved vis-a-vis remuneration

Role of Institute of Chartered Accountant of India

(i) To regulate the profession of Accountancy
(ii) Education & Examination of Chartered Accountancy
(iii) Exercise Disciplinary Jurisdiction
(iv) Input on Policy matters to Government
(v) Ensuring Standards of performance of Members
(vi) Formulation of Accounting Standards
(vii) Prescription of Engagement and Quality Control Standards
(viii) Laying down Ethical Standards
(ix) Continuing Professional Education
(x) Financial Report Review
(xi) Monitoring Quality through Peer Review
(xii) Conducting Post Qualification Courses
(xiii) Convergence with International Standards of Accounting and Auditing
(xiv) Review and Revision of Education and training curriculum
(xv) Launch of Post Qualification Courses Capacity building of firms
(xvi) Mandatory CPE Requirement
(xvii) Peer Review Mechanism
(xviii) Financial Report Review
(xix) Brand building - Nationally and Internationally
(xx) Focused approach on issues relating to Corp. Governance.
(xxi) Facilitating changes in regulatory frames.
(xxii) Vigorous pursuance of Mutual Recognition Agreements.
(xxiii) Arrangement with Universities for graduation qualification to CA students
(xxiv) Facilitating accounting reforms in various areas

4.2. Institute of Company Secretaries of India

The Institute of Company Secretaries of India (ICSI) is constituted under an Act of Parliament i.e. the Company Secretaries Act, 1980 (Act No. 56 of 1980). ICSI is the only recognized professional body in India to develop and regulate the profession of Company Secretaries in India. The Institute of Company Secretaries of India awards the certificate of bestowing the designation of Company Secretary(CS) to a candidate qualifying for the membership of the Institute. It was in 1960 that the Company Law Board started a course in Company Secretaryship leading to the award of Government Diploma in Company Secretaryship. As the number of students taking up the Company Secretaryship course grew, the Government promoted on 4th October, 1968, Institute of Company Secretaries of India under Section 25 of the Companies Act, 1956 for taking over from the Government the conduct of Company Secretaryship examination. The Institute of Company Secretaries of India (ICSI) has since been converted into a statutory body w.e.f. 1.1.1981 under the Company Secretaries Act, 1980. The Institute of Company Secretaries of India(ICSI) has on its rolls 21,042 members including 3,523 members holding certificate of the practice. The number of current students is over 1,50,000. The Institute of company Secretaries of India (ICSI) has its headquarters at New Delhi and four regional offices at New Delhi, Chennai, Kolkata and Mumbai. The Institute has four Regional Councils.

Membership of The Institute of Company Secretaries of India(ICSI) has been recognized for appointment to various superior posts and services under the Central Government. The affairs of the Institute of Company Secretaries of India (ICSI) are managed by a Council consisting of fifteen elected members and five nominees of the Central Government. Pursuant to section 383A of the Companies Act, 1956, companies having a paid -up share capital of Rs 5 crore or more, as prescribed by the Central Government, are statutorily required to appoint a whole-time Company Secretary. The major contribution of Company Secretary (CS) is in corporate sector. Company Secretary (CS) is an important professional aiding the efficient management of the corporate sector. Company Secretary (CS) is designated as an officer under the Companies Act. Company Secretary (CS) has to interact, coordinate, integrate and cooperate with various other functional heads in a company. A member of the Institute of Company Secretaries of India(ICSI) may also practise independently as a professional after obtaining a certificate of practice as provided in the Company Secretaries Act,1980.

Objectives and Functions:

1. Develops a cadre of highly competent Company Secretaries for ensuring corporate governance and effective management by registering Students with 10+2 and graduate qualifications for Foundation and Executive Programmes of Company Secretary ship Course respectively with course contents in Law, Management, Accounting and Finance disciplines;
2. Provides postal/oral / web-based coaching and training enabling Students to qualify as Company Secretaries;
3. Conducts Company Secretaryship Examination twice a year in June and December, at 68 centres spread all over India and an overseas centre at Dubai;
4. Arranges practical training for Executive/ Professional Programme pass Students with Companies/Practicing Company Secretaries empanelled with the Institute for the purpose;
5. Enrolls qualified persons as Associate/ Fellow Members of the Institute and issues Certificate of Practice to Members taking up practice;
6. Conducts Post Membership Qualification Courses for Members of the Institute;
7. Publishes widely read and highly acclaimed monthly journal 'Chartered Secretary' disseminating information, expeditiously.
8. Publishes 'Student Company Secretary' and 'CS Foundation Course Bulletin' for the benefit of Students;
9. Uploads on the website of the Institute (www.icsi.edu) CS Updates containing current notifications and circulars relating to various corporate and related laws generally on weekly basis;
10. Exercises professional supervision over the Members of the Institute both in practice and in employment in matters pertaining to Professional Ethics and Code of Conduct;
11. Undertakes research in Law, Management, Finance and Capital Market disciplines and brings out research publications;
12. Formulates Secretarial Standards and brings out Guidance Notes thereon;
13. Renders expert advisory services to Members on intricate issues relating to various corporate laws;
14. Organises Professional Development and Continuing Education Programmes, International! National! Regional Conventions and Conferences directly or through its Regional Councils and Chapters, Chambers of Commerce, Department of Public Enterprises, Sister Professional Institutes and other Professional Development/ Management Bodies;
15. Interacts with various National and Regional Chambers of Commerce with regard to various Government Policies and Legislations;
16. Interacts with Members of International Federation of Company Secretaries and Company Secretaries Institutes in other jurisdictions;
17. Bestows ICSI National Award for Excellence in Corporate Governance to best governed Companies;
18. Bestows ICSI Lifetime Achievement Award to eminent corporate personalities for Translating Excellence in Corporate Governance into Reality;
19. Conducts Investor Awareness Programmes throughout the country on behalf of the Investor Education & Protection Fund, Ministry of Corporate Affairs; and 20. Under takes Research Projects on behalf of Government and its Agencies/Institutions.

4.3. Institute of Cost and Work Accountant of India

It was during the early years of World War II, that the concept of cost as an independent entity made its beginning in the industrial circles of the world. Due to the prohibitive cost of defense operations, the then governments at war found it difficult to ascertain the price of defence purchases and thus evolved the concept of cost + contracts. This forced the contractors to submit the cost of the work to be undertaken by them, in order to be awarded the contract. 1945 brought the end of the war, and the nations ravaged by the effects of war began large-scale reconstruction of their economies through industrialisation. The end of colonialism meant that many nations gained their independence, and this process increased rapidly. The late forties and fifties can really be termed the golden era of industrialisation. The importance of cost accounting as being central to the formation of government policies provided the foundation of the rapid growth of the profession. What began as a mere exercise in estimating the cost later developed into a movement for efficiency and optimum utilisation of scarce resources. The profession was established by a special act of Parliament, namely, the Cost and Works Accountant Act, 1959. With the passing of the act, "The Institute of Cost and works Accountants of India" was established in 1944 and was registered as a company under the Companies act with the objectives of promoting, regulating, and developing the profession of Cost Accountancy.

It has since been continuously contributing to the growth of the industrial and economic climate of the country. The Institute of Cost and Works Accountants of India is the only recognized statutory professional organization and licensing body in India specialising exclusively in Cost and Management Accountancy. Cost Accountant is a person who offers to perform or perform services involving the costing or pricing of goods and services or the preparation, verification or certification of cost accounting and related statements.

Objectives of the Institute

(*a*) To develop the Cost and Management Accountancy function as a powerful tool of management control in all spheres of economic activities.

(*b*) To promote and develop the adoption of scientific methods in cost and management accountancy.

(*c*) To develop the professional body of members and equip them fully to discharge their functions and fulfill the objectives of the Institute in the context of the developing economy.

(*d*) To keep abreast of the latest developments in the cost and management accounting principles and practices, to incorporate such changes are essential for sustained vitality of the industry and other economic activities.

(*e*) To exercise supervision for the entrants to the profession and to ensure strict adherence to the best ethical standards by the profession.

(*f*) To organise seminars and conferences on subjects of professional interest in different parts of the country for cross-fertilisation of ideas for professional growth.

(*g*) To carry out research and publication activities covering various economic spheres and the publishing of books and booklets for spreading information of professional interest to members in industrial, education and commercial units in India and abroad.

In this way, national level councils meant for different leading profession are doing a commendable job in regulating the profession concerned. However, steps are required to make them more effective and purposeful.

Practice Questions

Objective Type Questions

1. East India Company was established in
   (*a*) 1600
   (*b*) 1630
   (*c*) 1650
   (*d*) 1665
2. Following degree is not a professional degree:
   (*a*) MBBS
   (*b*) MCA
   (*c*) MBA
   (*d*) MFA

3. Professional Management is based on:
   (*a*) Intuitions
   (*b*) Hunches
   (*c*) Scientific Analysis
   (*d*) Instincts
4. Sachar Committee was appointed in
   (*a*) 1977 (*b*) 1997
   (*c*) 1987 (*d*) 2007
5. Codes of ethics are formulated by:
   (a) Society
   (b) Professional Association
   (c) Government
   (d) Members themselves

Ans: 1. (a), 2. (d) 3. (c), 4. (b), 5. (b)

Short Answer Questions

1. What is profession?
2. What do you mean by professionals?
3. What is professional management?
4. What do you understand by code of ethics?
5. What is professional culture?
6. Who is a professional manager?
7. What do you mean by a professional association?

Long Answer Questions

1. What do you mean by professional management? Evaluate the factors responsible for the growth of professional management in India.
2. Is management a profession in India? Give arguments in support of your answer.
3. Discuss the nature of profession. Also examine its attributes.
4. Discuss the nature and functions of a professional manager.
5. What do you mean by professional manager? Also examine the requirements of a professional manager.
6. What is professional association? Examine its functions.
7. Examine the present status of Professional management in India. Suggest necessary steps to make the professional management in India more effective.

References

1. Cadbury Adrian, Corporate Governance and Chairmanship, A personal View, Oxford University Press, New York, 15t Indian Ed., 2003,p.2
2. Ray Arbind, The Indian Manager in Search of a Style, Economic and Political Weekly, Bombay, 1997.pA
3. Prakesh Tondon, Professional Management in India (Its Potential and Problems), Sri Ram Memorial Lecture Series in Management, 1974
4. op.cit- Ray Arbind, The Indian Manager in Search of a Style, p.5
5. Tripathi.A.N. Human Values.p.112.
6. Joseph.Towle; Theory of Professional Management, Richard D. Irwin Inc. Homwood Illinois.
   1973. p.14

7. Ray Arbind. The Indian Manages: In Search of Style, Asia Publishing House-Bombay, 1970.p.19 8. op.cit-Prakesh Tondon, Professional Management in India (Its Potential and Problems)
8. Sachar Committee Report, Para-5.3, 1997, p.14
9. Ibid.Para.5.6
10. Justice. Nain. J.L. Speech delivered at the 4th All India Convention of Company Sectaries held in Bombay in Feb.1976. He had quoted the related paragraph from the Judgement of the Bombay High court in the case of R.S. Deshpande Vs. Municipal Corporation of Greater Bombay (1975) 77 AIR 55.
11. op.cit-Prakesh Tondon, Professional Management in India (Its Potential and Problems) p.12-13 13. Moore, Wilbert: The Professions, Role and Rules, Russel Saga Foundation, New York, 1970 p.3
12. Sounders A M Carrand Wilson P.A. The Professions, Oxford, The Clarendés, Press 1973, p.298 15. Bush vannevar as quoted in the Annals of the American Academy of Political and Social Sciences, Volume No.297, Jan.1995., p.1
13. Ibid.pA8
14. op.cit-Prakesh Tondon, Professional Management in India (Its Potential and Problems), p.39
15. op.cit-Prakesh Tondon, Professional Management in India (Its Potential and Problems), p.39-40
16. Annual Report 2008-09, Department of School Education and Literacy & Department of Higher Education Ministry of Human Resource Development, Government of India.

4 CORPORATE GOVERNANCE

With the growing pace of the Indian economy and increase in the complexity of business operations, the forms of corporate organisations keep on changing. The thinking of corporate toward shareholders/stock holders have also been changed and now they are trying to fulfill the expectations of stakeholders. Business enterprises are required to fulfill the expectations of different stakeholders like wealth maximisation and social responsibility. It becomes imperative for them to attune their governing organs to these expectations. Corporate governance has succeeded in attracting a good deal of public interest because of its apparent importance for the economic health of company in particular and society in general. The concept of corporate governance covers a large number of distinct economic phenomenon. Liberalization and globalization initiatives have made it essential for the Indian corporate to make appropriate changes in their boards as well as their governance practices. Efforts to formulate standards for corporate governance took roots in countries like the United States and the United Kingdom and have subsequently spread to other countries.

Corporate Governance is the mechanism by which the values, principles, policies and procedures of a company are inculcated and manifested. The essence of corporate governance lies in promoting and maintaining integrity, transparency and accountability in higher echelons of the management. Corporate leaders need a set of tools which provide them a greater visibility into their organizations and strengthen the levels. The objectives *before* a business are to create wealth for the society, maintain and preserve that wealth efficiently and to share the wealth with the stakeholders. Corporate Governance is the method by which the aforesaid objectives are achieved. *The Rigveda,* the oldest book on record in the world, first coined the term as 'Harmony'. Thus, 'Symphony' amongst all the stakeholders was the *modus operandi.* The common corporate goal was "Prosperity to all."[1] According to the narration given in *Rigveda,* "Corporates should work like a honeybee, which takes the nectar of a flower without the flower losing its shape and fragrance and provided honey for the well being of the society."[2]

This message resembles the ethical theme followed by a 'good citizen' of the society, which has been given by our ancestors. The same theme has now been adopted in management of professional corporates of the new era. It is because of the strong social bondages of business with society that is ethically defined as for the society, from the society and by the society.

Origin of Corporate Governance

Corporate Governance is relatively a new discipline. This has attracted worldwide attention, particularly since the 1990s. The concept is assuming great importance of late due to the totally unexpected collapse of a few giant corporations in the United States such as world energy leader Enron and biggies like WorldCom, Adelphia, Tyco, Global Crossing, etc. Earlier, the United Kingdom (UK), had also witnessed several cases of corporate corruption and collapse, which led to setting up of Cadbury (1992), Greenbuiy, and Hampel (1997) Committees during the latter half of the 90s.

"India also experienced some financial scandals during 1950s (LIC), eighties and nineties and post-2001 period such as the Mundra's scam involving LIC (1957), Raj Sethia's scandal involving the Punjab National Bank (PNB) in early 1985, Harshad Mehta's mega swindle involving UTI, SBI and other institutions in 1992, Unit Trust of India's two episodes during its then Chairman Mr. Pherwani's period, and again in 2001, when Mr. Subramanium was Chairman,

Ketan Parekh's fraud involving Bank of India and Gujarat Cooperative Bank in 2001, Telgi's Stamp Paper scam and erstwhile Global Trust Bank's scam in early 2004."[3] Satyam Computers episode in 2008 is another failure of governance in India.

These developments have created an environment where we need to go in deep about the effective formulation process of corporate governance in India.

Conceptual Framework of Corporate Governance

"Governance is the process by which people in power make decisions that create, destroy or maintain social systems, structures and processes. Corporate Governance is therefore the process whereby people in power direct, monitor and lead corporations, and thereby either creates, modify or destroy the structures and systems under which they operate. Corporate governors are both potential agents for change and also guardians of existing ways of working. As such, they are therefore a significant part of the fabric of our society".[4]

Governance has proved an issue since people began to organize them for a common purpose. How to ensure the power of organization is harnessed for the agreed purpose, rather than diverted to some other purpose, is a constant theme. The institutions of governance provide a framework within which the social and economic life of countries is conducted. Corporate Governance concerns the exercise of power in corporate entities. Corporate Governance structure specifies the distribution of rights and responsibilities among different participants in the corporation, such as the board, managers, shareholders and other stakeholders, and spells out the rules and procedures for making decisions on corporate affairs. By doing this, it also provides the structure through which the company objectives are set and the means of attaining those objectives and monitoring performance.

The concept of "Corporate Governance primarily hinges on complete transparency, integrity and accountability of the management. There is also an increasingly greater focus on investor protection and public interest. The degree to which corporates observe basic principles of good Corporate Governance is becoming an increasingly important factor for making investment decisions."[5]

Corporate Governance is concerned with values, vision and visibility. It is about the value orientation of the organization, ethical norms for its performance, the direction of development and social accomplishment of the organization and the visibility of its performance and practices. It deals with the efficiency of the use of the resources, value addition and wealth creation within the broad parameters of the corporate philosophy inspired by the Corporate Governance.

Definitions of Corporate Governance

"In a narrow sense, Corporate Governance involves a set of relationships amongst the company's management, its board of directors, shareholders and other stakeholders."[6]

The shareholders are always eager to know whether the management is doing its best towards performance and profitability of the company and whether business is being conducted to promote their economic interests. This syndrome may be considered as one of the main contributions to the philosophy of corporate governance being witnessed today. Besides this, good corporate governance is committed to protect the interests of all segments of the society. So the essence of corporate governance lies in extending fairness to all the entities, i.e. shareholders, creditors, customers, employees and others associated with the working of the corporate in any capacity whether directly or indirectly; it covers all the entities being affected by its activities in some form or other.

It provides structure and incentives for the board and management to pursue objectives that are in the best interest of the company and its shareholders, and which can facilitate effective monitoring. A well-functioning board of directors can be good for the bottom line; companies perceived to be well governed will gain the confidence of shareholders, customers and other stakeholders, and have cheaper access of capital. "Corporate Governance integrates the interests of investors and managers and ensures that firms are run for the benefit of all classes of investors. In a broader sense, however, good corporate governance - the extent to which companies are run in an open and honest manner - creates overall market confidence, enhances efficiency of international capital and its allocation. It contributes ultimately to the nation's overall wealth and welfare."[7] "Corporate Governance deals with the ways in which suppliers of finance to corporations assure themselves of getting a return on their investment".[8]

Organization for Economic Cooperation and Development (OECD) has defined Corporate Governance to mean A system by which business corporations are directed and controlled. "Corporate Governance structure specifies the distribution of rights and responsibilities among different participants in the company such as board, management, shareholders and other stakeholders; and spells out the rules and procedures for corporate decision-making. By doing this, it provides the structure through which the company's objectives are set along with the means of attaining these objectives as well as for monitoring performance."[9]

The Cadbury Committee Report suggests, "Corporate Governance is the social, legal and economic process through which companies function and are held accountable."[10] Actually it is a system of structuring, operating and controlling a company with the following specific aims :

(*i*) Fulfilling long-term strategic goals of owners;

(*ii*) Taking care of the interests of employees;

(*iii*) A consideration for the environment and local community;

(*iv*) Maintaining excellent relations with customers and suppliers;

(*v*) Proper compliance with all the applicable legal and regulatory requirements.

Thus, Corporate Governance denotes the process, structure and relationship through which the Board of Directors oversees what the management does. It is also about being answerable to different stakeholders. In other words, Corporate Governance is a system by which the companies are run. It relates to the set of incentives, safeguards and disputes resolution processes that are used to control and coordinate the actions of the agents on behalf of the shareholders by the Board of Directors.

CII - Desirable Corporate Governance Code defined Corporate Governance as "Corporate Governance deals with laws, procedures, practices and implicit rules that determine the ability of a company to take informed managerial decisions vis-a-vis its claimants - in particular, its shareholders, creditors, customers, the state and employees. There is a global consensus about the objective of 'good' Corporate Governance: maximizing long-term shareholder value".[11] Thus, the way a company is organized and managed to ensure that all financial stakeholders (shareholders and creditors) receive their fair share of a company's earnings and assets.

The Institute of Company Secretaries of India has also defined the term Corporate Governance, as "corporate governance is the application of best management practices, compliance of law in true letter and spirit and adherence to ethical standards for effective management and distribution of wealth and discharge of social responsibility for sustainable development of all stakeholders".[12] It is an area of economics that emphasizes evolving institutional structures to regulate the contract, organizational designs and legislations. It motivates the shareholders and encourages the managers to deliver better returns on investments.

However, Corporate Governance has wider implications and is critical to economic and social well being, firstly in providing the incentives and performance measures to achieve business success, and secondly in providing the accountability and transparency to ensure the equitable distribution of the resulting wealth. According to World Bank, Corporate Governance is concerned with holding the balance between economic and social goals and between individual and communal goals. The governance framework is there to encourage efficient use of resources and equally to require accountability for the stewardship of those resources. The aim is to align as nearly as possible the interests of individuals, corporations and society.

In globalization era, Corporate Governance has become an increasingly important in determining the perception of international investor, managerial structures and credibility of business. There is a need for corporates in India to heed this tide of change. They must proactively design their culture-specific codes and effectively implement, instead of sit and wait for rules to be imposed from the government and regulatory agencies. There is ample evidence to establish that a single wrong doing is enough to ruin the reputation of a company, it took ages to build, while the culture of strict adherence to good governance practices keeps them ahead on sustainable basis.

The weak legal regime in many emerging markets can also pose a problem, as confidentiality and non-competition agreements may not work to constrain independent directors from misusing commercially sensitive information. Controlling shareholders may limit boards' access to information if they do not trust independent directors. Informal or social constraints on improper behavior may be more effective than legal ones, and so one way of addressing this problem is to appoint independent minded people who move in the social circles of the controlling shareholders. While this may work in the near-term, the long-term imperative is to strengthen the legal system so that the concept of the independent non-executive director can truly work in emerging markets.

The Cadbury committees report on Corporate Governance emphasized on the process, structure and relationship through which company functions and is held accountable. While the CII gave emphasis on global consensus about the objective of good Corporate Governance and maximizing long, term shareholders value, ICSI emphasized on adherence to ethical standards for effective management. SEBI committee headed by Shri N.R. Narayan Murthy emphasized on making distinction between personal and corporate fraud in the management of a company.

In the ultimate analysis, the crux of corporate governance relates to the manner in which the top management is entrusted with the fiduciary responsibility of administering the resources. The basic qualities expected in this regard are invariably trust, honesty, transparency etc.

Another issue, which was not covered, was the functioning of independent directors. As per the revised clause 49, for a company with an Executive Chairman, at least 50 per cent of the board should comprise independent directors. In the case of a company with a Non-Executive Chairman, at least one third of the board should comprise independent directors. The institution of independent directors to be successful requires that the independent directors are allowed to act independently. Similarly, independent directors should have courage to say no when things are not moving in the interest of the company and its stakeholders. Independence on paper is not enough in itself. The problem is not 'the number' of independents, but the quality of their contribution'. One solution is to recruit younger upcoming business leaders. Board members should also be able to provide sound business advice and real expertise, as well as engage effectively in-group settings. The independent directors must take pro-active steps to find solution to the problems of company and the investors. The independent directors are in a better position to make an impartial assessment regarding the matters of the company because in no way they are associated with the company.

Salient Features of Corporate Governance

Important features of corporate governance are as follows :

1. Transparency: A key element of good corporate governance is transparency, projected through a code of good governance, which incorporates a system of checks and balances between key players - boards, management, auditors and shareholders. Transparency in company's action may be ensured through making non-partisan disclosures and timely dissemination of information complete in all respect equally to all shareholders about results; Annual General Meetings (AGMs); quarterly updates on company's performance, risks, outlook, opportunities and threats etc.

2. Accountability : "Corporate governance is a way of life and not a set of rules. It is a way of life that necessitates taking into account the shareholders interests in every business decision. This has brought into focus the accountability of the Board of Directors of a company and their constituent responsibilities."[13]

(*a*) Towards Shareholders: It occurs when the company adopts an equitable and fair approach towards its shareholders, resorts to timely resolution of shareholder's complaints and grievances, rewards the shareholders on regular basis and constitutes dedicated cells in the organization to address shareholders grievances.

(*b*) Towards Society: Following are some of the ways by which a company can discharge its obligations towards the society:

(*i*) Providing assistance to victims during times of natural calamities;

(*ii*) Enlistment and education of the underprivileged and deprived;

(*iii*) Promotion of education and training in general;

(*iv*) Contributions, charity, donations for socially relevant causes;

(*v*) Steps for promoting welfare of mentally, physically or visually disabled;

(*vi*) Establishment of schools, hospitals, parks etc.

3. Trusteeship: "The doctrine of trusteeship is based on the *Bhagavad Gita.* The twin principles of 'aparigraha' (non-possession) and 'Sambhawa' (equalism) are the main principles of Bhagavad Gita.

Corporates are the trustee of the shareholders and their money; they should use their wealth for the welfare of the society and the community at large."[14] Trusteeship involves a strong code of discipline and ethical behaviour as well as equally strong principle of accountability.

4. Employees' Welfare: Good corporate governance is essentially concerned with company's human resource. The Annual Report could set out the initiatives taken by the company for employees' welfare in the following areas in particular:

(*i*) Training programmes organized for upgrading employees' skills;

(*ii*) Identification and rewarding of performances;

(*iii*) Focus on multi-skill programme where key executives are rotated to various functions to develop skills across different functions.

(*iv*) Housing schemes launched for employees;

(*v*) Launching of benevolent fund for employees;

(*vi*) Scholarships and/or educational facilities for children of the company's staff.

5. Environment Protection: Irrespective of whether a company is polluting or non-polluting, protection of environment should be concern of every socially responsible organization. Each company must take steps to make sustainable use of resources, establish a healthy and safe working environment, maintain ecological balance, take proactive steps to minimize waste generation and preserve the environment. The securing of ISO Certification for environmental protection could be highlighted in the Annual Report.

6. Meeting Social Obligations: There is a growing expectations that the business enterprise to be much more than a mere economic unit and be a good corporate citizen vigorously contributing to social issues and charity. It seeks to achieve the following objectives:

(*a*) A properly structured board capable of taking independent and objective decisions is in place at the helm of affairs;

(*b*) The board is balanced as regards the representation of adequate number of non-executive and independent directors who will take care of the interests and well-being of all the stakeholders;

(*c*) The board adopts transparent procedures and practices and arrives at decisions on the strength of adequate information;

(*d*) The board has an effective machinery to subserve the concerns of stakeholders;

(*e*) The board keeps the shareholders informed of relevant developments impacting the company;

(*f*) The board effectively and regularly monitors the functioning of the management team; and

(*g*) The board remains in effective control of the affairs of the company at all times.

The overall endeavor of the board should be to take the organization forward, to maximize long term value and shareholders' wealth.

Rationale of Corporate Governance

Rationale of corporate governances are as follows :

1. Need for Norms and Codes: Inadequacies and failures of an existing system often bring to the fore the need for norms and codes to remedy them. In the UK, deficiencies in the Accounting Standards became more evident after many companies, in their eagerness to increase earnings and accelerate growth, exploited the weaknesses in the accounting standards to show inflated profits and understate liabilities. Corporate governance develops norms and codes for board management regarding management of companies in the interest of stakeholders.

2. Agency Costs: The basic need for corporate governance arose due to agency costs. In the case of a public limited company, the shareholders are the owners or principals. But due to inherent nature of a public limited company, its large body of shareholders are scattered throughout the country and hence they themselves are unable to manage or run the company. Their interest mainly lies in getting reasonable return, based on the risk-profile of the company, year after year without any hindrance, whatsoever. To run their company, they have to appoint competent manager on market-related compensation package. These managers, thus, run the company on day-to-day basis as agents of their principals, i.e., the shareholders. While principals may feel that agents would be running the show in their interest, in actual practice things may not be often so. For example, the chief executive and other senior managers may even indulge in window-dressing of operational results of the company by fudging the firm's accounts.

3. Distribution of Rights & Responsibilities: Corporate Governance is a system, which directs and controls business corporations. The corporate governance structure specifies the distribution of rights and responsibilities among different participants in the corporation, such as the board, managers, shareholders and other stakeholders, and spells out the rules and procedures for making decisions on corporate affairs. By doing this, it also provides the structure through which the company objectives are set and the means of attaining those objectives and monitoring performance.

4. Mechanism of Transformation into Action: Corporate governance is the mechanism by which the values, principles, management practices and procedures of corporation are made manifest in the real world. Good corporate governance implies not only a mechanical compliance of legislations but also adding value to various stakeholders. Amidst the fierce competition in the wake of globalization and advent of knowledge economy, excellence is the only way of survival and growth. The essence of corporate governance involves the development of constructive relationship between different constituents of a corporate enterprise based on the principles of justice, lucidity, effectiveness and responsibility. Intensive competition, emerging new multilateral trading order and the need for sustainable development have generated extensive debate on the process and style of Corporate governance. "The need of the hour for the corporates is to follow corporate governance norms in their true spirit and practice the parameters of fairness, accountability, disclosure and transparency."[15]

5. Common Purpose: Governance has proved an issue since people began to organize them for a common purpose. How to ensure the power of organization is harnessed for the agreed purpose, rather than diverted to some other purpose, is a constant theme. The institutions of governance provide a framework within which the social and economic life of countries is conducted. Corporate governance concerns the exercise of power in corporate entities.

Elements of Good Corporate Governance

Elements of good corporate governance are as follows :

1. Role and Powers of Board: Good governance is decisively the manifestation of personal beliefs and values, which configure the organizational values, beliefs and actions of its Board. "The Board as a main functionary is primarily responsible to ensure value creation for its stakeholders. The absence of clearly designated role and powers of Board weakens accountability mechanism and threatens the achievement of organizational goals. Therefore, the foremost requirement of good governance is the clear identification of powers, roles, responsibilities and accountability of the Board, CEO, and the Chairman of the Board. The role of the Board should be clearly documented in a Board Charter."[16]

2. Legislation : Clear and unambiguous legislation and regulations are fundamental to effective corporate governance. Legislation that requires continuing legal interpretation or is difficult to interpret on a day-to-day basis can be subject to deliberate manipulation or inadvertent misinterpretation.

3. Management Environment : Management environment includes setting-up of clear objectives and appropriate ethical framework, establishing due processes, providing for transparency and clear enunciation of responsibility and accountability, implementing sound business planning, encouraging business risk assessment, having right people and right skill for the jobs, establishing clear boundaries for acceptable behavior, establishing performance evaluation measures and evaluating performance and sufficiently recognizing individual and group contribution.

4. Board skills: To be able to undertake its functions efficiently and effectively, the Board must possess the necessary blend of qualities, skills, knowledge and experience. Each of the directors should make quality contribution. A Board should have a mix of the following skills, knowledge and experience: Operational or technical expertise, commitment to establish leadership; Financial skills; Legal skills; and Knowledge of government and regulatory requirements.

5. Board Appointments: To ensure that the most competent people are appointed on the Board, the board positions should be filled through the process of extensive search. A well-defined and open procedure must be in place for reappointments as well as for appointment of new directors. Appointment mechanism should satisfy all statutory and administrative requirements. Priority should be given to an understanding of skill requirements of the Board particularly at the time of making a choice for appointing a new director. All new directors should be provided with a letter of appointment setting out in detail their duties and responsibilities.

6. Board Induction and Training: Directors must have a broad understanding of the area of operation of the company's business, corporate strategy and challenges being faced by the Board. Attendance at continuing education and professional development programmes is essential to ensure that directors remain abreast of all developments, which may impact their corporate governance and other related duties.

7. Board Independence: Independent board is essential for sound corporate governance. The goal may be achieved by associating sufficient number of independent directors with the board. Independence of directors would ensure that there are no actual or perceived conflicts of interest. It also ensures that the board is effective in supervising and where necessary, challenging the activities of management.

8. Board Meetings : Directors must devote sufficient time and give due attention to meet their obligations. Attending board meetings regularly and preparing thoroughly before entering the boardroom increases the quality of interaction in board meetings. Board meetings are the forums for decision-making. These meetings enable directors to discharge their responsibilities. The effectiveness of board meetings is dependent on carefully planned agendas and providing relevant papers and materials to directors sufficiently prior to board meetings. Also, in the present scenario, board meetings through modern means of communication like tele-conferencing, video conferencing may be expressly allowed under law.

9. Board Resources: Board members should have sufficient resources to enable them to discharge their duties effectively. It includes and access for director to independent legal and professional advice at the company's expense. The costs of supporting the board should be transparent and reported.

10. Code of Conduct : It is essential that the organization's explicitly prescribed norms of ethical practices and code of conduct are communicated to all stakeholders and are clearly understood and followed by each member of the organization. Systems should be in place to periodically measure, evaluate and if possible recognize the adherence to code of conduct.

11. Strategy Setting: The objectives of the company must be clearly documented in a long-term corporate strategy including an annual business plan together with achievable and measurable performance targets and milestones.

12. Business and Community Obligations: Basic activity of a business entity is inherently commercial but it should also take care of community's obligations. Commercial objectives and community service obligations should be clearly documented after approval by the board. The stakeholders must be informed about the proposed and ongoing initiatives taken to meet the community obligations.

13. Financial and Operational Reporting: The board requires comprehensive, regular, reliable, timely, correct and relevant information in a form and of a quality that is appropriate to discharge its function of monitoring corporate performance. For this purpose, clearly defined performance measures-financial and non-financial should be prescribed which would add to the efficiency and effectiveness of the organization. Reports and information provided by the management must be comprehensive but not so extensive and detailed as to hamper comprehension of the key issues. The reports should be available to board members well in advance to allow informed decision-making. Reporting should include status report about the state of implementation to facilitate the monitoring of the progress of all significant board approved initiatives.

14. Monitoring the Board Performance: The board must monitor and evaluate its combined performance and also that of individual directors at periodic intervals, using key performance indicators besides peer review. The board should establish an appropriate mechanism for reporting the results of board's performance.

15. Audit Committees: The Audit Committee is inter alia responsible for liaison with the management; internal and statutory auditors, reviewing the adequacy of internal control and compliance with significant policies and procedures, reporting to the board on key issues. The excellence of Audit Committee significantly contributes to the governance of the company.

16. Risk Management: Risk is an element of corporate functioning and governance that should not be neglected. There should be a clearly established process of identifying, analyzing and tackling risks, which could prevent the company from achieving its objectives effectively. It also involves establishing a link between risk-return and resourcing priorities. Appropriate control procedures in the form of a risk management plan must be put in place to manage risk throughout the organization. The plan should cover activities viz. review of operating performance, effective use of information technology, contracting out and outsourcing. The Board is ultimately responsible for identifying major risks to the organization, setting acceptable levels of risk and ensuring that senior management takes steps to detect, monitor and control these risks. The Board must satisfy itself that appropriate risk management system and procedure are apt to identify and manage risks. For this purpose the company should subject itself to periodic external and internal risk reviews.

Thus, the spirit of corporate governance should abide by the ancient wisdom of Shrimad Bhagawad Gita which defines yoga as "dexterity of work"[17] (YOGA KARMSU KAUSHLAM). The need of the hour is that we develop an attitude of poised efficiency in corporate governance. All the participants i.e. shareholders, directors and managers can usher in a culture that in turn can work well for the society as a whole. It transcends the common selfish interest. Efficiency of all participants is the touchstone of corporate governance.

Theories of Corporate Governance

Main theories of corporate governance are as follows:

1. Agency Theory : It assumes that managers will act opportunistically to further their own interest before shareholders. Number of shareholders is the function of the size of the firm. The result is that the shareholders lose effective control of large corporations due to dispersed ownership. When all shareholders own small minority interests to create diverse ownership, it is not rational for any investor to spend time and incur costs to supervise management as it provides a free ride for other investors. Small shareholders may lack the power and influence to extract information which could reveal expropriation or mismanagement. The reliance on the so-called 'professional managers' (the only one with the specialized knowledge to manage a company) gradually increases to virtual dependence. The separation of ownership from control increases the power of these managers and leaves them free to pursue their own aims. Agency theory states that "the value of a firm cannot be maximized because managers posses discretions, which allows them to expropriate value to themselves. Now, essentially the problem is whether these managers can be trusted or not. Shareholder interests can be compromised if managers maximize their self-interest at the expense of organizational profitability.

Agency theory insists that managers cannot be trusted; as managers are deemed to have short term, generally extrinsic financial aims. With such a tainted picture, the managers obviously should not be allowed to run the organization, simply on their own. "The theory deals with relationship that mirrors the basic agency structure of two major parties, a principal and an agent, who are engaged in cooperative behaviour, but have divergent interests and attitude towards risk. Accordingly, it meant for identifying and describing the governance mechanism that limits the agent's self-interest behaviour in situation where the principal and, agent have conflicting goals."[18] In the case of a corporation, the principals are the owners (shareholders), and the agents are the managers. Therefore, in order to reduce agent' opportunism, certain mechanisms need to be put in place here, comes into play the controlling role of the governing board or board of directors. With shareholders unable to engage in management, it becomes the responsibility of the board to represent shareholders' interests by keeping the management under control.

Thus organizations must have directors, who are independent of management influence in order to achieve maximum performance. "One way for the board to achieve independent control is by separating the initiation and implementation of decisions, i.e., decision management, from the ratification and monitoring of decisions, i.e. control. The board should takeover the function of decision control, and limit the management's function to decision management."[19] Hence the need and importance of independent directors is well emphasized. The consequences of this approach can be seen in current corporate governance codes that specify board composition in terms of number of outsiders, sometimes recommending a majority of the latter. Further, all these codes also incorporate the requirement for the formation of committees of the board; in particular, audit, remuneration and nomination committees, again staffed by a majority of outside directors. These board sub-groups are central for effective monitoring of the management.

'Agency Cost' is the inherent constituent of the agency theory. It is defined as the sum of the total costs of designing, implementing, and maintaining appropriate initiative and control systems, and the residual loss from not solving the problems completely."[20] Agency cost showed how investors of publicly traded corporations incur costs in monitoring and bonding managers in best serving shareholders. When the interests of the owners (shareholders) of a corporation will differ from those of management (agents), their attitude to risk will also be different. This difference in risk attitude between the two parties can give rise to an agency cost, either through missed opportunities by a risk-averse management, or at the other end of scale through management recklessness. "The best solution to such problems is to determine the most efficient contract governing the principal-agent relationship and an optimal incentive scheme to align the behaviour of the managers with the interests of the owners. To do so, a complete contract containing specifications of the agent duties, rewards and the rights of the principal to monitor their performance is required."[21] Agency theory, favours for adopting appropriate incentive systems to reward managers and it is a key solution to the agency problem. Corporate governance structures also represent such agency costs. Agency costs are the sum of the cost of monitoring management (the agent) banding the agent to the principal (shareholders/residual claimant) and residual losses. Basically, the central problem in corporate governance is to construct rules and incentives to effectively align the behaviour of managers (agents) with the desires of principles (owners).

2. Stakeholder Theory : It deals with the value of the firm. The firm is a system of stakeholders operating within the larger system of the host society that provides the necessary legal and market infrastructure for the firm's activities. "The purpose of the firm is to create wealth or value for its stakeholders by converting their stakes into goods and services. However, the purpose of the firm should be more widely defined than the maximization of the shareholder welfare."[22] The welfare of other parties that have a long-term interest in the firm's activities and its performance should also be considered. The stakeholders are not merely firm's shareholders and managers, but also its customers, creditors, employees etc. According to Freeman, a stakeholder is "any group or individual who can affect, or is affected by the achievement of company's purpose. These stakeholders have a legitimate claim on the firm, which is derived from the existence of an exchange relationship".[23] That is why there should be a sense of fairness in the way firms interact and conduct exchanges with other parties in maximizing the stakeholder's welfare. Moreover, fairness leads to socially efficient exchanges.

Stakeholder theory is also based on the notion that there are many groups in society, besides owners and employees to whom the corporation is responsible. The objectives of a corporation should only be achieved by balancing, often conflicting interests of these different groups.

Corporations can effectively to respond to the interests of society as a whole if they ensure the participation of stakeholders in their governing boards. The stakeholder approach to the role of the governing board expects the board to negotiate and compromise with stakeholders in the interests of the corporation. It recognizes the need for setting overall direction and thus it supports a coordinating role of the governing board. Company should try to encourage the long term employee ownership and encourage board representation by significant customers, suppliers, financial advisors, employees and community representatives.

3. Stewardship Theory : It says that the managers are good stewards of the corporation and diligently work to attain high levels of corporate profit and shareholders return. "The manager expected to work as a 'steward" whose aim is to do a good job. It follows that there is no motivation problem or nonalignment of interest between management and ownership. It stresses involvement rather than control, trust rather than monitoring, and performance enhancement rather than cost control."[24] It is also assumed that the "Managers are principally motivated by achievement, responsibility needs and given the needs of managers for responsible, self directed work, organisation may be served to free managers from subservience to non executive director dominated boards. It recognizes a range of non-financial motives for managerial behaviour. These include - the need for achievement and recognition, the intrinsic satisfaction of successful performance, respect for authority and work ethic. The rewards for 'stewards' are intrinsic in nature, like, opportunities for growth, achievement, affiliation, and self-actualization. Managers are viewed as interested in achieving high performance and capable of using a high level of discretion to act for the benefit of shareholders. "They are essentially good stewards of corporate assets, loyal to the company. In effect the individual becomes integrated with the organization, so aligning the interests of owners and management without the need for external control mechanisms."[25] Thus, theory deals with long-term rather than a short term orientation. Stewardship theory holds that a manager, when confronted with a course of action seen as personally unrewarding, will comply based on a sense of duty and identification with the organization. "Shareholders can therefore expect to maximize their returns when such an organizational structure is practiced. However, the inclination of individuals to act as stewards or self seeking agents may be contingent."[26] Hence, this theory fails to explain all situations.

Thus, in this perspective the board's involvement should be restricted to reviewing strategies that have been formulated by the management and to get involved in the performance oriented coalition with the latter, so as to achieve the corporate goals and missions. It is, therefore beneficial to have an active and participative board. The existence of such a relationship will make the management analyze and articulate their plans, proposals and suggestions in greater depth because of the high quality of discussions generated by the active and participative governing boards on any submissions for decisions. It encourages the reallocation of corporate control from owners to professional managers as a positive development towards managing the complexities of a modern corporation. The assumption that managers have a wide range of motives and behaviour beyond self-interest is the rationale for arguing that goal conflict may not be inherent in the separation of ownership from conflict. Actually, control empowers the managers to aim towards maximizing corporate profits. Hence, the role of the governing boards is to facilitate effective control by management.

Under the model of stewardship, insider-dominated boards are favoured for their depth of knowledge, access to current operating information, technical expertise etc. "The corporate governance codes gives guidelines on selection of directors, ensuring that the shareholders know about their directors' seriousness about being part of various committees e.g. in India, all listed companies have to give a report on corporate governance, which amongst other things should also include the number of meetings held in a year and the attendance of each director in those meetings (because unless there is participation, how would there be discussions, which is the very basis of this theory). The effect of this central proposition of stewardship theory is to predict that structures designed to increase the monitoring and control of management will be associated with lower company performance. Hence, the aspect of CEO duality receives a positive boost by the proponents of stewardship theory. CEO duality advocates that the position of the chairman and that of the chief executive officer is occupied by the same person".[27]

4. Resource Dependence Theory : "It examines certain aspects of the internal organization which are linked to inter-organization phenomenon."[28] Resource dependence approach is concerned with conceptual framework for understanding how firms view resources as the basic building block for the firm. It also provides a basis for organizational attempt to exert control over their environment by co-opting the resources needed to survive. It envisages the linking role of a governing board, which seeks to establish links, amongst corporations, which depend upon one another for access to valuable resources, thereby helping to regulate their interdependence. Resources may be financial, human, intangible, physical, organization, or technological. In this context, the firm is seen as a bundle of tangible and intangible resources and tacit know-how competences.

Boards can also be used as a mechanism to form links with external environment. Inter-organizational linkages, such as appointment of outside directors and board interlocks, can be used to manage environmental contingencies. An interlock is the social relation that is created between two corporations when one person is a member of the governing boards of both organizations. Directors who are prestigious in their professions and communities can be a source to timely information for executives. Sitting on the boards of companies, provides access to details of their finance and operations, as well as specific corporate information and this may ensure that the required resources will be allocated in favour of the interlocking corporation. Since governing boards help the organization to deal with its environment, enhance its legitimacy and assist in achieving its goals of efficiency and performance, they are seen as a critical link or an important linking instrument of the organization, to the external environment. It is argued that every firm has a narrow set of core or distinctive technology competencies and skills on which it should focus on. In the long run, a firm needs to focus its energies on a few key competencies to best exploit them. A detailed analysis of the firm's resources, capabilities and competencies will result in a better understanding of the sources of competitive advantage.

"The Board is required to guide the management in effectively accumulating, categorizing, developing and utilizing the firm's resources and skills over time."[29] "As the sustainability of a firm's competitive advantage depends on the ease with which resources can be imitated, directors should seek to foster distinctive capabilities such as leadership skills and reputation assets that are difficult for competitors to substitute or imitate."[30] Directors with superior leadership skills or competencies for handling the complexities of a global firm can better implement sustainable policies to enhance the firm's reputation with its multiple stakeholders. Thus, the governing boards are viewed as vehicles that corporations use to control other organization; to co-opt threats in their environment from competitors, suppliers, customers, and regulatory agencies, and generally to coordinate their business activities with other corporations. Moreover, interlocking directorates are often seen as media or channels of transmitting and communicating information.

Mechanisms of corporate governance

There are two types of mechanism generally used in corporate governance- Internal mechanism and external mechanism. These mechanisms are as follows:

A- Internal Mechanism

(*i*) **Ownership structure :** Agency theory says that separation of ownership and control incur some costs. Hence, owners need to find out various mechanisms to minimize these costs. That means owners can align the interests of managers and owners by adopting different mechanism. Based on this, it can be assumed that if owners are the managers then there will be no cost. But in the days of widespread ownership, it is not that easy. As majority of owners are with smaller holdings with which they cannot discipline managers. Hence, the structure of ownership is important in disciplining the managers. Owners, by virtue of the size of their equity positions, effectively have some control over the firms they own. Thus, ownership structure is a potentially important element of corporate governance.

Shareholdings by government, equity holdings by institutional investors, holdings by promoters and holding by pension funds etc, have differential influence on disciplining managers. In general, concentrated equity ownership is regarded as a bad mechanism in corporate governance since it gives the largest shareholders more discretionary powers of using firms resources in the areas that only serve their own benefits. It was find that cross holding and pyramidal ownership have been common in Asian economies. One consequence of such ownership arrangement is that the controlling shareholders are able to obtain more control at minimal capital expense, which makes "tunneling" much easier. On the other hand, since tunneling is usually inefficient for the firm as a whole, if the shareholding of the largest shareholders is very large and therefore there is high degree of congruence between his interest and the firm's interest, then ownership concentration may have positive effect. Widely dispersed share ownership, is that individual shareholders own very small fraction of an individual firms' share and therefore, have little or no incentive to expend significant resources to monitor managers or seek to influence decision making within the firm. Moreover, the free-rider problem reduces the incentives for these disparate shareholders to coordinate their actions. However, individual shareholders who have more significant ownership positions have greater incentives to expand resources to monitor and influence managers. So, the relationship between the firm performance and ownership concentration is expected to be U-shaped.

(ii) **Board of Director :** The board of directors is a mechanism through which shareholders can exert considerable influence on the behaviour of managers in order to ensure that the company is running in their interest. Corporation in most countries of the world have board of directors. The board exists primarily to hire, fire, monitor, and compensate management, all with an eye towards maximizing shareholders value. Major responsibilities of board of directors include determine the organizations mission and purpose, select the executives, support the executives and review the performance, ensure effective organizational planning, ensure adequate resources, manage resources effectively, determine and monitor the organisations programmes and services, enhance the organisations' public image, etc.

Board can be structured in such way that proper representation is given to independent directors, institutional directors and non-executives directors. A chairman who will lead the group heads the board. While the board is an effective corporate governance mechanism in theory, in practice its value is less clear. There are growing debate about like the effectiveness of board of directors, effectiveness of insider directors, board compensation, board structure etc. Executive compensation research is fundamentally concerned with the degree to which managers are compensated in ways that align their interests with those of their companies' shareholders.

(iii) **Executive compensation:** The third mechanism that ensures that managers pursue the interest of shareholders is executive compensation. If structured appropriately, it discourages the managers, who have control over the firm without investing in it, from acting against the interest of shareholders. The measures used to evaluate managers include both stock valuation and accounting based performance measures. However, Studies suggest that there is a positive relationship between executive pay and performance.

(iv) **Disclosure:** The absence of day-to-day control of operations of shareholder, disclosures by the management about company information has become very crucial for good governance. Honest managers will attempt to provide sufficient, accurate and timely information regarding the firms, operations, financial status, and external environment. Information about operational efficiency risks involved compliance to legal and regulatory matters, adherence to codes of conduct, environmental laws etc are mostly internal information to the company. The management needs to disclose the information to the concerned parties.

B. External mechanism

These mechanisms help in improving the governance of a corporation. External mechanism are as follows:

(i) **The market for corporate control:** The existence of an active market for corporate control is essential for efficient allocation of resources. When internal control mechanism fail to bridge the gap between the actual value of a firm and its potential value, will create incentive for outside parties to seek control of the firm. Changes in the control of firms virtually always occur at a premium, thereby creating value for the target firm's shareholders. Furthermore, the mere threat of a change in control can provide management with incentives to keep firm value high, so that the value gap is not large enough to warrant an attack from the

outside. Thus, the takeover market has been an important governance mechanism. It is assumed with the existence of market for corporate control, manager who are responsible for firm performance will be more cautious. If the firm is taken over by some body or sold by the existing shareholders due to bad performance will reflect on the managers mismanagement. Due to the fear of bad reputation, loss of job, managers try to put in their best to see that the firm performs well, and avoid take over by others. This found to be a good mechanism to align the interests of managers and shareholders. The market for corporate control can operate in three ways: proxy contests, friendly mergers and hostile takeovers. Proxy fights do not usually unseat the existing board of directors successfully because share holdings spread among many shareholders. Friendly mergers and takeovers occur in all countries and account for most of the transaction volume that occur. For hostile takeovers, they do occur frequently in the US and UK, however, much less so in Germany, France and Japan.

(ii) **Legal/Regulatory framework :** Legal environment play very crucial role in the standard of corporate governance of a country. Country's laws protect investors rights. Legal framework prevalent in a country helps disciplining managers and controlling shareholders' opportunistic behaviors. Extensive study done suggest that in countries with common law tradition, governance standards are generally higher and minority shareholders are relatively better protected. In contrast, countries pursuing continental law systems normally have poor minority shareholders protection and practice lower governance standards. Interestingly, they that cross-country differences in equity valuation, cost of capital and magnitude of external financing. It could be explained by a complained by a country's legal origin. Obviously, legal framework is an effective external mechanism that assures investors to get a fair return on their investment.

(iii) **Competition :** It is another powerful mechanism for solving a variety of agency problem is competition in product markets. If the managers of a firm waste resources, the firm will eventually fail in product markets. Hence, increased competition reduces managerial slack and may be helpful in limiting efficiency losses. The same logic implies that product competition helps curtail the "tunneling" activities of the controlling shareholders.

Thus, good corporate governance helps protect investors and ensures that investors get a fair return on their investment. An effective combination of the above internal and external mechanism influences the standards of good corporate governance.

Models of corporate governance

There are many different models of corporate governance around the world. These differ according to the economy model, political environment, variety of capitalism, awareness of investors and customers, legal framework of particular country. The coordinated model that one finds in Continental Europe and Japan also recognizes the interest of workers, managers, suppliers, customers and the community. Both models have distinct competitive advantage, but in different ways. Whereas the coordinated model of corporate governance facilitates incremental innovation and quality competition. The three important models of corporate governance are the Anglo-American model, the German model, the Japanese model. The brief about these models are given below:

(i) **The Anglo, American model:** The liberal model of corporate governance encourages radical innovation and cost competition. "The liberal model that is common in Anglo-American countries tend to give priority to the interests of shareholders. In the United States and UK, a corporation is governed by a board of directors, which has the power to choose an executive officer, usually known as a chief executive officer."[31] The CEO has broad power to manage the corporation on a daily basis, but needs to get board approval for certain major action, such as hiring his/her immediate subordinates, raising money, acquiring another company, major capital expansion, or other expensive projects. Other duties of the board may include policy settings, decision-making, monitoring management's performance, or corporate control.

The board of directors is normally selected by and responsible to the shareholders, but the byelaws of many companies make it difficult for all but the largest shareholders to have an effective influence over the makeup of the board. Normally, individual shareholders are not offered a choice of board nominee to sit on the board. Frequently, members of the boards of director are CEOs of other corporations.

The board appoints and supervises the managers who manage the day-to-day affairs of the corporation. While the legal system provides the structural framework, the stakeholders in the company will be suppliers, employees and creditors. However, creditors exercise their lien over the assets of the company. The policies are framed by the board of directors and implemented by the management. So there is clear separation of ownership and management, which minimize conflict of interest between the promoters and managers. Companies are run by professional managers who have negligible ownership stakes.

(ii) **The German Model :** According to this model shareholders own the company, but they do not entirely dictate the governance mechanism. Generally, shareholders elect 50 percent of members of supervisory board and the other half is appointed by labour unions.

In this way employees and workers also enjoy a share in the governance. The supervisory board is empowered to appoint and monitor the performance of management board. It also facilitate a reporting relationship between the supervisory board and management board. However, management board is independently authorized to conduct the day-to-day operations of the company. Special features of "German Model are as follows: (i) Banks and financial institutions have substantial stake in equity capital of companies.(ii) Labour relations officers is represented in the management board. Workers participation in management is practised. (iii) Both shareholders and employees have equal say in selecting the members of the supervisory board."[32]

(iii) **The Japanese Model :** In Japanese model, the financial institutions has accrual role in governance. The shareholders and the bank together appoint board of directors and the president. "Important features of Japanese Model are as follows: (i) Inclusion of president who consult both the supervisory board and the executive management. (ii) Importance of the lending bank is highlighted."[33]

(iv) **Indian Model :** India in its own right has a unique and epochal background of governance. In the ancient times, the King was always considered the representative of the people. The wealth of the state was not the personal wealth of the king. The principle of trusteeship is the backbone of corporate management. Kautilya's Arthasastra also provide deep insight with regard to good governance.

(a) Since beginning, India has been following mixed economy model. Here, government companies and private companies exist together. Basically, there is no difference in the governance structure of government companies and that of private companies.

(b) The Indian corporate sector is governed by the Indian Companies Act. The pattern of private companies is mostly that of closely held or dominated by a founder, his family and associates. In respect of public enterprises, central/state government is working as the promoter of the public enterprises and these governments are empowered to constitute individual governing board for each public enterprise.

In this context, two dimensions are quite noteworthy. Promoters are the deciding factor in constitution of governing board for public limited companies in private sector.

Features of Indian private sector companies as follows :

(a) Shareholdings are distributed among the promoters, specialized financial institutions, mutual funds, foreign institutional investors and retail or small investors.

(b) Promoter group controls the affairs of the companies even though in most of the cases they do not control more than fifty per cent shareholdings.

(c) Specialized financial institutions like LIC, GIC, IFCI, IDBI Banks, SFCs etc are controlled by the Government of India or State government. But these institutions have gentlemen agreements with these promoters and never intervene in the management unless their own interest is affected.

(d) Specialized financial institutions have a right to appoint their nominee directors on the board of these companies.

(e) Promoters with the help of specialized financial institutions fulfils the criteria of more than fifty percent shareholding they appoint their own directors on the board.

(f) Retail or small investors are quite dispersed all over the country and they do not take active interest even in attending the annual general meeting of the company where directors are to be appointed.

(g) Real power to appoint directors ultimately rests with the promoters and they hopefully follow all formalities in appointing directors but these directors are their own family members, relatives and friends.

(h) Clause 49 of listing agreement provides for the appointment of independent directors. In this case also, promoters have no problem and appoint their own men as so called professional as independent directors. who are ready to promote promoter's interest in the board meeting.

The distinctive feature of public sector companies are as follows :

a. Equity shares are owned wholly or substantially (51 per cent or more) by the government- central government, state government or local government.

b. Good deal of political and bureaucratic influences the board of directors. Bureaucrats and active politicians are generally appointed as directors of governing companies.

c. Organizations often viewed as a social entities.

d. The controlling administrative ministry appoints the board of directors.

e. Excessive emphasis on observing rules, regulations and guidelines. They do believe in red tapism.

f. Efficiency and performance are sacrificed at the altar of propriety.

Corporate Governance Rating (CGR) in India

Corporate Governance Rating is relatively a new approach with regard to corporate governance. Governance Metrics Inc., (GMI), a New York-based independent corporate governance Rating agency, was perhaps one of the first, which announced rating of the constituent companies of Japan's Nikkei 225 index in May 2003. This was the first international release by GMI, which intended to do similar studies of Australian and European companies in 2003. GMI is perhaps the only independent corporate governance-rating agency focusing on corporate accountability issues on a global scale. It's ratings are based on 600 data points per company and cover seven broad categories of analysis. These rating criteria are based on a number of known global CG codes, including those developed by the Organization for Economic Cooperation and Development (OECD). Corporate Governance rating is a symbolic representation by rating agencies about the relative level to which the rated company accepts and follows the codes and guidelines of corporate governance practices, not only as statutory compliance but also in spirit as well. It is based on core principles of fairness, transparency, accountability and responsibility. The variables that are analyzed while arriving at corporate governance rating for a corporate entity are shareholding structure, governance Structure and management process, board structure and processes, stakeholder relationship, transparency and disclosures and financial discipline.

Today, good Corporate Governance and social and environmental performance are increasingly important, and companies actually gain a competitive advantage if they demonstrate their compliance in the CG ratings. However, measuring the quality of Corporate Governance is a subjective exercise, and the inherent danger is that any survey will focus more on form - with a series of boxes to be ticked rather than substance. The companies are also expected to practice transparency in their financial and regulatory reporting, and compliance with the letter and spirit of laws and regulations of the 79 countries it operates in. On behalf of the customers they assess all major loan proposals for their environmental, ethical and social impact, and have guidelines about whom to lend and invest with.

The benefits of Corporate Governance Rating for the company, regulators and stakeholders need to be advocated. What restrains the corporate sector from embracing the Corporate Governance Rating is the fear that the regulators may decide to make it mandatory. Companies should be allowed to weigh the pros and cons of the Corporate Governance Rating model before adopting it. In fact, Corporate Governance norms should not be made mandatory. However, it should be recommendatory or voluntary in nature-left to the companies whether they want to adopt it or not. It is not mandatory for the companies in India to get themselves rated by any rating agency. SEBI's views are based on the fact that as ethical behavior, social responsibility of business or practicing honesty and courtesy cannot be mandated, so is the case with CG rating. Each company will have to decide for itself whether they would like to get their corporate governance practices rated by rating agencies like CRISIL, ICRA, etc. Both these credit rating agencies have now started this service from 2004.

Regulatory Framework of Good Corporate Governance in India: The Companies (Amendment) Act, 2000 has introduced good corporate governance leading to more transparent, ethical and fair business practice to be adopted by Corporates at large. The following highlights are given as under :

1. Section 217(2AA) deals with Directors Responsibility statement to be included in the Directors report.
2. Section 292A provides for constitution of Audit committee.

3. Section 274(1)(g) debars a person to act as a Director of a company if default in filling Annual Return / accounts or repayment of deposits/ interest /debentures / dividend has taken place.
4. Section 275 provides for appointment of a person as a director in a maximum of 15 companies.

1. Section 217 (2AA) : Section 217(2AA) deals with directors Responsibility statement to be included in the Directors Report shall now include a DRS on the following aspects:

(i) Applicable Accounting Standards have been followed in the preparation of financial statements along with proper reasons/explanations for material departures.

(ii) Accounting policies as prescribed are consistently applied.

(iii) Judgment and estimate are made in a reasonable and prudent manner to ensure true and fair view of the state of affairs and of the P & L account.

(iv) Adequate accounting records are maintained in accordance with the provisions of the companies Act 1956 for safeguarding the assets of the company and for preventing and detecting frauds and other irregularities.

(v) Financial statements have been drawn up on a going concern basis.

To bring out more transparency in accounting and auditing practices of the corporate the Act include Directors Responsibility Statement in the directors report as directors are representatives and accountable on the behalf of the company.

2. Section 292A: Every public company (listed or unlisted) having a paid up capital of at least Rs. 5 crore shall constitute a committee of the board to be known as Audit Committee. The provision in respect of the same is as follows :

(i) The committee shall have at least three (3) members.

(ii) Two-third (2/3) of the members shall be non-executive directors.

(iii) The Board of Directors shall prescribe the committee's terms of reference in writing.

(iv) The statutory auditor, the internal auditor and director- in charge of finance shall attend every meeting of the Audit Committee but shall not have the right to vote.

(v) Half-yearly and annual account will be discussed by the audit committee with auditors before presenting the same to the board.

(vi) The Audit Committee shall have the right to investigate any matters covered by the terms of reference.

(vii) The recommendations of the Audit Committee will be binding on the board. Though the board is a superior body, yet it cannot override the recommendation of the committee.

(viii) In case the board doesn't accept the recommendations of the Audit Committee, it will have to records the reasons and communicate the same to the shareholders.

(ix) The chairman of the audit committee shall attend the annual general meeting to provide clarifications on the matters relating to audit.

(x) The composition of the Audit Committee shall be disclosed in the annual report of the company.

(xi) The minutes of the audit committee are required to be placed before the next Board meeting.

(xii) Provisions regarding quorum of the Audit Committee, needs to be laid down by the Board by constituting the committee, if not spelt out, the whole of the committee, it appears must meet.

(xiii) Any default in, complying the provisions may entail prosecution up to one year or fine up to Rs. 50000 or both. The prosecution lies against the company and every officer of the company who is in default. Thus, offence is compoundable u/s 621A.

(xiv) The provisions in clause 49 of the Listing Agreements as required by the Stock Exchanges are not identical with the above provisions. It seems that all listed companies having a paid-up capital of minimum Rs. 5 crore will have to follow two sets of requirements.

Prominence to enhance the accountability of the board towards public disclosure regarding constitution of the Audit Committee and making it mandatory to follow the recommendations of Audit Committee also increases the status and significance of Audit Committee of Public Companies.

3. Section 274(1)(2) : Section 274(1) (g) debars a person to act as a Director of the company if default is filling Annual Returns/Accounts or repayment of deposits/ interest/ debentures/ dividend has taken place. Disqualifications of Directors –

(A) has not filed the annual accounts and annual returns for any continuous three financial years commencing on and after the first day of April, 1999; or

(B) has fail to repay its deposit or interest thereon on due date or redeem its debentures on due date or pay dividend and such failure continues for one year or more;

Provided that such person shall not be eligible to be appointed as director of any other public company for a period of five years from the date on which such public company in which he is a director failed to file annual accounts and annual returns under sub-clause (A) or has failed to repay its deposit or interest or redeem its debentures on due date or pay dividend referred to in clause (B). The Act disqualifies the directors on the grounds of denial on financial and legal issues and binds the directors of public companies to follow the requirements of full disclosure of their returns.

4. Section 275 : Section 275 provides for appointment of a person as a Director in a maximum of 15 companies.

No person to be a director of more than fifteen companies (substituted for "twenty companies" by the companies (Amendment) Act, 2000)-After the commencement of this Act, no person shall, save as otherwise provided in section 276, hold office at the same time as director in more than fifteen companies.

Above Section has retrenched the span of power and control of the individual director by reducing the number of his membership in other companies. The companies (Amendment) Act 2003 seeks to make far reaching changes in the companies Act, 1956. About 174 Sections are affected by the Act by way of an amendment, substitution of existing provisions as well as insertion of new provisions. The Amendment Act of 2003 is exclusive in many respects when compared to the earlier Amendment Acts of 1999, 2000 and 2002. Some of the major amendments are given below:

1. Section 292 A : In Section 292A of the principal Act, for sub-section (1), the following sub-sections shall be substituted namely:

(1) Every public company having paid-up capital of not less than crores of rupees shall constitute a committee of the Board known as Audit Committee which shall consist of not less than two independent directors and not more than such number of maximum independent directors, as the Central Government, may prescribe :
Provided that every Company which has consolidated the Audit Committee before the commencement of the companies (Amendment) Act, 2003 shall reconstitute within one year from such commencement, the Audit Committee consisting of independent directors in accordance with the provisions of this Act.

(1A) The members of the Audit Committee shall exercise such powers and perform such functions as may be prescribed."

2. Section 275 and 276 : For section 272 and 276 of the principal Act, the following sections shall be substituted, namely: "275. (1) No person shall, hold office at the same time as a director in more than fifteen companies: Provided that where any such person also holds office as managing director or whole -time director in any company, the limit specified in this sub-section shall be reduced to ten:

Provided that where any such person also holds office as a managing director or whole-time director in any company, the limit specified in this sub-section shall be reduced to ten:

Provided further that the Central Government may, specify, by the notification in the official Gazette, the percentage of shares which may be held by such director in a class or classes of companies wherein a person may be appointed as a director.

"276. (1) Any person holding office as director in more than fifteen companies or holding office as a managing director in more than ten companies, immediately before the commencement of the Companies (Amendment) Act, 2003 shall, within sixty days from such commencements.

(*a*) Choose not more than fifteen or as the case may be, ten of those companies, in which he wishes to continue to hold the office of director;

(*b*) resign his office as director in the other companies; and

(*c*) initiate the choice made by him under clause (a) to each of the companies in which he was holding the office of the director before such commencement, to the Registrar having jurisdiction in respect of each such company.

(2) Any resignation made in pursuance of clause (b) of sub-section (1) shall become effective immediately on the dispatch thereof to the company concerned.

(3) Where a person already holding the office of director in fifteen companies is appointed, after the commencement of the companies (Amendment) Act, 2003 as a director of any other company, the appointment

(*a*) Shall not take effect unless such person has, within fifteen days thereof, effectively vacated his office as director in any of the companies in which he was already a director; and

(*b*) Shall become void immediately on the expiry of the fifteen days, if he has not, before such expiry, effectively vacated his office as director in any of the other companies aforesaid".

3. Section 282 : In section 283 of the principal Act, in sub-section (2A), for the words, "punishable with fine", the words "punishable, with imprisonment for a term which may extend to three years and with fine" shall be substituted.

Practice Questions

Objective Type Questions

1. Concept of Corporate Governance is available in
   (*a*) Rigveda (*b*) Yajurveda
   (*c*) Atharveda (*d*) Samveda
2. Essence of Corporate Governance lies in except
   (*a*) Integrity (*b*) Transparency
   (*c*) Accountability (*d*) Delegation of Authority
3. Number of objectives of Corporate Governance given in Cadbury Committee Report
   (*a*) 8 (*b*) 7
   (*c*) 6 (*d*) 5
4. Resource Dependence Theory is linked to:
   (*a*) International Organisation
   (*b*) Inter organization
   (*c*) Intra organization
   (*d*) None of these
5. Stakeholder Theory deals with:
   (*a*) Price of the firm
   (*b*) Value of the firm
   (*c*) Profit of the firm
   (*d*) wealth of the firm

Ans: 1.(a), 2. (d), 3. (d), 4. (b), 5. (b)

Short Answer Questions

1. What is corporate governance?
2. What are the objectives of corporate governance?
3. What are the rationale of corporate governance?
4. What are the assumptions of stakeholders theory?
5. What do you mean by corporate governance rating?

Long Answer Questions

1. What is Corporate Governance? Examine its scope and objectives?
2. Discuss the role of board of directors in corporate governance.
3. What is corporate governance? Explain its scope and importance.
4. "The role of BOD is to govern and not to manage". Discuss the statement, bringing out the element of corporate governance.
5. Discuss the different approaches of corporate governance.

References

1. Singh Devi & Garg Subhash 'Corporate Governance' - Excel Books - New Delhi – 2001 p.7
2. ICSI National Award for Excellence in Corporate Governance, New Delhi, 2003
3. Singh Dr. S "Corporate Governance, Global Concepts and Practices" Excel Books, New Delhi, 2005, p. vii.
4. Lynn McGregor, The Human Face of Corporate Governance, Palgrave, New York, 2000, p.ll .
5. Narang.S.P.; Role in Corporate Governance, The ICFAI Journal of Corporate Governance, V oLIll, No.4, Hyderabad 2004 October, p.48
6. The Economic Times - 2004 "What's Corporate Governance" December 15
7. The Economic Times - 2004 "What's Corporate Governance" December 15
8. Shleifer and Vishny, The Journal of Finance, 1997, p.737
9. The Institute of Company Secretaries of India, New Delhi, 'Corporate Governance' (Modules of Best Practices), 2004 December, p.7
10. Ibid, p.7
11. "Desirable Corporate Governance - A Code", Confederation of Indian Industry, New Delhi, 1998 April, p.l
12. op.cit 'Corporate Governance', p.8
13. "Corporate Governance and Business Ethics, Excel Books, New Delhi, 1998, p.15
14. Ibid, p.15
15. ICSI National Award for Excellence in Corporate Governance, New Delhi, 2003
16. op.cit 'Corporate Governance', p.9-12
17. Tr. Swarupananda Swami - Shrimad Bhagawad Gita Advaita Ashram, Calcutta – 2000 Ch.2 -50-59.
18. Burton Peter,' Corporate Governance: Antecedents and Consequences, 2000, p. 194-203.
19. Fame E.F. and Jensen. M.C. Separation of ownership and control journal of Law and Economies 16, 1983, P. 301-325.
20. Jensen, M.C. and W.H. Meckling (1976), Theory of Firm, Managerial Behaviour, Agency Costs and Ownership Structure, Journal of Financial Economics, October, 305-306
21. Dodd. P.R. & J.B. Warner, "On Corporate Governance: A Study of Proxy Contests, Journal of Financial Economies, 11, 1983, p.401-433
22. Keasey, Corporate Governance Economic and Financial Issues, Oxford University Press, 1997, p.112. .
23. Hills & Jone:5, Stakeholders Agency Theory, Journal of Management Theory, 1992p.82
24. op.cit, Burton Peter, Corporate Governance., 2000, p.204
25. Argysic. C. Integrating the Individual and the organisation, 1990.

26. Muth, M.M. and Donaldson. L. Stewardship Theory and Board Structure: a Contingency Approach Corporate Governance. 6.1.1998.

27. Aggarwal, Neetu Role of Governing Bodies and Corporate Governance. Chartered Secretary, Jan, 2006, P.9

28. op.cit, Burton Peter, Corporate Governance, 2000, p.218

29. Moingeon, Ramanantsoa; Metais & Orton. 1998. Another look at Structure relationships: The Resource Based View, European Management Journal, 16, 3P, 297-305.

30. Petrick, Scherer, Brodzinski. Quinn and Ainia, 1999. Global Leadership skills and Reputational Capital: Intangible Resource for Sustainable Competitive Advantage: Academy of Management Executive (13.1.585).

31. Sujit Sikidar, Disclosure Transparency, Management Accountant, Institute of Cost and Work Accountant of India, V 01.31, No.2, Feb.1996, p.1 08

32. Rahul Bajaj, Corporate Governance, The Chartered Accountant, Journal of Institute of Chartered Accountant of India, Vo1.58, July 2009, p.44

33. D Geeta Eani & R K Mishra, Corporate Governance-Theory and Practice, Excel Books, New Delhi, 200g, p.57

5 CORPORATE GOVERNANCE COMMITTEES REPORTS

Today, Corporate Governance is being treated as panacea for all decisions in corporate management. We find valuable references about good governance system in our old Sanskrit literature -- Rigveda, Ramayan, Mahabharat, Chankaya's Arthshastra, Smrities and Puranas. So, perspective of corporate governance is quite strong. In present scenario, adoption and mechanism of corporate governance in India are totally based on the findings of various committee reports. Actually, recommendations of these committees constituted by different bodies and agencies are the basis for new enactments and necessary amendments in existing corporate laws. Now Indian corporates are also required to adopt, implement and execute these recommendations in their management behaviour. Keeping these requirements in mind, efforts have been made to present the summary of various Committee Reports and recommendations on Corporate Governance in two segments (A) International Scenario (B) Indian Scenario

A. International Scenario

1. Cadbury Committee Report (1992)

The Cadbury Committee was set up in May 1991 by the Financial Reporting Council, the London Stock Exchange and the accountancy profession to address the Financial aspects of Corporate Governance. Towards greater clarity to the respective responsibilities of director, shareholders and auditors it also strengthened trust in the corporate system. Companies whose standards of Corporate Governance are high are more likely to gain the confidence of investors and support the development of their businesses.

I. Terms of Reference :

To consider the following issues in relation to financial reporting and accountability and to make recommendations on good practice :

(*a*) Responsibilities of executive and non-executive directors for reviewing and reporting on performance, to shareholders and other financially interested parties; and the frequency, clarity and form in which information should be provided;

(*b*) The case for audit committees of the board, including their composition and role;

(*c*) The principal responsibilities of auditors and the extent and value of the audit;

(*d*) The links between shareholders, boards, and auditors;

(*e*) Any other relevant matter.

II. Composition of the Committee

The Committee was formed with members drawn from the CBI, the accountancy profession, finance directors, academia, the Bank of England, the Stock Exchange, the Institute of Directors, institutional investors, and the Law Society. The Department of Trade and Industry provided a secretary to the committee, who acted as their observer. Total number of the Committee members was sixteen and were as follows :

"(*i*) Sir Adrian Cadbury (chairman), (ii) Ian Butler, Council Member. CBI and former Chairman, CBI Companies, Committee, (iii) Jim Butler, Senior Partner, KPMG peat Marwick, (iv) Jonathan Charkham, Advisor-to the Governor; bank of England, (v) Hugh Collum, Chairman - Hundred Group of finance Directors, (vi) Sir Ron Dearing, Chairman, Financial Reporting Council, (vii) Adrew Likierman, Professor of Accounting and Financial Control, London Business School, (viii) Nigel Macdonald, Vice President, Institute of Chartered Accountants of Scotland, (ix) Mark Sheldon, President, law Society, (xi) Sir Andrew Hugh Smith, Chairman, London Stock Exchange, (xii) Sir Drmot de Trafford Bt, Chairman, Institute of Directors, Observers: (xiii) Mrs. Sarah Brown (until October 1991), (xiv) Mr. Arthur, Russell (from November 1991) Head of Companies Division, DTI; Secretary: (xv) Nigel Peace (on secondment from DTI), (xvi) Sir Christopher Hogg (Chairman, Reuters Holdings PLC, Courtaulds pic, and Courtaulds Textiles pic) acted as an adviser to the Committee."

III. Recommendations of the Committee

The main recommendations of the Cadbury Committee report were:

1. The board of all listed companies registered in the UK should comply with the Code of Best Practice.
2. Listed companies should make a statement about their compliance with the Code in the report and accounts and give reasons for any areas of non-compliance.
3. Companies' statements of compliance should be reviewed by the auditors before publication. The review should cover only those parts of the Compliance can be objectively verified. The Auditing Practices Board should cover only those parts of the compliance statements which relate to provisions of the Code where compliance can be objectively verified. The Auditing 'Practices Board should consider guidance for auditors accordingly.
4. All parties concerned with Corporate Governance should use their influence to encourage compliance with the Code. Institutional shareholders in particular, with the backing of the Institutional Shareholders' Committee, should use their influence as owners to ensure that the companies in which they have invested comply with the Code.
5. The committee's sponsors convened by the Financial Reporting Council, should appoint a new committee by the end of June 1995 to examine how far compliance with the Code has progressed, how far other recommendations have been implemented, and whether the Code needs updating, whether the sponsorship of the new Committee should be broadened and whether wider maters of Corporate Governance should be included in its brief.
6. The Companies Act should be amended to come into line with the requirements of the Code that directors' service contracts should not exceed three years without shareholders' approval.
7. Companies should expand their interim reports to include balance sheet information. The London Stock Exchange should consider amending the continuing obligations accordingly. There should not be a requirement for a full audit, but interim reports should be reviewed by the auditors and the Auditing Practices Board should develop appropriate guidance. The Accounting Standards Board in the accounting rules which companies should follow in preparing interim reports. The inclusion of cash flow information should be considered by the Committee's successor body.
8. Fees paid to audit firms for non-audit firms for non-audit work should be fully disclosed. The essential principle is that disclosure should enable the relative significance of the company's audit and non-audit fees to the audit firm to be assessed, both in a UK context and, where here appropriate, a worldwide context.
9. The accountancy profession should draw up guidelines on the rotation of audit partners.
10. Directors should report on the effectiveness of their system of internal control, and the auditors should report on their statement. The accountancy profession together with representatives of prepares of accounts should draw up criteria for assessing effective systems of internal control and guidelines for companies and auditors.
11. Directors should state in the report and accounts that the business is a going concern, with supporting assumptions or qualifications as necessary, and the auditors should report on this statement. The accountancy profession together with representatives of prepares of accounts should develop guidance for companies and auditors.
12. The question of legislation to back the recommendations on additional reports on internal control system and going concern should be decided in the light of experience.

13. The Government should consider introducing legislation to extend to the auditors of all companies the statutory protection already available to auditors in the regulated sector (banks, building societies, insurance and investment business) so that they can report reasonable suspicion of fraud freely to the appropriate investigatory authorities.
14. The accountancy profession together with the legal profession and representatives of prepares of accounts should consider further the question of illegal acts other than fraud.
15. The accounting profession should continue its efforts to improve its standards and procedures so as to strengthen the standing and independence of auditors.
16. Institutional investors should disclose their policies on the use of their voting rights.
17. The Companies gives its full support to the objectives of the Financial Reporting Council and the Accounting Standards Boards. It welcomes the action by the Financial Reporting Review panel over companies whose accounts fall below accepted reporting standards.
18. The Committee supports the initiative of the Auditing Practices Board on the development of an expended audit report. It also gives its full support to the lead which it is taking on the development of auditing practice generally.
19. The Committee welcomes the statement by the Institutional Shareholders' Committee on the Responsibilities of Institutional Shareholders in the UK.
20. Issues which the Committees has identified that its successor body may wish to review or consider in greater dept include: the application of the code to smaller listed companies; directors' training; the rules for disclosures of directors' remuneration, and the role which shareholders could play; a requirement for inclusion of cash flow information in interim reports and the procedures for putting forward resolutions at general meetings. The Committee and its successor will also keep watch on developments regarding the nature and extent of auditors' liability.

IV. The Code of Best Practice

The Committee had suggested the following Code of Best Practices :

(*i*) The Board should meet regularly, retain full and effective control over the company and monitor the executive management.

(*ii*) There should be clearly accepted divisions of responsibilities at the head of company, which will ensure a balance of power and authority, such that no individual has unfettered powers of decision. Where the chairman is also the chief executive, it is essential that there should be a strong and independent element on the board, with a recognized senior member.

(*iii*) The board should include non-executive directors of sufficient caliber and number for their views to carry significant weight in the board's decisions.

(*iv*) The board should have a formal schedule of matters specifically reserved to it for decision to ensure that the direction and control of the company is firmly in its hands.

(*v*) There should be an agreed procedure for directors in the furtherance of their duties to take independent professional advice if necessary, at the company's expense.

(*vi*) All directors should have access to the advice and services of the company secretary, who is responsible to the board for ensuring that board procedures are followed and that applicable rules and regulation are complied with. Any question of the removal of the company secretary should be a matter for the board as a whole.

(*vii*) Non-executive directors should bring an independent judgment to bear on issues of strategy, performance, resources, including key appointments, and standards of conduct.

(*viii*) The majority should be independent of management and free from any business or other relationship which could materially interfere with the exercise of their, independent judgement. Apart from their fees and shareholding. Their fees, should reflect the time which they commit to the company.

(*ix*) Non-executive directors should be appointed for specified terms and reappointment should not be automatic.

(*x*) Non-executive directors should be selected through a formal process and both this process and their appointment should be a matter for the board as a whole.

(*xi*) Directors' service contracts should not exceed three years without shareholders approval.

(*xii*) There should be full and clear disclosure of directors' total emoluments and those of the chairman and highest-paid UK director, including pension contributions and stock options. Separate figures should be given for salary and performance related elements and the basis on which performance is measured should be explained.

(*xiii*) Executive director's pay should be subject to the recommendations of a remuneration committee made up wholly or mainly non-executive directors.

(*xiv*) It is the board's duty to present a balanced and understandable assessment of the company's position.

(*xv*) The board should ensure that an objective and professional relationship is maintained with the auditors.

(*xvi*) The board should establish an audit committee of at least three non executive directors with written terms of reference which deal clearly with its authority and duties.

(*xvii*) The directors should explain their responsibility for preparing the accounts next to a statement by the auditors about their reporting responsibilities.

(*xviii*) The directors should report on the effectiveness of the company's system of internal control.

(*xix*) The directors should report that the business is a going concern, with supporting assumptions or qualifications as necessary.

We can say that committee has tried to develop a baseline for good Corporate Governance in Joint Stock Company. Power of decision in Corporates does not lie with any single person i.e. Head of the Company but with the board of the company. Appointment of non-executive directors is also vested with the Board. But the committee failed to recommend the exact number of non-executive directors to be appointed by the Board. The process of corporate governance investigation had a number of desirable features such as - a visionary chair who energetically promoted his recommendation; a committee which reflected the main stakeholders; a draft report and process of consultation; and a final report whose- recommendations were widely accepted. Cadbury Committee is not based on a universal code but takes care of the companies of UK only. We can also see that there is a big gap between shareholders and CEO as there is no proper channel of communication between them to strengthen their relationships. Some might contend that it is blind to ethical standards. Overall we can say that good governance gives expression to ethical norms. It is also adds to the prosperity of any society over the long-term.

2. Ronald Hampel Committee Report (1998)

The Hampel Committee was constituted in UK in 1995 on the initiative of the Chairman of the Financial Reporting Council, Sir Sydney Lip worth. This was followed by Cadbury Committee Report to examine how far compliance with code has progressed, how far other recommendations have been implemented and whether the updating of Code was needed. The task force of this committee was to consolidate the recommendations of the CADBURY Report in 1992 (focusing on Financial reporting) and the Greenbury Report in 1995 (focusing on director's remuneration), and prepare a 'Combined Code' on Corporate Governance. THE Code, published in 1998, was attached to the listing rules of the stock exchange with the requirement that companies must either declare their adherence to its provisions or explain any deviation from them.

I. Composition of the Committee

The Following members had constituted the Committee :

"(i) Sir Ronald Hampel- Chairman, (ii) Michael Coppel (Chairman, Airsprung Furniture GROUP PLC), (iii) Giles Henderson CBE(Senior Partner, Slaughter and May), (iv) Sir Nigel Mohns (Executive Chairman, Slough Estates plc), (v) Tony Richards TD (directors, Henderson Crosthwaite Ltd), (vi) Tom Ross (Principal and Actuary, Aon Consulting Limited), (vii) Peter Smith (Chairman, Coopers & Lybarnd), (viii) David Thomas (Director and General Manager (Investments) - The Equitable Life Assurance Society), (ix) Sir Clive Thompson (Chief Executive, Rentokil Intial Plc).

II. Terms of Reference

The committee sought to promote high standards of Corporate Governance in the interests of investor protection and in order to preserve and enhance the standing of companies listed on the Stock Exchange. Against this background the Committee-

a. conducted a review of the Cadbury code and its implementation to ensure that the original purpose be achieved, proposing amendments to and deletions from the code as necessary.

b. Kept under review the role of directors, executive and non-executive, recognizing the need for cohesion of board and the common legal responsibilities of all directors;

c. Prepared to pursue any relevant matter arising from the report of the Study Group on Directors' Remuneration chaired by Sir Richard Greenbury;

d. Addressed as necessary the role of shareholders in Corporate Governance issues.

e. Addressed as necessary the role of auditors in Corporate Governance issues; and

f. Dealt with any other relevant maters.

III. Recommendations of the Committee

Without impairing investor protection, the committee always kept in mind the need to restrict the regulatory burden on companies, e.g. by substituting principles for detail wherever possible. The main recommendations of the Committee are as follows :

(i) Investors to articulate their investment objectives to management.

(ii) Investors to be more open with managements in giving feedback on companies' strategies and performance;

(iii) Improved training for fund managers on industrial and commercial awareness;

(iv) Improved training from company managers involved in investor relations;

(v) Meetings between companies and institutional investors to be properly held, with a clear and agreed agenda.

(vi) Companies should include in their annual reports a narrative account of how they apply the broad principles.

Overall the report makes a good impression yet the report should clearly define the number of non-executive directors. The need is that a proper channel should be improved so the investor and the top level authorities can exchange the information in the interest of various stakeholders. The Committee has defined the legal responsibilities of all the directors to be nominated in the board as well as making provisions for the necessary role of shareholders in Corporate Governance of the Company. But Committee ignored the formulation of code of conduct for Corporate Governance. The gap between two board meetings has also not fixed by the Committee.

3. Blue Ribbon Report (1999)

Blue Ribbon Committee was set up by the Securities and Exchange Commission (SEC), US, in 1998. In February 1999, the Committee published the Report on Improving the Effectiveness of Corporate Audit Committees (the Blue Ribbon Report). The recommendations of the Blue Ribbon Committee were adopted and declared to be mandatory by the NYSE, the American Stock Exchange (Amex), Nasdaq and the American Institute of Certified Public Accountants (AICP A). The recommendations are not mandatory for foreign concerns; but are subject to their own national laws.

"On February 13, 2002, SEC Chairman Harvey Pitt asked the NYSE to review its Corporate Governance listing standards. In conjunction with that request, the NYSE appointed this Corporate Accountability and Listing Standard Committee to review the

NYSE's current listing standards, along with recent proposals for reform, with the goal of enhancing the accountability, integrity and transparency of the Exchange's listed companies.

I. Terms of Reference

The main purpose behind the setting up of the committee are as follows:

i. Increasing the role and authority of independent directors.

ii. Tightening the definition of "independent" directors and adding new requirements in audit committee qualification.

iii. Fostering a focus on good Corporate Governance by -

(*a*) Giving shareholders more opportunity to monitor and participate in the governance of their companies.

(*b*) Establishing new control and enforcement mechanisms.

iv. Encouraging all listed companies to establish an orientation program for new board members.

v. Recommendations included reforms in: (1) accounting and auditing, to ensure meaningful, accurate and credible financial reporting; (2) disclosure requirements, to ensure that material information is clearly and promptly disclosed; and (3) the methods of holding officers and directors of public' companies more accountable to their shareholders.

vi. Require listed companies to have a majority of independent directors.

vii. Empowering non-management directors to serve as a more effective check on management.

viii. Require listed companies to have a compensation committee composed entirely of independent directors.

ix. Increasing the authority and responsibilities of the audit committee, including granting it the sole authority to hire and fire independent auditors, and to approve any significant non-audit relationship with the independent auditors.

x. Require listed companies to adopt and disclose their Corporate Governance guidelines.

II. Recommendations

1. Require listed companies to have a majority of independent directors: All currently listed companies be required to achieve majority independence within 24 months of this rule's enactment. Companies newly listing must comply within 24 months. Additionally, given the importance of majority - independent boards, a company must publicly disclose when it becomes compliant with this requirement.

2. Tighten the NYSE definition of 'independent director': No director qualifies as "independent' unless the board of directors affirmatively determines that the director has no material relationship with the listed company (directly or as a partner, shareholder or officer of an organization that has a relationship with the company). Companies must disclose these determinations.

3. Empower non- management directors to serve as a more effective check on management.

(*a*) The non-management directors of each company must meet at regularly scheduled executive sessions without management.

(*b*) The independent directors must designate, and publicly disclose the name of, the director which will preside at the executive sessions.

4. Require listed companies to have a nominating/ corporate governance committee composed entirely of independent directors. The nominating / corporate governance committee must have a written charter that addresses:

(*a*) the committee's purpose- which, at minimum, must be to - identify individuals qualified to become board members, and to select, or to recommend that the board select, the director nominees for the next annual meeting of shareholders; and develop and recommend to the board a set of corporate governance principles applicable to the corporation.

(*b*) the committee's goals and responsibilities- which must reflect, at minimum, the board's criteria for selecting new directors, and oversight of the evaluation of the board and management.

(*c*) an annual performance evaluation of the committee.

5. Require listed companies to have a compensation committee composed entirely of independent directors. The compensation committee must have a written charter that addresses :

(*a*) the committee's purpose - which, at minimum, must be to discharge the board's responsibilities relating to compensation of the company's executives, and to produce an annual report on executive compensation for inclusion rules and regulations.

(*b*) the committee's duties and responsibilities - which, at minimum must be to review and approve corporate goals and objectives relevant to CEO compensation, evaluate the CEO's performance in light of those goals and objectives, and set the CEO's performance in light of those goals and objectives, and set the CEO's compensation level based on this evaluation.

6. Add to the 'independence' requirement the following new requirements for audit committee membership at listed companies :

(*a*) Directors' fees are the only compensation an audit committee member may receive from the company.

(*b*) A Director who meets the definition of "independence" mandated for all audit committee members, but who also holds 20% or more of the company's stock (or who is a general partner, controlling shareholder or officer of any such holder) cannot chair, or be a voting member of, the audit committee.

(*c*) The audit committee chair must have accounting or related financial management expertise.

7. Increase the authority and responsibilities of the audit committees, including granting it the sole authority to hire and fire independent auditors, and to approve any significant non- audit relationship with the independent auditors. The audit committee must have a written charter that addresses :

(*a*) the committee's purpose- which., at minimum, must be to assist board oversight of (i) the integrity of the company's financial statements, (ii) the company's compliance with legal and regulatory requirements, (iii) the independent auditor's qualifications and independence, and (iv) the performance of the company's internal audit function and independent auditors; and prepare the report that SEC rules require be included in the company's annual proxy statement.

(*b*) the duties and responsibilities of the audit committees- which, at minimum, must be to retain and terminate the company's independent auditors (subject, if applicable, to shareholder ratification).

(*c*) at least annually, obtain and review a report by the independent auditors describing: the firm's internal quality control procedures; any material issues raised by the most recent internal quality - control review, or peer review, of the firm, or by any material issues raised by the most recent internal quality- control review, or peer review, of the firm, or by any inquiry or investigation by governmental or professional authorities, within the preceding five years, respecting one or more independent audits carried out by the firm, and any steps taken to deal with any such issues; and (to assess the auditors independence) all relationships between the independent auditor and the company.

8. Increase shareholder control over equity-compensation plans.

(*i*) Shareholders must be given the opportunity to vote on all equity-compensation plans.

(*ii*) A broker may not vote a customers' shares on any equity compensation plan unless the broker has received that customer's instructions to do so.

9. Require listed companies to adopt and disclose their corporate governance guidelines such as Director Qualification standards, Director Responsibilities, Director access to management and, as necessary and appropriate independent advisors. Director Compensation, Director orientation and continuing education, Management succession, and Annual performance evaluation of the board should be addressed in the corporate governance guidelines.

10. Require listed companies to adopt and disclose a code of business conduct and ethics for directors, officers and employees, and promptly disclose any waivers of the code for directors or executive officers.

11. Require listed foreign private issuers to disclose any significant ways in which their corporate governance practices differ from those followed by domestic companies under NYSE listing standards.

12. Require each listed company CEO to certify to the NYSE each year:

(*i*) that the company has established procedures for verifying the accuracy and completeness of the information provided to investors; that those procedures have been carried out; and that, based upon the CEO's assessment of the adequacy of those procedures and of the diligence of those carrying them out, the CEO has no reasonable cause to believe that the information provided to investors is not accurate and complete in all material respects. The CEO must further certify that he or she has reviewed with the board those procedures and the company's compliance with them.

(*ii*) that he or she is not aware of any violation by the company of NYSE listing standards.

5. Enable the NYSE to issue a public reprimand letter to any listed company that violates an NYSE listing standard.

Board of directors is an apex body of the corporate Governance. Therefore, in the report, boards need a provision of strong independent directors who would be accountable to investors. As it is observed that a much needed auditors oversight body and members independent of the public accounting profession, fully investigate and possessing disciplinary powers, and independent funding are the key characteristics. The second area to reform is the public accounting. These are the areas where the NYSE and the NASD have failed totally. The Committee has recommend an increase of powers of Independent Directors by adding new requirements in Audit Committee i.e. granting the sole authority to 'hire and fire; independent directors. Necessary recommendations have also been made regarding material information disclosure. However, the Committee has ignored the employees' participation by the way of 'Whistle Blower Policy'. Ethical and Environmental norms to strengthen the good Corporate Governance have also been ignored.

4. King Committee Report (2002)

The King Report on Corporate Governance for South Africa (the 'King Report 2002') has been developed as an enterprise of the Institute of Directors in Southern Africa. The King Committee on Corporate Governance under the chairmanship of MERVYN E.KING S.C. represents a version and update of the King Report first published in 1994 and is an attempt to keep standards of Corporate Governance in South Africa in step with those as in the rest of the world. All companies listed on the Johannesburg Stock Exchange have to comply with the provisions of the Report.

I. Terms of Reference

The detailed terms of reference are:

1. To review the King Report 1994 and to assess its currency against developments, locally and internationally, since its publication on 29 November 1994;
2. To review and clarify the earlier proposal in the King Report 1994 for an 'inclusive approach' for the sustainable success of companies;
3. To recognize the increasing importance placed on non-financial issues worldwide, and to consider and to recommend reporting on issues associated with social and ethical accounting, auditing and reporting ("SEAAR") and safety, health and environment ("SHE"); and
4. To recommend how compliance with a new Code of Corporate Governance for South Africa can be measured and based on outcomes, that is, how the of companies can be measured through the "balanced scorecard" approach for reporting.

II. Recommendations :

Major recommendations of the Committee are:

1. To ensure that the existing quorum threshold for company meetings is sufficient to permit access to share owners to management through this forum.
2. To speed up communication and transmission of information through electronic communication that would improve governance and communication that would improve governance and communication between companies and their shareowners.
3. To introduce amendments in the existing Companies Act, regarding the accounting standard-setting, monitoring and enforcement processes.
4. Audit requirements of the Companies Act should be re-considered for dormant and inactive fully owned subsidies.
5. The Committee also recommended that the Companies Act should be amended to provide for summarized or abbreviated annual financial statements, otherwise termed Concise Financial Report, to be issued to shareowners.
6. Transparency in the dealing of institutional investor with other companies.
7. The question of directors' and officers liability insurance requires to be revisited, as the current section 247 of the Companies Act is ambiguous and does not fully cover the original King Committee 1994 recommendation.
8. Directors or officers may, by their acts of commission or omission, have contributed to a company's failure. Damages against auditors for company failures are becoming a matter of grave concern. Directors and auditors should only be held liable for damagers on a basis proportional to their contribution to the failure.

The king Committees report mainly deals with the amendments in the Companies Act. It favours utmost transparency in the dealings with institutional investors. Importance of the independent directors and the ethical norms and standards are ignored, that must be taken care of. As per the recommendations of the Committee directors and auditors will be accountable for the failure of the Company. However, the Scope of the Committee is quite limited and has also been ignored.

5. Sarbanes Oaxley Act (2002)

Following the Corporate Governance scandals in the U.S, the Sarbanes Oaxley Act was enacted which brought about fundamental changes in virtually every area of Corporate Governance and particularly in auditor's independence, conflict of interest, corporate responsibility and enhanced financial disclosure. "The Sarbanes Oaxley Act proved to be a model for India". Main Provisions of the Act are as follows:

1. Commission Rules and Enforcement: Section 3 deals with violation of Rules of the Public Company Accounting Oversight Board ("Board") is treated as a violation of the' 34 Act, giving rise to the same penalties that may be imposed for violations of that Act.

2. Board Membership: Section 101 states the Board will have five financially- literate members, appointed for five - years terms. Two of the members must be or have been certified public accountants, and the remaining three must not be and cannot have been CPA's the Chair may be held by one of the CPA members, provided that he or she has not been engaged as a practicing CPA for five years. The Board's members will serve on a full-time basis. No member may, concurrent with service on the Board, share in any of the profits of, or services payments from, a public accounting firm, other than fixed continuing payments, such as retirement payments. Members of the Board are appointed by the Commission, after consultation with the Chairman of the Federal Reserve Board and the Secretary of the Treasury. Members may be removed by the Commission 'for good cause'.

3. Auditing Quality Control, and Independence Standards and Rules: Section 103 states that the Board shall:

(*i*) register public accounting firms;

(*ii*) establish or adopt, by rule, auditing, quality control, ethics, independence, and other standards, relating to the preparation of audit reports for issuers;

(*iii*) conduct inspections of accounting firms.

(*iv*) Conduct investigations and disciplinary proceedings, and impose appropriate sanctions;

(*v*) Perform such other duties or functions as necessary or appropriate;

(*vi*) Enforce compliance with the Act, the rules of the Board, professional standards, and the securities laws relating to the preparation and issuance of audit reports and the obligations and liabilities of accountants with respect thereto;

(*vii*) Set the budget and manage the operations of the Board and the staff of the Board.

4. Auditing Standards: The Board would be required to 'cooperate on an on-going basis' with designated professional groups of accountants and any advisory groups convened in connection with standards- setting, and although the Board can 'to the extent that it determines appropriate' adopt standards proposed by those groups, the Board will have authority to amend, modify, repeal, and reject any standards suggested by the groups. The board must report on its standards- setting activity to the Commission on an annual basis.

The Board requires registered public accounting firms to prepare, and maintain for a period of not less than 7 years, audit work papers, and other information related to any audit report, in sufficient detail to support the conclusions reached in such report. The Board also requires a 2nd partner review and approval of audit reports registered accounting firms must adopt quality control standards.

The board must adopt an audit standards to implement the internal control review required by section 404(b). This standards must require the auditor evaluate whether the internal control structure and procedures include records that accurately and fairly reflect the transactions of the issuers, provide reasonable assurance that the transaction are recorded in a manner that will permit the preparation of financial statements in accordance with GAAP, and a description of any material weakness in the internal controls.

5. Mandatory Registration: Section 102 (a) states that Beginning 180 day after the date of the determination of the Commission under section 101 (d), it shall be unlawful for any person that is not a registered public accounting firm to prepare or issue, or to participate in the preparation or issuance of, any audit report with respect to any issuer.

6. Funding; Annual Accounting Support Fee for the Board: Section 109 (d) deals to audit a public company, a public accounting firm must register itself in the Board. The Board shall collect 'a registration fee' and 'an annual fee' from each registered public accounting firm, in amounts that are sufficient' to recover the costs of processing and reviewing applications and annual reports.

The board shall also establish by rule a reasonable 'annual accounting support fee' as may be necessary or appropriate to maintain the Board. This fee will be assessed on issuers only.

7. Inspection of Registered Public Accounting Firms: Section 104 deals with Annual quality reviews (inspections) must be conducted for firms that audit more than 100 issues, all others must be conducted every 3 years. The SEC and/or the Board may order a special inspection of any firm at any time.

8. Investigations and Disciplinary Proceedings; Reporting of Sanctions: Sections 105(d) deals with all documents and information prepared or received by the Board shall be confidential and privileged as an evidentiary matter and shall not be subject to civil discovery other legal proves) in any proceeding in any Federal or State court or administrative agency, unless and until presented in connection with a public proceeding or [otherwise] released in connection with a disciplinary action. However, all such documents and information can be made available to the SEC, the US Attorney General, and other federal and appropriate stage agencies.

Disciplinary hearings will be closed unless the Board orders that they be public, for good cause, and with the consent of the parties.

Sanctions can be imposed by the Board of a firm if it fails to reasonably supervise any associated person with regard to auditing or quality control standards, or otherwise. No sanctions report will be made available to the public unless stays pending appeal have been lifted.

9. Foreign Public Accounting Firms: Section 106 states that the bill would subject foreign accounting firms who audit a U.S. Company to registration with the Board. This would include foreign firms that perform some audit work, such as in a foreign subsidiary of a U.S. a company, which is relied on by the primary auditors.

10. Censure of the Board and other Sanctions: Section 107 (d) states that the SEC shall have oversight and enforcement authority over the Board. The SEC can, by rule or order, give the Board additional responsibilities. The SEC may require the Board to keep certain records, and it has the power to inspect the Board to keep certain records, and it has the power to inspect the Board itself, in the same manner as it can with regard to SROs such as the NASD.

The Board must notify the SEC of pending investigations involving potential violations of the securities laws, and coordinate its investigation with the SEC Division of Enforcement as necessary to protect an going SEC investigation. The SEC may, by order, censure or impose limitations upon the activities, functions, and operations of the Board if it finds that the Board has violated the Act or the securities laws, or of the Board has failed to ensure the compliance of accounting firms with applicable rules without reasonable justification.

11. Accounting Standards: With the power depicted by Section 108 the SEC is authorized to recognize, as 'generally accepted' any accounting principles" that are established by a standard - setting body that meets the bills criteria, which include requirements that the body-

(*i*) be a private entity.

(*ii*) Be governed by a board of trustees (or equivalent body), the majority of whom are not or have not been associated persons with a public accounting firm for the past 2 years;

(*iii*) be funded in a manner similar to the Board;

(*iv*) have adopted procedures to ensure prompt consideration of changes to accounting principles by a majority vote;

(*v*) considers, while adopting standards, the need to keep them current and the extent to which international convergence of standards is necessary or appropriate.

12. Services outside the Scope of Practice of Auditors; Prohibited Activities : According to Section 201, it shall be 'unlawful' for a registered public accounting firm to provide any non-audit service to an issuer contemporaneously with the audit, including: (i) bookkeeping or other services related to the accounting records or financial statements of the audit client; (ii) financial information systems design and implementation; (iii) appraisal or valuation services, fairness opinions, or contribution-in-kind reports; (iv) actuarial services; (v) Internal audit outsourcing services; (vi) management functions or human resources; (vii) broker or dealer, investment advisor, or investment banking services, (viii) legal services and expert services unrelated to the audit; (ix) any other service that the Board determines, by regulation, is impermissible. The Board may, on a case-by-case basis, exempt from these prohibitions any person, issuer, public accounting firm, or transactions, subject to review by the Commission.

The authority to pre-approve services can be delegated to 1 or more members of the audit committee, but any decision by the delegate must be presented to the full audit committee.

13. Audit Partner Rotation: Section 203 represents the lead audit or coordinating partner and the reviewing partner must rotate off of the audit every 5 years.

14. Auditors Reports to Audit Committees: Section 204 make a statement that the accounting firm must report to the audit committee all critical accounting policies and practices to be used all alternative treatments of financial information within [GAAP] that have been discussed with management ramifications of the use of such alternative disclosers and treatments, and the treatment preferred by the firm.

15. Conflicts of Interest: Section 206 states that the CEO, Controller, CFO, Chief Accounting Officer or person in an equivalent position cannot have been employed by the company's audit firm during the 1- year preceding the audit.

16. Study of Mandatory Rotation of Registered Public Accountants: Section 206 shows that the GAO will do a study on the potential effects of requiring the mandatory rotation of audit firms.

17. Consideration by Appropriate State Regulatory Authorities: Section 209 says that the state regulators are directed to make an independent determination as to whether the Boards standards shall be applied to small and mid -size non-registered accounting firms.

18. Corporate Responsibility for financial Reports: Section 302 express that the CEO and CFO of each issuer shall prepare a statement to accompany the audit report to certify the appropriateness of the financial statements and disclosures contained in the periodic report, and that those financial statements and disclosures fairly present, in all material respects, the operations and financial conditions of the issuers. A violations of this section must be knowing and international to give rise to liability.

19. Improper influence on Çonduct of Audits: Section 303 imparts that it shall unlawful for any officer or director of an issuer to take any action to fraudulently influence, coerce, manipulate, or mislead any auditor engaged in the performance of an audit for the purpose of rendering the financial statements materially misleading.

20. Officer and Director Bars and Penalties; Equitable Relief: Section 305 depicts that the SEC may issue an order to prohibit, conditionally or unconditionally, permanently or temporarily, any person who has violated section 10 (b) of the 1934 Act from acting as an officer or director of an issuer of the SEC has found that such person's conduct 'demonstrates unfitness' to serve as an officer or director of any such issuer.

In any action brought by the SEC for violation of the securities laws, federal courts are authorized to grant any equitable relief that may be appropriate or necessary for the benefit of investors.

21. Insider Trades During Pension Fund Black - Out periods Prohibited: Section 306 prohibits the purchase or sale of stock by officers and directors and other insiders during blackout periods. Any profits resulting from sales in violation of this section shall insure to and be recoverable by the issuer. If the issuer fails to bring suit or prosecute diligently, a suit to recover such profit may be instituted by the owner of any security of the issuer.

22. Disclosure in Periodic Reports; Disclosures Required: Section 401 (a) states that each financial report, which is required to be prepared in accordance with GAAP shall reflect all material correcting adjustments that have been identified by a registered accounting firm.

Each annual and quarterly financial report shall disclose all material off-balance sheet transactions and other relationships with 'unconsolidated entities' that may have a material current or future effect on the financial condition of the issuer.

The SEC shall issue rules providing that pro-from a financial information must be presented so as not to contain an 'untrue statement' or omit to state a material fact necessary in order to make the pro forma financial information not misleading.

23. Prohibition on Personal Loans to Executives: Section 492 (a) declares generally, it will be unlawful for an issuer to extend credit to any director or executive officer. Consumer credit companies may make home improvements and consumer credit loans and issue credit cards to its directors and executive officers if it is done in the ordinary course of business on the same terms and conditions made to the general public.

24. Disclosures of Transactions Involving Management and Principal Stockholders: Section 403 imparts that Directors, officers, and 10% owner must report designated transitions by the end of the seconds business day following the day on which the transactions was executed.

25. Management Assessment of Internal Controls: Section 404 requires each annual report of an issuer to contain an 'internal control report' which shall :

(*i*) state the responsibility of management for establishing and maintaining an Adequate control structure and procedures for financial reporting; and

(*ii*) contain an assessment, as of the end of the issuer's fiscal year, of the effectiveness of the internal control structure and procedures of the issuer for financial reporting.

26. Disclosure of Audit Committee Financial Expert: Section 407 declares that the SEC shall issue rules to require issuers to disclose whether at least 1 member of its audit committee is a 'financial expert'.

27. Real Time Disclosure: Section 409 states that the issuers must disclose information on material changes in the financial condition or operations of the issuers on a rapid and current basis.

28. Treatment of Securities Analysts by Registered Securities Associations: Section 501 deals with the National Securities Exchanges and registered securities associations must adopt conflict of interest rules for research analysts who recommend equities in research reports.

29. Appearance and Practice before the Commission: Section 602(a) says that the SEC may censure any person or temporarily bar or deny any person the right to appear or practice before the SEC if the person does not possess the requisite qualifications to represent others, lacks character or integrity, or has willfully violated Federal Securities laws.

30. Study and Report: Section 602(c) represents that SEC is to conduct a study of 'securities Professionals' (public accountants, public accounting firms, investment bankers, investment advisors, brokers, dealers, attorneys) who have been found to have aided and abetted a violation of Federal securities laws.

31. Corporate and Criminal Fraud Accountability Act of 2002: It is a felony to knowingly' destroy or create documents to 'impede, obstruct or influence' any existing or contemplated federal investigation. Auditors are required to maintain all audits or review work papers for five years. The statute of limitations on securities fraud claims is extended to the earlier of five years from the fraud, or two years after the Fraud was discovered, from three years one year, respectively.

Employees of issuers of accounting firms are extended 'whistle blower protection' that would prohibit the employer from taking certain actions against employees who lawfully disclose private employer information to, among others parties in a judicial proceeding involving a fraud claim. Whistle blowers are also granted a remedy of special damages and attorney's fees. For the crime in Securities fraud has penalties of fines and up to 10 years imprisonment.

32. White Collar Crime Penalty Enhancements: Maximum penalty for mail and wire fraud increased from 5 to 10 years. It promotes crime for tampering with a record or otherwise impeding any official proceeding. SEC has given authority to seek court freeze of extraordinary payments to directors, officer, partners, controlling persons, agents of employees. US Sentencing Commission to review sentencing guidelines for securities and accounting fraud is provided. SEC may prohibit anyone convicted of securities fraud from being an officer or director of any publicly traded company.

Financial Statements filed with the SEC must be certified by the CEO and CFO. The certification must state the financial statements and disclosures fully comply with provisions of the Securities Exchange Act and that they fairly present, in all material respect, the operations and financial condition of the issuer. Maximum penalties for willful and knowing violations of this section are a fine of not more than $ 5,00,000 and/or imprisonment of up to 5 years.

33. SEC Authority to Prohibit Persons from Serving as officers or Directors: Section 1105 declares that the SEC may prohibit a person from serving as an officer or director of a public company if the person has committed securities fraud.

When we go through the Act, was find that though SOX Act is broadly defined yet the Audit Committee lacks sufficient powers so the Board is not under any compulsion to follow the Committees' recommendations. It affects the accountability and responsibility of the Audit Committee a lot. The Committee has extended the Whistle Blower protection to employees of issuers and accounting firms. But it has made it optional for the Board to follow the Audit Committee recommendations. So, how can audit control be exercised in a Company is an important question which has been ignored by the Committees. The notion that 'Corporate irresponsibility' is relatively more widespread in the United States than elsewhere is based more on assertion than on any hard empirical evidence. Therefore, many would consider existing U.S. laws to be already on the conservative side when compared to other international corporate law regimes.

6. The Combined Code on Corporate Governance (2003)

This UK based code supersedes and replaces the Combined Code issued by Ronald Hampel committee on Corporate Governance in June 1998. It is derived from a review of the role and effectiveness of non-executive directors by Derek Higgs and a review of audit committees by a group led by Sir Robert Smith.

The report includes guidance on how to comply with particular parts of the Code: first, "Internal Control-Guidance from Director on the Combined Code, produced by the Turnbull Committee, which relates to code provisions on internal control and, second 'Audit Committees: Combined Code Guidance' , produced by the Smith Group, which relates to the provisions on audit committees and auditors. In Both cases, the guidance suggest ways of applying the relevant Code principles and of complying with the relevant Code provisions."

When the Combined Code of the Committees on Corporate Governance (the Code) was published, the institute of Chartered Accountants in England & Wales agreed with the London Stock Exchange that it would provide guidance to assist listed companies to implement the requirements in the Code relating to internal control. Principle D.2 of the Code states that the board should maintain a sound system of internal control to safeguard shareholders' investment and the company's assets. Provisions D.2.1 states that the directors should, at least, conduct annually, a review of the effectiveness of the group's system of internal control and should report to shareholders that they have done so. The review should cover all controls, including financial, operational and compliance which do not have an internal audit function should from time to time review the need for one. Paragraph 12.43A of the London Stock Exchange Listing Rules states that in the case of a company incorporated in the United Kingdom.

I. Terms of Reference

The terms of reference of the code intends to:

a. reflect sound business practice whereby internal control is embedded in the business processes by which a company pursues its objectives;

b. remain relevant over time in the continually evolving business environment;

c. enable each company to apply it in a manner which takes account of its particular circumstances.

II. Code provisions

1. Every company should be headed by an effective boards, which is collectively responsible for the success of the company. All directors must take decisions objectively in the interest of the company.

2. The board should meet sufficiently regularly to discharge its duties effectively. There should be a formal schedule of matters specifically reserved for its decision. The annual report should include a statement of how the board operates, including a high level statement of which types of decisions are to be taken by the board and which are to be delegated to management.

3. here should be a clear division of responsibilities at the head of the company between the running of the board and the executive responsibility for the running of the company's business. No one individual should have unfettered powers of decision.

4. The roles of chairman and chief executive should not be exercised by the same individual. The division of responsibilities between the chairman and chief executive should be clearly established, set out in writing and agreed by the board.

5. The board should include a balance of executive and non-executive directors (and in particular independent non-executive directors) such that no individual or small group of individuals can dominate the board's decision taking.

6. The board should identify in the annual report each non-executive director it considers to be independent. The board should determine whether the director is independent in character and judgement and whether there are relationships or circumstances which are likely to affect, or could appear to affect, the director's judgement. The board should state its reasons if it determines that a director is independent notwithstanding the existence of relationships or circumstances which may appear relevant to its determination.

7. There should be a nomination committee which should lead the process for board appointments and make recommendations to the board. A majority of members of the nomination committee should be independent non-executive directors. The chairman or an independent non-executive director should chair the committee, but the

chairman should not chair the nomination committee when it is dealing with the appointment of a successor to the chairmanship. The nomination committee should make available its terms of reference, explaining its role and the authority delegated to it by the board.

8. The chairman should ensure that new directors receive a full, formal and tailored induction on joining the board. As part of this, the company should offer to major shareholders the opportunity to meet a new non-executive director.

9. The board should state in the annual report how performance evaluation of the board, its committees and its individual directors has been conducted. The non-executive directors, led by the senior independent director, should be responsible for performance evaluation of the chairman, taking into account the views of executive directors.

10. All directors should be subject to election by shareholders at the first annual general meeting after their appointment, and to re-election thereafter at intervals of no more than three years. The names of directors submitted for election or re-election should be accompanied by sufficient biographical details and any other relevant information to enable shareholders to take an informed decision on their election.

11.The performance-related elements of remuneration should form a significant proportion of the total remuneration package of executive directors and should be designed to align their interests with those of shareholders and to give these directors keen incentives to perform at the highest levels.

12. The remuneration committee should have delegated responsibility for setting remuneration for all executive directors and the chairman, including pension rights and any compensation payments. The committee should also recommend and monitor the level and structure of remuneration for senior management. The definition of 'senior management' for this purpose should be determined by the board but should normally include the first layer of management below board level.

13. The directors should explain in the annual report their responsibility for preparing the accounts and there should be a statement by the auditors about their reporting responsibilities.

14. The board should, at least annually, conduct a review of the effectiveness of the group's system of internal controls and should report to shareholders that they have done so. The review should cover all material controls, including financial, operational and compliance controls and risk management systems.

15. The board should establish an audit committee of at least three, or in the case of smaller companies two members, who should all be independent non-executive directors. The board should satisfy itself that at least one member of the audit committee has recent and relevant financial experience.

16. The audit committee should have primary responsibility for making a recommendation on the appointment, reappointment and removal of the external auditors. If the board does not accept the audit committee's recommendation, it should include in the annual report, and in any papers recommending appointment or re-appointment, a statement from the audit committee explaining the recommendation and should Bet out reasons why the board has taken a different position.

17. The chairman should ensure that the views of shareholders are communicated to the board as a whole. The chairman should discuss governance and strategy with major shareholders. Non-executive directors should be offered the opportunity to attend meetings with major shareholders and should expect to attend them if requested by major shareholders. The senior independent director should attend sufficient meetings with a range of major shareholders to listen to their views in order to help develop a balanced understanding of the issues and concerns of major shareholders.

After studying the reports we find that The Combined Code on Corporate Governance only concentrates on internal control system while there is a demand of overall control system so as to develop a sound system. Moreover, sibling companies are often burdened with heavy procedures of corporate governance to get themselves registered under listing agreements. Keeping this in view, The Combined Code on Corporate Governance comes ahead with the objectives of making it easier for them. The Committee advocated the strengthening of internal control system. However, Committee ignores the important issues liker importance of Whistle Blower Policy, Ethical norms for good Corporate Governance and Environmental norms etc.

7. Higgs Report (2003)

A mainstay of the UK response to the Corporate Governance fallout from the US was to set up an independent review to be led by Derek Higgs of the role and effectiveness of non -executive directors. This was initiated by the Secretary of State for Trade and Industry and the Chancellor, in April 2002. Higgs was an executive director of Prudential plc, and a non-executive director of Allied Irish Bank plc, the British Land Company, Jones lang la sale inc, and Egg. He was also a senior advisor of USB Warburg Group. He was chairman of Partnerships UK, a now privatized government agency responsible for fostering PPP and PFI. He was a member of the Financial reporting Council, a Department of Trade and Industry committee to oversee financial reporting and company accounting, and a government advisory committee on business and the environment.

I. Terms of Reference

The detailed terms of reference were to asses:

(*i*) the population of non-executive directors in the UK- who are they-how are they appointed, how the pool might be widened, etc;

(*ii*) their 'independence,

(*iii*) their 'effectiveness';

(*iv*) Accountability; their relationship actual and potential - with institutional investors;

(*v*) Issues relating to non-executive director's remuneration;

(*vi*) The role of the Combined Code;

(*vii*) What, if anything, could be done- by individual boards, by institutional investors, by the Government or otherwise - to strengthen the quality, independence and effectiveness of non-executive directors.

II. Suggestions

The report reviewed the role and effectiveness of non-executive directors in the UK. The review further developed the UK framework of Corporate Governance, which commenced with the publication of the Cadbury report in 1992 and was taken forward by the Greenbury, Hampel and Trunbull reports.

The Higgs Report suggested following for the good practice:

(*a*) guidance for the chairman

(*b*) guidance for non-executive directors

(*c*) principal duties of the remuneration committee

(*d*) principal duties of the nomination committee

(*e*) pre-appointment due diligence checklist for new board members

(*f*) Non-executive director appointment.

The Committee has given a comprehensive provisions regarding role of non-executive directors and also reviewed the Cadbury Committee Recommendations. However, it has also ignored the importance of Audit Committee and Whistle Blower Policy etc. in its recommendations. We therefore, see the gap between the good governance and the effective board. Overall the review is useful for strengthening Corporate Governance.

8. ASX Corporate Governance Council Report (2003)

The ASX corporate governance council was formed on 15 August 2002, headed by Karen Leslie Hamilton bringing together 21 groups from disparate business backgrounds and carrying the varying aims and priorities that accompany those constituencies, with the objective of developing and delivering an industry-wide, supportable and supported framework for corporate Governance.

The enhancement of corporate accountability and the adoption of this framework for reporting is a major evolution in Corporate Governance practice in Australia. "In March 2003, the ASX Corporate Governance and best Practice Recommendations'. Compliance with the recommendations dealing with Audit Committees, but from 2004 listed entities are required to report in their annual report on whether they have complied during the year the subject of the report, or if they have not".

Recommendations: The major recommendations were :

(*a*) Formalize and disclose the functions reserved to the board and those delegated to management.

(*b*) A majority of the board should be independent directors.

(*c*) The chairperson should be an independent director.

(*d*) The roles of chairperson and chief executive officer should not be exercised by the same individual.

(*e*) The board should establish a nomination committee.

(*f*) Establish a code of conduct to guide the directors, the chief executive officer, the chief financial officer (or equivalent) and any other key executives.

(*g*) Disclose the policy concerning trading in company securities by directors, officers and employees.

(*h*) Require the chief executive officer (or equivalent) and the chief financial officer (or equivalent) to state in writing to the board that the company's financial reports present a true and fair view, in all material respects, of the company's financial condition and operational results and are in accordance with relevant accounting standards.

(*i*) Establish written policies and procedure designed to ensure compliance with ASX Listing Rule disclosure requirements and to ensure accountability at a senior management level for that compliance.

(*j*) Design and disclose a communications strategy to promote effective communication with shareholders and encourage effective participation at general meetings.

(*k*) The board or appropriate board committee should establish policies on risk oversight and management.

(*l*) Disclose the process for performance evaluation of the Board, its committees and individual directors, and key executives.

(*m*) Provide disclosure in relation to the company's remuneration policies to enable investors to understand (i) the costs and benefits of those policies and (ii) the link between remuneration paid to directors and key executives and corporate performance.

(*n*) Establish and disclose a code of conduct to guide compliance with legal and other obligations to legitimate stakeholders.

A deeper study of the report reveals that the ASX Council Report considered flexibility to optimize individual performance, however, be tempered by accountability -

The obligation to explain to investors why an alternative approach is adopted- the 'if not, why not?' Obligation. Also, the lack of the social responsibility is the drawback of the report, because the companies are the part of our society. The Committee has given a comprehensive provisions regarding role of non-executive directors and also reviewed the Cadbury Committee Recommendations. However, it has also ignored the importance of Audit Committee and Whistle Blower Policy etc. in its recommendations.

OECD Principles of Corporate Governance (2004)

The principles are intended to assist governments in their efforts to evaluate and improve the legal, institutional and regulatory framework for Corporate Governance in their countries, and to provide guidance and suggestions for stock exchanges, investors, corporations and other parties that have a role in the process of developing good governance. The organization for Economic Co-operation and Development (GECD) shall promote policies designed.

1. to achieve the highest sustainable economic growth and employment and a rising standard of living in members countries, while maintaining financial stability, and thus to contribute to the development of the world economy;
2. to contribute to sound economic expansion in member as well as non-member countries in the process of economic development; and
3. to contribute to the expansion of world trade on a multilateral, non-discriminatory basis in accordance with international obligations.

The original member countries of the GECD are Australia, Belgium, Canada, Denmark, Franch, Germany, Greece, Iceland, Ireland, Italy, Luxembourg, the Neatherlands, Norway, Portugal, Spain, Sweden, Switzerland, Turkey, the United Kingdom and the United States.

I. Composition of the Committee

The review of the Principles was undertaken by the OECD Steering Group on Corporate Governance under a mandate from OECD ministries in 2002. The review was supported by a comprehensive survey of how member countries addressed the different Corporate Governance challenges they faced, experts who contributed to the review, including: (i) Susan Bies, (ii) Susan Bray, (iii) Ron Blackwell, (iv) Alain -Xavier Briatte, (v) David Brown, (vi) Luiz Candtidiano, (vii) Maria Livanos Cattaui, (viii) Peter Clifford, (ix) Andrew crockett, (x) Stephen Davis, (xi) Peter Dey, (xii) Carmine Di Noia, (xiii) John Evans, (xiv) Jefrfrey Garten, (xv) Leo Goldschmidt, (xvi) James Grant, (xvii) Gerd Hausler, (xviii) Tom Jones, (xix) Stephen Joynt, (xx) Erich Kandler, (xxi) Michael Klein, (xxii) Igor Kostikov, (xxiii) Daniel Lenegue, (xxiv) Teruo Masaki, (xxv) II-Chong Nam, (xxvi) Taijii Okusu, (xxvii) Michel pebereau, (xxviii) Caroline Phillips, (xxix) Patricia Peter, (xxx) John Plender, (xxxi) Michel Prada, (xxxii) Ilain Richards, (xxxiii) Alastrair Ross Goobey, (xxxiv) Albrecht Schafer, (xxxv) Christian Strenger, (xxxvi) Barbara Thomas, (xxxvii) Jean - Claude tricher, (xxxviii) Tom Vant, (xxxix) graham Ward, (xl) Edwin Wright and (xli) Eddy Wrmeerch. In addition to participants from all OECD countries, the OECD Steering Group on Corporate Governance includes regular observers from the World Bank, the international Monetary Fund (IMF) and the Bank for International Settlements (BIS). For the purpose of the review of the Principles, The Financial Stability Forum (FSF), The Basel Committee on Banking Supervision, and the International Organization of Securities Commissions (IOSCO) were invited as ad hoc observers.

The OECD principles are intended to assist governments in their efforts to evaluate and improve the legal, institutional and regulatory framework for Corporate Governance in their countries, and to provide guidance and suggestions for stock exchanges, investors, corporations, and other parties that have a role in the process of developing good Corporate Governance. The Principles focus on publicly traded companies, both financial and non-financial.

II. Principles

The major revised principles are as follows:

1. The Corporate governance framework should be developed to view its impact on overall economic performance, market integrity and the incentives it creates for market participants and the promotion of transparent and efficient markets.
2. The legal and regulatory requirements that affect corporate governance practices in a jurisdiction should be consistent with the rule of law, transparent and enforceable.
3. The division of responsibilities among different authorities in a jurisdiction should be clearly articulated and ensure that the public interest is served.
4. Supervisory, regulatory and enforcement authorities should have the authority, integrity and resources to fulfill their duties in a professional and objective manner.
   Moreover, their rulings should be timely, transparent and fully explained.
5. Basic shareholders rights should include the right to:
   (*i*) secure methods of ownership registration;
   (*ii*) conveyor transfer shares;
   (*iii*) obtain relevant and material information on the corporation on a timely and regular basis;
   (*iv*) participate and vote in general shareholders meetings;
   (*v*) elect and remove members of the board; and
   (*vi*) share in the profits of the corporation.
6. Shareholders should have the rights to participate sin, and to be sufficiently informed on, decisions concerning fundamental corporate changes such as:
   (*a*) amendments to the statues, or articles of incorporation or similar governing documents of the company;
   (*b*) the authorization of additional shares; and
   (*c*) extraordinary transactions, including the transfer of all or substantially all assets, that in effect result in the sale of the company.
7. Shareholders should have the opportunity to participate effectively and vote in general shareholders meetings and should be informed of the rules, including voting procedures that govern general shareholders meetings:

(*i*) Shareholders should be furnished with sufficient and timely information concerning the date, location and agenda of general meetings, as well as full and timely information regarding the issues to be decided at the meeting.

(*ii*) Shareholders should have the opportunity to ask questions to the board, including questions relating to the annual external audit, to place items on the agenda of general meetings, and to propose resolutions, subject to reasonable limitations.

(*iii*) Effective shareholder participation in key corporate governance decisions, such as the nomination and election of board members, should be facilitated. Shareholders should be able to make their views known on the remuneration policy for board members and key executives. The equity components of compensation schemes for board members and employees should be subject to shareholders approval.

(*iv*) Shareholders should be able to vote in person or in absentia.

8. Capital structures and arrangements that enable certain shareholders to obtain a degree of control disproportionate to their equity ownership should be disclosed.

9. Markets for corporate control should be allowed to function in an efficient and transparent manner.

a. the rules and procedures governing the acquisition of corporate control in the capital markets, and extraordinary transactions such as mergers, and sales of substantial portions of corporate assts, should be clearly articulated and disclosed so that investors understand their rights and recourse. Transactions should occur at transparent prices and under fair conditions that protect the rights of all shareholders according to their class.

b. Anti-take-over devices should not be used to shield management and the board from accountability.

10. The exercise of ownership rights by all shareholders, including institutional investors, should be facilitated.

(*i*) Institutional investors acting in a fiduciary capacity should disclose their overall corporate governance and voting policies with respect to their investments, including the procedures that they have in place for deciding on the use of their voting rights.

(*ii*) Institutional investors acting in a fiduciary capacity should disclose how they manage material conflicts of interest that may affect the exercise of key ownership rights regarding their investments.

11. Shareholders, including institutional shareholders, should be allowed to consult with each other on issues concerning their basic shareholder rights as defined in the principles, subject to exceptions to prevent abuse.

12. All shareholders of the same series of a class should be treated equally.

(*i*) Within any series of a class, all shares should carry the same rights. All investors should be able to obtain information about the rights attached to all series and classes of shares before they purchase. Any changes in voting rights should be subject to approval by those classes of shares which are negatively affected.

(*ii*) Minority shareholders should be protected from abusive actions by, or in the interest of, controlling shareholders acting either directly or indirectly, and should have effective means of redress.

(*iii*) Votes should be cast by custodians or nominees in a manner agreed upon with the beneficial owner of the shares.

(*iv*) Impediments to cross border voting should eliminated.

(*v*) Processes and procedures for general shareholders meetings should allow for equitable treatment of all shareholders. Company procedures should not make it unduly difficult or expensive to cast votes.

13. Members of the board and key executives should be required to disclose to the board whether they, directly, indirectly or on behalf of third parties, have a material interests in any transaction or mater directly affecting the corporation.

14. The rights of stakeholders that are established by law or through mutual agreements are to be respected.

15. Where stakeholders interests are protected by law, stakeholders should have the opportunity to obtain effective redress for violation of their rights.

16. Performance - enhancing mechanisms for employees participation should be permitted to develop.

17. Where stakeholders participate in the corporate governance process, they should have access to relevant, sufficient and reliable information on a timely and regular basis.
18. Stakeholders, including individual employees and their representatives bodies, should be able to freely communicate their concerns about illegal or unethical practices to the board and their rights should not be compromised for doing this.
19. The Corporate governance framework should be complemented by an effective, efficient insolvency framework and by effective enforcement of creditors rights.
20. Remuneration policy for members of the board and key executives, and information about board meeting, including their qualifications, the selection process, other company directorships and whether they are regarded as independent by the board.
21. Information should be prepared and disclosed in accordance with high quality standards of accounting and financial and non-financial disclosure.
22. An annual audit should be conducted by an independent, competent and qualified, auditor in order to provide an external and objective assurance to the board and shareholders that the financial statements fairly represent the financial position and performance of the company in all material respects.
23. External auditors should be accountable to the shareholders and owe a duty to the company to exercise due professional care in the conduct of the audit.
24. Channels for disseminating information should provide for equal, timely and cost- efficient access to relevant information by users.
25. The Corporate governance framework should be complemented by an effective approach that addresses and promotes the provision of analysis or advice by analysts, brokers, rating agencies and others, that is relevant to decisions by investors, free from material conflicts of interest that might comprise the integrity of their analysis or advice.

III. Principles regarding Responsibilities of the Board

Principles regarding Responsibilities of the Board are as follows:

1. Board members should act on a fully informed basis, in good faith, with due diligence and care, and in the best interest of the company and the shareholders.
2. Where board decisions may affect different shareholders groups differently, the board should treat all shareholders fairly.
3. The board should apply high ethical standards. It should take into account the interests of stakeholders.
4. The board should fulfill certain key functions, including:
   (*i*) Reviewing and guiding corporate strategy, major plans of action, risk policy, Annual budgets and business plans; setting performance objectives; monitoring implementation and corporate performance; and overseeing major capital expenditures, acquisitions and diversitures.
   (*ii*) Monitoring the effectiveness of the company's governance practices and making changes as needed.
   (*iii*) Selecting, compensating, monitoring and, when necessary, replacing key executives and overseeing succession planning.
   (*iv*) Aligning key executive and board remuneration with the longer term interests of the company and its shareholders.
   (*v*) Monitoring and managing potential conflicts of interest of management, board members and shareholders, including misuse of corporate assets and abuse in related party transactions.
   (*vi*) Ensuring the integrity of the corporation's accounting and financial reporting systems, including the independent audit, and that appropriate system of control are in place, in particular, systems for risk management, financial and operational control, and compliance with the law and relevant standards.
   (*vii*) Boards should consider assigning a sufficient number of non-executive board members capable of exercising independent judgement to tasks where is a potential for conflict of interest. Examples of such key responsibilities are ensuring the integrity of financial and non-financial reporting, the review

of related party transactions, nomination of board members and key executives, and board remuneration.

(*viii*) When committees of the board are established their mandate, composition and working procedures should be well defined and disclosed by the board.

(*ix*) In order to fulfill their responsibilities, board members should have access to accurate, relevant and timely information.

The OECD Principles of Corporate Governance have given more emphasis on the protection of the interest of shareholders. The emphasis is given on shareholders ownership management that must be facilitated. Another aspect covered is the disclosure that the institutional investors must make. Besides shareholders, the role and responsibilities of the board is also reviewed and strengthened. But the report do not pay any need to the system of internal control i.e. internal audit control, internal financial controls etc. Besides, the ethical standards and the environmental norms are also ignored that constitute an important part of the OECD Principles.

(B) Indian Scenario

1. CII Code on Corporate Governance (1998)

It was in December 1995 that in India; the Confederation of Indian Industry (CII) took the initiative on corporate governance. A National Task Force set up a committee under the chairmanship of Mr. Rahul Bajaj, former President of CII and Chairman & Managing Director, Bajaj Auto Limited, included membership from industry, the legal profession, media and the economist in the group, Dr. Omkar Goswami, to prepare a comprehensive voluntary code of corporate governance.

The objective was to develop and promote a code that could be adopted and followed by Indian Companies, in the Private Sector Enterprises, Public Sector Enterprises and Banks or Financial Institutions, all of which are corporate entities, "As many as 2500 of the 3900 companies that got listed between 1991 and 1996 have completely disappeared; It is almost impossible to discover what happened to these corporations as there are no annual reports or any other form of published information about them.

This task force presented draft guidelines and code for Corporate Governance in April 1997 at the National Conference and Annual session of CII, and after due deliberation final code of Corporate Governance was recommended as follows:

I. Recommendations

A. Recommendations relating to 'Board of Directors'

1. There is no need to adopt the German System of two-tier boards to ensure desirable corporate governance. A single board, if it performs well, can maximize long-term shareholder value just as well as a two-or multi-tiered board. Equally, there is nothing to suggest that a two-tier boards, per se, is the panacea to all corporate problems.

2. Any listed company with a turnover of Rs. 100 crores and above should have professionally competent, independent, non-executive directors, who should constitute

(*a*) at least 30 percent of the board if the Chairman of the Company is a non-executive director, or

(*b*) at least 50 percent of the board if the Chairman and Managing Director is the same person.

3. No single person should hold directorships in more than 10 listed companies.

4.For non-executive directors to play a material role in corporate decision making and maximizing long term shareholders value, they need to

(*a*) become active participants in boards, not passive advisors;

(*b*) have clearly defined responsibilities within the board such as the Audit Committee; and-

(*c*) know how to read a balance sheet, profit and loss account, cash flow statements and financial ratios and have some knowledge of various company laws. This, of course, excludes those who are invited to join boards as experts in other fields such as science and technology.

5. To secure better effort from non-executive directors, companies should:

(*a*) Pay a commission over and above the sitting fees for the use of the professional inputs. The present commission if 1% of net profits (if the company has a managing director), or 3% (if there is no managing director) is sufficient.

(*b*) Consider offering stock options, so as to relate rewards to performance. Commissions are rewards on current profits. Stock options are rewards contingent upon future appreciation of corporate value. An appropriate mix of the two can motivate a non-executive director in keeping an eye on short term profits as well as longer term shareholder value.

6. While re-appointing members of the board, companies should duly consider the attendance record of the concerned director. If a director has not been present (absent with or without leave) for 50% or more meetings, then this should be explicitly stated in the resolution that is put to vote. As a general practice, one should not re-appoint any director who has not had the time to attend even one half of the meetings.

7. Key information that must be reported to, and placed before, the board must contain:

(*i*) Annual operating plans and budgets, together with up-dated long term plans.

(*ii*) Capital budgets, manpower and overhead budgets.

(*iii*) Quarterly results for the company as a whole and its operating divisions or business segments.

(*iv*) Internal Audit reports, including cases of thefts, and dishonesty of a material nature.

(*v*) Show cause, demand and prosecution notices received from revenue authorities which are considered to be materially important (Material nature if any exposure that exceeds 1 percent of the company's net worth).

(*vi*) Fatal or serious accidents, dangerous occurrences, and any effluent or pollution problems.

(*vii*) Default in payment of interest or non-payment of the principal on any public deposit, and/or to any secured creditor or financial institutions.

(*viii*) Defaults such as non-payment of inter-corporate deposits by or to the company, or materially substantial non-payment for goods sold by the company.

(*ix*) Any issue which involves possible public or product liability claims of a substantial nature, including any judgement or other which may have either past strictures on the conduct of the company, or taken an adverse view regarding another enterprise that can have negative implications for the company.

(*x*) Details of any joint venture or collaboration agreement.

(*xi*) Transactions that involve substantial payment towards goodwill, brand equity, or intellectual property.

(*xii*) Recruitment and remuneration of senior officers just below the board level, including appointment or removal of the chief Financial Officer and the Company Secretary.

(*xiii*) Labour problems and their proposed solutions.

(*xiv*) Quarterly details of foreign exchange exposure and the steps taken by management to limit the risks of adverse exchange rate movement, if material.

B. Recommendations relating to the need for Audit Committee are :

8. Recommendations relating to the need for Audit Committee contain the following:

(*i*) Listed companies with either a turnover of Rs. 100 crores or a paid up capital of Rs. 20 crores should set up audit committees within two years.

(*ii*) Audit committees should consist of at least three members, all drawn from a company's non-executive directors, who should have adequate knowledge of finance, accounts and basic elements of company law.

(*iii*) To be effective, the Audit Committees should have clearly defined Terms of Reference and its members must be willing to spend more time on the company's work vis-a-vis other non executive directors.

(*iv*) Audit committee should assist the board in fulfilling its functions relating to corporate accounting and reporting practices, financial and accounting controls, and financial statements and proposals that accompany the public issue of the financial reporting process.

(*v*) Audit committees should periodically interact with the statutory auditors and the internal auditors to ascertain the quality and veracity of the company's accounts as well as the capability of the auditors themselves.

(*vi*) For Audit Committees to discharge their fiduciary responsibilities with due diligence, is must be incumbent upon management to ensure that members of the committee, have full access to financial data of the company and its subsidiary and associated companies, including data on contingent liabilities, debt exposure, current liabilities, loans and investments.

C. Recommendations containing the Desirable Disclosures :

9. Under 'Additional Shareholder's Information', listed companies should given data on:

(*i*) High and low monthly averages of share prices in a major stock exchange where the company is listed for the reporting year.

(*ii*) Greater detail on business segments, up to 10% of turnover, giving shares on sales revenue, review of operations, analysis of markets and future prospects.

10. (A) Consolidation of Group Accounts should be optional and subject to,

(*i*) The FIs allowing companies to leverage on the basis of the group's assets, and

(*ii*) The Income Tax Department using the group concept in assessing the corporate income tax.

(B) If a company chooses to voluntarily consolidate, it should not be necessary to annex the accounts of its subsidiary companies under Section 212 of the Companies Act.

(C) However, if a company consolidates, then the definition of 'group' should include the parent company and its subsidiaries (where the reporting company owns over 50% of voting stake).

11. Major Indian Stock Exchanges should gradually insist upon a compliance certificate, signed by the CEO and the EFO, which clearly states that:

(*a*) The management is responsible for the preparation, integrity, and fair presentation of the financial statements and other information in the Annual Report, and which also suggest that the company will continue in business in the course of following year:

(*b*) The accounting policies and principles conform to standard practice, and where they do not, full disclosure has been made of any material departures.

(*c*) The board has overseen the company's system of internal accounting and administrative controls systems either directly or through its Audit Committee (for companies with a turnover of Rs. 100 crores or a paid-up capital of Rs. 20 crores).

12. For all companies with paid up capital of Rs. 20 crores or more, the quality or quantity of disclosures that accompanies a GDR issue should be the norm for any domestic Issue.

13. With regard to Capital Market Issues, the committees recommends that the government must allow far greater funding to the corporate sector against the security of shares and other papers.

D. Recommendations regarding Creditors right :

14. It would be desirable for FIs as pure creditors to re-write their covenants to eliminate having nominee directors excepts :

(*a*) in the event of serious and systematic debt default; and

(*b*) in the case of debtor company not providing six-monthly or quarterly operational data to the concerned FI(s).

15. To improve the quality of information given to the Indian investors the committee recommends:

(*i*) If any company goes to more than one credit rating agency, then it must divulge in the prospectus and issue document the ratings of all the agencies that did such an exercise.

(*ii*) It is not enough to state the ratings. These must be given in a tabular format that shows where the company stands relative to higher and lower ranking. It makes considerable difference to an investor to know whether the ranking agency or agencies placed the company in the top slots, or in the middle, or in the bottom.

(*iii*) It is essential that we took at the quantity and quality of disclosures that accompany issue of company bonds, debentures and fixed deposits in the USA and Britain - if only two learn what more can be done to inspire confidence and create an environment of transparency.

(*iv*) Finally, companies which are making foreign debt issues, cannot have two sets of disclosures norms: an exhaustive one for the foreigners, and a relatively minuscule for the Indian Investors.

16. Companies that default on fixed deposits and make inter-corporate loans or investments until the default is made good; and

A. accept further deposits and make inter-corporate loans or investments until the default is made good; and

B. declare dividends until the default is made good.

E. Recommendation Regarding Financial Institutions (FIs) and Nominee Directors :

17. Reduction in the number of companies where there are nominee directors, It has been argued by Financial Institutions (FIs) that are too many companies where they are on the board, and too few competent officers to do the task properly. So, in the first instance, FIs should take a policy decision to withdraw from boards of companies where their individual shareholding is 5% or less, or total FI holding is under 10%.

"Obviously not all well governed companies do well in the market place. Nor do the badly governed ones always sink. But even the best performers risk stumbling some day if they lack strong and independent boards of directors.

If we go through the reports, we can easily observed that CII code is quite in narrow form. We can also see that CII code does not consider Institutional investor as important. If only meditates on establishing the Corporate Governance Code and also there is no provision for putting heavy penalty and delisting procedure on companies for not doing timely disclosures and compliance of the Code. Also, Board of Directors and Audit Committee should be made responsible enough.

2. Kumar Mangalam Birla Committee Report on Corporate Governance

Preface

1.1 It is almost a truism that the adequacy and the quality of corporate governance shape the growth and the future of any capital market and economy. The concept of corporate governance has been attracting public attention for quite some time in India. The topic is no longer confined to the halls of academic and is increasingly finding acceptance for its relevance and underlying importance in the industry and capital markets. Progressive firms in India have voluntarily put in place systems of good corporate governance. Internationally also, while this topic has been accepted for a long time, the financial crisis in emerging markets has led to renewed discussions and inevitably focused them on the lack of corporate as well as governmental oversight. The same applies to recent high-profile financial reporting failures even among firms in the developed economies. Focus on corporate governance and related issues is an inevitable outcome of a process, which leads firms to increasingly shift to financial markets as the pre-eminent source for capital. In the process, more and more people are recognizing that corporate governance is indispensable to effective market discipline. This growing consensus is both an enlightened and a realistic view. In an age where capital flows worldwide, just as quickly as information, a company that does not promote a culture of strong, independent oversight, risks its every stability and future health. As a result, the link between a company's management, directors and its financial reporting system has never been more crucial. As the boards provide stewardship of companies, they play a significant role in their efficient functioning.

1.2 Studies of firms in India and abroad have shown that markets and investors take notice of well-managed companies, respond positively to them, and reward such companies, with higher valuations. A common feature of such companies is that they have systems in place, which allow sufficient freedom to the boards and management to take decisions towards the progress of their companies and to innovate, while remaining within a framework of effective accountability. In other words, they have a system of foods corporate governance.

1.3 Strong corporate governance is thus indispensable to resilient and vibrant capital markets and is an important instrument of investor protection. It is the blood that fills the veins of transparent corporate disclosure and high-quality accounting practices. It is the muscle that moves a viable and accessible financial reporting structure. Without financial reporting premised on sound, honest numbers, capital markets will collapse upon themselves.

1.4 Another important aspect of corporate governance relates to issues of insider trading. It is important that insiders do not use their position of knowledge and access to inside information about the company, and take unfair advantage of the resulting information asymmetry. To prevent this from happening, corporates are expected to disseminate the material price sensitive information in a timely and proper manner and also ensure that till such information is made public, insiders abstain from transacting in the securities of the company. The principle should be 'disclose or desist'. This therefore calls for companies to devise an internal procedure for adequate and timely disclosures, reporting requirements, confidentiality norms, code of conduct and specific rules for the conduct of its directors and employees and other insiders. For example, in many countries, there are rules for reporting of transactions by directors and other senior executives of companies, as well as for a report on their holdings, activity in their own shares and net year to year changes to these in the annual report. The rules also cover the dealing in the securities of their companies by the insiders, especially directors and other senior executives, during sensitive reporting seasons. However, the need for such procedures, reporting requirements and rules also goes beyond corporates to other entities in the financial markets such as Stock Exchanges, Intermediaries, Financial institutions, Mutual Funds and concerned professionals who may have access to inside information. This is being dealt with in a comprehensive manner, by a separate group appointed by SEBI, under the Chairmanship of Shri Kumar Mangalam Birla.

1.5 The issue of corporate governance involves besides shareholders, all other stakeholders. The Committee's recommendations have looked at corporate governance from the point of view of the stakeholders and in particular that of the shareholders and investors, because they are the raison de etre for corporate governance and also the prime constituency of SEBI. The control and reporting functions of boards, the roles of the various committees of the board, the role of management, all assume special significance when viewed from this perspective. The other way of looking at corporate governance makes to the efficiency of a business enterprise to the creation of wealth and to the country's economy. In a sense both these points of the committee, there was a clear convergence of both points of view.

1.6 At the heart of the committee's report is the set of recommendations which distinguishes the responsibilities and obligations of the boards and the management in instituting the systems for good corporate governance and emphasizes the rights of shareholders in demanding corporate governance. Many of the recommendations are mandatory. For reasons states in on the listed companies for initial and continuing, disclosures in a phased manner within specified dates, through the listing agreement. The companies will also be required to disclose separately in their annual reports, a report on corporate governance delineating the steps they have taken to comply with the recommendation of the Committee. This will enable shareholders to know, where the, companies, in which they have invested, stand with respect to specific initiatives taken to ensure robust corporate governance. The implementation will be phased, Certain categories of companies will be required to comply with the mandatory recommendations of the report during the financial year 2000-01, but not later than March 31, 2001, and others during the financial year 2001-2002 and 2002-2003. For the non-mandatory recommendation, the Committee hopes that companies would voluntarily implement these. It has been recommended that SEBI may write to the appropriate regulatory bodies and governmental authorities to incorporate where necessary, the recommendations in their respective regulatory or control framework.

1.7 The Committee recognized that India had in place a basic system of corporate governance and that SEBI has already taken a number of initiatives towards raising the existing standard. The Committee also recognized that the Confederation of Indian Industries had published a code entitled "Desirable Code of Corporate Governance" and was encouraged to note that some of the forward looking companies have already reviewed or are in the process of reviewing their board structure and have also reported in their 1998-99 annual reports the extent to which they have complied with the Code. The Committee however felt that under Indian conditions a statutory rather than a voluntary code would be far more purpose and meaningful, at least in respect of essential features of corporate governance.

1.8 The Committee however recognized that a system of control should not so hampering the companies so as to impede their ability to compete in the market place. The Committee believes that the recommendations made in this report mark an important step forward and if accepted and followed by the industry, they would raise the standards in corporate governance, strengthen the unitary boards system, significantly increase its effectiveness and ultimately serve the objective of maximizing shareholders value.

The Constitution of the Committee and the Setting for the Report

2.1 There are some Indian companies, which have voluntarily established high standards of corporate governance, but there are many more whose practices are a matter of concern. There is also an increasing concern about standards of financial reporting and accountability, especially after losses suffered by investors and lenders in the recent past, which could have been avoided, with better and more transparent reporting practices. Investors have suffered on account of unscrupulous management of the companies, which have raised capital from the market at high valuation and have performed, much worse than the past reported figures, leave alone the future projections at the time of raising money. Another example of bad governance has been the allotment of promoters shares, on preferential basis at preferential prices, disproportionate to market valuation of shares, leading to further dilution of wealth of minority shareholders. This practice has however since been contained.

2.2 There are also many companies, which are not paying adequate attention to the basic procedure for shareholders' service; for example, many of these companies do not pay adequate attention to redress investors' grievances such as delay in transfer of shares, delay in despatch of share certificate and dividend warrants and non-receipt of dividend warrant; companies also do not pay sufficient attention to timely dissemination of information to investors as also to the quality of such information. SEBI has been receiving large number of investor complaints on these matters. While enough laws exist to take care of many of these investor grievances, the implementation and inadequacy of penal provisions have left a lot to be desired.

2.3 Corporate governance is considered an important instrument of investor protection and it is therefore a priority on SEBI's agenda. To further improve the level of corporate governance need was felt for a comprehensive approach at this stage of development of the capital market, to accelerate the adaptation of globally acceptable practices of corporate governance. This would ensure that the Indian investor are in no way less informed and protected as compared to their counterparts in the best-developed capital markets arid economies of the world.

2.4 Securities market regulators in almost all developed and emerging markets have for sometime been concerned about the importance of the subject and of the need to raise the standard of corporate governance. The financial crisis in the Asian markets in the recent past have highlighted the need for improved level of corporate governance. The financial crisis in the Asian markets in the recent past have highlighted the need for improved level of corporate governance and the lack of it in certain countries have been mentioned as one of the causes of the crisis. Indeed corporate governance has been a wide If discussed topic at the recent meetings of the International Organization of Securities Commission (IOSCO). Besides in an environment in which emerging markets increasingly complete for global capital, it is evident that global capital will flow to markets, which are better regulated and observe higher standards of transparency, efficiency and integrity. Raising standards of corporate governance is therefore also extremely relevant in this context.

2.5 In the above-mentioned context, the securities and Exchange Board of India (SEBI) appointed the Committee on Corporate Governance on May 7, 1999 under the Chairmanship of Shri Kumar Managalam Birla, member SEBI Board, to promote and raise the standards of Corporate Governance. The Committee's membership is given in Annexure 1 and the detailed terms of the reference are as follows:

a. to suggest suitable amendments to the listing agreement executed by the stock exchanges with the companies and any other measures to improve the standards of corporate governance in the listed companies, in areas such as continuous disclosure of material information, both financial and non-financial, manner and frequency of such disclosures, responsibilities of independent and outside director.

b. to draft a code of corporate best practices; and

c. to suggest safeguard to be instituted within the companies to deal with insider information and insider trading.

2.6 A number of reports and codes on the subject have already been published internationally-notable among than are the Report of the Cadbury Committee, the Report of the Greenbury Committee, the Combined Code of the London Stock Exchange, the OECD Code on Corporate Governance and The Blue Ribbon Committee on Corporate Governance. In preparing this report, while the committee drew upon these documents to the extent appropriate, the primary objective of the committee was to view corporate governance from the perspective of the investors and shareholders and to prepare a Code to suit the Indian corporate environment, as corporate governance framework are not exportable. The Committee also took note of the various steps already taken by SEBI for strengthening corporate governance, some of which are;

- strengthening of disclosure norms for Initial Public offers following the recommendations of the Committee set up by SEBI under the Chairmanship of Shri Y H MALEGAM.
- providing information in director's reports for utilization of funds and variation between projected and actual use of funds according to the requirements of the Companies Act, inclusion of cash flow and funds flow statements in annual report;
- declaration of quarterly results;
- mandatory appointment of compliance officer for monitoring the share transfer process and ensuring compliance with various rules and regulations;
- timely disclosure of material and price sensitive information including details of all material events having a bearing on the performance of the company.
- dispatch of one copy of complete balance sheet to every household and abridged balance sheet to all shareholders;
- issue of guidelines for preferential allotment at market related prices; and
- issue of regulations providing for a fair and transparent framework for takeovers and substantial acquisitions.

2.7 The Committee has identified the three key constituents of corporate governance as the shareholders, the Board of Directors and the Management and has attempted to identify in respect if each of these constituents, their roles and responsibilities as also their rights in the context of good corporate governance. Fundamental to this examination and permeating throughout this exercise is the recognition of the three key aspects of corporate governance, namely; accountability, transparency and equality if treatment for all stakeholders.

2.8 The pivotal role in any system of corporate governance is performed by the board of director. It is accountable to the stakeholders and directs and controls the Management. It stewards the company, sets its strategic aim and financial goals and oversees their implementation, puts in place adequate internal controls and periodically reports the activities and progress of the company in the company in a transparent manner to the stakeholders. The shareholders' role in corporate governance is to appoint the directors and the auditors and to hold the board accountable for the proper governance of the company by requiring the board to provide them periodically reports, the activities and progress of the company in the company in a transparent manner to the stakeholders. The shareholders' role in corporate governance is to appoint the directors and the auditors and to hold the board accountable for the proper governance of the company by requiring the board to provide them periodically with the requisite information, in a transparent fashion, of the activities and progress of the company. The responsibility of the management is to undertake the management of the company in terms of the direction provided by the board, to put in place adequate control systems and to ensure their operation and to provide information to the board on a timely basis and in a provide information to the board on a timely basis and in a transparent manner to enable the board to monitor the accountability of Management to it.

2.9 Crucial to good corporate governance are the existence and enforceability of regulations relating to insider information and insider trading. These matters are being currently examined separately by a Group appointed by SEBI under the Chairmanship of Shri Kumar Mangalam Birla.

2.10 Adequate financial reporting and disclosure are the comer stones of good corporate governance. These demand the existence the implementation of proper accounting standards and disclosure requirements. A separate committee appointed by SEBI under the Chairmanship of Shri Y.H. Malagam (who is also member of this Committee) is examining these issues on a continuing basis. This Committee has advised that while in most areas, accounting standards in India are terms of coverage and content, there are a few areas where additional standards need to be introduced in India on an urgent basis. These matters are discussed in greater detail in para 12.1 of this report.

2.11 The Committee's draft report was made public through the media and also put on the website of SEBI for comments. The report was also sent to the Chambers of Commerce, financial institutions, stock exchanges, investor associations, the Association of Merchant Bankers of India, Association of Mutual funds of India, The Institute of Chartered Accountants of India, Institute of Company Secretaries of India, academicians, experts and eminent personalities in the Indian capital market, foreign investors. A copy of the draft report was also sent to Sir Adrian Cadbury who had chaired the Cadbury Committee on Corporate Governance set up by the London Stock Exchange, the Financial Reporting Council and the Accountancy Bodies in the U.K. in 1991.

2.12 The Committee has received comments from most of the above groups. Besides, Sir Adrian Cadbury, and several eminent persons in the Indian capital market, have sent detailed comments on the draft report. Separately, the Committee held meetings with the representatives of the Chambers of Commerce, Chairmen of the Financial Institutions, stock exchanges, investor associations. Thus, the Committee had the benefit of the views of almost all concerned entities that have a role in corporate governance. The Committee has taken into account the views and comments of these respondents in this final report.

2.13 The Committee puts on record its appreciation of the valuable inputs and painstaking efforts of Shri Anup Srivastava, Vice-President Corporate Strategy and Business Development of the Aditya Birla Group, Shri P. K. Bindlish, Division Chief, SEBI, Shri Umesh Kumar, and other officers of the SMDRP department of SEBI, in the preparation of this report.

The Recommendations of the Committee

3.1 This Report is the first formal and comprehensive attempt to evolve a Code of Corporate Governance, in the context of prevailing conditions of governance in Indian companies, as well as the state of capital markets. While making the recommendations the Committee has been mindful that any code of Corporate Governance must be dynamic, evolving and should change with changing context and times. It would therefore be necessary that this code also is reviewed from time to time, keeping pace with the changing expectations of the investors, shareholders, and other stakeholders and with increasing sophistication achieved in capital markets.

Corporate Governance- The Objective

4.1 Corporate governance has several claimants- shareholders and other stakeholders-which include suppliers, customers, creditors, the bankers, the employees of the company, the government and the society at large. This Report on Corporate Governance has been prepared by the Committee for SEBI, keeping in view primarily the interests of a particular class of stakeholders, namely, the shareholder, who together with the investors form the principal constituency of SEBI while not ignoring the needs of other stakeholders.

4.2 The Committee therefore agreed that the fundamental objective of corporate governance is the "enhancement of shareholder value, keeping in view the interests of other stakeholder". This definition harmonizes the need for a company to strike a balance at all times between the need to enhance shareholders' wealth whilst not in any way being detrimental to the interests of the other stakeholders in the company.

4.3 In the opinion of the Committee, the imperative for corporate governance lies not merely in drafting a code of corporate governance, but in practicing it. Even now, some companies are following exemplary practices, without the existence of formal guidelines on this subject. Structures and rules are important because they provide a framework, which will encourage and enforce good governance; but alone, these cannot raise the standards of corporate governance. What counts is the way in which these are put to use. The Committee is thus of the firm view, that the best results would be achieved when the companies begin to treat the code not as a mere structure, but as a way of life.

4.4 It follows that the real onus of achieving the desired level of corporate governance, lies in the proactive initiatives taken by the companies themselves and not in the external measures like breadth and depth of a code or stringency of enforcement of norms. The extent of discipline, transparency and fairness, and the willingness shown by the companies themselves in implementing the Code, will be the crucial factor in achieving the desired confidence of shareholders and other stakeholders and fulfilling the goals of the company.

Applicability of the Recommendations

Mandatory and non-mandatory recommendations

5.1 The Committee debated the question of voluntary versus mandatory compliance of its recommendations. The Committee was of the firm view that mandatory compliance of the recommendations at least in respect of the essential recommendations would be most appropriate in the Indian context for the present. The Committee also noted that in most of the countries where standards of corporate governance are high, the stock exchanges have enforced some form of compliance through their listing agreements.

5.2 The Committee felt that some of the recommendations are absolutely essential for the framework of corporate governance and virtually form its core, while others could be considered as desirable. Besides, some of the recommendations may also need change of statute, such as the Companies Act, for their enforcement. In the case of others, enforcement would be possible by amending the Securities Contracts (Regulation) Rules, 1957 and by amending the listing agreement of the stock exchanges under the direction of SEBI. The latter, would be less time consuming and would ensure speedier implementation of corporate governance. The Committee therefore felt that the recommendations should be divided into mandatory and non-mandatory categories and those recommendations which are absolutely essential for corporate governance, can be defined with precision and which can be enforced through the amendment of the listing agreement could be classified as mandatory. Others, which are either desirable or which may require change of laws, may, for the time being, be classified as non-mandatory.

Applicability

5.3 The Committee is of the opinion that the recommendations should be made applicable to the listed companies, their directors, management, employees and professionals associated with such companies, in accordance with the time table proposed in the schedule given later in this section. Compliance with the code should be both in letter and spirit and should always be in a manner that gives precedence to substance over form. The ultimate responsibility for putting the recommendations into practice lies directly with the board of directors and the management of the company.

5.4 The recommendations will apply to all the listed private and public sector companies, in accordance with the schedule of implementation. As for listed entities, which are not companies, but body corporates (e.g. private and public sector banks, financial institutions, insurance companies etc.) incorporate under other statutes, the recommendations will apply to the extent that they do not violate their respective statutes, and guidelines or directives issued by the relevant regulatory authorities.

Schedule of implementation

5.5 The Committee recognizes that compliance with the recommendations would involve restructuring the existing boards of companies. It also recognizes that some companies, especially the smaller ones, may have difficulty in immediately camp lying with these conditions.

5.6 The Committee recommends that while the recommendations should be applicable to all the listed companies or entities, there is a need for phasing out the implementation as follows:

- By all entities seeking listing for the first time, at the time of listing.
- Within financial year 2000-2001, but not later than March 31, 2001 by all entities, which are included either in Group 'A' , of the BSE, or in S&P CNX Nifty index as an January 1,2000. However, to comply with the recommendations, these companies may have to begin the process, of implementation as early as possible. These companies would cover more than 80%, of the market capitalization.
- Within financial year 2001-2002, but not later than March 31, 2002 by all the entities which are presently listed, with paid up share capital, of Rs. 10 crore and above, or net worth of Rs. 25 crore, or more any time in the history of the company.
- Within financial year 2002-2003, but not later than March 31, 2003 by all the entities, which are presently listed, with paid up share capital, of Rs. 3 crore and above.

Board of Directors

6.1 The board of a company provides leadership and strategic guidance, objective judgment independent of management to the company and exercises control over the company, while remaining at all times accountable to the shareholders. The measure of the board is not simply whether it fulfils its legal requirements but more importantly, the board's attitude and the manner it translates its awareness and understanding, of its responsibilities. An effective corporate governance system is one, which allows the board to perform these dual functions efficiently. The board of directors of a company, thus directs and controls the management of a company and is accountable to the shareholders.

6.2 The board directs the company by formulating and reviewing company's policies, strategies, "major plans, of action, risk policy, annual budgets and business plans, setting performance objectives, monitoring implementation and corporate performance and overseeing major capital expenditures, acquisitions and divestitures, change in financial control and compliance with applicable laws, taking into account the interests of stakeholders. It controls the company and its management by laying down the code of conduct, overseeing the process of disclosure and communications, ensuring that appropriate systems for financial control and reporting and monitoring risk are in place, evaluating the performance of management, chief executive, executive directors and providing checks and balances to reduce potential conflict between the specific interests of management and the wider interests of the company and shareholders including misuse of corporate assets and abuse in related party transactions. It is accountable to the shareholders for creating, practicing and enhancing wealth and resources for the company, and reporting to them on the performance in a timely and transparent manner.

However, it is not involved in day-to-day management of the company, which is the responsibility of the management.

Composition of the Board of Directors

6.3 The Committee is of view that the composition of the board of directors is critical to the independent functioning of the board. There is a significant body of literature on corporate governance, which has guided the composition, structure and responsibilities of the board. The Committee took note of this while framing its recommendations on the structure and composition of the board.

The composition of the board is important in as much as it determines the ability of the board to collectively provide the leadership and ensures that no one individual or a group is able to dominate the board. The executive directors (like director-finance, director-personnel) are involved in the day to day management of the companies; the non-executive directors bring external and wider perspective and independence to the decision making. Till recently, it has been the practice of most of the companies in India.

6.6 The Blue Ribbon Committee of the USA and other Committee reports have laid considerable stress on the role of independent directors. The law however does not make any distinction between the different categories of directors and all directors are equally and collectively responsible in law for the board's actions and decisions. The Committee is of the view that the non-executive directors, i.e. those who are independent and those who are not, help bring and independent judgement to bear on board's deliberations especially on issues of strategy, performance, management of conflicts and standards of conduct. The Committee therefore lays emphasis on the caliber of the non-executive directors, especially of the independent directors.

6.7 Good corporate governance dictates that the board be comprised of individuals with certain personal characteristics and core competencies such as recognition of the importance of the board's task, integrity, a sense of accountability, track record of achievements, and the ability to ask tough questions. Besides, having financial literacy, experience, leadership qualities and the ability to think strategically, the directors must show significant degree of commitment to the company and devote adequate time for meeting preparation and attendance. The Committee is also of the view that it is important that adequate compensation package be given to the non-executive independent directors so that these positions become sufficiently financially attractive to attract talent and that the non executive directors are sufficiently compensated for undertaking this work.

6.8 Independence of the board is critical to ensuring that the board fulfils its oversight role objectively and holds the management accountable to the shareholders. The Committee has, therefore, suggested the above definition of independence, and the following structure and composition of the board and of the committees of the board.

6.9 The Committee recommends that the board of a company have an optimum combination of executive and non-executive and non-executive directors with not less than fifty percent of the board comprising the non-executive directors. The number of independent directors (independence being as defined in the foregoing paragraph) would depend on the nature of the chairman of the board. In case a company has a non-executive chairman, at least one-third of board should comprise of independent directors and in case a company has an executive chairman, at least half of board should be independent.

6.10 The tenure of office of the directors will be as prescribed in the Companies Act.

Nominee Directors

7.1 Besides the above categories of directors, there is another set of director in Indian companies who are the nominees of the financial or investment institutions to safeguard their interest. The nominees of the institutions are often chosen from among the present or retired employees of the institutions or from outside. In the context of corporate governance, there could be arguments both for and against the continuation of this practice.

7.2 There are arguments both for and against the institution of nominee directors. Those who favour this practice argue that nominee directors are needed to protect the interest of the institutions who are custodians of public funds and who have high exposures in the projects of the companies both in the form of equity and loans. On the other hand those who oppose this practice, while conceding that financial institutions have played a significant role in the industrial development of the country as a sole purveyor of long term credit, argue that there is an inherent conflict when institutions through their nominees participate in board decisions and in their role as shareholders demand accountability from the board. They also argue that there is a further conflict because the institutions are often major players in the stock market in respect of the shares of the companies on which they have nominees.

7.3 The Committee recognizes the merit in both points of view. Clearly when companies are well managed and performing well, the need for protection of institution interest is much less than when companies are badly managed or under-performing. The Committee would therefore recommend that institutions should appoint nominees on the boards of companies only on a selective basis where such appointment is pursuant to a right under loan agreements or where such appointment is considered necessary to protect the interest of the institution.

7.4 The Committee also recommends that when a nominee of the institutions is appointed as a director of the company, he should have the same responsibility, be subject to the same discipline and be accountable to the shareholders in the same manner as any other director of the company. In particular, if he reports to any department of the institutions on the affairs of the company, the institution should ensure that there exist Chinese walls between such department and other departments which may be dealing in the shares of the company in the stock market.

Chairman of the Board

8.1 The Committee believes that the role of Chairman is to ensure that the board meetings are conducted in a manner which secures the effective participation of all directors, executive and non-executive alike, and encourages all to make an effective contribution, maintain a balance of power in the board, make certain that all directors receive adequate information, well in time and that the executive directors look beyond their executive duties and accept full share of the responsibilities of governance. The Committee is of the view that the Chairman's role should in principle be different from that of the chief executive, though the same individual may perform both roles.

8.2 Given the importance of Chairman's role, the Committee recommends that a non-executive Chairman should be entitled to maintain a Chairman's office at the company's expenses and also allowed reimbursement of the expenses incurred in performance of his duties. This will enable him to discharge the responsibilities effectively.

This is a non-mandatory recommendation.

Audit Committee

9.1 There are few words more reassuring to the investors and shareholders than accountability. A system of good corporate governance promotes relationships of accountability between the principal actors of sound financial reporting- the board, the management and the auditor. It holds the management accountable to the board and the board accountable to the shareholders. The audit committee's role flows directly from the board's oversight function. It acts as a catalyst for effective financial reporting.

9.2 The Committee is of the view that the need for having an audit committee grows from the recognition of the audit committee's position in the larger mosaic of the governance process, as it relates to the oversight of financial reporting.

9.3 A proper and well functioning system exists therefore, when the three main groups responsible for financial reporting the board, the internal auditor and the outside auditors- form the three-legged stool that supports responsible financial disclosure and active and participatory oversight. The audit committee has an important role to play in this process, since the audit committee is a sub-group of the full board and hence the monitor of the process. Certainly, it is not the role of the audit committee to prepare financial statements or engage in the myriad of decisions relating to the preparation of those statements. The committee's job is clearly one of oversight and monitoring and in carrying out this job it relies on senior financial management and the outside auditors. However, it is important to ensure that the boards function efficiently for if the boards are dysfunctional, the audit committees will do no better. The Committee believes that the progressive standards of governance applicable to the full board should also be applicable to the audit committee.

9.4 The Committee therefore recommends that a qualified and independent audit committee should be set up by the board of a company. This would go a long way in enhancing the credibility of the financial disclosures of a company and promoting transparency.

This is a mandatory recommendation.

9.5 The following recommendations of the Committee, regarding the constitution, functions and procedures of audit committee would have to be viewed in the above context. But just as there is no "one size fits all" for the board when it comes to corporate governance, same is true for audit committees. The Committee can thus only lay down some broad parameters, within which each audit committee has to evolve its own guidelines.

Composition

9.6 The composition of the audit committee is based on the fundamental premise of independence and expertise. The Committee therefore recommends that -

- the audit committee should have minimum three members, all being non executive directors, with the majority being independent, and with at least one director having financial and accounting knowledge;
- the chairman of the committee should be an independent director;
- the chairman should be present at Annual General Meeting to answer shareholder queries;
- the audit committee should invite such of the executives, as it considers appropriate (and particularly the head of the finance function) to be present at the meetings of the Committee but on occasions it may also meet without the presence of any executives of the company. Finance director and head of internal audit and when required, a representative of the external auditor should be present as invitees for the meetings of the audit committee;
- the Company Secretary should act as the secretary to the committee.

These are mandatory recommendations.

Frequency of meetings and quorum

9.7 The Committee recommends that to begin with the audit committee should meet at least thrice a year. One meeting must be held before finalisation of annual accounts and one necessarily every six months.

This is a mandatory recommendation.

9.8 The quorum should be either two members or one-third of the members of the audit committee, whichever is higher and there should be a minimum of two independent directors.

This is a mandatory recommendation.

Powers of the audit committee

9.9 Being a committee of the board, the audit committee derives its powers from the authorization of the board. The Committee recommends that such powers should include powers:

- To investigate any activity within its terms of reference.
- To seek information from any employee.
- To obtain outside legal or other professional advice.
- To secure attendance of outsiders with relevant expertise, if it considers necessary.
- This is a mandatory recommendation.

Functions of the Audit Committee

9.10 As the audit committee acts as the bridge between the board, the statutory auditors and internal auditors, the Committee recommends that its role should include the following :

- Oversight of the company's financial reporting process and the disclosure of its financial information to ensure that the financial statement is correct, sufficient and credible.
- Recommending the appointment and removal of external auditor, fixation of audit fee and also approval for payment for any other services.
- Reviewing with management the annual financial statements before submission to the board, focussing primarily on:
- Any changes in accounting policies and practices.
- Major accounting entries based on exercise of judgement by management.
- Qualifications in draft audit report.
- Significant adjustment arising out of audit.
- The going concern assumption.
- Compliance with accounting standards.
- Compliance with stock exchange and legal requirements concerning financial statements.
- Any related party transactions i.e. transactions of the company of material nature, with promoters or the management, their subsidiaries or relatives etc. that may have potential conflict with the interest of company at large. Reviewing with the management, external and internal auditors, the adequacy of internal control systems.
- Reviewing the adequacy of internal audit function, including the structure of the internal audit department, staffing and seniority of the official heading the department, reporting structure, coverage and frequency of internal audit.
- Discussion with internal auditors of any significant findings and follow-up thereon.
- Reviewing the findings of any internal investigations by the internal auditors into matters where there is suspected fraud or irregularity or a failure of internal control systems of a material nature and reporting the matter to the board.
- Discussion with external auditors before the audit commences, of the nature and scope of audit. Also post-audit discussion to ascertain any area of concern.
- Reviewing the company's financial and risk management policies.
- Looking into the reasons for substantial defaults in the payments to the depositors, debenture holders, share holders (in case of non-payment of declared dividends) and creditors.

This is a mandatory recommendation.

Remuneration Committee of the Board

10.1 The Committee was of the view that a company must have a credible and transparent policy in determining and accounting for the remuneration of the directors. The policy should avoid potential conflicts of interest between the shareholders, the directors, and the management. The overriding principle in respect of directors' remuneration is that of openness and shareholders are entitled to a full and clear statement of benefits available to the directors.

10.2 For this purpose the Committee recommends that the board should set up a remuneration committee to determine on their behalf and on behalf of the shareholders with agreed terms of reference, the company's policy on specific remuneration packages for executive directors including pension rights and any compensation payment.

This is a non-mandatory recommendation.

10.3 The Committee however recognized that the remuneration package should be good enough to attract, retain and motivate the executive directors of the quality required, but not more than necessary for the purpose. The remuneration committee should be in a position to bring about objectivity in determining the remuneration package while striking a balance between the interest of the company and the shareholders.

Composition, Quorum etc. of the Remuneration Committee

10.4 The Committee recommends that to avoid conflicts of interest, the remuneration committee, which would determine the remuneration packages of the executive directors should comprise of at least three directors, all of whom should be non-executive directors, the chairman of committee being an independent director.

10.5 The Committee deliberated on the quorum for the meeting and was of the view that remuneration is mostly fixed annually or after specified periods. It would not be necessary for the committee to meet very often. The Committee was of the view that it should not be difficult to arrange for a date to suit the convenience of all the members of the committee. The Committee therefore recommends that all the members of the remuneration committee should be present at the meeting.

10.6 The Committee also recommends that the Chairman of the remuneration committee should be present at the Annual General Meeting, to answer the shareholder queries. However, it would be up to the Chairman to decide who should answer the queries.

All the above recommendations in paragraphs 10.4 to 10.6 are non-mandatory.

10.7 The Committee recommends that the board of directors should decide the remuneration of non-executive directors.

Disclosures of Remuneration Package

10.8 It is important for the shareholders to be informed of the remuneration of the directors of the company. The Committee therefore recommends that the following disclosures should be made in the section on corporate governance of the annual report :

All elements of remuneration package of all the directors i.e. salary, benefits, bonuses, stock options, pension etc. Details of fixed component and performance linked incentives, along with the performance criteria. Service contracts, notice period, severance fees, stock option details, if any - and whether issued at a discount as well as the period over which accrued and over which exercisable.

This is a mandatory recommendation.

Board Procedures

11.1 The measure of the board is buttressed by the structures and procedures of the board. The various committees of the board recommended in this report would enable the board to have an appropriate structure to assist it in the discharge of its responsibilities. These need to be supplemented by certain basic procedural requirements in terms of frequency of meetings, the availability of timely information, sufficient period of notice for the board meeting as well as circulation of agenda items well in advance, and more importantly, the commitment of the members of the board.

11.2 The Committee therefore recommends that board meetings should be held at least four times in a year, with a maximum time gap of four months between any two meetings. The minimum information as given in Annexure 2 should be available to the board.

This is a mandatory recommendation.

The Committee further recommends that to ensure that the members of the board give due importance and commitment to the meetings of the board and its committees, there should be a ceiling on the maximum number of committees across all companies in which a director could be a member or act as Chairman. The Committee recommends that a director should not be a member in more than 10 committees or act as Chairman of more than five committees across all companies in which he is a director. Furthermore, it should be a mandatory annual requirement for every director to inform the company about the committee positions he occupies in other companies and notify changes as and when they take place.

This is a mandatory recommendation.

Accounting Standards and Financial Reporting

12.1 Over time the financial reporting and accounting standards in India have been upgraded. This however is an ongoing process and we have to move speedily towards the adoption of international standards. This is particularly important from the angle of corporate governance. The Committee took note of the discussions of the SEBI Committee on Accounting Standards referred to earlier and makes the following recommendations:

Consolidation of Accounts of subsidiaries

The companies should be required to give consolidated accounts in respect of all its subsidiaries in which they hold 51% or more of the share capital. The Committee was informed that SEBI was already in dialogue with the Institute of Chartered Accountants of India to bring about the changes in the Accounting Standard on consolidated financial statements. The Institute of Chartered Accounts of India should be requested to issue the Accounting Standards for consolidation expeditiously. Segment reporting where a company has multiple lines of business. Equally in cases of companies with several businesses, it is important that financial reporting in respect of each product segment should be available to shareholders and the market to obtain a complete financial picture of the company. The Committee was informed that SEBI was already in dialogue with the Institute of Chartered Accountants of India to introduce the Accounting Standard on segment reporting. The Institute of Chartered Accountants of India has already issued an Exposure Draft on the subject and should be requested to finalize this at an early date.

Disclosure and treatment of related party transactions

This again is an important disclosure. The Committee was informed that the Institute of Chartered Accountants of India had already issued an Exposure Draft on the subject. The Committee recommends that the Institute of Chartered Accountants of India should be requested to finalize this at the earliest. In the interim, the Committee recommends the disclosure set out in Clause 7 of Annexure 04.

Treatment of deferred taxation

The treatment of deferred taxation and its appropriate disclosure has an important bearing on the true and fair view of the financial status of the company. The Committee recommends that the Institute of Chartered Accountants of India be requested to issue a standard on deferred tax liability at an early date.

Management

13.1 In the view of the Committee, the over-riding aim of management is to maximize shareholder value without being detrimental to the interests of other stakeholders. The management however, is subservient to the board of directors and must operate within its boundaries and the policy framework laid down by the board. While the board is responsible for ensuring that the principles of corporate governance are adhered to and enforced, the real onus of implementation lies with the management. It is responsible for translating into action, the policies and strategies of the board and implementing its directives to achiever corporate objectives of the company framed by the board. It is therefore essential that the board should clearly define the role of the management.

Function of the Management

13.2 The management comprises the Chief Executive, Executive-directors and the key managers of the company, involved in day-to-day activities of the company.

13.3 The Committee believes that the management should carry out the following functions :

- Assisting the board in its decision making process in respect of the company's strategy, policies, code of conduct and performance targets, by providing necessary inputs.
- Implementing the policies and code of conduct of the board.
- Managing the day to day affairs of the company to best achieve the targets and goals set by the board, to maximize the shareholder value.
- Providing timely, accurate, substantive and material information, including financial matters and exceptions, to the boars, board-committees and the shareholders.
- Ensuring compliance of all regulations and laws.
- Ensuring timely and efficient service to the shareholders and to protect shareholder's rights and interests.
- Setting up and implementing an effective internal control systems, commensurate with the business requirements.
- Implementing and comply with the Code of Conduct as laid down by the board.
- Co-operating and facilitating efficient working of board committees.

13.4 As a part of the disclosure related to Management, the Committee recommends that as part of the directors' report or as an addition there to, a Management Discussion and Analysis report should form part of the annual report to the shareholders. This Management of Discussion & Analysis should include discussion on the following matters within the limit set by the company's competitive position:

- Industry structure and developments
- Opportunities and Threats
- Segment-wise or product-wise performance
- Outlook
- Risks and concerns
- Internal control systems and their adequacy
- Discussion on financial performance with respect to operational performance
- Material developments in Human Resources/Industrial Relations front, including number of people employed

13.5 Good corporate governance casts an obligation on the management in respect of disclosures. The Committee therefore recommends that disclosures must be made by the management to the board relating to all material financial and commercial transactions, where they have personal interest, that may have a potential conflict with the interest of the company at large (for e.g. dealing in company shares, commercial dealings with bodies, which have shareholding of management and their relatives etc.)

This is a mandatory recommendation.

Shareholders

14.1 The shareholders are the owners of the company and as such they have certain rights and responsibilities. But in reality, companies cannot be managed by shareholder referendum. The shareholders are not expected to assume responsibility for the management of corporate affairs. A company's management must be able to take business decisions rapidly. The shareholders have therefore to necessarily delegate many of their responsibilities as owners of the company to the directors who then become responsible for corporate strategy and operations. The implementation of this strategy is done by a management team. This relationship therefore brings in the accountability of the boards and the management to the shareholders of the company. A good corporate framework in one that provides adequate avenues to the shareholders for effective contribution in the governance of the company while insisting on a high standard of corporate behaviour without getting involved in the day to day functioning of the company.

Responsibilities of Shareholders

14.2 The Committee believes that the General Body Meetings provide an opportunity to the shareholders to address their concerns to the board of directors and comment on and demand any explanation on the annual report or on the overall functioning of the company. It is important that the shareholders use the forum of general body meetings for ensuring that the company is being properly stewarded for maximizing the interests of the shareholders. This is important especially in the Indian context. It follows from the above, that for effective participation shareholders must maintain decorum during the General Body Meetings.

14.3 The effectiveness of the board is determined by the quality of the directors and the quality of the financial information is dependent to an extent on the efficiency with which the auditors carry on their duties. The shareholders must therefore show a greater degree of interest and involvement in the appointment of the directors and the auditors. Indeed, they should demand complete information about the directors before approving their directorship.

14.4 The Committee recommends that in case of the appointment of a new director or re-appointment of a director the shareholders must be provided with the following information:

- A brief resume of the director;
- Nature of his expertise in specific functional areas; and
- Names of companies in which the person also holds the directorship and the membership of Committees of the board.

This is a mandatory recommendation.

Shareholders' Rights

14.5 The basic rights of the shareholders include right to transfer and registration of shares, obtaining relevant information on the company on a timely and regular basis, participating and voting in shareholder meetings, electing members of the board and sharing in the residual profits of the corporation.

14.6 The Committee therefore recommends that as shareholders have a right, to participate in, and be sufficiently informed on decisions concerning fundamental corporate changes, they should not only be provided information as under the Companies Act, but also in respect of other decisions relating to material changes such as takeovers, sale of assets or divisions of the company and changes in capital structure which will lead to change in control or may result in certain shareholders obtaining control disproportionate to the equity ownership.

14.7 The Committee recommends that information like quarterly results, presentation made by companies to analysts may be put on company's web-site or may be sent in such a form so as to enable the stock exchange on which the company is listed to put it on its own web-site.

This is a mandatory recommendation.

14.8 The Committee recommends that the half-yearly declaration of financial performance including summary of the significant events in last six-months, should be sent to each household of shareholders.

This is a non-mandatory recommendation.

14.9 A company must have appropriate systems in place which will enable the shareholders to participate effectively and vote in the shareholder's meeting. The company should also keep the shareholders informed of the rules and voting procedures, which govern the general shareholder meetings.

14.10 The annual general meetings of the company should not be deliberately held at venues or the timing should not be such, which makes it difficult for most of the shareholders to attend. The company must also ensure that it is not inconvenient or expensive for shareholders to cast their vote.

14.11 Currently, although the formality of holding the general meeting is gone through, in actual practice only a small fraction of the shareholders of that company do or can really participate therein. This virtually makes the concept of corporate democracy illusory. It is imperative that this situation which has lasted too long needs an early correction. In this context, for shareholders who are unable to attend the meetings, there should be a requirement which will enable them to vote by postal ballot for key decisions. A detailed list of the matters which should require postal ballot is given in Annexure 3. This would require changes in the

Companies Act. The Committee was informed that SEBI has already made recommendations in this regard to the Department of Company Affairs.

14.12 The Committee further recommends that to expedite the process of share transfers the board of the company should delegate the power of share transfer to an officer, or a committee or to the registrar and share transfer agents. The delegated authority should attend to share transfer formalities at least once in a fortnight.

This is a mandatory recommendation.

Institutional Shareholders

14.13 Institutional shareholders have acquired large stakes in the equity share capital of listed Indian companies. They have or are in the process of becoming majority stakeholders in many listed companies and own shares largely on behalf of the retail investors. They thus have a special responsibility given the weightage of their votes and have a bigger role to play in corporate governance as retail investors look upon them for positive use of their voting rights.

14.14 Given the weight of their votes, the institutional shareholders can effectively use their power to influence the standards of corporate governance. Practices elsewhere in the world have indicated that institutional shareholders can sufficiently influence because of their collective stake, the policies of the company so as to ensure that the company they have invested in, complies with the corporate governance code in order to minimize shareholders value. What is important in the view of the Committee is that, the institutional shareholders put to good use their voting power.

14.15 The Committee is of the view that the institutional shareholders

- Take active interest in the composition of the Board of Directors.
- Be vigilant
- Maintain regular and systematic contact at senior level for exchange of views on management, strategy, performance and the quality of management.
- Ensure that voting intentions are translated into practice.
- Evaluate the corporate governance performance of the company.

Manner of Implementation

15.1 The Committee recommends that SEBI writes to the Central Government to amend the securities Contract (Regulation) Rules, 1957 for incorporating the mandatory provisions of this Report.

15.2 The Committee further recommends to SEBI, that as in other countries, the mandatory provisions of the recommendation may be implemented through the listing agreement of the stock exchanges.

15.3 The Committee recognizes that the listing agreement is not a very powerful instrument and the penalties for violation are not sufficiently stringent to act as a deterrent. The Committee therefore recommends to SEBI, that the listing agreement of the stock exchange be strengthened and the exchanges themselves be vested with more powers, so that they can ensure proper compliance of code of Corporate Governance. In this context the Committee further recommends that the Securities Contract (Regulation) Act, 1956 should be amended, so that in addition to the above, the concept of listing agreement be replaced by listing conditions.

15.4 The Committee recommends that the Securities Contract (Regulation) Act, 1956 be amended to empower SEBI and stock exchange to take deterrent and appropriate action in case of violation of the provisions of the listing agreement. These could include power of levying monetary penalty both on the company and the concerned officials of the company and filing of winding-up petition etc.

15.5 The Committee also recommends that SEBI write to the Department of Company Affairs for suitable amendments to the Companies Act in respect of the recommendations, which fall within their jurisdiction.

15.6 The Committee recommends that there should be a separate section on Corporate Governance in the annual reports of companies, with a detailed compliance report on Corporate Governance. Non-compliance of any mandatory recommendation with reasons thereof and the extent which the non-mandatory recommendations have been adopted should be specifically highlighted. This will enable the shareholders and the securities market to assess for themselves the standards of corporate governance followed by a company.

This is a mandatory recommendation.

15.7 The Committee also recommends that the company should arrange to obtain a certificate from the auditors of the company regarding compliance of mandatory recommendations and annexe the certificate with the directors' report, which is sent annually to all the shareholders of the company. The same certificate should also be sent to the stock exchanges along with the annual returns filled by the company.

End Note

There are several corporate governance structures available in the developed world but there is no one structure, which can be singled out as being better than the others. There is no "one size fits all" structure for corporate governance. The Committee's recommendations are not therefore based on anyone model but designed for the Indian environment.

Corporate governance extends beyond corporate law. Its fundamental objective is not mere fulfillment of the requirements of law but in ensuring commitments of the board in managing the company in a transparent manner for maximizing long term shareholders value. The corporate governance has as many votaries as claimants. Among the latter, the Committee has primarily focused its recommendations on investors and shareholders, as they are the prime constituencies of SEBI. Effectiveness of corporate governance system cannot merely be legislated by law neither can any system of corporate governance be static. As competition increases, technology pronounces the death of distance and speeds up communication, the environment in which firms operate in India also changes. In this dynamic environment the systems of corporate governance also need to evolve. The Committee believes that its recommendations will go a long way in raising the standards of corporate governance in Indian firms and make them attractive destinations for local and global capital. These recommendations will also form the base for further evolution of the structure of corporate governance in consonance with the rapidly changing economic and industrial environment of the country in the new millennium.

Annexure 1

Names of the Members of the Committee

Kumar Mangalam Birla, chairman, Aditya Birla group Chairman of the Committee

1. Rohit Bhagat, Country Head, Boston Consulting Group
2. Dr. J. Bhagwati, Jt. Secretary, Ministry of Finance
3. Samir Biswas, Regional Director, Western Region, Department of Company Affairs, Government of India
4. S.P. Chhajed, President of Institute of Chartered Accountants of India.
5. Virendra Ganda, Ex-President of Institute of Company Secretaries of India.
6. Dr.. Sumantra Ghosal, Professor of Strategic Management, London Business School.
7. Vijay Kalantri, President, All India Association of Industries
8. Pratip Kar, Executive Director, SEBI - Member Secretary
9. Y.H. Malegam, Managing Partner, S.B. Billimoria & Co.
10. N.R. Narayana Murthy, Chairman and Managing Director, Infosys Technologies Ltd.
11. A.K. Narayanan, President of Tamil Nadu Investor Association
12. Kamal Parekh, Ex-President, Calcutta Stock Exchange (Shri J M Chaudhary-President Calcutta Stock Exchange)
13. Dr. R.H. Patil, Managing Director, National Stock Exchange Ltd.
14. Anand Rathi, President of the Stock Exchange, Mumbai
15. Ms. D.N. Raval, Executive Director, SEBI
16. Rajesh Shah, Former President of Confederation of Indian Industries
17. L.K. Singhvi, Sr. Executive, Director, SEBI
18. S.S. Sodhi, Executive Director, Delhi Stock Exchange

Annexure 2

Information to be Placed before Board of Directors

1. Annual operating plans and budgets and many updates.
2. Capital budget and any updates.
3. Quarterly-results for the company and its operating divisions or business segment.
4. Minutes of meetings of audit committee and other committee of the board.
5. The information on recruitment and remuneration of senior officers just below the board level, including appointment or removal of Chief Financial Officer and the Company Secretary.
6. Show cause, demand and prosecution notices which are materially important.
7. Fatal or serious accidents, dangerous occurrences, any material effluent or pollution problems.
8. Any material default in financial obligation to and by the company, or substantial non-payment for goods sold by the company.
9. Any issue, which involves possible public or product liability claims of substantial nature, including any judgement or order which, may have passed stricture on the conduct of the company or taken an adverse view regarding another enterprise that can have negative implications on the company.
10. Details of any joint venture or collaboration agreement.
11. Transactions that involve substantial payment towards goodwill, brand equity, or intellectual property.
12. Significant labour problems and their proposed solutions. Any significant development in Human Resources/Industrial Relations front like singing of wage agreement, implementation of Voluntary Retirement Scheme etc.
13. Sale of material nature of investments, subsidiaries, assets, which is not in normal course of business.
14. Quarterly details of foreign exchange exposures and the steps taken by management to limit the risks of adverse exchange rate movement, if material.
15. Non-compliance of any regulatory, statutory nature or listing requirements and shareholders service such as non-payment of dividend, delay in share transfer etc.

3. P.L. Sanjeev Reddy Report (2000)

Department of Company Affairs has been making necessary changes in the Companies Act, 1956 and the rules made there under to keep pace with the globalization process. The provisions relating to 'nomination facility for shareholders and deposit-holders; buy-back of securities', relaxation in norms relating to inter-corporate loans and investments', setting up of Investor Education and Protection Fund', allowing sweat equity' and certain important provisions introduced through Companies (Amendment) Act, 1999 (w.e.f. 31.10.1998) to provide initiatives and safeguards for improved investor protection and better corporate governance. The companies Act, 1956 has again been amended vide Companies (Amendment) Act, 2000 providing for Postal Ballot, Audit Committee, Directors Responsibility Statement, Debenture Trustees, Secretarial Compliance Certificates, Reduction of Time for Payment Dividend (including interim dividend), tenfold increases of fines and Option for Election of a Director by small shareholders etc.

The company Law Settlement Scheme, 2000 and Fast Track Scheme, 2000 launched by the Department of Company Affairs are other steps towards improved corporate governance. Through these schemes, successful attempts were made to create an environment of trust, confidence and partnership wherein companies in the past, came forward and availed one time declaration and settlement. The Companies Availing of the 'Fast Track Scheme, 2000' will be enormously benefited as it provides a simple 'exit route' for non functional companies saving them from protracted process of winding up.

Certain steps have also been initiated by SEBI for good corporate governance and investor protection.

(*i*) Composition of the Committee

In order to operationalize the concept of corporate governance / excellence on a sustained basis to sharpen India's global competitive edge and to further promote and develop corporate culture in the country. Towards this direction of achieving excellence, in May, 2000 the Department invited a group of leading industrialists, professionals, and academics i.e. (i) Shri Kumar Mangalam Birla, (ii) Shri M.R. Rao, (iii) Shri N.H. Mirza, (iv) Shri PM Narielvala, (v) Dr. MB Athreya, (vi) Shri Maninarayan Swami, (vii) Shri Mukesh Ambani, (viii) Shri Rajiv Chandrasekhar, (ix) Shri A. Ramaswamy, (x) Mr. S. Rajgopalan- President - ICAI, (xi) Dr. Subir Choudhary- president- ICSI, (xii) Shri B.M. Jain under the Chairmanship of Dr. P.L. Sanjeev Reddy to study and recommend measures to enhance corporate excellence in India. "This study group was formally constitute by Order No. 11/6/200 CL.V dates 15th May, 2000."

(*ii*) Recommendation

1. Direction and Management Distinguished : It is imperative to distinguish the nature of the two basic components of governance in terms of policy making and oversight responsibilities of the board of directors, and the executive and implementation responsibilities of corporate management comprising of the managing director and his or her team of executives including functional directors. Executives who are also on the board as directors of the company in effect wear two hats, one as part of the board and the other as part of the management. Directors derive their authority only when acting collectively as the board as directors of the company in effect wear two hats, one as part of the board and the other as part of the management. Directors derive their authority only when acting collectively as the board or when the board delegates specifically authorities to be exercised, such as for example in the case of managing directors. Managers, in the broadest sense of the term, have the responsibility to execute the policies under the supervision of the board, and for this purpose have the necessary authority to ensure compliance and implementation. The Task Force highlights this critical distinction particularly in the context of fixing responsibility for failure and the consequential liabilities that follow.

2. Role and Responsibilities of Corporate Boards and Directors : The Task force recommendation in this field calls for a greater role and influence for non-executive independent directors, a tighter delineation of independence criteria and minimization of interest - conflict potential, and some stringent punitive punishments for executive directors of companies failing to comply with listing and other requirements.

3. Managing & Whole-Time Directors: The Task Force felt that the shareholders and stakeholders of the company appointing them as their executives should have the benefit of their full attention and accordingly, has suggested some limitation on the nature and number of their other directorships.

4. Non-Compete Stipulations : Task Force opined and has accordingly recommended that there should be proper disclosure to the shareholders and the investing community.

5. Interested Shareholders : Accordingly, one of the most important recommendations of the Task Force is proposes the concept of interested shareholders who would be required to abstain from voting on specified matters that impact upon some but not all the shareholders. Task Force has recommended that this privilege be limited to few specific matters and even there with suitable provisions for breaking stalemate situations.

6. Measures Promoting Transparency and Informed Shareholder Participation : The task force recommendations addressing this issue relate to more meaningful and transparent accounting and reporting, improved annual reports concomitant with more detailed filing with regulatory authorities, and greater facilitation for informed participation using the advances in converging information and communications technologies.

7. National Listing Authority : The task force recommendation recognize this important signaling effect of listing, and provide for tougher listing and compliance regimen through a centralized National Listing Authority.

8. Measures Relating to Listing & Voluntary De-Listing : As a measure of investor protection and general upgrading of the status of listed companies both internationally and domestically. The Task Force recommendations apply the highest and toughest standards of corporate governance to listed companies.

9. Public Sector Enterprises : The Task force has recommended that such PSUs be relived from multiple surveillance agencies and simultaneously a commission be appointed to draft a suitable code of public behavior on the lines of Nolan (now Neil) Commission in the United Kingdom.

10. Corporate Social Responsibility : Task Force recommendations emphasis corporate social responsiveness and ethical business practices, seeking what might well turn out to be only the first small steps for better governance on this front but also the promise of a more transparent and internationally respected Corporate India of the future.

11. Centre for Corporate Excellence : There is a pressing need to set up an independent autonomous Centre for corporate Excellence that would function as a knowledge portal and repository in this field. The Task Force has recommended the constitution of such a Centre with three broad functions, Research and Studies, Education Promotion and Development, and Accreditation with respect to matters bearing upon corporate governance and excellence. After detailed considerations of alternative funding and sitting options, the Task force decided in favour of funding by the government and industry associations and professional bodies, and identified Bangalore as the preferred location.

12. Classification of Recommendation & Implementation : Recommendations of the Task Force have been grouped as essential, to be introduced immediately be legislation, and desirable, that can be left to the discretion of the companies and their shareholders in their wisdom. A model governance code incorporating both the essential and desirable measures has been recommended to be drafted and included as a Table in the companies Act, to be adopted at the option of the companies. Given the challenges of managing change, the Task Force has a recommended phased implementation of the essential measures, depending upon the size and capabilities of the companies on the one hand and on the other, the requirements of the market place. The Task Force is however convinced that the level of non-legislative and non-regulatory intervention is a function of the maturity of the market and the economy. Until acceptable levels of such maturity and market influence are reached, it may be necessary to support self-discipline and self-regulation with appropriate legislative and regulatory support with a provision for review after three years.

The Task Force on Corporate Governance gives prominence to the role of non-executive independent directors and at the same time, number and rights of managing and whole time directors have been decreased. The voting system in the context of Interested Shareholders needs more clarity in expression. Task Force recommends phased implementation of the norms of Corporate Governance while it should be at a time implementation to attain the true objectives of Corporate Governance.

4. Naresh Chandra Committee (2002)

After taking into consideration of Kumar Mangalam Birla Committee Report, "on 21st August, 2002, the Department of Company Affairs (DCA) under the Ministry of Finance and Company Affairs, Government of India appointed High Level Committee Naresh Chandra Committee to examine various Corporate Governance Issues to analysis and changes from different areas".

I. Terms of Reference

1. the statutory auditor-company relationship, so as to further strengthen the professional nature of this interface.
2. the need, if any, for rotation of statutory audit firms or partners;
3. the procedure for appointment of auditors and determination of audit fees;
4. restrictions, if necessary, on non-audit fees;
5. independence of auditing functions;
6. measures required to ensure that the management and companies actually present 'true and fair' statement of the financial affairs of companies;
7. the need to consider measures such as certification of accounts and financial statements by the management and directors;
8. the necessity of having a transparent system of random scrutiny of audited accounts;
9. adequacy of regulation of chartered accountants, company secretaries, and cost accountants; and other similar statutory oversight functionaries;
10. advantages, if any, of setting up an independent regulator similar to the Public Company Accounting Oversight Board in the SOX Act, and if so, its constitution; and
11. the role of independent directors, and how their independence and effectiveness can be ensured.

II. Recommendation

1. Disqualification for audit assignments : In line with international best practices, the Committees recommended an abbreviated list of disqualifications for auditing assignments, which includes:

(*i*) Prohibition of any direct financial interest in the audit client: by the audit firm, its partners or members of the engagement team as well as their 'direct relatives'.

(*ii*) Prohibition of receiving any loans and or guarantees: from or on behalf of the audit client by the audit firm, its partners or any member of the engagement team and their 'direct relatives'.

(*iii*) Prohibition of any business relationship: with the audit client by the auditing firm, its partners or any member of the engagement team and their direct relatives.

(*iv*) Prohibition of personal relationship: which would exclude any partner of the audit firm or member of the engagement team being a 'relative' of any of key officers of the client company, (as defined by section 5 of the Companies Act).

(*v*) Prohibition of services or cooling off period: under which any partner or member of the engagement team of an audit firm who wants to join an audit client, or any key officer of the client company wanting to join the audit firm, would only be allowed to do so after two years from the time they were involved in the preparation of accounts and audit of that client.

(*vi*) Prohibition of undue dependence on an audit client: A 'direct relative' is defined as the individual concerned, his or he spouse, dependent parents, children or dependent siblings. For the present, the term 'relative' is an defined under Schedule IA of the Companies Act. However, the Committee believes that the Schedule IA definition is too wide, and needs to be rationalized for effective compliance.

2. The committee recommends that the following services should not be provided by an audit firm to any audit client :

(*a*) Accounting and bookkeeping services, related to the accounting records or financial statements of the audit client.

(*b*) Internal audit services.

(*c*) Financial information systems design and implemented, including services related to IT system for preparing financial or management accounts and information flows of a company.

(*d*) Actuarial services.

(*e*) Broker, dealer, investment adviser or investment banking services.

(*f*) Outsourced financial services.

(*g*) Management functions, including the provision of temporary staff to audit clients.

(*h*) Any form of staff recruitment, and particularly hiring of senior management staff for the audit client.

(*i*) Valuation services and fairness opinion.

Further in case the firm undertakes any services other than audit, or the prohibited services listed above, it should be done only with the approval of the audit committee.

3. Independence standards for consulting and other entities that are affiliated to audit firms:

(*a*) Prohibition of undue dependence: Where an audit firm has subsidiary, associate or affiliated entities, yardstick of no more than 25 per cent pf revenues coming from a single audit client stated in Recommendation 2.1 should be widened to accommodate the consolidated entity should come from a single corporate client with whom there is also an audit engagement.

(*b*) The other prohibitions listed in Recommendation 2.1 should also apply in full to all affiliated consulting and specialized service entities of any audit firm that are either subsidiaries of the audit firm, or have common ownership of over 50 per cent with the audit firm.

4. Compulsory Audit Partner Rotation

(*a*) There is no need to legislate in favour of compulsory rotation of audit firms.

(*b*) However, the partners and at least 50 per cent of the engagement team (excluding article clerks and trainees) responsible for the audit of either a listed company, or companies whose paid up capital and free reserves exceeds Rs. 10 crore, or companies whose turnover exceeds Rs. 50 crore, should be rotated every five years. Also, in line with the provisions of the European Union and the IFAC, persons who are compulsorily rotated could, if need be, allowed to return after a break of three years.

5. Auditor's disclosure of contingent liabilities: The Committee recommends that management should provide a clear description in plain English of each material liability and its risks, which should be followed by the auditor's clearly worded comments on the management's view.

6. Auditor's disclosure of qualifications and consequent action

(*i*) Qualifications to accounts, if any Must form a distinct, and adequately highlighted, section of the auditor's report to the shareholders.

(*ii*) These must be listed in full in plain English- what they are (including quantification thereof), why these were arrived at, including qualification thereof, etc.

(*iii*) In case of a qualified auditor's report, the audit firm may read out the qualifications, with explanations, to shareholders in the company's annual general meeting.

(*iv*) It should also be mandatory for the audit firm to separately send a copy of the qualified report to the ROC, the SEBI and the principal stock exchange (for listed companies), about the qualifications, with a copy of this letter being sent to the management of the company.

7. Management's certification in the event of auditor's replacement

8. Auditor's annual certification of independence : Before agreeing to be appointed (along with 224(I)(b), the audit firm must submit a certificate of independence to the Audit Committee or to the board of directors of the client company certifying that the firm, together with its consulting and specialized services affiliates, subsidiaries and associated companies :

(*i*) are independent and have arm's length relationship with client company.

(*ii*) have not engaged in any non-audit services listed also prohibited in Recommendation above; and

(*iii*) are not disqualified from audit assignments by virtue of breaching any of the limits, restrictions and Prohibitions listed in Recommendations above.

9. Appointment of auditors : The Audit Committee of the Board of directors shall be the first point of reference regarding the appointment of auditors. To discharge this fiduciary responsibility, the Audit Committee shall :

(*a*) discuss the annual work programme with the auditor;

(*b*) review the independence of the audit firm in line with Recommendations above; and

(*c*) recommend to the board; with reasons, either the appointment/reappointment or removal of the external auditor, along with the annual audit remuneration.

10. CEO and CFO certification of annual audited accounts: For all listed companies as well as public limited companies whose paid-up capital and free reserves exceeds Rs. 10 crore, or turnover exceeds Rs. 50 crore, there should be a certification by the CEO (either the Executive Chairman or the Managing Directors) and the CFO (whole-time Finance Director or otherwise).

11. Setting up of independent Quality Review Board : There should be established, with appropriate legislative support three independent Quality Review Boards (QRB). Each for the ICAI, the ICSI and ICWAI to periodically examine and review the quality of audit, secretarial and cost accounting firms, and pass judgement and comments on the quality and sufficiency of system, infrastructure and practices.

12. Proposed disciplinary mechanism for auditors : Classification of offences and merging of schedules: At present there are two schedules of offences and misconduct- with the second requiring action by high Courts. These two schedules need to be merged, so that the Council is empowered to award all types of punishment for all types of offences.

I. Prosecution Directorate : An independent permanent directorate within the structure of ICAI shall be created, which shall act as the Prosecution Directorate. This office will exclusively deal with all disciplinary cases and, hence, expedite the process of enquiry and decision- making by fully devoting its time and energy towards processing these cases. The office should be headed by a person of the level of director, and should be one with a legal background and conversant with the provisions of The Chartered Accountants Act and its regulations.

II. Procedure for dealing with compliant cases

(*a*) The complaints received in the appropriate form, manner, and complete in all respects, shall be registered by the Prosecution Directorate, and sent to the member or firm within 15 days of registration such a complaint.

(*b*) Depending on the category of the complaint, the Prosecution Directorate shall ask for and obtain necessary documents. The time frame for this should be, under normal circumstances, no more than 60 days.

(c) On receipt of the relevant documents, the compliant, along with the views, if any, of the Prosecution Directorate, will be placed before the Disciplinary Committee. This has to be done within 20 days of receiving all relevant accompanying. This has to be within 20 days of receiving all relevant accompanying documents.

13. Procedure for dealing with information cases

(i) The prosecution Directorate shall examine information received. After forming his views, the Director of the Prosecution Directorate will place the matter before the Secretary of ICAI.

(ii) If the Secretary agrees with the view expressed by the Director, then the information case will be placed before the Disciplinary Committee.

(iii) In the event of the Secretary differing with the views of the Director, the matter would be placed before the President of ICIA and, thereafter, it would be discussed at a meeting between the president, secretary and the Director. If in this meeting, it is decided to refer the matter to the Disciplinary Committee, then reference is made accordingly.

(iv) After registering the 'information; case the procedure outlined for the compliant case may be followed mutatis mutandis.

14. Disciplinary Committee

(i) **Enquiries in relation** to misconduct of members shall be held by the Disciplinary Committee. To expedite decision - making, the Council of ICAI shall be empowered to constitute one or more bench of the Disciplinary Committees in cities where there are regional headquarters of ICAI.

(ii) **Composition :** Each bench should consist of five members. The President or the Vice-President of ICAI will be the Presiding Officer. The Committee recommended that, given their pre-occupation in the department, a sitting government official should not be nominated to the Disciplinary Committee. It is pointed out that for each stage in the process, strict time lines should be prescribed. This is especially important in respect of scrutiny of 'information cases'.

(iii) **Quorum :** Three of the five members.

(iv) **Tenure :** Co-terminus with the duration of the ICAI Council.

(v) **Functions :** The Disciplinary Committees shall hear the compliant and information cases referred by the Prosecution Directorate and record their decisions and conclusions in a report. This report shall also record the punishment to be awarded, if any, to the member, which can constitute (i) reprimand, (ii) removing the name of the member either permanently or for such a period as thought fit, (iii) monetary penalty, and / or (iv) a combination of any two.

15. Council : Any report submitted by the Disciplinary Committee should normally be considered by the Council within 45 days from the date of the report. It shall be the duty of the Council of ICAI to act upon the decisions of the Disciplinary Committee. While performing such a duty, the Council can :

(i) Endorse the decisions of the Disciplinary Committee, and implement them.

(ii) Refer any case back to the Disciplinary Committee for further enquiry, when it finds that certain issues need further enquiry. However, in doing so, the Council will have to frame the specific issues.

(iii) Direct the prosecution Directorate to place the case before the Appellate Body, in the event of the Council deciding to appeal against the decisions of the Disciplinary Committee.

16. Appellate Body: Headquartered in New Delhi, the Appellate Body shall consist of a Presiding Officer and four other members. The Presiding Officer shall be a retired judge of the Supreme Court or a retired Chief Justice of High Court. Two members shall be Past Presidents of ICAI, nominated by the Council. The remaining two shall be persons of eminence nominated by the DCA (but excluding any officer of the Department or member of the Council). The quorum shall be three.

17. Publication of decisions of the Disciplinary Committee : Due publicity shall be given by the Prosecution Directorate about the punishment ultimately awarded, through periodicals, newsletters, website and any other means considered appropriate.

18. Funding

(*i*) Appellate Body: Required funding arrangements should be made by the Central Government. This is essential for ensuring independence, and on the ground that the high Court stage can be said to have been always funded by the Government.

(*ii*) Disciplinary Committee: The expenses shall be borne by ICAI's Council, which shall also fix the emoluments, sitting fees, allowances, and other expenses of the members.

(*iii*) Prosecution Directorate: All expenses will be borne by the Council of ICAL.

(*iv*) Every complaint, other than a compliant made by or on behalf of the Central or any State Government shall be accomplished by a fee Rs. 5000, which will be returned as soon as the Disciplinary Committee recommends that case is not frivolous fees not refunded for frivolous cases will be used to partly defray the cost of investigation.

19. Defining an independent director : An independent director of a company is a non-executive director who :

(*i*) Apart from receiving directors' remuneration, does not have any material pecuniary relationships or transactions with the company, its promoters its senior management or is holding company, its subsidiaries and associated companies;

(*ii*) Is not related to promoters or management at the board level, or one level below the board (spouse and dependent, parents, children or siblings);

(*iii*) Has not been an executive of the company in the last three years;

(*iv*) Is not a partner or an executive of the statutory auditing firm, the internal audit firm that is associated with the company, and has not been a partner or an executive of any such firm for the last three years? This will also apply to legal firm(s) and consulting firm(s) that have a material association with the entity.

(*v*) Is not a significant supplier, vendor or customer of the company;

(*vi*) Is not a substantial shareholder of the company, i.e. owning 2 per cent or more of the block of voting shares;

(*vii*) Has not been a director, independent or otherwise, of the company for more than three terms of three years each (not exceeding nine years in any case);

The Committee recommended that the above criteria applicable for all listed companies, as well as unlisted public limited companies with a paid-up share capital and free reserves of Rs. 10 crore and above or turnover of Rs. 50 crore and above with effect from the financial year beginning 2003.

20. Percentage of independent directors : No less than 50 per cent of the board of directors of any listed company, as well as unlisted public limited companies. However, this will not apply to : (1) unlisted public companies, which have no more than 50 shareholders and which are without debt of any kind from the public, banks, or financial institutions, as long as they do not change their character, (2) unlisted subsidiaries of listed companies. Nominee will be excluded both from the numerator and the denominator.

21. Minimum board size of listed companies : The minimum board size of all listed companies, as well as unlisted public limited companies should be seven - of which at least four should be independent directors.

However, this will not apply to: (1) unlisted public companies, which have no more than 50 shareholders and which are without debt of any kind from the public, banks or financial institutions, as long as they do not change their character, (2) unlisted subsidiaries of listed companies.

22. Disclosure on duration of board meetings/Committee meetings : The minutes of board meeting and Audit Committee meetings and Audit Committee meetings of all listed companies, as well as unlisted public limited companies must disclose the timing and duration of each such meeting, in addition to the date and members in attendance.

23. Tele-conferencing and video conferencing : If a director cannot be physically present but wants to participate in the proceedings of the board and its committees, then minuted signed proceedings of a tele-conference or video conference should constitute proof of his or her participation.

24. Additional disclosure to directors : In addition to the disclosures specified in Clause 49 under 'Information to be placed before the board of directors'.

25. Independent directors on Audit Committees of listed companies : Audit Committees of all listed companies, as well as unlisted public limited companies should consist exclusively of independent directors.

26. Audit Committee charter :

(*a*) The Chairman of the Audit Committee must annually certify whether and to what extent each of the functions listed in the Audit Committee Charter were discharged in the course of the year. This will serve as the Committee's action taken report to the shareholders.

(*b*) Audit Committee should accept and recommended the financial statements with qualifications. The statement should also certify whether the Audit committee met with the statutory and internal auditors of the company without the presence of management, and whether such meetings revealed materially significant issues or risks.

27. Remuneration of non-executive directors :

(*a*) The statutory limit on sitting fees should be reviewed, although ideally it should be a mater to be resolved between the management and the shareholders.

(*b*) In addition, loss making companies should be permitted by the DCA to pay special fees to any independent director, subject to reasonable caps, in order to attract the best restructuring and strategic talent to the boards of such companies.

(*c*) The present provisions relating to stock options, and to the 1 per cent commission on net profits, is adequate and does not, at present, need any revision.

28. Exempting non-executive directors from certain liabilities : Time has come to insert provisions in the definitions chapter of certain Acts to specifically exempt non-executive and independent directors from such criminal and civil liabilities. An illustrative list of these Acts is the Companies Act, Negotiable Instruments Act, Provident Fund Act, ESI Act, Factories Act, Industrial Disputes Act and the Electricity Supply Act.

29. Training of independent directors

(*a*) DCA should encourage institutions of prominence including their proposed Centre for Corporate Excellence to have regular training programmes fro independent directors. In framing the programmes, and for other preparatory work, funding could possibly come from the IEPF.

(*b*) All independent directors should be required to attend at least one such training course before assuming responsibilities as an independent director, or considering that enough programmes might not be available in the initial years, within one year of becoming an independent director. An untrained independent directors should be disqualified under section 274(1) (g) of the Companies Act, 1956 after being given reasonable notice.

(*c*) Considering that enough training institutions and programmes might not be available in the initial years, this requirement may be introduced in a phased manner, so that the larger listed companies are covered first.

(*d*) The executing bodies must clearly state their plan for the year and their funding should be directly proportionate to the extent to which they execute such plans.

(*e*) There should be a 'trainee appraisal' system to judge the quality of the programmes and so help decide, in the second round, which should be dropped.

(III) Other Recommendations

1. SEBI and Subordinate Legislations

(*a*) SEBI may refrain from exercising powers of subordinate legislations in areas where specific legislation exists as in the Companies Act, 1956.

(*b*) If any additional requirements are sought to be prescribed for listed companies, then, in areas where specific provision exists in the Companies Act, it would be appropriate for SEBI to have the requirement prescribed in the Companies Act itself thorough a suitable amendment.

(*c*) In recognition of the fact that SEBI regulates activities in dynamics market conditions, the DCA should respond to SEBI's requirements quickly. In case the changes proposed by SEBI necessitate a change in the companies Act, the DCA should agree to the requirement being mandated in clause 49 of SEBI regulation until the Act is amended.

(*d*) It would be appropriate for SEBI to use its powers of subordinate legislation, in consultation with the DCA, and Vice versa. All committees set up either by SEBI or DCA to consider changes in law, rules or regulations should have representatives of both SEBI and DCA.

(*e*) A formal structure needs to be set up to ensure that the DCA, which regulates all companies, and SEBI, which regulates only listed companies, act in coordination and harmony.

2. Improving facilities in the DCA offices : The Government should increase the strength of DCA's offices, and substantially increase the quality and quantity of its physical infrastructure, including computerization.

3. Corporate Serious Fraud Office : A Corporate Serious Fraud Office (CSFO) should be set up in the Department of Company Affairs with specialists inducted on the basis of transfer I deputation and on special term contracts.

4. Penalties and Disqualification :

(*a*) Penalties ought to be rationalized, and related to the sums involved in the offences. Fess, especially late fees, can be related to the size of the company in terms of its paid-up capital and free reserves, or turnover, or both.

(*b*) Disqualification under section 274 (1) (g) of the Companies Act 1956 should be triggered for certain other offences than just non-payment of debt. However, independent directors need to be treated on a different footing and exempted as in the case of nominees directors representing financial institutions.

(*c*) A stricter regime should be prescribed for companies registered as brokers with SEBI. Greater accountability should be provided for with respect to transfer of money by way of Inter Corporate Deposits, or advances of any kind, from listed companies to any other company, as a necessary concomitant5 of the liberalization that section 372 A of the Companies Act, 1956 provides.

(*d*) DCA's prosecution wing needs to be considerably strengthened. Streamlined procedures be prescribed, in the Companies Act, on the lines of the recent amendments to the Code of Civil Procedure.

(*e*) To ensure that proceeds from illegal acts and frauds do not escape recovery, Companies Act needs to be amended to give DCA the powers of attachments of bank accounts etc., on the lines of the powers recently given to SEBI. I11 - gotten gains must be disgorged.

(*f*) Managers, Promoters should be held personally liable when found guilty of offences.

5. Pre-certification : DCA should consider reducing workload at offices of ROCs by providing for a system of 'pre-certification' by company secretaries; the system should provide for monetary and other penalties on company secretaries who certify incorrectly, even through error or oversight.

6. The Companies Act be amended to enable the DCA to order a 'compliance audit' , much in the same manner as it can order special audits under section 233-A of the Companies Act.

(*a*) MAOCARO should be amended to provide that auditors report certain violations.

(*b*) Section 293(1) (a) should be strengthened to prevent any unnatural stripping of assets, or sale of shares by management/promoters.

(*c*) ICAI should re-consider the limits it has set on the number of articles that a partner can train; something that has the unintended consequence of denying young prospective accountants the chance to train with the best in the profession.

(*d*) Companies should be required to establish, and publish, an Internal Code of Ethics.

(*e*) DCA should sponsor, and financially support, from the IEPF, research on corporate governance and allied subjects that have a bearing on investor/shareholder well being.

(*f*) ICAI should propose to the Government a regime and a regulatory framework that encourages the consolidation and growth of Indian firms, in view of the international competition they face, especially with regard to non-audit services.

(*g*) The Government should consider amending the Partnership Act to provide for partnerships with limited liability, especially for professions, which do not allow their members to provide services as a corporate body.

As Remy Manne has put it thus, “Management is a discrete economic service or function and the selection of individuals to perform that function; whether undertaken at the outset or during the later life of a company, is a part of the entrepreneurial job. Centralizing management serves simply to specialize these various economic functions and to allow the system to operate more efficiently”.

When we have a glance at the Report we see that exempting non-executive directors form certain criminal and civil liabilities would affect the culture of Corporate Governance. Earlier we see in Kumar Mangalam Birla Committee Report that the Corporate Social Responsibility is immensely taken care of while the present lacks this most essential norms.

5. N.R. Narain Murthy Committee (2003)

Good corporate governance is investor protection. The individual investors is at the end of a chain of financial information, stretching from corporate accountants and management, through Boards of Directors and audit committees, to independent auditors and stocks market analysts, to the investing public. Many of the links in this chain need to be strengthened or replaced to preserve its integrity.

SEB, therefore, believed that a need to review the existing code on corporate governance arise from two perspectives, (a) to evaluate the adequacy of the existing practices, and (b) to further improve the existing practices.

***(i)* Composition of the Committee:** After seeking the Naresh Chandra Committee Report SEBI established another committee in later part of 2002, which presented its report on February 8, 2003, "to review the Corporate Governance under the Chairmanship of Mr. N.R. Narayanmurthy, CEO, Infosys and the other member of the committee includes (i) Shri YH Malegam, Managing Partner, (ii) SB Billimoria & CO, (iii) Shri Ravi Narain, Managing Director, NSE, (iv) Shri AC Muthiah, president, FICCI, (v) Shri RK Somany, President, ASSOCHAM, (vi) Shri Ashok Soota, President, CII, (vii) Shri MK doogar, Representative, PHDCCI (viii) Shri Sumit Mazumder, President, BCCI, (ix) Shri Kamlesh S. Vikamsey, Member- Central Council, ICAI, (x) Shri S Gangopadhyay, President, ICSI, (xi) Shri T.R. Ramaswami, CEO, AMBI, (xii) Dr. Manoj Vaish, Executive Director, BSE, (xiii) Shri AK Narayan, President, Tamil Nadu Investors Association, (xiv) Shri Nitin Shingala, Investors Grievances, Forum, (xv) Prof. Manubhai Shah, Managing Trustee, CERC, (xvi) Shri Omkar Goswami, Chief Economist, (xvii) CII, Ms Sucheta Dalal, Consulting Editor, Financial Express, (xviii) Shri R Gopalakrishanan, Executive Director, Tata Sons Ltd. (xix) Shri D M Satwalekar, MD & CEO, HDFC Standard Life Insurance, (xx) Shri MK Chouhan, Chairman, Mahendra & Young Knowledge Foundation, (xxi) Ms. D N Raval, Executive Director, SEBI, (xxii) Shri Pratip Kar, Executive Director, SEBI, (xxiii) Shri PK Bindlish, General Manager, SEBI, Member Secretary."

***(ii)* Terms of Reference:** The terms of reference of the Committee are set out below.

(*a*) To review the performance of corporate governance; and

(*b*) To determine the role of companies in responding to rumour and other price sensitive information circulating in the market, in order to enhance the transparency and integrity of the market.

(*c*) The recommendations of the Committee are presented in this Report.

***(iii)* Recommendation**

A. Mandatory recommendations.

1. Audit committees of publicly listed companies should be required to review the following information mandatory:

(*i*) Financial statements and draft audit report, including quarterly/ Half - Yearly financial information;

(*ii*) Management discussion and analysis of financial condition and results of operations;

(*iii*) Reports relating to compliance with laws and to risk management;

(*iv*) Management letters / letters of internal control weakness issued by statutory/ internal auditors; and

(*v*) Records of related party transactions.

2. All audit committee members should be 'Financially literate' and at least one member should have accounting or related financial management expertise.

3. Management should place a report before the entire Board of Directors every quarter documenting the business risks faced by the company, measures to address and minimize such risks, and any limitation to the risk taking capacity of the corporation. The Board should formally approve this document.

4. Companies raising money through an Initial public Offering (IPO) should disclose to the Audit Committee, the uses/applications of funds by major category (capital expenditure, sales and marketing, working capital, etc), on a quarterly basis, the company shall prepare a statement of funds utilized for purposes other than those stated in the offer

document/ prospectus. The independent auditors of the company should certify this statement. The audit committee should make appropriate recommendations to the Board to take up steps in this matter.

5. It should be obligatory for the Board of a company to lay down the code of conduct for all Board members and senior management of a company. This code of conduct shall be posted on the website of the company. All Board members and senior management of a company. This code of conduct shall be posted on the website of the company.

All Board members and senior management personnel shall affirm compliance with the code on an annual basis. The annual report of the company shall contain a declaration to this effect signed off by the CEO and COO.

6. There should be no nominee directors. Where an institution wishes to appoint a director on the Board, the shareholders should make such appointment.

An Institutional director, so appointed, shall have the same responsibilities and shall be subject to the same liabilities as any other director. Nominee of the Government on public sector companies shall be similarly elected and shall be subject to the same responsibilities and liabilities as other directors.

7. All compensation paid to non- executive directors may be fixed by the Board of Directors and should be approved by Shareholders in general meeting. Limits should be set for the maximum number of stock options that can be granted to non-executive directors in any financial year and in aggregate. The stock options granted to the non-executive directors shall vest after a period of at least one year from the date such non-executive directors have retired from the Board of the Company.

8. Companies should publish their compensation philosophy and statement of entitled compensation in respect of non-executive directors in their annual report. Alternatively, this may be put up on the company's website and reference drawn thereto in the annual report. Companies should disclose on an annual basis, details of shares held by non-executive directors, including on an 'if-converted' basis.

9. Non- executive directors should be required to disclose their stock holding (both own or held by; for other persons on a beneficial basis) in the listed company in which they are proposed to be appointed as directors, prior to their appointment. These details should accompany their notice of appointment. The term 'independent director' is defined as a non- executive director of the company who:

(*i*) apart from receiving director remuneration does not have any material pecuniary relationships or transactions with the company, its promoters, its senior management or its holding company, its subsidiaries and associated companies;

(*ii*) is not related to promoters or management at the board level or at one level below the board;

(*iii*) has not been an executive of the company in the immediately preceding three financial years;

(*iv*) is not a partner or an executive of the statutory audit firm or the internal audit firm that is associated with the company, and has not been a partner or an executive of any such firm for the last three years. This will also apply to legal firm(s) and consulting firm(s) that have a material association with the entity.

(*v*) is not a supplier, service provider or customer of the company. This should include lessor-lessee type relationship also; and

(*vi*) is not a substantial shareholder of the company, i.e. owning two percent or more of the block of voting shares.

The Consideration as regards remuneration paid to an independent director shall be the same as those applied to a non-executive director.

10. Personnel who observe an unethical or improper practice (not necessarily a violation of law) should be able to approach the audit committee without necessarily informing their supervisors. Companies shall take measures to ensure that this right of access is communicated to all employees through means of internal circulars, etc. The employment and other personnel policies of the company shall contain provisions protecting 'whistle blowers' from unfair termination and other unfair prejudicial employment practices.

11. Companies shall annually affirm that they have not denied any personnel access to the audit committee of the company (in respect of matters involving alleged misconduct) and that they have provided protection to 'whistle blowers' from unfair termination and other unfair or prejudicial employment practices.

The appointment, removal and terms of remunerations of the chief internal auditors must be subject to review by the Audit Committee. Such affirmation shall form a part of the Board report on Corporate Governance that is required to be prepared and submitted together with the annual report.

12. The provision relating to the composition of the Board of Directors of the holding company should be made applicable to the composition of the Board of Directors of subsidiary companies. At least one independent director on the Board of Directors of the parent company shall be a director on the Board of Directors of the subsidiary company.

The Audit Committee of the parent company shall also review the financial statements. In particular the investments made by the subsidiary company. The minutes of the Board meetings of the subsidiary company shall be placed for review at the Board meeting of the parent company. The Board report of the parent company should state that they have reviewed the affairs of the subsidiary company also.

13. **SEBI should make rules for the following :**

A. Disclosure in the report issued by a security analyst whether the company that is being written about is a client of the analyst's employer or an associate of the analyst's employer, and the nature of services rendered to such company, if any;

B. Disclosure in the report issued by a security analyst whether the analyst or the analyst's employer or an associate of the analyst's employer hold or held (in the 12 months immediately preceding the date of the report) or intend to hold any debt or equity instrument in the issuer company that is the subject matter of the report of the analyst.

14. Disclosure of Contingent Liabilities: Management should provide a clear description in plain English of each material contingent liability and its risks, which should be accompanied by the auditor's clearly worded comments on the management's view. This section should be highlighted in the significant accounting policies and notes on accounts, as well as, in the auditor's report, where necessary. This is important because investors and shareholders should obtain a clear view of a company's contingent liabilities as these may be significant risk factors that could adversely affect the company's future financial condition and results of operations.

15. CEO/CFO Certification: For all listed companies, there should be a certification by the CEO (either the Executive Chairman or the Managing Director) and the CFO (whole-time Finance Director or other person discharging this function), which should state that, to the best of their knowledge and belief:

(*i*) They have reviewed the balance sheet and profit and loss account and all it schedules and notes on accounts, as well as the cash flow statements and the Directors' Report;

(*ii*) These statements do not contain any material untrue statement or omit any material fact nor do they contain statements that might be misleading;

(*iii*) These statements together present a true and fair view of the company, and are in compliance with the existing accounting standards and/ or applicable laws/ regulations;

(*iv*) They are responsible for establishing and maintaining internal controls and have evaluated the effectiveness of internal control systems of the company; and they have also disclosed to the auditors and the Audit Committee, deficiencies in the design or operation of internal controls, if any, and what they have done or propose to do to rectify these;

(*v*) They have also disclosed to the auditors as well as the Audit Committee, instances of significant fraud, if any, that involves management or employees having a significant role in the company's internal control systems, and

(*vi*) They have indicated to the auditors, the Audit Committee and in the notes on accounts, whether or not there were significant changes in internal control and/or of accounting policies during the year.

16. Definition of Independent Director has been adopted as it is from Naresh Chandra Committee.

17. Independence of Audit Committee: All audit committee members shall be non-executive directors.

18. Independent Directors Exemptions

(*i*) Legal provisions must specifically exempt non-executive and independent directors from criminal and civil liabilities under certain circumstances. SEBI should recommend that such exemptions need to be specifically spelt out for the relevant laws by the relevant departments of the Government and independent regulator's as the case may be.

(*ii*) However, independent directors should periodically review legal compliance reports prepared by the company as well as steps taken by the company to cure any taint. In the event of any proceedings against an independent director in connection with the affairs of the company, defense should not be permitted on the ground that the independent director was unaware of this responsibility.

B. Non- mandatory recommendation

1. Companies should be encouraged to train their Board members in the business model of the company as well as the risk profile of the business parameters of the company, their responsibility as directors, and the best ways to discharge them.

2. The performance evaluation of non-executive directors should be by a peer group comprising the entire Board of Directors, excluding the director being evaluated; and Peer group evaluation should be the mechanism to determine whether to extend/ continue the terms of appointment of non-executive directors.

After reviewing N.R. Narayanmurthy Committee Report, Department of Company Affairs under the Ministry of Finance, Government of India has implemented the Clause 49 of the Listing Agreement pertaining to corporate governance in India. The date for ensuring compliance with the revised Clause 49 of the listing agreement has been now extended up to December 31, 2005 (SEBI/CFD/DIL/CG/1I2005/29/3).

Whereas Birla Committee has strengthened the Corporate Social Responsibility, Murthy Committee ignored it. As the process of Indian judiciary system is very tedious, so there is a great demand to form a framework to make those fraud companies blacklisted who disobey the ethical norms. Murthy Committee also lacks the rules to check and abolish the IPO Offerings to safeguards the Interests of shareholders and investors. In India, we come to see that Listing Agreement and Companies Act still lack thoughtful debate on Corporate Governance. Murthy Committee should come ahead to bridge the gap. Murthy Committee denies appointing nominees directors while earlier committees have continued the norm. Also, along with the Annual Balance Sheet CEO/CFO certification should also be given on the basis of quarterly financial performance. Institutional investors are given no proper scope to progress in the way in the present report. Date of compliance should be extended to the day of financial year ending i.e. March 31, 2006 so that Clause 49 could be implemented in the maximum number of companies. Murthy committees has also taken no further steps in the direction of keeping the date online. This very negligence affects the transparency to a great extent.

6. Dr. J.J. Irani Committee Report on Company Law (2005)

On 31 May 2005, the J.J. Irani Committee made recommendations regarding to keep the number of independent directors at one-third of the total size of the board. The recommendation made by the committee to the ministry of company affairs on recasting the company law. The committee recommended that a minimum of one third of the total number of directors as independent directors should be adequate for a company with significant public interest irrespective of whether the chairman is executive or non-executive, independent or not, initially, this requirement should be extended to public listed companies and companies accepting public deposits. The requirements for other types of companies will be considered in due course.

The panel also said that there need not be a cap on the number of subsidiaries a company should have. So is the number of directors. "The new law will provide for professionals like chartered accountants and lawyers to form Limited Liability Partnership (LLPs). Partners of LLPs will not be personally liable for the defaults of the partnership.

Presence of independent director on the boards of companies having significant public interest would improve corporate governance. Law should recognize the principle of independent directors and spell out their attributes, role, qualifications, liability and manner of appointment along with the criteria of independence. However, prescription of the number and proportion of such directors in the Board may vary depending on size and type of company and may be prescribed through Rules.

(I) Recommendations :

The following "recommendations" are made by the committee:

1. The Committee recommended that in the Indian Context, it is important that the basic principles guiding the operation of corporate entities from registration to winding up or liquidation should be available in a single, comprehensive, centrally administered framework. The Committee also recommended a single corporate law framework for application to all companies.

2. The Companies Law may be so drafted that while essential principles are retained in the substantive law, procedural and quantitative aspects are shifted to the rules. This would enable the law to remain dynamic and to adapt to the changes in business environment.
3. The Committee recommended that the law should recognize the formation of a single person economic entity in the form of 'one Person Company'. Such an entity may be provided with a simpler regime through exemptions so that the single entrepreneur is not compelled to fritter away his time, energy and resources on procedural matters. The concept of "One Person Company' may be introduced in the Act with following characteristics :
   (*i*) OPC may be registered as a private company with one member and may also have at least one director;
   (*ii*) Adequate safeguards in case of death / disability of the sole person should be provided through appointment of another individual as Nominees Directors. On the demise of the original director, the nominee director will manage the affairs of the company till the date of transmission of shares to legal heirs of the demised member.
   (*iii*) Letters 'OPC' to be suffixed with the name of One Person Companies to distinguish it from other companies;
4. A Government Company should be clearly defined in law. It should be one whether there is a clear majority stake held by the state- i.e. Central and/ or State Government(s). There is no rationale for the definition of Government companies in course of their commercial activities.
5. Proper disclosures accompanied by mandatory consolidation of financial statements should address the concern attendant to the lack of transparency in holding -subsidiary structure.
6. Government may consider introduction of a separate Act to deal with the regulations of such "producer Companies'. Part IX A in the present Companies Act, which has hardly been resorted to and is more likely to create disputes of interpretation and may, therefore, be excluded from the Companies Act.
7. The Committee takes note of the e-governance initiative launched by MCA and recommends that it be implemented speedily. It recognized the immense potential of this programme to bring about ease of compliance at a lower cost. However, the Committee observes that e-Governance should be cost-effective to companies, including Small and One Person Companies, easy to use and accessible to all stakeholders and general public and enable the process of registration and filing for disclosures and retrieval of data efficiently and at a low cost. Further, the system should have adequate capacities to handle the likely growth in the corporate sector in India in the years to come as well as the increase in disclosure requirements that may be mandated by the legal and regulatory framework.
8. The Committee recommended that a separate Act be brought about to facilitate limited liability partnerships. The concepts need not be addressed in Co's Act.
9. The Board of Directors has to exercise strategies oversight over business operations. While directly measuring and rewarding management's performance. Simultaneously the Board has to ensure compliance with the legal framework, integrity of financial accounting and reporting systems and credibility in the eyes of the stakeholders through proper and timely disclosures.
10. Law should provide for minimum number of directors necessary for various classes of companies. There need not be any limit to the maximum numbers of directors that a Company may have. Limit to maximum number of directors should be decided by the company by/in the Articles of Association.
11. Government should not intervene in the process of appointment and removal of Directors in non-Government companies. It is important that role and powers of Government, under the present provisions to intervene in appointment of Directors be reviewed and revised, vesting the responsibility on the shareholders of the company.
12. It is recommended that requirement of obtaining the Central Government's approval under the Companies Act for non-resident managerial person should be done away with. Such person would continue to be subject to passport/visa, RBI and other Government requirements.
13. In view of the Companies, a minimum of one third of the total number of directors as independent directors should be adequate for a company having significant public interest, irrespective of whether the Chairman is executive or non-executive, independent or not.

14. The Committee felt that the issue of remuneration had to be decided by the shareholders in context of the circumstances of the company. The Committee also felt that the existing method of computation of net profits for the purpose of managerial remuneration, in the manner laid down in Sections 349 and 350 of the Act, should be done away with since the current provisions of the companies Act adequately ensure that a true and fair picture of the company's profit is presented.

15. The committee recommended relating to Audit Committee for Accounting and Financial matters are :

    (i) Majority of the Directors to be independent directors if the company is required to appoint Independence Directors;

    (ii) Chairman of the Committee also to be independent.

    (iii) At least one member of Audit Committee to have knowledge of financial management or audit or accounts;

    (iv) The Chairman of the Audit Committee should be required to attend the Annual General Meeting of the company to provide any clarification on matters relating to audit. If he is unable to attend due to circumstances beyond his control, any other member of the Audit Committee may be authorized by him to attend the Annual General Meeting on his behalf;

    (v) The recommendation of the Audit Committee if overruled by the Board should be disclosed in the Directors' Report along with the reasons for overruling.

16. To protect the shareholders of a listed company that opts to de-list, one buy-back offer by the company should be mandated within a period of 3 years of its de-listing from all the stock exchanges in India. Such an offer, taken in the background of the recommendations of ensuring fair valuations of shares, would also serve to protect minority interests.

17. The appointment and removal of the key managerial personnel i.e. Chief Executive Officer (CEO) / Managing Director, Company Secretary (CS) Chief Finance Officer (CFO) should be by the Board of Directors. In this continuation the following recommendations were also made :

    (i) The key managerial personnel including managing / (whole time) Executive Directors should be in the whole - time employment of only one company at any given time.

    (ii) Both the managing director as also the whole time directors should not be appointed for more than 5 years at a time.

    (iii) As Provided currently, the option to a company to appoint directors by proportional representation may be retained.

    (iv) The present requirement of having managing director/ Whole time director in a public company with a paid up capital of Rs. 5 crores may be revised to Rs. 10 crores by appropriate amendment of the Rules. The said limit could be reviewed from time to time.

    (v) Special exemptions may be provided for small companies from appointing such personnel on whole-time basis. Such companies may obtain services that may be considered mandatory under law from qualified professionals in practice.

18. The Committee considered the concept of exclusion of interested shareholders from participation in the General Meeting in the events of conflict of interest. The Committee felt that this was an aspect of good Corporate Governance which may be adopted by companies on voluntary basis by making a provision in the Article of Association of the Company.

19. There should also be a requirement of disclosure of director's background, education, training and qualifications, as well as relationships with managers and shareholders.

20. The Corporate should be encouraged to seek independent assessment/audit of the conduct of pools during general meetings of the company. Punishments for violation of fiduciary duties should be sufficiently severe so as to deter wrong doing.

21. The provisions of Section 265 (existing Act) could be made mandatory. The specific minority appointment director/ independent director could also play an important role in investor protection. The committee view was that the existing option may be retained.

22. The Committee recommended that if the companies seeking deposits were also compelled to obtain insurance coverage for deposits, this is a mechanism which would compel scrutiny into the credit-worthiness of the companies by the insurance companies in the interest of the depositors.
23. The Committee, therefore, feels that compensation to investors may be payable only in cases of established fraud, through a judicial process from the assets of the company or by lifting the corporate veil, those of the promoters or other beneficiaries of such fraud, accessed through a process of disgorgement.
24. The Committee recommends that Stakeholders Relationship Committee should be mandatory for a company having a combined shareholder/ deposit holder/ debenture holder base of 1000 or more.
25. Therefore, the Committee recommends that simultaneous to the harmonious regulatory approach providing for space to each regulator to operate effectively in their domain, provisions in the Companies Act allowing multiple jurisdiction may be done away with.

The initiative is seen as a timely move to introduce good Corporate Governance and insolvency law reforms, as the Indian economy assumes a significant position at the world center stage. It also offers a wonderful opportunity to bring the law in to par with international standards. This is the first time that such massive company law reforms are being undertaken since the company law came into being in 1956, and the effort is expected to change the landscape of Corporate Governance or any types of companies Act Prof-active, which still are active provisions. The Report also lacks such provisions, so as to check the independent directors from making misuse of material information provided to them. The report concentrates only on the role of independent directors.

Clause 49 - Corporate Governance Practices in India

The SEBI established another committee under the chairmanship of Mr. N.R. Narayan Murthi in later half of 2002, to review the performance of corporate governance; to determine the role of companies in responding to rumour and other price sensitive information circulating in the market, in order to enhance the transparency and integrity of the market. The committee has represented its report on February 08, 2003.

All the Stock Exchanges are directed to amend the listing Agreement by replacing the existing Clause 49 of the listing agreement (issued vide circulars dated 21st February, 2000, 9th March 2000, 12th September 2000, 22nd January, 2001, 16th March 2001 and 31st December 2001) with the revised Clause 49. SEBI circular no. SEBI/MRD/SE/3112003/26/08 dates August 26, 2003 (which has been since deferred) is withdrawn. The revised Clause 49 also specifies the reporting requirements for a company. This is a master circular which supersedes all other earlier circulars issued by SEBI on clause 49 of the listing agreements.

The provisions of the revised Clause 49 shall be implemented as per the schedule of the implementation given below:

(*a*) For entities seeking listing for the first time, at the time of seeking in-principle approval for such listing.

(*b*) For existing listing entities which were required to comply with Clause 49, which is being, revised i.e. those having a paid up share capital of Rs. 3 crores and above or net worth of Rs. 25 crores or more at any time in the history of the company, by **JANUARY 1, 2006.**

Companies complying with the provisions of the existing Clause 49 at present (issued vide circulars dated 21st February, 2000, 9th March 2000, 12th September 2000, 22nd January, 2001 16th March 2001 and 31st December 2001) shall continue to do so till the revised Clause 49 of the Listing Agreement is complied with till December 31, 2005, whichever is earlier.

The companies which are required to comply with the requirements of the revised Clause 49 shall submit a quarterly compliance report to the stock exchanges as per sub clause VI (ii), of the revised clause 49, within 15 days from the end of every quarter. The report shall be signed either by the Compliance Officer or the Chief Executive Officer of the company.

The revised clause 49 shall apply to all the listed companies in accordance with the schedule of implementation given above. However, for other listed entities, which are not companies, but body corporate (e.g. Private and Public Sector Banks, Financial Institutions, insurance companies etc.) incorporated under other statutes, the revised clause will apply to the extent that it does not violate their respective statutes and guidelines 0 directors issued by the relevant regulatory authorities. The revised clause 49 is not applicable to Mutual Funds.

The Stock Exchanges shall ensure that all provisions of the revised clause 49 have been complied with by a company seeking listing for the first time, before granting the principle approval for such listing. For this purpose, it will be considered satisfactory compliance if such a company has set up its board and its Board and Constituted Committees such as Audit Committee, Shareholders/ Investors Grievances Committee etc. in accordance with the revised clause before seeking in-principle approval for listing.

The Stock Exchanges shall setup a separate monitoring cell with identified personnel to monitor the compliance with the provisions of revised clause 49 on corporate governance the cell, after receiving the quarterly compliance report from the companies, which are required to comply with the requirements of the revised clause 49, shall submit a consolidate compliance report to SEBI within 60 days from the each quarter.

Clause 49- Corporate Governance in India

SEBI has issued guidelines regarding implementation of Clause 49 which are detailed below:

1. Board of Directors

(A) Composition of Board

(*i*) The board of directors of the company shall have an optimum of executive and non-executive directors with not less than fifty percent of the board of directors comprising of non-executives directors.

(*ii*) Where the chairman of the Board is a non-executive director, at least one-third of the Board should comprise of independent directors and in case he is an executive director, at least half of the Board should comprise of independent directors.

(*iii*) For the purpose of the Sub-clause (ii), the expression 'independent director' shall mean a non-executive director of the company who :

a. apart from receiving director's remuneration does not have any material pecuniary relationships or transactions with the company, its subsidiaries and associates which may affect independence of the director;

b. is not related to promoters or persons occupying management positions at the board level or at one level below the board;

c. has not been, an executives of the company in the immediately preceding three financial years;

d. is not a partner or an executive or was not partner or an executive during the preceding three years, of any of the following:

(*i*) the statutory audit firm or the internal audit firm that is associated with the company, and .

(*ii*) the legal firms (s) and consulting firm (s) that have a material association with the company,

e. is not a material supplier, service provider or customer or a lessor or lessee of the company, which may affect independence of the directors of the directors; and

f. is not a substantial shareholder of the company i.e. owning two percent or more of the block of voting shares.

Explanation : For the purposes of the sub-clause (3)

a. Associate shall mean a company which is an "associate" as defined in Accounting Standard (AS) 23, " Accounting for Investments in Associates in Consolidated Financial Statements", issued by the Institute of Chartered Accountants of India.

b. "Senior management" shall mean personnel of the company who are members of its core management team excluding Board of Directors. Normally, this would comprise all the members of management team excluding Board of Directors. Normally, this would comprise the members of management one level below the executive directors, including all functional heads.

c. "Relative" shall mean "relative" as defined in section 2(41) and section 6 read with schedule IA of the Companies Act, 1956.

(*iv*) Nominee directors appointed by an institution which have invested in or lent to the company shall be deemed to be independent directors.

(B) Non-executive Directors' Compensation and Disclosures: All fees/compensation, if any paid to non-executive directors including independent directors, shall be fixed by the board of directors and shall required previous approval of shareholders in general meeting. The shareholders, resolution shall specify the limits for the maximum numbers of stock options that can be granted to non-executive directors, including independent directors, in any financial years and in aggregate.

(C) Other provision as to board and committees

1. The board shall meet at least four times a year, with a maximum time gap of three months between any two meetings.
2. A director shall not be a member in more than ten committees or Act as chairman of more than five committees across all companies in which he is a director. For the more it should be a mandatory annual requirement for every director to inform the company about the committee position he occupies in other companies and notify changes as and when it take place.

(D) Code of Conduct

1. The Board shall lay down a code of conduct for all board members and senior management of the company. The code of conduct shall be put on the website of the company.
2. All Board members and senior management personnel shall affirm compliance with the code on an annual basis. The annual report of the company shall contain a declaration to this effect sign by the CEO.

II. Audit Committee

(A) Qualified and Independent Audit Committee

A qualified and independent audit committee shall be setup, giving the term of reference subject to the following :

1. The Audit shall have minimum three directors as members. Two-third of the menders of audit committee shall be independent directors.
2. All member of audit committee shall be financial literate and at least one member shall have a accounting or related financial management expertise.

(B) Meeting of Audit Committee: The audit committee should meet at least four times in a year and not more than four months shall elapse between two meetings. The quorum shall be either two members or one third of the members of the audit committee whichever is greater, but there should be a minimum of two independent present.

(C) Powers of Audit Committee: The Audit Committee shall have powers, which should include the following:

1. To investigate any activity within its term of reference
2. To seek information from any employee
3. To obtain outside legal or other professional advice
4. To secure attendance of outsiders with relevant expertise, if it considers necessary.

(D) Role of Audit Committee: The role of audit committee shall include the following;

1. Oversight of the companies financial reporting process and the disclosers of its financial information to ensure that the financial statement is correct sufficient and credible.
2. Recommending to the board, the appointment, reappointment and, if require, the replacement or removal of the statutory auditor and the fixation of audit fees.
3. Approval of payment of statutory auditors for any other services rendered by the statutory auditors.
4. Reviewing, with the management, the annual financial statements before submission to the board for approval, with particular reference to:
   a. Matters required being included in the Director's Responsibility Statement to be included in the Board's report in terms of clause (2AA) of section 217 of the Companies Act, 1956.
   b. Changes, if may, in accounting policies and practices and reasons for the same.
   c. Major accounting entries involving estimates based on the exercise of judgments by management.
   d. Significant adjustments made in the financial statements arising out of audit findings.
   e. Compliance with listing and other legal requirements relating to financial statements.
   f. Disclosure of any related party transactions.
   g. Qualification in the draft audit report.

5. Reviewing with the statement, the quarterly financial statements before submission to the board for approval.
6. Reviewing, with the management, performance of statutory and internal auditors and adequacy of the internal control systems.
7. Reviewing the adequacy of internal audit function, if any, including the structure of the internal audit departments, staffing and seniority of the official heading the department, reporting structure coverage and frequency of internal audit.
8. Discussion with internal auditors any significant findings and follow up there on.
9. Reviewing the findings of any internal investigations by the internal auditors into matters where there is suspected fraud or irregularity or a failure of internal control systems of a material nature and reporting the matter to the board.
10. Discussion with statutory auditors before the audit commences, about the nature and scope of audit as well as post-audit discussion to ascertain any area of concern.
11. Looking into the reasons for substantial defaults in the payment to the depositories, debenture holders, shareholders (in case of non-payment of declared dividends) and creditors.
12. To review the functioning of the Whistle Blower mechanism, in case the same exists.
13. Carrying out any other function as is mentioned in the terms of reference of Audit Committee.

Review of Information by Audit Committee

The Audit Committee shall compulsorily review the following information:

1. Management discussion and analysis of financial condition and results of operations;
2. Management of significant related party transactions (as defined by the audit committee), submitted by management;
3. Management letters / letters of internal control weakness issued by the statutory auditors;
4. Internal auditors reports relating to internal controls weakness; and
5. The appointment, removal and terms of remuneration of the Chief internal auditors shall be subjected to review by the Audit Committee.

III. Subsidiary Companies

1. At least one independent director on the Board of Directors of the Holding company shall be the director on the Board of Directors of a material non-listed Indian Subsidiary company.
2. The Audit Committee of the listed holding company shall also review the financial statements, in particular, the investment made by the unlisted subsidiary company.
3. The minutes of the board meeting of the listed holding company. The management should periodically bring to the attention of the Board of Directors of the listed holding company, a statement of all significant transactions and arrangements entered into by the unlisted subsidiary company.

Explanation 1: The term "material non-listed Indian Subsidiary" shall mean an unlisted subsidiary, incorporated in India, whose turnover or net worth (paid up capital and free reserves) exceeds 20% of the consolidated turnover or net worth respectively, of the listed holding company and its subsidiaries in the immediately preceding accounting year.

Explanation 2: The term "significant transaction or arrangement" shall mean any individual transaction and arrangement that exceeds or is likely to exceed 10% of the total revenues or total expenses or total assets or total liabilities, as the case may be, of the material unlisted subsidiary for the immediately preceding accounting year.

Explanation 3 : Where a listed holding company has a listed subsidiary, which is itself a holding company, the above provisions shall apply to the listed subsidiary in so far as its subsidiaries are concerned.

IV. Disclosures

(A) Basis of related party transactions

1. A statement in summary form of transactions with related parties, in the ordinary course of business shall be placed periodically before the Audit Committee.

2. Details of material individual transactions with related parties, which are not in a normal course of business, shall be placed before the audit committee.
3. Details of material individual transactions with related parties or other parties, which are not an arm's length basis, should be placed before the audit committee, together with Management's justification for the same.

(B) Disclosure of Accounting Treatment: Where in the preparation of financial statements, a treatment different from that prescribed in an Accounting Standard has been followed, the fact shall be disclosed in the financial statements, together with the management's explanation as to why it lives such alternative treatment is more representative of the true and fair view of the underlying business transaction in the corporate governance report.

(C) Board Disclosures-Risk Management : The Company shall lay down procedures to inform Board members about assessment and minimization procedures. These procedures shall be periodically reviewed to ensure that executive management controls risk through means of a properly defined framework.

(D) Proceeds from public issues, right issues, preferential issues etc.: When money is raised through an issue (public issues, right issues, preferential issues etc.), it shall disclose to the Audit Committee, the uses/ applications of funds by major category (capital expenditure' sales and marketing, working capital, etc.) on a quarterly basis as a part of their quarterly declaration of financial results. Further on an annual basis, the company shall prepare a statement of funds utilized for purposes other those stated in the offer document / prospects/notice and place it before the audit committee. Such disclosure shall be made. only till such time that the full money raised through the issue has been fully spent. This statement shall be certified by the statutory auditors of the company. The audit committee shall make appropriate recommendations to the Board to take up steps in this matter.

(E) Remuneration of Directors

1. All pecuniary relationship or transactions of the non-executive director's vis-a-vis the company shall be disclosed in the Annual Report.
2. Further the following disclosures on the remuneration of directors shall be made in the section on the corporate governance of the Annual Report:
   (*a*) All elements of remuneration package of individual directors summarized under major groups, "Such as salary, benefits, bonuses, stock options, pension etc.
   (*b*) Details of fixed components and performance linked incentives, along with the performance criteria.
   (*c*) Service contracts, notice period, severance fees.
   (*d*) Stock option details, if any-and whether issued at a discount as well as the period over which accrued and over which exercisable.
3. The company shall publish its criteria of making payments to non-executive directors in its annual report. Alternatively, this may be put up on the company's website and reference drawn thereto in the annual report.
4. The company shall disclose the number of shares and convertible instruments held by non-executive directors in the annual report.
5. Non-executive directors shall be required to disclose their shareholding (both own or held by/for other persons on a beneficial basis) in the listed company in which they are proposed to be appointed as directors, prior to their appointment. These details should be disclosed in the notice to the general meeting called for appointment of such director.

(F) Management

1. As part of the directors' report or as addition thereto, a Management Discussion and Analysis report should form part of the Annual Report to the shareholders. This Management Discussion & Analysis should include discussion on the following matters within the limits set by the company's competitive position:
   (*i*) Industry structure and development
   (*ii*) Opportunities and threats
   (*iii*) Segment-wise or product -wise performance
   (*iv*) Outlook
   (*v*) Risks and concerns
   (*vi*) Internal control systems and their adequacy

(vii) Discussion on financial performance with respect to operational performance

(viii) Material developments in human resources / Industrial relations front, including number of people employed

2. Senior management shall make disclosures to the board relating to all material financial and commercial transactions, where they have personal interest, that may have a potential conflicts with the interests of the company at large (e.g. dealing in company shares, commercial dealings with bodies, which have shareholding of management and their relatives etc.)

(G) Shareholders

1. In case of the appointment of a new director or re-appointment of a director the shareholders must be provided with the following information:

   (a) A brief resume of the director;

   (b) Nature of his expertise in specific functional areas;

   (c) Names of companies in which the persons also holds the directorship and the membership of committee of the Board: and

   (d) Shareholding of non-executive directors as stated in Clause 49 (IV) (E) (V) above

2. Quarterly results and presentations made by the company to analysts shall be put on company's website, or shall be sent in such a form so as to enable the stock exchange on which the company is listed to put it on its own website.

3. A board committee under the chairmanship of a non-executive director shall be formed to specifically look into the redressed of shareholders and investors complaints like transfer of shares, non-receipt of balance sheet, non-receipt of declared dividend etc. This committee shall be designated as 'Shareholders/ Investors Grievance Committee'.

4. To expedite the process of share transfer, the Board of the company shall delegated the power of share transfer to an officer or a committee or to the registrar and share agents. The delegated authority shall attend to share transfer formalities at least once in a fortnight.

V. CEO/CFO certification: The CEO, i.e. the managing director or manager appointed in terms of the Companies Act, 1956 and the CFO i.e. the whole -time Finance Director or any other heading the finance function discharging that function shall certify to the Board that:

1. They have reviewed financial statements and the cash flow statement for the year and that to the best of their knowledge and belief:

2. There are, to the best of their knowledge and belief, no transactions entered into by the company during the year which are fraudulent, illegal or violation of the company's code of conduct.

3. They accept responsibility for establishing and maintaining internal controls and that they have evaluated the effectiveness of the internal controls systems of the company and they have disclosed to the auditors and the Audit Committee, deficiencies in the design or operation of internal controls, if any, of which they are aware and the steps they have taken or propose to take to rectify these deficiencies.

4. They have indicated to the auditors and the Audit Committee.

   (i) Significant changes in internal control during the year;

   (ii) significant changes in accounting policies during the year and that the same have been disclosed in the - notes to the financial statements; and

   (iii) instances of significant fraud of which they have become aware and the involvement therein, if any, of the management or an employee having a significant role in the company's internal control system.

VI. Report Corporate Governance

1. There shall be a separate section on Corporate Governance in the Annual Reports of company, with a detailed compliance report on Corporate Governance. Non-compliance of any mandatory requirements of this clause with reasons thereof and the extent to which the mandatory requirements have been adopted should be specifically highlighted.

2. The companies shall submit a quarterly compliance report to the stock exchanges has within 15 days from close of quarter as per the format. The report shall be signed either by the Compliance Officer or the Chief Executive Officer of the company.

Format of quarterly Compliance Report on Corporate Governance

Name of the Company :

Quarter ending on :

Particulars	Clause of listing agreement	Compliance status Yes/No	Remarks
I. Board of Directors	491		
(A) Composition of Board	49 (IA)		
(B) None executive Directors' compensation & disclosures	49 (IB)		
(C) Other Provisions as to Board and Committees	49 (IC)		
(D) Code of Conduct	49 (ID)		
II. Audit Committee	49 (II)		
(A) Qualified & Independent Audit Committee	49 (IIA)		
(B) Meeting of Audit Committee	49 (IIB)		
(C) Powers of Audit Committee	49 (IIC)		
(D) Role of Audit Committee	49 (IID)		
(E) Review of Information by Audit	49 (IIE)		
III. Subsidiary Companies	49 (III)		
IV. Disclosures	49 (IV)		
(A) Basis of related party transactions	49 (IVA)		
(B) Board disclosures	49 (IVB)		
(C) Proceeds from public issues, rights issues, preferential issues etc.	49 (IVC)		
(D) Remuneration of Directors	49 (IVD)		
(E) Management	49 (IVE)		
(F) Shareholders	49 (IVF)		
V. CEO/CFO certification	49 (V)		
VI. Report on Corporate Governance	49 (VI)		
VII. Compliance	49 (VII)		

(1) The details under each head shall be provided to incorporate all the information required as per the provisions of the Clause 49 of the listing agreement.

(2) The non-mandatory requirements may be implemented as per the discretion of the company. However, the disclosures of the compliance with mandatory requirements and adoption (and compliance)/ non-adoption of the non-mandatory requirements shall be made in the section on corporate governance of the Annual Report.

Practice Questions

Objective Type Questions

1. The first committee constituted on corporate governance:
   (*a*) Cadbury Committee (*b*) Hamel Committee
   (*c*) Higgs Committee (*d*) Turn Bull Committee
2. Ronald Hampel Committee was set up in the year :
   (*a*) 1997 (*b*) 1998
   (*c*) 1999 (*d*) 2000
3. Clause 49 is based on the recommendations of committee headed by :
   (*a*) Mr. N.R. Narayan Murthi (*b*) Sri. Kumar Mangalam Birla
   (*c*) Sri Naresh Chandra (*d*) Mr. P.L. Sanjeev Reddy
4. The purpose behind setting up of the Green Bury Committee was to:
   (*a*) address the issue of internal control
   (*b*) recommend on the role and effectiveness of non-executive directors
   (*c*) remuneration of directors
   (*d*) assess the role of audit committee and the board composition
5. Constitution of Audit Committees of Public Listed Companies is a :
   (*a*) voluntary recommendation
   (*b*) legal recommendation
   (*c*) mandatory recommendation
   (*d*) None of these

Ans. : l. (a), 2. (b) 3. (a), 4. (c), 5. (c)

Short Answer Questions

1. What was the purpose behind setting up of Cadbury Committee?
2. Explain OECD principles regarding responsibility of the board.
3. Explain title functions of audit committee under CII code of corporate governance.
4. Explain the rationale of clause 49.
5. Explain title purpose of J J Irani Committee.

Long Answer Questions

1. Describe the main recommendation of the Cadbury committee.
2. Elaborate the OECD principles of Corporate Governance.
3. Describe the role and functions of remuneration committee of the board under CII code on corporate governance.
4. Examine the recommendations of Kumar Mangalam Birla Committee on corporate governance.
5. Critically evaluate the major recommendations of P.C. Sanjeev Reddy committee report.
6. Describe the recommendations of N.R. Narayan Murthy Committee Report.

6 GOVERNING BOARD

Governing Board or Board of Directors has been assigned a very crucial role in the management of a corporate entity. It is generally constituted with the help of various specialists, experienced and highly competent men, who are able to contribute substantially for the effective and successful functioning of companies. Success or failure of companies mostly depends upon the quality of head and heart of the board members. The main responsibility of the viable and successful operation of a company is vested in its board. Its composition reflects the representation on the body corporate. It also refers to the duly constituted authority which represent the owners of the enterprise. The Board stewards the company, sets its strategic aim and financial goals and oversees their implementation, puts in place adequate internal controls and periodically reports the activities and progress of the company in a transparent manner to the stakeholders. The shareholders' role in corporate management is to appoint the directors and the auditors and to hold the board accountable for the proper governance of the company. The board of a company provides leadership and strategic guidance, objective judgment and independent management to the company and exercises control over the company, while remaining at all times accountable to the shareholders. The measure of the board is not simply whether it fulfils its legal requirements but more importantly, the board's attitude and the manner it translates its awareness and understanding of its responsibilities.

The board directs the company, by formulating and reviewing company's policies, strategies, major plans of action, risk policy, annual budgets and business plans, setting performance objectives, monitoring implementation and corporate performance, and overseeing major capital expenditures, acquisitions and divestitures, change in financial control and compliance with applicable laws, taking into account the interests of stakeholders. It controls the company and its management by laying down the code of conduct, overseeing the process of disclosure and communications, ensuring that appropriate systems for financial control and reporting and monitoring risk are in place, evaluating the performance of management, chief executive, executive directors and providing checks and balances to reduce potential conflict between the specific interests of management and the wider interests of the company and shareholders including misuse of corporate assets and abuse in related party transactions. It is accountable to the shareholders for creating, protecting and enhancing wealth and resources for the company, and reporting to them on the performance in a timely and transparent manner. However, it is not involved in day-to-day management of the company, which is the responsibility of the management.

The governing structure of companies actually allows the shareholders to influence a company by exercising their voting rights. Traditionally, however, shareholders have been interested primarily in the return on their investment and have left the actual operation of the organization to its manager. But this type of shareholders thinking is now changing. Now they are interested to see how company is viable and efficient and to what extent it is compliance oriented in the eyes of laws. Thus, the shareholders of the company elect a board of directors to represent them in supervising the organisation's management and overall performance. "A board can appoint or remove top organization managers and approve major goals and plans. Directors play an important role by representing the shareholder's views, sharing their own professional expertise, and keeping management on its toes."[1]

Rationale of Government Board

Rationale of having governing board are as follows :

(i) It establishes a link between the owners of the enterprise, i.e. equity share holders and the executives who actually operate it, on the one hand and the general public, on the other.

(ii) A business entities is incorporated with an avowed objective to carry on the project within the broad framework of the mission and vision for the fulfillment of set corporate objectives. The board is required to interpret and enforce the corporate objectives effectively and successfully.

(iii) It provides a level to which the shareholders generally provide authority.

(iv) It develops leadership in a democratic way. In case of one-man leadership, other people are not in a position to get sufficient opportunities for their development.

(v) It maintains continuity of direction and policy in its functioning. In case of one-man management, business is to be effected by sudden change in the leadership by death, dismissal or retirement. This is not possible in Board Management.

(vi) It works as an efficient agency to evaluate and check the performance, of the Company.

(vii) It ensures decentralization of power and also delegates adequate authority to the lower levels.

Functions of the Board

Main functions of the Board are as follows :

(i) **Formulation of Basic Objectives and Policies :** The Board is responsible for laying down policies which include such questions as the determination of quality and quantity of product or services to be produced, pricing policy, re-organisation and development plans, human resources management and improvement of organisation structure etc. Reviewing key executive and board remuneration, and ensuring a formal and transparent board nomination process are also included in the job of the board. Board is required to look after the functions like monitoring and managing potential conflicts of interest of management, board members and shareholders, including misuse of corporate assets and abuse in related party transactions.

(ii) **Financial Administration:** Majority of the decisions of the Board have financial implications. So control over funds provides the Board an opportunity to give final decisions on these aspects. New capital investment decisions, risk policy, annual budgets and business plans, setting performance objectives, monitoring implementation and corporate performance, and overseeing major capital expenditure, acquisition and divestitures, change in financial control and compliance with applicable laws, taking into account the interests of stakeholders. It is also responsible for ensuring the integrity of the corporation's accounting and financial reporting systems, including the independent audit, and that appropriate systems of control are in place, in particular, systems for monitoring risk, financial controls, and compliance with the law.

(iii) **Human Resource Management :** It includes selecting, compensating, monitoring and, when necessary, replacing key executives and overseeing succession planning. It is the duty of the Board to select competent personnel to operate the company and to ensure the continuity of able management. The Board is free to create any post except at the Board level and to make appointments without any restriction of salary. But at the same time, the Board is also hound to follow the guidelines with regard to benefits to be made available to employees in respect of provident fund, retirement benefits, dearness allowance, house rent, company transport and other perquisites, etc. In addition, considerations of industrial relations, labour welfare and safety measures are to be discussed by the Board.

(iv) **Operational Management :** The Board is also responsible to monitor the effectiveness of the Corporate practices under which it operates and making changes as needed. It is expected to review the operation of the company continuously and revise policies, programmes, etc. as necessary by the circumstances prevailing in the organisation. The Board is also required to make contract, lay down future programmes for the production, formulation of schemes for distribution, their development and reorganisation in the interest of the organisation.

(*v*) **Public Relations :** It is the duty of the Board to maintain liaison with different stakeholders. Besides, it is also a job of the Board to consider and take decisions on questions relating to consumers and public from time to time so that their faith may be maintained in the company. Actually board is required to fulfill the social responsibilities towards producers, consumers and public at large as entrusted by the shareholders. Board is also required to oversee the process of disclosure and communication.

(*vi*) **Controlling Authority :** It controls the company and its management by laying down the code of conduct, overseeing the process of disclosures and communications, ensuring that appropriate systems for financial control and reporting and monitoring risk are in place, evaluating the performance of management, chief executive, executive directors and providing checks and balances to reduce potential conflict between the specific interests of management and the wider interest of the company and shareholders including misuse of corporate assets and abuse in related party transactions.

(*vii*) **Accountable to Shareholders :** It is accountable to the shareholders for creating, protecting and enhancing wealth and resources for the company, and reporting to them on the performance in a timely and transparent manner. However, it is not involved in day-to-day management of the company, which is the responsibility of the management.

Director as a Member of the Governing Board

The definition of the term 'director' given in the Companies Act does not throw light on the function and nature of duties performed by a director. So a director may be defined as an individual who directs, controls, manages or superintends the affairs of a company. As a body, they frame the general policy of the company, direct its affairs, appoint the company officers, ensure that they carry out their duties and recommend to the shareholders regarding distribution of dividend. The directors of a company collectively are referred to as the "Board of Directors" or 'Board'. Where a person functions as a director but without being lawfully appointed, he cannot be termed as a director.[2]

According to section 2(13) of the Companies Act, 1956, "director" includes any person occupying the position of director by whatever name called. According to section 303, any person in accordance with whose directions or instruction, the Board of directors of a company is accustomed to act shall be deemed to be a director of the company, except when the Board of directors so acts on advice given by him in professional capacity. [Section 7].

Nobody corporate, association or firm shall be appointed director of a company and only an individual shall be so appointed (Section 253). It is because the office of a director is to some extent an office of trust. There should be somebody readily available who can be held responsible for the failure to carry out the obligation of such an office. It will be difficult to fix that responsibility if the director is a body corporate, association of persons, or firm. 3 So shareholders have a right to appoint their nominees whom they trust as the director of the company. For all practical purposes, control over the majority of shareholding of the company decides the authority to appoint directors on the board. In some cases, nominee directors are also appointed but they are required to work as a part of the team for all purposes.

Nature of Board

It indicates the nature of board and how it is constituted. There are different types of directors who are generally appointed on the board. Effectiveness of the board is largely depends on the nature of directors who constitute it. Different types of the board are as follows:

1. Policy Board : It generally defined as a wisdom board and is more legislative, supervisory and advisory in character. The policy board is responsible for the governance of the company and thus it is only required to direct the company. Directing function involves formal and informal components. Formally, the board is involved in reviewing and screening executive decisions in the light of their environmental business and organizational implications. Informally, the board seeks to direct the organizations activities so that they are in accordance with the prevailing social, economic and political wilien.[3] The members of such a board in its pure form have no functional responsibility. These directors are generally drawn from disciplines of accounting, law, banking management, engineering etc. They are drawn from outside the organisation and exercise a sort of collective supervision. Leading entrepreneurs and business leaders are also nominated on the board. Thus, policy boards comprise men, mostly on part-time basis without having responsibility for any specialized functions of an executive head. Such a board is supervisory in nature and is by and large concerned simply with matters of general policy. It is also considered a vital link between the environment and the company.

Features : Following are the main features of the Policy Board -

(*i*) Part-time members are appointed on the Board only one or two members are appointed on full time basis.

(*ii*) The functioning of the board is of supervisory nature and it concerns itself merely with matters of general policy and not with operational details.

(*iii*) The members are not supposed to be experts or specialists in a particular branch or line of operations in the company.

(*iv*) It generally believes in collective supervision over the company. Members of the Board are expected to take a detached view of the managerial affairs, to consider the issues objectively to make policy decisions.

Merits : Following are the merits of the Policy Board-

(*i*) It gives greater freedom to company in making appointments. It can draw its appointees from any source it likes and its object, one presumes, should be to form a united team, a group of people capable of working together and giving collective direction to the company.

(*ii*) It generally takes an independent and critical view of management of the company. Not being involved in management, it can take a more objective view of the manager's performance.

(*iii*) It evaluates the affairs of the company from outside with a more comprehensive outlook and large vision and then formulates or modifies the policy. The members of a policy board not immersed in detail are perhaps better able to see the picture as a whole and to take board decisions."

(*iv*) It is suitable for promoting workers' participation in management and for conducting public relations effectively.

(*v*) It is in a better position to take and to issue commands properly.

(*vi*) It can easily interpret and execute the policy instructions of the promoter's groups issues in the larger interest of the company and stakeholders.

(*vii*) It is suitable for small companies because operational areas are quite limited. The Policy Board can work successfully in directing the affairs of a company.

Limitations : It has following limitations :

(*i*) In a policy board, those who are responsible for the formulation of policy are not responsible for carrying it out. If the board itself has to carry out the policy.

2. Functional Board : "A functional board consists predominantly of professional full-time managers drawn from within the company, each having a distinct top-level responsibility within the organisation." Thus, it consists of full-time members incharge of particular branches of work, viz., Production, Financial, Personnel, Marketing Management. The men on the functional board are there because of their expertise and experience in a particular branch of activities being carried on by the company.

Features : The following are the main features of functional board-

(*i*) It is constituted with full-time specialists. These members are generally holding the status of ahead in a particular functional area of the organisation.

(*ii*) Members of the board are selected on the basis of their specialized knowledge, and experience in a particular branch of activity, viz., Finance, Personnel, Production, Materials, Planning, Marketing and Research & Development.

(*iii*) Members of the board have defined responsibilities for specific functional areas and they have to work for the tasks assigned to them.

(*iv*) Members have a joint responsibility at the board level. They are jointly responsible for the decision taken in the board's meetings. They however, hold functional responsibility as a functional head.

(*v*) They have more effective control, knowledge and influence in the operations of the company because they are full time members.

Merits : Main advantages of a functional board are as follows:

(*i*) The board is useful because the members are responsible for policy formulation, planning and their execution at the same level and at the same time. It ensures better co-ordination at the board level.

(*ii*) It permits the existence of a small board because functional experts are employed on whole-time basis.

(*iii*) It encourages a sense of responsibility among individual members as they are accountable for the performance of their individual department.

(*iv*) It ensures better supervision and closer contact between top management and the point of actual operation.

(*v*) Its members are better placed to understand technical problems and to bring about technological improvements, whenever necessary.

Limitations: Limitations of functional board are as follows:

(*i*) It generally fails to take the macro approach towards the working of a company. The members who are too much busy in departmental details are apt "to see only the trees and not the forests."

(*ii*) The members of the board have, often, been found to be bad administrators taking only partisan and narrow view of the whole thing. They interfere too much with the work of their subordinates and tend to become vindictive and shortsighted.

(*iii*) The functional experts are often at loggerheads. They refuse to be considerate and accommodating. Hence, they cannot easily bring about that teamwork and harmony which are so necessary for the successful functioning of such board.

(*iv*) The functional members are unable to take prompt and smart decisions. There is a danger that the decisions may be arrived at by a process of rather 'unprincipled compromise' along the lines of "I will support what you want if you will support what I want."

(*v*) It lacks the necessary prestige and popular support (both within and outside the organisation) because "it gets involved in petty details and fails to take a broad view of the situation."

3. Mixed Board : Generally, policy boards and functional boards are not constituted in their purest form. Thus, a mixed board is being preferred by the leading Indian companies working in India. The mixed board consists of part-time and whole-time members. "There is a blend of full-time and part-time members, the former having specific fields of responsibility without being the heads of the department and the latter being men of wide experience to bring fresh air in the organisations with a more detached view. The mixed board, by nature, is 'policy-cum-functional' with some members having no portfolios assigned to them and others being responsible for certain functions or division of work.

Features : Main features are given below-

(*i*) It is constituted with the help of part-time members as well as full-time members. Ratio of the functional members generally depends on the size and functional areas of the company.

(*ii*) Part-time members, have no functional responsibilities. But full time members have a well-defined functional or departmental responsibilities in their specific area.

(*iii*) Functional members are generally insiders. They have to take the directors' responsibilities in addition to the responsibilities of a functional head in the company itself.

Merits : Merits of Mixed Board are as follows :

(*i*) It is compact and effective board. Members are matured, experienced and effective in their decision making process.

(*ii*) Part time members share their experiences with full time members. It makes the knowledge base of full time specialists more broad based and effective.

(*iii*) It encourages inter-corporate harmony as part time members are generally drawn from other companies who have wide experience in the corporate world.

(*iv*) It makes the coordination process more effective and viable. Nominees directors appointed by the financial institutions, regulatory authorities and other representatives of some of the stakeholders in the company can help the full time or functional members in achieving their goals.

(*v*) It ensures wider representation and consultation in the board meeting. Now companies are required to appoint independent directors on the board which itself indicate the necessity of mixed board.

Limitations : Limitations of mixed board are as follows:

(*i*) It increases the scope of having large size of the board.

(*ii*) It demoralizes the effectiveness of full time functional members as part time members are generally offensive in their behaviour.

(*iii*) It creates problems in the effective functioning of the company. Interest in casual briefs and frequent intervention by part time members create intra-group conflicts in the board meetings.

(*iv*) It fails to maintain secrecy as part time members may leak the deliberations to other interested parties.

Full-Time and Part-Time Members: The governing board may be constituted with the help of whole-time members. A board may consist of whole-time members only or it may consist of part-time members wholly or a board my consist of partly whole-time and partly part-time members. In practice, four types of members have been appointed on the board of private sector companies, viz., inside part-time members, outside part-time members, inside full-time members and outside full-time members.

Part-time Members : They may be inside part-time members or the outside part-time members:

1. The Inside Part-Time Members: A person who has some kind of operational responsibility within the company, viz., Finance Manager, Production Manager, Marketing Manager, Personnel Manager, and in addition to this, he is given the responsibility of being a member on the board, he may be taken as inside part-time member of the Board.

2. The Outside Part-Time Members: A person whose main sphere of activity lies outside the company of whose board he is a member. These members are generally drawn from the private sector managers, academicians, professionals, politicians, etc. These members are now called as independent member. Generally, they bring their rich experience in industry, trade, management, education and consultancy in the management of corporate entities.

Advantages of Part-Time Members : Following are the main advantages of part-time members:

(*i*) Part-time' appointments are made due to non-availability of suitable full-time members. The inside part-time members have the advantage that they are fully familiar with the company and its problems. They are also more easily available for appointments.

(*ii*) In the initial stages of the company, there is no need of full-time members because work pressure is quite low. At this stage, coordination is necessary which can be successfully carried out by part-time members. When the company has progressed well, it would be better and advantageous to have whole-time members.

(*iii*) A person, who has been appointed from outside the organisation, has the advantage that he can bring to bear upon the company and its problems a fresh approach and outlook, unbiased by having prolonged cooperation or connections with it.

In this regard, it has been rightly suggested that "it would also be advantageous to have a few part-time independent members who have proved their outstanding abilities in some area of industrial, commercial or financial enterprise or administration. They should be men who have faith in the success of the company and who do not have conflicting business interests with those of the companies to which they are nominated."

Limitations: Limitations of part-time members are as follows -

(*i*) Part-time members have inadequate time to work effectively as member of the board. These members are unable to play important role because they do not have sufficient time, energy or to improve the operational efficiency of the company. Similarly, outside part-time members are also busy with their own business work. It has been rightly pointed that "Part-time members, being too busy with their own business, may also lack that sense of responsibility and involvement which a company needs so much."

(*ii*) The part-time outside members do not have sufficient knowledge about the company to be really able to guide its destinies and they may not be interested enough to devote the necessary time to familiarize themselves. Even if interested, they do not be able to spare the time. According to Professor Robson, "The disadvantage of part-time members is that where the service is highly technical in character or surrounded with a mass of detail not easily mastered by a cursory survey of occasional memoranda. The part-time members are unlikely to posses adequate knowledge of the subject matter or sufficient grasp of the main problems to be able to play a part of real importance in influencing policy."

(*iii*) Part-time independent members are appointed by the promoters for coordination purposes. However, they do not have sufficient time to attend all the meetings of the boards on which they are represented or else they come to meetings almost unprepared and do not contribute anything substantial. They are also appointed on the boards of a large number of companies which make them unable to work effectively. Thus, the part-time independent members should not serve on a large number of boards. In this regard, it would be better to suggest that, "While appointing part-time independent directors to the board, the promoter should see that persons nominated do not have to serve on more than two or three boards and are not so burdened with their substantive work that they find it difficult to play a useful part in board meetings."

Full Time Members : They may be inside or outside members :

1. **The inside full time member:** A person, who has grown up within the company and has reached the highest position of the executive management, may be appointed as a member and then relieved of all executive responsibilities in the company. For example, finance manager of the enterprise may be appointed as Director of Finance on the board.
2. **The Outside Full-Time Member:** A person, ordinarily an expert in some field connected with the management of the company, is brought from outside and appointed as a full-time member. As an expert in particular field, he may be expected to help the board in its review and policy making functions especially relating to that field.

Merits : Merits of full time members are as follows :

(*i*) Full-time members have loyalty to and faith in the organisation and they are directly interested in the successful operation of the company.

(*ii*) Appointment of full-time members encourages the career appointment. In fact, as more and more persons are appointed from within the company, it will result in career appointments.

(*iii*) It also helps in keeping the morale of the executives quite high as their assessment is to be done by the full time members of the board.

Limitations: Limitations of full-time members are as follows:

(*i*) Appointment of full-time members generally results in a functional allocation of work among the various members of governing board. It would generate narrowness, division and aggravate the problems of coordination at the top level. Career appointments generally lead to inbreeding and shutting out new ideas. It also makes their dismissal difficult.

(*iii*) Outsider full-time appointments are generally criticized because they do not have loyalty to the organisation as they have short tenure on the board.

Normally, part-time and full-time members both are appointed on the board. Theoretically, the full-time board is by far the best, but under prevailing circumstances in India, the best way is to have part-time as well as full-time members on the board.

Size of Board

There are no hard and fast rules which can be laid down in connection with the size of the Board. It depends upon the nature of the industry or size of the company and on other factors. Sufficient care should be taken that Board should neither be too small to be dominated by a single man nor too large so that its members can "become in genuine team."

Thus, a functional Board with full-time members would have lesser number of members than the policy board comprising of mostly part-time members. Generally, the size of the Board is linked up with the question of giving representation to various groups. But this practice suffers from a serious defect-lack of necessary spirit for joint deliberations. Thus, "a Board should not have as many as to make free discussion impossible not so few that the necessary breath of viewpoint is not obtainable."

Section 252 provides that every public company must have atleast 3 directors and every private company must have atleast 2 directors. The Companies (Amendment) Act 2000 has inserted in Sec. 252(1) the following: Provide that a public company having-

(*a*) a paid up capital of 5 crore or more;

(*b*) one thousand or more small shareholders, may have a director elected by such small shareholders in the manner as may be prescribed.

In the above context, "small shareholder" means a shareholders holding shares of nominal value of twenty thousand rupees or less in a public company to which this section applies. This is the statutory limit and subject to it the Articles of a company may prescribe the maximum and the minimum number of directors for its board of directors. A company in a general meeting may by ordinary resolution increase or reduce the number of its directors within the limits fixed in that behalf by its articles (Section 258). Beyond such limits, a variation can be made by passing a special resolution. A company is not bound to appoint the maximum number of director required under Section 252, it may appoint any number within the maximum. Any increase beyond the limit fixed by the Articles must be approved by the Central Government except where the increase in the number of directors does not make the total number of directors more than twelve. Such an increase will become void if disapproved by the Central Government (Section 259). This provision is not applicable to a Government company and to a private company which is not a subsidiary of a public company and a company as per Section 25.

A Company's Articles of Association lay down the limit for the number of directors to be present on its board. The members can change this limit by passing a special resolution. Some boards may have only two directors while others may have twenty or more directors. The size of the board generally depends on the size of the company, larger the company, larger the size of the board. The size of board has a direct impact on the group dynamics of the board. Boards with more than seven or eight members may have problems in maintaining interpersonal relations. On larger boards members may form opposing groups due to differences in beliefs or opinions. But having smaller boards will leave the company with less experiences, knowledge and expertise to fall back on in times of crisis. In case of public sector companies the Estimates Committee has advocated for a Board of 3 to 4 members, one being the chairman. The Krishna Menon Committee has also favoured a small Board consisting of 5 to 9 members depending upon the size and nature of the enterprises. It is true that growing size of the unit requires the large-sized Board, because then specialized knowledge in different fields becomes necessary. But from the point of accountability, a small-size Board is more suitable.

A large-size Board simply increases the possibility of appointment of certain vested interests on the Board. The Indian Railways is the biggest enterprise in India. It has only 6 members on the Board. If such a giant enterprise can do with a small Board, there is every reason to think that the size of the board of companies should be reasonably balanced and of optimum size. A smaller Board with 3 to 7 members is likely to feel an adequate sense of responsibility which may make for quick disposal of business and harmonious working of the company. It is better to consider a board consisting of three to four full-time functional directors (including the chief executive), and three or four other part time member as independent directors, to be fairly balanced one. But, of course, there can be no pre-determined numbers; much would depend on the areas which need to be covered at the time of constitution of the board.

Tenure of Board Members

Efficient functioning of a Governing Board largely depends upon the tenure of the Board members. There is direct correlation between the stable top management and successful operation of the company. It is true that tenure of directors is governed by the discreation of the promoters. Members of the board are to retire by rotation and they are also eligible for re-nomination. But again it is decided by the promoters who have actual control over the shareholding of the company.

Appointment of subsequent directors is made at every annual general meeting of the company. Section 255 provides that not less than two third of the total number of directors of public company, or of a private company which is subsidiary of a public company must be appointed by the company in general meeting. These directors must be subject to retirement by rotation. The remaining directors of such a company and the directors generally of a purely private company must also be appointed by the company in general meeting. In other words, not more than one third of the total number of directors can act as non-retiring directors, i.e. not subject to retirement by rotation. (The object of Section 255 is to prevent the mischief of self perpetuating management).

At every subsequent annual general meeting one third of the directors of a public company or a private company which is not a subsidiary of a public company are liable to retire by rotation. Rotational director means a director retiring by rotation and does not include additional, alternate, debenture holder's or Central Government's nominee directors. Similarly, directors appointed by financial institutions in pursuance of the agreement entered into by these institutions with the company are not liable to retire by rotation. Such nominee directors are also not to be taken into account for computing one-third number of directors liable to retire. The directors cannot prolong their tenure by not holding an annual general meeting in time. They would automatically retire from office on expiry of the maximum permissible period within which such meeting ought to have been held.

In company form of organisation, it has been found that all directors (except full-time) retire at the Annual General Meeting. In some companies, the term of one year has now been changed and it has been extended to three years for part-time directors. Under Section 225 of the Indian Companies Act, 1956, there is a provision that all the part-time directors are appointed for a period of at least three years, one-third of whom would retire every year by rotation. The official directors have no fixed tenure and their tenures depend on the sole discretion of the promoters.

Short tenure of the members cannot help in improving the efficiency because in that short period, the members can only introduce themselves to the company and the company can introduce itself about their operations to the members. The members are unable to take concrete decision unless they are well-informed and well-versed with the operations of the enterprise. The tenure of members should aim at striking a balance between experience and new blood. While infusion of new blood from time to time is necessary, the process not be so rapid that the past experience is not properly reserved and utilised.

Qualifications of Board Members

It is quite useful that directors must have certain qualifications either in terms of industrial experience or in terms of professional experience. The qualification provision should be clearly mentioned in the Stature under which the companies have to be managed. It is suggested that part-time directors should have experience of industry or of industrial, commercial or financial matters, applied science, administration, or the organisation of workers and this could be prescribed in the statute.

As per the Indian Companies Act, 1956 a director need not hold any shares and need not be a member of a company. The Article of Association generally requires that the qualification of director shall be the holding of a specified number of shares known as qualification shares. The Articles generally provide for such qualification shares so that director may have personal interest in the company. Unless he is already qualified, he must obtain the qualification shares within two months after his appointment as a director. Any provision in the Articles of a company in so far as it requires a person to hold the qualification shares before his appointment as a director or to obtain them within a shorter time than two months will be void. The nominal value of these shares must not exceed Rs. 5,000 or the nominal value of one share where it exceed Rs. 5,000. Any provision requiring a director to hold as qualification shares more than this amount will be invalid. The holding of share warrant shall not be deemed to be the holding of qualification shares. (Sec. 270)

It is not essential for the director to buy his shares directly from the company. He must hold these shares in his own right. Until the required number of shares are registered in the name of the director, he is not qualified. If a person acts as a director of a company without holding the qualification shares, he will be punishable with fine, which may extend to Rs. 500 for every day between such expiry and the last day on which he acted as a director. (Sec. 272 as amended in 2000). Moreover by virtue of section 283, if a person fails to obtain the qualification shares as prescribed by the articles within the period specified, he automatically vacates office and cannot act as a director after the expiry of that period.

Composition of Board

The composition of the board of director is critical to its the independent functioning. The composition of the board is important in as much as it determines the ability of the board to collectively provide the leadership and ensures that no one individual or a group is able to dominate the board, The executive directors (like director-finance, director-personal) are involved in the day-do-day management of the companies; the non executive directors bring external and wider perspective and independence to the decision making. Till recently, it has been the practice of most of the companies in India to fill the board with representatives of the promoters of the company, and independent directors. This has undergone a change and increasingly the boards comprise of following groups of directors-promoter's director, executive and non-executive director, a part of whom are independent.

(i) **Independent director :** Independent directors are directors who apart from receiving director's remuneration do not have any other material pecuniary relationship or transactions with the company, its promoters, its management or its subsidiaries, which in the judgment of the board may affect their independence of judgment. Further, all pecuniary relationship or transactions of the non-executive directors should be disclosed in the annual report. It is important to note that "material pecuniary relationship affects the independence of a director". It should be the litmus test of independence and the board of the company would exercise sufficient degree of maturity when left to itself, to determine whether a director is independent or not.

The board be comprised of individuals with certain personal characteristics and core competencies such as recognition of the importance of the board's tasks, integrity, a sense of accountability, track record of achievements and the ability to ask tough questions. Besides having financial literacy, experience, leadership qualities and the ability to think strategically, the directors must show significant degree of commitment to the company and devote adequate time for meeting, preparation and attendance.

(*i*) The Board of directors of the company shall have an optimum combination of executive and non-executive directors with not less than fifty percent of the board of directors comprising of non-executive directors.

(*ii*) Where the Chairman of the Board is a non-executive director, at least one-third of the Board should comprise of independent directors and in case he is an executive director, at least half on the Board should comprises of independent directors.

(*iii*) For the purpose of the sub-clause (ii), the expression 'independent director' shall mean a non-executive director the company who :

(*a*) apart from receiving director's remuneration, does not have any material pecuniary relationships or transactions with the company, its promoters, its directors, its senior management or its holding company, its subsidiaries and associates which may affect independence of the director;

(*b*) is not in relation to promoters or persons occupying management positions at the board;

(*c*) has not been an executive of the company in the immediately preceding three financial years;

(*d*) is not a partner or an executive or was not partner or an executive during the preceding three years, of any of the following :

(*i*) the statutory audit firm or the internal audit firm that is associated with the company, and

(*ii*) the legal firm(s) and consulting firm(s) that have a material association with the company.

(*e*) is not a material supplier, service provider or customer or a lessor or lessee of the company, which may affect independence of the director; and

(*f*) is not a substantial shareholder of the company i.e. owning two percent or more of the block of voting shares.

***(ii)* Tenure for Independent Director :**

(*i*) An Individual may not remain as an Independent Director in a company for more than six years.

(*ii*) A period of three years should elapse before such an individual is inducted in the same company in any capacity.

(*iii*) No individual may be allowed to have more than three tenures as Independent Director in the manner suggested in 'i' and 'ii' above.

(*iv*) The maximum number of public companies in which an individual may serve as an Independent Director should be restricted to seven.

***(iii)* Nominee Director:** There is another set of director in Indian companies who are the nominees of the financial or investment institutions to safeguard their interest. Sec 255 permits one-third of the total number of director of a public company and of the private company which is a subsidiary of a public company to be appointed by parties other than shareholders on a non-rotational basis. The Articles may give the right to debenture holders, financial corporation or banking companies who have advanced loans to the company to nominate directors on the board of company. The number of directors so nominated should not exceed one-third of the total strength of the board. They are not liable to retire by rotation. These directors shall perform all the duties but they have for immunity from action from any liability.

Directors of a company are generally appointed by a simple majority of shareholders and a substantial minority cannot succeed in placing even a single director on the board. Section 265 intends to protect the interests of minority shareholders by giving an opportunity to place their nominee on the board. The Articles of a company may provide that the appointment of not less than 2/3 of the total number of director of a public company (or of a private company which is a subsidiary of a public company) shall be according to the principle of proportional representation, either by *the single transferable vote or by a system of cumulative voting* or otherwise. Such appointments shall be made once in three years and interim casual vacancies may be filled up according to Section 262.

Rationale : Nominee directors should be appointed on the following grounds :

(*i*) Financial institutions have played a significant role in the industrial development of the country as a sole purveyor of long term credit so they must have right to appoint their nominee directors on the board of assisted companies.

(*ii*) Nominee directors are needed to protect the interest of their institutions who are custodians of public funds and who have high exposures in the projects of the companies both in the form of equity and loans.

Limitations : Nominee directors have following limitations :

(*i*) There is an inherent conflict when institutions through their nominees participate in board decisions and in their role as shareholders demand accountability from the board.

(*ii*) There is a further conflict because the institutions are often major players in the stock market in respect of the shares of the companies on which they have nominees.

Thus, it would be better for the institutions to appoint nominees on the board of companies only on a selective basis where such appointment is pursuant to a right under loan agreement or where such appointment is considered necessary to protect the interest of the institution. However, when a nominee of the institutions is appointed as a director of the company, he should have the same responsibility, be subject to the same discipline and be accountable to the shareholders in the same manner as any other director of the company. In particular, if he reports to any department of the institutions on the affairs of the company, the institution should ensure that there exists Chinese walls between such department and other departments which may be dealing in the shares of the company in the stock market.

Appointment of Director

Director may be appointed in the following ways :

(*i*) By the articles as regard for first director (Section 254); (*ii*) By the Company in general meeting (Section 225 to 257, 263, 264), (*iii*) By the director (Section 260, 262, 313), (iv) By third parties (Section 225), (v) By the principle of proportional representation (Section 265), (*vi*) By the Central Government (Section 408).

(*i*) **First director by Articles :** The first directors are usually named in the Articles. The Articles may also provide that both the number and the names of the first directors shall be determined in writing by the subscribers to the Memorandum or a majority of them. Where the company has no Articles or the Articles are silent regarding the appointment of directors, the subscribers to the Memorandum who are individuals shall be deemed to be first directors of the company. They shall hold office until the directors are appointed at the first annual general meeting. If all the subscribers to the Memorandum happen to be bodies corporate, none of the subscribers can be deemed to be directors and company will have no directors until the first directors are appointed under section 254. Where the person named in the list of first directors do not assume office, for any reason (for example, death) then it is duty of the subscribers of the Memorandum to hold a meeting for appointment of directors.

(*ii*) **Appointment in the General Meeting :** If the number is not three or a multiple of three, then the number nearest one-third must retire from office. An example will make this rule clear. A company has 12 directors. Out of 12, 4 directors can be appointed as permanent directors if the company so desires. The remaining 8 directors will be liable to retire by rotation. Out of 8 directors, three directors shall retire in the first year, three in the second year and the remaining two in the third year. These vacancies shall be filled by the members at the annual general meeting. The directors to retire by rotation at every annual general meeting must be those who have been longest in office since their last appointment. As between persons who become directors on the same day, those who are to retire will, subject to any agreement among themselves, be determined by lot. [Sec. 256(1) and (2)].

To call annual general meeting is the duty of directors and by omitting to convene such meeting, they cannot take advantage of their own default. At the annual general meeting at which a director retires, the company may fill up the vacancy by appointing the retiring director or some other person thereto. The retiring director is deemed to be reappointed at the annual general meeting of adjourned meeting except in the following cases :

(1) at any previous meeting, a resolution for his re-appointment was put to vote, but was lost or

(2) the retiring director has, in writing, expressed his unwillingness to continue or

(3) he is not qualified or is disqualified for appointment or

(4) a special or ordinary resolution is necessary for his appointment by virtue of any provisions of the Companies Act, or

(5) It is resolved to fill two or more vacancies by a single resolution.

A person other than a retiring director is also eligible for appointment to the office of director subject to his necessary qualification. A notice in writing signifying his candidature must be left at the office of the company at least fourteen days before the date of the meeting along with a deposit of Rs. 500 which shall be refunded to such person or as the case may be to such member, if the person succeeds in getting elected as a director. The notice may be given either by the candidate himself or by his proposer. It shall not apply to a private company unless it is a subsidiary of a public company. The company shall inform the members at least seven days before the meeting about the candidature. A person who is being proposed as a candidate for the office of a director must sign and file with the company his consent in writing to act as a director if appointed. Such a person shall not act as a director unless he has within 30 days of his election, signed and filled with the Registrar his consent in writing to act a director. This requirement does not apply to a director retiring by rotation.

Appointment of directors of a public company must be voted individually by separate ordinary resolution, unless the company has in general meeting unanimously so resolved. In other words, each director shall be appointed by a separate resolution unless it is unanimously decided at the general meeting that more than one director may be appointed by a single resolution. Any resolution moved in contravention of this provision shall be void even if no objection was raised at the time of its being so moved.

***(iii)* Appointment by directors :** The directors are empowered to appoint- (i) Additional directors, (ii) Alternate directors, (iii) Directors filling casual vacancy.

(a) **Additional directors :** The board of directors may appoint additional directors from time to time if so authorized by its Articles. The number of directors and additional directors must not exceed the maximum strength fixed for the next annual general meeting. The purpose of section 260 is to enable the board to appoint competent persons who may otherwise find it difficult to come in by election. If the annual general meeting of the company is not held, or cannot be held, the person appointed as additional director vacates his office on the last day on which the annual general meeting should have been held in terms of section 166 of the Act. Additional director must possess or acquire qualification shares (if Articles so provide) within two months.

(b) **Alternate directors :** The board of directors may appoint an alternate director if authorized (a) by the articles or (b) by a resolution of the company at general meeting. An alternate director acts in the place of a director who is absent for more than three months from the State in which board meetings are held. He cannot hold office for a period longer than that permissible to the original director. (Sec. 313). Like other directors an alternate director has to perform same duties and he is subject to same liabilities. Where that Articles prescribe a share qualification for the office of director, the alternate director must possess or acquire the qualification as provided in section 270.

Where the office of any director appointed by the company in general meeting is vacated before the expiry of his term the director may fill up the vacancy at a meeting of the board. Any vacancy other than one caused by retirement of a director by rotation or by efflux of time is a casual vacancy. Such a vacancy may occur by reason of death, resignation, bankruptcy, disqualification or failure of an elected director to accept the office. The director so appointed will hold office till the end of the term of the director in whose place he is appointed. (Sec. 262) The term casual vacancy does not include vacancy caused by retirement by rotation. Procedure for filling casual vacancy is as follows : (1) Get the written consent of the person proposed to be appointed, (2) Call the meeting of the Board of director to fill casual vacancy, (3) Intimate the appointee of his appointment as director, (4) See that the person appointed to fill casual vacancy with the registrar his consent to act as director within 30 days, (5) Make sure that necessary entries are made in the Register of director and Register of directors shareholdings.

(c) **Casual Vacancies :** "In case of a public company or a private company which is a subsidiary of a public company, subject to any regulations in the articles of the company, the Board of directors at a meeting of the Board may fill in casual vacancy among the directors. A casual vacancies arises when the office of any director appointed by the company in a general meeting is vacated before his term of office expires in the normal course. Any person so appointed shall hold office only upto the date upto which the director in whose place he is appointed would have held office if it would not have been so vacated [Sec. 262].

A casual vacancy among directors arises by reason of death, resignation, disqualification or any other reason, than retirement of a director by rotation. If casual vacancy is not filled, it is presumed that the number of directors is presumed."[4]

***(iv)* Appointment by the Central Government :** The central government has power under Section 408 to appoint directors on an order passed by the Tribunal (earlier Company Law Board) to effectively safeguard the interest of the company or its shareholders or the public interest to prevent mismanagement or oppression. Such directors shall hold office for a period not exceeding three years on any one occasion. The power can be exercised by the Tribunal either on a reference made by the Central Government or on an application. (i) of not less than one hundred members of the company or (ii) of members of the company not holding less than one tenth of the total voting power therein.

The director appointed by the central government under section 408 (1) shall not be required to hold any qualification shares nor shall his period of office be liable to termination by retirement of directors by rotation. Such a director mayor may not be the member of the company. Any such director may be removed by the central government from his office and another person may be appointed in his place.

***(v)* Appointment by Proportional Representation :** "[Sec.255(1) & 265] Unless the articles provide for the retirement of all directors at every annual general meeting, not less than two-thirds of total number of directors of a public company, or of a private company which is a subsidiary of a public company, shall -

(*a*) be person, whose period of office is liable to determination by retirement of directors by rotation; and

(*b*) be appointed by the company in general meeting [Sec.255(1)].

The article of a company may provide for the appointment of not less than 2/3rds of the total number of directors of a public company or of a private company which is a subsidiary of a public company, according to the principles of proportional representation, whether by the single transferable vote or by a system of cumulative voting, or otherwise. The appointments must be made once in every three years and interim casual vacancies must be filled in by the Board of Directors in the Board meeting. [Sec.265]. Directors elected in accordance with proportional representation cannot be removed under the provisions of Sec. 284. To appoint directors by proportional representation, articles should provide so. The appointment is to be made once in three years."[5]

Restriction of Number of Directorships

Section 275 as amended by the Companies (Amendment) Act 2000 states that no person can be a director in more than fifteen companies. This number excludes directorship in private companies. Before the amendment, the limit was twenty companies. Choice on becoming director of more than 15 companies. Where a person already holding the office of a director in fifteen companies, making the total number of his directorships more than fifteen, he shall choose the directorships which he wished to continue to hold or to accept, so that number of the directorships, old and new, held by him shall not exceed fifteen. His new appointment will become void if he does not make a choice within fifteen days as aforesaid. [Sec. 277 (2)]. Exclusion of certain directorships for the purpose of 15 directorships. The following companies shall be excluded in calculating the number of companies of which a person may be a director :

(a) a private company which is neither a subsidiary nor a holding company of a public company; (b) an unlimited company; (c) an association not carrying on business for profit or which prohibits the payment of dividend; (d) a company in which such person is only an alternate director. [sec. 278 (1)]

The prohibition that a director shall not hold the office of a director in more than 15 companies does not extend to the holding of directorship in foreign companies as they do not come within the definition of "company" in the Act. Penalty for acting as director in more than 15 companies. Any person who holds office or acts as a director of more than 15 companies in contravention of the above provisions shall be punishable with fine which may extend to Rs. 50,000 in respect of each of those companies after the first 15 [Sec. 279 as amended in 2000].

Removal of Directors

A director may be removed from his office; (1) by the shareholders (Sec. 284); (2) by the central government [Sec. 388 B to 388 E]; (3) by the Tribunal [Sec. 402]

1. Removal by shareholders: Section 284 empowers the company to remove a director by ordinary resolution before the expiry of his period of office except in the following cases;

(a) A director appointed by the central government under section 408,(b) A director in case of a private company, holding office for life on 1st day of April, 1952. (A director for life subsequent to that date may be removed), (c) Directors appointed in accordance with the principle of proportional representation under section 265. This is to ensure that the directors appointed by the minority are not removed by a bare majority, (d) Directors appointed by Central Government under Industries (Development & Regulation) Act, 1951, (e) Special directors appointed under Sick Industrial Companies (Special Provisions) Act, 1985, (f) Directors appointed by financial institute under Statutory powers, (g) Nominee directors, (h) Directors appointed by Tribunal under section 402.

2. Removal by the central government: Section 388-B to 388-E empower the central government to remove managerial personnel including a director of a company from office on the recommendation of the Tribunal. The procedure prescribed for the removal of such person is that the central government will state a case against such a person and refer the same to the Tribunal with a request that the Tribunal may enquire into it and record a decision as to whether such a person is fit and proper person to hold the office of director or any other office connected with the conduct and management of a company.

3. Removal by the Tribunal : On an application to the Tribunal for prevention of oppression and mismanagement, the Tribunal may terminate, or set aside or modify any agreement between the company and the managing director or any other director or manager. (Sec. 402). On such termination, the director cannot serve the company in a managerial capacity for a period of five years from the date of the order of termination, without the permission of the Tribunal. The director on removed cannot sue the company for damages or compensation for loss of office.

Chairman of the Board

The main role of the Chairman is to ensure that the board meetings are conducted in a manner which secures the effective participation of all directors, executive and non-executive alike, arid encourages all to make an effective contribution, maintain a balance of power in the board, make certain that all directors look beyond their executive duties and accept full share of the responsibilities of governance. It is notable that the Chairman's role should in principle be different from that of the chief executive, though the same individual may perform both roles.

The Chairman is a necessary element of company meeting and is usually appointed by the Articles. Section 175 of the Companies Act, 1956 (the Act) provides that unless the Articles of company otherwise provide, the members personally present at the meeting shall elect one of themselves to be the chairman thereof on a show of hands. In the absence of any provision in the Articles of a company as regards the election of a chairman of its general meetings, the common law rule is that (a) the candidate for the office of chairman should not preside over the election meeting: and (b) that where an outgoing chairman seeks re-election, he should vacate the chair pending the election, unless on a show of hands he is re-elected without any controversy. The meeting may appoint a temporary or provision chairman to run the meeting until the chairman is elected. Any objection to the appointment of a chairman should be made immediately because otherwise any irregularity in the nomination may become cured by acquiescence.

Appointment of the Chairman : There are different provisions for the appointment of chairman of (i) Board meetings, (ii) Committee meetings and (iii) general meetings.

(i) **Board Meetings :** Most of the companies name in their Articles of Association the chairman of the meetings of the Board of directors. Certain other companies incorporate in their Articles a provision corresponding to the provision of Regulation 76 of Table A in Schedule I to the Companies Act, 1956, which provides; "(1) The Board may elect a chairman of its meetings and determine the period for which he is to hold office. (2) If no such chairman is elected or if any meeting the chairman is not present within five minutes after the time appointed for holding the meeting, the director present may choose one of their number to be chairman is not present within five minutes after the time appointed for holding the meeting, the director present may choose one of their number to be chairman of the meeting."

(ii) **Committee Meetings :** With regard to the chairman of the meetings of the various committees of the Board, Regulation 78 of Table A provides: "(1) A committee may elect a chairman of its meetings, (2) if no such chairman is elected or if at any meeting the chairman is not present within five minutes after the time appointed for holding the meeting, the members present may choose one of their number to be chairman of the meeting". As a matter of convention, the chairman of the meetings of the Board of director is a member on all the Board committees and he presides over all the committee meetings. In exceptional cases, however, the above provision of Regulation 78 or any corresponding provision in the articles of any company shall govern the appointment of committee chairman. Pursuant to Section 292A of the Act, an Audit Committee is

required to be constituted. Its chairman may be a managing or whole-time director or any other director, whereas in pursuance of clause 49 of the listing agreement, the Chairman of the Audit Committee shall be an independent director. The chairman of the Audit Committee must have to attend the annual general meeting to provide any clarification on matters relating to audit.

(iii) **General Meetings :** Usually the chairman of the meetings of the Board of directors, if named in the Articles of Association or if appointed by the Board of directors of a company for a specific period, presides over all the general meetings of the company. The Articles of Association of some companies contain provisions corresponding to the ones in Regulations 50, 51 and 52 of Table A about the appointment of chairman of the company's general meetings.

Management Director

Section 2(26) defines a managing director as "a director who, by virtue of an agreement with the company or a resolution passed by the company in general meeting or by its board of directors, or by virtue or its memorandum or article of association is entrusted with substantial powers of management which would not otherwise by exercisable by him, and includes a director occupying the position of a managing director, by whatever name called". The important features of a managing directors are as follows :

(i) A managing director must be an individual as nobody but an individual can be appointed as a director. A person, who is not a director cannot be appointed as a managing director. His appointment is automatically terminated if he ceases to act as director.

(ii) A managing director can be appointed under (a) an agreement with the company; or (b) a resolution passed by the company in general meeting; or (c) a resolution passed by its board of director; or (d) the Memorandum of Association of Company; or (e) the articles of association of the company.

(iii) A managing director is entrusted with substantial (not the whole) powers of management which would not otherwise be exercisable by him. But the power to do administrative acts of a routine nature when so authorized by the Board such as (1) affixing the common seal of the company to any document or (2) drawing and endorsing a cheque on the account of the company in any bank or any negotiable instrument or (3) signing any certificate of share or directing registration of transfer of any share will not make a director a managing director. In order to make a director, a managing director, it is necessary that the power exercisable by him constitute substantial power of management, which consists of laying down broad policies and objectives of the company.

(iv) The term 'Managing director' includes a director occupying the position of a managing director by whatever name called.

(v) A managing director of a company has to exercise his power subject to the superintendence, control and direction of the Board of directors [Sec.2(26)]. The Managing director is a servant of the company and remuneration payable to him is salary. But he is not a clerk or a servant so as to entitled to preferential payment.

Whole-Time Director

According to Explanation of Section 269(1), "Whole-time director includes a director in the whole time employment of the company." Thus, a whole-time director means a director who devotes all his time and attention to the carrying on of such of the affairs of the company as may be assigned to him by the board of directors and thereof. He is virtually a managing director though not so designated. Where a director is appointed to act as a Technical Adviser, Legal Adviser, Sales Manager, Works Manager, Finance Manager etc., on the full-time basis, he is treated as a whole time director. But a person who does not devote "substantially the whole of his time to the company" is not a whole time director.

Distinction between Managing Director and Whole time Director

Managing Director	Whole-Time Director
1. The appointment of a managing director need not necessarily be made with the consent of the members.	Appointment of a whole time director requires the sanction of the shareholders, by means of a special resolution.

Contd....

2. A managing director of company can be appointed for a maximum period of 5 years.	There is no such restriction regarding the term of appointment of a whole-time director.
3. A person can be managing director of 2 companies. However, the Central Government may permit any person to be appointed as a managing director of more than 2 companies if it is satisfied that it is necessary that companies should have common managing director for their proper functioning as a single-unit	
4. A managing director is entrusted with substantial power of management, i.e. discretionary power to take decision regarding some policy matters (e.g. pricing of product, adoption of new techniques, buying and selling policy etc.)	A whole-time director is just an ordinary employee having powers as per terms of employment.
5. A managing director and manager cannot exist simultaneously. (Sec. 197-A)	A whole-time director can be appointed together with the managing director or manager.

Manager

As per Section 2(24) "manager means an individual who, subject to the superintendence, control and direction of the Board of Directors, has the management of the whole, or substantially the whole, of the affairs of a company and includes a director or any other person occupying the position of a manager, by whatever name called, and whether under a contract of service or not." The important features of manager are as follows:

(*i*) Only an individual can be appointed as a manager of a company.

(*ii*) A manager shall have the management of the whole or substantially the whole of the affairs of a company. Further, manager is not an agent who is to do a particular thing, or a servant who is to obey orders, but a person who is entrusted with power to transact the whole of the affairs of the company.

(*iii*) A manager is subject to the superintendence, control and directions of the Board of directors.

(*iv*) Manager includes a director or any other person occupying the position of a manager, by whatever name called i.e. all de-facto managers.

(*v*) A manager may be appointed under a contract of service or otherwise.

(*vi*) A director may be a manager and in such a case if for any reason his office of director is vacated, the office of manager held by him is not affected but it is not so in case of managing director.

Distinction between manager and managing director

Manager	Managing Director
1. Manager may not be a director.	Managing director must be a director of the company.
2. There cannot be more than one manager in a company.	There may be more than one managing director in a Company.
3. A manager may be appointed under a contract of service or otherwise.	Managing director may be appointed by virtue of an agreement with the company or resolution passed by the company in general meeting or by the board of directors or the Memorandum or the Articles of Association of company.
4. Grounds of disqualifications remain effective only for 5 years.	Grounds of disqualification remain effective for the whole of life.
5. Conviction for moral turpitude by a foreign court is not a disqualification.	Conviction for moral turpitude by any Court in India or abroad is a disqualification.

Contd....

6. The Central Government may remove the disqualifications either generally or in relation to any company or companies by notification in the official gazette. (Sec. 385)	The Central Government has no such power to remove the disqualifications under Section 267.
7. The manager has management over whole or substantially the whole of the affairs of the company. Hence, the powers of a manager are wider than the powers of a managing director.	Managing director has substantial powers of management which would not otherwise be exercisable by him.
8. The maximum remuneration payable to a manager cannot exceed 5% of net profits.	Where more than one managing director is working in the same company, the maximum limit if fixed at 10% of the net profits.

Practice Questions

Objective Type Questions

1. Policy Board is constituted with the
   (*a*) Part time members
   (*b*) Mostly part time members
   (*c*) Full time members
   (*d*) All full time members
2. Provision of holding qualification shares is mentioned in
   (*a*) Articles of Association
   (*b*) Prospectus
   (*c*) Memorandum of Association
   (*d*) Indian Companies Act 1956
3. Additional directors are appointed by the
   (*a*) Company
   (*b*) Board of Directors
   (*c*) Article of Association
   (*d*) Tribunal
4. A person can hold directorship in number of companies
   (*a*) 10
   (*b*) 15
   (*c*) 20
   (*d*) 25
5. Managing Director of a company can be appointed for a maximum period of
   (*a*) 3 years
   (*b*) 5 years
   (*c*) 1 years
   (*d*) 7 years

Ans. : 1. (b), 2. (a), 3. (b), 4. (b), 5. (b)

Short Answer Questions

1. Who can be appointed as a director?
2. What do you mean by mixed board?

3. What is policy board?
4. What do you understand by functional board?
5. Define managing director.
6. Distinguish between managing director and whole time director.
7. Distinguish between managing director and manager.

Long Answer Questions

1. What role does the Board of Directors (BOD) play in strategic management of a company? What kind of relationship may the BOD have with the top management of the company? Examine and discuss.
2. Examine the functions of governing board. Also examine the representative character of governing board in India companies.
3. Examine the rationale of governing board in Indian corporate sector. Also give a comparative evaluation of different types of governing board.
4. Discuss the nature and scope of governing board. What is Board Corporate Governance?
5. What do you mean by Governing Board? Evaluate its functions and rationale.
6. Define Director. Also explain the procedures of appointment of a director.
7. What do you mean by the nature of Governing Board? Also examine its different types.
8. Discuss the procedures for constituting a Governing Board. Also distinguish between independent director and nominee director.

References

1. Courtland L. Bovee, John V. Thill, Marian Burk Wood, George P. Dovel, "Management", Mc Graw-Hill Inc, 1993, p.84
2. Ibid.p.89
3. Bhattacharya S.K. and N. Venkatraman, Managing Business Enterprise, Strategies, Structures and System. Vikas Publishing House, New Delhi, 1983, P.P. 166-69.
4. K.R. Bulchandani, Business Law for Management, Himalaya Publishing House, 2007, p.503
5. Ibid.p.505

7 MULTINATIONAL CORPORATION

Business organizations have their own relationship with the changing environment of the business organizational survival, growth and success requires an effective adjustment with the environment. Regulatory framework of business within the country, promotional support and participation of the government also decides the fate of the business organization. Continuous increase in the size of business organizations is the law of the day. It is the direct result of improvement in organizational operation's viability and effectiveness. Structural changes in organizations are affected by the requirement of the business environment. Movement of organisation from one region to another region and from one country to another country actually governed by the viable opportunities available in that particular region or country. Availability of large customer base, cheap labour force, supply of raw materials and other natural resources actually motivate the business organizations to undertake business operations in that particular country. Availability of productive and trading facilities and opportunities basically encourage and motivate the foreign companies to exfoliate them in the host countries. Establishment of East India Company in 1600 is the best example in this direction. There are two fundamental ways for companies and individuals to own assets in foreign countries viz. portfolio investment and direct investment. Portfolio investment gives companies and individuals a claim on profit of companies in foreign countries in which they have purchased shares. However, they do not have right to participate in the management. On the other hand, direct investment is nothing but a sort of buying and management of assets in foreign countries. The major difference between the portfolio investment and direct investment is the management and permanent ownership of assets through foreign outfits. Thus, portfolio investment is an investment in foreign assets whereby a company purchases shares in companies that own those assets. But direct investment is an investment in foreign assets whereby a company purchases assets that it manages directly. Eagerness of companies of home countries to purchase, control and mange the assets in host countries is the basis fro the development of multinational corporations.

Earlier, especially during 19th century, most companies restricted their operations to a single country. They were engaged in domestic business which deals with organizational activities that take place within the borders of one country. "It also included hiring employees, obtaining funds, arranging raw materials, selling finished goods and other businesses that could be performed within the home country. Actually home country is the nation where the company has its headquarter. There were certain firms that operated outside their home countries generally sent locally made goods to countries where those products were not available or received needed resources (such as raw material) from countries where such stables were plentiful"[1]. However, industrial revolution accelerated the pace of modern production systems and in the changed scenario; managers were not only able to make and sell products nationally but eventually to offer them in other countries. "By crossing national borders to acquire resources or to sell products these firms become involved in international business."[2] International business is concerned with those activities which take place across national borders in more than one country. Increasing level of business activities encourages the corporate enterprises to move beyond the domestic business activities and cross borders in search of resources or customers to conduct international business.

Nature of Multinational Corporation

The multinational corporation (MNC) has now become a household word. Although its definition is still the subject of debate what distinguishes an MNC from its predecessors, companies with foreign subsidiaries or affiliates, is direct investment abroad and direct interest in the business environment in which it has such investments."[3] In this context, it is important to say that the hallmarks of an MNC are control and integration of affiliates.[4] In practice, the concept of multinationality has different dimensions and due to this there is a problem in having a simple universally agreed definition of the term multinational corporation. However, "direct investment is characterized by an active involvement in the management of foreign investments typically through a multinational enterprise (MNE), a large corporation with operation and divisions spread over several countries but controlled by a central headquarter."[5]

According to the ILO Report. "The essential nature of the multinational enterprise lies in the fact that managerial headquarter is located in one country (referred to for convenience as the home country) while the enterprise carries out operations in a number of other countries as well (host countries)"[6]

Leonard Gomes also defined MNCs as "a corporation that controls production facilities in more than one country and such facilities having been acquired through the process of foreign direct investment. Firms that participate in international business, however large, they may be, soley by exporting or by licensing technology are not multinational enterprises."[7]

James C. Baker defines a multinational corporation as a company (i) which has direct investment base in several countries; (ii) which generally derives 20 to 50 percent of its net profit from foreign operations and (iii) whose management makes policy decisions based on the alternatives available anywhere in the world.

According to Bartlett and Ghoshal "the multinational organization is defined by the following characteristics: a decentralized federation of assets and responsibilities, a management process defined by simple financial control system overlaid on informal personal coordination and a dominant strategic mentality that viewed the company's worldwide operations as a portfolio of national business. In a multinational organization the decision obviously are decentralized."[8]

Thus, on the basis of above definitions multinational corporation can be defined as a corporation that produces goods or services in several countries and manages its global activities from organizational headquarter located in one country.

Features of Multinational Corporation

Multinational Corporation incorporates following features

1. Multi domestic management: It is an approach in which a company operating in several countries allows its local units to act independently and does not co-ordinate its international operations on a global basis. In each country, the local organization is self-contained and acts much like a separate domestic business might act. "Multidomestic management allows local managers to be highly responsive to environmental conditions in the host country."[9]

2. Host country: It is a nation outside the home country where an organization conducts its business activities. Headquarter or head office of a controlling organization is located or based on the home country. Host country is supposed to provide all legal and other environmental framework for external organizations generally called as MNCs. It is also required to formulate necessary guidelines for the purpose of direct investment. Conceptually, MNCs are also supposed to operate in a certain minimum number of nations five or six etc.

3. Direct investment: It is an arrangement in which a business organization acquires an ownership interest in the overseas company or invest in production and marketing facilities in another country called as host country. Direct investment is also characterized by an active involvement in the management of foreign investments. It is the tool by which MNCs develop their business outfits in host countries.

4. Headquarter in home country: It is a country where the company has its headquarter. It is the controlling place located in the home country to control different business outfits working in different host countries. Command system over business in the host country is regulated from the home country. It is also the central headquarter to formulate management policies for execution in home country as well as in the host countries. Development of centralized control mechanism is based at in the home country.

5. Bases of Production or service: MNCs are required to produce or provide services in host countries through direct investment MNC is interested to gain control over operations, to avoid any problematic trade barriers and to learn firsthand about the needs of its customers. Moreover, producing goods and services in the host countries where they will be sold enables the organization (MNC) to respond rapidly to environmental changes and at the same time, keeping marketing and distribution costs lower."[10]

6. Professional management team: MNCs in host countries are generally managed by professional team having geo-centric orientations. It is possible that an organization may be managed by family members in home country but it may be a limiting factor for itself. Due to the limitation, MNCs are generally managed by professionals in the host countries.

7. Income and workforce criteria: It is also suggested that a particular organization is to be called as MNC, if it fulfills the minimum percentage of its income and workforce. For example, it is suggested that MNCs must derive some minimum percentage of its income from foreign operations like 25 percent and have a certain minimum `ratio of foreign to total number of employees or of foreign total value of assets.

Factors Responsible for Companies Going International

Following factors generally encourage companies for going international:

1. To gain access to cheaper resources: Nature of business forces the companies like companies engaged in mining and petroleum business to have an access to more reliable or cheaper supply of raw materials in foreign countries. Similarly, manufacturing enterprises also try for cheap labour in host countries in comparison to costly labour available in the home country. Companies are eager to invest in developing foreign countries to avoid political instability at home or to gain access to a large pool of technological knowhow available in the host countries.

2. To increase return on investment: Companies are interested to increase their return through foreign investment. "Business is like individuals who shift their funds from areas where return on capital are lower to those where they are higher."[11] Companies also increase their chances for achieving a certain return on investment and stable or growing profits by expanding their overseas business.

3. To increase market share: According to Ramond Vernn's product cycle theory, companies that develop attractive new product sell them first in their home markets. Sooner or later, foreigners learn of these products, creating enough demand to justify exporting. If this demand continues to grow, it will eventually become more economical to invest in foreign manufacturing facilities."[12] Oligopolistic position of companies also positively improve the market share. According to Stevan Hymer, "companies that expand internationally tend to be oligopolistic that is, they tend to dominate their domestic market, either because their product are highly desirable or because their size lets them reap economies of scale. To continue growing, they will have to expand into international markets.[13]

4. To neutralize foreign tariffs and import quotas: Government of host country generally use tariff or import quotas to protect domestic business enterprises. In this enterprise, direct investment plays an important role in solving the problems created through the threat of foreign tariffs and import quotas. MNCs counter these threats by investing more and more in terms of direct investment in host countries.

Organisational Framework of Multinational Corporations

A multinational corporation can organize its operation in different countries through the following methods:

1. Branches: The easiest form of expanding business operations is to set up overseas branches. These branches are generally foreign outfits of the parent company located in the host countries. Legally, these branches are dependent on their parent company. As per the Indian Companies Act, 1956, all those companies, which are incorporated outside India and have developed business interest in India are called as foreign companies.

2. Subsidiaries: It is the popular method of direct investment generally used to start up or overtake total ownership and control of another company making the second company as a wholly owned subsidiary (developed in host country) of the parent company (headquartered in the home country). "Wholly owned subsidiary involves more investment, ownership control and risk than having only a partial interest in another company. But it can also allow the parent company the freedom to take whatever actions are necessary to make subsidiary perform as expected and to provide the parent with needed resources to improve its performance."[14]

3. Joint venture companies: "A joint venture is an arrangement in which two or more organizations cooperatively develop, produce or sell goods or services. The parent firms are independently of each other but share control over the joint venture. In some cases, one company supplies the materials and the products expertise, while the other supplies the knowledge to do business in the country they are targeting."[15] Thus, joint venture is a business enterprise or system in which domestic and foreign companies share the cost of developing new products or building production facilities in a foreign country. "A joint venture may be the only way to enter certain countries. Where by law, foreigners cannot own business. In other situations, joint ventures let companies pool technological knowledge and share the expense and risk of research that may not produce marketable goods."[16]

4. Franchise holders: It is fastest growing form of international licensing in which the licensor supplies a complete package of goods, services and materials generally accompanied by a well known brand name to the licensee. It is also a special kind of arrangement by which an affiliate working in the host country produces or markets the products of a multinational corporation after obtaining a license from it.

5. Global strategic partnership: It is an alliance formed by an organization with one or more foreign countries generally with an eye towards exploiting the other countries opportunities and towards assuming leadership in either supply or production. For the successful operations of global strategic partnership following conditions are to be fulfilled.[17]

(*i*) Each partner must believe the other has something it needs.

(*ii*) The partners must choose a strategy before they start to do business not afterward.

(*iii*) They must share the same attitude towards control of new business.

(*iv*) Working of partners should be effective in terms of operating styles, corporate cultures and moral values.

(*v*) They must agree to discard whatever organization forms that do not work.

(*vi*) There must be some ultimate decision maker and some of making decision stick. Otherwise, the new venture suffers from unclear lines of authority, poor communication and slow decision making.

Rationale of MNCs

Rationale of MNCs are as follows:

1. Financial strength: Finance is the lifeblood of a company; Huge financial resources are available with the MNCs. They are quite efficient in generation of funds in one country and investing them in another country. Thus, by this action, they are able to improve the level of investment in the host country. They are also successful in raising resources at international level as they hold good reputation in the market.

2. Product innovation: Product innovation is necessary to remain stay in the market for a long period. MNCs incur huge expenditure on developing R&D facilities in the host country as R&D facilities are required to provide for developing new products and superior design of existing products. Consumers can also be satisfied with the products and services being provided by the MNCs in the host country.

3. Effective technological background: In most of the cases, host countries are the underdeveloped or developing economies. They need accelerated pace of technological development in the country. Host countries need transfer of technology from MNCs to exploit their local resources in profitable way. In practice, MNCs are quite sensitive to these requirements and they transfer their technology to produce goods and services in the host countries.

4. Marketing strength: Since, MNCs are professionally managed, they hold more reliable and latest market information system. Market reputation of MNCs is also generally good and they feel less problem in selling their products. Effective advertising and sales promotion techniques also provide an additional advantage to these MNCs in marketing of their product or service in the host country.

5. Market expansion: Generally, MNCs operate their activities on large-scale basis and having a large sized structure, they try to build up international image of the host countries. With the help of their production bases and service network in the host country, they provide better export potentialities for the product being produced in the host countries. Thus, MNCs help the host country in its expansion of market territory.

Business Strategies of Multinational Corporations

Following are the major business strategies of Multinational Corporations :

1. Market Imperfections: MNCs generally creates market imperfections. The use of the market for coordinating the behaviour of agents located in different countries is less efficient than coordinating them by a multinational enterprise as an institution. The additional costs caused by the entrance in foreign markets are of less interest for the local enterprise. The existence of MNEs is reasoned by structural market imperfections for final products. The firms can maximize their joint income by a merger or acquisition which will lower the competition in the shared market. Due to the transformation of two separated companies into one MNE, the pecuniary externalities are going to be internalized. However, this doesn't mean that there is an improvement for the society. This could also be the case if there are few substitutes or limited licenses in a foreign market. The consolidation is often established by acquisition, merger or the vertical integration of the potential licensee into overseas manufacturing. This makes it easy for the MNE to enforce price discrimination schemes in various countries. Therefore, there is opportunity for the emergence of multinational firms as "an (negative) instrument for restraining competition between firms of different nations".

Market imperfections are generally considered as structural and caused by the deviations from perfect competition in the final product markets. Imperfections are originated from the control of proprietary technology and distribution systems, scale economies, privileged access to inputs and product differentiation. In the absence of these factors, market are fully efficient. It is claimed that market imperfections are inherent conditions in markets and MNEs are institutions that try to bypass these imperfections. The imperfections in markets are natural as the neoclassical assumptions like full knowledge and enforcement don't exist in real markets.

2. Tax Competition: Multinational corporations have played an important role in globalization. Countries and sometimes sub national regions must compete against one another for the establishment of MNC facilities, and the subsequent tax revenue, employment, and economic activity. To compete, countries and regional political districts sometimes offer to MNCs such as tax breaks, pledges of governmental assistance or improved infrastructure, or lax environmental and labnor standards enforcement. This process of becoming more attractive to foreign investment can be characterized as a race to the bottom, a push towards greater autonomy for corporate bodies, or both.

While multinationals certainly regard a low tax burden or low labor costs as an element of comparative advantage, studies suggest that MNCs deliberately avail themselves of tax environmental regulation or poor labour standards. Basically, MNC profits are tied to operational efficiency, which includes a high degree of standardisation. Thus, MNCs are likely to tailor production processes in all of their operations in conformity to those jurisdictions where they operate and maintain most rigorous standards. As for labor costs, while MNCs clearly pay workers in, e.g. Vietnam, much less than they would in the US it is also the case that they tend to pay a premium of between 10% and 100% on local labour rates. Finally, depending on the nature of the MNC, investment in any country reflects a desire for a long-term return. Costs associated with establishing plant, training workers, etc., can be very high; once established in a jurisdiction, therefore, many MNCs are quite vulnerable to predatory practices such as, e.g., expropriation, sudden contract renegotiation, the arbitrary withdrawal or compulsory purchase of unnecessary 'licenses,' etc. Thus, both the negotiating power of MNCs and the supposed 'race to the bottom' may be overstated, while the substantial benefits that MNCs bring (tax revenues aside) are often understated.

3. Market Withdrawal: Because of their size, multinationals can have a significant impact on government policy, primarily through the threat of market withdrawal. For example, in an effort to reduce health care costs, some countries have tried to pharmaceutical companies to license their patented drugs to local competetitors for a very low fee, thereby artificially lowering the price. When faced with that threat, multinational pharmaceutical firms have simply withdrawn from the market, which often leads to limited availability of advanced drugs. In these cases, governments have been forced to back down from their efforts. Similar corporate and government confrontations have occurred when governments tried to force MNCs to make their intellectual rights public in an effort to gain technology for local entrepreneurs. When companies are faced with the option of losing a core competitive technological advantage or withdrawing from a national market, they may choose the latter. Some MNCs like Coco Cola and IBM even left India in the late 1970s specially during Janta Party Government (after the announcement of Industrial Policy 1977) because these MNCs were not ready to accept the conditions as given in the New Industrial Policy of 1977.

This withdrawal often causes governments to change policy. Countries that have been the most successful in this type of confrontation with multinational corporations are large countries such as United States and Brazil which have viable indigenous market competitors.

4. Lobbying: Multinational corporate lobbying is directed at a range of business concerns, from tariff structures to environmental regulations. There is no unified multinational perspective on any of these issues. Companies that have invested heavily in pollution control mechanisms may lobby for very tough environmental standards in an effort to force non-compliant competitors into a weaker position. Corporations lobby tariffs to restrict competition of foreign industries. For every tariff category that one multinational wants to have reduced, there is another multinational that wants the tariff raised. Thus, it is quite serious and very hard and takes a lot of work for the owner. Multinational corporations such as Wal-mart and McDonald's benefit from government zoning laws, to create barriers to entry. Many industries such as General Electric and Boaing lobby the government to receive subsidies to preserve their monopoly.

5. Patents: Many multinational corporations hold patents to prevent competitors from arising. For example, Adidas holds many patents on the shoe designs, Siemens A.G. holds many patents on equipment and infrastructure and Mocrosoft benefits from software patents. The pharmaceutical companies lobby international agreements to enforce patent laws on others. Multinational companies through their subsidiaries are always trying to own these patents for penetrating in the foreign market.

6. Adjustments with Government Power: MNCs are generally interested to mould the governmental policies in their own favour. However, they always conscious enough to adjust with the government policies and programmes in case of need. Thus, in addition to efforts by multinational corporations to affect governments, there is much government action intended to affect corporate behavior. The threat of nationalization (forcing a company to sell its local assts to the government or to other local nationals) or changes in local business laws and regulations can limit a multinational's power. These issues become of increasing importance because of the emergence of MNCs in developing countries.

7. Micro Multinationals: Enabled by Internet based communication tools, a new breed of multinational companies is growing in numbers. These multinationals start operating in different countries from the very early stages. These companies are being called micro-multinationals. The point which differentiates micro-multinationals from the large MNCs is the fact that they are small businesses. Some of these micro-multinationals, particularly software development companies, have been hiring employees in multiple countries from the beginning of the Internet era. But more and more micro-multinationals are actively starting to market their products and services in various countries. Internet tools like Google, Yahoo, MSN, Ebay and Amazon make it easier for the micro-multinationals to reach potential customers in other countries. Service sector micro-multinationals, like Facebook, Alibaba etc. started as dispersed virtual businesses with employees, clients and resources located in various countries. Their rapid growth is a direct result of being able to use the internet, cheaper telephony and lower traveling costs to create unique business opportunities. Low cost SaaS (Software As A Service) suites make it easier for these companies to operate without a physical office. There's no longer a brain drain but brain circulation. People now doing startups understand what opportunities are available to them around the world and work to harness it from a distance rather than move people from one place to another."

Merits of MNCs

Merits of MNCs are as follows:

(*i*) They help in improving the investment level in host country. Consequently, there is more scope for further improvement in the level of income and employment.

(*ii*) They are effective vehicles for the transfer of technology to developing countries. With the help of technology, host countries are able to exploit their available resources in proper way.

(*iii*) They encourage professional management. They are able to demarcate a line between the ownership and management with the help of professional management. MNCs are basically managed by sophisticated management techniques.

(*iv*) They help host countries to have a core competency and cost effectiveness in their production/service system. Host countries are also able to maintain a favourable balance of payment due to foreign direct investment.

(*v*) They provide an effective system for integrating the different sectors of host economies. Growth of industrial sector is dependent on the agriculture sector and pace of agriculture sector is governed by the growth variables available in the industrial sector.

(vi) They invest huge amount in research and development activities. With the result, they make commendable contribution regarding inventions and innovations. Service sector caters the purpose of both these sectors.

(vii) They help the customers by improving the level of competition in the host economies. Domestic monopolies are to be eased out with the help of active participation of MNCs in the market. Customers are the biggest beneficiaries of MNCs, as they get relief from the clutches of domestic monopolistic or oligopolist.

(viii) They provide innovative marketing facilities to the customers. Licensing and franchising of brands, trademarks, patent etc enable the consumers of host countries to enjoy the product and services of MNCs.

Demerits of MNCs

Demerits of MNCs are as follows

(i) Technology being provided by the MNCs is meant for profit maximization and not for the developmental needs of host countries.

(ii) MNCs are quite financially powerful and flexible and they generally undermine the economic autonomy and control of host economies.

(iii) They are manipulative in their strategic activities and they may threaten the sovereignty of the nations in which they are doing their business. They are also generally accused of supporting repressive regimes: paying bribes to secure political influence; not respecting human rights; paying protection money to terrorist groups and destabilizing national governments of which they do not approve.[18]

(iv) They dump obsolete technology and bring in outdated products. Even polluting products banned in their home country are supplied to customers in the host country.

(v) They undermine local cultures and traditions and change the consumption habits for their benefits. Thus, they are generally against the long term interest of the local community, promote conspicuous consumption, dump harmful products in developing economies etc.

(vi) They are also accused of the environmental degradation, polluting the environment, not paying compensation for the environmental damages, causing harmful changes in the local living conditions and paying little regard to the rises of accidents causing major environmental catastrophes.[19]

(vii) They are generally engaged in consumer goods industries specially fast-moving consumer goods industries. They are not eager to invest in heavy or core industries, which required huge capital investment and long gestation period. So they retard growth of employment in the host country.

Suggestions

Following suggestions are required to be implemented by MNCs to avoid criticism.

(i) They should honour the national sovereignty of host countries and work as per the their regulatory framework of business and national ethos.

(ii) They should help in achieving the economic goals, development objectives and socio-cultural values of the host countries.

(iii) They should adopt business ethics and best business practices like timely payment of required taxes, abstention from involvement in anticompetitive practices, consumer and environmental protection and to work as a model employer.

(iv) They should be sensitive to human rights, corporate reporting, corporate governance, better competition etc.

(v) They should contribute in the development of science and technology in the host country. They should also work for the development of R&D facilities in the host country rather than transferring obsolete technology for production in the host country.

Distinction between Multinational Corporation and Transnational Corporation

In general terms, International Corporation, Multinational Corporation are often used as synonyms. But some prefer to draw a line of distinction between these terms. A company with manufacturing, investment or service operation in atleast one foreign country is called as an international corporation. A multinational corporation has a wider exposure and perspective. It must have direct investment in several countries and derive a substantial part of profits from foreign operations.

A transnational corporation is a multinational in which both ownership and control are so dispersed internationally that there is no principal domicile and no central source of power. The term global corporation is also generally used to mean more or less the same thing as the transnational corporation.

According to Theodore Levitt, the multinational corporation operated in a number of countries and adjusts its products and practices in each at a high relative cost; the global corporation operates with absolute constancy at a low relative cost; as if the entire world were a single entity; it sells the same thing the same way everywhere". Thus, according to this approach, entire world is a global village in which people desire the same products and life styles. However, transition phase of multinational entity has different stages at which they work as transnational or global corporation.

Regulatory Framework of MNCs in India

Earlier, specially before the liberalization, privatization and globalization (LPG) era, no serious efforts were made to attract foreign investment in India. Major thrust was given to the public sector industries in India. Even during the plan period, steel plants etc. were set up with the help of foreign collaborations and direct financial support of foreign countries. Government policy was also not conducive in favour of direct investment. The foreign Exchange Regulation Act, (FERA) 1973 required the foreign companies in India to dilute their foreign equity to 40 percent. However, certain exceptions were allowed in certain cases where high technology and export oriented sectors were considered in the interest of national economy. Some MNCs like Coco Cola and IBM even left India in the late 1970s specially during Janta Party Government (after the announcement of Industrial Policy 1977) because these MNCs were not ready to accept the conditions as given in the New Industrial Policy of 1977.

With the liberalization of foreign direct investment and removal of FERA restriction since 1991 a large number of MNCs have hiked their equity stake to 51 percent and acquired majority control in their Indian affiliates or outfits/subsidiaries. With the hike in equity, they acquire several strategic advantages. Enactment of foreign Exchange Management Act, 1999 further provided a liberal environment for the entry of MNCs in India. At present about 700 MNCs are working in different sectors of Indian Economy.

It is also important to note that Hindustan Lever, ITC, Bata India, ABB, P&G, Cadbury were the dominant MNCs working in our country. But after 1991, more and more MNCs are coming up in the country. Automobiles, Computers and Electronic equipments, Finance and Banks are the important emerging sectors where MNCs are taking growing interest due to liberalized framework of foreign direct investment. These MNCs also investing more and more in the sector like power and telecommunications. General Motors, Ford, Compaq, Motorola, Suzuki etc. have already joined the Indian Corporate Sector. The economic reforms have given considerable impetus for MNCs investment in India. Continuous relaxation in the maximum cap of foreign direct investment may attract more and more MNCs to have strategic partnership with Indian entrepreneurs.

MNCs have no doubt playing very important role in the economic development of our country. Over the years MNCs have perfected not only their products and services but also inculcate professional management in their activities. However, these MNCs are providing tough competition to Indian companies and they are not able to face these competition. These MNCs are also buying our popular Indian brands and companies and takeing over production facilities created over years by them. Brands like Limca, ThumsUp etc from Parle of Ramesh Chaouhan and Jai, Ok etc. from Tata Oil Mill Ltd. can be cited as an example. MNCs in India are not interested to invest in infrastructure sector which is at present needed urgently. Similarly, their entry into such areas as fast food and elite consumers goods does not have any rationale. In spite of above criticism in Indian context, it can be stated that in the face of stiff competition from MNCs, now Indian companies are being forced to upgrade their technology and quality of products for their survival in new business environment. In the era of economic reforms, Government of India itself providing liberal environment to them and they are entering in the country in big way. However, there should be some checks and counter checks on the operations of MNCs to protect the interest of Indian economy in general and Indian entrepreneurs in particular.

Destination India for Multinational Corporations

Following are the reasons for Multinational Companies to consider India as a preferred destination for business:

1. Huge market potential: India is a developing economy. Per capita income is increasing due to high growth rate in gross domestic product. Levels of saving, investment and employment opportunities are increasing at a faster rate. Rate of literacy is also improving. Life style is also under change. Due to these factors, MNCs are considering India as an emerging market for their products and services. Drugs and pharmaceuticals, capital goods, white goods automobiles, banking and financial services, food products and beverages are the major sectors where MNCs are playing their important roles.

2. FDI attractiveness: For quite a long time, India had a restrictive policy in terms of foreign direct investment. As a result, there was lesser number of companies that showed interest in investing in Indian market. However, the scenario changed during the financial liberalization of the country, especially after 1991. Government, nowadays, makes continuous efforts to attract foreign investments by relaxing many of its policies. As a result, a number of multinational companies have shown interest in Indian market.

Since 1991 Government of India has started the economic reform process in the economy. Liberlisation, privatization and globalization have created conducive environment for foreign investment specially foreign direct investment. Several sectors have been opened for FDI investment in terms of different scales. It has given favourable opportunities to multinational companies to invest huge fund under direct investment programme. The India as destination for FDI has been attracting huge amount for accelerating the pace of economic development.

3. Labour Competitiveness: Developing economy specially India is quite labour competitive in comparison to developed economies like USA. Availability of knowledge workers have also motivated MNCs to select India as an investment destination. With the result, MNCs are quite motivated to set up their production and service base in India in place of their host countries. Since labour is quite cheap here, MNCs are able to reduce their overall cost of production. Suzuki motors Corporation is best example which is quite successful in producing more motor car than in Japan. It is also successful in its export efforts of Suzuki Motor Car to developed nations.

4. Macro Economic Stability: Socio economic and political culture of India is quite harmonious and stable. Political stability of the country is good enough for attracting FDI. Availability of raw materials, labour, demand for products, capital formation, saving, investment ratio etc. are quite favourable. Economic policies are suitable and favourable for MNCs Continuous evaluation, monitoring and consequential adjustments in economic reforms process actually encourage the MNCs to treat India as their best investment destination.

Multinational Corporations in India

The multinational companies in India represent a diversified portfolio of companies from different countries. Majority of the MNC in India, are the American companies which account for about 37% of the turnover of the top 20 firms operating in India. However, the scenario has changed a lot off late. More enterprises from European Union like Britain, France, Netherlands, Italy, Germany, Belgium and Finland have come to India or have outsourced their works to this country. Finnish mobile giant Nokia has their second largest base in this country. There are also MNCs like British Petroleum and Vodafone that represent Britain. India has a huge market for automobiles and hence a number of automobile giants have stepped in to this country to reap the market. One can easily find the showrooms of the multinational automobile companies like Fiat, Piaggio, and Ford Motors in India. French Heavy Engineering major Alstom and Pharma major Sanofi Aventis have also started their operations in this country. The later one is in fact one of the earliest entrants in the list of multinational companies in India, which is currently growing at a very enviable rate. There are also a number of oil companies and infrastructure builders from Middle East. Electronics giants like Samsung and LG Electronics from South Korea have already made a substantial impact on the Indian electronics market. Hyundai Motors has also done well in mid-segment car market in India.

The list of multinational companies in India is ever-growing as a number of MNCs are coming down to this country has an increasing trend. Following are some of the major multinational companies operating their businesses in India:

(*i*) British Petroleum
(*ii*) Vodafone
(*iii*) Ford Motors
(*xvi*) Novartis pharma
(*xvii*) ABB cap goods
(*xviii*) Siemens cap goods

(iv) LG
(v) Samsung
(vi) Hyundai
(vii) Accenture
(viii) Reebok
(ix) Skoda Motors
(x) ABN Amro Bank
(xi) Hindustan Unilever consumer
(xii) ITC tobbaco and life style
(xiii) Procter and gamble consumer
(xiv) Pfizer pharma
(xv) Aventis pharma
(xix) Cadbury consumer
(xx) Nestle consumer
(xxi) Glaxo smith-kline [pharma and-consumer]
(xxii) Microsoft Software
(xxiii) IBM software
(xxiv) Coke drinks
(xxv) Pepsi-co food
(xxvi) Nokia communication

Present Perspective of MNCs

After going slow for long, multinational companies led by Siemens, MICO, ABB, Wartssila India, Denso Corporation are stepping up investment in India, buoyed by increased infrastructure spending and higher consumption from the rural sector. Most of the MNCs were resisting fresh investments for long, but have now changed course to announce big investments, seeing the immense potential. The MNCs have renewed their interest in India due to its buoyant economy and huge potential in the infrastructure and engineering sector. Recent announcements include Rs. 1800 crore investment by the Bosch Group's Indian arm Motor India Company Ltd (MICO), The Siemenss Ltd. has acquired Hyderabad based Elpro International's isolator (used in transmission and distribution lines) business and 50 per cent stake in Kharagpur based Flender Ltd. Siemen has also announced the setting up of an industrial steam turbine factor at Vadodara, Gujarat Engine maker Cummins India (where Cummins Inc. of the US holds 51 per cent) is setting up an additional manufacturing facility in Pune at an investment of Rs 15 crores while auto parts maker Bosch Chasis system (formerly Kalyani Brakes) has formed a joint venture with Brembo Spa of Italy for two wheelers brakes. Similarly, Ciba specially Chemicals has announced a Rs. 50 crore manufacturing plant at Goa and another Rs 70 crore investment in Gujarat through its fully owned subsidiary Diamond Dye Chem Ltd. Wartsila India promoted by Wartsila Corporation of Finland has also made fresh investment in India. On the FMCG front, Nestle India's new factory at Pantnagar has already started commercial production. The Hindustan Unilever meanwhile is increasing its rural focus further. Procter & Gamble is also expanding in the country though all the fresh investments are bringing done through its wholly owned arm P&G Home products. Different studies show that MNCs have showed down their investment between 1996 and 2003 but the scenario began to change from 2003. Many new MNC players have also made fresh investment in the Indian market and have done well while the existing MNCs players were found wanting as they postponed making commitments in terms of investments and exposure "Thinks have begun to change in recent times", "MNCs have not been on the news radar as these companies were focused on exports. However, with increased expenditure in the infrastructure front and the growing domestic consumption levels the MNCs in infrastructures and the FMCG sector are expanding and doing better. There is a re-rating of the share prices of MNCs happening at the moment, which indicates that investors are willing to pay higher price for the shares of MNC firms in the stock markets.

The rapid rise of multinational corporations has been a topic of concern among intellectuals, activists and laypersons who have seen these MNCs as a threat to Indian Industries. Studies suggest that multinationals create false needs in consumers and have had a long history of interference in the policies of sovereign nation states. Evidence supporting this belief includes invasive advertising (such as billboards, television ads, adware, stam, telemarketing, child-targeted advertising, guerrilla marketing), massive corporate campaign contributions in democratic elections, and endless global news stories about corporate corruption (Martha Stewart and Enron, for example). Anti-corporate protesters suggest that corporations answer only to shareholders, giving human rights and other issues almost no consideration.

Case Study

Read the following case study carefully and answer the following questions:

When Japanese companies first began manufacturing in the United States, many people smiled at oddities like prework exercise, but analysts were struck with the efficiency of the Japanese management style. Now, the Koreans are coming, setting up their own factories and bringing their version of management 'harmony'.

Dozens of South Korean Corporations have already opened offices in the United States, and two have began manufacturing operations. The Lucky-Goldstar Group opened a colour television factory in Huntsville, Alabama two and half years ago, and its now bustling with expansion plans. Last fall the Samsung Group also began producing colour televisions, at a factory in Roxbury 'Toenship,N.J.

In gambling that they can manufacture profitably in America, just when American manufactures are bitterly complaining and even going abroad because of foreign competition, the Koreans are counting on a blend of their own traditional management style with American business methods.

The Korean style is similar to the much better known Japanese approach, although experts say that Koreans are often more willing to blend their techniques with American methods. Korean management aims to foster a family atmosphere, in which employees interact freely with executives and share a strong commitment to the company's success.

Acting more as a gentle patriarch than as president of the Gold Star of America plant, P.W. Suh has taken concedes that there have been awkward moments – such as the reluctance of some American workers to wear uniforms – but in general employees and management alike appear to appreciate the results.

'You wouldn't believe what Gold star does for us.' Said Rachel Cothern, pausing form has job on the assembly line. My husband was in the hospital for major surgery, and some of the management came and sat with me through that Mr. Suh came and stayed with me in intensive care, and brought books and magaines." This carefully cultivated image of a friendly , caring company of one happy family typifies the Korean management style. But the friendship is not for nothing. It is intended to keep unions at bay and to foster a loyalty and enthusiasm in the work force that will generate more televisions per hour than American management can. One measure of its success is a daily absenteeism rate at Gold Star that averages 1 percent, compared with 5 percent in American companies. The idea is to import not Korean television but Korean management methods. These methods are associated with an economic miracle that produced even faster economic growth in South Korea over that last 25 years than in Japan. The Korean growth was three times faster than is the United States.

The principal weapon in the Korean armory is its management philosophy, what the Koreans call inhwa, or harmony. Even in South Korea, Lucky-Goldstar is an exemplar of philosophy.

'If we are in a hurry, we may ask employees for special consideration to do things differently', said H.D. Koo, president of overseas operations for the Lucky Goldstar Group, explaining the Koreans approach. 'And they will oblige. But in the United States may be they do not care that there is a hurry.'

Mr. Koo and his colleagues is the Lucky-Goldstar boardrooms want employees of the Huntsville plant to care, and so they are trying to transplant inhwa. 'I expect dedication and loyalty in the future, if we help our family', Mr. Suh said, using 'family' to refer to his work force.

Telling employees about company goals, and even asking for help, are cardinal principles of Goldstar. 'Family meetings' for all the staff, are held monthly, and quality discussions are scheduled for every two weeks. In addition, bonuses are used to build enthusiasm. About three days a week, workers get bonus – an hour of overtime pay – if their assembly line has increased output while maintaining quality levels. Employees also get $50 in cash if they do not miss a day of work for three months.

Similar management methods are used at the other Korean manufacturing plant in the United States. Samsung's in Roxbury township. The employees are also called a family, and interaction between workers and executives is stressed. Like the Japanese, the Koreans are coming to the United States largely because of feat that protectionists rules could keep out their exports. In February, 2004, the Commerce Department ruled that Korean electronics companies were dumping – or selling for less than fair value – colour television sets in the United States, Goldstar is now required to post cash deposits of 7.4% of the value of its shipments, although the final assessments may vary from that.

But in coming to America, the Koreans are also facing tough price competition. Although 2003 and 2004 were boom years for colour televisions , with about 16 million units sold last year, price competition has been reverse.

Although imports have been a major reason for the price competition, three out of four television sets sold in the United States are still made in this country. About two dozen manufactures continue to produce sets in the United States.

Charles K. Ryan, an analyst at Merrill Lynch and Company, said that Korean companies operating in South Korea and in the United States might come to dominate the lower level of the colour television market, for 13-inch and low priced 19-inch models, while more established companies produce larger, more complex televisions were the markup in higher.

One frustration for Gold Star is that because it lacks name recognition and a reputation, it has to sell at lower prices than its competition. Gold Star sells its televisions under its own name and under private brand names like Montgomery Ward, General Electric, and K-mart.

Notwithstanding the competition, Gold Star seems to be happy with its American experience. Since opening the factory in Huntsville, Gold Star has doubled its capacity and plans soon to add microwave ovens, computers and video-cassette recorders. Gold Star executives are buoyed by the finding that televisions produced in Huntsville can compete in price with sets produced in South Korea.

The basic wage in the Huntsville plant is $4.56 an hour, although bonuses and benefits and significantly to that. The comparable South Korean wage is $1.30. But mechanization has reduced the role of labour in the Alabama·plant, so that it costs only about $7 more to produce a television set in Huntsville than to build it in South Korea and ship it to the United States. The anti-dumping duty on Korean sets more than makes up that gap, Gold Star said.

Questions

1. Describe the Korean method of management. What advantages and disadvantages does it have over U.S. methods? How has it borrowed from U.S methods?
2. Why are Korean manufactures setting up manufacturing operations in the Unites States?
3. In your opinion, will the entry of foreign electronics manufactures have a positive or negative impact on the domestic electronics industry? Explain.
4. Can the recent success of Japanese and Korean MNEs be best explained by political, economic, or cultural factors?

Practice Questions

Objective Type Questions

1. Which was the first MNC worked in India:
   (a) East India Company
   (b) Dutch East India Company
   (c) Novaratrs
   (d) None of the above
2. ABB India is engaged in:
   (a) Capital goods industry
   (b) Fast moving consumer goods
   (c) White goods
   (d) Financial Service
3. Multinational Corporations generally prefer the route of:
   (a) Direct Investment
   (b) Portfolio investment
   (c) Indirect Investment
   (d) None of the above

4. Multinational Corporations generally believe in:
   (*a*) Strong production base
   (*b*) Strong brand base
   (*c*) Strong consumer base
   (*d*) Strong supply base
5. Multinational Corporations are concerned with except:
   (*a*) Direct investment
   (*b*) derive 20% to 50% their profit from host countries
   (*c*) control the management of company in host country
   (*d*) managerial headquarters at host countries

Ans: 1. (b), 2. (a) 3. (a), 4. (b), 5. (d)

Short Answer Questions

1. What do you mean by Multinational Corporation?
2. Explain the features of Multinational Corporation.
3. Examine the factors responsible for companies going international.
4. Discuss the rationale of MNCs.
5. Distinguish between Multinational Corporation and transnational corporation.

Long Answer Questions

1. Examine the role of Multinational Companies in India.
2. Discuss the various forms of foreign capital flows. Do you think entering of MNCs in less developed countries is rising?
3. Explain reasons for the rapid growth of Multinational Corporation in India.
4. What is Multinational Corporations? Discuss its merits and demerits.
5. Discuss the role of Multinational Corporations in India. How far foreign capital has been beneficial for the Indian economy?
6. "Multinational Corporations should not be encouraged in India". Comment.
7. What could be the broad approaches to control an Multinational Corporation? Analysing these approaches, present your own views.

References

1. James. F. Balt., Global Competitors: Some criteria for success. Business Horizon, January-February 1988. P. 34-41
2. Courtland L. Bovee, John V. Thill, Marian Burkwood and George P Dovel, Management, McGraw Hill Inc. NewYork, 1993. P 137
3. Prasad S.B. and Krishna Shetty Y, An Introduction to Multinational Management, Prentice-Hall., Englewood Cliffs, New Jersey, 1976,p 22
4. Behrman Jack N. Some Patterns In the Rise of Multinational Enterprise, Chapel Hill, N.C. University of North Carolina, 1969. P. XIV.
5. Robock Stefan H. and Simmonds Kenneth, International Business and Multinational Business, Homewood, Illinous, Irwin, 1983 P.7
6. ILO, Multinational Enterprises and Social Policy, ILO, Geneva, 1973. P.3
7. Leonard Gomes, International Economic Problems, Macmillan Press Ltd., London, 1978. P. 119
8. Christopher A Barlett and Sumamtra Ghoshal, Managing Across Borders, Boston, Havard Business School Press, 1998
9. Courtland L. Bovell etc. Ibid P. 138

10. Ibid P. 156
11. Yoshi, Tsurumi Multinational Management Business Strategy and Government Policy Cambride Mass Ballinger Publishing, 1977, P.76.
12. Stoner, James A.F. & Freeman R. Edward, Management Prentice Hall of India Private Limited, New Delhi, 1995, P. 132.
13. Yoshi Tsurumi Op cited., P.76.
14. op.cit. , Coutland L. Bovee John V-Thill, Marian Burk wood and George P. Dovel P. 157.
15. Ibid. P. 1555
16. op.cit., Stoner James A-F & Freeman R. Edward P. 135.
17. Perlmutter V. Howard and David A Heen an Cooperate to compete globally. Harvard Business Review by March April, 1986, P. 136-152.
18. Roger Bennett International business Addison wesley. Longman Delhi, 2000, P. 162.
19. Ibid, P. 162

8 COMPETITION AND COMPETITIVENESS IN INDIA

Everybody needs protection as its initial stage. At the time of independence, we had adopted the socialism as a base of economic development. Public sector was given dominant role and private sector and small sector were supposed to work in a protective umbrella. Role for each and every sector was defined under the various industrial policy statements. Thus, Indian industries were given protection in their operations. Their survival was totally governed by the protectionism approach adopted by the government in its policy framework. Different types of protections were granted to Indian industries. These include incentives and subsidies, preference in purchase of domestic supplies, capacity limitations, higher import duties export incentives reservation in product areas etc. They were also required to go by the control mechanism as per the guidelines of the government. Production and distribution controls were the main instruments in the hand of government. Thus, in the pre-reform era, various restraints to competition existed:[1] (i) investment restraints (licensing); (ii) control over acquisition of economic power through Monopolies and Restrictive Trade Practices Act (MRTP); (iii) public sector reservation for infrastructure and other industries creating monopolies in various areas; (iv) product reservation for the small-scale sector; (v) government procurement policies favouring public and small-scale sectors; (vi) trade restrictions and high tariffs; and (vii) restrictions on foreign direct investment. All these restraints (protective measures as well as controls) have been or are being relaxed now. In the present scenario, protection and controls are being replaced by a competitive and de-regulated open economic system.

Besides, the decontrol, deregulation and privatisation initiatives are being taken at a time when global economic environment is also undergoing a major change. The GATT-94 accord and the consequent setting up of the World Trade Organisation (WTO) have changed the rules of the game vis-a-vis world trade. Since 1991 government is trying to create competition in Indian Industries. "The objectives of competition is to create an active competitive environment, and aid and abett the process of creating globally competitive enterprises with enhanced investment and technological capabilities. Consequently, flexible regulatory framework in the areas of competition and competitiveness has been developed by the government. The regulatory framework includes competition law, policies relating to trade (market access, export subsidies, exchange rate, tariff and non-tariff barriers), investment (FDI, privatisation, tax, product reservation, interest rate) and technology development (IPRs, R and D, technology licensing and alliances)."[2] Actually, they come under the purview of 'competition policy', of the government incorporates all these dimensions insofar as they impinge on the process of competition. At the moment, competition policy describes the policy and programmes of the government towards competition and competitiveness in Indian industrial scene.

The developments in the working behaviour of industrial organisations during 1980s and 1990s have created some scepticism about the relationship between market concentration and market power and a greater recognition of the possible efficiency, enhancing role of vertical as well as horizontal agreements, mergers and acquisitions, core competency, capacity expansion, change in the product lines and product range and development of conglomerate enterprises. Consequently, general perception is changing and the most competition authorities today do not per se view large horizontal mergers, practices facilitating co-ordination, exclusionary practices, etc, as anti-competitive. Instrumentality of competitive flexibility like liberlisation has helped the Indian consumers to enjoy the benefit of growing competition in Indian market. Opening of sectors like telecom, civil aviation, banking and insurance, automobile sector, IT industries has really benefited the Indian consumers to a large extent.

Moreover, the competition authorities and courts have also shifted away from relying primarily on market share evidence for predicting the competitive consequences of business practices. "Market shares, though still quite important, are increasingly treated as only one element in a detailed economic analysis of the consequences of the particular conduct at issue. A large variety of factors including trade barriers, sunk costs, technology and product life cycles, rate of growth of demand, etc, are used to analyse the potential efficiency enhancing and market power effects of a business practice. Besides, both static and dynamic implications are sought to be ascertained."[3] These changes reflect the growing recognition that competition policy is extremely important in a globally integrated economy and needs to be properly integrated with other economic policies.

The present decade has indeed been one of the most challenging for the world economy. The unprecedented financial crises, acknowledged today as the worst since the Great Depression, has brutally shaken the foundations of some of the strongest economies in the world. Nearly 40 million jobs have been lost. Cumulative losses from bankruptcy. Closures and failed businesses are pegged at trillions of dollars. Though Governments across continents have responded speedily and in rare unison, the path of recovery is expected to be long and arduous. India has not been immune to this shock. "While at the aggregate level, our country has displayed remarkable resilience sustaining relatively high growth rates, several sectors have been adversely impacted. Though, there are sings today of a muted recovery, it is early days yet to signal a full-fledged revival. Despite this pall of gloom that bears on us, there are reasons to remain optimistic and confident. India's inherent strengths provide a strong foundation to better withstand the aftermath of the downturn in the global economy."[4]

Rationale of Competition Policy

The Indian corporate sector has developed a variety of strategies in the post-reform period to cope with the increasing competitive pressures due to internal and external liberalisation. With the maturing of the Indian oligopolies, the competition policy needs of the country are also undergoing changes. Some salient aspects of the changes in the Indian industrial sector are:

1. Restructuring Strategy: The Indian companies is vigorously restructuring itself. Restructuring is mainly geared towards consolidation in some important areas to correct the inefficiencies created by over-diversification in the pre-reform era.

2. Growing Pace for Acquisition: Multinational Corporations have actively participated in the merger and acquisition process to get market entry or to strengthen their presence. Acquisitions have been used by MNCs to quickly get access to various complementary assets. Indian companies are also getting overseas companies under their fold through acquisitions.

3. Competitive Access to Capital: MNCs are better placed vis-a-vis domestic firms in the acquisition game because of their deep pockets and relatively cheaper access to capital. The intentions to invest in India by MNCs are significantly influenced by these differences in the cost of capital.

4. Increasing Reliance on Foreign Technology: The reliance of the Indian companies on foreign technology purchase has increased. More and more technology flows are now tied with equity. Purchase of technology (especially foreign) is taking precedence over R and D; in house technology generation has taken a backseat. Besides, a large variety of inter-firm alliances are taking place.

5. Improving Manufacturing Capability: Indian companies are making efforts to improve manufacturing capability. This is being done through building alliances as well as through initiatives within the firm. Quality upgradation is now an important priority. However, these efforts at improving manufacturing capability may still prove to be inadequate to meet the competitive challenges. These inadequacies may also adversely affect India's chances of efficiency seeking FDI, the need for which has been emphasised.

6. Dominance of Product Differentiation Strategy: Product differentiation strategy is now dominating over other strategies of building distribution and marketing related complementary assets. Such a strategy helps Indian companies to stand up to multinationals with their strong and internationally recognised brands. Yet, because of inadequate attention to R and D and manufacturing Indian companies will not be able to improve their long term competitiveness.

7. Export Orientation: Export based growth strategies are being adopted by some Indian companies but such strategies are not widespread; export orientation increased appreciably in the early years of reform but have seen a major collapse since 1997-98. Overall, exposure to the international market is still inadequate to put the Indian companies on higher growth and learning trajectories. Quality upgradation and cost competitive should be used by Indian companies as a basic strategy in penetrating the foreign market.

Present Competition Policy

Silent features of the Competition Policy are as follows:[5]

1. Perspective of Economic Development: The Competition policy seeks to prevent restrictive business practices and market structures that significantly lessen competition. The objective of such a policy is to maintain and encourage competition in order to foster greater efficiency in resource allocation and maximise consumer welfare. The study shows that many mergers and acquisitions have taken place in India to access complementary assets like marketing, and distribution networks to reduce lags in market entry. Thus 'inefficient' domestic producers with complementary assets may become prime targets for mergers or acquisition by MNCs as economic liberalisation takes place. But these mergers may be transient or unstable and MNCs may dump the Indian partners as soon as they feel comfortable with the economic environment. In such situations, dynamic welfare effects of mergers (especially cross-border) become irrelevant though their assessment is quite difficult one.

2. Cost of Capital Advantage of MNCs : The FDI into India has been driven by the cost of capital differences corrected for expected exchange depreciation. Degree of ownership (and control) sought by MNCs are driven by the cost of capital factor. The ratio of distribution expense to all expense, which proxies for the strengths of existing (largely domestic) industry's distribution assets, had a negative influence over the desire for majority and dominant stake by the participating 'MNC'. Thus distribution assets are a countervailing strength to domestic business, and enable them to bargain for lower foreign ownership than what would otherwise have been possible. It is only the desire to be quickly off the ground that has made foreign companies with vast intangible assets or cost of capital advantage, to accommodate such local firms with significant distribution assets giving them some control through joint ventures, or otherwise.

FDI into India has been disproportionately large in capital using and infrastructure industries like power and telecom. In the power industry, the only advantage of the foreign firm is its lower cost of capital. In sectors where over and above the cost of capital advantage, intangible asset advantage also exists, the pressure on domestic firms have been too severe and many have succumbed to takeovers, or have sold out. In lifestyle associated product- markets, and in sectors which elsewhere are concentrated though not as yet in India, *i e*, sectors like fast moving consumer goods, in technology-intensive sectors, white goods and automobiles, takeovers, buyouts and investments that increase the equity stakes of foreign firms, have all increased dramatically. Financial sector reforms initiated in recent years do not seem to have mitigated the cost of capital advantages which the MNCs have vis-a-vis local firms. And therefore, unless the playing field is made more even, any competition policy initiative in India is likely to be biased in favour of the multinationals.

3. Micro-Economic Rigidities: For the policies relating to product reservation, credit, trade and tax have constrained the natural growth of a competitive small scale sector. Absence of a VAT system has also resulted in a situation that mutually beneficial linkages between small and large firms have not developed as much as they could have. If these choices are not open to domestic companies, to improve their competitiveness, competition policy alone would create large biases in favour of foreign firms. Enhancing the competitive potential of the Indian economy necessarily means higher and synergistic growth of the small scale sector and increasing inter-firm linkages especially the development of subcontracting.

4. Structural Changes in Public Sector Management: Many of the PSUs were created in India for strategic purposes. Unfortunately, they were protected from competition in a variety of ways. Absence of competitive pressures and the soft budget constraint meant that there were no pressures on these firms to be efficient. Most of the enterprises benefiting from the control and policy environment in this regard knew for certain that they would not be challenged in the domestic market. Thus, there was little incentive to work hard for the same. Thus, the great force of the market that shapes and drives firms even when present was not allowed to act. Even today, when privatisation is in the offing, most administrative ministries, at best, only dimly sense the need for competition in its most basic sense of firms being exposed to the market. Recent amendments have brought PSUs within the purview of the MRTP Act.

Besides, in the absence of managerial autonomy, the PSUs are not able to respond to the increasing competitive pressures from imports and other private domestic and foreign firms. The PSUs also carry a heavy baggage of rules and regulations which other firms do not have to carry. These constraints have to be relaxed if one expects PSUs to compete in the new environment. If this is not done, a competition policy may create a bias against the public sector. Thus, while it is important to see that public sector monopolies are not replaced by private sector monopolies, it is also necessary to create conditions wherein the PSUs, privatised or otherwise, are able to compete on 'equal' terms. To ensure that the competitive potential of the economy is unleashed to the fullest, to serve both the domestic, and the export markets, the task of privatisation should include the creation for competition in the post-privatised environment; since in that situation, even theoretically, the assumption that private monopolies would work to the common good cannot be made.

Disinvestment offers opportunities for creating competition, and strengthening the hand of potentially Indian MNCs and hence of competition and development of the industry in the long-run. But every situation is likely to be different, demanding, therefore, different solutions. The philosophy and approach of privatisation and disinvestment, at least with regard to critical public sector enterprises is, therefore, all the more urgent. Indeed, their liberation, would be necessary and vital in the industrialisation of the country itself. It would also be unfair to Indian business and to its managers to keep the current restrictions on, when they are under threat of being taken over or, their markets invaded by foreign firms. A disinvestment strategy for success would have to go beyond the current ad hocism, to integrally address, among other concerns, the issues of competition, and appropriate industry structure to ensure competition. This can only come with a fair, transparent, and publicly accepted and supported disinvestment mechanism.

5. Trade Policy as a Tool: Generally, trade liberalisation reduces the need for competition policy as anti-competitive practices are less feasible in an open economy, even when markets are concentrated. The trade policy-competition policy interface has acquired added significance in the context of the recent discussions in the WTO forums. Liberalised trade policy cannot substitute for competition law; the two complement one another in promoting trade, market access, global economic efficiency and consumer welfare. Therefore, enacting a law on competition policy is necessary, even where trade has been significantly liberalised. However, the timing or the sequencing of competition laws and other liberalisation initiatives is not very simple and needs to be thought through, in the context of the conditions prevailing in an economy. Use of 'trade disputes' to 'correct' behind the border anti-competitive practices has made the situation murky. Recent cases at the WTO highlight issues that are relevant for countries enacting or modifying their competition policies:[6]

(*i*) Given the complexities, the skill, data and resource requirements for dealing with such trade disputes through the WTO mechanism can be enormous, especially for a developing country. The coordination between departments dealing with WTO issues and competition authorities would become imminent. If a country opts for bilateral negotiations, political considerations may dominate such tasks, leading to practices like VERs and VIEs.

(*ii*) Virtually all policy instruments (*e.g*, those relating to distribution, public sector, small-scale industries, advertising), irrespective of when they were initiated, can be brought into the purview of WTO dispute settlement procedures through a so-called 'trade dispute'.

(*iii*) Such disputes not only question the freedom of the state to institute national policies but also raise doubts about what firms can or cannot do to organise their activities.

In this context, it is important to note that the Indian perspective on this issue should be that trade policy itself. It is concerned with access to markets; its aim is to remove artificial barriers to markets. Competition policy is concerned with firm behaviour in markets; it sets the rules under which firms compete with one another in markets. Economic organisation varies across countries. Neither 'firms' nor 'markets', particularly intermediate product markets, are necessarily the same in each country. Following this, policy induced closed markets need to be distinguished from 'restrictions on market access emanating from internationalization of markets' (or conversion of 'spot markets' into 'markets for long-term contracts') by firms. Competition policy does not lend itself very easily to incremental changes and certain policies that are pursued by governments may be perceived to be in the national interest.

6. Sequencing of Trade Liberalisation: The use of trade liberalization as a competition policy tool also needs to take into consideration, constraints on domestic firms that make the playing field uneven. If competition policy instruments are evenly employed to deal with anti-competitive practices across industry groups, the 'negative protection' faced by final goods producers will become even more significant. An industry specific implementation of competition policy instrument, which is increasingly the norm in most countries, will mitigate some of these problems but will increase the information, resource and skill intensity of competition law implementation. Lack of recognition of the role of macro-economic and exchange rate policy in determining a country's competitiveness is because of the excessive focus of traditional competition policy on the industry and industry structure and the hiatus between the pure and the monetary trade theories.

7. Inter-Firm Alliances: "The following suggestions provide useful pointers for policy-makers in India not only for R and D alliances but for competition policy in general."[7]

(*i*) The competition law should clarify that the rule of reason approach to be used for R and D alliances will explicitly take into account the appropriability regime, the pace of technological change, the diversity of the sources of new technology, the need to access complementary assets and technologies and the need to have cooperation for feedback across the technology supply chain.

(*ii*) Agreements covering technology development, standards etc among firms having moderate market share (20-25 per cent) should be explicitly exempt from anti-trust liability. The market share can even be higher in case of those product groups where import competition is possible.

(*iii*) Market definition should be tailored to the context of innovation and should focus primarily on the market for knowledge. Specific product markets should become relevant only when commercialization is included within the scope of the cooperative agreement. Even while analysing product market issues, extent of appropriability should be explicitly considered. The geographic market should be presumed to be worldwide, with the burden upon the challenger to demonstrate otherwise.

(*iv*) The competition law should not bias the selection of inter-firm organizational forms; integration by contract on alliance should be treated as favourably as full mergers.

(*v*) The law should explicitly include joint commercialisation efforts to exploit innovation as a part of R and D cooperation arrangements.

(*vi*) An administrative procedure should be created to evaluate cooperative arrangements among firms with higher (than 20-25 per cent) market shares for their dynamic efficiency gains and anticompetitive nature. Such administrative procedure should not be clearance oriented. Processes could be such as to result in sufficient incentives for regulatory bodies to detect and prove cases of abusive cooperative arrangements. Pro-competitive and efficient arrangements can be certified to pre-empt antitrust litigation in future. Inter firm alliances can be an important conduit for technological capability building in firms of developing countries.

8. IPRs Environment: With growing dependence on foreign sources of technologies such abuses may have a negative influence on technological capability building in developing countries. Therefore, countries like India should explicitly recognise the interplay between IPR and competition policies. Moreover, expenditure on R & D programmes are required to reduce the dependence of Indian Companies on foreign companies. Ultimately, technological capability will help the Indian companies to have a competitive strength in the long term.

9. Competition Law and its Administration: With the increase in the complexity of the issues at stake, skill requirements for the adequate functioning of a competition authority too, have risen significantly in recent years. it is extremely important to develop: (a) An independent competition law authority with adequate financial and skill resources at its disposal; (b) Institutional structures which minimise the overlap between various regulatory authorities and competition authority; and (c) Cooperative links with other agencies at the regional and the global level, to access to online data bases and help handle international cartels.

Overall, MRTPC is not seen as an agency which has the capability to do a fair, expeditious and transparent assessment of competition related problems. These factors and the absence of various other mechanisms in place in other countries, have been partly responsible for the distrust with which the regulatory authorities in India are seen by the general public.

Regulatory Framework of Competition in India

It is increasingly recognized that in a sound business climate, investors face relatively low entry and exit barriers and are protected against the risk of expropriation and abuse while consumers are protected against malpractices of trade and industry. The consumers are also ensured availability of acceptable quality goods and services in abundance and at affordable price. Laws have to change with the changing needs to the society. Old laws have to be altered, amended or repealed, while at times new laws have to be created to replace the existing laws. In other words, a law once enacted cannot remain a static piece of legislation, but has to respond to the needs of the time. The Government needs to keep a hawk like eye and ensure that the existing laws are constantly reviewed, changed repealed and replaced as may be the demands of the situation. Competition law is an example of the Government wanting to meet the needs of the changing times.

Historical Perspective

After the independence of the country in 1947, the Government of India adopted socialism as the cornerstone of Indian economy. As a result, instead of working on measures that would generate national wealth in the private and public sector, the Government of India was more interested in putting measures in place that would control and regulated trade and industry in the country. Profit was a dirty word in that era and big business was viewed with suspicion by the government. The government efforts were concentrated on ensuring that monopolistic business organizations were not created. To achieve that goal Government appointed a committee to provide necessary support.

Based on the report of the Committee, the Government enacted a law in 1969 called "Monopolies and Restrictive Trade Practices Act, 1969 (MRTP Act). The main object of the MRTP Act, as stated in the preamble, was to ensure that there was no concentration of economic power and there was control of monopolies and prohibition of monopolistic and restrictive trade practices. In other words, business should not become so big or resort to such policies that the consumer becomes the victim. Accordingly, a MRTP Commission was constituted to administer the Act. The MRTP Act was enacted in the era of licence and permit raj that believed in imposing control on trade and industry. Monopoly in trade and industry was regarded as bad in law. Though public interest and consumer welfare were at the core of the objectives of the said Act, as yet the concept of 'market economy, was not fully conceived then.

Need for Competition Law

Since 1970 the MRTP Act was amended several times to suit the conditions in the country. However, broadly the same situation continued right through the 70's and 80's. "It was only with the opening up of the economy in 1991 and the change in the philosophy of the government that brought about a dramatic shift in the economic scenario of the country. It was felt that the MRTP Act had outlived its utility and it no longer served the purpose in the changed environment. However, it was realized that there was no room for tinkering with the existing law and there was a need for a comprehensive competition law."[8]

(*i*) It was expected that the open market economy would ensure adequate competition, at the same time experience in other countries had indicated that some enterprises do try to undermine the market by resorting to anti-competitive practices for short term gain e.g. resorting to cartels, or companies with market power resorting to extortionist or predatory pricing. Hence, it was felt that such practices could nullify the gains from competition, which could be answered only by having a competition law.

(*ii*) There was a growing demand from the international community that India should not only do away with the MRTP Act, but also have specific law governing competition in business. To address this issue, the Government of India set up a Committee to review the provisions of MRTP Act. The Committee opined that it would not be enough to amend the MRTP Act and stressed the need for a new competition law to replace the MRTP Act.

(*iii*) "In the new economic era, it was found that the MRTP Act had "become obsolete in certain respects in the light of international economic developments relating more particularly to competition laws, and there (was) need to shift the focus from curbing monopolies to promoting competition." This led to enactment of the Competition Act, 2002.

Competition Act, 2002

The enactment of the Competition Act and its enforcement by an autonomous Commission is a key component in dealing with issues of competition. Competition Law & Policy result in equity among producers and reduce rent-seeking behaviour on their part. It is this imperative which has persuaded countries to either enact new law or to modernize their existing competition laws. The number of countries having a competition law has risen from 35 in 1995 to around 106 as on date. In line with the international trend and to cope with the changing realities, India has reviewed the Monopolies and Restrictive Trade Practices Act, 1969 and has enacted the Competition Act, 2002 (the Act) with many innovative features w.e.f 14 January 03. The Act seeks to repeal the M.R.T.P. Act and to dissolve the M.R.T.P. Commission from the date it is notified as such by the Central Government.

Accordingly, a new enactment was brought on the statute book namely, "The Competition Act, 2002", which received assent from the President of India on 13th January, 2003 and was published in the official gazette on 14th January, 2003. Interestingly, only some of the provisions were brought into force on 31st March, 2003, while some more provisions became from April.01, 2008. The Competition Act can be broadly divided into four parts:[9]

1. Anti-Competition Agreements
2. Abuse of Dominance
3. Combinations Regulation
4. Competition Advocacy

Unlike the MRTP Act, the thrust of the Competition Act is not on preventing growth, but ensuring that growth and size are not used to abuse the position in the market place.

The Competition Commission under the Act is to enquire into cases relating to Anti-Competitive Agreement, Abuse of Dominant position by an enterprise and Combinations through a process of Enquiry. The Commission is empowered to hold meetings at such times and places as per the procedures laid down in the regulations. All questions / issues that come up before any meeting of the Commission shall be decided by a majority of Members present through voting; in the event of equality of votes, the Chairperson (or presiding Member) shall have a second or casting vote. Every meeting of the Commission is required to have a quorum of three Members. The Commission is not bound by the Civil Procedure Code and has the power to regulate its own procedure.

After an Enquiry, in case the Commission finds that any agreement referred to in Section 3 or action of an enterprise in a dominant position is in contravention of Section 3 or 4, it may pass all or any of the following orders, namely:[10]

(i) direction to discontinue and not to re-enter such agreement or discontinue abuse of dominance;

(ii) impose penalty;

(iii) direct modification of agreement;

(iv) direction to abide by such other order including payment of costs;

(v) pass such other order as it may deem fit.

Likewise, the Commission is empowered to enquire into certain Combinations involving Enterprises, the turnover or assets of which exceed the threshold limits prescribed in the Act. The Commission after due procedure may approve, approve with modification or reject the proposed combination and declare the Combination Agreement as void.

The key factor in case of Anti-Competitive Agreements and Combinations is adverse appreciable effect on competition, in market, in India. The parameters to determine relevant market, relevant product market, relevant geographical market and factors to assess the appreciable adverse effect on competition in markets, in India have been prescribed in the Act itself and are to be determined by the Commission. A condition precedent to taking an action with respect to abuse of dominant position is that the alleged delinquent enterprise must have dominance in the relevant market. The factors which shall be taken into account to determine dominance and the situations when such dominance is to be construed as Abuse thereof are also prescribed in the Act.

The Commission is empowered to restrain any party from carrying on an act in contravention of sub-section (1) of Section 3 or sub-section (1) of Section 4 of the Act until the conclusion of such inquiry or until further orders, without giving notice to such party, where it deems it necessary. The Commission is assisted by a Director General who is under obligation, on the direction of the Commission, to carry out and furnish Investigation Reports into the contraventions of the provisions of the Act. He is to assist the Commission also in carriage of proceedings of Enquiries which are initiated by the Commission upon its own knowledge or information (suo motu) besides such other duties as are entrusted to it by the Commission.

The Commission is also assisted by the Secretary who besides being the custodian of the Records of the Commission is required to perform such other functions as are prescribed under the Act, Rules, and Regulations and such other duties as are entrusted to him by the Commission. Appeals against the orders of the Commission can be made before the Competition Appellate Tribunal. The Competition Commission of India is being guided by the following principles in its approach to its work:

1. To be in sync with markets; have good understanding of market forces.

2. To minimize cost of compliance by enterprises, and cost of enforcement by Commission.
3. To maintain confidentiality of business information; to maintain transparency in Commission's own operations.
4. To be a professional body, equipped with requisite skills.
5. To maintain a consultative approach.

Global Competitiveness

Global competitiveness of any nation is a function of joint effort made by its government, people and institutions. While there has been a major debate on the role of Government in opening the economy and accelerating the pace of economic reforms in the country, it is important to understand that these measures alone cannot enable India to become a competitive nation. However, effective action is required at the industry level and more specifically at the micro level. i.e. at the firm level.

The recent global financial meltdown is indeed an important wake up call for the world economy. It is more than evident today that Economic Growth and Sustainable Development are not necessarily the same thing. The last century and a half, since the Industrial Revolution, has witnessed unparallel material development. Unfortunately, such material development has come at a significant cost

It is indeed a tragedy that more than half of the global population is still plagued by the worst forms of poverty, hunger and disease. A UNDP Report prepared a few years ago, pointed out that 10% of the richest adults in the world own as much as 85% of the world's household wealth, while the bottom 50% have to contend with only 1% of household wealth. These widening income inequities are indeed a source of widespread discontent and social alienation. The specter of social unrest and terrorism threaten every corner of the world today. This divide is of even more concern to developing nations. With large numbers of people living on the edge of despair and insecurity, these disparities make them extremely vulnerable and create unstable societies.

Aggravating these inequities in the tremendous strain imposed on nature's life support systems. For decades, the growth process has paid scant attention to replenishing the rich natural resources inherited over many generations. As a consequence, in less than half a century, the world has lost the fourth of its topsoil and a third of its forest cover. In the last 35 years alone, a third of global bio-diversity was forfeited. Scientific evidence today confirms that humanity's demand on the planets living resources now exceeds its regenerative capacity by a wide margin. It now takes the earth one year and four months to regenerate resources used in a single year. And if this continues apace, the equivalent of the two Earths will be needed to support humanity's resource requirements by mid 2030. The current global economic model is therefore clearly unsustainable.

Indeed the world has been living far beyond its means. And in the process, the future has been seriously compromised. The global economic model has perpetuated a system of reward that focuses only on the generation of financial returns. In such an environment, the source of competitiveness for business is derived from a relatively narrow purpose of expanding consumer franchise and enhancing shareholder value. Conventional Balance Sheets and Profit and Loss Statements also do not take into account the cost burden of social inequities and ecological destruction. Unfortunately, such an approach has left a deferred cost burden to be borne by society and future generations. And that cost is today spiraling out of control, threading future economic progress.

A New Paradigm of Competitiveness

Changing scenario of environment requires business to shape a totally new paradigm of competitiveness. A strategic that will require business to build capabilities to addresses the stringent demand of a low-carbon global business environment. For a country, like India with millions below the poverty line and nearly 12 million people entering the job market every year, a competitive low carbon strategy of growth will also have to generate incremental employment and livelihoods. Therefore, for Indian business, this new paradigm of competitiveness will not only require the creation of "green businesses" but also the generation of "green livelihoods".

In the years ahead, a heightened level of consumer concern and greater social awareness will compel businesses to demonstrate their response to a low carbon regime through their products and practices. It is, therefore, entirely in the enlightened self interest of business to integrate this new paradigm in their business strategies. Going forward, competitiveness and profitability will be increasingly linked to the ability of business to make carbon reduction and the creation of sustainable livelihoods an integral part of their value propositions to their customers.

"Innovation, Incentivisation, and Inclusiveness hold the key to crafting this new dimension of competitiveness. Innovation in technology, processes and business models that enables achievement of a low carbon high growth economy. Incentives that encourage and reward the adoption of corporate strategies which go beyond the traditional frontiers of the market to achieve a larger societal contribution. Inclusiveness in aligning all forces be it public, private and people partnerships, or the power of supportive fiscal policies, financial initiatives and market institutions to achieve a common shared goal."[11]

Globally, energy constitutes the largest source of emissions contributing to global warming. India's challenges here is manifold. On the one hand, energy consumption needs to increase to fulfill India's developmental requirements as well as enlarge employment and income opportunities. On the other hand, affordable clean energy solutions are required to create a cost competitive low carbon economic environment. A larger emphasis on renewable sources is therefore imperative. The National Action Plan on climate change have launched several missions to address this extremely challenging tasks. The National mission on Solar Energy, Enhanced Energy Efficiency and Sustainable Habitants contain specific measures to move towards a low carbon strategy of growth.

The new paradigm of competitiveness makes it incumbent on businesses to progressively reduce its overall carbon footprint. Sustainable manufacturing competitiveness will require an aggressive strategy to reduce specific energy consumption.

Changing Perspective of Development and Competitiveness

The demands on businesses today to achieve a low carbon growth strategy that is also sustainable and inclusive, often makes it a tall order to follow. The primary reason is that markets seldom reward such long term endeavors. Markets, as they are constructed today, are attuned primarily, to reward financial performance irrespective of its carbon efficiency and capability to create sustainable and inclusive growth.

A recent global events have shown, markets on their own cannot be expected to deliver the imperatives of sustainable development. Therefore, it is time to craft a new path that places a premium on sustainable development. This obviously requires a completely new set of drivers and an enabling institutional framework. It is no longer a matter of choice. No single organ of society, be it the Government or Business, can meet the challenges on its own. These challenges can only be met by all sections of society joining hands to build a new paradigm of development. A new paradigm that creates new market drivers to propel sustainable growth strategy.

There are two important drivers that will enable a paradigm change:

(*i*) First and foremost is the imperative need to align the policies and regulations to encourage the conduct a business in a manner that results in the achievement of a positive carbon footprints and also supports the creation of societal capital If differential and preferential incentives, in the form of fiscal and financial benefits, were to flow to companies with sustainable business practices, powerful market drivers would emerge to support such endeavors of companies.

(*ii*) The second issue relates to a theme "Making Market Work for CSR". The most potent force that can trigger a complete rethink of corporate strategy and bring about transformational change lies in the power of the civil society. Civil society, by exercising their consumer franchise in favour of sustainable practices. Consumer preference for such responsible conduct will translate the commitments and investments made in building societal capital into financial rewards.

An aware civil society can therefore drive the creation of a market for responsible sustainable practices. However, such a market can only come about through enhanced education and heightened awareness. Particularly, awareness of the power that civil society can wield as Responsible Consumers and Investors. For this to happen, a creditable system of information must be made available to consumers so that they are able to make an informed and responsible choice. Financial Auditors and Credit Rating Agencies evaluate companies on their financial strengths and make such information available so that investors are able to make informed choices. Similarly, it is important to create s system of measurement and rating to evaluate the company's ecological and social impact. These ratings could be displayed on products and services enabling civil society to make an informed choice in favour companies that demonstrate sustainable business practices.

Factors Governing Global Competitiveness

The factors considered for global competitiveness by the World Economic Forum are:"[12]

(*a*) Openness: i.e. openness to foreign trade and investment, foreign direct investment and financial flows, exchange rate policy and ease of exporting.

(*b*) Government: This measures the role of the State in the economy. It includes the overall burden of government expenditures, fiscal deficits, rates of public saving, marginal tax rates and the overall competence of the civil service.

(*c*) Finance: This is a measure of how efficiently the financial intermediaries channel savings into productive investment, the level of competition in financial markets, the perceived stability and solvency of key financial institutions, levels of national saving and investment, and credit ratings given by outside observers.

(*d*) Infrastructure: This factor measures the quality of roads, railways, ports, telecommunications, cost of air transportation and overall infrastructure investment.

(*e*) Technology: This assesses computer usage, the spread of new technologies, the ability of the economy to absorb new technologies and the level and quality of research and development.

(*f*) Management: Management measures overall management quality, marketing, staff training and motivation practices, efficiency of compensation schemes and the quality of internal financial control systems.

(*g*) Labour: This factor measures the efficiency and competitiveness of the domestic labour market. It combines a measure of the level of a country's labour costs relative to international norms, together with measures of labour market efficiency (e.g. obstacles to hiring and firing of workers), the level of basic education and skills, and extent of disctoritionary labour taxes.

(*h*) Institutions: This factor measures the extent of corruption and vulnerability to organized crime.

Dimension of Global Competitiveness

Following dimensions are quite relevant in improving the Competitiveness of a nation:

1. Customer Centralism: One of the most important factors that make companies more competitive is their strong customer centralism. Customer is a human being with his own set of emotions, concerns and problems. The customer wants to buy only if somebody is willing to listen to him or her. "Various researches showed that the Indian housewife had different needs and hence required different products and brands for different use situations. The market generally segmented on the basis of demographic, psychographic, use situations, and decision criteria like price senility. On the basis of survey research the corporate management identified opportunities both at the low and the top end of the market. "[13] Customer centralism is not just introducing multiple brands and products for different markets. It goes beyond. It is a philosophy, which is geared to integrate the customer with the organization. Hence, the above-mentioned companies extensively use interactive technologies like Toll-free phone, CRM and e-CRM packages and have internalized one message, viz. speed in responding to the customer.

2. Products/Services quality: The global leaders are fetish about the quality of their products/services. This is one area where they do not wish to compromise. They know that the cost of replacement of a product or the cost of recovering lost moments in service industry is significantly high. These companies work at six sigma levels meaning virtually, a zero defect product or service. It creates a high degree of customer satisfaction and bondage. Quality in these companies is not just a statistical function. It is a part of the culture, which encourages quality in each and every facet of organizational life, be it recruiting, supplier selection, technology selection, manufacturing process, marketing and sales and service processes.

"Value maximization occurs only when firms are able to deliver world-class quality products and services to the customer at an affordable local price. The implication is that organizations will have to benchmark the quality of the products and services with the world's best and control the costs so as to enable the customer to buy them at a price he/she can afford."[14] Today Indian Companies are trying to offer premium quality products and services at the most affordable price, thereby creating a strong competition for even their American counterparts in the American market itself.

3. Volumes vs. Margins: With the technology changing the market and competition rules, there seems to be a lack of understanding that a firm has to achieve economies of scale and scope in production, marketing and almost in its entire operations. These economies of scale and scope cannot come about only by producing for the local markets. "What is needed today is to aggressively hunt for market opportunities in different countries. While it is a known fact that overseas marketing is a high cost/high risk alternative, the Indian firms have to understand that there is no other road. Perhaps they will have to examine the possibilities of strategic alliances, joint ventures and even consortium marketing to penetrate the foreign markets and create a niche for themselves. It is the volumes alone that will help Indian companies come out of the financial traps. This would obviously mean that the margins will have to be sacrificed and in some cases these companies will have to consider even contribution pricing strategy to penetrate overseas markets."[15] There is no point of looking at the government for solution or for help in reducing the cost of creating an entry barrier in the Indian market against foreign competition. The Government should bargain for an increased access to the overseas markets for the Indian products and services. In the domestic market, they will have to look at rural markets, and the ways to penetrate them through a change in packaging or a change in the price structures.

4. Innovation: The globally competitive companies understand that their national and international competitiveness rest squarely on a continuous improvement, innovation and change. Today the pressure for innovation on a continuing basis is substantially high. It is not merely important that the companies' products and services are available at the lowest cost or affordable prices in all markets but equally important is the fact that these are perceived as being innovative by the customers. Equally important is the fact that company and brand must continuously be perceived as contemporary, innovative and friendly. The pressure for innovation is also today from the markets. With the technology and customers changing rapidly, there is no other way but to be alive to these changes and continuously innovate.

"Innovation is a creative process. One of the most significant parameters that encourages creative thinking the organizational leadership that tolerates failure and is willing to invest in discovering unknown future. This obviously implies that the innovation process is both outward and inward looking simultaneously. The former involves continuous interaction between the research and marketing teams with the market place and the latter rests on organizational culture."[16] Innovation involves questioning the existing ways of doing the business and examining new ways of achieving the same. It is, therefore, the first reduction to practice of an idea in an organizational culture, and hence, more radical the idea, the more traumatic and profound its impact on organization. Even through organizations understand the importance of innovation they rarely try to encourage it. This is largely because often innovation creates ambiguities of which human beings are scared. Innovative organizations emphasis on building an atmosphere and a vision that encourages continuous change and innovative practices.

Today, an increasing variety of creative relationships exists in which innovative companies participate as joint ventures, consortium members, limited partners, major academic funding resource, venture capitalist spin off equity holders and so on. Innovative companies rely less on market researchers and more on interactive developments with lead customers. Their understanding is that formal market analysis continues to be useful for extending existing products lines but is often misleading in the case of rapid radical innovation. Thus, innovation process is not an incremental growth but a leapfrog strategy.

5. Entrepreneurial Spirit: Entrepreneurship is a driving force of all change and growth. In an entrepreneurial organization, leadership and strategic vision takes precedence. These organizations are value creators. The value creations logic rest on finding an answer to the question what is unique or distinct about the way in which we create the value. Value creation does not just imply maximizing shareholder value. Rather it is all about utility and functionality and hence refers to the value it delivers to those whom it serves, that is the stakeholders. "Profits and growth are the outcomes of an effective value creation process. Value creation can be achieved through the process of innovation. Once again innovation involves risk and entrepreneurs are those who thrive on risks. It is this entrepreneurship of entrepreneurial spirit in the organization that can make an organization competitive."[17]

6. Strategic Leadership: Global companies are quite successful due to their strategic leadership. Jack Welch, Bill Gates, late Shri HT Parekh, Adity Puri, KV Kamath, Narayana Murthy and Naresh Goel have one thing in common. They are all strategic and visionary leaders. Each of them has had a long-term vision of creating future and changing the paradigms in the industry. Not only so, they are the leaders who have created, in their own organizations, a vision community, who share the dream of taking the organization to the top of the rank, not only in their own industry but worldwide also.

7. Organizational Culture and Climate: Globally competitive organizations believe in empowering people and developing a learning culture. This obviously implies that they encourage their people to continuously learn from their experience and that of others both within industry and outside. These are the organizations that are open to ideas from all sources. Shared leadership and teamwork are another facet of these organizations. In fact, these are the organization where one feels always refreshed and charged. These are also the organization where learning and working is fun and one can sense and feel healthy organizational atmosphere.

Thus, the global competitiveness in Indian industry can be brought about only when the managements understand and internalize the processes of innovation, creativity, strategic leadership and customer centralism. There is no other alternative to survival. Indian companies and organizations will have to be globally competitive, which would even mean going global through strategic alliance, takeovers and B2B initiatives. The Indian industry has to act fast and in a decisive manner. This millennium will belong to entrepreneurial organizations that will dare to challenge to existing paradigms and create a new future. It will certainly not belong to the old conventional business leaders. For global competitiveness of entrepreneurial firms is far higher than the bureaucratic organizations.

The Competition Act, 2002

(No. 12 of 2003)

The Competition Act was enacted in 2002 and got the assent on 13-1-2003. It is an Act to provide, keeping in view of the economic development of the country, for the establishment of a Commission to prevent practices having adverse effect on competition, to promote and sustain competition in markets, to protect the interests of consumers and to ensure freedom of trade carried on by other participants in markets, in India, and for matters connected therewith or incidental thereto.

Salient features of the Act

Salient features of the act are as follows:

CHAPTER I
PRELIMINARY

1. Short title, extent and commencement : (1) This Act may be called the Competition Act, 2002.

(2) It extends to the whole of India except the State of Jammu and Kashmir.

(3) It shall come into force on such date as the Central Government may, by notification in the Official Gazette, appoint:

Provided that different dates may be appointed for different provisions of this Act and any reference in any such provision to the commencement of this Act shall be construed as a reference to the coming into force of that provision.

2. Definitions: In this Act, unless the context otherwise requires,—

(a) "acquisition" means, directly or indirectly, acquiring or agreeing to acquire—

(*i*) shares, voting rights or assets of any enterprise; or

(*ii*) control over management or control over assets of any enterprise;

(*b*) "agreement" includes any arrangement or understanding or action in concert,—

(*i*) whether or not, such arrangement, understanding or action is formal or in writing; or

(*ii*) whether or not such arrangement, understanding or action is intended to be enforceable by legal proceedings;

(c) "cartel" includes an association of producers, sellers, distributors, traders or service providers who, by agreement amongst themselves, limit, control or attempt to control the production, distribution, sale or price of, or, trade in goods or provision of services;

(d) "Chairperson" means the Chairperson of the Commission appointed under sub-section (1) of section 8;

(e) "Commission" means the Competition Commission of India established under sub section (1) of section 7;

(f) "consumer" means any person who

(i) buys any goods for a consideration which has been paid or promised or partly paid and partly promised, or under any system of deferred payment and includes any user of such goods other than the person who buys such goods for consideration paid or promised or partly paid or partly promised, or under any system of deferred payment when such use is made with the approval of such person, whether such purchase of goods is for resale or for any commercial purpose or for personal use;

(*ii*) hires or avails of any services for a consideration which has been paid or promised or partly paid and partly promised, or under any system of deferred payment and includes any beneficiary of such services other than the person who hires or avails of the services for consideration paid or promised, or partly paid and partly promised, or under any system of deferred payment, when such services are availed of with the approval of the first-mentioned person whether such hiring or availing of services is for any commercial purpose or for personal use;

(*g*) "Director General" means the Director General appointed under sub-section (1) of section 16 and includes any Additional, Joint, Deputy or Assistant Directors General appointed under that section;

(*h*) "enterprise" means a person or a department of the Government, who or which is, or has been, engaged in any activity, relating to the production, storage, supply, distribution, acquisition or control of articles or goods, or the provision of services, of any kind, or in investment, or in the business of acquiring, holding, underwriting or dealing with shares, debentures or other securities of any other body corporate, either directly or through one or more of its units or divisions or subsidiaries, whether such unit or division or subsidiary is located at the same place where the enterprise is located or at a different place or at different places, but does not include any activity of the Government relatable to the sovereign functions of the Government including all activities carried on by the departments of the Central Government dealing with atomic energy, currency, defence and space.

CHAPTER II
PROHIBITION OF CERTAIN AGREEMENTS, ABUSE OF DOMINANT POSITION AND REGULATION OF COMBINATIONS

Prohibition of agreements

3. Anti competitive agreements : (1) No enterprise or association of enterprises or person or association of persons shall enter into any agreement in respect of production, supply, distribution, storage, acquisition or control of goods or provision of services, which causes or is likely to cause an appreciable adverse effect on competition within India.

(2) Any agreement entered into in contravention of the provisions contained in subsection shall be void.

(3) Any agreement entered into between enterprises or associations of enterprises or persons or associations of persons or between any person and enterprise or practice carried on, or decision taken by, any association of enterprises or association of persons, including cartels, engaged in identical or similar trade of goods or provision of services, which

(*a*) directly or indirectly determines purchase or sale prices;

(*b*) limits or controls production, supply, markets, technical development, investment or provision of services;

(*c*) shares the market or source of production or provision of services by way of allocation of geographical area of market, or type of goods or services, or number of customers in the market or any other similar way;

(*d*) directly or indirectly results in bid rigging or collusive bidding, shall be presumed to have an appreciable adverse effect on competition:

Provided that nothing contained in this sub-section shall apply to any agreement entered into by way of joint ventures if such agreement increases efficiency in production, supply, distribution, storage, acquisition or control of goods or provision of services.

(4) Any agreement amongst enterprises or persons at different stages or levels of the production chain in different markets, in respect of production, supply, distribution, storage, sale or price of, or trade in goods or provision of services, including—

(*a*) tie-in arrangement;

(*b*) exclusive supply agreement;

(*c*) exclusive distribution agreement;

(*d*) refusal to deal;

(*e*) resale price maintenance, shall be an agreement in contravention of sub-section (1) if such agreement causes or is likely to cause an appreciable adverse effect on competition in India.

(5) Nothing contained in this section shall restrict—

(*i*) the right of any person to restrain any infringement of, or to impose reasonable conditions, as may be necessary for protecting any of his rights which have been or may be conferred upon him under—

(*a*) the Copyright Act, 1957 (14 of 1957);

(*b*) the Patents Act, 1970 (39 of 1970);

(*c*) the Trade and Merchandise Marks Act, 1958 (43 of 1958) or the Trade Marks Act, 1999 (47 of 1999);

(*d*) the Geographical Indications of Goods (Registration and Protection) Act, 1999 (48 of 1999);

(*e*) the Designs Act, 2000 (16 of 2000);

(*f*) the Semi-conductor Integrated Circuits Layout-Design Act, 2000 (37 of 2000);

(*ii*) the right of any person to export goods from India to the extent to which the agreement relates exclusively to the production, supply, distribution or control of goods or provision of services for such export.

Prohibition of abuse of dominant position

4. Abuse of dominant position: (1) No enterprise shall abuse its dominant position.

(2) There shall be an abuse of dominant position under sub-section (1), if an enterprise.—

(*a*) directly or indirectly, imposes unfair or discriminatory—

(i) condition in purchase or sale of goods or service; or

(ii) price in purchase or sale (including predatory price) of goods or service,

(*b*) limits or restricts—

(i) production of goods or provision of services or market therefore; or

(ii) technical or scientific development relating to goods or services to the prejudice of consumers; or

(*c*) indulges in practice or practices resulting in denial of market access; or

(*d*) makes conclusion of contracts subject to acceptance by other parties of supplementary obligations which, by their nature or according to commercial usage, have no connection with the subject of such contracts; or

(*e*) uses its dominant position in one relevant market to enter into, or protect, other relevant market.

5. Combination : The acquisition of one or more enterprises by one or more persons or merger or amalgamation of enterprises shall be a combination of such enterprises and persons or enterprises, if—

(a) any acquisition where—

(i) the parties to the acquisition, being the acquirer and the enterprise, whose control, shares, voting rights or assets have been acquired or are being acquired jointly.

(*ii*) the group, to which the enterprise whose control, shares, assets or voting rights have been acquired or are being acquired, would belong after the acquisition, jointly have or would jointly.

(b) acquiring of control by a person over an enterprise when such person has already direct or indirect control over another enterprise engaged in production, distribution or trading of a similar or identical or substitutable goods or provision of a similar or identical or substitutable service, if

6. Regulation of combinations: No person or enterprise shall enter into a combination which causes or is likely to cause an appreciable adverse effect on competition within the relevant market in India and such a combination shall be void.

CHAPTER III
COMPETITION COMMISSION OF INDIA

7. Establishment of Commission: (1) With effect from such date as the Central Government may, by notification, appoint, there shall be established, for the purposes of this Act, a Commission to be called the "Competition Commission of India".

(2) The Commission shall be a body corporate by the name aforesaid having perpetual succession and a common seal with power, subject to the provisions of this Act, to acquire, hold and dispose of property, both movable and immovable, and to contract and shall, by the said name, sue or be sued,

(3) The head office of the Commission shall be at such place as the Central Government may decide from time to time.

(4) The Commission may establish offices at other places in India.

8. Composition of Commission: (1) The Commission shall consist of a Chairperson and not less than two and not more than ten other Members to be appointed by the Central Government:

Provided that the Central Government shall appoint the Chairperson and a Member during the first year of the establishment of the Commission.

(2) The Chairperson and every other Member shall be a person of ability, integrity and standing and who, has been, or is qualified to be, a judge of a High Court; or, has special knowledge of, and professional experience of not less than fifteen years in international trade, economics, business, commerce, law, finance, accountancy, management, industry, public affairs, administration or in any other matter which, in the opinion of the Central Government, may be useful to the Commission.

(3) The Chairperson and other Members shall be whole-time Members.

9. Selection of Chairperson and other Members: The Chairperson and other Members shall be selected in the manner as may be prescribed.

10. Term of office of Chairperson and other Members : (1) The Chairperson and every other Member shall hold office as such for a term of five years from the date on which he enters upon his office and shall be eligible for re-appointment:

Provided that no Chairperson or other Member shall hold office as such after he has attained,—

(*a*) in the case of the Chairperson, the age of sixty-seven years;

(*b*) in the case of any other Member, the age of sixty-five years.

(2) A vacancy caused by the resignation or removal of the Chairperson or any other Member under section 11 or by death or otherwise shall be filled by fresh appointment in accordance with the provisions of sections 8 and 9.

(3) The Chairperson and every other Member shall, before entering upon his office, make and subscribe to an oath of office and of secrecy in such form, manner and before such authority, as may be prescribed.

(4) In the event of the occurrence of a vacancy in the office of the Chairperson by reason of his death, resignation or otherwise, the senior-most Member shall act as the Chairperson, until the date on which a new Chairperson, appointed in accordance with the provisions of this Act to fill such vacancy, enters upon his office.

(5) When the Chairperson is unable to discharge his functions owing to absence, illness or any other cause, the senior-most Member shall discharge the functions of the Chairperson until the date on which the Chairperson resumes the charge of his functions.

11. Resignation, removal and suspension of Chairperson and other members :(1) The Chairperson or any other Member may, by notice in writing under his hand addressed to the Central Government, resign his office:

Provided that the Chairperson or a Member shall, unless he is permitted by the Central Government to relinquish his office sooner, continue to hold office until the expiry of three months from the date of receipt of such notice or until a person duly appointed as his successor enters upon his office or until the expiry of his term of office, whichever is the earliest.

(2) Notwithstanding anything contained in sub-section (1), the Central Government may, by order, remove the Chairperson or any other Member from his office if such Chairperson or Member, as the case may be.

12. Restriction on employment of Chairperson and other Members in certain cases: The Chairperson and other Members shall not, for a period of one year from the date on which they cease to hold office, accept any employment in, or connected with the management or administration of, any enterprise which has been a party to a proceeding before the Commission under this Act:

13. Financial and administrative powers of Member Administration: The Central Government shall designate any Member as Member Administration who shall exercise such financial and administrative powers as may be vested in him under the rules made by the Central Government:

Provided that the Member Administration shall have authority to delegate such of his financial and administrative powers as he may think fit to any other officer of the Commission subject to the condition that such officer shall, while exercising such delegated powers continue to act under the direction, superintendence and control of the Member Administration.

14. Salary and allowances and other terms and conditions of service of Chairperson and other Members: (1) The salary, and the other terms and conditions of service, of the Chairperson and other Members, including travelling expenses, house rent allowance and conveyance facilities, sumptuary allowance and medical facilities shall be such as may be prescribed.

(2) The salary, allowances and other terms and conditions of service of the Chairperson or a Member shall not be varied to his disadvantage after appointment.

15. Vacancy, etc. not to invalidate proceedings of Commission : No act or proceeding of the Commission shall be invalid merely by reason of—10

(*a*) any vacancy in, or any defect in the constitution of, the Commission; or

(*b*) any defect in the appointment of a person acting as a Chairperson or as a Member; or

(*c*) any irregularity in the procedure of the Commission not affecting the merits of the case.

16. Appointment of Director General, etc. : (1) The Central Government may, by notification, appoint a Director General and as many Additional, Joint, Deputy or Assistant Directors General or such other advisers, consultants or officers, as it may think fit, for the purposes of assisting the Commission in conducting inquiry into contravention of any of the provisions of this Act and for the conduct of cases before the Commission and for performing such other functions as are, or may be, provided by or under this Act.

(2) Every Additional, Joint, Deputy and Assistant Directors General or such other advisers, consultantsand officers, shall exercise his powers, and discharge his functions, subject to the general control, supervision and direction of the Director General.

(3) The salary, allowances and other terms and conditions of service of the Director General and Additional, Joint, Deputy and Assistant Directors General or such other advisers, consultants or officers, shall be such as may be prescribed.

(4) The Director General and Additional, Joint, Deputy and Assistant Directors General or such other advisers, consultants or officers shall be appointed from amongst persons of integrity and outstanding ability and who have experience in investigation, and knowledge of accountancy, management, business, public administration, international trade, law or economics and such other qualifications as may be prescribed.

17. Registrar and officers and other employees of Commission : (1) The Commission may appoint a Registrar and such officers and other employees as it considers necessary for the efficient performance of its functions under this Act.

(2) The salaries and allowances payable to and other terms and conditions of service of the Registrar and officers and other employees of the Commission and the number of such officers and other employees shall be such as may be prescribed.

CHAPTER IV
DUTIES, POWERS AND FUNCTIONS OF COMMISSION

18. Duties of Commission : Subject to the provisions of this Act, it shall be the duty of the Commission to eliminate practices having adverse effect on competition, promote and sustain competition, protect the interests of consumers and ensure freedom of trade carried on by other participants, in markets in India:

Provided that the Commission may, for the purpose of discharging its duties or performing its functions under this Act, enter into any memorandum or arrangement with the prior approval of the Central Government, with any agency of any foreign country.

19. Inquiry into certain agreements and dominant position of enterprise : (1) The Commission may inquire into any alleged contravention of the provisions contained in subsection (1) of section 3 or sub-section (1) of section 4 either on its own motion or on—

(*a*) receipt of a complaint, accompanied by such fee as may be determined by regulations, from any person, consumer or their association or trade association; or

(*b*) a reference made to it by the Central Government or a State Government or a statutory authority.

(2) Without prejudice to the provisions contained in sub-section (1), the powers and functions of the Commission shall include the powers and functions specified in sub-sections (3) to (7).

(3) The Commission shall, while determining whether an agreement has an appreciable adverse effect on competition under section 3, have due regard to all or any of the following factors, namely:—

(*a*) creation of barriers to new entrants in the market;

(*b*) driving existing competitors out of the market;

(*c*) foreclosure of competition by hindering entry into the market;

(*d*) accrual of benefits to consumers;

(*e*) improvements in production or distribution of goods or provision of services;

(*f*) promotion of technical, scientific and economic development by means of production or distribution of goods or provision of services.

(4) The Commission shall, while inquiring whether an enterprise enjoys a dominant position or not under section 4, have due regard to all or any of the following factors, namely:—

(*a*) market share of the enterprise;

(*b*) size and resources of the enterprise;

(*c*) size and importance of the competitors;

(*d*) economic power of the enterprise including commercial advantages over competitors;

(*e*) vertical integration of the enterprises or sale or service network of such enterprises;

(*f*) dependence of consumers on the enterprise;

(*g*) monopoly or dominant position whether acquired as a result of any statute or by virtue of being a Government company or a public sector undertaking or otherwise;

(*h*) entry barriers including barriers such as regulatory barriers, financial risk, high capital cost of entry, marketing entry barriers, technical entry barriers, economies of scale, high cost of substitutable goods or service for consumers;

(*i*) countervailing buying power;

(*j*) market structure and size of market;

(*k*) social obligations and social costs;

(*l*) relative advantage, by way of the contribution to the economic development, by the enterprise enjoying a dominant position having or likely to have an appreciable adverse effect on competition;

(*m*) any other factor which the Commission may consider relevant for the inquiry.

(5) For determining whether a market constitutes a "relevant market" for the purposes of this Act, the Commission shall have due regard to the "relevant geographic market" and "relevant product market".

(6) The Commission shall, while determining the "relevant geographic market", have due regard to all or any of the following factors, namely:—

(*a*) regulatory trade barriers;

(*b*) local specification requirements;

(*c*) national procurement policies;

(*d*) adequate distribution facilities;

(*e*) transport costs;

(*f*) language;

(*g*) consumer preferences;

(h) need for secure or regular supplies or rapid after-sales services.

(7) The Commission shall, while determining the "relevant product market", have due regard to all or any of the following factors, namely:—

(*a*) physical characteristics or end-use of goods;

(*b*) price of goods or service;

(*c*) consumer preferences;

(*d*) exclusion of in-house production;

(*e*) existence of specialised producers;

(*f*) classification of industrial products.

20. Inquiry into combination by Commission: The Commission may, upon its own knowledge or information relating to acquisition referred to in clause (a) of section 5 or acquiring of control referred to in clause (b) of section 5 or merger or amalgamation referred to in clause (c) of that section, inquire into whether such a combination has caused or is likely to cause an appreciable adverse effect on competition in India:

21. Reference by statutory authority : (1) Where in the course of a proceeding before any statutory authority an issue is raised by any party that any decision which such statutory authority has taken or proposes to take. is or would be, contrary to any of the provisions of this Act, then such statutory authority may make a reference in respect of such issue to the Commission.

(2) On receipt of a reference under sub-section (1), the Commission shall, after hearing the parties to the proceedings, give its opinion to such statutory authority which shall thereafter pass such order on the issues referred to in that sub-section as it deems fit:

Provided that the Commission shall give its opinion under this section within sixty days of receipt of such reference.

22. Benches of Commission : (1) The jurisdiction, powers and authority of the Commission may be exercised by Benches thereof.

(2) The Benches shall be constituted by the Chairperson and each Bench shall consist of not less than two Members.

(3) Every Bench shall consist of at least one Judicial Member.

(4) The Bench over which the Chairperson presides shall be the Principal Bench and the other Benches shall be known as the Additional Benches.

23. Distribution of business of Commission amongst Benches : (1) Where any Benches are constituted, the Chairperson may, from time to time, by order, make provisions as to the distribution of the business of the Commission amongst the Benches and specify the matters, which may be dealt with by each Bench.

(2) If any question arises as to whether any matter falls within the purview of the business allocated to a Bench, the decision of the Chairperson thereon shall be final.

(3) The Chairperson may

(i) transfer a Member from one Bench to another Bench; or

(ii) authorise the Members of one Bench to discharge also the functions of the Members of other Bench:

24. Procedure for deciding a case where Members of a Bench differ in opinion : If the Members of a Bench differ in opinion on any point, they shall state the point or points on which they differ, and make a reference to the Chairperson who shall either hear the point or points himself o refer the case for hearing on such point or points by one or more of the other Members and such point or points shall be decided according to the opinion of the majority of the Members who have heard the case, including those who first heard it.

25. Jurisdiction of Bench : An inquiry shall be initiated or a complaint be instituted or a reference be made under this Act before a Bench within the local limits of its jurisdiction.

26. Procedure for inquiry on complaints under Section 19 : (1) On receipt of a complaint or a reference from the Central Government or a State Government or a statutory authority or on its own knowledge or information, under section 19, if the Commission is of the opinion that there exists a prima facie case, it shall direct the Director General to cause an investigation to be made into the matter.

(2) The Director General shall, on receipt of direction under sub-section (1), submit a report on his findings within such period as may be specified by the Commission.

(3) Where on receipt of a complaint under clause (a) of sub-section (1) of section 19, the Commission is of the opinion that there exists no prima facie case, it shall dismiss the complaint and may pass such orders as it deems fit, including imposition of costs, if necessary.

(4) The Commission shall forward a copy of the report referred to in sub-section (2) to the parties concerned or to the Central Government or the State Government or the statutory authority, as the case may be.

27. Orders by Commission after inquiry into agreements or abuse of dominant position : Where after inquiry the Commission finds that any agreement referred to in section 3 or action of an enterprise in a dominant position, is in contravention of section 3 or section 4, as the case may be, it may pass all or any of the following orders, namely:—

(*a*) direct any enterprise or association of enterprises or person or association of persons, as the case may be, involved in such agreement, or abuse of dominant position, to discontinue and not to re-enter such agreement or discontinue such abuse of dominant position, as the case may be;

(*b*) impose such penalty, as it may deem fit which shall be not more than ten per cent. of the average of the turnover for the last three preceding financial years, upon each of such person or enterprises which are parties to such agreements or abuse:

Provided that in case any agreement referred to in section 3 has been entered into by any cartel, the Commission shall impose upon each producer, seller, distributor, trader or service provider included in that cartel, a penalty equivalent to three times of the amount of profits made out of such agreement by the cartel or ten per cent. of the average of the turnover of the cartel for the last preceding three financial years, whichever is higher;

(*c*) award compensation to parties in accordance with the provisions contained in section 34;

(*d*) direct that the agreements shall stand modified to the extent and in the manner as may be specified in the order by the Commission;

(*e*) direct the enterprises concerned to abide by such other orders as the Commission may pass and comply with the directions, including payment of costs, if any: 15

(*f*) recommend to the Central Government for the division of an enterprise enjoying dominant position;

(*g*) pass such oilier order as it may deem fit.

28 Division of enterprise enjoying dominant position: The Central Government, on recommendation under clause (f) of section 27, may, notwithstanding anything contained in any other law for the time being in force, by order in writing, direct division of an enterprise enjoying dominant position to ensure that such enterprise does not abuse its dominant position.

29. Procedure for investigation of combination: Where the Commission is of the opinion that a combination is likely to cause, or has caused an appreciable adverse effect on competition within the relevant market in India, it shall issue a notice to show cause to the parties to combination calling upon them to respond within thirty days of the receipt of the notice, as to why investigation in respect of such combination should not be conducted.

30. Inquiry into disclosures under sub-section (2) of section 6: Where any person or enterprise has given a notice under sub-section (2) of section 6. The16 Commission shall inquire—

(a) whether the disclosure made in the notice is correct;

(b) whether the combination has, or is likely to have, an appreciable adverse effect on competition.

31. Orders of Commission on certain combinations: (1) Where the Commission is of the opinion that any combination does not, or is not likely to, have an appreciable adverse effect on competition, it shall, by order, approve that combination including the combination in respect of which a notice has been given under sub-section (2) of section 6.

(2) Where the Commission is of the opinion that the combination has, or is likely to have, an appreciable adverse effect on competition, it shall direct that the combination shall not take effect.

32. Acts taking place outside India but having an effect on competition in India : The Commission shall, notwithstanding that,—

(a) an agreement referred to in section 3 has been entered into outside India; or

(*b*) any party to such agreement is outside India; or

(*c*) any enterprise abusing the dominant position is outside India; or

(*d*) a combination has taken place outside India; or

(*e*) any party to combination is outside India; or

(*f*) any other matter or practice or action arising out of such agreement or dominant position or combination is outside India, have power to inquire into such agreement or abuse of dominant position or combination if such agreement or dominant position or combination has, or is likely to have, an appreciable adverse effect on competition in the relevant market in India.

33. Power to grant interim relief : (1) Where during an inquiry before the Commission, it is proved to the satisfaction of the Commission, by affidavit or otherwise, that an act in contravention of sub-section (1) of section 3 or sub-section (1) of section 4 or section 6 has been committed and continues to be committed or that such act is about to be committed, the Commission may, by order, grant a temporary injunction restraining any party from carrying on such act until the conclusion of such inquiry or until further orders, without giving notice to the opposite party, where it deems it necessary.

(2) Where during the inquiry before the Commission, it is proved to the satisfaction of the Commission by affidavit or otherwise that import of any goods is likely to contravene sub-section (1) of section 3 or subsection (1) of section 4 or section 6, it may, by order, grant a temporary injunction restraining any party from importing such goods until the conclusion of such inquiry or until further orders, without giving notice to the opposite party, where it deems it necessary and a copy of such order granting temporary injunction shall be sent to the concerned authorities.

(3) The provisions of rules 2A to 5 (both inclusive) of Order XXXIX of the First Schedule to the Code of Civil Procedure, 1908 (5 of 1908) shall, as far as may be, apply to a temporary injunction issued by the Commission under this Act, as they apply to a temporary injunction issued by a civil court, and any reference in any such rule to a suit shall be construed as a reference to any inquiry before the Commission.

34. Power to award compensation: Without prejudice to any other provisions contained in this Act, any person may make an application to the Commission for an order for the recovery of compensation from any enterprise for any loss or damage shown to have been suffered, by such person as a result of any contravention of the provisions of Chapter II, having been committed by such enterprise.

35. Appearance before Commission : A complainant or defendant or the Director General may either appear in person or authorise one or more chartered accountants or company secretaries or cost accountants or legal practitioners or any of his or its officers to present his or its case before the Commission.

36. Power of Commission to regulate its own procedure : (1) The Commission shall not be bound by the procedure laid down by the Code of Civil Procedure, 1908 (5 of 1908), but shall be guided by the principles of natural justice and, subject to the other provisions of this Act and of any rules made by the Central Government, the

Commission shall have powers to regulate its own procedure including the places at which they shall have their sittings, duration of oral hearings when granted, and times of its inquiry.

(2) The Commission shall have, for the purposes of discharging its functions under this Act, the same powers as are vested in a civil court under the Code of Civil Procedure, 1908(5 of 1908), while trying a suit, in respect of the following matters, namely:—

(*a*) summoning and enforcing the attendance of any person and examining him on oath;

(*b*) requiring the discovery and production of documents;

(*c*) receiving evidence on affidavits;

(*d*) issuing commissions for the examination of witnesses or documents;

(*e*) subject to the provisions of sections 123 and 124 of the Indian Evidence Act, 1872 (1 of 1872), requisitioning any public record or document or copy of such record or document from any office;

(*f*) dismissing an application in default or deciding it ex parte;

(*g*) any other matter which may be prescribed.

37. Review of orders of Commission : Any person aggrieved by an order of the Commission from which an appeal is allowed by this Act but no appeal has been preferred, may, within thirty days from the date of the order, apply to the Commission for review of its order and the Commission may make such order thereon as it thinks fit:

Provided that the Commission may entertain a review application after the expiry of the said period of thirty days, if it is satisfied that the applicant was prevented by sufficient cause from preferring the application in time:

Provided further that no order shall be modified or set aside without giving an opportunity of being heard to the person in whose favour the order is given and the Director General where he was a party to the proceedings.

38. Rectification of orders : (1) With a view to rectifying any mistake apparent from the record, the Commission may amend any order passed by it under the provisions of this Act.

(2) Subject to the other provisions of this Act, the Commission may make —

(*a*) an amendment under sub-section (1) of its own motion;

(*b*) an amendment for rectifying any such mistake which has been brought to its notice by any party to the order.

Explanation.– For the removal of doubts, it is hereby declared that the Commission shall not, while rectifying any mistake apparent from record, amend substantive part of its order passed under the provisions of this Act.

39. Execution of orders of Commission : Every order passed by the Commission under this Act shall be enforced by the Commission in the same manner as if it were a decree or order made by a High Court or the principal civil court in a suit pending therein and it shall be lawful for the Commission to send, in the event of its inability to execute it, such order to the High Court or the principal civil court, as the case may be, within the local limits of whose jurisdiction,—

(*a*) in the case of an order against a person referred to in sub-clause (iii) or sub-clause (vi) or sub clause (vii) of clause (l) of section 2, the registered office or the sole or principal place of business of the person in India or where the person has also a subordinate office, that subordinate office, is situated;

(*b*) in the case of an order against any other person, the place, where the person concerned voluntarily resides or carries on business or personally works for gain, is situated, and thereupon the court to which the order is so sent shall execute the order as if it were a decree or order sent to it for execution.

40. Appeal: L Any person aggrieved by any decision or order of the Commission may file an appeal to the Supreme Court within sixty days from the date of communication of the decision or order of the Commission to him on one or more of the grounds specified in section 100 of the Code of Civil Procedure, 1908 (5 of 1908):

Provided that the Supreme Court may, if it is satisfied that the appellant was prevented by sufficient cause from filing the appeal within the said period, allow it to be filed within a further period not exceeding sixty days: Provided further that no appeal shall lie against any decision or order of the Commission made with the consent of the parties.

CHAPTER V
DUTIES OF DIRECTOR GENERAL

41. Director General to investigate contravention : (1) The Director General shall, when so directed by the Commission, assist the Commission in investigating into any contravention of the provisions of this Act or any rules or regulations made thereunder.

(2) The Director General shall have all the powers as are conferred upon the Commission under subsection (2) of section 36.

(3) Without prejudice to the provisions of sub-section (2), sections 240 and 240A of the Companies Act, 1956 (1 of 1956), so far as may be, shall apply to an investigation made by the Director General or any other person investigating under his authority, as they apply to an inspector appointed under that Act.

CHAPTER VI
PENALTIES

42. Contravention of orders of Commission : (1) Without prejudice to the provisions of this Act, if any person contravenes, without any reasonable ground, any order of the Commission, or any condition or restriction subject to which any approval, sanction, direction or exemption in relation to any matter has been accorded, given, made or granted under this Act or fails to pay the penalty imposed under this Act, he shall be liable to be detained in civil prison for a term which may extend to one year, unless in the meantime the Commission directs his release and he shall also be liable to a penalty not exceeding rupees ten lakhs.

(2) The Commission may, while making an order under this Act, issue such directions to any person or authority, not inconsistent with this Act, as it thinks necessary or desirable, for the proper implementation or execution of the order, and any person who commits breach of or fails to comply with, any obligation imposed on him under such direction, may be ordered by the Commission to be detained in civil prison for a term not exceeding one year unless in the meantime the Commission directs his release and he shall also be liable to a penalty not exceeding rupees ten lakhs.

43. Penalty for failure to comply with directions of Commission and Director General : If any person fails to comply with a direction given by—

(*a*) the Commission under sub-section (5) of section 36; or

(*b*) the Director General while exercising powers referred to in sub-section (2) of section 41, the Commission shall impose on such person a penalty of rupees one lakh for each day during which such failure continues.

44. Penalty for making false statement or omission to furnish material information : If any person, being a party to a combination,—

(*a*) makes a statement which is false in any material particular, or knowing it to be false; or

(*b*) omits to state any material particular knowing it to be material, such person shall be liable to a penalty which shall not be less than rupees fifty lakhs but which may extend to rupees one crore, as may be determined by the Commission.

45. Penalty for offences in relation to furnishing of information : (1) Without prejudice to the provisions of section 44, if any person, who furnishes or is required to furnish under this Act any particulars, documents or any information,—

(*a*) makes any statement or furnishes any document which he knows or has reason to believe to be false in any material particular; or

(*b*) omits to state any material fact knowing it to be material; or

(*c*) wilfully alters, suppresses or destroys any document which is required to be furnished as aforesaid, the Commission shall impose on such person a penalty which may extend to rupees ten lakhs.

(2) Without prejudice to the provisions of sub-section (1), the Commission may also pass such other order as it deems fit.

46. Power to impose lesser penalty : The Commission may, if it is satisfied that any producer, seller, distributor, trader or service provider included in any cartel, which is alleged to have violated section 3, has made a full and true disclosure in respect of the alleged violations and such disclosure is vital, impose upon such producer, seller, distributor, trader or service provider a lesser penalty as it may deem fit, than leviable under this Act or the rules or the regulations:

Provided that lesser penalty shall not be imposed by the Commission in cases where proceedings for the violatio of any of the provisions of this Act or the rules or the regulations have been instituted or any investigation has been directed to be made under section 26 before making of such disclosure:

Provided further that lesser penalty shall be imposed by the Commission only in respect of a producer, seller, distributor, trader or service provider included in the cartel, who first made the full, true and vital disclosures under this section:

Provided also that the Commission may, if it is satisfied that such producer, seller, distributor, trader or service provider included in the cartel had in the course of proceedings,—

(*a*) not complied with the condition on which the lesser penalty was imposed by the Commission; or

(*b*) had given false evidence; or

(*c*) the disclosure made is not vital, and thereupon such producer, seller, distributor, trader or service provider may be tried for the offence with respect to which the lesser penalty was imposed and shall also be liable to the imposition of penalty to which such person has been liable, had lesser penalty not been imposed.

47. Crediting sums realised by way of penalties to Consolidated Fund of India: All sums realised by way of penalties under this Act shall be credited to the Consolidated Fund of India.

48. Contravention by companies: (1) Where a person committing contravention of any of the provisions of this Act or of any rule, regulation, order made or direction issued there under is a company, every person who, at the time the contravention was committed, was in charge of, and was responsible to the company for the conduct of the business of the company, as well as the company, shall be deemed to be guilty of the contravention and shall be liable to be proceeded against and punished accordingly: Provided that nothing contained in this sub-section shall render any such person liable lo any punishment if he proves that the contravention was committed without his knowledge or that he had exercised all due diligence to prevent the commission of such contravention.

(2) Notwithstanding anything contained in sub-section (1), where a contravention of any of the provisions of this Act or of any rule, regulation, order made or direction issued there under has been committed by a company and it is proved that the contravention has taken place with the consent or connivance of, or is attributable to any neglect on the part of, any director, manager, secretary or other officer of the company, such director, manager, secretary or other officer shall also be deemed to be guilty of that contravention and shall be liable to be proceeded against and punished accordingly.

Explanation.—For the purposes of this section,—

(*a*) "company" means a body corporate and includes a firm or other association of individuals: and

(*b*) "director", in relation to a firm, means a partner in the firm.

CHAPTER VII
COMPETITION ADVOCACY

49. Competition advocacy : (1) In formulating a policy on competition (including review of laws related to competition), the Central Government may make a reference to the Commission for its opinion on possible effect of such policy on competition and on receipt of such a reference, the Commission shall, within sixty days of making such reference, give its opinion to the Central Government, which may thereafter formulate the policy as it deems fit.

(2) The opinion given by the Commission under sub-section (1) shall not be binding upon the Central Government in formulating such policy.

(3) The Commission shall take suitable measures, as may be prescribed, for the promotion of competition advocacy, creating awareness and imparting training about competition issues.

CHAPTER VIII
FINANCE, ACCOUNTS AND AUDIT

50. Grants by Central Government : The Central Government may, after due appropriation made by Parliament by law in this behalf, make to the Commission grants of such sums of money as the Government may think fit for being utilised for the purposes of this Act.

51. Constitution of Fund : (1) There shall be constituted a fund to be called the "Competition Fund" and there shall be credited thereto—

(*a*) all Government grants received by the Commission;

(*b*) the monies received as costs from parties to proceedings before the Commission;

(*c*) the fees received under this Act;

(*d*) the interest accrued on the amounts referred to in clauses (a) to (c).

(2) The Fund shall be applied for meeting—

(*a*) the salaries and allowances payable to the Chairperson and other Members and the administrative expenses including the salaries, allowances and pension payable to the Director General, Additional, Joint, Deputy or Assistant Directors General, the Registrar and" officers and other employees of the Commission;

(*b*) the other expenses of the Commission in connection with the discharge of its functions and for the purposes of this Act.

(3) The Fund shall be administered by a committee of such Members of the Commission as may be determined by the Chairperson.

(4) The committee appointed under sub-section (3) shall spend monies out of the Fund for carrying out the objects for which the Fund has been constituted.

52. Accounts and Audit : (1)The Commission shall maintain proper accounts and other relevant records and prepare an annual statement of accounts in such form as may be prescribed by the Central Government in consultation with the Comptroller and Auditor-General of India.

(2) The accounts of the Commission shall be audited by the Comptroller and Auditor-General of India at such intervals as may be specified by him and any expenditure incurred in connection with such audit shall be payable by the Commission to the Comptroller and Auditor-General of India.

53. Furnishing of returns, etc., to Central Government : (1) The Commission shall furnish to the Central Government at such time and in such form and manner as may be prescribed or as the Central Government may direct, such returns and statements and such particulars in regard to any proposed or existing measures for the promotion of competition advocacy, creating awareness and imparting training about competition issues, as the Central Government may, from time to time, require.

(2) The Commission shall prepare once in every year, in such form and at such time as may be prescribed, an annual report giving a true and full account of its activities during the previous year and copies of the report shall be forwarded to the Central Government.

(3) A copy of the report received under sub-section (2) shall be laid, as soon as may be after it is received, before each House of Parliament.

National Manufacturing Competitiveness Council (NMCC)

Since 1991, the Indian economy is being progressively liberalized and its integration to the global economy is deepening. On one hand, the liberalization and globalization have provided unprecedented opportunity for the growth and expansion of the industry in general and the manufacturing in particular. On the other hand the Indian industry has to not only faced stiff competition from free imports but also continue its efforts to grow its export capability through competitiveness. There is a continuous need to benchmark the Indian manufacturing sector against the best in the world and enhance competitiveness of the manufacturing sector.

The National Manufacturing Competitiveness Council (NMCC) has been set up by the Government to provide a continuing forum for policy dialogue to energies and sustain the growth of manufacturing industries in India. The NMCC is expected to suggest various ways and means for enhancing the competitiveness of manufacturing sector including identification of manufacturing sectors which have potential for global competitiveness; current strengths and constraints of identified sectors, and recommend National level industry/sector specific policy imitative as may be required for augmenting the growth of manufacturing sector.

Rationale of the Council (NMCC)

1. The National Common Minimum Programme had identified the need to have a continuing forum consisting of representatives from Government, the Industry and the Academicia for policy dialogue to energize and sustain the growth of the manufacturing industry. Food processing, Textiles and Garments, Engineering, Consumer goods, Pharmaceuticals, Capital goods, Leather and IT hardware are among the priority items specifically mentioned in the Common Minimum Programme.

2. Globally the manufacturing activities are now acquiring a new dimension. The trend is to source products from low –cost countries (LCCs). This is gaining momentum. India with its past experience, large pool of skilled manpower, established raw material and supply base and growing domestic volumes has the potential to emerge as major manufacturing hub for the global market. To harness the opportunities and the potential, appropriate sector specific interventions with special focus is the need of the hour. Sectors like Textiles, Chemicals and Pharmaceuticals, Electrical and Electronics, Food processing and Leather and Handicrafts are some examples which offer immediate opportunities to garner a major share of the global market.

3. The average annual growth in GDP increased from 5.8% during 1980s to more than 6% during the nineties. The manufacturing sector grew at an average of 6.3% during 1991 to 2003. Industry contributes about 27% of GDP. The share of services has increased from 42% in 1991 to 51% in 2003 while the share of agriculture has decreased from 31% in 1991 to 22% in 2003. Manufacturing sector which is a part of the industry accounts for about 17% in India's GDP with a share of 12% in total employment (48 million persons). Manufacturing sector accounts for more than 75% share in India's total exports. East Asian economies, e.g., China (35%), Indonesia (25%), Malaysia (31%) and Thailand (34%) have a much higher contribution of manufacturing in their GDP.

4. India's share in the global trade is less than 1%, which is much below the potential. Five sectors viz., gems and jewellery, textiles, engineering goods, chemicals, leather and leather goods account for 75% of the India's exports. The two trading blocks, US and EU, receive more than 50% of exports from India.

5. Attaining competitive edge in 'manufacturing' depends critically on mitigating constraints; both the general constraints such as inadequate infrastructure, high transaction costs, higher interest, power and regulatory issues as well as sector specific constraints such as technology upgradation, market access, duty structure, managerial practices and competitive scales etc. Resolution of these constraints necessitates focused attention and action involving not only inter-Ministerial/Departmental co-ordination but also closer interaction amongst stakeholders viz; industry, input providers, financial institutions, education, research and management institutions.

6. Recognizing the importance of manufacturing in overall economic growth of a country and the need for enhancing its productivity, competitiveness and employment generation many countries have initiated institutional mechanism for a national approach on manufacturing.

7. In the above background and in line with the priorities laid down in the National Common Minimum Programme the Government has set up the National Manufacturing Competitiveness Council. This is an interdisciplinary and autonomous body at the highest level to serve as a policy forum for credible and coherent policy initiatives in manufacturing sector. The Council is expected to energize and sustain the growth of manufacturing industries in the Country and also help in implementation of strategy.

Scope of the Council

The area to be covered by the NMCC is very vast. In essence, it covers the entire gamut of Indian Economy and its competitiveness. It is difficult to divide the operations and deal with Manufacturing and Services as separate compartments as both are interlinked in many ways. The NMCC is, therefore, looking into the total area of manufacturing activities in the context of increasing need for employment opportunities and to unlock the full potential of Indian Industry.

Composition of the Council

The Council formed in October, 2004 is headed by Dr. V. Krishnamurthy, as Chairman at the Union Cabinet Minister Level and comprises of 25 members comprising of noted industrialists, economists and representatives from industry associations and the Government. Shri V. Govindarajan is the Member Secretary of the Council. The full composition of the Council is as under:

1.	Chairman of NMCC:	Dr. V. Krishnamurthy
2.	Member Secretary:	Mr. V. Govindarajan

Ex-Officio Members

(a) Government of India

3. Member-Industry, Planning Commission
4. Secretary/ Dept. of Industrial Policy & Planning

5. Secretary/ Finance.
6. Secretary/ Heavy Industries & Public Enterprises
7. Secretary/ Small Scale Industries
8. Director General, Council of Scientific and Industrial Research

(b) Apex Industrial Organizations

9. President-FICCI
10. President-CII
11. President-ASSOCHAM

Professional & Expert Members

(a) Management & Technical Institutions

12. Dr. Shekhar Chaudhuri: Director, IIM, Kolkata
13. Prof. M S Ananth: Director, IIM, Chennai

(b) Economists

14. Dr. Bibek Debroy
15. Dr. Isher Judge Ahluwalia: Director & Chief Executive, ICRIER

(c) Representatives of Various Industrial Sector

16. Mr. Ratan Tata: Chairman, Tata Sons.
17. Mr. Venu Srinivasan: CMD, TVS Motors
18. Mr. Mukul Kasliwal: Chairman, S Kumars Group
19. Mr. AM Naik: CMD, L&T
20. Mr. YC Deveshwar: CMD, ITC
21. Mr. Jamshed N. Godrej: MD. Godrej & Boyce Mfg.Co.
22. Mr. Baba N. Kalyani: CMD, Bharat Forge Ltd.
23. Mr. Suresh Neotia: CMD, Gujrat Ambuja Cements Ltd.
24. Mr. Habil Khorakiwala : CMD, Wockhardt.
25. Dr. Surinder Kapur: CMD, Sona Koya Steering Systems Ltd.
26. Ms. Uma Reddy: Chief Executive, Hitech Magnetics.

Role Assigned to the Council

Following role has been assigned to the council:

(*i*) Identification of manufacturing sectors, which have potential for global competitiveness, problems and constraints in such sectors with respect to structure and size of industry, technology gaps, modernization needs etc.;

(*ii*) Evolving sector specific strategies for enhancing competitiveness of manufacturing sector;

(*iii*) Recommending measures to create common infrastructure and facilities such as testing, quality, design, HRD, skills, training institutes, etc.; and

(*iv*) Providing forum for dialogue between the public and private sectors, labour and academic sectors.

Functions of the Council

The NMCC shall advise the Government on industrial and sector specific initiatives that may be required for enhancing competitiveness of industries. It would *inter alia* include:

(*a*) Sectoral and enterprise level initiatives;

(*b*) Innovation and technology development (R&D);

(*c*) Entrepreneurship promotion;

(*d*) Infrastructure and enabling facilities;

(*e*) Trade and fiscal policies; and

(*f*) Employment generation

Elements Governing Long Term Manufacturing Strategy

In order to achieve the objectives, NMCC is adopting the twin approach of drawing a National Strategy for Manufacturing which attempts to identify the areas of policy interventions and outlines the strategic directions that need to be pursued in order to realize higher levels of growth and employment and parallely concentrate on certain sub sectors of manufacturing where immediate policy interventions can unleash higher growth rates and expansion of markets. The NMCC has recommended a national level as well as sector level/ industry level specific policy initiatives as is required for augmenting the growth of manufacturing sector. Ten elements have been identified for attention by the NMCC as a part of its long term manufacturing strategy. These are:-

(*i*) Enhance Government focus on manufacturing competitiveness;

(*ii*) Creating conditions for investment in and growth of the manufacturing sector;

(*iii*) Lowering the cost of manufacturing;

(*iv*) Investing in innovations;

(*v*) Strengthening education and training at all levels;

(*vi*) Adoption of global best practices in manufacturing;

(*vii*) Right market framework, competition and regulation;

(*viii*) Issues relating to competitiveness in small and medium industries;

(*ix*) Competitiveness of public sector manufacturing industries; and

(*x*) Infrastructure development.

National Strategy for Manufacturing

The council after detailed discussions with the Industry, Economists, Academia, Government Departments concerned including Planning Commission, Economic Advisory Council of the Prime Minister and various stakeholders, has prepared and submitted "The National Strategy for Manufacturing" to the Government for its adoption and implementation. It attempts to identify the areas of policy and outlines the strategic directions that need to be pursued in order to realize higher levels of growth and employment. India has to aim at achieving a long term GDP growth rate of 8 to 10 percent to substantially improve the living conditions of its people for which the manufacturing sector should target an average growth rate of 12 to 14 per cent.

Sectors / Sub-Sectors of Engagement

The NMCC has identified the following sectors/ sub-sectors which have immediate potential for growth and employment:

(*i*) Textiles and garments

- Leather and Leather goods
- Auto components
- Drugs & pharmaceuticals
- Food processing
- Telecom equipment
- Gems and jewellery
- Handlooms and handicrafts
- Chemicals & Petrochemicals
- IT hardware/ electronics
- Skill Development
- Ports & Shipping industry
- Capital goods industry and

- Paper industry
- Biotechnology
- Cement
- Fertilizers
- Minerals & Metals
- Steel

The following sub-sectors have been studied in greater detail :

- Leather & Leather Goods
- IT Hardware & Electronics
- Small and Medium Enterprises (*SMEs*) – Financial & Venture Capital
- Textiles & Garments
- Food Processing Industries
- Auto Components
- Capital Goods
- Paper
- Chemicals & Petrochemicals
- Drugs & Pharmaceuticals
- Human Resource requirement in manufacturing sector
- Telecom Equipment sector
- Ports & shipping industry
- Handicrafts
- Telecom Equipment
- Innovation & R&D Policy
- Tax Issues
- Labour Issues

In the first round discussion, different stake holders, namely the Secretary of the Department concerned, the Industry Associations, the Academicians and the Industry captains in the sub-sector concerned participated. The discussions typically centered round, the growth potential of the sub-sector in a medium to long term, the actions to be taken by each of the stake holders to realize the potential by concentrating on improving the competitiveness of the sub-sector and indicative targets to be aimed at.

In addition, discussions are also proposed in the following areas:

- Gems & Jewellery
- Steel
- Minerals/Metals
- Biotechnology
- Fertilizers
- Cement
- University/Industry Coordination/Collaboration
- Infrastructure
- Offset Policy & Technology Transfer Issues

Promotion of ICT in Manufacturing

The NMCC and the Microsoft Corporation India Private Limited have launched collaboration for competitiveness enhancement programme for small and medium enterprise in Indian manufacturing sector. The Microsoft and the NMCC propose to create knowledge networks in identified clusters across the country to facilitate backward and forward linkages for the growth of the manufacturing sector. The networks will enhance access to markets, improve skills through relevant and focused training and provide for relevant and customized ICT solutions for the manufacturing sector. Microsoft and NMCC will work together to help create a self sustaining eco system of knowledge creation and sharing with industry associations. To start with pilot project in three clusters have been initiated for ICT intervention. These are: Ahmedabad Pharmaceuticals Cluster, Pune Auto Cluster and Tirupur Textile Cluster. A National manufacturing portal has been launched for helping the SME sector.

Setting up a High Level Committee on Manufacturing (HLCM)

1. The concern at all levels is in respect of implementation of the Strategy where too many agencies are involved. In order to ensure speedy resolution of the problems involving different agencies and effective implementation of the Strategy, Government has constituted a High Level Committee on Manufacturing, under the Chairmanship of the Hon'ble Prime Minister for resolving policy issues that may arise in the implementation of the National Manufacturing Initiative as may be adopted by Government as well as in the operationalisation of the plans for the growth of various sub-sectors of manufacturing.

2. The Members of the Committee include: Finance Minister, Commerce & Industry Minister, Deputy Chairman, Planning Commission, Chairman, Economic Advisory Council, Principal Secretary to PM and Ministers of sub-sectors concerned with the Chairman, NMCC being the Member/Convener. Member Secretary, NMCC along with Secretaries of Finance, Commerce, Industrial Policy & Promotion, Small Scale Industry, Heavy Industry & Public Enterprises and Economic Advisory Council are the permanent invitees to the above Committee. The Committee will be serviced by the PMO assisted by the NMCC.

3. With a view to facilitating the functioning of the HLCM, an Empowered Sub-committee has been constituted under the Chairmanship of Dr. V. Krishnamurthy, Chairman NMCC with Shri Ashwani Kumar, Minister of State (Industry) and Shri Anwarul Hoda, Member (Industry), Planning Commission as Members. The Chairman of the Empowered Committee may, from time to time, invite Ministers concerned for consultation. Member Secretary, NMCC; Finance Secretary; Secretary, Department of Expenditure; Secretary, Department of Commerce; Advisor to the Finance Minister and PMO Representative have been designated as the permanent invitees to the Empowered Sub-Committee of the HLCM. The Chairman may invite the Secretary of the Department concerned with the subject under discussion or any other officer to join the deliberations of the Sub-Committee.

4. The Empowered Sub-Committee was expected to undertake the following:

(*i*) Formulate/review/approve policy papers and proposals for submission to the HLCM;

(*ii*) Monitor the follow up on implementation of the decisions of HLCM; and

(*iii*) Undertake such other actions as may be necessary in furtherance of the objectives of the HLCM.

(*iv*) The Empowered Sub-Committee may be assigned such other tasks by the HLCM as may be found necessary from time to time.

5. The Empowered Sub Committee is also expected to act as the main executive body of the HLCM and submit its periodical reports for consideration of the HLCM. The Sub-Committee is to be serviced by the NMCC and concerned Ministries are expected to render required assistance to the Sub-Committee.

References

1. 5th UN Conference on Competition Policy 14-18 November, 2005. Belek (Antalya), Turkey., p.23-24
2. Business Standard, Sept 04, 2006,p.3
3. Competition Law Analysis and The Role of Economics Competition Commission of India, New Delhi (May 9, 2005), p.80
4. Business Line, July28, 2009,p.5

5. Rakesh Basant & Sebaastian Morris, "Competition Policy in India, Issues for Global Economy", Economic & Political Weekly, July 29, 2000,p.2735 – 2736
6. Ibid.p.2738-2739
7. T. Ramappa, Competition Law in India: Policies, Issues and Development, Oxford University Press 2006, p.56
8. Shri Vinod Dhall, Member, Competition Commission of India at Indian Paint Industry Conference, Mumbai. (January 15, 2005), p.85
9. Public Awareness on Competition Law & Policy Competition Commission of India, New Delhi, p.78
10. Approach Paper on Competition Advocacy with the State Governments- CCI
11. Business Line, July 28, 2009, p.5
12. Chartered Secretary, November, 2001, Volume No.XXXI,p.32-33
13. Ibid, p 45
14. Competition Law of India: Need to Go Slow and Steady- Anurag K. Agarwal- IIMA
15. Economic Times, New Delhi, Nov. 2009, p.4
16. Business Standard, Jan.2010, p.5
17. Ibid. p. 4

Practice Questions

Objective Type Questions

1. Following is not concerned with the regulation:
   (a) Investment restraints
   (b) Control over Mergers & Acquisitions
   (c) Disinvestment programmes
   (d) Product reservation for small scale sector
2. Competition Policy includes all of the following except:
   (a) Competition law
   (b) Policies relating to trade
   (c) FDI Investment
   (d) Brand Management
3. MRTP Act was repealed in:
   (a) 2000 (b) 2001
   (c) 2002 (d) 2003
4. Number of countries having a competition law increased to:
   (a) 104 (b) 106
   (c) 105 (d) 107
5. Relevant market is concerned with:
   (a) Domestic market
   (b) Foreign market
   (c) Asian Market
   (d) Geographic market

6. The National Manufacturing Competitiveness Council was set up in:
   (*a*) 2003 (*b*) 2004
   (*c*) 2005 (*d*) 2006
7. The National Manufacturing Competitiveness Council is comprises of:
   (*a*) 25 members (*b*) 26 members
   (*c*) 27 members (*d*) 28 members

Ans: 1.(*c*), 2. (d), 3.(c), 4.(b), 5.(d), 6.(b), 7. (b)

Short Answer Questions

1. What do you mean by Goods?
2. What do you know by an enterprise?
3. What is service?
4. What do you mean by anti competitive agreements?
5. What do you mean by abuse of dominant position?
6. What is combination?
7. What are the functions of Competition Commission of India?
8. What are the rationale of National Manufacturing Competitiveness Council?
9. What is the composition of the NMCC?
10. What are the functions of High level committee on Manufacturing?

Long Answer Questions

1. Discuss the nature and scope of Competition Policy in India. Explain its rationale.
2. Critically examine the salient features of the Competition Policy in India.
3. Critically examine the regulatory framework of competition in India.
4. What do you mean by global competitiveness? Also explain the factors governing global competitiveness.
5. Discuss the silent features of the Competition Act 2002.
6. Discuss the rationale and functions of National Manufacturing Competitiveness Council.
7. Examine the scope, composition and role of National Manufacturing Competitiveness Council.

9 MANAGERIAL REMUNERATION

Human factor is quite important factor in management of corporate sector. Gone are days when Indian corporate sector was managed by family managers and directors. These managers and directors were the part of the family system of promoters. Now companies are required to appoint professional managers and independent directors. Management personnel have been assigned a crucial role in corporate management. In the changed scenario, they are expected to give direction, ensure implementation, accountable for regulatory compliance and responsible for corporate disclosures and reporting. So there is need to compensate them properly as they have been appointed for operational direction and execution. Management personnel are also required to serve the purpose of stakeholders including stockholders. However, greater attention is to be paid on the wealth maximization of the shareholders. If shareholders are satisfied with their performance, naturally they will be liberal in approving managerial remuneration as per the provision of the Indian Companies Act, 1956 and necessary guidelines of the government. Basically, firms are required to fulfill two objectives: to maintain a high degree of current profitability; and to ensure high growth rates in future profitability. The relative emphasis on these two objectives depends on the various conditions prevailing in the environment in which firms are working. Management personnel are supposed to work for achieving these objectives. So, corporate performance can be defined and compared in terms of corporate efficiency and corporate growth. In most of the situations, corporate performance is the basis for deciding the level of managerial remuneration. Actually corporate performance is governed by the decisional capacity, hard work and coordinative approaches of management personnel. Thus, the managerial remuneration has an important role to play in the management of corporates. It tends to motivate managerial personnel to ensure efficient operation of the firm as well as chalkout efficient strategies for formulation and implementation of future plans.

Generally, companies pay huge amount to their management personnel. However, amounts differs from industry to industry, sector to sector and region to region. Diversities in managerial remuneration may create complexities in corporate management. Thus, the only option before the government is to develop and implement a systematic and uniform minimum remuneration system necessary for motivating the professional managers working in the Indian Corporate Sector. There are different forms of managerial remuneration viz., salary, sitting fee, commission, bonus etc. By whatever formulas these payments are made to the managerial personnel, it reflects the commitment of companies towards their management personnel. It also indicates that to what extent, companies are ready to share their earnings and profits in favour of management personnel.

The Government of India has developed a regulatory framework for ensuring uniformity in the payment of managerial remuneration. The Government has already systematized the managerial remuneration system by putting the Schedule XIII in Indian Companies Act, 1956. Besides Government also issues necessary guidelines with regard to payment of managerial remuneration. The Finance bill of the government also determines the tax implications of perquisites and fringe benefits etc.

Managerial Personnel

The Companies Act, 1956, contemplates five categories of managerial personnel

(*a*) an ordinary director, who is the director of the company;

(*b*) a part-time paid director, being a director in the part-time employment of the company;

(c) a whole-time director, being a director in the whole-time employment of the company;

(d) a managing director, being a director entrusted with substantial powers of management; and

(e) the manager, having the management of the whole, or substantially the whole, of the affairs of the company.

Definition of Remuneration

According to section 198 of Indian companies Act, 1956 'remuneration' includes the following:

(a) any expenditure incurred by the company in providing any rent-free accommodation or any other benefit or amenity in respect of accommodation, free of charge, to any of the persons specified in management personnel,

(b) any expenditure incurred by the company in providing any other benefit or amenity free of charge or at a concessional rate to any of the persons aforesaid;

(c) any expenditure incurred by the company in respect of any obligation or service which, but for such expenditure by the company, would have been incurred by any of the persons aforesaid; and

(d) any expenditure incurred by the company to effect any insurance on the life of, or to provide any pension, annuity or gratuity for, any of the persons aforesaid or hid spouse or child.

The remuneration payable to a director may take any one or more of the following forms

(a) sitting fee for each meeting of the Board, or a committee thereof, attended by him;

(b) monthly, quarterly or annual payments made to him; or

(c) a commission payable to him at specified percentage of the net profit of the company computed in the manner referred to in Section 198 (1).

Thus, the Companies Act enlarges the ordinary meaning of the word 'remuneration' as payment in money or otherwise for services rendered. A Chief Executive Officer (CEO) may be paid remuneration by way of a monthly payment and/or at a specified percentage of the company's net profits. While some companies prefer not to pay any commission and in lieu thereof absorb the element of commission into the monthly salary so as to ensure a steady income for the Chief Executive Officer (CEO) irrespective of fluctuations in the net profit of the company from year to year, others go to the extent of linking the CEO's pay with the share price of the firm by issuing employee stock options to him/her.

Section 198 of the Companies Act, 1956 limits the overall maximum managerial remuneration payable by a public company to persons entrusted with managerial functions to 11 per cent of the company's net profit (percentage of the net profit as contemplated by Section 198 (1) is to be computed in the manner laid down in Sections 349, 350 and 351 in the Companies Act). This percentage is exclusive of fees payable to directors for attending meetings of the board or committees thereof. The Section is concerned especially with managerial remuneration payable to managing directors. On the other hand, Section 309 is concerned with total remuneration payable to directors; whatever is the nature of such remuneration, managerial or otherwise. The Companies Act was amended from time to time as per demands from the industry chambers. Change in economic policy also prompts the change in the managerial remuneration.

Historical Perspective of Managerial Remuneration

The Administrative Guidelines, which were being followed by the Central Government, were made public on November 11, 1969. The Guidelines prescribed a ceiling of Rs. 90,000 per annum on the salary payable to a managerial person. They also provided for the payment of a commission of 1% on the net profits subject to a ceiling of Rs. 45,000 per annum. In addition, it provided for the payment of perquisites, the monetary value of which were evaluated as per the provisions of the Income-tax Act, 1961 and the rules made there under.

The 1969 Guidelines were revised in November 1978 by the Central Government. Earlier in 1973 the Central Government reviewed its policy with regard to payment of minimum remuneration to the managerial personnel consequent on the provisions contained in the Finance Act, 1971. While so revising the government spelt out its policy with regard to fixing of minimum remuneration in the following lines:

"The actual amount which should be allowed as minimum remuneration within the said ceiling will depend on various factors, that is size of the company, nature of the industry, sales and turnover, its profitability factors leading to the diminution or shrinkage of net profits and the future working prospects etc." The ceiling referred to above was Rs.

50,000 and the said guidelines specified that the ceiling could be pierced if such piercing is necessary for the efficient conduct of business of the company concerned.

In the light of the above, necessary revision was made taking into account the provisions of section 637AA which was inserted by the Companies (Amendment) Act, 1974 and the result of the review by the Central Government of the entire question of managerial remuneration. Actually, managerial remuneration was receivèd by the government in the context of socio-economic objectives of State Policy and the need for establishing a co-relation in managerial remuneration at comparable levels of responsibility in Government, public sector undertakings and public limited companies. The Government also took into account the recommendations of the Study Group on Wages, Incomes and Prices (Boothalingam Committee) whose report was published in May 1978 as well as the recommendations of the High Powered Expert under the chairmanship of Justice Rajinder Sachar. Due to these revisions in guidelines, the managerial remuneration was scaled down from Rs. 90,000 to 60,000 per annum. The commission was reduced from Rs. 45,000 to Rs. 12,000.00. The monetary value of perquisites were subjected to a ceiling of Rs. 60,000 per annum.

Judicial Scrutiny of Section 637AA and Revised Guidelines

The provisions of section 637AA of the Companies Act, 1956 and the revised guidelines 1978 came up for adjudication before a Division Bench of the Delhi High Court in Mahindra and Mahindra Limited and others v. Union of India -1983 (Delhi). The Delhi High Court in the said case observed as follows:

"After the decision of the Delhi High Court in Upper Doab Sugar Mills Ltd.'s case -1971 and before the decision of the Supreme Court-1977, reversing the decision of the Delhi High Court, Parliament had brought about a change in the Companies Act not by the amendment of section 198 or section 309 but by enacting section 637AA. Even section 637A was left as such on the statute book without either any amendment or being repealed. The result is that the power of the Central Government to accord approval etc., subject to conditions and to fix a limit with regard to remuneration is to be found not only in sections 198, 269 and 309 but also in 637A and 637AA. The Supreme Court has already upheld the power to fix remuneration and impose conditions under section 637AA. The Parliament was aware of the decision of the Delhi High Court in Upper Doab Sugar Mills Ltd.'s case and indeed it was as a result of that decision that section 637AA starts with a non obstante clause purporting to exclude the strict connotation of section 198 or section 309 or section 637A and so, gives a flexibility to governmental action. This flexibility given by parliament is not, however, absolute. In terms, the latter portion of section 637AA lays down that the Central Government is to fix the remuneration "within the limits specified in this Act, at such amount or percentage of profits of the company, as it may deem fit". The further guideline given to the Central Government by section 637AA in fixing the remuneration is mandatory for the section lays down that the Central Government shall (emphasis supplied) have regard to:

(*a*) the financial position of the company;

(*b*) the remuneration or commission drawn by the individual concerned in any other capacity, including his capacity as a sole-selling agent;

(*c*) the remuneration or commission drawn by him from any other company;

(*d*) professional qualifications and experience of the individual concerned;

(*e*) public policy relating to the removal of disparities in income."

Therefore, the Central Government cannot fix the remuneration of the person concerned nor can it formulate a policy nor can it give any administrative instructions except in accordance with the mandate of the section."

Thus, in the above judgment, the Delhi High Court struck down the 1978 guidelines. In 1983 the Government revised the guidelines and restored the ceiling on remuneration to pre 1978 levels. These guidelines were made operative with the approval of the Supreme Court before which an appeal against the judgement of the Delhi High Court in Mahindra & Mahindra's case was pending, in the case of those companies which gave positive consent to the fixation of remuneration under the 1983 guidelines.

Since 1983 there have been a number of changes in regard to appointment and payment of remuneration including minimum remuneration to the managerial personnel of companies. Now under section 269 of the Companies Act, 1956 a company can appoint and pay its managerial personnel if it conforms to the requirements set out in Schedule XIII appended to the Act. In case the appointment does not conform to the requirement then the same required the approval of the Central Government for which purpose an application will have to be submitted within 90 days of the appointment. As regards the minimum remuneration section 198 provides that 'notwithstanding anything contained in sub-section (1) to (3), but a subject to the provisions of section 269, read with schedule XIII, if, in any financial year, a company has no profits or its profits are inadequate, the company shall not pay to its directors, including any managing or whole-time director or manager, by way of remuneration any sum exclusive of any fees payable to directors under sub-section (2) of section 309, except with the previous approval of the Central Government'. As this provision has been made subject to the provision of section 269 and Schedule XIII appended to the Companies Act, 1956, the Central Government approval would be necessary only if Schedule XII does not specify the minimum remuneration proposed pierces the ceiling set out in Schedule XII.

Managerial Remuneration in Present Scenario

In the era of economic liberlisation companies have now been given freedom in the matter of appointment of management of managerial personnel. Companies with adequate profits have now full freedom to work out a suitable compensation package for their managerial personnel within the limit of 5% of the net profits if a company has one and within the limit of 10% of the net profits if a company has more than one managerial person. In the event of absence or inadequacy of profits a company can pay a remuneration ranging from Rs. 75,000 to Rs. 2 lacs per annum depending upon its effective capital, as minimum remuneration without the approval of the Central Government. Approval of the Central Government will be required only if the compensation package fixed is in excess of the aforementioned ceilings.

Therefore, these companies are required to approach the Central Government for its approval for payment of higher minimum remuneration. While profitability could be one of the criteria for fixing managerial remuneration it should not be the sole criterion. The other criteria could be the nature of the industry in which a company is engaged in, the turn over, the age of the plant and machinery installed, etc. Of late, the Central Government while approving the appointment of the managerial person, was allowing companies to pay remuneration in terms of Section II of Part of Schedule XIII i.e., allowing the companies to pay minimum remuneration as per Schedule XIII appended to the Act.

The remuneration payable to the directors is determined by the articles of the company or by a resolution or its the articles so require by a special resolution passed by the company in a general meeting. The directors cannot themselves fix the remuneration of all or any one of themselves. The expression managerial remuneration refers to the remuneration payable to the

(*a*) managing director;

(*b*) whole time director; or

(*c*) manager

It does not include executives who are not members of the board of directors irrespective of the salary paid to them.

Perquisites

"Perquisite" may be defined as any casual emolument or benefit attached to an office or position in addition to salary or wages. In essence, these are usually non-cash benefits given by an employer to employees in addition to cash salary or wages. However, they may include cases where the employer reimburses expenses or pays for obligations incurred by the employee. Perquisites are also referred to as fringe benefits. Broadly, "perquisite" is defined in the section 17(2) of the Income-tax Act as including:

(*i*) Value of rent-free or concessional rent accommodation provided by the employer.

(*ii*) Value of any benefit/amenity granted free or at concessional rate to specified employees etc.

(*iii*) Any sum paid by employer in respect of an obligation, which was actually payable by the assessee.

(*iv*) Any sum paid by the employer for assurance on life of the employee or to effect a contract for an annuity.

(*v*) Value of any other fringe benefit as may be prescribed.

Perquisites taxable in the hands of the employee as a part of salary income: "Broadly, in this system, the perquisites taxable in the hands of the employee as a part of salary income include:"[1]

(*i*) Value of rent-free or concessional rent accommodation provided by the employer.

(*ii*) Value of any benefit/amenity granted free or at concessional rate to specified employees, etc. Specified employees are company directors, employees with substantial interest in the company and any other employee whose salary income exclusive of non-monetary benefits and amenities exceeds Rs. 50,000/-.

(*iii*) Any sum paid by employer in respect of an obligation, which was actually payable by the assessee.

(*iv*) Any sum payable by the employer, directly or through a fund for assurance on life of the employee or to effect contract for an annuity. However, sums payable to recognised provident funds or approved superannuation funds, and certain other specified funds are exempt.

(*v*) Value of any other fringe benefit as may be prescribed (excluding fringe benefits subjected to the Fringe Benefit Tax).

Besides rent-free or concessional rent accommodation, other perquisites taxable in the hands of the employee include provision of services of a sweeper, a gardener, etc., supply of gas, electricity or water for household consumption, provision of free or concessional educational facilities for any member of the employee's household, provision of interest free or concessional loan, and benefit resulting from the use of any movable asset.

It has been clarified that the value of any leave travel concession or assistance received by an employee normally falls within the meaning of salary. It is, therefore, taxable in the hands of the employee subject to the exemption under clause (5) of section 10 of the Income-tax Act. However, leave travel concession not included in salary will be classified as an expense for the purposes of Fringe Benefit Tax and taxable in the hands of the employer. Other allowances falling within the meaning of salary like children education allowance and transport allowance, which are exempt subject to certain conditions are also to be considered part of salary income of the employee (Circular No. 8/2005). Certain perquisites and allowances, which are exempt, are listed in section 5 of this text. Salary income for the purposes of taxation and valuation of perquisites includes the pay, allowances, bonus or commission payable monthly or otherwise or any monetary payment, by whatever name called, from one or more employers, as the case may be, but does not include the following, namely:

(*i*) dearness allowance or dearness pay unless it enters into the computation of superannuation or retirement benefits of the employee concerned;

(*ii*) employer's contribution to the provident fund account of the employee;

(*iii*) allowances which are exempted from the payment of tax;

(*iv*) value of the perquisites specified in the concerned provision;

(*v*) any payment or expenditure specifically excluded.

Valuation Process of Perquisite

Valuation process of perquisites is given below:

Nature of perquisite	Valuation of perquisite
Unfurnished rent-free or concessional accommodation to Central or State Government Employees	License fee as determined by the government as reduced by the rent paid by the employee.
Unfurnished rent-free or concessional accommodation to non-Government Employees	w.e.f. 1/4/2002 to 31/3/2006- 10% of the salary in cities where population as per 1991 census is above 4 lakhs and 7.5% of salary in other cases. (w.e.f. 1-4-2005 to 31-3-2006 - 20% of salary in cities having population exceeding 4 lakhs as per 2001 census and 15% of salary in other cities) In case accommodation provided is not owned by the employer, but is taken on lease or rent, then actual amount of lease rent paid/payable by the employer or 10% of the salary, whichever is lower. w.e.f. 1/4/2006- 15% of the salary in cities where population as per 2001 census exceeds 25 lakhs, 10% of the salary in cities where population as per 2001 census exceeds 10 lakhs but does not exceed 25 lakhs and 7.5% of salary in other cases. In case accommodation provided is not owned by the employer, but is taken on lease or rent, then actual amount of lease rent paid/payable by the employer or 15% of the salary, whichever is lower. In both of above cases, the value of the perquisite would be reduced by the rent, if any, paid by the employee.

Contd....

Furnished Accommodation	Value of unfurnished accommodation as computed above, increased by 10% per annum of the cost of furniture (including TV/radio/refrigerator/ AC/other gadgets). In case furniture is hired from a third party, the value of unfurnished accommodation increased by hire charges paid/ payable by the employer. Any payment recovered from the employee towards the above would be reduced from this amount.
Hotel accommodation	24% of salary or the actual charges paid/payable to the hotel, whichever is lower. The above would be reduced by any rent actually paid by the employee. It may be noted that no perquisite would arise, if the employee is provided such accommodation on transfer from one place to another for a period of 15 days or less.
Motor car provided by the employer	W.e.f. 1-4-2008, if an employer providing such facility to his employee is not liable to pay fringe benefit tax, the value of such perquisite shall be : (*a*) Nil, if the motor car is used by the employee wholly and exclusively in the performance of his official duties. (*b*) Actual expenditure incurred by the employer on the running and maintenance of motor car including remuneration to chauffeur as increased by the amount representing normal wear and tear of the motor car and as reduced by any amount charged from the employee for such use (in case the motor car is exclusively for private or personal purposes of the employee or any member of his household). (*c*) Rs. 1200-(plus Rs. 600-, if chauffeur is also provided) per month (in case the motor car is used partly in performance of duties and partly for private or personal purposes of the employee or any member of his household if the expenses on maintenance and running of motor car are met or reimbursed by the employer). However, the value of perquisite will be Rs. 1600-(plus Rs. 600-, if chauffeur is also provided) per month if the cubic capacity of engine of the motor car exceeds 1.6 litres. (*d*) Rs. 400- (plus Rs. 600-, if chauffeur is also provided) per month (In case the motor car is used partly in performance of duties and partly for private or personal purposes of the employee or any member of his household if the expenses on maintenance and running of motor car for such private or personal use are fully met by the employee). However, the value of perquisite will be Rs. 600- (plus Rs. 600-, if chauffeur is also provided) per month if the cubic capacity of engine of the motor car exceeds 1.6 litres. If the motor car or any other automotive convenience is owned by the employee but the actual running and maintenance charges are met or reimbursed by the employer, the method of valuation of perquisite value is different. (See Rule 3(2)).
Provision of sweeper, gardener, watchman	Actual cost that is total amount of salary paid/ payable by the employer or any other person on by the employee.
Supply of gas, electric energy or water	Amount paid by the employer to the supplying agency or where supplied from resources owned by the employer, the manufacturing cost per unit incurred by the employer, less any amount paid by the employee.
Free or concessional educational facilities	Amount of expenditure incurred by the employer. In case where the educational institution is maintained or owned by the employer, or where provision is made in any other educational institution by reason of employee being in employment of that employer, the cost of such education in a similar institution in or near the locality (however, in this case

Contd....

	this sub-rule does not apply if the cost of education or the value of benefit per child does not exceed Rs. 1,000 per month). Any amount paid by or recovered from the employee is reduced from the value of the benefit.
Interest-free or concessional loan	Interest computed at rate charged per annum by the State Bank of India, in respect of loans for the same purpose, on the maximum outstanding monthly balance as reduced by the interest, if any, actually paid by the employee or any such member of his household. Exception is made for loans for specified medical treatment (amount of such exception is reduced by reimbursement from medical insurance) or where the amount of loans in aggregate is less than Rs. 20,000/-.
Free meals	The perquisite value in respect of free food and non-alcoholic beverages provided by the employer, not liable to pay fringe benefit tax, to an employee shall be the expenditure incurred by the employer as reduced by the amount paid or recovered from the employee for such benefit or amenity. However, no perquisite value will be taken if food and non-alcoholic beverages are provided during working hours and certain conditions specified under Rule 3(7)(iii) are satisfied.
Value of gift or voucher or token	The perquisite value in respect of any gift, or voucher, or token in lieu of which such gift may be received by the employee or member of his household from the employer, not liable to pay fringe benefit tax, shall be the sum equal to the amount of such gift, voucher or token. However, no perquisite value will be taken if the value of such gift, voucher or token is below Rs. 5000- in the aggregate during the previous year.
Credit Card provided by the employer	The perquisite value in respect of expenses incurred by the employee or any of his household members, which are charged to a credit card provided by the employer, not liable to pay fringe benefit tax, which are paid or reimbursed to an employee shall be taken to be such amount paid or reimbursed by such employer. However, no perquisite value will be taken if the expenses are incurred wholly and exclusively for official purposes and certain conditions mentioned in Rule 3(7)(v) are satisfied.
Club membership provided by the employer	The perquisite value in respect of amount paid or by the employer reimbursed to an employee by an employer, not liable to pay fringe benefit tax, against the expenses incurred in a club by such employee or any of his household members shall be taken to be such amount incurred or reimbursed by the employer as reduced by any amount paid or recovered from the employee on such account. However, no perquisite value will be taken if the expenditure is incurred wholly and exclusively for business purposes and certain conditions mentioned in Rule 3(7)(vi) are satisfied.
Use of any other movable asset	10% per annum of the actual cost of asset or the amount of rent or charge paid/payable by the employer as reduced by the amount, if any, paid or recovered from the employee. Laptops and computers are exempt.
Transfer of any movable asset	Actual cost of asset to the employer less the cost of normal wear and tear and as further reduced by the amount, if any, paid or recovered from the employee. The cost of normal wear and tear is calculated at 10% of cost for each completed year during which asset was put to use by the employer (normal wear and tear is calculated at 50% in the case of computers and electronic items and 20% in the case of motor cars by the reducing balance method).

Valuation of Perquisites Taxable in the Hands of the Employer under Provisions of Fringe Benefit Tax

The value of fringe benefits for purposes of levy of the Fringe Benefit Tax is computed as the aggregate of the valuations for the various fringe benefits provided or deemed to have been provided. The method of valuation of these fringe benefits is given below:

Nature of fringe benefit	Valuation of fringe benefit
Free/concessional ticket for private journeys of employees or their family members	100% of cost of free/concessional ticket as provided by the employer to the general public less amount paid/recovered from the employee/employees. Where the value of free/ concessional ticket is included in any other type of benefit mentioned below, the value of free/concessional ticket is reduced by the amount included in the other benefit.
Contribution made by employer to an approved superannuation fund	Actual amount of contribution in excess of Rs. 1 lakh per employee made by the employer.
w.e.f. 1/4/2008- Any specified security or sweat equity shares allotted or transferred, directly or indirectly, by the employer free of cost or at concessional rate to his employees (including former employees) This includes securities offered under Employees' Stock Option Plans	w.e.f. 1/4/2008- Fair market value (determined by method prescribed by Central Board of Direct Taxes in circular no. 9, dated 20/12/2007) of the specified security or sweat equity shares, on the date on which the option vests with the employee less the amount paid by or recovered from the employee in respect of such security or shares
Entertainment	20% of the expenses
Provision of hospitality (excluding food or beverages in office/factory or non transferable vouchers usable at eating joints/outlets)	20% of the expenses (Lower rate of 5% of the expenses for employer engaged in the business of a hotel) w.e.f. 1/4/2007-(Lower rate of 5% of the expenses for employer engaged in the business of carriage of passengers or goods by aircraft or ship)
Conference (excluding participation fee)	20% of the expenses
Sales promotion including publicity (excluding specified advertisement expenditures mentioned in para 4.2)	20% of the expenses
Employee welfare (excluding statutory obligations/ mitigation of occupational hazards/first aid) w.e.f. 1/4/2009-(excluding expenditure incurred or payment made to provide crèche facility for employees' children, sponsor an employee sportsman, or organize sports events for employees)	20% of the expenses
Conveyance	20% of the expenses (Lower rate of 5% of the expenses for employer engaged in the business of construction. Further, the value of fringe benefit is 5% of expenses for employer engaged in manufacture/production of pharmaceuticals or computer software)
Tour and travel (including foreign travel)	5% of the expenses
Use of hotel, boarding and lodging facilities	20% of the expenses

Contd....

	(The value of fringe benefit is restricted to 5% of expenses for employer engaged in manufacture/production of pharmaceuticals or computer software) (Lower rate of 5% of the expenses for employer engaged in the business of carriage of passengers or goods by aircraft or ship)
Repair, running (including fuel) of motor cars and depreciation thereon	20% of the expenses (Lower rate of 5% of the expenses for employer engaged in the carriage of passengers or goods by motor car)
Repair, running (including fuel) of aircraft and depreciation thereon	20% of the expenses ('Nil' in the case of employer engaged in the carriage of passengers or goods by aircraft)
Use of telephone (including mobile phone but excluding expenditure on leased telephone lines)	20% of the expenses
Maintenance of guest house accommodation (excluding accommodation for training purposes)	20% of the expenses w.e.f. 1/4/2009- Exempt
Festival celebrations	50% of the expenses w.e.f. 1/4/2009- 20% of the expenses
Use of health club and similar facilities	50% of the expenses
Use of any other club facilities	50% of the expenses
Gifts	50% of the expenses
Gifts and Scholarships	50% of the expenses

Schedule XIII to the Indian Companies Act, 1956

The Ministry of Companies Affairs has made important changes to schedule XIII to the Indian Companies Act 1956. These changes ensure greater flexibility for the companies to acquire better managerial skills.

The provisions of schedule XIII are applicable only to (a) a public limited company and (b) a private limited company which is subsidiary of a public company. The provisions of schedule XIII are not applicable to Government companies.

Practice Questions

Objective Type Questions

1. Section 198 is concerned with managerial personnel in relation to:
   (*a*) Appointment
   (*b*) Remuneration
   (*c*) Perquisites
   (*d*) Fringe Benefit
2. Number of categories of managerial personnel defined in the Indian Companies Act 1956:
   (*a*) 8 (*b*) 7
   (*c*) 6 (*d*) 5

3. Effective Capital means:
   (*a*) Paid up share capital
   (*b*) Reserves and Surpluses
   (*c*) Long term loans and deposits
   (*d*) Aggregate of all of the above
4. Remuneration Committee is given in:
   (*a*) Schedule XIII
   (*b*) Clause 49
   (*c*) Schedule XIV
   (*d*) None of the above
5. Schedule XIII is mandatory for companies with a paid up capital of:
   (*a*) Rs.5 crore or more
   (*b*) Rs.10 crore or more
   (*c*) Rs.15 crore or more
   (*d*) Rs.20 crore or more

Ans:1.(b), 2. (d), 3. (d), 4. (b), 5. (a)

Short Answer Questions

1. What is managerial remuneration?
2. Explain the scope of perquisite.
3. What do you mean by maximum managerial remuneration?
4. What are the rules regarding minimum remuneration in case of inadequate profits?
5. What are the determinants of managerial remuneration?

Long Answer Questions

1. What do you mean by managerial remuneration? Examine the provisions of Indian Companies Act 1956 with regard to managerial remuneration in India.
2. Critically examine the present guidelines with regard to managerial remuneration in India.
3. What do you mean by managerial remuneration? Examine its scope.
4. What do you know by perquisites? Explain its scope.
5. Critically examine the valuation process of perquisites.
6. What is managerial remuneration? Explain its limitations in detail.
7. Critically evaluate the rules regarding remuneration of director.

References

1. Amitabh Kumar, "Valuation of Perquisites", Tax Payer Information Series -36, Income Tax Department, New Delhi, 2008,p.1-2
2. Chinnasamy Ganesan, "Schedule XIII to the companies Act – A Practical Approach, Chartered Accountant Feb., 2003, p.832-833

10 SECURITIES & EXCHANGE BOARD OF INDIA (SEBI)

Saving is a function of national income and its level is determined by the level of investment environment. Conducive investment environment motivates the savers to save and invest the same under existing regulatory mechanism. Developing economies like India are facing resource crunch so that they should try to evolve effective strategies for resource mobilization. Development of conducive environment is one of these strategies. However, government is responsible for protecting the interest of fund providers for national development. Issuing companies are generally eager to mobilize resources from retail investors and promoters of these companies are not interested to protect the interest of retail investors. Retail investors are the backbone of the capital market. They provide depth to the market support and liquidity are also insured by the small investors. Thus, there is need for effective regulations to protect the interest of investors and also to maintain their confidence in the capital market to improve the market efficiency, enhance the transparency, prevent the unfair trade practices and bring the Indian capital market up to international standards. Indian capital market is an emerging market and efficient and effective regulatory mechanism is required to make the capital market more investor friendly.

After achieving independence in 1947 Government also alive to the problems of capital market and its proper development. Regulatory framework for capital issues was developed to: (i) to prevent the diversion of investible resources to non-essential projects, (ii) to regulate the issues of bonus shares, capital reorganization and the capital structure of companies with a view to discouraging the issue of shares with disproportionate voting rights and encouraging the adoption of sound methods and techniques in company floating, (iii) to recover disputed arrears of revenue to the Central Government, (iv) to enforce the payment of statutory dues to employees, and (v) to provide for measures to protect the interest of investors.

Historical Perspective of Regulatory Framework for Capital Issues

Earlier procedures of new issues were regulated by the Central Government as per the Capital Issues (Control) Act, 1947. The provisions of the Act were set to: (i) ensure that the investment should flow into productive channels (ii) promote a rational and healthy corporate sector, (iii) direct and distribute public subscription of new issues to avoid undue concentration in a particular sector or region, (iv) regulate capital re-organisation plans of companies for mergers and amalgamations,[1] (v) regulate the terms and conditions of foreign capital participation and of dilution or repatriation of foreign equity, and (vi) prevent development of new companies in overcrowded lines and/ or regions.

The Controller of Capital Issue was the most powerful controlling authority for capital issues (CCI)[2]. The capital issues refer to the issuing and creating any securities whether for each of otherwise and include the converting partly paid up shares into the fully paid up shares or increasing the par value of shares already issued.[3] The securities include (i) shares and stocks; (ii) debentures and bonds; (iii) mortgage deeds or other instruments creating or evidencing a charge or lien on the assets of the company, and (iv) instruments acknowledging loan to or indebtedness of the company.

The scope of the Act extended to all companies which made capital issues or renewed maturity or postponed repayment of any security of India or abroad.[4] The consent of the Controller of Capital Issue (CCI) was mandatory [5] where the issue of the capital was (i) in excess of Rs.1.00 crore during a period of 12 months. (ii) a public offer of securities at a premium or discount, (iii) issue of bonus shares of any amount by public or private companies, (iv) issue of preference shares carrying rights other than those privately placed with financial institutions, (v) issue of preference shares carrying conversion of participating rights, and (vi) issue of the securities involving relaxation of any of the conditions mentioned in the Capital Issues (Exemption) order, 1969 relating to (a) issue if shares arising from a revaluation of assets or creation of intangible assets, (b) rate of dividend on preference shares exceeding the specified limit, (c) promoter's share falling below the prescribed limit, (d) the preference share capital in excess of one-third of the equity capital, and (e) debt-equity ratio exceeding 2:1.

Under the Act following exemptions were made available to issuing companies (i) private companies provided these were not covered under the Monopolies and Restrictive Trade Practices (MRTP) Act, 1969, (ii) government companies provided no portion of their securities issues was offered to the general public, and (iii) banking, insurance concerns and provident fund societies incorporated as companies. However, these companies had to furnish initial and quarterly reports of the capital issues to the CCI when the capital issues exceeded Rs. 1.00 crore during a period of 12 months. The capital issues of securities at par upto Rs.1.00 crore by public limited companies within a period of 12 months. (ii) loan granted or bonds/debentures taken or guarantees given by public financial institutions, and (iii) loan, advances, overdrafts or guarantees given by the banking institutions.

The CCI was required to evaluate and review the cases as per the guidelines and policies formulated by the Central Government at the time of granting consent from time to time.[6] Various evaluating criteria were taken into account viz., adequacy of capital, sound capital structure, promoter's stake issue price, listing of the security, timing of issue, etc. The company had to submit detailed estimates of the projects costs, so as to ensure that the necessary financial resources would be raised by the companies easily may avoid approaching the capital market next time before the project was complete. In the case of time and cost overrun with regard to the project the scheme of finance was to be approved by the financial institutions and the same was to be accepted by the CCI. The adequacy of capital was ascertained by maintaining a balance capital structure.

The equity capital was composed of paid-up equity capital, irredeemable preference shares, redeemable preference shares within 12 months or more to run the company, share premium reserves and free reserves including development reserve. Debt includes all fixed interest bearing securities like debentures, redeemable preference shares with maturity period of less than 12 years, loans from the various financial institutions and deferred credit for the purchase of plant and machinery. The normal debt-equity ratio had been taken as 2:1[7] which was expected to be relaxed in case of capital intensive industries. However, normal equity preference ratio was fixed at 3:1[8]. The CCI was empowered to fix the rate of interest on debenture which was raised to 15% along with allowing a premium of 5% on the face value of debentures at the time of their redemption. It was also empowered to fix the rate of dividend on preference shares which was 15% at that time.

The CCI had to ensure a reasonable minimum stake by the promoters/directors in the capital to maintain public confidence and trust. The stake of promoters/directors was to be 15% in companies with capital upto Rs.1.00 crore; 12.5% in companies with capital upto Rs. 2 crore and 10% in companies with capital beyond Rs.2 crore. Promoters were required to subscribe these minimum amount of capital before going for public issue. The combined shareholdings of Indian promoters and foreign collaborators were fixed within the two-thirds limit of the total capital issues and the remaining one third could be offered to public if foreign collaborators were expected to participate in the equity.

Newly floated companies were not eligible to issue their shares at premium. The CCI also ensured that capital issues by a newly floated company could not be issued at premium. It was necessary to ensure liquidity, marketability, safety, price continuity and free transferability of capital. The CCI was also empowered to examine the arrangements for listing of securities as per the guidelines. It has also ensured that 40% of the capital issues were to be allotted to the promoters including their friends, associates, and interconnected companies and the remaining 60% to public financial institutions (11%) and public (49%). The CCI had tried to ensure that the capital issues were equitably distributed throughout the year. Rights or bonus shares were also allowed if an existing company desires to have additional capital issues for financing diversification, expansion, modernization, research and development programmes or desire to capitalize the reserves and surpluses.[9] The consent of CCI was also needed for such issues which was granted after paying attention to the value of assets, market price of shares, earning capacity of the company, growth prospects, dividend records, etc. Unsubscribed capital was to be equitably distributed among the applicants for additional shares. Matter with regard to issue of bonus shares was to be decided by the board of directors as per (i) the residual reserve test; (ii) the profitability test and (iii) on the time frequency test.

The validity of the consent order issued by the CCI was to be meant for 12 months unless it was specified otherwise or it was extended. The issuing companies were required to furnish the information on the amount subscribed and the amount received on the prescribed form. The limit for retention of oversubscription by public had uniformly scaled down to 15% for equity and debentures alike. In case the company desired for such retention of over subscription, it was to be stated in the original application meant for the CCI and its approval. However, there was a lot of criticism against the office of the CCI. Nepotism, corruption and interference were the major bases of criticism against the CCI. The Committee on Financial System (Narasimham Committee) observed that the growth of the newer forms of capital institutions is an indication of the growing volume and diversification of the capital market. For the business to grow on sound lines a framework of regulations, is however, necessary as a measures of investor's protection. The committee was of the view that the measure of control on capital market need urgent review.

The committee remarked that "the regulation of capital market should be aimed at protecting the investor's interest against possible risks and fraud. The Committee also proposed that SEBI should formulate a set of prudential guidelines to protect the interest of investors. This should replace the extant restrictive guidelines issued by the Controller of Capital Issues. The role of SEBI was envisaged as a market regulator to see that the market is functional on the basis of well laid down principles and guidelines and not get involved in routine functioning of the market as the CCI was doing in its regions. The role of regulation should be one to ensure timely compliance without excessive discretionary control as the main charge levied as the CCI.

In 1991 process of liberalization, privatization and globalisation was initiated and consequently the SEBI was established. A package of reforms was introduced in 1992. The package consisted of measures to liberalize, regulate and develop the securities market through establishment of Securities and Exchange Board of India (SEBI) as the market regulator responsible for regulation and development of the securities market in India. The practices of allocation of resources among different competing entities as well as its terms by a central authority, i.e., Controller of Capital Issues (CCI), was discontinued. Keeping the recommendations of Narasimham Committee in 1988 the Securities and Exchange Board of India (SEBI) was established by the Government of India through an executive resolution, and was subsequently upgraded as fully autonomous body (a statutory Board) in the year 1992 with the passing of the Securities and Exchange Board of India Act (SEBI Act) on 30th January 1992. A statutory and autonomous regulatory board with defined responsibilities and independent powers have been set up without having an intervention from the government. Now SEBI is responsible for development and the regulation of capital market. Actually, autonomous character of SEBI was also necessitated due to outcome of the Securities Scam of 1990-91.

Organisation of SEBI

The SEBI has been established as a body corporate, having perpetual succession and a common seal. The general superintendence, direction and management of the affairs of SEBI vests in a Board of members, which exercises all powers and do all acts and things which may be exercised or done by SEBI. Unless determined otherwise through regulations, the Chairman shall also have all these powers.

Section 4 (1) of SEBI Act provides that SEBI Board shall consist of the following members, namely:

(*a*) a chairman;

(*b*) two members from amongst the officials of the Ministry of the Central Government dealing with Finance and administration of the Corporate Act, 1956;

(*c*) one member from amongst the officials of the Reserve Bank;

(*d*) five other members of whom at least three shall be the whole time members, to be appointed by the central government.

The Chairman and the members are from amongst the persons of ability, integrity and standing who have shown capacity in dealing with problems relating to securities market or have special knowledge or experience of law, finance, economics, accountancy, administration or in any other discipline which, in the opinion of the Central Government, shall be useful to SEBI. The terms and conditions of service of Chairman and members are determined in the rules framed by Government in this regard.

Objectives of the SEBI

Major objectives of the SEBI are as follows:

(*i*) to protect the interests of investors in securities;

(*ii*) to promote the development of Securities Market;

(*iii*) to regulate the securities market and

(*iv*) for matters connected therewith or incidental thereto

Since its inception SEBI has been working and targeting the securities and is attending to the fulfillment of its objectives with commendable zeal and dexterity. The improvements in the securities markets like capitalization requirements, margining, establishment of clearing corporations etc. reduced the risk of credit and also reduced the market manipulation activities.

The SEBI has introduced the comprehensive regulatory measures, prescribed registration norms, the eligibility criteria, the code of obligations and the code of conduct for different intermediaries like, bankers to issue, merchant bankers, brokers and sub-brokers, registrars, portfolio managers credit rating agencies, underwriters and others. It has framed bye-laws, risk identification and risk management systems for Clearing houses of stock exchanges, surveillance system etc. which has made dealing in securities both safe and transparent to the end investor.

Two broad approaches of SEBI is to integrate the securities market at the national level, and also to diversify the trading products, so that there is an increase in number of traders including banks, financial institutions, insurance companies, mutual funds, primary dealers etc. to transact through the Exchanges. In this context, the introduction of derivatives trading through Indian Stock Exchanges permitted by SEBI in 2000 AD is a real landmark.

Objectives of Securities Market Regulation

An important feature of the securities market is the depth and breathe of public participation in the market. Millions of households and individual investors provide a pool of capital and a diversity of decision making that creates liquidity in the market and makes it dynamic. The securities markets are vital to the growth, development and strength of market economics. They support corporate initiatives, finance the exploitation of new ideas and facilitate the management of financial risk. Further, since retail investors are placing an increasing proportion of their money in mutual funds and other collective investments, securities markets have become central to individual wealth and retirement planning. Sound and effective regulation, and the confidence it brings, is important for the integrity, growth and development of securities markets. Appropriate regulations recognise the benefits of competition and facilitates capital formation and economic growth. Inappropriate regulation could impose an unjustified burden on the market and inhibit market growth and development.

The increasing internationalization of financial activities and the globalization of markets would ideally require a standard approach to address various regulatory issues across the globe. However, the different legislative and regulatory structures, reflecting local market conditions and historical developments, make it difficult to attain this goal. The particular manner in which a country structures the securities market regulatory framework often demands on the entire domestic context, including the relevant legal and commercial framework.

The three-core objective of securities market regulations are:

(*a*) Investor's protection.

(*b*) Ensuring fair, efficient and transparent markets.

(*c*) Minimizing systemic risk.

(*i*) Investors Protection

The basic objective of securities regulation is to protect investors from unfair and fraudulent practices, including insider trading, market manipulation, misleading advice and misuse of client assets.[8] The genuine investors' participation in the market can be increased only by building his confidence that he will be effectively protected against market abuses and lapses.

One of the most critical factors in sustainable development of securities market is confidence of the investor in the market mechanism. There can be no sustainable development in securities market unless highest priority is given to the creation of strong confidence among the common investors. Investors must be assured that they will be given a fair deal and will be adequately protected.[10] An investor should require protection through an external regulatory body, like SEBI, only when the market mechanism collapses due to fraudulent act of some ingenious market players.

Supervision of market intermediaries should also ensure investors' protection by setting minimum qualification standards for market participants. Investors should be detracted in a just and equitable manner by market intermediaries according to standards, which should be set out in rules of business conduct. There should be a comprehensive system of inspection, surveillance and compliance programs for regulation of intermediaries. It is also important that Investors should have access to a neutral mechanism such as arbitration, special courts or other such mechanisms of dispute resolution for redressal of their grievances.[11]

(*ii*) Fair, Efficient, and Transparent Market

Efforts are required to ensure a fair, efficient, and transparent securities markets in the country. Regulatory mechanism should closely link to investors' protection and, in particular, to the prevention of unfair trading practices. Market structure should not unduly favour some market users over others. Regulation should detect, deter and penalize market manipulation and other unfair trading practices. Regulation should aim to ensure that investors are given fair access to market facilities and market & price information. Regulation should promote market practices that ensure fair treatment of orders and reliable price discovery process. In an efficient market, dissemination of relevant information is timely and widespread and is reflected in the price discovery process. Regulation should promote market efficiency.

Transparency in market is defined as the degree to which information about trading (both for pre-trade and post-trade information) is made publicly available on a real-time basis. Pre-trade information concerns the posting of bids and offers as a means to enable investors to know, with some degree of certainty, whether and at what prices they can deal. Post-trade information is related to prices and volume of all individual transaction actually concluded. Regulation should ensure the highest levels of transparency. Market transparency is generally regarded as playing a central role in promoting fairness and efficiency of markets. It is however important to note that transparency in itself may not always be sufficient to ensure that market users get high quality price information. Competition delivers benefits to the overall market. Regulators may also need to review other factors such as market access, time-priority, order handling rules and reference pricing.

(*iii*) Minimizing systemic risk

The implementation of a strong and effective risk management and control system within securities firms promotes stability throughout the entire financial system. Aims of risk management and control system should be as follows:

(*a*) to protect firms against market, credit, liquidity, operational, and legal risks;

(*b*) to protect financial industry from systemic risk;

(*c*) to protect firm's customers from large non-market related losses (e.g., firm failure, misappropriation, fraud, etc.); and

(*d*) to protect firms and their franchise from suffering adversely from credibility risk.

Sound and effective risk management and controls promote both securities firm and industry stability, which in turn, inspires confidence in the investing public and counter parties. Securities firms thus have adequate economics and commercial incentives to employ strong risk management and internal control systems.

SEBI Administration

The Securities and Exchange Board of India Act, 1992 is having retrospective effect and is deemed to have come into force on January 30, 1992. Relatively a brief act containing 35 sections, the SEBI Act governs all the Stock Exchanges and the Securities Transactions in India.

Section 11 of the SEBI Act provides that to protect the interest of investors in securities and to promote the development of and to regulate the securities market by such measures, it is the duty of the Board. It has given power to the Board to regulate the businesses in Stock Exchanges, register and regulate the working of stock brokers, sub-brokers, share transfer agents, bankers to an issue, trustee of trust deeds, registrars to an issue, merchant bankers, underwriters, portfolio managers, investment advisers, etc., also to register and regulate the working of collective investment schemes including mutual funds, to prohibit fraudulent and unfair trade practices and insider trading to regulate take- over, to conduct enquiries and audits of stock exchanges, etc.

All the stock brokers, sub-brokers, share transfer agents, bankers to an issue, trustee of trust deed, registrars to an issue, merchant bankers, underwriters, portfolio managers, investment advisers and such other intermediaries who may be associated with the Securities Market are to register with the Board has the power to suspend or cancel such registration. The Board is bound by the directions vested by the Central Government each year, giving true and full account of its activities, policies and programmes. Any one of the aggrieved by the Board's decision is entitled to appeal to the Central Government.

Principles of Investment Environment

"There are different parties who are responsible for creating effective investment environment. They are required to go by the certain principles. These principles are as follows:"[12]

A. Principles relating to the regulators

(*i*) Responsibilities of the regulators should be clear and objectively stand

(*ii*) The regulators should be operationally dependent and accountable in exercise of its functions and powers.

(*iii*) The regulators should have adequate powers, proper resources and capacity to perform its functions and exercise its powers.

(*iv*) The regulator should adopt clear and consistent regulatory processes.

(*v*) The staff of the regulator should observe the highest professional standards including appropriate standards of confidentiality.

(*vi*) Principles of self-regulation.

(*vii*) The regulatory regime should make appropriate use of self-regulatory organizations (SRO) that exercise some direct oversight responsibility for their respective areas of competence and to the extent appropriate to the size and complexity of markets.

(*viii*) SROs should be subject to the oversight of the regulator and should observe standards of fairness and confidentiality when exercising powers and delegated responsibilities.

(*ix*) Principles for the enforcement of securities regulation.

(*x*) The regulator should have comprehensive inspection, investigation and surveillance powers.

(*xi*) The regulator should have comprehensive enforcement powers.

(*xii*) The regulatory system should ensure an effective and credible use of inspection, investigation, surveillance and enforcement powers and implementation of an effective compliance program.

B. Principles for co-operation in regulation

(*i*) The regulator should have authority to share both public and non-public information with domestic and foreign counterparts.

(*ii*) Regulators should establish information sharing mechanisms that set-out when and how they will share both public and non-public information with their domestic and foreign counterparts.

(*iii*) The regulatory systems allow for assistance to be provided to foreign regulators who need to make inquiries in the discharge of their functions and exercise of their powers.

C. Principles for Issuers

(*i*) There should be full, accurate and timely disclosure of financial results and other information, which is materials to investors' decisions.

(*ii*) Holders of securities in a company should be treated in a fair and equitable manner.

(*iii*) Accounting and auditing standards should be of a high and internationally acceptable quality.

D. Principles for collective investment schemes

(*i*) The regulatory system should set standards for eligibility and regulation of those who wish to market or operate a collective investment scheme.

(*ii*) The regulatory system should provide for rules governing the legal form and structure of collective investment schemes and the segregation and protection of client assets.

(*iii*) Regulation should require disclosure, as set forth under the principles for issuers, which is necessary to evaluate the suitability of a collective investment scheme for a particular investor and the value of the investor's interest in the scheme.

E. Principles for market intermediaries

(*i*) Regulation should provide for minimum entry standards for market intermediaries.

(*ii*) There should be initial and ongoing capital and other prudential requirements for market intermediaries that reflect the risks that the intermediaries undertake.

(*iii*) Market intermediaries should be required to comply with standards for internal organization and operational conduct that aim to protect the interests of clients, ensure proper management of risk, and under which management of the intermediary accepts primary responsibility for these matters.

(*iv*) There should be a procedure for dealing with failure of a market intermediary in order to minimize damage and loss to investors and to contain systemic risk.

F. Principles for the secondary market

(*i*) The establishment of trading systems including securities exchanges should be subject to regulatory authorization and oversight.

(*ii*) There should be ongoing regulatory supervision of exchanges and trading systems which should aim to ensure that the integrity of trading is maintained through fair and equitable rules that strike an appropriate balance between the demands of different market participants.

(*iii*) Regulation should promote transparency of trading.

(*iv*) Regulation should be designed to detect and deter manipulation and other unfair trading practices.

(*v*) Regulation should aim to ensure the proper management of large exposures, default risk and market disruption.

(*vi*) Systems for clearing and settlement of securities transactions should be subject to regulatory oversight and designed to ensure that they are fair, effective, efficient and that they reduce systematic risk.

Review of Regulatory Environment

Following agencies are involved in the regulatory environment of Indian capital market:

1. SEBI: Securities and Exchange Board of India (SEBI) was set up as an administrative arrangement in 1988. In 1992, the SEBI Act was enacted, which gave statutory status to SEBI. It mandates SEBI to perform a dual function: investor protection through regulation of the securities market and fostering the development of this market. SEBI has been vested most of the functions and powers under the Securities Contract Regulation (SCR) Act, which brought stock exchanges, their members, as well as contracts in securities which could be traded under the regulations of the Ministry of Finance. It has also been delegated certain powers under the Companies Act. In addition to registering and regulating intermediaries, service providers, mutual funds, collective investment schemes, venture capital funds and takeovers, SEBI is also vested with the power to issue directives to any person(s) related to the securities market or to companies in areas of issue of capital, transfer of securities and disclosures. It also has powers to inspect books and records, suspend registered entities and cancel registration.

The powers and functions of regulatory authorities for the securities market seem to be diverse in nature. SEBI is the primary body responsible for regulation of the securities market, deriving its powers of registration and enforcement from the SEBI Act. There was an existing regulatory framework for the securities market provided by the Securities Contract Regulation (SCR) Act and the Companies Act, administered by the Ministry of Finance and the Department of Company Affairs (DCA). SEBI has been delegated most of the functions and powers under the SCR Act and shares the rest with the Ministry of Finance. It has also been delegated certain powers under the Companies Act. RBI also has regulatory involvement in the capital markets regarding foreign exchange control, liquidity support to market participants and debt management through primary dealers. It is RBI and not SEBI that regulates primary dealers in the Government securities market. However, securities transactions that involve a foreign exchange transaction need the permission of RBI. So far, fragmentation of the regulatory authorities has not been a major obstacle to effective regulation of the securities market. Rather, lack of enforcement capacity by SEBI has been a more significant cause of poor regulation. But since the Indian stock markets are rapidly being integrated, the authorities may follow the global trend of consolidation of regulatory authorities or better coordination among them.

SEBI Act of 1992 has introduced self-regulatory organizations [SROs] for regulating various participants in the securities market. SEBI has already issued necessary guidelines for self regulatory for self regulatory organisations for effective compliance. However, at present the only market related SROs in India whose regulatory frameworks have been well established and which are actually functioning are the recognized stock exchanges.

2. RBI : Reserve Bank of India (RBI) has regulatory involvement in the capital market, but this has been limited to debt management through primary dealers, foreign exchange control and liquidity support to market participants. It is RBI and not SEBI that regulates primary dealers in the Government securities market. RBI instituted the primary dealership of Government securities in March 1998. Securities transactions that involve foreign exchange transactions need the permission of RBI.

3. Stock Exchanges: SEBI issued directives that require that half the members of the governing boards of the stock exchanges should be non broker public representatives and include a SEBI nominee. To avoid conflicts of interest, stock brokers are a minority in the committees of stock exchanges set up to handle matters of discipline, default and investor-broker disputes. The exchanges are required to appoint a professional, non member executive director who is accountable to SEBI for the implementation of its directives on the regulation of stock exchanges. SEBI has introduced a mechanism to redress investor grievances against brokers. Further, all issues are regulated through a series of disclosure norms as prescribed by SEBI and respective stock exchanges through their listing agreement. After a security is issued to the public and subsequently listed on a stock exchange, the issuing company is required under the listing agreement to continue to disclose in a timely manner to the exchange, to the holders of the listed securities and to the public any information necessary to enable the holders of the listed securities to appraise its position and to avoid the establishment of a false market in such listed securities.

Powers and Functions of SEBI

Chapter IV of SEBI Act, 1992 deals with the powers and functions of the Board. Section 11 of the Act lays down that it shall be the duty of the Board to protect the interests of the investors in securities and to promote the development of, and to regulate the securities markets by such measures as it thinks fit. These measures would include:

(i) regulating the business in stock exchanges and any other securities markets;

(ii) registering and regulating the working of stock brokers, share transfer agents, bankers to an issue, trustees of trust deeds, registrars to an issue, merchant bankers, underwriters, portfolio managers, investment advisers and such other intermediaries who may be associated with securities markets in any manner;

(iii) registering and regulating then working of the depositories, participants, custodians of securities, foreign institutional investors, credit rating agencies and such other intermediaries as the board may, by notification, specify in this behalf;

(iv) registering and regulating the working of venture capital funds and collective investment schemes, including mutual funds;

(v) promoting and regulating self-regulatory organizations;

(vi) prohibiting fraudulent and unfair trade practices relating to securities markets;

(vii) promoting investors' education and training of intermediaries of securities markets;

(viii) Prohibiting insider trading in securities;

(ix) Regulating substantial acquisition of shares and takeover of companies;

(x) Calling for information from, undertaking inspection, conducting inquiries and audits of the stock exchanges, mutual funds, other persons associated with the securities market, intermediaries and self-regulatory organizations in the securities market.

(xi) Calling for information and record from any bank or any other authority or board or corporation established or constituted by or under any central, state or provincial Act in respect of any transaction in securities which is under investigation or inquiry by the Board;

(xii) Performing such functions and exercising such powers under the provisions of the Securities Contracts (Regulation) Act, 1956, as may be delegated to it by the Central Government;

(xiii) Levying fees or other charges for carrying out the purpose of this section;

(xiv) Conducting research for the above purposes;

(xv) Calling from or furnishing to any such agencies, as may be specified by the Board, such information as may be considered necessary by it for the efficient discharge of its functions;

(xvi) Performing such other functions as may be prescribed.

Other Powers

Other powers of the SEBI are detailed below:

1. Power to Issue Directions : Section 11B of the Act provides that if SEBI is satisfied after making due enquiries, that it is necessary:

(*i*) in the interest of investors, or orderly development of securities market, or

(*ii*) to prevent the affairs of any intermediary or other persons referred of investors or securities market; or

(*iii*) to secure the proper management of any such intermediary or person, it may issue such directions-

(*a*) to any persons or class of persons referred to in section 12, or associated with the securities market;

(*b*) to any company in respect of matters specified in section 11 A, as may be appropriate in the interests of investors in securities and the securities market.

2. Powers to make Enquiry : SEBI has been given adequate powers to perform its functions. As per section 11B of the SEBI Act, if after making or causing to be made an enquiry, SEBI is satisfied that it is necessary:-

(*i*) in the interest of investors, or orderly development of securities market; or

(*ii*) to prevent the affairs of any intermediary or other persons referred to in section 12 being conducted in a manner detrimental to the interest of investors or securities markets; or

(*iii*) to secure the proper management of any such intermediary or person.

3. Power to make Rules : Section 29 empowers the Central Government to make rules for carrying out the purposes of this Act. Such rules may provide for all or any of the following matters namely,

(*i*) the term of office and other conditions of service of the chairman and the members of SEBI;

(*ii*) the additional functions that may be performed by SEBI under section 11 of the Act.

(*iii*) The manner in which the accounts of SEBI shall be maintained under section15;

(*iv*) The manner of inquiry by adjudicating officer;

(*v*) The salaries and allowances and other terms and conditions of service of the Presiding Officers, members and other officers and employees of the Securities Appellate Tribunal;

(*vi*) The procedure for the investigation of mis-behaviour or incapacity of the Presiding Officers or other members of the Securities Appellate Tribunal;

(*vii*) The form in which an appeal may be filed before the Securities Appellate Tribunal and the fees payable in respect of such appeal;

(*viii*) The form and the manner in which returns and report to be made to the Central Government under Section 18;l

(*ix*) Any other matter which is to be, or may be, prescribed, or in respect of which provision is to be, or may be made by rules.

4. Power to make Regulations : Section 30 empowers SEBI by notification to make regulations consistent with this Act and the rules made there under to carry out the purposes of this Act.

Such regulations may provide for all or any of the following matters, namely:

(*i*) the times and places of meetings of SEBI and the procedure to be followed at such meetings including quorum necessary for the transaction of business;

(*ii*) the term and other conditions of service of officers and employees of SEBI;

(*iii*) the matters relating to issue of capital, transfer of securities and other matters incidental thereto and the manner in which such matters shall be disclosed by the companies under section 11 A.

(*iv*) the conditions subject to which certificate of registration is to be issued, the amount of fee to be paid certificate of registration and the manner of suspension or cancellation of certificate of registration.

Responsibilities of the Board

The corporate governance framework should ensure the strategic guidance of the company, the effective monitoring of management by the board, and the board's accountability to the company and the shareholders. Board member should act on a fully informed basis, in good faith, in manner that is just and equitable, with due diligence and care, and in the best interest of the company and the shareholders. The board should ensure compliance with applicable law and take into account the interests of shareholders.

The key functions of the board should include:

1. Removing and guiding corporate strategy, major plans of action, risk policy, annual budgets and business plans; setting performance objectives; monitoring implementation and corporate performance; and overseeing major capital expenditure, acquisition and divestitures.
2. Selecting, compensating, monitoring and, when necessary, replacing key executive and overseeing succession planning.
3. Reviewing key executive and board remuneration, and ensuring a formal and transparent board nomination process.
4. Monitoring and managing potential conflicts of interest of management, board members and shareholders, including misuse of corporate assets and abuse in related party transaction.
5. Ensuring the integrity of the corporation's accounting and financial reporting systems, including the independent audit, and that appropriate systems of control are in place, in particular, systems for monitoring risk, financial controls, and compliance with the law.
6. Monitoring the effectiveness of the governance practices under which it operates and making changes as needed.
7. Overseeing the process of disclosure and communication.

The board should be able to exercise objective judgment on corporate affairs independent, in particular, from management. For this purpose boards should consider assigning a sufficient number of non-executive board members capable of exercising independent judgment to tasks where there is a potential for conflict of interest. Examples of such key responsibilities are financial reporting, nomination and executive and board remuneration. Board members should devote sufficient time to their responsibilities.

Registration of Intermediaries

Section 12 (1) of the Act provides that no stock- broker, sub- broker, share transfer agent, banker to an issue, trustee of trust deed, registrar to an issue, merchant banker, underwriter, portfolio manager, investment adviser and such other intermediary who may be associated with securities market shall buy, sell or deal in securities except under, and in accordance with, the conditions of a certificate of registration obtained from SEBI in accordance with the regulations made under this Act.

Co-operation between Various Agencies

The co-operation between major agencies responsible for regulation of securities markets and enforcement of law is achieved by nomination of representatives of RBI, Ministry of Law, Justice and Company Affairs, and Ministry of Finance of the Board of SEBI. However, of late need for a formal mechanism of co-operation between various regulatory agencies is been increasingly felt, particularly in view of a number of scams involving banks, non-banking finance companies and security brokers. Various suggestions made to the Government in this regard include the idea of setting up a 'super regulator' with a responsibility to co-ordinate the efforts of various regulatory agencies.

In January 2003, the Union Cabinet of India approves the establishment of a Serious Fraud Investigation Office (SFIO) within Department of Companies Affairs to investigate complicates financial frauds. The proposed office would utilize the expertise and experience of various investigations and enforcement agencies, including Central Bureau of Investigation (CBI) and SEBI to carry out a centralized and cohesive investigation into large multifaceted financial crimes. Insofa as the global co-operation is concerned, SEBI is a full member of the International Organization of Securities Commissions (IOSCO) and has been actively co-operating with regulators across the globe. SEBI has signs Memorandum of Understanding with the Securities and Exchange Commission (SEC) of USA, the Financial Service Commission (FSC) of Mauritius and Securities Commission of Malaysia.

Need for Making SEBI More Effective

Necessary measures are required to make SEBI more effective. In this context, government has been trying to strengthen the SEBI. SEBI has been given full operational independence. The general superintendence, direction and management of the affairs of SEBI have been vested in a Board of members. The Board consisting of a Chairman and eight other members exercise all the powers conferred upon SEBI under the SEBI Act. The Chairman also has the concurrent power of general superintendence and direction of the affairs of the SEBI and may also exercise all powers and do all acts and things, which may be exercised or done by SEBI. SEBI may also, by an order in writing, delegate any of its power or functions, as it may deem fit, to any member or officer of the Board, or any other person. Power to makes rules as per section 29 of the SEBI Act however cannot be delegated. He Central Government may issue directions to the SEBI on the policy matters. The Central Government may consider the views expressed by SEBI on such policy matter but its decision is final and binding on SEBI.

The Central Government also has the powers to supersede the Board for a period not exceeding six months, in any of the following circumstances:

(*a*) where on account of grave emergency, the Board is unable to discharge the functions and duties imposed on it by or under the provisions of this Act.

(*b*) Where the Board has persistently made default in complying with any direction issued by the Central Government under this Act or in the discharge of the functions and duties imposed on it by or under the provision of this Act and as a result of such default the financial position of the Board or the administration of the Board has deteriorated.

(*c*) Where circumstances exist making it necessary in the public interest so to do.

Securities Appellate Tribunal

The SEBI Act also provides for the establishment of the Securities Appellate Tribunals to consider appeals against SEBI's orders, of penalties. It is in order to afford proper appellate remedies to the affected parties by the decisions of the SEBI.

As per Section 15 K, the Central Government is empowered to establish by notifications one or more Appellate Tribunals, to be known as the Securities Appellate Tribunals to exercise the jurisdiction, power and authorities conferred on such Tribunal by SEBI Act or under the Act or any other law for the time being in force. The Central Government has set up a tribunal at Mumbai. According to Section 15 L, which deals with the composition of the Tribunal, the Securities Appellate Tribunals shall consist of a Presiding Officer and two other members to be appointed by the Central Government by notification.

Section 15 M prescribes that a person shall not be qualified for appointment as the Presiding Officer of Securities Appellate Tribunals unless he is a sitting or retired judge of the Supreme Court or a sitting or retired Chief Justice of a High Court. It has also been prescribed that the presiding officer of the Securities Appellate Tribunal shall be appointed by the Central Government in consulation with chief justice of India or his nominee. A person shall not be qualified for appointment as a member of Securities Appellate Tribunal unless he is a person of ability, integrity and standing who shown capacity in dealing with problems relating to securities market and has qualification and experience of corporate law, securities laws, finance, economics or accountancy.

A member of SEBI or any person holding a post at senior management level at SEBI cannot be appointed as presiding officer or member of Securities Appellate Tribunal during his service or tenure as such with the Board or within two years from the date on which he ceases to hold office as such in the Board. Section 15 N lays down that the Presiding Officer and every other member of Securities Appellate Tribunal shall hold office for a term of five years from the date he enters upon his office and is eligible for reappointment.

It has also been provided that the person attaining age of sixty eight years cannot hold office as the presiding officer of Securities Appellate Tribunal. Also a person who has attained the age of sixty two years cannot hold office as member of Securities Appellate Tribunal. Section 15-O lays down that salary and allowances payable to and the other terms and conditions of service (including pension, gratuity and other retirement benefits) of, the Presiding Officer and other members of a Securities Appellate Tribunal arte such as may be prescribed. It has also been provided that neither the salary and allowances nor other terms and conditions of service of the said Presiding Officer and other members of the Securities Appellate Tribunal shall be varied to their disadvantage after appointment.

Requirements for Appeal to the Tribunal

Sections 15 T and 15 U deal with the appeal procedure and power of Securities Appellate Tribunals.

1. Section 15T lays down that any person aggrieved:

(*a*) by an order of SEBI made, under this Act, or the ruled or regulations made there under; or

(*b*) by an order made by an adjudicating officer under this Act

may prefer an appeal to a Securities Appellate Tribunal having jurisdiction in the matter.

2. No appeal shall lie to the Securities Appellate Tribunals from an order made

(*a*) by SEBI

(*b*) by an adjudicating officer,

with the consent of the parties.

Powers of Securities Appellate Tribunal

The securities Appellate Tribunal shall have, for the purposes of discharging their functions under this Act, the same powers as are vested in a civil court under the Code of Civil Procedure, 1908, while trying a suit, in respect of the following matters, namely:

(*a*) Summoning and enforcing the attendance of any person and examining him on oath;

(*b*) Requiring the discovery and production of documents;

(*c*) Receiving evidence on affidavits;

(*d*) Issuing commissions for the examination of witnesses or documents;

(*e*) Reviewing its decisions;

(*f*) Dismissing an application for default or deciding it ex-parte;

(*g*) Setting aside any order of dismissal of any application for default or any order passed by its ex-parte;

(*h*) Any other matter which may be prescribed.

Role of SEBI

The securities market regulator has a very complex role to play. The regulator has the primary responsibility of attaining the three core objectives of securities regulation, viz., (a) protection of investors; (b) ensuring that markets are fair, efficient and transparent; and (c) reduction of systematic risk. At the same time the regulator also has to ensure that the regulation do not impose an unjustified burden on the market and inhibit market growth and development. The increasing globalisation of the securities trade has further complicated the role of regulator. The regulator thus has to maintain a tight balance between its roles as the regulator of local jurisdiction, promoter of domestic market development, and member of the international regulator community. The role of regulator has also to be understood in light of the following generally accepted principles regarding securities market regulator as enunciated on "Objectives and Principles of Securities Regulation", Report of IOSCO, Public Document No. 125, February, 2002.

1. The responsibilities of the regulator should be clear and objectively stated.
2. The regulator should be operationally independent and accountable in the exercise of its functions and powers.
3. The regulator should have adequate powers, proper resources and the capacity to perform its functions and exercise its powers.
4. The regulator should adopt clear and consistent regulatory processes.
5. The staff of the regulator should observe the highest professional standards including appropriate standards of confidentiality.

SEBI is doing commendable job to develop and strengthen the Indian capital market in proper perspective. Various roles being played by the SEBI are analysed below:

1. Research Activities : Knowledge management is the tool that helps the stakeholders to acquire the cutting edge in a globalished financial market. The guidelines for research initiative are incorporated in SEBI (Annual Report) Rules, 1994. Core activities of department of research includes preparation of reports, compilation of data for publication in monthly bulletin and generation of information and analysis on market trends as required by senior executives of SEBI from time to time. Concept papers in Greenfield areas of securities market are also part of the research profile. The Research Department published Handbook of Statistics on Indian Securities Market, which contains a vast collection of data on Indian securities market. The data published in the Handbook are consistent with the requirement of IMF under the special data dissemination standard.

Under the SEBI Act, 1992, SEBI is responsible for conducting research necessary for regulating and developing the securities market and protecting interests of investors in securities. Keeping this in view, and in order to promote quality research in the area of securities market in a cost effective manner. The SEBI instituted the "SEBI Award for Excellence in Research in the Area of Securities Market Initiative". Under the initiative, SEBI shall confers up to 3 (three) awards on the 3 (three) best researchers (individual/institutions) in securities market every year. The award includes a cash prize of Rs. 1,00,000 (Rupees One Lakh Only) and a citation.

2. Investor Awareness Education and Protection Programme

(i) **Redressal of Investor Grievances :** The SEBI has a comprehensive investor grievances processing mechanism. The Office of Investor Assistance and Education (OIAE) is the single window interface of SEBI with the investors. The OIAE accepts grievances of all investors who prefer to file their complaint with SEBI for matters falling within its jurisdiction. A standardized compliant format is available at all SEBI offices and on the SEBI website for the convenience of investors. Complaints are taken up with the concerned entities either directly by OAIE or by the investor complaint cell of the concerned department. SEBI officers also hold meetings with the company officials to impress upon them their obligations to redress the grievances of investors.

During the period 1991-92 to 2008-09, SEBI has received 26, 74,560 grievances from investors. Of this, a total of 25,03,560 grievances were redressed by respective entities, which indicate a redressal rate of 93.60 per cent. The cumulative status of investor grievances received by SEBI is given in Exhibit 10.1:

Exhibit 10.1

Redressal of Investor Grievances

Financial Year	Grievances Received		Grievance Redressed		Redressal Rate Percentage (cumulative)
	During the year	Cumulative	During the year	Cumulative	
1	2	3	4	5	6
1991-92	18,794	18,794	4,061	4,061	21.61
1992-93	1,10,317	1,29,111	22,946	27,007	20.92
1993-94	5,84,662	7,13,773	3,39,517	3,66,524	51.35
1994-95	5,16,080	12,29,853	3,51,842	7,18,366	58.41
1995-96	3,76,478	16,06,331	3,15,652	10,34,018	64.37
1996-97	2,17,394	18,23,725	4,31,865	14,65,883	80.38
1997-98	5,11,507	23,23,232	6,76,555	21,42,438	91.74
1998-99	99,132	24,34,364	1,27,227	22,69,665	93.24
1999-00	98,605	25,32,969	1,46,553	24,16,218	95.39
2000-01	98,913	26,29,882	85,583	25,01,801	95.13
2001-02	81,600	27,11,482	70,328	25,72,129	94.86
2002-03	37,434	27,48.916	38,972	26,11,101	94.99
2003-04	36,744	27,85,660	21,531	26,32,632	94.51
2004-05	54,445	28,40,095	53,361	26,85,993	94.57

Contd....

2005-06	40,485	NA	37,067	NA	NA
2006-07	26,473	2,56,2047	17,899	2,39,5895	93.51
2007-08	54,933	26,16,980	31,676	24,27,571	92.76
2008-09	57,580	26,74,560	75,989	25,03,560	93.60

Source: SEBI Annual Report different years.

(ii) **Securities Market Awareness Campaign** : The SEBI launched a comprehensive education campaign aimed at investors in securities market, which has been christened – "Securities Market Awakened Campaign".(SMAC). The motto of the campaign is –'An Educated Investor is a protected Investor'.

Following the national launch, the campaign has already been extended to 20 states and union territories. While the national as well as the state level launches were aimed at generating wide and adequate publicity for the campaign the structural foundation of the campaign is based on the continued and active participation of market participants, market intermediaries, investors' associations etc. who have under the aegis of SEBI undertaken to organize workshops at various cities/ medium and small towns in the country to spread SEBI's message of "Invest with knowledge".

3. Supervision : Implementation of the regulations entails a multi-stage process of supervision, enforcement through imitation of adjudication and enquiry against violation of rules and regulations and prosecution. Market intermediaries at varied levels have distinctive features and responsibilities. Therefore, supervision of different intermediaries requires individual approach that can serve a useful purpose. Effective supervision through on-site and off-site inspections, enforcement, and enquiry against violations of rules and regulations, and prosecutions are the essential features for effective enforcement of the Regulations. SEBI conducts inspections either directly or through stock exchanges, depositories, etc. Inspections on a periodic basis were conducted to verify the compliance levels of intermediaries. Specific/ limited purpose inspections were conducted on the basis of complaints, references, surveillance reports, specific concerns, etc. Stock exchanges and depositories were also directed by SEBI to carry out periodic/specific purpose inspections of their members/participants.

(i) **Promotion and Regulation of Self Regulatory Organizations :** SEBI (Self Regulatory Organizations) Regulations were notified on February 19, 2004 with the objective to promote organization of intermediaries representing a particular segment of the securities market as a self regulated entity/organization. Salient features of the regulations are:

(i) For any applicant to be recognized as SRO, it should be a company registered under Section 25 of Companies Act and have a minimum net worth of Rs. 1 crore;

(ii) The company shall make an application to SEBI in the prescribed format and provide a copy of the governing norms of the SRO along with a copy of the memorandum and articles of association;

(iii) The certificate of recognition as SRO shall be valid for a period of five years;

(iv) With the objective to ensure independence of the governing board of SRO, the regulations stipulate that majority of directors shall be independent directors;

(v) The regulations entrust SEBI with the right to undertake inspection of the books of accounts, other records and documents of the Self Regulatory Organization;

(vi) The Self Regulatory Organisation shall furnish periodical returns relating to its affairs to SEBI; and

(vii) In case of default, it is the obligation of the Board of Directors to take disciplinary action against a member.

(ii) **Development of Stock Exchanges as Self-Regulatory Organizations :** Stock exchanges are recognized under Section 4 of the Securities Contracts (Regulations) Act, 1956. These exchanges were recognized/set up over a period of time to stimulate the growth of the capital market by channelising the savings of households and others. These exchanges are suitably empowered by Section 9 of SC(R) Act, 1956 to make bye-laws for the conduct of business, regulation and enforcement of contracts. Risk-based inspection was carried out by SEBI and routine inspections of stock brokers/ sub-brokers and depository participants were conducted by stock exchanges and depositories. The quality of such inspections was overseen by SEBI by calling for periodic reports on inspections conducted, violations observed and actions taken.

4. Inspection of Market Intermediaries

(i) **Inspection of Brokers/Sub-brokers :** Details regarding inspection of brokers, sub-brokers and various actions taken during 2004-05 are given in Exhibit 10.2. The number of inspections conducted on sub-broking entities was higher at 140 during 2004-05 than that conducted on broking entities (93). It is significant to note that there was surge in the number of surprise/limited purpose inspections carried out on broking/sub-broking entities, which rose by 96 per cent to 57 during 2004-05 over 2003-04. During 2005-06, the number of regular inspections of stock brokers was 7 as compared to 93 in 2004-05. During 2006-07, inspections of stock brokers, sub-brokers were carried out as per various regulations of SEBI. During 2006-07, the number of regular inspections conducted on stock brokers was 30, compared to seven in the previous year. Like 2005- 06, no regular inspections of sub-brokers were conducted during 2006-07. However, there was a rise in the number of surprise/ limited purpose inspections carried out on stock brokers and sub-brokers. During 2007-08, the number of regular inspections of stock brokers was 16 as compared to 30 in the previous year No regular inspections of sub-brokers were conducted during 2007-08. The number of surprise/limited purpose inspections carried out on stock brokers increased to 47 in 2007-08 as compared to 37 in the previous year.

During 2008-09, the number of regular inspections of stock brokers was 33 as compared to 16 in the previous year There were two regular inspections of sub-brokers conducted during 2008-09. Further, three surprise/limited purpose inspections were carried out on stock brokers in 2008-09 as compared to 47 in 2007-08.

Exhibit 10.2
Inspection of Brokering/Sub-broking Entities

Year	Particulars			
	Regular inspections completed-Brokers	Regular inspections completed-Sub-Brokers	Inspections to verify financial aspects and level of brokerage-Brokers	Surprise/Limited Purpose Inspections-Brokers/Sub brokers
2003-04	176	83	202	29
2004-05	93	140	-	57
2005-06	7	Nil	-	32
2006-07	30	Nil	-	37*
2007-08	16	Nil	-	47
2008-09	33	2	-	3

* Includes limited purpose inspections of nine subsidiaries of stock exchanges to ascertain the implementation of the model tri-partite agreements and direct settlement of funds and securities by the main stock broker.

(ii) **Inspection of Other Intermediaries :** Section 11(2) of SEBI Act, 1992 provides that SEBI shall register and regulate the working of intermediaries. In fulfillment of the above, SEBI has completed the inspection of books and records of 47 depository participants and five registrars to an issue. Records of six merchant bankers (MBs) and nine bankers to the issue (BTIs) were also examined for alleged irregularities in the public issue procedure and allotment. During 2008-09, regular inspections were completed for 15 depository participants, two credit rating agencies and four registrars to an issue and share transfer agents.

(iii) **Inspection of Stock Exchanges :** SEBI inspected the stock exchanges to review the market operations, organizational structure and administrative control of the exchange so as to ascertain whether (i) the exchange provides a fair, equitable and growing market to investors; (ii) the exchange's organization, systems and practices are in accordance with the Securities Contracts (Regulation) Act (SC (R) Act), 1956 and rules framed there under; (iii) the exchange has implemented the direction, guidelines and instructions

issued by SEBI from time to time; and (iv) the exchange has complied with the conditions, if any, imposed on it at the time of renewal/grant of its recognition under Section 4 of the SC(R) Act, 1956.

During inspection of stock exchanges, a review of the market operations, organizational structure and administrative control of the stock exchange is made to ascertain as to whether:

(*a*) it provides a fair, equitable, transparent and growing market to the investors;

(*b*) its organisation, systems and practices are in accordance with the Securities Contracts (Regulation) Act, 1956 [SC(R) Act, 1956] and rules framed there under;

(*c*) it has implemented the directions. guidelines and instructions issued by SEBI / Government of India from time to time and

(*d*) it has complied with the conditions, if any, imposed on it at the time of renewal/ grant of its recognition under section 4 of the SC(R) Act, 1956.

During 2008-09, based on the turnover and other issues such as compliance with inspection observations, listing norms, etc. specific purpose inspections of equity segment of the following seven stock exchanges were carried out:

a. Bombay Stock Exchange Ltd.

b. Pune Stock Exchange Ltd.

c. Ahmedabad Stock Exchange Ltd.

d. Madhya Pradesh Stock Exchange Ltd.

e. Jaipur Stock Exchange Ltd.

f. Uttar Pradesh Stock Exchange Association Ltd.

g. Gauhati Stock Exchange Ltd.

Out of these, inspections of Bombay Stock Exchange Ltd., Pune Stock Exchange Ltd., Ahmedabad Stock Exchange Ltd. and Madhya Pradesh Stock Exchange Ltd. were specific purpose inspection to ascertain compliance status of previous inspection, administrating and monitoring control including control of subsidiaries of stock exchanges, compliance with status of investor grievances, etc. and the other three inspections were routine. In addition, during 2008-09, while considering the renewal of recognition of stock exchanges, special purpose inspection of the following stock exchanges was undertaken for ascertaining compliance levels:

a. Vadodara Stock Exchange Ltd.; and

b. Cochin Stock Exchange Ltd.

(*iv*) **Illegal Trading outside Stock Exchange :** SEBI, from time to time, received information about alleged illegal trading in securities by unregistered entities outside the stock exchanges. Illegal trading is a cognizable offence under section 19 of Securities Contract (Regulations) Act, 1956 within the meaning of Code of Criminal Procedure which does not fall within the regulatory jurisdiction of SEBI. Therefore, SEBI forwards such reference received by SEBI as well as press articles in this regard to chief ministers of respective states requesting them to look into the matter and to take action against those found to be involved in the illegal trading of securities. SEBI has also written letters to Chief Ministers of States requesting them to put the suitable action against any person/entity violating the provisions the provisions of SC(R)A.

There were some complaints regarding illegal trading outside stock exchange by registered entities also. On receipt of such complaint, concerned stock exchange have been asked to verify the complaint in order to ascertain the veracity of the allegations, and to take appropriate action. During the year, SEBI, in co-ordination with the respective stock exchanges carried out eight-surprise inspection of the intermediaries and appropriate enforcement action is being taken against the violators.

5. Inspection of Depositories : A special inspection of National Securities Depositories Limited was carried out during 2004-05. Inspection of depositories is conducted to:

(*a*) examine whether the procedures and practices of the depository are in compliance with the Depositories Act, 1996, SEBI (Depositories and Participants) Regulations, 1996, SEBI circulars, the bye-laws etc;

(*b*) check whether the books of account are being maintained by the depository, in the manner specified in SEBI (Depository and Participants) Regulations, 1996;

(*c*) look into the complaints received by depositories from participants, issuers, issuers' agents, beneficial owners or any other person; and

(*d*) ascertain whether violations and deficiencies pointed out in the last inspection report have been rectified.

As per Regulation 35 of SEBI (Depositories and Participants) Regulations, 1996 every depository needs to get inspected its controls, systems, procedures and safeguards and forward a copy of the inspection report to SEBI. During 2008-09, comprehensive systems audit of NSDL and CDSL including review of networks, security, Business Continuity Planning / Disaster Recovery, IT processes, application security, maintenance of IT infrastructure, data communication controls, etc. was performed by independent auditors as mandated.

6. Systems Audit : Trading settlement and risk management systems of stock exchange are almost completely automated. For this reason, it becomes very important that the systems do not have deficiencies which can impair their efficacy. It also becomes important to ensure that the stock exchanges have suitable Disaster Recovery Sites and Business Continuity Plans and that the systems are adequately secure. Active stock exchanges have been asked to carry out systems audit through external agencies competent to carry out systems audit exercise. SEBI does not follow up for rectification of deficiencies pointed out in the system audit report. In 2004-05 too, such follow up was done through off-site analysis of compliance reports from stock exchanges and meeting with the senior management of stock exchanges.

Considering the importance of systems audit in a technology driven securities market, SEBI directed all stock exchanges to conduct audit of their systems on an annual basis. The scope of systems audit encompasses audit of systems and processes related to examination of trading systems, clearing and settlement systems (clearing corporation/clearing house), risk management, databases, disaster recovery sites, business continuity planning, security, capacity management and information security audit. Accordingly, all stock exchanges were advised to conduct systems audit on an annual basis and place the systems audit, report and compliance status before the governing board of the exchange and submit the same to SEBI. Subsequently, follow up of observations brought out in the system audit reports of stock exchanges was done through correspondence as well as through meetings with senior management of stock exchanges, whenever required.

7. Surveillance

(*i*) Market Surveillance Mechanism : In order to ensure investor protection and to safeguard the integrity of the markets, it is imperative to have in place an effective market surveillance mechanism. The surveillance function is an extremely vital link in the chain of activities performed by the regulatory agency for fulfilling its avowed mission of protection of investor interest and development and regulations of capital markets. The surveillance system adopted by SEBI is two-pronged viz., Surveillance Cell in the stock exchange and the integrated Surveillance Department in SEBI.

(*ii*) Integrated Market Surveillance System : In order to enhance the efficiency of the surveillance function, SEBI has decided to put in place a world class comprehensive integrated market surveillance system (IMSS) across stock exchanges and across market segments (cash and derivative markets).

The proposed IMSS solution seeks to achieve the following objectives:

(*i*) An online data repository with the capacity to capture market transaction data and reference data from a variety of sources like stock exchanges, clearing corporation/ houses, depositories etc., in different formats for the securities and derivatives markets.

(*ii*) A research and regulatory analysis platform to check instances of potential market abuse and

(*iii*) Sophisticated alert engine that can work with various data formats (database, numeric and text data) to automatically detect patterns to abuse and then issue an alert. These include insider trading engine, fraud alert engine and market surveillance engine.

(*iii*) Interim Surveillance Arrangement : While the Integrated Market Surveillance System (IMSS) is in the process of being fully operationalised, an interim surveillance mechanism has been put in place since June 2003. A regular system of weekly surveillance meetings with major stock exchanges viz., NSDL, CDSL is now in place to provide a confidential platform for exchanges of views on areas of emerging concern-specific abnormalities and to consider pre-emptive actions and discuss general surveillance issues.

(*iv*) Inter Regulatory Alert Systems: In view of the growing linkages between the securities market and the banking system, it was felt desirable to set up an inter regulatory alert system between SEBI and RBI. Towards this end, a SEBI-RBI Group on Integrated System of Alerts has been set up to share information and to recommend suitable measures for co-coordinated action. In accordance with the recommendations made by the Groups, appropriate alerts and data have been identified. A system making use of the same has been put in place since February 2004 and the system is fully functional.

(*v*) **Surveillance Action:** Several preventive and proactive measures were taken by SEBI during the year for enhancing market safety and integrity. The surveillance measures taken during the year include shifting of scrips to trade-for-trade segment, reduction of circuit, filter, imposition of additional margins etc. Further the criteria for initiating such surveillance measure were also reviewed from time to time based on the prevailing market conditions. The year had witnessed spurt in mid-cap & low cap stocks and it was further observed that some of the defunct companies have become active. To arrest manipulative /speculative price rise in these scrips, various surveillance measures were taken up as and when considered necessary. The significant measures taken during the year were as under:

(*a*) SEBI observed that there were many instances of wash trades and circular trades in some illiquid scrips. In order to make the investors and brokers aware of such stocks, SEBI advised stock exchange to prepare and disseminate list of illiquid scrips, on monthly basis commencing from July 2008. Stock exchanges were also advised to intimate brokers to exercise additional due diligence while trading in these securities either on own account or on behalf of their clients.

(*b*) In order to increase awareness and facilitate better understanding of the risks involved in investing in derivative market, SEBI advised exchanges to include illustrative examples in the FAQs on derivatives so as to clearly bring out the extent of risk involved in derivatives' trading, especially the risk of loss of entire capital.

(*c*) To ensure that investors across the country are able to trade continuously and without difficulty, SEBI advised exchanges to take necessary steps to ensure that trading continues uninterrupted even during times of sun outage, which causes disruption in telecommunications.

(*d*) In order to protect the interest of those de-mat account holder who operate their accounts through power of attorney, SEBI stipulated that an SMS alert be sent to the account holder for debits from his accounts. This would reduce the scope for misuses of such de-mat accounts.

(*e*) SEBI advised depositories to close those nil balance de-mat accounts which were frozen due to non-furnishing of PAN in order to reduce the number of idle de-mat accounts in the system.

(*m*) Surveillance actions taken during 2008-09 are as follows:

During 2008-09, NSE initiated preliminary examination and investigation in 165 cases and BSE has initiated examination and investigation in 961 cases. Further, as surveillance measure, during the year NSE shifted 190 scrips to trade-for trade segment and BSE shifted 1,078 scrips to trade for- trade segment. NSE imposed a price band (2 per cent, 5 per cent and 10 per cent) on 942 instances whereas BSE imposed price band on 2,047 instances. Further, NSE and BSE verified 118 and 134 rumours respectively. The above mentioned actions are given in Exhibit – 10.3.

Exhibit-10.3

Surveillance Actions during 2008-09

Nature of Action	NSE	BSE
1	2	3
Scrips shifted to trade-for-trade Segment	209 (244)	842 (1,586)
No. of scrips in which price bands were imposed (2 per cent, 5 per cent, 10 per cent)	942 (1,098)	2,047 (3,971)
Preliminary Investigations taken up (NSE 164 and BSE 783)	165 (123)	961 (1,855)
Rumours verified from the Companies (NSE 301 and BSE 538)	118 (184)	134 (253)

Note: Figures in the parentheses pertain to 2007-08.

Source: SEBI Annual Report 2008-09.

8. Investigation: Investigations are undertaken with a view to examine alleged or suspected violations as well as to gather evidence and identify persons/entities behind irregularities and violations such as (a) price manipulation; (b) creation of artificial market; (c) insider trading; and (d) public issue related irregularities, takeover violations and other misconducts, etc.

Investigations involve the identification of persons involved in the violations, collection of elaborate data regarding primary issues, transactions in the secondary markets, trading details, followed by verification and analysis of the same. Pursuant to completion of investigation, various actions like administrative directions and penal actions under the SEBI Act and various SEBI Rules and Regulations are initiated. These actions include monetary penalties, warning, suspension of activities, cancellation of registration, prohibition of dealing securities and ban on access to the capital market etc.

(i) Stages of Investigation

(*a*) **Preliminary investigation :** Based on the facts contained in a reference and feedback obtained from exchanges/other sources of relevant information, preliminary investigation is made to check whether the matter warrants a formal investigation. At the preliminary investigation stage, information is sought and collected from all available sources including exchanges, depositories, secondary databases, company and brokers, if required. As this is only a preliminary investigation, production of documents and calling of information cannot be enforced. Based on available information, an assessment is made as to whether a formal investigation is needed to establishes charges of violations.

(*b*) **Formal Investigation :** Based on the findings of the preliminary investigation, a case is taken up for formal investigation. Once a case is taken up for formal investigation, the SEBI Act provides for calling for information; compelling production of documents; and examination of witnesses etc.

(*c*) **Post Investigative Proceedings :** After completion of investigation, action is taken by Enforcement Division as per the recommendations of the approving authority. The action may include issuing warning letter; initiating enquiry proceedings against registered intermediaries; initiating adjudication proceedings for levy of penalties; issuing directions under SEBI Act; and launching prosecution.

(ii) Trends in Investigation Cases : A total of 1,288 investigations have been undertaken by SEBI since 1992-93 and investigations have been completed in 1,223 cases. During 2008-09, 76 new cases were taken up for investigation and 116 cases were completed. More number of investigations was completed during 2007-08 as compared to the year 2008-09 as there was a backlog of cases during 2007-08 where substantial investigation was already completed in earlier year/s.

Exhibit-10.4
Investigation by SEBI

Numbers

Year	Particulars	
	Cases Taken up for Investigation	Cases Completed
(1)	(2)	(3)
1992-93	2	2
1993-94	3	3
1994-95	2	2
1995-96	60	18
1996-97	122	55
1997-98	53	46
1998-99	55	60

Contd....

1999-00	56	57
2000-01	68	46
2001-02	111	29
2002-03	125	106
2003-04	121	152
2004-05	130	179
2005-06	159	81
2006-07	120	102
2007-08	25	169
2008-09 (P)	76	116
Total	**1,288**	**1,233**

P : Provisional

Note: The pending cases are of the nature of preliminary scrutiny as well as of formal investigations

These cases are related with market manipulation and prices rigging; insider trading, take-overs and miscellaneous.

(*a*) **Nature of Investigation Cases Taken Up:** About 68 per cent of the cases taken up for investigation in 2008-09 pertain to market manipulation and price rigging as against 50 per cent of such cases taken up in the previous year. Other cases pertain to insider trading, takeover violations, irregularities in public issues, and other irregularities. Since, several investigation cases were taken up on the basis of multiple allegations of violations, strict classification under specific category becomes difficult. Such cases were classified on the basis of main charge/violations.

(*b*) **Nature of Investigation Cases Completed:** During 2008-09, about 74 per cent of the total 116 cases in which investigation was completed pertain to market manipulation and price rigging, misleading advertisements by the companies and unfair practices. Other cases in which investigation was completed pertain to insider trading, capital issue related irregularities, takeover violations, noncompliance of disclosure requirements etc.

(*iii*) Regulatory Actions Taken : After completion of investigation, further penal actions are initiated as per the recommendations made in the investigation reports and as approved by the competent authority. The action includes issuing warning letters, initiating enquiry proceedings for registered intermediaries, initiating adjudication proceedings for levying monetary penalties, passing directions under Section 11 of SEBI Act and initiating prosecution cases. Apart from completion of investigations, SEBI is also actively involved in post investigation enforcement actions and quasi judicial proceedings. Such actions include issuing show cause notices to the entities, examining their replies, organising and participating in the hearings of the entities before the Whole Time Members of SEBI, preparing draft orders, issuing press releases after orders are passed, briefings to advocates, coordinating the proceedings before Securities Appellate Tribunal (SAT) and before courts, coordination for cases filed in the courts, follow up for collection of penalty after orders passed by Adjudicating Officers, initiating prosecution for non-payment of penalties, processing of consent proposals filed by the entities, etc. Regulatory actions were taken against 461 entities in 2008-09. 230 prohibitive directions were issued under Section 11 of SEBI Act against various entities. 46 intermediaries were suspended during 2008-09 while warning was issued against 179 entities.

9. Enforcement of Regulations : Enforcement makes a regulatory system effective. Action follow up of cases of misconduct send out a tough signal to the market participants. Disciplinary actions in the form of justified penalties are indispensable for ensuring market integrity.

(*i*) **Enquiry and Adjudication Details :** During 2008-09, 310 orders were passed/ reports submitted; of which, 56 pertained to enquiries and 254 pertained to adjudications. Hearings were conducted for 601 cases, of which, 62 belonged to enquiries and 539 to adjudications. 1,517 show-cause notices were issued to different entities, of which, 97 pertained to enquiries and 1,420 cases pertained to adjudication.

(*ii*) **Market Intermediaries :** Enquiry proceedings were initiated against 17 stock brokers in 2008-09 as against five stock brokers in the previous year. Adjudication proceedings were initiated against 106 stock brokers in 2008-09 as against 23 stock brokers in 2007-08. 33 warnings were issued to stock brokers and 208 consent orders were passed.

(*a*) Enquiry proceedings were initiated against one registrar to an issue and share transfer agent whereas adjudication proceedings were initiated against two merchant bankers and three registrars to an issue and share transfer agent in 2008-09. Warning letters were issued to two depository participants and two registrars to an issue and share transfer agent.

(*b*) The SEBI has conducted enquiries and adjudication proceedings against the depository participant register to the issue, merchant bankers Overall position is indicated in Exhibit-10.5

Exhibit-10.5
Enquiry and Adjudication Proceedings against other Intermediaries

Numbers

Intermediary	Adjudication	Enquiry	Warning	Cease and Censure Pursuant to Enquiry	Warning Application Pursuant to Enquiry	Rejection of Application Pursuant to Enquiry
1	2	3	4	5	6	7
Depository Participant	-	-	2	-	-	-
Registrar to the Issue	3	1	2	-	-	-
Merchant Banker	2	-	-	-	-	-

Source: SEBI Annual Report 2008-09.

(*iii*) **Trends in Prosecution :** The number of prosecutions launched against companies, persons and entities have declined substantially in 2004-05 as compared to 2003-04. In 2004-05, prosecution was launched in 83 cases as compared with 464 cases in 2003-04. In 2003-04, SEBI launched prosecution against all CIS entities who had failed to comply with directions issued under Section 11B of SEBI Act, 1992. Total number of such cases was 332. This resulted in a substantial rise in the number of cases failed in the year 2003-04. 28 prosecutions were launched against 127 persons/ entities during 2008-09 as compared to 39 in 2007-08 (Table 3.25). Till 2008-09, region-wise, the highest number of prosecutions were launched in Western Region (556) followed by the Northern region (337) Overall position is indicated in Exhibit-10.6.

Exhibit-10.6
Prosecution Launched

Year	No. of cases in which prosecution has been launched	No. of persons/entities against whom prosecution has been launched
1	2	3
Up to and including 1995-96	10	58
1996-97	13	63
1997-98	11	81
1998-99	15	145
1999-00	23	121
2000-01	20	98
2001-02	115	613
2002-03	229	848

Contd....

2003-04	458	2,377
2004-05	84	410
2005-06	27	81
2006-07	21	149
2007-08	39	188
2008-09	28	127
Total	1,093	5,359

Source: SEBI Annual Report of different years.

28 prosecutions were launched against 127 persons/ entities during 2008-09 as compared to 39 in 2007-08 . Till 2008-09, region-wise, the highest number of prosecutions were launched in Western Region (556) followed by the Northern region (337).

Investors' Education and Training of Intermediaries

SEBI realizes that a cadre of securities market professionals is basic infrastructure for development of the securities market. It is essential not only to sustain the reforms undertaken so far but also to initiate further reforms and to maintain and enhance the confidence of investors/issuers in the market. The quality of personnel providing intermediation services determines the shape and health of the securities market, as the suppliers of funds/securities rely on knowledge and expertise of the intermediaries and look up to them for guidance and support.

As on March 31, 2005, SEBI had a total of 467 employees in various grades – 313 officers, 154 secretaries and other staff. With a view to encouraging deputation of its officers to overseas regulatory bodies and multilateral organizations, SEBI introduced a scheme for deputation/secondment/tour on duty/re-employment of SEBI officers to overseas regulatory bodies and multilateral organizations. Accordingly, 2 officers were sent on deputation to Capital Markets Authority, Sultanate of Oman and 2 officers were sent on deputation to Bahrain Monetary Authority under the scheme. During 2004-05, SEBI recruited 26 Trainee Officers, 1 Secretary and 3 Accounts Assistants.

In order to groom a cadre of professionals who understand the market and the regulations and can service the investors and the issuers improving thereby the competence of the intermediaries, a set of two complementary initiative namely training and certification is generally used. Keeping this in mind, SEBI has set up the 'National Institute of Securities Market' (NISM), which will undertake both initiative with creditability and efficiency. It would design and implement the entire gamut of educational initiative, including education, training, certification, research and consultancy in the area of securities market and allied subject for securities market, market professionals in India and neighboring countries. This would complement SEBI's statutory responsibility to:

(*i*) promote investor's education;

(*ii*) train intermediaries in the securities market; and

(*iii*) conduct research necessary for the discharge of its responsibilities.

Practice Questions

Objective Type Questions

1. SEBI was established on:

   (a) 1992 (b) 1990

   (c) 1988 (d) 1994

2. SEBI was enacted in:

   (a) 1992 (b) 1994

   (c) 1990 (d) 1996

3. Serious fraud Investigation office is working under the:

   (a) Ministry of Corporate Affairs (b) SEBI

   (c) Securities Appellant Tribunal (d) Ministry of Finance

4. SEBI board is composed of:
   (a) 8 members (b) 9 members
   (c) 10 members (d) 7 members
5. Integrated Market Surveillance system is concerned with following objectives except:
   (a) online data repository (b) research and regulatory analysis
   (c) control over depositories (d) developing sophisticated alert engine.

Ans: 1. (c), 2. (a) 3. (a), 4. (a), 5. (c)

Short Answer Questions

1. What is the rationale of securities regulation?
2. What are the functions of SEBI?
3. What do you mean by investors protection?
4. What are the powers of SEBI?
5. What are the functions of securities Tribunal Authority?
6. What do you mean by self regulatory organizations?
7. What is the composition of SEBI?

Long Answer Questions

1. Critically examine the role of SEBI in the regulation of capital market in India.
2. Define listed securities and permitted securities and distinguish between them.
3. Explain briefly the SEBI guidelines on pricing of equity shares by an issuer company.
4. "SEBI has not been able to regulate the capital market as it was expected to regulate." Do you think so? Give arguments in support of your answer.

References

1. Clause 4 (ii), The Capital Issues (Exemption) Order, 1969, Govt. of India, New Delhi
2. The control on capital issues has been abolished by an Ordinance issued by the President of India on May 29, 1992 which allowed the companies to issue securities freely after observing the Disclosures and Investors Protection Guidelines issues by the Security and Exchange Board of India (SEBI). This Ordinance has been replaced by an Act of Parliament since August 5, 1992.
3. Sec.2(1) (b) of Capital Issues (Control) Act, 1947.
4. Sec. 3(2) The Capital Issues (Control) Act, 1947.
5. Clause 9 The Capital Issues (Exemption) Order, 1969.
6. Guidelines for Issue of fresh share capital, Office of the Controller of Capital Issues, Ministry of India, New Delhi vide press note dated May 14, 1995, Aug.18, 1981, Sept.15, 1984, Aug19, 1985
7. Guidelines for Issue of Debentures by Public Limited Companies, The CCI vide circular No. S 11 (9) CCI (ii) dated Sept.15, 1984
8. Guidelines for Issue of fresh share capital, the CCI vide circular dated May, 14, 1975
9. Guidelines for Issue of Bonus Shares vide CCI circular dated 8 Aug, 1981.
10. Business Standard. Feb.02, 2010, p.1
11. Economic Times, Dec.2009, 0.3
12. Business Line. Oct.6, 2009

11 CAPITAL MARKET IN INDIA

Availability of capital is the lifeline of business organizations. Sufficient capital is required to accelerate the pace of economic development and growth of the country. Actually, channelisation of resources needs systematic procedures to minimize the risk involved in resource generation process, using resources and maintaining a peer standard of fund performance. The intense desire for resources and their relative scarcity creates the problem of priorities and choices before the management. "As for the capital, it is short in the underdeveloped economies both in the sense of real physical assets and also in terms of the funds with which their construction is financed. Such countries are supposed to be "poor because they are poor"[1] Moreover, capital is also indispensable for a developing economy particularly in the earlier stages of its economic development. Capital is nothing but it is a support system for development. In every economic system there is need of adequate capital to finance the economic development. "Capital imports usually come from the developed countries, which normally conceive of the developed-underdeveloped differing relations."[2] In practice, capital always flows from the place of excess to the place of deficiency. In an economy, capital is required to be invested into business by corporates as well as by the government to achieve developmental goals. Corporates need huge amount of capital to finance their operations and developmental programmes. The government also requires huge capital to invest in different welfare schemes and developmental activities. There are some potential investors who have excess of funds and they desire to invest their available funds into viable business operations. These investors usually follow the theme of liquidity, safety and profitability at a preferred level of risk prevailing in the economy at macro as well as micro level. Actually, risk-return trade off decides the volume of funds in the capital market. Financial market facilitates the two parties-investors and fund seeking enterprises with contrasting interest to meet their different objectives.

Financial Market

According to Poindexter and Jones "The financial markets permit both business and government to raise the needed funds by selling securities. Simultaneously, investors with excess funds are able to invest and earn a return, enhancing their welfare."[3] Thus, financial markets help in purchase and sale of financial assets.

"Financial Markets can be referred to be as those centres and arrangements which facilitate buying and selling of financial assets, claims and services."[4] It is important to note that "Financial markets deal with the exchange of different monies, the means by which people pay one another in different countries. In addition, financial markets trade claims as promises to pay in the future- and a variety of contingent contracts, where payments or exchanges depend on some future events. Claims include stocks and bonds, mortgaged loans, bank deposits, and many other instruments, whereas contingent contracts include futures and options, letters of credit, and forward contracts, among other things."[5]

The financial markets are generally to work as an intermediary between two parties of issuers to meet their financial needs and investors who have surplus fund at their disposal. Specific place or location is not defined for a financial market. Wherever a financial transaction takes place, it is deemed to have taken place in the financial market. Financial markets are pervasive in nature since financial transactions themselves are very pervasive in an economic system. Thus, the financial markets may be developed at any location where the two or more parties with contrast interest meet to exchange the values as per their matching requirements. Features of financial assets and services also tend to change as per the requirements of the market participants to meet the different requirements of the investors.

Role of Financial Market

Financial market ensures deal for the sale and purchase of financial securities. Financial securities with various risks are the main instruments of financial market. The financial markets serve as a focal point to facilitate the buying and selling of financial claims and services. The financial markets are the common platform for different stakeholders with varied interests of reducing risk of financial volatility, ensuring a riskless profit or gaining a higher profit through their viable strategies. The stakeholders operating in the markets are known as market participants where they trade in the financial market to achieve short as well as long-term financial objectives. Behaviour of stakeholders is governed by their short term, medium term and long term financial objectives.

"The participants on the demand and supply sides of financial markets are financial institutions, agents, borrowers and lenders. As an integral part of financial system, financial markets envisage transactions on all financial claims/instruments."[6] The corporations, financial institutions, individuals and governments trade in financial products in these markets either directly or through brokers and dealers on organised exchanges or off exchanges. Basically, there are two types of the financial markets. These are grouped into organised or un-organised markets. "In the organised markets, there are standardised rules and regulations governing their financial dealings. There is also a high degree of institutionalisation and instrumentalisation. These markets are subject to strict supervision and control by the regulatory bodies."[7] In the organised financial markets, the financial transactions take place in the well-established exchanges in the systematic and orderly structure or arrangements in the long as well as short term period.

Types of Financial Market : There are two types of organised financial market - money market and capital market.

A- Money Market

Money market is a place where the lending and borrowing of short-term funds are arranged. It includes the short-term credit instruments and the institutions and individuals who participate in the lending and borrowing business. "The stage of development of a money market serves as a barometer of the stage of development of an economy of a country where the money market is not developed, the economy of the country happens to be primitive."[8] "In a simple way, the money market transacts purchases and sells in money. In the money market the quantities supplied and demanded do not pertain to any ordinary commodity or service like wheat or labour service but to money."[9] The instruments traded in the markets are either money or equivalent to money. It is called as money or money equivalents. These assets are having short-term period to maintain the liquidity in the markets. "Money market is the market for dealing in monetary assets of short-term nature. Short term funds up to one year and for financial assets that are close substitutes for money are dealt in the money market."[10] Thus, the money market deals with financial assets having less than one year effective life cycle.

Features : Important features of money market are as follows:

(*i*) It is a centre for dealings in monetary assets having a short-term character. It meets the short-term requirements of the borrowers and provides liquidity or cash to lenders.

(*ii*) It is the place "where short-term surplus investible funds at the disposal of the financial and other institutions and individuals are bid by borrowers, again comprising of institutions and individuals and also by the government."[11]

(*iii*) The volume of each transaction is generally very high and requires fairness and transparency at high level. Big as well as small investors both are supposed to participate in the money market,

(*iv*) The money market is a wholesale market. The volumes are very large and generally transactions are settled on a daily basis. Trading in the money market is conducted over the telephone followed by written confirmation from both the borrowers and lenders.

(*v*) It caters the requirements of borrowers for short term funds and provides liquidity to the lenders of these funds.

(*vi*) The instruments used in the money market are highly liquid. Financial instruments are traded which are of close substitutes for money.

(*vii*) It is centre "where short term money instruments such as treasury bills, commercial papers, certificate of deposit, call money funds and commercial bills are supplied and demanded."[12]

Components of Money Market : Various components of money market are as follows:

(*i*) **Call Money Market:** The call money market is a highly liquid market for an extremely short period loan of one to fourteen days. These loans are repayable at the will of either borrower or the lender. The interest rate varies sharply on day-to-day, hour to hour and also centre to centre basis. Generally, it is highly volatile and sensitive to changes in demand and supply of call loans. The Indian call money market is associated with stock exchanges.

(*ii*) **Treasury Bills market:** "A treasury bill is a promissory note or a finance bill issued by the Government. It is highly liquid because its repayment is guaranteed by the government."[13] It is an instrument for short term borrowing. It is used by the government for a maturity period of 91 days, 182 days or 364 days. The treasury bills are of two types-ordinary or regular and ad-hoc treasury bills. The ordinary treasury bills are issued to the public, banks and other financial institutions to fulfill the short-term financial requirements of the central bank. The ad-hoc treasury bills are purchased by the central bank only.

(*iii*) **Commercial Bills Market:** Commercial bills market is the market for Bill of Exchange arising due to credit sale. The seller draws a bill on the buyer for a promise to pay the debt at a later date as specified in the bill. The seller discounts this bill through commercial banks to get the immediate payment. In India, The Discount and Finance House of India was set up in 1988 to promote the commercial bills market.

(*iv*) **Short Term Loan Market:** The short-term loan market facilitates the corporates to meet their working capital requirements. The commercial banks provide the temporary overdraft facility to the business houses and extend cash credit for one year to the entrepreneurs. The commercial banks play a crucial role in the short-term loan markets.

B- Capital Market

The requirement of capital depends on the changing structure of investment environment. Capital market refers to the market mechanism which provides institutional support system for marketing of long term and equity claims e.g. equity shares, preference shares, debentures, bonds, etc. "Structure of the capital market varies from country to country, depending upon a wide variety of factors-the history of the country, including banking history, the extent and type of business experience, the role of political factors, and the role of government."[14] The working of capital market also governed by the long term prospects of the economy. The capital market ensures the availability of proper channel for mobilising capital from different sources. "In the widest sense, it consists of a series of channel through which the savings of the community are made available for industrial and commercial enterprises, and public authories."[15] Thus, the capital market is a broad term which includes primary markets, secondary markets, term lending institutions, banks, investors and all those entities who are engaged in providing long-term capital to the corporate sector.

In an economy, the process of economic development requires continuous structural changes with changing scenario of global economy and its subsequent impact on the home country. The balanced growth of the economy can be achieved only with the proper support of strong capital market. "After independence, the rapid growth and expansion of the corporate and public enterprises has necessitated the development of the capital market in India. An ideal and sound capital market always tries to offer adequate quantity of capital to any industrial and business house at a reasonable rate which are expected to result high prospective yield to make the borrowing worthwhile."[16] It is necessary for the capital market to work for the supply of funds at minimum possible costs with high rate of return as yield.

Rationale of Capital Market : Capital market is required due to following reason:

(*i*) Determine a fair price for the securities it trades (price discovery)

(*ii*) Enable transactions to be made at this price quickly and easily (the provision of liquidity)

(*iii*) Enable transactions to be made at as low a cost as possible (minimization of trading costs).

The financial resources raised through the capital market is used for investment. Productive activities generate further outputs and incomes of the people and promote growth. Thus, economic growth and activities in the capital markets are closely related. Capital market performs two major functions of maintaining liquidity and fair pricing of securities available in the market. The term liquidity refers to the convenience and speed of converting assets into cash or transferring assets from one person to another without any loss of value. It facilitates the buying and selling of securities by a large number of investors continuously and instantaneously without incurring significant costs. It helps in reducing transaction costs. The availability of certain investors is must to ensure a required level of liquidity in the market. These investors are always ready to buy or sell securities. They are known as market makers and support to enhance the liquidity and reduce the transaction costs of the securities.

Functions of Capital Market : Functions of the capital market are as follows:

(*i*) It maintains liquidity and fair pricing of available securities in the market.

(*ii*) It facilitates the buying and selling of securities.

(*iii*) It helps to reduce transaction costs.

It ensures a required level of liquidity in the market;

It ensures availability of certain investors known as market makers.

Interdependence of Money and Capital Market

Money market and capital market are playing a crucial role in the financial market. Financial market needs both types of funds – short term funds as well as long term funds. Money market arranges short term funds while capital market is responsible for medium and long term funds. Both markets are supportive to each other and are inter dependent. "The existence of a capital market is dependent upon the existence of a well organized money market and capital market and the two markets together play an important role in the economic development of a country."[17] Both markets contribute to the flow of funds and liquidity in the varying periods. They affect and are also affected by each other. "a relative rise in the rate of interest in the money market may increase the demand in the capital markets, and a relative increase in the rate of interest or yield in the capital market will increase demand in the money market."[18] Thus, both money market and capital market play in tandem and provide strength to the financial market with continuity in operational behaviour.

Difference between Money Market and Capital Market : Difference between the money and capital market are as follows :

(*i*) Money market includes all agencies responsible for providing short-term capital to the industry at large. The investors once invested in the short-term instruments having less than 12 months maturity periods. Capital market is concerned with long term funds required by the industry. But it ensures liquidity to the instruments by providing trading facilities to them. It deals with those financial instruments which have maturities greater than one year.

(*ii*) Level of risk in money market is low as comparison to capital market.

(*iii*) Time to maturity and the financial soundness of issuers decides the level of risks in these two markets.

(*iv*) In the money market each single money market instrument is of large amount while in capital market each single instrument holds a small amount.

(*v*) Generally, money market instruments do not have any secondary market but capital market instruments have secondary markets.

(*vi*) In money market, there is no formal place for transactions while in capital markets the transactions take place in formal places like stock exchanges.

(*vii*) The instruments dealt in the money market are bills of exchanges, treasury bills, commercial papers, certificate of deposits etc. The instruments generally dealt in capital market are shares, debentures, government bonds etc.

(*viii*) In money markets, transactions have to be conducted without the help of brokers while in case of capital markets, transactions have to be conducted only through authorized dealers.

Constituents of Capital Market

There are two constituents of Capital market. These are Primary or New Issue Market and secondary market or Stock exchange.

1. Primary Market / New Issue Market : Primary market is one in which the company directly approaches investors for capital. The companies can approach for debt capital or equity capital or combination of both. It is a market of securities being issued by the issuer to investors. There is direct transactional relationship between the investors and issuing corporates. "Primary market or new issue market is mainly concerned with channelising the funds from savers to companies desirous of making investments in their ventures and for this it performs three distinct services namely, origination, underwriting, and distribution."[19] Origination function comprises investigation, analysis and processing of proposed new issues. New issues market also provides underwriting services to ensure the success of proposed issues. Distribution deals with the sale of securities to the ultimate investors.

In the new issue market, the issuing companies raise fund for long term objectives as for starting a new enterprise, expansion or diversification of existing businesses, research and development activities etc. This fund is directly provided by the public and financial institutions. Primary market contributes directly by matching the needs of companies and investors. The new issue market, therefore, functions as a direct link between the companies which require a provision for funds and the investing public. "When securities are initially offered to the public, they are said to be sold in the primary market. In the primary market, the proceeds of sale are used by the seller, perhaps a corporation, to make investments in real capital goods or for other purpose allowed under its corporate charter."[20] The issuer of the securities may be a new company or an existing company. The issues made by the companies also be of fresh security or the issue already made in the past. The Primary market deals with the raising of fresh capital either for cash or for consideration other than cash by companies, government and semi-government bodies, public sector units etc. and including all institutions dealing in the issue of fresh claims. "The primary market deals with those securities which are issued to the public for the first time. In the primary market, borrowers exchange new financial securities for long-term funds."[21] Thus, primary market is the place where a company makes its first contact with the public at large in search of capital. It facilitates the companies for capital formation. The forms in which these claims are incurred are equity shares, preference shares, debentures, rights shares, bonus shares, deposits, miscellaneous loans etc.

Process involved in Primary Market

Following process are involved in primary market:

(i) **Origination:** The origination is concerned with pre-issue management practices in which proper investigation, analysis and processing of new project proposals takes place. In this stage, a preliminary investigation is made by the sponsors of the issue about the technical, economic and financial feasibility to ensure viability of the project. Issuers generally engage advisory services to improve the quality of capital issues and ensure its success. These advisory services study the nature of the security, size of the issue, timings of floatation of issue, method of floatation of issue, pricing of the issue, etc. This function of origination is also performed by the merchant bankers who may be commercial banks, financial institutions or the private firms.

(ii) **Underwriting:** The underwriting process contracts makes the securities predictable and removes the element of uncertainty in the sale of securities. Underwriting is an agreement whereby the underwriter promises to subscribe a specified number of shares or debentures etc. in an issue if the probable investors do not subscribe to the issue. In case, the issue is fully subscribed, there is no liability for the underwriter. If a part of share issues remains unsold, it will be obligation of underwriter to buy such unsold shares.

(iii) **Distribution:** It refers to the sale of securities to the investors. It is carried out with the help of lead managers and brokers to the issues who maintain regular and direct contact with the ultimate investors. Actually, lead managers and brokers create market for the issue and make efforts for the success of the proposed issue.

Types of Floatations

Main types of floatations are as follows: (i) Prospectus (ii) Bought out deals/offer for sale (iii) Private placement (iv) Right Issue and (v) Book building.

(i) **Public Issue through Prospectus:** "Capital can be raised from the general public by the issue of prospectus. The prospectus is an invitation to the potential investors for subscribing the issue. The prospectus must contain various details regarding particulars of the company, its financial position etc."[22] This is the most common method practiced by companies to raise the capital through initial public offering (IPO). In public issues, the companies directly invite the general public or institutions to buy a fixed number of shares at a stated price through the document known as prospectus. According to the companies Act, 1985, the application forms for shares of a company must be accompanied by a prospectus. The companies are required to send the draft prospectus called as The Red Herring Prospectus to the stock exchanges where the shares of company are to be listed. The draft prospectus are scrutinized by

the stock exchanges and if there is need for any modification it has to be revised. "SEBI guidelines stipulate that in the case of a new company which does not have a three-year track record it cannot access the capital market, and if a new company is set up by an existing company with five year track record, the new company is free to determine the price of the shares."[23]

Exhibit 11.1

Issue of IPOs in Primary Market in India

Year	No. of Issues (IPOs)	Amount (Rs. Crore)	% Growth in No. of IPOS	% Growth in Amount
1989-90	186	2,522	--	--
1990-91	140	1,450	-24.73	-42.51
1991-92	195	1,400	39.29	-3.45
1992-93	526	5,651	169.74	303.64
1993-94	765	10,824	45.44	91.54
1994-95	N.A.	13,312	75.56	22.99
1995-96	1,423	8,882	5.96	-33.28
1996-97	740	4,671	-47.99	-47.41
1997-98	58	1,132	-92.16	-75.77
1998-99	22	504	-62.07	-55.48
1999-00	56	2,975	154.545	490.28
2000-01	115	2,479	105.35	-16.67
2001-02	06	1,082	-94.78	-56.35
2002-03	06	1,039	0	-3.97
2003-04	23	20,000	283.33	1,824.93
2004-05	23	12,382	0	-61.52
2005-06	79	10,936	71	- 11.67
2006-07	77	28,504	- 2.53	61.63
2007-08	85	42,595	10.38	49.43
2008-09	21	2,082	- 75.29	- 95.11

Source: Various Annual Reports, SEBI.

The prospectus contains the required details regarding name of the company, address of the registered office, existing and proposed activities of the company, location of the industry, name of directors, statutory provisions for the issue, programme of public issue such as opening, closing and earliest date of the issue, highlights and risk factors, capital structure, cost of the project, projected earnings, name of brokers/underwriters/ bankers/managers and registrars to the issue etc. Fund mobilized and number of IPOs in Indian Primary Market is shown in Exhibit-11.1

Thus, on the basis of above analysis there was a fluctuation in terms of number of IPOs and amount mobilized through number of IPOs. However, efforts are required to ensure stability in the primary market behaviour. It will encourage small investors to make more investment in Initial Public offerings. It will also ensure their active participation in the primary and secondary market.

***(ii)* Offer for Sale:** "Offer for sale is an offer through the intermediaries like issue houses or merchant bankers. The company sells the entire issue of shares or debentures to the issue houses at an agreed price which is generally below the par value and the shares then are resold by the issue house to the public"[24] In this process, the issuing company does not opt for retail distribution of issues to the public but directly sells the securities to the issue houses or share brokers at an agreed or negotiated price which is less than the par value and who resell the shares at a later stage at a high price. The difference in sale and resale price is known as turn or spread. Pricing is essential element to be decided by the dealers or merchant bankers. Generally, dealer decides the price by analyzing the viability and gestation period of the project, promoters' background and future projections. There are many advantages of offer for sale for the issuing company. These contracts helps the medium and small issuers to raise the funds in a short span of time with low cost of raising funds. This arrangement also helps in reducing the cost of raising funds. It also helps the entrepreneurs who are unfamiliar with the capital market but have the potential to raise and utilize the fund. Usually, in offer for sale contracts, the issues are sold at high premium to the public at large.

***(iii)* Private Placement:** There are certain intermediaries or agencies which are responsible for mobilizing funds for the companies. These agencies are financial institutions, mutual fund, insurance companies, merchant banking subsidiaries of commercial banks etc. Shares are generally sold by the companies to these agencies to reduce the time gap cost of issuing capital and other related formalities. The private placement market is a highly informal market and issues are placed with small number of financial institutions, corporate bodies and high net worth individuals. "A corporation sell the entire issue to a single purchaser (generally a financial institution or wealthy individual) or a group of such purchasers. This type of sale is known as a private (or direct) placement for the shares of company. In this method, company negotiates directly with the investor(s) over the terms of the offering, eliminating the underwriting function of the investment banker."[25] Thus, the private placement is a direct sale of securities by a company to the institutional investors at a suitable price. In this process, prospectus is not issued and there is no need of underwriting arrangements because the private placement itself resembles the underwriting process. "A private placement is different from the public offering of securities in terms of the regulatory requirements that must be satisfied by the issuer. If an issue qualifies as a private placement, it is exempt from the more complex registration requirements imposed on public offerings."[26] It also offers access to capital more quickly than the public issue. A public issue may take time of three months to four months while the private placement facilitates to raise the funds within two to three months.

(iv) Qualified Institutional Placement: Qualified institutional placement (QIP) is a capital raising tool, primarily used in India, whereby a listed company can issue equity shares, fully and partly convertible debentures, or any securities other than warrants which are convertible to equity shares to a Qualified Institutional Buyer (QIB). Apart from preferential allotment, this is the only other speedy method of private placement whereby a listed company can issue shares or convertible securities to a select group of persons. QIP scores over other methods because the issuing firm does not have to undergo elaborate procedural requirements to raise its capital. The Securities and Exchange Board of India (SEBI) introduced the QIP process through a circular issued on May 8, 2006, to prevent listed companies in India from developing an excessive dependence on foreign capital. Prior to the innovation of the qualified institutional placement, there was concern from Indian market regulators and authorities that Indian companies were accessing international funding via issuing securities, such as American depository receipts (ADRs), in outside markets. The complications associated with raising capital in the domestic markets had led many companies to look at tapping the overseas markets. This was seen as an undesirable export of the domestic equity market, so the QIP guidelines were introduced to encourage Indian companies to raise funds domestically instead of tapping overseas markets.

In order to make Indian markets more competitive and efficient, it has been decided by the SEBI to introduce an additional mode for listed companies to raise funds from domestic market in the form of "Qualified Institutions Placement" (QIP). Key features of the QIP are as under:

(a) **Issuer:** A company whose equity shares are listed on a stock exchange having nationwide trading terminals and which is complying with the prescribed requirements of minimum public shareholding of the listing agreement will be eligible to raise funds in domestic market by placing securities with Qualified Institutional Buyers (QIBs).

(b) **Securities:** Securities which can be issued through QIP are equity shares or any securities other than warrants, which are convertible into or exchangeable with equity shares (hereinafter referred to as "specified securities"). The specified securities shall be made fully paid up at the time of allotment. In case of a security which is convertible into or exchangeable with equity shares at a later date, the same may be converted/ exchanged in to equity shares at any time after the date of allotment of the security, no later than sixty months from the date of allotment.

(c) **Investors/Allottees**: The specified securities can be issued only to Qualified Institutional Buyers (QIBs). Such QIBs shall not be promoters or related to promoters of the issuer, either directly or indirectly. Each placement of the specified securities issued through QIP shall be on private placement basis. A minimum of 10% of the securities in each placement shall be allotted to Mutual Funds. Investors shall not be allowed to withdraw their bids / applications after closure of the issue. Allotment of specified securities issued shall be completed within twelve months from the date of passing of the resolution.

The resolution passed at the meeting of shareholders shall specify that the allotment is proposed to be made to QIBs and shall also specify the relevant date on the basis of which price of the resultant shares shall be determined. The placements made pursuant to authority of the same shareholders' resolution shall be separated by at least six months between each placement. The minimum number of allottees for each placement of specified securities made pursuant to this shall not be less than:

(*a*) two, where the issue size is less than or equal to Rs. 250 crores;

(*b*) five, where the issue size is greater than Rs. 250 crores.

Provided that no single allottee shall be allotted more than 50% of the issue size. Provided further that QIBs belonging to the same group or those who are under common control shall be deemed to be a single allottee for the purpose of this clause.

For the purpose of this clause –

(*i*) The expression 'QIBs belonging to the same group' shall derive meaning from the concept of 'companies under the same group' as provided in sub-section (11) of Section 372 of the Companies Act, 1956;

(*ii*) "Control" shall have the same meaning as is assigned to it by clause (c) of Regulation 2 of the Securities and Exchange Board of India (Substantial Acquisition of Shares and Takeovers) Regulations, 1997.

(*d*) **Issue Size:** The aggregate of the proposed placement and all previous placements made in the same financial year shall not exceed five times the net worth of the issuer as per the audited balance sheet of the previous financial year.

(*e*) **Placement Document:** Issuer shall prepare a placement document containing all the relevant and material disclosures. There will be no pre-issue filing of the placement document with SEBI. Specified securities shall be issued on the basis of a placement document. The placement document shall contain all material information, including the information specified in Schedule XXIA. The placement document shall be a private document provided to select investors, through serially numbered copies. The placement document shall also be placed on the website of the concerned stock exchange and of the issuer with a disclaimer to the effect that it is in connection with an issue to QIBs and that no offer is being made to the public or to any other category of investors. A copy of the placement document shall be filed with the Board for record purpose within 30 days of the allotment of specified securities.

(*f*) **Pricing:** The floor price of the specified securities shall be determined on a basis similar to that for GDR / FCCB issues and shall be subject to adjustment in case of corporate actions such as stock splits, rights issue, bonus issue etc. An issue of specified securities shall be made at a price not less than the higher of the following:

(*i*) The average of the weekly high and low of the closing prices of the related shares quoted on the stock exchange during the six months preceding the relevant date;

OR

(*ii*) The average of the weekly high and low of the closing prices of the related shares quoted on the stock exchange during the two weeks preceding the relevant date. Necessary explanation is given below:

(*a*) "relevant date" for the purpose of this clause means the day which is thirty days prior to the date on which the meeting of general body of shareholders is held, in terms of sub-section (1A) of Section 81 of the Companies Act, 1956 or other applicable provision to consider the proposed issue.

(*b*) "stock exchange" for the purpose of this clause means any of the recognised stock exchanges in which the equity shares of the issuer of the same class are listed and in which the highest trading volume in such shares has been recorded during the six months immediately preceding the relevant date.

Where securities which are convertible into or exchangeable with equity shares at a later date are issued, the issuer shall determine the price of the resultant shares in terms of stated above statement. The relevant date for the above purpose may, at the option of the issuer, be either the one referred as above or a day thirty days prior to the date on which the holder of the securities which are convertible into or exchangeable with equity shares at a later date becomes entitled to apply for the said shares. The specified securities allotted shall be made fully paid up at the time of their allotment.

The prices considered for determination of issue price of specified securities as shall be subject to appropriate adjustments if the issuer company:

(*a*) makes an issue of shares by way of capitalization of profits or reserves (other than by way of a dividend on shares);

(*b*) makes an issue of shares on rights basis;

(*c*) consolidates its outstanding shares into a smaller number of shares;

(*d*) divides its outstanding shares (including by way of stock split);

(*e*) re-classifies any of its shares into other securities of the company;

(*f*) is involved in such other similar events or circumstances, which in the opinion of the concerned Stock Exchange, requires adjustments.

(*g*) **Other procedural requirements :** The resolution approving QIP, passed under sub-section (1A) of Section 81 of the Companies Act, 1956 or any other applicable provision, will remain valid for a period of twelve months from the date of passing of the resolution. There shall be a gap of at least six months between each placement in case of multiple placements of specified securities pursuant to authority of the same shareholders' resolution. Issuer and Merchant Banker shall submit documents / undertakings, if any, specified in this regard in the listing agreement, for the purpose of seeking in-principle approval and final permission from Stock Exchanges for listing of the specified securities.

(*h*) **Involvement of Merchant Banker :** Any issue and allotment of specified securities shall be managed by Merchant Banker(s) registered with SEBI. The merchant banker shall exercise due diligence.

The issuer shall furnish a copy of the placement document to each stock exchange on which the same class of shares or other securities are listed. The issuer shall also furnish to each stock exchange on which the same class of shares or other securities are listed, a certificate stating that the issue is being made and complies with its requirements, along with the application made for seeking in-principle approval for listing of the specified securities. The issuer shall also furnish to each stock exchange on which the same class of shares or other securities are listed, the documents, undertakings, etc, if any, specified in the listing agreement for the purpose of seeking in-principle approval and final permission from Stock Exchanges for listing of the specified securities.

(*v*) Rights Issue: Rights issues are the shares, which are offered to the existing shareholders of a company in a proportion to their existing shareholding. According to section 81 of the Companies Act, 1956, if a public company wants to increase its subscribed capital by allotment of further shares after two years from the date of its formation or one year from the date of its allotment, whichever is earlier, should offer shares at first to the existing shareholders in proportion to the shares held by them at the time of offer. "A right issue involves selling securities in the primary market by issuing rights to the existing shareholders when a company issues additional equity capital; it has to be offered in the first instance to the existing shareholders on a pro-rate basis."[27] These issues are also transferable and saleable in the capital market. Even the shareholders are not legally bounded to accept the offer. The existing shareholders should also be given the time of at least 15 days to accept the offer. In this context, a notice regarding the number of shares allotted in the ratio of number of shares held to be issued by the company. It is right of Board of Directors to dispose the unsubscribed shares in their unanimous manner after the expiry of the time given in the notice.

(*vi*) Book-Building: "Book- building is an international practice which refers to collecting orders from investment bankers and larger investors based on an indicative price range."[28] The process of book-building was adopted in Indian capital market by the SEBI with the recommendations of the committee under the charimanship of Shri Y.H. Malegam in October, 1995. As per the SEBI guidelines, book-building is treated as an alternative method of pricing that portion of the issues which are reserved for the institutional as well as corporate investors. The book-building process involves firm allotment of the instrument to a syndicate created by the lead Managers who sell the issue later to the public at an acceptable price. The rest of issues offered to public are known as "net offer" to the public. The price of issues through book-building and net offer should be the same. The underwriting process takes place only after the fixation of price for book building as well as net offer process. The book-building process plays a crucial role in determining the fair price of issues and so help to enhance the investors' confidence. It also facilitate price discovery for the proposed issue.

Resource Mobilisation through Primary Market in India

Corporate sector is the most important beneficiary of the capital market. It generates resources from the primary market for capital investments. Joint stock companies of private sector as well as joint stock companies controlled and owned by the central and state governments to meet out their financial requirement through issue of their long-term securities. Besides, In Indian context, there are two types of securities generally issued by the issuers. These are corporate securities and government securities.

Corporate securities generally constitute issues from the private sector and government public companies, public sector undertakings bond, banks and financial institutions, private placements and Euro issues. Foreign issues if any have also constituted corporate securities.

During 2008-09, 47 companies accessed the primary market and raised Rs.16,220 crore through public (22) and rights issues (25) as against 124 companies which raised Rs.87,029 crore in 2007-08. All the public issues in equity instruments were initial public offerings (IPOs). There were only 21 IPOs during 2008-09 as against 85 during 2007-08. The amount raised through IPOs during 2008-09 was much lower at Rs.2,082 crore compared to Rs.42,595 crore during 2007-08. The share of public issues in the total resource mobilisation declined to 22.1 per cent during 2008-09 against 62.6 per cent in 2007-08. There was a public issue of nonconvertible debenture (Rs.1,500 crore) in 2008-09 after a long gap. During 2008-09, the share of rights issues in the total resource mobilisation was 77.9 per cent. The amount mobilised through rights issues during 2008-09 was Rs.12,637 crore compared to Rs.32,518 crore during 2007-08. The highest amount was mobilised in September 2008 (Rs.9,715 crore), followed by January 2009 (Rs.1,500 crore) and December 2008 (Rs.1,370). The number of issues was the highest in June 2008 (9) followed by September 2008 (8).

Exhibit-11.2

Resource Mobilisation through Public and Right Issues

Particulars	**2007-08**		**2008-09**		**Percentage share in total amount**	
	No.	**Amount**	**No.**	**Amount**	**2007-08**	**2008-09**
1	2	3	4	5	6	7
1. Public Issues (i) + (ii)	92	54,511	22	3,582	62.63	22.08
(*i*) Public Issues of which	92	54,511	21	2,082	62.63	12.84
IPOs	85	42,595	21	2,082	48.94	12.84
FPOs	07	11,916	00	00	13.69	0.00
(*ii*) Public Issues (Bond/NCD)	00	0.00	01	1,500	0.00	9.25
2. Rights Issues	32	3,518	25	12,637	37.37	77.91
3. Total	57	87,029	47	16,220	100.00	100.00
Memo Item: Offer for sale	7	2,152	3	48	2.47	0.30

Source: Sebi Annual Report 2008-09.

In order to facilitate quicker resource mobilisation by companies from institutional investors, Qualified Institutions' Placement (QIP) was introduced in 2006. However, QIP as a mode of resource mopping also declined in 2008-09 reflecting the general subdued trend in the primary markets. During 2008-09, only two companies resorted to QIP and garnered Rs.189 crore as compared to 36 listed companies which had raised Rs.25,525 crore during 2007-08.

Exhibit-11.3

Resource Mobilization through Qualified Institutional Investors

(Rs. crore)

Particulars	2007-08		2008-09	
	No.	Amount	No.	Amount
1	2	3	4	5
Total of which	36	25,525	2	189
Listed Companies at BSE	36	25,525	1	75
Listed Companies at NSE	34	24,679	2	189

Source: NSE, BSE.

Primary Market Norms

Relevant primary market norms in Indian capital market are given below:

(a) **Corporate Securities:** The issue of capital to public by Indian companies is governed by the Disclosure and Investor Protection (DIP) Guidelines of SEBI. The guidelines provide norms relating to eligibility for companies issuing securities, pricing of issues, listing requirements, disclosure, lock-in period for promoters' contribution, contents of offer documents, pre and post issue obligations, etc.

(b) **Government Securities:** The issue is governed by the terms and conditions specified in the general notification of the government and also the terms and conditions specified in the specific notification issued in respect of issue of each security. Government issues securities with fixed coupon rates, floating rate bonds, zero coupon bonds and securities with embedded derivatives. The securities are issued through auction either on price basis or on yield basis.

(c) **Mutual Funds:** Mutual fund is a kind of collective investment vehicle which pools the resources of small investors who generally lack expertise to invest on their own. Mutual fund invests in securities and distributes the returns among the investors on cooperative principles. It is set up in the form of a trust, which has sponsor, trustees, asset management company, and custodian. There are income funds, growth funds, balanced funds, liquid funds, gilt funds, index funds, sectoral funds, open ended, close ended and assured return funds. Thus, there is a fund for everybody. The mutual funds are regulated by SEBI regulations which prescribe a code of conduct as well as impose various investment restrictions in the interest of investors.

Policy Framework for Primary Market

A developed primary market is crucial for resource mobilisation by corporates to meet their growth and expansion plans. Indian primary market witnessed high activity in terms of resource mobilisation and number of issues during 2007-08, but the same pace could not be maintained during 2008-09. In view of the meltdown in equity markets, fewer companies entered the primary market and investors' response to public issues in 2008- 09 was tepid compared to 2007-08. However, the ongoing reforms in the primary market helped in maintaining the investors' confidence. Following are some major policy initiatives taken by SEBI to strengthen the primary market and making it more investor friendly.

(i) **Applications Supported by Blocked Amount (ASBA) :** The SEBI introduced a new mode of payment in public issues through book building wherein the application money remains blocked in the bank account of the applicant till allotment is finalised. The said process named ASBA is supplementary to the existing process of applying in public issues through cheque/draft.

(ii) **Eligibility of Shares for Promoters' Contribution and Offer for Sale:** The SEBI (DIP) guidelines provided that only those shares, which are held by shareholders for a period of at least one year at the time of filing of draft offer document for a public issue were eligible (i) to be included for computing promoters' contribution (except in cases where the shares have been issued at the same issue price during the preceding one year) and (ii) to be offered for sale. The shares issued pursuant to a restructuring exercise approved by

High Court(s), in lieu of business that had been in existence for a period of more than one year prior to the restructuring exercise were excluded. The amendments made such shares as eligible shares for offer for sale and for inclusion in the promoters' contribution.

(iii) **Reduction in Timelines for Rights Issues:** In order to mitigate market risks faced by issuers and investors and to enable listed companies to raise funds from its shareholders in a more time effective manner, the SEBI reduced the timelines in rights issues, starting from the notice period for calling a board meeting to the period stipulated for completion of allotment and listing. With these amendments in place time taken for completion of rights issues would reduce from 16 weeks to just about 6 weeks.

(iv) **Extension of Validity Period of SEBI Observations:** The validity period of the observations letter issued by the SEBI on draft offer documents filed for public/rights issues was increased from three months to a period of twelve months. This measure would give sufficient flexibility to issuer to plan for launching an issue. Every issues is required to file an updated offer document with SEBI and where updation includes significant changes in the offer document, such an updated Red Herring Prospectus/ Prospectus or Letter of Offer shall be filed with SEBI at least one month before filing the same with Registrar of Companies (RoC) or with Designated Stock Exchange as the case may be.

(v) **Announcement of Price Band before Initial Public Offer Opens:** The provisions in SEBI (DIP) guidelines mandated disclosure of the floor price or price band in an initial public offer through the book building process in the Red Herring Prospectus (RHP) filed with the RoC. Given that there is a time lag of about two weeks between the filing of the RHP with the RoC and issue opening date, this exposed the price band disclosed in the RHP to market conditions. In order to mitigate this, issuers making an initial public offer were permitted to announce the floor price or price band at least two working days before the issue opening date subject to fulfillment of certain disclosure requirements.

(vi) **Relaxation from Strict Enforcement of Rule 19(2)(b) :** In order to enable an unlisted company intending to list its shares issued to the shareholders of a listed company pursuant to a scheme of arrangement approved by a High Court, without making an initial public offer, the SEBI (DIP) Guidelines were amended to provide for relaxation from strict enforcement of requirements of rule 19(2)(b) of the Securities Contracts (Regulation) Rules, 1957 (SC(R)R) in case of proposal for listing of the following securities:

(*a*) Equity shares with differential rights as to dividend, voting or otherwise, offered through rights or bonus issue.

(*b*) Warrants issued along with Non Convertible Debentures through Qualified Institutions Placement.

(vii) **Pricing of Shares for Preferential Allotment to Qualified Institutional Buyers (QIBs) :** In order to facilitate eligible listed companies to raise funds from Qualified Institutional Buyers (QIBs) without going through the elaborate documentation process, it is prescribed that preferential allotment of shares to QIBs shall be priced at the last two weeks' average price. This is subject to the condition that the number of QIB allottees in such preferential allotment does not exceed five. For all other preferential allotments including those to QIBs exceeding five in number, the existing formula of the higher of six months' average price or two weeks' average price would continue to apply.

(viii) **Lock-in of Shares issued against Exercise of Warrants Issued on Preferential Basis:** As per the guidelines on preferential issues, warrants issued on preferential basis were subjected to lock-in for a period of one year or three years, as the case may be, and lock-in period of shares allotted on exercise of such warrants was adjusted to the extent of such period for which these warrants had already been locked-in. It is important that the shares so allotted pursuant to exercise of warrants would be subject to lock-in period of one year or three years, as the case may be, from the 'date of allotment' of such shares.

(ix) **Enhancement of Upfront Margin Payment on Allotment of Warrants Issued on Preferential Basis:** In terms of the guidelines on preferential issues, warrants could be allotted on preferential basis, subject to the allottees paying upfront amount equivalent to at least 10 per cent of the price fixed. It is decided to enhance the upfront amount so payable from 10 per cent to 25 per cent of the price fixed.

(x) **Non-applicability of Certain Provisions of Preferential Issue Guidelines:** The guidelines on preferential issues have been amended to provide that an issuer, which has been granted relaxation by SEBI in terms of regulation 29A of the SEBI (Substantial Acquisitions of Shares and Takeovers) Regulations, 1997, shall be exempted from certain provisions of preferential issue guidelines, i.e., pricing, certificate from statutory

auditors etc, subject to the condition that in the explanatory statement to the notice for the general meeting of the shareholders, issuer gives adequate disclosures about the details of the plan including the process proposed to be followed by it for identification of the allottees in addition to the disclosures required in other applicable laws.

(xi) **Issuance of Non-convertible Debentures with Warrants through QIP :** The guidelines for QIP have been amended to enable a listed company to make a combined offering of Non-Convertible Debentures (NCD) with warrants to Qualified Institutional Buyers (QIB). Under this, QIB can subscribe to the combined offering of NCD with warrants or to the individual instruments, i.e., either NCD or warrants, where separate books are run for NCD/ warrants. The company is, however, required to obtain relaxation from the applicability of the provisions of Rule 19(4) of the SC(R)R for listing/ trading of the warrants.

(xii) **Reduction in Timelines for Completion of Bonus Issues:** In continuation of its policy for rationalizing the time required for completion of issues, SEBI reduced the timeline for completion of bonus issues. Accordingly, where no shareholders' approval is required as per the Articles of Association of the issuer, the bonus issue shall be completed within 15 days from the date of approval by the board of directors. Where shareholders' approval is required for capitalisation of profits or reserves as per the Articles of Association of the issuer, the bonus issue shall be completed within 60 days from the date of meeting of board of directors wherein bonus was announced subject to shareholders' approval.

(xiii) **Eligibility of Nominee Directors for Employee Stock Option Scheme :** The SEBI (Employee Stock Option Scheme and Employee Share Purchase Scheme) Guidelines, 1999 have been amended to provide that a director, nominated by an institution as its representative on the Board of Directors of a company, is eligible to participate in the employee stock option scheme of the company, if the contract / agreement entered into between the nominating institution and the director so appointed specifically provides for acceptance of the employee stock option scheme of the company by such director and a copy thereof is filed with the company.

(xiv) **Accounting Treatment for Options Granted under Graded Vesting in Employee Stock Option Schemes:** The SEBI (Employee Stock Option Scheme and Employee Share Purchase Scheme) Guidelines, 1999 have been amended to bring the accounting treatment prescribed by SEBI, for options granted under graded vesting in an employee stock option scheme, in line with the accounting treatment provided by Institute of Chartered Accountants of India in this regard.

(xv) **Provisions Pertaining to Corporate Governance:** To enhance the standards of corporate governance for listed entities, amendments have been made in Clause 49 of the listing agreement by introducing new provisions such as:

- *(i)* requirement to have atleast one-half of the board as independent directors, if the non executive Chairman of the company is a promoter or is related to promoters or persons occupying management positions at the board level or at one level below the board,
- *(ii)* specifying the minimum age limit of 21 years for independent directors,
- *(iii)* specifying the maximum time gap (i.e., 180 days) between the retirement and resignation of an independent director and appointment of another independent director in his place, and
- *(iv)* requiring the listed companies to disclose the inter-se relationship between the directors in the filing made with stock exchanges.

(xvi) **'Fairness Opinion' of Independent Merchant Banker in Schemes of Arrangement:** In order to safeguard the interest of shareholders, SEBI amended clause 24 of the Listing Agreement to provide that the listed company as well as the unlisted company which are getting merged under a scheme of arrangement under section 391-394 of the Companies Act, 1956 shall be required to appoint an independent merchant banker for giving a 'Fairness Opinion' on the valuation done by valuers. Further, the 'Fairness Opinion' of the independent merchant banker shall be made available to the shareholders at the time of approving the resolution.

(xvii) Amendments to Provisions Pertaining to Submission of Quarterly Financial Reports by Listed Companies to Stock Exchanges: In order to bring more transparency in the disclosures of the financial results, SEBI amended Clause 41 of the listing agreement by:

(*a*) extending time limit for submission of consolidated financial results, from one month to two months from the end of the quarter;

(*b*) requiring the company to publish only consolidated financial results if it opts to submit consolidated financial results in addition to its standalone financial results;

(*c*) relaxing the requirement to place the limited review report on un-audited financial results before Board or Committee, only if the variation between un-audited financial results and its limited review exceeds 10 per cent; and

(*d*) requiring the company to submit the limited review report for the last quarter also, if it opts to submit un-audited financial results for the last quarter.

(xviii) Disclosure of Pledged Shares by Promoters/Promoter Group in Listed Companies: Clause 35 and clause 41 of the Listing Agreement were amended to provide for disclosure of details of shares held by promoters and promoter group entities in listed companies which are pledged or otherwise encumbered. This was done with a view to ensure that while deciding to invest in the company, the investors may factor in the information about the pledged or otherwise encumbered shares held by promoter/promoter group in the company, as the extent of pledge/ encumbrance may have a significant impact on the price of the shares.

2. Secondary Market

Investors need liquidity to their investment. Secondary market provides marketability, liquidity and security to investment. It enables the investors to offload their shareholdings for improving their liquidity. It is a place where an investor sells the existing securities to another investor. Newly floated securities are also listed on the stock exchanges for trading purposes. Since there are large number of sellers and buyers, the market is dynamic. The stock exchange provides a ready market for buying and selling of existing stocks routed through new issue market securities.

It is a market of existing securities being transacted among investors. The issuer may be a new company or an existing company. These issues may be of new type or the security used in the past. It is a well established organisation having proper rules and regulations for conduct of the business. The trading members have adequate knowledge regarding companies and continuous changes in the price of securities. It also develops price discovery to securities enabling the investors for knowing the real worth of their investments.

Nature of Stock Exchange

The Securities Contracts (Regulation) Act, 1956 defined a stock exchange as an association, organization or body of individuals, whether incorporated or not, established for the purpose of assisting, regulating and controlling business in buying, selling and dealing in securities. "The secondary market or stock exchange means anybody of individuals whether incorporated or not constituted for the purpose of assisting, regulating or controlling the business of buying, selling or dealing in securities."[29]

The secondary market, comprising stock exchanges, is a highly organised market for the purchase and sale of second hand quoted or listed securities through intermediaries, called stock brokers and sub-brokers. "The secondary market is also called stock market."[30] "The stock market provides a ready market for the purchase and sale of corporate securities. It is a two-way market in which investors and speculators' agents i.e. stock brokers are just as likely to be sellers as well as buyers. Besides, the stock market bridges the gap between governments and municipalities which need to borrow money for long periods or to raise permanent capital and investors who only wish to put up money for comparatively short time."[31] The secondary market ensures the liquidity in the capital market and contributes to capital formation. "The role of secondary market is to provide investors with liquidity for their investments, enabling them to move quickly, and without substantial loss in market value, from security to cash and from one security to another."[32] Thus, it plays a crucial role in quick transfer as well as exchange of securities into money or another security.

It would have been impossible for companies to raise long-term capital in the absence of an organized market enabling investors to exchange their shares for cash. The stock exchange provides a connecting link between existing investors who want to dispose of their investments because they need cash and potential investors who wish to invest because they have surplus cash available.

Historical Perspective of Stock Market in India

The history of the stock market in India is related to the establishment of East India Company, which started doing business in loan securities towards the close of the 18th century. This company was in fact dominating in those days in dealing in loan securities. Thereafter, by the year 1830, the business in corporate stocks and shares was also done. The shares of some of the banks were dealt in Bombay and similarly in Calcutta. The introduction of the concept of "limited liability" in the Companies Act in1850 brought about a revolution in establishment of Joint Stock Enterprises in India. Thereafter, the stock market in India went on expanding made with the passage of time.

The first organised stock exchange was established in India at Mumbai in 1887 and was named as 'The Native Share and Stock Brokers Association'. At that time it had 318 members on the list. The stock exchange in Mumbai was followed by other state exchanges as the 'Ahmedabad Share and Stock Brokers Association' in 1894, Calcutta Stock Exchange Association in 1908 and the Madras Stock Exchange Association (Private) ltd. in 1937. A number of other stock exchanges had started up during the First and Second World Wars. But most of these were makeshift stock exchanges and collapsed soon thereafter. When the Securities (Contracts) Regulation Act 1956 was passed only 7 stock exchanges, viz., Mumbai, Ahmedabad, Kolkata, Chennai, Delhi, Hyderabad and Indore, received recognition. Earlier, the number of stock exchanges in the country was 23. At the moment number of recognised stock exchanges comes to 20. In the past, floor trading was the only mechanism available to the parties to trade in securities but due to change in environment, screen based system was introduced. Overall position of the organizational structure of recognised stock exchanges was given in Exhibit-11.4.

Exhibit 11.4

Organization of Recognized Stock Exchanges in India

S. No.	Name of Stock Exchanges	Year of Establishment	Type of Association	Recognition			Entrance Fee/per Value of Share (Rs.)	No. of Members
				Original	Permanent			
				Date	Permanent	Date		
1.	Mumbai	1875	Voluntary nonprofit persons	31.8.87	Permanent	-	-	558
2.	Calcutta	1908 (Incorporated in 1923)	Public Limited Company	10.10.57	5 years	14.4.80	5,000	650
3.	Madras	1908 (Rcongnised on 29.4.57	Public Limited Company	15.10.75	5 years	15.10.92	25,000	168
4.	Ahmedabad	1984	Voluntary non-profit making association of persons	16.10.57	5 years	16.9.82	-	299
5.	Delhi	1947	Public Limited Company	9.12.57	5 years	9.12.82	4,000	321
6.	Hyderabad	1943	Company Limited by Guarantee	29.9.58	5 years	29.9.83	25,000	111
7.	M.P. (Indore)	1930	Voluntary non profit-making association of persons	4.12.58	5 years	24.12.88	5,000	184
8.	Bangalore	1957	Incorporated as a Pvt. Ltd. Co. & converted into a public Co. Ltd. on 3.4.1962.	16.2.63	5 years	16.2.83	1,000	126
9.	Cochin	1978	Public Limited Company	10.5.79	5 years	-	5,000	476
10.	UP (Kanpur)	1982	Public Limited Company	3.6.82	5 years	-	1,01,000	445
11.	Pune	1982	Company Limited by Guarantee	2.9.82	5 years	-	2,500	69
12.	Ludhiana	1983	Public Limited Company	29.4.83	5 years	-	10,000	220

Contd....

13.	Gauhati	1984	Public Limited Company	1.5.84	5 years	-	5,000	184
14.	Kanara (Mangalore)	1985	Public Limited Company	9.9.85	5 years	-	250	74
15.	Magadh	1986	Company Limited by Guarantee	11.12.86	5 years	-	5,000	189
16.	Jaipur	1983-84	Public Limited Company	9.11.89	1 years	-	2,500	500
17.	Bhubaneswar	1989	Company Limited by Guarantee	5.6.89	5 years	-	-	87
18.	Saurashtra Kutch	1989	Company Limited by Guarantee	10.7.89	5 years	-	10,000	300
19.	OTC Exchange of India	1989	Public Limited Company	Aug.89	5 years	-	N.A.	N.A.
20.	Vadodara (Baroda)	1990	Public Limited Company	5.11.90	5 years	-	25,000	176
21.	Coimbatore	1991	Public Limited Company	18.9.91	3 years	-	N.A.	N.A.
22.	Meerut	1991	Public Limited Company	20.11.91	3 years	-	N.A.	N.A.
23.	Inter Connected Stock Exchange of India Ltd							

Source: Bombay Stock Exchange, the Stock Market in India, Bombay 1992 and SEBI Report, 2001-02.

Change in Structural Framework: The SEBI is trying to strengthen and develop the stock exchanges in proper perspective. With the support of various committees recommendations, SEBI has taken various measures to make the stock exchanges more viable, efficient and investors friendly. Corporatisation and demutualization have changed the environment in which stock exchanges operated themselves. Latest position of working stock exchanges is given in Exhibit.11.5

Exhibit-11.5
Latest Position Of Stock Exchanges

(as on 30 June, 2010)

Sl. No.	Name of the Exchange	Valid Upto
1	Ahmadabad Stock Exchange Ltd.	Permanent
2	Bangalore Stock Exchange Ltd.	Permanent
3	Bhubaneswar Stock Exchange Ltd.	June 04, 2011
4	Bombay Stock Exchange Ltd.	Permanent
5	Calcutta Stock Exchange Ltd.	Permanent
6	Cochin Stock Exchange Ltd.	November 07, 2010
7	Coimbatore Stock Exchange Ltd. Due to pending litigation before the Hon'ble Madras High Court, Coimbatore Stock Exchange Ltd. (CSX) has not filed application for renewal of recognition which expired on 17.09.06. However, in terms of order dated 15.09.06 of the Hon'ble Court, the right of CSX to apply for renewal shall be subject to further orders of the court and the stock exchange shall not be entitled to oppose the renewal solely on the ground of lapse of time.	September 17, 2006
8	Delhi Stock Exchange Ltd.,	Permanent

Contd....

9	Gauhati Stock Exchange	April 30, 2011
10	Hyderabad Stock Exchange Ltd., The Hyderabad Stock Exchange Ltd. (HSE) failed to dilute at least 51% of its equity share capital to public other than shareholders having trading rights on or before the stipulated date i.e. August 28, 2007. Consequently, in terms of section 5(2) of the Securities Contracts (Regulation) Act, 1956, the recognition granted to HSE stands withdrawn with effect from August 29, 2007.	
11	Interconnected Stock Exchange of India Ltd.	November 17, 2010
12	Jaipur Stock Exchange Ltd.	January 08, 2011
13	Ludhiana Stock Exchange Ltd.,	April 27, 2011
14	Madhya Pradesh Stock Exchange Ltd	Permanent
15	Madras Stock Exchange Ltd.	Permanent
16	Magadh Stock Exchange Ltd. "SEBI vide order dated September 3, 2007 refused to renew the recognition granted to Magadh Stock Exchange Ltd."	
17	* Mangalore Stock Exchange As per Securities Appellete Tribunal order dated October 4, 2006, the Mangalore Stock Exchange is a de-recognized Stock Exchange under Section 4 (4) of SCRA	
18	MCX Stock Exchange Ltd	September 15, 2010
19	National Stock Exchange of India Ltd.	Permanent
20	OTC Exchange of India	August 22, 2010
21	Pune Stock Exchange Ltd.	September 01, 2010
22	Saurashtra Kutch Stock Exchange Ltd. SEBI vide order dated July 06, 2007 has withdrawn the recognition granted to Saurashtra Kutch Stock Exchange Limited.	
23	U.P. Stock Exchange Limited	June 02, 2011
24	United Stock Exchange of India Limited	March 21, 2011
25	The Vadodara Stock Exchange Ltd.	January 03, 2011

Thus, the information given in exhibit 11.5 shows that five regional stock exchanges have been made by the SEBI as non function as they were involved in different irregular activities and non compliance of rules and directives.

Organization and Management of Stock Exchanges

The Securities Contracts (Regulation) Act, 1956 regulates stock exchange operations and trading rules for the securities. These acts in conjunction with the Companies Act, 1956 are envisaged to create those basic conditions on which the edifice of the sound revitalized private sector is to be built up. Most of the stock exchanges in India has been organised in company form of Organisation- Company form of organisation includes public limited companies and company limited by guarantee. The Securities Contracts (Regulation) Act, 1956 came into force in February 20, 1957, which provides for:

(*a*) Recognition of stock exchanges;

(*b*) General control over their trading practices;

(*c*) Regulations of contracts and options in securities; and

(*d*) Procedures for listing of the securities by the public companies.

The Central Government set up on April 12, 1988 "Securities and Exchange Board of India (SEBI)" in Bombay to promote orderly and healthy development of the securities market and to provide adequate investors protection. The Securities and Exchange Board of India seeks to create an environment to facilitate mobilization of adequate resources through the securities market. This environment includes rules and regulations, institutions and their interrelationship, instruments, practices, infrastructure and policy framework. These objectives are proposed to be accomplished by being responsive to the need of securities issuers, the investors and the market intermediaries. Certain dimensions of stock exchanges are given below:

(*i*) Membership Arrangement : Business at Stock Exchanges can be transacted by the members of the stock exchange only. Membership is restricted to persons who are financially sound and possess adequate experience. Further, members of the recognized stock exchanges are subject to authorization and registration by the SEBI and have to pay certain fee to stock exchanges and SEBI as an annual charge. A member can transact business on his behalf or on behalf of his clients. A non – member can deal in shares only through members. The relationship between client and member is fiduciary in nature. Member act as a custodian and handles securities of his clients as per their instructions. The Government has also prescribed new norms for selection of members for the guidance of duly constituted committee. The criteria which is to be followed includes:

(*i*) Professional and other educational qualifications.

(*ii*) Experience relevant to securities market.

(*iii*) Financial Status.

(*iv*) Performance in the interview.

(*v*) Written test.

According to the circular issued by SEBI in May 1993 in respect of membership of stock exchange, Corporate bodies (both Indian as well as foreign) are now allowed to get themselves registered as the broker member of recognized stock exchanges in the country. The SEBI setup a committee headed by Justice M.H. Kania in March 2002, to evolve a roadmap for the conversion of these exchanges into new governance mechanisms, with a separation between ownership, management and trading rights. The implementation of these new governance mechanisms is already under progress.

(*ii*) Listing of Securities on Stock Exchanges : Listing means admission of securities of any incorporated company, central and state governments, quasi governmental and other financial institution/corporations, municipalities, electricity, housing boards etc. to dealings on a recognised stock exchanges. Every recognised stock exchange i.e., a stock exchange which is for the time being recognised by the central government under section 4 of the Securities Contracts (Regulation) Act, 1956, has the power to make bye-laws for the listing of securities on the stock exchange, the inclusion of any security for the purpose of dealings and the suspension or withdrawal of any such securities and the suspension or prohibition of trading in any specified securities. This power to make bye-laws is subject to the prior approval of the central government. Further, the central government has the power to make or amend bye-laws of recognized stock exchanges either on a request by the governing body of a stock exchange or on its own motion. Securities are bought and sold in recognized stock exchanges through members who are known as brokers. The prices at which the securities are bought and sold on a recognized stock exchanges are known as 'official quotation'. In November 2002, SEBI approved the establishment of a 'Central Listing Authority' (CLA), which centralizes the listing functions. However, it currently takes place at the exchange level. Once CLA is fully functional, it may take up ongoing monitoring of compliance of listing requirements by firms.

(*iii*) Settlement Process: Necessary steps involved in settlement process are given below:

(*a*) **Settlement Cycle:** The trades accumulate over a trading cycle of one day and at the end of the day, these are clubbed together, and positions are netted and payment of cash and delivery of securities settle the balance after 2 working days. All trades executed on a day 'T' are settled on T+2 day. Earlier stock exchanges were required to necessarily complete their settlement within seven days and to conduct the auction immediately i.e. not later than eight days, after the completion of the relevant trading period. In those cases, where members have failed to give the delivery, as on date, the exchanges have a weekly settlement cycle. Trades are executed on screen and matched trade details are linked to settlement system electronically, and hence matching and confirmation of trades for direct participants are instantaneous. All communications relating to securities settlement is fully electronic and automated.

(*b*) **Negotiated Dealing System (NDS):** It facilitates screen based negotiated dealing for secondary market transactions in government securities. NDS members concluding deals outside NDS system in government securities are required to report the deal on NDS system within 15 minutes of concluding the deal. The deals reported/negotiated on NDS without the use of brokers, are required to be settled on T+0 or T+1. The deals executed through brokers need to be reported to exchanges and can be settled on T+0 T+5 basis. The system is designed to maintain anonymity of buyers and sellers but only the vital information of a transaction viz., number of the security, nomenclature, amount (face value), price/rate and/or indicative yield, in case applicable, are disseminated to the market. NDS interfaces with Clearing Corporation of India (CCIL) for settlement of government securities transactions for both outright and repo trades done/reported by NDS members.

(*c*) **Clearing Corporation of India Limited:** It facilitates settlement of transactions in government securities (both outright and repo) on Delivery Versus Payment (DVP-II) basis which provides for settlement of securities on gross basis and settlement of funds on net basis simultaneously. It acts as a central counterparty for clearing and settlement of government securities transactions done on NDS.

(*iv*) **VaR based margin:** The Stock Exchanges are advised to comply with the following provisions regarding collection of VaR based margin.

(*i*) The VaR based margin shall be collected on an upfront basis at the time of trade (instead of T+1 day).

(*ii*) The VaR based margin shall be collected/adjusted against the additional capital/collateral deposited by the member in the form as specified in circular prescribed by the SEBI from time to time.

(*iii*) The margin so collected may be realised along with the pay-in.

(*v*) **Rolling Settlement:** In order to enhance liquidity and to shorten the carry forward cycle and to make feasible the availability of alternative hedging mechanism in the form of derivatives, the SEBI introduced rolling settlement in respect of shares wherein compulsory dematerialized trading for all the investors has been introduced.

(*vi*) **Trading Practices:** A listed security is available for trading on the exchange. A security listed on other exchanges is also permitted for trading. The stock exchanges levy listing fees- initial fees and annual fees from the listed companies. It is a major source of income for many exchanges. A listed company can voluntary delist its securities from a stock exchange after providing an existing opportunity to holders of securities at a price determined through reverse book building. An existing opportunity is not necessary, if the security remains listed on an exchange having nationwide trading terminals. An exchange can, however, delist the securities compulsorily following a very stringent procedure.

(*vii*) **Trading Mechanism:** The exchanges provide an on-line fully- automated screen based trading system (SBTS) where a member can punch into the computer quantities of securities and the prices at which he likes to transact and the transaction is executed as soon as it funds a matching order from a counter party. The SBTS electronically matches order on a strict price/time priority and hence cuts down on time, cost and risk of error, as well as on fraud resulting in improved operational efficiency.

(*viii*) **Trading Rules:** The SEBI has framed regulations to prevent insider trading as well as unfair trade practices. The acquisitions and takeovers are permitted in a well-defined and orderly manner. Thresholds of shareholding, which require disclosure or public offer, have been prescribed. The companies are permitted to buy back their securities to improve liquidity and enhance the shareholders' wealth.

(*ix*) **Price Bands:** Stock market volatility is generally a cause of concern for both policy makers as well as investors. To curb excessive volatility, SEBI has prescribed a market wide circuit breaker system which brings about a coordinated trading halt in all equity and equity derivatives markets nation-wide, when the index moves either way by 10%, 15% and 20%. The movement of either S&P CNX Nifty or Sensex, whichever is breached earlier, triggers the breakers. As an additional measure of safety, exchanges have imposed individual scrip wise price bands, as high as 20% in some securities. However, in respect of securities for which derivative products are available or those included in indices on which derivative products are available, a daily price limit of 10% is applicable.

An Overview of Equity Market

(i) **Major Indicators:** Equity markets witnessed downward and volatile trend during 2008-09. The domestic. markets largely reflected the uncertainties in international financial market in the financial year. Markets were characterised by severe bouts of volatility during the year. The BSE Sensex and S&P CNX Nifty depreciated by 37.9 per cent and 36.2 per cent, respectively, over March 31,2008 . The BSE Sensex declined 5936 points to close at 9709 on March 31, 2009 from 15644 on March 31, 2008. The S&P CNX Nifty also declined 1714 points to close at 3021 at the end of March 2009 over 4735 at the end of March 2008. Indian markets had recorded severe volatility at the close of 2007-08. However, towards the beginning of the 2008-09, indices recovered and registered gains during April-May 2008. Better than expected fourth quarter results of 2007-08 declared by IT majors, net purchases by FIIs in the Indian equity market till May 20, 2008, and some easing of international crude oil prices helped the recovery. However, in June 2008, markets reversed due to hike in domestic and international fuel prices, rise in inflation rate, net FII sales in the equity segment, rupee depreciation and a general decline in international stock markets. Notwithstanding the deteriorating international financial crisis, the Indian equity markets performed in orderly manner in the second quarter of 2008-09. Domestic stock markets recovered with intermittent corrections in the second quarter till mid-September 2008. Since then, bankruptcy of world's largest financial institutions had its sway on Indian financial markets. Added to these were the heavy net sales by FIIs, domestic inflation, depreciation of rupee and slowdown in the industrial growth as shown by IIP. In third quarter of the financial year, weak trend continued in the markets as there was a sharp fall in the share prices. Concerns over the world economy plunging into recession added to the downswing. Substantial net outflows by FII, poor second quarter corporate results, depreciation of rupee and concerns of Indian economy falling into recession on account of weak industrial growth and decline in exports accentuated the downtrend. The subdued and volatile trend continued in the fourth quarter of 2008-09 mainly reflecting the international equity markets. The BSE Sensex touched a low of 8160 on March 9, 2009. Thereafter, a slight recovery was seen in consonance with the improvements in world equity markets towards the end of 2008-09. In tandem with the decline in stock prices in 2008-09, there was a fall in turnover and market capitalisation across the board.

Exhibit-11.6

Major Indicators of Indian Stock Markets

Item	2007-08	2008-09	Percentage Variation 2007-08	Percentage Variation 2008-09
1	2	3	4	5
A. Indices				
BSE Sensex				
Year-end	15,644	9,709	19.68	- 37.94
Average	16,569	12,366	35.00	- 25.37
S&P CNX Nifty				
Year-end	4735	3,021	23.89	- 36.20
Average	4,897	3,731	37.08	- 23.81
S&P CNX Nifty				
Year-end	3,826	2,295	21.64	- 40.02
Average	4,097	2,951	37.85	- 27.97
B. Volatility (per cent)				
BSE Sensex	30.55	43.58	-	-
S&P CNX Nifty	32.09	41.54	-	-
C. Total Turnover (Rs.cr.)				
Cash Segment(All-India)	51,30,816	38,52,579	76.74	- 24.91
of which				

Contd....

BSE	15,78,857	11,00,075	65.12	- 30.32
NSE	35,51,038	27,52,023	82.55	- 22.50
Derivative Segment	1,33,32,787	1,10,22,257	79.80	-17.33
BSE	2,42,309	11,775	310.64	-95.14
NSE	1,30,90,478	1,10,10,482	77.95	-15.89
D. Market Capitalization (Rs.cr.) @				
BSE	51,38,014	30,86,075	44.94	- 39.94
NSE	48,58,122	28,96,194	44.27	- 40.38
E. P/E Ratio@				
BSE Sensex	20.11	13.65	-	-
S&P CNX Nifty	20.63	14.30	-	-
S&P CNX Nifty	17.86	13.13	-	-

* Volatility is measured in terms of standard deviation of returns on index.

@ As on March 31 of the respective year.

Source: Various Stock Exchanges.

(ii) **Turnover Performance:** In tandem with the downward spiral of equity prices, there was a decline in the trading volumes in stock exchanges in 2008-09. During 2008-09, turnover of all stock exchanges in the cash segment declined by 24.9 per cent to Rs. 38,52,579 crore compared to Rs. 51,30,816 crore in 2007-08. BSE and NSE together contributed more than 99.9 per cent of the turnover, of which NSE accounted for 71.4 per cent in the total turnover in cash market. Apart from NSE and BSE, the only two stock exchanges which recorded turnover during 2008-09 were Kolkata Stock Exchange and UPSE.

Exhibit11.7

Turnover in the stock exchanges in India

Stock Exchange	2007-08	2008-09	Percentage Share
1	2	3	4
Ahmedabad	Nil	Nil	Nil
BSE	15,78,857	11,00,075	28.55
Bangalore	Nil	Nil	Nil
Bhubaneswar	Nil	Nil	Nil
Cochin	Nil	Nil	Nil
Coimbatore	Nil	Nil	Nil
Delhi	Nil	Nil	Nil
Gauhati	Nil	Nil	Nil
ISE	Nil	Nil	Nil
Jaipur	Nil	Nil	Nil
Kolkata	446	393	0.01
Ludhiana	Nil	Nil	Nil
Madras	Nil	Nil	Nil
MPSE	Nil	Nil	Nil

Contd....

NSE	35,51,037	27,52,023	71.43
OTCEI	Nil	Nil	Nil
Pune	Nil	Nil	Nil
UPSE	475	89	0
Vadodara	Nil	Nil	Nil
Total	51,30,816	38,52,579	100.00

Source: Various Stock Exchanges.

The exhibit-11.7 shows that there was hardly any transaction on other stock exchanges. Month-wise, BSE and NSE recorded the highest turnover in July 2008 followed by May 2008 and April 2008. Despite the declining volumes, Indian exchanges maintained their positions vis-à-vis major exchanges of the world. As per the data released by World Federation of Exchanges (WFE), NSE was ranked fourth and BSE was ranked seventh among the top most exchanges in terms of the number of trades in equity shares for the calendar year 2008. In terms of the value of shares traded, NSE was ranked 18th among the top-most exchanges for the calendar year 2008.

Activities in Stock Exchanges

Over the years, NSE and BSE have emerged as the nation-wide stock exchanges of the country contributing more than 99 per cent of the total turnover. Apart from NSE and BSE, only Calcutta and UPSE recorded some transactions. Four stock exchanges viz., Hyderabad, Magadh, Saurashtra Kutch Stock Exchange (SKSE) and Mangalore, have recently been de-recognised by SEBI. The number of shares traded and delivered declined at BSE, NSE, Calcutta and UPSE. The value of shares delivered also declined at these stock exchanges. Of the total shares traded, NSE's share was 65.7 per cent, followed by BSE which constituted 34.3 per cent of the total shares traded. NSE had a share 72.6 per cent in the total value of shares delivered followed by BSE (27.4 per cent)

Developments in Secondary Market in India

Major developments of secondary market in India are as follows:

1. De-mat Trading: Scripless trading is a method of securities trading in which the settlement of transactions take place via book entry instead of physical exchange and delivery of securities certificates. The major objective of introducing scripless trading is to ensure the safety of securities certificates and to improve the liquidity position of the stock markets both in primary and secondary markets. The major advantages of dematerialised trading system are as follows:

(*a*) Reduction in paper work of stockbrokers and stock exchanges.

(*b*) Ensuring safety of certificates from theft, fake certificates, multination, department etc.

(*c*) Reduction in cumbersome share transfer procedures as being followed now.

(*d*) Greater speed in exchange and delivery of securities certificates.

(*e*) Improves liquidity of both the individual scrips and stock market position.

The SEBI has introduced trading of shares in dematerialisation form during 1995-96 to control the growing menance of bad deliveries. Dematerialization of securities is one of the major steps for improving and modernising market and enhancing the level of investor protection through elimination of bad deliveries and forgery of shares, and expediting the transfer of shares. Recognizing the far reaching benefits that would accrue to the market through the removal of physical securities, the speeding up of dematerialisation process has been high on the agenda of the SEBI.

There are in place two fully developed depositories which maintain and transfer ownership records in electronic form for the entire range of securities. These depositories are Central Depositories Services Ltd and National Securities Depositories Ltd. They encourage broadest direct and indirect industry participation. A large variety of instruments including all securities and money market instruments are held in depositories. These are held in dematerialized form. Investor is sovereign under the depository legislation which gives him right to hold the securities in physical form or demat form. All securities which investor likes to hold in demat form, are held in depositories. All active securities are traded and settled in demat form. The depositories operate under the Depositories Act, 1996, and the systems are in place for smooth inter-depository transfer of securities. Stamp duty on transfer of demat securities have been abolished. Securities held in depositories are freely transferable. Demat securities are preferred collateral in the market. The admission to a depository for dematerialisation of securities has been made a prerequisite for making a public or rights issue or an offer for sale. All new IPOs are compulsorily traded in demat form. It has also been made compulsory for public listed companies making IPO of any security for Rs. 10 crore or more to do the same only in dematerialised form.

2. Depositories Network: Depository institutions include commercial banks (or simply banks), savings and loan associations (S & Ls), savings banks, and credit unions. All are financial intermediaries that accept deposits can join depositories network. Their income is derived from two sources: (i) the income generated from the loans they make and the securities they purchase and (ii) fee income. Depository institutions are highly regulated because of the important role that they play in the country's financial system. Demand deposit accounts are the principal means that individuals and business entities use for making payments, and government monetary policy is implemented through the banking system. All depository institutions face this interest rate risk. Managers of a depository institution who have particular expectations about the future direction of interest rates will seek to benefit from these expectation. Those who expect interest rates to rise may pursue a policy to borrow funds for a long time horizon (that is, to borrow long) and lend funds for a short time horizon (to lend short). If interest rates are expected to drop, managers may elect to borrow short and lend long.

3. Inter-Connectivity between NSDL and CDSL: In order to establish inter-connectivity of National Securities Depositories Limited (NSDL) and Central Depositories Services Limited (CDSL), it is decided that settlement of market transactions should begin with the clearing members opening accounts in both depositories and the clearing house or corporations for effecting the same pay-out of shares of each depository as a pay-in of shares in that depository.

Corporatisation and Demutualisation of Indian Stock Exchanges

The stock exchanges world over have been generally formed as 'mutual' organisations. The trading members not only provide broking services., but also own, control and mange such exchanges for their mutual benefit. They don't generally distribute profit among themselves and therefore, termed as 'not-for-profit' organizations. Stock exchanges owned by members may work towards the interest of members alone which may be detrimental to the rights of other stakeholders. There could also be conflict of interest between ownership and management. In order to eliminate conflict of interest, there is need to segregate the management functions from ownership and trading rights through demutualisation. Moreover, stock exchanges should ideally work as body corporate similar to any other 'for-profit' corporate entity.

The SEBI constituted a Committee on Corporatisation and Demutualisation of Stock Exchanges under the Chairmanship of Justice M.H. Kania, former Chief Justice of India, in 2002 for advising SEBI on corporatisation and demutualisation of exchanges and to recommend the steps that need to be taken to implement the same.

In the meantime, the Securities Laws (Amendment) Act, on January 7, 2005 was enacted on October 12, 2004, which amended the Securities Contracts (Regulation) Act, 1956 to facilitate the corporatisation and demutualisation of Stock Exchanges. The Act makes it mandatory that all stock exchanges, if not already corporatised and demutualised, shall be corporatised and demutualised on or before the appointed date so notified in the official gazzette by SEBI, a scheme for corporatisation and demutualisation to SEBI for approval.

Exchanges were also advised to adhere to the time schedule. A press release indicating tentative time schedule of C&D was issued on January 7, 2005. Thereafter, SEBI had several rounds of discussions with all the stock exchanges to clarify and sort out their specific issues and to guide them to prepare their schemes in compliance with the SCRA. The discussions were quite protracted, as there were several legal issues involved. The exchanges were advised to submit their final schemes to SEBI for approval latest by January 31, 2005. With the submission of the scheme by BSE on March 9, 2005, the schemes from all the exchanges were received. The Corporatisation and Demutualisation of the BSE was notified on May 20, 2005.

As provided in the SC(R) A, SEBI vide notification dated March 23, 2005, has specified that the National Stock Exchange of India Limited, which is already corporatised and demutualised would not be required to submit a scheme to SEBI for approval, subject to the following conditions:(a) The National Stock Exchange of India Limited shall not change its current corporate and demutualised structure, without prior approval of SEBI; and (b) The National Stock Exchange of India Limited shall comply with further conditions as may be imposed by SEBI in this regard from time to time.

The process of C and D involves transfer of assets from the exchanges which are Associations of Persons/Companies limited by Guarantee/Not-for-profit Companies to the emerging corporate demutual exchange and such transfer attracts stamp duty. To facilitate the process of corporatisation and demutualisation and to make it tax-neutral, the Government, has decided a one-time exemption from payment of stamp duty on notional transfer of assets from the exchanges which are Association of Persons/Companies limited by Guarantee/Not-for-profit Companies to the emerging corporate demutual exchange.

The process of demutualisation involves the bifurcation of members' rights in a stock exchange into 2 segments-ownership rights and trading rights. It thereby changes the relation between members and the stock exchanges and alters the position of stock exchanges, as they would not retain their voluntary, not- for-profit character, but become 'for profit' corporate bodies. The process of transition from a mutually-owned association to a company owned by shareholders or, in other words, the transformation of the legal structure from a mutual from to a business corporation is referred to as 'demutualisation'. The company so constituted as a result of the process may be listed or unlisted.

Rationale of Corporatisation and Demutualisation

(*i*) Developments in computing power and application have changed markets to a great extent. Technological advancements and developments have changed the conditions of competition in the securities markets, and as a result, stock exchanges are facing growing domestic and international competition from other firms. This has put an increasing requirement on stock exchanges to be cost efficient, transparent and more widely accountable.

(*ii*) Market reforms are resulting in exchanges, i.e., clearing, settlement and listing are under potential competitive threat. To meet these threats, exchanges are being driven to organize themselves and behave like commercial enterprises. This, in turn, calls for the modernisation, demutualisation and a radical change of the organisational structure and outline of the existing exchanges, thereby allowing a more rapid response to these developments.

(*iii*) Exchanges need to meet the demand from their customers for lower transaction costs, more efficient services and new products. The only credible way to meet the requirements of the customer is by investing in new technology that would reduce the role of the brokers.

(*iv*) A mutualised exchange in all cases subject to conflict of interest. In such cases, the decisions of the exchange could affect the interest of the members either individually or collectively.

(*v*) The basic objective of demutualisation of stock exchanges is to do away with the involvement of brokers in the management of the Exchanges, to convert the Exchanges into business entities so that they are professionally managed, to eliminate insider trading and an effort to continue capital market reforms. This idea would also ensure that the Government has greater control in the administration of the country's capital market.

Features of Demutualisation

Important features of demutualisation are as follows:

(*a*) **Governance:** One of the issues regarding the governance is whether the demutualised corporate structure would compromise the position of the stock exchanges as a public entity. The inclusion of outside directors would be useful to serve as a check and would promote integrity.

(*b*) **Transferability of Shares:** The issues that would arise is whether the shares of the listed stock exchange would be freely transferable like the stocks of any other listed company. If these shares would be transferable, the question that is raised is about the consequences if, after a takeover, the interests of the new shareholder are not aligned with the role of the exchange as a public entity.

(*c*) **Self-listing:** A conflict of interest may arise if the exchange lists its shares on itself. An exchange may benefit by listing its own shares due to the enhanced visibility and reputation, accountability, transparency and market discipline. The question that arises is whether the exchange can be self-regulated and whether this, in turn, would conflict with the other competing companies that are also listed on the exchanges.

Regional Stock Exchanges in India

The technology drives today the stock markets the world over. India is no exception. Establishment of National Stock Exchange of India Ltd., (NSE) in 1994 with an all-India spread and expansion of operations of Bombay Stock Exchange (BSE) throughout the country, both of which have their trader work stations at over 400 centres in the country today, have led to the virtual extinction of all the 19 Regional Stock Exchanges (RSEs) spread across the length and breadth of the country. Indian securities market has large number of stocks. With the recent reforms in securities settlement in the Indian securities markets, regional stock exchanges lost their business making it harder for them to provide the liquidity.

Factors Responsible for Decline of Regional Stock Exchanges In India

1. Abolition of badla with effect from July 2, 2001, which acted as the backbone of trading at the Calcutta, Delhi, Ahmedabad and Ludhiana Stock Exchanges and also at a few other exchanges, which conducted badla trading but in a clandestine manner, dealt a serious blow to trading at the Regional Stock Exchanges (RSEs). Introduction of uniform trading cycles at all the stock exchange, also effective from July 2, 2001, reduced further the volume of trading at the RSEs due to diminished opportunities for arbitrage transactions. Introduction of compulsory rolling settlements, initially in a few securities and subsequently in all securities effective from December 31, 2001 on a T+5 basis accelerated the reduction in turnover at the RSEs. The switch over of the rolling settlement to T+3 effective from April 1, 2002 and to T+2 with effect from April 1, 2003 sealed the fate of the RSEs.
2. All the major operators at the RSEs have acquired memberships of either NSE of BSE or of both, while most others acquired the sub-brokerships of members of NSE/BSE and all of them switched over their operations completely to NSE and BSE. In spite of the fact that trading at the RSEs has ground to a halt, RSEs have managed to survive so far because of the annual listing fees that are being received from the listed companies. The circulars issued by the Ministry of Finance on April 23, 2003 withdrawing its earlier circulars which required all companies including existing listed companies, to be listed on the stock exchanges located in the State where the registered office or the main works/fixed assets of the company are situated has driven the last nail into the coffin of RSEs as companies have started lining up one after the other to get themselves delisted from the RSEs. With the incomes drying up almost completely, RSEs saw a totally deserted look with no activity whatever.
3. A host of factors like low capital base of listed companies, (there are about 2,000 listed companies with a paid up capital of Rs. 3 crore and below), progressive reduction in public offer from 60 percent of the issued capital to 25/10 percent for eligibility for listing, switch-over to proportionate allotment of securities, free pricing of shares, introduction of book-building in respect of IPOs, introduction of order-driven system and of rolling settlement etc., have all cumulatively been responsible for the present state regional Indian stock markets.

Present Scenario of Regional Stock Exchanges

Four regional stock exchanges (Hyderabad, Magadh, Saurashtra and Kutch stock exchange out of the 22 recognised stock exchanges in India (SEBI has refused renewal of recognition to Mangalore Stock Exchange), NSE and BSE account for almost 100% of the total turnover. As far as RSEs are concerned, except for the Calcutta Stock Exchange (CSE) and the Uttar Pradesh Stock Exchange (UPSE), there is no trading on any other stock exchange and even on the CSE and UPSE, the business is down to a trickle. The financial condition of the RSEs is by and large also weak. This state of affairs has been prevailing for the past several years. The factors responsible for this condition includes the advent of automated trading and extension of nationwide reach of BSE and NSE which offered a large and liquid market to investors across the country, the introduction of uniform rolling settlement from June 2001 in place of account period settlement with varying settlement cycles and the abolition of the concept of regional listing.

The share of 19 RSEs, which was as much as 45.6 per cent of the total all India turnover of Rs.2.39 lakh crore in 1995-96, declined progressively year after year and in 2001-02, it was just 8.4 per cent of the total volume of Rs. 8.96 lakh crore. At present, there is virtually no trading at any of the RSEs. Trading in the cash segment is thus confined to NSE and BSE only, with the share of the latter, which used to account for over 70 percent of the all-India volume of trading till 1995, is also progressively declining. Currently, BSE accounts for about 30 per cent of the aggregate volume of trading on NSE and BSE in the cash segment. In the derivatives segment, while NSE clocks in about Rs. 2000 crore daily, the turnover on BSE has been progressively declining virtually to the zero level.

Exhibit-11.8

Turnover of The RSEs

(Rs. in crores)

SEs\Year	2000-01	01-02	02-03	03-04	04-05	05-06
Bhubaneswar	0.02	0	0	0	0	0
Calcutta	355035	27074	6539	1927	2714	2800
Coimbatore	0	0	0	0	0	0
Cochin	26	1	0	0	0	0
Pune	6171	1150	2	0	0.37	0
Vadodra	0.85	10	260	0	0	0
Ahmedabad	54035	14644	15482	5044	8	0
Uttar Pradesh	24741	13337	14763	13130	5343	1487
Jaipur	0	0	0	0	0	0
OTCEI	126	4	0.54	16	0.01	0.01
Ludhiana	9154	857	0	0	0	0
Madras	109	24	38	99	27	5
Hyderabad	978	41	5	3	14	97
Magadh	1	0.0041	1	0.09	0	91
Saurashtra Kutch	0	0	0	0	0	0
Bangalore	1087	934	0.11	0.1	0	0
Delhi	82996	5526	11	3	0	0
Gauhati	0	0	0	0	0	0
Madhya Pradesh	4	10	0	0	0	0
Inter-connected	237	69	24	0.034	0	0

Source: Business Line, as on 2.06.06, p.2.

The RSEs of the country and their members had spent over Rs. 200 crore in automating their trading, clearing and settlement systems, largely driven by regulatory compulsions, sadly to witness them lying idle at present. In the year 2005-06, the trading took place only at 5 regional stock exchanges viz., Calcutta, Uttar Pradesh, Hyderabad, Magadh and Madras, which very meager when compared with the trading at NSE and BSE. The Calcutta Stock exchange and Uttar Pradesh exchange showed a good performance in 2000-01 but the figure continued to decrease year after year and it reached at only 2800 crore and 1487 crore respectively. Due to this decline in the figure of trading at the RSE, the market regulators were required to take action and decide whether to revive these exchanges or close it down.

Suggestion for Revival of Regional Stock Exchange

1. All the RSEs may be given a regulatory mandate to consolidate and form a third stock exchange, in addition to BSE and NSE.
2. The un-utilized funds lying with the RSEs may all be pooled in and transferred to a common "stock exchange fund" that could be used for funding securities market transactions.

3. Efforts are required to consolidate stock exchanges on region wise basis. An active market for trading in commodities could be developed by the stock exchanges in the southern region. Similarly, stock exchanges in the northern, eastern and western regions could be consolidated.
4. RSEs may be encouraged to consider any revival initiatives including corporate restructuring by merger with any of the premier stock exchanges subject to mutual agreement. There is need for effective and efficient stock exchange for small and medium enterprises. The RSEs may not be able to survive independently in view of the changed circumstances in the Indian securities market.
5. RSEs may be permitted to establish a platform for book building, both for initial public offerings (IPOs) and follow-on public offerings (FPOs) and also for delisting of companies.

Policy Framework for Secondary Market

(i) **Short Selling and Securities and Lending Borrowing Scheme (SLB):** The broad framework for short selling and securities lending and borrowing scheme for all market participants was specified by SEBI in December 2007. This framework was operationalised with effect from April 21, 2008. Pursuant to feedback from the market participants, the scheme for Securities Lending and Borrowing was revised. Key modifications made to SLB were:

(i) increasing the tenure of SLB,

(ii) extending the duration of SLB session

(iii) allowing margins in SLB to be taken in the form of cash and cash equivalents and

(iv) clarifying how to deal with corporate actions.

(ii) **Margining of Institutional Trades in the Cash Market:** With a view to bring about a level playing field in the cash market among all categories of investors and to strengthen the risk management framework, margining for institutional trades was made mandatory by SEBI w.e.f., April 21, 2008. Margins were collected from institutional investors on a T+1 basis. Institutional investors were permitted to maintain their entire margin in the form of approved securities. Further, members were allowed to make early pay-in of funds and to adjust pay-in obligations from the cash component of liquid assets deposited by them.

(iii) **Exit Option to Regional Stock Exchange:** Broad guidelines were specified by SEBI to provide an exit option to Regional Stock Exchanges (RSEs) whose recognition was withdrawn and/or renewal of recognition was refused by SEBI or for RSEs who would want to surrender their recognition.

(iv) **Introduction of Direct Market Access (DMA):** With a view to increase liquidity, bring about greater transparency, lower impact cost for large orders and reduce risk of error associated with manual execution of client orders, the facility of Direct Market Access (DMA) was introduced. This facility allows brokers to offer its clients direct access to the exchange trading system through the broker's infrastructure without manual intervention by the broker. The DMA framework places onus on the broker to do proper risk assessment of clients before providing DMA facility and broker is responsible for risk management, setting trading/ exposure/ positions limits and maintaining adequate audit trails. The facility was initially provided to institutional investors. It was clarified that Institutional investors may use DMA facility through investment managers after due authorisation and upon furnishing to the broker/exchange suitable agreements/ undertakings between the institution and investment manager stating, *inter alia*, that the institutional investor shall be responsible for all actions undertaken by its authorized investment manager. Such investment managers may execute necessary documents on behalf of the institutional investor.

(v) **Mandatory Requirement of PAN:** The Central government has exempted the persons resident in Sikkim from Direct Income taxes. In view of this, SEBI exempted investor residing in the state of Sikkim from the mandatory requirement of PAN for their investments in mutual funds. In view of Rule 114 C (1) (c) of Income Tax Rules, requirement of PAN was also relaxed in the case of securities market transactions undertaken on behalf of Central and State Governments and by the officials appointed by the Courts e.g., official liquidator, court receiver etc. (under the category of Government). The SEBI has made it mandatory for all securities transactions to indicate the PAN of the parties involved. From August,16 it is also mandatory for Depositories companies to indicate the PAN of their clients.

Trading in Retail Debt: In order to enable the retail investors to participate in the trading and investing in Government Securities, the Bombay Stock Exchange has launched the screen based Retail Trading in government securities on January 16, 2003. With this initiative, the Indian Fixed Income Securities Market, which until recently was mainly dominated by the wholesale investors like Banks and Insurance companies, etc. was made accessible to the retail investors. This initiative was possible mainly due to some path-breaking initiative by the government of India- Ministry of Finance, RBI and SEBI. The retail trades in government securities under the Retail Debt Segment (REDS) are executed on electronic order matching BOLT System of the Exchange based on price-time priority. The BOLT system of the Exchange spans across the country. Thus, retail investors across the country can participate in this segment. The trades in this segment are settled on T+2 basis w.e.f. April 1, 2003 along with the trades in the equities segment. The government securities can be held and transferred through the same beneficiary Demat accounts of investors at both the Depositories as is used for equities. The Retail trades in Government Securities through the BOLT system are guaranteed by the Exchange and a separate Trade Guarantee Fund has been set up for this purpose with an initial contribution of Rs. 5 crores from the Exchange. Bombay Exchange has conducted seminars and investor meetings on the Retail Debt Market in Ahmedabad, Vadodara and Cochin. The Exchange has also conducted training programme on the Retail Debt Market at Chennai, Hyderabad and Bangalore. Thus, the SEBI has been engaged in regulating the functioning of participants in primary market as well as secondary market operations. However, effective measures are required to safeguard the interest at large.

Practice Questions

Objective Type Questions

1. Money market is concerned with:
   (*a*) short term funds
   (*b*) Medium term funds
   (*c*) Ling term funds
   (*d*) All of the above
2. Maturity period of Treasury bill is of:
   (*a*) 91 days
   (*b*) 182 days
   (*c*) 364 days
   (*d*) All of the above
3. New Issue market is with issue of except:
   (*a*) IPO
   (*b*) FPO
   (*c*) Right Issue
   (*d*) Bonus shares
4. ASBA is concerned with:
   (*a*) Money market
   (*b*) Primary market
   (*c*) Secondary Market
   (*d*) None of the above
5. Private Placement is concerned with:
   (*a*) selling entire issue to a single purchaser
   (*b*) selling entire issue to a group of purchaser
   (*c*) amount is raised without issuing prospectus
   (*d*) All of the above

Ans: 1. (a), 2. (d) 3. (d), 4. (b), 5. (d)

Short Answer Questions

1. Discuss the role and importance of stock market index in the Indian capital market.
2. State the regulatory measures to promote investors confidence in Indian Capital market.
3. What is placement memorandum?
4. What is insider trading?
5. What do you mean by demutualization of stock exchanges?

Long Answer Questions

1. 'Stock exchange is instrumental to economic growth of a country." Comment. Highlight the roe of stock exchanges in India.
2. What is stock exchanges? Describe the services rendered by an Indian Stock Exchange.
3. Describe the salient features of Indian Capital Market. Give suggestions to make it more effective.
4. "Stock Exchange is the barometer of any country's prosperity." Discuss.
5. What is primary market? How does it different from secondary market? Also explain the reasons for capital boom in recent months.

References

1. Nurkse, R., "Problems of Capital Formation in Underdeveloped Countries", P.63.
2. Hanson, A.H., "Public Enterprise and Economic Development", Rutledge & Kegan Paul Ltd., London, 1954, P.5.
3. Poindexter, J.C. and Jones, C.P., Money, "Financial Markets and the Economy", West Publishing Company, St. Paul, Minn., 1980, P. 317.
4. Gordon, E. & Natarajan, K., Financial Markets and Services, Himalaya Publishing House, Mumbai, 1999, P. 8.
5. Giddy, Ian H., Global Financial Markets, AITBS Publishers & Distributors, New Delhi, 1997, P.5.
6. Subramonion, P., Capital Market and Financial Services- Theory and Operations, Kalyani Publishers, New Delhi, 2001, P. 6.
7. Op.cit., Gordon, E. and Natarajan, K., Financial Markets and Services, P.8.
8. Vaish, M.C., Money, Banking and International Trade, New Age International (P) Limited, New Delhi, 1996, P. 306-307.
9. Ibid.p.304
10. Machiraju, H.R., Indian Financial System, Vikas Publishing House Pvt. Ltd., New Delhi, 2002. P.45.
11. Reserve Bank of India, Reserve Bank of India: Function and Working, RBI, Mumbai, 2002-03.
12. Subramonion, P., Capital Market and Financial Services- Theory and Operations, Kalyani Publishers, New Delhi, 2001, P. 12.
13. Op.cit- Gordon, E. and Natarajan, K., Financial Markets and Services, P. 15
14. Rosen, George, Some Aspects of Industrial Finance in India, Asia Publishing House, Bombay, 1962, P.1.
15. Kuchhal, S.C., Corporation Finance Principles and Problems, Chaitanya Publishing House, Allahabad, 1996, P. 270
16. Dhar, P.K., Indian Economy Its Growing Dimensions, Kalyani Publishers, New Delhi, 2003, P. 767.
17. Gangadhar, V. and Ramesh Babu, G., Investment Management, Anmol Publications Pvt. Ltd., New Delhi, 2003, P. 99.
18. S.C. Kuchhal, Corporation Finance Principles and Problems, Chaitanya Publishing House, Allahabad, 1996, P. 270-271
19. Briston, R.J and Liversidge, J., Practical Approach to Business Management Decision, MacMillan, London, 1979,p.75

20. Haugen, Robert A., Modern Investment Theory, Pearson Education (Singapore) Pte. Ltd., New Delhi, 2001, P. 20.
21. Op.cit., Gordon, E. and Natarajan, K., Financial Markets and Services, P.10.
22. Mishra, S.K. and Puri, V.K., Economic Environment of Business, Himalaya Publishing House, Mumbai, 2003, P. 672.
23. Op.cit-Machiraju, H.R., Merchant Banking Principles and Practice P. 147.
24. Op.cit-Machiraju, H.R., Merchant Banking Principles and Practice, P. 156.
25. Horne, Van, Investments, Prentice Hall of India Limited, 1992, P. 534.
26. Fabozzi, P., Frank, S., Modigliani, Franco, Jones, Frank J. and Derri, Michael, G., Foundations of Financial Markets and Institutions, Pearson Education (Singapore) Pte. Ltd., Delhi, 2002. P. 274.
27. Chandra, Prasanna, Financial Management Theory and Practice, Tata McGraw- Hill Publishing Company Limited, New Delhi, 1995, P. 548.
28. Op.cit-Machiraju, H.R., Merchant Banking Principles and Practice, P. 203.
29. Ball, Ray, Share Market and the Portfolio Theory, Queensland University of Queensland Press, Queensland, 1980, P. 132.
30. Reilly, F.K., Investments, C.B.S College Publishing, New York, 1982, P.60.
31. Srivastava, R.M. Essentials of Business Finance, Himalaya Publishing House, Bombay, 1995, P. 327.
32. Haugen, Robber, A.: Modern Investment Theory, Pearson Education (Singapore) Pte. Ltd., New Delhi, 2001, P.21.

12 DEVELOPMENT FINANCIAL INSTITUTION IN INDIA

The economic development of any country depends on the availability of adequate financial resources. Financial system has been assigned to mobilize and allocate resources efficiently and effectively. A typical structure of financial system in any economy consists of financial institutions, financial markets, financial instruments and financial services. An efficient and robust financial system acts as a powerful engine of economic development by mobilising resources and allocating the same to their productive uses. It reduces the transaction cost of the economy through provision of an efficient payment mechanism, helps in pooling of risks and making available long-term capital through maturity transformation. An efficient financial system also helps in the process of alleviating poverty. Financial system acts as a catalytic agent for providing financial support for entrepreneurial activity. It also ensures economic reforms and growth.

The emerging economies in post colonial era experienced the difficult choice of appropriate mechanism for channelising resources into the development efforts. Large number of these economies had inherited capital starved primitive financial systems. These systems were not efficient to allocate resources among competing demands in the economy. "The task of institution building was too important and not to be left at the mercy of the market forces at the nascent stage of development. In such a situation several governments in Continental Europe and East Asian economies decided to take matters into their hands and established institutions specifically to cater to the requirements of financial resources for developmental efforts. Such institutions were called Development Financial Institutions."[1] Development financing in developing economies is a risky as well as uncertain business. It involves financing of industrial and infrastructure projects which usually have long gestation period and lower expected rate of return. The long term nature of these loans has associated with its uncertainty as to performance of the loan assets is generally not up to the mark. The repayment of the long term project loans is dependent on the viability and performance of the project and cash flows arising from it rather than the realisability of the collaterals. Technological obsolescence, market competition, change of government policies, natural calamities, poor management skills, poor infrastructure etc may be important reasons for project failure. Thus, the markets and banking institutions were highly averse to such uncertainty involved in project funding. These institutions were also unable to possess enough information and skills to predict with certainty about the performance of the projects. "There were also the cost considerations associated with such risky ventures. The long term loan comes with a higher price tag due to the term premium loaded into the pricing. In such a situation the long term financing would be scarce as well as costly so as to render the project financially unviable."[2]

Development Financial Institutions (DFIs) were established with the Government support for underwriting their losses as also the commitment for making available low cost resources for lending at a lower rate of interest than that demanded by the market for risky projects. In the initial years of development it worked well. Process of infrastructure building and industrialization got accelerated. The financial system was improved considerably as per the needs of projects. Appraisal system of long term projects had also been strengthened due to improvement in availability of information and skills. Thus, the DFIs improved their appetite for risk associated with such projects. "The intermediaries like banks and bond markets became sophisticated in risk management techniques and wanted a piece of the pie in the long term project financing. These intermediaries also had certain distinct advantages over the traditional DFIs such as low cost of funds and benefit of diversification of loan portfolios"[3]. The government support to DFI was also declining due to fiscal reasons or building the market more competitive and efficient. Thus, the heydays of DFIs were towards the end of twentieth century over and they started working in isolation. Similarly, DFIs were either restructured and repositioned or they just faded away from scene in several economies, having attained their developmental goals. The Indian experience also indicates the same story. Fiscal imperatives and market dynamics has forced the government to undertake reappraisal of its policies and strategy with regard to the role of DFIs in Indian system.

However, it is important to note that our country has not achieved its development goals even then due to unavoidable circumstances like economic reforms we are trying to restructure the DFIs in different shape.

Role of Development Finance

Role of development finance may be evaluated in following ways:

(*i*) It is supposed to identify the gaps in efficacy of institutions and markets and act as a 'gap-filler'.

(*ii*) It makes up for the failure of financial markets and institutions to provide certain kinds of finance to economic agents who are really interested to improve the working of economy.

(*iii*) It targets at economic activities or agents, which are rationed out of market. It motivates the agent to take risky business with venture finance.

(*iv*) It helps the funds seekers by providing concessional funds at lower rate of return. Social return of DFIs is quite high. Keeping these facts in mind, central banking system also supports development financial institutions.

(*v*) It is specialized in nature and involved long term finance. It is exclusively meant for infrastructure and industry, finance for agriculture and small and medium enterprises (SME) development and financial products for certain sections of the people who needs funds for development perspectives.

Nature of Development Financial Institutions (DFIs)

Diamond William, (1957) defines development institutions as "an institution to promote and finance enterprises in the private sector".[4] According to Boskey Shirley, "the development banks are, "institutions, public/private, which have one of their principal functions, as the making of medium and long term investment in the industrial projects".[5] According to Nyhart and Janssens development banks are "those institutions, which provide general medium-term and long-term financial assistance to a developing economy".[6]

The World Development Report (1989) defines, "financial intermediaries are those, which emphasis the provision of capital (loans and equity) for development. It may specialize in particular sector, for example, industry, agriculture or housing".

Hook (1976), also suggests, that the development banks have two functions to perform i.e. banking and development."[7] As a banker, the development banks are expected to finance those projects, which are "Bankable". A project is bankable if it is in the nature of self financing. Elaborating self financing projects, Kane J.A., says that "a project is self-financing, if it is able to generate enough income within a specified period of time to (i) cover the cost of operations, (once the plants begin the operations), (ii) repay the principle and interest charges thereon and (iii) lease a residual profits enough to remain in the operations."[8]

It is specialized mode of extending development finance and it is generally called as development financial institution (DFI) or development bank. A DFI is defined as "an institution promoted or assisted by government to provide development finance to sectors of the economy. The institution distinguishes itself by a judicious balance as between commercial norms of operation, as adopted by any private financial institution, and developmental obligations; it emphasizes the "project approach" - meaning the viability of the project to be financed – against the "collateral approach"; apart from provision of long-term loans, equity capital, guarantees and underwriting functions, a development bank normally is also expected to upgrade the managerial and the other operational pre-requisites of the assisted projects. Its insurance against default is the integrity, competence and resourcefulness of the management, the commercial and technical viability of the project and above all the speed of implementation and efficiency of operations of the assisted projects. Its relationship with its clients is of a continuing nature and of being a "partner" in the project than that of a mere "financier".

These definitions outlined the pervasive nature of the development banks. There are different types of promoters for DFIs. Some DFIs are found to be the government sponsored, others are privately owned, and still others are in both hands. These DFIs are engaged in providing different types of services. Promotional and entrepreneurial services are the main theme of these DFIs. These services carry a commitment towards faster growth and fulfillment of the aspirations of the economy.

On the basis of above analysis, it may be stated that the DFIs are necessary for long-term finance and other assistance for activities or sectors of the economy where the risks may be higher than that the ordinary financial system is unable to bear the risks involved. They have also been playing effective role in stimulating equity and debt markets by (i) selling their own stocks and bonds; (ii) helping the assisted enterprises float or place their securities and (iii) selling from their own portfolio of investments.

Thus "a development bank is intended to provide a necessary capital, enterprise, managerial and technical know-how where these are inadequate on non-available and also assist in building up the financial and socio-economic infrastructure, favorable to quick economic development. The emphasis on its various activities has shifted from one country to another according to its peculiar needs and circumstances. In some countries, the stress has been on finance; in some others, one promotion; yet in others on technical skill and advice; and again elsewhere on economic planning itself."[9]

Historical Perspective of DFIs

DFIs are created in developing countries to resolve market failures, especially with regard to financing of long-term investments. The DFIs played a very significant role in rapid industrialisation of the Continental Europe. Many of the DFIs were sponsored by national governments and international agencies. The first government sponsored DFI was created in Netherlands in 1822. In France, significant developments in long-term financing took place after establishment of DFIs such as Credit Foncier and Credit Mobiliser, over the period 1848-1852. In Asia, establishment of Japan Development Bank and other term-lending institution fostered rapid industrialisation of Japan.

Another "society de generate de Belgigue" was setup in 1882 in Belgium with a specific object of project financing operational and promotional activities. The success of these institutions, provided strong impetus for creation of DFIs in India after independence, in the context of the felt need for raising the investment rate. RBI was entrusted with the task of developing an appropriate financial architecture through institution building so as to mobilise and direct resources to preferred sectors as per the plan priorities. While the reach of the banking system was expanded to mobilise resources and extend working capital finance on an ever-increasing scale, to different sectors of the economy, the DFIs were established mainly to cater to the demand for long-term finance by the industrial sector. The first DFI established in India in 1948 was Industrial Finance Corporation of India (IFCI) followed by setting up of State Financial Corporations (SFCs) at the State level after passing of the SFCs Act, 1951. A detailed historical perspectives of DFIs in India is given below:

1. Financial Institutions set up between 1948 and 1974 : Besides IFCI and SFCs, in the early phase of planned economic development in India, a number of other financial institutions were set up, which included the following. The ICICI Ltd. was set up in 1955, LIC in 1956, Refinance Corporation for Industries Ltd. in 1958 (later taken over by IDBI), Agriculture Refinance Corporation (precursor of ARDC and NABARD) in 1963, UTI and IDBI in 1964, Rural Electrification Corporation Ltd. and HUDCO Ltd. In 1969-70, Industrial Reconstruction Corporation of India Ltd. (precursor of IIBI Ltd.) in 1971 and GIC in 1972. It may be noted here that although the powers to regulate financial institutions had been made available to RBI in 1964 under the newly inserted Chapter IIIB of RBI Act, the definition of term 'financial institution' was made precise and comprehensive by amendment to the RBI Act Section 45-I (c) in 19745.

2. DFIs set up after 1974 and Notification of certain institutions as Public Financial Institutions : Another important change that took place in 1974 was the insertion of Section 4A to the Companies Act, 1956 where under certain existing institutions were categorised as 'Public Financial Institutions' (PFI) and the powers of Central Government to notify any other institution as PFI were laid down. In exercise of these powers GOI has been notifying from time to time certain institutions as PFIs. As on date, under the Section 4A, six specified institutions are regarded as PFI and it has been provided that the Securitisation Company or Reconstruction Company which has obtained a certificate of registration under sub-section (4) of Section 3 the Securitisation and Reconstruction of Financial Assets and Enforcement of Security Interest Act, 2002 shall also be regarded as a PFI. Besides these institutions, GOI has been notifying, from time to time, certain other FIs as PFIs and as on date additional 46 institutions have been so notified. Thus, in all 52 institutions have been categorised as PFIs.

The FIs set up after 1974 have been as follows. NABARD was set up in 1981, EXIM Bank (functions carved out of IDBI) in 1982, SCICI Ltd. in 1986 (set up by ICICI Ltd. in 1986 and later merged into ICICI Ltd. in 1997), PFC Ltd. and IRFC Ltd. In 1986, IREDA Ltd. in 1987, RCTC Ltd. and TDICI Ltd. (later known as IFCI Venture Capital Funds Ltd. and ICICI Venture Funds Management Ltd.) in 1988, NHB in 1988, TFCI Ltd. (set up by IFCI) in 1989, SIDBI (functions carved out of IDBI) in 1989, NEDFi Ltd. in 1995 and IDFC Ltd. in 1997.

A wide variety of DFIs have come into existence and they perform the developmental role in their respective sectors. Apart from the fact that they cater to the financial needs of different sectors, there are some significant differences among them. While most of them extend direct finance, some extend indirect finance and are mainly refinancing institutions viz., SIDBI, NABARD and NHB which also have a regulatory / supervisory role. DFIs can be broadly categorised as all-India or state / regional level institutions depending on their geographical coverage of operation. Functionally, all-India institutions can be classified as:

(*i*) term-lending institutions (IFCI Ltd., IDBI, IDFC Ltd., IIBI Ltd.) extending long-term finance to different industrial sectors,

(*ii*) refinancing institutions (NABARD, SIDBI, NHB) extending refinance to banking as well as non-banking intermediaries for finance to agriculture, SSIs and housing sectors,

(*iii*) sector-specific / specialised institutions (EXIM Bank, TFCI Ltd., REC Ltd., HUDCO Ltd., IREDA Ltd., PFC Ltd., IRFC Ltd.), and

(*iv*) investment institutions (LIC, UTI, GIC, IFCI Venture Capital Funds Ltd., ICICI Venture Funds Management Co Ltd.). State / regional level institutions are a distinct group and comprise various SFCs, SIDCs and NEDFi Ltd.

Development Banks have encouraged entrepreneurship in various sectors of the national economy wherever they are functioning. Actually, they have generated a development revolution. "By adopting the practices of promotional, innovating and entrepreneurial banking in world's economy, these institutions provided a model to some of the developing countries including India, which were in search of suitable machinery for providing the much needed financial support to the industries according to the national plan priorities for economic development."[10]

In the development of DFIs, the Government had chosen Japan as model. The model, the industrial Bank of Japan, formed in 1902, was deliberately set up in the lines of credit mobiliser of finance. During the first fifteen years of independence (1948-63), a number of financial institutions namely IFCI, ICICI, NSIC, SFCs etc. were set up in India. "However, the growth of these financial institutions were not backed by any effective mechanism to coordinate and integrate their activities. It was also felt that the totality of their contribution would not be adequate in terms of magnitude as well as range and pattern of financing in relation to requirements of rapid and diversified industrial development."[11]

Thus, "to co-ordinate the workings of various institutions and to develop a cohesive financial structure adapted to the changing needs of the emerging industrial structure, the presence of a central development financial institutions was felt essential. The Central development Bank could provide dynamic leadership in the task of promoting a widely diffused and diversified and yet viable process of industrialization. This bank would be connected directly or indirectly with all problems or questions relating to long and medium term financing of industries and would adopt and enforce a system of priorities in promoting the industrial growth. In response to the above needs, a battery of such institutions came into existence after independence. A bill for the establishment of the industrial financial corporation for providing medium and long-term finance to industries in India was introduced in 1946 of the legislative assembly, the IFCI Act, was passed by the dominion parliament on 13th February 1948 and IFCI was born in July, 1948. At present, the entire gamut of such institutions comprises 12 institutions at the national level and 46 at the state level."[12]

Rationale of DFIs in India

The DFIs were set up in India on the following rationale:

(*i*) **Improving rates of Savings and Investment:** Rate of capital formation is low. At the time of independence saving rate was around at 5 per cent of national income. India had a fairly diversified industrial base for an developing country, with a number of well established industrial houses at the time of independence. So level of saving mobilization was to be by the expedited by the DFIs. So necessary guarantee was expected from the DFIs otherwise entrepreneurs and promoters would have not been able to generate resources from the market.

(ii) **Infancy Stage of Capital Market:** The capital market was at infancy stage and industries had to depend on their own profits and banks for financing for further development programmes. That is why these bonds funds institutions, investment institutions, other trusts, etc. has been declared as DFIs in terms of public financial institutions, (PFI) under Section IVA of companies Act, 1956.

(iii) **Risk Averse Commercial Bank:** Commercial banks were not interested in venture financing as they are quite risky one. DFIs are specialised financial institutions and well equipped in risky venture.

(iv) **Arrangement of Loan in Foreign Currency:** DFIs till the shift in the policy regime, had access to lines of credit in foreign currencies from various multilateral and bilateral agencies at low rates of interest mainly for project financing. Earlier, foreign currency risks due to fluctuation in the exchange rates was borne by the central government, and so they did not have an incentive to develop a system of risk management otherwise it would added to their costs of operation.

(v) **Specialized Credit Support System:** DFIs could sanction and disburse credit at fixed / assured rates spread over their borrowing rates till the early 1990. Moreover, under the existing industrial licensing policy system obtaining a license itself was taken as license to get credit from DFIs, without the investor going through the elaborate procedures normally associated with projected appraisal for credit sanction based on commercial judgement and viability.

(vi) **Arrangement of Priority Sector Financing:** DFIs did not have competition in deploying their funds to public companies. However, some commercial banks had started providing term capital from about the latter part of the 1970s. As priorities for investments in various sectors in the economy were given, along with targets set in successive plans.

(vii) **Project Evaluation and Funding:** Some DFIs had also conducted economic potential surveys of regions or states and provided considerable support to a number of development projects. When projects costs were high and could not be financed by one DFI, they formed loan consortia with commercial banks whereby DFIs could provide large sized loans thereby reducing the incidence of risks.

(viii) **Coordinating Financing Agencies:** The DFIs were expected to work as conduits between the government/ other financing agencies and the ultimate borrowers for an assured margin. They also acquired skills and expertise to study the viability and technical efficiency of projects which was called as the directly productive activities'.

Objectives behind setting up of the DFIs

A. All India FIs

- **(*i*) Term lending institutions (IFCI, ICICI Ltd., IDBI, IDFC Ltd., IRCI Ltd.) :** The first FI to be established in India was IFCI. It was established by statute in 1948 for the purpose of making medium and long-term credit more readily available to medium and large industrial concerns in corporate and co-operative sectors in India. The setting up of the next all India term lending FI was sponsored by the World Bank when Industrial Credit and Investment Corporation of India Ltd. was established in 1955 as a company established under the Indian Companies Act, 1913 and with the primary objective of promoting industries in the private sector and meeting their foreign exchange requirements. On July 1, 1964, IDBI was established under Industrial Development Bank of India Act, 1964, as the principal financial institution for industrial development in the country for co-ordinating, in conformity with the national priorities, the working of institutions engaged in financing, promotion and development of industry and assisting the development of such institutions for providing credit and other facilities for the development of industry. IDBI had taken over the functions of the erstwhile Refinance Corporation for Industries Ltd., set up in 1958. Besides providing direct finance by way of term loans, IDBI also refinances term loans given by eligible institutions specified in the IDBI Act to medium and large-scale units and rediscounts/discounts bills of exchange and promissory notes arising out of the sale/purchase of machinery and equipment. It operates special products for technology upgradation, energy conservation and pollution control and provided venture capital not only for development and use of indigenous technology and adaptation of imported technology but also to leverage new opportunities thrown open by developments in emerging sectors like information technology, biotechnology, etc. It provides a wide range of merchant banking and advisory services, which includes issue management, project advisory, credit syndication, valuation and corporate restructuring. It also extends loans to various financial intermediaries and invests in their shares and bonds. EXIM Bank and SIDBI, which were established as statutory bodies in 1982 and 1990, respectively took over certain functions from IDBI. While EXIM Bank took over the export finance function of the IDBI and began functioning on March 1, 1982, SIDBI commenced its operations in April 1990 by taking over the outstanding portfolio and activities of IDBI pertaining to the small-scale sector. Much later, IDFC Ltd. was incorporated in January 1997 as a non-government company to foster the growth of private capital flows for infrastructure finance, on a commercially viable basis with a mandate to lead capital to infrastructure sector. In 1997, IIBI Ltd. was incorporated as a government company and it took over business and functions of the erstwhile Industrial Reconstruction Bank of India established under IRBI Act, 1984 (which itself was originally set up as Industrial Reconstruction Corporation of India in 1971) to function as the principal credit and reconstruction agency for industrial revival and to co-ordinate the work of other institutions engaged in a similar activity, assisting and promoting industrial development and rehabilitating sick and closed industrial concerns. Besides project finance, IIBI also provides short duration non-project asset-backed financing in the form of underwriting/direct subscription, deferred payment guarantees and working capital/other short-term loans to companies to meet their fund requirement.

***(ii)* Refinancing institutions (NABARD, NHB, SIDBI) :** NABARD was established in December 1981, under the National Bank for Agriculture and Rural Development Act 1981, as an Apex institution at the national level, for providing credit for the promotion of agriculture, small scale industries, cottage and village industries, handicrafts, other rural crafts and other allied economic activities in rural areas, with a view to promoting integrated rural development and securing the prosperity of rural areas. Prior to setting up of NABARD some of its functions were being discharged by RBI through its Agriculture Credit Department set up in 1935 and Agricultural Refinance Corporation set up by an Act of Parliament in 1963 which was renamed as and Agricultural Refinance and Development Corporation (ARDC) by an amendment to Act in 1975. NHB was set up as per the provisions of National Housing Bank Act, 1987 and it started functioning from July 9, 1988. NHB is wholly owned subsidiary of RBI and, apart from being a refinancing institution, is also the regulator and supervisor of housing finance companies. Its primary responsibility is to promote and develop specialized housing finance institutions for mobilizing resources and extending credit for housing. It has powers to grant loans and advances and provides other financial support to housing finance institutions and scheduled banks and has various other important functions. SIDBI was set up in 1990 under an Act of Parliament (SIDBI Act, 1989) as a wholly owned subsidiary of IDBI. It is the principal financial institution for promoting and financing development of industry in the small scale sector as also for co-ordinating the functions of institutions engaged in similar activities. As stated earlier, SIDBI commenced its operations in April 1990 by taking over the outstanding portfolio and activities of IDBI pertaining to the small-scale sector.

***(iii)* Investment institutions (LIC, UTI, GIC, IFCI Venture Capital Funds Ltd., ICICI Venture Funds Management Co. Ltd.) :** The nationalisation of insurance business in the country resulted in the establishment of Life Insurance Corporation of India (LIC) in 1956 as a wholly owned corporation of the Government of India. The broad objectives of LIC are to spread life insurance across the country, particularly in the rural areas and to the socially and economically backward classes.

Unit Trust of India (UTI), the largest mutual fund organisation in India, was set up in 1964 by an Act of Parliament to fulfill the objectives of mobilising retail savings, investing them in the capital market and passing on the benefits accrued from the acquisition, holding, management and disposal of securities to the small investors. The General Insurance Corporation of India was formed on January 1, 1973 as a holding company, with four subsidiary companies (now de-linked) and has been operating a number of need-based insurance schemes to meet the diverse and emerging needs of various segments of society and provides financial assistance to industrial projects. GIC is now in the process of implementing comprehensive strategies to meet the opportunities and challenges emanating from private sector participation in the insurance and reinsurance business. IFCI Venture Capital Funds Ltd. (IVCF) and ICICI Venture Funds Management Co. Ltd. were set up in 1988 as venture capital finance companies. While IVCF was previously known as Risk Capital and Technology Finance Corporation Ltd. (RCTC), ICICI Venture Funds Management Company Ltd. was known as TDICI Ltd.

***(iv)* Sector Specific/specialised institutions (EXIM Bank, SCICI Ltd., TFCI Ltd., REC Ltd., HUDCO Ltd., IREDA Ltd, PFC Ltd., IRFC Ltd.):** EXIM Bank, wholly owned by the GOI was established under the EXIM Bank Act, 1981 with a view to promoting India's international trade and for all matters connected therewith. SCICI Ltd. was set up by ICICI Ltd. in 1986 was later merged back into ICICI Ltd. in 1997. TFCI Ltd. was set up in February 1989 as a specialised all-India Development Financial Institution catering to the needs of the tourism industry by IFCI, some nationalised banks, and other FIs. RECL was established in 1969-70 as a Government company to facilitate availability of electricity for rural and semi-urban population and to act as an organization for financing and promoting projects covering generation, conservation, transmission and distribution of power in the country. HUDCO Ltd. was set up in 1969-70 as a company, initially for financing of public sector housing agencies such as Housing Boards and

Development Authorities. Later, in mid-seventies, it diversified into financing of co-operative housing and subsequently also undertook financing of corporates – both in public and private sector.

It has further diversified into financing real estate builders and is progressively moving towards provision of individual housing loans as also extending techno-financial assistance to individuals. HUDCO Ltd., being a HFC is being regulated IREDA Ltd. was incorporated as a company with effect from 11 March 1987 primarily as one of the instruments for promoting, developing and financing New and Renewable Sources of Energy (NRSE) technologies and thereby accelerating the momentum of development and help in large-scale utilisation of renewable energy sources. PFC Ltd. was established in July 1986 as a company to act as DFI dedicated to the Power Sector. It, along with REC Ltd., provides financial assistance / services for the power projects, raises resources from international and domestic sources, lends to power projects in India, to acts as catalyst to bring improvement in the functioning of state power utilities and assists state power sectors in carrying out reforms.

IRFC Ltd. was incorporated in 1986 as Central Government Company to acquire the "Rolling Stock" (i.e. the locomotives, freight wagons and passenger coaches) for leasing out to Indian Railways for which it mobilises funds from various sources. The lease rentals from the Indian Railways form its principal source of income.

B. State level / Regional Institutions (SFCs, SIDCs, NEDFi Ltd.)

State Financial Corporations Act, 1951 was enacted by the Parliament to provide institutional framework for financing medium and small-scale industries, which fell outside the operational scope of IFCI. After enactment of the Act, SFCs were set up in the various States over a period of time. The Act provides special role for the State Governments in the promotion and management of the affairs of the SFCs. At present, there are 18 SFCs of which 17 were set up under the SFC Act, 1951 while the Tamil Nadu Industrial Investment Corporation Ltd. was incorporated under the Companies Act, 1956 but still functions as SFC. Their main objectives are to finance and promote small and medium enterprise in the States concerned for achieving balanced regional growth, catalyse investment, generate employment and widen the ownership base of industries by way of providing term loans, direct subscription to equity / debentures, extending guarantees, discounting of bills and providing special / seed capital, etc.

State Industrial Development Corporations (SIDCs) are State level institutions established under the Companies Act 1956 as wholly owned undertakings of State governments for promotion and development of medium and large industries in the respective States. Most of the SIDCs have not yet been notified by the government as PFIs under the Companies Act, 1956 but being companies and engaged in making loans and advances, fall within the definition of non-banking financial companies under the RBI Act, 1934, and were subject to the RBI (DNBS) Directions till recently. These Corporations provide financial assistance in the form of rupee loans, underwriting /direct subscriptions to shares/debentures and guarantees and also undertake a range of promotional activities. SIDCs are also involved in setting up of medium and large industrial projects in the joint sector /assisted sector in collaboration with private entrepreneurs or as wholly owned subsidiaries. In keeping with the changing environment, many SIDCs are trying to diversify their activities and enter into areas of equipment leasing, merchant banking, venture capital and mutual funds. As on 31 December 1999, there were 28 SIDCs of which 11 SIDCs – in eight States and three Union Territories – also function as SFCs to provide assistance to small and medium enterprises and act as promotional agencies. NEDFi Ltd. was incorporated on August 9, 1995 under the Companies Act, 1956 for development in the North Eastern states of India. It was promoted by IDBI, ICICI Ltd., IFCI Ltd., SIDBI, LIC, GIC and its subsidiaries, UTI and SBI, which own the FI's entire paid up capital of Rs.100 crore. NEDFi Ltd. was conceptualised in the Borathakur Committee Report in 1994 to cater to the needs of the North-Eastern Region which was endowed with rich natural resources and nearly one-third of the country's hydro power potential (84,000 MW) but was yet to experience industrial development on a scale achieved by other regions of the country. NEDFi Ltd. aims to be a dynamic and responsive organization to catalyse the economic growth of the Northeast. It will assist in the efficient formation of fixed assets by identifying, financing and nurturing eco friendly and commercially viable industrial, infrastructure, agro-horticulture, fishery and animal-husbandry projects in the region.

Changing Environment of DFIs in India

Historically, low-cost funds were made available to DFIs to ensure that the spread on their lending operations did not come under pressure. DFIs had access to soft window of Long Term Operation (LTO) funds from RBI at concessional rates. They also had access to cheap funds from multilateral and bilateral agencies duly guaranteed by the Government. They were also allowed to issue bonds, which qualified for SLR investment by banks. For deployment of funds, they faced little competition as the banking system mainly concentrated on working capital finance. With initiation of financial sector reforms, the operating environment for DFIs changed substantially. The supply of low-cost funds was withdrawn forcing DFIs to raise resources at market-related rates. On the other hand, they had to face competition in the areas of term finance from banks offering lower rates. The change in operating environment coupled with high accumulation of nonperforming assets due to a combination of factors caused serious financial stress to the term-lending institutions.

Challenges before DFIs

In the changed environment, DFIs are facing the following challenges:

(*i*) **Problems in Mobilisation of Resources:** The DFIs have to mobilize funds from the market but they suffered from structural inflexibility as they did not have good network of branches all over the country, unlike the commercial banks. There are restrictions on the amount of funds that could float in the market. With the removal of the framework of regulations on the interest rate regime, the need arose for aligning the interest rates (borrowing as well as lending) of DFIs with those of the market.

(*ii*) **Problem of Competitive Interest Rate:** The DFIs have to also cut down their lending rates to levels set by commercial banks and also provide access to their funds as liberally as the banks without, a matching reduction in their own borrowing costs. DFIs are not habitual of flexible interest rates and they are loosing their business from the corporate sector.

(*iii*) **Removal of Concessional Rate Regime:** DFIs' access to borrowings from the central government at a highly concessional rate of interest was withdrawn in a phased manner, since the fiscal deficit which led to the external current account deficit. Since 1991 banking sector reforms have changed the business environment of DFIs. RBI's measure of bringing down the SLR ratio to the statutory minimum in respect of all scheduled commercial banks. It has also affected the DFIs' ability to mobilise adequate funds, as banks are the major subscribers of bonds issued by the DFIs.

(*iv*) **Flexible Mode of Fund Generation:** DFIs access to short term sources of funds is quite limited. Studies suggests that Term deposits, certificates of deposits, term money borrowing inter-corporate deposits and commercials papers all put together are equivalent to their Net Owned Fund. Thus, it is inflexible as well as expensive for DFIs.

(*v*) **Competitive Environment:** As part of banking reforms, bank were given considerable freedom to extend term loans, project finance etc. Earlier, it was exclusive domain of DFIs. Thus, DFIs are facing stiff competition from bank in disbursement of term capital.

(*vi*) **Adverse Liquidity Position:** The merger in the 1990s of many domestic firms for improving competitiveness and introducing new technologies had also an impact on DFIs adversely, since some of the older firms that could not compete effectively could not stay in the market. Therefore, they could not repay their dues on schedule, placing enormous pressure on the DFIs liquidity position.

(*vii*) **Stringent Prudential Norm:** The severe strain on the financial position of the DFIs increased when the institutions were brought under the purview of regulation and supervision of the RBI. The regulation and supervision required the DFIs to comply with internationally recognized stringent prudential norms relating to asset classification, capital adequacy, provisioning and income recognition and standards relating to risk management of their portfolios and market exposures.

(*viii*) **Discriminatory Government Support System:** Due to change in Government policy there was adverse impact on the performance of DFIs. The NABARD, SIDBI and NHB continued to receive governmental support even after the shift in the policy regime. Remaining DFIs are not under the list of discriminatory government support.

Regardless of this deviation, DFIs in general undertook a number of measures to reposition and reorient their operations as warranted by the competitive environment. Accordingly, a number of innovative non-traditional products and services were offered, viz, investment banking, stock broking, custodial services, technical advice, etc. with a view to reduce the risks by exploiting the economies of scale. They also established management teams to handle finances, market products, and reduce delays in decision-making, even though such initiatives entailed additional costs.

Growth of DFIs in India[13]

Indian economy was facing long and medium term credit to industry. The Indian economy from the very beginning of the First World War. To fill up the vacuum, vigorous attempts were made: firstly, in the wake of Swadeshi Movement (1906-13) and subsequently in the immediate post world war- I period. The India industrial commission (1916-18), headed by Sir T.H. Holland, gave a great deal of thought to the problem of financial provisions for industrial enterprises. The report of the commission was published in the year 1918. It recommended for the establishment of special financial institutions to meet out financial needs of industries. It emphasized the utility of forming industrial banks. The Japanese bank was the only bank of its kind at that time. The Indian industrial conference held in Bombay in 1915 had also advocated the establishment of industrial banks. In 1924 External Capital Committee proposed establishment of a specialist institution for meeting the problems of industrial finance in India. The committee observed, "India possesses a vast store of dormant capital awaiting development, in order to make this available for investment, banking facilities must be increased and extended". Subsequently the central banking enquiry committee studied the financial problems of industries in India. The central banking inquiry committee in 1931 expressed view in favour of provincial banks. Various provincial banking inquiry committees were also appointed in 1929. All these committees emphised the need for making banking more useful to industries and no less than five of them proposed for the creation of specialized banking institutions.

However, no serious efforts were made for the establishment of industrial banks as recommended by the various committees. Towards the end of the world war – II, the question of industrial finance once again came to draw the attention of the government. In 1940 the emphasis shifted from a purely industrial mortgage bank to that of industrial finance corporation. After independence, large number of financial institutions came into existence. At present, the entire gamut of such institutions comprises 12 institutions at the national level and 46 at the state level. Overall position of financial institutions in India is given in exhibit-12.1.

Exhibit-12.1

Financial Institutions in India
(with the years of establishment)

Development Banks				Investment Institutions		Specialized Financial Institutions	
National Level		State Level					
IFCI	1948	SFCs	1951-60	LIC	1956	RCTC	1988
ICICI	1955	SIDCs	1960-70	UTI	1964	TDICI	1988
IDBI	1964	TCOs	1970-80	GIC	1973	TFCI	1988
IRBI	1985						
SCICI	1986						
SIDBI	1990						

Thus, it was in free India, viable efforts were made to establish DFIs in the country to arrange financial support to corporate sectors. Analytical framework of phase wise growth and development of DFIs are as follows:

Phase I: Institutionalization Era (1948-55)

The development banking took its birth in India in the year 1948 with the setting up of Industrial Financial Corporation of India (IFCI) on July 01, 1948 to provide medium and long term credit to industrial unit in the public and cooperative sectors. It was set up as a statutory corporation, was provided by the central government, the Reserve Bank of India, commercial banks and other financial institutions.

The government has also enacted the State Financial Corporation (SFC) Act, 1951; as a result 18 SFCs are engaged in financing and promotion of small and medium enterprises in various states of India today. National Small Industries Corporation (NSIC) was also set up in 1955, with development of small scale sector as its main objective. It has been promoting the interests of the small industries in the country primarily by assisting them in procurement of machineries and various inputs as well as marketing of their output. Besides, it has also been assigned to train technical personnel and offer consultancy services to other developing countries.

The creation of the Industrial Credit and Investment Corporation of India (ICICI) in 1955 is the another landmark in the history of development banking in India. Its main thrust has been on financing of private sector through provision of foreign currency loans, equity participation and underwriting of public issues. The ICICI was setup as a public limited company without any direct equity participation from the government or the RBI. The IBRD had also played an active role in its formation; about 30% of its initial equity capital was subscribed by foreign investors constituting UK 20 percent and USA 10 percent.

Phase II: Expansion Era (1955-64)

The expansion of operations by the existing DFIs and fresh additions to the institutional infrastructure comprise the major development in the second phase. The demand for institutional support increased considerably and the DFIs had tried their best to meet out growing requirements by expanding the scope and coverage of their activities. For instance, IFCI extended its assistance to hotels, introduced underwriting facilities and provided guarantees for deferred payments and foreign currency loans. In the same way with the foreign exchange crisis in 1957-58, foreign currency loans provided by ICICI became the main source of payment for imported equipments.

The Life Insurance Corporation of India (LIC) was setup in 1956 due to nationalisation of the life insurance business. Although LIC is not a DFI, it was assigned, as a part of its business, the role of providing industrial finance through underwriting and direct purchase of industrial shares, bonds as well as debentures. In 1958 another institution, the Refinance Corporation for Industry Ltd. (RCI), was established by RBI, LIC and commercial banks. Its primary objective was to provide refinance to commercial banks (and later to SFCs) in respect of term loans to the industrial units in terms of private sector. However, it was merged with IDBI in 1964.

And the state level, State Small Industries Development Corporations (SSIDCs) were setup in1971 to cater to the primary developmental needs of the small, tiny and village industries. Besides SSIDCs, the State Industrial Development Corporation (SIDCs) was setup to act as catalyst for industrial development in their respective states. They undertakes financial, promotional and developmental activities, viz. provision of term loans and underwriting / direct subscription of share / debentures, conducting feasibility studies and entrepreneurship development programmes, developing industrial estates and setting of medium and large project in the joint / assisted sector or as wholly owned subsidiaries. Out of 28 SIDCs in the country, 11 function as SIDCs-cum-SFCs at present.

Phase-III: Consolidation and Innovation Era (1964-76)

By the early 1960s, the country had developed an elaborate network of financial institutions, which served with fair degree of success, for the growing needs of industrial development. However, institutional machinery was required to:

(*a*) garner the savings from the house-hold sector (b) effectively coordinate and integrate the functioning of the diverse institutions in the field and (c) finance the gigantic projects of national importance, envisaged in the third and fourth five year plans (1961-74) which the existing institutions were either unwilling or unable to finance.

To fulfill the above requirement, the Unit Trust of India (UTI) was set up in February 1964 to mobilize and channelise the community savings towards corporate shares and debentures. The IDBI was established in July 1964, as the apex DFI of the country. The IDBI was set up as a wholly owned subsidiary of RBI. However, in 1976 its ownership was transferred to the government of India. It was vested with responsibilities which RBI vis-à-vis industrial financial institutions did earlier in the country. In 1971, the Industrial Reconstruction Corporation of India (IRCI) was set up by the IDBI, LIC and banks for reconstruction and rehabilitation of sick and closed industrial units. The General Insurance Corporation of India (GIC) and its four subsidiaries had also joined in consortium financing arrangements with other all India financial institutions after their nationalization in 1973.

The DFIs have also taken major innovative measures to strengthen the base of industrial development in the country. These measures were comprised of:

(*a*) Introduction of consortium financing approach with common loan application form and common project appraisal,

(*b*) Rediscounting of machinery bills to boost up the nascent domestic capital goods industry

(*c*) Industrial potential services in backward areas

(*d*) Concesional finance for notified backward areas

(*e*) Creation of Technical Consultancy Organizations (TSOs) and the Management Development Institute (MDI)

(*f*) Introduction of loan convertibility clause and appointment of nominee directors in assisted units

(*g*) financing of public / joint sector units; and

(*h*) introduction of, merchant banking services by ICICI

Phase IV: Stability of Growth Era (1976-84)

The fourth phase of development banking can be termed as the phase of stability and substantial growth. Autonomy was also provided to IDBI to ensure its growth in volume of business. These Development Financial Institutions have formulated their strategy for improving quality of their operations, viz., simplification of procedures to expedite sanctions and disbursements, liberalization of landing policies for modernization and technological upgradation, increased flow of assistance to projects located in backward areas and provision of bridge loans against public issues. They have made serious efforts for promotion of entrepreneurship. The network of TCOs was further extended and a national institute – The Entrepreneurship Development Institute of India (EDII) – was set up at Ahmedabad in 1983, with a view to introducing various subsidy scheme and venture funds / seed capital schemes. Sanctions and disbursement of the major DFIs (like IFCI, ICICI, IDBI, IRCI, SFCs, and SIDCs) have also increased substantially during this period.

Phase V: Era of Diversification & Change (1984-1992)

This phase was marked by the creation of new institutions, change in operational policies, growth and diversification in the operations of financial institutions. The Industrial Investment Bank of India Ltd. (IIBI), North-Eastern Finance Corporation (NEDFC), ICICI Venture, Tourism Finance Corporation of India ltd. (TFCI), Infrastructure Development Finance Company Ltd. (IDFC) and Small Industries Development bank of India (SIDBI) were set up during 1984-1992. The basic purpose of establishing these institutions to strengthen the existing institutional infrastructure in the country thus, by 1992 the country was being served by well integrated network of 59 development finance institutions; six all India DFIs, four specialized financial institutions, three investment institutions, 18 SFC and 28 SIDCs. however, the three all India industrial development banks (AII DBS), namely IFCI, ICICI and IDBI comprised the core of industrial financing system; there share being nearly three – fifth of total finance disbursed by the a four mentioned institutions.

The AIIDBs introduced new financial product/ services and expanded the scope of their activities. Ensuring substantial growth and diversification were the basic theme of their operations in this period. The emphasis got shifted from projected finance to provision of fund and fee based financial services, viz. leasing, installment credit, equipment finance, bridge loans, buyer/ suppliers credit guarantees, underwriting merchant banking and allied services.

The Risk Capital and Technological Finance Corporation Ltd. (RCTC) and Technology Development and Information Company of India ltd. (TDICI) was also setup in 1992 and 1993 respectively to strengthen the efforts for financing and promotion of new technologies/entrepreneurship. These were the steps required to accelerate the pace of technological development in the country.

Moreover, many significant changes as policy initiatives by the Government took place in this period. In 1984, the government issued first guidelines for the appointment of nominees directors in the assisted companies. Some relaxation was also announced in the policy regarding conversion of loans into equity. However, the practice was abandoned in 1992. Similarly the project finance participation certificate (PFPC) scheme, extended in 1984 to all projects irrespective of their cost, was gradually liberalized and finally abolished in 1992. Other important policy developments of the period include deregulation of interest rates and withdrawal of concessional finance scheme for backward areas.

Phase VI: Reorientation Era (1992-98)

In 1991, the government initiated economic reforms to correct the macro-economic imbalances and to effect structural adjustments with the objective of making the real sector of the economy more competitive and efficient. The process necessitated reorientation on the part of the Indian DFIs to meet the challenges of the emerging competitive environment as outlined by the Narasimham Committee.

The DFIs on their part responded to changing requirements by introducing a variety of new products/ services and enlarged the scope of the existing ones. In the meantime, the government withdrew tax benefits to IDBI and changed the character of IFCI from a statutory corporation to a company. Further, with decline in the traditional sources of low cost funds, the DFIs were forced to go to the capital market to augment their financial resources. This phase witnessed a significant increase in the activities of the capital market. New financial regulatory institutions; SEBI, rating agencies, etc. were created to regulate the activities of various players in the capital market. Besides FIIs' dedicated debt funds, many other intuitional players were allowed to operate both in the primary and secondary capital market.

Phase VII: Universal Banking Era (1998 Onwards)

The financial sector reforms have effected significant changes in the operating environment of banks and financial institutions. The deregulations of interest rates, emergence of disintermediation process arising out a liberalized capital market and increasing participation by banks in project finance significantly altered the operating environment of banks. With DFIs in turn, making the forays into the realm of working capital financing, the traditional operating divisions between banks and DFIs became increasingly blurred. "harmonizing the role of DFIs and banks" issued by the RBI. Earlier, there were the Khan Committee report and the classic proposals of the Narasimham Committee (II).

Khan Committee Report

The RBI constituted the working group in December last year. Headed by IDBI chairman SH Khan, the panel comprised SBI chairman MS Verma, ICICI managing director and CEO KV Kamath, IFCI chief KD Agrawal, Bank of India CMD MG Bhide, Union Bank chief AT Pannir Selvam and RBI executive director V Subrahmanyam. The working group headed by the IDBI chairman SH Khan submitted a summary of recommendations to then RBI governor Bimal Jalan on 24-4-1998.

Recommendations having Long Term Implications[14]

Recommendations having long term implications are as follows:

(i) Full banking licences should be given to the development financial institutions (DFIs) and called for mergers between strong banks and institutions.

(ii) A "super-regulator" is require to established to supervise and coordinate the activities of multiple regulators in order to ensure uniformity in treatment to various sections of the financial world.

(iii) The cash reserve ratio (CRR) should be reduced for banks within a timeframe and phasing out the statutory liquidity ratio (SLR) in line with international practice.

(iv) DFIs in India are operating on commercial considerations and if these institutions are required to assume any developmental obligations, the government should provide "an appropriate level of financial support".

(v) The DFIs till the time the DFIs are given full banking licences, they should be permitted to have wholly-owned banking subsidiaries.

(vi) A universal bank can be a single company, a holding company with wholly-owned subsidiaries, a group of entities with cross-holdings or even a flagship company which may or may not have independent shareholders.

(vii) The appropriate corporate structure should not be imposed by the regulator.

(viii) The regulatory framework should be enable to ensure the transition towards universal banking. A function-specific and institution-neutral regulatory framework must be developed. "This concept of neutrality should be applicable to both foreign and local entities."

(ix) The supervisory authority should focus on off-site supervision based on periodic reporting by banks and DFIs and on-site supervision should be undertaken only in exceptional cases.

(x) A risk-based supervisory framework should be developed keeping in tune with international practice. The banks and institutions should be supervised on a consolidated basis.

(xi) The application of CRR should be confined to cash and cash-like instruments in case of existing reserve ratio requirement and it should be brought down progressively.

(xii) The SLR should be phased out.

(xiii) A standing committee to harmonise the roles of banks and institutions as these is considerable amount of overlapping between the business of banks and the institutions. The group should convinced the RBI to waive all restrictions on institutions' resource mobilisation as they run counter to the spirit of financial sector liberalisation.

Recommendations having Short Term Implications[15]

Interim recommendations having short term implications are as follows:

(*i*) Suitable level of SLR may be stipulated for institutions on incremental outstanding fixed deposits raised from public;

(*ii*) CRR should not be imposed as institutions as they are not permitted to access cash and cash-like instruments;

(*iii*) Inter-bank and institutional investments and deposits should be free from reserve requirements to develop the term money market;

(*iv*) A uniform risk-weightage of 20 per cent may be assigned for banks' investments in triple-A rated institutional bonds; and

(*v*) Banks may be permitted to exclude investments in SLR securities issued by an institution while calculating the exposure to that institution.

(*vi*) Priority sector should be defined by including certain industries within its ambit.

(*vii*) "The priority sector obligation should be linked to the net bank credit at the end of the previous financial year as it would facilitate efficient loan disbursals

(*viii*) Non-inclusion of infrastructure lendings should be done in the definition of "net bank credit" used in computing the priority sector obligations.

The recommendations of the Khan working group echo the Narasimham committee report's observation that the financial structure is evolving towards a continuum of institutions rather than discrete specialisation. Universal banking is the model espoused by both the committees. Given this objective, the problem then becomes one of providing a level playing field between the various players in the financial sector. The Khan committee has tried to do this in various ways. One of the most interesting ones is the suggestion to explore ways of merging banks and financial institutions, which could be one solution to the problem of weak banks.

Thus, in the light of these recommendations, the Reserve Bank of India prepared a discussion paper in January 1999 to address the various issues concerning the universalisation of banking and elimination of the specific functional role of specialized financial institutions. One of the major issues addressed in the discussion paper relates to the conversion of DFIs either into commercial banks or NBFCs "the issues of transformation of a DFIs into a bank should be considered after elapse of reasonable period of time. In the interim DFIs could tailor needs to become either a bank or a NBFC, depending on institutions-specific consideration and their comparative advantages. If a DFI chooses to become a bank or NBFC, then it should be prepared to fully confirm to the entire amount of prudential, regulatory and supervisory norms applicable to banks / NBFCs".

RBI Working Group Report

Reserve Bank of India has constituted another Working Group on May 2004 for Development Financial Institutions (DFIs) under the supervision of:

(*i*) Sh. N. Sadasivan, Banking Ombudsman for Maharashtra and Goa, Chairman Sh. S.S. Gangopadhyay.

(*ii*) Chief General

(*iii*) Manager, RBI, Member

(*iv*) Sh. O.P. Aggarwal.

(*v*) Chief General Manager.

(*vi*) RBI, Member

(*vii*) Sh. Deepak Mohanty, Adviser, RBI, Member

(*viii*) Sh. Amarendra Mohan, General Manager, RBI, Member

(*ix*) Sh. M.K. Samantaray, General manager, RBI, Member

Summary of Recommendations of the Working Group is as follows: [16]

1. In view of the banking system having acquired the skills of managing risks in extending finance to different sectors of the economy including long term finance and the capital market, (both equity and debt taken together) providing significantly larger resources to the corporate sector, the need for DFIs as the exclusive providers of development finance has diminished. The banks may be encouraged to extend high risk project finance with suitable Government support with a view to distributing risks and funding sources as also developing appropriate credit appraisals and monitoring skills across the financial system. Banks may also be permitted to raise long term resources through issuance of development bonds for the purpose of long term project finance so that problems of asset liability management can also be taken care of.
2. In a purely market driven situation, the business model of any DFI which raises long term resources from the market at rates governed by the market forces and extends only very long term credit to fund capital formation of long gestation is unlikely to succeed on account of threat to its spreads from high-cost of funds and high propensity to accumulate NPAs owing to exposures to very high credit risks. DFIs are, therefore, crucially dependent for their existence on Government commitment for continued support. Central Government need to decide after a detailed social cost benefit analysis on the areas of activities which require development financing and only those DFIs which the Central Government decides to support, for the time being, may continue as DFIs. The rest of the DFIs must convert to either a bank or a NBFC as recommended by the Narasimham Committee and should be subject to full rigour of RBI regulations as applicable to the respective categories. Further, no DFI should be established in future without the Central Government support.
3. Many of the institutions notified as PFIs under Section 4A of the Companies Act, 1956 have become financially weak and act without any assurance of Government support. The bonds issued by these PFIs and their certain other liabilities are treated as eligible investments for insurance companies, PFs, mutual funds and RNBCs. Such exposures on select PFIs also qualify for concessional risk weight of 20% for banks, FIs, NBFCs and RNBCs under RBI guidelines. The eligibility of resources raised by these entities as 'approved investments' and concessional risk weight of 20% allowed for exposure by banks, FIs, NBFCs and RNBCs are based on a perception of safety merely on account of the PFI status being conferred on them and the same should be done away with.
4. In the current scenario, SFCs have outlived their utility and should be phased out within a definite time frame. The credit gap, if any, created by the exit of the SFCs from the market can be filled up by banks and also by suitably repositioning SIDBI.
5. The DFIs which convert into banks are expected to comply with all the regulations applicable to banks from the date of conversion. However, on grounds of practical considerations the entities may need exemption / relaxations in regard to certain norms relating to equity holdings and priority sector lending for a period of 3-5 years after conversion depending on the situation in which they are placed. No relaxations should be granted unless mandated by statute in respect of requirements such as minimum capital, income recognition, asset classification and provisioning, capital adequacy, maintenance of CRR and SLR, drawing of accounts and building of reserves, permissible banking business etc.
6. The DFIs being non banks are more akin to NBFCs and, therefore, should as a general rule be subject to NBFC guidelines. However, while the dominant theme of the NBFC guidelines is to protect the depositors' interest and ensure the viability of the NBFCs for that purpose, such regulatory or supervisory concerns from the view point of protecting depositors' interest are very much less in respect of DFIs, most of which do not accept public deposits or even if they do, have very small proportion of public deposits as compared to their total resources raised. Yet, failure of any of the larger DFIs could have adverse effect on the entire financial system as these entities raise resources on large scale, by issuance of bonds, from domestic banks, PFs, insurance companies, trusts as also the general public. The regulation of these DFIs should, therefore, be so designed as to ensure that the regulatory framework along with the Government support available to the DFIs works towards ensuring their financial soundness so that the overall systemic stability is not endangered.
7. Of all India DFIs established by statute, IDBI is converting itself into a bank. After such transformation, only four viz. Exim Bank and three Refinancing Institutions NABARD, SIDBI and NHB will continue to function as DFIs established by statute. These institutions work as instruments of public policy and as such

their functions arising out of implementation of public policy may be overseen by Central Government. Considering their systemic importance RBI may continue to regulate the financial and related aspects of these DFIs irrespective of whether they accept public deposits or not. All the recommendations for regulation made for Development Finance Companies (DFC) except recommendations relating to registration with RBI, entry-point norms and composition of Board of Directors should be made applicable to these four DFIs. It is observed that RBI has ownership interest in two DFIs viz. NABARD and NHB. As there is a scope for conflict of interest, RBI may divest its ownership stakes in these two institutions.

8. In varying degrees three refinancing institutions NHB, SIDBI and NABARD shoulder responsibilities of regulating and / or supervising the financial intermediaries falling under their respective domains viz. Housing Finance Companies in case of NHB, SFCs and SIDCs in case of SIDBI and State Co-operative Banks, District Central Co-operative Banks and RRBs in case of NABARD. RBI may ensure that the standard of regulations or supervision exercised by the NHB, SIDBI and NABARD over the institutions falling under their respective domains are broadly at par with that maintained by RBI. Till the state level, DFIs established by statute such as SFCs are phased out, suitable regulatory and supervisory powers in respect of these entities may be vested in SIDBI.
9. DFIs which have been constituted as companies and are performing developmental roles should be classified as a new category of NBFCs called 'Development Financial Companies' (DFCs) and subjected to uniform regulation.
10. Considering the structural, functional and operational flexibility available to companies as opposed to statutory bodies, as a general policy, all DFIs that may be set up in future may be constituted as companies (DFCs). As a category of NBFCs, DFCs will be required to be registered with RBI like all other NBFCs.
11. Considering the nature of business of development financing, the entry point norms for DFCs should be set sufficiently high at NOF of Rs.100 crore.
12. DFCs accepting public deposits should maintain liquid assets as prescribed for other NBFCs in terms of Section 45-IB of the RBI Act. Similarly, DFCs will also be statutorily required to transfer certain proportion of annual profits to reserve funds, as required in terms of provision of Section 45-IC of the RBI Act.
13. With a view to enabling the DFCs to access short term and medium term resources to a larger extent and thereby reducing their cost of funds, the present prescription of limiting such access to the extent of NOF may be done away with in respect of those DFCs which have the minimum CRAR of 15%, net NPAs not exceeding 5% of total assets and are fully complying with the ALM guidelines issued by RBI restricting the gap limits to 10 and 15% for the first two time buckets of 1-14 days and 15-28 days respectively subject to the condition that public deposit will not exceed 1.5 times of NOF as prescribed for loans / investment companies. Restrictions will continue to remain in force for DFCs which do not satisfy the above requirements.
14. Keeping in view their systemic importance, the DFCs may be subjected to the guidelines laid down by RBI for the select FIs in respect of their investments and credit portfolio.
15. The extant prudential norms relating to income recognition, asset classification, provisioning, capital adequacy and single and group exposures etc. applicable to select FIs currently regulated by RBI flow from their functions as DFCs and not from their institutional forms and as such, the same may be adopted for DFCs. Thus, DFCs may be required to maintain CRAR of 9% only instead of 15% as prescribed for NBFCs in general.
16. Considering their systemic significance, the DFCs may be required to submit their audited annual accounts to RBI within a specified time frame after the end of each accounting year. They may also be required to obtain prior approval of RBI before appointing / re-appointing / removing the statutory auditor / auditors.
17. Keeping in view the systemic importance of DFCs, RBI should have the powers to prescribe composition of Board of Directors of DFCs so as to ensure inclusion in the Board, of professionals having special knowledge or practical experience in the matters of finance, accountancy, management, industry or any other area of importance which RBI might consider useful to the DFCs. RBI may also consider issuing suitable guidelines on the broad principles of corporate governance to be adopted by DFCs.

18. The supervisory process in respect of the select DFIs established following the recommendations of the Informal Advisory Group on Regulation and Supervision of FIs is working satisfactorily. The same may be extended to supervision of all DFCs as well.

19. Even though the non public deposit taking companies are slated to be excluded from the purview of Financial Companies Regulations Bill 2000, RBI should put in place as an initial measure, a system of periodical collection of all information relevant to the systemic concerns pertaining to large sized non public deposit taking companies say with total assets of Rs. 500 crore and above. The information system may include, besides submission of annual financials, quarterly reporting of specific details of the company's assets and liabilities which focus on their linkages to the market, inter-corporate / intercompany and capital market exposures and all other sensitive information. This system may also be specified for public deposit taking companies to the extent required.

20. The scope that exists for unlimited access to public deposits by RNBCs poses serious concerns relating to the depositors' interest. A cap in terms of NOF may, therefore, be fixed for mobilization of public deposits by RNBCs. To avoid any hardship to the existing RNBCs, the cap on public deposits may be fixed at a level of 16 times of NOF, as an initial measure along with a direction that the RNBCs will ultimately have to conform to the norms for raising of public deposits for NBFCs in general i.e. four times or 1.5 times of NOF as applicable. The time of such transition should preferably be not more than five years, although extension of time may be warranted by, among other reasons, the future cash flows arising out of the deposit contracts already entered into by the respective RNBCs and the nature of fixed expenses built into their operations.

21. RNBCs are at present required to deploy to the extent of 80% of their deposits funds mobilized in some specified categories of investments and have the freedom to deploy funds only to the extent of 20% of their deposit liabilities or 10 times of NOF, whichever is lower so as to ensure protection to the depositors. With the progressive reduction of the cap on deposits in terms of NOF, commensurate progressive increase in the discretion for deployment of funds may be allowed to RNBCs so that on completion of transition they would comply with the norms for raising public deposits while enjoying the freedom to use the deposit and other funds in the manner applicable to other NBFCs.

22. To ensure that the quality of investments by RNBCs remains good during the period of transition, unlisted and unrated bonds issued by any company / institution including PFI should not be part of the investments. Further, investments in unlisted but rated bonds and debentures should be only to the extent of 5% of their total investments in debt securities. Suitable caps may be fixed by RBI for exposures to capital market, real estate, unlisted but rated securities and units of equity oriented mutual funds. Above all, the directed investments may comprise only the rated and listed securities or the units of debt oriented mutual funds as per prudential guidelines for non-SLR securities for banks besides the Government Bonds and listed and rated Government guaranteed bonds. If rating of any of the investments in the directed category is downgraded below the prescribed grade, the same should be shifted to discretionary category with immediate effect and no fresh investment should be made in the discretionary category until any resultant shortfall in the directed investment is made good.

23. Keeping in view the conscious policy of moving away from the administered interests rate regime and also the prevalent interest rate, the floor limit on the rate of interest which can be offered by the RNBCs to the depositors may be removed.

24. RNBCs are allowed to levy service charges for collection of deposits as per the extant guidelines. The benefit of higher yield on assets, consequent upon progressive freedom to be granted to RNBCs in respect of their investments / lending operations may be passed on to the depositors at the time of maturity payment in the form of interest to compensate for the service charges levied.

25. In order to minimize the rate of discontinuity in collection of installments relating to recurring deposits mobilized by RNBCs, the commission structure should be uniform for collection of all deposit instalments and the agency agreements should provide for dis-incentives to agents for failure to collect all instalments.

Major Development Financial Institutions in India

Nature and functions of major developmental financial institutions are given below:

1. Industrial Finance Corporation of India (IFCI Ltd.) : It is India's first development finance institution, was set up in 1948 on July 01 under the Industrial Finance Corporation Act 1948 as a statutory corporation to pioneer industrial credit to medium and large scale industries. The constitution of IFCI was changed in May 1993 from a statutory corporation to a company under the Companies Act, 1956 providing the institutions with greater flexibility to respond to the needs of the rapidly changing financial system as also greater access to the capital markets.

The operations of IFCI's comprise project finance, financial services and corporate advisory services. It is providing long-term financial support to all the segments of the Indian Industry, export promotion, import substitution, entrepreneurship development, pollution control, energy conservation and generation of both direct and indirect employment. It provides custodial and investor services, rating and venture capital services through its subsidiaries / associate companies.

2. Industrial Credit and Investment Corporation (ICICI) : It was established in 1955. It facilitated industrial development in line with economic objectives of the time. It evolved several new products to meet the changing needs of the corporate sector. It provided a range of wholesale banking products and services, including project finance, corporate finance, hybrid financial structures, syndication services, treasury- based financial solutions, cash flow based financial products, lease financing, equity financing, risk management tools as well as advisory services. It also played a facilitating role in consolidation in various sectors of the Indian industry by funding mergers and acquisitions. In the context of the emerging competitive scenario in the financial sector ICICI Ltd. have been integrated into a single full-service banking company as ICICI Bank in May 2002.

3. Industrial Development Bank of India (IDBI) : It was established on 1st July 1964 under an act of parliament as a wholly owned subsidiary of the Reserve Bank of India. In February 1976, its ownership was transferred to the government of India and it was made as the principal financial institutions for coordinating the activities of institutions engaged in financing, promoting and developing industries in the country. Current shareholding of the Government of India is 58.47%.

During the last five decades it was instrumental in not only establishing a well developed, diversified and efficient industrial and institutional structure but also adding a qualitative dimension to the process of industrial development in the country. Over the years, IDBI has enlarged its basket of products and services, covering almost the entire spectrum of industrial activities, including manufacturing and services. It provided financial assistance, both in rupee and foreign currencies, for green- field projects as well as for expansion, modernisation and diversification purposes. In the wake of financial sector reforms unveiled by the government since 1992, it evolved an array of funds and fee based services to meet the entire gamut of financial and corporate advisory requirements of its clients. It also provided indirect financial assistance by way of refining of loans extended by State-level financing institutions and banks and by way of rediscounting of bill of exchange arising out of sale of indigenous machinery on deferred payments terms.

Due to change in operating environment, Government of India decided to transform IDBI into a commercial bank. The IDBI (Transfer of Undertaking and Repeal) Act 2003 was consequently enacted by parliament in December 2003. The Act provides for repeal of IDBI Act, corporatisation of IDBI and transformation into a commercial bank. The provisions of the Act have come into force from 2 July 2004 in terms of a Government Notification to this effect. The IDBI has already commenced banking business in accordance with the provisions of the new Act in addition to the business being transacted under IDBI Act, 1964.

4. Industrial Investment Bank of India Ltd. (IIBI) : It was set up in 1971 for rehabilitation of sick industrial companies. It was again reconstituted as industrial reconstruction bank of India in 1985 under the IRBI Act, 1984. With a view to converting the institutions, IRBI was incorporated under the Companies Act, 1956, as Industrial Investment Bank of India Ltd. (IIBI) in March 1997. It offers a wide range of products and services, including term loan assistance for project finance, short duration non-project backed financing, working capital/ other short term loans to companies, equity subscription, asset credit, equipment finance and investment in capital market and money market instrument.

5. Infrastructure Development Finance Company Ltd. (IDFC) : It was incorporated in 1997. It was conceived as a specialized institutions to facilitate the flow of private finance to commercially viable infrastructure projects through innovative products and processes. Telecom, power, roads, ports, railways, urban structure together with food and agriculture –related infrastructure. Besides, it assists the development of urban water and sanitation sectors. It has also taken new initiatives in the areas of tourism, healthcare and education. It provides assistance by way of debt and equity support, mezzanine structures and advisory services. It encourages banks to participate in infrastructure projects through take-out financing for a specific term and at a preferred risk profile.

Financial operation of DFIs in India[17]

All India financial institutions in general and DFIs in particular have attained commendable achievement in contributing financial assistance for rapid industralisation of our country. The industrial progress achieved by the private sector in the last six decades since 1950-54 was largely due to the funds supplied by these DFIs. Since 1980-81, the loan assistance sanctioned and disbursed by DFIs had picked up rapidly. The financial assistance sanctioned by DFIs grew to Rs.116461 crores in 2000-01 from Rs. 2713.6 crores in 1980-81 and in the similar manner, disbursements increased proportionately from Rs. 1865.4 crores to Rs. 76439.8 crores during the same period. However, there was steep decline in sanctions and disbursements from 2000-01 onwards with an exception to the year 2003-04.

The rapid decline in DFIs financial assistance from 2000-01 may be attributed to recession and other equally important factors. The ICICI was merged ICICI Bank and ceased to be a development financial institute. The IDBI has also been merged with IDBI Bank in 2004. The major DFIs, viz. IDBI and IFCI have also suffered due to large NPAs and are unable to mobilise funds from the market for their lending operations.

Exhibit-12.2

Trends of Assistance sanctioned and Disbursed by AIFIs

(Rs. crore)

Year	Sanctions	Growth Rate (%)	Disbursements	Growth Rate (%)	DSR
1980-81	2713.6		1865.4		68.7
1981-82	2966.9	9.3	2149.5	15.2	72.4
1982-83	3096.3	4.4	2293.6	6.7	74.1
1983-84	3874.7	25.1	2945.5	28.4	76.0
1984-85	5177.7	33.6	3367.3	14.4	65.0
1985-86	6168.6	19.1	4649.5	38.1	75.4
1986-87	7540.1	22.2	5367.3	15.4	71.2
1987-88	9085.4	20.5	6626.1	23.5	72.9
1988-89	10967.3	20.7	7227.1	9.1	65.9
1989-90	13984.4	27.5	9099.6	25.9	65.1
1990-91	18329.1	31.1	12156.5	33.6	66.3
Post liberlisation period					
1991-92	21059.6	14.9	15386.6	26.6	73.1
1992-93	32054.0	52.2	22362.7	45.3	69.8
1993-94	39770.6	24.1	25682.8	14.8	64.6
1994-95	55108.4	38.6	31970.6	24.5	58.0
1995-96	56135.8	1.9	36507.5	14.2	65.0
1996-97	48192.7	-14.1	42540.3	16.5	88.3
1997-98	71475.0	48.3	54186.0	27.4	75.8
1998-99	79774.3	11.6	59099.5	9.1	74.1
1999-00	100437.5	25.9	70930.0	20.0	70.6

Contd....

2000-01	116461.0	16.0	76439.8	7.8	65.6
2001-02	79001.4	-32.2	63822.2	-16.5	80.8
2002-03	39621.0	-49.8	33258.9	-47.9	83.9
2003-04	63609.2	60.5	40439.5	21.6	63.6
Cumulative up to end of March 2004	906371.3		657221.4		
CAGR (1980-81 – 1984-85		17.5		15.9	
CAGR (1985-86 – 1989-90)		22.7		18.3	
Post Liberlisation period					
CAGR(1990-91 – 1994-95)		31.7		27.3	
CAGR(1995-96 – 1999-00)		15.7		18.1	
CAGR(2000-01 – 2003-04)		-14.0		-14.7	

Sources: Compiled from Annual Reports of AIFIs.

Thus, structured changes have been ensured in some of DFIs. Merger of ICICI, IDBI and UTI etc has eroded the base of DFIs in the country. Now these institutions are working as a commercial banks.

Plan-wise Assistance Sanctioned and Disbursed

The DFIs in India are playing very important role in providing financial assistance to different sectors of the economy. The volume of sanctions aggregated to Rs. 919655.9 crores and that of disbursements to Rs. 651109.2 crores during 1948-2006. The disbursement to sanction ratio (DSR) stood at 70.7 percent for the entire period of study. A plan-wise analysis of financial assistance sanctioned and disbursed by DFIs is presented in exhibit 12.3. During the First-five year plan, the volume assistance by DFIs recorded an increase of almost 4.6 and 2.6 fold respectively in sanctions and disbursements over the Pre-plan period (1948-51). This might be due to remarkable expansion in the operation of IFCI and the setting up of State Level Fianace Corporations (SFCs) in some states of the country. From Rs. 37.47 crores, the sanctions increased to Rs. 212.24 crores during the second five year loan and disbursement enhanced from Rs.15.22 crores to Rs.142.02 crores as compared to the first plan period. Moreover, during the same period disbursement to sanction ratio (DSR) increased from 40.6 to 66.9.

It is important to note that the grant of financial assistance not only gathered momentum during second plan period, but also it picked up the pace. It may be due to expansion in scope and coverage DFIs activities. For instance, IFCI extended its assistance to hotels, introduced underwriting facility by providing guarantees for differed payments and foreign currency loans. Similarly with foreign exchange crisis in 1957-58, foreign currency loans provided by ICICI became the main source of payment for imported equipments. Establishment of Refinance Corporation for Industry Ltd (RCI) in 1958 is another significant cause for growth of assistance by DFIs.

Exhibit-12.3

Assistance Sanctioned and Disbursed during different plan periods

(Rs.crore)

Plan Period	Periods	Amount Sanctioned	Amount Disbursed	DSR (%)
Pre-Plan Period	1948-51	8.13	5.79	71.2
First-Five Year Plan	1951-56	37.47	15.22	40.6
Second-Five Year Plan	1956-61	212.24	142.02	66.9
Third -Five Year Plan	1961-66	471.9	422.84	89.6
Three-Annual Plans	1966-69	374.78	335.93	89.6

Contd....

Fourth -Five Year Plan	1969-74	1452.61	984.2	67.8
Fifth -Five Year Plan	1974-80	4737.9	3092.1	65.3
Sixth-Five Year Plan	1980-85	14680.4	10326.8	70.3
Seventh-Five Year Plan	1985-90	49375.3	34208	69.3
Post-liberalization period				
Two-Annual Plans	1990-92	40367.4	26231.3	65.0
Eight-Five Year Plan	1992-97	25472.8	164033.9	64.4
Ninth-Five Year Plan	1997-02	447149.2	324477.5	72.6
Tenth-Five-Year Plan	2002-07	103230.2	73698.4	71.4

Sources: Compiled from Annual Reports of AIFIs.

During the third five-third plan, the amount of assistance by all India financial institutions doubled in terms of sanctions and more than three times in terms of disbursements in comparison to the second plan. The steep rise in the amount of assistance during third plan may be attributed to establishment of IDBI in July 1964 as the Apex DFI of the country and UTI in February 1964 to mobilize and channelise the community savings into corporate shares and debentures. Three Annuals Plans (1966-69) showed the sanctions and disbursements of Rs. 374.78 crores and Rs. 335.93 crores respectively, which is less than the third five year plan. The total assistance recorded an increase of more than three times in sanctions and more than two times in disbursements in fourth five year plan period over the third plan period. This increase in assistance was due to elaborate network of financial institutions, which served with fair degree of success. IDBI, UTI and other state level financial institutions started their operations at massive scale, which gave adequate momentum to industrial finance in India during 1969-74. During 4th plan total amount disbursed was Rs.984 crore against the sanctioned amount of Rs.1453 crore.

The financial assistance extended by the AIFIs became quite encouraging during Fifth-five year plan (1974-80) as the total sanctions amounted to Rs. 4347.9 crores and disbursements to Rs. 3092.1 crores with 65.3% utilization rate. Actually, simplification of procedures to expedite sanctions and disbursements, liberalizations of lending policies for modernization and technical upgradation, increased flow of assistance to projects located at backward areas and provision of bridge loans against public issues by major DFIs (IFCI, ICICI, IDBI, IRCI, SFCs, and SIDCs) are responsible for major increase in financial assistance.

During the sixth and seventh five year plan (1980-90) assistance provided by DFIs recorded an increase of more than three times in comparison to their respective previous plans. While the aggregate of sanctions arrived at Rs. 14680 crores at the end sixth five year plan, it crossed Rs. 49375 crores during the seventh five year plan. However, the disbursement rate remained around 70% in both the plan periods. There was a plan –holiday for two years and two annual plans were introduced during 1990-92. During this period, the sanctions and disbursement too remained higher than the reasonable utilization rate of 65%.

The unprecedented growth in financial assistance during sixth and seventh five year plan periods might be due to establishment of six new institutions, namely industrial investment Bank of India (IIBI), North Eastern Finance Corporation (NEDFC), ICICI ventures, Tourism Finance Company lTD. (TFCI), Infrastructure Development Bank of India (SIDBI). Besides substantial growth and diversification was probably the most spectacular aspect of their operations during this plan period.

The eight five – year plan (1992-97) showed an increasing trend, with the sanctions and disbursement reached at a considerable height of Rs. 254728 crores and Rs. 164033.9 crores respectively. it is a record, which is six times higher than the previous plan period. However from 70%, the utilization rate dropped to 64.4%. The fall in disbursement / utilization rate may be caused due to following reasons: in 1991, the Government started the process of economic process in the financial sector which necessitated reorientation With decline in the traditional sources of low-cost funds, the DFI's were forced to go to capital market to augment their financial resources even at higher cost.

During the Ninth five year plan period (1997-02) the financial assistance of AIFIs to industrial sector was twice over the eighty five year plan. While sanctioned amount reached at Rs. 447149.2 crores, the disbursement at Rs. 324477.5 Crores further from 64.4%, the disbursement-sanction ratio rose to 72.6% during this plan period.

A significant acceleration in overall growth momentum across quarters was the hall mark of India's economic resurgence during the Tenth five year plan (2002-07). Several policy directives for Development Financial Institutions (DFIs) were intended to facilitate the process of their transition to becoming banks for their sustained viability. These included measures aimed at financial restructuring provision of regulatory relaxation for restructured investments of creditor's banks as well as providing Government support and transfer of stressed assets of DFIs to asset reconstruction companies for managing their NPA levels. As a part of harmonization of the prudential norms between banks and DFIs, the 90 days NPA norms was extended to DFIs on a prospective basis. Similarly guidelines issued to banks to prevent slippage of Accounts in Sub-standard category to doubtful category were also extended to DFIs. Financial assistance sanctioned and disbursed by AIFIs during 2002-06 witnessed growth of 23.08% and 22.71% respectively as compared to the previous plan period although utilization rate of assistance sanctioned from 72.6% to 71.4%.

The remarkable buoyancy in overall GDP in Ninth and Tenth Five-Year Plan periods, after a relatively subdued performance in the previous plan periods, underpinned inter alia by a pronounced strengthening of industrial activity and exports and incipient signs of improvement in business confidence, which usually translate into bulge in industrial investment intentions going forward, resulted in a generally improved performance of financial institutions during two last plan periods, reversing the consecutive downturn of the past three plans periods. The capital market in India in spite of significant improvement, has not witnessed increasing volume of trading in the light of the underdevelopment of the debt market which is mostly confined.

Problems of Development Financial Institutions in India

Since 1991, there has been a qualitative shift in the emphasis of the government from social goals maximization to commercial viability and competitive efficiency. Due to changed environment, the Development Financial Institutions (DFIs) were forced to adapt their lending strategies and activities towards realization of these objectives. Some of the major problems and challenges faced by DFIs in post reforms era are given below:

(i) **Deregulated Market Environment:** Before the 1991, DFIs were operating in a protected market with the administered rate of interest on their loans, but after 1991, they have been forced to enter in to the deregulated market environment. Now Market related rate of interest is the operational base for the DFIs.

(ii) **Crisis of Creditability**: The DFIs is facing the crisis of creditability in the wake of economic liberlisation, globalization and changing business environment. NPA of these DFIs is increasing and is adversely affecting their profitability.

(iii) **Growing Competition in Financial Market**: The free market economy during the 1990's also witnessed the keen competition for DFIs from the commercial banks, NBFCs and others. At present, the commercial banks are financing both short-term and long-term finance to the corporate sector so it has created a problem for the DFIs to increase and diversify their client base. It became easy for their commercial banks to finance both kinds of loans and accept deposits and transforms them to loans. But for the DFIs, these types of facilities are not available and they basically depend on the market their resource mobilization and financing.

(iv) **Easy Access to Capital Market**: The liberalisation and globalization process started in the Indian economy ash revived the capital market and opened the door for the corporate sector to raise their resources directly from the market. The corporate sector is not interested in the financial assistance of DFIs. This disintermediation process in the Indian economy also adversely affected the functioning of the development banks.

(v) **Competitive Interest Rates**: The DFIs have already entered into the capital market to raise their resources. These resources are generally raised with the market rate of interest that is higher than the previously administered rate of interest, so it result in an increase of their cost of borrowings. The DFIs are also being forced to reduce their lending rates due to competition. There is also the problem of greater risk exposure and consequent higher NPA in their traditional investment portfolio. These factors have resulted in the decline of their income, which obviously is squeezing of their spread and force the DFIs to enter into other types of activities specially, the fee based activities.

(vi) **Accountability to Stakeholders**: The increasing access of the DFIs to the Indian capital market has created a new type of problem for them with which they were not acquainted earlier. Thus, the management of most of the DFIs in this competitive economy is always on their toes because of this increasing accountability from the public and more specifically from their private shareholders. Now DFIs are required to accountable to their stakeholders for transparency and reporting.

(*vii*) **Universal Banking System:** The concept of universal banking, which has been recommended by the Khan Committee, has put the DFIs into a fix. Now the concept of development banking is slowly going out of fashion. They have now converted into an NBFC or an universal bank.

Development Financial Institutions have been assigned a crucial role in the development of the country. They have played their role in the promotion of industrial units and entrepreneurial environment. However, due to change in economic environment since 1991 continuous dilution is occurred in their working. New economic policy of the government since 1991 has made some of the development financial institutions irrelevant in the present context of development. Structural changes have been made in the role and objective of some of the development financial institutions. Even today some of the financial institutions are still playing their role in proper perspective.

Practice Questions

Objective Type Questions

1. IFCI was established in:
   (*a*) 1947 (*b*) 1948
   (*c*) 1950 (*d*) 1950
2. Indo Industrial Commission was headed by:
   (*a*) Sir T.H. Holland
   (*b*) Diamond William
   (*c*) Sir T.N. Sapru
   (*d*) Boskey Shirley
3. IDBI was incorporated in:
   (*a*) 1962 (*b*) 1964
   (*c*) 1960 (*d*) 1966
4. S H Khan Committee was set up to :
   (*a*) enquire about the viability of development banks
   (*b*) restructure the working of development banks
   (*c*) harmonizing the roles and operations of development banks
   (*d*) transformation of DFI's into banks
5. SIDBI was setup in:
   (*a*) 1990 (*b*) 1992
   (*c*) 1994 (*d*) 1996

Ans: 1. (b), 2. (a) 3. (c), 4. (c), 5. (a)

Short Answer Questions

1. Explain the diversified activities of All India Financial Institutions?
2. State the functions of Industrial Finance Corporation.
3. Explain the objectives and working of Industrial Bank of India.
4. Explain the functions and working of Small Industrial Development Bank of India.
5. Discuss the objectives and functions of State Financial Corporation.
6. Critically appraise the working of Industrial Credit & Investment Corporation of India. (ICICI)
7. Discuss the objectives functions and working of Development banks in India.
8. What is universal banking?
9. What do you know by the term lending functions of Financial Institutions in India?
10. What do you mean by Development Banking? State the evolution of development banking in India.

Long Answer Questions

1. Discuss the significance of financial institutions in the development of Indian economy.
2. What do you mean by development banks? Briefly spell out various promotional activities conducted by development banks in India.
3. "The success of any development bank depend upon availability of resources which in turn is influenced by ability of savers and their attitude and attitude of institutions and its capacity to make attractive offers of their financial assets." Explain and also state the resource mobilization policy of Indian development banks.
4. "Khan Committee had foreseen diminishing rate of development banks." Comment on the statement and discuss the objectives, functions and major policies of development banks in India.
5. "IDBI not only acts a coordinator of functions and operations of all other All India Financial Institutions but also provides working capital to the projects assisted." Comment.

References

1. Business Line, Jan.14, 2008, p.7
2. Economic Times, Nov. 24, 2009, p.4
3. Business Standard, Feb. 15, 2010, p.2
4. Diamond William, Development Banks, Baltimore, John Hopkeins press, 1957, p -5-7
5. Boskey, Shirley; Problems and Practices of Development Banks, Baltimore, Johan Hopkins Press, 1959, p -9
6. Nyhart, J.d., Janassenss, E.F., A Global Directory of Development Finance Institutions in Developing Countries, OECD, Paris.
7. Hook, J.T.D., Financing and Problem of Development Banking, New York, Fredrick A. Pager Publisher, 1976, p.2
8. Kane, Joseph. A., Development Banking, Laxington Books, D.C. Health and Company, 1975, p.14-15
9. Basu, S.K., Theory and Practice of Development Banking, Bombay, Asia Publishing House, 1965, p.-1
10. Bert, F. Hoselitz (ed). The Progress of Under Developed Areas, Chicago, University of Chicago, 1952, p.3
11. Paul E. Robert, Jr., "Development Banking: The Issue of Public and Private Banking," Economic Development and Public and Cultural Change, Vol.xix, Pril 1971, p.427
12. Sharma, P.K. Development Banks and Entrepreneurship Promotion in India, Mittal Publication , New Delhi, 1972, p.16
13. Bholanath Kamila, Ph.D Thesis on Emerging Role of Development Financial Institutions in Post Reform Era, submitted to F.M.University Balasore, 2008, p. 33
14. Copyright © 1998 Indian Express Newspapers (Bombay) Ltd. p.4
15. Ibid. p.5
16. Report of the Working Group on Development Financial Institutions, Reserve Bank of India Department Of Banking Supervision, Financial Institutions Division, May 2004
17. Op.cit- Bholanath Kamila, Emerging Role of Development Financial Institutions in Post Reform Era, p.73

13 FOREIGN INVESTMENT IN INDIA

Economic development of the country is generally governed by the development of certain institutions, attitudes and conditions within which it can sustain its growth. Developing countries like India are facing resource crunch for accelerating their growth process. Foreign investment helps them to build an institutional framework required for such type of development. With the globalization of financial markets, private capital has now been moving around the world in search of highest returns. Capital crosses border of a country most easily than labour. The growth in the flow of foreign capital has become possible only because investment policies in the western countries have changed to allow foreign investment including portfolio investments abroad. The structural adjustments following economic reforms, reduction in budgetary deficits, restructuring of public sector, relaxation of trade and exchange controls etc. have created a favourable climate for capital inflows into many developing countries like India.

Foreign investment is generally treated as instrument of international policy to boost up the growth prospects. Time tested Indian financial institutions, flexible regulatory authorities and vibrant corporate enterprises now offer foreign investors a transparent investment environment. Macroeconomic stability, structural adjustments, appropriate price and investment policies have created an enabling environment for foreign investment. Dynamic and highly competitive corporate sector in India has long been the backbone of its economic activity and offers considerable scope for foreign investment.

"The advantages of India as an investment destination rest upon strong fundamentals, which include a large and growing market; world-class scientific, technical and managerial manpower; cost effective and highly skilled labour; abundant natural resources; a large English speaking population; independent judiciary, etc. This is now recognized by a number of global investors who have either already established a base in India or is in the process of doing so. Ongoing initiatives, such as further simplification of rules and regulations, improvement in infrastructure is expected to provide necessary impetus to increase foreign investment inflows in country."[1] The inflows of foreign investment depend on domestic economic conditions, world economic trends, and strategies of global investors. The government, on its part, is fully committed to creating strong economic fundamentals and an increasingly proactive foreign investment policy regime. The positive efforts of the government to improve the investment climate, including sustained improvement on infrastructure front, have led to renewed optimism about India as an emerging investment destination. Now, it is policy of the government to attract productive foreign investment which significantly contribute to industrialization and socio-economic development. Actually, foreign investment supplements the domestic capital and technology.

Rationale of Foreign Investment in India

Following arguments are advanced in favour of foreign investment:

(i) **Increase in Level of Capital:** In underdeveloped countries, rate of capital formation is quite low. They do not have funds for their industrialization. Foreign investments helps them to raise the level of their capital substantially.

(ii) **Complementing the Technological Gap:** Level of literacy education, professional and technical education is poor in underdeveloped countries. They have very low level of technology as compared to the advanced

countries. It becomes necessary for importing technology from the developed countries. Technical assistance received from abroad in India has helped in filling up the technological gap in the following three way: (i) provision of expert services, (ii) training of Indian personnel abroad; (iii) provision of education, research and training institutions in the country.

(iii) **Meeting Initial Risk:** Underdeveloped countries generally suffer from acute scarcity of private entrepreneurs. They are unable to assume risk as their appetite for risk is low. It creates obstacles in the industrialization process. But once the industrialization process gets started with the initiative of foreign capital, domestic industrial activity starts picking up, as more and more people of the host country enter the industrial field.

(iv) **Exploitation of the Natural Resources:** A number of underdeveloped countries posses huge mineral resources which await exploitation. Required technical skill and expertise are not available in these countries. As a result, they have to depend upon foreign capital to undertake the exploitation of the resources. They undertake foreign collaboration route to exploit natural resources.

(v) **Development of Basic Economic Infrastructure:** The economic infrastructure includes system of transport and communications, power development of irrigation facilities etc. Due to lack of adequate resources underdeveloped countries are unable to build up economic infrastructure of country on its own. Thus, they need the assistance of foreign capital to undertake this task.

(vi) **Improvement in the Position Balance of Payments:** To accelerate the process of economic development underdeveloped countries require more imports in the form of machinery, capital goods, raw materials, spares and components etc., as compared to their exports. Generally, they face adverse balance of payments. Foreign capital provides a short-term solution to the problem in the form of foreign exchange.

Types of Foreign Investment

With reference to foreign investment, foreign investment may be categorized into:

1. Foreign Direct Investment
2. Portfolio Investment
3. Non Resident Indian Deposits
4. External Commercial Borrowings

1. Foreign Direct Investment

Foreign direct investment is called 'direct' if it provides actual control to the investor (usually a multinational company) in the invested-in enterprise. The control over the enterprise doesn't merely involve the control of the investment capital; it is control in terms of actual power of management and effective decision-making in the major aspect of the working of the invested-in enterprise including finance, production, technology, marketing, staffing and further promotion. The most distinguishing feature of FDI is to exercise the control over decision-making in an enterprise located in one country (say India) by investors located in another country (say France). Although individuals or partnerships may make such investments, most of them are made by enterprises, a large part by MNCs.

Nature of Foreign Direct Investment (FDI)

FDI refers to investment in foreign country where the investor retains the control over the investment. It typically takes the form of starting a subsidiary, acquiring a stake in an existing firm or starting a joint venture in the foreign country. Direct investment and management of the firms concerned normally go together.

FDI is the process whereby residents of one country (the home country) acquire ownership of assets for the purpose of controlling the production, distribution and other activities of a firm in another country (the host country).

"International Monetary Fund (IMF) and Organization for Economic Cooperation and Development(OECD) define FDI similarly as a category of cross border investment made by a resident in one economy (the direct investor) with the objective of establishing a 'lasting interest' in an enterprise (the direct investment enterprise) that is resident in an economy other than that of the direct investor. The motivation of the direct investor is a strategic long term relationship with the direct investment enterprise to ensure the significant degree of influence by the direct investor in the management of the direct investment enterprise. Direct investment allows the direct investor to gain access to the direct investment enterprise which it might otherwise be unable to do."[2] The objectives of direct investment are different from those of portfolio investment whereby investors do not generally expect to influence the management of the enterprise. In the Indian context, FDI is defined in Para 2.1.12 of this Circular.

Motives of FDI

Following are the main motives of FDI:

(*i*) Resources Seeking
(*ii*) Market Seeking
(*iii*) Efficiency Seeking

(*i*) Resource Seeking : Historically, the most important motivation of FDI has been exploitation of natural resources. Foreign firms are generally interested to seek cheap labour viz. labour and capital or other material resources. This reduces production costs which can make the firms competitive in developing economies or under developed economies. Cheaper resources could be the result of low wage price profile of the economy, idle or unutilized resources or state subsidies available for the purpose.

(*ii*) Market Seeking : Generally, home country protects its market from international competition by making the tariffs quite high or quotas. Large population provide a good attraction to FDI motives. Market access is the predetermining motive for investing in the manufacturing sector of under developed economics. The growing importance of the service sector has also been resulting an increase in FDI as most services are not tradable and, therefore, the only way to deliver them to foreign markets is through establishment abroad.

(*iii*) Efficiency Seeking : Low cost of production, deriving mostly from cheap labour, is the driving force of many FDIs in developing countries. Export processing has been developed by developing countries mostly to take advantage of the efficiency seeking FDI flows.

Essentials of Foreign Direct Investment

Essentials of FDI are as follows:

(*i*) **Stable, predictable macro-economic policy:** Companies must have the confidence that the economy in which they make an investment will be managed in a competent and predictable way. Simply investors must believe that the rules of the game will not change in the middle of a contest.

(*ii*) **An effective and honest government:** Foreign investors must be convinced about the integrity of the host government and its ability to maintain law and order. Proactive government is necessary for attracting FDI in the country.

(*iii*) **A large and growing market:** The size and potential for growth of a country's domestic market, especially the purchasing power of its customers are key. Companies do not seek to invest in a market where there is little potential to make a profit.

(*iv*) **Freedom of Activity in the market:** The strength of the competition, as well as the degree of government (their and ours) interference to enter a country's market, are important factors. The freer the market, the more attractive it becomes as an investment site for international investors.

(*v*) **Minimal government regulations:** The cost of government regulation and intervention in the affairs and private companies must be kept to a minimum. Excessive regulatory mechanism hampers the inflows of foreign investments.

(*vi*) **Property rights and protection:** Private property must be protected. Proper use of company's real or intangible (patent, copyright, etc.) property will be ensured in the host country.

(*vii*) **Reliable "infrastructure":** The ability to consummate transactions and get products and service to market is also critical. Transportation, power generation, insurance and accounting services, a competent financial system or other basic factors are necessary for making the foreign investment more viable and operative.

(*viii*) **Availability of High-quality factors of production:** While the investor brings capital, technology and management to the host country, the quality of the indigenous work force and the availability of local raw materials are also key ingredients in the recipes for success.

(*ix*) **A strong local currency:** The local currency must retain its value. If Investment is made in dollars and then the local assets (valued in the local currency) are devalued then foreign investors will get reduced.

(*x*) **The ability to remit profits, dividends and interest:** Basic motive behind foreign investment is the earning of income in terms of profit, dividends and interest. Foreign investors generally get interested in repatriation of their income to home country. They must be allowed to do like this for promoting foreign investment.

(*xi*) **A favourable tax climate:** Tax incentives attract initial investment in the developing country like India. Final investment decision of a company is usually based on how a country's taxation will affect the normal operating environment once the venture is off the ground.

(*xii*) **Freedom to operate between markets:** A company must be able to source goods and service from its operating environment once the venture is off the ground. Optimisation of resource utilization is the basic purpose behind this requirement.

(*xii*) **Freedom to operate between markers:** A company must be able to source goods and services from its operating unit in one market in order to serve other markers to maximize its global efficiency by trading among its operating entities in different countries to "round out" its product lines.

Objectives of FDI

The objectives of foreign direct investment are as follows:

(*i*) To acquire latest technology

(*ii*) Receive foreign exchange

(*iii*) Generate competition

(*iv*) Increase the rate of investment

(*v*) Reduce dependence on imports, and

(*vi*) Boost the overall health of economy.

Organizational Framework of FDI in India

The Government has created following authorities to streamline the FDI movement in India:

1. Department of Industrial Policy & Promotion (DIPP): The Department of Industrial Policy and Promotion was established on 1995 and has been reconstituted in the year 2003 with the merger of the Department of Industrial Development. Earlier separate Ministries for Small Scale Industries & Agro and Rural Industries (SSI & A&RI) and Heavy Industries and Public Enterprises (HI & PE) were created in October, 1999.

With progressive liberalization of the Indian economy, initiated in July 1991, there has been a consistent shift in the role and functions of this Department. From regulation and administration of the Industrial sector, the role of the Department has been transformed into facilitating investment and technology flows and monitoring industrial development in the liberalized environment.

2. Role and Functions of (DIPP): The role and function of the Department of Industrial Policy and Promotion primarily include:

(*i*) Formulation and implementation of industrial policy and strategies for industrial development in conformity with the development needs and national objectives.

(*ii*) Monitoring the industrial growth, in general and performance of industries specifically assigned to it, in particular, including advice on all industrial and technical matters;

(*iii*) Formulation of Foreign Direct Investment (FDI) Policy and promotion, approval and facilitation of FDI;

(*iv*) Encouragement to foreign technology collaboration at enterprise level and formulating policy parameters for the same;

(*v*) Formulation of policies relating to Intellectual Property Rights in the field of Patents, Trademarks, Industrial Designs and Geographical Indications of Goods and administration of regulations, rules made there under;

(*vi*) Administration of industries (Development & Regulation) Act, 1951;

(*vii*) Promoting industrial development of industrially backward areas and the North Eastern Region including International Co-operation for industrial partnerships and

(*viii*) Promotion of productivity, quality and technical cooperation.

3. Secretariat for Industrial Assistance (SIA): Secretariat for Industrial Assistance (SIA) has been set up by the Government of India in the Department of Industrial Policy and Promotion in the Ministry of Commerce & Industry to provide a single window service for entrepreneurial assistance, investor facilitation, receiving and processing all applications which requires Government approval, conveying Government decisions on applications field, assisting entrepreneurs and investor in setting up projects (including liaison with other organizations and State Governments) and in monitoring implementation of projects. It also notifies all Government Policy Decision relating to investment and technology, collects and publishes monthly production data for selected industry groups.

(*i*) **Promotional Activities :** As an investor friendly agency, it provides information and assistance to Indian and foreign companies in setting up industry and making investments. It guides prospective entrepreneurs and disseminated informations and data on a regular basis through its two monthly newsletters the "SIA Newsletter" and the SIA Statistics" as also through its Website address, i.e. http://dipp.nic.in. It also assists potential investors in finding joint venture partners and provides complete information on relevant policies and procedure, including those, which are specific to sectors and the State Government.

(*ii*) **Public Relation & Complaint (PR&C) :** Public Relation & Complaint (PR &C) Section functioning under the Secretariat for Industrial Assistance, Department of Industrial Policy and Promotion provides assistance to entrepreneurs on various subjects concerning investment decision. PR& C receives all paper/applications related to industrial approvals i.e. IEMs, Industrial License, Foreign Investment, Foreign Technology Agreements, 100% EOUs, EHTP, STP Schemes, etc. and immediately issues a computerized acknowledgement, which also has an identity/reference number. All correspondence with the SIA should quote this number. The Unit also provides information regarding the current status of applications filed for various industrial approvals.

(*a*) **Publication :** Secretariat For Industrial Assistance (SIA) Newsletter is a monthly publication and covers information on data relating to Foreign Direct Investment, NRI investment, sectoral break-ups, country wise break-up, all approvals accorded for Foreign Direct Investment, and NRI investment during the month.

(*b*) **Other Publications :** These publications include Manual as well as sector specific publications, such as on the Indian Automobile industry, Cement Industry, Engineering industries, Leather industries, etc. A set of publications relating to the Infrastructure sector with specific volumes on Ports, Roads, Power, Telecom, and Railway is also published. Other publication includes information on Current taxation and duty structure, Entry options for business in India and the like. All or any of these publications are available through the EAU of the SIA, the Investment Promotion and Infrastructure Development Cell, as also Indian Missions abroad.

(*c*) **Statistics :** This is also a monthly publication which constrains data relating to Industrial License, approvals granted for setting up 100 per cent Export Oriented Units, details of approvals for Industrial License, EOUs, Foreign Technical Collaboration etc., monthly data on industrial production select industry groups, as well as policy announcements by Government during the month. Annual issues of SIA Statistics are also available.

(*iii*) **Entrepreneurial Assistance Unit (E.A.U.) :** The entrepreneurial assistance unit functioning under the Secretariat for industrial assistance, Department of Industrial Policy and Promotion provide assistance to entrepreneurs on various subjects concerning investment decisions. The unit receives all paper/application related to industrial approvals and immediately issued a computerized acknowledgement, which also has an identify/reference number. All correspondence with the SIA should quote this number.

The unit also attends to enquiries from entrepreneurs relating to a wide range of subjects concerning investment decisions. It furnishes clarifications and arranges meetings with nodal officers in concerned Ministeries/Organisations. The Unit also provides information regarding the current status of applications filled for various industrial approvals.

4. Foreign Investment Implementation Authority (FIIA) : Foreign Investment Implementation Authority (FIIA) was established on 9.8.1999 to assist the foreign investors in getting necessary approvals and thereby facilitating quick translation of Foreign Direct Investment (FDI) approvals into implementation. Fast Track Committees have set up in 30 Ministries/Departments for regular review of FDI mega projects (with proposed investment of Rs. 1 billion and above), and resolution of any difficulties in consultation with the concerned Ministries/State Government. Unresolved issues are brought before FIIA. Details of the Fast Track Committees set up in various Ministries/ Departments is available at the website www.dipp.nic.in. FIIA to facilitate the process of translating FDI into implementation. The agency provides services to foreign investors to help obtain necessary approvals, sort out operational problems and seek intervention of various government agencies to find solution to their problems.

The functions of the FIIA are as under:

(*i*) Expediting various approvals/permissions;

(*ii*) Fostering partnership between investors and government agencies concerned;

(*iii*) Resolved difference in perceptions;

(*iv*) Enhance overall credibility;

(*v*) Review policy framework; and

(*vi*) Liaise with the Ministry of External Affairs for keeping India's diplomatic missions abroad informed about translation of FDI approvals into actual investment and implementation.

5. Investment Promotion and Infrastructure Development Cell (IP &ID) : In order to give further impetus to facilitation and monitoring of investment, as well as for better coordination of infrastructural requirement for industry, the IP & DI cell has been setup.

The functions of the Cell include:-

(*i*) Dissemination of information about investment climate in India;

(*ii*) Investment facilitation;

(*iii*) Developing and distributing multimedia presentation materials and other publications;

(*iv*) Organising Symposiums, Seminars , etc. on investment promotion;

(*v*) Liaison with State Governments regarding investment promotion;

(*vi*) Documentation of single window systems followed by various states;

(*vii*) Match making service for investment promotion;

(*viii*) Coordination of progress of infrastructure sectors approved for investment /technology transfer, power, telecom, ports, roads, etc.;

(*ix*) Facilitating Industrial Model Town project and Industrial Parks, etc;

(*x*) Promotion of Private Invesment including Foreign Investment in the infrastrucutre sector;

(*xi*) Compilation of sectoral policies, strategies and guidelines of infrastructure sectors, both in India and abroad; and

(*xii*) Facilitating preparation of a perspective plan on infrastructure requirements for industry.

6. State Level Project Implementation Agencies : India has evolved a comprehensive organisational structure at the state level for industrial development. In most states the organisations present to assist and promote industries are:

(*i*) Investment Promotion Agencies (IPA)

(*ii*) State Industrial Development Corporation (SIDC)

(*iii*) Small Scale Industries Development Corporation (SSIDC)

(*iv*) State Financial Corporation (SFC)

(*v*) District Industries Centre (DIC)

(*vi*) Single Window Service and Escort Service

Several state government have set up single window services (SWS) and investor escort services (ES). SWS aim at providing the investors a single point of contact to meet all regulatory requirements and get the required individuals is assigned from one of the state government agencies to the investor. ES is targeted at large and medium sized projects and one investor. ES seeks to help the investors in information collection, identification of project sites, arranging feasibility studies, clearance of the project by financial institutions, etc.

7. Foreign Investment Promotion Council (FIPC) : Apart from making the policy framework investor-friendly and transparent, promotional measures are also taken to attack Foreign Direct Investment into the country. The Government has constituted a Foreign Investment Promotion Council (FIPC) in the Ministry of Commerce and Industry. This comprises professionals from Industry and Commerce. It has been set up to have a more target-oriented approach towards Foreign Direct Investment promotion. The basic function of the Council is to identify specific sectors/projects within the country that require Foreign Direct Investment and target specific regions/countries of the world for its mobilization.

Benefits of FDI

Following benefits are available from FDI:

(*i*) It helps in increasing the investment level and thereby the income and employment in the host country.

(*ii*) The transnational corporations have been used as vehicles for the transfer of technology especially to the developing country.

(*iii*) It popularizes managerial revolution in the host countries through professional management and the employment of highly sophisticated management techniques.

(*iv*) It enables the host countries to increase their exports and decrease their import requirements.

(*v*) It works to equalize the cost of factors of production around the world.

(*vi*) It provides an efficient means of integrating economies. It easily integrates the host economies with the global economies.

(*vii*) It also enables the host country to have very efficient research and development system.

(*viii*) It helps to increase competition and break domestic monopolies.

Limitations of FDI

The following are the limitations of direct foreign investment:

(*i*) The technologies brought in by the foreign investors may not be adaptable in the host country because of the (a) difference in consumption needs; (b) size of the domestic markets, (c) resource availabilities, (d) stage of the development of the economy.

(*ii*) Private foreign capital tends to flow to high profit areas rather than to priority sectors of the economy.

(*iii*) Foreign capital sometimes interferes in national politics through their economic tools.

(*iv*) Multinational corporations can evade or undermine economic autonomy and control through their power and flexibility. Their activities may be injurious to the national interests of particular countries.

(*v*) Foreign investments, sometimes have an unfavourable effect on the Balance of Payments of a country because the drainage of foreign exchange by way of royalty, dividends etc. is greater than the investment by the foreign concerns.

(*vi*) Foreign investors sometimes engage in unfair and unethical trade policies and governments of home countries pressurize the governments of host countries to free these MNCs from penal actions.

Barriers in FDI Movement in India

Following are the main barriers in FDI movement in India-

(i) Poor infrastructure

(ii) Higher level of taxation

(iii) Redtapism

(iv) Rigid and protective labour laws

(v) Absence of good governance

(vi) Ineffective intellectual property regime

(vii) Defective macro-economic policies

Initiatives taken to Promote FDI in India

Several steps have been initiated to facilitate increased FDI inflows are as follows:

(*i*) On the policy front, while the FDI policy is already very liberal, it is being further progressively rationalised. An exercise has been initiated for integration of all prior regulations on FDI, contained in FEMA, RBI circulars, various Press Notes etc., into one consolidated document, so as to reflect the current regulatory framework. The draft consolidated FDI framework has been launched by Department of Industrial Policy & Promotion on 24.12.2009 and is available at DIPP's website (www.dipp.nic.in) for comments.

(ii) On the investment promotion front, the Department organizes 'Destination India' and 'Invest India' events in association with CII and FICCI.

(iii) DIPP has been undertaking concerted efforts for improving the business environment in the country. The business reforms aimed at improving the business environment include setting up of single windows, online registrations, computerization of information, simplification of taxes and payments, reduction of documents through developing single forms for various licences/permissions and reduction of inspections etc.

(iv) As a step towards promoting an online single window at the national level for business users, the Department has undertaken the eBiz project, which is one of Mission Mode Projects (MMPs) under the National e-Governance Plan (NeGP). The objectives of setting up of the e-Biz Portal are to provide a number of services to business users covering the entire life cycle on their operation. The project aims at enhancing India's business competitiveness through a service oriented, event-driven G2B interaction.

(v) The National Manufacturing Competitiveness Council (NMCC) has been set up to provide a continuing forum for policy dialogue to energize and sustain the growth of manufacturing industries.

(vi) The Department has regular interaction with foreign investors. Such interactions have been held in bilateral/ regional/ international meets such as Indo-ASEAN, Indo-EU, Indo-Japan, etc. Meetings with individual investors were also held on a regular basis.

(vii) The Department website (www.dipp.nic.in) has been made both comprehensive and informative with online chat facility. About 4500 investment related queries were replied during the year.

N.K. Singh Committee Report

The Steering Committee was formed under the chairmanship of Sri N.K. Singh Member Secretary Planning Commission.

Terms of Reference

The terms of reference of the Committee were as follows:

(i) To suggest policy and governance reforms necessary for attracting private investment, both domestic and foreign.

(ii) To identify factors which inhibit higher FDI flows and suggest remedial steps.

(iii) To examine policy reforms towards mergers and acquisition for attracting FDI.

(iv) To suggest changes in institutional apparatus and organizations, both in Centre and States, for attracting the FDI flows.

(v) To suggest Policy reforms in Export Processing Zones for attracting higher FDI flows.

(vi) To suggest policy and governance reforms to attract NRIs for making higher FDI.

(vii) To examine the factors responsible for the success of other countries like China in attracting FDI and make suitable recommendations based on the experience of other successful countries.

Major Recommendations of the Committee[3]

The major "recommendations" of the Steering Committee are as follows:

(i) Consider the enactment of a Foreign Investment Promotion Law that incorporates and integrates aspects relevant to promotion of FDI.

(ii) Urge States to enact a special investment law relating to Infrastructure to expedite all investment in infrastructure sectors and remove hurdles to production in this critical sector.

(iii) Empower the Foreign Investment Promotion Board to give initial Central level registrations and approvals where possible, with a view to speeding up the process of project implementation.

(iv) Change government's Rules of Business to empower FIIA to expedite the processing of administrative and policy approvals.

(v) The aggregate FDI target for the 10th Plan should be dis-aggregated in terms of sectors and relevant administrative ministries/department, to increase accountability. This could help ensure that the policy pre-requisites for increasing domestic private investment and FDI are expedited by the concerned departments.

(vi) Sectoral FDI caps should be reduced to the minimum and entry barriers eliminated. With the exception of 'Defense industry' FDI caps can be removed in all manufacturing and mining. Caps can also be eliminated in Advertising, Private Banks and Real Estate and raised in Telecom, Civil Aviation, DTH/KU broadcasting, Insurance and Plantations (other than tea).

(vii) The existing strategy for attracting FDI should be overhauled. The relative emphasis must shift from a broad (scatter shot) approach to one of targeting specific companies in specific sectors. The Foreign Investment Promotion Council should be reformed to implement this strategy. It should be chaired by a person with global credibility and involve Minister level functionaries who can interact with the heads of the Fortune 500 companies.

(viii) The informational aspects of the strategy should be refined in the light of the perceived advantage and disadvantage of India as an investment destination and should use information technology and modern marketing techniques.

(ix) The Special Economic Zones should be developed as the most competitive destination for export related FDI in the world, by simplifying applicable laws, rules and administrative procedure and reducing red tape to the level found in China. The focus should be on accelerated/immediate implementation of reforms that may take a much longer time in the country as whole and not on tax sops.

(x) Domestic Policy Reforms in the Power Sector, Urban Infrastructure and Real Estate and de-control/de-licensing should be expedited to promote private domestic and foreign investment.

The role of Foreign Direct Investment (FDI) in the upgradation of technology, skills and managerial capabilities is now well accepted. Additional investments, over and above the investments possible with the available domestic resources, help in providing much needed employment opportunities.

Present FDI Policy

The government has announced its consolidated FDI Policy in March, 2010. It will be effective from April 01, 2010[4] Salient features of Consolidated FDI Policy are as follows:

It is the intent and objective of the Government to promote foreign direct investment through a policy framework which is transparent, predictable, simple and clear and reduces regulatory burden. The system of periodic consolidation and updation is introduced as an investor friendly measure. Efforts have been made to consolidate the FDI Policy Framework in the proper perspective legal edifice is also built on the regulatory mechanism developed by RBI under FEMA from time to time.

1. Origin of Investment In India

(A) A non-resident entity (other than a citizen of Pakistan or an entity incorporated in Pakistan) can invest in India, subject to the FDI Policy. A citizen of Bangladesh or an entity incorporated in Bangladesh can invest in India under the FDI Policy, only under the Government route.

(B) NRIs resident in Nepal and Bhutan as well as citizens of Nepal and Bhutan are permitted to invest in the capital of Indian companies on repatriation basis, subject to the condition that the amount of consideration for such investment shall be paid only by way of inward remittance in free foreign exchange through normal banking channels.

(C) OCBs have been derecognized as a class of Investors in India with effect from September 2003. Erstwhile OCBs which are incorporated outside India and are not under the adverse notice of RBI can make fresh investments under FDI Policy as incorporated non-resident entities, with the prior approval of Government of India if the investment is through Government route; and with the prior approval of RBI if the investment is through Automatic route.

(D)(i) An FII may invest in the capital of an Indian company either under the FDI Scheme/Policy or the Portfolio Investment Scheme. 10% individual limit and 24% aggregate limit for FII investment would still be applicable even when FIIs invest under the FDI scheme/policy.

(ii) The Indian company which has issued shares to FIIs under the FDI Policy for which the payment has been received directly into company's account should report these figures separately under item no. 5 of Form FC-GPR (Post-issue pattern of shareholding) so that the details could be suitably reconciled for statistical/ monitoring purposes.

(*iii*) A daily statement in respect of all transactions (except derivative trade) have to be submitted by the custodian bank in floppy / soft copy in the prescribed format directly to RBI to monitor the overall ceiling/sectoral cap/statutory ceiling.

(E) No person other than registered FII/NRI as per Schedules II and III of Foreign Exchange Management (Transfer or Issue of Security by a Person Resident Outside India) Regulations of FEMA 1999, can invest/trade in capital of Indian Companies in the Indian Stock Exchanges directly i.e. through brokers like a Person Resident in India.

(F) A Foreign Venture Capital Investor (FVCI) may contribute upto 100% of the capital of a Venture Capital Fund/Indian Venture Capital Undertaking and may also set up a domestic asset management company to manage the fund. All such investments are allowed under the automatic route subject to SEBI & RBI regulations and FDI Policy. However, FVCIs are also allowed to invest as non-resident entities in other companies subject to FDI Policy.

2. Types of Instruments

(A) Indian companies can issue equity shares, fully, compulsorily and mandatorily convertible debentures and fully, compulsorily and mandatorily convertible preference shares subject to pricing guidelines/valuation norms prescribed under FEMA Regulations. The pricing of the capital instruments should be decided/ determined upfront at the time of issue of the instruments.

(B) Other types of Preference shares/Debentures i.e. non-convertible, optionally convertible or partially convertible for issue of which funds have been received on or after May 1, 2007 are considered as debt. Accordingly, all norms applicable for ECBs relating to eligible borrowers, recognized lenders, amount and maturity, end-use stipulations, etc. shall apply. Since these instruments would be denominated in rupees, the rupee interest rate will be based on the swap equivalent of London Interbank Offered Rate (LIBOR) plus the spread as permissible for ECBs of corresponding maturity.

(C) The inward remittance received by the Indian company vide issuance of DRs and FCCBs are treated as FDI and counted towards FDI.

(D) Issue of shares by Indian Companies under FCCB/ADR/GDR

(*i*) Indian companies can raise foreign currency resources abroad through the issue of FCCB/DR(ADRs/ GDRs), in accordance with the Scheme for issue of Foreign Currency Convertible Bonds and Ordinary Shares (Through Depository Receipt Mechanism) Scheme, 1993 and guidelines issued by the Government of India there under from time to time.

(*ii*) A company can issue ADRs / GDRs if it is eligible to issue shares to persons resident outside India under the FDI Policy. However, an Indian listed company, which is not eligible to raise funds from the Indian Capital Market including a company which has been restrained from accessing the securities market by the Securities and Exchange Board of India (SEBI) will not be eligible to issue ADRs/GDRs.

(*iii*) Unlisted companies, which have not yet accessed the ADR/GDR route for raising capital in the international market, would require prior or simultaneous listing in the domestic market, while seeking to issue such overseas instruments. Unlisted companies, which have already issued ADRs/GDRs in the international market, have to list in the domestic market on making profit or within three years of such issue of ADRs/GDRs, whichever is earlier. ADRs / GDRs are issued on the basis of the ratio worked out by the Indian company in consultation with the Lead Manager to the issue. The proceeds so raised have to be kept abroad till actually required in India. Pending repatriation or utilization of the proceeds, the Indian company can invest the funds in:-

(*a*) Deposits, Certificate of Deposits or other instruments offered by banks rated by Standard and Poor, Fitch, IBCA, Moody's, etc. with rating not below the rating stipulated by Reserve Bank from time to time for the purpose;

(*b*) Deposits with branch/es of Indian Authorized Dealers outside India; and

(*c*) Treasury bills and other monetary instruments with a maturity or unexpired maturity of one year or less.

(*iv*) The ADR / GDR proceeds can be utilized for first stage acquisition of shares in the disinvestment process of Public Sector Undertakings / Enterprises and also in the mandatory second stage offer to the public in view of their strategic importance.

(*v*) Voting rights on shares issued under the Scheme shall be as per the provisions of Companies Act, 1956 and in a manner in which restrictions on voting rights imposed on ADR/GDR issues shall be consistent with the Company Law provisions.

(*vi*) The pricing of ADR / GDR issues should be made at a price determined under the provisions of the Scheme of issue of Foreign Currency Convertible Bonds and Ordinary Shares (through Depository Receipt Mechanism) Scheme, 1993 and guidelines issued by the Government of India and directions issued by the Reserve Bank, from time to time.

(*vii*) The pricing of sponsored ADRs/GDRs would be determined under the provisions of the Scheme of issue of Foreign Currency Convertible Bonds and Ordinary Shares (Through Depository Receipt Mechanism) Scheme, 1993 and guidelines issued by the Government of India and directions issued by the Reserve Bank, from time to time.

(E) (*i*) Two-way Fungibility Scheme: A limited two-way Fungibility scheme has been put in place by the Government of India for ADRs / GDRs. Under this Scheme, a stock broker in India, registered with SEBI, can purchase shares of an Indian company from the market for conversion into ADRs/GDRs based on instructions received from overseas investors. Re-issuance of ADRs / GDRs would be permitted to the extent of ADRs / GDRs which have been redeemed into underlying shares and sold in the Indian market.

(*ii*) Sponsored ADR/GDR issue: An Indian company can also sponsor an issue of ADR / GDR. Under this mechanism, the company offers its resident shareholders a choice to submit their shares back to the company so that on the basis of such shares, ADRs / GDRs can be issued abroad. The proceeds of the ADR / GDR issue are remitted back to India and distributed among the resident investors who had offered their Rupee denominated shares for conversion. These proceeds can be kept in Resident Foreign Currency (Domestic) accounts in India by the resident shareholders who have tendered such shares for conversion into ADRs / GDRs.

3. Eligibility of FDI In Resident Entities

(A) FDI in an Indian Company

(*i*) Indian companies including those which are micro and small enterprises can issue capital against FDI.

(B) FDI in Partnership Firm / Proprietary Concern

(*i*) A Non-Resident Indian (NRI) or a Person of Indian Origin (PIO) resident outside India can invest by way of contribution to the capital of a firm or a proprietary concern in India on non-repatriation basis provided;

(*a*) Amount is invested by inward remittance or out of NRE/FCNR(B)/NRO account maintained with Authorized Dealers / Authorized banks.

(*b*) The firm or proprietary concern is not engaged in any agricultural/ plantation or real estate business or print media sector.

(*c*) Amount invested shall not be eligible for repatriation outside India.

(*ii*) Investments with repatriation benefits: NRIs/PIO may seek prior permission of Reserve Bank for investment in sole proprietorship concerns/partnership firms with repatriation benefits. The application will be decided in consultation with the Government of India.

(*iii*) Investment by non-residents other than NRIs/PIO: A person resident outside India other than NRIs/PIO may make an application and seek prior approval of Reserve Bank for making investment by way of contribution to the capital of a firm or a proprietorship concern or any association of persons in India. The application will be decided in consultation with the Government of India.

(*iv*) Restrictions: An NRI or PIO is not allowed to invest in a firm or proprietorship concern engaged in any agricultural/plantation activity or real estate business (i.e. dealing in land and immovable property with a view to earning profit or earning income there from) or engaged in Print Media.

(C) FDI in Trusts: FDI in Trusts other than VCF is not permitted.

(D) FDI in other Entities: FDI in resident entities other than those mentioned above is not permitted.

4. Conditions on Issue/Transfer of Shares

(A) The capital instruments should be issued within 180 days from the date of receipt of the inward remittance or by debit to the NRE/FCNR (B) account of the non-resident investor. In case, the capital instruments are not issued within 180 days from the date of receipt of the inward remittance or date of debit to the NRE/FCNR (B) account, the amount of consideration so received should be refunded immediately to the non-resident investor by outward remittance through normal banking channels or by credit to the NRE/FCNR (B) account, as the case may be.

(B) Issue price of shares – Issue price of shares to persons resident outside India under the FDI Policy, shall be on the basis of SEBI guidelines in case of listed companies. In case of unlisted companies, valuation of shares has to be done by a Chartered Accountant in accordance with the guidelines issued by the erstwhile Controller of Capital Issues (CCI).

(C) Foreign Currency Account – Indian companies which are eligible to issue shares to persons resident outside India under the FDI Policy may be allowed to retain the share subscription amount in a Foreign Currency Account, with the prior approval of RBI.

(D) Transfer of shares and convertible debentures

(*i*) Subject to FDI sectoral policy, foreign investors can also invest in Indian companies by purchasing/acquiring existing shares from Indian shareholders or from other non-resident shareholders. General permission has been granted to non-residents/NRIs for acquisition of shares by way of transfer subject to the following:

(*a*) A person resident outside India (other than NRI and erstwhile OCB) may transfer by way of sale or gift, the shares or convertible debentures to any person resident outside India (including NRIs).

(*b*) NRIs may transfer by way of sale or gift the shares or convertible debentures held by them to another NRI.

(*c*) A person resident outside India can transfer any security to a person resident in India by way of gift.

(*d*) A person resident outside India can sell the shares and convertible debentures of an Indian company on a recognized Stock Exchange in India through a stock broker registered with stock exchange or a merchant banker registered with SEBI.

(*e*) A person resident in India can transfer by way of sale, shares/ convertible debentures (including transfer of subscriber's shares), of an Indian company in sectors other than financial services sectors (i.e. Banks, NBFC, Insurance, ARCs, CICs, infrastructure companies in the securities market viz. Stock Exchanges, Clearing Corporations, and Depositories, Commodity Exchanges, etc.) under private arrangement to a person resident outside India.

(*f*) General permission is also available for transfer of shares/convertible debentures, by way of sale under private arrangement by a person resident outside India to a person resident in India.

(*ii*) The sale consideration in respect of equity instruments purchased by a person resident outside India, remitted into India through normal banking channels, shall be subjected to a Know Your Customer (KYC) check by the remittance receiving AD Category – I bank at the time of receipt of funds.

(*iii*) Escrow: AD Category – I banks have been given general permission to open Escrow account and Special account of non-resident corporate for open offers / exit offers and delisting of shares. The relevant SEBI (SAST) Regulations or any other applicable SEBI Regulations/ provisions of the Companies Act, 1956 will be applicable.

(E) Prior permission of RBI in certain cases for transfer of capital instruments

(*i*) The following instances of transfer of capital instruments from resident to non-residents by way of sale require prior approval of RBI:

(*a*) Transfer of capital instruments of an Indian company engaged in financial services sector (i.e. Banks, NBFCs, Asset Reconstruction Companies, CICs, Insurance companies, infrastructure companies in the securities market such as Stock Exchanges, Clearing Corporations, and Depositories, Commodity Exchanges, etc.).

(*b*) Transactions which attract the provisions of SEBI (Substantial Acquisition of Shares & Takeovers) Regulations, 1997.

(*c*) The activity of the Indian company whose capital instruments are being transferred falls outside the automatic route and the approval of the FIPB has been obtained for the said transfer.

(*d*) The transfer is to take place at a price which falls outside the pricing guidelines specified by the Reserve Bank from time to time.

(*e*) Transfer of capital instruments where the non-resident acquirer proposes deferment of payment of the amount of consideration, prior approval of the Reserve Bank would be required, as hitherto. Further, in case approval is granted for a transaction, the same should be reported in Form FC-TRS, to an AD Category – I bank for necessary due diligence, within 60 days from the date of receipt of the full and final amount of consideration. The link office of the AD Category-I Bank will consolidate such Form FC-TRS details and report the same to the Central Office of RBI.

(*ii*) The transfer of capital instruments of companies engaged in sectors falling under the Government Route from residents to non-residents by way of sale or otherwise requires Government approval followed by permission from RBI.

(*iii*) A person resident in India, who intends to transfer any capital instrument, by way of gift to a person resident outside India, has to obtain prior approval from Reserve Bank. While forwarding applications to Reserve Bank for approval for transfer of capital instruments by way of gift.

(F) Conversion of ECB/Lumpsum Fee/Royalty into Equity

(*i*) Indian companies have been granted general permission for conversion of External Commercial Borrowings (ECB) (excluding those deemed as ECB) in convertible foreign currency into shares/preference shares.

(*ii*) General permission is also available for issue of shares/preference shares against lump sum technical know-how fee, royalty, under automatic route or SIA/FIPB route, subject to pricing guidelines of SEBI/CCI and compliance with applicable tax laws.

5. Issue of Instruments

(A) Issue of Rights/Bonus Shares – FEMA provisions allow Indian companies to freely issue Rights/Bonus shares to existing non-resident shareholders, subject to adherence to sectoral cap, if any.

(B) Prior permission of RBI for Rights issue to erstwhile OCBs- OCBs have been derecognized as a class of investors from September 16, 2003. Therefore, companies desiring to issue rights share to such erstwhile OCBs will have to take specific prior permission from RBI. As such, entitlement of rights share is not automatically available to erstwhile OCBs. However, bonus shares can be issued to erstwhile OCBs without the approval of RBI.

(C) Additional allocation of rights share by residents to non-residents – Existing nonresident shareholders are allowed to apply for issue of additional shares/ fully, compulsorily and mandatorily convertible debentures/ fully, compulsorily and mandatorily convertible preference shares over and above their rights share entitlements. The investee company can allot the additional rights share out of unsubscribed portion, subject to the condition that the overall issue of shares to non-residents in the total paid-up capital of the company does not exceed the sectoral cap.

(D) Acquisition of shares under Scheme of Merger/Demerger/Amalgamation: Mergers/demergers/ amalgamations of companies in India are usually governed by an order issued by a competent Court on the basis of the Scheme submitted by the companies undergoing merger/ demerger/ amalgamation.

(E) Issue of shares under Employees Stock Option Scheme (ESOPs)

(*i*) Listed Indian companies are allowed to issue shares under the Employees Stock Option Scheme (ESOPs), to its employees or employees of its joint venture or wholly owned subsidiary abroad who are resident outside India, other than to the citizens of Pakistan. ESOPs can be issued to citizens of Bangladesh with the prior approval of FIPB. Shares under ESOPs can be issued directly or through a Trust subject to the condition that:

(a) The scheme has been drawn in terms of relevant regulations issued by the SEBI, and

(b) The face value of the shares to be allotted under the scheme to the non-resident employees does not exceed 5 per cent of the paid-up capital of the issuing company.

(ii) Unlisted companies have to follow the provisions of the Companies Act, 1956. The Indian company can issue ESOPs to employees who are resident outside India, other than to the citizens of Pakistan. ESOPs can be issued to the citizens of Bangladesh with the prior approval of the FIPB.

(iii) The issuing company is required to report the details of such issues to the Regional Office concerned of the Reserve Bank, within 30 days from the date of issue of shares.

6. Entry Route, Caps, Entry Conditions, etc of Investment : (1) Calculation of Total Foreign Investment I.E. Direct and Indirect Foreign Investment in Indian Companies.

(A) Investment in Indian companies can be made both by non-resident as well as resident Indian entities. Any non-resident investment in an Indian company is direct foreign investment. Investment by resident Indian entities could again comprise of both resident and non-resident investment. Thus, such an Indian company would have indirect foreign investment if the Indian investing company has foreign investment in it. The indirect investment can also be a cascading investment i.e. through multi-layered structure.

(B) For the purpose of computation of indirect Foreign investment, Foreign Investment in Indian company shall include all types of foreign investments i.e. FDI; investment by FIIs(holding as on March 31); NRIs; ADRs; GDRs; Foreign Currency Convertible Bonds (FCCB); fully, compulsorily and mandatorily convertible preference shares and fully, compulsorily and mandatorily convertible Debentures regardless of whether the said investments have been made under Schedule 1, 2, 3 and 6 of FEMA (Transfer or Issue of Security by Persons Resident Outside India) Regulations.

(C) Guidelines for calculation of total foreign investment i.e. direct and indirect foreign investment in an Indian company.

(i) Counting the Direct Foreign Investment: All investment directly by a non- resident entity into the Indian company would be counted towards foreign investment.

(ii) Counting of indirect foreign Investment:

(a) The foreign investment through the investing Indian company would not be considered for calculation of the indirect foreign investment in case of Indian companies which are 'owned and controlled' by resident Indian citizens and/or Indian Companies which are owned and controlled by resident Indian citizens.

(b) For cases where condition (a) above is not satisfied or if the investing company is owned **or** controlled by 'non-resident entities', the entire investment by the investing company into the subject Indian Company would be considered as indirect foreign investment.

Entry Routes for Investment

(A) Investments can be made by non-residents in the shares/fully, compulsorily and mandatorily convertible debentures/ fully, compulsorily and mandatorily convertible preference shares of an Indian company, through two routes; the Automatic Route and the Government Route. Under the Automatic Route, the foreign investor or the Indian company does not require any approval from the RBI or Government of India for the investment. Under the Government Route, prior approval of the Government of India through Foreign Investment Promotion Board (FIPB) is required.

(B) Investment would be subject to the 'Existing Venture/ tie-up condition' as defined below:

(i) With effect from January 12, 2005 the joint venture agreements are expected to include a 'conflict of interest' clause to determine/ safeguard the interests of joint venture partners in the event of one of the partners desiring to set up another joint venture or a wholly owned subsidiary in the same field of economic activity.

(ii) Where a foreign investor has an existing joint venture/ technology transfer/ trademark agreement in the same field, prior to January 12, 2005, the proposal for fresh investment/technology transfer/technology collaboration/trademark agreement in a new joint venture for technology transfer/technology collaboration/trademark agreement would have to be under the Government approval route through FIPB/ Project Approval Board.

(*iii*) The following investments, however, will be exempt from the requirement of Government approval even though the foreign investor may be having a joint venture or technology transfer/ trademark agreement in the same filed:

(*a*) Investments to be made by Venture Capital Fund registered with the Securities and Exchange Board of India (SEBI); or

(*b*) Investments by Multinational Financial Institutions like Asian Development Bank(ADB), International Finance Corporation(IFC), Commonwealth Finance Corporation (CDC), Deutsche Entwicklungs Gescelschaft (DEG) etc.; or

(*c*) where in the existing joint venture, investment by either of the parties is less than 3 per cent; or

(*d*) where the existing joint venture / collaboration is defunct or sick; or

(*e*) for issue of shares of an Indian company engaged in Information Technology sector or in the mining sector, if the existing joint venture or technology transfer / trade mark agreement of the person to whom the shares are to be issued are also in the Information Technology sector or in the mining sector for same area/mineral.

(C) Guidelines for transfer of ownership or control of Indian companies in sectors with caps from resident Indian citizens to non-resident entities in sectors with caps:

In sectors with caps, including *inter-alia* defence production, air transport services, ground handling services, asset reconstruction companies, private sector banking, broadcasting, commodity exchanges, credit information companies, insurance, print media, telecommunications and satellites, Government approval/ FIPB approval would be required in all cases.

Caps on Investments

Investments can be made by non-residents in the capital of a resident entity only to the extent of the percentage of the total capital as provided/permitted in the FDI policy. Thus, while investment are prohibited in some sectors/activities, there are restrictions/ conditions/caps on the investment in certain other sector/activities.

Entry Conditions on Investment

Investments can be permitted to be made by non-residents in the capital of a resident entity in certain sectors/activity with entry conditions. These entry conditions would be applicable for investment only by non-resident entities. Such conditions may include norms for minimum capitalization, lock-in period, etc.

Downstream Investment by Indian Companies

(A) The Policy for downstream investment by Indian companies seeks to lay down and clarify about compliance with the Foreign investment norms on entry route, conditionalities and sectoral caps. The 'guiding principle' is that downstream investment by companies 'owned' or 'controlled' by non-resident entities would require to follow the same norms as a direct foreign investment i.e. only as much can be done by way of indirect foreign investment through downstream investment.

(B) The Guidelines for calculation of total foreign investment, both direct and indirect in an Indian company, at every stage of investment including downstream investment, have been detailed in earlier pages.

(C) Guidelines for downstream investment by Investing Indian Companies 'owned or controlled by non-resident entities'

(*i*) The Policy on downstream investment comprises policy for (a) only operating companies (b) operating-cum-investing companies (c) only investing companies as below:

(*ii*) Only operating companies: Foreign investment in such companies would have to comply with the relevant sectoral conditions on entry route, conditionalities and caps with regard to the sectors in which such companies are operating.

(*iii*) Operating-cum-investing companies: Foreign investment into such companies would have to comply with the relevant sectoral conditions on entry route, conditionalities and caps with regard to the sectors in which such companies are operating. Further, the subject Indian companies into which downstream investments are made by such companies would have to comply with the relevant sectoral conditions on entry route, conditionalities and caps in regard of the sector in which the subject Indian companies are operating.

(*iv*) Investing companies: Foreign Investment in Investing Companies will require the prior Government/ FIPB approval, regardless of the amount or extent of foreign investment. The Indian companies into which downstream investments are made by such investing companies would have to comply with the relevant sectoral conditions on entry route, conditionalities and caps in regard of the sector in which the subject Indian companies are operating.

(D) For infusion of foreign investment into such companies which do not have any operations and also do not have any downstream investments, Government/ FIPB approval would be required.

Guidelines for Consideration of FDI Proposals by FIPB

(A) The following guidelines are laid down to enable the FIPB to consider the proposals for FDI and formulate its recommendations.

(*i*) All applications should be put up before the FIPB by its Secretariat within 15 days and it should be ensured that comments of the administrative ministries are placed before the Board either prior to/or in the meeting of the Board.

(*ii*) Proposals should be considered by the Board keeping in view the time frame of thirty (30) days for communicating Government decision.

(*iii*) In cases in which either the proposal is not cleared or further information is required in order to obviate delays presentation by applicant in the meeting of the FIPB should be resorted to.

(*iv*) While considering cases and making recommendations, FIPB should keep in mind the sectoral requirements and the sectoral policies vis-à-vis the proposal (s).

(*v*) FIPB would consider each proposal in its totality

(*vi*) The Board should examine the following while considering proposals submitted to it for consideration.

(*a*) Whether the items of activity involve industrial licence or not and if so the considerations for grant of industrial licence must be gone into;

(*b*) Whether the proposal involves any export projection and if so the items of export and the projected destinations.

(*c*) Whether the proposal has any strategic or defence related considerations.

(B) While considering proposals the following may be prioritised.

(*i*) Items falling in infrastructure sector.

(*ii*) Items which have an export potential.

(*iii*) Items which have large scale employment potential and especially for rural people.

(*iv*) Items which have a direct or backward linkage with agro business/farm sector.

(*v*) Items which have greater social relevance such as hospitals, human resource development, life saving drugs and equipment.

(*vi*) Proposals which result in induction of technology or infusion of capital.

(C) The following should be especially considered during the scrutiny and consideration of proposals.

(*i*) The extent of foreign equity proposed to be held (keeping in view sectoral caps if any.

(*ii*) Extent of equity from the point of view whether the proposed project would amount to a holding company/wholly owned subsidiary/a company with dominant foreign investment (i.e. 76% or more) joint venture.

(*iii*) Whether the proposed foreign equity is for setting up a new project (joint venture or otherwise) or whether it is for enlargement of foreign/NRI equity or whether it is for fresh induction of foreign equity/NRI equity in an existing Indian company.

(*iv*) In the case of fresh induction offerings/NRI equity and/or in cases of enlargement of foreign/NRI equity, in existing Indian companies whether there is a resolution of the Board of Directors supporting the said induction/ enlargement of foreign/NRI equity and whether there is a shareholders agreement or not.

(v) In the case of induction of fresh equity in the existing Indian companies and/or enlargement of foreign equity in existing Indian companies, the reason why the proposal has been made and the modality for induction/ enhancement (i.e. whether by increase of paid up capital/authorized capital, transfer of shares (hostile or otherwise) whether by rights issue, or by what modality.

(vi) Issue/transfer/pricing of shares will be as per SEBI/RBI guidelines.

(vii) Whether the activity is an industrial or a service activity or a combination of both.

(viii) Whether the items of activity involves any restriction by way of reservation for the Micro & Small Enterprises sector.

(ix) Whether there are any sectoral restrictions on the activity.

(x) Whether the proposal involves import of items which are either hazardous, banned or detrimental to environment (e.g. import of plastic scrap or recycled plastics).

Constitution of FIPB

(A) FIPB comprises of the following Core Group of Secretaries to the Government of India:

(i) Secretary to Government, Department of Economic Affairs, Ministry of Finance – Chairperson

(ii) Secretary to Government, Department of Industrial Policy & Promotion, Ministry of Commerce & Industry

(iii) Secretary to Government, Department of Commerce, Ministry of Commerce & Industry

(iv) Secretary to Government, Economic Relations, Ministry of External Affairs

(v) Secretary to Government, Ministry of Overseas Indian Affairs.

(B) The Board would be able to co-opt other Secretaries to the Central Government and top officials of financial institutions, banks and professional experts of Industry and Commerce, as and when necessary.

Approval Levels for Cases under Government Route

The following approval levels shall operate for proposals involving FDI under the Government route i.e. requiring prior Government approval:

(i) The Minister of Finance who is in-charge of FIPB would consider the recommendations of FIPB on proposals with total foreign equity inflow of and below Rs.1200 crore.

(ii) The recommendations of FIPB on proposals with total foreign equity inflow of more than Rs. 1200 crore would be placed for consideration of CCEA. The FIPB Secretariat in DEA will process the recommendations of FIPB to obtain the approval of Minister of Finance and CCEA.

(iii) The CCEA would also consider the proposals which may be referred to it by the FIPB/ the Minister of Finance (in-charge of FIPB).

Policy on Route, Caps and Entry Conditions

Prohibition on Investment in India

(A) FDI is prohibited in the following activities/sectors:

(a) Retail Trading (except single brand product retailing)

(b) Atomic Energy

(c) Lottery Business including Government /private lottery, online lotteries, etc.

(d) Gambling and Betting including casinos etc.

(e) Business of chit fund

(f) Nidhi company

(g) Trading in Transferable Development Rights (TDRs)

(h) Real Estate Business or Construction of Farm Houses

(i) Activities / sectors not opened to private sector investment.

Besides foreign investment in any form, foreign technology collaboration in any form including licensing for franchise, trademark, brand name, management contract is also completely prohibited for Lottery Business and Gambling and Betting activities.

Agriculture

(A) Agriculture & Animal Husbandry

100% FDI is allowed under automatic route in Floriculture, Horticulture, Development of Seeds, Animal Husbandry, Pisciculture, Aquaculture and Cultivation of Vegetables & Mushrooms under controlled conditions and services related to agro and allied sectors.

Note: Besides the above, FDI is not allowed in any other agricultural sector/activity.

(B) For companies dealing with development of transgenic seeds/vegetables, the following conditions apply:

(*i*) When dealing with genetically modified seeds or planting material the company shall comply with safety requirements in accordance with laws enacted under the Environment (Protection) Act on the genetically modified organisms.

(*ii*) Any import of genetically modified materials if required shall be subject to the conditions laid down vide Notifications issued under Foreign Trade (Development and Regulation) Act, 1992.

(*iii*) The company shall comply with any other Law, Regulation or Policy governing genetically modified material in force from time to time.

(*iv*) Undertaking of business activities involving the use of genetically engineered cells and material shall be subject to the receipt of approvals from Genetic Engineering Approval Committee (GEAC) and Review Committee on Genetic Manipulation (RCGM).

(v) Import of materials shall be in accordance with National Seeds Policy.

(C) Tea Plantation

100% FDI is allowed in the Tea sector including tea plantations under Government route subject to the conditions of :

(*i*) Compulsory divestment of 26% equity of the company in favour of an Indian partner/Indian public within a period of 5 years

(*ii*) Prior approval of the State Government concerned in case of any future land use change.

Note: Besides the above, FDI is not allowed in any other plantation sector/activity.

Industry

(A) Mining

(*i*) 100% FDI is allowed under the automatic route in Mining and Exploration of metal and non-metal ores including diamond, gold, silver and precious ores but excluding titanium bearing minerals and its ores; subject to the Mines and Minerals (Development & Regulation) Act, 1957.

(*ii*) Coal and Lignite

(*a*) 100% FDI is allowed under the automatic route in Coal & Lignite mining for captive consumption by power projects, iron & steel and cement units and other eligible activities permitted under and subject to the provisions of Coal Mines (Nationalization) Act, 1973.

(*b*) 100% FDI is allowed for setting up coal processing plants like was heries subject to the condition that the company shall not do coal mining and shall not sell washed coal or sized coal from its coal processing plants in the open market and shall supply the washed or sized coal to those parties who are supplying raw coal to coal processing plants for washing or sizing.

(*iii*) Mining and mineral separation of titanium bearing minerals and ores, its value addition and integrated activities.

(*a*) India has large reserves of beach sand minerals in the coastal stretches around the country. Titanium bearing minerals viz. Ilmenite, rutile and leucoxene, and Zirconium bearing minerals including zircon are some of the beach sand minerals which have been classified as "prescribed substances" under the Atomic Energy Act, 1962.

(*b*) FDI up to 100% is allowed under Government route in mining and mineral separation of titanium bearing minerals & ores, its value addition and integrated activities subject to sectoral regulations and the Mines and Minerals (Development and Regulation Act 1957)

(*c*) FDI for separation of titanium bearing minerals & ores will be subject to the following additional conditions viz.:

(A) value addition facilities are set up within India along with transfer of technology;

(B) disposal of tailings during the mineral separation shall be carried out in accordance with regulations framed by the Atomic Energy Regulatory Board.

(d) FDI will not be allowed in mining of "prescribed substances" listed in the Notification No. S.O. 61(E) dated 18.1.2006 issued by the Department of Atomic Energy.

(B) Manufacturing

(*i*) Manufacture of items reserved for production in Micro and Small Enterprises (MSEs).

Any industrial undertaking which is not a Micro or Small Scale Enterprise, but manufactures items reserved for the MSE sector would require Government route where foreign investment is more than 24% in the equity capital.

(*ii*) Alcohol – Distillation & Brewing: 100% FDI is allowed under the automatic route.

(*iii*) Cigars & Cigarettes Manufacture: 100% FDI is allowed under Government route and subject to the obtaining of Industrial licence under the Industries (Development & Regulation) Act 1951.

(*iv*) Coffee & Rubber processing and warehousing: 100% FDI is allowed under the automatic route.

(*v*) Defence Industry

FDI is permissible up to 26%, under Government route subject to Industrial license under the Industries (Development & Regulation) Act 1951 and the following conditions:

(a) Licence applications will be considered and licences given by the Department of Industrial Policy & Promotion, Ministry of Commerce & Industry, in consultation with Ministry of Defence.

(b) Cases involving FDI will be considered by the FIPB and licences given by the Department of Industrial Policy & Promotion in consultation with Ministry of Defence.

(*c*) The applicant should be an Indian company / partnership firm.

(*d*) The management of the applicant company / partnership should be in Indian hands with majority representation on the Board as well as the Chief Executives of the company / partnership firm being resident Indians.

(*e*) There would be a three-year lock-in period for transfer of equity from one foreign investor to another foreign investor (including NRIs & erstwhile OCBs with 60% or more NRI stake) and such transfer would be subject to prior approval of the FIPB and the Government.

(*f*) Arms and ammunition produced by the private manufacturers will be primarily sold to the Ministry of Defence.

(*vi*) Drugs & Pharmaceuticals including those involving use of recombinant technology - 100% FDI is allowed under the automatic route

(*vii*) Hazardous chemicals viz. hydrocyanic acid and its derivatives; phosgene and its derivatives; and isocyanates and di-isocyanates of hydrocarbon - 100% FDI is allowed under the automatic route and subject to the obtaining of Industrial licence under the Industries (Development & Regulation) Act 1951.

(*viii*) Industrial Explosives - 100% FDI is allowed under the automatic route and subject to the obtaining of Industrial licence under the Industries (Development & Regulation) Act 1951 and regulations under Explosives Act 1898.

(*ix*) Power

Electric Generation, Transmission, Distribution and Trading: FDI upto 100% is permitted under automatic route for:

(*a*) Generation and transmission of electric energy produced in-hydro electric, coal/lignite based thermal, oil based thermal and gas based thermal power plants.

(*b*) Non-Conventional Energy Generation and Distribution.

(*c*) Distribution of electric energy to households, industrial, commercial and other users and

(*d*) Power Trading

The above would be subject to the provisions of the Electricity Act 2003.

Note: Above items do not include generation, transmission and distribution of electricity produced in atomic power plant/atomic energy since private investment in this sector/activity is prohibited and is reserved for public sector.

Services Sector

(A) Advertising and Films

(*i*) 100% FDI under the automatic route is allowed in Advertising sector

(*ii*) 100% FDI under the automatic route is allowed in Film Industry including film financing, production, distribution, exhibition, marketing and associated activities related to film industry.

(B) Civil Aviation Sector

The Civil Aviation sector includes Airports, Scheduled and Non-Scheduled domestic passenger airlines, Helicopter services / Seaplane services, Ground Handling Services, Maintenance and Repair organizations; Flying training institutes; and Technical training institutions.

Policy for FDI in Civil Aviation sector

(*i*) Airports:

(*a*) Greenfield projects- FDI upto 100% is allowed under the automatic route.

(*b*) Existing projects- FDI upto 100% is allowed. The investment upto 74% is under the automatic route and beyond 74% under the Government route.

(*ii*) Air Transport Services:

(*a*) Air Transport Services would include Domestic Scheduled Passenger Airlines; Non- Scheduled Airlines; Chartered Airlines; Cargo Airlines; helicopter and seaplane services.

(*b*) No foreign airlines would be allowed to participate directly or indirectly in the equity of an Air Transport Undertaking engaged in operating Scheduled, Non-Scheduled, and Chartered airlines.

(*c*) Foreign airlines are allowed to participate in the equity of companies operating Cargo airlines, helicopter and seaplane services.

(*iii*) FDI ceilings in Air Transport Services:

(*a*) Scheduled Air Transport Service/ Domestic Scheduled Passenger Airline - FDI up to 49% and investment by Non-resident Indians (NRI) up to 100% allowed on the automatic route.

(*b*) Non-Scheduled Air Transport Service/ Non-Scheduled airlines, Chartered airlines, and Cargo airlines- FDI up to 74% and investment by Non-resident Indians (NRI) up to 100% allowed. FDI in on the automatic route upto 49% and on the Government route beyond 49% and upto 74%.

(*c*) Helicopter services/seaplane services requiring DGCA approval- FDI up to 100% allowed on the automatic route.

(*iv*) FDI ceilings in other services under Civil Aviation sector

(*a*) Ground Handling Services- FDI up to 74% and investment by Non-resident Indians (NRI) up to 100% allowed. FDI under the automatic route upto 49% and through the Government route beyond 49% and upto 74%. This will be subject to sectoral regulations and security clearance.

(*b*) Maintenance and Repair organizations; flying training institutes; and technical training institutions - FDI up to 100% allowed on the automatic route. 5.15.4 The policy for FDI in the Civil Aviation Sector would be subject to the Aircraft Rules, 1934 as amended from time to time, Civil Aviation Requirements, and Aeronautical Information Circulars as notified by the Ministry of Civil Aviation.

(C) Asset Reconstruction Companies:

(*i*) 'Asset Reconstruction Company' (ARC) means a company registered with the Reserve Bank of India under Section 3 of the Securitisation and Reconstruction of Financial Assets and Enforcement of Security Interest Act, 2002.

(*ii*) Persons resident outside India, other than Foreign Institutional Investors (FIIs), can invest in the equity capital of Asset Reconstruction Companies (ARCs) registered with Reserve Bank only under the Government Route. Automatic Route is not available for such investment. Such investments have to be strictly in the nature of FDI. Investments by FIIs are not permitted in the equity capital of ARCs and FDI is restricted to 49 per cent of the paid-up capital of the ARC.

(*iii*) However, FIIs registered with SEBI can invest in the Security Receipts (SRs) issued by ARCs registered with Reserve Bank. FIIs can invest upto 49 per cent of each tranche of scheme of SRs, subject to the condition that investment by a single FII in each tranche of SRs shall not exceed 10 per cent of the issue.

(*iv*) Any individual investment of more than 10% would be subject to provisions of section 3(3) (f) of Securitization and Reconstruction of Financial Assets and Enforcement of Security Interest Act, 2002.

(D) Banking

(*i*) Private sector

(*a*) FDI limit in Private Sector Banks is 74 % including investment by FIIs. This will include FDI investment under the Portfolio Investment Scheme (PIS) by FIIs, NRIs and shares acquired prior to September 16, 2003 by erstwhile OCBs, and continue to include IPOs, Private placements, GDR/ADRs and acquisition of shares from existing shareholders. FDI as above upto 49% is under the automatic route and beyond that upto 74% on the Government route.

(*b*) The aggregate foreign investment in a private bank from all sources will be allowed up to a maximum of 74 per cent of the paid up capital of the Bank. At all times, at least 26 per cent of the paid up capital will have to be held by residents, except in regard to a wholly-owned subsidiary of a foreign bank.

(*c*) The permissible limits under portfolio investment schemes through stock exchanges for FIIs and NRIs will be as follows.

(*ii*) Banking- Public Sector

(*a*) FDI and Portfolio Investment in nationalized Banks are subject to overall statutory limit of 20% under Government route as per section 3(2D) of the Banking Companies (Acquisition & Transfer of Undertakings) Acts 1970/80. The same ceiling is also applicable to the State Bank of India and its associate Banks.

(E) Broadcasting

(*i*) Terrestrial Broadcasting FM (FM Radio): Foreign investment, including FDI, NRI and PIO investments and portfolio investments are permitted up to 20% equity for FM Radio's Broadcasting Services with prior approval of the Government.

(*ii*) Cable Network: Foreign investment, including FDI, NRI and PIO investments and portfolio investments are permitted up to 49% for Cable Networks under Government route subject to Cable Television Network Rules, 1994.

(*iii*) Direct–to-Home: Foreign investment, including FDI, NRI and PIO investments and portfolio investments are permitted up to 49% for Direct to Home under Government route. Within the limit of 49%, FDI will not exceed 20%.

(*iv*) Headend-In-The-Sky (HITS) Broadcasting Service:

(*a*) The total direct and indirect foreign investment including portfolio and foreign direct investment in HITS shall not exceed 74%. FDI upto 49% would be on automatic route and beyond that under government route.

(*v*) Setting up hardware facilities such as up-linking, HUB etc.

FDI policy in the Up-linking of TV Channels is as under:

- Foreign investment of FDI and FII up to 49% would be permitted under the Government route for setting up Up-linking HUB/ Teleports;
- FDI up to 100% would be allowed under the Government route for Up linking a Non- News & Current Affairs TV Channel;
- Foreign investment of FDI and FII up to 26% would be permitted under the Government route for Up-linking a News & Current Affairs TV Channel subject to the condition that the portfolio investment from FII/ NRI shall not be "persons acting in concert" with FDI investors,

(F) Commodity Exchanges

(*i*) Futures trading in commodities are regulated under the Forward Contracts (Regulation) Act, 1952. Commodity Exchanges, like Stock Exchanges, are infrastructure companies in the commodity futures market. With a view to infuse globally acceptable best practices, modern management skills and latest technology, it was decided to allow foreign investment in Commodity Exchanges.

(*ii*) Policy for foreign investment in Commodity Exchanges

(*a*) There is composite ceiling of 49% for foreign investment under Government route as follows:

- Investment upto 26% as Foreign Direct Investment (FDI) under the FDI Scheme incorporated as Schedule 1 under regulation 5 (1) of the Foreign Exchange Management (Transfer or Issue of Security By a Person Resident Outside India) Regulations, 2000 (FEMA Regulations)
- Investment upto 23% by registered FII under the Portfolio Investment Scheme incorporated as Schedule 2 under Regulation 5(2) of the FEMA Regulations,

(*b*) FII purchases shall be restricted to secondary market only.

(*c*) No foreign investor/ entity, including persons acting in concert, will hold more than 5% of the equity in these companies.

(G) Construction and maintenance

(*i*) 100% FDI is allowed under the automatic route in Construction and maintenance of-roads, rail-beds, bridges, tunnels, pipelines, ropeways, runways, waterways & water reservoirs, hydroelectric projects, power plants and industrial plants.

(*ii*) 100% FDI is allowed under the automatic route in construction and maintenance of Roads and highways offered on BOT basis including collection of toll.

(*iii*) 100% FDI is allowed under the automatic route in construction and maintenance of Rural Drinking Water Supply Projects, Package Water Treatment Plants, Rain and Rain Water Harvesting Structures, Waste-Water Recycling And Re-Use Techniques And Facilities, Rain-Water Re- Charging And Re-Use Techniques Of Ground Water.

(*iv*) Ports and Harbours: 100% FDI is allowed under the automatic route.

FDI upto 100% is permitted on the automatic route for Mass Rapid Transport Systems in all Metropolitan Cities including associated commercial development of real estate. The conditions at para 5.23.1, 5.23.2 and 5.23.3 would not apply.

(H) Development of Townships, Housing, Built-up infrastructure and Construction development projects.

(*i*) FDI up to 100% under the automatic route in townships, housing, built-up infrastructure and construction-development projects (which would include, but not be restricted to, housing, commercial premises, hotels, resorts, hospitals, educational institutions, recreational facilities, city and regional level infrastructure) is allowed.

(*ii*) The investment would further be subject to the following conditions:

- Minimum capitalization of US$10 million for wholly owned subsidiaries and US$ 5 million for joint ventures with Indian partners. The funds would have to be brought in within six months of commencement of business of the Company.

(*iii*) At least 50% of the project must be developed within a period of five years from the date of obtaining all statutory clearances.

(*iv*) Hotels & Tourism, Hospitals and SEZ's are exempted from the provision of J (iii and iii). Provision of J (iii and iii) would also not apply in case of investment by NRIs,

(*v*) 100% FDI is allowed under the automatic route in development of Special Economic Zones (SEZ) without the conditionalities at J (i) &(iii)

(*vi*) FDI is not allowed in Real Estate Business.

(I) Courier services for carrying packages, parcels and other items which do not come within the ambit of the Indian Post Office Act, 1898.

(*i*) 100% FDI is allowed under the Government route.

(*ii*) This will be subject to existing Law i.e Indian Post Office Act 1898 and exclusion of activity relating to the distribution of letters.

(J) Credit Information Companies (CIC)

(*i*) Foreign investment in Credit Information Companies is subject to the Credit Information Companies (Regulation) Act, 2005.

(*ii*) Foreign investment consisting of FDI and FII upto 49% is permitted under the Government route, subject to regulatory clearance from RBI.

(*iii*) Investment by a registered FII under the Portfolio Investment Scheme would be permitted up to 24% only in the CICs listed at the Stock Exchanges, within the overall limit of 49% for foreign investment.

(*iv*) Such FII investment would be permitted subject to the conditions that:

(*a*) No single entity should directly or indirectly hold more than 10% equity.

(*b*) Any acquisition in excess of 1% will have to be reported to RBI as a mandatory requirement; and

(*c*) FIIs investing in CICs shall not seek a representation on the Board of Directors based upon their shareholding.

(K) Health and Medical Services: 100% FDI is allowed under the automatic route

(L) Hotels and Tourism related Industry

(*i*) 100% Foreign Investment is allowed under automatic route.

(M) Industrial Parks - both setting up and already established Industrial Parks

(*i*) FDI up to 100% is permitted under the automatic route in Industrial Parks.

(*ii*) FDI up to 100% on the automatic route is allowed in Construction development projects,

(N) Insurance

(*i*) FDI up to 26% in the Insurance sector, as prescribed in the Insurance Act, 1999, is allowed under the automatic route.

(O) Infrastructure Company in the Securities Market:

Foreign investment is permitted in infrastructure companies in Securities Markets, namely, stock exchanges, depositories and clearing corporations, in compliance with SEBI Regulations and subject to the following conditions:

(*i*) There is a composite ceiling of 49 per cent for Foreign Investment, with a FDI limit of 26 per cent and an FII limit of 23 per cent of the paid-up capital;

(*ii*) FDI will be allowed under the Government route; and

(*iii*) FII can invest only through purchases in the secondary market.

(P) Non-Banking Finance Companies (NBFC)

(*i*) 100% foreign investment in NBFC is allowed under the automatic route in the following activities: Merchant Banking, Under Writing, Portfolio Management Services, Investment Advisory Services, Financial Consultancy, Stock Broking, Asset Management, Venture Capital , Custodian Services, Factoring, Credit Rating Agencies, Leasing & Finance, Housing Finance, Forex Broking, Credit Card Business, Money Changing Business, Micro Credit, Rural Credit

(*ii*) Investment would be subject to the following minimum capitalisation norms:

(*a*) US $0.5 million for foreign capital upto 51% to be brought upfront.

(*b*) US $5 million for foreign capital more than 51% and upto 75% to be brought upfront.

(*c*) US $50 million for foreign capital more than 75% out of which US $7.5 million to be brought upfront and the balance in 24 months.

(*d*) 100% foreign owned NBFCs with a minimum capitalisation of US $50 million can set up step down subsidiaries for specific NBFC activities.

(*e*) Joint Venture operating NBFCs that have 75% or less than 75% foreign investment can also set up subsidiaries for undertaking other NBFC activities, subject to the subsidiaries also complying with the applicable minimum capitalisation norm mentioned in (i), (ii) and (iii) above and (vi) below.

(*f*) Non- Fund based activities : US $0.5 million for all permitted non-fund based NBFCs irrespective of the level of foreign investment subject to the following condition:

It would not be permissible for such a company to set up any subsidiary for any other activity, nor it can participate in any equity of an NBFC holding/operating company.

(iii) Credit Card business includes issuance, sales, marketing & design of various payment products such as credit cards, charge cards, debit cards, stored value cards, smart card, value added cards etc.

(Q) Venture Capital Fund (VCF): A Foreign Venture Capital Investor (FVCI) may contribute upto 100% of the capital of an Indian Venture Capital Undertaking and may also set up a domestic asset management company to manage the fund. All such investments can be made under automatic route.

(R) Petroleum & Natural Gas Sector

(*i*) FDI up to 100% under the automatic route is permitted in exploration activities of oil and natural gas fields, infrastructure related to marketing of petroleum products, actual trading and marketing of petroleum products, petroleum product pipelines, natural gas/LNG pipelines, market study and formulation and Petroleum refining in the private sector.

(*ii*) FDI up to 49% is permitted under the Government route in petroleum refining by the Public Sector Undertakings (PSU). This should not involve any divestment or dilution of domestic equity in the existing PSUs.

(S) Print Media

(*i*) Publishing of Newspaper and periodicals dealing with news and current affairs: Foreign investment, including FDI and investment by NRIs/PIOs/FII, up to 26%, is permitted under the Government route.

(*ii*) Publication of Indian editions of foreign magazines dealing with news and current affairs: Foreign investment, including FDI and investment by NRIs/PIOs/FII, up to 26%, is permitted under the Government route.

(*iii*) Publishing/printing of Scientific and Technical Magazines/specialty journals/ periodicals: 100% FDI is permitted under the Government route.

(*iv*) Publication of facsimile edition of foreign newspapers: FDI up to 100% is permitted under Government route in publication of facsimile edition of foreign newspapers provided the FDI is by the owner of the original foreign newspapers whose facsimile edition is proposed to be brought out in India.

(T) Security Agencies in Private sector

The 'Private Security Agencies (Regulation) Act, 2005' regulates the operations of private security agencies. Under Section 6(2) of the above Act, "A company, firm or an association of persons shall not be considered for issue of a licence under this Act, if, it is not registered in India, or is having a proprietor or a majority shareholder, partner or director, who is not a citizen of India". As such, under the provisions of this Act: majority shareholder cannot be a foreigner-i.e. foreign shareholding would be restricted to a maximum of 49% under the Government route.

(U) Satellites – Establishment and operation:
FDI upto 74% is allowed under Government route.

(V) Storage and Warehouse Services: 100% FDI is allowed under the automatic route in Storage and Warehousing including warehousing of agricultural products with refrigeration (cold storage).

(W) Telecommunication

(*i*) Telecom services: Foreign Direct Investment limit in telecom services is 74 percent subject to the following conditions:

(*a*) This is applicable in case of Basic, Cellular, Unified Access Services, National/ International Long Distance, V-Sat, Public Mobile Radio Trunked Services (PMRTS), Global Mobile Personal Communications Services (GMPCS) and other value added Services.

(*b*) Both direct and indirect foreign investment in the licensee company shall be counted for the purpose of FDI ceiling. Foreign Investment shall include investment by Foreign Institutional Investors (FIIs), Non-resident Indians (NRIs), Foreign Currency Convertible Bonds (FCCBs), American Depository Receipts (ADRs), Global Depository Receipts (GDRs) and convertible preference shares held by foreign entity. In any case, the `Indian' shareholding will not be less than 26 percent.

(*c*) FDI up to 49 percent is on the automatic route and beyond that on the Government route FDI in the licensee company/Indian promoters/ investment companies including their holding companies shall require approval of the Foreign Investment Promotion Board (FIPB) if it has a bearing on the overall ceiling of 74 percent. While approving the investment proposals, FIPB shall take note that investment is not coming from countries of concern and/or unfriendly entities.

(*d*) FDI upto 100% is allowed for the following activities;

- Infrastructure provider providing dark fibre, right of way, duct space, tower (IP Category I)
- Electronic Mail
- Voice Mail

(*ii*) The investment upto 49% is under the automatic route and beyond 49% under the Government route.

(X) Trading

(*i*) 100% FDI is permitted under the automatic route for trading companies for the following activities:

(*a*) Cash & Carry trading Wholesale Trading/ Wholesale Trading.

Cash & Carry Wholesale trading/Wholesale trading, would mean sale of goods/merchandise to retailers, industrial, commercial, institutional or other professional business users or to other wholesalers and related subordinated service providers.

(*b*) Guidelines for Cash & Carry Wholesale Trading/Wholesale Trading (WT): For undertaking WT, requisite licenses/registration/ permits, as specified under the relevant Acts/Regulations/ Rules/Orders of the State Government/ Government Body/Government Authority/Local Self-Government Body under that State Government should be obtained.

(*c*) Trading for exports. E-commerce activities: E-commerce activities refer to the activity of buying and selling by a company through the e-commerce platform. 100% FDI is permitted under the Government route for trading companies

(Y) Transport and Transport Support Services: 100% FDI under the automatic route is allowed for:

(*i*) Pipeline transport, ocean and water transport, inland water transport.

(*ii*) Transport Support Services

(Z) Other Sectors: In sectors/Activities not listed above, FDI is permitted upto 100% on the automatic route subject to applicable laws/sectoral rules/regulations.

2. Portfolio Investment

If investor has only a sort of property interest investing the capital in buying equities, bonds, or other securities abroad. It is referred to as Portfolio Investment. Investor uses his capital in order to get a return on it, but has not much control over the use of the capital. 'Foreign Institutional Investor'(FII) means an entity established or incorporated outside India which proposes to make investment in India and which is registered as a FII in accordance with the SEBI (FII) Regulations 1995. Foreign institutional investment also means that investment made by foreign institutions such as pension funds, mutual funds, investment trust, asset management companies and other specified institutions, in the securities traded on the domestic primary and secondary markets. In the case of India, securities includes shares, debentures, warrants, other schemes floated by domestic mutual funds and other securities specified by the government of India from time to time. These are regarded as portfolio investments from the point of view of Foreign Institutional Investors since they do not grant them any managerial control. Although Government of India treats Investments in Foreign Currency Convertible Bonds and Global Depositary Receipts underlying equity shares by FIIs as direct investments, these are portfolio investments from the point of view of FIIs.

Historical Perspective of FII Investment Policy

India embarked on a gradual shift towards capital account convertibility with the launch of the reforms in the early 1990s. Although foreign natural persons – except NRIs – are prohibited from investing in financial assets, such investments were permitted by FIIs and Overseas Corporate Bodies (OCBs) with suitable restrictions. Ever since September 14, 1992, when FIIs were first allowed to invest in all the securities traded on the primary and secondary markets, including shares, debentures and warrants issued by companies which were listed or were to be listed on the Stock Exchanges in India and in the schemes floated by domestic mutual funds, the holding of a single FII and of all FIIs, Non-resident Indians (NRIs) and OCBs in any company were subject to the limit of 5 per cent and 24 per cent of the company's total issued capital, respectively. Furthermore, funds invested by FIIs had to have at least 50 participants with no one holding more than 5 per cent to ensure a broad base and preventing such investment acting as a camouflage for individual investment in the nature of FDI and requiring Government approval.

Initially the idea of allowing FIIs was that they were broad-based, diversified funds, leaving out individual foreign investors and foreign companies. The only exception were the NRI and OCB portfolio investments through the secondary market, which were subject to individual ceilings of 5 per cent to prevent a possible "take over." Individuals were left out because of the difficulties in checking on their antecedents, and of their lack of expertise in market matters and relatively short-term perspective. OCB investments through the portfolio route have been banned since November, 2001.

In February, 2000, the FII regulations were amended to permit foreign corporates and high net worth individuals to also invest as sub-accounts of Securities and Exchange Board of India (SEBI)-registered FIIs. Foreign corporates and high net worth individuals fall outside the category of diversified investors. FIIs were also permitted to seek SEBI registration in respect of sub-accounts for their clients under the regulations. While initially FIIs were permitted to manage the sub-account of clients, the domestic portfolio managers or domestic asset management companies were also allowed to manage the funds of such sub accounts and also to make application on behalf of such sub-accounts. Such sub-accounts could be an institution, or a fund, or a portfolio established or incorporated outside India, or a broad-based fund, or a proprietary fund, or even a foreign corporate or individual. So, in practice there are common categories of entities, which could be registered as both FIIs and sub-accounts. However, investment in to a sub account is to be made either by FIIs, or by domestic portfolio manager or asset management company, and not by itself directly.

In view of the recent concerns of some unregulated entities taking positions in the stock market through the mechanism of Participatory Notes (PNs) issued by FIIs, the issue was examined by the Ministry of Finance in consultation with the Reserve Bank of India (RBI) and SEBI. Following this consultation, in January 2004, SEBI stipulated that PNs are not to be issued to any non-regulated entity, and the principle of "know your clients" may be strictly adhered to. SEBI has indicated that the existing non-eligible PNs, will be permitted to expire or to be wound-down on maturity, or within a period of 5 years, whichever is earlier. Besides, reporting requirement on a regular basis has been imposed on all the FIIs.

Eligibility Criteria

The following entities, established or incorporated abroad, are eligible to be registered as FIIs: (a) Pension Funds, (b) Mutual Funds, (c) Investment Trusts, (d) Asset Management Companies, (e) Nominee Companies, (f) Banks, (g) Institutional Portfolio Managers, (h) Trustees, (i) Power of Attorney holders, (j) University funds, endowments, foundations or charitable trusts or charitable societies. Besides the above, a domestic portfolio manager or domestic asset management company is now also eligible to be registered as an FII to manage the funds of sub accounts. The FIIs can also invest on behalf of sub-accounts. The following entities are entitled to be registered as sub-accounts: i) an institution or fund or portfolio established or incorporated outside India, ii) a foreign corporate or a foreign individual.

Registration

FIIs registered with SEBI fall under the following categories:

(*a*) Regular FIIs – those who are required to invest not less than 70 per cent of their investment in equity-related instruments and up to 30 per cent in non-equity instruments.

(*b*) 100 per cent debt-fund FIIs – those who are permitted to invest only in debt instruments.

Restructuring of Approval Process

(*i*) A Working Group for Streamlining of the Procedures relating to FIIs constituted in April, 2003 by the Government, inter alia, recommended streamlining of SEBI registration procedure, and suggested that dual approval process of SEBI and RBI be changed to a single approval process of SEBI. This recommendation has since been implemented.

(*ii*) Forward cover in respect of equity funds for outstanding investments of FIIs over and above such investments on June 11, 1998 was permitted. Subsequently, forward cover up to a maximum of 15 per cent of the outstanding position on June 11, 1998 was also permitted. This 15 per cent limit was liberalized to 100 per cent of portfolio value as on March 31, 1999 in January 2003.

(*iii*) Like in other countries, the restrictions on FII investment have been progressively liberalized. From November 1996, any registered FII willing to make 100 per cent investment in debt securities were permitted to do so subject to specific approval from SEBI as a separate category of FIIs or sub-accounts as 100 per cent debt funds. Such investments by 100 per cent debt funds were, however, subject to fund-specific ceilings specified by SEBI and an overall debt cap of US $1-1.5 billion. Moreover, investments were allowed only in debt securities of companies listed or to be listed in stock exchanges. Investments were free from maturity limitations.

(*iv*) From April 1998, FII investments were also allowed in dated Government securities. Treasury bills being money market instruments were originally outside the ambit of such investments, but were subsequently included from May, 1998. Such investments, which are external debt of the Government denominated in rupees, were encouraged to deepen the debt market. From April, 1997, the aggregate limit for all FIIs, which was 24 per cent, was allowed to be increased up to 30 per cent by the Indian company concerned by passing a resolution by its Board of Directors followed by a special resolution to that effect by its General Body.

(*v*) While permitting foreign corporates/high net worth individuals in February, 2000 to invest through SEBI registered FII/domestic fund managers, it was noted that there was a clear distinction between portfolio investment and FDI. The basic presumption is that FIIs are not interested in management control. To allay fears of management control being exercised by portfolio investors, it was noted that adequate safety nets were in force, for example, (i) transaction of business in securities on the stock exchanges are only through stock brokers who have been granted a certificate by SEBI, (ii) every transaction is settled through a custodian who is under obligation to report to SEBI and RBI for all transactions on a daily basis, (iii) provisions of SEBI (Substantial Acquisition of Shares and Takeovers) Regulations, 1997 (iv) monitoring of sectoral caps by RBI on a daily basis.

(*vi*) In 1998, the aggregate portfolio investment limits of NRIs/PIOs/OCBs and FIIs were enhanced from 5 per cent to 10 per cent and the ceilings of FIIs and NRIs/OCBs were declared to be independent of each other.

(*vii*) Aggregate FII portfolio investment ceiling was enhanced from 30 per cent to 40 per cent of the issued and paid up capital of a company [March 01 2000]. The enhanced ceiling was made applicable only under a special procedure that required approval by the Board of Directors and a Special Resolution by the General Body of the relevant company. The FII ceiling under the special procedure was further enhanced [March 08

2001] from 40 per cent to 49 per cent. Subsequently, the FII ceiling under the special procedure was raised up to the sectoral cap in September, 2001.

Role of FII Investment

Role of FII assessment can be assessed in following ways:

(*i*) "Various supply and demand factors have made investing via institutions a rapidly growing sector in many developed countries".[5] There is enhanced supply of funds from investors to institutions because of the aging of population, funded pension systems, and growing wealth. Institutions are also able to give better services and attractive returns because of ease of diversification, better corporate governance, liquidity, deregulation and fiscal incentives. Given this background, there is likely to be a large and growing demand for Indian stocks by FIIs.

(*ii*) It is of some importance to note that the bouts of liberalization of the FII regime has coincided with pressure on the foreign exchange and balance of payments fronts, for example, in the aftermath of the 1991 crisis and around the 1997 East Asian crisis. Now that there is no apparent balance of payments problem, the critical question is whether there are any reasons for liberalizing the FII regime.

(*iii*) FIIs have a natural advantage in processing information. One of the problems noted for such investment in emerging markets consists in the lower amount of reliable and quality information available in such countries relative to developed ones. It can be expected that with rapid progress in disclosure norms, accounting standards, shareholder rights, legal framework, and corporate governance in general, FII investments are going to accelerate in India. FII investments in some companies are already at their ceiling level, and the ceiling is much below the stakes that FIIs have acquired in some of the top Korean chaebols.

(*iv*) Countries that have liberalized their FII regimes did not do it out of balance of payments compulsions. Taiwan, for example, removed all restrictions – previously 10 per cent individually and 25 per cent collectively until March 1998, and 15 per cent and 30 per cent until January 1, 2001 – from the beginning of 2001. People's Republic of China, without a balance of payments problem, opened itself up to FII investment in 2003. Swiss Bank UBS, by buying into four of China's A-share stocks – Baoshan Iron and Steel, Shanghai Port Container, Sinotrans Air, and ZTE Corp – became the first FII to enter the Chinese market on Wednesday, July 9, 2003.

Advantage of FII Investment

The advantages of having FII investments can be broadly classified under the following categories.

(*i*) **Enhanced flows of equity capital:** FIIs are well known for a greater appetite for equity than debt in their asset structure. For example, pension funds in the United Kingdom and United States had 68 per cent and 64 per cent, respectively, of their portfolios in equity in 1998. Thus, opening up the economy to FIIs is in line with the accepted preference for non-debt creating foreign inflows over foreign debt. Furthermore, because of this preference for equities over bonds, FIIs can help in compressing the yield-differential between equity and bonds and improve corporate capital structures. Further, given the existing savings-investment gap of around 1.6 per cent, FII inflows can also contribute in bridging the investment gap so that sustained high GDP growth rate of around 8 per cent targeted under the 10th Five Year Plan can materialize.

(*ii*) **Managing uncertainty and controlling risks:** Institutional investors promote financial innovation and development of hedging instruments. Institutions, for example, because of their interest in hedging risks, are known to have contributed to the development of zero-coupon bonds and index futures. FIIs, as professional bodies of asset managers and financial analysts, not only enhance competition in financial markets, but also improve the alignment of asset prices to fundamentals.

(*iii*) **Good and Effective Informational Base:** Institutions in general and FIIs in particular are known to have good information and low transaction costs. By aligning asset prices closer to fundamentals, they stabilize markets. Fundamentals are known to be sluggish in their movements. Thus, if prices are aligned to fundamentals, they should be as stable as the fundamentals themselves. Furthermore, a variety of FIIs with a variety of risk-return preferences also help in dampening volatility.

(*iv*) **Improving capital markets:** "FIIs as professional bodies of asset managers and financial analysts enhance competition and efficiency of financial markets. Equity market development aids economic development."[6] By increasing the availability of riskier long term capital for projects, and increasing firms' incentives to supply more information about themselves, the FIIs can help in the process of economic development.

(*v*) **Improved corporate governance:** Good corporate governance is essential to overcome the principal-agent problem between share-holders and management. Information asymmetries and incomplete contracts between share-holders and management are at the root of the agency costs. Dividend payment, for example, is discretionary. Bad corporate governance makes equity finance a costly option. With boards often captured by managers or passive, ensuring the rights of shareholders is a problem that needs to be addressed efficiently in any economy. Incentives for shareholders to monitor firms and enforce their legal rights are limited and individuals with small share-holdings often do not address the issue since others can free-ride on their endeavour. What is needed is large shareholders with leverage to complement their legal rights and overcome the free-rider problem, but shareholding beyond say 5 per cent can also lead to exploitation of minority shareholders.

(*vi*) **Professional Working Behaviour**: FIIs constitute professional bodies of asset managers and financial analysts, who, by contributing to better understanding of firms' operations, improve corporate governance. Among the four models of corporate control – takeover or market control via equity, leveraged control or market control via debt, direct control via equity, and direct control via debt or relationship banking – the third model, which is known as corporate governance movement, has institutional investors at its core. In this third model, board representation is supplemented by direct contacts by institutional investors. Institutions are known for challenging excessive executive compensation, and remove underperforming managers. There is some evidence that institutionalization increases dividend payouts, and enhances productivity growth.

Apprehensions About FIIs

The two common apprehensions about FII inflows are the fear of management takeovers and potential capital outflows.

A. Management control

(*i*) FIIs act as agents on behalf of their principals – as financial investors maximizing returns. There are domestic laws that effectively prohibit institutional investors from taking management control. For example, US law prevents mutual funds from owning more than 5 per cent of a company's stock.

(*ii*) According to the International Monetary Fund's Balance of Payments Manual 5, FDI is that category of international investment that reflects the objective of obtaining a lasting interest by a resident entity in one economy in an enterprise resident in another economy. The lasting interest implies the existence of a long-term relationship between the direct investor and the enterprise and a significant degree of influence by the investor in the management of the enterprise. According to EU law, foreign investment is labeled direct investment when the investor buys more than 10 per cent of the investment target, and portfolio investment when the acquired stake is less than 10 per cent.

(*iii*) Institutional investors on the other hand are specialized financial intermediaries managing savings collectively on behalf of investors, especially small investors, towards specific objectives in terms of risk, returns, and maturity of claims.

(*iv*) All take-overs are governed by SEBI (Substantial Acquisition of Shares and Takeovers) Regulations, 1997, and sub-accounts of FIIs are deemed to be "persons acting in concert" with other persons in the same category unless the contrary is established. In addition, reporting requirement have been imposed on FIIs and currently Participatory Notes cannot be issued to un-regulated entities abroad.

B. Potential capital outflows

(*i*) FII inflows are popularly described as "hot money", because of the herding behaviour and potential for large capital outflows. Herding behaviour, with all the FIIs trying to either only buy or only sell at the same time, particularly at times of market stress, can be rational.[7] With performance-related fees for fund managers, and performance judged on the basis of how other funds are doing, there is great incentive to suffer the consequences of being wrong when everyone is wrong, rather than taking the risk of being wrong when some others are right. The incentive structure highlights the danger of a contrarian bet going wrong and makes it much more severe than performing badly along with most others in the market. It not only leads to reliance on the same information as others but also reduces the planning horizon to a relatively short one. Value at Risk models followed by FIIs may destabilize markets by leading to simultaneous sale by various FIIs, as observed in Russia and Long Term Capital Management 1998 (LTCM) crisis. Extrapolative expectations or trend chasing rather than focusing on fundamentals can lead to destabilization. Movements in the weightage attached to a country by indices such as Morgan Stanley Country Index (MSCI) or International Finance Corporation (W) (IFC) also leads to en masse shift in FII portfolios.

(*ii*) Another source of concern are hedge funds, who, unlike pension funds, life insurance companies and mutual funds, engage in short-term trading, take short positions and borrow more aggressively, and numbered about 6,000 with $500 billion of assets under control in 1998.

(*iii*) Some of these issues have been relevant right from 1992, when FII investments were allowed in. The issues, which continue to be relevant even today, are: (i) benchmarking with the best practices in other developing countries that compete with India for similar investments; (ii) if management control is what is to be protected, is there a reason to put a restriction on the maximum amount of shares that can be held by a foreign investor rather than the maximum that can be held by all foreigners put together; and (iii) whether the limit of 24 per cent on FII investment will be over and above the 51 per cent limit on FDI. There are some other issues such as whether the existing ceiling on the ratio between equities and debentures in an FII portfolio of 70:30 should continue or not, but this is beyond the terms of reference of the Committee.

(*iv*) It may be noted that all emerging peer markets have some restrictions either in terms of quantitative limits across the board or in specified sectors, such as, telecom, media, banks, finance companies, retail trading medicine, and exploration of natural resources. Against this background, further across the board relaxation by India in all sectors except a few very specific sectors to be excluded, may considerably enhance the attractiveness of India as a destination for foreign portfolio flows. It is felt that with adequate institutional safeguards now in place the special procedure mechanism for raising FII investments beyond 24 per cent may be dispensed with.

Committee on FIIs Portfolio Investment

Originally, Committee on FII's Portfolio Investment was constituted on March 13, 2002 under the Chairmanship of Dr. Rakesh Mohan, then Advisor to Union Finance Minister. However, committee was reconstituted on May17, 2004 with the following members:

(*i*)	Dr. Ashok K. Lahiri, Chief Economic Adviser	Chairman
(*ii*)	Shri U.K. Sinha, Joint Secretary (Capital Markets), Dept. of Economic Affairs, Ministry of Finance, Government of India	Member
(*iii*)	Sri Umesh Kumar, Joint Secretary, Dept. of Industrial Policy and Promotions, Government of India.	Member

Main Recommendations of the Committee

Given the necessity of boosting agricultural growth through development of agro processing, and expanding industry by at least 10 per cent per year to integrate not only the surplus labour in agriculture but also the unprecedented number of women and teenagers joining the labour force every year, there is an urgent need to scale up investment in the economy. FII inflows can help in augmenting the investible resources in the economy, and the following measures may be considered for increasing the availability of stocks eligible for such portfolio investments:-

A. Recommendations in para A will apply, in general, to all sectors.[8]

(*i*) In general, FII investment ceilings, if any, may be reckoned over and above prescribed FDI sectoral caps. The 24 per cent limit on FII investment imposed in 1992 when allowing FII inflows was exclusive of the FDI limit. The suggested measure will be in conformity with this original stipulation.

(*ii*) Special procedure for raising FII investments beyond 24per cent upto the FDI limit in a company may be dispensed with by amending the relevant SEBI (FII) Regulations.

(*iii*) In order to provide dispersed investments and prevent concentration, the existing limit of 10 per cent by a FII in a single company may continue.

B. Specific recommendations are being made for the following sectors keeping in mind their special nature:

(*i*) For telecommunications services, defence production, public sector banks and insurance companies, where composite limits on FDI and FII investments apply, the following is recommended:-

(*a*) Telecom services: As recommended by the earlier Group of Ministers to the Union Cabinet and taking into account security considerations, while the Composite cap may be maintained, it may be enhanced to 74 per cent of the paid up capital without separate sub-ceilings.

(*b*) Defence production: In this strategic sector a limit of 26 per cent applies on FDI. A composite cap of 49 per cent may be imposed with no sub ceiling for FDI and FII.

(*c*) Public sector banks: In public sector banks where a composite cap of 20 per cent for foreign investments applies, FII investment up to 20 per cent over and above the existing cap of 20 per cent should be allowed. However, FIIs will have no representation on the board of these banks. If necessary, the statutes may be amended for this purpose.

(*d*) Insurance companies: In insurance companies, a composite cap of 26 per cent for FDI and FII investments applies. Like in defence production, this composite cap may be enhanced to 49 per cent by amending the relevant statutes.

(*ii*) In print media, FII investment is prohibited under regulation 5(2) of FEMA notification No.20 dated May 3, 2000, (as amended in terms of FEMA Notification No.35/2001-RB dated February 16, 2001). The same may continue for the time being

(*iii*) Similarly, gambling, betting, lottery, which are areas of dubious value added and where FDI is prohibited, may also be kept out of bounds for FII investments.

(*iv*) In retail trading currently FDI is prohibited. FII investments, however, are permitted up to 24 per cent in all listed companies, except in print media companies. Accordingly, FII investments in retail trading cannot exceed 24 per cent as no FDI is permitted. This restriction may continue, as it will help develop supply chains in a wide range of products, including that of agriculture.

(*v*) Sectors which are not yet open for private investments, e.g., terrestrial broadcasting and postal services (delivery of letters) should explicitly be prohibited for FII investments, as no investible securities are available.

Sector with Portfolio Investment Limits[9]

Committee has analysed the current guidelines and proposed the following sector wise Portfolio investment limits given in Exhibit-13.1

Exhibit-13.1
Current and Proposed Portfolio Investment Limits

Sl. No.	Sector	FDI Limits (S/A) S = Statutory A= Administrative	Current FII Limits	Proposed FII Limits
1.	Agriculture (including plantation)	The FDI Cap is Administrative. No FDI/NRI investment is permitted other than Tea Plantation.	100 percent in Tea Plantation.	100 in Tea Plantation.
2.	Atomic minerals	The FDI Cap is Administrative. Mining and mineral separation Value addition per se to the products of (a) above. Integrated activities [comprising of both (a) and (b) above.]	74 percent	100 percent
3.	Broadcasting	The FDI Cap is Administrative. Broadcasting a) Setting up hardware facilities, such as unlinking, HUB, etc. b) Cable Network c) Direct-to-Home d) Terrestrial Broadcasting FM e) Terrestrial TV	49 per cent Inclusive of FDI 49 percent Inclusive of FDI 49 percent Inclusive of FDI limit of 20 percent Nil	100 per cent 100 per cent 100 per cent 100 per cent Nil
4.	Coal and Lignite	The FDI Cap is Administrative. i) Non-PSUs ii) PSUs	74 percent 49 percent inclusive of FDI	100 percent 49 percent inclusive of FDI
5.	Defence and strategic industries	The FDI Cap is Administrative. Foreign Direct Investment is permitted up to 26 per cent with prior Government approval.	26 percent	49 percent (inclusive of FDI)
6.	Domestic Airlines	The FDI Cap is Administrative. (Detailed guidelines have been issue by Ministry of Civil Aviation) In the Domestic Airlines (i) FDI upto 40 percent (ii) 100 percent investment by NRI	40 percent	80 percent (inclusive of FDI)
7.	Establishment and Operation of	The FDI Cap is Administrative.	74 percent	100 percent

Contd....

	Satellite			
8.	Housing and Real Estate	The FDI Cap is Administrative.	24 percent	24 percent
9.	Lottery business, gambling and betting	Government has reiterated prohibition of foreign direct investment (FDI) / Foreign technical collaboration (FTC) in any form in lottery business, gambling and betting sector.	Nil	Nil
10.	Mining	The FDI CAP is Administrative. i. For exploration and mining of diamonds and precious stones FDI is allowed up to 74 per cent under automatic route	74 percent	100 percent
11.	Petroleum	The FDI Cap is Administrative (excluding PSU refineries) PSUs	100 percent (excluding PSUs) 26 percent	100 percent (excluding PSUs) 49 percent Inclusive of FDI
12	Postal services Courier services excel distribution of letters	The FDI Cap is Administrative.	100 percent	100 percent
13.	Print Media	The FDI Cap is Administrative.	Nil	Nil
14.	Private Sector Banking	The FDI Cap is Administrative. 74 per cent from all sources on the automatic route.	74 percent	100 percent
	Public Sector Banking	The FDI Cap is Statutory. 20 per cent from all sources	20 percent inclusive of FDI	40 percent inclusive of FDI
	Insurance	The FDI Cap is Statutory. FDI up to 26 per cent in the Insurance sector is allowed on the automatic route subject to obtaining license from Insurance Regulatory & Development Authority (IRDA)	26 percent inclusive of FDI	49 percent inclusive of FDI
15.	Telecommunication	The FDI Cap is Administrative. i) In basic, cellular, value added services and global mobile personal communications by satellite, FDI is limited to 49 per cent subject to licensing and security requirements (FDI +FII put together.) ii) In ISPs with gateways, radio-paging and end-to end bandwidth, FDI is permitted up to 74 per cent	49 percent inclusive of FDI 74 percent Inclusive of FDI	74 per cent inclusive of FDI 74 per cent inclusive of FDI
16.	Retail Trading	The FDI Cap is Administrative. FDI is not permitted in retail trading activity.	24 percent	24 percent
17.	Venture Capital	The FDI Cap is Administrative. Offshore Venture Capital Funds/Companies are allowed to invest in domestic Venture Capital Fund (VCF) and undertaking as well as other companies through the automatic route, subject only to SEBI Company(VCC) regulations and sector Venture Capital specific caps on FDI.	Nil	Nil

Restriction on Foreign Ownership[10]

Following restriction have been imposed on foreign ownership as given in Exhibit-13.2.

Exhibit-13.2

Restrictions on Foreign Ownership in the Emerging Markets

Sl.No.	Country	Investment Restrictions
1.	India	1. Each FII (investing on its own) or sub-account cannot hold more than 10 per cent of the paid-up capital of a company. A sub account under the foreign corporate/individual category cannot hold more than 5 per cent of the paid up capital of the company. 2. The maximum permissible investment in the shares of a company, jointly by all FIIs together is 24 per cent of the paid-up capital of that company. 3. This limit of 24 per cent can be raised to 30 per cent, 40 per cent, 49 percent or up to the FDI limits specified for that particular sector, subject to approval from the shareholders and the RBI. 4. In the case of public sector banks, the foreign ownership limit is 20 percent.
2.	China	1. Subject to the approved investment quota, QFII can invest on the following financial instruments: • Shares listed in China's stock exchanges (excluding B shares); • Treasuries listed in China's stock exchanges;* • Convertible bonds and enterprise bonds listed in China's stock • exchanges;* • Other financial instruments as approved by CSRC.** 2. QFII should observe the following requirements in A shares: • Shares held by each QFII in one listed company should not exceed • 10 per cent of total outstanding shares of the company; • Total shares held by all QFII in one listed company should not exceed • 20 per cent of total outstanding shares of the company. 3. No restriction on investment in B shares. 4. QFIIs are restricted or prohibited from investing in some industries or businesses (e.g. medicine manufacturing, mining, telecommunications, etc.)
3.	Taiwan	1. Foreign institutional investors (FINIs) have no limit on investment while foreign individual investors (FIDIs) are subject to a US $5 million investment quota. 2. Foreign investors may invest up to 100 per cent of public-listed companies. However, foreign ownership limitation remains for some public listed companies per the regulations and rules of relevant governing authorities e.g. banking industry where individual ownership cannot exceed 25 per cent for a single investor, and telecommunications companies, except the staterun Chunghwa Telecom stayed capped at 20 per cent, the foreign ownership of which cannot exceed 49 per cent. 3. Foreign investors are allowed to put 30 per cent of their investment capital in TWD fixed deposits, margins or premiums of futures or options trading, and money market instruments (including bankers' acceptances, commercial papers and repos).
4.	South Korea	Foreign ownership limits on listed stocks have mostly been abolished. However, there are now 22 stocks that still have foreign ownership ceilings. Those include stocks issued by public companies and companies in specific industries such as broadcasting, aviation and telecommunications.
5.	Hongkong	There is no restriction on foreign investment except the Hong Kong Television Broadcast stock that foreigners cannot hold more than 10 per cent and 49 per cent in aggregate.

Contd....

6.	Indonesia	Currently, there are no restrictions on foreigners or non-residents investment in listed securities except for media stocks, in which the aggregate foreign ownership limit of 20 per cent applies.
7.	Thailand	Company whether listed or not. Foreign ownership may be limited by laws governing investment promotion licenses, concession permits, a particular company's memorandum/ Articles of Association or some specific areas of business, such as commercial banks and finance companies where the limit on foreign ownership is 25 per cent.
8.	Malaysia	Foreign investors are allowed to freely invest in any securities listed on the Stock Exchange. However, there are companies with foreign ownership limits. There are currently 36 companies listed on the MSEB which have foreign shareholding limit. Foreign shareholdings limit can range between 25 percent to 79 percent although the general limit is 30 percent. For banks and finance companies, the limit for foreign interest in local companies is 30 percent.
9.	Philippines	Different industries are subject to different limits for foreign ownership. These limits range from zero to 60per cent of the total equity of the enterprise: • No foreign equity participation is allowed in mass media, engineering, medicine & other professional activities, retail trading, small scale mining etc. • Upto 20 per cent foreign equity is allowed in private radio communication • Upto 25 per cent and 30per cent foreign equity is allowed in private recruitment, locally funded public works; and advertising respectively • Upto 40 per cent foreign equity is allowed in Exploration, development. • and utilization of natural resources, real estate, public utilities, education institutes, Operation of deep sea commercial fishing vessels etc. • Upto 40 per cent foreign equity is allowed in financing companies and investment houses regulated by the SEC.
10.	Sri Lanka	Foreign ownership limits are: • Banking – 60 per cent • Insurance – 90 per cent • Stock broking Firms Licensed by the SEC – 100 per cent

* On 2 December 2002, the Shanghai Stock Exchange and Shenzhen Stock Exchange announced in their "Implementing Rules for Securities Trading of Qualified Foreign Institutional Investors" that QFIIs cannot trade in corporate bonds and treasury bond repurchases until further notice.

** According to the CSRC, QFIIs can also invest in open-end or closed-end investment funds approved by the CSRC, initial public offers, rights issues, additional share issues and convertible bond issues.

Role of Foreign Institutional Investors in Indian Portfolio Investments

Foreign Institutional Investors (FIIs) invest in various countries including emerging market in order to reduce risk through portfolio diversification and also to receive additional returns. Country-specific factors are important determinants of such institutional investment.

A scheme for attracting portfolio from Foreign Institutional Investors (FIIs) has been operational since September, 1992. Under this scheme, FIIs including institutions such as Pension Funds, Mutual Funds, Investment Trusts, Asset Management Companies, Nominee Companies and Incorporated/ Institutional Portfolio Managers or their power of attorney holders are allowed to invest in all the securities traded on the primary and secondary markets. Such securities would include shares, debentures and warrants issued by companies which are listed/to be listed on the Stock Exchanges in India and the schemes floated by domestic mutual funds. FIIs are permitted to invest in Government securities including Treasury Bills. FIIs who register themselves as debt Funds with SEBI are permitted to make 100% of their investment in Debt securities of Indian companies. Such portfolio investments by FIIs are subject to investment ceilings as indicated below:

A. Individual FIIs/Sub-account: 10% of the issued and paid-up capital in a company.

B. Aggregate by all FIIs: 24% of the issued and paid up capital in a company.

The aggregate ceiling for FII portfolio investments through the secondary market could be raised beyond the normal level of 24% upto the sectoral cap/statutory ceiling as applicable, subject to compliance with the specific procedure prescribed. The aggregate ceiling is separate and exclusive of NRI portfolio ceiling.

Guidelines for Investment by Foreign Institutional Investors

The Government of India has formulated following guidelines regarding portfolio investment.

(i) Foreign institutional investors (FIIs) including institutions such as Pension Funds, Mutual Funds, Investment Trusts, Asset Incorporated/Institutional Portfolio Managers or their power of attorney holders (providing discretionary and non-discretionary portfolio management services) and non-discretionary portfolio management services) would be welcome to make investments under these guidelines.

(ii) FIIs would be welcome to invest in all the securities traded on the Primary and Secondary markets, including the equity and other securities/instruments of companies which are listed/ to be listed on the Stock exchange in India including the OTC exchange of India. These would include shares, debentures, warrants, and the schemes floated by domestic Mutual Funds. Government may even like to add further categories of securities later from time to time.

(iii) FIIs would be required to obtain an initial registration with Securities and Exchange Board of India (SEBI), the nodal regulatory agency for securities market, before any investment is made by them in the securities of companies listed on the stock exchange in India, in accordance with these guidelines. Nominee companies, affiliates and subsidiary companies of a FII will be treated as separate FIIs for registration with SEBI.

(iv) Since there are foreign exchange controls also in force, for various permissions under exchange control, along with their application for initial registration FIIs shall also file with SEBI another application addressed to RBI for seeking various permissions under FERA, in a format that would be specified by RBI for this purpose. RBIs general permission would be obtained by SEBI before granting initial registration and RBIs FERA permission together by SEBI, under a single window approach.

(v) For granting registration to the FIIs, SEBI shall take in to account the track record of the FII, its professional competence, financial soundness, experience and such other criteria that may be considered by SEBI to be relevant. Besides, FII seeking initial registration from the Securities Commission, or the regulatory organization for the stock market in the country of domicile/incorporation of the FII.

(vi) SEBI's initial registration would be valid for five years. RBI's general permission under FERA to the FII will also hold good for five years. Both will be renewable for similar five-year periods later on.

(vii) RBI's general permission under FERA would enable the registered FII to buy, sell and realize capital gains on investments made through initial corpus, remitted to India, subscribe/ renounce rights offerings of shares, invest on all recognized stock exchanges through a designated bank branch, and to appoint a domestic Custodian for custody of investments held.

(viii) This General Permission from RBI shall also enable the FII to:

a. Open foreign currency denominated accounts in a designated bank. (There can even be more than one account in the same bank branch each designated in different foreign currencies, if it is so required by FII for its operational purpose);

b. Open a special non-resident rupee account which could be credited all receipts from the capital inflows, sale proceeds of shares, dividends and interests;

c. Transfer sums from the foreign currency accounts to the rupee account and vice-versa, at the market rate of exchange;

d. Make investments in the securities in India out of the balances in the rupee account;

e. Transfer repatriable (after tax) proceeds from the rupee account to the foreign currency account(s);

f. Repatriate the capital, capital gains, dividends, incomes received by way of interest, etc. and any compensation received towards sale/renouncement of rights offerings of shares subject to the designated branch of a bank/the custodian being authorized to deduct withholding tax on capital gains and arranging to pay such tax and remitting the net proceeds at market rates of exchange;

g. Register FII's holdings without any further clearance under FERA.

(*ix*) There would be no restriction on the volume of investment minimum or maximum-for the purpose of entry of FIIs, in the primary/secondary market. Also there would be no lock-in-period prescribed for the purpose of such investments made by FIIs. It is expected that the differential in the rates of taxation of the long-term capital gains and short-term capital gains would automatically induce the FIIs to retain their investments as long-term investments.

(*x*) Portfolio investments in primary to a ceiling of 30% of issued share capital for the total holdings of all registered FIIs, in any one company. The ceiling would apply to all holdings taking into account the conversions out of the fully and partly convertible debentures issued by the company. The holding of a single FII in any company would also be subject to a ceiling of 10% of total issued capital. For this purpose, the holdings of an FII group will be counted as holdings of a single FII.

(*xi*) The maximum holdings of 24% for all non-resident portfolio investments, including those of the registered FIIs, will also include NRI corporate and non-corporate investments, but will not include the following:

1. Foreign investments under financial collaborations (direct foreign investments), which are permitted upto 51% in all priority areas.
2. Investments by FIIs through the following alternative routes:
   a. offshore single/regional funds;
   b. Global Depository Receipts;
   c. Euro convertibles

(*xii*) Disinvestments will be allowed only through stock exchange in India, including the OTC Exchange. In exceptional cases, SEBI may permit sales other than through stock exchanges, provided the sale price is not significantly different from the stock market quotations, where available.

(*xiii*) All secondary market operations would be only through the recognized intermediaries on the Indian Stock Exchange, including OTC Exchange of India. A registered FII would be expected not to engage in any short selling in securities and to take delivery of purchased and give of sold securities.

(*xiv*) A registered FII can appoint as Custodian an approved by SEBI to act as custodian of securities and for confirmation of transactions in Securities, settlement of purchase and sale, and for information reporting. Such custodian shall establish separate account for detailing on a daily basis the investment capital utilization and securities held by each FII for the RBI and SEBI semi-annually as part of its disclosure and reporting guidelines.

(*xv*) The RBI shall make available to the designated bank branches a list of companies where no investment will be allowed on the basis of the upper prescribed ceiling of 30% having been reached under the portfolio investment scheme.

(*xvi*) Reserve Bank of India may at any time request by an order a registered FII to submit information regarding the records of utilization of the inward remittances of investment capital and the statement of securities transactions. Reserve Bank of India and/or SEBI may also at any time conduct a direct inspection of the record and accounting books of a registered FII.

(*xvii*) FIIs investing under this scheme will benefit from a concessional tax regime of a flat rate tax of 20% on dividend and interest income and a tax rate of 10% on long term (one year or more) capital gains.

Types of FIIs

Entities eligible to invest in India via the FII route are:

Categories of FIIs

1. Pension Funds
2. Mutual Funds
3. Insurance Companies
4. Investment Trusts
5. Banks

6. University Funds
7. Endowments
8. Foundations
9. Charitable Trusts/Societies

Further, following entities proposing to invest on behalf of broad based funds are also eligible to be registered as FIIs:

1. Asset Management Companies
2. Institutional Portfolio Managers
3. Trustees
4. Power of Attorney Holders

(i) As FIIs: Overseas pension funds, mutual funds, investment trust, asset management companies, nominee companies, banks, institutional portfolio managers, university funds, endowments, foundations, charitable trusts, charitable societies, a trustee or power of attorney holder incorporated or established outside India proposing to make proprietary investments or investments on behalf of a broad-based fund (that is, fund having more than 20 investors with no single investor holding more than 10 per cent of the shares or units of the fund).

(ii) As sub-accounts: A sub-account is generally the underlying fund on whose behalf the FII invests. The following entities are eligible to be registered as sub-accounts: Partnership firms, private companies, public companies, pension funds, investment trusts, and individuals.

(iii) Domestic entity: A domestic portfolio manager or a domestic asset management company shall also be eligible to be registered as an FII to manage the funds of sub-accounts.

FIIs Investment in India

The main information available on FII pertains to the inflows and outflows. The key information pertains to the current market value of investments and the share of the FIIs in the trading are indicated in exhibit 13.3.

Exhibit-13.3
Investments by FIIs

Year	Gross Purchases (Rs. crore)	Gross Sales (Rs. crore)	Net Investment (Rs. crore)	Net Investment (US $ Mn.)	Cumulative Net Investment (US $ Mn.)
1	2	3	4	5	6
1992-93	17	4	13	4	4
1993-94	5.593	466	5,126	1,634	1,638
1994-95	7,631	2,835	4,796	1,528	3,167
1995-96	9,694	2,752	6,942	2,036	5,202
1996-97	15,554	6,979	8,574	2,432	7,634
1997-98	18,695	12,737	5,957	1,650	9,284
1998-99	16,115	17,699	-1,584	-386	8,898
1999-00	56,856	46,734	10,122	2,339	11,237
2000-01	74,051	64,116	9,934	2,159	13,396
2001-02	49,920	41,165	8,755	1,846	15,242
2002-03	47,061	44,373	2,689	562	15,805
2003-04	1,44,858	99,094	45,765	9,950	25,755
2004-05	2,16,951	1,71,071	45,880	10,352	36,293

Contd....

2005-06	3,46,976	3,05,509	41,467	9,363	45,657
2006-07	5,20,507	4,89,665	30,841	6,821	52,477
2008-09	6,14,579	6,60,389	- 45,811	- 9,837	59,081
2009-10 (Apr-Feb)	7,61,208	6,47,987	1,13,220	23,787	82,868

Discrepancies in total figures, if any, are due to rounding off.

The data presented above is compiled on the basis of reports submitted to SEBI by custodians.

Note: The data pertains to all the activities undertaken by FIIs in Indian Securities Market, including trades done in secondary market, primary market and activities involved in right/bonus issues, private placement, merger & acquisition, etc.

Source: SEBI.

Exhibit- 13.3 significance shows the FIIs' share of the overall market turnover. It also enables an assessment of the impact of the foreign institutions on Indian economy. The Economic Survey suggests that the FII turnover could be around 12-15 per cent of the total market turnover. The Government is keen on FII inflows as that is thought to better value our markets as also speed up the process of integrating with developed markets.

This is all the more important as rupee might start appreciating in the context of large foreign flows and the economy's growth prospects and there would be pressure from the domestic export lobby to mitigate the situation. Such a monitoring would go a long way in protecting the country's interests and hopefully will not be considered "draconian" or "oppressive" by the wise men of the West.

Critical Evaluation of FIIs in Indian Context

There is an intense debate amongst policy makers currently over whether India should discourage substantial parts of the foreign portfolio investment coming into Indian stock markets. The Reserve Bank of India reportedly believes that foreign institutional investments that have occurred so far through participatory notes (PNs) must be wound down forthwith as these could be hot monies with no proper record of the end investor. India has received net FII inflows of over $22 billion in the past three years. A good chunk- over 40% by one estimate- of such inflows may have come through PNs. The FIIs registered in India issue participatory notes to entities/individuals abroad who otherwise cannot invest in the Indian market. This entitles provide funds such entities to invest through the FIIs registered in India. Often it is difficult to track the end investor as there are layers of such entities.

Both the RBI and Sebi would like the identity of the end investor to be known and want such entities to be regulated in the country where they reside. Investigation in some recent cases has shown that these end investors are Indians living abroad. A lot of Indian money is coming back because India is now seen by the rest of the world as the long-term growth story offering sustained returns on capital. Such returns get further enhanced because of the view that the Indian currency will appreciate over the longer term as incremental productivity explodes in this region.

It is true that the antecedents of such monies would be somewhat ambiguous. Over the decades our businesses, not confident of India's innate economic strength, had incentives to take money out of the country to keep them in safe dollar havens. This was done through various tried and tested methods such as gold-plating project costs and showing inflated imports. Tax payers' money lent to businesses by public financial institutions and banks found their way into bank accounts abroad. Exporters too under invoiced to keep part of their proceeds aboard. All this happened in the decades before the 1990s when India was seen as a poor Third World economy with no future.

But when things dramatically changed for the better, especially in recent years, such funds want to come back to India. In the past few years, India had received about 30% of all foreign portfolio investments that came into the emerging markets. Even if 20% of such inflows were to move out in a short span, there could be financial crises. Such a fear is essentially derived from the old crisis-prone mindset of expecting the worst all the time. India needs to develop some of that confidence now. There is no reason to fear that there could be a massive flight of capital from India. In fact, the expert group set up by the finance ministry to study foreign portfolio investments has given interesting statistics on how the FIIs were net buyers during all crisis periods in recent years.

The findings of the expert group clearly point out that during all market crashes in recent years, the FIIs were net buyers. Whether it was the stock market crash of 2001, the market collapse after India's nuclear test in 1998 or the meltdown after the Asian financial crises of 1997, the FIIs were largely net buyers in India. Ironically, the domestic investors were net sellers during such crisis periods.

In this context, the expert group is emphatic that India has followed the policy of progressively liberalizing foreign investment flows. And this must continue with adequate safeguards in place. "To avoid the pitfalls of throwing the baby with the bath water, there cannot be a turnaround from the avowed policy of gradual liberalization, including the capital account."

Remedial Measures by the SEBI to Improve FIIs Working

Offshore derivative instruments (ODI) have been a constant source of irritation for Indian regulators over the last few years. Experience shows that imposing restrictions on these instruments can destabilize financial markets, forcing the regulator a backtrack. The only recourse left to prevent misuse of these instruments is to enforce stricter compliance with the existing guidelines. The recent instance of the Securities and Exchange Board of India (SEBI) banning Barclays Bank and Societe Generale from issuing ODIs appears to be an efforts in that direction. This directive should send a strong signal other foreign institutional investors (FIIs) who issue ODIs that the days when the regulator looked the other way while the guidelines were blatantly flouted are over. ODIs, or P-notes, as they are more popularly called, are offshore instruments issued by FIIs with underlying Indian Securities to overseas investors.

Investors who do not wish to register with Indian regulatory authorities prefer this route to take an exposure to the Indian capital market. What complicates the issue is that these instruments can be issued onward by the clients of FIIs to other entities. The Reserve Bank of India has consistently voiced its reservation against these instruments on the ground that this route was being used for money-laundering. The copious inflow through this route in 2007 that led to sharp appreciation in the rupee resulted in restrictions being imposed on these instruments in October 2007. But these restrictions were withdrawn a year later, following fear of large-scale unwinding by P-note holders, leading to sharp erosion in rupee and stock prices.

Onus on Foreign Investors

SEBI has mandated that the P-notes must be issued only to entities regulated by relevant regulatory authority in the countries of their incorporation. And it has put the onus of ensuring this on the FIIs primarily issuing the P-note. These foreign investors are also required to comply with "know your client" (KYC) guidelines while issuing the ODIs. Since ODIs are not transacted through any exchange and are mainly over-the counter contracts between two entities, SEBI has to rely entirely on the FIIs to comply with the guidelines laid down by it. Compliance is ensured by requiring FIIs to make periodic disclosures of all the relevant details of ODIs transacted by them. The prescribed form also includes columns asking for the information on back-to-back issuance of ODIs, name of the regulator who regulates the entity to whom the ODIs have been further issued and the nature of the investor –whether hedge fund, individual, pension fund and so on. This information ensures that FIIs are aware of the end beneficiaries of these instruments whether they are regulated entities and so on.

The recent skirmish involving two big names in the financial world, Barclays Bank and Societe Generale, however, shows that foreign institutions are paying scant regard to the SEBI guidelines, Barclays Bank had issued ODIs with Reliance Communications as the underlying to Hythe Securities. But in its periodic disclosures to SEBI, it had mentioned the counterparty as UBS AG and had entirely omitted Hythe from the disclosure form.

Further, is had also omitted to disclosure that the same ODIs had been further issued to Pluri, that is an unregulated entity. The Societe Generale (SG) case is very similar and the counterparty involved is, again, Hythe Securities. On SEBI raising a query regarding SG's dealing with Hythe, SG revealed that of the 48 transactions with Hythe, 14 were strongly reported. On further questioning regarding the end beneficiary of the ODI, SG denied any knowledge of further issuance of the ODI stating that it was transacting only with Hythe on 'principal' basis. On further scrutiny Hythe confirmed that these ODIs were onward issued to opportunity S.A. and further to Pluri.

Both Barclays and SG have not only misrepresented facts and made false disclosures, the end beneficiaries of the ODIs is an unregulated entity about which much not is stated. This is gross violation of the guideline requiring FIIs to ensure that only entities regulated by relevant authorities were issued with ODIs and raises serious doubts about the kind and color of money flowing into the stock market through this conduit. These two instances could just be the tip of the ice berg as far as flouting the P-note guidelines go. Mukier details could be revealed as the regulator digs deeper. But by claming down on two of the big names SEBI is sending a strong signal that the days of a lax ODI regime are over. FIIs have now to either comply or stop transacting in these instruments.

Suggestive Framework

Following suggestions have been made to make the FIIs investment more effective:

(*i*) Government must be alert about the funds particularly in the context of the large hedge funds that are not regulated in many territories.

(*ii*) SEBI and the Reserve Bank of India should set up a group of experts to monitor the FIIs and their activity in the market, especially if they have any hand in the volatility.

(*iii*) Government Policy should be formulated to protect the interest of exporters.

3. NRI Investment

'Non Resident Indian' (NRI) means an individual resident outside India who is a citizen of India or is an individual of Indian origin. To attract foreign investment in India, Government is offering several facilities to Non Resident Indians (NRIs), Persons of Indian Origin (PIO) and Overseas Corporate Bodies (OCBs). NRIs/PIOs/OCBs/ are permitted to open bank accounts in India out of funds remitted from abroad, foreign exchange brought in from abroad or out of funds legitimately due to them in India, with authorised dealer.

Reserve Bank has granted general permission to NRIs/PIOs, for undertaking direct investments in Indian companies, under the Automatic Route purchase of shares under Portfolio Investment Scheme, investment in companies and proprietorship/partnership concerns on non-repatriation basis and for remittances of current income. NRIs/PIOs do not have to seek specific permission for approved activities under these schemes.

Direct Investment Opportunities Available to NRIs/PIOs/OCBs

(*i*) **Automatic Route Of RBI With Repatriation Benefits:** NRIs/OCBs can invest in shares/convertible debentures of Indian companies under the Automatic Route without obtaining Government or RBI permission except for a few sectors where FIPB/SIA permission is necessary, or where the investment can be made only up to a certain percentage of paid up capital.

(*ii*) **Investment With Government Approval:** Investments not eligible under the Automatic Route, are considered by the Foreign Investment Promotion Board (FIPB) a high Powered inter-ministerial body under the chairmanship of Secretary, Department of Industrial Policy & Promotion, SIA, subject to sectoral limits/norms. These investments also enjoy full repatriation benefits.

(*iii*) **Other Investments With Repatriation Benefits**

(*a*) Investment in Domestic Mutual Funds

(*b*) Investment in Bonds Issued By Public Sector Undertakings

(*c*) Purchase of Shares of Public Sector Enterprises (By NRIs/PIOs/OCBs)

(*d*) Deposits with Companies (For A Minimum Period of Three Years)

(*e*) Investment in Government Securities/Shares

(*iv*) **Investment Upto 100% Equity without Repatriation Benefits**

(*a*)	Capital Contribution to any Proprietary or Partnership Concern	NRIs can invest by way of capital contribution in any proprietary or partnership concern in India provided the firm or the proprietary concern is not engaged in any agricultural/plantation activities or real estate business or Print Media on non-repatriation basis subject to the certain conditions.
(*b*)	New Issues of Shares/ Debentures of Indians Companies	NRIs/OCBs has been granted general permission to subscribe to the shares/convertible debentures of an Indian company on non-repatriation basis, and to an Indian company to issue shares or convertible debentures by way of new/rights/bonus issue to NRIs/OCBs on non-repatriation basis provided that the investee company is not engaged in agricultural/ plantation activities or real estate business (excluding real estate development i.e. development of property or construction of houses) or chit fund or is not a Nidhi company.

(*v*) **Other Investments by NRIs/OCBs without Repatriation Benefits**

(*a*) Investment in Non Convertible Debentures

(*b*) Money Market Mutual Funds

(*c*) Deposits With Companies

(*d*) Commercial Papers (OCBs are presently not permitted

The general policy and facilities for FDI are applicable to NRIs as well. In addition, Government has extended some additional facilities to NRIs, which include investment in the real estate and civil aviation sectors up to 100 per cent, besides a liberal investment regime on non repatriation basis.

4. External Commercial Borrowings (ECB)

External Commercial Borrowings (ECBs) include bank loans, suppliers' and buyers' credits, fixed and floating rate bonds (without convertibility) and borrowings from private sector windows of multilateral Financial Institutions such as International Finance Corporation. Euro-issues include Euro-convertible bonds and GDRs. In India, External Commercial Borrowings are being permitted by the Government for providing an additional source of funds to Indian corporates and PSUs for financing expansion of existing capacity and as well as for fresh investment, to augment their sources available domestically. ECBs can be used for any purpose (rupee-related expenditure as well as imports) except for investment in stock market and speculation in real estate. External Commercial Borrowings (ECB) are defined to include Commercial bank loans, buyer's credit, supplier's credit, securitised instruments such as floating rate notes, fixed rate bonds etc., credit from official export credit agencies, commercial borrowings from the private sector window of multilateral financial institutions such as IFC, ADB, AFIC, CDC etc. and Investment by Foreign Institutional Investors (FIIs) in dedicated debt funds.

Applicants are free to raise ECB from any internationally recognised source like banks, export credit agencies, suppliers of equipment, foreign collaborations, foreign equity - holders, international capital markets etc.

Regulator

The department of Economic Affairs, Ministry of Finance, Government of India with support of Reserve Bank of India, monitors and regulates Indian firms access to global capital markets. From time to time, they announce guidelines on policies and procedures for ECB and Euro-issues.

ECB Guidelines

The important aspect of ECB policy is to provide flexibility in borrowings by Indian corporates, at the same time maintaining prudent limits for total external borrowings. The guiding principles for ECB Policy are to keep maturities long, costs low, and encourage infrastructure and export sector financing which are crucial for overall growth of the economy.

The ECB policy focuses on three aspects:

(*i*) Eligibility criteria for accessing external markets.

(*ii*) The total volume of borrowings to be raised and their maturity structure.

(*iii*) End use of the funds raised.

Silent features of ECB policy are as follows:

1. On a review of the prevailing macroeconomic conditions and developments in international financial markets, Reserve Bank of India (RBI) has modified so the aspects of the ECB policy as indicated below:

(*i*) **All-in-cost ceilings:** As per the extant policy, the all-in-cost ceilings have been dispensed with, under the approval route, until December 31, 2009. In view of the improvement in the credit market conditions and narrowing credit spreads in the international markets, it has been decided to withdraw the existing relaxation in the all-in-cost ceilings under the approval route with effect from January 1, 2010. Accordingly, the all-in-cost ceilings under the approval route for the ECBs, where Loan Agreements have been signed on or after January 1, 2010 will be as under:

Average Maturity Period All -in-cost Ceilings over six month Libor*

Three years and up to five years - 300 basis points

More than five years - 500 basis points

*for the respective currency of borrowing or applicable benchmark.

Eligible borrowers proposing to avail of ECB after December 31, 2009, where the Loan Agreement has been signed on or before December 31, 2009 and where the all-in-cost exceed the above ceilings, should furnish a copy of the Loan Agreement. Such proposals would continue to be considered under the approval route.

(ii) **Integrated township:** As per the extant policy, corporates, engaged in the development of integrated township, as defined in Press Note 3 (2002 Series) dated January 04, 2002, issued by the Department of Industrial Policy and Promotion (DIPP), Ministry of Commerce & Industry, Government of India are permitted to avail of ECB, under the approval route, until December 31, 2009. On a review of the prevailing conditions, it has been decided to extend the current policy until December 31, 2010, under the approval route. All other terms and conditions, stipulated in the A.P. (DIR Series) Circulars referred to above, remain unchanged.

(iii) **Buyback of the Foreign Currency Convertible Bonds (FCCBs):** In terms of A.P. (DIR Series) Circular No. 39 dated December 8, 2008, read with A.P. (DIR Series) Circular No. 58 dated March 13, 2009 and A.P. (DIR Series) Circular No. 65 dated April 28, 2009, Indian companies have been allowed to buy back their Foreign Currency Convertible Bonds (FCCBs) both under the automatic route and approval route until December 31, 2009. Keeping in view the prevailing macroeconomic conditions and global developments, especially the improvements in the stock prices, it has been decided to discontinue the facility with effect from January 1, 2010.

(iv) **ECB for the NBFC Sector:** As per the current ECB norms, Non-Banking Finance Companies (NBFCs), which are exclusively involved in the financing of the infrastructure sector, are permitted to avail of ECBs from multilateral / regional financial institutions and Government owned development financial institutions for on-lending to the borrowers in the infrastructure sector under the approval route. In view of the thrust given to development of infrastructure sector, it has been decided with immediate effect to allow NBFCs exclusively involved in financing the infrastructure projects to avail of ECB from the recognized lender category including international banks under the approval route, subject to complying with the prudential standards prescribed by the Reserve Bank and the borrowing entities fully hedging their currency risk. The AD Category-I bank should certify the compliance with the prudential norms by the borrowing NBFCs.

(v) **ECB for Spectrum in the Telecommunication Sector:** As per the extant policy, as indicated in A.P. (DIR Series) Circular No. 26 dated October 22, 2008, payment for obtaining license/permit for 3G Spectrum is considered an eligible end - use for the purpose of ECB under the automatic route. It has now been decided to permit eligible borrowers in the telecommunication sector to avail of ECB for the purpose of payment for Spectrum allocation. This modification will come into effect with immediate effect. All other aspects of ECB policy such as USD 500 million limit per company per financial year under the automatic route, eligible borrower, recognised lender, end-use, average maturity period, prepayment, refinancing of existing ECB, reporting arrangements and terms and conditions stipulated in the A.P. (DIR Series) Circulars shall remain unchanged.

2. As per the extant policy, eligible borrowers in the telecommunication sector are permitted to avail of ECB for the purpose of payment for spectrum allocation, under the automatic route. Keeping in view the large outlay of funds required to be paid directly to the Government within a limited period of time, it has been decided to make a one-time relaxation in the end-use conditions of the ECB policy.

(i) The payment for spectrum allocation may initially be met out of Rupee resources by the successful bidders, to be refinanced with a long-term ECB, under the approval route, subject to the following conditions: The ECB should be raised within 12 months from the date of payment of the final installment to the Government; The designated AD - Category I bank should monitor the end-use of funds; Banks in India will not be permitted to provide any form of guarantees; and All other conditions of ECB, such as eligible borrower, recognized lender, all- in-cost, average maturity, etc, should be complied with.

(ii) Eligible borrowers in the telecommunications sector proposing to fund the payment for Spectrum allocation directly out of the proceeds of the ECBs may continue to avail of the ECBs under the automatic route as per the extant policy.

(iii) All other aspects of ECB policy, such as USD 500 million limit per company per financial year under the automatic route, eligible borrower, recognised lender, end-use, average maturity period, prepayment, refinancing of existing ECB and reporting arrangements remain unchanged.

3. As per the extant ECB procedures, any changes in the terms and conditions of the ECB after obtaining the Loan Registration Number (LRN) from the Department of Statistics and Information Management (DSIM), Reserve Bank, require the prior approval of the Reserve Bank. Accordingly, the requests of the borrowers for changes in the terms and conditions, such as, drawdown / repayment schedules, currency of borrowing and changes in designated AD bank, name of the borrowing company, etc. are referred to the Reserve Bank for necessary approval. As a measure of simplification of the existing procedures, Reserve Bank of India has decided to delegate powers to the designated AD category-I banks to approve the following requests from the ECB borrowers, subject to specified conditions:

(*i*) Changes / modifications in the drawdown / repayment schedule Designated AD Category – I banks may approve changes / modifications in the drawdown / repayment schedule of the ECBs already availed, both under the approval and the automatic routes, subject to the condition that the average maturity period, as declared while obtaining the LRN, is maintained. The changes in the drawdown / repayment schedule should be promptly reported to the DSIM, Reserve Bank in Form 83. However, any elongation / rollover in the repayment on expiry of the original maturity of the ECB would require the prior approval of the Reserve Bank.

(*ii*) Changes in the currency of borrowing Designated AD Category I banks may allow changes in the currency of borrowing, if so desired, by the borrower company, in respect of ECBs availed of both under the automatic and the approval routes, subject to all other terms and conditions of the ECB remaining unchanged. Designated AD banks should, however, ensure that the proposed currency of borrowing is freely convertible.

(*iii*) Change of the AD bank Designated AD Category - I banks may allow change of the existing designated AD bank by the borrower company for effecting its transactions pertaining to the ECBs subject to No-Objection Certificate (NOC) from the existing designated AD bank and after due diligence.

(*iv*) Changes in the name of the Borrower Company Designated AD Category - I banks may allow changes in the name of the borrower company subject to production of supporting documents evidencing the change in the name from the Registrar of Companies.

The modifications to the ECB guidelines have come into force with immediate effect. All other aspects of the ECB policy, such as USD 500 million limit per company per financial year under the automatic route, eligible borrower, recognised lender, end-use, all-in-cost ceiling, average maturity period, prepayment, refinancing of existing ECB and reporting arrangements remain unchanged.

4. On a review of the policy, it has been decided to modify the extant ECB policy in respect of the Infrastructure Finance Companies (IFCs) i.e. Non Banking Financial Companies (NBFCs) categorised as IFCs by the Reserve Bank. As per the extant norms, IFCs have been permitted to avail of ECBs for on-lending to the infrastructure sector, as defined in the extant ECB policy, under the approval route.

As a measure of liberalisation of the existing procedures, it has been decided to permit the IFCs to avail of ECBs, including the outstanding ECBs, up to 50 per cent of their owned funds under the automatic route, subject to their compliance with the prudential guidelines already in place. ECBs by IFCs above 50 per cent of their owned funds would require the approval of the Reserve Bank and will, therefore, be considered under the approval route. Designated Authorized Dealer banks should ensure compliance with the extant norms while certifying the ECB application both under the automatic and approval routes. All the other aspects of ECB policy such as USD 500 million limit per company per financial year under the automatic route, eligible borrower, recognised lender, end-use, average maturity period, prepayment, refinancing of existing ECB and reporting arrangements remain unchanged.

Foreign Investment in India

Generally foreign investment constitutes four dimensions like- FDI investment, Portfolio investment, NRIs Investment and ECB investments. Overall position of foreign investment inflows is given in Exhibit-13.4, 13.5 and 13.6.

Exhibit-13.4
Foreign Investment Inflows

(US$ million) **As on July 13, 2010**

Item		1995-96	1996-97	1997-98	1998-99	1999-00	2000-01	2001-02	2002-03	2003-04	2004-05	2005-06	2006-07	2007-08	2008-09 (P)	2009-10 (P)
1		2	3	4	5	6	7	8	9	10	11	12	13	14	15	16
A.	Direct Investment (I+II+III)	2,144	2,821	3,557	2,462	2,155	4,029	6,130	5,035	4,322	6,051	8,961	22,826	34,835	35,180	37,182
	I. Equity (a+b+c+d+e)	2,144	2,821	3,557	2,462	2,155	2,400	4,095	2,764	2,229	3,778	5,975	16,481	26,864	27,995	27,149
	a. Government (SIA/FIPB)	1,249	1,922	2,754	1,821	1,410	1,456	2,221	919	928	1,062	1,126	2,156	2,298	4,699	3,471
	b. RBI	169	135	202	179	171	454	767	739	534	1,258	2,233	7,151	17,127	17,998	18,990
	c. NRI	715	639	241	62	84	67	35	—	—	—	—	—	—	—	—
	d. Acquisition of shares *	11	125	360	400	490	362	881	916	735	930	2,181	6,278	5,148	4,632	3,148
	e. Equity capital of unincorporated bodies #	..	..	..	..	..	61	191	190	32	528	435	896	2,291	666	1,540
	II. Reinvested earnings +	..	..	..	..	..	1,350	1,645	1,833	1,460	1,904	2,760	5,828	7,679	6,428	8,080
	III. Other capital ++	..	..	..	..	..	279	390	438	633	369	226	517	292	757	1,953
B.	Portfolio Investment (a+b+c)	2,748	3,312	1,828	–61	3,026	2,760	2,021	979	11,377	9,315	12,492	7,003	27,271	–13,855	32,375
	a. GDRs/ADRs # #	683	1,366	645	270	768	831	477	600	459	613	2,552	3,776	6,645	1,162	3,328
	b. FIIs **	2,009	1,926	979	–390	2,135	1,847	1,505	377	10,918	8,686	9,926	3,225	20,328	–15,017	29,047
	c. Offshore funds and others	56	20	204	59	123	82	39	2	—	16	14	2	298	—	—
	Total (A+B)	**4,892**	**6,133**	**5,385**	**2,401**	**5,181**	**6,789**	**8,151**	**6,014**	**15,699**	**15,366**	**21,453**	**29,829**	**62,106**	**21,325**	**69,557**

Exhibit-13.5

(US $ million)

Item		2010-11 (P)		
		Apr.	May	Apr-May
1		2		
A.	Direct Investment (I+II+III)	2,179	2,213	4,392
	I. Equity (a+b+c+d)	2,179	2,213	4,392
	a. Government (SIA/FIPB)	440	555	995
	b. RBI	1,361	1,274	2,635
	c. Acquisition of shares *	378	384	762
	d. Equity capital of unincorporated bodies #	..		
	II. Reinvested earnings +	..		
	III. Other capital ++	..		
B.	Portfolio Investment (a+b+c)	3,315	-364	2,951
	a. GDRs/ADRs # #	156	127	283
	b. FIIs **	3,159	-491	2,668
	c. Offshore funds and others	—	—	—
	Total (A+B)	**5,494**	**1,849**	**7,343**

Exhibit-13.6

(US $ million)

Item		Apr.	May	Jun.	Jul.	Aug.	Sep.	Oct.	Nov.	Dec.	Jan.	Feb.	Mar.	2009-10 (P) Apr.— Mar.
	1	2	3	4	5	6	7	8	9	10	11	12	13	14
A.	Direct Investment (I+II+III)	2,339	2,095	2,471	3,476	3,174	1,512	2,332	1,700	1,542	2,042	1,717	1,209	37,182
	I. Equity (a+b+c+d)	2,339	2,095	2,471	3,476	3,174	1,512	2,332	1,700	1,542	2,042	1,717	1,209	27,149
	a. Government (SIA/FIPB)	931	101	85	248	643	111	302	179	51	588	93	139	3,471
	b. RBI	1,150	1,916	2,337	1,757	2,477	1,355	1,726	1,367	1,233	1,292	1,364	1,016	18,990
	c. Acquisition of shares *	258	78	49	1,471	54	46	304	154	258	162	260	54	3,148
	d. Equity capital of unincorporated bodies #	..	..	..	..	..	..	..	..	..	..	..	..	1,540
	II. Reinvested earnings +	..	..	..	..	..	..	..	..	..	..	..	..	8,080
	III. Other capital ++	..	..	..	..	..	..	..	..	..	..	..	..	1,953
B.	Portfolio Investment (a+b+c)	2,278	5,639	353	3,032	1,574	5,095	2,922	1,274	1,533	3,139	230	5,306	32,375
	a. GDRs/ADRs ##	33	—	10	965	1,603	96	—	381	94	46	—	100	3,328
	b. FIIs **	2,245	5,639	343	2,067	-29	4,999	2,922	893	1,439	3,093	230	5,206	29,047
	c. Offshore funds and others	—	—	—	—	—	—	—	—	—	—	—	—	—
	Total (A+B)	**4,617**	**7,734**	**2,824**	**6,508**	**4,748**	**6,607**	**5,254**	**2,974**	**3,075**	**5,181**	**1,947**	**6,515**	**69,557**

* Relates to acquisition of shares of Indian companies by non-residents under Section 6 of FEMA, 1999. Data on such acquisitions have been included as part of FDI since January 1996.

** Represents inflow of funds (net) by Foreign Institutional Investors (FIIs).

Figures for equity capital of unincorporated bodies for 2009-10 are estimates.

Represents the amount raised by Indian Corporates through Global Depository Receipts (GDRs) and American Depository Receipts (ADRs).

+ Data for 2009-10 are estimated as average of previous two years.

++ Data pertain to intercompany debt transactions of FDI entities.

Notes : 1. Data on FDI have been revised since 2000-01 with expanded coverage to approach international best practices.

2. These data, therefore, are not comparable with FDI data for previous years.

3. Monthly data on components of FDI as per expanded coverage are not available.

Thus, the overall performance of foreign investment inflows is quite satisfactory. These inflows are necessary to keep up the development process at higher growth rate. Each and every segment of foreign investments have their own advantages and limitations. Regulatory authorities are required to develop flexible rigorous and effective regulatory mechanism so that foreign investment inflows can play their role in economic development of the country in proper perspective.

Case Study

Read the following case study carefully and analyse it in terms of your responses to the questions given at the end.

Electrolux Acquisitions

Electrolux is Sweden's largest manufacturer of electrical household appliances and was one of the world's pioneers in the marketing of vacuum cleaners. However, not all the products bearing the Electrolux name are controlled by the Swedish firm. Electrolux vacuum cleaners sold and manufactured in the United States, for example, have not been connected with the Swedish firm since the US subsidiaries were sold in the 1960s. The Swedish firm reentered the U.S. market in 1994 by purchasing National Union Electric, which manufactures Eureka vacuum cleaners.

Electrolux pursued its early international expansion largely to gain economies of scale through additional sales. The Swedish market was simply too small to absorb fixed costs as much as the home markets from competitive firms from larger countries. When additional sales were not possible by exporting, Electrolux was still able to gain certain scale economies through the establishment of foreign production. Research and development expenditures and certain administrative costs could thus be spread out over the additional sales made possible by foreign operations. Additionally, Electrolux concentrated on standardized and rationalization of parts.

Until the late 1980s, Electrolux concentrated primarily on vacuum cleaners and the building of its own facilities in order to effect expansion. Throughout the 1970s, though, the firm expanded largely by acquiring existing firms whose product lines different from those of Electrolux. The compelling force was to add appliance lines to complement those developed internally. Its recent profits ($220 million in 1983) have enabled Electrolux to go on an acquisitions binge. Electrolux acquired two Swedish firms that made home appliances and washing machines. Electrolux management felt that it could use its existing foreign sales networks to increase the sales of those firms. In 1993, Electrolux acquired another Swedish firm, Facit, which already had extensive foreign sales and facilities. Vacuum cleaner producers were acquired in the United States and in France; and to gain captive sales for vacuum cleaners, Electrolux acquired commercial cleaning service firms in Sweden and in the United States. A French kitchen equipment producer, Arthur Martin, was bought, as was a Swiss home appliance firm. Therma, and a U.S. cooking equipment manufacturer, Tappan.

Except for the Facit purchase, the above acquisitions all involved firms that produced complementary lines that would enable the new parent to gain certain scale economics. However, not all the products of acquired firms were related, and Electrolux sought to sell off unrelated businesses. In 1998, for example, a Swedish firm, Husqvarna, was bought because of its kitchen equipment lines. Electrolux was able to sell Husqvarna's motorcycle line but could not get a good price for the chain saw facility. Reconciled to being in the chain saw business, Electrolux then acquired chain saw manufactures in Canada and Norway, thus becoming one of the world's largest chain saw producers. The above are merely the most significant Electrolux acquisitions; the firm made approximately fifty acquisitions in the 1990s.

In 2000, Electrolux announced a takeover that was very different from those of the 1990s. It offered $175 million, the biggest Electrolux acquisition, for Granges, Sweden's leading metal producer and fabricator. Granges was itself a multinational firm (1999 sales of $1.2 billion) and made about 50 percent of its sales outside of Sweden. The managing directors of the two firms indicating that the major advantage of the takeover would be the integration of Granges' aluminium, copper, plastics, and other materials into Electrolux's production of appliances. Many analysts felt that the timing of Electrolux's bid was based on indications that Beijer invest, a large Swedish conglomerate, wished to acquire a non-ferrous metals mining company. Other analysts felt that Electrolux would be better off to continue international horizontal expansion, as it had in the 1990s. The analysts pointed to large appliance makers such as AEG Telefunken of West Germany that were likely candidates for takeover because of the recent poor performance.

Practice Questions

Objective Type Questions

1. Foreign investment is an instrument of:
   (*a*) Global capital market
   (*b*) International Policy
   (*c*) WTO agreement
   (*d*) IMF assistance programme
2. In FDI, investors expect to influence:
   (*a*) management of the enterprise
   (*b*) investment of the enterprise
   (*c*) environment of the enterprise
   (*d*) performance of the enterprise
3. Following is not the main motive of FDI:
   (*a*) resource seeking
   (*b*) profit seeking
   (*c*) market seeking
   (*d*) efficiency seeking
4. Department of Industrial Policy and Promotion was established in:
   (*a*) 1993 (*b*) 1994
   (*c*) 1995 (*d*) 1996
5. Secretariat for Industrial (S/A) has been set up to provide: :
   (*a*) licence to industrial undertaking
   (*b*) project financing
   (*c*) Entrepreneurial development programme
   (*d*) single window service for entrepreneurial assistance.

Ans: 1. (b), 2. (a) 3. (b), 4. (c), 5. (d)

Short Answer Questions

1. What are the functions of Department of Industrial Policy and Promotion?
2. How does foreign direct investment is different from portfolio investment?
3. What do you mean by non-resident Indians?
4. What are the functions of foreign investment implementation authority?
5. What are the objectives of FDI?

Long Answer Questions

1. What is foreign investment? Also examine its rationale in Indian context.
2. What do you mean by foreign investment? Examine its different types.
3. What is foreign direct investment? Examine its essentials.
4. Critically examine the main recommendations of N.K. Singh Committee report.
5. Critically evaluate the organizational framework of FDI in India.

Questions

1. What are Electrolux's reasons for direct investment in other countries?
2. How has Electrolux's strategy changed over time? How has this affected its direct investment activities?
3. Which of the company's foreign investments would be horizontal which could be vertical? What are the advantages of each?
4. What do you see as the main advantages and possible problems of expanding internationally primarily through acquisitions as opposed to building one's own facilities?
5. Should the company take over Granges? Justify.

References

1. Economic Times, Dec. 20, 2009, p.2
2. Consolidated FDI Policy, Department of Industrial and Promotion, Ministry of Commerce and Industry, Government of India, p.5
3. N.K. Singh Committee Report on Foreign Direct Investment
4. Consolidated FDI Policy, Department of Industrial and Promotion, Ministry of Commerce and Industry, Government of India, p.14-25
5. E. Philip Davis: "Institutional Investors, Financial Markets and Financial Stability", Discussion Paper PI-0303, The Pensions Institute, Birkbeck College, London, January 2003.
6. Demigrüç-Kunt, A. and R. Levine (1996): "Stock Market Development and Financial Intermediaries: Stylized Facts", World Bank Economic Review, Vol. 10, pp. 341-69.
7. Bikhchandani, S and S. Sharma (2000): "Herd Behaviour in Financial Markets", Working Paper No. WP/00/48, International Monetary Fund, Washington DC, 2000.)
8. Dr. Ashok k. Lahiri, Shri U.K. Sinha and Shri umesh kumar, Report of the committee on liberalization Of Foreign institutional investment, Department of economic affairs, Ministry of finance, Government of India, June 2004, p.15-17
9. Ibid.p.30-32
10. Ibid.p.33-34

14 CORPORATE RESTRUCTURING

Business world is a dynamic world. Managers working in business organizations are required to adjust themselves in changing business scenario. They have to develop their own mental models about the ways of doing business in an organisation. Necessary assumptions applicable to a particular business scenario help them in their decision-making process. Mental models represent the knowledge of managers who have intensive experience about the industry and the organisation and how specific action relates to desired outcomes."[1] Assumptions generally deal with "(i) environment, specifically markets, customers and important technologies (ii) the mission or purpose (iii) core (content) competencies required to fulfill the mission"[2]. These mental models and assumptions are generally derived from experience with past successes and failures contributing to the overall picture of the firm.[3] In practice, these mental models and assumptions are useful in the short run for further managerial decision-making and strategic management. But in the long run each and every system is governed by the change and these mental models and assumptions are not so useful in the changed scenario. So it would be unviable for the managers to stick to these models and assumptions as they became obsolete, irrelevant and may harm the functioning of the enterprise. Keeping the changing requirements of dynamic world, mental models and assumptions are required to be refined, revised and readjusted for making more viable and productive to the corporate environment.

Powerful change forces affect the business environment. Change in transportation and communications have resulted in effective changes in internationalization of markets. Development of deregulatory framework is the direct result of globalisation of competition and its increased intensity. Massive change forces are working in each and every segment of business scenario. Industry, trade, transport, communication, service sector, agriculture sector all are under the impact of powerful change forces. Thus, there is a need for business firms to continue their adjustment process to the strong change forces. "The way of doing business will continue to change. The forms of competition will continue to multiply and its intensity will continue to increase. Relations with suppliers, workers, consumers and other stakeholders will continue to evolve."[4] So there is always a need to adjust with the changing process for an effective operation of a business firm. The sweeping wave of economic reforms and liberalization has transformed the business scenario all over the world. The most significant development has been the integration of national economies with market oriented globalised economy. The multi lateral trade agenda and the World Trade Organisation have been facilitating easy and free flow of technology, capital and expertise across the globe.

Also, globalisation has opened many choices for the consumers – technologies are changing, established brands, are being challenged by value for money products, inter-country trade has increased and entry barriers are reduced. In this international scenario, there is heavy accent on the quality, range, cost and reliability of product and services. This necessitates companies world over to reshape and reposition themselves to meet the challenges and seize opportunities thrown open by globalisation. The management strategy in such turbulent times is to focus on core competencies – selling loss making or low contribution activities/companies and acquiring those, which can contribute to profit and growth of the group. The underlying objective is to achieve and sustain superior performance.

With the opening up of the economy, and absence of strict regulations about the size and volume of business, businesses are encouraged to grow in size, reduce costs make prices internationally competitive and provide the consumer a wider choice. As the size of the shrinks, it becomes extremely difficult for all companies to survive, unless they cut costs and maintain prices. In such a situation, corporate restructuring eliminates duplication of expenses, prevents price war in a shrinking market and reduces the number of competitors.

After all, these forces will remain forceful for a long period. Their degrees may be different at a particular point of time. But, certainly they will guide the working of business firms under these circumstances. However, under the changing scenario, the only option available before the business firms to restructure and reorient their working for survival and growth. In this context, corporate restructuring has been assigned to play its role. It is a vehicle for adjustment of environmental changes. Thus, in a modern corporate culture, corporate restructuring is defined as a process of adjustment, necessitated by the environmental changes available or taking place in a business scenario. Basically, structuring deals with the process of revision and adjustment in mental models and assumptions of managers.

In the context of Indian scenario, the words of Jusitce Dhananjaya Y. Chandrachud are quite important one. According to him, corporate restructuring is one of the means that can be employed to meet the challenges which confront business. The unleashing of Indian economy has opened up lucrative and dependable opportunities to business community as a whole. The absence of strict regulations about the size and volume of business encouraged the enterprises to opt for mergers and amalgamation so as to produce on a massive scale, reduce costs of production, make price internationally competitive. Companies, by merging and amalgamation, reduce the number of competitors, increase their market share, provides economies of scale, reduction in production, administration, setting, legal and professional expenses, provides the benefit of integration, tax advantage, strengthen its financial strength, revival of weak or sick company, synergistic operational advantage, competitive advantage, optimum use of capacities and factors of production, advantage of brand equity, and diversification.

In modern corporate culture, corporate restructuring is a comprehensive process by which a company can consolidate its business operations and strengthen its position for achieving its short term and long term corporate objectives – synergetic, dynamic, continuing as a competitive and successful entity. It is concerned with arranging business activities of the corporate as a whole so as to achieve certain pre-determined objectives at corporate level. These objectives include orderly redirection of the firms' activities, deploying surplus cash from one business to finance profitable growth in another, exploiting interdependence among present or prospective businesses with the corporate portfolio, risk deduction and development of core competencies. It aims at improving the competitive position of an individual business and maximizing its contribution to corporate objectives. It also aims at exploiting the strategic assets accumulated by a business i.e., to enhance the competitive advantage, thereby enhancing shareholder's wealth. Wealth maximization of shareholders is the most important objective of modern corporate culture.

Nature of Corporate Restructuring

Corporate Restructuring is concerned with redesigning of business activities to ensure fulfillment of certain pre-determined objectives at corporate level. Stability, liquidity and profitability are the basic objectives of business firms. These basic objectives ultimately guide the business firms to ensure their survival and growth in changing business scenario. Corporate restructuring is a mechanism to achieve survival and growth. According to oxford dictionary, restructuring means to give a new structure to rebuild or rearrange. In this way, corporate restructuring deals with rearranging the business for increased efficiency and profitability. It is generally concerned with business level restructuring that is, with the business portfolio changes that firms undertake in order to either deal with the problem they face or to create a more profitable enterprise. Business portfolio changes could lead to the firm acquiring some business and divesting some others.

Thus, the corporate restructuring deals with the significant changes in the strategies and policies of business firm with regard to its assets, composition and liability and equity pattern as well as operations.

Rationale of Corporate Restructuring: Rationale of corporate restructuring are as follows-

(*i*) It focuses on core strengths, operational synergy and efficient allocation of managerial capabilities and infrastructure.

(*ii*) It attempts to analyze the changes in the environment and the organization and relate such changes to strategic actions that organizations need to take.

(*iii*) It helps in consolidation and economies of scale by expansion and diversification to exploit extended domestic and global markets.

(*iv*) It acquires constant supply of raw materials and occurs to scientific research and technological development.

(*v*) It ensures an appropriate mix of loan and equity capital to reduce the cost of servicing and improve return on investment.

(*vi*) It improves corporate performance to bring the company at par with competitors by adopting the radical changes brought out by information technology.

(*vii*) It revives and rehabilitates a sick unit by adjusting losses of the sick unit with profits of a healthy company.

Objectives of Corporate Restructuring: Objectives of corporate restructuring are as follows-

(*i*) To meet the growing needs of global competition.

(*ii*) To encourage implementation of risk reduction programmes in business operations.

(*iii*) To address the agency problem of conflict of interest between managers and shareholders. It helps to better align the interests of managers and shareholders.

(*iv*) To help in movement of assets to owners who can utilize them more effectively. It also helps the economic system to move assets to their highest valued uses.

(*v*) To improve the competitive position of an individual business and maximise its contribution to corporate objectives.

(*vi*) To enable the company to exploit the strategic assets accumulated by a business i.e. natural monopolies, goodwill, exclusively through licensing etc. to enhance the competitive advantages.

(*vii*) To ensure orderly redirection of the firms activities.

(*viii*) To deploy surplus cash from one business to finance profitable growth in another business.

(*ix*) To exploit inter dependence network facilities of present or prospective businesses within the existing corporate portfolio.

(*x*) To execute development of core competencies.

Kinds of Corporate Restructuring: Main types of corporate restructuring are as follows:

1. **Financial Restructuring:** It deals with changes in the equity pattern, equity holdings and cross holding pattern, debt-servicing schedule etc. Thus, it is concerned with restructuring of capital base and arranging finance for projects. It also involves decisions with regard to acquisitions, mergers, joint ventures and strategic alliances.

   When during the life time of a company, any of the following situations arise, the Board of Directors of a company is compelled to think and decodes on the company's restructuring:

   (*i*) necessity for injecting more working capital to meet the market demand for the company's products or services.

   (*ii*) When the company is unable to meet its current commitments.

   (*iii*) When the company is unable to obtain further credit from the suppliers of raw materials, consumable stores, bought out components etc. and from other parties like those doing job work for the company.

   (*iv*) When the company is unable to utilize its full production capacity for lack of liquid funds.

Generally, company faces two types of situations viz., under capitalization and over capitalization.

An under-capitalized company may consider restructuring its capital by taking one or more of the following corrective steps:

(*a*) Injecting more capital whenever required either by resorting to right issue or additional public issue.

(*b*) Resorting to additional borrowings from financial institutions, banks, other companies etc.

(*c*) Issuing debentures, bonds etc., or

(*d*) Inviting and accepting fixed deposits from directors, their relatives, businesses associates and public.

If a company is over capitalized, it can consider restructuring its capital by taking following corrective measures:

(*a*) Buy back of own shares.

(b) Paying back surplus share capital to shareholders;
(c) Repaying loans to financial institutions, banks etc;
(d) Repaying fixed deposits to public; etc.
(e) Redeeming its debentures, bonds, etc.

2. Organization restructuring: It is concerned with changes in the organisation. It also involves developing internal structures and procedures for improving the capability of personnel in an organization to respond to changes. Actually, it incorporates changes in the structure of the organization reducing hierarchies, or delivering, reducing the number of employees or downsizing, redesigning positions and altering reporting relationships. Generally, people resist to change. Redesigning of organisation relationship is requires to facilitate the process of financial and technological restructuring. Managers and employees are responsible for running the company and they have to make the company more viable on a continuous basis. If they failed to ensure this mission they have to face the consequences of failures. Ultimately, necessary changes are required to be integrated in the organizational culture of the company.

3. Technological Restructuring: It relates with technical collaborations of company with foreign companies to improve its technical capabilities. Basic purpose behind technical collaboration is to exploit the technical expertise of foreign collaborators in domestic production system. Technological restructuring is generally meant for up gradation of existing technology or introduction of advanced technology, acquiring technical know-how and facilitating transfer of technology. Foreign technology collaboration may involve agreement for highering technical knowhow, engineering services in respect of specific projects, patent or trade mark agreement and agreement for supply of plant, machinery and other business equipment. Technical collaborations are considered on the basis of annual royalty payments which are linked with the value of actual production.

4. Market Restructuring: It enables the company to improve core competency through market segmentation, reduction or additions in product lines or product range. Brand acquisitions or sale is also the part of market restructuring strategy of the company. Market restructuring is to be implemented by keeping in mind the following questions:

(i) What do our customers wants?
(ii) What is our business?
(iii) Who are our customers?
(iv) What is existing and potential customers?
(v) How far can we go in serving customer needs?
(vi) What profit margins can we expect?
(vii) What basic form should our strategy take?
(viii) What advantages do we have in serving customers needs?
(ix) Do we wish to develop our own new products?
(i) Do we wish to be a product leader?
(i) How much will not customers buy at what price?

Thus, market restructuring is implemented through adjusting its own marketing policy to the changed circumstances.

Illustration-1

Gemini Copper Ltd. is a public limited company in which Government of India holds 99.4% equity and remaining equity is held by public including financial institutions, banks and public at large. The company is into the business of copper mining and manufacturing various copper products with huge potential due to increased global demand of copper at good price. Company was running into losses of financial year ended on 31st March, 2010. Following is the balance sheet of the company as on 31st March, 2010.

Liabilities	Rs. in Crores	Assets	Rs. in crores
Equity share capital	800	Fixed assets	350
Preference shares		Current assets :	

Contd....

(subscribed by Central Govt.)	180	Loans and advances	100
Loan (given by Central Govt.)	50	Profit and loss account	630
Current liabilities and provisions	50		
	1,080		1,080

In the current year, the company is doing exceedingly well and hopes to continue profitable performance in years to come due to all round increased demand and price of copper. This company is the only company in the country to have copper mines.

To accelerate improved financial performance and to increase shareholders' value the company is planning to expand its mining operations substantially and for that to invite technical –cum –financial partners from overseas market to meet funds requirements and technical support.

The shares of the company are listed in Indian Stock market and ruling price per share is about Rs. 100 of Rs. 10 face value share. Due to huge mining potential and huge copper reserves in the mines, the company is not willing to offer the shares to financial partner at current market price but wants to charge a very high premium. Due to huge losses in the balance sheet, it is not possible for the company to approach the foreign investors for a premium issue, which may be overcome by financial restructuring as per the advice of the merchant banker. The board of directors of the company is willing to appoint you as financial advisor to give road map to the Board of Directors. In this regard, answer the following questions-

(i) How will the financial restructuring be possible?

(ii) Would the Government be able to maintain its market capitalization?

(iii) Do you think that market price of shares shall fall after restructuring?

(iv) If the company has to mobilize Rs. 3,000 crore more after restructuring, what possible ways, you would suggest for the same and at what premium?

(C.S. Final, Dec. 2007)

Solution:

(i) For financial restructuring of the Company, the balance sheet of the Company has to be improved. Losses should be removed. For that, since Government is major shareholder, it may agree for reducing the face value and paid-up value of the share from Rs. 10 to Rs. 4 per share. In this way, Rs. 480 crores may be used to write off losses. Remaining losses can be written off against preference shares.

(ii) Even with these losses the market price of shares is Rs. 100 per share, hence with writing off losses, the market perception will further improve and price is not likely to go down even for Rs. 4 face value shares. To meet eventuality of price going down and to meet the loss of preference share capital, remaining preference share capital and government loan can be converted into equity at a premium, which will give government cushion against any drop of market capitalization of government stake.

(iii) No, market price of shares shall not fall after restructuring because of the two main reasons. First is that company is on profitability path. The second reason is because of huge hidden wealth of the company.

(iv) For mobilizing Rs. 3000 crores, best options may be to go for ECB, which may be capitalized into equity with the consent of parties, convertible bonds and GDRs/ ADRs subject to compliance of the Securities & Exchange Board of India Rules and regulations, Securities & Exchange Board of India (Depositories and Participants) Regulations, 1996, Securities and exchange Board of India (Substantial Acquisition of shares and takeovers Regulations, 1997 and Foreign exchange Management Act, 1999 provisions.

Tools of Corporate Restructuring

Important tools of corporate restructuring are as follows-

1. Amalgamation
2. Merger
3. Demerger
4. Acquisitions
5. Takeover

6. Joint Venture
7. Disinvestment
8. Strategic Alliances
9. Franchises
10. Buy Back of Shares

1. Amalgamation: Amalgamation is "an arrangement by which the assets of two or more companies become vested in under the control of one of the existing companies or a newly formed company. The share capital of the combined company will spread amongst the shareholders of the original companies."[5] It contemplates two or more companies deciding to pool their resources to function either in the name of one of the existing companies or to form a new company to takeover the businesses and undertakings including all other assets and liabilities of both the existing companies.

According to the Halsbury's Law of England, the term "amalgamation is a blending of two or more existing undertakings into one undertaking, the shareholders of each blending company becoming substantially, the shareholders in the company which is to carry on the blending undertakings. "Amalgamation is generally possible either by transfer of two or more undertakings to a new company or by the transfer of one or more undertakings to an existing company."[6]

Sometimes, "under an amalgamation 'two or more companies are merged, either by consolidation of their undertakings or defect by the acquisition of a controlling interest in the capital of one undertaking by the other or of the capital of both by a new company."[7] Thus, amalgamation also covers acquisition. However, Weinberg, makes a distinction between merger/consolidation and acquisition of controlling interest. "There is another approach which deals with a situation where an amalgamation can be a case of merger of one company with another or the takeover of the two or more companies by one new company."[8] Thus, it provides more wider coverage to the acquisitions as it may take the form of amalgamation. It is notable that for the purpose of Indian Companies Act, 1956. Merger and Amalgamation are synonymous. Besides, Section 390-396A contains provisions on compromise, arrangements and reconstruction. Amalgamation is also an arrangement or reconstruction.

Section 2(1B) of the Income Tax Act, 1961 also defines amalgamation in relation to companies, as the merger of one or more companies with another company or merger of two or more companies to form one company in such a manner that (i) all the property of the amalgamating company or companies immediately before the amalgamation becomes the property of the amalgamated company by virtue of the amalgamation; (ii) all the liabilities of the amalgamating company or companies immediately before the amalgamation become the liabilities of the amalgamated companies by virtue of amalgamation; (iii) shareholders holding not less than $9/10^{th}$ in the value of shares in the amalgamating company or companies become shareholders of the amalgamated company by virtue of amalgamation; this does not however, include shares already held by the shareholders of the amalgamating company in the amalgamated company.

Features of Amalgamation

Important features of amalgamation are as follows-

(*i*) It provides blending of two or more existing undertakings wherein, the shareholders of each blending company become substantially shareholders in the company which is to carry on the blended undertakings[9] or

(*ii*) It ensures transfer of two or more undertakings to a new company or transferring of one or more undertakings to an existing company.[10]

(*iii*) It contemplates a state of things under which two companies are so joined as to form a third entity or one company is absorbed into and blended with another company.

(*iv*) It transfers property, assets and liabilities of one or more companies to another company. Thus, properties, assets and liabilities are absorbed by and transferred to an existing company or a new company. The transferor company merges into or integrates with the transferee company. The transferor company losses its legal identity and is dissolved (without winding up).

Thus, amalgamation involves fusion of two or more companies. Generally, two companies lose their identity and a new company comes into existence for the specific purpose. Firms of equal size generally prefer this type of combination.

2. Merger : Merger is a combination of two or more companies into a single company. It combines of two or more companies in which one company survives under its own name while the other ceases to exist as a legal entity. It is defined "as an arrangement whereby the assets of two (or more) companies become vested in or under the control of one company (which may or may not be one of the original two companies) which has as its shareholders, all or substantially all the shareholders of the two companies.[11] Absorption is another type of merger where a small company integrates with large company. Smaller company ceases to exist after its merger with large company. The recent merger of Bank of Rajasthan with ICICI Bank is the case of absorption. After the merger, Bank of Rajasthan ceased to exist while the ICICI Bank expanded and continued.

Reverse merger takes place when a healthy company merges into a financially weak company. In the context of Companies Act, 1956 there is no distinction between a merger or reverse merger because in either case one company merges with another company. Reverse merger like an amalgamation or merger is carried out through High court route under the provisions of section391 to 394 of the Companies Act 1956. When the reverse merger of the sick company becomes effective, the name of sick company may be changed to that of the healthy company and the transferee company becomes entitled to various tax benefits.

Objectives of Mergers: Following are the major objectives of a merger. [12]

(*i*) It helps in horizontal growth to achieve optimum size or to carve out greater market share or to curb competition or to use the unutilized capacity of another company.

(*ii*) It economies cost, eliminates avoidable sales tax and to excise duty payment specially in vertical combination.

(*iii*) It ensures product diversification.

(*iv*) It mobilises financial resources by utilizing idle funds lying with another company.

(*v*) It improves free flow of cash in case of merger of an export company/ an investment company/ a trading company with an industrial company.

(*vi*) It also improves cash flow by merging subsidiary with holding company.

(*vii*) it activates industrial activity as taking over a small company which may have necessary industrial license but the promoters do not wish to proceed with the project.

Conditions for Successful Mergers

The main parameters required for success of any merger are given below:

1. The earning performance of the merged company can be measured by return on total assets and return on net worth. Generally, probability of the success or failure in economic benefits is very high among concentric mergers.
2. Merger may be able to sustain the increase in earnings if the merged company yields larger net profit than before, or a higher return on total funds employed on the merged company.
3. The capitalization of the company determines its success or failure. Similarly, dividend rates and payouts also determine the success or failure.
4. Merged company creates larger business for acquiring company its means it has helped in survival and growth of the acquiring organisation.
5. Comparison of the performance of merged company with the performance of the similar sized company in the same industry in respect of (i) Sales, (ii) assets, (iii) net profit, (iv) earnings per share and (v) market price of shares should be undertaken to get better comparison.
6. Gains to shareholders are measured in terms of increase or decrease in share prices of the merged company. However, share prices are influenced by many factors other than the performance result of the company.
7. Some mergers also increase in size of capital base and market segments of the merged or amalgamated company. They also increase the resources which enable the firm to optimize its size.
8. Fair market value is one of the valuation criteria for measuring the success of post merger company. Fair market value is defined as the value in the hands between a willing buyer and willing seller, each having reasonable knowledge of all the pertinent facts and neither being under pressure nor compulsion to buy and sell. Such valuation is generally made in pre-merger cases.

9. Some other factors like improved debtors realization, reduction in non-performing assets, improvement due to economies of larger scale production and application of superior management techniques and cheap finance, labour and materials should also be assessed for the success or failure of merger.

Merger, Consolidation, Amalgamation, Acquisition

Merger is a combination of two or more companies in which one company survives under its own name while the other ceases to exist as a legal entity. Consolidation is a combination of two or more companies in which all companies cease to exist as legal entity and a new company is created. Thus, there is a difference between merger and consolidation.[13] However, there is a technical distinction between the two. Consolidation is an absorption and merger is called as amalgamation.[14] However, consolidation and merger are treated as amalgamation in terms of Section 391 and 394 of Indian Companies Act, 1956.

Types of Merger: Important types of mergers are as follows:

1. Horizontal Merger: When two companies of the same line of business merges together, it is called horizontal merger. It involved two firms operating and competing in the same kind of business activity. The principle benefit from this type of merger are economies of scales in production and distribution, and possible increase in market power in a more concentrated industry. Acquirer is the most important beneficiary of this merger as it strengthens the product market position.

"It also involves joining together of two or more companies which are producing essentially the same products or rendering same or similar services or their products directly come to in the market with each other."[15] Actually, it is a merger between competitors who are manufacturers or distributors of the same type of products or who render similar or same type of products or who render similar or same type of services for profit. Testing criteria for this merger is that combination is possible among the competitors who are engaged in production or distribution of same product or service with an objective of reducing the number of competition companies as well as the level of competition in an industry. It also improves the scope of economies of scale and limitations of duplicate facilities.

Thus, the horizontal merger is a growth strategy that involves the acquisitions of one or more competitors. It also involves expansion by broadening the reach of the current product lines and eliminating the threats presented by the acquired competitor's position. It is generally a step toward increasing organizational sales, profits and market share.

Limitations of the horizontal Merger: Following are the major limitations of the horizontal merger:

(*i*) It promotes monopolistic trend in the industry as it decreases the number of firms working in an industry.

(*ii*) It helps the operating firms in an industry to develop cartel for monopoly profits.

(*iii*) It enables the combined forms to engage in anti competitive practices.

(*iv*) It adversely affects the survival of small firms, as they are unable to compete with dominating firm.

(*v*) It discourages the development of first generation entrepreneurship in an industry.

2. Vertical Merger: It involves different stages of production operations. In this case, merger takes place among the companies having different levels of production process of the same product or same line of business. The acquiring and target companies both are working in the same industry having strong supplier buyer relationship. The acquired company is either a supplier or customer of the acquiring company. It is usually undertaken when the market of the intermediate product is imperfect. These are different reasons for vertical merger.

(*i*) availability of technological economies.

(*ii*) elimination of searching cost for prices, contracting payment collection and advertising.

(*iii*) improvement in planning for inventory and production due to efficient internal information flow.

(*iv*) accomplishment of expropriation by demanding the supply of goods or services produced from the specialized assets at a price below its average cost.

Thus, vertical merger is also a part of growth strategy that involves the acquisition of one or more organizations that are suppliers, distributors or customers of the firm products. Actually, it involves expansion through the supply chains or the distribution channels that serve the organisation.

Limitations of Vertical Merger: Limitations of vertical mergers are as follows:

(*i*) If upstream firms obtain a high level of vertical integration into an associated retail market, this may facilitate collusion in the upstream market by monitoring retail prices.

(*ii*) The elimination by vertical merger of a disruptive buyer in a downstream market may facilitate collusion in the upstream market.

(*iii*) Non-horizontal mergers by monopoly public utilities may be used to evade rate regulation.

3. Conglomerate Mergers: It involves those firms that are engaged in unrelated types of business activity. In this merger, merging companies operates in unrelated markets having no functional relationship. The main focus of the conglomerate merger is on how the acquiring entity can enhance the overall stability and balance the total portfolio in the market. However, these deals are not intended at sharing resources technologies, synergies or product market strategies, but they enable the acquiring company to enhance its overall stability and balance the total portfolio in terms of better use of resources and generation of revenue. Two important characteristics define a conglomerate firms (i) a conglomerate firm controls a range of activities in various industries that require different skills in the specific managerial functions of research, applied engineering productions, marketing (ii) the diversification is achieved mainly by external acquisitions and mergers not by internal development.[16] The basic feature of conglomerate merger is to develop a self contained division or subsidiary company by acquiring another company. Each self contained division or subsidiary company is delegated the authority to choose and serve its own customers, using its own technology to produce its own goods and services. However, these divisions and subsidiaries have to work for the micro objectives of holding companies.

Thus, the basic purpose of conglomerate merger is to ensure overall stability of the acquirer company and creates balancing acts in the company's total portfolio of diverse products and production processes and thereby reduces the risk of instability of cash flows.

Limitations of Conglomerate Merger: Limitations of conglomerate merger are as follows-

(*i*) It lacks commonality either in its end product or in the rendering of any specifically of service to the society.

(*ii*) It creates fewer interdependency among divisions due to diversities exist in different operating units or divisions.

(*iii*) It requires a lot of efforts to monitor divisional performance for achieving the overall organizational goals.

4. Cogeneric or Concentric Merger: It is the part of growth strategy which involves focusing organizational resources on the growth of one product or a small group of related products. It is also called as market penetration strategy where merger ensures a good way for acquiring company to improve its market position. It involved a process where acquirer and target companies are related through the basic technologies, productions process or markets. The acquired company represents an extension of product line, market participation or technologies of the acquiring company from its current set of business into contigenrous business. The acquiring company derives benefits by exploitation of strategic resources and from entry into a related market having higher return that is employed earlier. The potential benefit of the congeneric merger is high because these transactions offer opportunities to diversity around a common core of strategic resources.[16] Actually, it is a merger in which there is carry over in specific management functions (e.g. marketing) or complementarily in relative strengths rather than carry over/complementarities is only generic management functions (e.g. planning). Thus, if the activities of the segment brought together are so related that there is carryover of specific management function (research, manufacturing, finance, marketing, personnel and so on or complementarity in relative strengths among these specific management functions) the merger should be termed concentric rather conglomerate."[17]

There are three types of concentric merger[18]:

(*i*) When a similar type of products is offered with the help of unrelated technology, e.g. a company in the sewing machine businesses diversifies into kitchen ware and household appliances, which are sold through a chain of retail stores to housewives.

(*ii*) When a similar type of product (or service) is provided with the help of related technology, e.g. a raincoat manufacturer makes other-rubber based items such water proof shoes and rubber gloves sold through the same retail outlets.

(*iii*) When a new type of product or service is provided with the help of related technology, e.g., a leasing firm offers hire-purchase services to institutional customers and consumer financing for purchase of durables to individual customers.

Motivating Factors for Mergers: Following factors are responsible for mergers:

1. **Availability of Economies of Scale:** Economies of scale is concerned with the volume of production which leads to reduction in cost of production per unit. It is cost effectiveness, which is generally associated with the manufacturing operations where ratio of output to input improves with the volume of operations. Mergers help the companies to expand the volume of production without a corresponding increase in fixed costs. Optimum utilization of management resources and systems of planning, budgeting, reporting and control also help in ensuring economies of scale.
2. **Operating Economies:** Mergers also help the combined firm to avoid overlapping of functions and facilities. Various functions may be consolidated and duplicate channels may be eliminated by implementing an integrated planning and control system.
3. **Financial Benefits:** Financial benefits include financial synergies and benefits such as eliminating financial constraints, deployment of surplus cash, enhancing debt capacity and lowering the costs of financing. Sometimes cash rich companies are unable to use their surplus cash for profitable purposes as internal growth is not possible. In that case, it would be better for these companies to improve the market value of their shares by using their surplus cash in purchase of another company. A combined company can easily ensure stability of cash flows; enhance the capacity of servicing a larger account of debt, and getting a higher interest tax shield to improve the shareholders wealth.
4. **Market Leadership:** Mergers enable the merging companies to have a greater number of market resources. With the additional combined market share a company can afford to control the price in a better manner with the consequent increase in profitability. Since combined firm has a better bargaining power, it can easily deal with labour, suppliers and buyers at favourable terms. Mergers also enable the combined firms to develop effective R&D facilities and it can also export technological breakthrough against obsolescence and price wars.
5. **Diversification:** It implies growth through the combination of firms in unrelated business. Merger are also performed to diversify the company's dependence on a number of segments of the economy. It also reduced the risk involved in a particular segment of economy. All businesses go through cycles and if the fortunes of company were linked to only one or a few products then in the decline stage of their product life cycles, the company would find it difficult to sustain itself. Actually, diversification is also a growth strategy that involves the acquisition of companies working in other industries or in other lives of business. Thus, merger helps the business firms to expand into different product lines. One reason for this type of merger to diversify is to counter the effects of the effects of external environmental conditions such as economic changes and seasonal changes. The company therefore looks for either related or unrelated diversification and may decide to do that so not internally, but by setting up new products, externally by merging with companies, of the desired product profile. Such diversification helps to widen the growth the opportunities for the company and smoothen the ups and down of their life cycles.
6. **Synergy:** It deals with combined activity of two or more sub-systems that's results in better performance than when the units work in isolation. It represents the two plus two equals five (2+2=5) effect. With the help of this approach, combined firm is more valuable than the sum of individual combining firms (2+2=4). It enables the combining firms to create a unique level of integration spanning the entire value chain in the line of business. It also helps the merged entity to achieve cost effectiveness, increase in earnings potential etc. Besides, focused operational efforts, rationalization, standardization and simplification of business process, productivity improvements, improved procurements and the elimination of duplication are the major benefits of synergic environment.
7. **Purchase of New Product or Brand Name:** Strategically, companies purchase new products or brands to reduce the gestation period or time lag in product development or brand development. Merger, would provide readymade facilities, which would provide a quicker entry for encashing the comparative advantage of the new product before new entrants make the market much more competitive and much less profitable.
8. **Strategic Integration:** Some companies' oftenly have a complementary nature of businesses viz. commercial strengths, geographic profiles and site integration etc. Merger helps the merged entity to conduct operations in the most cost effective and efficient manner. It also enables the firm for optimal utilization of various infrastructural and manufacturing assets, utilities and other site facilities.

9. **Taxation or Investment Incentives:** Tax incentives also attract merger of companies. A company, which has incurred losses in previous years, can carry such losses forward and offset them against future taxable profits and reduce tax liabilities. In this situation, if loss-making company merges with a company with large taxable profits would help to absorb the tax liability of the latter. Modernization and huge investment in plant and machinery also entitle the company to enjoy substantial investment connectives. But it is possible only when the company has sufficient taxable profit to offset these incentives. Acquiring or merging such a company with a highly profitable company ensures full use of the investment incentives.

Illustration-2

X Ltd is considering the proposal to acquire Y Ltd. and the financial information is given below:

	X Ltd.	Y Ltd.
No. of equity shares	10,00,000	6,00,000
Market price per share (Rs.)	30	6,00,000
Market capitalization (Rs.)	3,00,00,000	1,08,00,000

X. Ltd. intends to pay Rs.1,40,00,000 in cash for Y ltd. If Y Ltd market price reflects only its value as a separate entity, calculate the cost of merger when merger is financed by cash. **(C.S. Final, June, 2007)**

Solution:

When merger is financed by cash cost of merger is

= (cash – MVy) + (MVy – PVy)

MVy = Market Value of Y Ltd.

PVy = True/Intrinsic value of Y Ltd.

Cost of merger = (14,000,000 – 108,000,00 – 108,000,00)

= Rs.32,00,000

(Note: Market value and intrinsic value assumed to be same.)

If cost of merger becomes negative then shareholders of X Ltd. will get benefited by acquiring Y Ltd. in terms of market value.

Illustration-3

IDBI Bank Ltd. (IDBI) has finally walked away with United Western Bank (UWB), the Satara-based private sector bank. There were 17 commercial banks including public sector banks, private sector banks and foreign banks, who had bid for UWB. There was also one restructuring proposal from UWB, which envisaged the help of the Maharashtra Government in association with SICOM, HDFC and its subsidiaries as associates and IDFC. These investors together had offered to pump in around Rs. 350 crore into the bank.

IDBI has offered Rs. 28 per share to all UWB shareholders. The major institutional shareholders in UWB is SICOM's acquisition price. The IDBI's offer price works out to 1.8 times of the book value. This is higher than the average of 1.25 times for public sector banks' but lower than the average of three for the top 4 new private sector banks:

	IDBI	UWB
No. of Branches	195	230
Deposits (Rs. in crores)	26,000	6,480
Advances (Rs. in crores)	52,518	4,006
NPAs (in %)	1.01	5.66

It is a win-win situation for IDBI, as they will be able to acquire a branch network of around 230 and around 3,000 employees of UWB. The employee acquisition, according to analysts, is equally important for IDBI as it has a high attrition rate and this acquisition will give it access to around 3,000 professional bankers at one go.

In the light of above details and other factors, answer the following questions:

(*i*) What is the meaning of 'amalgamation' according to Accounting Standard-14?

(*ii*) Why were there so many suitors despite UWB being in poor health?

(*iii*) Can IDBI handle post-merger cultural issues?

(*iv*) How does this merger fits into IDBI Bank's strategic management?

(*v*) Classify the 'merger'. In which category would you like to put UWB's merger with IDBI Bank?

(C.S. Final, June, 2007)

Solution:

(*i*) According to AS-14 issued by Chartered Accountant of India, amalgamation means an amalgamation pursuant to the provisions of the Companies Act, 1956 or any other statute which may be applicable to companies. Under the said AS-14, two methods of amalgamation have been contemplated, viz., (a) amalgamation in the nature of mergers, and (b) amalgamation on the nature of purchase.

In the said case the amalgamation is in the nature of merger.

(*ii*) Some of the reason which has attracted many suitors despite UWB being in poor health:

First, over the past couple of years there has been a rediscovery world wide of the centrality of the branch network to a bank's performance. Branches are vital for customer acquisition, for assessing stable, low costs deposits and for cross selling of products. Secondly, the rural retail market is attractive and it can take care of initial costs. Once a bank gets familiar with the terrain, it can tap into SMEs, trade financing etc. Thirdly. Credit has been growing at 30% for the three years in a row and this changes economics of branches earlier thought unattractive.

(*iii*) The cultural issues are likely to be less acute with a Public Sector Bank than with a private sector or foreign sector bank. Besides, a crisis situation tends to make the cultural and people issues like deployment of staff, closure of branches, more manageable.

(*iv*) The merger has the potential to add greater value to IDBI, itself coming out of the troubled time. The addition to branches means a lot to IDBI. Secondly, IDBI has positioned itself at the upper end of the retail. The merger gives it a chance to move market and broad base its customer profile. Thirdly, since the IDBI has a high attrition rate; this acquisition provide access to around three thousand professional bankers.

Strategic fit in general often occurs by way of economies of scale, elimination of competition, better use of resources, better use of complimentary resources, use of surplus funds and diversification.

(*v*) Classification of Merger:

(*a*) Horizontal (Merger between businesses of similar types).

(*b*) Vertical (merger between businesses engaged in different stages of production operation).

(*c*) Conglomerate (merger between in unrelated fields).

(*d*) Others

- Cash merger (some shareholders receiving cash for their shares and other to get their shares in the continuing firm)
- De-facto merger (merger cost in the form of an acquisition if assets)
- Downstream merger (merger of parent company into its subsidiary)
- Up stream merger (merger of subsidiary into its parent company)
- Short from merger
- Triangular merger

Illustration-4

Kangan Ltd. is considering merger with Payal Ltd. Kangan Ltd.'s shares are currently traded at Rs. 25 per share. It has 2,00, 000 shares outstanding and its earnings after taxes (EAT) amount to Rs. 4,00,000. Payal Ltd. has 1,00,000 shares outstanding; its current market price is Rs. 12.50 per share and its EAT is Rs. 1,00,000. The merger will be effected by means of a stock-swap (exchange). Payal Ltd. has agreed to a plan under which Kangan Ltd. will offer the current market value of Payal Ltd.' shares.

(*i*) What are the pre-merger earnings per share (EPS) and P/E ratios of both the companies?

(*ii*) What must the exchange ratio be for Kangan Ltd.'s pre-merger and post-merger EPS to be the same?

(*iii*) If Payal Ltd. P/E ratio is 8, what will be its current market price? What will be the exchange ratio? What will Kangan Ltd.'s post-merger EPS be?

(C.S. Final, Dec. 2007)

Solution:

(*i*)

Company	Kangan Ltd. Rs.	Payal Ltd. Rs.
Market price of equity shares	25.00	12.50
No. of equity shares outstanding	2,00,000	1,00,000
Earning after tax	4,00,000	1,00,000
EPS =	Rs. 4,00,000/ 2,00,000 shares = 2.00	Rs.1,00,000/ 1,00,000 shares = 1.00
P/E ratio =	Rs. 25/2= 12.5	12.50/1 = 12.5

(*ii*) In such cases the number of shares will be: (Total earnings) Rs. 5,00,000 / (EPS) Rs. 2 = 2,50,000 equity shares. It means 50,000 shares of Kangan Ltd. will have to be issued to the shareholders of Payal Ltd. One share of kangan Ltd. will be issued for every two shares held by shareholders of Payal Ltd.

Then pre-merger and post – merger EPS of Kangan Ltd. will be same as follows;

Pre-merger EPS of Kangan Ltd. Rs. 2.00

Post-merger EPS of Kangan Ltd. Rs. 5, 00, 000/ 2, 50,000 equity shares = Rs. 2.00

(*iii*) (i) If Payal Ltd. P/E ratio is 8, its current market price will be Rs. 8 only (8 × 1)

(*ii*) Then the exchange ratio will be 8/25 i.e. 32/100. For every 100 shares of Payal Ltd. 32 shares of Kangan Ltd. will be issued (1, 00,000 × 32)/ 100 = 32,000 shares of Kangan Ltd. will be issued to all the shareholders of Payal Ltd.

(iii) Post merger EPS of Kangan Ltd. = Total earning/ Total shares = 5, 00,000 / 2, 32,000

Equity shares = Rs. 2.16

3. Demerger : It is generally used to describe division or separation of an undertaking of a business, functioning with or under a common corporate umbrella. Actually, it is a corporate partition of a company into two undertakings, thereby retaining one undertaking with it and by transforming the other undertaking to the resulting company.

It involves "spinning of unrelated business/division/unit in a diversified company into a standalone company along with a free distribution of its shares to the existing shareholders of the original company."[19] In demerger, the demerged company sells and transfers one or more of its undertakings to the resulting company for an agreed consideration. The resulting company issues its shares at the agreed exchange ratio to the shareholders of the demerged company.

According to Income Tax Act 1961 (Section 2 Subsection 19AA) also states that demerger in relation to companies means transfer, pursuant to a scheme of arrangement under section 391 to 394 of the companies Act 1956 by a demerged company of its one or more undertakings to any resulting company in such a manner that:

(*i*) all the property of the undertaking being transferred by the demerged company, immediately before the demerger, becomes the property of the resulting company by virtue of the demerger;

(*ii*) all the liabilities relatable to the undertaking, being transferred by the demerged company, immediately before the demerger, become the liabilities of resulting company by virtue of the demerger;

(*iii*) the property and the liabilities of the undertaking or undertakings being transferred by the demerged company are transferred at values appearing in its books of account immediately before the demerger;

(*iv*) the resulting company issues, in consideration of the demerger, its shares to the shareholders of the demerged company on a proportional basis;

(v) the shareholders holding not less than three fourths in value of the shares in the demerged company (other than shares already held therein immediately before the demerger or by a nominee for, the resulting company or companies by virtue of the demerger, otherwise than as a result of the acquisition of the property or assets of the demerged company or any undertaking thereof by the resulting company;

(vi) the transfer of the undertaking is on a going concern basis.

(vii) the demerger is in accordance with the conditions, if any, notified under Sub-section (5) of Section 72A of the Income Tax Act 1961 by the Central Government in this behalf.

Conditions for demerger: Generally demerger takes place in following conditions

(i) When a division or unit no longer fits into the company's plans;

(ii) When company itself wants to rationalize specialize its operation in core area.

(iii) When affecting family settlement is required.

(iv) When a scheme of arrangement under section 391 to 394 of the companies Act required.

(v) When selling the undertaking on disjunctive basis is required.

Sub-Systems of Demerger : There are following sub-system of demerger by which efforts are generally made to unlock the value of the business firms in favour of their shareholders. These are as follows:

(i) Spin offs

(ii) Splits off

(iii) Split ups

(iv) Equity Carve Outs

(i) **Spin offs:** It is a process under which a company creates a subsidiary whose shares are distributed on a pro-rata basis to the shareholders of the parent company. Hence, the shareholders proportional ownership of the shares is the same in the new legal subsidiary as available in the parent firm. The new subsidiary has its own management and is run independently from its parent company. The number of shares of subsidiary company varies in relation to the parent's share varies. Generally, parent companies retains 10% to the 20% of the shares in the new subsidiary. However, to qualify for tax exemptions on a spin off, the parent company must own 80% of voting rights of spinned off subsidiary company. Recent spin-off by Grasim Industries of its cement business to Samruddhi cement company is the popular example of spin off.

A spin off subsidiary has an advantage of independent stock price that directly reflects the market's valuation to management initiatives and more links compensation to performances. To a certain extent spin offs also help in increasing the number of securities for a given number of possible states of the world if financial markets are not complete. It also facilitates mergers when the bidder is interested in only in one part of the target firm's operations. Spin off of cement division of L&T company to Ultra teck of Birla Group is the classic case of this type of merger. Moreover, spin offs are the best when a parent company has no potential to create value through skills, systems, or synergies. Spin off occurs when a division of company or organisation becomes an independent business. Spin off is a demerger when an existing parent company distributes on a pro-rata basis, all the shares it owns in a controlled subsidiary to its own shareholders by which it is enable to make the two of them, a single company or corporation. There is no money transaction, no revaluation of subsidiary assets and the transaction is treated as a tax-free exchange. The value of their shares in the original company will be adjusted by the market to take account of the spin off. Both companies exist and carry on the business. It does not alter ownership proportion in any company.

(ii) **Split Offs:** Under this process, a new company is created to takeover the business of an existing division or unit. A portion of the existing shareholders receives shares in newly created subsidiary company in exchange of shares of the parent company. Split offs generally undertaken to control the effects of over capitalization. Consequently, equity base of the parent company is reduced. It is a process of downsizing of the business firm. However, it does not reflect the shareholding of the parent firm in relation to shareholding of the newly created subsidiary company. It also does not provide any help in increasing the cash inflows of the parent company.

(iii) **Split ups:** Split ups are used by the business firms to create two or more separate entities. Actually, under this process, entire firm is broken up in series of spin offs so that the parent company no longer exists and only the new off-springs are come into existence. The process of spilt ups creates a new class of shares for each of the subsidiaries and ensuring a payment of current dividend to each new class of shareholders. At last, parent company is to be dissolved. Shareholders in the new companies may be different from the shareholders of the parent company as they may have exchanges their shares for shares in one or more of the spin-offs. The spin ups are generally taken by initial carve outs and spin offs of individual parts from one or more core activities. The success of the split ups is depends on the market value of the firm.

(iv) **Equity Carve Out:** It is the initial public offering (IPO) of a portion of the equity shares of a wholly owned subsidiary. Equity carve out is also referred to as "Split off IPOs". In IPO of the equity of the subsidiary resembles a seasoned equity offering of the parent company in cash which is received from a public sale of equity shares. The parent company generally retains majority control. Equity carve outs are for firms who can easily separate their subsidiaries. Equity carve outs are more successful for those subsidiaries who hold high margin and a high growth compared to their competitors. Capital gain through carveout can also be used for acquisition purposes. Carve outs allow companies to have better access to capital market. Parents debt rating also helps the subsidiaries to generate resources from the market. Carve outs allow division managers to take primary responsibility for financial and investment decisions. Managers can go to capital markets for money rather than trying to over state budgeting needs to the parent company. The IPO of the equity shares of the subsidiary initiates public trading in a new and distinct set of equity claims on the assets of the subsidiary company.

However, there is basic difference between equity carve outs and spin offs. In spin-off, a distribution is made pro-rata to the shareholders of the parent company as a dividend. It is a non cash payments to the shareholders of the parent company. In an equity carve out, the shares of the subsidiary sold in the capital market for cash is to be received by the parent company. Similarly, in a spin off the parent company has no control over the subsidiary assets. In a carve out, the parent generally sells only a minority interest in its subsidiary company and remain in control of subsidiary assets and its operations.

Steps to be taken to effectuate a scheme of demerger[20]

(i) Study the operational, legal and taxation process of the demerger.

(ii) Prepare the division or unit wise balance sheet so that the assets and liabilities of the undertakings or business to be demerged could be studied itemwise.

(iii) Prepare a comprehensive scheme of demerger in consultation with all the interested parties.

(iv) Place it for approval of the Board of Directors, Prepare a calendar of all major and minor pre-demerger and post merger activities.

(v) Appoint an expert for valuation of shares for determining share exchange ratio.

(vi) Appoint an advocate for appearance before High Court/Tribunal.*

(vii) Make an application to the High Court/Tribunal* under section 391/(1) for an order to convene and hold meetings of members /creditors or any class of them by a judge's summons in form 33 and affidavit in form 34 of the companies (Court) Rules, 1959.

(viii) On obtaining the Court/Tribunal's* order, convene the meetings in the manner prescribed and get the merger approved by the prescribed majority in value of the creditors or number of members, as the case may be. The notice should be sent in form 36 by the person authorized by the Court/Tribunal.*

(ix) The notice of the meeting shall be published in such newspapers as the judge may direct, not less than 21 days from the date fixed for the meeting in form 38.

(x) The chairman appointed for the meeting shall file an affidavit showing that the directions regarding issue of notices and advertisements have been duly compiled with.

(xi) On the date of the meeting, hold the same and chairman of the meeting shall submit the report stating accurately the number of creditors/members present and in person or proxy, their individual values and the way they voted.

(xii) The report shall be submitted in Form 39 within 7 days of the meeting to the Court/Tribunal*.

(xiii) When the scheme is approved by the required majority, make the petition in Form 40 and file it with Tribunal/Court*. The Tribunal/Court* will fix the date for hearing of the petition and notice of hearing shall

be advertised in the same newspaper in which notice of the meeting was advertised not less than 10 days before the date of hearing.

(*xiv*) Obtain an order of the Tribunal/Court* and file its certified copy with the registrar of companies within 14 days from the date the order or such time as may be fixed by the Tribunal/Court*.

(*xv*) The said order after filling the Registrar of Companies will be binding on all the creditors and members or, in the case of Company being wound up, on the liquidator and distributaries of the company.

Reconstruction: It is usually concerned with the transfer of an undertaking or business of a company to one or more other companies, specially formed for the purpose. It is also called as special purpose vehicle. The old company goes into liquidation and its shareholders, instead of being repaid their capital are issued and allotted equivalent shares in the new company. Consequently, the same shareholders carry on almost the same undertaking or enterprise in the name of a new company. "In this way reconstruction of business involves the idea of substantially the same person carrying on substantially the same business."[21]

Halsbury's Laws of England defines reconstruction as follows:

"While an undertaking being carried on by a company is in substance transferred, not to an outsider, but to another company consisting substantially of the same shareholders with a view to its being continued by the transferee company, there is a reconstruction. It is also reconstruction, where, after the transfer of a part of the company's undertaking the stockholders in the new company comprise a majority in number, but less than half in value of the shareholders in the original company."

Thus, "reconstruction" involved the winding up of an existing company and the transfer of its assets and liabilities to a new company formed for the purpose of taking over the business and undertaking of the existing company. Shareholders in the existing company become shareholders in the new company. The business, undertaking and shareholders of the new company are substantially the same as those of the old company. The new company may have a different capital structure from that of the old one, or have different objects, or be incorporated in a different country, but an essential features of a reconstruction is that the new company's membership is substantially the same as that of the old company.

Difference between Demerger and Reconstruction

Demerger means transfer, pursuant to a scheme of arrangement under Section 391 to 394 of the Companies Act, 1956 by the demerged company of its one or more undertaking to a new company formed for the purpose, known as the resulting company, in such a manner that all the property of the undertaking, being transferred by the demerged company become the liabilities of the resulting company by virtue of the demerger; all the liabilities relatable to the undertaking, being transferred by the demerged company becomes the liabilities of the resulting company by virtue of the demerger; the property and the liabilities of the undertaking or undertakings being transferred by the demered company are transferred at values appearing in its books of account immediately before the demerger.

In the case of reconstruction, a new company is formed, the existing company is dissolved by passing a special resolution for members voluntary winding up and authorizing the liquidator to transfer the undertaking, business, assets and liabilities of the transferor company to the transferee company. The transferee company pays the consideration by issue and allotment of its shares to the shareholders of the transferor company in accordance with the pre-determined share exchange ratio. In this process, the old company is liquidated and is reconstructed in the form of a new company with substantially the same shareholders, same undertaking and business.

Illustration-5

DEF Ltd was incorporated with a capital of Rs. 70 crore, promoted by a well known group HIJ Ltd. Unfortunately, DEF Ltd was incurring heavy losses right from incorporation and its accumulated losses as on 31st March, 2003 stood at Rs. 95 crore. The major finished products of DEF Ltd were the raw materials of HIJ Ltd. A summarized position of the financial condition of both these companies given below:

	(Rs. In Crore)	
Liabilities	DEF Ltd.	HIJ Ltd.
Share Capital	70	34
Reserves	--	173

Contd....

Other Liabilities	50	--
	120	207
Assets		
Total Assets	25	207
Losses	95	--
	120	207

Assuming that provisions of the Sick Industries Companies (Special Provision Act), 1985 are not applicable, advice the management of HIJ Ltd., the most tax efficient and company law friendly method of reconstruction of the company which would be in the longs term interests of both the companies. HIJ Ltd. and DEF Ltd., the financial institutions, shareholders and the employees involved. **(C.S. Final, Dec. 2003)**

Solution:

From the fact given in the question it is clear that the complete paid up capital of DEF Ltd. has eroded. The ideal solution would be to dissolve DEF Ltd., as even its assets are not enough to pay its creditors. But since it is stated to belong to a well known group HIJ Ltd. a scheme of reconstruction has to be worked which will help DEF Ltd. To tide over the present difficulties and repay the loans over a rescheduled time period. This would be workable as it is also given in the question that the major finished products of DEF Ltd. were the raw materials of HIJ Ltd., so a proper scheme of arrangement appears to be the savior of all concerned i.e., all shareholders, institutions, suppliers, employees etc.

To make the reconstruction proposal viable to both the transferor and transferee, it is necessary first to write down the capital of DEF Ltd. by following the process of capital reduction but the scheme of arrangement and not under section 100. Then a reverse merger may be resorted to since in a reverse merger the loss making company is transferee company into which the profit making company merges. The name of the loss making company can thereafter be changed to that of the profit making company to protect brand equity of profit making company. Such an arrangement may be beneficial on the following grounds:

(i) As the raw materials of the profit making company are the finished products of the loss making company, it would be forward integration to DEF Ltd.

(ii) Pooling of resources would afford stronger resilience to with stand competition.

(iii) Combined operations would result in economies of scale, reductions of costs and integrated operations.

(iv) Integration of all activities leading to increased professionalism, streamlined management, sizeable reduction in management costs and avoidance of duplication in management set-up.

(v) The creditor who could otherwise have lost out would agree for a moratorium for a couple of years and then would be able to recover all their outstandings.

(vi) Employees of the loss making company who would have lost their jobs would find renewed enthusiasm for work since the company would not close down.

4. Acquisitions : Acquisition refers to the process in which a person or firm acquires controlling interest in another firm. Acquisition is the purchase of a controlling interest in a firm, generally via a tender offer for the target shares. For the purpose of Takeover and Substantial Acquisitions Regulations 10 and 11, acquisition means and includes: (a) direct acquisition in a listed company to which the Regulations apply; (b) indirect acquisition by virtue of acquisition of companies, whether listed or unlisted, whether in India or aboard. Generally, acquisition process involves following actions:

a. Strategic processes for growth in value

b. The economics of the industry

c. The firm's organization system

d. Multiple strategies for value growth

e. Search processes

f. Economic basis-synergy potentials

g. Restructuring potentials

h. Due diligence-both legal and business

i. Cultural factors

j. Valuation

k. Negotiation

l. Deal Structuring

m. Implementation

n. Reviews and renewal processes

Acquisition in general sense is acquiring the ownership in a property. In the context of business combination, an acquisition is the purchase by one company of a controlling interest in the share capital of another existing company. Company go in for acquisitions for a number of strategic or tactical reasons, like growth orientation, access to raw materials, technology, cheaper labour, innovations, reduction in dependence on exports. It can be enforced through an agreement with the persons holding a majority interest in the company's management or through purchasing shares in the open market or purchasing new shares by private treaty or by making a takeover offer to the general body of shareholders. Acquisition basically differs from amalgamation in terms of implementation procedure. Acquisition may take place either by outright purchase of assets or by acquisition of shares. The terms acquisition thus includes merger and consolidation."[22] There are other forms of acquisitions:

(*i*) Leveraged Buyout (LBO): It is defined as an acquisition by a small group of investors, financed largely by borrowing. This acquisition may be either of all stock or assets, of a public company. The buying group forms a shell company to act as the legal entity making the acquisition. This buying group may enter into stock purchase deal or asset purchase deal. Under the stock purchase device the shareholders sell their stock in the target company to the buying group and then the two firms may be merged. Under the asset purchase mode, the target company sells its assets to the buying group. This exercise aims at generating enormous increases in the market value and value gains for shareholders both who own the firm before the restructuring and after the restructuring.

The leveraged buyouts differ from the ordinary acquisition in following ways: (i) a large fraction of purchase price is debt financed through junk bonds. (ii) the shares of LBOs are not traded on open markets. In a LBO programme, the acquiring group consists of a small number of persons/ organizations/ sponsored by buyout specialists etc. This group, with the help of certain financial instruments like high yield high debt instruments, private placement instruments, bridge financing etc. acquire all or nearly all of the outstanding shares of the target firm. An attractive candidate for acquisition through leveraged buyout should posses three basic attributes: (a) It must have a good position in Industry with sound profit history.(b) The firm should have a relatively low level of debt and high level of 'bankable' assets. (c) It must have stable and predictable cash flows and adequate working capital.

(*ii*) Management Buyout (MBO): It is simply a transaction through which the incumbent management buy outs all or most of the other shareholders. The management may take on partners, it may borrow funds or it can organize the entire restructuring on its own. A MBO begins with arrangement/ raising of finance. Thereafter, an offer to purchase all or nearly all of the shares of a company not presently held by the management has to be made which may necessitate a public offer and even delisting. Consequent upon this, restructuring may be affected and once targets have been achieved, then the company can go public again.

(*iii*) Management buy-in: This is the situation when a group of managers from outside the business wish to buy into the business and run it, or buy into a division of the existing company.

5. Takeover : Takeover is a corporate device whereby one company acquires control over another company, usually by purchasing all or a majority of its shares. It is an acquisition of shares carrying voting rights in a company with a view to gaining control over the management of the company. It takes place when an individual or a group of individuals or a company acquires control over the assets of a company either by acquiring majority of its shares or by obtaining control of the management of the business and affairs of the company. Thus, the takeover is a strategy of acquiring control over the management of another company either directly by acquiring shares or indirectly by participating in the management. The objective is to consolidate and acquire large share of the market.

When an "acquirer" takes over control of the "target company", it is termed as takeover. When a company acquires "substantial quantity of shares or voting rights" of the target Company, it results into substantial acquisition of shares. Where the shares of the company are closely held by a small number of persons, a takeover may be effected by agreement with the holders of those shares. However, where the shares of a company are widelyheld by the general public, it involves the process as set out in the SEBI (Substantial Acquisition of Shares and Takeovers) Regulations, 1997.

If shares of company are under quoted on the stock market, the company may be under a constant threat of takeover. In fact every company is vulnerable to a takeover threat. The takeover strategy has been conceived to improve corporate value, achieve better productivity and profitability by making optimum use of the available resources in the form of men, material and machines. Ordinarily, a larger company takes over a smaller company. In a reverse takeover, a smaller company acquires control over a larger company. However, takeover of management is quite distinct from takeover or possession for the purpose of sale of establishment. In case of takeover of management the underlying view is to rehabilitate the establishment by providing better management. But in case of takeover of the company, minimum purchase of majority shares of is essential.

Objects of takeover: Main objectives of a takeover are as follows:

(*i*) To effect savings in overheads and other working expenses on the strength of combined resources;

(*ii*) To achieve product development through acquiring firms with compatible products and technological/manufacturing competence, which can be sold to the acquirer's existing marketing areas, dealers and end users;

(*iii*) To diversify through acquiring companies with new product lines as well as new market areas, as one of the entry strategies to reduce some of the risks inherent in stepping out of the acquirer's historical core competence;

(*iv*) To improve productivity and profitability by joint efforts of technical and other personnel on the strength of improved efficiency in administration, management production, finance and marketing of goods and services as a consequence of unified control;

(*v*) To create shareholder value and wealth by optimum utilization of the resources of both companies;

(*vi*) To achieve economy of numbers by mass production at economical costs;

(*vii*) To avail advantage of vertical combination;

(*viii*) To secure substantial facilities available to large companies compared to smaller companies;

(*ix*) To avail market development benefits in terms of new geographical territories or segments;

(*x*) To facilitate an increase in market share of the company by attaining dominant position by eliminating competition.

Kinds of Takeover: Main kind of takeover are follows:

(*i*) **Friendly Takeover:** Friendly takeover is possible with the consent of taken over company. It is based on negotiated settlement through bargaining between the two parties. In friendly takeover, there is an agreement between the management of two companies through negotiations and the takeover bid may be with consent of majority or all shareholders of the target company. This kind of takeover is done through negotiations between two groups. Therefore, it also called negotiated takeover. Before a bidder makes an offer for another company, it usually first informed the company board of director. If is felt that accepting the offer serves shareholders better than rejecting it, it recommends the offer better be accepted by the shareholders.

(*ii*) **Hostile Takeover:** When an acquirer company does not offer the target company the proposal to acquire its undertaking but silently and unilaterally pursues efforts to gain control against the wishes of existing management, such acts of acquirer are known as 'hostile takeover'. It is an unwanted offer made by a potential acquirer which is strongly opposed by the target company. Such takeovers are hostile on the management and are thus called hostile takeover. A hostile takeover allows a suitor to a target company's management unwilling to agree to a merger or takeover. A takeover is considered "hostile" if the target company's board rejects the offer, but the bidder continues to persuit it, or the bidder makes the offer without informing target company's board before hand. Generally, aggressive tactics viz., bear hug, proxy contest, tender offer are used by the potential acquirer to get over the control of the target company.

(*i*) **Bear Hug:** In a bear hug, a letter is mailed indicating acquisition proposal to the management of the target company. This type of letter is issued by the potential acquirer without warning. The letter contains a demand for immediate decision from the target company.

(*ii*) **Proxy Contest:** A proxy contest is an effort or movement by a group of effort dissident shareholders for seeking representation of their men on the governing board or to change the by-laws of the company.

(*iii*) **Tender Offer:** A tender offer is a takeover tactic in which the potential acquirer approaches directly to the shareholders of the target company with an offer to purchase their shares.

Offer Price: The offer price in case of hostile takeover shall be the highest of -

- The negotiated price under the agreement referred in Regulation 14(1);
- Price paid by the acquirer or persons acting in concert with him for acquisition, if any, during the 26 week or average of the daily high and low of the closing prices of the shares during the 2 weeks preceding the date of public announcement, whichever is higher.

There are different ways for conducting hostile takeover:

(*a*) A tender can be made where the acquiring company makes a public offer at a fixed price above the current market price.

(*b*) A proxy fight through which acquiring company tries to persuade enough shareholders usually a simple majority to replace the management with a new one which will prove the takeover.

(*c*) Open market purchase of enough shares quietly to effect a change in management. It is also known as a creeping tender offer.

The main consequence of a bid being considered hostile is practical rather than legal. If the board of the target company cooperates the bidder can conduct due diligence into the affairs of the target company. It can find out exactly what it is taking on before it makes a commitment. But a hostile bidder knows only publicly available information about the target company and so takes a risk. Also, banks are less willing to back hostile bids with the loan that are usually needed to finance the takeover. However, some investors may proceed with hostile takeovers because they are aware of mismanagement by the board and are trying to force the issue into public and potentially legal scrutiny.

(*iii*) **Bail out Takeover:** Takeover of a financially sick company by a profit earning company to bail out the former is known as bail out takeover. Such takeover normally takes place in pursuance to the scheme of rehabilitation approved by the financial institutions or the scheduled banks, who have already lent money to the sick company. The lead financial institutions, evaluates the bids received in respect of the purchase price track record of the acquirer and his financial position. This kind of takeover is generally done with the approval of the financial institutions and banks.

Takeover Bids

"Takeover bid" is an offer to the shareholders of a company, whose shares are not closely held, to buy their shares in the company at the offered price within the stipulated period of time. It is a technique, which is adopted by a company for taking over control of the management and affairs of another company by acquiring its controlling shares. Bids are offered to the shareholders with a view to acquiring sufficient number of shares for gaining control of the target company. It is usually expressed to be conditional upon a specified percentage of shares being the subject to acceptance by or before a stipulated date. There are three types of bids. These bids are mandatory, partial or competitive bids.

(*a*) **Mandatory Bid :** SEBI (Substantial Acquisition of Shares and Takeovers) Regulations 1997 as amended by Second Amendment Regulations, contain provision for making public announcement i.e. mandatory bid vide Regulations 10, 11 and 12 in the following cases:

(*a*) for acquisition of 15% or more of the shares or voting rights;

(*b*) for acquiring additional shares or voting rights to the extent of 5% of the voting rights in any financial year ending on 31st March if such person already hold not less than 15% but not more than 75% of the shares or voting rights in a company;

(*c*) for acquiring shares or voting rights along with persons acting in concert to exercise more than 75% of voting rights in a company.

(*d*) for acquiring control over a company.

(*b*) **Partial Bid :** Partial bid covers a bid made for acquiring part of the shares of a class of capital where the offeror intends to obtain effective control of the offered company through voting power. Such a bid is made for equity shares carrying voting rights. In other words, the offeror bids for the whole of issued shares of one class of capital in a company other than equity share capital carrying voting rights, partial bids come to the fore. Regulation 12 of SEBI (Substantial Acquisition of Shares) Regulations, 1997 qualifies partial bid in the form of acquiring control over the target company irrespective of whether or not there has been any acquisition of shares or voting rights in a company. For such acquisition, it is necessary to make public announcement in accordance with the Regulations.

(*c*) **Competitive Bid :** Competitive bid is an offer made by a person other than the acquirer who has made the first public announcement. Competitive bid can be made by any person within 21 days of public announcement of the offer made by the acquirer. Such bid shall be made through public announcement in pursuance of Regulation 25 of the SEBI Takeover Regulations 1997. Such public announcement of the competitive offer for acquisition is made for acquisition of shares of the same target company [Regulation 25 (a)]. Any competitive offer by an acquirer shall be for such number of shares which when taken together with shares held by him along with persons acting in concert with him shall be atlest equal to the holding of the first bidder including the number of shares for which the present offer by the first bidder has been made. No person shall make a competitive bid for acquisition of shares of a financially weak company where once lead financial institution has evaluated the bid and accepted the bid the acquirer who has made the public announcement in pursuance of Regulation 35 of SEBI Takeover Regulations, 1997.

Consideration for Takeover: Following options are generally used for the payment of takeover consideration:

1. **Consideration in the form of cash:** Takeover by an offeror company of an offeree company may be affected by a cash consideration, either for all or in part of the equity capital through a bid directly from the equity holders or through the stock market. The offeror company can have the new shares in sufficient number allotted to it or its directors to gain controlling voting power in the offeree company and also purchase for cash, block of shares from the persons in control of the offeree company, carrying effective voting rights and thereby enabling its nominees on the Board to control the affairs of the company.

2. **Consideration in the form of Shares:** When consideration is offered in the form of shares by the offeror in own company to shareholders of the target company various courses of action are available:

   (*a*) Share-for-share takeover bid in which the offeror company in exchange for shares of offeree provides fully paid up shares on a stated basis. Apart from this, share-plus-cash or share-plus-loan stock, convertible or non-convertible, shares or loan stock with a cash option could be a mode of consideration.

   (*b*) Reverse bid wherein the offeree company makes share-for-share bid for the whole of the equity capital of the offeror company where the offeror company has a large capital base. This alternative is more suitable when the offeree company is listed as a growing concern and capable of acting as a better holding company by pursuing its policies etc. Also, this mode offers sufficient tax advantages.

   (*c*) Combinations of various modes may be resorted to, for discharging the consideration. For instance, acquisition by private deal of a block of shares from the existing Board of Directors or larger controlling interest shareholders of the offeree company or acquisition of all or part of the assets of the offeree company for shares of offeror company or reverse acquisition with offeree company etc.

   Thus, the decision about the proper mix of alternatives should be taken through expert advice, having considered the relative quoted market prices of shares of offeror and offeree, their dividend yield, gearing level, security cover, voting strength, net assets value, etc.

3. **Acquisition through a new company:** A new company may be formed by acquiring shares in two target companies and the shares of the new company may be issued to the shareholders of both target companies, in consideration for acquisition of share capital or undertakings in whole or in part.

4. **Acquisition of Minority held shares of a subsidiary:** The offerer, if already holds more than 50% of issued capital in the offeree company and plans to acquire the balance equity of the offeree will have to resort to takeover tactics subject to the restrictions placed by the Indian Company Law and also SEBI guidelines.

Illustration- 6

Adroit Ltd. is run and managed by an effective team that insists on reinvesting 60% of its earnings in projects that provides a return on equity (ROE) of 10% despite the fact that the firm's capitalization rate (k) is 15%. The firm's current year's earnings is Rs.10 per share.

(*i*) At what price will the share of Adroit Ltd. sell?

(*ii*) What is the present value if growth opportunities?

(*iii*) Why would such a firm be a takeover target?

(C.S. Final, June 2007)

Solution:

(*i*) Calculation of Market Price per share at which Adroit Ltd. share will be sold (P)

$$= \frac{E(1-b)}{Ke-br}$$

Where, E = Earnings per share (Rs.10)

B = Retention ratio =0.60

r = Capitalisation rate or cost of equity = 15% or 0.15

or, g = Dividend growth or Growth rate of the firm i.e., Return on Equity (r) x

Retention ratio (b) i.e. = 10 × .60 or 6% or 0.06

Substituting the available information in the question in the above formula, we may get as under:

$$P = \frac{10(1-0.60)}{0.15-0.60} \quad \frac{10 \times 0.40}{.09} \quad \frac{4}{0.09}$$

Or, Rs.44.44

Note: Market Price per share may also be worked out by using other methods and accordingly the answer will change.

(*ii*) Calculation of Present value of Growth Opportunities (PVGO)

= Market price per share when the firm retention rate is 60% - Market price per share when the payout ratio is 100% or retention ration is 0%.

= Rs.*66.67 – Rs.44.44

= (-) Rs.22.23 (Negative)

$$P* = \frac{dividend}{Ke} = \frac{10}{0.15} = Rs.66.67$$

Thus, in this case the firm will have negative present value of growth opportunities because it is a declining firm having capitalization rate which is 15% higher than rate of return on equity which is 10%.

(iii) Reasons for the firm to be takeover target

Negative Present Value of Growth Opportunities (PVGO) implies that the net present value of the firm's projects is negative. The rate of return on those assets is less than the opportunity cost of capital. Such a firm would be subject to takeover target because another firm could buy the firm at a market price of Rs. 44.44 per share and increase the value of the firm by changing its investment policy. For example, if the new management simply pay out all earning as dividend, the value of the firm would increase up to its no growth value of Rs. 66.66.

Creeping Acquisition

The term 'creeping acquisition' encompasses a range of situations. While it can refer to a series of acquisitions over time that individually do not raise competitive concerns, but when taken together, the acquisition have a significant competitive impact.

The term creeping acquisition refers to a firm with substantial market power enhancing its market power through one or more acquisitions which individually do not lessen competition. Actually, creeping acquisition is described as conduct that comprises the accumulated effort of a number of small individual transmissions which, when considered in isolation at the time that each transaction occurred would not breach the fixed limit. Thus, the each transaction considered in isolation at the time it may have a limited impact on competition, and would therefore would not fall with the scope of a particular fixed limit but over a longer period a series of transactions may have the cumulative effect of substantially lessening competition in the market. Creeping Acquisition means incremental acquisition of shares by an existing shareholder during a given period. Creeping acquisition does not trigger the takeover code i.e. the SEBI (Substantial Acquisition of Shares & Takeover) Regulations 1997. In terms of Regulation 11 of the SEBI (Substantial Acquisition of Shares Takeovers) Regulations 1997 a person holding 15% or more but less than 75% of the shares or voting rights in a listed company can acquire further upto 5% shares or voting rights in any financial year ending 31st March without having a public announcement to acquire shares in accordance with the Regulations.

Illustration-7

Mittal Steels, owned by L.N. Mittal & Family, has its headquarters in London and Rotterdam. It has plants in 14 countries spread across Europe, Asia, North America and Africa. Its first acquisition took place in 1989.

Arcelor was founded in 2002 by merger of Abred of Luxembourg, Arcelia of Spain and Usinor of France. Its turnover is valued at 33 billion. Its plants, joint ventures and subsidiaries are spread across 60 countries.

In the year 2006, Mittal steel made an offer to acquire Arcelor. Its original offer to Areclor was for 17.5 billion. In May it increased the offer to 24 billion and the final offer was 26.9 billion. Mittal's final offer was accepted. Mittal paid 40.37 a share for Acrelor nearly double the price. It was trading before the first bid was made.

When metal made first bid, Arcelor rejected with vengeance. It recommended to shareholders not to sell shares to Mittal as the two companies did not share the same strategic vision, business model and values.

A couple of European governments did not like the idea of an Indian taking over an European company. The French foreign minister felt it would affect 28,000 jobs and that the bid was ill-prepared and hostile. However, Mittal Steel set jobs would be safeguard. Arcelor took the matter to regulators to that the takeover. But the regulators did not find any antitrust provisions being violated and asked arcelor not to issue shares to anyone without investors' explicit consent.

To begin with Arcelor refused to meet Mittal until a string of demands were met and simultaneously orchestrated a 13 billion deal with Severstal of Russia to keep Mittal away.

A shareholders wrath grew over the Severstal agreement and pressures for other quarters increased, Arcelor accepted Mittal's final bid. Arcelor had to pay 130 million as a fine to Servestal for breaching the contract.

Ultimately, L N Mittal succeeded in acquiring Arcelor. The combined capacity of Arcelor Mittal is 109.7 million tonnes.

Questions

(*i*) Was this takeover 'hostile' of 'friendly'? Distinguish between hostile takeover and friendly takeover.

(*ii*) Why did the executives of Arcelor defend Mittal's bid to takeover?

(*iii*) What normally happens once a hostile takeover is completed?

(*iv*) Do you think that the executives of Arcelor created defences against the Mittal keeping the best interest of stockholders in mind?

(*v*) Anti-takeover strategies can be of two types, viz. preventive and reactive. Explain them.

(*vi*) Evaluate defense strategies adopted by target firms to hostile takeover.

(C.S. Final, June 2007)

Solution:

(*i*) Acquisition of Arcelor by L.N. Mittal was a hostile takeover.

In a hostile takeover, an acquirer company does not offer the target company the proposal to acquire its undertaking but silently and unilaterally peruses efforts to gain control against the wishes of existing management. Such takeovers are hostile on the management and are thus called hostile takeover.

Friendly takeover is with the consent of the taken over company. In friendly takeover, there is an agreement between the managements of two companies through negotiations and the takeover bid may be with the consent of majority or all shareholders of the target company. This kind of takeover is done through negotiations between two groups. Therefore, it is also called negotiated takeover.

(*ii*) The executives of a target company, being Arcelor in the given case, defend hostile takeover on account of –

(*a*) Desire to retain autonomy or management;

(*b*) The preference for an alternative partner;

(*c*) The belief in the traditional setup that could be compromised by induction of new management; and

(*d*) The desire to negotiate a more favourable financial takeover.

In this case, the Arcelor executives tried to defend the hostile takeover on account of differences in the following respects:

(*a*) Strategic vision;

(*b*) Business model and values

(*c*) Cultural differences

(*d*) Nationalism [Mittal being owned by an Indian]

(*e*) Fear of loss of job and loss of control

(*iii*) Normally, once a hostile takeover is completed, a major restructuring takes place by way of –

(*a*) Divestitures of business units,

(*b*) Extensive layoffs, major changes in strategic direction, and

(*c*) Disruptions in the communities in which firm operates.

However, in case of Mittal- Arcelor not much of the above had happened except that the feeling of few top executives of Arcelor and some European governments have been hurt.

(*iv*) No, the executives of Arcelor did not create defences against the Mittal keeping the best interest of stakeholders in mind. In hostile takeovers, executives are generally motivated by their self preservation thereby subordinating the priority of stockholders by value.

In the case, the payment of 130 million to Severstal as fine for breaching the contract was a net loss to the shareholders. Had the shareholders worth not grown over the Severstal agreement, the executives would not have accepted Mittal's offer. Further, Mittal's offer of 40.37 a share for Arcelor was nearly double the price, it was trading before the first bid.

(*v*) Preventive strategies are constructed when executives since that the company is vulnerable to attack because of its depressed stock price, competitive weakness, market conditions or financial exigencies.

Preventive Strategies

(*i*) **Poison Pill:** In poison pill strategy the target company aims at making its own stock less attractive to the acquirer. It allows existing shareholders (except the bidding company) to buy more shares at a discount, with the goal to dilute the shares held by the bidder and make the takeover bid more difficult and expensive. This type of poison pill is usually written into the company's shareholder rights plan.

(*ii*) **Wright knight:** White Knight is a company (the "good guy") that gallops into make a friendly takeover offer to a target company that is facing a hostile takeover from another party (a "black knight") The white knight offers the target firm a way out with a friendly takeover.

(*iii*) **Golden Parachutes:** Golden Parachute is a measure in which lucrative benefits are offered to the current top executives of the company which include items such as stock options, bonuses, liberal severance pay and so on. Golden parachutes can be worth millions of dollors and can cost the acquiring firm a lot of money and therefore act as a strong deterrent to proceeding with their takeover bid.

(*iv*) **Dual Capitalisation:** If the law of land permits a second class of stock for the purpose of diminishing voting power of existing shareholders may be issued.

Reactive defenses are created when the target firm does not believe in creating permanent barriers to hostile takeovers.

Reactive Strategies

(*i*) **Litigation:** The target company may persue a legal injunction and restraining order against a pursuer to bar the acquirer till the time he can prove legally that the justification for the injunction is unfounded. The target company can levy three charges on the attacker that the acquisition would be anti-competitive that the bidder was not disclosed already available information that the pursuer deliberately misrepresented facts to deprive stockholders of their rights. Litigation results into extension of the negotiation period and the ensuring negotiations often lead to sweetening of the initial bid and a higher probability of a friendly takeover.

(*ii*) **Greenmail:** If the goal of aggressor is short term profit rather than long term corporate control, then the target company repurchases the shares acquired by the aggressor at a premium in exchange for an agreement of no takeover. This is also known as "bon voyage bonus" or a goodbye kiss.

(*iii*) **Standstill Agreements:** It is a contract between the aggressor and the target company in which the pursuer agrees not to acquire any more shares of a target firm for a specified time in exchange of certain a fee.

(*iv*) **Capital Structure Changes:** The target company has four options – recapitalization (paying shareholders a super dividend through taking additional loan), assuming additional debt to the balance sheet, approving the sale of additional stock to increase voting power of executives or to dilute shareholders equity in favour of a management friendly investor and buy-back of existing shares by way of tender offer equivalent to the raider.

Defence Strategy	Popular to target firm	Effectiveness as Defence	Stockholders' wealth effects
Poison pills	High	High	Positive
White knight	Medium	Medium	Positive
Golden Parachutes	Medium	Low	Negligible
Litigation	Medium	Low	Positive
Greenmanil	Very Low	Medium	Negative
Standstill	Low	Low	Negative

6. Joint Ventures : Joint ventures are new enterprises owned by two or more participants. They are typically formed for special purposes for a limited duration. It is an arrangement in which two or more organizations cooperate to develop, produce or sell product and services. The parent firms are independent of each other but share control over the joint venture. In some cases one company supplied the materials and the product expertise, while the other supplied the knowledge to do business to do business in the country they are targeting. It brings the participants essentially into a medium to long-term contract that is both specific and flexible. It is a contract to work together for a specified period of time. Each participant expects to gain from the activity but also must make a contribution.

Joint ventures may be used to acquire complementary technological or management resources at lower cost of or benefit from economies of scale, critical mass, and the learning curve effect-all elements of strategic alliances. They also offer more direct control over international operations than licensing or exporting and they allow organizations to tap the expertise of others as they expand in to overseas markets. They also allow organisations to spread the rise of entering a new market developing a new technology, or building a new plant. But joint ventures do not always perform as expected. Joint venture participants continue to exist as separate firms with a joint venture representing a newly created business enterprise. The joint venture may be organized as a partnership, a corporation, or any other form of business organization the participating firms might choose to select.

Characteristics of Joint Venture

Characteristic of Joint Ventures are as follows:

(*i*) Contribution by partners of money, property, effort, knowledge, skill, or other asset to a common undertaking.

(*ii*) Joint property interest in the subject matter of the venture.

(*iii*) Right of mutual control or management of the enterprise.

(*iv*) Expectation of profit, or presence of "adventure."

(*v*) Right to share in the profit.

(*vi*) Limited to the objective to a single undertaking or adhoc enterprise.

Each partner must have something unique and important to offer the venture and simultaneously provide a source of gain to the other participants. However, the sharing of information and/or assets required to achieve the objective need not extend beyond the joint venture. Hence, the participants' competitive relationship need not be affected by the joint venture arrangement. Sometimes the joint arrangement is relatively informal, involving only an exchange of ideas and information while the participants work on similar challenges.

Failure of Joint Ventures: Following reasons are responsible for the failure of joint ventures:

(*i*) Possibility of management disagreement between the partners operational and personnel problems.

(*ii*) Incompatible goals and methods of joint ventures.

(*iii*) Existence of an imbalance in the competence or the investment level of the partners.

(*iv*) Insufficient sales or profits generated through the ventures.

(*v*) Changes in the market structure of the joint venture.

(*vi*) Joint ventures are of limited scope and duration.

(*vii*) It involves small fraction of each participant's total activities.

7. Divestment : It involved a sale of a segment of a company (assets, a product line, a subsidiary) to a third party for cash or securities or both. Thus in a divestment, the organisation decides to get out of certain business and sells off units or divisions.

Reasons for divestment: Reasons for divestment are given below:

1. **Inadequate Market Share of Growth:** There is inadequate market share or growth potential for the existing business of the company. It is largely due to the environmental pressure on the working of the company.
2. **Irregular Cash inflows:** Continuous irregular or negative cash flow from a particular business create financial problems for the whole enterprise. It creates the need for divestment of a particular business of the firm to other company.
3. **High Cost of Technical Change:** There is technical change which requires high investment. If it is beyond the capacity of the organization then it would be better for it to go for divesture.
4. **Growing Competition:** Severity of competition and the inability of a firm to cope with the situation encourage the company to undertake divesture.
5. **Unmanageable Business:** The present business is unmanageable by the organisation because there are some testing troubles due to which company is facing problems in its operations. Large size of the business, wrong conception of the project, labour unrest, shortage of raw materials are responsible factors that forces the company for divesture.
6. **Part of Merger Plan:** Divestment by one firm may be a part of a merger plan executed with another firm where nuptial exchange of unprofitable decision may take place. The assumption is that such an exchange is in mutual strategic interest.
7. **Necessity of Survival:** Divestment is necessary because by selling off a part of a business the company may be in a position to survive in the long.

Motives for Divestitures: Divestitures are generally undertaken with the following motives:

(*i*) Dismantling of conglomerate structure

(*ii*) Abandoning the core business

(*iii*) Need for restructuring or change in strategies

(*iv*) Sale to group company for value addition

(*v*) Inability to finance additional investment required

(*vi*) Harvesting of past successes

(*vii*) Sale of unwanted businesses from prior acquisitions

(viii) Sale of business to finance prior acquisitions

(ix) Safeguard to takeover threats

(x) Fulfillment of regulatory requirements

(xi) Selling businesses to their managers

(xii) Sale of unrelated businesses

(xiii) Sale of low margin product lines

(xiv) Purchase of shares in another firm

(xv) Rectification of mistakes in future

(xvi) Learning divesture as a part of strategy

8. Strategic Alliance : It is a relationship among companies that are something short of establishing a joint venture entity. It is defined as "an associations to further the common interests of the members" or intercorporate agreements covering a wide gamut of functions ranging from component sourcing through research and development to production and marketing. Alliances are used to enter new markets, access new technologies and achieve economies of scale faster and cheaper than any other acquisition method."[23] It is "an agreement between two or more individuals or entities stating that the involved parties will act in a certain way in order to achieve a common goal. Strategic alliances usually make sense when the parties involved have complementary strengths".[24] Any arrangement or agreement under which two or more firms cooperate in order to achieve certain commercial objectives is referred to as strategic alliance. A true strategic alliance is a written arrangement between two companies that complement each other in a particular identified area. It is not a partnership, and neither company has legal power to control or obligate the other. Instead, it is commitment by the two companies to provide capabilities or cross servicing in certain identified areas. By properly utilizing a strategic alliance, companies can expand their product and service offerings substantially, without the usual corresponding investment in staff equipment, and facilities.

Strategic alliances may be defined in terms of following characteristics: "[25]

(i) "Two or more firms unite to pursue a set of agreed upon goals but remain independent subsequent to the formation of the alliance?

(ii) The partner firms share the benefits of the alliance and control over the performance of assigned tasks perhaps the most distinctive characteristics of alliances of assigned tasks- perhaps the most distinctive characteristics of all alliances and that makes so difficult to manage.

(iii) The partner firms contribute on a continuing basis in one or more key strategic areas, for example, technology, production and so forth."

Strategic alliance may also indicates a cooperative agreement between two or more companies where.[28]

(i) A common strategy is developed in unison and win-win attitude is adopted by all parties.

(ii) The relationship is reciprocal, with each partner prepared to share specific strengths with each other, thus leading power to the enterprise.

(iii) A pooling of resources, investments, and risks occurs for mutual (rather than individual) gain."

Alliances between companies have become a crucial weapon in the battle for competitive advantage. A "strategic alliance" is an excellent vehicle for two companies to work together profitably. Managed wisely, a strategic alliance can help companies develop and exploit their unique strengths. For example, a large company can break down the marketing barriers that face a small company, which in turn brings entrepreneurial creativity to the partnership. An alliance can also be a powerful tool for accessing new technology and developing domestic or international business opportunities. Alliances can rapidly meet a company's need for key resources such as most customers, additional capital, new/better products, new distribution channels, additional facilities, increased production capacity, or competent personnel etc.

Features of Strategic Alliance: Important features of strategic alliance are as follows[27]:

(i) No need to create new entity.

(ii) The relative sizes of the firms may be highly unequal.

(iii) It may involve relations with competitors.

(iv) Synergic value creation is possible by combining different resources.

(*v*) More value addition to the partnering firms by creating an organizational mechanism that aligns better decisions authority.

(*vi*) Pooling of resources and expertise is possible among partner firms.

(*vii*) It facilitates evolution of relationship.

(*viii*) Adaptability and change are required overtime.

(*ix*) Deliberate efforts are required to change the direction of at least one partner.

(*x*) It blesses corporate boundaries.

(*xi*) It encourages multiple partnership.

(*xii*) It requires mutual trust.

(*xiii*) It increases speed of change.

(*xiv*) It enables the participating companies to move in other emerging areas and attractive possibilities emerge

(*xv*) It provides access to creative people who want to work with smaller firms. A strategic alliance with small firms enable the larger firms to attract and provide incentives to more creative people.

Types of Alliances: Different types of alliances are as follows.[28]

(*i*) **Collisions between competitors:** The companies having core businesses of two strong and direct competition form an alliance. They are short lived because of competitive tensions and fail to achieve their strategic and financial goals.

(*ii*) **Alliance of the weak:** Two weak companies join forces in the hope that they will improve their mutual performance. But the weak grow weaker and the alliance fails.

(*iii*) **Disguised Sales:** There is possibility that a weak company joins with a strong competitor. Strong competitor never help the weaker company strategically. The alliance is short lived and the weak is acquired by the strong.

(*iv*) **Bootstrap Alliance:** The performance of weak company may be improved by forming an alliance with a strong company But the natural partnership must be developed into a alliance of equals.

(*v*) **Evolution to a sale:** Two strong and initially compatible partners initiate the alliance. This type of alliance may succeed in meeting the initial objectives and exceed the seven years average life span for alliance. But when tensions develop among the competitors, one partner ultimately sells out to the other.

(*vi*) **Alliance of complementary equals:** Alliance is a game of complementarily and compatibility. It can lead to mutually beneficial relationships. But its average life generally comes to 7 years. Any exercise of partner generally mark the future of alliance.

Rationale of Strategic Alliance: Rationale of strategic alliances are as follows:

(*i*) **Satisfy customers demand:** In many market customer demand profile is changing. Popularity of "systems solutions" force the customers to rely on a single company to service all equipments required by them. Strategic alliance easily ensures system solutions.

(*ii*) **Share R & D Costs:** High financial stakes and a cut-throat global market have fuelled a spate of competitive alliances in a number of industries.

(*iii*) **Fill Knowledge Gaps:** Participants generally prefer to reduce their costs by sharing the R&D costs. Big companies generally use alliances to capture new developments, and innovations. So, they always try to keep their technological resource based innovations ahead of competition.

(*iv*) **Make Scale Economies:** Alliances generally enable the participants to amortise their huge investments in shortest possible time as their scale of operations are quite high.

(*v*) **Market Scope Economies:** Scope of operations of a company can also be increased with the help of alliances. Alliances focusing on the scope help counter the ever-shorter product cycle of modern technology.

(*vi*) **Jump Market Barriers:** A company can easily sells its products in the home market but it may not possible for it to sell these products in the international markets. Alliance Marketing, franchising, distribution and licensing deals generally unable a development-focused company to concentrate on its new products. So, they prefer strategic alliance for products.

(vii) **Speed Product Introduction:** The narrowing of the development-to-market lead time has been a crucial feature of entrepreneurship. In many sectors, the first company to introduce a new product enjoys the dominant market position and stands the best chance of recouping costs before the competition arrives at the scene to drive prices down-or-before patent protection expires.

(viii) **Pre-empt Competitive Threats:** Generally, a few large players who increasingly dominate the market in some industries are trying to preempt the competitive threats. So there may be some companies resort to an "if you can't beat them, join them". Approach.

(ix) **Use excess capacity:** Larger number of companies use the restructuring effect of manufacturing alliances to soak up their excess capacity. It reduces costs as well as revenues.

(x) **Cut Exit Costs:** Participants can use alliances to cut the costs of leaving a business alliance, exit process is easy, flexible and less time consuming.

Scope of Strategic Alliance: Scope of Strategic Alliance is given below:

(i) **Development of new network:** It may be beneficial for an exporter to ally with a local partner to understand the functioning and behaviour of a local market network.

(ii) **Removal of regulatory barriers:** Alliances offer suitable options to foreign firms to have alliance with local partners or firms of host country. Local partners are supposed to have already removed the regulatory barriers available in the local market.

(iii) **Diversification:** It may be advantageous to enter into an alliance, with established business leaders as they guide to minimize pitfalls in a new business territory specially in host countries.

(iv) **Minimise competition:** An alliances minimizes the competition. Generally, it is entered into with a market leader who hold more competitive strength in local market.

(v) **Development of new products and restructuring:** An alliance in the form of a research and development alliance may focus at the development of new products. It also enables the firm to adapt to a more effective organisational structure.

(vi) **Meeting need for key resources:** Alliances can also help a company to cater its key resources such as most customers, additional capital, new/better products, new distribution channels, additional facilities, increased production capacity, or competent personnel etc on a competitive price and at higher volume.

(vii) **Environmental benefits:** It enable the strategic partners to seize the opportunities before they appear from the market. It also helps in ensuring greater flexibility, increasing company's market share and getting access to new markets. Effective respond to change, getting core competency, and removal of weaknesses are also the other benefits of strategic alliances.

Forms of Strategic Alliances: Forms of Strategic alliances are as follows:

(i) Pro-competitive alliance
(ii) Non-competitive alliance
(iii) Competitive alliance
(iv) Pre-competitive alliance

(i) **Pro-competitive alliance:** This situation arises due to the low interaction and low conflict between the strategic partners. Here, both the co-operation as well as competition between the firms are low. There are many cases of vertical value chain relationships between manufacturers and their suppliers or distributors and they are inter industry. In this alliance, firms actually are not investing their resources for manufacturing inputs. They are distributing finished or semi-finished goods together. One of the examples in this case is a supplier and buyer firm entering for long-term contracts.

(ii) **Non-competitive alliance:** This arises out of high co-operation and low competition. This is intra industry i.e. they are within the same industry, the alliance here is between non competitive firms. Firms generally enter into an alliance are from the same industry, yet they do not consider each other as rivals. They conduct themselves in different areas of activities hence giving less change for competition to arise. E.g. firms that work in different/distinct areas-geographically.

(iii) **Competitive alliance:** It arises due to high co-operation and high competition. The competitive alliance could be either inter-industry or intra-industry. The involved partners are rivals engaged in a cooperative arrangement where intense interaction is a must, e.g. many foreign companies operating independently in India or entering into a cooperative arrangement with local rival companies for definite purposes.

(iv) **Pre-competitive alliance:** It arises because of the low co-operation and high competition for e.g. Joint research and development activities, mass awareness campaigns etc. In this case, two firms from different or unrelated industries come together to develop new products or technology. It could also be to create awareness about new products or ideas among the stakeholders of the products.

Precautions in Strategic Alliances

There are 3 C's which are to be borne in mind while selecting prospective partners' for entering into successful alliances are: (i) compatibility (ii) capability and (iii) commitment

(i) **Compatibility:** For ascertaining the compatibility the following points need to be considered:

(a) How much compatibility exists among management practices and organization structures?

(b) Whether the management are centralized or decentralized?

(c) Whether both managements are flexible enough and committed to overcome the potential /probable conflicts?

(d) Are both managements flexible enough and committed enough to overcome potential conflicts? Also, how compatible are customer service policies and philosophies Is there any difference in production strategies.

(e) How do practices in labour relations compare? Are relations smooth or strike prone? How do managements view their employees?

(f) The compatibility on production policies, customer policies, quality management, employees policies, etc.

(g) Compatibility as to financial strength, risk orientation; corporate cultures dividend policies, reinvestment debt equity ratio, currency management etc. Are the partners publicly held, privately held state owned etc.

(h) How compatible are polices on ethics and health, safety and environment?

(i) What is potential partner's alliance record?

(j) Considerations such as interpersonal relationships are equally important to success. Even when the above factors fit well, the alliance can fail miserably if the people involved cannot get along.

(ii) **Capability:** As regard capability a dossier may be complied on each partner to evaluate their strengths and weaknesses and a team of experts preferably should undertake a feasibility study of the relationships. The following areas may be examined and evaluated:

(a) Stability and consistency of management.

(b) How does reality accord with a potential partners own projection of itself?

(c) Has a multifunctional team scrutinized the capabilities?

(d) Is the potential partner's management stable and coherent? The management structure of an ally may today appear capable of running the alliance but tomorrow it may prove to be otherwise.

Commitment: Finding a partner with an equal sense of commitment to the alliance is the third key stone to success. Even if partners appear to be capable and compatible, unless they are willing to invest the time, energy and resources to make the chances of the alliance to change the market conditions are slim.

(i) Does the alliance falls within a core business of product line of the partners? If the proposed alliance is in a business area that is only peripheral to the partners main stream activities, several dangers may exist. First, the partner may not devote the time and resources necessary to making the venture succeed, and secondly the partner could easily withdraw from the alliance and leave to your disadvantage.

(ii) Whether the relationship will continue? In other words, it should be determined as to how difficult it would be for potential partners to withdraw.

Illustration-8

During the year 2006, Corporation Bank, Oriental Bank of Commerce and Indian Bank have decided to form a strategic business alliance. The Boards of the three nationalized Banks informed the Bombay Stock Exchange on 14th

September, 2006, that the proposed 'strategic business alliance' of these three PSU Banks is only a 'technical alliance' and will not involve inter-bank transfer of staff. The bank employees unions have also been kept informed of the proposed alliance to share information.

In the light of above, answer the following questions:

(*a*) What do you understand by the term 'strategic business alliance'?

(*b*) Why alliances are becoming popular?

(*c*) What are the important criteria in the selection of alliance partners?

(*d*) How does an alliance lead to synergy?

(*e*) Why did the three PSU Banks, in your opinion, formed a strategic business alliance instead of amalgamation/merger? **(C.S. Final, June 2007)**

Solution:

(*a*) Strategic business alliance means any arrangement or agreement under which two or more firms cooperate in order to achieve certain commercial objectives. A true strategic alliance is a written arrangement between two companies that complement each other in a particular area.

In the given case, strategic alliance has three distinguishable charactertics :

- The three banks have united to pursue a set of goals agreed upon but remain independent entities.
- The partner banks share the benefits of the alliance and control over the performance of assigned tasks.
- The partner banks contribute on a accounting basis in one or more key strategic areas, e.g., technology, products and so forth.

(*b*) Alliances popularity can be attributed to business becoming more competitive and challenging, technology become more expensive and exciting, and the environment becoming more complex and volatile.

Alliances help to deal with these challenges by allowing firms to-

- share resources, facilities and competencies
- share technology, knowledge and information;
- share costs and risks;
- achieve better access to exciting a new markets; and
- reduce competition

(*c*) The three criteria to be used for selecting a partner are :

A. Compatibility: The compatibility of the partner can be judged by considering the following aspects of a prospective partners:

(*i*) partner's strategy

(*ii*) difference in corporate cultures

(*iii*) financial strength, risk orientation, dividend policies, reinvestment, debt-equity ratios, currency management.

(*iv*) policies on ethics and health, safety and environment

B. Capability : The capabilities of the potential candidates are obviously of prime importance, and companies may want to compile a dossier on each and evaluate their strengths and weaknesses. Among the issues to be considered are:

(*i*) complementary strengths

(*ii*) feasibility study of the relationships

(*iii*) management stability and coherent.

C. Commitment : Finding a partner with a equal sense of commitment to the alliance is the third keystone to the success. Even if partners appear capable and compatible, unless they are willing to invest the time, energy and resources to make the alliance a success, the chances of the alliances being able to change the market conditions are slim. Two important tips on how it can be tested whether their potential partners share a sufficient degree of commitment to the alliance:

(1) Does the alliance fall within a core business or product line of the partner? If the proposed alliance is in a business area that is only peripheral to the partner's mainstream activities, several dangers may exist. First, the partner may not devote the time and resources necessary to making the venture succeed. Secondly, the partner could easily withdraw from the alliance and leave to you disadvantage.

(2) Determine how difficult it would be for a potential partner to withdraw from the alliance. One partner may incorporate the objectives into it global strategy, pour in considerable effort and resources, and suddenly be left high and dry if the other partner suddenly leaves.

(*d*) The concept of synergy refers to situations where the combined value of two assets is greater than separate value. Synergy results from using assets in ways that increase their efficiency, effectiveness, or value. An alliance is an excellent vehicle for two companies to work together profitably. Though two or more firms unite to pursue a set of agreed upon goals, they remain independent subsequent to the formation of an alliance. Alliance leads to synergy. It results in overcoming legal or regulatory barriers, diversification, avoiding competition focusing on new products and restructuring, sharing of risks, increasing efficiency through economies of scale, specialization, updating technology etc.

(*e*) The three banks namely Corporation Banks, Oriental Bank of Commerce and Indian Bank have been working for a long time and have their presence and brand value recognition in different geographical pockets. It is easier for banks to form an alliance than to go for amalgamation /merger which requires lot of negotiations, post execution efforts apart from nod from the government and the RBI.

9. Franchises : A licensing arrangement in which the licensor supplies a complete package of goods, services and materials to the licensee. It is a type of licensing arrangement in which a company sells a package containing a trademark, equipment, materials and managerial guidelines. "A franchising agreement allows, an independent organization, an enterprise called the franchisee, to operate a business, under the name of another, called the franchisor in return for a fee".[29] The franchisor provides trademarks, operating system and well-known product reputations, as well as continuous support services and such as advertising, training, reservation services (for hotel operations) and quality assurance programs etc to the franchisee. Some companies opt for the benefits of franchising, which include an established brand name and company identity, well defined policies and procedures and assistance in both starting up and managing the enterprise. Franchising efforts the opportunity to reduce the risks of starting a business by using proven methods and selling goods or services that have an established image in the minds of customers. This is also a special form of licensing. However, in this case the franchisor has more control over the franchisee and provides more support than all licensor-licensee relations. Franchising is a way of entering foreign market. These agreements are in the form of formal contracts. Sometimes, companies may find that franchisee's eventually learns about their operations to operate independently to become direct competitors. Actually, it is a convenient way to expand quickly into larger territories.

Characteristics of Franchise: The following are the characteristics of franchisees

(*i*) The Franchisor holds popular products, brands, trademark etc under his control.

(*ii*) The franchiser have a proven success in franchising in its domestic market, before venturing abroad.

(*iii*) Franchise is the combined result of certain factors like lower prices, efficiency, product appeal, popularity for the products etc. Brands encourage the franchise to get into the contacts.

(*iv*) Unique products and operating procedure and system are the part of franchisee business.

(*v*) A royalty apart from fixed pay exists for the use of the franchisor's operating procedures, formulas, trademarks right to use franchisors name. It is normally based on the franchisee's sales.

(*vi*) The franchisor provides the franchisee faith in, its corporate image, expertise, advertising, help in establishing the business and favourable negotiations with suppliers.

(*vii*) The franchisee agrees to the franchisor's requirement for financial reporting, operating procedures etc.

(*viii*) The franchisor is required to bring necessary changes in their products or services to suit customer tastes and preferences. The franchisee is also requires necessary supply information, about the local markets customs and cultures.

10. Buy Back : It is popular form of financial structuring. Good corporate governance requires proper utilization of shareholders money. When a company has surplus funds which it cannot, in the given circumstances and in the given state of money market, deploy in a growth process from which it would be able to maintain an average return on capital employed and earnings per share, the company's finances need to be restructured by balancing the same. Buy back results in a return of shareholdings and the reduction of floating stock of the company's securities in the market while at the same time creating value for the remaining equity. Thus, both demerger and buy back, using different methods of restructuring, at aim at increasing shareholders wealth.

Buyback of share is a financial strategy that allows a company to buy its equity shares and other specified securities. When equity is costlier than debt, buy-back helps in reducing the overall cost of capital. At the same time, a buy-back helps in maintaining shareholders value by return of surplus cash to shareholders, in reducing the overall capital cost. At the same time buyback helps in maintaining shareholders value by return of surplus cash to the shareholders, in reducing the overall capital cost of the corporate. In other words, buy-back results in the return of the shareholders money and the redirection of the floating stock of the companies securities in the market, while at the same time creating value for the remaining equity.

According to Section 77A(1) of the of the Companies Act, 1956, a company may purchase its own shares or other specified securities out of (i) its free reserves or; (ii) the securities premium account or (iii) the proceeds of any shares or other specified securities. However, no buy back of any kind of shares or other specified securities can be made out of the proceeds of an earlier issue of the same kind of shares or securities.

As per Section 77A (2), a buy back must be authorized by the articles of association of the company, else the articles will have to be amended . In terms of the Section 77A(2) (b) the buy-back must be approved by a special resolution passed in general meeting. However, if the buy back is or less than 10% of the total paid-up equity capital and free reserves of the company and such buy-back is authorized by the Board of Directors at its meeting by a resolution, special resolution is not required. Further, no offer of buy-back can be made within a period of 365 days reckoned from the date of the preceding offer of buy-back, if any.

According to Section 77A(2)(c) a buy-back may be equal to or less than 25% of the total paid up capital and free reserves of the company. Also, the buy-back of equity shares in any financial year should not exceed 25% of its total paid up equity capital in that financial year. According to Section 77A (2)(e) all the shares or other securities for buy-back must be fully paid-up. Further according to Section 77A (2) (f) the buy-back of shares/other specified securities listed on any recognised stock exchange must be in accordance with SEBI regulations in this behalf. According to Section 77A(4) every buy-back must be completed within twelve months from the date of the passing of the necessary resolution. Section 77A(5) provides the various methods of buy back. Further, the security certificates so bought back are to be extinguished and destroyed within 7 days of completion of buy-back. No further issue of same kind of shares /securities can be made within a period of 6 months of buyback except by way of bonus issue. Section 77AA requires transfer of a sum equal to the nominal value of the shares purchased out of free reserves to be transferred to the capital redemption reserve account of the company and details of such transfer to be disclosed in the balance sheet.

Section 77B(1) lays down that no company shall directly or indirectly purchase its own shares or specified securities:

- through any subsidiary company including its own subsidiary companies; or
- through any investment company or group of investment companies; or
- if a default by the company in repayment of fixed deposits or interest payable thereon, redemption of debentures or preference shares or payment of dividend to any shareholder or repayment of any term loan or interest payable thereon to any financial institution or bank is subsisting.

Buy-back through Book building route: A company can buy-back its securities through the book-building route under Regulation 17 of (SEBI(Buy-back of securities), Regulations, 1988) by the following procedures:

(*i*) The maximum price at which the buy-back will be made is to be specified in the resolution.

(*ii*) The company should appoint a merchant banker.

(*iii*) Escrow Account as per Regulation 10 to be opened and deposit therein shall be made before the date of public announcement.

(*iv*) The copy of public announcement has to be filed with SEBI within two days of announcement along with stipulated fees.

(v) Book building process should be made through an electronically linked transparent facility.

(vi) Bidding centres to be opened which shall not be less than 30 days in number and at least one electronically linked terminal should be there at all bidding centres.

(vii) Offer of the buy-back should remain open for a period of not less than 15 days and not exceeding 30 days.

(viii) The buyback price shall be based on the acceptances received and the highest price accepted in the bidding process should be paid to all holders whose securities have been accepted for buy-back.

Illustration-9

In October 2006, OCL, a listed company, made a right issue of 18 lakh zero coupon convertible debentures (ZCCD) to the shareholders of the company. As per the terms of the offer, each ZCCD was automatically and compulsorily converted into one equity share of Rs.10 on 1 Jan-2007. Further, each ZCCD Ltd had one detachable warrant attached thereto which entitles the holder thereof to apply for and seek allotment of one equity share of the company. The company now proposed that an offer be made by the warrant holders for buy back of the entire 18,00,000 warrants. In light of above case, answer the following questions confined to Section 77A and the SEBI (Buy back of securities) Regulations, 1988:

(i) Whether the provisions of the section 77A will be applicable to buy back of warrants?

(ii) Whether the provisions of the SEBI (buy back of securities) Regulations, 1988 will be applicable to the proposed buy back of warrants?

(iii) Are partly paid-up securities eligible for buy-back?

(C.S. Final, Dec. 2007)

Solution:

(i) Section 77A of the Act applies to Buy-back of company's own shares or "other specified securities". Section 77A does not define "securities" nor is it defined elsewhere in the Act, however, under Section 77A company is allowed to buy its securities (other than shares) only if they are "specified securities". Explanation (a) at the end of the Section provides that "specified securities" includes Employees Stock Option other Securities as may be notified by the Central Government from time to time. Since no securities have been notified by the Central Government so far, buy-back of warrants are not covered by Section 77A.

(ii) In the case of listed companies, a buy back of the shares or other specified securities listed on any recognised stock exchange shall be in accordance with the SEBI (Buy Back of Securities) Regulations, 1998. The Regulations will not apply to buy back of the warrants. In this case, since Section 77A itself is not applicable as clarified above. It may be noted that the regulations, which are made under Section 77A of the Companies Act do not apply to transactions not covered under section 77A.

(iii) According to Section 77A (e) of the Companies Act, 1956, all the shares or other specified securities to be brought-back must be fully-paid at the time of buy-back. If any of the securities which are which are proposed to be bought back are partly paid, steps must be taken to make them fully paid before a buyback of such securities.

Valuation of Shares

Valuation of each shares of each company involved in reconstruction, merger or takeover is imperative. A number of factors affect valuation including inter-alia : (i) current market price; (ii) profits earned and dividend paid over the past few years; (iii) future prospects (iv) reserves positions; (v) realizable value of net assets of the company; (vi) age of plant and machinery; (vii) net worth of the company; (viii) public perception of the management of the company with regard to integrity, fair business practices, efficiency, etc.

Based on the above factors a number of methods of valuation of shares have come to be recognised. As reliance only on one method of valuation can be misleading, it is universally recognised that while valuing the shares of the company, it is advisable not to depend upon any single method but to resort to a combination of three well recognised methods. These are as follows: (a) net assets value method, (b) earning per share method and (c) market price method for arriving at a fair and reasonable value.

Methods of Valuation of shares: The three methods of valuation stated above are as follows:

(a) **Net Asset Method:** In this method, adding the value of all the assets of the company and substracting the value of the liabilities, leaves net assets valuation which can determine the value of the business. To achieve the fair exchange ratio the combination of above methods is used by giving appropriate weightage, to the financial status and various factors involved in respect of the concerned transferor and transferee companies. But this has to be done on a going concern concept. i.e. at not less than normal or reasonable profit. However, this method does not take into account (i) off balance sheet financing (ii) current replacement cost of assets.

The assets based valuation may be further based on (a) book value of the assets where as the tangible book value of a company is obtained from the balance sheet by taking adjusted, historical cost of assets and subtracting the liabilities; (b) Replacement Costs which reflects expenditures required to replicate the operations of the company; (c) appraisal vale or excess earnings i.e, comparisons of earnings of businesses before and after sale; and (d) Excess earnings, wherein a premium is added to the appraised value of net assets. A combination of these methods would be a representative value.

(*b*) **Earning Method:** The purpose of valuation based on earnings is to determine the annuity available to the buyer for his outlay which he would expect to be commensurate with the price paid. From the last earnings decleared items such as tax, preference dividend if any are deducted and net earnings are taken. An alternate to this method is the use of price earning ratio instead of the rate of return.

(*c*) **Market price method:** The share market price in case of a listed company takes into account all the other factors affecting the share price and hence is a good measure of valuation subject to speculation discount of share prices. However, this method has little relevance in the case of unlisted companies where earning of similar companies have to be taken into account.

Open Market Valuation

Open market value refers to a price of the assets of the company which could be fetched or realized by negotiating sale provided there is a willing seller, property is freely exposed to market, sale could materalise within a reasonable period, orders will remain static throughout this period and without interruption from any purchaser giving an extra ordinary higher bid. Each asset of the company is normally valued on the basis of liquidation a resale item rather than on a going concern basis. The assets if the company, which are not subject to regular use/sale, could be assessed on depreciated or replacement cost. Besides intangible assets are also assessed according to normal practices and recognised conventions.

An alternate to this method is the use of price-earning (P/E) ratio instead of the rate of return.

Net Assets Value/Valuation based on assets

This method is based on the simple assumption that adding the value of all assets of the company and subtracting the liabilities, leaving a net asset valuation, can best determine the value of business.

Discounted Cash Flow: Discounted cash flow analyses consist of projecting future cash flow, deriving a discount rate and applying this discount rate to the futures cash flows and terminal values.

This detailed analysis depends upon accurate financial projection and discount rate assumption. The resulting company valuation is the sum of discounted future cash flows and the discounted terminal value.

Practice Questions

Multiple Choice Questions

1. Merger of Reliance Petroleum Ltd with Reliance Industries Ltd is a case of:
   (*a*) Horizontal Merger
   (*b*) Vertical Merger
   (*c*) Conglomerate Merger
   (*d*) Concentric Merger
2. Merger of Associated Glass Ltd with Hindustan Sanitary ware Ltd is an example of:
   (*a*) Horizontal Merger
   (*b*) Vertical Merger
   (*c*) Conglomerate Merger

(*d*) Concentric Merger

3. Merger of Bank of Rajasthan with ICICI Bank is a case of:
   (*a*) Horizontal Merger
   (*b*) Vertical Merger
   (*c*) Conglomerate Merger
   (*d*) Concentric Merger
4. Alliance fail to improve
   (*a*) flexibility
   (*b*) market share
   (*c*) competence
   (*d*) internal weaknesses
5. Demerger takes place not in a following condition:
   (*a*) a division or unit no longer fits into the company operation
   (*b*) a division or unit no longer fits into the company's plans
   (*c*) company itself wants to rationalize or specialize its operation in core area.
   (*d*) a division or unit no longer viable in present business environment.

Ans: 1. (c), 2. (d) 3. (a), 4. (d), 5. (d)

Short Answer Questions

1. What is merger?
2. What do you mean by amalgamation?
3. What is reconstructing?
4. What do you mean by consolidation?
5. What do you mean by strategic alliances?

Long Answer Questions

1. What do you mean by corporate restructuring? Examine its rationale and limitations.
2. Discuss the different tools of corporate restructuring.
3. Discuss the advantages and disadvantages of Mergers and Acquisitions in India.
4. "The objective of mergers has changed from gaining new market access for existing products to technology exchange, global competition, industry convergence and economies of scale." Comment on this statement.
5. "Mergers, demergers, takeovers or combinations or acquisitions take place as a vehicle for achieving faster corporate growth." Discuss.
6. Corporate restructuring increases shareholders' wealth." Critically examine this statement.

References

1. Walsh J.P. "Managerial and Organisation Cognition" organization science. Vol. 6, 1995, PP. 280-32.
2. Drucker. P.F. "The Theory of Business" Harvard Business Review, 70 (5) PP. 95-104.
3. Harrison J.G. and St. John. C.H. "Strategic Management of Organisation and Stakeholders" South Western College Publishing Ohio 1998, P-272.
4. Weston J. Fred, Siu Juan, Johnson Brian A, Takeover, Restructuring & Corporate Governance p.xxvii
5. Weinberg. M.A, 'Takeover and Amalgamation', 2nd edition, PP. 3-4.
6. Ramaiya. A. Guide to the Companies Act, Wadhwa and Company Pvt. Ltd., 1986. p. 843.
7. Grower, 'Modern Company Law', 2nd edition, p. 550.
8. Breadsell and Company Pvt. Ltd. vs. State of Madras, 28 Company Cases, 1968 (I) Company, L.J.102. The Madras High Court.

9. Halsbury's Laws of England.
10. Mandal Ranjit Kumar, 'Corporate Mergers in India', Opcited, p.4.
11. The ICSI, Corporate Restructuring: Law and Practice, p.21.
12. Puri. L.K., Company Amalgamation and Merger, ICSI Conference, 1981.
13. Van Horne, James C, Financial Management and Policy, Prentice Hall Publication, New Delhi, 1979 p,625
14. Chakraborthy H., Advance Accountancy, Oxford University Press, Calcutta, 1978, p. 949
15. Weston J Fred, Chung Kwang S and Hung Susan E, Takeovers, Restructuring and Corporate Governance, Prentice Hall of India Private Ltd., New Delhi, 1996. p. 85
16. Lorange Peter, Kotlar Chuk, Eugene and Singh H., "Corporate Acquisitions: A Strategic Perspective" in Rock Milton(ed.) The Management Acquisition Handbook. McGraw-Hill Book Co. 1987. pp 3.13.
17. Weston J Fred, Chung Kwang S and Hoag Susan E, op.cit, p. 85.
18. Ved Prakash, Strategic Management, Anmol Publication Pvt. Ltd, New Delhi, 2005, p. 434)
19. Venketeswaran, N. "Restructuring of Corporate India" The Emerging Scenario. Vikalpa (22) 3:7.
20. ICSI Guidelines Answer, June 2006 p.20
21. Textile machinery Corporation Lts vs. CIT (1977) 107, ITR 195 (Sc)
22. Madal Ranjit Kumar, Corporate Merger in India, Kanishka Publishers Distributors,1995, New Delhi, p. 2.
23. Merriam Webster Collegiate Dictionary, tenth edition.
24. Azhar Kazmi, Strategic Management Published by John Wiley and Sons, Inc. | Publication date : April 2002
25. Yoshino, M.Y. & Rangan, U.S. (1995). Strategic Alliances: An Entrepreneurial Approach to Globalization. Boston: Harvard Business School Press
26. Lando Zeppei, managing partner of Booz, Allen and Hamilton,
27. Weston J. Fred, Siu Juan, Johnson Brian A, Takeover, Restructuring & Corporate Governance, p. 431.
28. Bleeke Joeal and David Ernst. "Is your strategic alliance Really a Scale?" Harvard Business Review, 73JanFGeb, 1995, pp.97-105
29. Phillip Kotlar, Marketing Management, 1997, p.12

15 MERGERS AND ACQUISITIONS IN INDIA

The basic purpose of a company is to survive and expand its business horizon in an existing environment. Shareholders of the company are the owners of the company and they do beehive in wealth maximization through the value of their shares. The promoters have also their long-term interest in their companies to promote and try to maximize the value of firm. In the process, company is expected to accelerate their growth in existing and emerging business areas. For this purpose, company can adopt different growth strategies viz. expansion strategy or diversification strategy. Companies generally engage themselves in wide range of activities like expansion, shrinkage, restructuring of assets and ownership structures. Internal expansion is the most important source of corporate growth. However, it has its own limitations in existing structural framework. If a company decides to strengthen its base in existing system or in favour of moving into emerging areas also, then it has to analyse various options to achieve its goals like (i) formation of a new company, (ii) acquisition of an existing company and (iii) merger with an existing company. But these options are governed by the internal factors, which are available in the company itself. These factors are (i) the cost that it is prepared to incur (ii) the likelihood of success that is expected and (iii) the degree of managerial control that it requires to retain. For the companies desiring immediate growth and quick returns, mergers and acquisitions offer an attractive opportunity as they obviate the need to start from scratch and reduce the cost of entry into an existing business. However, this will need to be weighed against the fact that part of the ownership of the existing business remains with the former owners.

Mergers and Acquisitions (M & As) activities throughout history have been related to the economic and cultural characteristics of their time and place. "In the United States and the United Kingdom, merger and acquisitions become a popular strategy for growth and diversification during the sixties and the seventies. The merger wave came late to India although sporadic cases of merger cannot be uncommon. In fact, the merger wave reached India during the eighties when large number of mergers took place. Interestingly, all economic categories of mergers rather and sprawling number of sick industrial companies were brought to the fold of profitable companies."[1] The increasing pull of M & As throughout the world in recent years is related to the powerful change forces like liberalization, privatization and globalization, technological changes, level of competition and competitiveness of the firm, changes in industry organization, individual entrepreneurship, boom in the stock market, low interest rate regime and strong fundamentals for economic growth.

Conceptual Framework of Mergers and Acquisitions

The words merger and acquisition are frequently used but the distinctions are not precise. In general, Merger is a combination of two or more companies in which one company survives under its own name while the other ceases to exist as a legal entity. Actually, it is the fusion or absorption of one thing or right into another. It is also an arrangement whereby the assets of two (or more) companies become vested in or under the control of one company (which may or may not be one of the original two companies), which has its shareholders all, or substantially all, the shareholders of the two companies. Acquisition is defined as the purchase of a controlling interest in a firm generally via a tender offer for the target shares. So in practice acquisition and tender offer both are synonymous to each other. Tender offer usually means that one firm or person is making an offer directly to the shareholders to sell (tender) their shares at specified prices.

Merger and acquisition involve the external approach to expansion. Generally, "there is no basic difference in the three terms, merger, takeover and acquisition and they are frequently used synonymously. However, a technical distinction can be made in these terms. "While mergers take place when the objectives of the buyer firm and the seller firm to acquire."[2] Takeover is a common way for acquisition and may be defined as "the attempt (often sprung as a surprise) of one firm to acquire ownership or control over another firm against the wishes of the latter's management (and perhaps some of its stockholders."[3] But in practice, takeover may not have any element of surprise and may not necessarily be against the wishes of the acquired firm. It is notable that there are two types of takeover: hostile takeovers and friendly takeover. Hostile takeovers relate with a situation when an acquirer company does not offer the target company the proposal to acquire its undertaking but silently and unilaterally pursues efforts to gain control against the wishes of existing management. Friendly takeover develops an agreement between the management of two companies through negotiation and the takeover bid may be with the consent of majority or all shareholders of the target company.

"In general, mergers reflect various forms of combining companies through some mutuality of negotiations. In tender offer, the bidder directly contracts shareholders inviting them to sell (tender) their shares at an offer price. The directors of the company may or may not have endorsed the tender offer proposal. In a practical sense mergers and tender offers are two forms of takeovers. So it would be appropriate to refer merger and acquisition activities as takeovers or M & A. activity."[4]

Objectives of Mergers and Acquisitions

Main objectives of mergers and acquisitions are as follows:

(*i*) To limit competition

(*ii*) To utilize underutilized market power

(*iii*) To overcome the problem of slow growth and profitability in one's own industry

(*iv*) To achieve diversification

(*v*) To gain economies of scale and increase in income with proportionately less investment

(*vi*) To establish a transnational bridge head without excessive start up costs to gain access to foreign market

(*vii*) To utilize underutilized resources, human and physical and managerial skills

(*viii*) To displace existing management

(*ix*) To circumvent government regulations

(*x*) To create an image of aggressiveness and strategic opportunism, empire building and to access vast economic powers of the company

(*xi*) To increasing the value and efficiency of resources by ensuring optimal uses thereby increasing the shareholders value

(*xii*) To maintain or increase the company's growth especially where internal growth is restricted due to scarcity of resources

(*xiii*) To ensure healthy expansion of business firms as they evolve through successive stages of growth and development

(*xiv*) To increase or enhance the profitability through cost reduction resulting from economies of scale, operating effectiveness and synergy

(*xv*) To effect complementarities in internal and external growth necessary in long-range evolution of firms

(*xvi*) To diversify the risks by segregating them into systematic risk and unsystematic risk

(*xvii*) To help in successful entry of the firm into new product markets and into new geographic markets

(*xviii*) To accelerate the company's market power and reducing the severity of competition

(*xix*) To ensure success in competition in international markets

(*xx*) To reduce tax liability of acquiring firm under as Income Tax Act provision to set off the losses of target company.

Acquisition Process: It comprises the following activities.

1. Formulation of Strategy: It defines the character and scope of the firm. It also seeks to meet different challenges relating with complex, ill-structured dynamic environmental changes in competitive thrusts etc. before the firm. Firms are supposed to formulate central methodological procedure by which it can easily identify and eliminate the weaknesses and improve the resources and capabilities for ensuring more strength.

2. Nature of the Industry: It is defined as economic characteristics of the industry concerned. There are different parameters for classification of an industry like nature of products, durability of products, functional distribution of products like, products, services and information, product life cycle, tangibility of the product and level of technological involvement etc. Similarly, business activities in the industry are also influenced by the economic, political and cultural environments. Responses to change are also governed by the features of the industry. Relative opportunities and advantage of large and smaller firms are also influenced by the nature of the industry in which they are working.

3. Organization system of the firm: A firm is supposed to develop an organizational structure suitable for its strategies and operational requirements. Resources and capabilities of the firm should also be consistent with its products market activities. Development of an effective information flow system is necessary for meaningful performance measurement of the firm. Firm is required to formulate its compensation systems so that they can fulfill the criteria of contribution to value creation. There are two popular forms of organization viz. Unitary (U) form and multidivisional (M) form. "Unitary (U) form of organization is based on functions such as production, marketing, geographic areas. They must change as the scope of a firm's activities expands. The multi-dimensional (M) form provides a more flexible framework for expanding products and widening geographic areas of operation."[5] A firm are required to clearly articulate strategic vision and strong organizational framework for embracing the expanded and new activities. In addition, operational efficiency must be achieved. The firm must have a solid basis for adding capabilities and resources to align more effectively to changes and opportunities through acquisitions. But if the firm is under performing, it's more likely to be a target for a takeover.

4. Multiple strategies for value growth: There are different growth strategies before the firm. Internal growth strategy can be achieved through product expansion and new product launching. Alliances and joint ventures provide growth opportunities requiring low level of investments. Licensing from other firms provide revenues with small incremental direct costs. Divestures enables the firm to harvest successes or correct mistakes. Fund availability can be improved with the help of spin-offs strategy. Intensive corporate focus can also be ensured by opting for spin offs. Buy back of shares may also enable the firm to improve its value.

5. Search Processes: Acquisitions ensure growth and it should be an ongoing activity of the firm. In this context, firm is expected to develop a dedicated core group having experience and expertise in acquisition process. Besides, core group should also be responsible for developing a work force that is expected to work as a source of research information on potential acquisition candidates. Necessary information regarding potential candidates for acquisition purposes can be collected through customers, suppliers and competitors. "Customers can provide information on product and marketing effectiveness in relation to competitors. Continued surveillance of competitors provides information on whether the firm is in the forefront of best practices. Interaction with suppliers can be source of information on potential product improvements and may uncover opportunities for vertical integration of operations. Trade shows and technical forums provide information. Financial analysis and market analysts develop considerable knowledge about the best practices and superior performance."[6]

6. Economic Environment: Changing face of economic environment encourages mergers. Liberalization, privatization and globalization stimulate acquisition programmes, alliances and joint ventures. Deregulation usually reflects new technologies and intensified competition, which puts pressure on incumbent firms to improve their performance. Existing companies in the industry has to adjust new technologies, new forms of competition to reinvest itself. The high technology area generally stimulates acquisitions programmes based on a critical set of technological capabilities expanded and improved by acquisitions. Globalization is also responsible for creating pressure for cross border mergers. "Economic reversals in developing countries have resulted in invasions of the bargain snatchers. Industry rolls up represent the consolidation of a highly fragmented industry through aggressive programmes of acquiring similar businesses. Industry characteristics favourable for a roll up include initial fragmentation, substantial industry annual revenues. Companies with robust cash flows and economies of scale."[7]

7. Cultural environment: Corporate culture is defined as an organization's values, traditions, norms, beliefs and behaviour patterns. It is generally articulated in formal statements of organization values and aspirations. It can also be expressed as informal relationships network and company's operating style. Moreover, corporate culture may be conveyed by the kinds of behaviour that are rewarded in an organisation. So it would be better for the companies to manage its own corporate culture effectively before engaging in merger activity. Different types of differences are generally available in organisation culture. (i) strong top leadership versus team approach (ii) management by formal paperwork versus management by wandering around. (iii) Individual decision versus group consensus decisions. (iv) Rapid evaluation based on performance versus long term relationship based on loyalty. (v) Rapid feedback for change versus formal bureaucratic rules and procedures. (vi) Narrow career paths versus movement through many areas. (vii) Risk taking encouraged versus one mistake and you are out. (viii) Big stakes (bet your company) decisions versus low risk activities. (ix) Learn from the customer versus we know what is best for the customer. (x) Narrow responsibility assignment versus everyone in this company is a source of new or improved product ideas or sources of sales effort or sources of cost efficiencies and so on.

It is notable that these differences are certain to be developed when companies are combined. However, firm should try to recognize these cultured differences and to respect them. Efforts are required to generate information on how the acquiring firm has managed cultured environment in the past and how the firm has managed organizational change.

8. Valuation process: It helps in providing a rational procedure for arriving at a acquisition price. If the price is inadequate or low then the target firm may resist and that may seek to interest bidders. Similarly, if the price is high then it will be difficult for the firm to recover the premium already paid from post merger synergies. So firm should be careful. Mergers or acquisitions increase value when value of the combined firm is greater than the firm's premerger values of the independent entities. For this purpose, a valuation model is given below:

$$NVI = V_{BT} - (V_B + V_T)$$

Where

NVI = Net value increase

V_B = Value of bidder alone

V_T = Value of target alone

V_{BT} = Value of firms combined.

9. Negotiation: M & As provide opportunities for principled negotiation. Both the parties will be able to fulfill their purpose if they are ready to use the standards of fairness. Moreover, it would be better for them to produce agreements that build good future relationships. Acquiring firms are supposed to assess its strengths and weaknesses. It should try to identify its resources and capabilities required and what it brings to the deal. A key factor in M & As is realistic identification of gains, synergies and their sources, whether in revenue enhancement and/or cost reduction and/or possibilities for new and strengthened strategies. This is the basis for developing a solid quantification of the firm's BATNA- Best Alternative To a Negotiated Agreement. In merger valuation, quantification of BATNA is facilitated. Value relationships can be analysed with reference to comparable companies and comparable transactions.

10. Deal structuring: It deals with those variables, which help, in deal finalization. These are (i) understanding the tax consequences of combining firms. (ii) understanding the accounting treatment employed for assessing the economic consequences, (iii) methods of payment in cash, shares, debentures or a combination there of (iv) use of contingency payout and formulation of standard for the bonus or penalty.

11. Implementation: It starts with the signing of the merger agreement. There is difference of opinion about this approach. Some authors say that implementation starts as a condition for thinking about M & As. However, firm is required to implement all aspects of effective operations before it can effectively combine organisations. Efforts are also required for ensuring shareholders value orientation in the implementation process. Companies should prefer only those mergers that are fit for its corporate strategy like strengthening weaknesses, filling gaps, developing new growth opportunities, extending capabilities etc. For this purpose, firm should have integration leadership. The integration leader should have management experience with external constituencies and participants. Firms should also create cross-functional teams to devote more attention to the issues involved in the integration process. However, they are also expected to make a balance between speed and disruption as slow integration process adversely affects the M & A deals. Advance integration plans can be helpful in achieving the goals of M & A programmes.

12. Monitoring Process: It deals with review of environmental changes affecting the integration process. No plan or set of policies can remain in force without change for very long. So firm is expected to adjust with new opportunities and challenges. For this purpose, broad strategy is necessary for guiding the success of business operated by the firm. Continuous organizational growth is necessary to retain executives for a long-term basis. Launching new products, promoting strong brands and expanding the business horizon should be the guiding star for faster growth of combining firm.

Theories of Mergers & Acquisitions : Major theories of mergers and acquisitions are as follows-

1. Efficiency Theories: These theories assume that mergers and other form of acquisitions have the potential for social benefits. They generally involve improving the performance of incumbent management or achieving a form of synergy. Basic assumption of efficiency theories is that the productivity of the firm can be improved through the improvement in economies of scale. M & As provide a mechanism to make the capital more efficient and productive. Efficiency theories incorporate following related theories:

(i) **Differential Managerial Efficiency:** Efficiency improvements can result from combining firms of unequal managerial capabilities. "A relatively efficient bidder may acquire a relatively inefficient target value can be increased by improving the efficiency of the target firm. In the same way, the bidder may seek a merger with a target firm because the management of the target firm can improve the efficiency of the bidder. The target firm may have relatively better growth opportunities than the bidder or vice versa."[8]

The theory suggests that there are firms with below average efficiency or that are not operating upto their potential however defined. In other words, some firms operate below their potential and as a result have below average efficiency. Firms operating in similar kind of business activity would be most likely to be the potential acquirers. They would have the background for detecting below average or less than full potential performance and have the managerial know how for improving the performance of the acquired firm.

(ii) **Inefficient Management Theory:** The inefficient management theory is based on the assumption that inefficient management is simply not performing up to its potential. In other words, inefficient management may simply represent incompetent management. So, it provides opportunities to another control group to manage the assets of the firm more effectively.

Since, general belief is that almost anyone could do better so it would be an effective rationale for conglomerate mergers. Thus, inefficient management theory develops scope for mergers between firms with unrelated businesses. However, it also assumes that owners (or shareholders) of acquired firms are unable to replace their own managers and therefore, it is necessary to invoke costly mergers to replace inefficient managers.

(iii) **Operating Synergy Theory:** It assumes that the economies of scale and economies of scope do exist in the industry and that prior to the merger the firms are operating at levels of activity that fall short of achieving the potential for economies of scale. The economies of scale is concerned with spreading of the fixed cost over increasing levels of production. Similarly, economies of scope refer to using a set of skills or an asset which is currently being used to produce a specific product or service or to produce related products or services. These economies generally arise because of individualities such as people, equipment and overheads, which provide increasing returns if, spread over a large number of units of output. Thus, in manufacturing operations heavy investments in plant and equipment typically produce such economies. Economies available in the areas of production, research and development, marketing and finance are treated managerial economies. Operating synergy may be available in horizontal, vertical and even in conglomerates mergers.

(iv) **Diversification Theory:** It deals with preservation of organizational and reputational capital and securing financial and tax advantages. "Diversification of the firms can provide managers and other employees with job security and opportunities for promotion and other things being equal, results in lower labour costs."[9] Generally, executives and other employees do not have opportunities to diversify themselves to other firms due to their specialized knowledge. They expect that firm should make specific investments and any knowledge acquired by them while working for the firm may be valuable to the firm but not for others. So merger provides them opportunity to use their acquired specialized knowledge and get higher pay. This situation is possible only when the firm opt for diversification through conglomerate mergers. The owner-manager is not interested to offload their shares in the firm for reasons of corporate control. However, in case of undiversified firm they have to bear a high-risk premium in their investments. So diversification through merger enables them to reduce their risk premium and enjoy a higher expected rate of return. Goodwill or reputation is generally acquired overtime through firm's specific investments viz. ethical

behaviour in advertising, research and development, fixed assets, personnel training, organizational development etc. Goodwill/reputation of the firms enable the customers, suppliers and employees to have an effective relationship with it. Diversification through merger also helps the firm to preserve its goodwill or reputational capital for a long period.

(v) **Financial Synergy Theory :** It states that when the rates of cash flows of the acquirer is greater than that of the acquired firm, capital is reallocated to the acquired firm and hence it can take up viable investment opportunities. In business, there are two types of firms (i) firms with large internal cash flows and small investment opportunities have excess cash inflows. (Cash rich companies) (ii) firms with low internal funds generation and large growth opportunities have a need for additional financing (Cash starved companies). Merger of these two companies may result in advantages from the lower costs of internal funds availability. Similarly, "debt capacity of the combined firm can be greater than the sum of the two firms' capacities before their merger and this provide tax savings on investment income. Merger also enables the firm to enjoy the benefits of economies of scale in floatation and transaction costs of securities.[10]

(vi) **Strategic Realignment Theory:** It provides M & A as a strategy to the firm for adjusting the changes available in the external environment. It is concerned with acquiring new management skills to augment the capabilities of the firm in relation to new growth areas or to meet new competitive threats. In this context, "strategic planning approach to mergers appears to imply either the possibilities of economies of scale or utilization of unused capability in the firm's present managerial capabilities."[11] Firms can also acquire management skills to augment their present capabilities by external diversifications. It is also true that new capabilities and new markets could be developed internally. But timing is most important in capturing growth opportunities. The speed of adjustment through merger would be quicker than internal development so it would be better for the firms to realize synergies in managerial capabilities. "On the other hand, a competitive market for acquisitions implies that the net present value from merger and acquisition investments is likely to be small. Nonetheless, if these investments exploit synergy, opportunities and can be used as a base for still additional investments with positive net present values, the strategy may succeed."[12]

(vii) **Under Valuation Theory:** Under valuation of the target firms motivates mergers and acquisitions. It refers to target firm being worth more than what is it actually valued at. Sometimes, acquirers have inside information and under valuation is the difference between the market value of the assets and their replacement costs. It is also termed as q Ratio. The q ratio is defined as the ratio of the market value of the firm's shares to the replacement costs of the assets represented by these shares. If potential acquirer wants to develop additional capacity to produce a particular product, it could achieve additional capacity by acquiring of firm and a they may place a higher value on the shares than the current market price (CMP). Since acquirers or bidders have special information regarding the real strength of the company, which the general market does not have, then they are better placed in quoting higher price than the current market price of shares of the target company. Current market price of shares is governed by different factors like, current performance of the firm, image of the management, perception of the shareholders about the company so bidders can avail the benefits of the under valuation of shares available in the market in comparison to their intrinsic values.

In practice inflation has double-barreled impact. Firstly, increasing rate of depression depresses the stock prices and secondly, inflation also improves the current replacement costs of assets in comparison to their historical book values. There twin effects result in a decline of the q ratio. "If a company wished to add to capacity in producing a particular product, it could acquire the additional capacity more cheaply by buying a company that produces the product rather than building brick and mortar from scratch. If firm A seeks to add capacity, this activity implies that its marginal q ratio is greater than 1, but if other firms in its industry have average q ratio of less than l, it is efficient for firm A to add capacity by the purchase of other firms. For example, if the q ratio is 0.6 and if in a merger the premium paid over market value is 50 percent, the resulting purchase price is 0.6 times 1.5, which equals 0.9. This means that the average purchase price would still be 10 percent below the current replacement costs of the assets acquired. This potential advantage would provide a broad basis for the operation of the under valuation theory in recent years when the q ratio was low."[13]

2. Information Theory: It is based on the hypothesis that new information is generated as a result of the tender offer and revaluation is permanent.[14] A tender offer in the acquisition spreads the information that the shares of the target firm are undervalued and immediately the market revalues those shares even the offers turns out to be unsuccessful. Thus, the information hypothesis provides two forms of information[15]— (a) tender offer disseminates information that the target shares are undervalued and the offer prompts the market to revalue those shares "No particular action by the target firm or any other is necessary to cause the revaluation. This behaviour is treated as sitting on a goldmine explanation (b) the offer inspires target firm management to implement a more efficient business strategy on its own. This is stated as "Kick in the pants" explanation. No outside input other than the offer itself is required for the upward revaluation."[16] However, "a permanent revaluation of the target shares occurs when the target resources are combined with the resources of an acquiring firm or at least when the control of the target resources is transferred to the acquiring firms".[17]

3. Signaling Theory: It states that particular actions may convey other significant forms of information. Actually, it is based on the theory of signaling propounded by Spence, which is related with labour market. "According to him, higher quality labour in terms of intelligence or aptitudes would receive greater returns from education and training than lower quality labour. Hence, the level of education of a labourer was a signal not only of more training but also of higher innate abilities. Lower quality labour would have negative returns on investment in education and training. Thus, it was advantageous for some to signal but disadvantageous for others"[18]. Therefore, using the signal conveys meaningful and correct information. Signaling may also be involved in mergers and tender offers in a number of ways. The fact that a firm has received a tender offer may signal to the market that hither to unrecognized extra values are possessed by the firm or that future cash flow streams are likely to rise. When a bidder firm uses common stock in buying another firm, this may be taken as a signal by the target and others that the common stock of the bidder firm is overvalued. "When business firms repurchase their shares, the market may take this as a signal that management has information that its shares are undervalued and that favourable new growth opportunities will be achieved."[19]

4. Hubris Hypothesis: The hubris hypothesis assumes strong form of efficiency of markets. Stock prices reflect all (public and non public) information, redeployment of productive resources cannot bring gains, and management cannot be improved through reshuffling or combinations across firms. Actually, the efficiency theories of takeovers are based on some form of market inefficiency. According to Roll, hubris hypothesis serves the role of benchmark for comparison and is the null against which other hypothesis should be compared. Managers may have good intentions but can make mistakes in judgment. They presume their tender valuations are correct though the market valuation may be otherwise. The ego and pride of the management may compel them to believe their valuation is superior to the market. Hubris is responsible for higher valuation of the bidders (over the target's true economic value). Thus, the Hubris indicates the excessive self confidence (pride, arrogances) of the bidders and due to this, they have to cough up higher price for the bids. Generally, severe competition between bidders forces them to pay too much for the bids. Even there is single bidder, he may again to pay too much due to potential competition of other bidders. Roll hypothesis indicates that "managers commit errors of over optimism in evaluating merger opportunities due to excessive pride, animal sprits or hubris."[20]

The concept of winner's curse is related with auctions. When there are many bidders or competitors for an object of highly uncertain value, a wide range of bids is likely to result. Thus, the Hubris hypothesis is relevant with competitive tender offer. The competitors competing in the bidding process may raise the bid upward time and again. The temptation to win the game often results in the winner curse. Actually, the problem involved in the process is difficulties in estimation of the correct valuation of the asset. In the absence of the correct valuation, the highest bidder will bid and typically pay in excess of the expected value of the asset. The winning bidder is therefore cursed in the sense that its bid exceeds the value of the object or asset so the firm loses money. Hubris spirit is governed by the desire to avoid loss of face, media praise, desire to be projected as aggressive firm, inexperience, overestimation of synergies, etc. Thus, the winners curse ultimately compels the winner to be cursed by paying more than what the target firm is actually worth.

5. Agency Problem: Agency problem arises due to conflict of interest available between the principal (shareholders) and agent (managers). The agents have an incentive to act in his own self interest as he bears less than the total costs of his actions. It is generally called as an agency problem. Actually agency problem arises when managers own only a fraction of the ownership shares in the company. This partial ownership discourages them to work hard and enjoy more perquisites like luxurious offices, cars, club memberships etc. at the cost of the company. The basic idea in their mind is that majority owners bear most of the cost. Similarly, in big corporations having dispersed ownership sufficient incentives for individual owners are not available to use substantial resources required to monitor the behaviour of managers.

Agency problems are the direct result of contractual obligation between managers (decision or control agents or risk takers) and owners risk bearers. These contracts cannot be written and enforced at no cost. Resulting (agency) costs include (i) cost of structuring a set of contracts (ii) costs of monitoring and controlling the behaviour of agents by the principal (iii) cost of bonding to guarantee that the agents will make optimal decision or principals will be compensated for the consequences of sub-optimal decisions and (iv) the residual loss, that is the welfare loss experienced by principals, arising from the divergence between agents decisions and decision to maximize principals' welfare. This residual loss can arise because the costs of full enforcement of contracts exceed the benefits.[21]

However, agency problems may be efficiently tackled by some organizational and market mechanism. Generally, big companies are characterized by separation of ownership and control. They are represented by the decision variables. Decision management, which is responsible for imitation and implementation and decision control, is accountable for ratification and monitoring. These variables are necessary to limit the power of individual decision agents to expropriate shareholders interests. Central functions are delegated to a board of directors by the shareholders, who retain approval rights on important matters, including board membership, mergers and new stock issues."[22] "It is also notable that "compensation arrangement and the market for managers may also mitigate the agency problem. Compensation is generally linked with performance like bonus payments and executive stock option schemes. Managers are expected to maintain their own reputation as well as labour market determines the level of compensation as per their performance reputation."[23]

Stock market is the barometer for the performance of the economy. It also work as an external monitoring device since quality of decision made by the managers is reflected in the stock price. Thus, the stock prices of the company as such also summarize the decisional performance of its managers. Low stock prices force the managers to change their operational behaviour and fulfill the expectation of existing shareholders. However, when these measures fail to control the agency problems, the market for takeovers provides an external control device of last resort. A takeover through a tender offer or a proxy fight enables outside managers to gain control of the decision process of the target while circumventing existing managers and the Board of directors."[24] M & A helps the outside managers to gain control of the decisional processes of the target firm while avoiding existing managers. M & A generally rescue the target firm from its inefficient managers and agency problems.

6. Managerialism Hypothesis: This hypothesis is formulated by Mueller which suggests that managers make combinations solely to increase firm size and their own compensation. According to this hypothesis, managers are motivated to increase the size of their firms. It is also assumed that the compensation to managers is a functions of the size (sales) of the firm and managers therefore adopt a lower investment hurdle rate and they create unprofitable investment through M & As. The managerialism theory argues that the agency problem is not solved and that merger activity is a manifestation of the agency problems of inefficient, external investment by managers.[25] However, study also suggests that managers compensation is significantly correlated with the firms profit rate not its level of sale."[26]

7. Free Cash Flow Hypothesis: Free Cash Flow hypothesis suggests that M & As takeover takes place because of the conflicts between managers and shareholders over the payout of free cash flows. "According to Jensen "Free cash flow is the cash flow in access of the amount required to fund all projects that have positive net present values when discounted at the applicable cost of capital."[27] It is for the management of the firm to timely ensure the payment of this free cash flow (FCF) to shareholders if the firm is to be efficient and to maximize share price. However, it reduces the resource availability under the control of managers and thereby reduces their power. Besides "they are further subject to monitoring by the capital markets when they seek to finance additional investment with new capital."[28]

Managers are also required to ensure an effective payout future cash flow. An effective way to do this is by issuing bonds or debentures without retention of the proceeds of the issue. Generally, issue of debentures or bonds in place of equity shares, management is under obligation to promise payout future cash flows more effectively rather than having a dividend policy in place. Jensen further emphasised that the control functions of debt is more important in organization that generate large cash flows but whose outlook involves low growth or an actual reduction in size. It also increases risks of bankruptcy/liquidation costs as well as agency costs of the debt. Some highly risky projects, generally benefit shareholders at the expense of bond holders. Thus, efforts are required to have an optimal debt/equity ratio where the marginal costs of debt is equal to the marginal benefits of the debt.

8. Redistribution Hypothesis: It includes different forms of redistribution like tax gains and market power. It examines the redistribution of income from government to acquiring firm or redistribution of power from target firm to acquiring firm.

(*i*) **Tax Gains:** Availability of tax savings or benefits due to tax exemptions, incentives or other forms of subsidies made available by the government also creates conducive environment for mergers. It represents a form of redistribution of income from the government. Mergers may be used to substitute capital gains for ordinary income tax. A company which has incurred losses in the past can carry such losses forward and offset them against future taxable profits and reduce tax liabilities. Such a company when merged with a company with large taxable profits would help to absorb the tax liability of the later. A similar advantage also exists when a company is modernizing or investing heavily in plant and machinery, which entitles it to substantial investment incentives but has not much taxable profits to off set with them. Acquiring or merging such a company with a highly profitable company would help make fully use of the investment incentives for the acquirer.

(*ii*) **Market Power:** Merger increases the market share of acquiring firm in the industry in which it is working. Increasing market share really mean increasing the size of the firm relative to other firms in an industry. It also increases the concentration of the firm in the particular industry. It is called as monopoly power. Product differentiation entry barriers and market share are the three important sources which improve the market power of the acquiring firm. Market power helps the acquiring firm to set the prices that are not suitable in a more competitive market. Horizontal mergers are the best course of action for improving the market share. Increased concentration is generally the result of active and intense competition. It is also important to note that the intense competition continues among large firms in concentrated industry because the dimensions of decision making over prices, outputs, types of products, quality of product, service and so on are so numerous and of so many gradation that collusion among the firm simply is not feasible.

Mergers & Acquisitions in India

India is emerging as a vibrant player in the world of mergers and acquisitions (M & A). In many areas, India is emerging at the top. As a leader in Information Technology, India was designated the third most attractive research and development centre in the world by UNCTAD (United Nations Conference on Trade and Development) in its world. The most important benefit that the developing and transition economies derive from outward investments is increased competitiveness. This strengthens the arms of local companies and of the MNCs to survive in a competitive environment. Therefore, the more the domestic industries invest abroad, the more the benefits to the home economy.

Factors Driving Developing Nations to Go Global: Following factors are responsible for developing nations to go global-

(*i*) It helps market penetration. Indian multinational corporations looking for niche markets- such as IT services and pharmaceutical products- gained substantially through outbound investments.

(*ii*) Rising labour costs at home push Indian MNCs abroad.

(*iii*) Competitive pressures in the domestic economy force Indian MNCs to invest abroad.

(*iv*) Home government policy liberalisation stimulates outbound investments; indeed, since 2003 Indian government has taken various steps to liberalise overseas investments.

Various Committee Report on Takeover

Various committee reports on takeover are as follows:

Justice P.N. Bhagwati Committee Report On Takeovers

Takeover of companies is a well accepted and established strategy for corporate growth. International experience of takeovers and mergers and amalgamations has been varied. Nonetheless, one of its important lessons is that, its appeal as an instrument of corporate growth has usually been the result of an admixture of corporate ethos of a country, shareholding pattern of companies, existence of cross holdings in companies, cultural conditions and the regulatory environment.

In India, however, "the market" for takeovers has not yet become significantly active, though following economic reforms, there is now a discernible trend among promoters and established corporate groups towards consolidation of market share, and diversification into new areas, albeit in a limited way through acquisition of companies, but in a more pronounced manner through mergers and amalgamations. The latter course is outside the purview of SEBI and constitutes a subject matter of the Companies Act, 1956, and the courts of law, and there are well laid down procedures for valuation of shares and protection of the rights of investors. This Report and the SEBI Regulations for Substantial Acquisition of Shares and Takeovers do not deal with the subject of mergers and amalgamations.

In common parlance, a takeover bid is generally understood to imply the acquisition of shares carrying voting rights in a company in a direct or indirect manner with a view to gaining control over the management of the company. Generally speaking, there cannot be a change in the control of a company simpliciter, unaccompanied by acquisition of shares, though there have been cases before SEBI where management control has changed from one group of persons to another without any overt acquisition of substantial quantities of shares. It would therefore be correct to state that, takeover or gaining control over a company, as opposed to pure investment, is the most common leitmotif for substantial acquisition of shares. Such takeovers could take place through a process of friendly negotiations or in a hostile manner in which, the existing management resists the change in control. It is for this reason that substantial acquisition of shares in a listed company and change in control of a listed company have both been addressed in this Report. In a market driven economy, where free competition should thrive without relying on the protective hand of bureaucratic intervention, it is important that such critical processes as substantial acquisition of shares and takeovers, which can significantly influence corporate growth and contribute to the wealth of the economy through rational allocation and optimal utilisation of resources, take place within the orderly framework of regulations and that such a framework should be one which comports with principles of fairness, transparency and equity, and above all with the need to protect the rights of the shareholders.

The first attempts at regulating takeovers were made in a limited way by incorporating a clause, viz. Clause 40, in the listing agreement which provided for making a public offer to the shareholders of a company by any person who sought to acquire 25% or more of the voting rights of the company. This allowed for the passive participation of shareholders of the company that is being taken over, in the takeover process. But the clause used to be easily circumvented and its basic purpose frustrated by the acquirers, simply by acquiring voting rights a little below the threshold limit of 25% for making a public offer. Besides it was also noted that it was possible to acquire control over a company in the Indian context with even holding 10% directly. There was therefore a case for lowering of the threshold from 25%. In 1990, even before SEBI became a statutory body, Government, in consultation with SEBI, amended Clause 40 by -

(*i*) lowering the threshold acquisition level for making a public offer by the acquirer, from 25% to 10% ;

(*ii*) bringing within its fold the aspect of change in management control under certain circumstances (even without acquisition of shares beyond the threshold limit), as a sufficient ground for making a public offer;

(*iii*) introducing the requirement of acquiring a minimum of 20% from the shareholders;

(*iv*) stipulating a minimum price at which an offer should be made;

providing for disclosure requirements through a mandatory public announcement followed by mailing of an offer document with adequate disclosures to the shareholders of the company; and

(*vi*) requiring a shareholder to disclose his shareholding at level of 5% or above to serve as an advance notice to the target company about the possible takeover threat.

These changes helped in making the process of acquisition of shares and takeovers transparent, provided for protection of investors' interests in greater measure and introduced an element of equity between the various parties concerned by increasing the disclosure requirement. But the clause suffered from several deficiencies - particularly in its limited applicability and weak enforceability. Being a part of the listing agreement, it could be made binding only on listed companies and could not be effectively enforced against an acquirer unless the acquirer itself was a listed company. The penalty for non-compliance was one common to all violations of a listing agreement, namely, delisting of the company's shares, which ran contrary to the interest of investors. The amended clause was unable to provide a comprehensive regulatory framework governing takeovers; nonetheless, it made a positive beginning.

The SEBI Act enacted in 1992, empowered SEBI to regulate substantial acquisition of shares and takeovers, and made substantial acquisition of shares and takeovers a regulated activity for the first time. The SEBI Regulations for Substantial Acquisition of Shares and Takeovers were notified by SEBI in November 1994. Clause 40(A & B) of the listing agreement also remained in force. The Regulations preserved the basic framework of Clause 40 (A & B) by retaining the requirements of - initial disclosure at the level of 5%, threshold limit of 10% for public offer to acquire minimum percentage of shares at a minimum offer price and making of a public announcement by the acquirer followed by a letter of offer. But the Regulations did make a significant departure from Clause 40(A & B) by dropping "change in management" simpliciter as a ground for making a public offer. On the other hand, several new provisions were introduced enabling both negotiated and open market acquisitions, competitive bids, revision of offer, withdrawal of offer under certain circumstances and restraining a second offer in relation to the same company within 6 months by the same acquirer. These provisions were used later by some acquirers to launch hostile and competitive bids. Additionally, the Regulations enhanced the level of investor protection in several ways. Being statutory in nature, violation of its provisions attracted several penalties. These inter alia included SEBI's right to initiate criminal prosecution under section 24 of the SEBI Act, issue directions to the person found guilty not to further deal in securities, prohibit him from disposing of any securities acquired in violation of the regulations, or direct him to sell shares acquired in violation of the Regulations and take action against the concerned intermediary who is registered with SEBI. The SEBI Act also empowered SEBI to adjudicate fines as penalties for certain violations of the Regulations. Indeed, there have already been a number of instances, where SEBI has initiated penal action against the acquirers under these provisions for violation of the Regulations.

The process of substantial acquisition of shares and takeovers is complex. SEBI has now gained considerable experience and insight into the complexities in this area through the administration of the Regulations and Clause 40 A & B of the listing agreement. It has also helped SEBI focus attention on certain areas in the regulatory framework which not only required clarity but also needed to be addressed specifically. For example, the provisions for open market acquisition of shares, competitive bid and revised offer in the Regulations allowed hostile takeovers and competitive offers to be launched, and the consequent revision of offers to take place for the first time in the Indian market; nonetheless, these offers demonstrated with certain degree of acuity, the deficiencies in the existing provisions. These needed to be specifically addressed in the extant Regulations to make the regulatory framework more comprehensive and equitable.

A Committee was therefore set up by SEBI in November 1995, under the Chairmanship of Justice P.N. Bhagwati, former Chief Justice of India, to review the Securities and Exchange Board of India (Substantial Acquisition of Shares and Takeovers) Regulations, 1994. The terms of reference of the Committee were :

(*i*) to examine the areas of deficiencies in the existing Regulations; and

(*ii*) to suggest amendments in the Regulations with a view to strengthening the Regulations and making them more fair, transparent and unambiguous and also protecting the interest of investors and of all parties concerned in the acquisition process.

The Committee was constituted with wide representation from the Chambers of Commerce and Industry, Investors Associations, Stock Exchanges, Merchant Bankers, Institute of Chartered Accountants and Legal Experts. The members of the Committee were as follows:

1. **Justice P.N. Bhagwati - Chairman**

   Chambers of Commerce & Industry were represented by
2. Sh. Adi Godrej, representing Confederation of Indian Industry (CII)
3. Sh. Bipin Jhaveri, representing Associated Chambers of Commerce and Industry (Assocham)
4. Sh. Rajendra S. Lodha, representing Federation of Indian Chambers of Commerce and Industry (FICCI)

   Investors Associations were represented by
5. Prof. M. D. Limaye, representing Lokmanya Seva Sangh
6. Prof. Manubhai Shah, representing Consumer Education and Research Centre (CERC).

   Merchant Bankers were represented by
7. Sh. Udayan Bose, Chairman, Lazard Creditcapital Ltd.
8. Sh. Shitin Desai, Vice Chairman & Managing Director, DSP Merrill Lynch Ltd.
9. Sh. Nimesh Kampani, Chairman, J.M. Financial & Investment Consultancy Services Ltd.

   Stock Exchanges were represented by
10. Sh. Kamal Kabra / Sh. M.G. Damani (President, The Stock Exchange, Mumbai)

    Legal Experts were represented by
11. Sh. J.R. Gagrat of Gagrat & Co.
12. Sh. R.A. Shah of Crawford Bayley & Co.
13. Sh. Shardul Suresh Shroff of Amarchand Mangaldas & Suresh A. Shroff & Co.

Institute Chartered Accountants of India was represented by

14. Sh. Y.M. Kale / Sh. T. S. Vishwanath (President, Institute of Chartered Accountants of India (ICAI))

SEBI was represented by

15. Kum. D.N. Raval, Executive Director
16. Sh. Pratip Kar, Executive Director and Member Secretary.

PART I

1. The Approach of the Committee

(*i*) The Committee was of the view that the Regulations for substantial acquisition of shares and takeovers should operate principally to ensure fair and equal treatment of all shareholders in relation to substantial acquisition of shares and takeovers. While on the one hand the Regulations should not impose conditions which are too onerous to fulfill and hence make substantial acquisitions and takeovers difficult, at the same time, they should ensure that such processes do not take place in a clandestine manner without protecting the interests of the shareholders. A balance must necessarily be struck between the two considerations. The objective of the Regulations should therefore be to provide an orderly framework within which such processes could be conducted. The Regulations should also help in evolving good business standards as to how fairness to shareholders can be achieved, as maintenance of such standards is of importance to the integrity of the financial markets, and they should not concern themselves with issues of competition, or financial or commercial advantages or disadvantages of a takeover. The committee also noted that the process of substantial acquisition of shares and takeovers is so intertwined with the warp and weft of the industry, especially in the wake of economic reforms, that it would be unrealistic to make Regulations in this area without taking into account the ground realities of the Indian industry.

(*ii*) The Committee also recognised that the process of takeovers is complex and is interrelated to the dynamics of the market place. It would therefore be impracticable to devise regulations in such detail as to cover the entire range of situations which could arise in the process of substantial acquisition of shares and takeovers. Instead there should be a set of General Principles which should guide the interpretation and operation of the Regulations, especially in circumstances which are not explicitly covered by the Regulations. These principles are -

(*a*) Equality of treatment and opportunity to all shareholders.

(*b*) Protection of interests of shareholders.

(*c*) Fair and truthful disclosure of all material information by the acquirer in all public announcements and offer documents.

(*d*) No information to be furnished by the acquirer and other parties to an offer exclusively to any one group of shareholders.

(*e*) Availability of sufficient time to shareholders for making informed decisions.

(*f*) An offer to be announced only after most careful and responsible consideration.

(*g*) The acquirer and all other intermediaries professionally involved in the offer, to exercise highest standards of care and accuracy in preparing offer documents.

(*h*) Recognition by all persons connected with the process of substantial acquisition of shares that there are bound to be limitations on their freedom of action and on the manner in which the pursuit of their interests can be carried out during the offer period.

(*i*) All parties to an offer to refrain from creating a false market in securities of the target company.

(*j*) No action to be taken by the target company to frustrate an offer without the approval of the shareholders.

2. The "definitions" section should by and large set the tone for interpretation of its substantive provisions. Very often, imprecision in the definition of the terms results in difficulties in interpretation of regulations. To the extent possible, definitions should be clear, precise and unambiguous and definitions of key terms and concepts which form the basis of the regulations should be laid down.

(*i*) **Definition of 'Acquirer'** : The Committee recommends that (*a*) not only acquisition of shares but also voting rights in a company or control over a company, howsoever such control be exercised -directly or indirectly- must be covered under the Regulations and the present definition of "acquirer " expanded to include these situations;

(*b*) The term 'control' be defined to include " the right to appoint majority of the directors or to control the management or policy decisions, exercisable by person or persons acting individually or in concert, directly or indirectly, including by virtue of their shareholding or management rights or shareholders agreements or voting agreements, or in any other manner.

(*c*) as the expansion of the definition of "acquirer" in the Regulations would render Clause (40 A & B) of the listing agreement redundant, it may now be replaced by a clause requiring compliance of the SEBI Regulations as a condition of listing.

(ii) **Definition of 'Persons acting in concert' :** The Committee recommends that

(*a*) the present definition of "persons acting in concert" be expanded to include mutual funds, their sponsors, asset management companies and trustees, venture capital funds, their sponsors, foreign institutional investors, banks, financial advisers and stock brokers with a provision to exclude banks which provide normal commercial banking services to an acquirer;

(*b*) sub-clause (iv) of clause (d) of regulation 2 of the existing Regulations be re-worded to bring out the role of investment companies in cases where such companies are used as vehicles to make substantial acquisition of shares or voting rights in a company;

(*c*) the term "associate" which has been used in the Regulations in the context of "person acting in concert" be defined;

(*d*) public financial institutions which are at present included in the list of persons deemed to be acting in concert be excluded. The inclusion of "venture capital funds and sponsors" in the definition of "persons acting in concert" and the definition of the term 'associate' were in response to the feedback received by the Committee on the draft Report.

(iii) **Burden of proof on 'persons acting in concert' :** The Committee recommends that

(*a*) in the definition of persons acting in concert, the persons be grouped in such a manner in the same group or category that they bear such relationship amongst themselves as could justify raising of a presumption in the normal course of affairs that they are acting in concert. For example, a sponsor of a mutual fund could be presumed to be acting in concert with the trustee company or asset management company of the same mutual fund; similarly a merchant banker may be presumed to be acting in concert with his client as acquirer. But no presumption may be made that persons in one group are acting in concert with persons in another group. It has to be proved by evidence that they are acting in concert. (Reference : Part II of the Report- sub-clause (e) of sub-regulation (1) of regulation 2).

(iv) **Definition of 'Offer Period' :** The Committee recommends that

(*a*) the offer period be defined as the period from the date of the first public announcement of the first offer till the date of the closure of that offer.

(v) **Definition of 'Promoter' :** The Committee recommends that

(*a*) the definition of the term 'promoter' may be based substantially on the recommendations from the Malegam Committee Report as accepted by SEBI, which has already been widely accepted for the purpose of disclosure.

(vi) **Definition of 'Public Shareholding' :** The Committee recommends that

(*a*) the term may be defined to mean shareholding in the hands of any person other than the acquirer and persons acting in concert with him.

(vii) **Definition of 'Shares' :** The draft report retained the definition of shares as per the existing Regulations which included any security which entitles the holder to receive shares with voting rights at a future date. The Committee decided to retain the same definition. The Committee, however, noted that mere acquisition of securities which would confer voting rights at a later date should not trigger the code at the point of acquisition of the securities before voting rights are acquired and that the Regulations would be attracted only at the point of time when the securities are converted into shares with voting rights and this should be clearly brought out in the Regulations.

(*viii*) **Definition of 'Target company'** : The Committee recommends that the listed company which is the subject matter of acquisition or takeover may be defined as the target company.

(*ix*) **Definition of the remaining terms :** The Committee recommends that the definitions of the remaining terms in the existing Regulations be retained.

3. Applicability of the Regulations : The Committee recommends that : SEBI should appoint a Panel comprised of experts and officers of SEBI and the recommendations of the Panel may be taken into account by SEBI while considering exemptions in cases which would not be covered by the circumstances specifically enumerated in the Regulations. The Committee therefore recommends that: the requirement to make a public offer be exempted for acquisitions made under firm allotment in public issues and preferential offers, with full disclosure as to who the allottees are and the consequences, if any, on the control of the company; acquisitions by the shareholder pursuant to rights issue to the extent of his entitlement and additional entitlement subject to certain conditions; inter se transfers among group companies within the definition of group in the MRTP Act; inter se transfer among promoters and foreign collaborators, among relatives, among government companies, among state level financial institutions and private co-promoters in joint sector projects; acquisitions pursuant to schemes of arrangement or reconstruction including amalgamation or merger or demerger under any law or Regulation, Indian or foreign; acquisition of shares by market makers during the course of market making, acquisition of shares by financial institutions in the ordinary course of their business in view of the special role in the Indian context or as pledgees.

(*i*) **Rights Issues** : The Committee recommends that: instead of fully exempting rights issue as was proposed in the draft Report, apart from acquisitions made by a shareholder pursuant to an application made to the extent of his entitlement, additional allotments within the limit of the acquisitions permitted in any period of 12 months and additional allotments to the persons currently in control of the company, provided he had disclosed in the letter of offer that he intends to take up additional shares if the issue is undersubscribed, be excluded.

(*ii*) **Preferential Offers :** *The Committee recommends that:* the acquisition of shares covered under section 81 (1A) of the Companies Act be exempt from the applicability of the regulations subject to full disclosure in the notice for the extraordinary general meeting called for consideration of preferential issue, including identity of the acquirer and consequent changes in shareholding pattern and control of the company etc.

(*iii*) **Market Makers** : The Committee recommends that: Acquisition of shares in the ordinary course of business by a registered market maker of a Stock Exchange in respect of shares for which he is the market maker during the course of market making be exempt.

(*iv*) **Indirect acquisition** : The Committee recommends that: concept of indirect acquisitions be brought in. This has been done in the definition of acquirer in clause (b) of sub regulation (1) of regulation (2); in the definition of persons acting in concert in sub clause (1) of clause (e) of sub regulation (1) of regulation (2); further while excluding unlisted companies from the purview of the Regulations in clause (k) of sub-regulation (1) of regulation 3.

(*v*) **Chain principle** : *The Committee recommends that:* indirect acquisition of control of a company should require compliance to the Regulations and this needs to be clarified by way of suitable explanation.

(*vi*) **Residual Cases and Takeover Panel** : The Committee recommends that: SEBI may be vested with power to grant exemption in residuary cases and for this purpose SEBI shall set up a Panel. The Panel would be recommendatory in nature. Any order granting or refusing exemption passed by the Board shall be a reasoned order and shall be published. This, procedure, while bringing transparency, would also serve to create precedents and help develop jurisprudence on the subject through case law.

(*vii*) **Reporting of Exemptions to Stock Exchange and SEBI** : The Committee recommends that: in order to ensure transparency in the transaction and assist in the monitoring, all the exempted transactions should be subject to reporting requirements to the concerned stock exchanges in advance of the proposed acquisition and to SEBI. (Reference : Part II of the Report - sub-regulation (3) and (4) of Regulation 3).

4. Power to remove difficulties : The Committee recommends that: the Board be vested with power to remove difficulties in the interpretation or application of the Regulations. (Reference : Part II of the Report - Regulation 5).

5. Disclosure of shareholding and control in a listed company : The Committee recommends that: apart from disclosures about individual holdings, disclosures about persons in control of management of the company and their shareholding interest in the company should also be called for.

6. Substantial Acquisition of shares and acquisition of control of the company:

(i) **Acquisition of shares or voting rights**

(a) **Negotiated vs. open market acquisition** : The Committee recommends that: as the manner of initial acquisition which would trigger public offer has no relevance as far as performance of obligations under the Regulations are concerned, the two provisions should be combined into a single provision.

(b) **Threshold Limit for Mandatory Public Offer** : In the draft Report, the Committee had decided to retain the present threshold of 10%. The rationale which has been explained in the Preface to the Report was accepted by the Committee and it was decided to retain this threshold. A large number of public comments received supported retention of this threshold, though there were a few who suggested the raising of the threshold to at least 26%. It was felt that under Indian conditions hardly any person as investor would invest in more than 10% in any company unless he has an intention of taking over the company at some point of time and the Committee therefore decided to retain the existing threshold limit of 10%.

The Committee recommends that:

(A) having regard to the Indian situation in which it is possible to acquire control of a company with a lower percentage of holding, the present threshold of 10% for public offer be retained;

(B) the present ambiguity about the applicability of the Regulations to persons who acquire shares beyond the threshold limit of 10% without initially holding any share be removed by adding the words "together with shares or voting rights held, if any".

(ii) **Consolidation of holdings :** The Committee felt that introducing such differential limits would not be in the interest of the shareholders and moreover would not be justifiable on any rational basis. It was therefore decided to remove this differentiation and permit acquisitions upto 2% in any 12 month period, to all persons who hold shares above the threshold limit of 10%. The Committee decided that substantial acquisition till an acquirer gains absolute control level of 75% may be brought within the scope of the Regulations.

The Committee recommends that:

(A) person(s) holding not less than 10% but not more than 75% may acquire upto 2% shares in any period of twelve months, without attracting the mandatory public offer requirement.

(B) The Committee also felt that it would be desirable to clarify that the provisions of these Regulations will not be applicable to any person who holds 75% or more at the time of notification of these Regulations and also to any acquirer who has reached the level of 75% without any breach of the provisions of the Regulations in force from time to time.

(iii) **Takeovers** : The Committee recommends that:

(A) the term 'control, may be defined by giving an inclusive definition and also, the consequences of change in control be included in the substantive portion of the Regulations, through provision for disclosure of person(s) in control of the company at periodical intervals which could indicate change in control over the company, when it occurs;

(B) mandatory public offer consequent upon change in control over the company be also provided.

(iv) **Relevance of Clause 40 A & B of the Listing Agreement** : The Committee recommends that: clause 40 A & B of the listing agreement may be replaced by a clause requiring compliance with the SEBI Regulations on Takeovers.

(v) **Appointment of Merchant Banker** : The Committee recommends that: only a Category I Merchant Banker, not being a group company or associate of the acquirer or the target company, be appointed for the purpose.

(vi) **Timing of public announcement of offer** : The Committee recommends that :

(A) the public announcement of offer be made not later than four working days of the agreement.

(B) in case of acquisition of securities (including GDRs / ADRs) which would entitle the acquirer to voting rights at a later date, the public announcement be made not later than four working days before conversion, or exercise of option, as the case may be leading to acquisition of shares with voting rights exceeding the threshold limit.

(vii) Public announcement of offer : The Committee recommends that

(A) Public announcement be released in all editions of an English national daily with wide circulation, one Hindi national daily with wide circulation and a regional language daily having circulation at the place where the registered office of the target company is situated and at the place of the stock exchange where the shares of the target company are most frequently traded.

(B) Public announcement be submitted to SEBI two working days in advance of its release.

(C) Public announcement be sent to all the stock exchanges on which the shares of the company are listed and to the target company at its registered office.

(D) Once the public announcement is made, the public offer shall be deemed to have been made.

(viii) Contents of public announcement of offer : The Committee recommends that

(A) The highest and average price paid by the acquirer or persons acting in concert with him for acquisition, if any, of shares of target company during the twelve month period prior to the date of the public announcement be disclosed in public announcement (Reference : Part II of the Report - Regulation 16 (viii)).

(B) The future plans of the acquirer, if any, for the target company, including whether the acquirer proposes to strip or dispose of or otherwise encumber any of the assets of the target company during the next succeeding 2 years be disclosed in the public announcement and in the absence of such disclosure, the acquirer shall be debarred from doing so. Where the public announcement sets out future plans, the acquirer shall also state how he proposes to implement such future plans.

(C) Public announcement should contain disclosure on financial arrangements for implementing the offer.

(D) Persons holding unregistered shares should be enabled to participate in the offer.

(E) The statutory approvals required to give effect to the offer be spelt out, with a declaration that no other approvals other than those mentioned in the public announcement are required for giving effect to the offer.

(F) Offer conditional as to minimum level of acceptances may be allowed, subject to checks and balances.

(G) The acquirer should be required to accept minimum of 20% irrespective of whether the conditional offer has elicited response to the level of acceptances desired by the offeror, but a lower price, which shall not be less than the minimum offer price as per the Regulations, can be offered for the minimum mandatory acceptances.

(ix) Approval of Board for Letter of Offer : The Committee recommends that

(A) disclosure requirements be clearly and elaborately specified by the Board (Reference : Part II of the Report - sub-regulation (1) of Regulation 18)

(B) offer document be filed with SEBI within fourteen days of public announcement and if no comments are communicated within twenty one days, the offer document may be circulated to the shareholders.

(x) Specified Date : The Committee recommends that

(A) concept of 'record date' may be replaced with 'specified date', which can be any date as may be decided by the acquirer and indicated in the public announcement subject to the condition that such date shall not be later than the thirtieth day from the date of public announcement.

(xi) Minimum offer price and payment of consideration other than in cash : The Committee recommends that

(A) the acquirer be permitted to pay consideration by way of cash or by exchange of securities,

(B) The existing formula for minimum offer price be retained with the additional parameter namely the highest price paid by the acquirer for any acquisition of shares of the target company during the twelve months prior to the date of public announcement.

(C) Where a preferential offer is made to an acquirer during the twelve month period ending with the date of closure of the offer, the price at which the preferential allotment has been made will also be taken into account in determining the offer price.

(D) The minimum offer price shall be fixed in consultation with the merchant banker in case of infrequently traded shares, to be justified on parameters specified in the regulations.

(E) Infrequent trading be defined.

(F) In case of acquisitions made by the acquirer during the offer period in any manner either from the market or from any particular investor(s), the highest price paid for such acquisition be paid to the shareholders under the public offer, unless it is less than the minimum offer price.

(xii) **Minimum Offer and Minimum Holding after the Offer :** The Committee recommends that

(A) The minimum offer as stipulated in the present regulations may continue but with a proviso allowing minimum offer of only 10% for consolidation of holdings by persons presently in control of the company.

(B) An offer may be made for 100% of the shares of the target company.

(C) The acquirer may be given an option to buy out the remaining shares if the public shareholding were to fall below 10% consequent upon a public offer which would have the effect of deemed delisting; or

(D) Alternatively, the acquirer may undertake to bring the public shareholding to a level as would satisfy the listing requirements through an offer for sale, with suitable disclosure in the offer document.

(xiii) **General Obligations of the Acquirers**

(a) **Participation in the open offer by outgoing management** : The Committee recommends that: persons other than parties to the agreement, in the case of negotiated takeovers, may participate in the open offer.

(b) **Offer to GDR / ADR holders and holders of convertibles or warrants** : The Committee recommends that

(A) the letter of offer should be sent to the custodians of GDR / ADR holders;

(B) the letter of offer should also be sent to the holders of warrants or convertibles issued pursuant to a domestic issue, where the period for exercise of option or conversion falls within the offer period.

(c) **Offer to be completed within specified time :** The Committee recommends that

(A) the time limit for each activity should be spelt out, as an obligation of the acquirer, so that the takeover process is completed promptly. These are -

(B) Filing of offer document with SEBI within fourteen days of the date of public announcement.

(C) Mailing of letter of offer so as to reach the shareholders, within forty five days of the date of public announcement.

(D) Offer to open within sixty days of the date of public announcement (E) Offer to close within a maximum of 105 days of the date of public announcement (F) Consideration to be mailed within thirty days of the date of (G) SEBI may permit extension of time limit under certain circumstances, subject to acquirer agreeing to pay interest for delayed period.

(d) **Acquisitions during offer period** : The Committee recommends that: except where an offer is made conditional as to minimum level of acceptances, the acquirer may be allowed to make acquisitions during offer period subject to the condition that highest price paid for such acquisition be paid to the shareholders under the public offer, unless it is less than the minimum offer price.

(e) **Escrow Account** : The Committee recommends that

(A) an escrow deposit as under shall be made for the value of the public offer

(B) For consideration payable under the public offer upto and including Rs. 100 crore - 25%; and for consideration exceeding Rs. 100 crore - 25% upto Rs.100 crore and 10% thereafter.

(C) amount to be adjusted whenever there is a revision in offer price;

(D) the amount will be used for payment of consideration to shareholders or refunded upon timely fulfillment of the obligations and forfeited, if not.

(E) to ensure that this escrow account which is in the interest of investors does not become too onerous a burden on the acquirer especially where the acquisition could involve large sums, the acquirer should also be allowed the option of depositing the escrow amount otherwise than in cash i.e. by way of bank guarantee or approved securities with appropriate margin as determined by the merchant banker.

(*f*) **Financial arrangements for fulfillment of obligations** : The Committee recommends that: the acquirer shall make firm arrangements for finance required and disclose full details of the arrangements both in the public announcement and in the letter of offer.

(*g*) **Procedure for payment of consideration to shareholders** : The Committee recommends that: an obligation to open a separate bank account may be cast on the acquirer and the procedure for payment of consideration may be laid down in the Regulations (Reference : Part II of the Report - sub-regulation (12) of Regulation 22 and Regulation 29).

(*h*) **Cooling Period** : The Committee recommends that

(*a*) if an offer made by an acquirer has been withdrawn, the acquirer should not be allowed to make a bid for the same company within a period of 6 months from the date of the public announcement or withdrawal or closure of the offer.

(*b*) In the event of non-fulfillment of obligations under Chapter III or IV of the Regulations, the acquirer shall not make an offer for acquisition of shares of any company or a period of twelve months from the date of closure of the offer.

(*i*) **Obligations of the target company :** The Committee recommends that

(*a*) till the offer formalities are completed, the target company shall be precluded from inducting any person or persons nominated by the acquirer or belonging to his group into the board of the target company or in management of the target company during the offer period.

(*b*) the target company shall exclude any person or persons connected with the acquirer from participating in any matter(s) relating to or arising from the offer.

(*c*) management changes can be made after closure of the offer and deposit of full amount in a special account with the bank.

(*d*) to begin a healthy trend as obtaining in developed markets, the board of directors of the target company, if they so wish, may send their unbiased comments on any bid to their shareholders keeping in view the fiduciary responsibility of the directors and for that purpose, seek the opinion of an independent merchant banker or a committee of independent directors. The directors of the target company shall be liable for any mis-statement or concealment of material information in the discharge of this function.

(*e*) the board of directors of the target company shall facilitate the acquirer in verification of securities tendered for acceptances.

(*f*) once the acquirer fulfills his obligations under the regulations as certified by the merchant banker, the target company shall -

(*g*) transfer the shares in the name of the acquirer;

(*h*) allow proportional representation on the board to the acquirer or give control over the company, as the case may be.

(*xv*) **Obligations of merchant bankers :** The Committee recommends that

(*a*) obligations of the merchant bankers be specifically laid down in the Regulations and penalties for non-compliance by the merchant bankers be provided.

(*b*) Merchant banker shall be liable to make good the shortfall, if any, in the escrow account.

(*xvi*) **Competitive bid :** The Committee recommends that

(*a*) A competitive bid can be for some or all of the shares of the target company the outer time limit within which a competitive can be made may be increased to 21 days.

(*b*) No bid for the target company can be made during the offer period, after twenty one days from the date of public announcement of the first offer.

(c) Subject to minimum offer requirement, any competitive offer by an acquirer shall be for such number of shares which, when taken together with shares held by him shall be at least equal to the number of shares for which the first public announcement has been made.

(d) Consequent upon a competing bid or bid(s), the acquirer(s) under the earlier offer should have the freedom either to revise their terms of offer or withdraw from the offer with the prior approval of the Board, within fourteen days of the announcement of the competing bid and if no such announcement is made, the offer on original terms shall subsist and be binding the acquirer.

(e) The competing bidders shall have the freedom to revise their offer price upwards anytime upto seven working days prior to the date of closure of the offer.

(f) If more than one bid subsist at the end of thirty five days from the date of public announcement of the first offer, it would be the shareholders' prerogative to choose one over another and to facilitate shareholders exercise of option in such an event, the competing offers shall close on the same date.

(xvii) **Revision of offer** : The Committee recommends that: upward revision in price and number of shares sought to be acquired may be permitted, irrespective of whether or not there is a competitive bid, upto seven working days prior to the date of closure of the offer, subject to public announcement in respect of such changes and consequent changes in the escrow.

(xviii) **Withdrawal of Offer** : The Committee recommends that the circumstances under which withdrawal of offer can be made could be clearly spelt out.

7. Bail out Takeovers : *The Committee recommends:* retention of the existing provisions with marginal changes for enhanced clarity and operational simplicity. Additionally, competitive bid would not be allowed for bail out takeovers as the selection of the incumbent in the management has been made through a process of competitive bidding.

8. Penalties for non-compliance : The Committee therefore recommends that SEBI Act be amended to

(a) expand the scope of adjudication and levy of monetary penalties;

(b) increase the amount of monetary penalties to make the penalties meaningful;

(c) provide for forfeiture and auction of shares acquired in violation of Regulations;

(d) provide for award of interest, cost and damages, if any, to the aggrieved party(ies) in case of violation of any of the provisions of these Regulations ;

(e) render null and void acquisition of shares made in violations of the Companies Act, 1956, regulation 3, 10, 11 and 12 of the Regulations or of any conditions imposed by SEBI while granting exemption under Regulation 4;

(f) strengthen the criminal sanctions for violations of any of the regulations.

Additionally, the Committee also recommends that provisions should be made in Company Law for personal disqualification of directors of the acquirer who violates the provisions of the Regulations.

The above penalties would be in addition to the penalties already existing in the SEBI Act and Regulations.

SECURITIES AND EXCHANGE BOARD OF INDIA (SUBSTANTIAL ACQUISITION OF SHARES AND TAKEOVERS) REGULATIONS, 1997

According to Substantial Acquisition of shares and takeover regulations, 1997:

(a) "Act" means the Securities and Exchange Board of India Act, 1992 (15 of 1992);

(b) "acquirer" means any person who, directly or indirectly, acquires or agrees to acquire shares or voting rights in the target company, or acquires or agrees to acquire control over the target company, either by himself or with any person acting in concert with the acquirer;

(c) "control" shall include the right to appoint majority of the directors or to control the management or policy decisions exercisable by a person or persons acting individually or in concert, directly or indirectly, including by virtue of their shareholding or management rights or shareholders agreements or voting agreements or in any other manner.

(*d*) "person acting in concert" comprises—

(1) persons who, for a common objective or purpose of substantial acquisition of shares or voting rights or gaining control over the target company, pursuant to an agreement or understanding (formal or informal), directly or indirectly co-operate by acquiring or agreeing to acquire shares or voting rights in the target company or control over the target company.

(2) Without prejudice to the generality of this definition, the following persons will be deemed to be persons acting in concert with other persons in the same category, unless the contrary is established :

(*i*) a company, its holding company, or subsidiary or such company or company under the same management either individually or together with each other;

(*ii*) a company with any of its directors, or any person entrusted with the management of the funds of the company;

(*iii*) directors of companies referred to in sub-clause (i) of clause (2) and their associates;

(*iv*) mutual fund with sponsor or trustee or asset management company;

(*v*) foreign institutional investors with sub-account(s);

(*vi*) merchant bankers with their client(s) as acquirer;

(*vii*) portfolio managers with their client(s) as acquirer;

(*viii*) venture capital funds with sponsors;

(*ix*) banks with financial advisers, stock brokers of the acquirer, or any company which is a holding company, subsidiary or relative of the acquirer: Provided that sub-clause

(*x*) shall not apply to a bank whose sole relationship with the acquirer or with any company, which is a holding company or a subsidiary of the acquirer or with a relative of the acquirer, is by way of providing normal commercial banking services or such activities in connection with the offer such as confirming availability of funds, handling acceptances and other registration work;

(*xi*) any investment company with any person who has an interest as director, fund manager, trustee, or as a shareholder having not less than 2 per cent of the paid-up capital of that company or with any other investment company in which such person or his associate holds not less than 2 per cent of the paid-up capital of the latter company.

(*e*) "panel" means a panel constituted by the Board for the purpose of regulation 4;

(*f*) "promoter" means—

(*a*) any person who is in control of the target company;

(*b*) any person named as promoter in any offer document of the target company or any shareholding pattern filed by the target company with the stock exchanges pursuant to the Listing Agreement, whichever is later;

and includes any person belonging to the promoter group as mentioned in

Explanation I: Provided that a director or officer of the target company or any other person shall not be a promoter, if he is acting as such merely in his professional capacity.

Explanation I. For the purpose of this clause, "promoter group" shall include:

(*a*) in case promoter is a body corporate—

(*i*) a subsidiary or holding company of that body corporate;

(*ii*) any company in which the promoter holds 10% or more of the equity capital or which holds 10% or more of the equity capital of the promoter;

(*iii*) any company in which a group of individuals or companies or combinations thereof who holds 20% or more of the equity capital in that company also holds 20% or more of the equity capital of the target company; and

(*b*) in case the promoter is an individual—

(*i*) the spouse of that person, or any parent, brother, sister or child of that person or of his spouse;

(*ii*) any company in which 10% or more of the share capital is held by the promoter or an immediate relative of the promoter or a firm or HUF in which the promoter or any one or more of his immediate relative is a member;

(*iii*) any company in which a company specified in (i) above, holds 10% or more, of the share capital; and

(*iv*) any HUF or firm in which the aggregate share of the promoter and his immediate relatives is equal to or more than 10 per cent of the total.

Explanation II.– Financial Institutions, Scheduled Banks, Foreign Institutional Investors (FIIs) and Mutual Funds shall not be deemed to be a promoter or promoter group merely by virtue of their shareholding:

Provided that the Financial Institutions, Scheduled Banks and Foreign Institutional Investors (FIIs) shall be treated as promoters or promoter group for the subsidiaries or companies promoted by them or mutual funds sponsored by them;]

(*c*) "public shareholding" means shareholding held by persons other thanpromoters as defined under clause (h);]

(*d*) "target company" means a listed company whose shares or voting rights or control is directly or indirectly acquired or is being acquired;

1. Applicability of the regulation: (1) Nothing contained in regulations 10, 11 and 12 of these regulations shall apply to:

(*a*) allotment in pursuance of an application made to a public issue:

(*b*) allotment pursuant to an application made by the shareholder for rights issue, (i) to the extent of his entitlement; and (ii) up to the percentage specified in regulation 11:

(*c*) allotment to the underwriters pursuant to any underwriting agreement;

(*d*) inter se transfer of shares amongst—

(*i*) group coming within the definition of group as defined in the Monopolies and Restrictive Trade Practices Act, 1969 (54 of 1969) where persons constituting such group have been shown as group in the last published Annual Report of the target company;]

(*ii*) relatives within the meaning of section 6 of the Companies Act, 1956 (1 of 1956);

(*iii*) (*a*) Qualifying Indian promoters] and foreign collaborators who are shareholders;

(*b*) [qualifying promoters]:

[Provided that the transferor(s) as well as the transferee(s) have been holding shares in the target company for a period of at least three years prior to the proposed acquisition.]

[*Explanation*: For the purpose of the exemption under sub-clause (iii) the term ["qualifying promoter"] means—

(*i*) any person who is directly or indirectly in control of the company; or

(*ii*) any person named as promoter in any document for offer of securities to the public or existing shareholders or in the shareholding pattern disclosed by the company under the provisions of the Listing Agreement, whichever is later; and includes,

(*a*) where the [qualifying promoter] is an individual,—

(A) a relative of the [qualifying promoter] within the meaning of section 6 of the Companies Act, 1956 (1 of 1956);

(B) any firm or company, directly or indirectly, controlled by the [qualifying promoter] or a relative of the [qualifying promoter] or a firm or Hindu undivided family in which the [qualifying promoter] or his relative is a partner or a copartner or a combination thereof:

Provided that, in case of a partnership firm, the share of the [qualifying promoter] or his relative, as the case may be, in such firm should not be less than fifty per cent (50%);

(*b*) where the [qualifying promoter] is a body corporate,—

(A) a subsidiary or holding company of that body; or

(B) any firm or company, directly or indirectly, controlled by the [qualifying promoter] of that body corporate or by his relative or a firm or Hindu undivided family in which the [qualifying promoter] or his relative is a partner or coparcener or a combination thereof:

Provided that, in case of a partnership firm, the share of such [qualifying promoter] or his relative, as the case may be, in such firm should not be less than fifty per cent (50%);]

(*iv*) the acquirer and persons acting in concert with him, where such transfer of shares takes place three years after the date of closure of the public offer made by them under these regulations.

(*v*) the International Finance Corporation, Asian Development Bank, International Bank for Reconstruction and Development, Commonwealth Development Corporation and such other international financial institutions;

(*vi*) a merchant banker or a promoter of the target company pursuant to a scheme of safety net under the provisions of the Securities and Exchange Board of India (Disclosure and Investor Protection) Guidelines, 2000 in excess of limit specified in sub-regulation (1) of regulation 11;]

(*vii*) a merchant banker or nominated investor in the process of market making and subscription by the nominated investor to the unsubscribed portion of issue, in terms of Chapter XA of the Securities and Exchange Board of India (Issue of Capital and Disclosure Requirements) Regulations, 2009:

2. Takeover panel : (1) The Board shall for the purposes of this regulation constitute a panel of majority of independent persons from within the categories mentioned in sub-section (5) of section 4 of the Act.

(2) For seeking exemption the acquirer shall file an application with the Board, giving details of the proposed acquisition and the grounds on which the exemption has been sought.

(3) The acquirer shall, along with the application pay a fee of [fifty thousand rupees] to the Board, either by a banker's cheque or demand draft in favour of the Securities and Exchange Board of India, payable at Mumbai.

(4) The Board shall within 5 days of the receipt of an application forward the application to the panel.

(5) The panel shall within 15 days from the date of receipt of application make a recommendation on the application to the Board.

(6) The Board shall after affording reasonable opportunity to the concerned parties and after considering all the relevant facts including the recommendations, if any, pass a reasoned order on the application within 30 days thereof.

(7) The order of the Board under sub-regulation (6) shall be published by the Board.

3. Power of the Board : In order to remove any difficulties in the interpretation or application of the provisions of these regulations, the Board shall have the power to issue directions through guidance notes or circulars:

CHAPTER II

DISCLOSURES OF SHAREHOLDING AND CONTROL IN A LISTED COMPANY

1. Transitional provision: (1) Any person, who holds more than five per cent shares or voting rights in any company, shall within two months of notification of these regulations disclose his aggregate shareholding in that company, to the company.

(2) Every company whose shares are held by the persons shall, within three months from the date of notification of these regulations, disclose to all the stock exchanges on which the shares of the company are listed, the aggregate number of shares held by each person.

(3) A promoter or any person having control over a company shall within two months of notification of these regulations disclose the number and percentage of shares or voting rights held by him and by person(s) acting in concert with him in that company, to the company.

(4) Every company, whose shares are listed on a stock exchange shall within three months of notification of these regulations, disclose to all the stock exchanges on which the shares of the company are listed, the names and addresses of promoters and/or person(s) having control over the company, and the number and percentage of shares or voting rights held by each such person.

2. Acquisition of 5 per cent and more shares or voting rights of a company: (1) Any acquirer, who acquires shares or voting rights which (taken together with shares or voting rights, if any, held by him) would entitle him to more than five per cent or ten per cent or fourteen per cent 2[or fifty four per cent or seventy four per cent] shares or voting rights in a company, in any manner whatsoever, shall disclose at every stage the aggregate of his shareholding or voting rights in that company to the company and to the stock exchanges where shares of the target company are listed.]

(1A) Any acquirer who has acquired shares or voting rights of a company shall disclose purchase or sale aggregating two per cent or more of the share capital of the target company to the target company, and the stock exchanges where shares of the target company are listed within two days of such purchase or sale along with the aggregate shareholding after such acquisition or sale.]

(2) The disclosures mentioned in sub-regulations (1) [and (1A)] shall be made within [two days] of, —

(*a*) the receipt of intimation of allotment of shares; or

(*b*) the acquisition of shares or voting rights, as the case may be.

(2A) The stock exchange shall immediately display the information received from the acquirer on the trading screen, the notice board and also on its website.]

(3) Every company, whose shares are acquired shall disclose to all the stock exchanges on which the shares of the said company are listed the aggregate number of shares held by each of such persons referred above within seven days of receipt of information.

3. Continual disclosures: (1) Every person, including a person mentioned in regulation 6 who holds more than per cent shares or voting rights in any company, shall, within 21 days from the financial year ending March 31, make yearly disclosures to the company, in respect of his holdings as on 31st March.

(2) A promoter or every person having control over a company shall, within 21 days from the financial year ending March 31, as well as the record date of the company for the purposes of declaration of dividend, disclose the number and percentage of shares or voting rights held by him and by persons acting in concert with him, in that company to the company.

(3) Every company whose shares are listed on a stock exchange, shall within 30 days from the financial year ending March 31, as well as the record date of the company for the purposes of declaration of dividend, make yearly disclosures to all the stock exchanges on which the shares of the company are listed, the changes, if any, in respect of the holdings of the persons and also holdings of promoters or person(s) having control over the company as on 31st March.

(4) Every company whose shares are listed on a stock exchange shall maintain a register in the specified format to record the information received under the relevant regulations.

4. Disclosure of pledged shares: (1) A promoter or every person forming part of the promoter group of any company shall, within seven working days of commencement of Securities and Exchange Board of India (Substantial Acquisition of Shares and Takeovers) (Amendment) Regulations, 2009, disclose details of shares of that company pledged by him, if any, to that company.

(2) A promoter or every person forming part of the promoter group of any company shall, within 7 working days from the date of creation of pledge on shares of that company held by him, inform the details of such pledge of shares to that company.

(3) A promoter or every person forming part of the promoter group of any company shall, within 7 working days from the date of invocation of pledge on shares of that company pledged by him, inform the details of invocation of such pledge to that company.

(4) The company shall disclose the information received to all the stock exchanges, on which the shares of company are listed, within 7 working days of the receipt thereof, if, during any quarter ending March, June, September and December of any year,—

(*a*) aggregate number of pledged shares of a promoter or every person forming part of promoter group taken together with shares already pledged during that quarter by such promoter or persons exceeds twenty five thousand; or

(*b*) aggregate of total pledged shares of the promoter or every person forming part of promoter group along with the shares already pledged during that quarter by such promoter or persons exceeds one per cent of total shareholding or voting rights of the company,— whichever is lower.]

5. Power to call for information: The stock exchanges and the company shall furnish to the Board information with regard to the disclosures made under regulations 6, 7 and 8 as and when required by the Board.

CHAPTER III
SUBSTANTIAL ACQUISITION OF SHARES OR VOTING RIGHTS IN AND ACQUISITION OF CONTROL OVER A LISTED COMPANY

1. Acquisition of fifteen per cent or more of the shares or voting rights of any company: No acquirer shall acquire shares or voting rights which (taken together with shares or voting rights, if any, held by him or by persons acting in concert with him), entitle such acquirer to exercise fifteen per cent or more of the voting rights in a company, unless such acquirer makes a public announcement to acquire shares of such company in accordance with the regulations.

2. Consolidation of holdings: (1) No acquirer who, together with persons acting in concert with him, has acquired, in accordance with the provisions of law, [15 per cent or more but less than fifty five per cent (55%) of the shares or voting rights in a company, shall acquire, either by himself or through or with persons acting in concert with him, additional shares or voting rights entitling him to exercise more than 5% of the voting rights with post acquisition shareholding or voting rights not exceeding fifty five per cent in any financial year ending on 31st March unless such acquirer makes a public announcement to acquire shares in accordance with the regulations.

(2) No acquirer, who together with persons acting in concert with him holds, fifty-five per cent (55%) or more but less than seventy-five per cent (75%) of the shares or voting rights in a target company, shall acquire either by himself or

Provided that in a case where the target company had obtained listing of its shares by making an offer of at least ten per cent (10%) of issue size to the public (75%), the words and figures 'ninety per cent (90%) were substituted.

Provided further that such acquirer may, notwithstanding the acquisition made without making a public announcement under these Regulations, acquire, either by himself or through or with persons acting in concert with him, additional shares or voting rights entitling him upto five per cent. (5%) voting rights in the target company subject to the following:-

(*i*) the acquisition is made through open market purchase in normal segment on the stock exchange but not through bulk deal /block deal/ negotiated deal/ preferential allotment; or the increase in the shareholding or voting rights of the acquirer is pursuant to a buyback of shares by the target company;

(*ii*) the post acquisition shareholding of the acquirer together with persons acting in concert with him shall not increase beyond seventy five per cent.(75%).]

(2A) Where an acquirer who (together with persons acting in concert with him) holds fifty-five per cent (55%) or more but less than seventy-five per cent (75%) of the shares or voting rights in a target company, is desirous of consolidating his holding while ensuring that the public shareholding in the target company does not fall below the minimum level permitted by the Listing Agreement, he may do so 3[***] by making a public announcement in accordance with these regulations :

3. Acquisition of control over a company: Irrespective of whether or not there has been any acquisition of shares or voting rights in a company, no acquirer shall acquire control over the target company, unless such person makes a public announcement to acquire shares and acquires such shares in accordance with the regulations:

Provided that nothing contained herein shall apply to any change in control which takes place in pursuance to a special resolution passed by the shareholders in a general meeting :

Provided further that for passing of the special resolution facility of voting through postal ballot as specified under the Companies (Passing of the Resolutions by Postal Ballot) Rules, 2001 shall also be provided.

Explanation.—For the purposes of this regulation, acquisition shall include direct or indirect acquisition of control of target company by virtue of acquisition of companies, whether listed or unlisted and whether in India or abroad.

4. Appointment of a merchant banker: Before making any public announcement of offer referred to in regulation 10 or regulation 11 or regulation 12, the acquirer shall appoint a merchant banker in Category I holding a certificate of registration granted by the Board, who is not an associate of or group of the acquirer or the target company.

5. Timing of the public announcement of offer: (1) The public announcement shall be made by the merchant banker not later than four working days of entering into an agreement for acquisition of shares or voting rights or deciding to acquire shares or voting rights exceeding the respective percentage specified therein:

(2) The public announcement referred to in regulation 12 shall be made by the merchant banker not later than four working days after any such change or changes are decided to be made as would result in the acquisition of control over the target company by the acquirer.

(3) In case of indirect acquisition or change in control, a public announcement shall be made by the acquirer within three months of consummation of such acquisition or change in control or restructuring of the parent or the company holding shares of or control over the target company in India.

6. Public announcement of offer: (1) The public announcement to be made under regulation 10 or 11 or 12 shall be made in all editions of one English national daily with wide circulation, one Hindi national daily with wide circulation and a regional language daily with wide circulation at the place where the registered office of the target company is situated and at the place of the stock exchange where the shares of the target company are most frequently traded.

(2) Simultaneously with publication of the public announcement in the newspaper a copy of the public announcement shall be,

(*i*) submitted to the Board through the merchant banker,

(*ii*) sent to all the stock exchanges on which the shares of the company are listed for being notified on the notice board,

(*iii*) sent to the target company at its registered office for being placed before the Board of Directors of the company.

(3) The offer under these regulations shall be deemed to have been made on the date on which the public announcement has appeared in any of the newspapers referred to in sub-regulation (1).

7. Contents of the public announcement of offer: The public announcement shall contain the following particulars, namely:—

(*i*) the paid-up share capital of the target company, the number of fully paid-up and partly paid-up shares;

(*ii*) the total number and percentage of shares proposed to be acquired from the public, subject to a minimum as specified in sub-regulation (1) of regulation 21;

(*iii*) the minimum offer price for each fully paid-up or partly paid-up share;

(*iv*) mode of payment of consideration;

(*v*) the identity of the acquirer(s) and in case the acquirer is a company or companies, the identity of the promoters and, or the persons having control over such company(ies) and the group, if any, to which the company(ies) belong;

(*vi*) the existing holding, if any, of the acquirer in the shares of the target company, including holdings of persons acting in concert with him;

(*vii*) the existing shareholding, if any, of the merchant banker in the target company;]

(*viii*) the salient features of the agreement, if any, such as the date, the name of the seller, the price at which the shares are being acquired, the manner of payment of the consideration and the number and percentage of shares in respect of which the acquirer has entered into the agreement to acquire the shares or the consideration, monetary or otherwise, for the acquisition of control over the target company, as the case may be;

(*ix*) the highest and the average price paid by the acquirer or persons acting in concert with him for acquisition, if any, of shares of the target company made by him during the twelve months period prior to the date of public announcement;

(*x*) the object and purpose of the acquisition of the shares and future plans, if any, of the acquirer for the target company, including disclosures whether the acquirer proposes to dispose of or otherwise encumber any assets of the target company in the succeeding two years except in the ordinary course of business of the target company:

(*xi*) the specified date as mentioned in regulation 19;

(*xii*) the date by which individual letters of offer would be posted to each of the shareholders;

(*xiii*) the date of opening and closure of the offer and the manner in which and the date by which the acceptance or rejection of the offer would be communicated to the shareholders;

(*xiv*) the date by which the payment of consideration would be made for the shares in respect of which the offer has been accepted;

(*xv*) disclosure to the effect that firm arrangement for financial resources required to implement the offer is already in place, including details regarding the sources of the funds whether domestic, i.e., from banks, financial institutions or otherwise or foreign, i.e., from Non-Resident Indians or otherwise;

(*xvi*) provision for acceptance of the offer by person(s) who own the shares but are not the registered holders of such shares;

(*xvii*) statutory approvals, if any, required to be obtained for the purpose of acquiring the shares under the Companies Act, 1956 (1 of 1956), the Monopolies and Restrictive Trade Practices Act, 1969 (54 of 1969), the Foreign Exchange Regulation Act, 1973 (46 of 1973), and/or any other applicable laws;

(*xviii*) approvals of banks or financial institutions required, if any;

(*xix*) whether the offer is subject to a minimum level of acceptances from the shareholders; and

(*xx*) such other information as is essential for the shareholders to make an informed decision in regard to the offer.

8. Brochures, advertising material, etc. : The public announcement of the offer or any other advertisement, circular, brochure, publicity material or letter of offer issued in relation to the acquisition of shares shall not contain any misleading information.

9. Submission of letter of offer to the Board: (1) Within fourteen days from the date of public announcement made the acquirer shall, through its merchant banker, file with the Board, the draft of the letter of offer containing disclosures as specified by the Board.

(2) The letter of offer shall be dispatched to the shareholders not earlier than 21 days from its submission to the Board.

(3) The acquirer shall, while filing the draft letter of offer with the Board under sub-regulation (1), pay a fee as mentioned in the following table, by bankers' cheque or demand draft drawn in favour of the 'Securities and Exchange Board of India', payable at Mumbai:

Offer size	Fee (Rs.)
Less than or equal to ten crore rupees.	One lakh rupees (Rs. 1,00,000)
More than ten crore rupees, but less than or equal to one thousand crore rupees.	0.125 per cent of the offer size.
More than one thousand crore rupees, but less than or equal to five thousand crore rupees.	One crore twenty five lakh rupees (Rs. 1,25,00,000) plus 0.03125 per cent of the portion of the offer size in excess of one thousand crore rupees (Rs. 1000,00,00,000).
More than five thousand crore rupees.	A flat charge of three crore rupees (Rs. 3,00,00,000).]

10. Specified date: The public announcement shall specify a date, which shall be the "specified date" for the purpose of determining the names of the shareholders to whom the letter of offer should be sent: Provided that such specified date shall not be later than the thirtieth day from the date of the public announcement.

11. Offer price: (1) The offer to acquire shares under regulation 10, 11 or 12 shall be made at a price not lower than the price determined as per sub-regulations (4) and (5).

(2) The offer price shall be payable—

(*a*) in cash;

(*b*) by issue, exchange and/transfer of shares (other than preference shares) of acquirer company, if the person seeking to acquire the shares is a listed body corporate; or

(*c*) by issue, exchange and, or transfer of secured instruments of acquirer company with a minimum A' grade rating from a credit rating agency registered with the Board;

(*d*) a combination of clause (a), (b) or (c) : Page 39 of 75 amount to be paid in cash as mentioned in any announcement or the letter of offer is not reduced.

(3) In case the offer price consists of consideration payable in the form of securities issuance of which requires approval of the shareholders, such approval shall be obtained by the acquirer within seven days from the date of closure of the offer:

Provided that in case the requisite approval is not obtained, the acquirer shall pay the entire consideration in cash.

(4) For the purposes of sub-regulation (1), the offer price shall be the highest of—

(*a*) the negotiated price under the agreement referred to in sub-regulation (1) of regulation 14;

(*b*) price paid by the acquirer or persons acting in concert with him for acquisition, if any, including by way of allotment in a public or rights or preferential issue during the twenty-six week period prior to the date of public announcement, whichever is higher;

(*c*) the average of the weekly high and low of the closing prices of the shares of the target company as quoted on the stock exchange where the shares of the company are most frequently traded during the twenty-six weeks or the average of the daily high and low of the prices of the shares as quoted on the stock exchange where the shares of the company are most frequently traded during the two weeks preceding the date of public announcement, whichever is higher:

(5) Where the shares of the target company are infrequently traded, the offer price shall be determined by the acquirer and the merchant banker taking into account the following factors:

(*a*) the negotiated price under the agreement referred to in sub-regulation (1) of regulation 14;

(*b*) the highest price paid by the acquirer or persons acting in concert with him for acquisitions, if any, including by way of allotment in a public or rights or preferential issue during the twenty-six week period prior to the date of public announcement;

(*c*) other parameters including return on net worth, book value of the shares of the target company, earning per share, price earning multiple vis-à-vis the industry average :

(6) In case of disinvestment of a Public Sector Undertaking, whose shares are infrequently traded, the minimum offer price shall be the price paid by the successful bidder to the Central Government or the State Government, arrived at after the process of competitive bidding of the Central Government or the State Government for the purpose of disinvestment.

(7) Notwithstanding anything contained in the provisions where the acquirer has acquired shares in the open market or through negotiation or otherwise, after the date of public announcement at a price higher than the offer price stated in the letter of offer, then, the highest price paid for such acquisition shall be payable for all acceptances received under the offer:

(8) Any payment made to the persons other than the target company in respect of non- compete agreement in excess of twenty-five per cent of the offer price arrived at shall be added to the offer price.

(9) In case where shares or secured instruments of the acquirer company are offered in lieu of cash payment, the value of such shares or secured instruments shall be determined in the same as duly certified by an independent merchant banker (other than the manager to the offer) or an independent chartered accountant of a minimum ten years standing or a public financial institution.

(10) The offer price for partly paid up shares shall be calculated as the difference between the offer price and the amount due towards calls-in-arrears or calls remaining unpaid together with interest, if any, payable on the amount called up but remaining unpaid.

(11) The letter of offer shall contain justification or the basis on which the price has been determined.

Explanation.— (*i*) The highest price under clause (b) or the average price under clause (c) of sub-regulation (4) may be adjusted for quotations, if any, on cum-rights or cum-bonus or cum-dividend basis during the said period.

(*ii*) Where the public announcement of offer is pursuant to acquisition by way of firm allotment in a public issue or preferential allotment, the average price under clause (c) of sub-regulation (4) shall be calculated with reference to twenty-six week period preceding the date of the board resolution which authorised the firm allotment or preferential allotment.

(*iii*) Where the shareholders have been provided with an option to accept payment either in cash or by way of exchange of security, the pricing for the cash offer could be different from that of a share exchange offer or offer for exchange with secured instruments provided that the disclosures in the letter of offer contains suitable justification for such differential pricing and the pricing is subject to other provisions of this regulation.

(*iv*) Where the offer is subject to a minimum level of acceptance, the acquirer may, subject to the other provisions of this regulation, indicate a lower price for the minimum acceptance up to twenty per cent, should be the offer not receive full acceptance.

(12) The offer price for indirect acquisition or control shall be determined with reference to the date of the public announcement for the parent company and the date of the public announcement for acquisition of shares of the target company, whichever is higher.

12. Acquisition price under creeping acquisition: (1) An acquirer who has made a public offer and seeks to acquire further shares under sub-regulation (1) of regulation 11 shall not acquire such shares during the period of 6 months from the date of closure of the public offer at a price higher than the offer price. (2) Sub-regulation (1) shall not apply where the acquisition is made through the stock exchanges.

13. Minimum number of shares to be acquired: (1) The public offer made by the acquirer to the shareholders of the target company shall be for a minimum twenty per cent of the voting capital of the company:

(2) If the acquisition made in pursuance of a public offer results in the public shareholding in the target company being reduced below the minimum level required as per the Listing Agreement, the acquirer shall take necessary steps to facilitate compliance of the target company with the relevant provisions thereof, within the time period mentioned therein.

(3) Where the public offer is made the minimum size of the public offer shall be the lesser of the following—

(*a*) twenty per cent of the voting capital of the company; or

(*b*) such other lesser percentage of the voting capital of the company as would, assuming full subscription to the offer, enable the acquirer, together with the persons acting in concert with him, to increase his holding to the maximum level possible, which is consistent with the target company meeting the requirements of minimum public shareholding laid down in the Listing Agreement.

(4) The letter of offer shall state clearly the option available to the acquirer.

(5) For the purpose of computing the percentage the voting rights as at the expiration of 2[fifteen] days after the closure of the public offer shall be reckoned.

(6) Where the number of shares offered for sale by the shareholders are more than the shares agreed to be acquired by the person making the offer, such person shall accept the offers received from the shareholders on a proportional basis, in consultation with the merchant banker, taking care to ensure that the basis of acceptance is decided in a fair and equitable manner and does not result in non-marketable lots:

14. Offer conditional upon level of acceptance: (1) Subject to the provisions of sub-regulation (8) of regulation 22, an acquirer or any person acting in concert with him may make an offer conditional as to the level of acceptance which may be less than twenty per cent:

15. General obligations of the acquirer: (1) The public announcement of an offer to acquire the shares of the target company shall be made only when the acquirer is able to implement the offer.

(2) Within 14 days of the public announcement of the offer, the acquirer shall send a copy of the draft letter of offer to the target company at its registered office address, for being placed before the board of directors and to all the stock exchanges where the shares of the company are listed.

(3) The acquirer shall ensure that the letter of offer is sent to all the shareholders (including non-resident Indians) of the target company, whose names appear on the register of members of the company as on the specified date mentioned in the public announcement, so as to reach them within 45 days from the date of public announcement:

(4) The date of opening of the offer shall be not later than the fifty fifth day from the date of public announcement.

(5) The offer to acquire shares from the shareholders shall remain open for a period of twenty days.

(5A) The shareholder shall have the option to withdraw acceptance tendered by him up to three working days prior to the date of closure of the offer.

(6) In case the acquirer is a company, the public announcement of offer, brochure, circular, letter of offer or any other advertisement or publicity material issued to shareholders in connection with the offer must state that the directors accept the responsibility for the information contained in such documents.

(7) During the offer period, the acquirer or persons acting in concert with him shall not be entitled to be appointed on the board of directors of the target company.

(8) Where an offer is made conditional upon minimum level of acceptances, the acquirer or any person acting in concert with him—

(*i*) shall, irrespective of whether or not the offer received response to the minimum level of acceptances, acquire shares from the public to the extent of the minimum percentage specified in sub-regulation (1) of regulation 21: Provided that the provisions of this clause shall not be applicable in case the acquirer has deposited in the escrow account, in cash, 50 per cent of the consideration payable under the public offer;

(*ii*) shall not acquire, during the offer period, any shares in the target company, except by way of fresh issue of shares of the target company, as provided for under regulation 3;

(*iii*) shall be liable for penalty of forfeiture of the entire escrow amount, for the non-fulfilment of obligations under the regulations.

(9) If any of the persons representing or having interest in the acquirer is already a director on the board of the target company or is an—insider within the meaning of the Securities and Exchange Board of India (Insider Trading) Regulations, 1992, he shall refuse himself and not participate in any matter(s) concerning or—relating to the offer including any preparatory steps leading to the offer.

(10) On or before the date of issue of public announcement of offer, the acquirer shall create an escrow account as provided under regulation 28.

(11) The acquirer shall ensure that firm financial arrangement has been made for fulfilling the obligations under the public offer and suitable disclosures in this regard shall be made in the public announcement of offer.

(12) The acquirer shall, within a period of 1[fifteen] days from the date of the closure of the offer, complete all procedures relating to the offer including payment of consideration to the shareholders who have accepted the offer and for the purpose open a special account as provided under regulation 29 :

(13) Where the acquirer fails to obtain the requisite statutory approvals in time on account of wilful default or neglect or inaction or non-action on his part, the amount lying in the escrow account shall be liable to be forfeited and dealt with in the manner provided in clause (e) of sub-regulation (12) of regulation 28, apart from the acquirer being liable for penalty as provided in the regulations.

(14) In the event of withdrawal of offer in terms of the regulations, the acquirer shall not make any offer for acquisition of shares of the target company for a period of six months from the date of public announcement of withdrawal of offer.

(15) In the event of non-fulfilment of obligations under Chapter III or Chapter IV of the regulations the acquirer shall not make any offer for acquisition of shares of any listed company for a period of twelve months from the date of closure of the offer.

(16) If the acquirer, in pursuance of an agreement, acquires shares which along with his existing holding, if any, increases his shareholding beyond 15 per cent, then such agreement for sale of shares shall contain a clause to the effect that in case of non-compliance of any provisions of this regulation, the agreement for such sale shall not be acted upon by the seller or the acquirer.

(17) Where the acquirer or persons acting in concert with him has acquired any shares in terms of sub-regulation (7) of regulation 20 at a price equal to or less or more than the offer price, he shall disclose the number, percentage, price and the mode of acquisition of such shares to the stock exchanges on which the shares of the target company are listed and to the merchant banker within 24 hours of such acquisition and the stock exchanges shall forthwith disseminate such information to the public.

(18) Where the acquirer has not either, in the public announcement, and, or in the letter of offer, stated his intention to dispose of or otherwise encumber any assets of the target company except in the ordinary course of business of the target company, the acquirer, where he has acquired control over the target company, shall be debarred from disposing of or otherwise encumbering the assets of the target company for a period of two years from the date of closure of the public offer.

(19) The acquirer and the persons acting in concert with him shall be jointly and severally responsible for fulfillment of obligations under these regulations.

16. General obligations of the board of directors of the target company: (1) Unless the approval of the general body of shareholders is obtained after the date of the public announcement of offer, the board of directors of the target company shall not, during the offer period,—

(*a*) sell, transfer, encumber or otherwise dispose of or enter into an agreement for sale, transfer, encumbrance or for disposal of assets otherwise, not being sale or disposal of assets in the ordinary course of business, of the company or its subsidiaries; or

(*b*) issue or allot any authorised but unissued securities carrying voting rights during the offer period; or

(*c*) enter into any material contracts.

(2) The target company shall furnish to the acquirer, within seven days of the request of the acquirer or within seven days from the specified date whichever is later, a list of shareholders or warrant holders or convertible debenture holders as are eligible for participation under Explanation (ii) to sub-regulation (3) of regulation 22 containing names, addresses, shareholding and folio number, and of those persons whose applications for registration of transfer of shares are pending with the company.

(3) Once the public announcement has been made, the board of directors of the target company shall not,—

(*a*) appoint as additional director or fill in any casual vacancy on the board of directors, by any person(s) representing or having interest in the acquirer, till the date of certification by the merchant banker as provided under sub-regulation (6) below.

(*b*) allow any person or persons representing or having interest in the acquirer, if he is already a director on the board of the target company before the date of the public announcement, to participate in any matter relating to the offer, including any preparatory steps leading thereto.

(4) The board of directors of the target company may, if they so desire, send their unbiased comments and recommendations on the offer(s) to the shareholders, keeping in mind the fiduciary responsibility of the directors to the shareholders and for the purpose seek the opinion of an independent merchant banker or a committee of independent directors. Provided that for any mis-statement or for concealment of material information, the directors shall be liable for action in terms of these regulations and the Act.

(5) The board of directors of the target company shall facilitate the acquirer in verification of securities tendered for acceptances.

(6) Upon fulfillment of all obligations by the acquirers under the regulations as certified by the merchant banker, the board of directors of the target company shall transfer the securities acquired by the acquirer, whether under the agreement or from open market purchases, in the name of the acquirer and/or allow such changes in the board of directors as would give the acquirer representation on the board or control over the company.

(7) The obligations provided for in sub-regulation (16) of regulation 22 shall be complied with by the company in the circumstances specified therein.

17. General obligations of the merchant banker: (1) Before the public announcement of offer is made, the merchant banker shall ensure that—

(*a*) the acquirer is able to implement the offer;

(*b*) the provision relating to escrow account referred to in regulation 28 has been made;

(*c*) firm arrangements for funds and money for payment through verifiable means to fulfil the obligations under the offer are in place;

(*d*) the public announcement of offer is made in terms of the regulations;

(*e*) his shareholding, if any in the target company is disclosed in the public announcement and the letter of offer.

(2) The merchant banker shall furnish to the Board a due diligence certificate which shall accompany the draft letter of offer.

(3) The merchant banker shall ensure that the public announcement and the letter of offer is filed with the Board, target company and also sent to all the stock exchanges on which the shares of the target company are listed in accordance with the regulations.

(4) The merchant banker shall ensure that the contents of the public announcement of offer as well as the letter of offer are true, fair and adequate and based on reliable sources, quoting the source wherever necessary.

(5) The merchant banker shall ensure compliance of the regulations and any other laws or rules as may be applicable in this regard.

(5A) The merchant banker shall not deal in the shares of the target company during the period commencing from the date of his appointment in terms of regulation 13 till the expiry of the fifteen days from the date of closure of the offer.

(6) Upon fulfillment of all obligations by the acquirers under the regulations, the merchant banker shall cause the bank with whom the escrow amount has been deposited to release the balance amount to the acquirers.

(7) The merchant banker shall send a final report to the Board within 45 days from the date of closure of the offer.

18. Competitive bid: (1) Any person, other than the acquirer who has made the first public announcement, who is desirous of making any offer, shall, within 21 days of the public announcement of the first offer, make a public announcement of his offer for acquisition of the shares of the same target company.

(2) No public announcement for an offer or competitive bid shall be made after 21 days from the date of public announcement of the first offer.

(2A) No public announcement for a competitive bid shall be made after an acquirer has already made the public announcement pursuant to entering into a Share Purchase or Shareholders' Agreement with the Central Government for acquisition of shares or voting rights or control of a Public Sector Undertaking.

(2B) No public announcement for a competitive bid shall be made after an acquirer has already made the public announcement pursuant to relaxation granted by the Board in terms of regulation 29A.

(3) Any competitive offer by an acquirer shall be for such number of shares which, when taken together with shares held by him along with persons acting in concert with him, shall be at least equal to the holding of the first bidder including the number of shares for which the present offer by the first bidder has been made.

(4) Upon the public announcement of a competitive bid or bids, the acquirer(s) who had made the public announcement(s) of the earlier offer(s), shall have the option to 5[make an announcement revising the offer.

(6) The acquirers who have made the public announcement of offer(s) including the public announcement of competitive bid(s) shall have the option to make upward revisions in his offer(s), in respect of the price and the number of shares to be acquired, at any time up to seven working days prior to the date of closure of the offer.

19. Upward revision of offer: Irrespective of whether or not there is a competitive bid, the acquirer who has made the public announcement of offer may make upward revisions in his offer in respect of the price and the number of shares to be acquired, at any time up to seven working days prior to the date of the closure of the offer.

20. Withdrawal of offer: (1) No public offer, once made, shall be withdrawn except under the following circumstances:—

(*a*) the statutory approval(s) required have been refused;

(*b*) the sole acquirer, being a natural person, has died;

(*c*) such circumstances as in the opinion of the Board merit withdrawal.

(2) In the event of withdrawal of the offer under any of the circumstances specified under sub-regulation (1), the acquirer or the merchant banker shall—

(*a*) make a public announcement in the same newspapers in which the public announcement of offer was published, indicating reasons for withdrawal of the offer;

(*b*) simultaneously with the issue of such public announcement, inform - (i) the Board; (ii) all the stock exchanges on which the shares of the company are listed; and (iii) the target company at its registered office.

21. Provision of escrow: (1) The acquirer shall as and by way of security for performance of his obligations under the regulations, deposit in an escrow account such sum as specified in sub-regulation (2).

(2) The escrow amount shall be calculated in the following manner—

(*a*) For consideration payable under the public offer—

up to and including Rs. 100 crores	25 per cent
exceeding Rs. 100 crores	25 per cent;

up to Rs.100 crores and 10 per cent thereafter.

(*b*) For offers which are subject to a minimum level of acceptance, and the acquirer does not want to acquire a minimum of 20 per cent, than 50 per cent of the consideration payable under the public offer in cash shall be deposited in the escrow account.

(3) The total consideration payable under the public offer shall be calculated assuming full acceptances and at the highest price if the offer is subject to differential pricing, irrespective of whether the consideration for the offer is payable in cash or otherwise.

(4) The escrow account referred to in sub-regulation (1) shall consist of—

(*a*) cash deposited with a scheduled commercial bank; or

(*b*) bank guarantee in favour of the merchant banker; or

(*c*) deposit of acceptable securities with appropriate margin, with the merchant banker; or

(*d*) cash deposited with a scheduled commercial bank in case of clause (b) of sub-regulation (2) of this regulation.

(5) Where the escrow account consists of deposit with a scheduled commercial bank, the acquirer shall while opening the account, empower the merchant banker appointed for the offer to instruct the bank to issue a banker's cheque or demand draft for the amount lying to the credit of the escrow account, as provided in the regulations.

(6) Where the escrow account consists of bank guarantee, such bank guarantee shall be in favour of the merchant banker and shall be valid at least for a period commencing from the date of public announcement until 1[twenty] days after the closure of the offer.

(7) The acquirer shall, in case the escrow account consists of securities empower the merchant banker to realise the value of such escrow account by sale or otherwise provided that if there is any deficit on realisation of the value of the securities, the merchant banker shall be liable to make good any such deficit.

(8) In case the escrow account consists of bank guarantee or approved securities, these shall not be returned by the merchant banker till after completion of all obligations under the regulations.

(9) In case there is any upward revision of offer, consequent upon a competitive bid or otherwise, the value of the escrow account shall be increased to equal at least 10 per cent of the consideration payable upon such revision.

(10) Where the escrow account consists of bank guarantee or deposit of approved securities, the acquirer shall also deposit with the bank a sum of at least 1 per cent of the total consideration payable, as and by way of security for fulfilment of the obligations under the regulations by the acquirers.

(11) The Board shall in case of non-fulfilment of obligations under the regulations by the acquirer forfeit the escrow account either in full or in part.

(11A) In case of failure by the acquirer to obtain shareholders' approval required under sub-regulation (3) of regulation 20, the amount in escrow account may be forfeited.

(12) The escrow account deposited with the bank in cash shall be released only in the manner as given in regulations 27 & 29.

(13) In the event of non-fulfilment of obligations by the acquirer, the merchant banker shall ensure realisation of escrow amount by way of foreclosure of deposit invocation of bank guarantee or sale of securities and credit proceeds thereof 1[to the Investor Protection and Education Fund established by the Board].

22. Payment of consideration: (1) For the amount of consideration payable in cash, the acquirer shall, within a period of 2[seven] days from the date of closure of the offer, open a special account with a banker to an issue registered with the Board and deposit therein, such sum as would, together with 90 per cent of the amount lying in the escrow account, if any, make up the entire sum due and payable to the shareholders as consideration for acceptances received and accepted in terms of these regulations and for this purpose, transfer the funds from the escrow account.

(2) The unclaimed balance lying to the credit of the account referred to in sub-regulation (1) at the end of three years from the date of deposit thereof shall be transferred to the investor protection fund of the regional stock exchange of the target company.

(3) In respect of consideration payable by way of exchange of securities, the acquirer shall ensure that the securities are actually issued and despatched to the shareholders.

Relaxation from the strict compliance of provisions of Chapter III in certain cases.

29A. The Board may, on an application made by a target company, relax any or more of the provisions of this Chapter, subject to such conditions as it may deem fit.

CHAPTER IV
BAIL OUT TAKEOVERS

1. Bail out takeovers. (1) The provisions of this Chapter shall apply to a substantial acquisition of shares in a financially weak company not being a sick industrial company, in pursuance of a scheme of rehabilitation approved by a public financial institution of a scheduled bank (hereinafter referred to as "the lead institution").

(2) The lead institution shall be responsible for ensuring compliance with the provisions of this Chapter.

(3) The lead institution shall appraise the financially weak company taking into account the financial viability, and assess the requirement of funds for revival and draw up the rehabilitation package on the principle of protection of interests of minority shareholders, good management, effective revival and transparency.

(4) The rehabilitation scheme shall also specifically provide the details of any change in management.

(5) The scheme may provide for acquisition of shares in the financially weak company in any of the following manner:

(*a*) outright purchase of shares, or

(*b*) exchange of shares, or

(*c*) a combination of both:

Explanation.—For the purpose of this Chapter, the expression "financially weak company" means a company, which has at the end of the previous financial year accumulated losses, which has resulted in erosion of more than 50 per cent but less than 100 per cent of its net worth as at the Page 65 of 75 beginning of the previous financial year that is to say of the sum total of the paid-up capital and free reserves.

2. Manner of acquisition of shares: (1) Before giving effect to any scheme of rehabilitation the lead institution shall invite offers for acquisition of shares from at least three parties.

(2) After receipt of the offers under sub-regulation (1), the lead institution shall select one of the parties having regard to the managerial competence, adequacy of financial resources and technical capability of the person acquiring shares to rehabilitate the financially weak company.

(3) The lead institution shall provide necessary information to any person intending to make an offer to acquire shares about the financially weak company and particularly in relation to its present management technology, range of products manufactured, shareholding pattern, financial holding and performance and assets and liabilities of such company for a period covering five years from the date of the offer as also the minimum financial and other commitments expected of from the person acquiring shares for such rehabilitation.

3. Manner of evaluation of bids: (1) The lead institution shall evaluate the bids received with respect to the purchase price or exchange of shares, track record, financial resources, reputation of the management of the person acquiring shares and ensure fairness and transparency in the process.

(2) After making evaluation as provided in sub-regulation (1), the offers received shall be listed in order of preference and after consultation with the persons in the affairs of the management of the financially weak company accept one of the bids.

4. Person acquiring shares to make an offer: The person acquiring shares who has been identified by the lead institution under sub-regulation (2) of regulation 32, shall on receipt of a communication in this behalf from the lead institution make a formal offer to acquire shares from the promoters or persons in charge of the affairs of the management of the financially weak company, financial institutions and also other shareholders of the company at a price determined by mutual negotiation between the person acquiring the shares and the lead institution.

5. Person acquiring shares to make public announcement: (1) The person acquiring shares from the promoters or the persons in charge of the management of the affairs of the financially weak company or the financial institution shall make a public announcement of his intention for acquisition of shares from the other shareholders of the company.

(2) Such public announcement shall contain relevant details about the offer including the information about the identity and background of the person acquiring shares, the number and percentage of shares proposed to be acquired,

offer price, the specified date, the date of opening of the offer and the period for which the offer shall be kept open and such other particulars as may be required by the Board.

(3) The letter of offer shall be forwarded to each of the shareholders other than the promoters or the persons in charge of the management of the financially weak company and the financial institutions.

(4) The letter of offer shall state clearly the option available to the acquirer under sub-regulation (4).

(5) For the purposes of computing the percentage referred to in sub-regulation (4), the voting rights as at the expiration of 1[twenty] days after the closure of the public offer shall be reckoned. (7) While accepting the offer from the shareholders other than the promoters or persons in charge of the financially weak company or the financial institutions, the person acquiring shares shall offer to acquire from the individual shareholder his entire holdings if such holding is up to hundred shares of the face value of rupees ten each or ten shares of the face value of rupees hundred each.

6. Competitive bid: No person shall make a competitive bid for acquisition of shares of the financially weak company once the lead institution has evaluated the bid and accepted the bid of the acquirer who has made the public announcement of offer for acquisition of shares from the shareholders other than the promoters or the persons in charge of the management of the financially weak company.

7. Acquisition of shares by a State level public financial institution: Where a proposal for acquisition of shares in respect of a financially weak company is made by a State level public financial institution, the provisions of these regulations in so far as they relate to scheme of rehabilitation prepared by a public financial institution, shall apply except that in such a case the Industrial Development Bank of India, a corporation established under the Industrial Development Bank of India Act, 1964 (10 of 1964), shall be the agency for ensuring compliance with these regulations for acquisition of shares in the financially weak company.

CHAPTER V
INVESTIGATION AND ACTION BY THE BOARD

1. Board's right to investigate: The Board may appoint one or more persons as investigating officer to undertake investigation for any of the following purposes, namely:—

(*a*) to investigate into the complaints received from the investors, the intermediaries or any other person on any matter having a bearing on the allegations of substantial acquisition of shares and takeovers ;

(*b*) to investigate suo motu upon its own knowledge or information, in the interest of the securities market or investors' interest, for any breach of the regulations ;

(*c*) to ascertain whether the provisions of the Act and the regulations are being complied with for any breach of the regulations.

2. Notice before investigation: (1) Before ordering an investigation under regulation 38, the Board shall give not less than 10 days notice to the acquirer, the seller, the target company, the merchant banker, as the case may be.

(2) Notwithstanding anything contained in sub-regulation (1), where the Board is satisfied that in the interest of the investors no such notice should be given, it may, by an order in writing direct that such investigation be taken up without such notice.

(3) During the course of an investigation, the acquirer, the seller, the target company, the merchant banker, against whom the investigation is being carried out shall be bound to discharge his obligation as provided in regulation 40.

3. Obligations on investigation by the Board: (1) It shall be the duty of the acquirer, the seller, the target company, the merchant banker whose affairs are being investigated and of every director, officer and employee thereof, to produce to the investigating officer such books, securities, accounts, records and other documents in its custody or control and furnish him with such statements and information relating to his activities as the investigating officer may require, within such reasonable period as the investigating officer may specify.

(2) The acquirer, the seller, the target company, the merchant banker and the persons being investigated shall allow the investigating officer to have reasonable access to the premises occupied by him or by any other person on his behalf and also extend reasonable facility for examining any books, records, documents and computer data in the possession of the acquirer, the seller, the target company, the merchant banker or such other person and also provide copies of documents or other materials which, in the opinion of the investigating officer are relevant for the purposes of the investigation.

(3) The investigating officer, in the course of investigation, shall be entitled to examine or to record the statements of any director, officer or employee of the acquirer, the seller, the target company, the merchant banker.

(4) It shall be the duty of every director, officer or employee of the acquirer, the seller, the target company, the merchant banker to give to the investigating officer all assistance in connection with investigation, which the investigating officer may reasonably require.

4. Submission of report to the Board: The investigating officer shall, as soon as possible, on completion of the investigation, submit a report to the Board.

5. Communication of findings: (1) The Board shall, after consideration of the investigation report referred to in regulation 41, communicate the findings of the investigating officer to the acquirer, the seller, the target company, the merchant banker, as the case may be, and give him an opportunity of being heard.

(2) On receipt of the reply, if any, from the acquirer, the seller, the target company, the merchant banker, as the case may be, the Board may call upon him to take such measures as the Board may deem fit in the interest of the securities market and for due compliance with the provisions of the Act and the regulations.

6. Appointment of auditor: Notwithstanding anything contained in this regulation, the Board may appoint a qualified auditor to investigate into the books of account or the affairs of the person concerned.

7. Directions by the Board: Without prejudice to its right to initiate action under Chapter VIA and section 24 of the Act, the Board may, in the interest of securities market or for protection of interest of investors, issue such directions as it deems fit.

8. Manner of Service of summons and notices issued by the board: A summons or notice issued by the Board under these regulations may be served in the manner provided in regulation 22 of the Securities and Exchange Board of India (Procedure for Holding Enquiry by Enquiry Officer and Imposing Penalty) Regulations, 2002.

9. Penalties for non-compliance: (1) Any person violating any provisions of the regulations shall be liable for action in terms of the regulations and the Act.

(2) If the acquirer or any person acting in concert with him, fails to carry out the obligations under the regulations, the entire or a part of the sum in the escrow account shall be liable to be forfeited and the acquirer or such a person shall also be liable for action in terms of the regulations and the Act.

(3) The board of directors of the target company failing to carry out the obligations under the regulations shall be liable for action in terms of the regulations and the Act.

10. Appeal to the Central Government: Any person aggrieved by an order of the Board made, on and after the commencement of the Securities Laws (Second Amendment) Act, 1999, (i.e., after 16th December, 1999), under these regulations may prefer an appeal to a Securities Appellate Tribunal having jurisdiction in the matter.

11. Repeal and saving : (1) The Securities and Exchange Board of India (Substantial Acquisition of Shares and Takeovers) Regulations, 1994, are hereby repealed.

JUSTICE P. N. BHAGWATI REPORT ON SUBSTANTIAL ACQUISITIONS OF SHARES AND TAKEOVERS

The SEBI (Substantial Acquisition of Shares and Takeovers) Regulations, 1997 dealt primarily with issues such as consolidation of holdings, conditional offers, change in control, formation of Takeover Panel, competitive offers, and not the least important increased, investor protection. Numerous new provisions were included in the Regulations with a view to dealing with these issues. During the course of administration of the Regulations, it was observed by SEBI that by and large these provisions served well in fulfilling the object and purpose of harmonising interests of economic growth with those of investor protection. The Regulations in fact spurred takeover activity as evidenced by the large number of public offers, cases of automatic exemption and references to the Takeover Panel under the provisions of the Regulations during the years following upon the coming into force of the Regulations. However, it was found as a result of the experience of the working of the Regulations that some provisions were open to diverse interpretations while some others were not sufficiently precise and could be used to achieve unintended results. Moreover, new challenges in the light of on-going economic reforms, which arose consequent on liberalisation, needed to be satisfactorily met. The challenges were accentuated in view of the irreversible integration of the Indian economy in general and the capital market in particular with the world markets. It was, therefore, realised that in order to make the Regulations efficient and effective for achieving the object and purpose for which they were made as also to meet the challenges resulting from economic reforms and liberalisation, it was necessary to take a fresh look at the Regulations and make a dispassionate, well informed review of the provisions of the Regulations in the light of the experience gained as a result of working the Regulations, so as to better subserve investor interest, consistent with fostering economic growth. The need for review of the Regulations arose as early as June 1998.

SEBI, with a view to addressing these concerns, reconstituted the same Committee, which was instrumental in drafting the 1997 Regulations. The terms of reference of the Committee are:-

1. To review the working of the Regulations.
2. To consider suitable suggestions for further refinement of the Regulations in the light of experience gained so far.

The Committee comprised of the following members:-

Justice P.N. Bhagwati – Chairman

Chambers of Commerce & Industry were represented by:-

Shri Bipin Jhaveri, representing Associated Chambers of Commerce and Industry (Assocham).

Shri Adi B. Godrej (upto December 2000) and Shri N. A. Soonawala (from December 2000) representing Confederation of Indian Industry (CII)

Shri R.S. Lodha, representing Federation of Indian Chambers of Commerce and Industry (FICCI)

Institute of Chartered Accountants of India was represented by its President,

Shri Rahul Rai (upto February 1999),

Shri S P Chhajed (from March 1999 to February 2000),

Shri G Sitharaman (from March 2000 to February 2001),

Shri N D Gupta (from March 2001 to February 2002) and

Shri Ashok Chandak (from March 2002).

Stock Exchanges were represented by the Executive Director of The Stock Exchange, Mumbai,

Late Shri M G Damani (upto January 2000),

Shri A Rathi (from January 2000 to March 2001) and

Shri A.N. Joshi (from April 2001).

Legal Experts were represented by:- Shri J.R. Gagrat of Gagrat & Co.

Shri R.A. Shah of Crawford Bayley & Co.

Shri Shardul S. Shroff of Amarchand & Mangaldas & Suresh A. Shroff & Co.

Investors Associations were represented by:

Prof. Manubhai Shah, representing Consumer Education and Research Centre

Prof. M.D. Limaye representing Lokmanya Seva Sangh (Shri Limaye however did not attend any of the meetings citing personal reasons). Merchant Bankers were represented by

Shri Nimesh Kampani, Chairman, JM Morgan Stanley Pvt. Ltd.

Shri Shitin Desai, Vice Chairman & Managing Director, DSP Merrill Lynch Ltd.

Shri Udayan Bose, Chairman, Lazard India Limited

Shri Vallabh Bhansali, Enam Financial Consultants Pvt. Ltd. (Special Invitee)

SEBI was represented by:

Shri O.P. Gahrotra, Ex Senior Executive Director (upto February 2001)

Shri Pratip Kar, Executive Director

Shri R.M. Joshi, Executive Director

Ms. D.N. Raval, Executive Director and Member Secretary

Takeover Panel

1. The Committee was informed that The Panel set up by SEBI in terms of Regulation 4(1) for examining applications for exemption and to give recommendations has been in operation since April 11, 1997. The Panel consists of eminent people drawn from various fields who meet regularly and have given valuable inputs to the

decision making process of SEBI on exemption cases. The Panel had as on 31.3.2002 considered and given recommendations in 120 cases and SEBI had in almost all cases accepted the recommendations of the Panel. The Panel has thus helped in setting healthy precedence.

2. The Committee considered the various issues raised. The Committee noted that there are certain issues which are purely procedural and others which require consideration by the Committee. While opining that the existing procedure may continue, the Committee recommended certain changes. The decisions of the Committee in this regard as well as the rationale are as follows:

Constitution of the Panel

The Committee recommends that the constitution of the Panel may be left to SEBI. The Committee also recommends that the present practice of including a former member of the judiciary in the Panel be continued. As regards the terms of appointment, the Committee recommends that the term of each member shall be for 3 years and the member will be eligible for reappointment.

Scope of the Panel

The Committee recommends that the scope of the Panel may be enhanced by deleting the word "*such*" appearing in Regulation 3(1)(l). However, the Committee also recommends that the scope of the Panel cannot be extended to relax the conditions which are stipulated as part of regulatory provisions. The Committee, therefore, recommends that the Regulations may be amended to make a provision for enabling SEBI to make reference to the Panel for interpretation of the Regulations.

Hearing by the Panel

The Committee recommends that the Panel may not be required to grant hearing to the applicant but may seek further information where considered necessary.

Remitting back the applications to the Panel

The Committee recommends that the Panel should have the benefit of all correspondence in respect of the matter before them for consideration.

Certification of facts in the application

The Committee recommends that the facts given in the application should be certified through an affidavit and where a company makes the application, the authority of the person making the application should be backed by a board resolution or a valid authorization by the board.

Communication of Panel's recommendations to the applicant

The Committee recommends that the reasons for rejection of application in case the Panel were to recommend rejection of application should be advised to the applicant in advance of the hearing before the SEBI.

Rejection of applications by SEBI

The Committee recommends that where the applications are found to be technically deficient, SEBI may not reject but would give the applicant an opportunity to remove the defects within the specified time period and resubmit.

2. Publishing Of SEBI's Order: The Committee recommends that the SEBI's order should be posted on SEBI's website.

3. Consolidation of holdings

(i) **Creeping acquisition in professionally managed companies :** Committee was of the considered opinion that any differentiation among a group of shareholders militated against the principle of "equality of treatment and opportunity to all shareholders", which is the corner stone of the Takeover Regulations. In view of the above, the Committee was not in favor of any special treatment to professionally managed companies. The Committee recommends that the requirement of approval of the Board of the Target company / Government for any acquisition by foreign companies (excluding NRI OCBs) may be included in the Regulations.

(ii) **Creeping acquisition by acquirers holding 15% and above but less than 75%:** The Committee recommends that the creeping acquisition limit of 10% should be retained upto March 2004.

(iii) **The Committee recommends that the creeping acquisition limit may** be reckoned with respect to financial year ending March 31.

(*iv*) **Creeping acquisition by acquirers holding 75% and above:** The Committee recommends that any acquisition by acquirers holding 75% and above should be in a transparent manner through open offers for minimum 20% and accordingly proviso to Regulation 21(1) may be deleted.

4. Control : The decisions of the Committee with reference to issues regarding "control" and the rationale therefore is as follows:

(*i*) **Acquisition of control :** The Committee recommends that change in control can be brought about only pursuant to a special resolution passed by the shareholders in a General Meeting and postal ballot should be allowed in respect of such meetings.

(*ii*) The Committee recommends that the modified explanation to the word "control" which should appear in Regulation 2 shall read as under:

(*a*) Where there are two or more persons in control over the target company, the cessor of any one such person from such control shall not be deemed to be a change in control of management nor shall any change in the nature and quantum of control amongst them constitute change in control of management. Provided that a transfer from joint to sole control shall not constitute change in control subject to such transfers being effected in accordance with Regulation 3 (1)(e) relating to interse transfer.

(*b*) Where any person or persons are given joint control, such control shall not be deemed to be a change in control - a) if the control given is equal to or less than the control exercised by person(s) presently having control over the company, and b) such change in control is effected in accordance with Regulation 3.

(*iv*) **Acquisition of control through preferential allotment:** The Committee recommends that the present exemption for preferential allotment be continued subject to the condition that any resolution for preferential issue should provide for postal ballot to enable greater shareholder participation.

(*v*) **Inter-se transfers:** The Committee recommends that

(*a*) As regards interse transfer amongst the relatives, the existing provisions may continue.

(*b*) Regarding group, interse transfer amongst constituents of the group as disclosed to the stock exchange atleast a month before the date of proposed acquisition and falling within the definition of the word "group" as defined in the MRTP Act may be exempt.

(*c*) While the minimum 3 year holding period may be retained for transfers amongst 2 different groups of promoters, the 5% holding as a condition for such transfers may be deleted.

(*d*) interse transfer amongst different promoters or groups of promoters made at a price not exceeding 25% price as determined in terms of Regulation 20(2) or Regulation 20(3) alone would merit automatic exemption. Other cases may be referred to the panel.

5. Minimum offer size: The Committee recommends that no change in the minimum offer size is required to be made at this juncture.

6. 100% exit to small shareholders: The Committee recommends that it would not be equitable to have a 100% exit option to one class of shareholders alone.

7. Institutional funding for takeovers: In the context of lack of institutional funding for takeovers, the Committee recommends that banks /financial institutions should be encouraged to consider financing takeovers. The Committee desires that SEBI may consider taking up the matter with the Reserve Bank of India for facilitating such funding.

8. Offer Price: The Committee's views and recommendations on the various issues are:

(*i*) **Minimum offer price v/s offer price :** The Committee recommends that the word "minimum" appearing in the title and body of Regulation 20 be deleted. The Regulations should be amended so that

(*a*) obligations under the Regulations with regard to payment of consideration are applicable to the total consideration offered and

(*b*) the offer price shall not be lower than the price determined in accordance with Regulation 20.

(*ii*) **Parameters for determining offer price:** The Committee recommends that

(*a*) the average market price in terms of Regulation 20(2)(d) may be calculated on the basis of 26 weeks or 2 weeks average, whichever is higher, preceding the date of public announcement.

(b) price paid by the acquirer for any acquisitions during 26 weeks period may be considered.

(c) Any payment in respect of non-compete agreement in excess of 25% of consideration paid to persons other than the target company shall be deemed to form part of the consideration paid for acquisition of shares and should be factored in for the purpose of reckoning offer price.

(d) The offer price for partly paid shares may be calculated as per difference between the offer price less the amount unpaid/ calls in arrears together with interest, if any, payable on the amount called up remaining unpaid.

(iii) **Mode of payment:** The Committee recommends that

(a) The offer price may be paid by issue of securities.

(b) Change in mode of payment may be permitted only in case of upward revision in offer price/ size.

(c) Following an upward revision, where the mode of payment is changed to cash cum security, composition could be allowed to be changed as long as the cash component is not reduced by subsequent changes.

(d) Where mode of payment is changed subsequently, if, for whatever reasons, the acquirer is unable to fulfill the conditionalities flowing out of such change in mode, the acquirer shall be required to pay the entire amount of consideration in cash.

(e) Where the mode of payment involves issuance of securities, the approval of the shareholders should be obtained within 21 days from the date of closure of the offer, so that the merchant banker can ensure that the special account is funded in cash in case the shareholders approval has been refused.

9. Infrequently traded shares: The Committee recommends that

(a) The shares of the target company may be deemed to be infrequently traded if on the stock exchange, the annualized trading turnover in that share during the preceding 6 calendar months prior to the month in which the Public Announcement is made is less than 5% (the number of shares) of the shares listed on the stock exchange.

(b) As regards SEBI seeking independent valuation wherever considered necessary, while the Committee had no objection in SEBI doing so in respect of infrequently traded shares, the opinion of the Committee was divided in respect of the shares which were to be classified as frequently traded. Majority of the members of the Committee had objection to SEBI seeking independent valuation for shares classified as frequently traded.

10. Conditional offers: In view of the above, the Committee recommends that –

(a) An offer should always be for 20% or above; but the offer may be subject to an acceptance level of less than 20%.

(b) An offer can be conditional upon the success of restructuring by parent or holding company.

(c) When the offer is pursuant to a MoU, the acquirer may be allowed to make an offer conditional as to level of acceptances, only if the acquirer binds himself to rescind the MoU in case the desired level of acceptances is not received.

(d) There is no need to distinguish between obligated and nonobligated offers.

11. Obligations of target company: The Committee recommends that the public/rights issue for which the offer document has been filed with the Registrar of Companies/ the Stock Exchange(s) should be allowed to be proceeded ahead with. The Regulation 23(1)(b) may be amended to include not only issue but also allotment.

12. Competitive bids: The various issues which have been raised for consideration are: the minimum size of a competitive bid vis a vis the original bid, whether the competing offer could open subject to various approvals and should the competitive bidder be allowed to withdraw the offer after the first bidder had withdrawn or revised the offer following the competitive bid.

(i) **Size of competitive bid:** The Committee recommends that the competitive bid shall be for such number of shares which, when taken together with shares held by competitive bidder along with persons acting in concert with him, shall be at least equal to the post offer target of the original bidder. This stipulation may be complied with at least at the time of making a first competitive bid.

(*ii*) **Approvals for competing offers:** The Committee recommends that except for shareholders approval, (which in any case has to be obtained within 21 days from the date of the closure of the offer) the open offer could be made which is subject to statutory approvals. There is no need for the acquirer to defer the open offer till the statutory approvals are obtained. The Committee further recommends that in case the acquirer fails to obtain the shareholders approval within 21 days from the date of closure of offer, the escrow amount may be forfeited.

(*ii*) **Withdrawal of offer following competitive bid:** The Committee recommends that the provision relating to withdrawal of offer following a competitive bid contained in Regulation 27(1)(a) be deleted.

13. Payment of consideration through exchange of shares: Considering the above, and keeping in view the shareholders interest the Committee recommends that

(*a*) The acquirer may be permitted to offer shares of a third listed company, subject to the condition that the shares of that company are included in the list of A Group / specified shares of the Stock Exchange, Mumbai or shares grouped under S & P CNX Nifty of the National Stock Exchange.

(*b*) Shareholders approval should be taken within 21 days from the date of closure of the offer. If, for whatever reasons, the shareholders approval cannot be obtained, the acquirer shall pay the entire consideration in cash.

(*c*) If the process involves fresh issue of capital by the Acquirer Company, such fresh issue should conform to the Preferential Issue Guidelines of SEBI.

(*d*) Preference shares shall not be allowed to be issued.

14. Open offer process: The Committee recommends that

(*a*) Working days mean working days of SEBI.

(*b*) there is no need for the copy of public announcement to be submitted to anyone at all. It would suffice if the public announcement is given simultaneously in newspapers/ stock exchanges/ target company and SEBI.

(*c*) SEBI should have the power to call for submission of revised letter of offer etc. but the Regulations should clearly specify the circumstances under which a resubmission would be called for.

(*d*) SEBI should convey its comments on the letter of offer within 7 days of the date of receipt of additional information / resubmission.

(*e*) SEBI should also have the power to reschedule date of opening/ closure, in cases where the offer becomes subjudice or involves some investigation by SEBI etc. or as a consequence of any revised resubmission.

15. Disclosure requirements: The Committee recommends that

(*a*) Disclosures should be made at every stage when the acquirer crosses the limit of 5%, 10% and 14%;

(*b*) For acquirers holding 15% and above, purchases or sales at every 2% level should be disclosed.

(*c*) The reporting of acquisitions/ sales should be made to the stock exchanges and the target company within 2 days.

(*d*) The acquirers are obligated to ensure that the necessary disclosures reach the company and the stock exchanges.

(*e*) The exchange shall immediately flash the information received on the trading screen/ notice board and also post such information on its website. Such information should be retained on the website for a period of atleast one year.

(*f*) The percentage level referred to should be computed on a gross purchase basis at any point of time to decide whether the Regulations are attracted.

(*g*) Any non-compliance of the requirement should be viewed seriously and appropriate action should be initiated.

16. Applicability of the Regulations

(*i*) **Acquisition by pledgees other than banks and financial institutions:** The Committee recommends that

(*a*) In case of acquisition through pledge, Takeover Panel may decide if exemption should be granted based on the facts of each case.

(*b*) At the time of creation of pledge, disclosures should be made by the pledgees to the company and the stock exchanges so as to keep the public adequately informed.

(ii) **Acquisitions pursuant to a scheme of arrangement:** The Committee recommends that the words 'of arrangement' appearing at Regulation 3(1)(j)(ii) may be deleted.

(iii) **Acquisition of shares by Government Companies:** The Committee was informed that based on the proposals received from the Ministry of Disinvestment, and approved by SEBI, suitable amendments in the Regulations have already been made.

(iv) (a) **Transfers by acquirers after open offer:** Interse transfer of shares amongst acquirers who have made the open offer. The Committee recommends that automatic exemption may be considered in respect of interse transfer amongst the acquirer and persons acting in concert with him only where the proposed acquisition takes place after 3 years from the date of closure of open offer. In other cases, reference may be made to the Panel.

(b) **Transfer of shares from SFCs to acquirers after open offer:** The Committee recommends that the automatic exemption currently available under Regulation 3(1)(i) for transfer of shares from state level financial institutions; including their subsidiaries, to co promoters of the company pursuant to an agreement between such financial institution and such co-promoter(s) should be extended to include successors / assignees of the co promoters of the company.

(v) **Applicability of the Regulations to Foreign Institutional Investors:** The Committee recommends no change in the existing provisions.

(vi) **Miscellaneous exemptions:** The Committee was informed that under the current Regulations the acquisition of shares by

(a) persons in exchange of shares tendered under an open offer

(b) in excess of creeping acquisition limit pursuant to offer of safety net for acquisition of shares by promoters/ merchant bankers

(c) international development organisations such as Asian Development Bank (ADB), Commonwealth Development Corporation (CDC), International Financial Corporation (IFC) and other international organizations are not exempt under the automatic route from the requirement of making an open offer.

The Committee felt that the above referred acquisition arising as a result of receipt of consideration for open offers in terms of the Regulations are passive acquisitions and hence require to be exempted from the applicability of the Regulations. It was also felt that safety net i.e. acquisition by a promoter or through a merchant banker is for the benefit of investors and therefore anyone providing safety net and thereby crossing the threshold limit, should not be burdened with open offer obligations. This may also encourage promoters /merchant bankers to offer safety net to investors. Regarding the acquisitions by International financial organisations like IFC, ADB etc., it was felt that these organisations have an important role to play and are akin to Indian financial institutions. Since such institutions may not have an interest in gaining control, their acquisitions may be exempt from the Regulations.

While on the subject of exemption, Shri Manubhai Shah, on behalf of CERC, strongly stated that granting of exemption to the acquirers from making public offers is overwhelmingly anti small investor and it defeats the very purpose of the Regulations. He, therefore, opined that as far as possible, there should be no room for exemption or any contingency or any possible permutation or combination where exemption should be allowed whereby acquirers are not required to make public offer to the shareholders. He stated that the obligation of the acquirers to make public offer should be the rule and not the exception.

The Committee recommends that the scope of Regulation 3 i.e. the exemption provisions should be expanded to cover acquisitions

(a) by a person in pursuance to an open offer for exchange of shares.

(b) in excess of creeping acquisition limit pursuant to offer of safety net made by promoters/ merchant bankers.

(c) by international development organisations such as IBRD, ADB, CDC, IFC.

It was also felt that safety net i.e. acquisition by a promoter or through a merchant banker is for the benefit of investors and therefore anyone providing safety net and thereby crossing the threshold limit, should not be burdened with open offer obligations. This may also encourage promoters /merchant bankers to offer safety net to investors. Regarding the acquisitions by International financial organisations like IFC, ADB etc., it was felt that these organisations have an important role to play and are akin to Indian financial institutions. Since such institutions may not have an interest in gaining control, their acquisitions may be exempt from the Regulations. While on the subject of exemption, Shri Manubhai Shah, on behalf of CERC, strongly stated that granting of exemption to the acquirers from making public offers is overwhelmingly anti small investor and it defeats the very purpose of the Regulations. He, therefore, opined that as far as possible, there should be no room for exemption or any contingency or any possible permutation or combination where exemption should be allowed whereby acquirers are not required to make public offer to the shareholders. He stated that the obligation of the acquirers to make public offer should be the rule and not the exception.

The Committee recommends that the scope of Regulation 3 i.e. the exemption provisions should be expanded to cover acquisitions

(*a*) by a person in pursuance to an open offer for exchange of shares.

(*b*) in excess of creeping acquisition limit pursuant to offer of safety net made by promoters/ merchant bankers.

(*c*) by international development organisations such as IBRD, ADB, CDC, IFC.

17. Reporting to SEBI: Under the current Regulations, certain acquisitions which are exempted under the Regulations are to be reported to SEBI within 21 days of the acquisition. The Committee deliberated on whether this requirement should continue. The Committee recommends that there is no need to dispense with the present requirement of reporting.

18. Date of proposed acquisition: The Committee deliberated on what should be the reference date in case of securities which are convertible. The Committee recommends that the date of conversion of the securities should be the reference date for determining the applicability of the Regulations.

19. Definitions: (*i*) The Committee after discussions and experience shared by SEBI, recommends that the following may be clarified:

(*a*) The term acquirer also includes 'persons acting in concert'.

(*b*) The acquirers /persons acting in concert are all jointly and severally responsible for fulfillment of obligations under the Regulations.

(*c*) The term 'voting rights' which is not defined in the Regulations would carry the meaning as per definition in the Companies Act, 1956.

(*ii*) Offer period: In the light of the above, the Committee recommends that, 'Offer period' may be reckoned to be from the date of the MOU, if any, to the date of completion of all formalities.

(*iii*) Promoter: The Committee recommends that the definition of 'promoter' may be redrafted as under :

"Promoter" means -

(*i*) the person or persons who are (in control of the company) directly or indirectly whether as a shareholder, director or otherwise, over the company; or

(*ii*) person or persons named in any offer document as promoters.

(*iii*) where the promoter is an individual –

(*a*) a relative of the promoter within the meaning of section 6 of the Companies Act, 1956 (1 of 1956);

(*b*) any firm or company, directly or indirectly, controlled by the Promoter or a relative of the Promoter or a firm or Hindu undivided family in which the Promoter or his relative is a partner or co-parcener or a combination thereof; Provided that in case of partnership firm the share of the promoter or relative of the promoter is not less than 50%.

(*iv*) where the promoter is a corporate body:-

(*i*) subsidiary or holding company of that body; or

(*ii*) any firm or company, directly or indirectly, controlled by the Promoter of that body corporate or his relative or a firm or Hindu undivided family in which the Promoter or his relative is a partner or co-parcener or a combination thereof."

Provided that in case of a firm, the share of a promoter or relative of a promoter is not less than 50%.

(*iv*) Public shareholding: The Committee recommends that in a particular situation, if the definition is not found to hold good, SEBI may intervene and issue suitable directions.

(*v*) Shares: The Committee recommends that for the purpose of these Regulations, the term 'shares' would not include preference shares.

***(vi)* Date of Acquisition:** The Committee noted that in a demat environment, the issue may not have much relevance. The Committee also noted that the Regulations are also applicable in case of intention to acquire shares which would imply that registration of shares is not a prerequisite for determining acquisition of shares.

20. Asset Stripping: The Committee recommends that:

(*a*) The offer document should include an undertaking from the acquirer not to strip substantial assets except with the prior approval of the shareholders of the target company.

(*b*) Any non compliance thereto should be treated as a mis-statement in the offer document inviting appropriate action by SEBI.

(*c*) As a measure of investor protection, SEBI may consider extending the same principle to the listed companies in general by making such an undertaking as a part of listing agreement.

21. Indirect acquisition of a company through chain principle. The Committee recommends that

(*a*) The offer for a company which gets acquired as a result of acquisition of a target company can be subsequent to the successful completion of the takeover of the target by the acquirer. It should be made within 3 months of consummation of restructuring or arrangement by parent or holding company.

(*b*) The price shall be determined as highest of the two prices determined as per the provisions of the Regulations, with reference to the date of the public announcement for the target company and the date of public announcement for the company which is consequently acquired.

22. Acquisition of Indian listed company by virtue of acquisition of an Overseas Company: The Committee recommends that it may be clarified that the obligation to make an open offer would rest on the entity one level above the Indian listed company.

23. Permitting change in management pending completion of offer Formalities: The Committee recommends that

(*a*) acquirers may be allowed to enter the management after the period of competitive bidding is over.

(*a*) such changes may be allowed only when 100% of consideration payable, assuming full acceptances, is deposited in escrow in cash where the consideration payable is in cash; or in the form of securities where the consideration payable is by way of issue, exchange and/or transfer of securities.

24. Withdrawal of acceptances tendered: The Committee recommends that the investors may be allowed to withdraw the form of acceptance tendered upto 3 working days prior to the date of closure of offer.

The Committee recommends that the investors may be allowed to withdraw the form of acceptance tendered upto 3 working days prior to the date of closure of offer. The Committee recommends that acquisitions during offer period, irrespective of the price at which it was acquired must be disclosed to the stock exchanges. The Committee also recommends that the information received by the stock exchanges shall be immediately posted on the trading screen for information of the public. The Committee recommends that the acquirers may not be permitted to acquire shares at a price higher than offer price for a period of six months. This restriction however will not apply to market purchases.

25 Acquisition during and subsequent to public offer: The Committee recommends that acquisitions during offer period, irrespective of the price at which it was acquired must be disclosed to the stock exchanges. The Committee also recommends that the information received by the stock exchanges shall be immediately posted on the trading screen for information of the public.

The Committee recommends that the acquirers may not be permitted to acquire shares at a price higher than offer price for a period of six months. This restriction however will not apply to market purchases.

26. Delisting pursuant to an offer under the Regulations: The Committee recommends that a suitable clarification to this effect may be incorporated in the Regulations.

27. Compression of time taken for open offers: The Committee recommends that suitable amendments may be made in the Regulations wherever possible.

28. Penalties: The Committee, in the light of above discussions, recommends as follows:

(*i*) A new Regulation 12A may be inserted clearly spelling out the following:

(A) Any acquisition of shares in breach of Regulation 10, 11 or 12 of the Takeover Regulations shall be null and void.

(B) So also, where exemption under Regulation 3 is not available for any reasons whatsoever and an acquisition is made in breach of Regulations 10,11 or 12, such acquisition shall be null and void.

(*ii*) Where it is not possible to restore status quo ante for any reason, SEBI should direct appointment of a merchant banker for the purpose of causing disinvestment of shares acquired in breach of Regulations either through public auction or market mechanism, in its entirety or in small lots, or through offer for sale.

(*iii*) Any profit made in the process should be put in the Investor Protection Fund.

(*iv*) Where an acquisition of shares pursuant to an allotment is null and void due to breach of Regulations 3, 10, 11 or 12, SEBI shall report the same to the target company, and the stock exchanges. The target company shall cancel the shares which are null and void and shall report to SEBI and stock exchanges about the cancellation of such shares. The depository shall freeze further transfer of such shares.

(*v*) Where SEBI is satisfied that as a result of acquisition of any shares, violation of Regulations 10, 11 or 12 is likely to take place, SEBI may direct the target company or the depository not to give effect to transfer of any such shares and not to permit the acquirer or any nominee or any proxy of the acquirer, to exercise any voting or other rights attaching to such shares.

(*vi*) Violators and their associates may be debarred from accessing or dealing in the capital market for such period as may be determined by the SEBI.

(*vii*) For non compliance with the disclosure requirement in Regulation 6,7 & 8, the SEBI may have the power to direct disinvestment of such shares as are in excess of the trigger point for reporting requirement, as well as to impose monetary penalty.

(*viii*) In exceptional cases, such other remedies as considered appropriate may be granted by SEBI.

(*ix*) This is without prejudice to any other penalty as may be levied by SEBI.

29. Power to remove difficulties: The Committee, therefore, recommends that the Regulations be amended so that if any difficulty arises from certain offers being subject to more than one jurisdiction, SEBI is empowered to issue directions for the purpose of resolving the conflict of laws, if any.

REPORT OF THE INTERNAL GROUP ON SEBI (SUBSTANTIAL ACQUISITION OF SHARES AND TAKEOVERS) REGULATIONS, 1997

Background

An internal group was formed to closely look into the provisions of the Regulations and suggest measures which may take care of the interest of the investors. The Group deliberated and finalized their recommendations. The recommendations of the Group in this regard are placed at Annexure. **The views expressed by the Group are mainly of the group and not necessarily of SEBI.**

Recommendations of the Group

1. Offer Price : However, such a restriction of lower threshold limit may hamper the process of strategic investments, such as, acquisition through preferential allotment pursuant to a special resolution passed u/s 81(1A) of the Companies Act, 1956. Thus, the group felt that such an acquisition may be exempted from the obligation of the open offer subject to acquirer making upfront disclosure in the notice of the shareholders to the effect that in the event of the acquirer acquiring more than 5% but less than 15%, the acquirer would not be obligated to make an open offer.

Further, an acquirer should not be permitted to cross the 5% limit through an acquisition made through off market. In other words, where an acquirer who holds, say 1% in a target company, could acquire additional shares upto a maximum of 4% through off market transactions. If an acquirer already holds 5% or more, he could acquire further shares only through stock market mechanism (except through preferential allotment as referred to above), failing which the Takeover Code would be triggered.

The Group, therefore, recommends as under :

a. The threshold limit for acquisition through off market transactions shall be limited to 5% of shares or voting rights and any acquisition beyond this through off market transactions would trigger the open offer obligation.

b. An acquirer who holds more than 5% but less than 15% shares or voting rights shall acquire additional shares or voting rights, only through stock market mechanism and otherwise, the acquisition would trigger the open offer obligation.

c. However, acquisition through preferential allotment pursuant to a special resolution passed u/s 81(1A) of the Companies Act, 1956 would be exempted. This would be subject to the condition that the shareholders pass a separate special resolution to the effect that the prospective acquirer would not be required to make an open offer in terms of the provisions of the Regulations, pursuant to the said acquisition. In the event of such a resolution being defeated, the acquirer shall be required to comply with the open offer obligations under the Regulations, if he acquires the shares beyond the threshold limit of 5%. This would be in addition to other categories of exemption already provided under Regulation 3.

The existing provisions of Reg.10 shall be modified suitably.

2. Reduction in Time for completion of open offer : The group observed that at present open offer formalities ideally take 120 days to complete from the date of public announcement. It was felt that the same should be reduced as it would be in line with the time period prevailing in other countries. In this regard, considering the major structural changes and developments in the secondary market such as the introduction of dematerialisation of shares, speedy information dissemination etc, and following representations from the market players, the group recommends that the current time cycle of the offer may be reduced from 120 days to 90 days. It was felt that the proposed reduction of time cycle would facilitate quick realization of consideration by the shareholders regarding the shares tendered and accepted in the open offer and the acquirer would also be in a position to acquire the shares/control in the target company, as per the objective of the offer.

3. Restriction of Sale during the offer period: In view of the above, the group recommends that the Regulations may be amended by incorporating a specific provision under "General obligations of the Acquirer" to put a restriction on the sale of shares by the acquirer during the offer period.

4. Independent advice by the board of Target Company: The Group, therefore, recommends that the Regulations may be amended suitably by incorporating a clause thereby obligating the board of the target company to comment on the general affairs of the target company and future plans if any by way of a notice/comments letter to the shareholders of the target company.

The group also recommends that the Target company may be obligated to provide such information as may be sought by the acquirer for the purpose of making adequate disclosures in the letter of offer as specified in the standard format by the Board.

5. Time frame for completion of acquisition through the MOU which triggers the code: However, as regards the time limit for completion of MOUs, it was decided that since it is a contractual obligation of acquirer and seller, SEBI may not intervene in the issue. It is for the concerned parties to decide when they wish to exercise their right regarding acquisition of shares.

6. Participation of Merchant Banker in the Open Offer and disclosure of the same to all the shareholders: The group observed that the regulations are not explicit on the said issue and recommends that the regulations may be suitably amended under the heading obligations of Merchant Banker thereby providing for the following:

- Merchant Banker should not be allowed to deal in the scrip of Target Company during the period commencing from date of appointment of MB as manager to the issue till the 15 days from the closure of the offer.
- Shareholding of Merchant Banker in the target Company, if any, shall be disclosed in the public announcement as well as in the letter of offer.

Achuthan Committee Report on Takeovers

The existence of an efficient and smooth-functioning market for takeovers plays an important role in the economic development of a country. It is a widely recognized fact that one of the key elements of a robust corporate governance regime in any country is the existence of an efficient and well-administered set of Takeover Regulations. Regulations on takeovers seek to ensure that the takeover markets operate in a fair, equitable and transparent manner.

In keeping with the foregoing, India also has seen a steady evolution of a set of capital market regulations in respect of substantial acquisition of shares and takeovers. While the initial threads of regulation were incorporated in the late 1980s through Listing Agreement, provisions for a legal framework was provided in 1992 by a statute, viz. the SEBI Act, 1992. The SEBI Act, 1992 expressly mandated SEBI to regulate substantial acquisition of shares and takeovers by suitable measures. Accordingly, SEBI provided a legal framework by making the Takeover Regulations of 1994, which came into force on November 4, 1994.

In November 1995, SEBI appointed a committee to review the Takeover Regulations of 1994 under the chairmanship of Justice P.N. Bhagwati (the Bhagwati Committee). The said committee submitted its report in January 1997. Taking into consideration its recommendations, the Takeover Regulations of 1997 were notified by SEBI on February 20, 1997, repealing the Takeover Regulations of 1994. These regulations were periodically amended in response to events and developments in the marketplace, regulatory and judicial rulings as well as evolving global practices as considered appropriate. In 2001, a review of the Takeover Regulations of 1997 was carried out by a reconstituted committee chaired by Justice P.N. Bhagwati. The reconstituted Bhagwati committee submitted its report in May 2002. Based on the same, further amendments were made to the Takeover Regulations of 1997. So far, the Takeover Regulations of 1997 have been amended 23 times.

Composition of the Committee: The composition of the Committee is as under:

(*a*) **Mr. C. Achuthan**, Former Presiding Officer, Securities Appellate Tribunal – **Chairman**.

(*b*) **Mr. Kumar Desai**, Advocate, High Court.

(*c*) **Mr. Somasekhar Sundaresan**, Advocate; Partner, J. Sagar Associates.

(*d*) **Mr. Y. M. Deosthalee**, Group Chief Financial Officer, Larsen and Toubro Ltd.

(*e*) **Mr. Koushik Chatterjee**, Group Chief Financial Officer, Tata Steel Ltd.

(*f*) **Mr. Raj Balakrishnan**, Managing Director - M&A, DSP Merrill Lynch Ltd.

(*g*) **Mr. Sourav Mallik**, Executive Director - M&A, Kotak Mahindra Capital Company Ltd.

(*h*) **Mr. A. K. Narayan,** President, Tamil Nadu Investors' Association.

(*i*) **Prof N. Venkiteswaran,** Professor, Indian Institute of Management, Ahmedabad.

(*j*) **Ms. Usha Narayanan**, Executive Director, Corporation Finance Department, SEBI.

(*k*) **Mr. J. Ranganayakulu**, Executive Director, Legal Department, SEBI, and

(*l*) **Ms. Neelam Bhardwaj**, General Manager, Division of Corporate Restructuring, **SEBI** – Member Secretary.

Approach of the Committee: Substantial acquisition of shares in, or takeover of, a listed company impacts a host of stakeholders, such as, the acquirer, the target company, the management and the public shareholders. It is critical that the legal framework regulating such substantial acquisition of shares and takeovers is precise, unambiguous and predictable, and balances multiple, and at times, conflicting interests of such stakeholders. For instance, the public shareholder of the target company would be keen to get the highest possible price for his shares, while the acquirer would want to shoulder the least possible financial and regulatory burden. The target company may wish to support, oppose or remain neutral to, a transaction, often depending on who the acquirer is. It then falls upon the regulator to balance the interests of various stakeholders and to provide for a fair, equitable and transparent regime that addresses the concerns of all stakeholders.

In drafting the Proposed Takeover Regulations, the Committee adopted an approach of balancing and calibrating such conflicting objectives. While the Committee believes that the Proposed Takeover Regulations, by and large, strike such a balance, the Regulations do recognize and accord primacy to the goal of protection of the interests of the public shareholders in takeover situations. The Committee also recognizes that no regulation would be able to provide for every situation that may arise in the domain of economic activity. However, if the regulatory intent, purpose and underlying philosophy are clearly understood and articulated, these can provide guidance even in ambiguous situations. The Committee believes that the stated objectives of the Takeover Regulations of 1997 continue to remain valid and relevant. As the Committee is recommending substantive changes to the Takeover Regulations of 1997, it decided to draft a new text of Takeover Regulations.

Fundamental Objectives of Proposed Takeover Regulations : The fundamental objectives of the Proposed Takeover Regulations are as follows:

(*i*) To provide a transparent legal framework for facilitating takeover activities;

(*ii*) To protect the interests of investors in securities and the securities market, taking into account that both the acquirer and the other shareholders or investors and need a fair, equitable and transparent framework to protect their interests;

(*iii*) To balance the various, and at times, conflicting objectives and interests of various stakeholders in the context of substantial acquisition of shares in, and takeovers of, listed companies.

(*iv*) To provide each shareholder an opportunity to exit his investment in the target company when a substantial acquisition of shares in, or takeover of a target company takes place, on terms that are not inferior to the terms on which substantial shareholders exit their investments;

(*v*) To provide acquirers with a transparent legal framework to acquire shares in or control of the target company and to make an open offer;

(*vi*) To ensure that the affairs of the target company are conducted in the ordinary course when a target company is subject matter of an open offer;

(*vii*) To ensure that fair and accurate disclosure of all material information is made by persons responsible for making them to various stakeholders to enable them to take informed decisions;

(*viii*) To regulate and provide for fair and effective competition among acquirers desirous of taking over the same target company; and

(*ix*) To ensure that only those acquirers who are capable of actually fulfilling their obligations under the Takeover Regulations make open offers.

Key Recommendations

1. Offer Size

Current Provisions: The Regulations currently require that on acquisitions resulting in triggering regulations 10, 11 and 12, the acquirer is mandatorily required to make an open offer for a minimum of 20% of the voting capital (reckoned as on the fifteenth day after closure of the offer).

Recommendation: The Committee recommends that every open offer pursuant to a substantial acquisition of shares in, or change of control over a target company under the Takeover Regulations ought to be for every share held by all the shareholders of the target company, as on the expected date of the close of the tendering period. Holders of equity-linked instruments eligible to be converted into equity shares prior to the aforementioned date may do so and tender their equity shares in the open offer.

2. Minimum Public Shareholding Requirements

Current Provisions: The Takeover Regulations currently provide that if the acquisition made pursuant to an open offer results in the public shareholding in the target company falling below the minimum level required as per the listing agreement, the acquirer shall take necessary steps to facilitate compliance with the relevant provisions thereof, within the time period specified therein.

Recommendation

(*i*) The Committee recommends that the target company should stand delisted, should the acquirer have stated its intention to delist the target company and the response to the open offer is such that the acquirer's shareholding crosses the delisting threshold.

(*ii*) The Committee recommends that in the event the shares of the target company stand delisted pursuant to the open offer, every shareholder who has not tendered an acceptance of the open offer shall be entitled to require the acquirer to acquire his shares at the offer price at any time within a period of twelve months from the fifteenth day from the date on which the shares are delisted from the stock exchanges. This exit window would also be available to the holders of all equity-linked instruments in the company. The company and the acquirer shall take necessary steps to facilitate the provision of an option to such holders to accelerate the conversion / vesting of such instruments during the period of this exit window.

(*iii*) The Committee also recommends that should the acquirer's shareholding reach a level between the maximum permissible non-public shareholding and the delisting threshold, such acquirer be given an option to proportionately reduce the acquisitions. The acquisitions that are proportionately reduced would be those under the open offer, the agreement (if any) and immediate past purchases (except acquisitions due to allotments by the target company). Such reduction would enable the acquirer not to breach the maximum permissible non-public shareholding.

3. Initial Threshold

Current Provisions: The Takeover Regulations currently provide that if an acquirer acquires or agrees to acquire shares or voting rights such that his voting rights exceed 15% of the voting capital of the target company, he is required to make an open offer.

Recommendation: The Committee therefore recommends that the initial acquisition threshold for a mandatory open offer be raised to 25% of the voting capital of the target company.

4. Creeping Acquisitions

Current Provisions

(*i*) The Takeover Regulations currently provide that if an acquirer already holds more than 15% but less than 55%, he may acquire additional shares carrying not more than 5% of voting rights within a financial year without having to make an open offer.

(*ii*) Further, where the holding is above 55% but less than 75%, a one-time allowance to increase their shareholding by 5% through market purchases or pursuant to a Buy back by the target company, without having to make an open offer, has been permitted since October 28, 2008 provided that post acquisition holding of acquirer does not go beyond 75%.

Recommendation: The Committee recommends a creeping acquisition limit of 5% per financial year computed on a gross basis for all shareholders holding more than 25% so long as the maximum non-public shareholding limit is not breached.

5. Voluntary Offers

Current Provisions: Currently, the Takeover Regulations provide for consolidation of shareholding by an acquirer who is desirous of maximizing his shareholding without breaching the minimum public shareholding requirements. The offer size for an open offer under this provision is the lower of 20% or the maximum permissible acquisition without breaching the minimum public shareholding requirement.

Recommendation: The Committee therefore recommends that acquirers collectively holding shares entitling them to exercise 25% or more voting rights in the target company may voluntarily make an open offer to consolidate their shareholding. The Committee has proposed a minimum open offer size of 10% consistent with the rationale of consolidation option outside the creeping route. Voluntary offers should not, however, be of a size that could lead to breach of the maximum permissible non-public shareholding.

6. Control

Current Provisions: The Takeover Regulations currently provide for inclusive definition of "control". It is provided under the Takeover Regulations that control shall include the right to appoint majority of directors or to control the management or policy decisions exercisable by a person or persons acting individually or in concert, directly or indirectly, including by virtue of their shareholding or management rights or shareholder agreements or voting agreements or in any other manner.

Recommendations: The Committee recommends that the definition of "control" be modified to include "ability" in addition to "right" to appoint majority of the directors or to control the management or policy decisions would constitute control. It is also clarified that a director or officer of the target company would not be regarded as being in control merely by virtue of holding such position.

7. Offer Price

Current Provisions

(*i*) The Takeover Regulations currently provide the parameters to be considered for determining the minimum offer price depending on whether or not the shares of the target company are "frequently traded" (shares which have annualized trading volume of 5% or more of the listed share capital during a period of 6 calendar months preceding the month in which the public announcement is made). Such parameters for frequently traded shares include the price under the agreement for acquisition that attracted the open offer, any price paid by the acquirer or persons acting in concert during a 26-week period preceding the public announcement (termed as the "look back period"), and the historical market average price of the shares for a proximate past period.

(*ii*) For "infrequently traded" shares, the Takeover Regulations require the computation of the offer price on the basis of financial parameters such as return on net worth, industry price-earnings multiples and the like, apart from any price actually paid by the acquirer or persons acting in concert during the look back period, or in the transaction that triggers the open offer obligation.

(*iii*) The Takeover Regulations also require addition to the open offer price, of any amount paid towards non-compete fee in excess of 25% of the open offer price.

Recommendation

(*i*) The Committee therefore recommends that the minimum offer price for direct acquisitions should be the highest of:

(*a*) the highest negotiated price per share of the target company for any acquisition under the agreement attracting the obligation to make a public announcement of an open offer;

(*b*) the volume-weighted average price paid or payable for any acquisition, whether by the acquirer or by any person acting in concert with him during the fifty-two weeks immediately preceding the date of the public announcement; and

(*c*) the highest price paid or payable for any acquisition, whether by the acquirer or by any person acting in concert with him during the twenty-six weeks immediately preceding the date of the public announcement; and

(*d*) the volume-weighted average market price, for frequently traded shares, during 60 trading days immediately preceding the date of the public announcement, computed based on market prices on the stock exchange where the shares of the company are most frequently traded during that period.

(*ii*) The Committee recommends that frequently traded shares should now be defined as shares which have a trading volume of 10% or more of the total number of shares during a period of 12 calendar months preceding the month in which the public announcement is made.

(*iii*) In addition, the Committee also recommends that the clause relating to non-compete fee be deleted from the Takeover Regulations, and any consideration paid in any form inclusive of all ancillary and collateral agreements shall form part of the negotiated price.

8. Indirect Acquisitions

Trigger for indirect acquisitions

Current Provisions: The Takeover Regulations currently provide that acquirer has to make an open offer for shares of the target company when there is direct or indirect change of control of the target company irrespective of any direct acquisition of shares of the target company. The regulations also provide for deferment of open offer obligations till consummation of the original transaction.

Recommendation: The Committee recommends that irrespective of whether the target company is material to the parent transaction, open offer obligations have to be triggered. Where a change in control over the target company occurs, shareholders of the target company ought to rightfully get an adequate exit opportunity.

9. Timing and Offer Price

Current Provisions

(*i*) The Takeover Regulations currently provide that in case of indirect acquisition of shares or change of control, a public announcement may be made by the acquirer at any time from the date of the initial announcement of the intention to acquire or entering in to the acquisition agreement, until completion of three months after the consummation of such acquisition or change in control or restructuring of the parent or the company holding shares of or control over the target company.

(*ii*) The Takeover Regulations currently do not differentiate between open offers arising due to direct acquisitions vis-à-vis indirect acquisitions for computation of offer price and the same offer price formula prescribed for direct acquisitions is used for indirect acquisitions as well, and the practice is to compute the offer price as of the date of the announcement of primary acquisition and as of the date of the public announcement for the target company, whichever is higher.

Recommendation: (i) With regard to the pricing of open offers triggered on account of indirect acquisitions, the Committee recommends the following:

(A) Where the proportionate net asset value, or the sales turnover, or the market capitalization of the indirectly-acquired listed company represents more than 80% of the net asset value, sales turnover or the deal value for the parent business or company, the acquirer must specify the value of the stake in the Indian company and the basis of such valuation that would have been factored in, and the Takeover Regulations would treat such acquisitions as if they were direct acquisitions in all respects.

(B) For indirectly acquired target companies, the minimum offer price ought to be the highest of: 1) The highest negotiated price per share, if any, of the target company for any acquisition under the agreement attracting the obligation to make a public announcement of an open offer;

(a) Where the proportionate net asset value, or the sales turnover, or the market capitalization of the indirectly acquired listed company represents more than 15% of the net asset value, or the sales turnover, or the deal value for the parent business or company, the acquirer shall be required to compute and disclose the per share value of the target company taken into account for the acquisition of the parent business or company and the basis of such valuation.

(b) Where the proportionate net asset value, or the sales turnover, or the market capitalization of the indirectly acquired listed company represents less than 15% of the net asset value, or the sales turnover, or the deal value for the parent business or company, the acquirer shall not be necessarily required to make the computation as above, but to factor in the same if the same has been carried out.

(*ii*) The volume-weighted average price paid or payable for any acquisition, whether by the acquirer or by any person acting in concert with him during the fifty-two weeks immediately preceding the date on which the intention or the decision to make the primary acquisition was announced in the public domain or any agreement was entered into;

(*iii*) The highest price paid or payable for any acquisition, whether by the acquirer or by any person acting in concert with him during the twenty-six weeks immediately preceding the date on which the intention or the decision to make the primary acquisition was announced in the public domain or any agreement was entered into; and The highest price paid or payable for any acquisition, whether by the acquirer or by any person acting in concert with him between the date on which the intention or the decision to make the primary acquisition was announced in the public domain or any agreement was entered into and the date of the public announcement;

(C) For frequently traded shares, the volume-weighted average market price on the stock exchange for a period of 60 trading days preceding the date on which the intention or the decision to make the primary acquisition was announced in the public domain or any agreement was entered into, as traded on the stock exchange where the maximum volume of trading in the shares of the target company are recorded during such period.

(D) The price offered as of the date of public announcement (to be calculated as detailed above) shall have to be increased by 10% per annum for the period between the announcement of primary acquisition and date on which the detailed public statement is actually made.

(*iv*) With regard to the timing of the issue of public announcement, the Committee recommends that for transactions where the proportionate net asset value, or the sales turnover, or the market capitalization of the indirectly-acquired listed company represents more than 80% of the net asset value, sales turnover or the deal value for the parent business or company, the public announcement be made on the earlier of the date on which the intention or the decision to make the primary acquisition was announced in the public domain or any agreement was entered into. In all other cases, the public announcement can be made within four business days of such date, and in such cases the detailed public statement should be issued within five business days of the consummation of the primary acquisition.

10. Withdrawal of open offer

Current Provisions: The Takeover Regulations currently provide that no open offer, once made, shall be withdrawn except under the following circumstances:

(*a*) the statutory approval(s) required have been refused;

(*b*) the sole acquirer, being a natural person, has died;

(*c*) such circumstances as in the opinion of SEBI merits withdrawal.

Recommendation: The Committee recommends that, in addition to the grounds currently existing, an open offer may be withdrawn where any condition stipulated in the agreement for acquisition attracting the obligation to make the open offer is not met for reasons outside the reasonable control of the acquirer, and such agreement is rescinded

11. Competing Offers

Current Provisions: The Takeover Regulations currently provide the opportunity to any person other than the acquirer to make a competing offer within 21 days of the public announcement of the first offer. The Takeover Regulations also provide that any competitive offer by an acquirer shall be for such number of shares which, when taken together with shares held by him shall be at least equal to the holding of the first bidder including the number of shares for which the present offer by the first bidder has been made.

Recommendation: Therefore, with a view to rationalize the time lines for making a competing offer, the Committee recommends that a competing offer may be made within 15 business days from the date of the original detailed public statement instead of 21 calendar days from the date of the original public announcement. No further offer should be allowed to be made after the expiry of the said period of 15 business days until the completion of all the competing offers.

(*i*) An open offer made by a competing acquirer shall not be regarded as a voluntary open offer and therefore all provisions of Takeover Regulations, including relating to offer size, shall apply accordingly.

(*ii*) The Committee also recommends that an acquirer, who has made a competing offer, shall be entitled to acquire the shares acquired by the other competing acquirers in their respective competing open offers within 21 business days of the expiry of the offer period without attracting an obligation to make another open offer. However, such an acquisition shall not be made at a price exceeding the offer price in the competing offer made by the acquirer who buys shares in such transaction. Moreover, such an acquisition ought not to take the shareholding of the acquirer beyond the maximum permissible non-public shareholding limit.

(*iii*) The Committee also considered certain other conditions specific to competing offers and recommended the following:

a. During the pendency of competing offers, no appointment of additional directors ought to be made on the board of directors of the target company.

b. The ability of an acquirer to proportionately reduce his acquisitions such that the holding does not exceed the maximum permissible non-public shareholding ought not to be available where competing offers are underway. This is critical to ensure that competing acquirers compete on an identical end-objective and shareholders are truly able to compare them on the offer price.

c. Unless the open offer first made is an open offer conditional as to the minimum level of acceptances, no open offer made by a competing acquirer may be conditional as to the minimum level of acceptances.

d. The schedule of activities and the tendering period for all competing offers shall be carried out with identical timelines and the dates for tendering shares shall be revised to the dates for tendering shares in acceptance of the competing offer last made.

12. Obligations of the Target Company

Material Actions

Current Provisions: The Takeover Regulations currently provide that the target company shall not, during the offer period sell, transfer, encumber or otherwise dispose of assets of the company or its subsidiaries or enter into any material contracts.

Recommendation: The Committee, therefore, recommends retaining restrictions on the target company during the offer period from carrying out material transactions outside the ordinary course of business except with the consent of the shareholders through a special resolution. The Committee recommends that such restrictions would also cover the subsidiaries of the target company, and such actions in respect of subsidiaries would also require approval of the shareholders of the target company.

13. Composition of the Board

Current Provisions: The Takeover Regulations currently provide that till the offer formalities are completed, the target company shall be precluded from inducting any person or person nominated by the acquirer or belonging to his group into the board of the target company other than in cases, where acquirer deposits full consideration in an escrow account.

Recommendation: 1. The Committee recommends that the acquirer or persons acting in concert with him may be represented on the board only after the expiry of a period of 15 business days from the date of the detailed public statement and provided the entire consideration payable under the open offer is deposited in cash in the escrow account required under the Takeover Regulations and the offer is not subject to any conditions other than regulatory approvals.

2. The Committee also recommends that if a competing offer is made, there ought to be no appointments of directors during the offer period, and only casual vacancies arising out of death or incapacitation may be filled with prior approval of shareholders.

14. Timelines for the Open Offer process

Current Provisions: The Committee discussed the current timelines for an open offer under the existing Takeover Regulations and reviewed the same with a view to shorten the timelines.

Recommendation: The Committee recommends the following:

(*i*) A short public announcement should be made on the same date as the date of transaction which triggered the open offer through a notice to the Stock Exchange, followed by a detailed public statement within 5 business days of the public announcement.

(*ii*) Post submission of draft letter of offer, all timelines are dependent on issue of comments by SEBI, thus the Committee recommends to link timelines (post submission of draft letter of offer) to the date of receipt of SEBI comments on the draft letter of offer.

(*iii*) The letter of offer should be sent to the most recent set of shareholders. Therefore, the Committee recommends that date for reckoning the shareholders to whom the letter of offer shall be sent should be ten business days prior to commencement of the tendering period.

(*iv*) Most shareholders tender their shares on the last few days of the offer period, after the date of final revision in price has been carried out, and hence the initial part of the offer period is virtually redundant. Hence, the overall time frame of the tendering period has been reduced to ten business days, and the last date for upward revision of offer price has been moved up to three business days prior to commencement of the tendering period.

(*v*) Since the last date of upward revision is prior to the opening of the open offer, shareholders are expected to be in receipt of all information to enable them to decide on the open offer. Therefore, there is no requirement to permit withdrawal of shares tendered in response to the open offer. This would also make the process more efficient.

(*vi*) The acquirer shall issue an advertisement 1 business day prior to the opening of the tendering period announcing the schedule and procedure for tendering acceptances.

(*vii*) The entire open offer process from the public announcement to the payment of consideration can now be done within fifty seven business days.

(*viii*) A summary of the revised timelines and activity chart for an open offer pursuant to a direct acquisition is set out below:-

15. Mode of Payment

Current Provisions: The Takeover Regulations currently provide that offer consideration shall be payable either (a) by way of cash; (b) by issue, exchange and, or transfer of shares (other than preference shares) of acquirer company, if the person seeking to acquire the shares is a listed body corporate; or (c) by issue, exchange and, or transfer of secured instruments of acquirer company with a minimum 'A' grade rating from a credit rating agency registered with the Board; or (d) a combination of clause (a), (b) or (c).

Recommendation: The Committee recommends the following:

(*i*) The offer price may be paid (a) in cash; (b) by issue, exchange or transfer of frequently traded shares of the acquirer or of the persons acting in concert with the acquirer; (c) by issue, exchange or transfer of listed secured debt instruments issued by acquirer or the persons acting in concert with him with minimum rating of investment grade; (d) by issue, exchange or transfer of convertible debt securities entitling the holder to acquire listed shares of the acquirer or of the person acting in concert with him; or (e) a combination of (a), (b), (c) and (d).

(*ii*) In cases where the acquirer or persons acting in concert with him, proposes to pay the offer consideration by way of issue of its listed shares, the acquirer or PAC as the case may be, may take its shareholder approval for the purpose of allotment of shares up to a specified percentage of the equity capital of the issuer and any allotment of shares pursuant to such resolution may be made within a period of one year from the date of passing of the resolution or till the date next AGM, whichever is earlier.

(*iii*) ICDR Regulations may be appropriately amended to facilitate such open offers.

(*iv*) Where the acquirer has acquired more than 10% of the voting rights in the target company in cash during the fifty two weeks prior to the public announcement, the shareholders of the target company should be provided an option to receive the payment of offer consideration in cash.

(*v*) The Committee also recommends due certification from an independent merchant banker or by a chartered accountant with a minimum of 10 years standing on valuation of shares of the issuer and the basis for arriving at the relevant exchange ratio.

16. Exemptions from open offer obligations

Current Provisions: The Takeover Regulations currently provide for fourteen categories of transactions which are exempted from the requirement to make an open offer subject to satisfying the conditions specified therein, if any, without the need to seek SEBI's approval for the same. Further, for the transactions that are not covered in the aforesaid fourteen categories, an application can be made for seeking exemption from SEBI. Such applications are referred to a takeover panel for its recommendations. SEBI considers the recommendations received and passes an appropriate order.

Recommendation: The Committee has classified the exemptions on the basis of the specific charging provisions which deal with the obligation to make an open offer, and has sought to distinguish between acquisitions involving change in control and those involving only consolidation of shareholding. The deliberations in brief and the recommendations of the Committee on the same are discussed below under separate heads.

A- Exemption from open offer obligations in case of acquisition of shares and / or control

(*i*) Acquisitions arising out of *inter-se* transfer of shares among "qualifying parties" as specified under the Regulations would be exempt from making an open offer. The nature and type of such qualifying parties has been spelt out with the underlying principle being that such transfers do not represent a typical acquisition carrying an economic value, which ought to result in providing an exit opportunity to all shareholders. The only circumstance where this principle has been deviated from is to permit transfer between co-promoters, or persons acting in concert, who have been disclosed as such for at least three years, and that too only if the premium being paid to the exiting party is less than 25% of the volume weighted average price over the 12 weeks period and subject to the parties having complied with all their disclosure obligations.

(*ii*) Acquisition of shares in the ordinary course of business by stock brokers, under-writers, merchant bankers, and specific persons performing specific routine commercial roles should be out of the purview of an open offer obligation.

(*iii*) In respect of inter-se transfers amongst certain "qualifying parties" as listed and defined under the Takeover Regulations, the Committee recommends that, in order to curb the abuse of introduction of new entities as qualifying parties, in most cases a requirement of pre existing relationship of at least three years has been prescribed. In particular, the current exemption on Group Companies which does not have this three year requirement has been restricted to transfers between co-subsidiaries and their parents where there is no change in control.

(*iv*) In respect of schemes of re-arrangement approved by a court or other competent authority, the Committee felt that where the schemes entail a transformation of the target company, it would be desirable to continue to provide for an exemption from the obligation to make an open offer.

(*v*) The Voting rights that accrue on preference shares in proportion to the paid up preference share capital, when dividend remains unpaid beyond the periods set out in Section 87(2) of the Companies Act, 1956, would not attract an obligation to make an open offer. Such voting rights are temporary in nature and upon dividend being paid, cease to exist. Moreover, even the voting rights on equity shares would vary when voting rights accrue on the preference shares and abate when dividend is paid.

B- Exemption from open offer obligations in case of acquisition of shares only and not control

(*i*) Corporate Debt Restructuring under the scheme prescribed by the RBI provides a means by which funds can be infused into a financially weak company. Presently there is no specific provision under the Takeover Regulations that explicitly exempts such schemes. Consequently, the Board receives a number of applications seeking exemptions.

(*ii*) The acquisitions pursuant to such schemes may be exempted from triggering the open offer obligation under the Takeover Regulations only if the scheme has been authorized by the shareholders by way of a special resolution passed by postal ballot, and no change in control over the target company takes place through such acquisition.

C- Exemption from open offer obligations in case of acquisition of substantial stake

(*i*) Companies routinely avail of loans from the banks and financial institutions for their working capital requirements and other funding needs. Often, such acquisitions involve the pledging of shares of a target company, and these pledges do get invoked in the event of loan default or otherwise. Normally, the shares so pledged with an individual bank would be well within the enhanced threshold specified under Regulation 3(1). In view of this, it would be appropriate to exempt acquisition of shares by a consortium of banks pursuant to invocation of a pledge.

(*ii*) Share buy-backs may be undertaken by a company as a way of returning value to the shareholders. Such passive increase in shareholding resulting in a stake exceeding the trigger in Regulation 3(1) is possible, but given that that this trigger is to be considered sacrosanct, no one should be entitled to retain a stake above such threshold. Therefore, the Committee recommends that such shareholders be given ninety days to reduce their stake to a level below the threshold set out in Regulation 3(1).

D- Exemption from open offer obligations in case of acquisition of shares beyond the creeping threshold

(*i*) Certain acquisitions may be exempted from making an open offer under Regulation 3(2) considering the level of creeping acquisition permitted. However, the same type of acquisition ought not to be exempted under Regulation 3(1), where the threshold of the trigger is enhanced and is sacrosanct.

Special Exemptions

(*ii*) The SEBI currently has the powers to grant exemption from the obligation to make an open offer and recommends retention of the same. It would be open to SEBI to seek advice of an expert Panel before granting an exemption from an open offer obligation.

(*iii*) The Board may also grant an exemption or relaxation from strict compliance from specific requirements only under special circumstances. Any exemption or relaxation may be made only in exceptional cases and that too in the broader interests of the investors in securities and the securities markets. In all such cases, an order with justification should be published by SEBI.

(E) Whitewash Provisions: The Takeover Regulations currently provide for whitewash in case of change in control of the target company i.e. an open offer would not be required if the shareholders of the target company were to pass a special resolution waiving the open offer in case of change in control.

(*i*) The Committee observed that providing for whitewash only for change in control and not for substantial acquisition of shares or voting rights (without change in control) apparently is an unintended anomaly. The Committee examined the possibility of introducing a whitewash provision in the Takeover Regulations on the lines of international practice i.e. an open offer would not be required if a material majority of the shareholders of the target company were to pass a resolution waiving the open offer. The rationale for such a framework is that an open offer is ultimately made for the benefit of the shareholders and it is well within the shareholders' rights to renounce such a benefit if they so desire.

(*ii*) Whitewash provisions may be required in situations where (a) the transaction is triggered by an asset or share acquisition by the target company, where consideration was paid by issuing shares of the target company; (b) the transaction is a preferential allotment or other primary infusion which breaches the relevant thresholds; (c) the transaction is a bail-out takeover; (d) acquirer's acquisition of voting rights is due to receipt of shares/ voting rights as gift; or (e) acquisition is made in an environment where the liquidity is scarce. In such circumstances, it is possible that a transaction that a majority of shareholders desire and support may be rendered infeasible due to the need to make an open offer. In such cases, whitewash provisions may provide the acquirer an opportunity to take control of the target company or to cross the relevant substantial acquisition or creeping acquisition limits, with the approval of shareholders of the target company who repose their faith and confidence in the acquirer.

(*iii*) The Committee considered imposing strict conditions such as a high positive waiver vote requirement (say, 90%) and a minimum voter participation threshold. Some members felt that the absence of such a framework would make the Takeover Regulations onerous with no room to exempt from an open offer even where the shareholders themselves do not desire it. It was however observed that in the absence of robust regulations on proxy solicitation, and given the realities of the Indian market, any provision for shareholder waiver for an open offer may not be in the best interests of investors at large. Moreover, some members of the Committee felt strongly against a majority of the shareholders exercising the power to waive an open offer imposing their will on an out-voted minority.

(*iv*) The Committee observed that SEBI is taking certain steps to promote institutional voting, and that it is also pursuing means to operationalise electronic-voting. It was therefore felt that the market is not yet ready for a whitewash mechanism for automatic exemptions from open offers. In any case, as observed, the shareholders always have option not to tender their shares if they so desire. While SEBI does have discretionary powers to grant exemptions from open offers, it would be open to SEBI to take into account whether a significant majority has waived the right to an open offer, when considering an application for exemption.

(*v*) The Committee is of the view that although whitewash provisions are, in principle, not undesirable, the time is not yet ripe to introduce the same in India. Therefore, the current whitewash provision in case of change in control of the target company has not been retained.

17. Recommendation by the independent directors of the Target Company

Current Provisions: The Takeover Regulations currently provide that the board of directors of the target company may, if they so desire, send their unbiased comments and recommendations on the offer(s) to the shareholders, keeping in mind the fiduciary responsibility of the directors to the shareholders.

Recommendation: The Committee recommends that the independent directors on the board of directors of the target company ought to make a reasoned recommendation on the open offer. For the making of such a recommendation, the board of the target company ought to appoint a committee of independent directors with freedom to consult and engage external advisors such as merchant bankers, chartered accountants and lawyers at the expense of the target company. Such committee of independent directors ought to make a reasoned recommendation and such recommendation ought to be sent to all the stock exchanges where the shares of the target company are listed and be published in the same newspapers where the relevant detailed public statement of the open offer was published.

18. Obligations of the Acquirer Disposal of assets of the Target Company

Current Provisions: The Takeover Regulations currently provide that where the acquirer has not stated his intention to dispose of or otherwise encumber any assets of the target company except in the ordinary course of business of the target company, the acquirer shall be debarred from disposing of or otherwise encumbering the assets of the target company for a period of 2 years from the date of closure of the public offer.

Recommendation: The Committee recommends that unless acquirer has declared an intention in the detailed public statement and the letter of offer, the acquirer shall be debarred from alienating any material assets of the target company (including its subsidiaries) for a period of two years after the offer period. However, where such alienation is necessary despite no such intention having been expressed by the acquirer, the target company shall require a special resolution passed by the shareholders by way of a postal ballot.

19. Obligations of the Merchant Banker

Current Provisions: The Takeover Regulations currently provide that the merchant banker shall ensure compliance of the Takeover Regulations and any other laws or rules as may be applicable in this regard and provide other specific obligations under Regulations 24 of the current Takeover Regulations.

Recommendation: The Committee recommends that the merchant banker would be expected to demonstrate the application of due skill, care and diligence in the discharge of professional duties cast on him and the obligations of the merchant banker ought to be construed accordingly. It is perhaps likely that despite following best practices and full application of diligence, skill and care, an acquirer could end up defaulting under the Takeover Regulations. In such circumstances, the Committee believes that, in the least, the expectation from a merchant banker would be a demonstration of the *bona fide* efforts undertaken by him in professionally and diligently discharging the role envisaged for the merchant banker under the regulations.

20. Disclosure Obligations

Current Provisions: The current Takeover Regulations obligate any acquirer who crosses the specified thresholds to disclose at every stage his aggregate shareholding or voting right to the company concerned and to the stock exchanges where shares of the company are listed. It also obligates a promoter / majority shareholder to annually disclose to the company and the concerned stock exchange regarding the number and percentage of shares or voting rights held by him along with PACs.

Recommendation: The Committee recommends that the acquirer promoter / shareholders shall be asked to disclose their acquisition on periodic as well as transaction specific basis upon crossing the limits specified therein to the Stock Exchange. Further, such disclosures shall be of the aggregated shareholding and voting rights of the acquirer and every person acting in concert with him. Moreover, the acquisition and holding of any security or instrument that would entitle the acquirer to receive shares in the target company, including warrants and convertible debentures, shall also be required to be disclosed.

21. Present Tax regime: 1. The Committee discussed about the tax treatment provided to the shareholders in an open offer vis-à-vis a transaction through the stock exchanges. It was noted that the present tax regime in India is more favorable towards the open market transactions as against open offer transactions. For taxation purposes, an open offer transaction is considered akin to an off-market deal, which in the view of the Committee is not desirable.

2. Off-market deals, by their very nature, are entered into between private individuals in a non-transparent and largely unregulated manner. On the other hand, open offer, as an activity, is highly regulated and all the parties involved in the process are required to follow the provisions laid down in the Takeover Regulations, including various disclosures requirements. Also, the basic objective of an open offer is to benefit investors at large by granting them a just and fair exit opportunity. It would perhaps not be correct to club a regulated and investor friendly activity like open offers in the same bracket as an off-market deal.

Recommendations: There is a need to bring parity in the tax treatment given to the shareholders who tender their shares in an open offer and those who are selling the same in the open market. The SEBI may like to suitably take up this issue with the concerned authorities in the Government.

Critical Evaluation of Achuthan Committee Report

With a Securities and Exchange Board of India (Sebi) panel recommending pushing the open offer trigger level from 15 per cent to 25 per cent, India has inched closer to the norms in major world economies, where the threshold is 30 per cent or above. In the UK, the first trigger point is 30 per cent. Initial trigger points in other countries like Singapore, Hong Kong, European Union and South Africa are in the range of 30 per cent to 35 per cent. In India, according to the Companies Act, anyone holding in excess of 25 per cent can block special resolutions. The Takeover Regulations Advisory Committee, in its report to Sebi, said the threshold of 15 per cent was fixed in an environment where the shareholding pattern in corporate India was such that it was possible to control listed companies with a shareholding of as low as 15 per cent. According to the report, the mean and median of promoter shareholdings in listed companies are 48.9 per cent and 50.5 per cent of the total equity capital, respectively. Moreover, the number of companies declared to be controlled by promoters holding 15 per cent or less is below 8.4 per cent. On the Bombay Stock Exchange (BSE), only 6.1 per cent listed companies have promoter shareholding of between 15 per cent and 25 per cent. The trigger levels in other countries were set primarily based on the level at which a potential acquirer could exercise positive control over a company. "Taking into account both the ability of promoters to exercise de facto control at 25 per cent and the law governing special resolutions, a 30 per cent threshold would be too high," said the committee. According to the Committee the existing trigger threshold of 15 per cent has outlived its contextual relevance and requires an upward revision. A significant change in the shareholding pattern in listed companies has been observed over the last few years.

"Despite the increase in the mean level of promoter shareholding, there are a number of prominent companies in India which are controlled by shareholders holding between 25 per cent and 30 per cent of the voting capital of the company," said the report. This trend, the report added, suggested that promoters would be capable of exercising de facto control at the 25 per cent level. In this context global best practices are as follows:

(*i*) In the UK, the threshold is 30%.

(*ii*) In Singapore, Hong Kong, the EU & S Africa, it is 30-35%.

(*iii*) Less than 8.4% listed companies are controlled by promoters holding 15% or less.

(*iv*) Mean and median of promoter shareholdings in listed companies at 48.9 per cent and 50.5 per cent, respectively.

(*v*) In India, anyone holding in excess of 25% can block special resolutions.

The new takeover code guidelines offer larger opportunity for investment in India, as it increases the threshold for open offers to 25 per cent from 15 per cent. The proposed change is a potential game changer for ultra high growth mid-sized (UHMS) Indian companies — a segment that always deserved to be rewarded by policy makers. You will now see Carlyle engage more pro-actively with such companies. The old threshold limit prevented, unintentionally, exceptionally high growth companies from receiving commensurately large capital from global PE funds like Carlyle. With the proposed change in the open offer threshold, this constraint to the growth of UHMS Indian companies will be eased. Carlyle could now provide larger equity funding to such valuable companies, alongside its expertise. Illustratively, in the Rs 1,200-crore market capitalisation range, we can now provide Rs 400-crore equity funding to a galloping company, whereas in the past such a company would have been able to seek around half the amount. So, a valuable new segment opens up to us. But more importantly, this change is good for the best companies in India and so is a positive for the economy. While the change in threshold is only 60 per cent (from 15 per cent to 25 per cent), the amount of capital a company would now be able to take from a PE fund without breaching trigger limits would increase by 89 per cent. But keep in mind that PE funds' interest in PIPEs is by and large confined to exceptional companies.

The binding constraint to buy-outs in India was never the takeover code or delisting rules. The real constraint is Press Note 4 (PN 4) of 2009 clause 6(d) that places a blanket restriction on any borrowing by any holding company in India, if it is majority owned by a foreign entity. Its earlier avatar was PN 9 of 1999. Since January 2009, around 25 Indian entrepreneurs tried to sell companies founded by them to one or the other of the top four PE funds operating in India. They came to PE funds, because they knew PE buyers would invest in and grow their companies, orient them to capturing global markets, retain the management team built by the entrepreneurs (unlike in a trade sale to a local competitor who would strip out the management team) and professionalise the company in every respect. Not one of the deals could be consummated, because regulations do not permit PE funds to design an optimal capital structure for buy-outs. It meant a potential loss to the economy, to entrepreneurship and to employment and I did wonder who gained.

Investments will go where investments can be absorbed, which means the highest growth sectors. At eight-nine per cent, GDP (gross domestic product) growth, almost every sector needs growth capital in India. So in India, PE is in the happy situation of being able to choose its menu of sectors, where it believes growth would create the largest value and invest in those sectors.

Major M & A Deals in India

Major M & As deal are given below:

***(i)* Tata Corus Deal:** An Indian company Tata Steel has made the bid for a European steel company much larger than itself. It is something which has never happened. Tatas kayoed Brazil's CSN to pick up Corus at 608 pence a share in an all cash deal costing $ 12.1 billion (Rs. 53361 crore). The company had to increase its original offer of 455 pence a share for Corus by about 34 per cent to 608 pence to trip its Brazilian rival CSN in the race for the Anglo-Dutch steel maker. At 608 pence a share, the enterprise value of Corus works out to $710 per tonne. Today, to set up a green field capacity, going downstream as much as Corus has in terms of tin plate capacity, galvanizing capacity and construction solutions anywhere in the world, would cost somewhere between $1200 and $1300 per tonne". The Corus acquisition immediately added 19 million tonnes of capacity to Tata Steel, apart from giving it access to the "growth markets" of Europe, where quality of products and service are important. Deal was guided by the 53 : 47 debt-equity ratio and exposure would be $4.1 billion through a mix of debt and equity. Remaining would be through loans and ring finance by special purpose vehicle. It is a case of horizontal merger.

***(ii)* Jet-Sahara Deal:** Jet airways has purchased Air Sahara for Rs. 1,450 crore. Jet Airways has already paid Rs. 500 crore as deposit to Air Sahara which in turn has accepted a generously stagged payment schedule that will end only in 2011. Jet will pay only Rs. 400 crore on or before April 20, 2007. The remaining Rs. 550 crore will be paid in interest free equal installments (Rs. 137.50 crore each) from March 30, 2008 to 2011. Taking the saving on interest (at existing rates), the net present value of the deal will be is Rs. 1,200 crore. Enterprise value was derived after including around Rs. 550 crore in adjustments which includes the cost of four helicopters and immovable property that will be returned to the Sahara promoters, an investment of Rs. 180 crore made by Jet to run the airline, and other interest payments, which it had made. However Jet has paid only Rs. 300 crore less than what it had promised in January, 2006, when the deal was first signed.

***(iii)* Hindalco-Novelis Deal:** Hindalco industries has now expanses the Global Indian takeover of the US, sealing $ 6 billion all cash deal to acquire Atlanta based Novelis. The acquisition immediately takes Hindalco into in the Fortune 500 list and makes it one of the top five integrated aluminium players globally. This is the biggest ever acquisition by an Indian company in North America and of a US company. The acquisition also makes Hindalco one of the largest integrated aluminium players globally and the largest producers of flat-rolled products (FRP). The Atlanta based Novelis is the largest players with a 19% share of the global market.

***(iv)* Vedanta Sesa Goa Deal:** Non-ferrous metals major Vedanta Resources appears to be preparing itself to get inot steel making business to make itself a completely diversified metals and mining. Vedanta has elbowed aside steel giant Arcelor Mittal and the Aditya Birla Group in the race of Mitsui's controlling stake in Sesa Goa. Sesa Goa is an iron ore mining company, which was under Italian management before being acquired by Mitsui in 1996, produces about 10 million tonnes of iron ore from mine across Goa, Karnataka and Orissa. It exports about 90 per cent of its production to China, Europe and Japan. At the current production rates, Sesa's iron ore reserves and resources of 207 million tonnes may support over 20 years of mined production. The company also operates a 2.5 mtpa pig iron and metallurgical coke facilities.

The Anil Agarwal-founded Vendanta Resources, a London listed company flagged off its new pursuit on 24.4.2007 by acquiring a controlling stake of 51% in Sesa Goa Ltd. Vedanta is in the process of expanding its existing businesses in the aluminum, copper and zinc segments to one million tonne production capacity each with an investment of $8 billion. Vedanta, which owns 72.3% stake in Sterlite Industries announced the acquisition of the 51% stake in Sesa Goa owned by Japan's Mitsui for $981 million (around Rs. 4,070 crore), implying a price of Rs. 2,036 per share.

The company has already made an open offer to the public shareholders of Sesa Goa to acquire an additional 20 per cent holding in the company at the same price. It is expected to announce the open offer in the next four days, with the offer remaining open till July. The total cash consideration for the 71% stake (including the open offer) was $1.37 billion. The acquisition was be financed through a mix of newly committed bank debt facilities of $1.1billion and the existing cash resources of the company. Mr. Agarwal said the company would consider adding value to its newly acquired iron ore business by getting into steel making. Explaining the rationale for this, he said traditionally metal mining and production are two different businesses. Mining companies entered into steel production only through joint ventures with a partner that had the know-how for steel making.

***(v)* Essar Algoma Steel Deal :** It is a case of horizontal merger. Essar Global, through its wholly owned subsidiary Essar Steel Holdings and Canada's Algoma Steel Inc announced that they have signed a definitive agreement providing for acquisition by Essar of all of the common shares of Algoma for Canadian $56.00 per share, or an aggregate equity value of $1.8 billion ($1.58 billion or approximately Rs. 6,800 crore) payable in cash. The offer price represents a premium of 48 per cent to Algoma's volume weighted average stock price for the 20-day period ending February 14, 2007 when Algoma confirmed that it was in discussion regarding a potential takeover. Under the terms of the agreement, Algoma will undertake a court approved plan of arrangement pursuant to which an Essar subsidiary will acquire all of the share of Algoma in consideration for C$56.00 in cash per share. The arrangement must be approved by Algoma's shareholders by the affirmative vote of at least 66 percent ($2/3^{rd}$) of the votes cast, in person or by proxy, at a shareholders meeting, and is subject to customary closing conditions including necessary regulatory approvals. The support agreement provides for payments to Essar in the event that the acquisitions is not completed under certain circumstances.

This transaction will also benefit Algoma's employees and the city of Sault Ste Marie, Ontario, as it will result in new ownership that is committed to investment in Algoma's facilities to support growth and business sustainability." Shashi Ruia, chairman, Essare Global, said, "Algoma acquisition fits in with our global steel vision of having world class low-cost assets, with a global footprint. Algoma provides us with an excellent platform for the Canadian and North American markets."

***(vi)* Tata Power PL Kaltim Prima Coal** and PT Arutmin Indonesia Deal: It is a case of vertical merger. The Tata Power Company has signed a $1.1-billion (Rs. 4,950 crore) deal to buy 30 per cent stakes in two Indonesian coal companies, and in a related coal trading company, all promoted by PT Bumi Resources Tbk (Bumi), Indonesia. PL Kaltim Prima Coal and PT Arutmin Indonesia are two of Indonesia's largest coal mines which together produced 53.5 million tonnes in 2006, of which 95 per cent was exported. Together the companies are among the top three coal exporting thermal coal mines in the world. In addition, the companies have excellent transport infrastructure for shipping coal for exports. Kaltim Prima is reported to have reserves of nearly 3.6 billion tonnes of coal. The transaction cost of $1.1 billion is prior to working capital and other adjustments. The seller PT Bumi Resources could get as much as $200 million more from these adjustments, getting $1.3 billion from the deal.

"The acquisition specifically address fuel requirements of the Mundra Ultra Mega Power Project, the Trombay project and the coastal power project in Maharashtra. It is complementary and supports the assumptions made in the bid for Mundra UMPP. "This move not only secures fuel requirements in the light of the aggressive growth plans charted out by the company, but also opens up opportunities for Tata Power to own and operate a range of world class, competitive and profitable electricity and energy businesses in India and overseas. Tata Power will make this acquisition through an offshore special purpose vehicle. Funding will be done through a combination of debt in the SPV, internal accruals and borrowings from Tata Power. The funding details cannot currently be specifically described since the company is finalising a funding package that would include other projects, including the Mundra UMPP.

The company will require 21mt of imported coal for all these planned projects. The Indonesian deal will take care of 50 per cent of Tata Power's requirements, which would be capped there. "From a risk point of view, we don't want to get more than 50 per cent of our requirements from one country. The financial impact of the acquisition on Tata Power will be positive over a five-year time frame; however it would be under marginal pressure for one to two years. But, on a consolidated basis, the deal will be positive from day one, the acquiree companies being profit making ones.

***(vii)* Matsushita Anchor Electricals: Joint Venture Deal:** Matsushita Electric Works (MEW) of Japan, owners of the National and Panasonic brands, has acquired 80 percent equity stake in the privately held Anchor Electricals for Rs. 2,000 crore. The deals is the largest overseas buy out for MEW, the previous one being a German company for around Rs. 1,000 crore. Anchor is the market leader in the Indian electrical accessories and wiring devices market with annual sales exceeding Rs. 900 crore. It is in the form of joint venture Following the transaction, Anchor will become a consolidated subsidiary of Matsushita Electric Works, Ltd. "There is no option to acquire 100 per cent stake." said Mr. Atual Shah, Managing Director. Anchor Electricals Pvt. Ltd. After the deal, there will be six members on the board from MEW and four from Anchor Electricals. MEW will introduce new products such as home appliances, lighting, home automations, interior design solutions and security systems and security products in India. It will also look at improving the manufacturing efficiency. Post the joint venture, the Anchor brand name and logo will continue. Mr. Shah said the focus will be to expand the market share and bring products which will fetch higher margins. The funds will also be used to help the consumer business of Anchor grow. Anchor is eyeing 100 percent growth in the next four years and a 500 per cent growth in the next 100 years. The price-earnings ratio for the deal is 15 times the 2006-07 earnings. However, the deal valuation cannot be compared to any other player in the space as the electrical accessories and wiring market is in the unorganized sector Achor currently enjoys between 60-70 per cent market share in India. "The strategy of MEW is to gain top market share in wiring devices with Anchor," said Mr. Toshihide ARIL, Chairman of the new joint venture. "We expect 20 per cent year-on-year growth after the joint venture. Anchor Electricals Pvt. Ltd. recorded net sales of Rs. 922 crore for the year ended March 2006 and net profit of Rs. 187 crore. MEW's sales stood at%13.7 billion for the year ended march 2006.

***(viii)* United Breweries (UB) Deccan Aviation Deal:** Bangalore based Deccan Aviation, which runs the country's largest budget carriers, Air Deccan, was divested its 26 per cent stake to its competitors and full service airlines Kingfisher Airlines, a subsidiary of Vijay Mallaya promoted liquor company UB Group. The board of Deccan Aviation approved the proposal to make preferential allotment of Kingfisher Airlines at Rs. 155 per share. Now Air Deccan is a subsidiary of Kingfisher Airlines.

***(ix)* Thomas Cook India and TCI & TTE Takeover:** Travel Corporation (India) Pvt. Ltd. (TCI) was purchased by Thomas cook India for Rs. 182.45 crore. In addition to acquiring TCI, Thomas cook acquired TT Enterprises visa services for Rs. 16.9 crore. Both transactions are of all cash deals The deal was funded through a combination of internal accruals and debt. While TCI has a significant presence in the inbound tourism marker, Thomas Cook does not. That was the primary reason why Thomas Cook decided to buy the company. He also said that TCI's inbound tourism accounted for 48 per cent of its turnover. In contrast, for Thomas Cook, it was only 5 per cent. The deal also gives Thomas Cook access to TCI's 11 international offices. They will serve as selling and distribution offices for the group. TCI will become a wholly owned subsidiary of Thomas Cook. Thomas Cook's acquisition of TT Service- a visa outsourcing service providers in India, Sri Lanka, Nepal & and Philipines – allows the company to offer one stop travel arrangement for its customers. TT Service currently has nine office in India. A company which needs to be serious about outbound traffic should also be able to provide better visa services. TT Enterprises is in the process of demerging its visa services from its cargo and forex businesses. It is only after the dermerger that Thomas Cook will take control.

The deal increases Thomas Cook's purchasing power (leverage) with airlines and hotels. The combined traffic of the two entities also propels Thomas Cook to number one position in the inbound tourism market in India.

***(xi)* Indian Hotels Company Ltd (IHCL) And Ritzz Carlton Hotel Deal:** Indian Hotels owners of the Taj Group of hotels, has purchased the Ritzz-Carlton hotel in Boston for $170 million (Rs. 765 crore), concluding a transaction for which it had signed a letter of intent recently. Taj Hotels Resorts and Palaces has signed a share purchase agreement with Millennium Partners, owners of the Boston Hotel. The equity components of the deal was be financed from the company's unutilised FCCB proceeds. The 273 room hotel, set up in 1927 is located on Arlington Street near Boston's Public Garden. It is the oldest Ritz Carlton hotel in continous operation in the US. The TAj Boston becomes the company's second hotel property in the US. In 2005, Taj Hotels entered into a 30-year management contract agreement to operate and manage the Pierre on New York's fifth Avenue. It is definitely a good move because the management wants to turn Taj into global brand. As far as the valuation of the hotel is concerned, it is hard to say because financials are not outright now. But it is definitely one step forward from a management perspective. The addition of this hotel to the Taj Group's growing international portfolio reinterates its commitments to establishing a significant presence for the Taj Hotels Resorts and Palaces brand in key destination across the globe.

Selected Outbound M & A Transactions of over US $100 million (as of Mid 2008)

Acquirer	Foreign Target	Target Industry	Target Country	Approximate Deal Value (US$)
Tata Steel Ltd.	Corus Group PLC	Steel	U.K	14.85 billion
Hindalco Industries Ltd.	Novelis Inc.	Aluminum	Canada	6 billion
Sterlite Industries India Ltd.	Aserco Inc.	Mining	U.S.	2.6 billion
Tata Motors Ltd.	Ford Motors Co.'s Jaguar Ltd and Land Rover Holdings	Automotive	U.K	2.3 billion
Essar Steel Ltd.	Algoma Steel Inc.	Steel	Canada	1.57 billion
United Spirits Ltd.	Whyte and Mackay Ltd.	Food and Beverages	U.K	1.18 billion
Tata Power Company Ltd.	30% stake each in PT Kaltim Priam Coal and PT Artumin Indonesia	Energy	Indonesia	1.1 billion
Tata Chemicals	General Chemical Industrial Products	Chemicals	U.S	1.0 billion
Tata Sons Ltd Tata Tea Ltd.	30% stake in Energy brands Inc	Food and Beverages	U.S	677 million
Dr. Reddy's Laboratories Ltd.	Betapharm Arzneimittel GmbH	Pharmaceuticals	Germany	571 million
Wirpo Technologies Ltd.	Infocrossing Inc.	Technology	U.S.	568 million
Suzion Energy Ltd. through its subsidiary AE-Rotor Holding BV	Hansen Transmission International NV	Industrial Machinery	Belgium	521 million
Ranbaxy Laboratories Ltd.	Terapia S.A	Pharmaceuticals	Romania	324 million
Videocon Appliances Ltd	Thomson Multimedia cathode ray tube business	Technology	France	292 million
Jubilant Organosys Ltd.	Draxis Health Inc.	Pharmaceuticals	Canada	258 million

Contd....

Tata Coffee Ltd.	The Eight O'Clock Coffee Co.	Food and Beverages	U.S.	220 million
Aditya Birla Nuvo Ltd.	Minacs Worldwide Inc.	Technology	Canada	172 million
United Phosphorous Ltd.	Cerexagri S.A	Chemicals	France	142 million
Subex Systems Ltd	Azure Solutions Ltd.	Technology	U.K.	140 million
United Phosphorous Ltd.	Advanta Netherlands Holdings BV	Food and Beverages	The Netherlands	119 million

Source: Rajpal, D. and S.Parekh, "India Looks Outward: Cross-Border M&A by India Corporations–Canadian Considerations", Stikeman, October 2008.Based on data from Capital IQ.

Case Study

Read out the following cases and answer the following Questions:

Case Study 1. HOEL, target company, is a company whose shares are listed in the NSE and BSE, BEIL, acquirer company, entered into a share purchase agreement (SPA) with UIC on 14th February, 2005 to acquire 100% equity of UBL, a person acting in concert (PAC), a wholly owned subsidiary of UIC. In turn, UBL held 1,52,81,633 shares of HOEL, consulting 26.01% of HOEL's equity. As the aforesaid constituted indirect acquisition of shares and control of HOEL, the acquirer company and UBL made a public announcement on 15th February, 2005 in terms of the SEBI (Substantial Acquisition of shares and takeovers) Regulations, 1997 to acquire 1,17,48,990 shares of the target company, i.e., HOEL constituting 20% of its equity.

Meanwhile, UBL replaced two of its nominees on the Board of directors of HOEL with two directors who were appointed on UBL's Board on 14th Feb., 2005 (which is the date of SPA and also the first day of the offer period) by the BEIL. In turn, they were appointed as directors of HOEL also, on the same day, in this context, answer the following questions-

(*i*) Define the offer period in terms of the SEBI (Substantial Acquisition of shares and takeovers) Regulations, 1997.

(*ii*) What is the period of offer in the instant case?

(*iii*) Who is required to make public announcement and when it is required to be made?

(*iv*) Is the appointment of directors valid under the SEBI (Substantial Acquisition of shares and takeovers) Regulations, 1997?

(C.S. Final Examination, December 2003)

Answer

(*i*) According to regulation 2 (f) of the Takeover Code "offer period" means the period between the date of entering into Memorandum of Understanding or the public announcement, as the case may be and the date of completion of offer formalities relating to the offer made under SEBI (Substantial Acquisition of shares and takeovers) Regulations, 1997.

(*ii*) Memorandum of Understating (MOU) is not defined under SAST Regulations, However, it is observed that MOU is an agreement/ contract recorded in writing in which the terms of contract are recorded. Share Purchase Agreement and Memorandum of Understanding both the words convey the same meaning and legally speaking both constitutes an agreement. Therefore, since the SPA was signed on 14.02.2005, the offer period shall commence from this date until the completion of all the offer formalities relating to the offer made under SAST Regulations, 1997.

(*iii*) The acquirer is required to appoint Merchant Banker (MB) registered with SEBI before making a Public announcement (PA.) PA is required to be made through the said MB. The acquirer is required to make the PA within four working days of the entering into an agreement to acquire shares or deciding to acquire shares/ voting rights to the target company or after any such change (s) as would result in change in control over the target company.

(*iv*) As per Regulations 22 (7) of SAST Regulations, 1997 during the offer period, the acquirer or persons acting in concert with him shall not be entitled to be appointed on the board of directors of the target company. Since appointment of directors was made on 14.02.2005 which is the date of offer, the default in the instance case has been committed.

Case Study 2. Anjana Ltd. wants to acquire the shares of Good Luck Ltd., a listed company. Enumerate the obligations of the acquirer company under the SEBI Takeover Code.

(C.S. Final, Dec. 2008)

Answer

Regulations 22 lays down the following general obligations of the acquirer, Anjana Ltd.:

The acquirer must make public offer only when he is able to implement the offer. The acquirer must send draft letter of offer, within 14 days of the public announcement, to all the stock exchanges where the shares of the company are listed. The acquirer must ensure dispatch of letter of offer to all the shareholders of the target company, whose names appear in the register of members of the company on the specified date so as to reach them within 45 days of the public announcement.

The acquirer must also ensure dispatch of letter of offer to the custodians of Global Depository Receipts or American Depository Receipts to enable such persons to participate in the open offer, if they are entitled to do so. The acquirer must also ensure dispatch of letter of offer to warrant holders and convertible debenture holders, where the period of exercise of option or conversion falls within the offer period.

Where the public announcement is made pursuant to an agreement to acquire shares or control over the target company, the acquirer should send the letter of offer only to those shareholders who are not parties to the agreement. The acquirer should also ensure that the offer remains open for a period of 30 days. The shareholder shall have the option to withdraw acceptance tendered by him up to three working days prior to the date of closure of offer.

The announcement of offer and all publicity material issued to shareholders must state the directors accept the responsibility for the information contained therein. If any director desires to exempt himself from the responsibility for the information in such document, he should issue a statement to that effect with reasons. During the offer period, the acquirer or persons acting in concert with him should not get himself appointed on the board of Directors of the target company. In case of acquisition of shares or voting rights or control of Public Sector Undertaking under Regulation 14 (1), provision of Regulation of 23 (8) shall apply. Also, where the acquirer, other than acquirer who has made offer conditional upon level of acceptance (Regulation 21 A), after assuming full acceptance, has deposited in the escrow account, hundred percent of consideration if it was payable in cash, and in the form of securities where consideration was payable by way of issue, exchange or transfer of securities or combination after a period of twenty one days from the date of public announcement. The acquirer shall acquire shares to the extent of the specified minimum percentage, where the offer is made conditional upon minimum level of acceptances. The acquirer shall not acquire, during the offer period, any shares in the target company, except by way of fresh issue of shares. On or before the date of issue of announcement, the acquirer should open an escrow account. The acquirer should ensure firm financial arrangement for fulfilling the obligations under the public offer and this should be disclosed in the public announcement.

In the event of withdrawal of offer, the acquirer should not make any offer for acquisition of shares of the target company for a period of six months from the date of public announcement of withdrawal of offer.

Case Study 3. Vinod is having 14% of shares or voting rights of Ambitious Ltd., a listed company. Vinod wants to further acquire 40% of shares in Ambitious Ltd. What are the steps he is required to take?

Answer

When any person acquires or agrees to acquire any securities exceeding 15% of the voting rights in any company or if any person who holds securities which in aggregate carries less than 15% of the voting rights of the company and seeks to acquire the securities exceeding 15% of the voting rights, such person shall not acquire any securities exceeding 15% of the voting rights, such person shall not acquire any securities exceeding 15% of the voting rights of the company without complying with the relevant provisions of the SEBI (Substantial Acquisition of Shares and Takeovers) Regulations, 1997.

In accordance with regulation 10, no acquirer is authorized to acquire shares or voting rights which (taken together with shares or voting rights, if any, held by him or by persons acting in concert with him), entitle such acquirer to exercise fifteen percent or more of the voting rights in a company without making a public announcement to acquire shares of such company in accordance with the Regulations. In the present case, Vinod can further acquire 40% of shares in Ambitious Ltd. by making a public announcement in accordance with the provisions of these Regulations.

Regulations 13 to 29 contain several important procedural matters in relation to making a public announcement.

Case Study 4. Sunshine Ltd. is amalgamated with Best Ltd. The scheme is approved by requisite majority. Ministry of corporate Affairs (MCA) has raised an objection for the merger. Is the court bound to go by the opinion of the Regional Director, MCA?

Answer

The Court under section 394 A shall give notice of every application made to it under section 391 or 394 to the Central Government and shall take into consideration the representations, if any, made to it by the government before passing any order under any of these section.

If Regional Director raises on objection for the merger, the court is not bound to go by it and it can form its independent opinion over the matter as decided in the case Sakamari Steel & Alloys Ltd.

Practice Questions

Objective Type Questions

1. M & A deals involve:
   (*a*) external approach to expansion
   (*b*) internal approach to expansion
   (*c*) informal approach to expansion
   (*d*) None of the above
2. Options available in emerging areas are not concerned with the following:
   (*a*) formation of new company
   (*b*) acquisition of new company
   (*c*) merger with existing company
   (*d*) increasing production capacity
3. Economies of scale concerned with:
   (*a*) Increasing the fixed cost over increasing levels of production
   (*b*) decreasing the fixed cost over increasing levels of production
   (*c*) Spreading of the fixed cost over increasing levels of production
   (*d*) stagnating of the fixed cost over increasing levels of production
4. Hubris hypothesis is concerned with:
   (*a*) No payment for M & As
   (*b*) higher payment for acquisition
   (*c*) Lower payment for acquisition
   (*d*) None of these
5. The concept of winner's curse is concerned with:
   (*a*) Agency problem
   (*b*) Hubris Hypothesis
   (*c*) Signaling Theory
   (*d*) information Theory
6. Pro competitive alliance is an alliance where:
   (*a*) low interaction and low conflict between the strategic partners
   (*b*) High cooperation and low competition between the strategic partners

(c) high cooperation and high competition between the strategic partners
(d) low cooperation and high competition between the strategic partners

7. Corporate Control means right to:
   (a) appoint majority of directors on the board of the target company
   (b) control management of the target company
   (c) policy decision affecting the target company
   (d) All of the above
8. Can an acquirer make an offer for more than
   (a) 5%
   (b) 10%
   (c) 15%
   (d) 20%

Ans: 1. (a), 2. (d) 3. (c), 4. (b), 5. (b), 6. (a), 7.(d), 8.(d)

Short Answer Questions

1. Distinguish between takeover and acquisition.
2. What are the objective of merger and acquisition?
3. What do you mean by winner's curse?
4. What do you mean by diversification strategy?
5. What do you mean by inefficient management?
6. What is control?
7. What do you mean by person acting in concert?
8. What do you mean by promoter?

Long Answer Questions:

1. What do you mean by mergers and acquisitions? Explain their objectives.
2. Discuss the steps involved in acquisition process.
3. Examine the different theories of mergers and acquisitions.
4. Discuss the nature and scope of Hubris hypothesis.
5. What do you mean by creeping acquisition? Give SEBI Guideline with regard to this.
6. Discuss the SEBI guidelines with regard to disclosure of takeover transaction.
7. Describe the SEBI guidelines with regard to acquisition of control over a company.
8. Discuss the contents of the public announcement of an offer for takeover.
9. Examine the SEBI guidelines regarding calculation of offer price.
10. Discuss the general obligation of an acquirer.
11. What do you mean by escrew account? Also, examine the SEBI guidelines relating with escrew account.

References

1. Mandal Ranjit Kumar, Corporate Mergers in India, Kauishka Publishers Distributors, New Delhi, 1995, P.225.
2. Glueck W.F. and Jauch L.R. Business Policy and Strategic Management, New York, McGraw Hill, 1984, 4th Ed., P. 24.
3. Thompson AA Jr. and Strickland AJ III, Strategic Management, Plano, Texas, Business Publication, 1984, 3rd Ed., P.90.

4. Weston J. Fred, Siu, Juan A. and Johnson Brian A. Takeovers, Restructuring & Corporate Governance, Pearson Education Asia, New Delhi, 2002, P.6
5. Ibid,.p.-636
6. Ibid., p. 640.
7. Ibid., p-120
8. Ibid., p-140.
9. Ibid., p- 143.
10. Levy H and Sarnat M. "Diversification; Portfolio Analysis and the Uneasy Care for Conglomerate Mergers. Journal of Finance, September, 1970, p. 795-802.
11. op. cit, p. 143, Weston. J. Fred, Siu, Juan. and Johnson Brain A.
12. Weston J. Fred, Chung S.Kwang and Hoag Susun. E, Mergers, Restructuring, and corporate control, Prentice Hall of India Private Ltd., New Delhi, 1996, p. 198.
13. Ibid.p-199
14. Bralley, M. Inter firms Tender offers and the Market for Corporate Central Journal of business October 1980. PP. 345-376.
15. Desai A. and Kim E.H. "The Rationale Behind Inter-firm Tender offers: Information or Synergy?" Journal of Financial Economics, April 11, 1903. p. 183-206.
16. Desai. A and Kim E.H. Synergistic Gains from Corporate Acquisitions and Their Division between the Stake holders of Target and Acquiring Firms. Journal of Financial Economics 21, 1988. p 3-40.
17. op.cit, P. 144, Weston J. Fred, Siu Juan A. & Johnson Brian A.
18. Spence a. Michael. Job Market Signaling Guarter Journal of Economics, 87 August 1973, PP. 355-379.
19. op.cit, P. 201, Weston J. Fred, Siu Juan A. & Johnson Brian A.
20. Roll. E.C., "The Hubris Hypothesis of Corporate Takeovers" Journal of Business 59, 1986, PP. 197-216.
21. opcit.p.146, Weston. J. Fred, Siu, Juan A. and Johnson Brian A. Takeovers
22. Ibid P.146.
23. Fama E.C. "Agency Problems and theory of the Firms, Journal of Political Economy, 88 April, 1980, PP. 288-307.
24. Marine H.C, "Mergers and Market for corporate control" Journal of Political Economy 73, April 1965 PP110-120.
25. op. cit., P.203 Weston. J. Fred, Chung, Kwang, S. and Hoag, Susan, E.
26. Lewellen W.G. and B. Huntsman, "Managerial Pay and Corporate Performance" American Economic Review, Sept.1970, p.710-720
27. Jensen M.C., Agency Costs of Free Cash Flow, Corporate Finance and Takeovers. American Economic Review 76, May 1986, PP 323-329
28. Jensen M.C., The Takeover Controversy: Analysis and Evidence "Chapter 20 in Knight, Raiders Rose Ackerman, ed. New York, Oxford University Press, 1988 PP 403-414.

16 CORPORATE FINANCIAL REPORTING IN INDIA

Traditionally, the focal point of the literature of accounting has been the needs and the viewpoints of investors. Indeed, it was based on the premise that the maximization of shareholders' 'wealth is an appropriate guide for how the firm should act. Equally corporate reports also attempted to provide relevant information to decision makers but it was largely confined to the decisions about investors and creditors. But there are other parties also expect from the corporate world. They want to know the policy implications of the corporate decision making process. Management workers, suppliers, government, regulatory authorities and society at large. The changing social environment has been concerned with the social imbalance between those having wealth and controlling society through the influence of wealth and those whose political influence in numerical terms has secured the return of governments committed to reforms and the gradual redistribution of wealth. In effect, this imbalance is reflected in the growing significance of stakeholders in place of stockholders in present-day scenario. Management is now supposed to communicate adequate and necessary information to those who have stake in the firm: investors, creditors, bankers, employees, government, society etc. Management is also required to disclose relevant information due to authoritative pronouncements, regulatory rules or custom or because it considers it useful to stakeholders and discloses it voluntarily. Keeping the charging pace of these requirements, efforts are being made by Indian corporate sector to focus on the following emerging issues.

There are different stakeholders who have stake in the working of a company. Shareholders, investors, management, employees, suppliers, customers, government, regulatory authorities and society etc. are the key stakeholders in the company. They need detailed information to assess to what extent company is serving their stakes. Timely information enable them to assess, reorient and change their strategies about the company. Corporate financial reporting that ensures timely and adequate information to them. In India, Indian Companies Act, 1956 directives and policy guidelines of Ministry of Corporate Affairs SEBI guidelines and guidelines formulated by other regulatory authorities force the companies to provide detailed information to their stakeholders.

Corporate Financial Reporting aims at serving the stakeholders by providing relevant information so that they judge the performance of the company. Generally speaking, the term 'financial reporting' is used to mean general purpose external financial reporting. Often it is said that the purpose of financial reporting is the preparation of general purpose reports for external users. Financial reports are mainly intended (legally) for shareholders, but they can also be used by a number of other interested parties who have stake in the company.

Rationale of Corporate Financial Reporting: Rationale of corporate financial reporting is given below:

(*a*) **Investors:** They are concerned with the risk involved in, and return, available on their investments. They need information to determine whether they should buy, hold, or sell the security. Shareholders are also interested in information which enables them to access the ability of the enterprise to pay dividends. Financial reporting helps the investors about assessing the stability, liquidity and profitability of the company.

(*b*) **Employees:** Financial reporting provides information about the past, present and future trend of economic performance of the company. Employees and their unions are interested in the information about the stability and profitability of company. They are also interested in information which enables them to access the ability of company to provide remuneration, retirement benefits and employment opportunities.

(*c*) **Lenders:** Credit worthiness of the company develops confidence among the lenders or creditors. Lenders are interested in information which enables them to determine whether their loans, and the interest thereon, will be paid in time. Assets of the company serve the payment base of loans provided by the lenders.

(*d*) **Suppliers and creditors:** Suppliers and creditors are interested in information that enables them to determine whether amounts owing to them will be paid in time.

(*e*) **Customers:** They have a long-term involvement with company. Customers have an interest in information about the continuance of a company. Customers can assess the company through the information available in the annual report.

(*f*) **Government:** Government is also interested in the allocation of resources and, therefore the activities of company. It also require information in order to regulate the activities of company, determine taxation policies and as the basis for national income.

(*g*) **Society:** Companies affect members of the society at large. Financial statements assist the public by providing information about the trends and recent developments in the prosperity of companies and the range of its activities.

Special Purpose Report

General purpose financial reporting aims to satisfy the information needs of all potential users. Company law provisions in almost all countries of the world have consistently accepted the utility of general purpose financial reporting. However, company can also prepare specific purpose report to serve the industrial stakeholders.

Specific purpose reports are criticized on following grounds:

(*i*) the cost of developing the specified reports to satisfy special requirements of specific users may exceed the benefits when the company financial reporting policy is determined in its totality.

(*ii*) specialized needs of specific users can not be ascertain with any degree of certainty.

(*iii*) issuing multiple reports about the financial results of an enterprise can create confusion among various users.

(*iv*) multiple reports may not be desirable and practicable from the standpoint of information economics.

Characteristics of Accounting Information

International Accounting Standard Committee (IASC) has outlined the following characteristics of an accounting information:

1. Relevance: Relevance is closely and directly related to the concept of useful information. Relevance implies that all those items of information should be reported that may help the users in making decisions and/ or predictions. In general, information that is given greater weight in decision making more relevant. Specially, it is information's capacity to make a difference that identifies its relevant to a decision. Relevance is defined as "the primary standards and requires that information must bear upon or be usefully associated with actions it is designed to facilitate or results desired to be produced".[1]

"Relevant Accounting information must be capable of making a difference in a decision by helping users to form predictions about the outcomes of past, present and future events or to confirm or correct expectations."[2]

2. Reliability: Reliability makes the accounting information useful for decision making. Reliable information is required to form judgments about the earning potential and financial position of a business firm. Reliability is that quality which permits users of data to depend upon it with confidence as representative of what is purports to represent. "The reliability of a measure rests on the faithfulness with which it represents, coupled with an assurance for the user that it has that representational quality. To be useful, information must be reliable as well as relevant. Degrees of reliability must be recognised. It is hardly ever a question of black or white, but rather of more reliability or less. Reliability rests upon the extent to which the accounting description or measurement is verifiable and representationally faithful. Neutrality of information also interacts with these two components of reliability to affect the usefulness of information."[3]

3. Understandability: Understandability is a quality of information that enables users to perceives its significance. The benefits of information may be increased by making it more understandable and hence useful to wider circle of users. Presentation of information should not only facilitate understanding but also avoid wrong interpretation of financial statements. Thus, understandable financial accounting information presents data that can be understood by the users of the information and is expressed in form and with terminology adapted to the user's range of understanding. The Corporate Reports observes: "Understandability does not necessarily mean simplicity, or that information must be presented in elementary terms, for that may not be consistent with the proper description of complex economic activities. It does mean that judgments need to be applied in holding the balance between the need to ensure that all material matters are disclosed and the need to avoid confusing users by the provision of too much detail. Understandability calls for the provision, in the clearest form, of all the information which the reasonably instructed reader can make use of and the parallel presentation of the main features for the use of the less sophisticated."

4. Comparability: Economic decisions requires making choice among possible courses of actions. In making decisions, the decision-maker has to make comparisons among available alternatives. This process which is facilitated by financial information. Comparability implies to have like things reported in a similar fashion and unlike things reported differently. The "primary objective of comparability should be to facilitate the making of predictions and financial decisions by creditors, investors and others."[4]

5. Consistency: Consistency of method over a period a period of time is valuable quality that makes accounting numbers more useful. Consistent use of accounting principles from one accounting period to another enhances the utility of financial statements to users by facilitating analysis and understanding of comparative accounting data. Lack of consistency produces lack of comparability. The value of inter-company comparisons is substantially reduced when material differences in income are caused by variations in accounting practices.

6. Neutrality: Neutrality is also known as a quality of "freedom from bias" or objectivity. Neutrality means that, in formulating or implementing standards, the primary concern should be the relevance and reliability of the information that results, not the effect that the new rule may have on a particular interest on user(s). A neutral choice between accounting alternatives is free from the bias towards a predetermined result. The objectives of (general purpose) financial reporting serves many different information users who have diverse interests, and no one predetermined result is likely to suit all usres' interests and purposes. Therefore, accounting facts and accounting practices should be impartially determined and reported with no objective of purposeful bias toward any user or user group. If there is no bias in selection of accounting information reported, it cannot be said to favour one set of interests over another. It may, in fact, favour certain interests, but only because the information points that way.

7. Materiality: It implies that not all financial information need or should be communicated in accounting reports-only material information should be reported. Information should be disclosed in the annual report which is likely to influence economic decisions of the users. Information that meets this requirement is material. Magnitude of the item by itself, without regard to the nature of the item and the circumstances in which the judgment has to be made, will not generally be a sufficient basis for a materiality judgment. Materiality judgments are primary and qualitative in nature. They are described as the relative quantitative importance of some piece of financial information to a user, in the context of the decision to be made.

8. Timeliness: Timeliness means having information available to decision-makers before it loses its capacity to influence decisions. Timeliness is an ancillary aspect of relevance. If the information is either not available long after the reported events that it has no value for future action, it lacks relevance and is of little or no use. Timeliness alone cannot make information relevant, but a lack of timeliness can rob information of relevance it might otherwise have had.

9. Verifiability: "Verifiable financial accounting information provides results that would be substantially duplicated by independent measures using the same measurement methods."[5] The quality of verifiability contributes to the usefulness of accounting information because the purpose of verification is to provide a significant degree of assurance that accounting measures represent, what they purport to represent.

10. Conservatism: Conservatism is generally referred to as a the conventions that many accountants believe to be appropriate in making accounting decisions. According to APB (USA) Statement 4:

"Frequently, assets and liabilities are measured in a context of significant uncertainties. Historically, managers, investors and accountants have generally preferred that possible errors in measurements be in the direction of understatement rather than overstatement of net income and net assets. This has led to the convention of conservatism.

Significance of Company Annual Report: Significance of company annual report are as follows:

(*i*) It is a medium of corporate reporting.

(*ii*) Annual report is regarded as an important source of information about a company's affairs.

(*iii*) Annual report is relatively more and easily assessable than any other source of information.

(*iv*) Annual report contains audited information which creates confidence among the public.

(*v*) Annual report provides detailed information including financial statements. Other important information also includes historical summary, statistical data, important business results, company's plans and policies which are not available in other sources of information.

(*vi*) Annual reports and statements therein help the professional analyst and rating agencies etc. to predict company's future share prices and the related cash flows to the investors.

Benefits of Financial Reporting: Benefits of financial reporting are as follows:

1. Help in Decisions Making: Mautz and May observes: "Financial disclosure is essential to the functioning of a free enterprise economy. One aspect of a market oriented economy is the allocation of capital on a market basis. Financial disclosure is required to support a viable capital market. Indeed, without adequate financial disclosure there is real question whether significant amounts of capital could be formed. In addition, a viable capital market is essential to resource allocation within the economy. It is the capital market that a major portion of the nation's resources are allocated to those company which serve customers effectively, and capital is refused to those companies who do not serves customers effectively."

2. Cost of Capital: Adequate disclosure in annual reports to enhances the market price of shares of the company share in the long run. Full disclosure have a favourable impact on the company's cost of capital. Thus, as investment or confidence in the company is high. High share prices help the company to enjoy the benefits of the capital market like charging premium on issue of equity capital or pay lower or competitive rate of interest on debt capital. It also enhances the future marketability of subsequent issue of company's shares.

"Consistently good financial reporting should have a favorable long run effect's on the company's cost of capital – Over a period of time, good reporting leads to informed investors who, because they understand the company, will pay a fair price for its securities..... Minimum or inconsistent reporting often leads to some loss of investor's confidence in the quality of company information and, ultimately in the price they will pay in the market. Credibility is a subtle intangible of great importance to any company, corporate reporting practices have a major effect on it. We have often observed this connection between credibility, corporate reporting, and the cost of capital. Good corporate reporting is a log term policy applicable to good times and bad."[6]

3. Control on volatility of share prices: Adequate disclosure help in controlling volatility in the share prices of the company. Fluctuations in share prices occur because of the ignorance prevailing in the investment market. Fluctuations show an element of uncertainty in investment decisions. If the securities market are in possession of full information, the ignorance and uncertainty will be reduced and share prices will tend to maintain equilibrium. It also help in preventing fraud and manipulations and control the chances of their occurrences.

4. Managerial Regulating Decisions: Financial reports help in regulating the behaviour of managers of companies. Shareholders prefer accounting procedures that mirror economic events as closely as possible. However, shareholders also must be concerned that managers might manipulate the reported data to increase their compensation.

Interim Financial Reporting

The aim of interim reports is to provide users with more timely information about companies so as to alleviate the disadvantages of the time lag between annual reports. The financial reports play an important role in security investment decisions. Changes in share prices, following the disclosure of quarterly earnings are greater than share average price changes during the year.

Thrust Areas of Corporate Financial Reporting

1. MDA Reporting: Disclosures about the 'Management Discussions and Analysis' are to ensure that there is transparency in company's financial performance and provide the investors with the disclosure necessary to evaluate a company and to make informed investment decisions. The financial statements along with brief accompanying footnotes alone are not sufficient to judge the quality of earnings and the likelihood of past performance being indicative of future performance. The ordinary investor needs narrative explanations to understand the performance and the environment in which the firm operates. 'The Management Discussion and Analysis' part in the annual report fulfils this objective as it explains the performance and actions of the company in descriptive terms. MD & A is intended to give the investor an opportunity to look at the company through the eyes of management by providing both short-and long-term analysis of the business of the company. The item asks management to discuss the dynamics of the business and to analyze the financials.

The MD & A is a very important section of an annual report, especially for those analyzing the fundamentals which include management and management style. Although this action contains useful information, but investors must be cautious as the section is unaudited. Among other things, the MD & A provides an overview of the previous year of operation and how the company fared in that time period. Management will usually also touch on the upcoming year, outlining future goals and approaches to new projects. As a preface to the financial statements, a company's management discussion and analysis (MD & A). Report regarding management discussion and analysis contains forward looking statement which may be identified by their use of words like plans; expects; will, anticipates, believes; intends, projects, estimates or other words having similar meaning. All statements that address expectations or projections about the future, including but not limited to statements about the company's strategy for growth, product development, market position, expenditures, and financial results, are forward-looking statements.

Clause 49 of listing agreement between a company and the stock exchange in which the securities of the company are listed requires the publication of the MD & A and specific that, within the limit set by the companies competitive position, it should discuss the following: industry structure and developments; opportunities and threats; segment-wise and product-wise performance; outlook; risks and concerns; internal control systems and their accuracy; discussion on financial performance with respect to operational performance; and material developments in human resources/industrial relations front, including the number of people employed.

Given this broad scope, the inclusion of MD & A in the annual report definitely has the potential of immensely increasing transparency in corporate reporting. This is the result of a lack of any specific disclosure norms in Clause 49 beyond the mere specification of the issues to be discussed.

The fundamental expectation from MD & As is that they will present an analysis of the business as seen through the eyes of the board of directors. Therefore, it is appropriate that elements of information used in managing the company, including subsidiary companies, should be disclosed in the report. In taking managerial decisions, board of directors use non-financial information extensively. Unfortunately, companies are extremely reluctant to disclose this non-financial information unless compelled by a specific regulatory directive.

In May 2005, the Accounting Standards Board (ASB) of the UK issued Reporting Standard-1 that set out the reporting standard for Operating and Financial Review (OFR)- a report similar to our MD & A. The standard, requires listed companies to provide information similar to that required by the Indian Clause 49. However, this standard goes beyond regulations like Clause 49 in two important ways. First, it also requires listed companies to provide information about environmental matters and about social and community issues. This will help shareholders of a company to know whether their company gives only lip service to 'sustainability and development' or really incorporates these concerns in its business strategy. It is also expected that the standard will force companies to provide quantitative details of investment in 'corporate social responsibility', thereby allowing a more transparent evaluation of its actual commitment towards 'social responsibility'.

Even more importantly, the standard goes beyond just listing heads under which information should be provided to specifying concrete requirements that ensure the quality of disclosure. It requires listed companies to disclose key performance indicators (KPI) and to provide information that enables members (shareholders) to understand each KPI disclosed in the OFR. It requires that for each KPI disclosed in the OFR a company should provide the following information: the definition and its calculation method should be explained; its purpose should be explains; the source of underlying data should be disclosed and, where relevant, assumptions should be explained; quantification and commentary on future targets should be provided; where information from the financial statements has been adjusted for inclusion in the OFR, that fact should be high-lighted and a reconciliation should be provided; where available, corresponding amount for the financial year immediately preceding the current year should be disclosed; and any changes to KPIs should be disclosed and the calculation method used compared to previous financial years, including significant changes in the underlying policies adopted in the financial statements, should be identified and explained.

In preparing MD & As, companies should comply with the spirit of the requirement rather than a legalistic approach to compliance. In absence of a 'safe harbour' clause, the report is addressed to shareholders and not to investors in general to enforce accountability, but to avoid liability. The safe harbour clause protects directors from liabilities arising from an untrue statement of a material fact or omission of a material fact necessary to make the forward looking statement not misleading. Moreover, each company adds a cautionary statement that 'actual results could differ materially from those expressed or implied' to limit the potential liability of its board of directors. Therefore, companies should take innovative approach in presenting the report.

Forward-looking statements are based on certain assumptions and expectations of future events. The company cannot guarantee that these assumptions and expectations are accurate or will be realized. The company's actual results, performance or achievements could thus differ materially from those projects in any such forward-looking statements. The company assumes no responsibility to publicly amend, modify or revise the forward-looking statements, on the basis of any subsequent development, information or events.

2. Corporate Governance Report: SEBI code of Corporate Governance requires listed companies to include a separate section of corporate Governance in their annual reports. This section should include a detailed compliance report on Corporate Governance. The code provides the following suggested list of items to be included in the report: Composition and category of directors, number and attendance of Board of Directors (BOD) meeting and last Annual General Meeting (AGM). Term of reference, composition, meeting and attendance of the Audit committee. remuneration committee. Shareholders' grievances and redresses. Information on general body meetings. Disclosures on materially significant related party transactions and details of non-compliance by the company, penalties, and strictures imposed on the company by Stock Exchange or SEBI or any statutory authority. Information on means of communication to the shareholders and investors.

1. There shall be a separate section on Corporate Governance in the Annual Reports of company, with a detailed compliance report on Corporate Governance. Non-compliance of any mandatory requirement of this clause with reasons thereof and the extent to which the non-mandatory requirements have been adopted should be specifically highlighted.
2. The companies shall submit a quarterly compliance report to the stock exchanges within 15 days from the close of quarter as per the format. The report shall be signed either by the Compliance Officer or the Chief Executive Officer of the company.

Format of Quarterly Compliance Report on Corporate Governance

Name of the Company:

Quarter ending on:

Particulars	Clause of Listing agreement	Compliance Status Yes/No	Remarks
I. Board of Directors	49(I)		
(A) Composition of Board	49 (IA)		
(B) Non-executive Directors' compensation & disclosures	49 (IB)		
(C) Other provisions as to Board and Committee	49 (IC)		
(D) Code of Conduct	49 (ID)		
II. Audit Committee	49 (II)		
(A) Qualified & Independent Audit Committee	49 (IIA)		
(B) Meeting of Audit Committee	49 (IIB)		
(C) Powers of Audit Committee	49 (IIC)		
(D) Role of Audit Committee	49 (IID)		
(E) Review of Information by Audit Committee	49 (IIE)		
III. Subsidiary Companies	49 (III)		

Contd....

IV. Disclosures	49 (IV)		
(A) Basis of related party transactions	49 (IVA)		
(B) Board Disclosures	49 (IVB)		
(C) Proceeds from public issues, rights issues, preferential issues etc.	49 (IVC)		
(D) Remuneration of Directors	49 (IVD)		
(E) Management	49 (IVE)		
(F) Shareholders	49 (IVF)		
V. CEO/CFO Certification	49 (V)		
VI. Report on Corporate Governance	49 (VI)		
VII. Compliance	49 (VII)		

Compliance Process

1. The company shall obtain a certificate from either the auditors or practicing company secretaries regarding compliance of conditions of corporate governance as stipulated in this clause and anex the certificate with the directors' report, which is sent annually to all the shareholders of the company. The same certificate shall also be sent to the stock Exchanges along with the annual report filed by the company.
2. The non-mandatory requirements may be implemented as per the discretion of the company. However, the disclosures of the compliance with mandatory requirements and adoption (and compliance)/non-adoption of the non-mandatory requirements shall be made in the section on corporate governance of the Annual Report.

3. Quality Financial Reporting (QFR): Quality Financial Reporting refers to financial reporting which reflects the economics of the transactions undertaken by the enterprises in a reliable, transparent, understandable and comparable way. The quality of financial reporting information affects the functioning of the capital markets. High quality financial reporting strengthens investors' confidence, which allows them to reduce the risk premium they demand for investing money in corporate securities. This reduction in risk premium is translated into lower cost of capital for companies. Deficiencies in financial reporting foster uncertainty. Uncertainty creates risk, which motivates investors to demand a higher rate of return. This results in a higher cost of capital and lower security prices. The quality of corporate financial reporting is determined by many factors. Included among these factors are-the quality of generally accepted accounting principles (GAAP), the effectiveness of the financial regulatory authorities.

It is important to note that standards should be principles-based. It is not new. One of the key concerns raised by US accounting scandals like Enron was that US accounting standards had become 'rules-based', filled with specific details in an attempt to address as many potential contingencies as possible. This made standards longer and more complex, and led to arbitrary criteria for accounting treatments that allow companies to structure transactions to circumvent un-favourable reporting. Also, many standards specified so-called 'bright-line' accounting rules, which made the choice of treatment depend on percentage tests. For example, the US GAAP requires consolidation of financial statements where the investor holds more than 50 per cent of voting rights in the investee company. This shifted the goal of professional judgment from consideration of the best accounting treatment to the goal to achieve technical compliance.

4. Global Reporting Initiative (GRI): The Global Reporting Initiative (GRI) is long term multi stakeholders, international undertaking whose mission is to develop and disseminate globally applicable sustainability reporting guidelines for voluntary use by organization reporting on the economic, environmental and social dimensions of their activities, products and service. The GRI's sustainable reporting guidelines issued in June 2000 encompass the three linked elements of sustainability as they apply to an organization.

(i) **Economic:** Including for example, wages and benefits, labour productivity, job creation, expenditure on outsourcing and investment in training and other forms of human capital.

(ii) **Environmental:** Including for example, impact of processes products and services on air, water, land, biodiversity and human health.

(*iii*) **Social:** Including, for example, work place, health and safety, employee retention, labour rights and wages and working conditions at out sources operations.

In the current guidelines, these three elements are largely treated as separate reporting elements. However, GRI plans to move towards a reporting framework that links the economics, environmental and social elements to form a more integrated reporting structure.

5. International Financial Reporting Norms: The steady expansion of International Financial Reporting Standards (IFRS) as the way the world's companies report results continues apace. The days of troubles over implementation are past. But, with the great upheaval survival, companies are wondering if they are seeing all the benefits they had been promised and for which they had hoped.

"One of the biggest benefits is that the process of moving of IFRS in a multi-national has been a good learning process, identifying subtle differences which they had not realized before". "The process made people go back and look again at things they had been doing for years. They have discovered lots of items that had been assumed to be the same, but were not."

"Analysts can learn more about a company by seeing the options it takes in reporting as it embarks on a new financial path." "Understanding the rationale for making various financial reporting choices they require more time in reading the notes, and the implications of new reporting on data trends will most likely not be clear for two or three more years." The original goals of comparability and transparency around the world are still clung to but it is now obvious the full effects will take longer to emerge than was originally expected.

"On a general global scale there have clearly been moves towards comparability," "But financial statements are getting so complex that you can't see the wood for the trees. There is greater transparency but it can be less useful because of the increase in detail." And this has not helped the analyst community. "They seek the complexity as a nuisance," And the politics of implementation have not gone away either. "Standard-setting is about change management".

The Corporate Report (UK)

It is an important discussion paper covering the scope and aims of published financial reports. It deals with public accountability of economic entity, working concepts as a basis for financial reporting, and most suitable means of measuring and reporting the economic position, performance and prospects of the business entity. The Corporate Report's main findings are as follows:

(*i*) The basic philosophy and starting point of The Corporate Report is that financial statements should be appropriate to their expected use by potential users. In other words, they should attempt to satisfy the information needs of their users.

(*ii*) The report assigned responsibility for reporting to the 'economic entity' having an impact on society through its activities. The economic entities are itemized as: limited companies, listed and unlisted; pension schemes, charitable and other trusts, and not for profit organization; non-commercially oriented Central Government departments and agencies, partnership and other forms of unincorporated business enterprises; trade unions and trade and professional associations; local authorities and nationalized industries and other commercially oriented public sector bodies.

(*iii*) The report defined users as those having a reasonable right to information and whose information needs should be recognized by corporate reports. The users are identified as the equity investor group, the loan creditors group, the employee group, the analyst-adviser group, the business contact group, the government, and the public.

(*iv*) There are seven desirable characteristics are cited, namely, that the corporate report be relevant, understandable, reliable, complete, objective, timely, and comparable. These characteristics satisfy the fundamental objectives of annual reports set by the basic philosophy,

(*v*) Limitations of current reporting practices mentioned to make the users aware about the constraints of the report:

(*a*) A statement of value added, showing how the benefits of the efforts of an enterprise are shared among employees, providers of capital, the state and reinvestment.

(*b*) An employment report, showing the size and composition of the work force relying on the enterprise for its livelihood, the work contribution of employees, and the benefits earned.

(*c*) A statement of money exchanges with government, showing the financial relationship between the enterprise and the state.

(*d*) A statement of transactions in foreign currency, showing the direct cash dealing, between the United Kingdom and other countries.

(*e*) A statement of future prospects, showing likely future profit, employment, and investment levels.

(*f*) A statement of corporate objectives showing management policy and medium-term strategic targets.

(*vi*) There are six measurement bases (historic cost, purchasing power, replacement cost, net realization value, value to the firm, and net present value) against the three criteria (theoretical acceptability, utility , and practicality) of the report. However, it is accompanied by the use of general index adjustment.

Special features of corporate reporting practices as in India

Following are the special features of corporate reporting practices as in India:

1. Consolidated Financial Highlights: The scope of financial highlights includes extra ordinary internal financial developments, and integrated financial achievement performance with regard to operating revenue, net sales and services, earnings before interest and depreciation and amortization (EBIT)TA), profit before tax (PBT), return on capital employed (ROCE), profit after tax (PAT), minority interest, share of associate companies and extra ordinary items (PATMISACEI), return on net worth (RON), These information are available on comparative basis- -previous and Current Year. Graphical presentation of information is also available so that relevance parties can analyse the information and draw a conclusion thereof.

2. Chairman's Letter and Speech: It deals with introduction about global scenario, specific global scenario of industry in which company is working, domestic market condition, financial highlights of results, efforts already made to make the company more efficient and viable, precautions, proposed strategies, major breakthrough achieved by the company etc.

3. Corporate Information: It provides information with regard to the list of members of the Board of Directors. Generally names of chairman, managing director, non-executive independent director, chief financial officer, company secretary, auditors, solicitors, bankers and registered office of the company, are included in the corporate information.

4. Management Discussion and Analysis: It provides relevant information regarding major breakthrough, global acquisition, investment and divestment, market branding, market share and initiatives, company philosophy, key performance highlights, consolidated performance, key domestic and global developments, brands, product and services, research and development activities, quality initiatives, human resources, corporate social responsibility, fund raising technical initiatives, financial performance, consolidated performance, risk management, internal control outlook, cautionary statements states that the management of the company has prepared and responsible for the financial statements that appear in this report. These are in conformity with accounting principles generally accepted in India and, therefore may include, amounts based on informed judgements and estimates. The management also accepts responsibility for the preparation of other financial information that is included in this report. Statements in this Management Discussions and Analysis describing the company's objectives, projections, estimates and expectations may be 'forward looking statements' within the meaning of applicable laws and regulations. Management has based these forward looking statements on its current expectations and projections about future events. Such statements involve known and unknown risks, significant changes in the political and economic environment in India or key markets abroad, tax laws, litigations, labour relations, exchange rate fluctuations, interest and other costs and may cause actual results to differ materially.

5. Ten Years Financial Highlights: It makes a provision of financial highlights of last ten years. It is indicated on comparative basis. It is categorized on different segments like the earnings, what the company owned, network of the company and ratios. It facilitates the stakeholders specially investors and analysts to judge the performance of the company on the basis of its ten year performance.

6. Directors Report: It is addressed to the shareholders of the company. It includes reporting on global perspective and domestic scenario of the industry in which company is working. Company's operations-physical and financial achievements, acquisitions, investment and divestmen, issue of bonus /right shares, dividend and reserves, change in directorate, promoter group and research development, subsidiary companies, consolidation, Conservation of energy, technology absorption and foreign exchange earnings outgo. Particulars of employees, directors responsibility statements, auditors fixed deposits, share registrar and transfer agents, environment, health and safety, acknowledgements , Annexure to Directors Report-c List of group companies and information required under section 217 (1) (e) of the Indian Companies Act, 1956.

7. Corporate Governance: It highlights the company's philosophy's on corporate governance composition of the board of directors and meetings and audience of the members. Directors compensation, Committees of the Board like-audit committee, remuneration committee shareholders/investors grievances committee, Management-management discussion and analysis report, disclosure of material translation, accounting policies, insider trading, shareholders-disclosure regarding appointments and /or reappointment of directors, directors membership in other companies, information on general body meeting, details of capital market non compliance if any, unclaimed shares and dividends, governance of subsidiaries, CEO/CFO certification, auditors certificate on corporate governance, report on corporate governance etc.

8. Additional Shareholder Information: It is exclusively relate with the shareholders of the company. It deals with information like annual general meeting, financial calendar, dates of book closure, unclaimed dividend s for the last 7 years. Registrar and agents, share transfer system, GDR/ADRs. stock codes, listing details, market price date – stock exchange wise distribution of shareholding, categories of shareholders, plant location, address for correspondence, non mandatory requirements like- chairman's office, remuneration committee, financial results, whistle blower policy and auditors certificate on corporate governance, compliance with code on conduct, managing directors and chief financial officer certificate on corporate governance.

Certificate on Corporate Governance

To

The Members

ABC Co. Ltd.

Mumbai-400 030

Dear Sirs, We have examined the compliance of conditions of Corporate Governance by Crompton Greaves Limited, for the year ended 31 March 2010, as stipulated in Clause 49 of the Listing Agreement entered into by the Company with the Stock Exchanges.

The compliance of conditions of Corporate Governance is the responsibility of the Management. Our examination was limited to a review of the procedures and implementations thereof, adopted by the Company for ensuring compliance with the conditions of Corporate Governance as stipulated in the said clauses. It is neither an audit nor an expression of opinion on the financial statements of the Company.

In our opinion and to the best of our information and according to the explanations given to us and the representations made by the Directors and the Management, we certify that the Company has complied with the conditions of Corporate Governance as stipulated in Clause 49 of the above mentioned Listing Agreement.

We further state that such compliance is neither an assurance as to the future viability of the Company nor of the efficiency or effectiveness with which the Management has conducted the affairs of the Company.

For XYZ & Co.

Chartered Accountants

Registration No. 11000

Rammohan

Partner

Membership No.21000

Mumbai, 13 May 2010

Declaration of Compliance with Code of Conduct

This is to certify that all the Members of the Board of Directors and Senior Management (i.e. one level below the Executive Directors i.e. Vice President level) of the Company, have confirmed compliance with the Company's Code of Conduct during April 2009 to March 2010. The Company's Code requires every Member of the Board and Senior Management to:

- Fulfill the functions of their office with integrity as well as professionalism and exercise the powers attached thereto, with due care and diligence.
- Act in the best interests of, and fulfill their fiduciary obligations to the Company's shareholders, whilst also considering the interests of other stakeholders.
- Take informed business decisions based on independent judgment and in the best interests of the Company, not influenced by personal interest or gain.
- Respect the confidentiality of information and use utmost discretion whilst deciding its disclosure or dissemination, ensuring that no personal advantage or detriment to the Company results from the same.
- Make available to, and share information with fellow Directors/Executives when considered expedient in the best interests of the Company.
- Protect and use the Company's assets for legitimate business purposes and be alert to situations that could lead to loss or misuse of these assets.
- Minimise any situation or action that can create conflict of interests of the Company vis-à-vis personal interest or interests of associated persons, and make adequate disclosures, where necessary.
- Act in a manner that will protect the Company's reputation.
- Encourage reporting of behaviour, which is contrary to the Company's "Values", and ensure that the person reporting such violation is not aggrieved in any manner.
- Comply, in letter and spirit, with all applicable laws, rules and regulations, and also honour the philosophy of "good faith", guided by one's sense of right and wrong.
- Abide by the relevant terms of the Insider Trading Code formulated by the Company, and any other Code that may be formulated from time to time, as applicable.
- Adhere to the terms of the powers delegated by the Board.
- Whilst entering into contracts with Service Providers and Consultants, protect the arrangement for disclosure or dissemination of confidential information.
- Establish processes and systems for storage, retrieval and dissemination of documents, both in physical and electronic form, so that the obligations of this Code of Conduct are fulfilled.
- Raise concerns, if any, on the above issues, at a Board Meeting.

Sri Devdas

Managing Director

Mumbai, 13 May 2010

Management Director's and Chief Financial Officer's Certificate on Corporate Governance

To

The Board of Directors

ABC Co. Ltd

CERTIFICATE

We have reviewed the stand-alone and Consolidated financial results and the cash flow statement of ABC Co. Ltd for the financial year ended 31st March, 2010. and certify that:

(*a*) These results and statements, to the best of our knowledge and our belief:

(*i*) do not contain any materially untrue statement or omit any material fact or contain statements that might be misleading;

(*ii*) present a true and fair view of the Company's affairs and are in compliance with existing accounting standards, applicable laws and regulations.

(*b*) To the best of our knowledge and belief, there are no transactions entered into by the Company during the year, which are fraudulent, illegal or volatile of the Company's Code of Conduct.

(*c*) We accept responsibility for establishing and maintaining internal controls and have evaluated the effectiveness of the internal control systems of the Company and have disclosed to the Auditors and the Audit Committee, deficiencies in the design or operation of internal controls of which we are aware, and the steps taken and proposed to be taken to rectify these deficiencies.

(*d*) We have also indicated to the Auditors and the Audit Committee:

(*i*) significant changes in the internal controls with respect to financial reporting during the year and the achievement of adequate internal controls within the Company's ERP systems;

(*ii*) significant changes in accounting policies during the year, and these have been disclosed in the notes to the financial statements.

(*e*) To the best of our knowledge and belief, there are no instances of significant fraud involving either the Management or employees having a significant Role in the Company's internal control systems with respect to financial reporting.

Syam Gopal

Managing Director

Madan Gopal

Chief Financial Officer

Mumbai, 13 May 2010

9. Auditors Report: It deals with the audit report on the financial statement submitted by the company's auditors under section 227 of the Indian Companies Act 1956. Auditor is also required to submit an annexure dealing the a various aspects of the auditor's report. Format of auditor's report is given below:

We have audited the attached Balance Sheet of Crompton Greaves Limited as at 31st March, 2010, the Profit and Loss Account and also the Cash Flow Statement for the year ended on that date, annexed thereto. These financial statements are the responsibility of the Company's management. Our responsibility is to express an opinion on these financial statements based on our audit. We conducted our audit in accordance with auditing standards generally accepted in India. Those Standards require that we plan and perform the audit to obtain reasonable assurance about whether the financial statements are free of material misstatement. An audit includes examining, on a test basis, evidence supporting the amounts and disclosures in the financial statements. An audit also includes assessing the accounting principles used and significant estimates made by management, as well as evaluating the overall financial statement presentation. We believe that our audit provides a reasonable basis for our opinion.

In accordance with provisions of Section 227 of the Companies Act, 1956, we report that:

1. As required by the Companies (Auditor's Report) Order, 2003 and as amended by the Companies (Auditor's Report) (Amendment) Order, 2004 issued by the Central Government of India in terms of Section 227 (4A) of the Companies Act, 1956, we enclose in the Annexure, a statement on the matters specified in paragraphs 4 and 5 of the said Order.

2. Further to our comments in the Annexure referred to above, we report that:

(*a*) we have obtained all information and explanations, which to the best of our knowledge and belief were necessary for the purposes of our audit;

(*b*) in our opinion, proper books of account as required by law have been kept by the Company, so far as appears from our examination of those books;

(*c*) the Balance Sheet, the Profit and Loss Account and the Cash Flow Statement dealt with by this report are in agreement with the books of account;

(*d*) in our opinion, the Balance Sheet, the Profit and Loss Account and the Cash Flow Statement dealt with by this report comply with the accounting standards referred to in Section 211 (3C) of the Companies Act, 1956; and

(*e*) on the basis of the written representations received from directors of the Company as on 31st March, 2010, and taken on record by the Board of Directors, we report that none of the directors is disqualified as on 31st March, 2010, from being appointed as a director in terms of Section 274 (1)(g) of the Companies Act, 1956.

In our opinion, and to the best of our information and according to the explanations given to us, they said accounts, read together with the Significant Accounting Policies in Schedule 'A' and the Notes on the Balance Sheet and Profit and Loss Account in Schedule 'B', give the information required by the Companies Act, 1956, in the manner so required and give a true and fair view in conformity with the accounting principles generally accepted in India:

(*i*) in the case of the Balance Sheet, of the state of affairs of the Company as at 31st March, 2010;

(*ii*) in the case of the Profit and Loss Account, of the profit for the year ended on that date; and

(*iii*) in case of the Cash Flow Statement, of the cash flows for the year ended on that date.

For ABC & Co
CHARTERED ACCOUNTANTS
Registration No.11000
Rammohan
PARTNER
Membership

Mumbai, 13th May, 2010
No.21000

10. Financial Statements: Financial Statements include Balance Sheet, Profit and Loss Account, Cash flow statements and different schedules forming part of the balance sheet like schedule – 1. Share Capital Schedule 2. reserves and surpluses schedule. 3. Secured loans and schedule Unsecured loans and schedule 4. Fixed Assets Schedule 5. Investments.

Practice Questions

Objective Type Questions

1. Corporate Reporting is meant for:
   (*a*) General Purpose
   (*b*) Specific Purpose
   (*c*) Government Purpose
   (*d*) Social Purpose
2. Characteristics of Accounting Information does not deal with as per 9 ASC:
   (*a*) Relevance
   (*b*) Reliability
   (*c*) Profitability
   (*d*) Comparability
3. Section 217(1)(e) of Indian Companies deals with:
   (*a*) Corporate governance report
   (*b*) environmental report
   (*c*) list of group companies
   (*d*) forward looking statements

4. Auditor's Report is concerned with the section of Indian Companies Act:
   (*a*) 225 (*b*) 226
   (*c*) 227 (*d*) 228
5. Certificate on Corporate governance is to be signed by:
   (*a*) Managing Director and Company Auditor
   (*b*) Managing Director and Chief Finance Officer
   (*c*) Chief Finance Officer and Company and Auditor
   (*d*) Chief Finance Officer and Independent Director

Ans: 1. (a), 2. (c) 3. (c), 4. (c), 5. (b)

Short Answer Questions

1. What is corporate financial reporting?
2. What do you mean by special purpose report?
3. What do you mean by cautionary statement?
4. What is risk management committee?
5. What do you know by certificate of corporate governance?

Long Answer Questions

1. What is corporate financial reporting? Examine its rationale and limitations.
2. What is accounting information? Explain its characteristics.
3. Critically examine the corporate financial reporting practices in India.
4. What do you mean by Director's report? Explain its features and contents.
5. What do you mean by declaration of compliance with code of conduct? Explain its features.

References

1. American Accounting Association's Committee, A Statement of Basic Accounting Theory.
2. Financial Accounting Standards Board in its Concept No.1 (para 47, 1978).
3. FASB Concept No.2.
4. Hendriksen.
5. The Accounting Principles Board of USA.
6. A report for Arthur Anderson and Company.
7. Prof. Jawahar Lal, Corporate Financial Reporting, Theory and Practice, Taxman, 2nd edition, July 2005, p.449.

17 CORPORATE SOCIAL RESPONSIBILITY IN INDIA

Business enterprises are the basic cells of modern economic life and their phenomenal success in converting natural resources into economic wealth is quite important. These business enterprises are playing active role in transformational process of social and physical environment in the interest of society at large. Basically they are the institutional members of society. If individual members have an obligation to improve the level and standard of society, then corporates have also responsibility to enrich the society as per its requirements. They are also the citizens and citizens have civic duties and responsibilities. The corporate performance affects the economy and creates social problems. An equal amount of social responsibility is needed to match their social power. Business enterprises are expected to perform its role in an orderly manner so that they can have a claim for the well being of the society. Thus, the measurement and reporting of social performance of profit- oriented firms form the core of Corporate Social Responsibility (CSR).

Nature of Corporate Social Responsibility

The term Corporate Social Responsibility reflects the impact of a corporation's activities on society. This embodies the performance of its economic function and other actions taken to contribute to the quality of life. These activities may extend beyond meeting the letter of law due to the pressures of competition or the requirements of contracts.

'Corporate Social Responsibility is operating a business in a manner which meets or excels the ethical, legal, commercial and public expectations that a society has from the business.'

The term corporate social responsibility refers to the concept of business being accountable for how it managers the impact of its processes on stakeholders on a voluntary basis.

The NAA Committee (1977:2) has identified four major areas of social performance: community development, human resources, physical resources and environmental contribution, and product or service contributions. The responsibility of business itself indicates the desire to ensure the optimum use of resources, development and expansion, operation and management, promotion of research environment, and environmental management etc. Since corporates have to draw on the community in which they operate for all resources, they also have obligations to their multiple stakeholders. Stakeholders are defined as those who get affected by corporate policies and practices. It is acknowledged fact that business has not just financial accountability but also has the social and environmental responsibility. It is generally known as the triple bottom-line of good governance. The license to operate in the societies trust that an organisation will work in the best interest of the society. Society itself is increasingly being critical about the operating norms in the industry. Business cannot be seen as aggravating the problems of the merger, poverty, depletion of natural resources or inequities. Entry barriers, adverse judgment from judiciaries or Earlier, business was expected to serve the purpose of its stockholders as a creator of financial wealth. But now business is assigned to fulfill the expectations of different stakeholders like consumers, employees, shareholders, society, community, environment and government etc.

Need for Corporate Social Responsibility

The Indian corporate sector has seen the current decade as a period of high growth and the emergence of a strong India Inc. having a significant global footprint. The decade also saw the financial crisis that shook the global markets. While the corporate sector is recovering from the jolt of the global financial crisis, the future is looking bright. However, the corporate sector is also standing in the midst of a sustainability crisis that poses a threat to the very existence of business. What we have before us is a cross-road where one path leads us to inclusive growth and the other may lead to unsustainable future. However, the first path will require careful nurturing for which all stakeholders need to assume and discharge their respective responsibilities. Business sector generating wealth and value for the shareholders in the last sixty years, but simultaneously we also have the problems of poverty, unemployment, illiteracy, malnutrition etc. facing the nation. The corporate growth is sometimes seen as widening the gap between the India and Bharat through its income – skewing capability. This gap needs to be bridged. While the Government undertakes extensive developmental initiatives through a series of sectoral programmes, the business sector also needs to take the responsibility of exhibiting socially responsible business practices that ensures the distribution of wealth and well-being of the communities in which the business operates. The Indian business has traditionally been socially responsible. From inactive philanthropy to the incorporation of the stakeholders' interest in the business model, the Indian business sector practices various methods of discharging its social responsibility. While a lot of human and economic energy is available for utilization in this area, a suitable mechanism is required to channelize this energy for which the Government, corporate sector and the communities need to partner together.

The subject of Corporate Social Responsibility has evolved during last few decades from simple philanthropic activities to integrating the interest of the business with that of the communities in which it operates. By exhibiting socially, environmentally and ethically responsible behaviour in governance of its operations, the business can generate value and long term sustainability for itself while making positive contribution in the betterment of the society. Although, we have seen a period of sustained economic growth in the current decade, we still continue to face major challenges on the human side in India. The problems like poverty, illiteracy, malnutrition etc. have resulted in a large section of the population remaining as "un-included" from the mainstream. We need to address these challenges through suitable efforts and interventions in which all the state and non-state actors need to partner together to find and implement innovative solutions. Indian business has traditionally been socially responsible and some of the business houses have demonstrated their efforts on this front in a laudable manner. However, the culture of social responsibility needs to go deeper in the governance of the businesses.

Approaches Towards CSR

Approaches towards CSR are as follows:

1. Profit maximisation approach: The first approach originates in classical economic theory as expressed in the hypothesis that the firm has one and only one objective, which is to maximize profit. By extension, the objective of a company should be to maximize shareholders' wealth. In striving to attain this objective within the constraints of existing legal and ethical framework, business corporations are acting in the best interests of society at large. This classical interpretation of the concept of corporate social responsibility has been advocated as-there is one and only one social responsibility of business- to use its resources and engage in activities designed to increase its profit, as long as it stays within the rules of the game. Participation of corporates in open and free competition, without deception or fraud may be considered as an important aspect of the social responsibility. "Few trends could so thoroughly undermine the very foundations of our free society as the acceptance by corporate officials of a social responsible firm other than to make as much money for their shareholders as possible."[1]

2. Social objective approach: It was developed in the 1970s, recognizing the significance of social objectives in relation to the maximization of profit. According to this approach, corporate managers should make decisions which maintain an equitable balance between the claims of stakeholders viz., shareholders, employees, customers, suppliers and the general public. The corporation represents, therefore, a coalition of interests, and the proper consideration of the various interests of this coalition is the only way to ensure that the corporation will attain its long-term profit maximization objective.

3. Balancing approach: It regards profit as a means to an end, and not as an end in itself. The promoters/executives of a company have the problem of reconciling the demands of employees for more wages and improved benefit plans, customers for lower prices and greater values, shareholders for higher dividend and greater capital appreciation— all within a framework that will be constructive and acceptable to society. Balancing stakeholders needs understanding their concern, priporitising them and making them a part of the business process is essential. It is generally believed that industry cannot be an island of prospering in a sea of prosperity. Accordingly, "organizational decisions should be concerned with the selection of socially responsible alternatives. Instead of seeking to maximize profit generally, the end result should be a satisfactory level of profit which is compatible with the attainment of a range of social goals."[2]

Trusteeship model of Mahatma Gandhi also advocates that whereby the wealth you create has to be ploughed back for the benefit of society. In fact, today the debate is not about whether corporates need to take on social responsibility, because that is taken as given, but how this responsibility is to be discharged and how it is to be measured, audited and continuously improved upon. It is a fact that, the success of companies is measured by their turnover, size, market capitalization, profit after tax or shareholder value created. But the real purpose of business corporations is to improve the quality of life in society. How and to what extent corporates have improved the life of society al large is to be analysed, interpreted and reported in proper manner is one of the main theme of modern business.

Scope of CSR

Ernst and Ernst have identified six areas in which corporate social responsibility is expected: [3]

Environment. (ii) Energy (iii) Fair business practices (iv) Human resources (v) Community involvement (vi) Product.

(i) **Environment:** This area involves the environmental aspects of production, covering pollution control in the conduct of business operations, prevention or repair of damage to the environment resulting from processing of natural resources and the conservation of natural resources. Corporate social objectives are to found in the abatement of the negative external social effects of industrial production, and in adopting more efficient technologies to minimize the use of irreplaceable resources and the reduction of waste.

(ii) **Energy:** This area covers conservation of energy in the conduct of business operations and increasing the energy efficiency of the company's products.

(iii) **Fair business practices:** This area concerns the relationship of the company to special interest groups. In particular it deals with:

(*a*) Employment of minorities, (b) advancement of minorities, (c) employment of women (d) advancement of women (e)employment of other special interest groups (f) support for minority business (g) socially responsible practices abroad.

(iv) **Human resources:** This area concerns the impact of organizational activities on the people who constitute the human resources of the organization. These activities include:

(a) Recruiting practices, (b) training programmes, (c) experience building- job rotation, (d) job enrichment, (e) wage and salary levels, (f) fringe benefit plans, (g) congruence of employee and organizational goals, (h) mutual trust and confidençe, (i) job security, stability of workforce, layoff and recall practices, (j) transfer and promotion policies, (k) occupational health.

(v) **Community involvement:** This area involves community activities, health-related activities, education and the arts and other community activity disclosures.

(vi) **Products:** This area concerns the qualitative aspects of the products, for example their utility, life-durability, safety and serviceability, as well as their effect on pollution. Moreover, it includes customer satisfaction, truthfulness in advertising, completeness and clarity of labeling and packaging. Many of these considerations are already important from a marketing point of view. It is clear, however, that the social responsibility aspect of the product contribution extends beyond what is advantageous from a marketing angle.

Objectives of CSR

Objectives of CSR are as follow:

1. To identify and measure the periodic net social contribution of an individual firm, which includes not only the social costs and benefits internalized to the firm, but also those arising from externalities affecting different social segments;

2. To help in determining an individual firm's strategy and practices, which directly affect the relative resource and power status of individuals, communities, social segments and generations are consistent with widely shared social priorities, on the one hand and individuals' legitimate aspirations on the other; and

3. To make available in an optimal manner to all social constituents relevant information on a firm's goals, policies, programmes, performance and contribution to social goals.

There has been a long-standing debate over scope of the corporate social responsibility but it is a fact that its scope is affected by the change available in the business environment. Social responsibility of business is a continuous process as the business is a regular and on-going activity and it is composed of two-way traffic. The business as well as the different sections of the society have mutual interests.

Conceptual Framework of Corporate Citizenship

The growing domination of global economic forces is pushing business to acquire greater responsibility for social well-being. As a result, a new concept is emerging in the new millennium: 'Corporate Citizenship' resembling the 'Corporate Social Responsibility.' A company's reputation in terms of corporate citizenship can be a key asset in attracting and retaining customers, opening up new markets, and attracting and retaining a loyal and productive workforce. Corporates which fail to undertake this social responsibility face the prospects of shrinking consumer base and consequently profits. Some of the world's most successful companies, including Shell, Nike, Union Carbide and Exxon, operating entirely within the law have experienced devastating public relations and disasters due to negative public perceptions of their social responsibility. These perceptions have hurt the reputation and credibility of these companies, and correspondingly shareholders' value.

"CSR encourages increased understanding and active participation of corporates in equitable social development as an integral part of good business practice. It focuses on finding ways for corporates to behave in a manner that maximizes their society's wealth and consequently stake holders' value."[4] Corporate Social Responsibility is a continuing commitment by business to behave ethically and contribute to economic development while improving the quality of life of the workforce and their families as well as of the local community and society at large. Corporate Social Responsibility is considered a must for any company under the public gaze.

CSR is not a concept Indian corporates are unfamiliar with, though their activities may not always have borne the CSR tag. For instance, as long back as the 1920s, Tata Steel was engaged in philanthropic activities like maternity benefits, payment of provident fund, working hours etc. on which legislation was later enacted by government. Today, in post-liberalisation era, more companies have begun thinking on similar lines. With MNCs (multi-national corporations) focusing on CSR, many Indian corporates now keep aside sums ranging from 0-15 per cent of their profits after tax for CSR. Understanding of Corporate Social Responsibility is a fledgling area of serious economic activity.

"Corporate responsibility norms seem to rise as wealth increases. Growing demand for more responsible corporate behaviour creates business opportunities. Firms that meet the demand at an early stage stand to win; laggards are put at risk."[5] A company that puts the interests of its stakeholders first through good corporate governance finds its stock more attractive to investors.

The manner in which the business community is contributing to the developmental issues is also undergoing a change. The old style paternalistic philanthropy of 'doing for the community'— building schools and hospitals in the name of the company's founder– is giving way to the idea of 'working with the community'. These ideas include: sharing marketing, technical and managerial skills; using communities as channel members to distribute the company's products; setting up ancillary units managed by communities and supplying products and using employees as volunteers, trainers and mentors. In simple terms, being socially responsible makes good business sense and firms could be rewarded by increased patronage. Corporates are expected to continuously improve their social, environmental and financial performance. The criteria of CSR as considered by companies includes environment, health and safety, sustainable development, human rights, ethics, gender equity, customer relations, etc. The World Business Council for Sustainable Development in its publication "Making Good Business Sense" clearly stated how Companies behaviour affects many people, including the flora and fauna, and not just the shareholders. A company should be a responsible member of the society in which it operates. That means contributing to sustainable development by working to improve the quality of life of employees, their families, the local community and stakeholders up and down the supply chain. It can mean a day-care facility for working mothers, a new clinic, health insurance, playgrounds; it can also mean bio-degradable packaging, cleaner fuel for buses and trucks, community tree plantation drives, reduced water and energy consumption.

Regulatory Base of CSR: Regulatory base of CSR is given below:

1. **Legislation:** It outlaws undesirable social activities. Many examples exist of public concern with undesirable features of business activity, and of legislation to suppress such activities. For example, legislation relating to child labour in India has made employment of a child less than 14 years as illegal.
2. **Licensing systems:** They may be employed to limit the extent of activities which are useful to society, but present a potential social problem. The licensing of lorries, for example, has been made the subject of certificates of road-worthiness, and attention is now being paid to the control of exhaust emission. Thus, licensing may be qualitative as well as quantitative.
3. **Taxation:** Taxation is a convenient manner of internalising external social costs of activities having negative effects on society. The objective is to impose taxes on the firm equal in magnitude to the damage sustained by society from the firm's activities. The obvious purpose of such taxes would be to encourage firms to abate the effects of such activities or, alternatively, to finance public programmes for controlling these effects. There should be a tariff of taxes designed to encourage firms to locate an area where their methods of production would do least harm to the environment. Environment Protection Control Act, 1988 has made necessary provisions with regard to pollution control process in India.

Corporate Social Communication Process

Social Performance Reports are the latest trend in corporate communication indicating the level of compliance of social responsibility. The growing popularity of corporate social reporting and organisations' desire to know their stakeholders' view on corporate social performance suggests two possibilities.

(*i*) that stakeholders are interested in corporate behaviour, and business attitudes are changing from a predominantly managerial emphasis to collaborative one.

(*ii*) that there is an infrastructure of management information systems underpinning the whole process of reporting and providing the information behind organisationl decision-making. Social accounting systems identify and measure social performance. If an organization then chooses to disclose this information in the interests of transparency and openness, its stakeholders must be confident that the information is true.

Reliable information systems reduce the risk that reporting of inaccurate information could damage the firm's reputation. Many organizations collect information that is pertinent to stakeholder groups, but all of them do not disclose it. Corporate attitudes towards stakeholders are changing; rather than holding stakeholders at arm's length, many organizations are now seeking to engage with them. It is a definite change from the hostile encounters that gave rise to early forms of social auditing and reporting. Stakeholders are becoming more articulate about their interests and concerns, and organizations are getting better at communicating about social performance issues. "Corporate social reporting is increasingly popular for communicating data about social performance of corporates to multiple constituents. The wave of corporate communication is under-pinned by existing management information system. But while popular management accounting tools are being used for social responsibility decision-making, they require skillful adaptation if they are to demonstrate transparency and accountability. They have to perceive the value of business as holistic and not additive."[6] The organizations take advantage of their good social reputation in their marketing campaigns.

Social image of organisations is extremely important for several stakeholder groups. The groups they identified are similar in all forms of organizations: communities, customers, employees, environment, shareholders and suppliers. But the priority given to different stakeholder groups varies. The organizations are planning to develop links between the externally- reported measures and their internal reporting. But, despite lacking such a system, the firms are concerned about their social performance. Barry H. Spicer suggest that following measures are required to ensure effective compliance of social responsibility. "[7]

Action Plan for CSR

(*i*) Establish an implementation team that includes a management accountant and managers. A manager should lead this. Consult managers about the social information and performance measures they need, (ii) develop links between the organization's mission statement/objectives and its internally reported social performance measures, (iii) develop internal social performance measures for each of organisation's stakeholder groups, (iv) check that the internally reported social performance measures include both input and output measures, (v) set up a system for the internal monitoring and management of social performance, (vi) develop explicit links between managers' evaluation and their contribution to the organisation's social performance.

"The social values and culture of an organization are critical factors affecting its social performance- often through informal group control and self-control."[8] External social reporting is important, but so is management information on social performance. Ultimately, it is the strategic and operating decisions of managers and other employees that determine the social performance of an organization.

Voluntary Guidelines for Corporate Social Responsibility

The Ministry of Corporate Affairs has issued voluntary guidelines for the corporate social responsibility in 2009. These guidelines are as follows: [9]

Preamble

The 21st century is characterized by unprecedented challenges and opportunities, arising from globalization, the desire for inclusive development and the imperatives of climate change. Indian business, which is today viewed globally as a responsible component of the ascendancy of India, is poised now to take on a leadership role in the challenges of our times. It is recognized the world over that integrating social, environmental and ethical responsibilities into the governance of businesses ensures their long term success, competitiveness and sustainability. This approach also reaffirms the view that businesses are an integral part of society, and have a critical and active role to play in the sustenance and improvement of healthy ecosystems, in fostering social inclusiveness and equity, and in upholding the essentials of ethical practices and good governance. This also makes business sense as companies with effective CSR, have image of socially responsible companies, achieve sustainable growth in their operations in the long run and their products and services are preferred by the customers. Indian entrepreneurs and business enterprises have a long tradition of working within the values that have defined our nation's character for millennia. India's ancient wisdom, which is still relevant today, inspires people to work for the larger objective of the well-being of all stakeholders. These sound and all-encompassing values are even more relevant in current times, as organizations grapple with the challenges of modern-day enterprise, the aspirations of stakeholders and of citizens eager to be active participants in economic growth and development.

CSR is not philanthropy and CSR activities are purely voluntary- what companies will like to do beyond any statutory requirement of obligation. To provide companies with guidance in dealing with the abovementioned expectations, while working closely within the framework of national aspirations and policies, following Voluntary Guidelines for Corporate Social Responsibility have been developed. While the guidelines have been prepared for the Indian context, enterprises that have a trans-national presence would benefit from using these guidelines for their overseas operations as well. Since the guidelines are voluntary and not prepared in the nature of a prescriptive road-map, they are not intended for regulatory or contractual use. While it is expected that more and more companies would make sincere efforts to consider compliance with these Guidelines, there may be genuine reasons for some companies in not being able to adopt them completely. In such a case, it is expected that such companies may inform their stakeholders about the guidelines which the companies have not been able to follow either fully or partially. It is hoped that "India Inc." would respond to these Guidelines with keen interest.

After considering the experience of adoption of these guidelines by Indian Corporate Sector and consideration of relevant feedback and other related issues, the Government may initiate the exercise for review of these Guidelines for further improvement after one year.

Guidelines

Fundamental Principle

Core Elements: Each business entity should formulate a CSR policy to guide its strategic planning and provide a roadmap for its CSR initiatives, which should be an integral part of overall business policy and aligned with its business goals. The policy should be framed with the participation of various level executives and should be approved by the Board.

The CSR Policy should normally cover following core elements:

1. Care for all Stakeholders: The companies should respect the interests of, and be responsive towards all stakeholders, including shareholders, employees, customers, suppliers, project affected people, society at large etc. and create value for all of them. They should develop mechanism to actively engage with all stakeholders, inform them of inherent risks and mitigate them where they occur.

2. Ethical functioning: Their governance systems should be underpinned by Ethics, Transparency and Accountability. They should not engage in business practices that are abusive, unfair, corrupt or anti-competitive.

3. Respect for Workers' Rights and Welfare: Companies should provide a workplace environment that is safe, hygienic and humane and which upholds the dignity of employees. They should provide all employees with access to training and development of necessary skills for career advancement, on an equal and non-discriminatory basis. They should uphold the freedom of association and the effective recognition of the right to collective bargaining of labour, have an effective grievance redressal system, should not employ child or forced labour and provide and maintain equality of opportunities without any discrimination on any grounds in recruitment and during employment.

4. Respect for Human Rights: Companies should respect human rights for all and avoid complicity with human rights abuses by them or by third party.

5. Respect for Environment: Companies should take measures to check and prevent pollution; recycle, manage and reduce waste, should manage natural resources in a sustainable manner and ensure optimal use of resources like land and water, should proactively respond to the challenges of climate change by adopting cleaner production methods, promoting efficient use of energy and environment friendly technologies.

6. Activities for Social and Inclusive Development: Depending upon their core competency and business interest, companies should undertake activities for economic and social development of communities and geographical areas, particularly in the vicinity of their operations. These could include: education, skill building for livelihood of people, health, cultural and social welfare etc., particularly targeting at disadvantaged sections of society.

Implementation Guidance

1. The CSR policy of the business entity should provide for an implementation strategy which should include identification of projects/activities, setting measurable physical targets with timeframe, organizational mechanism and responsibilities, time schedules and monitoring. Companies may partner with local authorities, business associations and civil society/non-government organizations. They may influence the supply chain for CSR initiative and motivate employees for voluntary effort for social development. They may evolve a system of need assessment and impact assessment while undertaking CSR activities in a particular area. Independent evaluation may also be undertaken for selected projects/activities from time to time.

2. Companies should allocate specific amount in their budgets for CSR activities. This amount may be related to profits after tax, cost of planned CSR activities or any other suitable parameter.

3. To share experiences and network with other organizations the company should engage with well established and recognized programmes/platforms which encourage responsible business practices and CSR activities. This would help companies to improve on their CSR strategies and effectively project the image of being socially responsible.

4. The companies should disseminate information on CSR policy, activities and progress in a structured manner to all their stakeholders and the public at large through their website, annual reports, and other communication media.

Recommendations of Standing Committee of Parliament on Finance (SCF)

The standing committee of Parliament on finance which has thoroughly examined the Companies Bill 2009 on the extent which of Corporate Social Responsibility (CSR) being undertaken by corporates and the need for a comprehensive CSR policy, the Ministry of Corporate Affairs have agreed that the Bill may now include provisions to mandate that every company having [(net worth of Rs. 500 crore or more, or turnover of Rs.1000 crore or more)] or [a net profit of Rs. 5 crore or more during a year] shall be required to formulate a CSR Policy to ensure that every year at least 2% of its average net profits during the three immediately preceding financial years shall be spent on CSR activities as may be approved and specified by the company. The Directors shall be required to make suitable disclosures in this regard in their report to members. In case any such company does not have adequate profits or is not in a position to spend prescribed amount on CSR activities, the directors would be required to give suitable disclosure/reasons in their report to the members.

While welcoming the Ministry's acceptance of the Committee's suggestion to bring Corporate Social Responsibility (CSR) in the statue itself, the Committee feels that separate disclosures required to be made by companies in their Annual Report by way of CSR statement indicating the company policy as well as the specific steps taken there under will be a sufficient check on non-compliance.

Practice Questions

1. CSR is:
   (*a*) The integration of social and environmental concerns in to the daily business of the company
   (*b*) The same as business ethics
   (*c*) A theory about ethics
   (*d*) The title of a Government committee
2. A difference between corporate and unit objectives is:
   (*a*) Multiple objectives might well be more common at the unit rather than the corporate level.
   (*b*) Unit level objectives will be more financially focused.
   (*c*) Corporate level objectives will be less financial.
   (*d*) Unit level objectives will be set by corporate managers
3. Voluntary guidelines for corporate social responsibility was issued in:
   (*a*) 2007 (*b*) 2008
   (*c*) 2009 (*d*) 2010
4. Number of areas identified by the Ernest and Ernest in corporate social responsibility are:
   (*a*) 4 (*b*) 5
   (*c*) 6 (*d*) 7
5. Making Good Business sense was published by:
   (*a*) Indian Development Council
   (*b*) UNO Council for Social Development
   (*c*) World Business Council
   (*d*) American Institute of Policy Research

Ans: 1. (a), 2. (a), 3. (c), 4. (c), 5. (c)

Short Answer Questions

1. What is Corporate Social Responsibility?
2. Examine the different approaches of corporate social responsibility.
3. Explain the scope of corporate social responsibility.
4. Discuss the objective of corporate social responsibility.
5. What is corporate citizenship?
6. What do you mean by corporate social communication process?
7. Explain the major problems in corporate social responsibility.

Long Answer Questions

1. "Corporate should be socially accountable" Comment on this statement.
2. What do you mean by Corporate Social Responsibility? Examine its different approaches.
3. What is Corporate Social Responsibility? Evaluate its scope.
4. Explain the nature of Corporate Social Responsibility. Also examine its objectives.
5. What do you mean by corporate citizenship? Examine the regulatory base of corporate social responsibility.
6. Examine the process of corporate social communication. Also evaluate the issues involved in corporate social responsibility.
7. Critically examine the different aspects of corporate social responsibility in Indian scenario.

References

1. Friedman, M, Capitalism and Freedom, Chicago: University of Chicago Press, (1962), p.123
2. Ramnathan, K.V., "Towards a Theory of Corporate Social Accounting," The Accounting Review, July, 1996
3. Ernst, & Ernst, Social Responsibility Disclosure— Survey. Cleve land, Ohio, (1978), p.70
4. Dewhurst, J., "The Green Resource Audit," The Accountant, October, (1989), p.89
5. Accounting Standards Committee, "The Corporate Report" Institute of Chartered Accounts in England and Wales, (1975), p.102
6. Ditzler, Patricia "Corporate Social Performance," Management Accountant, February, (1983), p.119
7. Spicer, Barry H. "Investors' Corporate Social Performance and Information Disclosure", The Accounting Review, January, (1978), p.145
8. Rearce, D.W.A. Markandaya and E.B. Barlier, "Blueprint for a Green Economy", Earth Scan, (1989)
9. Voluntary Guidelines on Corporate Social Responsibility, Ministry of Corporate Affairs, 2009, p.7-10

18 MANAGEMENT DISCUSSIONS AND ANALYSIS

Traditionally, the centric approach of accounting has been to fulfill the needs and expectations of investors. Indeed, it was based on the premise that the maximization of shareholders' 'wealth is an appropriate guide for achieving the objective of the firm. Similarly, financial reports also tried to provide relevant information to management but it was largely confined to the decisions about investors and creditors. "The changing social environment has been concerned with the social imbalance between those having wealth and controlling society through the influence of wealth and those whose political influence in numerical terms has secured the return of governments committed to reforms and the gradual redistribution of wealth."[1] In effect this imbalance has forced the management to go for stakeholders interest in place of stockholders interest. Management is now supposed to communicate adequate and necessary information to those who have stake in the firm: investors, creditors, bankers, employees, government, society etc. Management is also required to disclose relevant information due to authoritative pronouncements, regulatory rules, or custom or because it considers it useful to stakeholders and discloses it voluntarily. It is notable that financial statements alone are not sufficient to communicate overall performance of an entity. Senior management, boards of directors and investors now turn to a broad array of information in order to explain and evaluate the overall performance and prospects of an organization. In this context, Management's Discussion and Analysis (MD & A) being used as the communication package for external reporting purposes. Management Discussion and Analysis is mandatory for the companies to disclose under SEBI Listing Agreement, Clause 49.

The modern corporate behaviour is based on a system of trust and confidence of stakeholders. However, corporates are also required to fulfill the objective of long term sustainability and shareholders value. The system of corporate stewardship works effectively only when shareholders have a high level of confidence that their representatives are managing the affairs of company in their interest. "To win this level of confidence corporate leaders need a set of tools that provides greater transparency and insight into the working of management. Management Discussion and Analysis (MD & A) reporting provide a sound base for satisfying the need of stakeholders. Strong corporate governance practices have set a model for corporate disclosure. The corporate governance has also helped in improving the financial reporting structure. Existing investors and potential investors both expect information in an analytical form and want to see the inner picture of the company through the eyes of management. The financial statements along with the brief accompanying footnotes alone are not sufficient to judge the quality of earnings and the likelihood of past performance being indicative of the future performance. The shareholders and related parties are always eager to know whether the management is doing its best towards performance and profitability of the company or whether the business is conducted to promote their economic interest. These requirements actually created a platform for the Development of Discussion and Analysis Reporting through the eyes of management.

The 'Management Discussion and Analysis' form a part in the annual report to fulfill the above objective as it explains the performance and actions of the company in descriptive terms. The MD & A is intended to give the investor an opportunity to look at the company through the eye of management by providing both short and long term analysis of the business of the company. It also asks the management to discuss the dynamics of the business and to analyze its financial implications." Disclosures under the 'Management Discussions and Analysis' are to ensure that there is transparency in company's financial performance and also provide sufficient information to the investors for evaluating a company and thus making informed investment decisions.

The MD & A is a very important section of an annual report, especially for those analyzing the fundamentals of the company. It also include management perception and its style. However, investors must be cautious as the section is unaudited. The MD & A provides an overview of the previous year of operation and how the company fared in that time period. Management usually also touches on the upcoming year, outlining future goals and approaches to new projects. By the virtue of being family owned and managed, in most Indian companies, in 1920's and 1930's the executives and directors were either the promoters themselves or their kith and kin – people they trusted. However, the regulators still lacks the teeth to police the markets effectively. There is no alternative to truly independent watch dogs. It is because auditors, rating agencies, and the banks faced conflicts of interest that they failed to blow the whistle. Corporate management needs to clear up their acts and draw-up plans to tackle their conflicts of interests.

The purpose of the MD & A is to enhance financial reporting, mainly in the Annual Report, by providing a high level overview of the financial results and health of a company. The MD & A is information that accompanies financial statements as part of an entity's financial reporting. It explains the main trends and factors underlying the development, performance and position of the entity's business during the period covered by the financial statement. It also explain the main trends and factors that are likely to affect the entities future development, performance and position. "The MD & A report, when prepared properly provides users of financial statements with additional information and data, explaining the company's results of operations and financial conditions for those periods being reported. Management's discussion is candid and open and free of boilerplate messages, which explains and elaborates on the company's financial performance and condition." The disclosure in MD & A is of paramount importance in increasing the transparency of company's financial performance and providing investors with the disclosure necessary to evaluate a company and to make informed investment decisions. MD & A also provides a unique opportunity for management to provide appreciation of what the financial statements shows and not show, as well as important trends and risks that have shaped the past or reasonably likely to shape the future. It provides forward looking information about the company's operations and strategic plan to achieve certain operating targets. MD & A enables users of financial statement to predict future earnings and / or cash flows with more accuracy, and improve their ability to make well informed investment decisions.

Conceptual Framework of MD & A

A section of Annual Report where the company's management provides insight as to expected future developments, analysis of result of operations, and its financial positions, including cash flows, liquidity, and capital resources. Every publicly listed company in India is required to supplement financial statements in its annual reports with a Management Discussion and Analysis Report (MD & A) covering the performance and prospects of the firms in non financial terms.

"Clause 49 (Corporate Governance) of the listing agreements between the company and the stock exchange in which the securities of that companies are listed requires the publication of the MD & A and specifies that, within the limits set by the companies competitive positions, it should discuss' industries structure and development ; opportunities and threats ; segments- wise and product-wise performance; outlook; risks and concerns; internal control system and their accuracy; discussion on financial performance with respect to operational performance ; and material development in human resources/ industrial relations front, including the number of people employed" given this broad scope, the inclusion of MD & A in the annual report definitely has the potential immensely increasing transparency in corporate reporting. This is the result of a lack of any specific disclosure norms in Clause 40 beyond the mere specification of the issues to be discussed. Corporate Governance is the mechanism by which the values, principles, management's practices and procedure of corporation are made manifest in the real world. Good corporate governance ensures not only a mechanical compliance of legislation but also adding value to various stakeholders. Globalization and advent of knowledge economy have motivated the companies to work for excellence. Excellence is the only way of survival and growth. The essence of corporate governance involves the development of constructive relationship between the different constituents of a corporate enterprise based on the principles of justice, lucidity, effectiveness and responsibility.

The Fundamental expectation from MD & A is that it will presents an analysis of the business as seen through the eyes of board of directors. Therefore, it is appropriate that elements of information used in managing the company, including subsidiary companies, should be disclosed in the report. The board of directors generally use non financial information for decision making process. Unfortunately boards are extremely reluctant to disclose this non financial information unless compelled by a specific regulatory directive."

MD & A is "intended to provide, in one section of a filing, material historical and prospective textual disclosure enabling investors and other users to access financial condition and results of operations of the company with particular emphasis on prospects for the futures." MD & A provides forward looking information "where there are known trends. Uncertainties other factors enumerated in the rules that will results on or that are reasonably likely to result in, a material impact on the company's liquidity, capital resources revenues and results of operations, including income from continuing operations."

"The underlying principle stated by regulators is that an MD & A report should enables readers to view the past results and future prospects of an issuer "through the eyes of management". This fundamental "first principle" underlies six others, namely that MD & A reports should;

(*a*) Complement as well as supplement financial statements;

(*b*) Have a for word - looking orientation;

(c) Focus on long term value creation;

(*d*) Integrate long- short term perspectives;

(*e*) Present information material to the decision- makers need;

(*f*) Embody the quantities of reliability, comparability, consistency, relevance and understandability.

Nature of Management Discussion and Analysis

Management discussion and analysis is a forward looking statements which may be identified by their use of words like plans; expects; will, anticipates, believes; intends, projects, estimates or other words having similar meaning. All statements that address expectations or projections about the future. Statements about the company's strategy for growth, product development, market position, expenditures, and financial results, are also included in forward— looking statements.

Forward-looking statements are based on certain assumptions and expectations of future events. The company cannot guarantee that these assumptions and expectations are accurate or will be realized. The company's actual results, performance or achievements may be changed due to change in business environment.

Characteristics of MD & A

(*a*) It gives the investor an opportunity to look at the company through the eyes of management by providing both a short and long term analysis of the company.

(*b*) It discloses known trends or any known demands, commitments, events or uncertainties that will result in or likely to affect the liquidity of the company.

(*c*) It provides information regarding known trends and uncertainties that the company reasonably expects will have a material impact on net sales, revenues, income from continuing operations.

(*d*) It presents material events and uncertainties known to management that would cause reported information not to be necessarily indicative of future operating results or of future financial condition.

(*e*) It explains the significance of the accounting estimates to the company financial condition, changes in financial condition, results of operations and, where the material, an identitification of line items in the company's financial statements affected by the accounting estimates.

(*f*) It summarises the qualitative discussions of changes in overall financial performance and, to the extent material, line item in the financial statements if the were to assume that the accounting estimate were changed, either by using reasonably possible near-term changes in most material assumption(s) underlying the accounting estimates or by using the reasonably possible range of the accounting estimates.

(*g*) It also evaluates the quantitative and qualitative discussions and any material changes made to the accounting estimates in the past three years, the reasons for the changes, and effect on lying items in the financial statements and overall financial performance.

(*h*) It presents a statement of whether or not the company's senior management has discussed the development and selection of the accounting estimates and the necessary disclosure regarding it, with the audit committee of the company's board of directors.

(*i*) It facilitates the identification of the segments of the company's business and their relative performance.

(*j*) It presents necessary discussions of the accounting estimate on a segment basis, to the extent that a failure to present that information would result in an omission that renders the disclosure materially misleading.

Elements of Good MD & A Reporting

Following elements are required for a good MD & A reporting:

1. Emphasis on Financial information : The sebi states that companies should explain the underlying reasons or implications with respect to known trends, events, demands, commitments and uncertainties. If there is a reasonable likelihood that reported financial information is not indicative of a companies future financial conditions or operating performance, appropriate disclosure should be considered in MD & A. Thus, the companies are encouraged to disclose not only information responsive to MD & A requirements but also an analysis that explains managements view of the implications and significance of the information.

2. Known material trends and uncertainties : The SEBI notes that companies must identify known trends, events, demands, commitments and uncertainties that are reasonably likely to have a material effect on financial condition or operating performance. Companies should consider both quantitative and qualitative disclosure of the material effects of known trends and uncertainties.

3. Keys performance indicators, including non-financial indicators : The Sebi stresses that companies should discuss key performance indicators; including non financial performance indicators that their management uses to manage the business and that would be useful to investors. If companies disclose material information other than their filed documents (such as press releases), they should evaluate whether that information should also be included in MD & A. Disclosure should provide a balanced view of the material underline dynamics of the business, including both a description of the companies successes and instances when it failed to achieve goals.

4. Liquidity and capital resources : The SEBI suggests that companies should consider enhanced analysis of the sources and uses of cash. It also outlined the notes the need for companies to consider enhance disclosure regarding debt instruments, guarantees and related covenants. Companies should consider disclosure about funds necessary to complete projects and achieve stated objectives and plans, as well as commitments for capital or other expenditures. Companies must provide disclosure regarding their material financial agreements and the importance to cash flows. Where a company has decided to raise or seeks to raise material external equity or debt financing or is reasonably likely to do so in the future, discussions and analysis of the amounts or ranges involved, the nature and term and features of the financing and impact of the companies cash positions and liquidity should also be considered. Companies should also consider the impact of covenants on their ability to undertake additional financing.

5. Critical accounting estimates : The SEBI encourages companies to consider enhanced discussion and analysis that supplements, but does not duplicate the description of accounting policies in the notes to financial statements and provides greater insight into the quality and variability of information regarding financial condition and operating performance companies should analyze such factors as how they arrived at estimates, how accurate the estimates / assumptions have been in the past, how much the estimates / assumptions have changed in the past, and whether the estimates / assumptions are reasonably likely to change in the future.

Historical Perspective of MD & A

The history of Management Discussion and Analysis dates back to 1968 when Securities and Exchange Commission (SEC) of United States of America (USA) made MD & A as part of the Guides for Preparation and Filing of Registration Statements (SEC Securities Act release 334936). In 1974, the SEC directed that corporate annual reports include a discussion and analysis of the summary of operations (SEC Securities Act release IC- 8175). In 1980 the SEC adopted the MD & A as a separate requirement and changed the focus from operating results to the financial statements as a whole (SEC Exchange Act release 34-17114). With this 1980 amendment began the formal requirement for a discussion of issues and trends relating to liquidity, capital resources and the results of operations. Later many modifications were made on the requirements of MD & A and recent one was the modifications to elaborate on off-balance sheet disclosures (SEC Exchange act release 33-8182; 34-47664). The crisis in investor confidence in capital markets following several unprecedented corporate collapses and scandals in 2001 and 2002 caused tough new governance and financial disclosure requirements already introduced in the USA. The MD & A was originally devised by the Securities and Exchange Commission (SEC) in the United States as part of a regulatory filing to provide disclosure that supplement financial statements. In other countries also, particularly the developed countries, the market regulators made it compulsory for the companies to include MD & A report in their annual reports. The requirements of disclosures under MD & A vary to a great extent in the matured markets. But the objective of MD & A is the same in every regulatory environment, that is, the management of companies should provide the most relevant information and provide it in a language and formats that investors can be expected to understand. Typically the MD & A requirements adopted by the regulators in developed countries are intentionally general as the business requirements of industries differ a lot. The regulators believed that a flexible approach elicits more meaningful disclosure. The past is not necessarily indicative of future results. Because valuation looks to the future as well as past and present. The market has to analyze and interpret the reported information. and, ultimately, investors have to judgements based on the reports. It is a road that has many obstacles which provide a base to build a building named MD & A.

The MD & A was first introduced by Canadian Securities regulators in 1989 (Ontario). Since then, the Canadian Securities Administrators have made MD & A a requirement in all Canadian securities jurisdictions. The MD & A and the financial statements annual and interim- together are being recognized as the core business reporting package. Further, the role and responsibilities of audit committees for overseeing the integrity of corporate disclosures — financial statements and MD & A alike – are becoming more rigorous and demanding than ever.

MD & A in Indian Scenario

Given the increasing awareness about corporate governance, the corporate governance reports prepared in India also contained the regulations on the disclosure of MD & A. The Kumaramangalam Committee report in 1999 talked about the disclosure of Management Decision and Analysis in section 13.4 and 13.5, both of which were mandatory. Accepting the suggestions, the SEBI made it mandatory for the companies to have certain details in the MD & A report. In early 2002, the Securities and Exchange Board of India (SEBI), under the listing agreement, made it mandatory for listed companies to incorporate Management Discussions and Analysis (MD & A) has a part of their annual report. The requirement is that company's include discussions regarding industry structure and development, opportunities and threats, segments -wise or product- wise performance, outlook, risks and concerns, internal control systems and adequacy and financial performance as a part of its financial report. Management has to provide key financial and non financial performance indicators that provide a look at a company through the 'eyes of management' along with the disclosures describing what happened, why it happened, and its effect.

The SEBI Listing Agreement Clause 49: states that the annual report should have a section titled "Management Discussion and Analysis Report" (as part of or in addition to the director's report) and should include the following: (i) Industry structure and development, (ii) Opportunities and threats, (iii) Segment— and product— wise performance, (iv) Outlook, (v) Risks and concern, (vi) Internal Control systems and their adequacies, (vii) Discussion on financial performance with respect of operational performance, (viii) Material development in HR including number of people employed.

Disclosure should be made by the management to the board relating to all material, financial and commercial transactions including areas of personal interest or potential conflict with the interest of company at large. The major idea behind the MD & A disclosure in India is to explain the performance of the company in narrative terms and keep the investors informed about the SWOT of the company. It differs from the MD & A requirements laid by SEC in USA, which reflect the matured market condition there. Besides, there is an overlap between the requirements of Directors report and MD & A in the Indian context. The mandatory requirement under SEBI regulations does not clearly indicate the issues to be disclosed under each heading. It does not differentiate clearly between financial statements and off-balance sheet arrangement. SEBI's intentions of keeping the requirements very broad have actually made the requirements very vague.

Objective of MD & A

Objectives of MD & A reporting are as follows:

(*i*) communicate management insights about the reporting entity.

(*ii*) To increase the understandability and usefulness of the annual report.

(*iii*) To provide understandability about the entity and its operations, services levels, success, challenges and future.

(*iv*) To present a narrative explanation of company's financial statements that enables investors to see the company through the eyes of management.

(*v*) To improve overall financial disclosure and provide the context with in which financial statements should be analyzed.

(*vi*) To provide information about the quality of, and potential variability of, a company's earnings and cash flow, so that investors can ascertain the likelihood of that past performance of indicative of future performance.

(*vii*) To provide a narrative explanation, through the eyes of management, of how an entity has performed in the past, its financial condition, and its future prospects.

(*viii*) To provide investors with information to help them decide whether to invest or continue to invest in an entity.

(*ix*) To ensure complete and adequate information for current and prospective investors to rating agencies, lenders, customers, competitors, employees, suppliers, and government authorities.

Importance of MD & A Disclosures

Importance of MD & A can be assessed on the following grounds:

1. It is a powerful tool for management to communicate how the entity has created value and how it plans to continue doing so.
2. It communicates with investors. With better communication investors will be in position to understand underlying potential and prospects of the company.
3. It is helpful in disclosure which leads to a lower cost of capital and a more appropriate risk premium.
4. It critical and sufficient useful information in the report which permit users to assess investment opportunities.
5. It provides an opportunity for an entity to communicate the effectiveness of its stewardship of resources, and, further, progress towards its stated strategic objectives.
6. It integrates and accumulates important information about the entity that investors need to know.
7. It helps in orienting new directors and others interested in knowing about an entity's performance and prospects. The internal processes, systems and discipline are required to prepare an effective reporting structure.
8. It provides new insights into key performance drivers, promoting accountability and control, and facilitating benchmarking of performance.
9. It provides financial managers with the opportunity to present both short-term and long-term analysis of the company's financial activities that is based on the currently known facts, decisions or conditions.
10. It discusses the current year results in comparison with the prior years, with emphasis on the current year. This fact based discussion and analysis present the positive and negative aspects of the comparison with the prior year.

Requirements of MD & As Reporting

Requirement of MD & A reporting are as follows:

1. Through the Eyes of Management: An entity should disclose information in the MD & A that enables readers to view it through the eyes of management. The "MD & A is a narrative explanation, through the eyes of management, of how the company performed during the period covered by the financial statements, and of company's financial condition and future prospects." "Through The Eyes of Management" is therefore fundamental to MD & A reporting. This principle requires disclosure of appropriate elements of the information used by the management for internal purposes and recognizes the need to align internal and external reporting. The information that is relied on in managing the entity, including that which forms the basis of presentations to the board of directors, is precisely the information investors need to view the entity through the eyes of management. In determining the nature and extent of internal information to be reported, entities need to balance the benefit of disclosure against competing demands, while recognizing that they have disclosure obligations. Public disclosure reduces the risk of selective disclosure by providing the information to all current and potential investors and minimizes the risk of inappropriate use of undisclosed material information. While this principle calls for disclosures to reflect management's perspective, MD &

As, for all reporting issuers, are subjected to review by the board of directors and/or audit committee to ensure completeness and balance.

2. Integration with Financial Statements: MD & As should complement as well as supplement financial statements. The MD & A and the financial statements are key to understanding an entity's financial performance. This principle reinforces securities regulations, namely, that the MD & A "complements and supplements your financial statements, but does not form part of your financial statements." The MD & A supplements financial statements by providing analysis of historical performance data. It complements financial statements by presenting contextual and prospective information that financial statements do not provide. In supplementing financial statements, disclosure in the MD & A should (i) explain the conditions and events that shaped the results reflected in the financial statements and (ii) help in understanding how past conditions and events may give rise to future financial consequences. In complementing financial statements, the MD & A should provide useful qualitative and quantitative information about the business and its performance that is not reported in financial statements, but which is relevant to the evaluation of past results and assessment of future prospects.

3. Completeness and Materiality: MD & As should be complete, fair and balanced, and provide information that is material to the decision-making needs of users. An MD & A should present faithfully the substance of what it purports to represent. It needs to be fair, avoiding promotional language and exaggeration. It is critical for management credibility that the MD & A be balanced in its disclosures, being free from deliberate or systemic bias, and openly reporting bad news as well as good news, thus avoiding the creation of overly optimistic or pessimistic expectations. The MD & A should be transparent and discuss the complete range of possibilities and possible outcomes. Completeness calls for management to identify, address, and communicate the qualitative and quantitative information necessary for users to understand and evaluate the entity's strategy, business, results, financial condition, risks and prospects. This would include information about off-balance sheet arrangements. To enable readers to see the entity through the eyes of management, all appropriate information should be disclosed within the MD & A.

4. Forward -Looking Orientation: A forward-looking orientation is fundamental to useful MD & A reporting. A forward- looking orientation calls for the MD & A to explain past events, decisions, circumstances and performance in the context of whether they are reasonably likely to be indicative of, and have a material impact on, future prospects. It also calls for an MD & A to describe management's strategy and future events, decisions, circumstances, opportunities and risks that management considers likely to materially impact future prospects. Forward-looking information is an important element of the forward-looking orientation that is the foundation of a good MD & A. Forward-looking information is broadly defined as — "disclosure regarding possible events, conditions or results of operations that is based on assumptions about future economic conditions and courses of action and includes future-oriented financial information with respect to prospective results of operations, financial position or cash flows that is presented either as a forecast or a projection".

5. Strategic Perspective: The focus in MD & As should be on management's strategy for generating value for investors over time. MD & A disclosure should provide the information that a reasonable investor would want to know in making an investment decision with a view to value accruing over time. This will involve integrating quantitative and qualitative information in a way that communicates the business model and strategy for generating value for investors over time. MD & As should discuss performance against milestones that show progress towards achievement of longer-term goals. The nature of the industry will affect management's determination of an appropriate long-term perspective for MD & A reporting.

6. Usefulness: To be useful, MD & As should be understandable, relevant, and comparable. To be understandable, MD & As should be written in plain language, with candour and without promotional language or exaggeration. Entities should consider using graphics and tables with explanatory narratives where these would enhance understanding. The MD & A should present relevant information that readers would want to know in making a decision to invest or continue to invest in the entity. Information most important to MD & A readers should receive appropriate prominence. It should focus on those matters that management perceives to be the most important, together with its approach to those matters. Information is comparable when sufficient commentary and disclosure have been provided so that similarities and differences among entities can be discerned and evaluated, including disclosures about accounting policies and changes therein. Comparability facilitates benchmarking among entities and business segments. Comparability includes consistent reporting over successive reporting periods and enables meaningful trend identification and analysis. Any changes in matters being reported or in their computation, should be explained unless irrelevant or immaterial.

Recommended Practice for MD & A

The MD & A should communicate information that helps users understand past performance and future prospects. Five key elements of the disclosure framework to achieve this are:

1. Businesses and strategy;
2. Key performance drivers;
3. Capability to deliver results;
4. Results and outlook; and
5. Risk.

1. Business and Strategy: MD & As should disclose the underlying rationale, context and factors considered by management in developing strategy. This rationale would relate to both internal and external factors, and to opportunities and risks. Disclosures of key assumptions upon which the strategy depends should indicate in appropriate detail how changes in them could impact the implementation of strategy. It includes a description of each core business in which the entity operates, including the total size of the business, its growth, and other relevant features. Besides, a description of those aspects of each core business that are distinctive to the entity is also included.

An overview of management's strategy for each core business, including each significant segment, and for the entity as a whole, including: significant long term business objectives, goals or targets and shorter term priorities, as appropriate; attitude to and tolerance for risk; extent to which each core business is managed at the local level or through central oversight; strategy for developing, maintaining or reducing productive capacity; in determining the optimal capital structure, targeted debt to equity ratios, and any hedging strategies; the strategic direction and financing implications behind acquisitions and dispositions; outsourcing practices, strategic business relationships and related finance implications; the entity's focus regarding research and new product development; and marketing, distribution, pricing and customer credit arrangements.

2. Key Performance Drivers: MD & A disclosure framework introduces the concept of disclosure of key performance drivers and associated performance measures and indicators: The MD & A should: (a) identify the key performance drivers for the company, and each of its core businesses and segments; (b) explain their significance to strategies and results; and (c) define and discuss the related performance measures, and, to the extent useful to readers, leading indicators.

Key performance drivers are defined as "those activities, competencies and qualities in which superior performance and favorable results are essential for the company, core businesses and segments. Readers of MD & As need to understand the performance drivers that are critical to successful implementation of the entity's strategy and achievement of its goals. They also need to know the key performance indicators used by management to monitor progress on these key performance drivers. The MD & A should: (a) identify the key performance drivers for the entity, and each core business, including each significant segment; (b) explain their significance to strategies and results; and (c) define and discuss the related key performance indicators. Key performance drivers may be external to the organization and largely outside management's direct control, or they may be internal. Internal performance drivers are those activities, competencies and qualities for which superior performance and favourable results are essential to enable the entity, core business, or segment to achieve its strategic goals. Key performance drivers may differ among entities, core businesses and segments. Examples of external performance drivers include raw material prices, foreign exchange rates, and interest rates. Examples of internal performance drivers in which performance is measured, include: market share; sales pricing; overheads; working capital; research and development and new product development; supply chain management; cost containment and operating efficiency; workforce; customer satisfaction; leadership and governance; capacity and utilization; innovation; technology; reputation and brand equity; financing; safety; and environmental responsibility, including greenhouse gas emissions. SEBI offers examples of areas which may identify as key performance drivers and in which performance are accordingly measured and reported these areas includes "environmental responsibility" and "social responsibility". Other examples in this same section are work force, work place organization and culture, customer's satisfaction, leadership and governance, reputation and safety.

3. Capability to Deliver Results : The MD & A should incorporate key information needed by investors, including that which has been disclosed in other regulatory filings. It is a cornerstone of continuous disclosure. The MD & A ensures that the information is distributed to investors and is subjected to appropriate audit committee and board of director oversight. An entity should use MD & A reporting, annual and interim, to gather, integrate and present information significant to investors, including key information that has previously been communicated through other channels. In addition, entities should update, as necessary, previous disclosures about strategy, key performance drivers, capabilities, risks and results. In this way, all significant information is disclosed and kept current through the MD & A.

4. Results and Outlook: The MD & A is written primarily for current and prospective investors, but at the same time recognizing that there is a wide range of other readers. Its purpose, as originally stated by the regulators, is to give a reader the ability to look at the issuer through the eyes of management. It is intended by the regulators to supplement financial statements by providing historical and prospective analysis and discussion of the business of the issuer as a contact for better understanding its results and future outlook. Certain MD & A requirements are specific to particular industry sectors, notably mining, oil and gas companies. The MD & A is now, in the eyes of the regulators, a key element of the continuous disclosure regiment for reporting issuers in Canada. The quality and readability of MD & A reporting and its consistency with other elements of corporate disclosure is monitored and reported periodically by Canadian regulatory bodies as part of their oversight of continuous disclosure practices.

5. Risk: A dimension of risk is that information used internally by management and boards of directors or information disclosed externally may be an error. Either occurrence can have adverse consequences to the entity or to its shareholders. This risk applies to MD & As, as well as other disclosures, and accordingly MD & A readers need assurance that appropriate risk management steps have been taken. Management is responsible for the existence and effectiveness of systems, controls and procedures to ensure that information used internally by management and disclosed externally is reliable and timely. "Risk disclosures are essential to enable readers to the company through the "eyes of Management." "A company should disclose its principal risks and describe related risk management systems to enable the MD & A report readers to understand and evaluate the company's risks and its decisions regarding the management of such risks. Such disclosure should include:

(*i*) the principal risks and uncertainties facing the company and its core business and segments, as appropriate;

(*ii*) the strategies and process employed for managing these risks.

(*iii*) the potential specific impact of these risk on results and capabilities including capital resources and liquidity

Quantitative information on risks and potential impact on future prospects of the business should be presented along with qualitative information. In particular, it should provide specific quantitative information about the potential variability of results depending on the outcome of the disclosed risks. Sebi provides clear direction as to what information is useful and complete MD & A should provide about any other risks that has strategic or operational significance to the companies business and future prospects.

Aspects of MD & A

Following are the important aspects of Management Discussion and Analysis:

1. General disclosure principles: There are six principles that provide the foundation underpinning MD & A disclosures.

(*i*) Complement as well as supplement financial statements;

(*ii*) be reliable, complete, fair and balanced, providing material information— that is, information important to an investor, acting reasonably, in making a decision to invest or continue to invest in the company;

(*iii*) Have a forward –looking orientation;

(*iv*) Focus on management's strategy for generating value for investors over time; and

(*v*) Be written in plain language, with candour and without exaggeration, and

(*vi*) Embody the qualities of clarity, relevance, comparability and consistency over reporting periods.

2. The disclosure framework: It advocates that companies should structure and integrate their MD & A disclosures within a broad disclosure framework. Much of the information called for under this approach may already be available within a company but it is rarely presented in single, succinct disclosure document. The analysis of past result and discussion of future prospects should be framed within the context of the five key elements of the disclosure framework. These are: (i) the company's vision, core business and strategy; (ii) key performance drivers; (iii) capabilities (capital and other resources) to achieve desired results; (iv) results – historical and prospective analysis; and (v) the risks that shape strategy and may affect the achievement of results.

It is also important to note that MD & A explains the "why" behind both past performance and future prospects by "connecting the dots" between otherwise separate pieces of internal and external information. MD & As should communicate not only financial information but also relevant and material non-financial information. Any disclosure and discussion of targets should be presented within a longer term strategic context and, in subsequent periods, be compared to actual results achieved.

3. Continuous disclosure: It indicates that MD & As – annual and interim – need to be seen as integral elements of the continuous disclosure regiment. A company should use MD & A reporting to gather, integrate and present information significant to investors, including information that has previously been communicated through other channels. In addition, companies should update, as necessary, previous MD & A disclosure about strategy, key performance drivers, capabilities, risks and results. Failure to update MD & As may result in investors being misled if they rely upon out-dated information. Analysis of actual results in MD & As should include a discussion of progress against previously disclosed goals, objectives or targets. In this way all significant information is disclosed and updated, as necessary through the MD & As.

4. Integrity of disclosure: It suggests that reporting issuers provide a statement about the responsibility of management for the existence of appropriate information system, procedures and controls to ensure that information used internally and disclosed externally is complete and reliable. The MD & A should include a statement about the 'oversight' role of the board of directors and audit committee to ensure the integrity of the reported information.

Responsibilities of Boards of Directors

Entities should provide a statement about the oversight role of the audit committee in reviewing the MD & A and the role of the board of directors in approving the MD & A. Management naturally has a bias that the audit committee and board need to bear in mind contents the MD & A should provide the view through the management's eyes. It should be an objective analysis and provide a proper sense of events taking place in the entity. Accordingly, the audit committee and board need to assess whether the MD & A is consistent with information they have received from management. They should pay particular attention to any information that has been omitted from the MD & A because of issues such as confidentiality. The oversight role played by the audit committee and board of director regarding annual and interim MD & As should be disclosed. Audit committees and boards of directors need to ascertain whether, in preparing the MD & A, management has applied the general disclosure principles.

Critical Evaluation of MD & A Reporting

It does give investors a clearer picture of what the company does. It also points out some key areas where the company has performed well. As the management's analysis is at their discretion, it would be better to take it for what it is worth. In this context following considerations are referred: (i) How candid and accurate are the management comments? (ii) Does management discuss significant financial trends over past couple of years? (iii) How clear are management's comments? If executives try to confuse with high-sounding words and jargon, perhaps they have something to hide. (iv) Do they mention potential risks or uncertainties moving forward?

Disclosure is the name of the game. If a company gives a fair amount of information in the MD & A, it is likely that management is being upfront and honest. It should raise a red flag if the MD & A portion of the financial statement ignore serious problems that the company has been facing. Withholding important information not only deceives those who read the financial statements but, in extreme cases, also makes the company liable for lack of disclosure.

Guidance Notes Regarding MD & A

In November 2002, the Canadian Performance Reporting Board of the Canadian Institute of Chartered Accountants issued Management's Discussion and Analysis: Guidance on Preparation and Disclosure (the CICA Guidance)[2] to help companies in preparing MD & As. The CICA Guidance provides 20 questions for audit committees and boards of directors to ask in discharging their MD & A oversight responsibility. This publication also provides important information for directors about developments in MD & A reporting.

The CICA Guidance is revised from time to time in the light of changes in securities regulations. It focuses on MD & A disclosure requirements, change in accounting standards and trends in business reporting practices. In addition, corporate governance requirements, trends and practices may, over time, indicate the need for revision of those parts of the CICA guidance that address management's responsibility for and the board's oversight of, the integrity of disclosures. Such revisions may, in turn, trigger the need for revisions to this 20 Questions publication from time to time. These 20 questions are given below:

1. Do the disclosures comply with regulatory requirements: Sometimes, certain regulatory requirements call for subjective judgments of the by management in order to decide on appropriate disclosure. Management should be asked to indicate such instances and explain the rationale for the chosen form and extent of disclosure in question. Legal counsel may be asked by management to review the MD & A for compliance with regulatory requirements. The audit committee would then ask for the opinion of the counsel regarding regulatory compliance.

2. To what extent has the CICA Guidance been followed in preparing the MD & A? If any significant aspects of that guidance have not been followed, have the reasons been satisfactorily explained: It is concerned with the management perception about the company's corporate disclosure policy (approved by the board), its financing needs and its goals for relations with capital markets. The basis for management's decision regarding the use of the CICA Guidance should be explained. The audit committee or board will also want to be informed as to the extent, if any, to which the regulators are encouraging or expecting reporting issuers to follow the CICA Guidance.

3. Has management provided a representation about the reliability of the underlying systems and processes on which information is based: MD & A disclosures of performance measures should be based on measurement and reporting systems appropriate for the subject matter in question. Actually It is not concerned with the accounting systems underlying the financial statements. Management information systems used in providing operational information and reports to management and for management reporting to the board of directors or to external authorities should also be the basis for factual MD & A disclosures. Systems and processes for tracking consistency and comparability of MD & A disclosures from period to period are also important. Management should be expected to provide a representation about the integrity and reliability of systems and processes underlying MD & A disclosures.

4. What has been management's approach to determining materiality in preparing the MD & A: The CICA Guidance advocates a test based on significance to investor decision-making when considering the materiality of matters, quantitative or qualitative, to be included in the disclosures. This test is increasingly favoured by the regulators. Impact on market prices, follows investor decision making based upon what is disclosed to them. Completeness and Materiality Principle in the CICA Guidance states: "To be reliable, MD & As should be complete, fair and balanced, and provide information that is material to the decision-making needs of users. "

5. Is there any information that management has omitted from the MD & A due to competitive concerns and if so, what is management's rationale for such omission and does the board agree: The CICA Guidance presents a view that concerns about the impact of disclosures on competitive advantage need to be challenged and carefully evaluated. Such concerns may be valid and justifiable for some companies in certain circumstances and industry sectors, including those that are regulated. In many cases such concerns are not only justified, but also show that more disclosure rather than less is more effective in building market& place understanding of and confidence in a company's future prospects. A company should disclose the appropriate level of strategic information to enable an investor to make an informed investment decision. Management should be asked to provide and explain its justification for any information that it has withheld from the MD & A. Possible courses of action to decide which better serves the best interest of shareholders: disclosure for the sake of transparency and more informed investment decision versus potential harm to the company and loss of shareholder value that may be caused by inadequate disclosure.

6. Are there any disclosures presented in previous periods' MD & As that are not addressed in this draft MD & As, and if so, why: The MD & As should be written in plain language, with candour and without exaggeration and embody the qualities of understandability, relevance, comparability and consistency over reporting periods. To be consistent over reporting period, significant information should be updated and explained unless it becomes irrelevant or inappropriate. If the information is no longer relevant or appropriate, why this is so should be explained. Companies should not avoid discussion and update of a previously raised issue by simply omitting it from a subsequent MD & A report. Consistency in reporting also enhances comparability. Comparable information is information about which sufficient commentary and disclosure has been provided so that similarities and differences among time periods and/or companies can be discerned and evaluated. Management should be asked to provide a clear and factual representation as to whether there are any disclosures in prior periods' MD & A that are not addressed in the current MD & A, indicate what such disclosures were and explain why they are not now addressed.

7. Are the principal business risks disclosed and discussed in the MD & A consistent with those that management has reviewed with us for other purpose? Risk disclosures in the MD & A should be consistent with what has previously been presented to and reviewed with the board by management concerning business risks and their implications for strategy and results.

The CICA Guidance recommends that a company should disclose its principal risks and describe related risk management systems to enable MD & A report readers to understand and evaluate the company's risks and its decision regarding the management of such risks. Such disclosure should include: (a) the principle risks and uncertainties facing the company and its core businesses and segments, as appropriate; (b) the strategies and processes employed for managing these risks; (c) the potential specific impact of these risks on results and capabilities, including capital resources and liquidity. There should be continuity from one period to another regarding risk disclosures and how the risk impacts on results.

8. Have precious disclosures to the markets in any form (websites, previous MD & A, press releases) been reviewed in the light of intervening events and up-dates as necessary in the current MD & A to ensure that investors are not misled? The CICA Guidance states that a company should use MD & A reporting, annual and interim, to gather, integrate and present information significant to investors, including information that has previously been communicated through other channels. In addition, companies should update, as necessary, previous disclosure about strategy, key performance drivers, capabilities, risks and results. In this way, all significant information is disclosed and kept current through the MD & As. Where a company has determined that a change has occurred and has disclosed this to the market place and /or regulators, its subsequent MD & A report (annual or interim) should incorporate and reflect that disclosure and provide appropriate further analysis, as necessary, as to the effect of the change on the company's view going forward. Companies should ensure that forward-looking disclosures in previous MD & A are updated as necessary to reflect subsequent events or changes. This is important to maintain reliability and credibility in MD & A reporting.

9. Are there any ways in which the MD & A disclosures are inconsistent with information provided in the financial statements or notes thereto and further, are the MD & A disclosures consistent with the company's disclosure policy and with other disclosures and releases made to the public, including prior periods' MD & As? The CICA Guidance states that MD & As should complement as well as supplement financial statements. In supplementing financial statements (an existing regulatory requirement), disclosure in the MD & A should (i) explain the conditions and events that shaped the information contained in the financial statements and (ii) help in understanding how past conditions and events may give rise to future financial consequences. In complementing financial statements, the principle of providing information "to give a reader the ability to look at the issuer through the eyes of management" should drive disclosure.

10. If alternative financial performance measures have been disclosed, has their relevance been satisfactorily explained? Where such measures are derived from GAAP financial statements, have reconciliation to the financial statements been provided? The CICA Guidance states that to the extent that non-GAAP measures of financial performance are reported in the MD & A, companies should define the non-GAAP measures, explain their significance, and, for measures provided as GAAP-based alternatives, provide a reconciliation of these to related measures disclosed in the financial statements. Management uses its discretion in deciding the most useful way of communicating results to the market place. Investors are entitled, however, to understand how alternative financial performance measures relate to GAPP financial statements, audited or otherwise, and why such alternative measures are relevant to an adequate understanding of the company's performance and prospects.

11. How does the company's MD & A compare with MD & As of other companies within the same industry sector and/or other relevant benchmarks? In the interests of continually improving the usefulness of its own MD & A disclosures, management of a reporting issuer may monitor the MD & As of other companies in the same industry sector or monitor other companies' disclosures on specific issues such as risk or key performance drivers and measures. Members of audit committees and boards of directors typically serve on other boards, and therefore may be able to bring the benefit of their own knowledge of reporting practices in other companies. The combination of management's and board members' knowledge of MD & A reporting practices by other companies can be a useful resource for enhancing the quality and usefulness of a given company's MD & As.

12. What feedback, if any, has been received from regulators about the adequacy of the company's MD & A and/or other disclosures such as press releases and financial statements? Regulators are required to monitor the performance of MD & A reporting. They review the compliance, and take necessary feedback from the stakeholders about the MD & A compliance. Sometimes companies receive communications from regulators enquiring about or expressing concern about a management or the audit committee about any such communications received from regulatory bodies, what action has been taken or is proposed in response, and where the matter currently stands.

13. What feedback, if any, has been received from institutional or other significant investors or their proxies about the adequacy of the company's MD & A and other disclosures? Management should also be required to bring to the attention of the audit committee any communication from institutional or other investors or analysts (as proxies for investors) about the MD & A. This is especially important if such communication expressed concern or misunderstanding about an MD & A report or some other disclosure. The degree of significance of the concern should be explained by management, as well as the action taken or proposed in response, and where the matter currently stands.

14. Have legal counsel reviewed the MD & A and if so, what comments do they have? Legal counsel typically review a company's MD & A before release, usually in order to advise management regarding the appropriateness of any forward-looking information and related cautionary language, and also to identify and disclosures that have implications regarding potential harm to the company's competitive advantage. Legal counsel may also advise about expected or possible future legal and regulatory matters that may significantly affect the company in terms of strategy and/or risk and should therefore be disclosed and discussed in the MD & A.

15. Have the external auditors reviewed the MD & A and, if so, what comments do they have? This approach may be particularly appropriate where the audit committee's review and approval of the MD & A is done in conjunction with its review and approval of the related financial statements and the auditors' report thereon. External auditors read information (such as MD & As) published in reports that contain financial statements upon which they are expressing an audit opinion, in order to ensure that there are no inconsistencies between the financial statements and that other information. The audit committee may consider engaging the external auditor to carry out specified audit procedures regarding particular parts of the MD & A to assist the audit committee in satisfying itself about the reliability of MD & A disclosures.

16. Is the information contained in the MD & A consistent with that which has been previously presented to the audit committee and board of directors? Members of audit committees and boards of directors throughout the year receive from management a wide range of information regarding matters that include strategic direction, availability of resources, company performance and evaluation of management performance. The MD & A review by the audit committee should include a step whereby audit committee members individually and collectively review and consider information given previously to them, and assess whether there are any inconsistencies between such information and any part of the MD & A as a whole. Minutes of previous audit committee and board meetings should also be reviewed for these purposes. To the extent the audit committee detects or suspects any inconsistencies, management should be asked to confirm or explain the matter and, if necessary, adjust the MD & A.

17. Does the MD & A report include all significant issues that management has previously raised with us? If not, what is missing and why? It focuses on "errors of omission" rather than inconsistencies between actual information items in MD & As compared to earlier presentations of the same information. Minutes of previous audit committee and board meetings should also be reviewed for these purposes. Again, to the extent that the audit committee detects or suspects any omission of information about an issue that would be significant to an investor, management should be asked to confirm or explain the matter, and, if necessary, adjust the MD & A.

18. Is the MD & A written in clear, plain language and does it present with candour and without exaggeration a fair and balanced picture, including "bad news" as well as "good news"? If "yes", fine. If "no", then in what way does the MD & A appear inadequate, and what needs to be done to remedy the problem?

19. Does the MD & A provide a complete and integrated view of the company's historical results, prospective analysis, and financial condition explaining the "why" behind performance and prospects? If "yes". fine. If "no", then in what way does the MD & A appear inadequate, and what needs to be done to remedy the problem?

20. Does the MD & A, together with the financial statements, provide the necessary information to enable readers of the MD & A to reach an informed judgement about investing or continuing to invest in the company? If "yes", fine. If "no", then in what way does the MD & A appear inadequate, and what needs to be done to remedy the problem?

On the above guidance notes, companies can ensure better understandability of their M&A reporting. Interests of stakeholders is suppress and it can be protected with the MD & A reporting to a certain extent.

Asian Paints

Management Discussion and Analysis 2009-10

The financial year 2009-10 began with several apprehensions about the global as well as the domestic global environment. To cope with the global financial cries, which impacted the world economy in 2008-09, central banks as well as governments across developed and many emerging economies reacted quickly with large interest rate cuts, massive injection of liquidity and fiscal stimulus programmes. These measures helped in reducing uncertainty, reducing uncertainty, increasing confidence, fostering improvement in financial conditions and allaying fears of a global depression. Whatever may be individual views on the measures taken, these has helped recovery across most part of the world; certainly the specter of a global depression receded fairly rapidly. While the major emerging markets bounced back quickly, even the developed world economies have seen a gradual or slow rebound from the recessionary trend seen last year. There are serious imbalances in Southern Europe that are major concerns; even so, the world is probably on course for resumption of economic growth with the pace being different from region to region. The major emerging economies of China, India and Brazil have recovered well, growing only marginally lower than earlier years. As prospects improved, commodity prices staged a comeback from lows reached earlier and the world trade is beginning to look up.

From the beginning of financial year 2009-10, an upswing in economic activity was seen. Industrial output saw a recovery with the Index of Industrial Production (IIP) registering growth of 10.4% for the period April 2009-March 2010 significantly up from the 2.6% growth recorded in the previous year. The Rupee also saw an uptrend and appreciated from levels of Rs. 51 per USD in April, 2009 to around Rs. 45 per USD in March, 2010. The decisive mandate in the general elections also helped in bringing about political stability and removing the uncertainty that was prevalent in the country. Accordingly, the Indian economy is expected to record a GDP growth of about 7.5% in financial year 2009-10. This is in spite of poor monsoon in 2009.

1. Products and Markets : The performance of the Indian Paint Industry in 2009-10 was much better anticipated at the beginning of the financial year. The first half of the year was better than expected and in the second half the Indian growth story was seen in all sectors of the economy. Construction activity revived and capital expenditure revived across sectors. A combination of good demand and lower than expected raw material prices helped the paint industry excellent growth in revenues and even better growth in profits. The market for all paints produced by companies in India, both big and small, is estimated to have grown by about 18% by value over the previous year. The growth for both decorative paints and industrial paints would be high with industrial paints growing significantly in the automotive and durable segments.

Decorative Paints

Decorative paints account for over 75% of the overall paint market in India and include wall finishes for interior and exterior use, enamels, wood furnishes and ancillary products such as primers, putties, etc. The company shown a robust performance this year. Demand for decorative paints was very good throughout the year.

The key feature of the financial year 2009-10, other than the remarkable growth, was the fact that the factors like benign raw material prices and appreciating rupee resulted in expansion of margins in this segment.

Net sales grew ahead of volume sales due to lower excise duty in the year and a richer product mix. Emulsion paints for interiors have been growing much faster than distempers over the last decades. The trend continues in 2009-10. The company tie-up with DoPort USA to co-brand the Royale range of Emulsions with Teflon worked to its advantage with the product doing extremely well across markets. Exterior Emulsions too continued to grow much faster than the overall paint demand powered by the company's leading brands, Apex Ultima, Apex and Ace.

The Company's signature stores "Colour with Asian Paints" at Bandra in Mumbai continued to attract a large number of consumers, who were able to experience the possibilities with colour. The stores has attracted many consumers from Mumbai and other cities, professional decorators, architects and designers resulting in many leads for home solutions.

The company continued to expand its network and provide several customer friendly services so as to improve the quality of service to the end consumer. The company made considerable investments in upgrading the ambience of its dealers by refurbishing them with new visual branding. The company has began to establish a new chain of stores called 'Colour Ideas'. These are existing dealers with whom your company partners is making an investment to makeover the shops to offer a slice of the 'Signature Store' to consumers across the country who can thereby experience the same inspiration to experiment with colours. There are now 12 'Colour Ideas' stores across the country. These have met with a very enthusiastic from the consumers. The company is now in the process of further expanding this network of colour ideas across the country.

A CRM (Customer Relationship Management) system has been developed to improve the customer compliant handling process to ensure that complaints are addressed and closed quickly and customer satisfaction is enhanced.

The company has continued to develop capability in colour and décor marketing. The colours tools introduced have proved to be popular. Training programmes for the dealers have been conducted at many locations to facilitate their usage. The company continued to invest in the are of colour with the launch of Colour Next 2010. Several Colour Guides and Décor booklets are available to consumers at retail outlets to enable them to make an informed decision.

The expression of the Colour World network continues unabated and today the company has more than 15,000 Colour Worlds offering a wide range of products and shades to consumers even in many small towns across the length and breadth of the country. The company expects that within 5 years, substantial part of its sales would come from the Colour World across the country.

Prices of raw materials were lower than expected in the first nine months of the year. However, there were signs of increase in raw materials in the last quarter. This coupled with the increase in excise duty in the budget, reduced margins. The company expects raw materials prices to rise during the year 2009-10.

In order to build supply chain further to cater to the growth envisaged in future, the first phase of the sixth Decorative Paint at Rohtak, Harayana, has been commissioned on 12th April 2010, as scheduled, at a cost of approximately Rs. 500 crore with an initial capacity of 150,000 KL per annum. The capacity of this state-of-art Plant, located at the Industrial Model Town (IMT) developed by Harayana State Infrastructure and Industrial Development Corporation (HSIIDC) will be expanded in the stages to 4,00,000 KL per annum. The plant has been developed in the area of 130 aces of which 43 aces is green belt. The construction of this project was stared in July 2008 and was completed in 21 months.

The capacity of the company's Sriperumbudur Plant in Tamil Nadu, has been raised to 1,40,000 KL per annum and emulsion making capacity in the plant was enhanced to meet the requirements fully. The distribution centre at Sriperumbudur plant has been commissioned and land for the centre at Patancheru plant has been procured. With the completion of the Distribution Centre at Patancheru Plant over the next none months, the company would have modernised its vast distribution system, making it possible to service its 30,000 strong distribution base more effectively, with lower levels of inventory.

Industrial Coatings

Automotive Coatings: Asian PPG Industries Limited

In 1997 the company and PPG Industries Inc. formed Asian PPG Industries Limited (APPG), a 50:50 joint venture, which services the Automotive OEM, Auto Refinish and certain industrial coatings markets in India.

Domestic sales of passenger vehicles grew impressively during the year 2009-10. Automakers supported this performance by introducing new models and offering attractive pricing. Exports too complimented the domestic growth story by registering a growth of 33%. The low base effect of the previous year was also visible in the growth figures. Indian Two Wheeler Industry crossed the 10 milllion mark in 2009-10, on the back of upsurge in domestic demand as well as exports.

The impact of continuing efforts by customers to reduce costs in view of rising new material costs was arrested through product development, formulation efficiency, effective sourcing, substitution and costs reduction measures. These developments have resulted in improved sales as well as bottom line performance during the year under review.

Total gross sales after discounts but before excise duty increased to Rs. 476.88 crores from Rs. 420.94 crore in the previous year- a growth of 13.3%. The profit after tax increased to Rs. 28.52 crore from Rs. 14.43 crores representing a rise of 98%. The consolidated sales were Rs. 490.39 crore and the profit after tax was Rs. 30 crore. The sales of Faaber Paints Private Limited (FPPL), a wholly owned subsidiary of APPG, grew by 35.8% to Rs. 15.01 from Rs. 11.05 crore: Profit before tax of Rs. 2.13 crores was up from Rs. 0.28 crore in the previous year. The company feels that the business will continue to see good growth and remains optimistic about the prospects of APPG's performance in future.

Non Auto Industrial Coatings

The auto industrial coatings market is serviced by your company through its Growth Business Unit and a wholly owned subsidiary, Asian Paints Industrial Coatings Limited (APICL). The company is present in several major product segments in this market to harness the potential growth opportunities in these segments.

Although, the Indian economy started showing signs of resurgence from the second quarter of financial year 2009-10 capital expenditure expands by corporate followed with a lag. Business from maintenance painting declined compared with the 2008-09 and the Industrial Coatings business of the company mirrored this industry trend. However, there has been an improvement in sales in the second half of the year in Industrial Liquid Paints.

Business from the larger products and from engineering contractors and fabricators has been important contributor to the industry growth. Pitching for business involving medium to high value protecting coating projects in specific project, has been an important feature during the financial year 2009-10. Business generation efforts from OE (Original Equipment) customers manufacturing light and heavy industrial goods have shown some results in the second half of the year. There has been an intense competition for business among the major companies in the larger projects.

The profit from the Industrial Liquid Paints business were good in the year. There has been a conscious and successful effort to improve the gross contribution from the entire range of Industrial Liquid Paints by increasing the entire range of Industrial Liquid Paints by increasing the range of higher range products. Material costs were also benign for most part of the year and the tight control was exercised over costs. There has been an increase in material costs primarily in the last quarter of the year under review, which is likely to continue through the financial year 2010-11. This will impact the margins and contributions, as price increases are implemented in industrial coatings with a considerable lag.

The Industrial Paints plant at Taloja near Mumbai completed its third year of operation in Feburary 2010, and has today developed the capability to satisfactorily manufacture the entire range of industrial products. The ISO 14001 environmental certification audit was conducted at the plant by personnel from BVQI and the plant has been awarded this certification.

Asian Paints Industrial Coatings Limited

Asian Paints Coatings Limited (APICL), the wholly owned subsidiary of the company, is engaged in the manufacture and sale of Powder Coatings.

The size of the domestic powder coating market is estimated at around 38.700 MT in the financial year 2009-10. While the demand was subdued in the initial part of the financial year 2009-10, the market saw improved demand in the second half of the year, with white and brown goods dealing the way. Higher focus on business from OEM manufacture increased the Company's share of business and share of growth in these accounts. Some business was generated from emerging product technology domains such as fast cure and low bake powder coatings. Material costs were benign, aided by the appreciation of the Rupee against the Dollar during the year 2009-10. The Powder Coating Plants at Sarigam in Gujarat and Baddi in Himachal Pradesh have an integrated quality and Environment Management System and are certified under the ISO 9000 and ISO 14001 standards, APICL also received the DSIR (Department of Science and Industrial Research) recognition for its Research and Development facility at Sarigam.

International Operations

The impact of the financial crisis was more marked in countries where the company has international operations than in India. Although, the situation improved as the year progressed. It severely impacted demand for paints across most markets. Despite this, the performance of the International operations has been good.

During the year, Berger International Limited (BIL) the company's subsidiary, has divested its stake in its subsidiaries in Malaysia, Thailand and Hong Kong after evaluating the prospects of its operations in these countries. Likewise, the subsidiary in China was divested in April 2010.

Asian Paints International Limited, the Mauritius based wholly owned subsidiary of the company, bought back 4.1 mn of its shares held by the company for a consideration of Rs. 19.5 crores resulting an exceptional income of Rs. 5.8 crore for the company.

The focus in international operations during the year was an realigning the portfolio by divesting identified units, strengthening the position in the market place by expanding the network, installing additional dealer tinting systems and introducing new products, managing credit risk and improving internal efficiencies in all areas including working capital. Customer service level, reduction in material losses in manufacturing, implementing standard practices and enhancing overall safety standards. Material prices remained low for a greater part of the year due to the global slowdown and have started firming up towards the end of the year.

The international operations for period January to December 2009 have earned a profit before tax (PBT) of over Rs. 100 crore for the first time. The subsidiary in Oman declared a dividend for the first time, during the year.

During the 15 month period (January 2009-March 2010), paint sale was Rs. 1,201 crore. For the 12 month period (January 2009-December 2009), sale increased by 9% to Rs. 986 crore. Adjusted for exchange rate impact, the revenue growth from the paint sale is flat for the period January 2009-December2009. New product sale in volume terms constituted approximately 2.7% of total paint sales and over 1400 dealers tinting systems have been installed so far in various subsidiaries.

Profit after tax for overseas operations of the group during the 15 month period is Rs. 115 crores. Corresponding figure for the 12 month period (January 2009-December 2009) is Rs. 95.2 crore compare to Rs. 42.8 crores during the 2009-10. The divestments of subsidiaries during the year resulted in an exceptional gain of Rs. 1.2 crores.

The revenue from paint sales of BIL, a subsidiary listed on Singapore Stock Exchange, for the 15 month period was S$160 million (equivalent to Rs. 536 crores). The revenue from paint sales for the 12 month period (January 2009-December 2009) has decreased by 13% to S$135 million (equivalent to Rs. 455 crores partly due to the divestments made during the year. BIL has earned a profit after tax for the 12 month period (January 2009-December 2009) of S$3.4 million (equivalent to Rs. 12 crores) as compared to S$2.8 million (equivalent to Rs. 9 crore) during the previous year. The profit after tax for the 15 month period (January 2009 – March 2010) is S$4.0 million equivalent to Rs. 13.5 crore.

The group posts the divestments, operates in the following geographies:

Region	Countries
Caribbean	Barbados, Jamaica, Trinidad, Tobago
Middle East	Egypt, Oman, Bahrain, and UAE
South Asia	Bangladesh, Nepal, Sri Lanka
South East Asia	Singapore
South Pacific	Fiji, Solomon Islands, Tongo and Vanuatu

The region wise performance is detailed below:

Caribbean : During the 15 month period (January 2009-March 2010) the region achieved a sale of Rs. 196 crore. The global economic meltdown had a severe impact on the Caribbean economies and hence the performance of the region was adversely affected. The revenue from paint sales has increased by 2% to Rs. 167 crore in the 12 month period (January 2009-December 2009). Adjusted for exchange rate impact, the revenue from paint sales has decreased by 1%. PBIT (profit before interest and tax) for the region has increased by 108% to Rs. 12 crore during this period. All the subsidiaries in the region have made profit. The higher profit is due to the substantially better performance of the subsidiaries in Jamaica and Barbados.

Middle East: During the 15 month period (January 2009-March 2010) the region achieved a sale of Rs. 652 crores. For the 12 month period (January 2009-December 2009), the revenue from paint sales has increased by 15% to Rs. 534 crores. Adjusted of exchange rate impact the revenue from paint sales has increased by 3%. Although, all the economies in the region have been impacted by the global recessionary trend, the impact has been most prolonged in Emirates. PBIT for the region has increased by 80% to Rs. 101 crores in the 12 month (January 2009-December 2009).

The Middle East region has the largest operating region for the group ourside India, The region now contributes 54% of the revenue from overseas operations. All the subsidiaries in the region have performed well.

South Asia: During the 15 month period (January 2009-March 2010) the region achieved a sale of Rs. 187 crores. For the 12 month period (January 2009 –December 2009) revenue from paint sales increased by 28% to Rs. 147 crores. Adjusted for exchange rate impact, the revenue from paint sales has increased by 18% during this period. The PBIT for the region has increased by 115% to Rs. 18 crore during this period.

All subsidiaries in the region have performed well. Expansion of the ColourWorld dealers network and increased influencer interactions through painters –dealer meets has helped all the subsidiaries to achieve health sales growth.

South East Asia: During the year under review, the economies in the region were severely impacted by the global meltdown. The subsidiaries in China, Malaysia, Hong Kong and Thailand were divested. On account of divestments being effected at different points of time during the year. Sales figures were not comparable with those of the 2008-09. During the 15 month period (January 2009-March 2010), the region achieved a sale of Rs. 96 crores.

The subsidiary in Singapore had performed well and revenue during the 15 month period (January 2009-March 2010) was Rs. 61 crores. For the 12 month period (January 2009-December2009), the sales has increased to Rs. 49 crore. The subsidiary has achieved a PBIT growth of 38% over the previous year for this period.

South Pacific: During the 15 month period (January2009-March 2010) the region achieved a sale of Rs. 85 crores. For the 12month period (January 2009 –December 2009), paint sales increased by 7% to Rs. 67 crores. Adjusted for exchange rate impact, the revenue from paint sales has increased by 9%. The PBIT for the region has increased by 54% to Rs. 9 crore during this period. As mentioned in the last annual report, the management will continue to take all feasible steps to enhance the operating performance and the cash flows from the overseas subsidiaries.

Others: Company has chemical business consisting of Phthalic Anhydride and Pentaerythritol. Manufactured at Ankleshwar in Gujarat and Cuddalore in Tamil Nadu, respectively. These units were sets up as backward integration initiatives in the late eighties. They are not seen as growth drivers for the company and continue to be managed for value. During the year, 56% of Phthalic Anhydride and 52% of Pentaerythritol production was consumed in-house and the balance was sold in the open market.

The Phthalic Anhydride business showed good recovery from the steep drop in demand experienced in 2008-09 and reported good profits in 2009-10. The production and sales of Pentaerythritol was also satisfactory during the year. A zero discharge system and a captive power plant was installed in the Pentaerythritol plant. The new captive power plant meets almost the entire power requirement of the plant. While generating all the steam required for production process. This has led to substantial savings in the expense earlier incurred on power drawn from the state electricity board.

II. Environment, Health and Safety

Environment, Health and Safety (EHS) is one of the primary focus areas for the company. The Company's EHS policy is to consider compliance to statutory EHS requirements as the minimum performance standards as is committed to go beyond and adopt stricker standard wherever appropriate. The company focuses on pollution abatement, resource optimization and waste minimization, which leads to sustainable development. The company also gives priority and attention to the health and safety of its employees to work as per prescribed procedures designed to meet all EHS requirements of the company. The company endeavors to educate its customers and the public and safe use of its products, on a continuous basis.

Due to continued focus, Sriperumbudur plant was presented with the Tamil Nadu State Safety Award by Inspectorate of factories, Tamil Nadu for outstanding safety performance. The Research and Technology centre for Asian Paints at Turbhe, Navi Mumbai, was certified for ISO 18001 safety standards. The plant at Bhandup, Mumbai was formally appreciated by Mutual Aid Response Group, Mumbai sub region for doing excellent work in the area of safety.

The company's newly commissioned plant at Rohtak, Haryana, has been built to nary exacting and contemporary environment, health and safety standards. Based on the British Safety Council safety standard, several safety features have been incorporated in the design of the plant.

Company has always been an environmentally conscious manufacturing Company and believed in resource conservation. After achieving 'Zero Discharge' of Industrial effluent, minimization of waste through reduction of source and recycle/reuse was the key focus areas for company during the year 2009-10. This resulted in reduction in specific generation of effluents and solid waste.

The Rohtak plant was designed for 'Zero Discharge' of industrial effluent. The plant has a state of the art effluent treatment system, a reverse osmosis plant and a multi effect evaporator that allows the pant to recycle more than 99% of the effluent back into the process. The plant has provided about 43 aces of green belt and roof-top rain water harvesting structures to harvest 35 million litre of water every year. Solar PV panels have been installed which will light 75 LED street lights in the plants saving around 25,000 units of electricity every year. Also, a solar water hearing system has been installed generating 45,000 liters of hot water every day for process applications which is not the standard industrial practice. The administration building of the Rohtak plant has been build as per the green building standards.

Company's six paint plants and the two chemical plants have ISO 14001 environmental certification, with Taloja plant being the most recent among them to join the ISO 14001 certification during the year 200-10. The Sriperumbuddur plant was awarded consents for expansion by the Tamil Nadu Pollution Control Board without any increase in the environmental pollution load. The Penta plant at Cuddalore became a 'Zero Discharge' facility by commissioning Reverse Osmosis unit followed by the Multiple Effect Evaporator and Agitated thin-film dryer. This implies that your company's five paint plants and one chemical plant have achieved 'Zero Industrial Discharge, capability.

The Ankleshwar Plant was honoured with Gujarat Cleaner Production Award by the Gujarat Cleaner Production Center and Department of Environment and Forest, Government of Gujarat. Ankleshwar plant was also presented with the award in the chemical sector for outstanding achievement in environmental management by Greentech foundation India.

III. Human Resources

The employees of the company are important and valuable assets and have contributed significantly in achieving sustained growth over the years. During the year 20009-10, significant advancements were made on multiple fronts in different Human Resources (HR) processes. To enable better interface, initiatives like introduction of HR Help Desk, Employee Self Service and e-Learning applications were done during the year.

People development has been a key element in the DNA of the company. While each and every plays a part in scripting her/his 'Development', certain focused activities are also carried out to ensure synergy and growth.

e-Learning was introduced in the Company during the year 2009-10 to meet the ever growing diverse developmental needs of the organisation that is spread across multiple locations. The year also saw stabilization of the Performance Management System that was put during the place during the 2008-09 with greater ownership and competence.

During the year, the industrial relations at all the plants of the company continued to be cordial. The year that went by has seen the company move many notches in putting in place the basics that automatically sets the company ups for continuing and augmenting superlative people oriented action in the year to come.

IV. Corporate Social Responsibility

Today business environment demand that corporates play a pivotal role in shouldering social responsibility. We will be happy to learn that in the year under review the company executed several Corporate Social Responsibility (CSR) programmes for the benefit of the company where we operates. The company CSR initiatives primarily focus on three core areas: Water conservation, Aged Care and Education.

The Total Water Management (TWM) Centre located in the premises of the company's manufacturing facility at Bhandup, Mumbai has been championing the issue of water conservation; informing and demonstrating techniques of water harvesting to the public at large. A large number of concerned citizens ranging from representatives of government bodies, housing societies, corporate and even school students have visited the TWM centre to obtain a holistic perspective on water management. The company has also organized and participated in the numerous seminars to create awareness on this fast depleting natural resource.

The company continues to operate mobile Medicare Units around the Patancheru (Andra Pradesh), Kasna (Uttar Pradesh), Sriperumbudur (Tamil Nadu), and Ankleshwar (Gujarat). Plants also provides health care to the elders in the villages. In the area around the Sriperumbudur plant, this initiative being administer in collaboration with Help Age India, an NGO. Additionally, other aids like dentures, cataract surgeries, hearing aids, wheel chairs, walking sticks, etc. are also being provided to the elderly. Camps are also held to involve the elders in activities which provide them joy and feeling of inclusion within the society. The company is also actively involved in upgrading the infrastructure facilities in schools near its plants to facilitate proper and unhindered education of children staying in villages in the vicinity of the plants.

V. Information Technology

During 2009-10, the company has set up and stabilized two centralized Customer Contact Centers for improving servicing to its dealers. The contact centres have been provided with advanced telephony solutions with integration with the company's backend applications. This has allowed the Company to standardize the order taking process and provide dealers with a uniform, agile, and improved experience of interacting with the company. This has also given the capability to improve the speed of enabling new services being offered to the dealers and end consumers.

The Rohtak Plant which has commissioned in April 2010, has been implemented using Advanced Manufacturing Execution Systems which optimizes the material flow controls used in paint manufacturing. This will improve the throughput of the plant and rovide real time information visibility of operations.

As stated above, with the increasing global focus on the environment and the preservation, the company has implemented an environment, health and safety (EHS), system to streamline the processes, monitor compliance to standards and report of various control parameters.

While the company continues to strengthen existing systems and processes to drive efficiencies, during the year under review, the Company has also invested towards building a robust infrastructure to manage structured and unstructured information in the organisation. This will be implemented in phases in the next 18 months.

VI. Research and Development

The Company is executing an integrated strategy for technology development and deployment. The technology function supporting the company's strategy around for missions: technology development, development of substantially new products, productivity improvement and cost reduction. The focus of the Company in the financial year 2009-10 had been to exploit and leverage the results of technology development and platform programmes and set the stage for a shift towards eco friendly products. A number of those new concepts will be incorporated in products to be launched next year. This is to allows the company to meet its mid and long term strategic goals. Those capabilities, build on the technology trends and customers requirements made possible development of substantially new products and productivity improvements in manufacturing. The technology group also puts a reward emphasis on rejuvenating the products portfolio in support of the joint venture. Furthermore, the integration of the overseas technical groups has continued and their support has increased to leverage the Company capabilities. The removal of lead has been extended to products sold in overseas units.

Your company will continue to strengthen collaboration with research organizations to accelerate progress. Some of those programmes are bearing fruits and will enhance the overall technical capabilities in the area of resins and emulsions development. The company has been successful in increasing its presence in international forums through publications in peer review journals. The recognition of work of its scientists has helped shape an image of the organization that attracts competent and committed scientists. The company scientists were recognised with the Gordon award for their work in the area of self cleaning paints.

VII. Internal Control Systems and their Adequacy

The company is committed to ensuring comprehensive internal controls across its operations to ensure that all assets are safeguarded and protected against loss from unauthorized use or disposition. Towards the end, it has deployed:

(i) A well-defined control structure using a mix of manual and automated control systems.

(ii) Well defined procedures to carry put and approve financial transactions.

(iii) Well defined review mechanisms at different levels in the hierarchy in all aspects of company performance.

(iv) Shared services model implemented for the company with the objective of improving control and centralizing payments.

(v) Independent internal audit department continuously monitoring and reporting on the adequacy or otherwise of internal control processes across the business units.

(vi) A risk based approach towards developing an Audit Plan for the Company and its subsidiaries which is presented to the audit committees for their approval and feedback.

(*vii*) A blend of process audit and operational audits covering both domestic and international operations to ensure true and fair reporting and compliance with regulatory requirements as well as internal policies.

(*viii*) A mechanism to bring significant observations along with any action plan identified by the management to the attention of the audit committee for review and guidance at periodic intervals.

VIII. Risk and Outlook

The forces that are driving the current rebound are partly temporary in nature, including major fiscal stimulus and central banks' support for credit markets. A significant risk could be a premature exit from the accommodative monetary and fiscal policies currently in place. In general, the global economy still seems vulnerable with the ongoing upheaval on account of sovereign debtor crisis in the European Union, a pointer to the imbalances prevalent in the world economy. If the growth trajectory achieved so far is not sustained, it could have a significant impact on sentiments and adversely impact consumer demand and consumption both in the Indian as well as International markets. Interest rates have already started picking across the world. This can have an adverse impact on demand, particularly in the interest rate sensitive sectors like housing and automobiles. Also, if as a result of adverse geopolitical, economic or natural conditions, the economies of countries where the company has significance presence do not perform well, the performance of the company can get affected. These risks are continually monitored while managing the Company's overall operations.

However, the overall outlook for 2010-11 appears to be positive but nevertheless challenging. In many of the emerging and developing economies, activity is expected to be buoyant, largely driven by good internal demand as well as the upturn in demand in the advanced regions. In most of the advanced economies, the economic recovery is expected to continue, albeit at a lower rate than in the past. While there are concerns with regard to substantive reforms, infrastructure bottleneck, insurgent activities within the country, spiraling inflation on account of the food price increases etc. The Company believes that the economy would remain buoyant in the medium term and is optimistic that the Indian economy will be able to achieve a GDP growth in excess of 7.5%. Also, with early prediction of normal monsoon in India, the company expects rural economy to perform well and support paint demand in rural areas. In addition, policy initiatives like increasing the slabs of income tax exemption and renewed thrust on infrastructure sector is expected to provide further support to paint demand. The progress on key reforms, especially on taxation, needs to be watched.

The company is optimistic about its performance in 2010-11, given that these factors augur well for demand of paints in India as well as the other international markets where the Company has presence. However, rising input prices could make the operating margins achieved in the past year unsustainable.

Practice Questions

Objective Type Questions

1. MD & A Reporting in India was launched by the:
   (*a*) Ministry of Corporate Affairs
   (*b*) RBI
   (*c*) Ministry of Finance
   (*d*) SEBI
2. MD & A Reporting is mandatory under listing agreement clause:
   (*a*) 40 (*b*) 44
   (*c*) 49 (*d*) 53
3. MD & A Reporting was recommended by the:
   (*a*) Kumarmangalam Birla Committee
   (*b*) J J Irani Committee
   (*c*) CIC Committee
   (*d*) None of the above

4. Performance drivers are not concerned with:
   (*a*) Core competency
   (*b*) Qualities of superior performances
   (*c*) Social Responsibility
   (*d*) Entrepreneurship
5. Number of guidance notes issued by the Canadian Institute of Chartered Accountant are :
   (*a*) 18 (*b*) 20
   (*c*) 22 (*d*) 24

Ans: 1. (d), 2. (c), 3. (a), 4. (d), 5. (b)

Short Answer Questions

1. What is MD & A reporting?
2. What do you mean by forward-looking statements?
3. Explain the scope of MD & A reporting.
4. What do you know by Caveat regarding MD & A reporting?
5. Explain the rationale of MD & A reporting.

Long Answer Questions

1. What do you mean by Management Discussion & Analysis? Examine its regulatory framework.
2. Explain the nature of Management Discussion and Analysis. Also give critical comments about it.
3. Evaluate the historical perspective of Management Development and Analysis.
4. Examine the rationale and different aspects of MD & A reporting.
5. Give in brief about the questions set in guidance notes issues by the Canadian Institute of Chartered Accountants.

References

1. Glautier M and Underdow, B. Accounting Theory and Practice. Pitman Publishing, London, 1982, p. 409.
2. Guidance Notes Issues by Canadian Institute of chartered Accounts (CICA).
3. Asian Paints, Annual Report, 2009-10.

19 INDUSTRIAL SICKNESS IN INDIA

Problem of industrial sickness is not specific to any industry or country. In developed economies with better social security systems and abundant capital. The approach to sickness is to restore a unit to normalcy through restructuring devices within a short period of time or else close it down. Such easy and straight forward options are not available to labour abundant economies like India which can ill afford large scale unemployment either of labour or of valuable productive assets caused by sickness. Further, sizeable funds of banks and financial institutions and blocked up in sick units which impair the banks profitably and their ability to recycle fund in other productive areas. This has an adverse effect on the economy of country like India. Thus, industrial sickness is a result of faulty management policies as well as fiscal problems. Under such circumstances, isolated fiscal reforms programme with a determined management and relevant management policies for revival of sick industries.

"Industrial development is identified as the effective means to the economic growth in any country. Industrial sickness has become a common feature of the large scale sector as well as small scale sector. In spite of the enactment of special legislations and various steps taken by the government and RBI to deal with the problem, industrial sickness is growing. The liberalization of the economy resulting into increased competition has added to the problem of industrial sickness."[1] "Closures of business units and corporate failures resulting in bankruptcies have become a normal feature in market economies the world over."[2] Growing competition and the ever-changing international economic environment often lead to high incidence of corporate failures in developed market economies. However, these economies have the resilience to absorb the economic disturbances brought about by the closure of industrial units. In order to combat the problem of industrial sickness, a comprehensive assessment of the magnitude of industrial sickness and an analysis of the main factors which bring about sickness are necessary. Both prevention and cure of industrial sickness would depend on our ability to identify sickness as early as possible and analyse its causes. Faulty or delayed identification would reduce the effectiveness of the remedial action such as restoring the financial viability of sick units and protecting units which would become sick.

The problem of industrial sickness is nothing peculiar to our economy or any developing country. It is also present in the advanced countries, but there it is considered prudent to shut down the units if they are sick. But in developing countries, like India, one cannot afford to do so as it will lead to substantial national block capital to go waste and create unemployment of those already employed, when additional employment is a crying need of the hour. Even 'not so fit' or 'unfit' industries may have to be rendered a helping hand to raise and stand on their own, to avoid wastage or total loss of funds and other resources already invested therein.

Criteria for Identification of Sick Units

The Reserve Bank of India identifies sick industrial units on the basis of a mix of criteria including continued cash losses, imbalances in the financial structure, and deterioration in liquidity. "A unit may be considered sick if it has incurred cash losses for one year and, in the judgement of the Bank (RBI), it is likely to continue to incur cash losses for the current year as well as the following year and the unit has an imbalance in its financial structure such as current ratio of less than 1:1 and worsening debt equity ratio."[2]

Term lending institutions identify sickness on the following criteria:

(*i*) continuous defaults in meeting four consecutive half-yearly installments of interest or principal of institutional loans.

(*ii*) continuous cash losses for a period of two years or continued erosion in the net worth by 50 per cent or more mounting arrears on account of statutory or other liabilities for a period of one or two years. The most stringent definition is given in the Sick Industrial Companies (Special Provisions) Act of 1985, which defined a sick unit as "An industrial company (being a company registered for not less than seven years), which has at the end of any financial year accumulated losses equal to or exceeding its entire net worth and has also suffered cash losses in such financial year and the financial year immediately preceding such financial year," These definitions view sickness in terms of extreme deterioration in the financial health of the unit. However, the criteria do not warn sufficiently well in advance about the impending closure of a unit. For instance, the wiping out of the entire net worth of a unit accompanied by at least two consecutive years of cash loss clearly signals extreme form of sickness which would in fact take the enterprise to the brink of closure. Similarly, severe cash losses with persistent defaults in institutional debt servicing also indicate fairly advanced stage of sickness on the part of the industrial unit, though this stage would certainly precede the stage of complete erosion of the net worth of the unit. The criteria, in fact, delay the identification process by at least a couple of years or more.

Concept of Weak Units

The recent RBI guidelines facilitate the detection of sickness at the incipient stage but only for large and medium units. An industrial unit will be termed as "weak," if at the end of any accounting year it has:

(*i*) accumulated losses equal to or exceeding 50 per cent of its peak net worth in the immediately preceding five accounting years.

(*ii*) a current ratio of less than 1:1.

(*iii*) suffered a cash loss in the immediately preceding accounting year.

Incipient sickness: If the downfall in the smooth functioning of various operational areas of the unit continues unabated. The actual process of sickness then starts. Such a stage is considered to be incipient sickness and is identified by reference to the following symptoms:

(1) There are continuous such losses from year to year and the trend is expected to continue in future.

(2) Deterioration is expected in the current ratio in the current financial year, even though the same may have been more than one in the previous financial year.

(3) There is gradual erosion in the net worth during the previous and current financial year and is expected to continue in future also.

(4) Deterioration continues in the debt-equity position in the current financial year and subsequently also.

In a nutshell, it may be seen that incipient industrial sickness is that stage where the unit incurs cash losses; however the position of financial structure may not be very much alarming. This is the time to take certain corrective measures to prevent the unit from turning into sickness. This will, however require proper identification, care and follow-up programme.

According to Section 3 (O) of the Sick Industrial Companies Act, 1985, a sick industrial company is an industrial company (being a company registered for not less than 5 years) which has at the end of any financial year accumulated losses equal to or exceeding its entire net worth. The condition of 7 years have reduced to 5 years and the condition regarding cash losses has been omitted by the 1993 amendment.

With regard to potentially sick industrial companies the SICA has provisions for identifying impending sickness as of 50% or more of the net worth. If the accumulated losses of an industrial company in any financial year have resulted in erosion of 50% or more of its net worth during the immediately preceding 4 years (5 years reduced to 4 years by the 1993 Amendment), it is considered as potentially sick and in such cases the company shall within a period of 60 days from the date of finalization of the duly audited accounts of the company for the relevant financial year report to this effect to the Board and held a general meeting of the shareholders of the company for bringing the fact to their notice.

Criteria to Identify Sickness / Incipient Sickness

In order to measure sickness, information on, whether the unit has outstanding source(s) of the loan (institutional/non-intuitional), whether there was delay in institutional loan for more than 12 months and whether there was erosion in the extent of 50 per cent of the net worth during the previous accounting year, was collected in the Census. On the basis of this information, the definition given by the Kohli Committee measure sickness. In other to measure incipient sickness, the continuous decline in three consecutive years was identified as a suitable indicator, and so information given was continuous decline in gross output compared to the previous two financial data collected. Thus, the following criteria was adapted to identify sick / incipient sick Census:

(*i*) Continuous decline in gross output compared to the previous two financial years,

(*ii*) Delay in repayment of institutional loan, for more than 12 months, and

(*iii*) Erosion in the net worth to the extent of 50 percent of the net worth during the accounting year.

Sickness/incipient being a leading question, the enumerators were asked from the entrepreneurs of the units satisfying at least one of the above criteria, and has not been running satisfactorily.

By the Companies (second amendment Act) 2002

Define a sick company as one :

(*i*) Which has accumulated losses if any financial year equal to 50% or more of its average net worth during four years immediately preceding the financial year in question, or

(*ii*) Which has failed to repay its debts within any three consecutive quarters on demand for repayment by its creditors.

Potential Sickness Industry Company

"An industrial company whose accumulated loss is more than 50% or more of its peak net worth during the immediately preceding four financial years."

Signals and Symptoms of Sickness

Sick companies start throwing up signals, which need to be identified and monitored before the unit becomes gravely sick. In the early stages of sickness, the warning signals in several functional areas are termed as signals. The persistence of these signals over a long period become symptoms of sickness. An industrial unit tends to show signs of financial distress starting with short term liquidity problems, revenue losses, operating losses and moving in the direction of over use of external credit until it reaches a stage where it is overburdened with debt and not being able to generate sufficient funds to meet its obligation. The signals gradually merge into symptoms and get related to plant performance, capacity utilization, financial ratios, share market price, practices in the area of finance, production, marketing and labour relations etc.

While the existence of the signals and symptoms is a ground for suspecting that the industrial unit concerned is prone to sickness, the magnitude of sickness cannot be predicted on these grounds alone. An objective analysis of units (sick vs. healthy) financial condition over a time period is necessary.

Stages of Sickness[3]

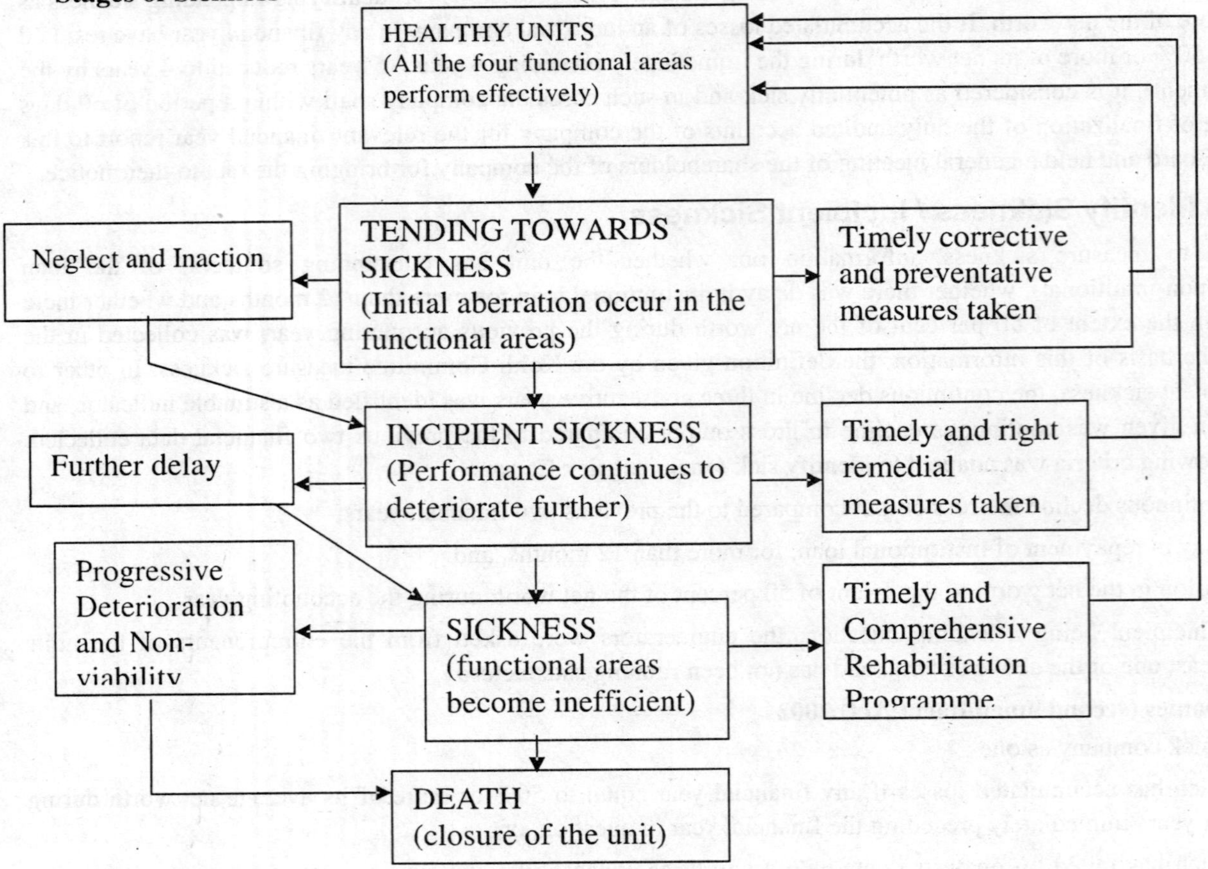

Rehabilitation

Rehabilitation is a remedy considered for industrial units, which had already become sick and are on the verge of virtual collapse. Some viable policy measures are required to revive the sick units.

Rehabilitation has been discussed under two heads:

(*i*) What has been done at various levels – the union government, the RBI, and financial institutions- to rehabilitate sick units?

(*ii*) What should be done to revive sick units?

Rehabilitation Programme

The rehabilitation programme will involve the following major issues which have to be sorted out after it has been decided that the sick unit is viable and should be rehabilitated:

(*a*) Change of management.

(*b*) Development of a suitable management information system.

(*c*) A settlement with the creditors for payment of their dues in a phased manner, taking into account the expected cash generation as per viability study.

(*d*) Determination of the sources of additional funds needed to refinance.

(*e*) Modernisation of plant and equipment or expansion of an existing programme or even diversification of the products being manufactured.

(*f*) Concession or reliefs or assistance to be allowed by the state level corporation, financial institutions and central government.

Board for Industrial and Financial Reconstruction (BIFR)

The Board for Industrial and Financial Reconstruction (BIFR) was set up in January 1987 under the Sick Industrial Companies (Special Provision) Act, 1985 (SICA). It has been established with a view to revive potentially viable sick industrial companies or recommend the closure of totally non-viable companies. The BIFR became operational from 15th May 1987.

Earlier, only sick units in private sector could be referred to it but after amendment in the SICA in December, 1991, public enterprises have also been brought under its purview.

Objectives of BIFR

The principle objectives of BIFR are as follows:

(*a*) To evaluate the techno-economic viability of sick industrial companies with a view to either rehabilitating them or to closing them down.

(*b*) To stop continues drain of public and private resources; and

(*c*) To protect employment, as far as it is practicable.

Operational Procedure

When a sick industrial company is registered with the BIFR, it is dealt with by the BIFR in the following manner: (a) In the first stage, an enquiry has to be held to determine whether the company is sick. (b) If so determined, the BIFR has to determine whether the company can make its net worth positive through its own efforts. (c) If that is not possible, a finding has to be recorded as to whether it is in the public interest to attempt to rehabilitate the company. The measures which the BIFR can take are outlines in SICA. (d) The rehabilitation effort commences by commissioning an Operating Agency to prepare techno-economic viability report. Operating Agencies comprise the all India financial institutions and selected Banks the latter on the basis of RBI's advice, (e) Based on the viability report and such other measures (such as merger, change of management) as may be appropriate, BIFR can proceed to draw a draft scheme of rehabilitation. Such scheme has to be agreed by the parties which are called upon to give relief and concessions in respect of past liabilities and to give fresh funds by way of long-term capital or working capital. (f) It is advertised inviting comments and objections. Therefore, the scheme can be sanctioned with or without modification by the BIFR.

Ultimately, the BIFRA may recommend for rehabilitation of sick unit or its taking over by the workers' co-operative or its sale or its closure.

Functioning of Operating Agency under SICA

Under the provision of the SICA, an operating agency performs the following function:

1. Conducting inquiry: In respect of a sick industrial company and make a report with respect to such matters as may be specified by the BIFR. The enquiry should be completed as expeditiously as possible and an endeavour should be made to complete the enquiry within 60 days from the commencement of the enquiry. [Section 16(2) and (3)]

2. Preparation of Scheme: The operating agency has to prepare the schemes as specified in sub-section (3) of Section 17 of SICA and sub-section (1) of Section 18. The scheme should be prepared quickly and ordinarily within a period of 90 days from the date of the order of BIFR.

3. Recommending to BIFR various steps to be taken to remove the difficulties in the implementation of the scheme sanctioned by the BIFR [Section 18(9)].

4. To implement the sanctioned scheme if so ordered by BIFR.

5. The operating agency may be appointed as the liquidator by the High Court (Section 30(3)).

6. To prepare detailed list of assets, liabilities, shareholders, etc. with respect to a company as may be required by the BIFR. Section 21 for the proper discharge of the function, empowers the BIFR to require any operating agency to prepare with respect to a company:

(*a*) A complete inventory of:

(*i*) all assets and liabilities of whatever nature;

(*ii*) all book of accounts, registers, maps, plants, records, documents of title or ownership of property and all other documents of whatever nature relating thereto.

(*b*) a list of shareholders and list of creditors showing separately in the list of creditors, the secured creditors and unsecured creditors.

(*c*) a valuation report in respect of the shares and assets in order to arrive at a reserve-price for the sale of the industrial undertaking to the company or for fixation of lease rent or share exchange ratio.

(*d*) an estimate for reserve price, lease rent or share exchange ratio and

(*e*) proforma accounts, where no up-to-date audited accounts are available.

Working of the BIFR

At present, the BIFR is overburdened with the perusal of rehabilitation package forwarded to it for revival of enterprises which are sick. On an average, it takes two or three to finalize the package resulting in apprehension of workers about their future and blockage of funds which leads to further decline in the state of sickness of the enterprise. The government has decided that the enterprises whose cases are pending with the BIFR would continue to get financial assistance from the banks. However, with the amendment of SICA, 1985 the PEs have also been brought under the purview of the BIFR resulting in further increase in burden on the BIFR which is already capable of handling the amount of work it has in hand. As such, the government has to think of ways and means to process the cases for rehabilitation in a speedy manner by providing the necessary infrastructure to the BIFR.

All companies served with closure orders by the Board have been referred to state High Courts before finally winding them up. As these cases take over five years before a final settlement is arrived at, none of these winding-up orders have been implemented. It is not just the High Court which are making the BIFR orders ineffective. According to industry point of view, while an exit policy does exist at present in the form of BIFR, not much has been achieved in this direction as the Board also does not have enough powers to rehabilitate or wind up a sick company. It is important to note that the Board has sought changes in SICA to arm itself with powers to revive or wind up ailing companies as the present process is very cumbersome. The Board has always had problems in hastening the process of rehabilitation or winding up as it cannot take physical possession of a unit. The All India Financial Institution like IFCI, IDBI and ICICI also cannot take possession of a unit despite their heavy financial involvement in the companies. This hinders immediate winding up or rehabilitation process. It is important to note that BIFR is taking more time in deciding the cases referred to it. There has been two important reasons for such delay:

(i) BIFR is a quasi-judicial body, which emphasizes consensus from all and gives veto power to anyone; and

(ii) parties often wriggle out of commitments made by them. There is a need for developing a system to decide case expeditiously and timely.

In fact, the labour class suffers a lot due to this delay as it has no say and not much staying power. It is urgently needed that not only sickness is detected early but sickness is cured sooner and in economically cheaper way. Keeping this fact in mind, the Goswami Committee has recommended that danger signal for sickness should flash when there is a 180-days default in term-lending dues or a 180- days irregularity in last-credit or working capital. This will save the nation from growing sickness and help in early cure of sickness. if any.

Since its inception in May, 1987 till the end of August, 2005, the Board for Industrial and Financial Reconstruction (BIFR) received 6,991 references under the Sick Industrial Companies (Special Provision) Act (SICA), 1985. These references included 296 reference from Central and State PSUs (CPSUs and SPSUs). Out of the reference received 5,412 references were registered under section 15 of SICA. 1987 references were dismissed as non-maintable under the Act, 748 rehabilitation schemes, by appellate authority for industrial and financial recommendation (AAIFR) or Supreme Court (SC), where sanctioned and 1,306 companies were recommended to be wound up. 385 companies were declared 'no-longer sick' and were discharged from the purview of SICA on the year net worth turning positive after the implementation of the schemes. Among the 296 references for PSUs, 213 (91 CPSUs and 122 SPSUs) were registered up to September 30, 2006. Rehabilitation schemes were sanctioned for 28 CPSUs and 26 SPSUs. It was recommended that 29 CPSUs be wound up, 9 CPSUs and 14 SPSUs were declared 'no-longer sick'.

Exhibit 19.1

References to BIFR as on September 30, 2006						
Sl. No.	**Status**	**Private**	**Central PSUs**	**State PSUs**	**Total PSUs**	**Total**
1	References received	6,695	108	188	296	6,991
2	Registration declines	1,484	17	66	83	1,567
3	Under Scrutiny	12	0	0	0	12
A 4	References registered	5,199	91	122	213	5,412
DISPOSALS						
5	Dismissed					
	(i) as non-maintainable	1,660	11	36	47	1,707
	(ii) as multiple registered	218	0	0	0	218
6	Rehabilitation schemes approved/sanctioned					
	(i) by BIFR	695	27	26	53	748
	(ii) by AAIFR/SC	11	1	0	1	12
7	Declared on longer sick out of Sl No. 6	462	9	14	23	485
8	Winding up recommended to the concerned high courts	1,234	29	40	69	1,303
9	Dropped now	119	5	3	8	127
B	Total (5+6+8+9)	3,937	73	105	178	4,115
C	PENDING					
10	Draft schemes circulated	42	2	0	2	44
11	Winding up notice issued	85	1	4	5	90
12	Pending for sickness determination	357	2	1	3	360
13	Declared sick	678	11	10	21	699
14	Schemes failed and reopened	8	1	0	1	9
15	Pending cases remanded by AAIFR	43	1	2	3	46
16	Stay ordered by courts	46	0	3	3	49
	Total (C =A-B)	1,262	18	17	35	1,297

Source: BIFR, Department of Economic Affairs, Ministry of Finance.

Constraints and Problems

The BIFR has listed the following constraints and problems which inhibits its smooth functioning:

1. Delay in submission of reports by operating agencies.

2. Lack of prompt and final response from the concerned governments and their agencies in the matter of reliefs and concessions and further infusion of funds for rehabilitation of potentially viable units in the public sector.
3. Greater reluctance on the part of banks and FIs to support sick companies in the wake of the RBI guidelines on provisioning against NPA (Non-performing Assets) and delays in the release of working capital.
4. Prolonged delays on the part of promoters in a large number of cases to bring in promoters contribution in time and according to the prescribed percentage.
5. Appeals registered with the AAIFR against BIFR orders total 730 till end 1999. Time in taken in deciding these appeals. It would appear that most of the decisions of the BIFR have been appealed in AAIFR.
6. Several cases of appeal against BIFR decisions have been made to High Courts, where they linger on for fairly long periods.

Restructuring of Legal Framework for Industrial Sickness

The SICA was enacted in 1985 to tackle the grave problem of industrial sickness in India. But it became a tool of rampant abuse in the hands of delinquent promoters, who partied merrily under the umbrella of protection provided by the now infamous Section 22 of the Act. while the frustrated creditors and lenders watched, helplessly. Such promoters even managed to obtain and further benefit from additional activities carried on in such establishment or undertaking or any unit thereof is an industry and the other activity or each of the other activities carried on in such establishment or undertaking or unit thereof is not severable from and is, for the purpose of carrying on, or aiding the carrying on of, such predominant activity or activities, the entire establishment or undertaking or, as the case may be, unit thereof shall be deemed to be an industrial establishment or undertaking."

As the Bill merely refers to an 'industrial undertaking' without clearly defining it as is done by the SICA, an amendment to the definition in the Bill for the said term will be the only way for avoidance of what could be a ground for litigation.

The definition of 'industrial undertaking talks about an undertaking 'pertaining to any industry'. The term 'industry' is not defined in the Companies Act, 1956. It is also riot defined under the Depositories Act, 1996 read with Section 2-A of the Act. Whereas the term used and defined in the SICA is 'scheduled industry', a similar term and definition are absent from the Bill. Therefore, difficulties about interpretation of the term 'industry' may arise. A Seven-Judge Bench of the Supreme Court *in-Bangalore Water Supply & Swwerage* Board AIR 1978 SC 548 had the opportunity to analyze the meaning and scope of the term 'industry' under the Industrial disputes Act, 1947. A study of the far-reaching judgment could be an eye-opener in understanding how difficult it is to understand the true meaning of the term 'industry' in the absence of a clear-cut definition.

The intention of the Government as to where it wants the existing definition of 'industrial undertaking' as contained in the SICA to continue is not clear. If only 'scheduled industrial undertakings' as contained in the SICA read with the IDRA are to be brought within the definition, it will be fit and proper to incorporate the same definition of industrial undertaking, scheduled industry, factory, etc, in the Bill also.

Factory- Though the definition of 'industrial undertaking' in the Bill uses the word 'factory', there is no definition for the term 'factory' in the Companies Act, 1956. The SICA also does not define 'factory. However, for the purpose of the SICA, the definition of 'factory' as contained in Section 3(c) of the Industries (Development and Regulation) Act, 1951 as premises where a manufacturing process is carried on may be referred to. There is no nexus between the manufacturing process and the number of workers employed nor is there any reference to the use of power. In the Factories Act, 1948, a 'factory' is defined on the same lines as in the IDRA which is relevant for the SICA except for the difference that the number of workers is 10 and 20 respectively instead of 50 and 100 workers in the IDRA definition. Thus, it will be noticed that different Acts define the term 'factory' differently and in the absence of a specific definition to be followed for the purpose of the Companies Act, 1956, confusion and avoidable litigation will be the end-result.

Unit The definition of 'industrial undertaking' also uses the word 'units' in the definition. There is no definition for the term 'unit or units' in company law. It may be noted here that the term 'unit' is defined in the *Explanation* to the definition of the term 'undertaking' in Section 2(v) of the Monopolies and 'Restrictive Trade Practices Act. 1969. However, reference to the MRTP Act, 1969, without a corresponding reference in the Companies Act. 1956 itself cannot always be resorted to.

Sick Industrial Company- The Bill has a revised definition of 'sick industrial company' which recognizes failure to pay debts as a criterion for determining sickness. The erosion of net worth continues to be another recognised criterion for determining sickness.

Operating agency- The definition of the term 'operating agency' has also undergone a change. A group of experts consisting of persons having special knowledge of' business or industry, henceforth will be the operating agency. No doubt, public financial institutions, State level institutions, scheduled banks or any other person to be specified by the National Company Law Tribunal will also be an 'operating agency'.

Company Amendment Bill, 2001

Sick Industrial Companies (Special Provisions) Repeal Bill, 2001 has been introduced in the Parliament on August 23, 2001 to repeal the Sick Industrial Companies (Special Provisions) Act, 1985 (SICA). The bill will be taken up in the Parliament soon, and when passed, it shall come into force on a date to be announced by the Central Government, by notification in the Official Gazette.

The Sick Industrial Companies (Special Provisions) Act, 1985 (1 of 1986) (the Act) was enacted on January 9, 1986 to tackle the problem of industrial sickness. This act was amended during the year 1993. The Act contains, among other things, provisions for:

(*i*) Preparation and sanction of the scheme of rehabilitation. If any by the Board (Section 18)

(*ii*) Procedure for winding up of sick industrial companies found to be non-viable (Section 20)

(*iii*) Suspension of legal proceedings, contracts etc. during the specified period when the matter is pending before the Board for Industrial and Financial Reconstruction (BIFR/Appellate Authority for Industrial and Financial Reconstruction (AAIFR) (Section 22)

Even though 15 years have been completed the working of the BIFR could not be considered satisfactory because of the enormous delay in disposal of the cases. The necessity of consensus amongst secured creditors before finalization of the revival schemes was the main factor took shelter under the umbrella of the BIFR. Excessive protection to sick industries has been hetherto available under Section 22 of the SICA which provides for automatic stay of all proceedings. Hence, financial institutions found it difficult to proceed to take legal action against the mechanism the Government has accepted the recommendations of the Eradi Committee and agreed to scrap the SICA. Accordingly the Government introduced the Bill in the Parliament to repeal SICA.

Main features of the SICA Repeal Bill

The main features of the Sick Industrial Companies (Special Provisions) Repeal Bill, 2001 are as follows :

(*i*) The Bill seeks to repeal the Sick Industrial Companies Act, 1985 (1 of 1986)

(*ii*) The Bill envisages dissolution of the BIFR and the AAIFR : and

(*iii*) All proceedings pending before the BIFR and the AAIFR prior to their dissolution shall stand abated.

However, the repealed enactment shall not affect the following:

(*i*) any other enactment in which the repealed enactment has been applied, incorporated or referred to :

(*ii*) the previous operation of the repealed enactment or anything duly done or suffered thereunder:

(*iii*) any right, privilege, obligation or liability acquired, accused or incurred under the repealed enactment ;

(*iv*) any other made by the Board for preparation and sanction of the schemes.

The proposed new framework

The task of rehabilitating sick industrial units is proposed to be vested in the National Company Law Tribunal (NCLT) proposed to be constituted by amending the Companies Act, 1956. The Central Government while introducing the bill for repealing the SICA has simultaneously introduced the Companies (Amendment) Bill, 2001 (the CAB 2001), with the aim, inter alia, of constituting the National Company Law Tribunal (Tribunal).

The Tribunal will be set up to exercise the powers and jurisdiction presently being exercised by various bodies, viz., the CLB, the BIFR and the AAIFR and High Courts and consequently the multiplicity of litigation before various Courts or quasi-judicial bodies or forums regarding revival or rehabilitation or merger or amalgamation or winding up and insolvency will be avioded and the matter will be decided by the proposed Tribunal.

In the CAB 2001 a new Part VI-A has been inserted after the existing Part VI. The new Part VI-A contains the provisions relating to revival and rehabilitation of sick industrial companies. In view of this amendment new section from 424-A to 424-L will be inserted in the Companies Act, 1956 relating to matters concerning sick industrial companies. Besides winding-up procedures will also be under the purview of Tribunal. A new section 433 will be substituted in place of existing Section 433 of the Companies Act, 1956. The new section 433 related to circumstances in which a company may be wound up if the Tribubal is of the opinion that the company should be wound up under the circumstances specified in Section 424-G of the CAB, 2001.

As per this provision, if the Tribunal is of the opinion that the sick industrial company is not likely to make its net worth exceed the accumulated losses within a reasonable time while meeting all its accumulated losses and that the company as a result thereof is not likely to become viable in future and that it is just and equitable that the company should be wound up, it may record its finding and order winding up of the company.

A comparison is given below in respect of provisions relating to revival and rehabilitation (not relating to winding up) of sick industrial companies of the SICA and the CAB 2001:

Sl.No.	Reference Section in the Companies (Amendment) Bill, 2001	Subject	Reference Section in SICA
1	2	3	4
1.	46-AA	Definition of Sick Industrial Company	3(O)
2.	31-AA	Definition of Operating Agency	3(1)
3.	424-A	Reference to the Tribunal	15
4.	424-B	Inquiry into the working of sick industrial companies	16
5.	424-C	Powers of the Tribunal to suitable order on completion of enquiry	17
6.	424-D	Preparation and sanction of scheme	18
7.	424-E	Rehabilitation by giving financial assistance	19
8.	424-F	Arrangement for continuing operations etc. during inquiry	19A
9.	424-G	Winding up of sick industrial company	20
10.	424-H	Operating Agency to prepare complete inventory etc.	21
11	424-I	Direction not to dispose off assets	22A
12.	424-J	Power of Tribunal to call for periodic information	23B
13.	424-K	Misfeasance proceedings	24
14.	424-L	Penalty for certain offences	33
15.	10 FQ	Appeal	25

Note: In the above sections, wherever 'Board' is mentioned in SICA, it has been replaced by the Tribunal I the CAB, 2001.

Changes brought in by the CAB, 2001

The following are the important changes brought in by the CAB, 2001:

1. **Definition of Operating Agency:** As per Section 3(1) of the SICA, 'Operating Agency" means any public financial institutions, state level institution, scheduled bank or any other person as may be specified by general order or special order as its agency by the Board.

In accordance with Section 31-AA of the CAB, 2001, 'Operating Agency' means any group of experts consisting of persons having special knowledge of business or industry in which the sick industrial company was engaged and includes public financial institution, state level institution, scheduled bank or any other person as may be specified as the operating agency by the Tribunal.

2. **Definition of Sick Industrial Company:** As per Section 3(o) of the SICA, 'sick industrial company' means an industrial company (being a company registered for not less than five years) which has at the end of any financial year accumulated losses equal to or exceeding its entire net worth.

   As per Section 46-AA of the CAB, 2001, 'Sick Industrial Company' means an industrial company which has-

   (*i*) accumulated losses in any financial year equal to fifty per cent or more of its average net worth during four years immediately preceding such financial year, or

   (*ii*) failed to repay its debt within any three consecutive quarters on demand for its repayment by a creditor or creditors of such company.

3. **Expeditious completion of inquiry:** In the proposed Section 424-B of the CAB, 2001 relating to the preparation and sanction of schemes, the operating agency shall complete its enquiry as expeditiously as possible and submit its report to the Tribunal within twenty-one days from the date of such order prepare the scheme within a period of sixty days (Earlier ninety days) from the date of order of the Tribunal.

4. **Government Companies:** As per the SICA Government companies are not exempted. As per Section 424-A of the CAB, 2001 reference is not required to be made in respect of a Government company. However, a Government company may make a reference to the Tribunal with the previous approval of the Central Government or the State Government as the case may be.

5. **Certificate from auditor:** The application to the Tribunal for reference shall be accompanies by a certificate from an auditor from a panel of auditors prepared by the Tribunal indicating—

   (*a*) the reasons of the net worth of such company being less than fifty per cent ; or

   (*b*) the default in repayment of its debt making such company a sick industrial company as the case may be.

6. **Repayment of debt:** The scheme normally covers payments of debt. However Section 424(d) of the CAB, 2001 now specifically provides for repayment of debt.

7. **Copy of Scheme to be filed with the Registrar:** In accordance with Section 424(9) of the CAB, 2001, a copy of the sanctioned scheme shall be filed with the Registrar within a prescribed time by the company to which such scheme relates.

8. **Creditors may also prepare a scheme:** The creditors of a sick industrial company may also prepare a scheme for revival or rehabilitation of that company and submit the same to the Tribunal for its sanction. However, no scheme shall be submitted by the creditors to the Tribunal unless such scheme by the Tribunal shall, as far as may be, apply to the scheme. The scheme if sanctioned by the Tribunal, shall be binding on all the creditors and no others concerned.

9. Penalty for certain offences-In accordance with Section 33 of the SICA whoever violates the provisions of the Act or any scheme, or any order of the Board or the appellate authority and whoever makes a false statement or gives false evidence to the Board or appellate authority shall be punishable with simple imprisonment for a term which may extend to three years and shall also be liable for fine. In the CAB, 2001, the provision relating to penalty for certain offences is same as in the SICA except that the punishment is simple imprisonment which may extend to three years or shall be liable to fine not exceeding ten lakh rupees.

Certain definitions

A side-by-side presentation of the relevant definitions relating to sick companies as proposed in the Bill and the corresponding definitions in the SICA below:

Definitions in the Bill	Definitions in SICA
'Industrial Company' means a company, which owns one or more industrial undertakings. [Clause 2 (19-AA)] 'Industrial undertaking' means any undertaking, pertaining to any industry carried on in one or more factories or units by any company, as defined in clause (aa) of Section 3 of the Industries (Development and Regulation) Act, 1951 but does not include a small-scale industrial undertaking as defined in clause (j) of that section; [Clause 2 (19-AB)]	'Industrial Company' means a Company which owns one or more Industrial Undertakings. [Section 3(1)(e)] 'Industrial undertaking' means any undertaking pertaining to a scheduled industry carried on in one or more factories by any company but does not include- (i) an ancillary industrial undertaking as defined in clause (aa) of Section 3 of the Industries (Development and Regulation) Act, 1951 (65 of 1951); and (ii) a small scale industrial undertaking as defined in clause (j) of the aforesaid section 3. [Section 3(1)(f)].
'Factory'- No definition.	'Factory'- means any premises, including the precincts thereof, in any part of which a manufacturing process is being carried on or is ordinarily so carried on- (i) with the aid of power, provided that fifty or more workers are working or were working thereon on any day of the preceding twelve months; or (ii) without the aid of power, provided that one hundred or more workers are working or were working thereon on any day of the preceding twelve months and provided further that in no part of such premises any manufacturing process is being carried on with the aid of power; [Section 3(2)(b) read with Section 3(c) of IDRA]
'Sick Industrial Company' means an industrial company which has- the accumulated losses in any financial year equal to fifty per cent, or more of its average net worth during four years immediately preceding such financial year; or failed to repay its debts within any three consecutive quarters on demand for its repayment by a creditors or creditors of such company; [Clause 2(46-AA)]	'Sick Industrial Company means an industrial company (being a company registered for not less than five years) which has at the end of any financial year accumulated losses equal to or exceeding its entire net worth. *Explanation*: For the removal of doubts, it is hereby declared that an industrial company existing immediately before the commencement of the Sick Industrial Companies, (Special Provision) Amendment Act, 1993, registered for not less than five years and having, at the end of any financial year accumulated losses equal to or exceeding its entire net worth, shall be deemed to be a sick industrial company. [Section 3(1)(o)]

'Operating Agency means any group of experts consisting of persons having special knowledge of business or industry in which the sick industrial company is engaged and include public financial institutions, State level institutions, scheduled bank or any other person as may be specified as the operating agency by the Tribunal. [Clause 2(31-AA)]	'Operating Agency' means any public financial institutions, State level institutions, scheduled bank or any other person as may be specified by general or special order as its agency by the board.

Critical Explanation of Terminologies

"Industrial Undertaking"- This term is defined in the Bill to mean and undertaking as defined in clause (aa) of Section 3 of the Industries (Development and Regulation) Act, 1951. However, clause (aa) of Section 3 of the Industries (Development and Regulation) Act, 1951 defined the term 'ancillary industrial undertaking'. Clause (aa) of Section 3 of the industries (Development and Regulation) Act, 1951 (herein referred to as 'IDRA') is not therefore correct. It is not the intention to call and industrial undertaking as an ancillary industrial undertaking. In view of this, the definition of 'Industrial undertaking as contained in the Bill requires amendment.

In the context of the above, it is relevant to note that the Sick Industrial Companies (Special Provision Act, 1985 contains a clear definition of the term 'Industrial Undertaking'. The term 'Industrial Undertaking' in the SICA is understood with reference to a 'scheduled industry' as defined in the IDRA. Further, under the SICA an ancillary industrial undertaking and a small scale industrial undertaking are excluded from the definition of 'industrial undertaking' in the Bill neither refers to scheduled industry as mentioned in the IDRA, there is also a definition for 'industrial establishment' or 'undertaking' in the Industrial Dispute Act, 1947. As per section 2(ka) of The Industrial Disputes Act, 1947: "Industrial establishment or undertaking" means an establishment or undertaking in which any industry is carried on: Provided that where several activities are carried on in an establishment or undertaking and only one or some of such activities is or are an industry or industries, then:

(*a*) if any unit of such establishment or undertaking carrying on any activity, being an industry, is severable from the other unit or units of such establishment or undertaking, such unit shall be deemed to be a separate industrial establishment or undertaking;

(*b*) if the predominant activity or each of the predominant activities carried on in such establishment or undertaking or any unit thereof is an industry and the other activity or each of the other activities carried on

as the bill merely refers to an 'industrial undertaking' without clearly defining it as is done by the SICA, an amendment to the definition in the bill for the said term will be the only way for avoidance of what could be a ground for litigation.

The definition of 'industrial undertaking' talks about an undertaking 'pertaining to any industry'. The 'industry' is not defined in Companies Act 1956. It is also not defined under the Depositories Act, 1996 read with Section 2-A of the Act, Whereas the term used and defined in SICA is 'scheduled industry' a similar term and definition are absent from the bill. Therefore, difficulties about the interruption of the term 'industry' may arise. A seven Judge bench of the supreme court in Bangalore Water Supply and Swwerage Board AIR 1978 SC 548 had the opportunity to analyse the meaning and scope of the term 'industry' under the Industrial Disputes Act, 1947. A study of the far reaching judgment could be an eye-opener in understanding how difficult it is to understand the true meaning of the term 'industry' in the absence of clear cut definition.

The intention of the Government as to where it wants the existing definition of 'industrial undertaking' as contained in the SICA to continue is not clear, If only 'scheduled undertaking' as contained in the SICA read with the IRDA are to be brought within the definition, it will be fit and proper to incorporate the same definition of industrial undertaking, scheduled industry, factory etc. in the bill also.

Factory: Though the definition of ;industrial undertaking' in the Bill uses the word 'factory' there is no definition for the term 'factory' in the Companies Act, 1956. The SICA also does not define 'factory. However, for the purpose of the SICA. The definition of factory as contained in section 3(c) of the Industries (Development and Regulation) Act, 1951 as premises where the manufacturing process as carried on may be referred to. There is no nexus between the manufacturing process and the number of workers employed nor is there any reference to the use of power. In the Factories Act, 1948, a 'factory' is defined on the same lines as in the IRDA which is relevant for the SICA except for the difference that the number of workers is 10 and 20 respectively instead of 50 and 100 workers in the IDRA definition. Thus, it will be noticed that different acts define the term 'factory' differently and in absence of a specific definition to be followed for the purpose of the Companies Act, 1956, confusion and avoidable litigation will be the end result.

Unit: The definition of 'industrial undertaking' also uses the word units' in the definition. There is no definition for the term 'units or units' company law. It may be noted here that the term, 'unit' is defined in the explanation to the definition of the term 'undertaking' in section 2(v) of the Monopolies and Restrictive Trade Practices Act, 1969. However, reference to the MRTP Act, 1969, without a corresponding reference in the Companies Act, 1956 itself cannot always be resorted to.

Sick Industrial Company- The bill has a revised definition of 'sick industrial company' which recognizes failure to pay debt as a criteria for determining sickness. The erosion of net worth continues to be another recognised criteria for determining sickness.

Operating agency- The definition of the term 'operating agency' has also undergone a change. A group of experts consisting of persons having special knowledge of business or industry, henceforth will be the operating agency. No doubt, public financial institutions, state level institutions, scheduled banks or any other person to be specified by the National Company Law Tribunal will also be an 'operating agency'.

BIFR. AAIFR to be dissolved

Consequent on the repeal of the SICA by the Sick Industrial Companies (Special Provisions Repeal Bill, 2001, the Board for Industrial and Financial Reconstruction ('BIFR') and the Appellate Authority for Industrial and Financial Reconstruction ('AAIFR') will stand dissolved. However, the National Company Law Tribunal to be constituted as per clause 10-FB of the Bill will be the authority to hear and decide matters pertaining to sick industrial companies.

Fate of existing BIFR companies

The repeal Bill is silent about existing BIFR cases. It states that 'All proceedings pending before BIFR and AAIFR prior to their dissolution shall stand abated. In fact absence of explicit provision in the repeal enactment is a bolt from the blue for the existing BIFR companies.

In the CAB 2001, nothing is mentioned about the transfer of pending BIFR cases to the Tribunal whereas in accordance with the proposed new Section, 647-A of CAB, 200 I, pending winding up proceedings will be transferred to the Tribunal. According to this section where the winding up of a company has commenced, subject to the supervision of the District Court or High Court before the commencement of the Companies (Amendment) Act. 2001 such winding up shall continue to be under the supervision of the District Court, or the High Court as the case may be and the company shall be wound up in the same manner and in the same incidents as if the Companies (Amendment) Act, 2001 had not been passed.

In this regard, the following possibilities may arise :-

(*i*) The Government may issue notification under the repealed exactment for automatic transfer of all pending cases to the Tribunal. This is a must because the BIFR companies cannot be left out abruptly. Otherwise these companies may file writ petitions in the High Court against the Government.

(*ii*) Existing BIFR companies may have to register afresh with the Tribunal.

Similarly, a decision is awaited on the ailing public sector undertakings registered with the BIFR.

Rehabilitation Fund

The CAB 2001 proposes levy and collection of cess on turnover or gross receipt of companies for the purposes of rehabilitation, revival or prosecution of sick industrial company. A levy by way of cess shall be imposed at such rate not less than.005 percent and not more than 0.1 percent of the value of annual turnover of every company or its annual gross receipt, whichever is more, as the Central Government may, from time to time, specify in the Official Gazette. (Section 441-A of CAB, 2001).

The Fund shall be applied by the Tribunal for the purposes of –

(*a*) Making interim payment of workmen's dues pending the revival or rehabilitation of the sick industrial company; or (*b*) Payment of workmen's dues due to the workmen, referred to in sub-section (3) of section 529 of the sick industrial company; or

(*c*) protection of assets of sick industrial companies; or

(*d*) revival or rehabilitation of sick industrial company which in the opinion of the Tribunal are necessary or expedient for the said purposes.

If any cess payable by a company is not paid within the stipulated time it shall be deemed to in arrears and the same shall be recovered by the Tribunal in the manner as may be prescribed. The Tribunal may also impose a penalty not exceeding ten times the amount in arrears.

Salient Features of the CAB: Salient features of the CAB are given below:

1. Quick disposal: The Tribunal will work through benches. There shall be ten special benches which will deal with the matters relating to revival or rehabilitation etc. The Tribunal can decide the matter on merits including introduction of its own scheme. This will shorten the time-span of the entire process to about two years which presently takes several years in the matter of winding up of the companies.

2. New definition of sick industrial company: The definition of sick industrial company has undergone through a significant change. As per the new definition for an industrial company to be sick the accumulates losses in any financial year are to be equal to fifty percent or more of its average net worth during four years immediately preceding such financial year or it should have failed to repay is debt within any three consecutive quarters on demand for its repayment by a creditor or creditors of such company. Section 23 of the SICA relates to potentially sick companies and this has been taken for the purpose of definition of sick industrial company. Accumulated losses reaching fifty per cent of the net worth is a common phenomenon and perhaps this may lead to early detection of sickness. Non-payment of debt for three-quarters will make the Company to apply to the Tribunal failing, which the company would attract penalty under Section 424-L of the CAB 2001. Since " section 424-L of the CAB 2001 is a penal provision, this Will be applicable prospectively. This is a bank to the banks because companies will hesitate to make default in repayment of debts.

3. Protective against distress: In the SICA, Section 22 gives protection to sick industrial companies against distress. This section has been omitted in the CAB, 2001. It does not mean that the banks and financial institutions can take legal action easily against the company in a civil court. In accordance with Section 10-GB of the CAB, 2001 no civil court shall have any jurisdiction to entertain any suit or proceeding in respect of any matter which the Tribunal or the Appellate Tribunal is empowered to determine and no injunction shall be granted by any Court or any authority in respect of any action taken or to be taken in pursuance of any power conferred by or under this Act or any other law for the time being in force. In view of this, the banks or any financial institutions or creditor can move the Tribunal.

4. Creditor's scheme : As per the CAB, 2001, the creditors can prepare the scheme but the scheme submitted by the creditors should be approved by at least two-thirds of the creditors. It is most unlikely that the scheme submitted by the creditors would be acceptable to the company.

5. Quick decision on privatization of Government Companies: Under the CAB, 2001, the reference to the Tribunal in respect of Government companies is optional not mandatory. This will help the Government to take quick decisions in privatizing the future sick public sector units, as there is no need to refer the sickness of the unit to the Tribunal.

6. Tribunal power: Compared to the BIFR, the Tribunal under the CAB, 2001, is vested with greater powers. All the parties will be bound by the Tribunal's orders and in case of non-availability of a workable proposal for revival or rehabilitation etc., the Tribunal can decide the matter on merits including introduction of its own scheme.

7. Greater scope of professional practice for chartered accountants/cost accountants/company secretaries: As per Section 10-GD of the CAB, 2001, the applicant or appellant may either appear in person or authorize one or more chartered accountants or cost accountants or company secretaries or legal practitioners to present his or its case before the Tribunal or the Appellate Tribunal, as the case may be. This gives, more scope for the practicing company secretaries and cost accountants to exercise their professional talents.

8. Copy of scheme to be given to Registrar: A copy of the scheme has to be given to the Registrar of Companies. The purpose of this requirement is not known. This will add to the administrative work of Registrar of Companies.

9. Quicker winding up procedure: For non-viable units under Section 20 of the SICA, the BIFR has to refer the matter of winding up to the High Court. Now this function can be discharged by the Tribunal. This Will reduce considerable time in deciding the winding up of the companies by the Tribunal in case viability/rehabilitation cannot be established.

10. Levy of cess: a disturbing feature: Another disturbing feature of the amendments proposed in the CAB, 2001, is the rehabilitation cess to be levied on the turnover of a company. When the company becomes sick, the company has to take measures to restructure its debts by sale of its assets and negotiating with creditors. On the other hand, the compulsion that companies should contribute to the rehabilitation fund looks like a punishment and it is not at all justified.

No doubt repeal of the SICA is a blow to the existing sick industrial companies but it is definitely a boon to financial institutions and banks as they could see a way out for sick industrial companies pending with the BIFR for a long time. In line with international practices the Companies Act has been remodelled. The delay involved in deciding the cases would be considerably reduced in future.

The Tribunal under the CAB will have ample powers. Since individual affidavits will be filed with the Tribunal. which will have powers of contempt of Court, there will be an in-built seriousness in its proceedings. As Government companies do not come under the purview of compulsory reference to the Tribunal, the Government may privatise future sick companies which would otherwise be under the threat of winding up.

The provisions in the CAB, 2001 relating to revival and rehabilitation of sick industrial companies are better than those in the SICA, because although under the SICA, the benefit of rehabilitation, and protection against distress was available, but under the new provisions besides a quicker revival/rehabilitation of' sick companies protection of workers interests will also be taken care of and pending worker will be paid out of the rehabilitation funds proposed to be created.

The investors who have invested in the sick industrial company need not wait for a long time for rehabilitation of the company. This is a welcome measure. Thus the creditors, corporate, banks, investors and the economy as a whole will stand to benefit. Before the bill to repeal the SICA is passed, the Government should take care of the problems of the existing BRFR companies and ensure a quick decision of their cases.

Practice Questions

Objective Type Questions

1. Industrial Sickness should not be concerned with the following:
   (*a*) continuous default in meeting four consecutively half yearly installments of interests or principal of institutional loans.
   (*b*) continuous losses for a period of two years or continuous erosion in the net worth by 50 per cent or more.
   (*c*) continuous cash losses for a period of two years or continued erosion in the net worth by 50 percent or more.
   (*d*) mounting areas on account of statutory of other liabilities for a period of one or two years.
2. Incipient sickness is not an indication of:
   (*a*) continuing cash losses from year to year and trend is expected continue in future.
   (*b*) continuous losses for last 2 years.
   (*c*) Deterioration in the current ratio.
   (*d*) Gradual erosion in the net worth during the previous and current financial year.
3. RBI identified a unit as sick if it has not fulfilled the following conditions:
   (*a*) confirmed cash losses.
   (*b*) imbalances in the financial structure.
   (*c*) positive net worth.
   (*d*) deterioration in liquidity.

4. BIFR becomes operational form:
   (*a*) 1st April, 1987
   (*b*) 15 April, 1987
   (*c*) 1st July, 1987
   (*d*) 30th September, 1987
5. Operating agency is not concerned with the following:
   (*a*) Public financial institutions
   (*b*) State level institutions
   (*c*) Scheduled banks
   (*d*) SEBI
6. Rehabilitation fund is not meant for:
   (*a*) making interim payments of workman's dues
   (*b*) protection of assets of sick industrial companies
   (*c*) construction of labour colony
   (*d*) revival or rehabilitation of sick industrial company

Ans: 1. (b), 2. (b) 3. (c), 4. (b), 5. (d), 6.(c)

Short Answer Questions

1. Examine the changing role of BIFR.
2. What are the main functions of operating agency?
3. What is industrial sickness?
4. Discuss the causes of sickness in SSIs.

Long Answer Questions

1. Discuss the causes of industrial sickness and describe the role of BIFR in this regard.
2. "Sick Companies are those companies which are unable to earn profits." Discuss.
3. "BIFR itself is a sick organisation". Discuss.
4. What is industrial sickness? Distinguish between confirmed sickness and potential sickness as given in SICA Act. Do you think that BIFR is quite effective in controlling industrial sickness?
5. Discuss various impediments in industrial rehabilitation in India. Give suggestions for tackling the problem of industrial sickness.
6. What are the causes of industrial sickness? What remedies would you suggest for preventing it?

References

1. Pro.(Dr.) Sreeranganadhan & Miss Roshna Varghese, "Management of Industrial Sickness, 2004, p. 23.
2. Slatter S, Corporate Recovery: Successful Turnaround Strategies and Their Implications, Harmoundsworth: Penguin Books, 1984.
3. Mathur, Satish, B., Sickness in Small Scale Sector: Causes and Cures, Concept Publishing Company Limited, New Delhi, 1999.

20 TURNAROUND MANAGEMENT

Business organizations are required to formulate and implement different strategies for their survival, rehabilitation, expansion and diversification. These strategies include stability strategy, expansion strategy, retrenchment strategy, combination strategy etc. A retrenchment strategy is implemented when an organization aims at contraction of its activities through substantial reduction or the elimination of the scope of one or more of its business in terms of their respective customer grants, customer functions or alternative technologies. These strategies are used to improve the overall performance of the business entity. In practice, there is confusion about the appropriateness of nomenclature of the strategy as it has different context. The word 'Retrenchment' is generally used in the area of human resource management. It deals with separation of employees due to decreasing trend in workload on account of recession or reorganization of work. However, it has different connotation in strategic management. Retrenchment strategy does not always involve for any of large number of reasons a business can find itself with declining profits. Economic recessions, production inefficiencies and innovative breakthrough by competitors are also responsible for the declining profit. In many cases, strategic managers believe that the firm can survive and eventually recover if a concerted effort is made over a period of few years to fortify basic distinctive competencies.[1] Actually, retrenchment strategy is one where an enterprise decides to improve its performance in reaching its objectives by (i) focusing on functional improvement, specially reduction in cost, (ii) reducing the number of functions it performs by becoming a captive company, or (iii) reducing the number of the products and markets it serves up to and including liquidation of business.[2] So retrenchment strategy provides various options, specially to deal with last stage of the product life cycle. Product Life Cycle (PLC) analyses the situation where every product, whether it is a tangible item or a service, passes through a series of marketing stages that make up the product's life cycle. These stages are product development stage, introduction, growth, maturity and decline. At each stage managers must consider how to maximize sales and profit. Decline stage is the most challenging phase before the business organizations.

Scope of retrenchment strategy includes three forms turnaround, divestment and liquidation. Management is required to adopt the turnaround strategy to control the declining trend available in business operations. But before implementing the turnaround strategy, it would be better to identify the symptoms. These symptoms are declining profitability, fluctuating cash flows, decreasing sales and market share, and increasing debt burden. These symptoms require effective monitoring control mechanism and launching recovery programme. There are following types of recovery situations.[3]

The present business scenario is governed by the constant changes available in business environment. For any firm to survive in any industry, it requires continuous monitoring and improvement of the systems and operations. Survival of a firm in any industry is essential. Severe resource crunch, consistent downtrend in operating profits or net worth may lead the firm to insolvency. Appropriate actions, both internal and external, are required to change the future prospects. This process of bringing about a revival in the firm's fortunes is termed as "Turnaround Management".

Nature of Turnaround Management

Turnaround management refers to the management measures, which reverse the negative trends in the performance indicators of the company. In other words, turnaround management refers to the management measures which turn a sick company back to a healthy one or those measures which reverse the deteriorating trends of the performance indicators such as falling market share, sales (in constant rupees) and profitability and worsening debt-equity ratio.

Criteria for Adopting Turnaround Management: Following criteria are to be tested before the launching of turnaround management in the company.

***(i)* Continuous negative cash flow:** It deals with comparison of operating costs and operating revenues. If revenue realization is less than the cash incurred on operating costs it means company is facing liquidity crunch. Increasing bad debts, blocking of funds in inventories, problems in raising price tags etc. are the important factors responsible for negative cash lows. Sometimes, non-operating incomes also help the company to ease its liquidity problem but it is not a normal feature in each case.

***(ii)* Negative profits:** It is concerned with poor viability of the company. It also means to say that the company is not able to generate profit from its operational behaviour. Poor capacity utilization, poor brand image, shortage of orders, poor cost control process, rising salary and wage structure, shortage of raw materials and their rising prices are some of the important variables which are responsible for higher operating cost against the revenue generated from the sales. With the result, company is forced to incur losses from year to year and thereafter net worth indicates a declining trend.

***(iii)* Declining market share:** It shows the position of company's product in the industry concerned. If market share of the product being produced by the company shows a declining trend its mean product concerned is loosing its shine in the market and competitors are growing at the cost of the company in the market. Ineffective product mix and marketing mix, poor R & D efforts, failure in launching of innovative product poor capacity utilization etc. are responsible for declining market share.

***(iv)* Deterioration in physical facilities:** Efficiency of production system is also governed by the physical facilities available in the company. Effective maintenance of plant and machinery, storage facilities for raw materials as well as final product, timely arrangement of ancillary parts or spare parts, water supply road & transport facilities, availability of effective supply chain management are necessary elements for better productive behaviour of the company. If company is facing problems on these counts, it shows that production and sales performance will be adversely affected in the long term.

***(v)* Poor human resource management:** In case of growth or expansion phase, companies generally employ more and more human resources to fulfill the manpower requirements. However, they fail to inculcate organizational commitment and dedication among these employees. HRD programmes are also the casualty. At the time of saturation, stagnation or declining phase, there human resources are just become liability on financial resources of the company. Change in technology and product orientation also forces the companies to identify some employees as surplus. Competitors in the industry are also making efforts for luring senior executives and other middle level managers to switch over to them. Increasing trend in employee turnover ratio also indicate that company is loosing its grip over its high performing employees. With the result, morale of employees is going down and ultimately labour productivity is quite low leading to financial disaster for the company.

***(vi)* Un-competitive products or services:** Companies are expected to have a continuous touch with their customers. Consumers survey is the best technique for gauging the mood and behaviour of the consumers about the products being produced by the company. On the basis of feedback technique, necessary changes are required to be made in the product mix, R & D programme and price etc. Changes are also to be ensured in line of production, product range and price range etc. If companies are unable to do these things in time their products and services becomes uncompetitive and they will adversely affect the market share of the product or services.

***(vii)* Mismanagement:** Managers are the change agent in the company and they are supposed to carry the mission and vision of the company for a long-term perspective. Effective cost management, arrangement of cheap finance, product innovation, professional behaviour, effective marketing strategies, growing market share, committed workforce, better brand equity and good public image are some of the important considerations by which managers have to test their effectiveness. If managers fail on their counts, they fail to deliver the goods in right perspective and they may be responsible for mismanagement. If a particular company or an organization faces one or more of their problems is need of the turnaround management.

Scope of Turnaround Management

It focuses on the short-and long-term financing needs (*as* banks and financial institutions do) as well as on strategic issues to ensure success of turnaround strategy. Scope of turnaround management includes

(1) Analysis of product, market, production processes, competition, and market segment positioning.

(2) Clear thinking about the market place and production logic.

(3) Implementation of plans by target-setting, feedback, and remedial action.

Phases of Turnaround Management: There are 3 phases in any Turnaround Management.

1. Identification of Danger Signal
2. Selection of Appropriate
3. Implementation of change process.

Phase I: Identification of danger signal

Companies do not turn sick overnight and do not qualify as potential candidates for turnaround. They become sick slowly, and process of sickness can be stopped by timely corrective action. But in reality, most companies do not recognize this fact. The following are some of the universally accepted danger signals, which a company should watch out for:

(*i*) Decreasing market share / Decreasing constant rupee sales

(*ii*) Decreasing profitability

(*iii*) Increased dependence on debt / Restricted dividend polices

(*iv*) Failure to plough back the profits into business/Wrong diversification at the expense of the core business.

(*v*) Lack of planning

(*vi*) Inflexible CEO/Management succession problems/Unquestioning Board of Directors

(*vii*) A management team unwilling to learn from competitors.

Phase II: Selection of appropriate Strategy

Turnaround Management classifies into two broad categories. They are

1. Strategic Turnaround: As the name itself suggests, strategic turnaround choices may force the company to completely change its current way of operations. The choices under this method are:

(*a*) A new way to compete in the existing business

(*b*) Entering into an altogether new business

Under the first choice, the focus is either on increasing the market share in a given product market frame work or in repositioning the product market relationship. The increase in market share can be achieved by improving product quality perception through dealer push or by a consumer pull. Alternatively, entering a new business as a turnaround strategy can be approached through the process of product portfolio management.

2. Operating Turnarounds: Main operating turnaround strategies are also follows:

(*i*) **Asset reduction strategies:** If a firm is operating much below the Breakeven level, it must take steps to reduce its assets. This will reduce the level of fixed costs and help in reducing the total costs of the firm.

(*ii*) **Revenue increasing strategies:** If the firm is operating substantially but not extremely below its breakeven level, then the appropriate turnaround strategy is to generate extra revenues.

(*iii*) **Cost cutting strategies:** If the firm is operating around or above the breakeven level, cost reduction strategies are preferable as they are easy to carry out and the firms' profits rise once the unnecessary costs are cut down.

(*iv*) **Combination strategies:** Operating closer but below breakeven levels calls for application of combination strategies. Under this method all the three namely cost reducing, revenue generating and asset reduction actions are pursued simultaneously in an integrated and balanced manner. Combination strategies have a direct favourable impact on cash flows as well as on profits.

Phase III: Implementation of change process

Implementation plays an important role in any turnaround management. Identification of an appropriate strategy by itself will not guarantee success. Similarly partial adoption of a strategy is also not useful. The selected strategy needs to be pursued relentlessly and with all out effort to make it work. The success or otherwise of a Turnaround strategy depends on the commitment shown by the top management as also the operating management.

Methods of Managing Turnaround

There are three methods by which turnarounds can be managed:

1. **Turnaround by existing management team:** In this turnaround the existing management team handles the entire turnaround strategy with the advisory support of a specialist external consultant. This method is successful only when the chief executive has a reasonable amount of creditability left with the banks and financial institutions and a qualified consultant is available. This form of turnaround management is not so popular.
2. **Turnaround by specialist:** In this turnaround, the existing team withdraws temporarily and executive consultant or turnaround specialist is employed to complete the turnaround programme. This person is usually deputed by the banks and financial institutions and, after the job is over, reverts to the original position. This method is also a rare phenomenon in India.
3. **Turnaround by new management team:** It involves the replacement of the existing team, specially the chief executive, or merging the sick organization with a healthy one. It is the most difficult method but oftenly used in India.

Turnaround Strategy

It is a retrenchment strategy intended to reverse a negative trend. Actually, it is an effective tool to reverse the process of decline. Turnaround strategies derive their names from the action involved that is reversing a negative trend and regain profitability. Since the underlying purpose of retrenchment is to reverse current negative trends, the method is often referred to as a turnaround strategy. In turnaround situations, management may reduce the payroll or trim employee benefits, cut the number of operating facilities, or eliminate unprofitable products and markets. But turnaround managers also try to increase the level of customer satisfaction and to adjust pricing for better profitability.

Turnaround strategy implies planning and taking action with a view to turn a sick unit into a healthy one. Most companies during their history are likely to face symptoms of sickness. Some companies which have a meteoric rise and then collapse, need adoption of turnaround strategy. Some smaller companies make efforts to rise above certain level, and never reaches that level, instead show a poor performance. On the other hand, there may be companies which may be quite mature, may be even professionally managed but they run into difficulties for some reason or the other and have to adopt the turnaround strategy to survive and goods again. It is concerned with strategic actions, which an organization takes to compete in the same business in turnaround situations. Turnaround situations may be improvement in organizational lower performance caused by downward trend which is not controllable by present actions of management.

Conditions Required for Turnaround Strategy

The various conditions required for any turnaround strategy are as follows:

(*i*) A competitive, viable core operation or thrust on which can be built a viable business.

(*ii*) Bridge capital to finance turnaround.

(*iii*) A competent and top management with the authority to act. It is quite essential that the top management should have clear-cut vision, commitment to vision and will, to achieve the vision. Only then turnaround strategy would proceed.

1. Features of Turnaround Strategy: Following are the basic features of the turnaround strategy:

(*i*) It is a part of retrenchment strategy.

(*ii*) It ensures the success of principle: "hold the present business and cut the costs."

(*iii*) It involves improvement in declining organizational profitability.

(*iv*) It is accomplished with the help of (a) cost reduction (b) asset reduction.

(*v*) If focuses on improved asset utilization.

(*vi*) It involves the change in the organization's strategy to compete in the present business generally called as strategic turnaround. It consists of determination of organization's share in the market, no change in the market share or change in market share by certain percentages.

(*vii*) It also involve actions ensuring increasing revenue through regaining lost position rather than increased penetration of the market, decreasing costs, decreasing assets or a combination effort. It is called as operating turnaround.

2. Danger Signals for Declining Performance: Johan M. Harris has listed following danger signals of impeding declining trend in performance.

(*i*) Deteriorating performance indicators: These indicators deals with decreasing market share, decreasing amount of sales at constant prices and decreasing profitability. Decreasing trend in market share indicates the inability of the company to compete with other players working in the same industry. It also shows company's declining competitive strength. Declining trends in sales and profits also indicates that the company is unable to earn a competitive rate of return on its sales as well as investment etc.

(*ii*) Deteriorating financing problems: These problems are responsible for adverse trend in capital structure and dividend policies. Excessive use of trading on equity, growing volume of debt, lopsided debt equity ratio and lower credit rating cause a damaging effect on the credit worthiness of the company. In this situations, banks and other lenders apply restriction on the loan taking process of these companies. These steps further aggravate financial problems before these companies. Similarly, restriction on dividends to conserve cash or satisfy debt conditions also adversely affect the perception of shareholders towards their companies.

(*iii*) Inadequate Investment: Companies are required to ensure continuity in reinvestment in plants, equipments, maintenance system and replacement of other plants and equipments. These steps generally help in maintaining competitive strength of companies in the market. If they are unable to do so in time, it means they are preparing the groundwork for their failure. Some companies are also habitual of inviting troubles by ignoring their basic or core business and rely on new, easier, grey and risky areas of new businesses.

(*iv*) Lack of Planning: Business environments is always a dynamic and ever-changing process. Under this process, companies are expected to formulate effective planning for their survival, growth and diversification, But unability to do so in time or for lack of proper planning companies are inviting trouble for themselves. Companies are expected to formulate short-run as well as long-run policies for facing the challenges in the future.

(*v*) Problem at the top management levels: Some companies are also facing problems relating with their top management, which adversely affect their effective functioning. Similarly, there is a tendency among them to aggressively carry through their own ideas without critically evaluating their future implications. Ultimately, these tendencies affect their operational behaviour and profitability. Some of these problems are lack of receptiveness of chief executive, ineffective management succession plans, differences of opinion among the promoters family members, ineffective coordination and lack of trust among the members of the governing board, and in- effective management team etc.

With the help of above danger signals, one can easily assess the need for formulating and implementing turnaround strategy. Thus, turnaround management is the process which incorporates these stages: formulating and implement the turnaround strategy.

Approaches of Turnaround Management: Following approaches are generally useful in turnaround management:

1. Surgical approach: It involves a tough attitude and the pattern of action initiated is also the same. The new chief executive is expected to assert his authority by issuing necessary orders and directives for structural changes, centralized function, retrenchment and closing down the non-viable plants and divisions or product lines etc. Necessary changes are also expected in product mix for improving the product viability in the market. Replacement of obsolete machinery and equipments and strengthening process of R & D, marketing and financial controls are also expected under this approach.

2. Non-surgical process: It is human in nature and governed by the behavioural change. It is aimed at improving work-culture and morale in the companies. It deals with understanding of the problems, eliciting opinions, need for conciliatory attitude and negotiated settlements among different factions of stakeholders.

There has been cases of "harsh" is "surgical turnarounds and non-surgical" or "humane" turnarounds (without tears). There have also been instance of "low cost turnarounds" and high cost turnarounds". According to Pradeep N. Khandwalla, "The surgical and non-surgical varieties shared a few strategic elements in common, notably staff incentives and motivation, gathering stakeholders support, and restructuring. These three when pressed into service, may provide a distinctive colour to both type of turnarounds. But there were differences, too. Management by mission, raising of capital, and non-automation and non-training based attempts at improving productivity and its related functions were strategic elements for surgical turnarounds but not for non-surgical turnarounds. Building management systems, for grater operations controls and effectiveness, formal disqualifies activities, innovation, modernization and plant, and above all, attempts at creating confidence in management, collective problem solving, and building teamwork were options that were strategic in non-surgical turnarounds but not in surgical turnarounds."

Tools of Turnaround Management

Turnaround management consists of following tools:

1. **Change in management:** It is concerned with identification process whether present management is justifiable in present scenario of the company. However, if change in management is desirable then it should be analyzed that what are their wrong doings and how have they managed the company. Continuance of present top management or its change depends on the quality it possesses. If it is observed that in the present context, certain skills and qualities are desirable and present top management does not have that qualities, it should be changed. But efforts should be made towards appointing experienced and professionals on the top management so that company may be brought to on the track in shortest possible time.

2. **Technical analysis:** Sometimes, business has a strong current operating health but the company has lost its position in the market strategically. Technical analysis deals with analysis of major declines in sales and market share. Methods of turnaround process are determined on the basis of magnitude of the sales and market reversal sought. It this context, three alternatives are generally used.

(*i*) maintenance or even reduction of market share concentrating on one or more viable product or market segment.

(*ii*) Marginal increase in market share by trying to convert dropout position into a follower position, follower position competitor position or competitor position to a market leader position.

(*iii*) Substantial increase in market share by making offensive efforts to reach from drop out position to a competitor position or from follower position to a market leader position.

3. **Operating systems.** There systems are concerned with designing operating turnarounds. These systems enable the company to make itself efficient. In this context, following alternatives are important.

(*i*) Revenue generating process: In this process, company is expected to focus on its existing line of products. If there is need for supplementary products, that have to be produced or arranged to make the existing line of products more viable. Efforts are also required to initiate price-cutting, offensive advertising and launching of direct sales to reach more and more potential customers. These steps will enable the company to generate more sales and consequently more revenues for its operation.

(*ii*) Cost Cutting Process: This process is popular specially in the short run to overcome the problem of high direct labour costs, advertising cost, R & D costs, human resources development costs, inventory costs etc. Effective cost control techniques can easily help the company to reduce its costs in the short run. Direct labour costs can be minimized by offering voluntary retirement package to employees. Advertising costs can be restricted to products only. Better inventory management practices may be more beneficial in controlling inventory costs. Some measures can also adopted in reducing the R & D costs as well as human resource development costs etc.

(*iii*) Asset Reduction Process: It is governed by the long-term prospects of the business and the criticality of its financial position. This process can be initiated if company thinks that there is no better prospects of its sales performance in near future or long term prospects of sales performance is quite weak in comparison to its production capacity. However, it also depends on the sale ability of different assets and financial requirements of the company.

(*iv*) Combination Process: It is the balancing act of revenue generating process, cost-cutting process and asset reduction process. This process is generally preferred when the company is working on breakeven point.

Combination process increases the cash flow in the company in comparison to individual effect of these processes. However, combination process is quite complex so far as managerial jobs are concerned.

Factors of Turnaround Management

Following factors are commonly employed in turnaround management:

1. Management factor: In-efficient management is the most important factor affecting overall performance of the company. Improvement in management process is the first requisite condition for launching turnaround management. In this context, the general trend is the replacement of current chief executive by new efficient chief executive officer (CEO). The new chief executive is supposed to streamline the existing management system and ensuring a change in organizational culture of the company.

2. Human resource factor: Ineffective human resource development generally makes the human resources redundant, demoralized and a liability on the financial resources of the company. In one way or other, these resources are surplus in implicit sense and doing nothing regarding labour productivity. So turnaround management provides a remedial measure through which surplus manpower is to be got rid of, morale is to be restored and the quality of the manpower is to be improved through effective human resource practices. Appointment of competent and professional people is also to be made in key positions of management hierarchy of the company.

3. Production mix modifications: Outdated production facilities, lack of innovative products and poor R & D facilities adversely affect the volume of sales, curtail the customership base and lower down the profitability. In this context, as a part of turnaround management programme, thrust should be given on the development of better R & D facilities, creating intrapreneurship culture among the employees and managers and bringing modification in the product mix. Unviable products are to be phased out and innovative products are to be launched. If existing products need modifications or innovativeness they have to be carried out in an effective way.

4. Production facilities: Absence of effective maintenance system of plants and equipment affects their productivity adversely. Similarly, lack of modernization and related improvement of plant and machinery also adversely affect the capacity utilization and quality of products, and they by decreasing trend in sales and profit volume. Turnaround management deals with modernization of plants and equipments and their effective maintenance. These steps can also easily help the management to achieve uninterrupted production flow and better capacity utilization. It will help in the process of cost reduction higher production and better profit realization.

5. Financial management: Declining trend in capacity utilization, production, productivity sales and profit performance is responsible for poor credit-worthiness of the company. Companies working under these situations are also unable to get sufficient financial support from financial institutions. Turnaround management provides a base for financial restructuring and consequently due to this arrangement banking and other financial institutions can be persuaded for further lending programme.

6. Marketing strategy: Lack of effective marketing strategy is another major factor for poor performance of some companies. Formulation and implementation of effective marketing strategy as a part of turnaround management enable the management to improve the sales performance. Product mix modifications and marketing mix modifications programmes can be easily integrated to develop an effective marketing strategy for the company as such. It will also help the company in developing new customership, entering the new market and withdrawing from the unviable market.

7. Other measures: Some companies are also facing problems in managing assets specially fixed assets and landed property effectively and having some divisions as loss making propositions. Side by side companies also face severe resource crunch. Under these situations, turnaround management provides several measures like liquidation of assets

Which are not in use, closing or selling down some non-viable divisions and lines of businesses freezing the salary and perquisites of employees, and stream lining the process of raw material supply etc.

Turnaround Elements

Several essential elements of turnaround have been identified by researchers from time-to-time. According to Hofer (1980), asset reduction, revenue increasing, cost cutting, change in market share, change in key functional areas emphasis, change in top management and change in business are essential elements of turnaround. According to Pradip N. Khandwalla (1981, 1989), induction of change agents at the top, credibility building by the change agents, mobilization of the organization, quick way-off action, reprieve from external pressures, opportunistic harnessing of external environment, strengthening of mechanisms for influencing external environments, selective change in product-mix, selective professionalisation of management function, motivational strategy, co-ordination strategy, performance control strategy, and management styles are essential elements of turnarounds. According to Mukherji (1989), diagnosing, problem solving and trouble shooting, organizational design, short-term actions, creditability building, organization development, culture-management, management of change etc., are the essential elements of turnaround strategy.

Elements of Turnaround Management

Following are the main elements of turnaround management-

(*i*) Change in top management
(*ii*) Initial Credibility Building action
(*iii*) Neutralizing external pressures.
(*iv*) Initial Central
(*v*) Identifying quick pay off activities
(*vi*) Quick cost reductions
(*vii*) Revenue generation
(*viii*) Asset liquidation for generating cash
(*ix*) Mobilisation of the organization
(*x*) Better internal coordination

Stages of Turnaround

Following are the six turnaround stages which have to be crossed to achieve turnaround:

1. **Evaluation stage:** In this stage, preliminary study, survey, discussion etc. have to be undertaken. Meetings have to be held with customers, suppliers, banker etc. to assess the situation and seek their co-operation. The markets and competition with other companies have to be studied and evaluated. The cost, productivity, and efficiency have to be analyzed thoroughly. Arrange meetings with people of the company itself, discuss with them, explain to them and seek their co-operation. All factors which inhibit turnaround have to be identified.
2. **Building the team:** In the second stage, an efficient team have to be built which may be helpful in achieving the turnaround. This would require strong leadership. In the absence of strong leadership, staff of the organization may be demoralized, and the leader has to boost their morale. As select band of workers have to be organized and motivated.
3. **Emergency measures:** In this stage, several emergency measures have to be taken without waiting for reduction in competition or technological breakthrough. Such measures may cover cost-cutting efficiency involvement, asset reduction, revenue generation, raising money and bringing about organizational changes whenever necessary.
4. **Motivating the team:** At this stage, the leader has to be very careful in motivating the team to work efficiently according to strategy chalked out. Clear-cut responsibility and accountability has to be laid down, the employees have be duly inspired, climate of eventual success and urgency have to be created and the purse strings have to be contracted effectively. The leader has also to take tough action whenever necessary. Compensation deals may have to be entered into to enthuse the employees. The leader has to demonstrate a vision, commitment to vision and will to achieve that vision to the employees.
5. **Stabilization stage:** When the committed and motivated teams works hard and the turnaround has been attained, the announcement of the end of the crisis has to be made. There should be public acknowledgement of help given all concerned and involved. The strength has to be identified and advantages from the same can be obtained. Expansion plan may be undertaken which can be managed effectively. Those areas have to be avoided where the firm is likely to be at disadvantage.
6. **Return to normal growth:** In this stage, all efforts have to be made to market the product quite effectively. Efforts should be made to influence the threat of entry, develop appropriate market strategy, and assess the

bargaining power of the supplies as well as customers. The top management must make efforts not only to protect the market share but also to expand it.

Practice Questions

Multiple Choice Questions

1. Forms of retrenchment strategy exclude the following:
   (*a*) turn around
   (*b*) buy back of shares
   (*c*) divestment
   (*d*) liquidation
2. Need of turnaround strategy requires symptom analysis of the following:
   (*a*) declining profitability
   (*b*) fluctuating cash flows
   (*c*) high turnover of labour
   (*d*) decreasing sales
3. Turn around management does not deals with the following:
   (*a*) diagnosis of the impending troubles
   (*b*) choosing appropriate turnaround strategy
   (*c*) implementation of the change process and its monitoring
   (*d*) taking remedial measures
4. Methods of managing turnaround exclude the following:
   (*a*) turnaround by existing management team
   (*b*) turnaround by workers
   (*c*) turnaround by specialists
   (*d*) turnaround by new management team
5. Turnaround strategy is concerned with the following:
   (*a*) reversing a negative trend
   (*b*) reversing a positive trend
   (*c*) reversing a revival trend
   (*d*) reversing rehabilitation trend

Ans: 1. (b), 2. (c) 3. (d), 4. (b), 5. (a)

Short Answer Questions

1. What is turnaround management?
2. Explain the methods of managing turnaround.
3. Examine the scope of turnaround management.
4. Discuss the features of turnaround strategy.
5. Evaluate the different approaches of turnaround management.
6. Explain the elements of turnaround management.
7. Explain the various key factors in turnaround strategy.

Long Answer Questions

1. What do you mean by turnaround management? Also examine the criteria for adopting turnaround management.
2. What is turnaround strategy? Examine its features and rationale.

3. Discuss the danger signals for declining performance of the firm. Does they help in turnaround programme?
4. What is turnaround management? Examine its various tools.
5. Why firms are interested to reverse the negative trend in their performance? Also explain the factors commonly employed in turnaround management.
6. What is turnaround management? Examine its various tools.
7. Explain the objectives of turnaround management. Also discuss the various stages of turnaround management.

References

1. Prasad, L.M, Business Policy: Strategic Management Sultan Chand & Sons, New Delhi, 2003, p. 264.
2. Johan. A. Pearce II & Richard B. Robinson, J.R. Strategic Management; 3rd Edi A.I.T.B.S. Publishers & Distributors 1996 (Regd.) New Delhi, p. 265.
3. Slatter, S., Corporate Recovery: Successful Turnaround Strategies and Their Implementation, New York, Penghin, 1984. Also quoted in Ajhar Kazmi Business Policy and Strategic Management. Tata Mc Graw Hill Publishing Company Ltd., New Delhi, 2002. p.200.
4. Francis Cherunilam, Strategic Management, Himalya Publishing House, Mumbai, 1998, p. 192.

21 PUBLIC ENTERPRISES IN INDIA

Historically, Public Enterprises (PEs) played an important part in the development of Indian industry and economy. At the time of independence, it was considered that political independence without self reliance could be detrimental to the country sovereignty and autonomy in policy making. The massive investments which were made in the early decades after independence to build public sector was more out of historical necessity than from adherence of any political ideology. The basic objectives of setting up of the PEs were to build infrastructure for economic development, create employment opportunities, promote balanced regional development and to generate investable resources for development. At that time, Hanson rightly stated that, "Whatever the ultimate perspective may be, the country anxious to develop economically has no alternative but to use public enterprise on a considerable scale, at the very least in order to get things going."[1] He has also gone to the extent of saying that "Public enterprise without a plan can achieve something: a plan without public enterprise is likely to remain on paper."

Keeping these facts in mind, in India Public Enterprises (PEs) were structured as an instrument of government policy and not designed for purely commercial gains or profit making. They were also required to fulfill several other objectives such as provision for basic infrastructure, basic goods and services, development of backward areas, providing employment and promoting welfare of people, especially the weaker section of the society. Also as required by Article 39 of the constitution, the public sector was mean to help develop an economic system which did not result in the concentration of wealth and means of production to the detriment of the common man – and to ensure that the ownership and control of material resources of the community were so distributed as to subserve the common good. The massive investments required for developing the infrastructure and basic goods and services, at that time could only be provided by the government. To undertake these massive developments, PEs were created as separate corporations or companies so that these organisations could be kept away from government procedures and run on commercial lines.

Public Enterprises (PEs) represents one of the most solid and enduring creations of independent India. The strong industrial base that our country enjoys today which has enabled India. India time and again to withstand both domestic and global shocks is largely a contribution of vibrant public enterprises.

However, today, in the competitive environment there is urgent need to redefine the public sector philosophy so that the achievements attained painstakingly over decades are not squandered away simply because the response of PEs to changing scenario was delayed. Now, there is growing need to review the government priorities in the light of current demands of Indian economy and to initiate steps to move away from the "governing of business to the business of governing."

Nature of Public Enterprises

The major definitions given by the authorities on Public Enterprises are as follows:

A.H. Hanson states that "Public enterprises mean state ownership and active operations of industrial, agricultural, financial and commercial undertakings."[2] The term has been used here in a more familiar sense and the coverage of enterprises is very specific.

Encyclopedia Britannica: "The term usually refers to government ownership and active operation of agencies engaged in supplying the public the goods and services which alternatively might be supplied by privately owned profit motivated firms (private enterprise)."[3] The definitional has laid emphasis on government ownership and absence of profit motive.

N.N. Mallya has laid more emphasis on the autonomous character and stated as follows: "Public enterprises are autonomous or semi-autonomous corporations and companies established, owned and controlled by the state and engaged in industrial and commercial activities."[4]

S.S. Khera contends that "By public enterprise is meant the industrial, commercial and economic activities carried on by the central government or by a state government or jointly by the central government and a state government and in each case either solely or in association with private enterprise, so long as it is managed by a self-contained management."[5] The definition has stressed the following points:

(*i*) It covers the industrial, commercial and economic activities.

(*ii*) State ownership whether by the Centre or by the state is essential.

(*iii*) It is managed by a self-contained managerial cadre?

Friedmann defines public enterprise as "an institution operating a service of an economic or social character, on behalf of the government, but as an independent legal entity, largely autonomous in its management, through responsible to the public, government and Parliament and subject to some direction, by the government, equipped on the other hand with independent and separate funds of its own and the legal and commercial attributes of a commercial enterprise." The definition is comprehensive and has covered almost all the important features of PE, i.e., government ownership, autonomous functioning, accountability to public through government and Parliament, separate financial system, etc.

Main Characteristics of PEs[6]

Main characteristics of public enterprises:

1. Public Ownership: The public enterprises should either be wholly owned by the central government or state government (s) or local authority or jointly owned by two more of them, Government ownership means that more than 50% of the equity is being held by a public authority. If the enterprise is owned by the government and private persons, the state must have the predominant share (at least 51%) in the ownership of such enterprises. Section 617 of the Indian Companies Act clearly specifies that 'Government company means nay company in which not less than fifty one per cent of the paid up share capital is held by the central government or by any state government or central government partly and partly by one or more state governments.' Further, the public corporations and the department undertakings are fully owned by the government. It has to be kept in mind that the public enterprises do not include the enterprises functioning under cooperative sector. Recently, the state government of Uttar Pradesh, however, has included the cooperative enterprises under public sector fold.

2. Government Control and Management: Public enterprises are managed by the government or the public authority. If a public enterprise is operating under the management of private institutions, it does not mean that it has become a private enterprise. The essential condition for a PE is that the government has got a right to manage and control the affairs of the enterprise. In the USA, the Atomic Energy Commission is managed by private institutions and even then it is called a PE.

3. Public Accountability: The enterprises are provided funds from the public exchequer. It becomes imperative that they should be accountable to the public through Parliament, whose funds are invested to carry on the activities of the enterprises. This goal is achieved through ministers, government, Parliament, audit bodies, etc.

4. Public Purpose: The private enterprise is essentially a business proposition in which public purpose finds a subsidiary or peripheral position and in no case supersedes business considerations. In PE, social aspects can well precede, supersede and even completely engulf business considerations. The public interest in various forms and shape provides an under-current for all its strategic decisions.

5. Wide Coverage of Activities: The public enterprises are not established for a specific line of activity or manufacture. They cover varied range of activities. "If we exclude agriculture, home trade, and a few other areas, mostly in the unorganized sectors like lorry transportation, it pervades the economy world today." In India, especially after independence, the PEs are operating in almost every area, viz, construction, marketing, agriculture, finance, development, mining etc.

6. Economic Enterprise: In a public enterprise, the price charged for its goods and services is expected to cover the cost. In some cases, the price charged may not cover the cost, but the aim is that in the long run the enterprise as a whole would at least break even. Hospitals, universities and a few public utilities like railways, posts and telegraphs charge a fee for their service, but as it does not cover, and it is also not intended to cover, the cost, such activities are not PE, though owned and managed by the state.

7. Autonomous Functioning: In spite of the initial huge investment made by the government, the PEs are provided sufficient autonomy to manage their affairs in their own fashion. The self-contained management has the right to manage the affairs on the basis of sound business considerations ad prudent commercial practices. The government does not interfere in their day-to-day activities. The finances of these enterprises are kept separate from the public exchequer. Departmental undertakings are exception to this financial autonomy.

Thus, public enterprise can be defined "as an activity of the government, whether central, state or local, involving manufacturing or production of goods including agriculture, or making available the services, it has a sound blending of public purpose, public accountability, autonomous functioning and inherent right to manage and control the enterprise by the government."

Rationale Public Enterprises: Rationale of Public Enterprises are as follows:

1. Instrument for Success of Planning: It is usually said that the success of a planned economy is based on the growth of public enterprises. Modern economy has inevitably to be a planned economy and the responsibility of planning is to be discharged by the government which necessarily leads to the participation of the state in the actual management of the enterprises in addition to the regulation of commerce and industry managed by private entrepreneurs. In this connection, Hanson has rightly stated that "Public enterprise without a plan can achieve something; a plan without public enterprise is likely to remain on paper." This is so because the answers to various problems, which arise, cannot normally be found unless the Government and Government undertakings have direct experience of managing such enterprises. They can also share greater responsibility of achieving the objectives laid down in the plans.

2. Provision of Infrastructure: To transform the 'colonial' economy into a 'national' economy and form a background to developed one, the basic requisite is to provide infrastructural facilities. Railways, road, telecommunications, power, shipping, airlines, postal, banking and insurance facilities have to be developed for the rapid advancement of the country. The general experience of various countries is that these facilities have to be developed for the rapid advancement of the country. The general experience of various countries is that these facilities cannot be provided efficiently and economically by the private entrepreneurs. This, the Government has been forced to take up active interest in provision of these basic facilities which may ultimately encourage the rapid growth of agriculture and industries in the country.

3. Development of Key and Basic Industries: It has been the experience of various developing economies, including India, that private entrepreneurs have mainly engaged themselves in commercial and less riskily ventures. They do not take sufficient: interest in the development of key and basic industries, mainly because they do not have sufficient capital and other resources for it and also that they do not want to take risks involved in it. With the result, Governments of these economies have been forced to come forward to develop such key and basic industries to achieve self-reliance and faster development of the economy.

4. Balanced regional Growth: Private entrepreneurs are guided mainly by profit motive. They establish industries in those areas where they expect a high rate of profit and security of their investment. They are also not in position to exploit the natural resources effectively. These things have forced the Government to intervene in the economic activities through a planned dispersal of industries, which will ensure balanced regional growth of the country. It is only through the state the development of relatively backward areas can be affected.

5. Establishment of a Socialist and Welfare Oriented Society: The functions of the Government which were originally limited to the maintenance of law and order, defense of the country, etc., have considerably been expanded in recent years. A Government, which is wedded to the establishment of a socialist and welfare-oriented society, is increasingly compelled to enter directly into industrial and commercial activities to achieve this objective. It is the duty of the state to protect the society from the exploitation of industrialists of private capitalists by establishing PEs and thereby providing sufficient opportunities to all concerned to develop themselves.

6. Preventing Concentration of Economic Power: It has become the major duty of the state to remove the inequalities of income and wealth prevailing in the society as much as possible. It was felt that the economic systems should be so changed which may not be conducive to the accumulation of wealth and economic power in a fewer hands. By establishment PEs, this objective can also be achieved satisfactorily. It has been pointed out that "Private enterprise leads to vast inequalities in the distribution of wealth which are not desirable on social grounds and also on economic grounds to the extent they are the result of unearned income." It artificially creates the paradox of 'poverty in the midst of plenty.' Producers, on the one hand, complain of gluts and surpluses while consumers, on the other hand, are under-fed, under-clothed and under-sheltered.

7. Meeting Defence Requirements: Industries connected with the production of arms and ammunition or supply of services essential to the defence of the country have always been considered fit to be set up in the public sector. Obviously, private production cannot possibly be depended upon from the point of view of the national security and safety. Besides, there is a need for utmost secrecy which could be secured only when the industry is under state ownership and control.

8. Effective Implementation of Government Policies: The Government policy has an important bearing on the nature of the product to be manufactured, the management of the undertaking, pricing of products, scale of operations and personnel, etc. The private enterprises are mainly concerned with their own self-interest and may not pay due attention on the Government policies effectively. On the other hand, the PEs are to be run in the larger interest of the national. Therefore, they are careful in proper interpretation and effective implementation of Government policies.

9. Model Employer: State participation in commerce and industry is an important instrument of attaining the objective of serving as model employer. By establishing PEs, the state is in a position to set up ideals in the areas of non-retrenchment of surplus staff, housing provisions, management and technical training, fixation of reasonable level of wages for workmen and introduction of workers' participation in management. There is ample scope for leadership on the part of the state to act as a model employer.

10. Contribution to National Exchequer: The surpluses generated by the PEs could be profitably utilized for social benefits. They may also contribute towards further investment and growth of the economy. If these enterprises are left in the hands of private entrepreneurs, the profits would be pocketed by them and the surpluses could not be utilized in the larger interests of the economy. In India, the state has had laid upon it, by Directive Principles of State Policy, the responsibility for the total socio-economic welfare of the people. In this changed context, taxation has proved inadequate for the tasks of raising the total revenues. By active participation of the state in business and commerce, funds can be accumulated for its multifarious responsibilities.

11. Stimulation of Research and Development Activities: It is the primed duty of the state to stimulate Research and Development activities and to build up indigenous technologies leading to optimum self-reliance. Private entrepreneurs consider the expenditure on R & D as wasteful expenditure. It is through PEs that the Government can discharge its responsibility of stimulating research and development efforts more effectively.

12. Strengthening Foreign Exchange Resources Position: In order to meet the development needs, under-developed countries lay stress on the strengthening of the foreign exchange resources position either by exporting the surplus goods and services of the country or by making vigorous efforts in substituting imported products. In India, the basic industries were established mainly to save enormous amount of foreign exchange. State has established a good number of enterprises to promote exports and encourage import substitution.

13. Augmentation of Employment Opportunities: Large-scale participation by state in industrial and commercial field is bound to increase the employment opportunities directly and it would stimulate other related activities to generate additional employment indirectly. The employment, whether generate directly or indirectly, will increase the national dividends of the country considerably.

14. Promotion of Standard of Living : The socialist pattern of society, which has been accepted as a national goal, promises a higher standard of living for the vast majority of masses. If poverty is to be eliminated and if each citizen is to enjoy essentials of life, e.g., food, shelter, clothing, etc., there is an urgent need to step up production of goods and services relevant to the consumption by the masses. This can be achieved at a faster rate through the promotion of PEs rather than through private ones.

Types of Public Enterprises

PEs are engaged in the manufacture of goods and provision of services in almost all the important spheres of economic activity. A categorization on the above basis will give the following types of PEs.

1. Commercial Public Enterprises: They are not engaged in the manufacture of any product or service. They actively participate in trading and marketing activities. The State Trading Corporation of India Ltd., the Minerals and metals Trading Corporation Ltd., the Food Corporation of India, the Indian Oil Corporation and the Cotton Corporation of India are the examples of such enterprises.

2. Manufacturing Public Enterprises: Majority of the PEs can be put in this category. They produce capital as well as consumer goods. They provide infrastructural facilities to provide an investment base to private entrepreneurs. Enterprises engaged in the manufacture of steel, oil, machinery, chemicals, fertilizers, engineering equipments, transportation equipments, minerals, etc., may be kept in this category.

3. Financial Public Enterprises: These government-owned enterprises are engaged in the provision of finance for industries. Industrial Development Bank of India, Industrial Finance Corporation of India, Unit Trust of India, State Finance Corporations, State Bank of India, Nationalized Commercial Banks, etc., are providing funds to commercial and industrial enterprises in public and private sector.

4. Promotional Public Enterprises: A few PEs are engaged in the promotion of industries specially in SSI sector. The activities of National Small Industries Corporations are related to promotion of SSI units. Further, the activities of National Industrial Corporations are related to promotion of SSI units. Further, the activities of National Industrial Development Corporation Ltd. and Indian Mines Bureau are promotional by nature. At present, financial PEs are also engaged in promotional activities.

5. Public Utilities: A few public utilities like Doordarshan, Akashavani, Road Transport Corporations, State Electricity Boards, Railways, Post and Telegraphs etc. are providing services to general public. Their services are essential by nature. They are operating under monopolistic conditions but they have to keep the 'public interest' uppermost.

Historical Perspective of Public Sector Enterprises

It has been found necessary by developing countries of the world to set up PEs to bring about rapid economic growth. The state intervention of an active kind has become a cardinal feature of the Indian economy since the end of the British colonial rule. Earlier, the policy of the British government ruling in India was to maintain India as a predominantly agricultural economy only and exploit it as its colony. The construction of an extensive network of railways and irrigation work was designed mainly to transform India into an agricultural colony of British industry and to fulfill certain political ends. During the First Word War, there was a desire to enlist support to Indian industries when the fighting strength was weakened due to non-availability of military supplies. "During the inter-war period, all-through the government adopted a policy of limited industrialism, political and constitutional situation entailed the Government of India for giving more weight in formulating its proposals to British interest." The state monopoly enterprises like Railways and Posts & Telegraphs, etc., were administered by the government to suit the interests of British capitalism. The establishment of the Board of Industrial and Scientific Research in 1940, Reconstruction Committee in 1941 and Planning & Development Division in 1944 gave a momentum to the industrial development of India. This marked the state interference in the industrial development of the country.

Government Policy Framework for PEs

On 21st April, 1945 the Planning and Development Division had issued a policy statement specifying a crucial role for the industrial development of the country. "Certain industries must be taken under central control in the interests of coordinated development. Government should play an active part in the industrial development of the country." It was also stated in the policy statement that basic industries of national importance might be nationalized provided (i) adequate capital was not forthcoming and (ii) it was regarded essential in the national interests to promote such industries.

Industrial Policy Resolution, 1948

The role which the state had to play in the economic life of the country was defined in the statement in the following words: "There can be no doubt that the state must play a progressively active role in the development of industries but ability to achieve the main objectives should determine the immediate extent of state responsibility and the limits to private enterprise." It was stated in the statement that the manufacture of arms and ammunition, the production and control of atomic energy, the ownership and management of railway transport would be the exclusive monopoly of the central government. In case of coal, iron and steel, aircraft, ship-building, manufacture of telephone, telegraph and wireless apparatus excluding radio receiving sets, and mineral oils, the state "will be exclusively responsible for the establishment of new undertakings." The state would always have an inherent right to acquire any existing undertaking in public interest. But the existing units in the above fields were allowed to operate for a term of ten years and thereafter the whole matter is reviewed for acquisition. In the last category, eighteen industries were listed which were subject to central regulation and control in as much as "their location must be governed by economic factors of all India importance" or they "require considerable investment and a high degree of control." The other industries were left to be developed in the private sector. Here also "the state will progressively participate in this field, nor will it hesitate to intervene whenever the progress of an industry under private enterprise is unsatisfactory." The approach of the government was realistic in this policy statement to achieve the basic objectives of maximum protection, full employment and social justice and the state was assigned a progressively increasing role. But the resolution was not clear and definite as regards the areas of private sector.

Industrial Policy Resolution, 1956

By 1954, the social thinking of mixed economy was diverted into socialist pattern of society. The Directive Principles of State Policy stated that "the state shall strive to promote the welfare of the people by securing and protecting as effectively as it may be a social order in which justice, social, economic and political, shall inform all the institutions of the nation life."

The main objectives of the new Policy Resolution were:

(*i*) to accelerate the rate of economic growth and speed up industrialization;

(*ii*) to develop heavy industries and machine-making industries;

(*iii*) to expand the public sector;

(*iv*) to build up a large and growing cooperative sector;

(*v*) to reduce disparities in income and wealth; and

(*vi*) to prevent private monopolies and the concentration of economic power in different fields in the hands of a few individuals.

"All industries of basic and strategic importance or in the nature of public utility services should be in the public sector. Other industries which are essential and require investment on a scale which only the state in present circumstances could provide have also to be in the public sector." The industries had been listed in Schedule 'A' if this resolution, which included the industries of arms and ammunition; atomic energy; iron and steel; heavy castings and forgings of iron and steel: heavy plant and machinery for basic industries; heavy electrical plants; coal and lignites, the machinery for basic industries; heavy electrical plants; coal and lignites, the minerals oils; mining and processing of copper, lead, zinc, tin, chrome ore, sulphur and etc; aircraft; air and railway transport; ship building; generation and distribution of electricity; and telecommunication equipments. In the second category, there were twelve industries listed in Schedule "B" which would be progressively state owned and in which the state would generally take the initiative in establishing new undertaking. In this category, the private sector was also allowed to develop industrial enterprises of its own or with state participation. The third category comprised all other industries not listed in schedules "A" and "B". They had, in general, been left to the initiative and enterprise of the private sector. It had, however, been made clear in the Resolution that the state would be free to start any industry in this category. The state would continue to provide increased financial assistance and special assistance would be given to enterprises organized on cooperative lines. The private sector would be subject to control and regulation in terms of the Industries (Development and Regulation) Act to fit into the framework of the social and economic policy of the state.

"The division of industries into separate categories does not imply that they are being placed in water-tight compartments. Inevitably, there will not only be an area of overlapping but also a great deal of dovetailing between industries in the private and public sectors." The state could start any industry not included in Schedule 'A' and Schedule 'B' and in appropriate cases, privately owned units might be permitted to produce an item falling within Schedule 'A' for meeting their own requirement or as by-products.

It was expected that PEs would increase the revenue of the state and provide resources for reinvestment. These enterprises were to be judged by their total results not only with the sole criterion of profitability. The resolution of 1956 had not made any material departure from the earlier policy of 1948. The role of the state had further been extended to certain new areas which were earlier left to private entrepreneurship.

Industrial Policy Resolution, 1973

On 2nd February, 1973, the government had issued at Press note on industrial policy in the light of the experience in the implementation of Industrial Licensing Policy of 1970 and approach to the Fifth Five-Year Plan. As regards the role of the public sector, the stand taken by the earlier resolution of 1956 would be followed. In order to reduce the concentration of economic power, the concept of joint sector was introduced as a promotional instrument. Actually speaking, this policy statement was a supplementary statement to the Industrial Policy Statement of 1956. It mainly contained the provisions of the government pertaining to the joint sector and re-emphasized the objectives of the resolution of 1956.

Industrial Policy Resolution, 1977

The industrial policy of the Janata Government announced on 23rd December, 1977, recognized the crucial problems of unemployment, rural-urban disparities and low level of increase in the national income. As compared to population growth in India, the growth rate of per capital national income was low during the last decade. The objective of this new industrial policy must, therefore, be directed towards removing the distortions of the past, so that the genuine aspirations of the people can be met within a time-bound programme of economic development.

Regarding public sector, it was pointed out that it would not only be the product of important and strategic goods of basic nature but it would also be used effectively as a establishing force for maintaining essential supplies for the consumers. It would be charged with the responsibility of encouraging the development of a wide range of ancillary industries, and contributing to the growth of decentralized production by making available its expertise in technology and management to small-scale and cottage industry. The government would revise the prices of the products of public sector in upward direction to generate adequate internal resources as the expansion and diversification plans of PEs would have to be financed by their own internal resources.

Industrial Policy Resolution, 1980

In this resolution of 23rd July, 1980, the task of raising the pillars of economic infrastructure in the country was entrusted to the public sector for reasons of its greater reliability. It also pointed out that the 1956 resolution still forms the basis of our industrial policy. Referring to the public sector, it was stated "An unfortunate development during the recent political vacuum in the country has been an erosion of faith in the public sector which has been reflected in its poor performance in recent years. Public sector, which was conceived to provide the pillars of the country's economic infrastructure, was rendered hollow." In order to rehabilitate faith in the public sector, the policy stated that "we have not only to restore people's faith in the public sector but also evolve effective operational systems of management in the public sector not as nobody's sector." Regarding efficiency, the government had decided to launch a drive to revive the efficiency of public sector undertakings. Industrial undertakings in this sector would be closely examined on a unit by unit basis and corrective action would be taken in terms of time-bound programme, wherever necessary. It is also proposed to take effective steps on developing managerial cadres in functional fields such as operations, finance, marketing and information system.

Industrial Policy Resolution, 1990

The Government of India announced its New Industrial Policy on 31st May, 1990. In this policy, the Government has not made any substantial change regarding the role of PEs. It implies that the earlier policies would continue. However, the Government has opened the door of steel production to the private sector. This is, undoubtedly, a major policy change. Generation of power has also been opened to the private sector.

Industrial Policy Resolution, 1991

The Government has decided to take a series of measures to unshackle the Indian industrial economy from the cobwebs of unnecessary bureaucratic control. In this context, following aspects were highlighted in the Resolution with regards to public sector.

(*i*) Portfolio of public sector investments will be reviewed with a view to focussing public sector on strategic high-technical and essential infrastructure. Whereas some reservation for the public sector is being retained there would be no bar for areas of exclusivity to be opened to the private sector selectively. Similarly, the public sector will also be allowed entry in areas not reserved for it.

(*ii*) Public enterprises which are chronically sick and which are unlikely to be turned around will, for the formulation of revival/rehabilitation schemes, be referred to the Board for Industrial and Financial Reconstruction (BIFR), or other similar high level institutions created for the purpose. A social security mechanism will be created to protect the interests of workers likely to be affected by such rehabilitation packages.

(*iii*) In order to raise resources and encourage wider public participation, a part of the Government's shareholding in the public sector would be offered to mutual funds, financial institutions, general public and workers.

(*iv*) Boards of public sector companies would be made more professional and given greater powers.

(*v*) There will be a greater thrust on performance improvement through the Memorandum of Understanding (MOU) system through which management would be granted greater autonomy and will be held accountable. Technical expertise on the part of the Government would be upgraded to make the MOU negotiations and implementation more effective.

(*vi*) To facilitate a fuller discussion on performance, the MOU signed between Government and the public enterprise would be placed in Parliament. While focussing on major management issues, this would also help to place matters on day-to-day operations of public enterprises in their correct perspective.

It is being felt that labour may not accept this policy in view of anticipated retrenchments. Further, it has been said that the closure of public enterprises through BIFR would further delay the implementation of the Government decision to close the sick and unviable enterprises. Critics argue that the excessive reliance on MOUs may not bring results.

New Orientation of Policy Framework

Keeping the changing business scenario in mind the Government of India had announced the adoption of a new approach towards the public sector on July, 1991. This was an important part of the new industrial policy. Silent features of new approach towards public enterprises given in the said Industrial Policy are as follows:

(*i*) Portfolio of public sector investments will be viewed with a view to focus the public sector on strategic, high-tech, and essential infrastructure. Whereas some reservation for the public sector is being retained there would be no bar for areas of exclusivity to be opened up to the private sector selectivity. Similarly, public sector will also be allowed entry in areas not reserved for it.

(*ii*) Public sector which are chronically sick and which are unlikely to be turned around will, for the formulation of revival/rehabilitation schemes, be referred to the Board for Industrial and Financial Reconstruction (BIFR), or other similar high level institutions created for the purpose. A social security mechanism will be created to protect the interests of workers likely to be affected by such rehabilitation packages.

(*iii*) In order to raise resources and encourage wider public participation, a new part of the government's shareholding in the public sector will be offered to mutual funds, financial institutions, general public and workers.

(*iv*) Boards of public sector companies would be made more professional and given greater powers.

(*v*) There will be a greater thrust on performance improvement through the Memorandum of Understanding (MoU) system through which management would be given greater autonomy and will be held accountable. Technical expertise on the part of the government would be upgraded to make the MoU negotiation and implementation more effective.

(*vi*) To facilitate fuller discussion on performance, the MoU signed between Government and the public enterprises would be placed in parliament. While focusing on major management issues, this would also help to place matters on day to day operations of public enterprises in their correct perspective.

Performance of Public Enterprises

Performance of PEs has been evaluated in terms of investment, sales, profit and employment.

1. Investment: The aggregate investment in PEs grew from Rs. 29 crore in 5 enterprises in 1951-52 to Rs. 528951 crore in 246 enterprises in 2008-09. The financial investment in PEs during 2008-09 over 2007-08, moreover, increased by Rs. 73584. Overall growth in investment in PEs is given in exhibit- 21.1

Exhibit 21.1

Growth in Investment #

Particulars	Total Investment (Rs. in crore)	Enterprises (No.)
1	2	3
At the commencement of the 1st five year plan (1.4.1951)	29	5
At the commencement of the 2nd five year plan (1.4.1956)	81	21
At the commencement of the 3rd five year plan (1.4.1961)	948	47
At the end of 3rd five year plan (31.3.1966)	2410	73
At the commencement of the 4th five year plan (1.4.1969)	3897	84
At the commencement of the 5th five year plan (1.4.1974)	6237	122
At the end of 5th five year plan (31.3.1979)	15534	169
At the commencement of the 6th five year plan (1.4.1980)	18150	179
At the commencement of the 7th five year plan (1.4.1985)	42673	215
At the end of 7th five year plan (31.3.1990)	99329	244
At the commencement of the 8th five year plan (1.4.1992)	135445	246
At the end of 8th five year plan (31.3.1997)	213610	242
At the end of 9th five year plan (31.3.2002)	324614	240
At the end of 10th five year plan (31.3.2007)	420476	245
At the end of First year of Eleventh Five Year Plan (31.3.2008)	455409	242
At the end of second year of Eleventh Five Year Plan (31.3.2009)	528951	246

As in the Balance Sheet

Source: Public Enterprise Survey, Vol. I of the concerned years.

While the Central Government has the majority equity holding in PEs (84.49%) investment in terms of both equity and long term loans has been forthcoming from other parties as well, such as, the financial institutions, banks, private parties (both India and foreign), State Governments and holding companies. However, there is drastic change in 'sources of investment' that is a significant change in 2004-05 to 2008-09. Whereas the share of Central Government in total investment stood at 37.78 per cent in 2004-05, it declined to 29.83 per cent in 2008-09. The share of financial institutions / banks (and 'others'), on the other hand, that was 39.89 per cent in 2004-05 has gone up to 54.09 percent in 2008-09. In a way this shows the greater confidence of FIs and banks in the PEs. The share of 'foreign parties' in total financial investment has also shown increase from 8.37 per cent in 2004-05 to 8.52 per cent in 2008-09.

Components of Investment

The structure of financial investment in PEs shows some change during the period 2002-03 Exhibit 21.2. While the share of paid up capital in total (financial) investment was 32.57 percent during 2002-03, it declined to 26.25 percent in 2008-09. The share of long term loans, on the other hand, went up from 66.56 percent in 2002-03 to 73.02 percent in 2008-09.

Exhibit 21.2
Components of financial Investment

(Rs. in crore)

Year ending	Paid-up capital	Share application money	Long term loans	Investment (3+4+5)
1	2	3	4	5
As on 31.3.2003	109306 (32.57)	2933 (0.87)	223408 (66.56)	335647 (100)
As on 31.3.2004	111874 (31.96)	7087 (2.02)	231033 (66.01)	349994 (100)
As on 31.3.2005	117551 (32.84)	6494 (1.81)	233894 (65.34)	357939 (100)
As on 31.3.2006	120844 (1.54)	6204 (29.93)	276658 (68.53)	403706 (100)
As on 31.3.2007	125323 (29.76)	6306 (1.50)	288847 (68.74)	420476 (100)
As on 31.3.2008	131232 (28.81)	3090 (0.08)	321087 (70.51)	455409 (100)
As on 31.3.2009	138843 (26.25)	3867 (0.73)	386241 (73.02)	528951 (100)

Source: Public Enterprise Survey, Vol. I of the concerned years.

There were altogether 246 PEs under the administrative control of various ministries/ departments as on March 31, 2009. The cumulative investment (paid-up capital plus long-term loans) in all the PEs together stood at Rs 5,28,951 crore as in end-March 2009. The largest share in this investment belonged to the service sector (46.1 per cent) followed by electricity (26.2 per cent), manufacturing (18.1 per cent) and mining (8.8 per cent). A great deal of investment in PEs is being made through internal resources rather than through investment from outside. 9.48 Of the total, 158 PEs made net profit and 54 net loss in 2008-09. The year witnessed severe financial under-recoveries by public-sector Oil Marketing Companies (OMCs) as they had to keep the prices low on sale of petroleum products in the domestic market. The foreign exchange outgo exceeded the foreign exchange earnings of PEs during 2008-09.

Exhibit-21.3
Performance of PEs during 2008-09

(Rs crore)

Sl.	Particulars	2007-08	2008-09	Per cent change over previous year
1.	Investment (long-term loan + equity)	4,55,367	5,28,951	16.2
2.	Capital Employed (net fixed assets + working capital)	7,23,719	7,93,096	9.6
3.	Total Turnover	10,94,484	12,63,405	15.4
4.	Profits of Profit-making PEs	91,571	98,652	7.7
5.	Losses of Loss-making PEs	10,257	14,424	40.6
6.	Net Worth	5,18,530	5,84,072	12.6
7.	Dividend Declared	28,081	25,493	-9.2
8.	Corporate Tax	1,65,994	1,51,728	-8.6

Contd....

9.	Interest Paid	32,200	40,330	25.2
10.	Contribution to Central Exchequer	1,65,994	1,51,728	-8.6
11.	Foreign Exchange Earnings	67,678	74,184	9.6
	Oil Companies	46,051	48,422	5.1
	Other Companies	21,627	25,762	19.1
12.	Foreign Exchange Outgo	3,68,228	4,28,821	16.5
	Oil Companies	2,57,723	2,78,989	8.3
	Other Companies	1,10,505	1,49,832	35.6

Source: Department of Public Enterprises.

Exhibit 21.3 shows that the investment in 2008-09 was increased by 16.2% over the previous year 2007-08. However, contribution of PEs in terms of dividends, corporate tax and contribution to national exchequer declined over the previous year 2007-08 by 9.2, 8.6 and 8.6 respectively.

2. Sales Performance of PEs: The volume of the sales of public enterprises has been growing over the period. The sales of Rs. 1,33,906 crores during 1991-92 have increased to Rs. 3,89,199 crores during 1999-00 and rs.5,86,140 crores during 2003-04. The figures showing the absolute and relative position of turnover for the year 1991-92 and onwards have been shown in Exhibit-21.4

Exhibit-21.4
Sales Performance of PEs

Year	(Rupees in crore)		Turnover to Capital Employed (%)	Growth of Turnover (%)
	Turnover/Operating Income	Capital Employed		
1991-92	1,33,906	1,17,991	113.49	12.83
1992-93	1,47,266	1,40,110	105.11	9.98
1993-94	1,58,049	1,59,836	98.88	7.32
1994-95	1,87,355	1,62,450	115.33	18.54
1995-96	2,26,919	1,73,948	130.45	21.12
1996-97	2,60,735	2,31,178	112.79	14.90
1997-98	2,76,002	2,49,855	110.46	5.86
1998-99	3,10,179	2,65,093	117.01	12.38
1999-2000	3,89,199	3,02,867	128.50	25.48
2002-03	5,35,165	4,17,931	128.05	19.58
2003-04	5,86,140	4,52,250	129.61	9.53
2004-05	7,44,307	5,04,826	139.83	19.39
2005-06	8,32,584	5,81,250	140.00	
2006-07	9,64,410	NA	145.90	15.28
2007-08	10,94,484	7,23,719	151.09	13.43
2008-09	12,63,405	7,93,096	159.10	15.43

Source: Public Enterprise Survey, Vol. I of the concerned years.

It may be seen from the above exhibit that the public sector enterprises have shown consistent growth in the turnover/operating income. It has increased form Rs. 1,33,906 crores in 1991-92 to Rs. 3,89,199 crores during 1999-2000. The increase in turnover during this period works out to 19.1% and 25.5%. It is to be noted that turnover was Rs. 28,635 crore during 1981-82 which has crossed 1,00,000 crore mark during 1989-90. During 2005-06, the turnover is increased to Rs. 8,32,584 crores. As a percentage of capital employed, it is highest at 140%. The turnover increased to Rs. 9,64,419 crore.

3. Profitability of Public Enterprises: Pre-tax profits assume greater importance as a yardstick for judging the operational efficiency of management since the level of tax rate at any given point of time is determined by the government and therefore, constitutes an extraneous factor beyond the control of the management. The investors, however, are more concerned with the post-tax profits that are available to compensate against the capital provided by them. The related figures have been shown in Exhibit-21.5.

Pre-tax Profits and Post tax Profits
Exhibit-21.5

Year	(Rs. in crores)	
	Pre-tax profits	Post tax Profits
1975-76	306	19
1980-81	1,025	446
1985-86	3,100	1,771
1990-91	3,500	2,272
1995-96	13,621	9,574
1998-99	19,702	13,203
1999-2000	22,037	14,331
2000-01	24,967	15,653
2001-02	38,233	25,978
2002-03	49,831	32,399
2003-04	75,290	53,168
2004-05	85,550	64,963
2005-06	84,250	70,288
2006-07	1,11,527	77,175
2007-08	1,20,487	79,748
2008-09	84,250	70,288

Source: Public Enterprise Survey, Vol. I of the concerned years.

The pre-tax profits have recorded substantial improvement during 1975-2000. From a figure of Rs. 306 crores in 1975-76 it has been risen to Rs. 22,262 crore in 1999-2000 more than 72 times during last 24 years. The post tax profits have also increased substantially from Rs. 19 crore in 1975-76 to Rs. 14,555 crores in 1999-2000. In terms of percentage, the returns are insignificant during 1975-76 to 1990-91. But thereafter it increased to about 9% on investment in 1999-2000. Similarly, post tax profit on equity comes to 17.65 percent in 1999-2000 in comparison to 13.70 percent in 1995-96. During 2005-06, post-tax profit increased to Rs. 70,288 crores.

4. Human Resource Management in PEs: Large scale employment by public enterprises has over the years, led to a situation where some of the enterprises are saddled with over employment or excess manpower resulting in low level of per capita productivity. Government has initiated a voluntary retirement scheme in public enterprises to help them shed excess manpower and to improve the age mix and the skill mix. Emphasis is also being given to training and re-training programmes to bring about overall improvement in per capita productivity. As on 31.3.2009, the 246 PEs employed over 15.35 lakh people (excluding casual workers). One-fourth of the manpower was in managerial and supervisory cadres. The PEs have thus a highly skilled workforce, which is one of their basic strengths. The PEs, in turn, provide lifetime employment to their employees. As the PEs operate under dynamic market conditions, while, some of them may face shortage of people, others may have excess manpower. The Government, therefore, initiated a Voluntary Retirement Scheme (VRS) to help these enterprises to shed excess manpower. The continuous increase in the total number of employees, their salaries and wages and their wage level of PEs in India may be seen from Exhibit-21.6.

Exhibit-21.6
Employment and Average Annual Emoluments

Year	No. of Employees In lakh	Average Annual per capita emoluments in Rs.	% Increase in Average Annual emoluments
1967-68	5.54	3,978	-
1975-76	15.05	8,953	-
1985-86	21.54	25,887	-
1989-90	22.36	43,665	-
1991-92	21.79	56,508	14.90
1992-93	21.52	64,983	15.00
1993-94	20.70	72,043	10.86
1994-95	20.62	82,517	14.54
1995-96	20.52	1,06,876	29.52
1996-97	20.08	1,10,662	3.54
1999-2000	18.06	1,68,339	21.83
2000-01	17.40	2,19,272	30.49
2001-02	19.92	1,93,554	- 11.72
2002-03	18.66	2,25,986	16.75
2003-04	17.66	2,48,481	9.95
2004-05	17.00	2,86,112	15.14
2005-06	16.49	2,84,123	-0.69
2006-07	16.14	3,98,496	40.25
2007-08	15.66	4,10,802	3.0
2008-09	15.35	5,39,150	- 31.24

Source: Public Enterprise Survey, Vol. I of the concerned years.

The basic parameters of the model Voluntary Retirement Scheme which were notified by the Government vide DPE's OM dated 5.10.88 and 6.1.89 was in force since 1988 till April 2000. Government has improved upon the existing scheme and introduced a new scheme of VRS on 5.5.2000 and again on 6.11.2001. As per the available information, about 3.03 lakh employees opted for Voluntary Retirement Scheme (VRS), till 31.3.2009. A good many PEs, are faced with a high rate of 'attrition', as employees are leaving to join other organizations on account of higher salaries being offered elsewhere. The total number of employees in PEs that was 15.65 lakhs in 2007-08 came down further to 15.35 lakhs in 2008-09.

Organizational Structure

The Public Enterprises (PEs) belong to either of the two broad classifications of 'statutory corporations' or 'Government companies'. While the Corporation form of PEs have their objectives and scope defined in the legislation/Act of Parliament, the Company form of PEs have their functions articulated based on the Articles of Association. These Government companies are, moreover, registered with the Registrar of Companies under the Companies Act, 1956. The PEs are mostly commercial enterprises. Some PEs, such as, National Film Development Corporation, National Research Development Corporation, National Small Industries Corporation Ltd., Jute Corporation of India Ltd. and Handicrafts & Handloom Export Corporation India Ltd. etc. are, however, 'promotional' in nature.

In general, these are large scale enterprises requiring appropriate organizational structure, with particularization of functions and delegation of authority (from top to bottom). With a view to bring about unity of purpose, moreover, there is always the need for co-ordination. Necessary planning is called vis-à-vis order booking / demand forecasting, sales network, man-and-machine utilization, design and research, welfare measures and job satisfaction of employees. Different PEs have been taking various HR initiatives for employee involvement, knowledge acquisition, career and succession planning etc for improving the performance in their respective organizations. Essentially, these initiatives revolve around building competency levels followed by commitment to the organization and systems improvement, and finally evolving a vibrant corporate culture. The Department of Public Enterprises (DPE), Government of India has been, furthermore, formulating guidelines in respect of organizational structure, corporate governance, wage and salary policy, executive development programme etc., which are applicable to all the PEs. The paragraphs below discuss some of these guidelines issued by the DPE.

Organizational Structure of PEs

The Department of Public Enterprises (DPE) formulates policy guidelines on the Board structure of Public Enterprises and advises on the shape and size of organizational structure of PEs. The public enterprises are categorized in four Schedules namely 'A', 'B', 'C' and 'D' based on various quantitative, qualitative and other factors. The quantitative factors are: investment, capital employed, net sales, profit before tax, number of employees, number of units and value added per employee. Qualitative factors are: national importance, complexities of problems, level of technology, prospects for expansion and diversification of activities and competition from other sectors, etc. The other factors relate to the strategic national importance of the corporation. The pay scales of Chief Executives and full time Functional Directors in PEs are determined as per the Schedule of the concerned enterprise.

As on 31.3.2009, there were 247 PEs in the country. Out of the 247 PEs, there are 58 Schedule 'A', 70 PEs in Schedule 'B', 46 PEs in Schedule 'C' and 6 PEs Schedule 'D'. The rest are covered under the uncategorized category. The details of the Board level posts (whole time) in the categorized PEs are given in the exhibit below :

Exhibit-21.7
Details of Board level posts in CPSE

Schedule	Chief Executive		Whole Time Director	
	2008	2009	2008	2009
Schedule A	56	58	-	-
Schedule B	74	70	202	213
Schedule C	47	46	185	183
Schedule D	06	06	67	67
Total	183	180	454	463

Source: Public Enterprise Survey, Vol. I of the concerned years.

Proposals received from various administrative Ministries/Departments for initial categorization /upgradation of PEs in appropriate schedule, personal upgradation, creation of posts in PEs, etc. are considered in DPE in consultation with the Public Enterprises Selection Board (PESB). During 2008-09, 2 PEs were initially categorized in appropriate Schedule, 3 PEs were upgraded to higher Schedule and one post of Chief Executive and 9 posts of Functional Directors were created.

Corporate Governance in PEs

The concept of Corporate Governance has generated extensive debate during the last few years due to the fast changing economic scenario all over the world. The term Corporate Governance includes the policies and procedures adopted by a corporate entity in achieving its objectives in relation to shareholders, employees, customers and suppliers, regulatory authority and the community at large. In general parlance, it means a code of corporate conduct in relation to all the stakeholders, whether internal or external. Corporate Governance implies transparency of management systems and encompasses the entire mechanics of the functioning of the company. It provides a system by which corporate entities are directed and controlled, besides attempting to put in place a system of checks and balances between the shareholders, directors, auditors and the management.

In India, all listed companies including listed PEs are covered by the SEBI guidelines. To further improve Corporate Governance standards in India, SEBI revised the code of Corporate Governance based upon the recommendations of N.R. Narayana Murthy Committee set up in 2002. Clause 49 of SEBI guidelines mandates a listed company to comply with the various provisions relating to corporate governance. The Organization for Economic Cooperation and Development (OECD), which is a forum of the Governments of 30 democracies also took initiatives to address governance issues and it suggested principles of Corporate Governance. India is not a member of OECD. In September 2005, the OECD circulated guidelines on Corporate Governance of State-owned enterprises. These guidelines cover issues like (i) ensuring an effective legal and regulatory framework for State-owned enterprises; (ii) the State acting as an owner; (iii) equitable treatment of shareholders; (iv) relations with stakeholders; (v) transparency and disclosures; and (vi) responsibilities of the Boards of State-owned enterprises.

The post-1991 period has witnessed significant changes in the public sector policy. The areas reserved for public sector were reduced. The Public Enterprises (PEs) were expected to look for internal resources and borrowings and concentrate on improvement in operations and efficiency on commercial lines of operation aimed at earning profit. In pursuance of the Industrial Policy Statement of 24.7.1991, detailed guidelines on composition of Board of Directors were issued by the Department of Public Enterprises (DPE) in March 1992. These guidelines inter-alia provided that at least one-third of the Directors on the Board of a PE should be non-official Directors. The Navratna and Miniratna schemes evolved by the Government in 1997 provided that these PEs should set up Audit Committees. Based on the SEBI guidelines, further instructions were issued by DPE in November 2001 stating that at least half of the Board of listed PEs with executive Chairman should be Independent Directors.

Formulation of Guidelines on Corporate Governance

In August, 2005, the Government enhanced the powers delegated to Navratna, Miniratna and other profit making PEs. Further, 9 more CPSEs were granted Navratna status in 2007 and 2008. As a result, the public accountability of the PEs has increased. In this context, Government had approved the implementation of guidelines on corporate governance for PEs. These guidelines were formulated by DPE keeping in view relevant laws, instructions and procedures. The views of various stakeholders such as administrative Ministries/ Departments, PEs, nodal Ministries like Company Affairs, Finance (Expenditure), Comptroller and Auditor General (C & AG), Securities and Exchange of Board of India (SEBI), Institute of Chartered Accountants of India (ICAI), Institute of Company Secretaries of India (ICSI), Institute of Cost & Works Accountants of India (ICWAI), National Foundation for Corporate Governance (NFCG), Institute of Public Enterprise, etc. were taken into account while formulating these Guidelines. These guidelines are applicable to listed as well as un-listed PEs and cover issues like composition of Boards, Audit Committee, Subsidiary companies, disclosures, Code of conduct and ethics, risk management and These guidelines are applicable to listed as well as unlisted PEs and cover issues like composition of Boards, Audit Committee, Subsidiary companies, disclosures, Code of Conduct and ethics, risk management and compliance.

Composition of Board

In respect of the Board composition, these Guidelines provide that the number of functional Directors should not exceed 50% of the actual strength of Board and the number of Government nominee Directors shall be restricted to maximum of two. In case of listed PEs with executive chairman, the number of non-official Directors shall be at least 50% of Board members. In case of unlisted PEs and listed PEs with non-executive chairman, at least one-third of the Board Members shall be non-official Directors. The Government has also laid down pre-defined criteria in terms of educational qualifications, age and experience in respect of persons to be considered for appointment as non-official Directors. As in clause 49 of SEBI, relevant clauses have been incorporated in these guidelines to ensure 'independence' of nonofficial Directors and avoid potential conflict. It has also been provided that the Directors nominated by any institution other than public financial institution will not be treated as non-official Directors. It has been further mandated that the Board meetings are to be held at least once in every 3 months and at least 4 such meetings in a year and all relevant information is required to be given to the Board. Further, the Board should lay down code of conduct for all members and senior management. In this regard, a model Code has been incorporated in the Guidelines to assist the PEs. The Guidelines inter alia provide that the Board should ensure integration and alignment of risk management system and the company should undertake suitable training programmes for its new Board members.

Audit Committee: The provisions relating to Audit Committee require a qualified and independent Audit Committee to be set up by PEs with minimum three Directors as members. Further, two-thirds of the members of this Committee should be independent Directors with chairman to be independent Director. The Audit Committee has been given extensive powers with regard to financial matters of company and it should meet at least 4 times in a year.

Subsidiary Companies: With regard to subsidiary companies, it has been provided that at least one independent Director of holding company should be Director on the Board of subsidiary company, and the Audit Committee of holding company should review the financial statements of subsidiary company. All significant transactions and agreements of subsidiary company are required to be brought to the notice of the Board of Directors of holding company.

Disclosures : The provisions regarding disclosures require all transactions to be placed before the Audit Committee. The Guidelines mandate that while preparing financial statements, treatment of data should be as per prescribed Accounting Standard and if there are any deviations, the same are to be explicitly mentioned. Further, the Board is to be informed about risk assessment and minimization procedures, and the Management is to make disclosures to the Board relating to all financial and commercial transactions where they have personal interest or may have a potential conflict.

Compliance: It has also been mandated in the Guidelines that there should be a separate section on Corporate Governance in Annual report of company with details of compliance. The PEs will have to obtain a certificate from auditors/company secretary regarding compliance with these Guidelines. Chairman's speech in AGM will also carry a section on compliance with Corporate Governance Guidelines and will form part of the company's Annual Report.

Implementation and Grading: The DPE will grade PEs on the basis of their compliance with Guidelines and such grading will be used for MOU Awards. Keeping in view the importance of Corporate Governance in State Level Public Enterprises (SLPEs), all States have also been advised to implement these Guidelines. The proposal for extension of guidelines on Corporate Governance is under consideration of the Government of India.

Appointment of Functional Directors of PEs

Functional Directors including Chief Executives of the PEs are appointed by the concerned Administrative Ministries/Departments on the basis of recommendations of Public Enterprises Selection Board (PESB). The Public enterprises Selection Board is a high powered body constituted by the Government of India vide its Resolution dated 3.3.1987. The PESB has been set up with the objective of evolving a sound managerial policy for the Public Sector Enterprises and, in particular, to advise Government on appointments to their top management posts. As per GOI Resolution, the PESB shall consist of a part-time or full-time chairperson and three fulltime Members. The Chairperson and Members are persons who have had a long and distinguished career in management of public or private corporations or public in administration, and have had a proven record of achievements, preferably, in the field of personnel, finance, production or marketing. The Government has decided that candidates from State Level Public Sector Enterprises (SLPEs) and the 'private sector' will also be considered for selection to the post of functional directors in CPSEs as non-internal candidates along with the candidates of Public Sector Enterprises subject to fulfilling the eligibility criteria. The Government has recently revised the procedure for obtaining CVC clearance in respect of candidates recommended by PESB for Board level posts in PEs so as to reduce delays. It has been furthermore prescribed that CVC will directly grant its clearance or otherwise convey the same to the concerned Administrative Ministry/Department within 15 days of the receipt of the recommendations of PESB.

Professionalization of Boards of PEs

The DPE formulates policy guidelines on the Board structure of PEs. In pursuance of the public sector policy being followed since 1991, several measures have been taken by the Department of Public Enterprises to professionalize the Boards of public enterprises. The guidelines issued in 1992 mention that outside professionals should be inducted on the Boards of PEs in the form of part-time non-official Directors and that the number of such Directors should be at least 1/3rd of the actual strength of the Board. In the case of listed PEs headed by an executive Chairman, the number of non-official Directors (Independent) should be at least half the strength of the Board. The guidelines also provide that the number of Government Directors on the Boards should be not more than one-sixth of the actual strength of the Board subject to a maximum of two. Apart from this, there should be some functional Directors on each Board whose number should not exceed 50% of the actual strength of the Board. In regard to selection and appointment of non-official (Independent) Directors on the Boards of PEs, the following eligibility criteria is being adopted:

a. **Age :** Age band should be between 45-65 years (minimum/maximum limit). This could however be relaxed for eminent professionals for reasons to be recorded, being limited to 70 years.

b. **Qualification :** Minimum qualification for part time non official (Independent) Directors would be graduate degree from a recognized university.

c. **Experience :** Persons of eminence with proven track record from industry, business or agriculture; CMD/MD in corporate sector/PSE; Professor level in an academic institution or professionals of repute like eminent Chartered Accountants/Cost Accountants at the level of Directors of Institutes/Heads of Department; persons having experience of not less than 10 years at the level of Joint Secretary and above in the Government.

The proposals for appointment of non-official (Independent) Directors are initiated by the concerned Administrative Ministries/Departments. In so far as Navratna and Miniratna PEs are concerned, the selection of non-official Directors is made by the Search Committee consisting of Chairman, PESB), Secretary, DPE, Secretary of the administrative Ministry/Department of the PEs, Chief Executive of the concerned PEs and non-official Members. In the case of remaining PEs (other than Navratna/Miniratna PEs), Public Enterprises Selection Board (PESB) makes the selection of non-official (Independent) Directors. The concerned Administrative Ministry/Department appoints the non-official (Independent) Directors on the basis of recommendations of Search Committee/PESB after obtaining the approval of the competent authority.

The Navratna scheme provides that the Boards of these companies should be professionalised by inducting a minimum of 4 non-official Directors before their Boards can exercise the enhanced powers. Similarly, in the case of Miniratna CPSEs also the induction of minimum 3 non-official Directors is pre-condition for the exercise of delegated powers under the Miniratna Scheme.

During the last three years (2006, 2007 and 2008), the Search Committee and PESB have recommended the names of 387 persons for appointment as non-official (Independent) Directors on the Boards of PEs. During the year 2009 (till October, 2009), the names of 67 persons have been recommended by the Search Committee/PESB in this regard.

The functional Directors, on the other hand, are appointed by the administrative Ministry on the recommendations of PESB and with the approval of the Competent Authority. The Government Directors are appointed in ex-officio capacity and their choice vests with the concerned administrative Ministries/ Departments. In order to ensure timely appointment of requisite number of non-official Directors on the Board of PEs, the DPE has formulated proposals and submitted the same to the Government for approval. DPE's proposal to expedite the process of selection and appointment of non-official (Independent) Directors on the Boards of PEs is being considered by the Government.

Executives Development Programme (EDP)

As the nodal Department for PEs, the Department of Public Enterprises is supplementing the efforts of these enterprises for human resource (HR) development by organizing Executive Development Programmes (EDPs) for senior and middle level executives. The PEs design their in-house HR development programmes for upgrading the skills and knowledge of their executives. These initiatives are further supplemented by training programmes conducted by premier management / training institutes in the country in collaboration with the Department of Public Enterprises.

The EDPs are conducted for a duration of 2-5 days. While 23 such programmes were conducted during 2008-2009, 15 such programmes are planned for the year 2009-10. These programmes are organized in collaboration with institutes, such as, the Institute of Company Secretaries, the Institute of Cost and Works Accountants of India, National Institute of Micro Small and Medium Enterprises, the National Institute of Financial Management, Institute of Chartered Accountants of India, Indian Society for Training and Development, the Institute of Company Secretaries of India and the Indian Society of Health Administration, etc. The subjects covered under these programmes include financial management, leadership challenge, effective marketing management, total quality management, information technology & e-commerce, management information systems, communication skills, corporate governance, corporate social responsibility, MOU principles & practices, project management, capital market reform & risk management, negotiation strategies & skills, health and stress management, industrial relations & labour issues, international taxation/ international finance, accounting standards, project planning and monitoring, etc. Secretary, DPE is a member on the Board of Governors of IIM (Kolkata) and the Institute of Public Enterprise (Hyderabad). Secretary, DPE is also a member of the Executive Board of the Standing Conference of Public Enterprises (SCOPE), New Delhi. Furthermore, India is a founder member of the International Centre for Promotion of Enterprises (ICPE), Ljubljana, Slovenia which is an intergovernmental organization. India has doubled its annual contribution to ICPE from the year 2007-2008. Senior and middle executives from PEs have been going to ICPE for different training programmes. Currently, India is the President of ICPE Council. ICPE also conducts a full year MBA Course.

Practice Questions

Objective Type Questions

1. Number of working PEs in India as on 31-3-2008 was
   (*a*) 240 (*b*) 246
   (*c*) 242 (*d*) 251
2. Number of workers employed in PEs in India as on 31-3-09 was
   (*a*) 15.53 lakh
   (*b*) 16.10 lakh
   (*c*) 15.35 lakh
   (*d*) 14.53 lakh
3. Amount of investment already made in PEs in India as on 31-3-2010
   (*a*) 528951
   (*b*) 455367
   (*c*) 455637
   (*d*) 528591
4. Forms of PEs do not include the following:
   (*a*) Public Corporation
   (*b*) Holding Company
   (*c*) Public Company
   (*d*) Departmental Undertaking

5. Scope of PEs do not include the following:
   (*a*) PEs cover all Industrial Commercial and Economic Activities
   (*b*) State Ownership
   (*c*) PEs have professional management
   (*d*) PEs are managed by a self contained management centre.

Ans: 1.(*b*), 2. (b), 3. (a), 4. (b), 5. (c)

Short Answer Questions

1. What are salient features of PEs Policy of 1991?
2. What is the position of Corporate Governance in PEs in India?
3. What do you mean by professionalisation of Boards of PEs?
4. What do you understand by Executive Development Programme in PEs?
5. What do you mean by Public accountability of PEs?

Long Answer Questions

1. What do you mean by Public Enterprises? Explain its significance in the economic development of India?
2. What is desirability of public enterprises in India's context?
3. What are the objectives of public enterprises? Have Public Enterprises achieved these objectives in India?
4. "The various objectives of public enterprises are unclear and conflicting". Explain it and point out whether they have achieved the set objectives?
5. Discuss the various of facets of growth of public enterprises in the light of post independence industrial policy.

References

1. Hanson.A.H., "Public Enterprises and Economic Development", Routledge and Kegan Paul Ltd., 1954, p.23
2. op.cit. Hanson.A.H., "Public Enterprises and Economic Development", p.115
3. Encyclopedia, Volume 18, Encyclopedia Britanica Inc., Chicago, 1965,p.738
4. Mallya, N.M., Public Enterprises in India, The Institute of Constitutional and Parliamentary Studies, New Delhi,1971,p.1
5. Khera. S.S., Management and Control in Public Enterprises, Asia Publishing House, Bomaby,1964.p.10
6. Jagdish Prakash, Nageshwar Rao, Mata Badal Shukla, Administration of Public Enterprises in India, Himalaya Publishing House, Mumbai, 2010, p.2)

22 RESTRUCTURING OF PUBLIC ENTERPRISES IN INDIA

The Public Enterprises (PEs) have made tremendous contributions to the development of the country at a time when the private sector was almost in infancy. In the last two decades, private sector enterprises have tried to march forward and they are getting success in their operations. Introduction of Liberalisation, Privatisation and Globalisation (LPG) has given private sector enterprises a broader framework for their operations. However, in the changed scenario public enterprises are facing severe constraints. In terms of quality or competence, the PEs are no way inferior to private sector companies. Efficiency is not dependent on ownership. There are efficient PEs as well as not so efficient ones. Just on there are successful private sector companies and not so successful ones. Today, the image of public sector is poor not because of lack of concerted efforts in communicating the achievements and activities of the public sector. There has been a campaign from the private sector organizations for privatization of PEs which has not been confronted effectively. There is need to improve communication system and to acquire latest skills in order to convey right image of PEs and of the public sector as a whole. "The general image of the public sector is that it is white elephant, loss making, but this has arisen because of a few organisations and most of them are taken over from the private sector." These PEs are inefficient due to continuous government intervention, overstaffing, poor labour productivity, and social obligations. In the changed scenario, they have to compete with private sector enterprises and they need level playing field with them. They need immediate attention from the government. covering organizational, financial, personnel and marketing issues Liberalization, Privatization and Globalisation have changed the whole scenario of PEs working environment. The government of India has taken several initiatives to restructure the PEs and result forth coming are quite positive. But these efforts need continuity to remove the constraints being faced by the PEs. They now need restructuring process.

Change in PEs Working Environment

"The concept of globalisation underlines the advantages of procuring goods and services from each and every part of the globe where they are produced with best technology, to best quality, and at competitive price. To meet the aspirations of the people and the globe compulsions, policies had to be revised. Liberlisation of rules and regulations and scrapping of controls followed suit."[1] These PEs have moved over from a protectionist regime to a more open regime. Competition in every field has generated concerns which were unknown to them for many decades. Besides the new priorities of growth and profit rolled out for the PEs recently, they find that there is increasing competition too, which compounds the situation. The seller's market has given place to a buyer's market. It is the customer who dictates terms today. Customers, competitors, and constant change drive Organisations crazy. They have pushed managements from the realms of products to processes for self-renewal and re-engineering.

Organisations who have understood the rationale for these changes in time, have restructured themselves to retain their market share and survive the competition. Others have fallen by the wayside. The changes needed are conceptually simple. But the journey towards change proves to be arduous and halting. The PEs have perforce to focus on customers and give them products they need. With the change in technology, processes of PEs have to change. The costs of PEs have to be competitive which means they should increase their productivity and eliminate inefficiencies.

They have to deploy and redeploy the resources including the work force for achieving the optimum benefit. It is indeed quite a job to pull up the sinking organizations, turn them round and transform them for healthy operations.

Restructuring can be achieved only through cooperation and understanding. A company has not only to do things right. It has also to do right things to stay alive. This requires careful scanning of the market, anticipation and guts. Restructuring requires strategic plans which are practicable and bold. The objectives of the strategic plans should be SMART viz. Specific, Measurable, Achievable, Realistic and Timely. Restructuring is thus easy to wish and difficult to realize. Survival demand that these difficulties have to be overcome. Pre-requisites for restructuring are –the courage to identify current deficiencies and the will to correct them even at the cost of public exchequer. Innovations are imperative to infuse new life and revitalize the Organisations. Companies which are unable to modernize face the bleak prospect of carrying their people who were earlier destined to carry the organisation towards growth and profits. Many such companies produce turnover without profits and profits without cash. Unless the trend is revered and the companies are transformed, they become a drag on the economy and the society.

Need of Restructuring Process

"Restructuring is required in both profit making and loss making public enterprises because of changing competitive environment and changes in government policies."[2] Restructuring is coming to PEs as a compulsion and in next five years there will be no option but to undergo organizational changes. It should originate from within the organisation so that the employees could join hands to make it more effective. Disinvestment and privatization, another dimensions of restructuring, are coming up very fast and in a large way. "Restructuring is essential for enterprises manufacturing goods – capital equipment or capital goods – as it is for those engaged in services."[3] Restructuring is as a relevant intervention for public enterprises, as it is for private ones. In the past – before the launch of the economic reforms programme both public and private enterprises were relatively inflexible. Both considered, no doubt for different reasons, that there were no real compulsions for change. Today, restructuring more rampant in the private sector than it is in the public sector. Both need it urgently and continuously. The business environment, metamorphosed by globalisation, IT and telecom, has made restructuring necessary for the survival.

Major Issues for Restructuring Programme

In the context of overall problem of restructuring and cases of sick enterprises in the public enterprises, the major issues which emerge are:

(*i*) How do we distinguish between revivable and non-revivable enterprises?

(*ii*) What are the options available for non-revivable enterprises?

(*iii*) Is it possible to merge the non-revivable enterprises with other units?

(*iv*) If yes, what will be the fast track mechanism?

(*v*) If the non-revivable enterprises are closed down, what about the manpower engaged?

(*vi*) Are there safety nets available or could these be created?

(*vii*) How can PEs, to be turnaround (or to be closed), attract worker support and cooperation?

(*viii*) Can some non-revivable PEs be handed over to workers?

(*ix*) What are the priorities for revivable units?

(*x*) What strategy can be adopted for PEs which cannot stand alone or are vulnerable units to be left alone to be forced to terminal sickness?

(*xi*) What can be the best mechanism to expedite the operation?

(*xii*) What about incipient sickness?

(*xiii*) If revivable PEs and PEs with incipient sickness are to be revived where will the funding come from?

(*xiv*) What impact will the closure of BIFR have on the PEs which are referred to it and others which may be referred?

(*xv*) What strategies should be followed to deal with (a) non revivable PEs, (b) revivable (PEs which call for immediate ICU (intensive care treatment), (c) loss making enterprises which have the potential for gaining competitive strengths, and (d) PEs which are performing but run the risk of becoming sick in the global environment.

(*xvi*) How does privatization programme affect the future and future course of action of non-performing PEs?

Scope of Restructuring Process

Restructuring is just business renewal. It can be either total or partial. It can be structural, strategic or operational touching the following:

(*i*) Transformation of corporate vision, which may involve change in work culture.

(*ii*) Technology substitution and upgradation.

(*iii*) Strategic change involving expansion, diversification, integration – backward or forward hiving off.

(*iv*) Corporate renewal: encompassing intra-corporate organisation.

(*v*) Leveraging capital, right –sizing capital or rationalizing capital resource.

(*vi*) Human resource revamp: involving right sizing or establishing new relationships or developing and realigning new skills.

(*vii*) Functional rationalizations involving business process reengineering including organizational restructuring.

(*viii*) Market restructuring which may include changes of product mix, product development, re-segmentation or new competition thrust.

(*ix*) Cost reduction focusing on asset structure or operating costs.

Objectives of Restructuring Process

"The goals for restructuring process inter-alia would include: technological upgradation, improvement in productivity and quality, profit maximization, cost reduction, shedding of non-productive areas etc. Each organisation has its own individual entity and characteristics and, therefore, non common prescription can be given to all public enterprises."[4] It is imperative, therefore to take restructuring exercises on case to case basis to improve their performances.

The broad objectives of restructuring would include:

(*i*) Clear business goals

(*ii*) Improved work ethos and culture

(*iii*) Cost reduction

(*iv*) Improved profitability

(*v*) Motivated and trained manpower

(*vi*) Market oriented approach

(*vii*) Technological upgradation

Each of the public enterprise must carry out an introspection and draw up strategic plans to meet the challenges of the market. This would call for adopting a holistic approach to productivity encompassing areas e.g. finance, marketing, technology, HRD, together with optimization of resources–physical and financial. It is generally recognised that modernization of industries is essential to improve productivity and reduce costs. Development of human resources is – key factor in modernization. The level of technology sophistication has an overwhelming influence on productivity. The speed of technological changes is forcing the organisations to continuously redesign, modify, innovate the products/services in order to be competitive in the global market.

Formulation of Restructuring Strategy

The strategy to be adopted for restructuring of public enterprises will be enterprise-specific. Restructuring process in general is depicted in figure 22.1. SWOT analysis consisting of identification of strength, weaknesses, opportunities and threats of the enterprise is the first step in restructuring process.

Figure -22.1
RESTRUCTURING PROCESS

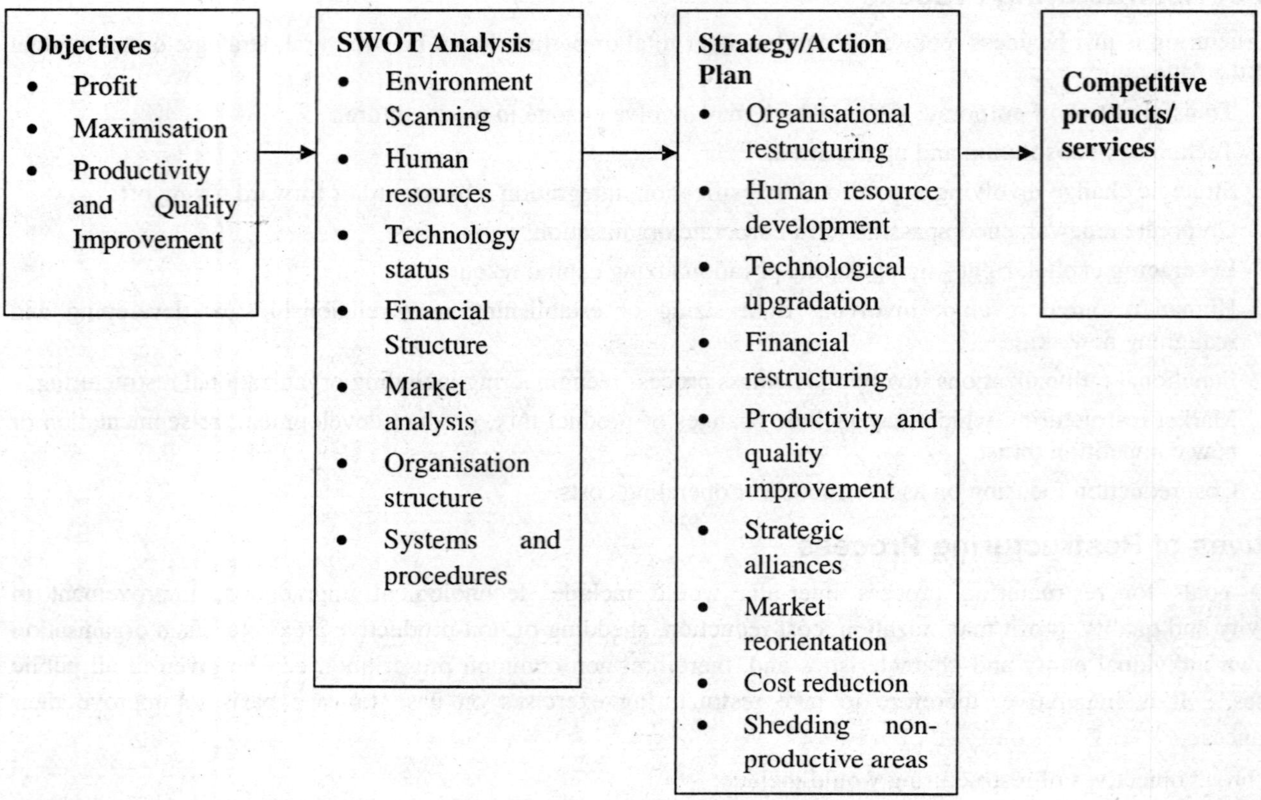

Necessary action plan will bring out the financial and physical resources required to achieve the goals spelt out in strategic plan. Strategic alliances will be spelt out that could be considered in the related areas. Time frame, modalities of implementation, organizational requirements and mechanism for monitoring the progress will be detailed out. It is expected that such restructuring process will chart out course for individual public enterprise which may emerge as market oriented, lean and flexible organisation to respond effectively to the competitive environment.

Thus, the Public enterprises in the sector have to be competitive in the emerging environment of globalisation and economic liberalization. Quality and productivity should be improved through technological upgradation, human resource development and organizational improvements. These call for restructuring of public enterprises. Restructuring process has to be enterprise specific and should be done with a view to:

(*i*) search globally for opportunities and resources possibly through strategic alliances;
(*ii*) maximize returns on all assets;
(*iii*) perform only those functions that can be performed quicker, more effectively and at lower costs;
(*iv*) outsource those areas which can be more economically and effectively done by others;
(*v*) close down those areas which are non-productive.

Strategically, this would necessitate redesign of work places, recognise the work practice and restructure the physical and financial assets to cater to the changing market needs. This is the task by itself and can be accomplished internally by managers, deployed exclusively for the purpose with assistance from an external management consultant.

Government Initiatives in Restructuring of Public Enterprises

"Government is committed to reform and restructure the Public Sector Enterprises so that they stand poised with the best of their kind in the world. Government's strategy towards public enterprises will continue to encompass a judicious mix of strengthening strategic units, privatizing non-strategic ones through gradual disinvestment or strategic sale and devising viable rehabilitation strategies for weak units."[5] Efforts in this direction would include:

(*i*) Revival through the process of BIFR.

(*ii*) Mergers, Contractions, diversifications as circumstances dictate.

(*iii*) Financial restructuring wherever to appropriate.

(*iv*) Joint venture formation by induction of partner(s) capable of providing technical, financial and marketing inputs.

(*v*) Manpower rationalization, including introduction of voluntary separation scheme in non-viable PEs.

Sickness in Public Enterprises

Some of the Central Public Sector Enterprises (PEs) have been incurring losses continuously for the last several years. The accumulated loss in many of these cases have exceeded their net worth. Sickness in PEs has been the continuing concern of the Government. There has, nonetheless, been significant improvement in the overall condition of these enterprises over the years. In comparison to 105 loss making PEs in March 200, there were 54 loss making PEs in March, 2009. Overall position of loss making public enterprises is given in Exhibit 22.1.

Exhibit-22.1
Loss making PEs
(2002-03 to 2008-09)

Year	No. of Loss making PEs, during the year	Aggregate Loss, during the year (Rs. in crore)	No. of sick PEs*	No. of sick PEs**	Accumulated losses of sick PEs** (Rs. in crore)
(1)	(2)	(3)	(4)	(5)	(6)
2002-03	105	10972	–	111	76721
2003-04	89	8522	–	100	73487
2004-05	73	9003	81	90	82352
2005-06	63	6845	75	81	83554
2006-07	61	8526	83	74	89064
2007-08	52	10257	78	67	93781
2008-09	54	14424	–	65	85968

Note: *As per the definition of BRPSE ** As per the definition of BIFR.

Source: Public Enterprise Survey, Vol. I of the concerned years.

Thus, the Exhibit 22.1 shows that PEs are sick and their accumulated loss is quite huge of Rs. 85968. It is important to note that closure of sick PEs is not the solution. They need effective restructuring programme.

Factors Responsible for Sickness in PEs

Factors Responsible for Sickness in PEs are as follows:

1. Historical Reasons: The reason for sickness varies from enterprise to enterprise. In some cases, the cause of sickness is historical; textile companies which were taken over from the private sector on social consideration for protecting employment of workers in early seventies could not be modernized quickly. British India Corporation, Bird Jute & Exports and NTC belong to this group.

2. Lack of Modernization: here have been other enterprises that were taken over from the private sector but could not be modernized. These include engineering and refractory enterprises like Andrew Yule & Co, Bharat Wagons & Engineering, Biecco Lawrie, Praga Tools, Burn Standard, Braithwaith & Co., Richardsan and Crudass Ltd., drug companies like Bengal Chemicals and Pharmaceuticals Ltd., transportation/ shipping companies like Hooghly Dock & Port Engineering Ltd., Central Inland Water Transport Corporation and consumer goods companies like Tyre Corporation of India and Hooghly Printing Co. Ltd.

3. High Cost of Operations: These became sick over the years on account of high manpower cost, high cost of production due to inefficiencies and competition from private sector. These include fertilizer companies like Fertilizer Corporation of India, Hindustan Fertilizer Corporation, Pyrites, Phosphates and Chemicals Ltd., chemicals and drugs companies like Indian Drugs & Pharmaceuticals Ltd., Hindustan Insecticides Ltd., and Hindustan Antibiotics Ltd.

4. Macro Economic Objectives: Some of the loss making companies, such as, the Nagaland Pulp & Paper Company Ltd., Manipur State Drugs & Pharmaceuticals Ltd., and North Eastern Regional Agricultural Marketing Corporation Limited etc, have had macro-economic objectives to serve like development of backward areas providing remunerative prices to farmers, etc.

5. Other reasons: Adverse market/stiff competition, obsolete technology/ machines, high manpower costs, weak marketing strategies and slow decision making process.

Strategies for revival/restructuring : Some of the strategies adopted for restructuring/ revival of sick CPSEs are mentioned below:

(i) **Financial Restructuring:** Financial restructuring involves investment in PEs by the Government in the form of equity participation, providing loan, (plan/ non-plan) grants and/or write-off of past losses as well as changing the debt equity ratio. Measures such as waivers of loan/interest, panel interest, conversion of loan into equity, conversion of interest including panel interest into loan, moratorium on payment of loan/interest, Government guarantee, sale of fixed assets including excess land, scarifies by state government, one-time settlement with banks/financial institutions, etc.

(ii) **Business restructuring:** Business restructuring involves change of management, organizational restructuring, hiving off viable units from PEs for formation of separate company, closure of unviable units, formation of joint ventures by induction of partners capable of providing technical, financial and marketing inputs, change in product mix, improving marketing strategy, etc. are the steps taken under the business restructuring process as per need on case to case basis.

(iii) **Manpower Rationalisation:** Salaries and Wages are often a major component of cost for an enterprise. In order to shed excess man power, PEs have often resorted to the Voluntary Retirement Scheme (VRS) from time to time. In case of PEs found unviable and decided to be closed, the Voluntary Separation Scheme is introduced in such units. Retrenchment of employees is adopted as the last resort in exceptional circumstances.

The revival packages granted by the Government amounting to Rs. 5221.65 in 2005-06, Rs. 2438.89 crore in 2006-07, Rs. 769.94 crore in 2007- 08 and Rs. 6698.49 crore in 2008-09 has helped these enterprises in a big way in improving their conditions. Some of the sick and loss making enterprises have turned around and recorded profit during the last two years.

Sick Industrial Companies (Special Provisions) Act, 1985 (SICA)

Net loss in a company means excess of expenditure (including depreciation, interest, taxes, extra ordinary items, prior period adjustments but before providing appropriations to reserves) over operating income. If, however, the enterprise incurs 'cash loss', that is 'net loss' along with 'provision for depreciation', then it is usually considered a fit case for recommending closure. The PEs were brought under the purview of Sick Industrial Companies (Special Provision) Act, 1985 (SICA) which was subsequently amended in 1991 and made effective from 1992. Under the provisions of Sick Industrial Companies (Special Provisions) Act, 1985 (SICA), the industrial PEs whose accumulated losses are equal to or have exceeded their net worth, may be referred to the Board for Industrial and Financial Reconstruction (BIFR). The BIFR may either sanction suitable revival/rehabilitation schemes (in case of enterprises which are viable) or recommend winding up/closure (in respect of enterprises considered unviable). During the period of the last seventeen years, that is, 1992-93to 2008-09, 65 PEs have been referred to the BIFR (Exhibit-22.2). The year-wise registration of PEs with BIFR is given below :

Exhibit-22.2
Registration of PEs with BIFR

Year	No. of PE	Year	No. of PE
1992	30*	2001	2
1993	2*	2002	3

Contd....

1994	4*	2003	2
1995	1	2004	4*
1996	2	2005	2
1997	3	2006	1
1998	3	2007	1
1999	3	2008	0
2000	2	2009	0
		Total	65

* This includes the subsidiaries of NTC, which has been registered again in 2008 after merger.

Source: Public Enterprise Survey, Vol.I of the concerned years

Exhibit 22.2 shows that the number of PEs registered with the BIFR is declining. It is also important to note that now BIFR is default body that is why no new cases are being referred to the BIFR for providing sufficient necessary support systems.

Present position of PEs with BIFR

Out of the 65 PEs registered with BIFR till 30.6.2009, 3 PEs namely Scooters India Limited, Vignyan Industries Limited & North Eastern Regional Agricultural Marketing Corporation Limited, have since been declared 'No Longer Sick' by the Board. This does not include Indian Iron Steel Co. Limited as it has been merged with Steel Authority of India Limited. In addition, Bharat Immunologicals and Biologicals Corporation Limited, Hindustan Salts Limited, Maharashtra Elektrosmelt Limited, Hindustan Insecticides Limited and Hindustan Organic Chemicals Limited have been dropped from the list of 'sick industrial PEs' by BIFR on their net worth becoming positive. Cases of four PEs have been declared as 'Non-maintainable' by the Board as either the matter had become time barred for reference to the Board or on account of the net worth of the PE becoming positive or the PE was found not fulfilling the conditions of being industrial company as defined under SICA or on some other grounds. Moreover, one of these companies, namely, Manipur State Drugs and Pharmaceuticals Limited has been closed. The status of the 65 sick industrial PEs registered with BIFR as on 30.6.2009 is given at Exhibit-21.3

Exhibit-22.3
Status of CPSEs registered with BIFR

Sl. No.	Particulars	Number
1.	Revival scheme sanctioned	11
2.	Draft Scheme circulated/under examination/ under process	14
3.	Declared no longer sick	3
4.	Dropped on net worth becoming positive	5
5.	Dismissed as non-maintainable	4
6.	Winding up recommended and closed	15
7.	Winding up recommended	5
8.	Winding notice issued	1
9.	Sanctioned by AAIFR	1
10.	Failed and re-opened	2
11.	Pending determination of sickness	1
12.	Deregistered with BIFR	3
	Total	**65**

Source: Public Enterprise Survey, Vol. I, 2008-09

The BIFR has already disposed of 48 cases of PEs either through sanctioning revival schemes (11 cases), or recommending winding up (21 cases) or declaring 'no longer sick' (3 cases) or dropping due to net worth becoming positive (5 cases) or dismissing the cases as non-maintainable (4 cases). The BIFR is yet to take any view on 17 cases of PEs. The process of appointment of Official Liquidator (OL) for winding up of PEs has been also slow. The process of sanctioning of revival /rehabilitation schemes has also been slow on account of involvement of multiple agencies, delay in finalization of revival schemes, lack of funds, lack of adequate powers with BIFR, lack of proper monitoring of sanctioned revival schemes, delay in winding up of sick companies, etc.

Board for Reconstruction of Public Sector Enterprises (BRPSE)

The Government set up a Board for Reconstruction of Public Sector Enterprises (BRPSE) in December, 2004 to advise the Government inter alia on the measures to be taken to restructure/revive of PEs. The Board comprises of a part-time Chairman, three part-time Non-Official Members and three part-time Official Members including Secretary, Department of Expenditure, Secretary, Department of Disinvestment and Secretary, Department of Public Enterprises. There is a full-time Secretary for BRPSE in the level of Additional Secretary to the Government of India. In addition, Chairman, Public Enterprises Selection Board, Chairman, Standing Conference on Public Enterprises and Chairman, Oil and Natural Gas Corporation Limited are the permanent invitees in the meetings of the BRPSE. Secretaries to the Government in the Administrative Ministry /Department concerned with the PEs under consideration by the Board are special invitees. There is a full time secretary to the Government for BRPSE in the level/rank of Additional Secretary to the Government of India. The Board is located in the Department of Public Enterprises (DPE). The DPE provides necessary secretarial assistance to the Board.

Strategies for Revival or Restructuring of PEs.

Strategies for Revival or Restructuring of PEs are as follows:

1. The purpose of making reference to BRPSE, a company is considered 'sick' if it has accumulated losses in any financial year equal to 50% or more of its average net worth during 4 years immediately preceding such financial year, and/or a company which is a sick company within the meaning of Sick Industrial Companies (Special Provisions) Act, 1985 (SICA). The concerned administrative Ministries/ Departments are required to send proposals of their PEs identified as 'sick' for consideration of BRPSE. Other loss making PEs may be considered by the Board either suo moto or upon reference by the administrative Ministry, if it is of the opinion that revival/restructuring is necessary for checking the incipient sickness (incurring loss for two consecutive years) and making the PE profitable, keeping the industry specific business environment in view. The Board is expected to make its recommendations within 2 months of the date of receipt of the complete proposal from the administrative Ministry/ Department.
2. As per the definition of sick PEs given above and the performance evaluation of PEs for 2007-08 and previous years, 78 PEs were referable to BRPSE. Up to September, 2009, cases of 64 sick PEs have been referred to BRPSE; out of which the Board has made recommendations in respect of 58 cases. In addition, the Board has also recommended to the Government to accord "in principle" approval for rescinding of its earlier decision to close the units of Fertilizers Corporation of India (FCIL) and Hindustan Fertilizers Corporation Ltd. (HFCL) and to explore various options for their revival. The Board during the period from November, 2008 to September, 2009 reviewed the status of implementation of revival package sanctioned by Government to 5 PEs namely (i) Mineral Exploration Corporation Ltd. (ii) Central Inland Water Transport Corporation Ltd., (iii) Heavy Engineering Corporation Ltd., (iv) Bengal Chemicals & Pharmaceuticals Ltd. and (v) Fertilizers & Chemicals (Travancore) Ltd. and also the status of its recommendations in respect of 3 PEs namely (i) Hindustan Cables Ltd., (ii) Brahmaputra Valley Fertilizer Corporation Ltd. and (iii) Madras Fertilizers Ltd.
3. Out of these 58 cases, the Government has approved revival proposals in respect of 36 cases of PEs and winding up of two enterprises namely Bharat Opthalmic Glass Limited and Bharat Yantra Nigam Ltd. as on 30.9.2009. Out of the 36 cases of revival approved by the Government till September, 2009, 15 were approved during 2005-06, 11 cases were approved during 2006-07, 6 cases have been approved during 2007-08, 4 cases have been approved during 2008-09, and 2 cases have been approved during 2009-10 (upto September, 2009). The restructuring/revival proposals approved by the Government involved a total expenditure of Rs. 16253.36 crore including Rs. 2920.71 crore as cash assistance and Rs. 12332.65 crore as

non cash assistance. The enterprise-wise details of cash and non-cash assistance in respect of approved proposals are given in Annex-12.2. Government have approved on 26.11.2007 transfer of Bharat Heavy Plates and Vessels Ltd. to BHEL and merger of Bharat Refractories Ltd. with SAIL on 24.4.2008. BIFR approved on 13.6.2008 merger of Praga Tools Ltd. with HMT Machine Tools Ltd.w.e.f.1.4.2007. Government also approved on 7.2.2008 for transfer of Bharat Wagon & Engineering Co. Ltd. (BWEL) from D/o Heavy Industries to M/o Railways and administrative control of it was transferred w.e.f. 13.8.2008.

4. In addition to the above, Government have already approved revival package for Nagaland Pulp & Paper Co. Ltd. with a total assistance of Rs. 787.54 crores (Rs. 552.44 crores cash and Rs. 235.10 crores as non-cash). Government have also approved second revival package for Heavy Engineering Corporation (HEC) on 4th September, 2008 at a total cost of Rs. 615.43 crores (Rs. 310 crores as cash and Rs. 305.43 crores as non-cash). Similarly, the Government have approved on 7.2.2008 a onetime interim grant of Rs. 200 crores as non-plan funds to Fertilizer & Chemicals (Travancore) Ltd (FACT) to enable it to sustain its operation till 31.3.2008. This package is in addition to the revival package approved in March, 2006. In order to revive, ITI Ltd., the Government have sanctioned a sum of Rs. 1427 crores (Rs. 1403 crores as cash and Rs. 24 crores as non-cash) from December, 2004 till January, 2009. Further, the Government has also approved on 20.2.2009, inter alia, Rs. 3000 crores towards revival of ITI Ltd. Government have also approved 2nd revival package on for NTC for Rs. 6129.75 crores by way of waiver of Government of India loans and interest thereon. The Government have also approved proposal of converting Semi-Conductor Complex Ltd. into a Society under the Department of Space on 23.2.2006. The proposal for transfer of assets, liabilities and manpower of National Instruments Ltd. (Kolkata) to Jadhavpur University, Government of West Bengal was approved on 8.2.2007 (Table 12.4). Government have also approved revival of Hindustan Fertilizer Corpn. Ltd. (Barauni Unit) on October 30, 2008 through Special Purpose Vehicle to be promoted by Fertilizer PSUs/ Fertilizer Co-operatives. The Government have established an Empowered Committee of Secretaries (ECS) with the mandate to evaluate all options of revival of closed units of FCI and HFCL, and to make suitable recommendations for consideration of the Government.

Voluntary Retirement Scheme (VRS)

As a result of the ongoing restructuring in the sick and loss making industries PEs, several policy reforms have been initiated by the Government. Right sizing of manpower is one of the measures adopted. Consequently, the Voluntary Retirement Scheme (VRS), was announced in October, 1988. It was further liberalized and a comprehensive package was notified by the Department of Public Enterprises (Government of India) in May, 2000. In view of the difficulties faced by the CPSEs where the wage revision of 1992 or 1997 (as the case may be) could not be effective, the VRS was liberalized through subsequent notification of November, 2001. This notification, inter-alia provides for 100% additional compensation for the employees where wage revision of 1992 could not be made effective. Similarly, 50% additional compensation was allowed for employees where wage revision of 1997 under VRS to employees following CDA pattern at 1986 scales of pay has been enhanced by 50% w.e.f. 26.10.2004. These increases in VRS compensation are to be computed based on the existing pay of employees. Since the introduction of VRS in October 1988 to March 2009, approximately 6.10 lakh employees have been released under this scheme.

(i) **VRS in CPSEs that can support the scheme on their own:** Enterprises, which are financially sound and can sustain VRS on their own, can frame their own schemes of VRS and make it attractive enough for employees to opt for it. They may offer as compensation upto 60 days salary (only Basic Pay + DA) for every completed year of service. However, such compensation will not exceed the salary for the balance period of service left.

(ii) **VRS in marginally profit or loss making/sick/ unviable PEs:** Marginally profit /loss making PEs as well as sick and unviable units may adopt :

- *(i)* either the Gujarat Model, under which the compensation is computed by allowing 35 days salary for every completed year of service and 25 days for each year of the balance service left until superannuation subject to conditions that the compensation shall not exceed the sum of salary for the balance period left for superannuation, or
- *(ii)* The VRS package of Department of Heavy industry (DHI) model, under which ex-gratia payment equivalent to 45 days emoluments Pay + DA) for each completed year of service are the total emoluments for the balance period f service, whichever is less, is applicable.

The employees who have completed not less than 30 years of service will be eligible for a aximum of 60 (sixty) month's salary/wage as compensation and this will be subject to the mount not exceeding the salary/wage for the balance period of service left.

Scheme of Counselling, Retraining and Redeployment (CRR)

Restructuring of enterprises is a global phenomenon, particularly in the context of liberalized economy. There has been thrust on restructuring the PEs, both at macro as well as micro level. In the process, rationalization of manpower has also become a necessity. But this affects in some cases the interest of the workers. As such, the policy of the Government has been to implement reforms with a humane face and provide adequate safety net for the affected workers.

Considering the emerging need to have safety net, Government established the National Renewal Fund (NRF) in February, 1992 broadly to cover the expenses of VRS and to provide retraining to workers in the organized sector. In the wake of ongoing restructuring exercises in the central enterprises, focus was given on the need of PEs. The NRF was abolished in February, 2000. The retraining activity was administered earlier by Department of Industrial Policy & Promotion until 31st March, 2001. The scheme for Counselling, Retraining and Redeployment (CRR) of rationalized employees of CPSEs is under implementation since 2001-02. The scheme for Counselling, Retraining and Redeployment (CRR) inter-alia aims :

(*i*) to provide opportunity for self-employment.

(*ii*) to reorient rationalized employees through short duration programmes.

(*iii*) to equip them for new avocations.

(*iv*) to engage them in income generating self-employment.

(*v*) to help them rejoin the productive process.

The main elements of the CRR programme are Counselling, Retraining and Redeployment. Besides, a new element of sensitization programme has also been included under CRR programme. Counselling helps the rationalized employees to absorb the trauma of leaving the organization, to properly manage their funds including compensation and to motivate them to face the challenges and to re-join the productive process. Similarly, retraining strengthens their skill/expertise. Selected training institutes impart need-based training of 30 days / 45 days / 60 days modules. The faculty support is both internal and external, and the approach is to provide classroom lectures as well as field experience. In the process, trainees interact with experts from various fields and are being helped in preparation/finalization of project reports. The retraining should lead to redeployment mostly through self-employment. In the present scheme, the objective is to maximize the rate of self-employment. The Nodal Agencies, therefore, provide need-based support, linkage with credit institutions and continuously follow up with the retrained personnel. In order to further broad base the coverage and re-employability, certain modifications have been brought out in the CRR scheme. Modified scheme is being implemented from 2007-08. For monitoring the CRR programme, the inbuilt mechanism involves field visits and inspections by the concerned officers of DPE. Coordination.

Committees at local level have also been formed. The Scheme also provides for inter-ministerial Review Committee under Secretary (PE) with members from selected concerned Governments/agencies/PEs. The Nodal Training Agencies are required to counsel VRS optees, impart training and reorientation programme, develop curriculum /materials, prepare feasibility report market survey, post training follow up, interface with credit institutions, support in self employment, regular liaison with PEs, convening meeting of Coordination Committee etc. PEs are the key to the success of the scheme. They are supposed to extend all possible support for the welfare of the separated employees by clearing their compensation/dues before release. Long association with employees puts PEs in a better position to identify their retraining needs.

Year wise number of persons trained under the scheme is shown in exhibit-22.4 :

Exhibit-22.4
Number of Persons Trained

Year	No. of persons trained
2001-02	8064
2002-03	12066

Contd....

2003-04	12134
2004-05	28003
2005-06	32158
2006-07	34398
2007-08	9728
2008-09	9772
Total	146324

Source: Public Enterprise Survey, Vol.I of the concerned years

A Plan Fund of Rs. 8 crore was allocated initially during 2001-02, which was enhanced to Rs. 10 crore during 2002-03 and 2003-04. The plan fund substantially increased to Rs. 30 crore during 2004-05 and 2005-06 and further enhanced to Rs. 31.50 crore during 2006-07. During 2007-08, Rs. 10.00 crore was allocated and during 2008-09, plan allocation was Ws. 8.70 crores for implementation of CRR scheme. In 2008-09, 19 nodal agencies were operational with 46 Employees Assistance Centres (EACs).

Delegation of Enhanced Financial Powers to PEs

1. Mahanavratna Scheme: Maha Navratna PSUs are the biggest public sector undertaking (PSU)'s of India. Presently, only Indian Oil, ONGC, SAIL and NTPC have been declared as Maha Navratna. But only NTPC will be able to exercise the authority since the other companies are not having the requisite numbers of independent directors in their boards. These companies shall be allowed to take decisions on projects independently of Government of values up to Rs. 5,000/- crores.

2. Navratna scheme: Under this scheme, the Government has delegated enhanced powers to PEs having comparative advantage and the potential to become global players. Navratna PEs are as under:

(*i*) Bharat Electronics Limited
(*ii*) Bharat Heavy Electricals Limited
(*iii*) Bharat Petroleum Corporation Limited
(*iv*) Coal India Limited
(*v*) GAIL (India) Limited
(*vi*) Hindustan Aeronautics Limited
(*vii*) Hindustan Petroleum Corporation Limited
(*viii*) Mahanagar Telephone Nigam Limited
(*ix*) National Aluminium Company Limited
(*x*) NMDC Limited
(*xi*) Power Finance Corporation Limited
(*xii*) Power Grid Corporation of India Limited
(*xiii*) Rural Electrification Corporation Limited
(*xiv*) Shipping Corporation of India Limited

The powers presently delegated to the Boards of Navratna PEs are as under :

(*i*) **Capital Expenditure:** The Navratna PEs have the powers to incur capital expenditure on purchase of new items or for replacement, without any monetary ceiling.

(*ii*) **Technology Joint Ventures and Strategic Alliances**: The Navratna PEs have the powers to enter into technology joint ventures or strategic alliances and obtain by purchase or other arrangements, technology and know-how.

(iii) **Organizational Restructuring:** The Navratna PEs have the powers to effect organizational restructuring including establishment of profit centers, opening of offices in India and abroad, creating new activity centers, etc.

(iv) **Human Resources Management:** The Navratna PEs have been empowered to create and wind up all posts up to E-6 level and make all appointments up to this level. The Boards of these PEs have further been empowered to effect internal transfers and re-designation of posts. The Board of Directors of Navratna PEs have the power to further delegate the powers relating to Human Resource Management (appointments, transfer, posting, etc.) of below Board level executives to subcommittees of the Board or to executives of the PE, as may be decided by the Board of the PE.

(v) **Resource Mobilization:** These PEs have been empowered to raise debt from the domestic capital markets and for borrowings from international market, subject to condition that approval of RBI/Department of Economic Affairs, as may be required, should be obtained through the administrative Ministry.

(vi) **Joint ventures and Subsidiaries:** The Navratna PEs have been delegated powers to establish financial joint ventures and wholly owned subsidiaries in India or abroad with the stipulation that the equity investment of the PE should be limited to the following amounts :

(i) Rs. 1000 crore in any one project.

(ii) 15% of the net worth of the PE in one project.

(iii) 30% of the net worth of the PE in all joint ventures/ subsidiaries put together.

(iv) Mergers & Acquisitions (M&A).

(vii) **The Navratna PEs** have been delegated powers for Mergers and Acquisitions subject to the conditions that

(i) it should be as per the growth plan and in the core area of functioning of the PE,

(ii) conditions/limits would be as in the case of establishing joint ventures/ subsidiaries, and

(iii) the Cabinet Committee on Economic Affairs would be kept informed in case of investments abroad. Further, the powers relating to Mergers and Acquisitions (M & A) are to be exercised in such a manner that it should not lead to any change in the public sector character of the concerned PE.

(viii) **Creation/Disinvestment in subsidiaries:** The Navratna PEs have powers to transfer assets, float fresh equity and divest shareholding in subsidiaries subject to the condition that the delegation will be in respect of subsidiaries set up by the holding company under the powers delegated to the Navratna PEs and further to the proviso that the public sector character of the concerned PE (including subsidiary) would not be changed without prior approval of the Government and such Navratna PEs will be required to seek Government approval before exiting from their subsidiaries.

3. Miniratna scheme: In October 1997, the Government had also decided to grant enhanced autonomy and delegation of financial powers to some other profit making companies subject to certain eligibility conditions and guidelines to make them efficient and competitive. These companies, called Miniratnas, belong to two categories, namely, Category- I and Category-II. The eligibility conditions and criteria are:

(i) Category-I PEs should have made profit in the last three years continuously, the pre-tax profit should have been Rs. 30 crores or more in at least one of the three years and should have a positive net worth.

(ii) Category-II PEs should have made profit for the last three years continuously and should have a positive net worth.

(iii) These PEs shall be eligible for the enhanced delegated powers provided they have not defaulted in the repayment of loans/ interest payment on any loans due to the Government.

(iv) These public sector enterprises shall not depend upon budgetary support or Government guarantees.

(v) The Boards of these PEs should be restructured by inducting at least three nonofficial Directors as the first step before the exercise of enhanced delegation of authority.

(vi) The administrative Ministry concerned shall decide whether a Public Sector Enterprise fulfilled the requirements of a Category-I/ Category-II company before the exercise of enhanced powers.

The delegation of decision-making authority available at present to the Boards of these Miniratna PEs is as follows:

(i) **Capital Expenditure:**

a. For PEs in category I: The power to incur capital expenditure on new projects, modernization, purchase of equipment, etc., without Government approval upto Rs. 500 crore or equal to net worth, whichever is less.

b. For PEs in category II: The power to incur capital expenditure on new projects, modernization, purchase of equipment, etc., without Government approval upto Rs. 250 crore or equal to 50% of the Net worth, whichever is less.

(ii) **Joint Ventures (JVs) and Subsidiaries**

a. Category I PEs: The power to establish joint ventures and subsidiaries in India with the stipulation that the equity investment of the PE in any one project should be limited to 15% of the networth of the PE or Rs. 500 crore, whichever is less. The overall ceiling on such investment in all projects put together is 30% of the networth of the PE.

b. Category II PEs: The power to establish joint ventures and subsidiaries in India with the stipulation that the equity investment of the PE in any one project should be 15% of the networth of the PE or Rs. 250 crore, whichever is less. The overall ceiling on such investment in all projects put together is 30% of the networth of the PE.

(iii) **Mergers and Acquisitions (M & A):** The Board of Directors of these PEs have the powers for Mergers and Acquisitions (M & A), subject to the conditions that (a) it should be as per the growth plan and in the core area of functioning of the PE, (b) conditions/limits would be as in the case of establishing joint ventures/subsidiaries, and (c) the Cabinet Committee on Economic Affairs would be kept informed in case of investments abroad. Further, the powers relating to Mergers and Acquisitions (M & A) are to be exercised in such a manner that it should not lead to any change in the public sector character of the concerned PEs.

(iv) **Scheme for HRD:** To structure and implement schemes relating to personnel and human resource management, training, voluntary or compulsory retirement schemes, etc. The Board of Directors of these PEs have the power to further delegate the powers relating to Human Resource Management (viz., appointments, transfer, posting, etc.) of below Board level executives to subcommittees of the Board or to executives of the PE, as may be decided by the Board of the PE.

MOU System in PEs

The Memorandum of Understanding (MoU) as applicable to public sector enterprises is a negotiated document between the government and the management of the enterprise specifying clearly the objectives of the agreement and the obligations of both the parties. It was first introduced in France in two phases, that is, as '*contracts de programme*' in 1970 and as '*contracts d'* Enterprise' in 1979 consequent to the Simon Nora Committee Report (1967). The main purpose of the MoU system is to ensure a level playing field to the public sector enterprises vis-à-vis the private corporate sector.

MoU system in India was first introduced in 1986 as a result of the recommendations of the Arjun Sengupta Committee Report (1984). The Committee laid emphasis on medium term contract between the Government and the Public Enterprises (PEs) and recommended a five-year agreement that may be reviewed annually. Moreover, since the PEs have been set up as part of the national/central plan, the Committee favoured MoUs especially in respect of PEs in the core sectors of steel, coal, power, petroleum, fertilizer and petro-chemicals.

Autonomy and Accountability

The 'management' of the enterprise is, nevertheless, made accountable to the government through promise for performance or 'performance contract'. The government continues to have control over these enterprises through a priori supervision through 'setting targets' in the beginning of the year and through a posteriori 'performance evaluation' at the end of the year.

In order to grant autonomy to public sector enterprises vis-à-vis control of the government, the Arjun Sengupta Committee identified three areas of Government-PSE interaction, namely (a) price fixation, (b) investment planning and (c) financial management.

In regard to price fixation the Committee observed that price control/ administered price/ retention price may be retained only in areas where the nature of product so justifies. It further stated that wherever PEs are operating under competitive market conditions, the PEs should be left on their own to fix the price of their output. While fixing prices for products of PEs operating *under monopoly conditions*, these should be benchmarked with international prices. The gradual dismantling of Administered Price Mechanism (APM) since 1991 has increasingly helped these enterprises to fix the output prices on market principles.

In regard to autonomy for investment planning, greater powers were subsequently delegated to the Board of Directors as recommended by the Committee. The Board of Directors of MoU signing PEs can therefore sanction capital expenditure without the prior approval of the government, especially so if the required funds could be found from the internal resources of the enterprise. In regard to financial management especially with reference to 'auditing', the Arjun Sengupta Committee was of the view that subsequent to evolving of appropriate accounting standards by the Comptroller and Auditor General of India (CAG), supplementary audit by CAG for the non-core sector should be given up. In the case of the enterprises in the core sector, however, the Committee recommended that company audit by the CAG may continue.

The Committee further observed that Ministries should not interfere in areas of decision making which are within the delegated powers of PEs. Accordingly, numerous 'administrative controls' emanating from different 'government circulars' issued over the years and pertaining to public sector enterprises were dispensed consequent to the review exercises undertaken in the Department of Public Enterprises in 1996 and in 2000.

MOU System 'Process and Principles'

The process of finalizing the MoUs starts with the issue of detailed Guidelines by the Department of Public Enterprises (DPE) on the basis of which the PEs submit their draft MoU after getting them approved by the respective Boards and the Administrative Ministries. The draft MOUs indicate the (five) performance targets on a five point scale for the ensuing financial year. These draft MoUs are then discussed, improved and finalized during the MoU negotiation meetings. The MoU negotiations are attended by the Chief Executives of the PEs, Senior Officers from the administrative Ministries and the representatives of the nodal Government agencies such as Planning Commission and Ministry of Finance. The Task Force on MoU set up by DPE, moreover, provides the oversight during the MoU negotiations.

(i) **Task Force and Syndicates:** The MoU Task Force comprise former Civil Servants, CMDs of the Public Enterprise, financial and technical professionals, Chartered Accountants and academics. They are selected by DPE. Currently, there are 90 Task Force members who are divided into sector-wise Syndicate Group. Each Syndicate consist of 6-7 members. One of the members of the Syndicate acts as the Convener. The rich experience and knowledge of the TF members in different fields provides the necessary technical input and enables the Syndicate in fixing more realistic targets. The DPE issues the Minutes of MoU negotiation meetings to the PEs (and the Ministry/Department concerned) for finalizing the MoUs which are authenticated in the DPE to ensure that those are in accordance with the decisions on targets as agreed upon during the meeting. Subsequently, all MoUs have to be signed before 31st March for implementation during the succeeding financial year.

(ii) **High Power Committee on MoU:** The High Power Committee (HPC) on MoU is a Committee of Secretaries (COS) set up by the Government as the Apex Committee to assess the performance of MoU signing PEs with reference to the commitments made by them in the MOU and also to assess how far the Administrative Ministries/ Departments have been able to give the necessary support as committed by them in the MoU. HPC is headed by the Cabinet Secretary. Secretary, Department of Public Enterprises is the Member- Secretary of this committee. The other members comprise, Finance Secretary, Secretary (Expenditure), Secretary (Planning Commission), Secretary(Statistics & Programme Implementation). Chairman Public Enterprises Selection Board, Chief Economic Advisor, Department of Economic Affairs and Chairman Tariff Commission. The Apex Committee of Secretaries on MoU has been from time to time giving directions in regard to the determination of the principles and parameters for evaluating the performance of PEs.

Aims and Objectives of MoU system in PEs

The aims and objectives of the MoU system are broadly the followings:

(*a*) To improve the performance of public sector enterprises by increasing autonomy of Management of the Company.

(*b*) To remove the fuzziness in goals and objectives of public sector enterprises.

(*c*) To evaluate the performance of management through objective criteria.

(*d*) To provide incentive for better performance in future.

The incentives under the present system take two forms, namely 'monetary' and 'non-monetary' incentives. As per the Second Pay Revision Committee recommendations (for the executives of PEs) vide DPE OM No. 2(70)/08-DPE (WC)-GL-XV/08 dtd. 26.11.2008, the variable Performance Related Pay (PRP) would be payable in the case of profit making PEs at 100% eligibility levels if the PE achieves the MoU rating as "Excellent". If the PE's MoU is rated as "Very Good", the eligibility of PRP would be 80% of the basic pay. In respect of "Good" and "Fair" ratings, the eligibility levels would be 60% and 40% respectively. However, there will be no PRP irrespective of the profitability of PE, in case it is rated as "Poor". (Moreover, 60% of the PRP will be given with the ceiling of 3% of Profit Before tax (PBT) and 40% of the PRP will come from 10% of incremental profit. Further, the PRP has been linked to the performance of the individual executives, which will be based on a robust and transparent Performance Management System). The non-monetary incentives comprise the MoU Awards. These awards are also an expression of commitment of the policy makers to the MoU system. While excellent performing PEs are awarded with the MoU (Excellent) Awards with Trophies and Excellence Merit Certificates, the remaining excellent performing PEs are recognized with Excellence Merit Certificates.

MoU Targets and Performance Evaluation

Performance evaluation at the end of the year indicates the extent to which the mutually agreed Targets agreed upon at the beginning of the year were achieved by the enterprise.

MoU Targets

The exercise of fixing MoU targets involves the following steps:

(*i*) Preparation of MoU Guidelines, which are issued by DPE in the month of October/ November.

(*ii*) Submission of draft MoU by PEs through Administrative Ministry on the basis of the MoU guidelines.

(*iii*) Examination of draft MoUs by the MoU Division and preparation of critiques to be circulated to the Task Force Members.

(*iv*) Fixing of dates and venue for MoU negotiation meetings that starts from January/February.

(*v*) Holding the MoU negotiation meetings to finalize the MoUs in the presence of the Task Force (January – March) each year.

(*vi*) Preparation and circulation of the Minutes of the MoU negotiation meetings to PEs and concerned administrative Ministry after approval of the Convener.

(*vii*) Submission of the revised MoU by PEs through administrative Ministries as per the Minutes.

(*viii*) Examination of revised MoUs for authentication by DPE.

(*ix*) All MoU has to be signed before 31st March of every year.

Evaluation methodology

The MoU system was revamped in 1989 and further refi ned in 2004. Under the current MoU Guidelines, equal weights (50% + 50%) are assigned to 'financial' and 'non-financial' parameters. These are done on the lines of 'balanced score card' approach of performance evaluation. The 'financial' parameters generally relate to profit related, size related and productivity related parameters. The 'non-financial parameters' are further sub-divided into 'dynamic parameters', 'enterprise-specific parameters' and 'sector-specific parameters'. Examples of 'dynamic' parameters are project implementation, investment in R & D and extent of globalization etc. The 'composite score' is thus an index of the performance of the enterprises. The grading of the 'composite score' is done in the following manner :

Exhibit-22.5

MoU Composite Score	Grading
1.00-1.50	Excellent
2.51-3.50	Very Good
1.51-2.50	Good
3.51-4.50	Fair
4.51-5.0	Poor

Source: Public Enterprise Survey, Vol.I of the concerned years

Similarly, while the 'sector-specific' parameters refer to macroeconomic factors like change in demand and supply, price fluctuations, variation in interest rates etc, (that are, factors beyond the control of the management), the 'enterprise-specific' parameters relate to issues such as safety and pollution etc. Performance targets for MoUs are framed on a five point scale.

Coverage of PEs under the MoU system

The MoU system that was started with four PEs signing MoU in the year 1986-87 increased its coverage to 144 PEs in the year 2008-09. The exhibit-22.6 below provides the coverage of PEs over the years under the MOU system.

Exhibit-22.6
MoU signing CPSEs

Year	MOUs signed*(Nos.)	Year	MOUs signed*(Nos.)
1987-88	4	1998-99	108
1988-89	11	1999-2000	108
1989-90	18	2000-01	107
1990-91	23	2001-02	104
1991-92	72	2002-03	100
1992-93	98	2003-04	96
1993-94	101	2004-05	99
1994-95	100	2005-06	102
1995-96	104	2006-07	113
1996-97	110	2007-08	144
1997-98	108	2008-09	144
		2009-10	197

* Until 2008-09, only Independent/Holding Companies have been signing MoU with their respective Ministries. The Subsidiary Companies were to sign MoUs with their Holding Companies. However, from 2009-10, the Subsidiary Companies have also to sign MoUs directly with the respective Ministries.

Source: Public Enterprise Survey, Vol.I of the concerned years

The number of PEs opting for MOU is growing and is also indicates its popularity. However, there is need to monitor their performance to what extent they are getting necessary autonomy etc in their actual behaviour.

MoU ratings of PEs during the last five years

MoU rating of PEs during the last five years shown in the table below :

Exhibit-22.7
MoU Ratings

(in nos.)

Rating	2003-04	2004-05	2005-06	2006-07	2007-08
Excellent	54	45	44	46	55
Very Good	21	31	36	37	34
Good	10	12	14	13	15
Fair	11	10	08	06	08
Poor	00	01	00	00	00
Total	96	99	102	102	112

Source: Public Enterprise Survey, Vol.I of the concerned years.

Exhibit-22.7shows that about 50% PEs covered under the MOU system are excellent one. Number of PEs rated as excellent comes to 55 out of 112 in 2007-08. Similarly, about 30% PEs are very good in terms of MOU rating system. However, efforts are required to get feedback to what extent they are maintaining their rating status. If they are improving their rating grade it should be treated as that they are doing well and will be given more up-gradation in terms of Navratna to Maharatna status.

Disinvestment in Public Enterprises

In Public Enterprises (PEs), government fundings or budgetary provisions are the most important source of finance. The Government has invested huge funds in these PEs but return on investment is not so encouraging. It comes to around 4% in 2008-09. Contribution to public exchequer by the PEs is also not up to the mark. There was significant decline in total contributions of PEs to the public exchequer from Rs. 165994 crore in 2007-08 to Rs. 151728 crore in 2008-09. This is the overall scenario of PEs during the last three decades. In this situation, government has its own limitations in extending financial support to these PEs. They have to be made competitive, productive, efficient and self dependent. Disinvestment is one of the most important tool in the hands of the government to make these PEs more responsive and responsible in their operational behaviour.

So, the Government has initiated disinvestment programme in these PEs as a major part of public sector reforms. "The government has found out an important source to mobilize funds through sale of its equity-holding in PEs to meet its budgetary deficits. There are two approaches to disinvestment programme. According to first approach, whenever, Government sells its equity holdings in PEs to public, private parties, financial institutions and mutual funds etc., it is called as disinvestment. According to second approach when PEs are generally directed by the Government to issue their equity shares to the public, private parties, financial institutions and mutual funds with a view to reduce its control, that is also called as disinvestment."[6]

Disinvestment is an expedient that will be accompanied by reinvestment for redesign and revamping of the economy. The disinvested proceeds will go to create fresh assets in sectors with which government should concern itself most. Disinvestment is thus positive concept. The programme of disinvestment will be founded on increasing the efficiency, eliminating losses, infusing modern technology and enriching management skills in a competitive environment that maximizes capital gains. The considerations governing disinvestment should be:"[7]

(i) the organisation should thereby become stronger, be capable of growing faster, acquire competitive edge globally and expand it exports.

(ii) It must conduce constant induction and updation of technologies

(iii) It should catalyse abiding and genuine foreign investments.

(iv) It should not create monopolies but end them.

(v) It should enhance indigenous technological capabilities and augment investment on R&D within the country.

(vi) The return through disinvestment must be commensurate with the value of the assets.

(vii) The procedure should be totally transparent.

Objectives of the Disinvestment

The government has been disinvesting its equity holding in PEs since November, 1991. The major objectives of the disinvestment can be stated as under:

1. **Revenue Collection:** The government is making a virtue out of the necessity to raise revenue for bringing down the fiscal deficit as commitment made to the IMF.
2. **Improvement in Efficiency**: This is being undertaken to ensure greater accountability and improved efficiency. The financial institutions and mutual funds are expected to off-load them into the secondary market. This will enable to the investors to demand more accountability and efficiency from the management of PE concerned.
3. **Resources Mobilization:** With the help of disinvestment programme, government would be in a position to garner sufficient resources. One of such funds, Government can make available some funds as loan to the PE concerned.
4. **Direct Participation by Public:** Such disinvestment would enable the public, in general, to participate in the equity of PEs. So far, their investment is highly indirect.
5. **Encourage Employee Ownership:** This would enable and encourage the employees to buy shares of PEs and thereby become their owners also. This would ultimately develop the series of belonginess among them. It may motivate them to work harder and improve the work culture.

Need for a Long Term Disinvestment Strategy

The public sector in Indian continues to be more important component of the Indian Industries even after liberalization unlike the experience in many other countries which went in for wholesale privatization. Therefore, The PEs in general must be managed on sound commercial lines and must generate surpluses and make contributions commensurate with the quantum of public resources invested in them. Specially, in the strategic sector, the public sector is expected to have a commanding presence. PEs will be called upon to play an important role in certain core sectors of the economy. However, this should be achieved with minimum dependence on budgetary researches while government policies should provide a level playing field for PEs to compete with the private sector.

Government's withdrawal from non-core sector is indicated on considerations of long-term efficient use of capital, growing financial unviability and the compulsions for these PEs to operate in an increasing competitive and market-oriented environment. A large number of PEs in these sectors is either marginally profitable or loss making. Budgetary support to these loss making PEs has been a recurring feature over the last several years. Increased competitive pressure have adversely affected some PEs which were earlier profitable. Growing financial stringency will reduce the capacity of Government to support them and consequently lead to their closure with loss of employment in large numbers. Thus, in all profitably loss making PEs will continue to be an increasing drain on the budget unless available policy on disinvestment is evolved and implemented on them.

Viewed in this scenario disinvestment has larger implications that just selling government equity at the best price in profitable enterprises as these alone may not provide long term budgetary benefits unless the questions of loss making PEs is also addressed. The essence of a long term disinvestment strategy should therefore be not only enhance budgetary receipts but also minimize budgetary support towards loss making units while ensuring their long term viability and sustainable levels of employment in them.

Disinvestment as a strategy should aim at wide dispersal of government shareholding in the domestic market and broad based ownership in the process. This off course will be subject to limitation of the capital market in the capacity to absorb the proposed disinvestment and private sectors capital requirement from the same market. Sale of shares in the foreign markets may therefore also become necessary and the extent would be determined on a case basis depending upon the market conditions etc.

Public Sector Disinvestment Commission

The Ministry of Industry (Department of Public Enterprises) vide its resolution dated 23rd August, 1996, constituted a Public Sector Disinvestment Commission for a period of three years with Mr. G.V. Ramakrishna as its full time Chairman. The term of the Commission was further extended till 30th November, 1999. The Commission submitted its (12) reports on 58 PEs. The Commission was reconstituted in July, 2001 for a period of two years with Dr. R.M. Patil as its (part-time) Chairman. The term of this Commission was subsequently extended till October, 2004. The reconstituted Commission submitted its reports on 41 PEs, including review cases of earlier Commission's recommendations on 4 PEs. The term of the Commission expired on 31st October, 2004 and the Commission was wound up.

Department of Disinvestment, Ministry of Finance

The Department of Disinvestment (Ministry of Finance) was formed on 10th December, 1999 to handle the following functions:

a. (*i*) All matters relating to disinvestment of Central Government equity in PEs.

(*ii*) All matters relating to sale of Central Government equity through offer for sale or private placement, in the erstwhile PEs.

b. Decisions on the recommendations of the Disinvestment Commission on the modalities of disinvestment, including restructuring.

c. Implementation of disinvestment decisions, including appointment of advisers, pricing of shares, and other terms and conditions of disinvestment.

d. Matters relating to Disinvestment Commission.

e. Issues relating to PEs for purposes of disinvestment of Government equity only.

f. Financial policy in regard to the utilization of the proceeds of disinvestment, channelised into the National Investment Fund.

The Department was later elevated in 2001 and became the Ministry of Disinvestment. Subsequently from 2004, it has once again been turned into a Department of the Ministry of Finance.

Evolution of Disinvestment Policy

The policy of disinvestment has largely evolved through the policy statements of Finance Ministers in their Budget Speeches. The policy, as evolved, is enumerated below:

(*i*) In the Interim budget 1991-92, it was announced that the Government of India would divest upto 20% of its equity in selected PE's in favor of mutual funds, financial and institutional investors belong to the public sector.

(*ii*) In the budget speech of 1992-93, the cap of 20% was re-instated and the list of eligible investor was enlarged to include FII's, employees and OCB's.

(*iii*) In April, 1993, the Rangarajan Committee recommended for divestment upto 49% of PE's equity for industries explicitly reserved for the public sector and over 74% in other industries. The Government did not, however, take any decision on its recommendations.

(*iv*) As per the Common Minimum Programme, the Finance Minister in his Budget Speech announced the setting up of Disinvestment Commission for 3 years. The Common Minimum Programme also emphasized on greater transparency in the disinvestment process.

(*v*) In the Budget Speech of 1998-99, the Government announced that shareholding in PEs may be brought down to 26% on a case to case basis, excluding strategic PEs (where Government would retain majority shareholding). It was also stated that the interest of workers will be protected in all cases. On 16th March, 1999, the Government accordingly classified these enterprises into strategic and non strategic PEs. Enterprises belonging to the following areas were declared as strategic PEs;

(*vi*) Arms and ammunition (and the allied items of defence equipment), defence aircrafts and warships;

(*vii*) Atomic energy (except in the areas related to the generation of nuclear power and applications of radiation and radio-isotopes to agriculture, medicine and non-strategic industries);

(*viii*) Railway transport. (All other PE's were to be considered non strategic).

(*ix*) In the Budget Speech of 1999-2000, it was announced that the Government will continue to strengthen the strategic PEs and "privatize" the non-strategic ones through gradual disinvestment or strategic sale and will devise viable rehabilitation strategies for the weak units.

(*x*) In the Budget Speech of 2000-01, the Government stressed on restructuring and revival of viable PEs; on closing down of PEs which cannot be revived and to bring down Government shareholdings in nonstrategic PEs to 26% or lower, if necessary. It was further announced that the receipts from disinvestment will be used for social sectors, restructuring of PEs and for retirement of public debt.

(*xi*) In May, 2004, the Government adopted the National Common Minimum Programme (NCMP), which outlined the policy of the Government with respect to PEs as mentioned below:

a. The Government pledged to devolve full managerial control and commercial autonomy to successful, profit-making companies operating in competitive environment. It was declared that PEs will not be privatized. The 'Navratna' PEs were allowed to raise resources from the capital market. It was also announced that efforts will be made to modernize and restructure 'sick public sector companies'.

b. Sale of small proportions of Government equity through IPO/FPO was favoured, without changing the character of (PE's. In this regard, it approved listing of unlisted profit table PE's subject to residual equity of the Government remaining atleast 51% and Government retaining the control over the management.

c. The Government also constituted the 'National Investment Fund' NIF. The proceeds from disinvestment of PE's was channelized into NIF. It was, furthermore, declared that 75% of annual income of NIF will be used to finance selected social sector schemes in education, health and employment, and the rest 25% of the annual income to meet the capital investment requirements of profit table and revivable PE's.

d. On 27th January, 2005 the Government, approved in principle the following:

a. Listing of currently unlisted profitable PEs, each with a net worth in excess of Rs. 200 crore, through an Initial Public Offering (IPO) either in conjunction with a fresh equity issue by the PE concernedor independently by the Government on a case to case basis, subject to the residual equity of the Government remaining at least 51 per cent and the Government retaining management control of the PE;

b. Sale of minority shareholding of the Government in listed and profitable PEs either in conjunction with a Public Issue of fresh equity by the PE concerned or independently by the Government subject to the residual equity of the Government remaining at least 51 per cent and the Government retaining management control of the PE; and

c. Constitution of a "National Investment Fund".

d. On 25th November, 2005, Government decided, in principle, to list unlisted, profitable PEs on domestic stock exchanges and to selectively sell small portions of equity in these PEs (other than the Navratna PEs).

The current policy on disinvestment emanate from the President's Address to the Joint Session of both the Houses of Parliament (4.6.2009) where it was stated, as under: 'Our fellow citizens have every right to own part of the shares of public sector companies while the Government retains majority shareholding and control. My Government will develop a roadmap for listing and people-ownership of public sector undertakings while ensuring that Government equity does not fall below 51%'. The Hon'ble Finance Minister in his Budget Speech (6.7.2009), furthermore, announced, as under: "Public Sector Undertakings (PSUs) are the wealth of the nation, and part of this wealth should rest in the hands of the people. While retaining at least 51 per cent Government equity in our enterprises, I propose to encourage people's participation in our disinvestment programme. Here, I must state clearly that public sector enterprises, such as, banks and insurance companies will remain in the public sector and will be given all support, including capital infusion, to grow and remain competitive'. The Department of Disinvestment, Ministry of Finance, in consultation with Ministries/Departments will accordingly identify cases for disinvestment in select PEs. The focus will first be on profitable PEs that are listed with less than 10% public shareholding (and make them compliant through Follow-on Public Offerings). Profitable unlisted companies will be also listed on stock exchanges through Offer for-Sale or through Issue of Fresh Equity by the companies or both in conjunction.

Components of Disinvestment Policy

Following are the main components of Disinvestment strategy:

1. Strengthen PEs

(*i*) Strengthen profitable PEs to promote greater competitiveness and profitability to enable payment of higher dividends to enhance share values.

(*ii*) Strengthen other marginally profitable PEs and reduce their future dependence on the budget.

(*iii*) Financially restructure and revive loss making PEs to invite private capital for long-term turn-around.

2. Protect Employee Interest

(*i*) Sustaining long term employment by financial turnaround of loss making PEs.

(*ii*) Providing adequate and fair competition through VRs to surplus workforce.

(*iii*) Provide for employee participation in Management.

3. Broad Base Ownership

(*i*) Enhance retail reach of PEs of shares to small investor.

(*ii*) Offering of shares at suitable price discount as compared to the institutional investor.

4. Augment receipts for Government

(*i*) Enhance Government receipts by disinvestment in profitable PEs.

(*ii*) Eliminate the need for budgetary support for loss making PEs.

5. To Reduce Bureaucratic Control

(*i*) With the reduce holding of the government in the equity of PEs, the bureaucratic hold and control would also be reduced considerably. It may provide more autonomy to the management of these PEs, which they are clamouring for.

The need to lay a sound foundation for the disinvestment process impinged upon the three major components of the strategy.

(*i*) The selection of the companies to be offered.

(*ii*) The pricing of the equity, and

(*iii*) The rationale of the disinvestment mechanism.

(*i*) The selection of the companies to be offered: In practice, the list of companies offered in the first phase of disinvestment had to be limited to choose companies which were prima-facie, such that the investment market could appreciate without much difficulty and price reasonably. Later on companies were categorized in three categories – Cat.- A, Cat.-B and Cat. – C. The Categorisation in these categories was based on NAV. Those whose net assets value of Rs. 10/-. Shares was above 50good, Category B as good and Category C as no so good but with good track record. It was the decision of the government not to offer only the best but also some not so good but with good track record companies.

(*ii*) The pricing of the equity: The pricing formula adopted for the referral price was average of NAV and PECU (Profit Earning Capacity Value) at 10% industry capitalization rate.

This was in accordance with the guidelines of the CCI which was in existence at that time

(*iii*) The rationale of the disinvestment mechanism: A direct offer of shares to the public was not feasible because even with the most sophisticated valuation skill, a fair issue price on Company by Company basis was impossible to determine since the PEs were unknown to the market. The risk of over-pricing or under-pricing on a Company-Specific basis was real but clearly unaffordable. The Government, therefore took a fundamental view of reality and decided to: (a) offer randomly structured portfolios of shares, each with a national reserve price based on a complex valuation procedure, and (b) decided to off-load the shares to institutional investors as a buffer between the government and the stock market. It was the argument of the government that institutional investors would be able to handle these risks much more efficiently than individual investors because of their ability to invest substantial amount of money and buy and hold a large number of public sector shares.

Current Policy on Disinvestment

The current policy on disinvestment emanate from the following pronouncements by the Government:

(*i*) 'Our fellow citizens have every right to own part of the shares of public sector companies while the Government retains majority shareholding and control. My Government will develop a roadmap for listing and people-ownership of public sector undertakings while ensuring that Government equity does not fall below 51%'. (President's Address to Joint Session of both the Houses of Parliament dtd. 4.6.2009).

(*ii*) "Public Sector Undertakings (PSUs) are the wealth of the nation, and part of this wealth should rest in the hands of the people. While retaining at least 51 per cent Government equity in our enterprises, I propose to encourage people's participation in our disinvestment programme. Here, I must state clearly that public sector enterprises such as banks and insurance companies will remain in the public sector and will be given all support, including capital infusion, to grow and remain competitive. (FM's Budget Speech dtd. 6.7.2009).

Objective of Listing

There are inherent advantages in the listing of shares of profit table PEs on the stock exchanges. This process will enhance shareholder's value in such PEs and bestow the following benefits on these listed companies:

a. Higher disclosure levels will bring greater transparency, liquidity and credibility to their stocks;

b. Enhance corporate governance through induction of independent directors' on the Boards of these PEs, which is mandatory for listed companies;

c. Higher levels of public scrutiny will enforce ethical conduct of business in these PEs and thus improve corporate culture;

d. Expectations of investors / shareholders will bring pressure upon the management to perform and to unlock the true value of these enterprises;

e. Listing will enable wider shareholding of PE stocks, and people-ownership of PEs.

Broad Approach to Disinvestment

The Department of Disinvestment in consultation with Ministries/Departments will to identify cases for disinvestment. The focus will first be on profitable PEs that are listed with less than 10% public shareholding (and make them compliant through Follow-on Public Offerings). Profit table unlisted companies will be also listed on stock exchanges through Offer-for-Sale or through Issue of Fresh Equity by the companies or both in conjunction.

Disinvestment in PEs

(i) The Government approved disinvestment of 5.25% equity of National Thermal Power Corporation Limited (NTPC) on 12th July, 2004 (out of Government's shareholding) in conjunction with the IPO by the Company. The IPO that was completed in October 2004 fetched an amount of Rs. 2684.07 crore.

(ii) The Government sold 8% equity in Maruti Udyog Limited (MUL) in January 2006 out of its residual shareholding of 18.28% to public sector financial institutions (FIs) and public sector banks through a differential pricing method. The Government realized, in the process, Rs. 1567.60 crore from this sale. In March 2006, 0.01% equity of the Company was sold to the employees and the Government realized an amount of Rs. 2.08 crore. On 21st December 2006, the Government decided to disinvest its entire residual shareholding of 10.27% in Maruti Udyog Limited. The shareholding of 10.27% was finally disinvested in May 2007 though the differential pricing method to Indian public sector FIs, public sector banks and Indian Mutual Funds. The Government realized in the process Rs. 2277.62 crore from this disinvestment.

(iii) In February, 2007, the Government decided to piggy-back with an 'Offer-for-Sale' of 10 per cent, 5 per cent and 5 per cent of the pre-issue paid-up capital of REC, PGCIL and NHPC respectively. Overall position about the disinvestment programme is indicated in Exhibit-22.8:

Exhibit-22.8
Disinvestment in PEs

(Rs. In crores)

Year	Target	Actual
1991-92	2,500	3,037.74
1992-93	2,500	1,912.51
1993-94	3,500	-
1994-95	4,000	4,843.10
1995-96	7,000	168.48
1996-97	5,000	379.67
1997-98	4,800	910.00
1998-99	5,000	5371.11
1999-00	10,000	1,860.14
2000-01	10,000	1,871.26
2001-02	12,000	5,657.69
2002-03	12,000	3,3,47.98
2003-04	14,500	15,547.41
2004-05	4,000	2,764.87
2005-06	No target fixed	1,569.68
2006-07	No target fixed	-
2007-08	No target fixed	4,181.39
2008-09	No target fixed	-
2009-10	No target fixed	4,259.90

Source: Public Enterprise Survey, Vol.I of the concerned years

The IPO of PGCIL was completed in October 2007 and the Government realized an amount of Rs. 994.82 crore. The IPO of REC was completed in March, 2008 and the Government realized an amount of Rs. 819.63 crore. The IPO of NHPC was completed in August, 2009 and the Government realized an amount of Rs. 2012.85 crore. In August, 2007, the Government approved disinvestment of 10% equity in Oil India Ltd, out of its shareholding along with fresh issue of equity of 11% of the post-issue paid-up capital of Oil India Limited and simultaneous disinvestment of 10% equity of Government in favour of IOC, HPCL and BPCL in the ratio of 2:1:1, at the market discovered price. The IPO was completed in September, 2009 and the Government realized an amount of Rs. 2247.046 crore. The total receipts from disinvestment over the period 1st April. 1999 till 30th September, 2009, amounted to Rs. 57,682.93 crore.

National Investment Fund

The Government decided to constitute a "National Investment Fund" (NIF) on 27th January 2005. The Fund is maintained outside the Consolidated Fund of India, and into which the realisation from sale of minority shareholding of the Government in profitable PEs would be channelized. The income from the Fund will be used for the broad objectives of (a) Investment in social sector projects and programmes which promote education, health care and employment; and (b) Investment in select profit table and revivable public sector enterprises that promise adequate returns, through enlarging their capital base.

The salient features of NIF are mentioned below :

(*i*) The proceeds from disinvestment of PEs will be channelized into the National Investment Fund which is to be maintained outside the Consolidated Fund of India.

(*ii*) The corpus of the National Investment Fund will be of a permanent nature.

(*iii*) The Fund will be professionally managed to provide sustainable returns to the Government, without depleting the corpus. Select public sector Mutual Funds have been entrusted with the management of the corpus of the Fund.

(*iv*) 75 per cent of the annual income of the Fund will be used to finance select social sector schemes that promote education, health and employment. The residual 25 per cent of the annual income of the Fund will be used to meet the capital investment requirements of profit table and revivable PEs that yield adequate returns, in order to enlarge their capital base to finance expansion/diversification.

Fund Managers of NIF

The following Public Sector Mutual Funds have been appointed (initially) as Fund Managers to manage the funds of NIF under the 'discretionary mode' of Portfolio Management Scheme which is governed by SEBI guidelines, namely.

(*i*) the UTI Assets Management Company Ltd.

(*ii*) the SBI Funds Management Company (Pvt.) Ltd.

(*iii*) the Jeevan Bima Sahayog, Asset Management Company Ltd.

Corpus of NIF

The present corpus of the Fund is Rs. 1814.45 crore being the proceeds from the disinvestment in Power Grid Corporation of India Limited and Rural Electrification Corporation. While the pay out on NIF, in the first year, stood at Rs. 84.81 crores, it was Rs. 206.21 crores in the second year. (Average income works out to 8.47% in the first year and 10.02% in the second year). The average income for the two years, therefore, works out to 9.245%, against the hurdle rate of 9.25%.

SUMMARY OF RECEIPTS FROM DISINVESTMENT: (1991-92 – 30.09.2009)

Year	Budgeted receipt (Rs. crore)	Receipts through sale of minority shareholding in PEs (Rs. crore)	Receipts through sale of majority shareholding of one PEs to another PEs (Rs. crore)	Receipts through Strategic sale (Rs. crore)	Receipts from other related transactions (Rs. crore)	Receipts from sale of residual shareholding in disinvested PE's/companies(Rs. crore)	Total receipts (Rs. crore)	Transactions
(1)	(2)	(3)	(4)	(5)	(6)	(7)	(8)	(9)
1991–92	2,500	3,037.74	–	–	–	–	3,037.74	Minority shares sold in Dec,1991 and Feb, 1992 by auction method in bundles of "very good" and "average" companies.
1992–93	2,500	1,912.51	–	–	–	–	1,912.51	Shares sold separately for each company by auction method.
1993–94	3,500	–	–	–	–	–	–	Equity of 6 companies sold by auction method but proceeds received in 94-95
1994–95	4,000	4,843.10	–	–	–	–	4,843.10	Shares sold by auction method.
1995–96	7,000	168.48	–	–	–	–	168.48	Shares sold by auction method
1996–97	5,000	379.67	–	–	–	–	379.67	GDR-VSNL
1997–98	4,800	910.00	–	–	–	–	910.00	GDR-MTNL
1998–99	5,000	**5371.11	–	–	–	–	5371.11	GDR-VSNL; Domestic offerings of CONCOR and GAIL, Cross purchase by 3 Oil sector companies i.e., GAIL, ONGC and IOC.
1999–00	10,000	**1479.27	–	105.45	275.42	–	1,860.14	GDR-GAIL; Domestic offering of VSNL; capital reduction and dividend from BALCO; Strategic sale of MFIL
2000–01	10,000	–	1,371.23	554.03	–	–	1,871.26	Sale of KRL, CPCL BRPL to CPSEs; Strategic Sale of BALCO and LJMC
2001–02	12,000	–	–	3,090.09	2,567.60	–	5,657.69	Strategic sale of CMC, HTL, VSNL, IBP, PPL, hotel properties of ITDC and HCI, slump sale of Hotel Centaur, Juhu Beach, Mumbai, and leasing of Ashok Bangalore; Special dividend from VSNL, STC and MMTC, sale of shares to VSNL employees

2002–03			–	2252.72	1095.26	–	3,3,47.98	Strategic sale of HZL, IPCL, hotel properties of ITDC, slump sale of Centaur Hotel Mumbai Airport, Mumbai, Premium for renunciation of rights issue in favour of SMC; Put Option of MFIL, sale of shares to employees of HZL and CMC.
2003–04	14,500	12,741.62	–	342.06	–	2,463.73	15,547.41	Strategic sale of JCL; Call option of HZL; Offer for sale of MUL, IBP, IPCL, CMC, DCI, GAIL, and ONGC, Sale of shares of ICI Ltd.
2004–05	4,000	2,700.06	–	–	64.81	–	2,764.87	Offer for sale of NTPC; sale of shares to IPCL employees
2005–06	No target fixed	–	–	–	2.08	1,567.60	1,569.68	Sale of MUL shares to Indian Public Sector Financial Institutions and banks and employees
2006–07	No target fixed	–	–	–	–	–	–	
2007–08	No target fixed	1,814.45	–	–	–	2,366.94	4,181.39	Sale of MUL shares to Indian public sector financial institutions, public sector banks and Indian Mutual Funds and sale of PGCIL and REC shares through Offer for Sale.
2008–09	No target fixed	–	–	–	–	–	–	
2009–10	No target fixed	4,259.90	–	–	–	–	4,259.90	(Rs. 2012.85 - NHPC and Rs. 2247.05 - OIL)
Total		39,617.91	1,317.23	6,344.35	4,005.17	6,398.27	57,682.93	

* Out of Rs. 5371.11, Rs. 4184 crore constitute receipts from cross purchase of shares of ONGC, GAIL and IOC,

** Out of Rs. 1479.27, Rs. 459.27 crore constitute receipts from cross purchase of shares of ONGC, GAIL and IOC

Suggestions

Some specific suggestions in this regard are as follows:

(i) **Under One Ministry:** The present ministerial control and interventions arise mainly because of the concept of administrative ministries. If a real solution is to be found to get out of this system, then an alternative has to be considered. For the purpose of parliamentary and other accountability, there will have to be some ministry concerned with PEs. One alternative could be to place all or most of the PEs under one Ministry, say, Dept. of Public Enterprises. The role of DPE could be more of information collection, policy coordination etc. rather than looking into day to day management.

(ii) **Government Directors:** Only one government director nominee of the Ministry concerned with the subject may to be appointed on Board in order to provide policy inputs and ensure the association of concerned sectoral/subject ministries, but without any informal 'veto' power.

(iii) **Chief Executive and full time Director:** The government should appoint only the Chief Executive (CMD) as selected by PESB and approved by ACC. Full time directors should be appointed by Boards (which can constitute specific committees for the purpose). These full time directors will be fully accountable to CMDs/Boards. The full time directors of the subsidiary PEs should be appointed by the Board of the holding PEs.

(iv) **Delegation of Powers:** Boards should have complete decision making powers, covering all areas such as investment decision making, joint ventures, market borrowing etc. without reference to government as long as no net budgetary support is involved. Boards should have complete freedom of operation, without PEs or any Chief Executives having to refer matters to the ministries.

(v) **Withdrawal of Guidelines:** Even after withdrawing 696 guidelines, about 300 guidelines still exist and more guideline are being issued from time to time. Government should withdraw all such guidelines which affect day to day activities/ operations of PEs. Any new guidelines or instructions can be issued in exceptional circumstances concerning overall government policy. The PEs should develop their own guidelines on corporate governance and ethics which may govern their functioning.

(vi) **Accountability by Results:** This is the major change being suggested. Instead of procedures and individual actions, the accountability should be judged by performance and results. For this purpose, MoU system may be converted into a long range corporate plans based directional and performance planning system. That may be used for accountability for results instead of individual activities. The system should be streamlined, made more effective and extended to al PEs. An annual rolling review should be undertaken by independent groups consisting of professionals (such as the Adhoc Task Force Syndicates in the Present MoU system) in order to determine the direction and the progress of the company, keeping in mind its long term corporate objectives. As in the private sector, excellent performance of Chief Executives /full time directors (including turning around of sick enterprises)should be suitably rewarded, while poor performance be penalized. Even part time Directors should be held accountable for results and suitably rewarded for excellent performance.

(vii) **Performance related Incentives to Employees:** While government as the owner, has been deciding the pay scales for executives and limits for the compensation packages, the managements should have full freedom to give performance related incentives and profit sharing (upto a pre-decided percentage). For loss making PEs also such incentives should also be permitted as long as these led to improvement of performance and reduction in wages and turnaround.

(viii) **Parliamentary Control:** The importance of parliamentary controls cannot be undermined. However, to given greater freedom to PEs, this control may be exercised through only one committee of parliament (say COPU). It should also take care of policy related questions or queries to be raised by MPs. However, no other questions such as those related to day-to-day operations need to raised. This aspect will have to be considered by the parliament.

(ix) **Internalize Audit and Vigilance:** These aspects should be looked largely by PEs themselves through effective internal systems. CAG and CVC/CB1 may have mainly cross-check and supervisory role to be performed in a commercially oriented system and organisation. Some of these aspects have been discussed with CVC and a separate Chapter on 'vigilance' for PEs have been introduced soon. Similarly, discussion have also been held with CAG and a small group is presently working on the improvements which can be brought in the present system. The main idea is to bring commercial orientations, while ensuring effective accountability.

Practice Questions

Objective Type Questions

1. Number of PEs registered with BIFR till 30.06.09 was:
   (*a*) 55 (*b*) 45
   (*c*) 65 (*d*) 75
2. The Board for Reconstruction of Public Enterprises was established in:
   (*a*) 2003 (*b*) 2005
   (*c*) 2004 (*d*) 2006
3. Composite score for MOU rating includes number of grading:
   (*a*) 2 (*b*) 3
   (*c*) 4 (*d*) 5
4. Number of Mahanavratna PEs is as on 31-3-2010:
   (*a*) 3 (*b*) 4
   (*c*) 5 (*d*) 6
5. Number of Navratna PEs is as on 31-3-2010:
   (*a*) 2 (*b*) 3
   (*c*) 4 (*d*) 5

Ans: 1. (c), 2. (c) 3. (d), 4. (b), 5. (d)

Short Answer Questions

1. What are the factors responsible for sickness in PEs?
2. What are the functions of BRPSE?
3. What do you mean by voluntary retirement scheme in PEs?
4. What do you understand by Mahanavratna scheme of PEs?
5. What do you know by POU in PEs?

Long Answer Questions

1. What do you mean by Restructuring of PEs? Examine its rationale.
2. Critically examine the strategies for revival or rehabilitation of PEs.
3. What do you mean by Ratna Schemes of PEs? Explain its process and grading.
4. Explain the nature of Memorandum of Understanding in PEs. Examine its procedures and benefits.
5. Discuss the different steps adopted by the government to restructure the PEs in India.

References

1. Kaleido SCOPE, Vol.19, October 1999, p..9
2. Kaleido SCOPE, Vol. 20, June 2000, p..21
3. Kaleido SCOPE, Vol. 21, Sept.2001)
4. Kaleido SCOPE, Vol. 15, September 1995p.6
5. Kaleido SCOPE, Vol. 15, December, 1999
6. Jagdish Prakash, Nageshwar Rao, Mata Badal Shukla, Administration of Public Enterprises in India, Himalaya Publishing House, 2010, p.418)
7. Kaleido SCOPE, Vo. 19, June 2000, p.11

23 COORDINATING AND FACILITATING CORPORATE AGENCIES

Private sector and public sector enterprises have been assigned a crucial role in the development of Indian economy. These enterprises of both the sectors have actually trying to achieve commanding heights in the Indian economy. To coordinate the growth activities in proper perspective, some coordinating and facilitating agencies has been established and they are doing well. These important agencies are CII, FICCI, ASSOCHAM, AIAI and SCOPE.etc. These agencies are responsible for coordinating and facilitating the activities of member enterprises with the government and ensuring intra enterprise coordination on the other hand. These organisations are playing an important role in the formation of an informed public opinion in the developing country like India.

The most popular name of these coordinating and facilitating agencies is the chamber. In India, most of these agencies are working as chamber of commerce. A chamber of commerce, therefore serve as a central agency for individuals, firms, companies and trade associations for promoting and protecting business interests. It is through this central agency that varied interest groups deal with common problems and develop a collective thought."[1]. Besides promoting the economic interest of the members, these organisations are also interested in promoting the social and economic welfare of the country. Ethical, social and moral motives are of paramount importance in the working of these organisations. It is for these reasons, that these voluntary organisations have become instruments of economic and social progress; it is also on this account that these organisations enjoy a privileged status.

A chamber of commerce resembles a trade association but the two are basically different. A chamber is concerned with diversified a diversified activities aimed at protecting the interest of trade, as well as, industry rather than of any one economic group. A chamber of commerce tries to advance the general interest of all the economic groups under its umbrella rather than serving any one particular economic group. A chamber of commerce, therefore develops a broader outlook on economic issues which affect diversified interests of the various classes of members. As a result of its diversified membership a chamber of commerce has very often to reconcile the conflicting interests of different economic groups within the membership fold. There are local, regional and apex organisations in the chamber of commerce areas.

A trade association, on the other hand, is a voluntary non-profit organisation which draws its members, individuals, firms and companies from a specific field of business or industry. Members of a trade association are brought together by mutuality of interest and they create an agency to render a number of mutual aid services and to improve the trades and industry's position generally. Traders including retailers, wholesalers and other distributors, though competitors in a particular trade may form a trade association. Merchants interested in a particular products or manufacturer manufacturing a particular product may also from such an association. Trade associations may be formed at the local, regional and national level. The variety of interests in the Indian economy is best reflected in the wide variety of trade associations. Naturally, there are great differences in type, structure and organisations in ever changing functional needs. These associations are quite effective and successful in putting the issues of member enterprises before the government and getting the things done in their favour. In international scenario, these associations are also engaged in serious dialogues with other international agencies.

1. The Confederation of Indian Industry (CII)

The history of CII is the story of the transformation of a miniscule association, representing a small segment of industry, to the premier business association of modern India. The journey began in 1895 when 5 engineering firms, all members of the Bengal Chamber of Commerce and Industry, joined hands to form the Engineering and Iron Trades Association (EITA). The Confederation of Indian Industry (CII) works to create and sustain an environment conducive to the growth of industry in India, partnering industry and government alike through advisory and consultative processes. CII is a non-government, not-for-profit, industry led and industry managed organisation, playing a proactive role in India's development process. Founded over 115 years ago, it is India's premier business association, with a direct membership of over 8100 organisations from the private as well as public sectors, including SMEs and MNCs, and an indirect membership of over 90,000 companies from around 400 national and regional sectoral associations. With 64 offices in India, 9 overseas in Australia, Austria, China, France, Germany, Japan, Singapore, UK, and USA, and institutional partnerships with 223 counterpart organisations in 90 countries, CII serves as a reference point for Indian industry and the international business community.

Functions of CII

(*i*) CII catalyses change by working closely with government on policy issues, enhancing efficiency, competitiveness and expanding business opportunities for industry through a range of specialised services and global linkages.

(*ii*) It provides a platform for sectoral consensus building and networking. Major emphasis is laid on projecting a positive image of business, assisting industry to identify and execute corporate citizenship programmes. Partnerships with over 120 NGOs across the country carry forward our initiatives in integrated and inclusive development, which include health, education, livelihood, diversity management, skill development and environment, to name a few.

(*iii*) CII has taken up the agenda of "Business for Livelihood" for the year 2010-11. Businesses are part of civil society and creating livelihoods is the best act of corporate social responsibility. Looking ahead, the focus for 2010-11 would be on the four key Enablers for Sustainable Enterprises: Education, Employability, Innovation and Entrepreneurship. While Education and Employability help create a qualified and skilled workforce, Innovation and Entrepreneurship would drive growth and employment generation.

***(i)* Engineering and Iron Trades Association (EITA):** EITA was set up at the end of 1895 with the aim of pressurising the colonial government to place government orders for iron and steel and engineering goods with companies based in India. At that time the practice was to place all government orders with firms based in UK.

***(ii)* Engineering Association of India (EAI):** Till 1942 IEA was the only all-India association of engineering industry and represented mainly big engineering companies, particularly the British firms. This led to a situation where the interests of the Indian firms (mainly medium and small scale) were not sufficiently represented. Thus, the Engineering Association of India (EAI) was established in 1942 as an affiliate of the Indian Chamber of Commerce. EAI represented small and medium engineering firms mostly owned and promoted by Indians, and had different origins and management styles from the IEA.

***(iii)* Confederation of Engineering Industry (CEI):** Foreseeing the upcoming challenges in the future, the leadership at AIEI felt the need for greater consolidation and solidarity that would put the industry on a stronger footing and would help it meet the challenges of competition and globalisation. Thus, in 1986 there was a change in name from AIEI to the Confederation of Engineering Industry (CEI), reflecting the growth and expansion of the organisation since 1974. CEI now became an apex body for manufacturing industries at the national level.

***(iv)* Indian Engineering Association (IEA):** The change in name from EITA to IEA in 1912 reflected the association's decision to exclude traders from the membership and concentrate fully on promoting the cause of manufacturers. By this time, many more manufacturers had come into being and there was a conflict of interest between traders, who preferred government orders to be placed with companies in the UK, and manufacturers of engineering goods, who sought industry promotion through public orders.

***(v)* Association of Indian Engineering Industry (AIEI):** After Independence of India in 1947, the public sector assumed the lead role in industrial development. By 1970s, a new base of heavy industries had been built, but private companies faced restrictions through licensing requirements for new units and /or expansion. Keeping in view the greater interests of the Engineering industry in the country, in April 1974, the two associations - IEA and EAI - merged to form the Association of Indian Engineering Industry (AIEI). For the engineering industry the merger meant a stronger association capable of harnessing larger resources and providing a wider range of services.

Confederation of Indian Industry (CII)

In 1991, industrial licensing was abolished and economic reforms on a wide scale started taking shape. With effect from 1st January 1992, in keeping with the government's decision to opt for the liberalisation of the Indian economy, the name of CEI was changed to Confederation of Indian Industry (CII). In a new policy environment, it was natural that there would be inter-sectoral integration through a process of diversification and expansion, where the engineering units would diversify into non-engineering units and vice-versa. Since 1992, through rapid expansion and consolidation, CII has grown to be the most visible business association in India.

Divisions and Councils of CII

Economies around the world are aligning themselves to the requirements of rapid globalisation. In a global village, where market accessibility is no longer a hurdle, the tough part is capturing market shares and retaining them. Only those, who have adopted global quality standards leveraging their intellectual capital have managed this feat. Guided by this fact, CII has embarked on smarter initiatives that enhance competitiveness of Indian industry by underlining the need for rapid up gradation on parameters like quality, corporate governance, knowledge management, energy efficiency and environment management. All this, not only to increase productivity and profitability but also to enhance the quality of life of the community. Different divisions and councils of CII develop and undertake new services for the business community and beyond are as follows:

(i) **Specialised Services Division** aims to provide solutions to organizations not just for their competitiveness needs, but also to help them become more self reliant by helping them develop flexible strategies that cater to changing needs. **Corporate Services Group** assists companies maximise corporate and shareholder value through a range of activities covering: Consulting, Research Projects, Knowledge Based Events and Research Papers.

(ii) **Energy Management Division** provides its expertise to domestic as well as overseas organisations. The range of services offered includes : comprehensive energy audits, in-house and centre-wise intensive training programmes, specific energy consumption norms, 'Energy Conservation (Encon)' missions and international conferences / exhibitions on trends in energy efficiency.

(iii) **Environment Management Division** facilitates the utilisation of national and international expertise through seminars, workshops and training programmes. It undertakes a wide range of programmes & awareness activities covering legal and technical aspects including design and implementation of Environment Management systems as per ISO 14001, OHSAS 18001 and SA 8000. Pollution Prevention and Waste Minimization Initiatives, Green Supply Chain Management, Environmental Performance Evaluation, Strategic Environmental Assessment, Sustainable Development and Environmental Planning, Hazardous Waste Management, Site Feasibility Assessment etc. are some of the other services offered. **Green Services Division** operates through the **Green Business Centre (CII-GBC),** offering niche Green Services to Indian industry. The objective of the CII-GBC is to promote Green Concepts leading to sustainable development, efficiency and equitable growth. Services offered: Green Process Certification, Green Building Certification (advisory services on construction of green buildings and award of Green Building certificate), Technology Centres, Training Programmes on Green related topics and business incubation – facilitating entrepreneurs in developing and marketing new and innovative Green products for commercialisation.

(iv) **Technology Services Division** offers the following services to members : Technology Audit, Technology Export, technology transfer and problem solving skills from R&D and academic institutions (through CII TDB Technology Transfer Centres). Total Cost Management is offered as a company-wide systematic and structured approach, which involves providing a holistic framework to control, reduce and eliminate costs, across the value chain. Managing the financial outcome of activities prevails over all operations, both internally and externally; and is one of the most powerful tools that corporations can use in their quest for competitive advantage.

(v) **Total Quality Management Division,** working in tandem with the CII Institute of Quality in Bangalore, provides a comprehensive range of services to members : multi-client training and awareness programmes,

in-company training, individual company counseling and advisory services, seminars and focussed missions within India and overseas to study and share best practices. 'Quality of life' is not the privilege of a few, but the birthright of every human being. And the responsibility of taking it to the underprivileged lies with the privileged, more so with profit making organizations. Towards this end, CII's Social Development and Community Affairs Council (SDCA) has pledged the allegiance of all members, taking the 'More for India' slogan to their boardroom agenda. SDCA's various initiatives cover issues like education, child rehabilitation, women empowerment, rural development, human rights, population, healthcare and the control of HIV/AIDS.

(*vi*) **Trade Fairs** organised by CII act as windows to the world, showcasing all that is current and more that could be expected. They serve as effective platforms for technology transfer and business development. The Made in India Show has traveled to several countries and is the largest overseas exposition of Indian goods and services. International Engineering & Technology Fair (IETF) and Auto Expo are two reputed biennial fairs held in Delhi, now into their 15th and 7th editions respectively. Other trade fairs cover diverse sectors, ranging from biotechnology, information technology and railways to water.

(*vii*) **International Conferences** organised by CII work towards keeping its members abreast of contemporary global standards and emerging trends. With a firm belief in the credo 'Confer to Prosper', CII has been instrumental in bringing together decision makers, thought leaders, influencers and policy makers on common platforms to pool in their intellectual resources for the good of all. The **Partnership Summit** has established itself as India™s most important business event. Other conferences cover a variety of themes like leadership, marketing, entertainment, fashion, retail and the environment, to name a few.

(*viii*) **Other initiatives:** In the last few years, CII has also stepped up its engagement on a wide range of issues that it identifies as being of national concern and priority. 4 Missions and 2 Campaigns have been launched: on Manufacturing Innovation, Knowledge and Skills Development, Sustainable Growth and Inclusive Growth. The Campaigns are on Brand India and Integrity India.

(*a*) The Mission on **Manufacturing Innovation** was begun to inculcate Innovation as a way of life in Indian business. Global competitiveness is being promoted through global partnerships for learning sessions with leading international practitioners in innovation.

(*b*) The Mission on **Knowledge and Skills** looks to "Promote a Sustainable Framework that would assist Industry across sectors in developing Knowledge and Skills abilities in its Workforce to International standards."

(*c*) The Mission on **Sustainable Growth** proposes to promote and champion sustainable growth in Indian Industry, without compromising on high and accelerated Growth."

(*d*) The Mission on **Inclusive Growth** facilitates Inclusive Growth for Sustainable and Equitable Growth. The Bihar Project focuses on the Samastipur district, one of the 100 most backward districts. Yet another unique project is the Art-North-East Project, an initiative by CII and NEDFi to provide market linkages for handlooms and handicraft products from North East. The project has had direct and indirect benefits for 7100 families. The Rural Business Hubs project is taking off with the institution of many partnerships. 4 RBH Pilots projects initiated range from fruits in Nainital, Jathropa Cultivation for Bio diesel in Haryana to carpet weaving and 'Blue Pottery' from Rajashthan.

(*e*) Through the **Brand India Campaign**, CII strives to Build Brand salience for India by positioning it as a "Globally Competitive and sound Investment destination and as a Reliable Partner to do business with."

(*f*) The **Integrity India Campaign** takes on the challenge of "working to improve probity in public life by putting the issue of Integrity on the front burner."

Perspective

CII strongly believes that partnership and cooperation between industry, government and civil society is the key to economic and social development of India. At CII, all efforts are directed towards harnessing and leveraging the power of technology to change communication, business and business procedures, connect knowledge to procedures and hence, impact profits and the lives of common citizens for the better. Essential prerequisites for this to happen are wider, more holistic perspectives and greater participation in policy formulation by all concerned groups. The policy advisory and consultative services of CII cover intra and inter-industry discussions, industry-community parleys and industry-government meetings, all aimed at giving the whole policy making process a better business focus and more representative hue. The CII have over the years created several credible, géneric and focused fora for meaningful dialogue covering various aspects such as finance and taxation, foreign direct investment, banking, insurance, WTO and international trade, disinvestment, small and medium enterprises, defence, elections and industrial relations.

(i) **CII's Annual National Conference** has established itself as the major interface between all sections of government, academia, society and industry. It is here that policy and opinion makers come together on a common platform to discuss and brainstorm on issues relevant to sustained development and its equitable distribution. The event provides a unique opportunity to take stock of initiatives taken over the past year, unveil new plans and set the charter for the year ahead.

(ii) **India Economic Summit** organised annually since 1984, in partnership with World Economic Forum is South Asia's most prominent annual gathering of decision makers, industry and thought leaders, senior representatives of leading global corporations and international investors. Deliberations at the Summit centre around India's ongoing reforms process, the opportunities and concerns. Informal discussions and opinions shared here serve as a global barometer for the same. Infrastructure is the yarn that weaves the fabric of an economy. Investments in telecommunications, surface transport, roads, highways, ports and airports have emerged as key imperatives in India's efforts to derive maximum benefits from economic reforms. CII's Infrastructure Council seeks to establish public-private partnerships for sound strategising and faster operationalisation of plans, the idea being to dovetail corporate managerial skills and expertise with government financial resources and reach. Investor friendly legal and regulatory policy frameworks, risk mitigation, resource mobilisation and centre-state harmonisation are critical issues that CII continuously addresses during its interactions with governments and institutions.

(iii) **Council for MNCs** has been set up in recognition of the crucial role being played by multinational corporations in global integration and overall development of the Indian economy. The council looks after the interests of over 498 organisations and holds regular discussions with key government officials. It has made a strong case for a single window clearance system for all investment projects as a step towards making India a more attractive destination for foreign direct investment. Small and medium enterprises are key drivers of the Indian economy. They generate substantial employment and have earned global recognition for cost effectiveness and technology adaptation. CII works towards keeping small industry at the forefront of change with updates on latest technologies, market opportunities and finance. Our MoU with the Small Industries Development Bank of India (SIDBI) helps promote ancillary linkages. CII has also evolved a unique, tailor-made cluster approach to help SMEs implement ISO 9000 quality systems.

WTO Advisory Services are provided by experts at the International Trade Policy Division who track all relevant developments at international fora. Participation at all WTO Ministerials held thus far and ongoing exchanges with counterparts in Europe, Japan and the USA add value to their opinions and shared perspectives. In addition to providing key inputs to government representatives at multilateral negotiations, the division also assesses WTO asymmetry and compliance at individual companies and undertakes detailed studies of WTO impact on specific sectors and companies.

(iv) **Public Policy Committee** strives to build consensus on contentious economic, political and social issues. Firm in its belief that an economy built on consensus is an economy headed for success, the committee engages in dialogue with Members of Parliament, political parties and NGOs on issues as diverse as electoral reforms, impact of globalisation, good governance, patents regime, WTO and communication convergence.

(v) **National Committee on Defence** works very closely with the Ministry of Defence towards achieving self-reliance in this sector. It seeks to establish a strong partnership with the defence services to enlarge the role of Indian industry in defence production and supplies. A major achievement of CII's sustained efforts has been the opening up of defence production to the private sector in certain categories. We have also organised CEO Missions overseas and domestic vendor development programmes to explore business opportunities.

Roles of CII

The primary goal of CII is to develop Indian industry and to ensure that government and society as a whole, understand both the needs of industry and its contribution to the nation's well being. The CII has been trying to play following roles:

(i) To identify and strengthen industry's role in the economic development of the country.

(*ii*) To act as a catalyst in bringing about the growth and development of Indian Industry.

(*iii*) To reinforce industry's commitment to society.

(*iv*) To provide up-to-date information and data to industry and government.

(*v*) To create awareness and support industry's efforts on quality, environment, energy management and consumer protection.

(*vi*) To identify and address the special needs of the small sector to make it more competitive.

(*vii*) To promote cooperation with counterpart organisations.

(*viii*) To work towards the globalisation of Indian industry and integration into the world economy.

This is done by adopting a proactive and partnership approach with the government on various national and international issues concerning the Indian economy. It closely interacts on policy issues at both the central and state levels. Extensive dialogue and interaction with members and all sections of the community to build consensus are held.

Strategies being Persuaded by CII

The strategies for holistic integration of industry with the needs of society are built around the four prongs of Key Initiatives / Information, global integration, commitment to society and competitiveness of industry. The common factor in all its activities is partnership across a cross-section of organizations, including government, non-governmental organizations and international bodies. Working with and learning from diverse institutions, CII has strengthened the services it provides to its members as well as society at large. In an e-enabled world, economic well-being of nations and their people is determined by the degree of their integration with the global fraternity. As businesses have transcended frontiers, marked by the free movement of people, goods, capital and information, international work processes have become more cohesive. Economic realignments and geo-political developments have brought in their wake opportunities as well as uncertainties.

The International works towards providing membership of the CII clearer strategies based on deeper insights and analytical perceptions of emerging realities. At the forefront in helping Indian business connect and interact with global business, CII has activated a multi-pronged strategy for global networking. Meeting heads of state and government, decision makers, networking with counterpart organisations, multilateral and academic institutions and other policy making bodies, CII's alternate diplomacy ensures continued access to emerging opportunities for its membership. The network of 15 overseas offices helps us disseminate vital information related to markets and joint venture possibilities to Indian and foreign companies.

India's economy is a mirror image of our pluralistic, democratic polity and is marked by heterogeneity of both character and scale. Policy related to one industry is more than likely to have an impact on several others in a domino like effect. The clear strategy here is to manage complementary and conflicting interests to the benefit of all concerned sectors. This is a task that CII's Agriculture, Manufacturing and Services Councils have performed with rare aplomb since their very inception. Better known collectively as ASCON (Associations Council), it walks the proverbial tightrope seeking to build consensus among its membership of 114 sectoral associations, 23 sector specific divisions and 14 committees. The single most important benefit of deliberations at an umbrella body like ASCON is the convergence of opinions and views. It provides members the much needed opportunity of exploring symbiotic inter-sectoral synergies.

Sectors of Operations

It includes the following:

(*i*) Agriculture

(*ii*) Infrastructure

(*iii*) Manufacturing

(*iv*) Services

(*v*) Industrial competitiveness

Development Initiatives of CII

Following development initiatives have been taken by the CII:

(i) **Affirmative Action:** Responding to Prime Minister Dr Manmohan Singh's call to Indian Industry to take Affirmative Action to create education and employment opportunities for the weaker sections of society, CII formed task force subsequently proposed concrete steps to be taken by Indian Industry for creating education and employment opportunities for people belonging to Scheduled Caste and Scheduled Tribe. Affirmative Action for the Scheduled Castes and Scheduled Tribes communities is defined as a voluntary commitment by Indian companies to help the Government and civil society in the national endeavour to ensure equal opportunity to members of the Scheduled Castes and Scheduled Tribes communities. The progress is being made on 4 Es i.e., (i) Entrepreneurship Development; (ii) Employability; (iii) Education; and (iv) Employment for the Scheduled Castes and the Scheduled Tribes. This has been well received by industry. In addition, CII developed a Code of Conduct on Affirmative Action, which is being followed by companies. The Code relates to non-discrimination, assistance, and transparency with respect to employees/ applicants/ vendors from the SC & ST communities. This is a voluntary commitment. Needless to say member companies have been proactive and enthusiastic, energized by CII's Mission mode. Various companies have evolved different programmes and there is an enthusiasm about greater engagement with society and the underprivileged. CII has received spontaneous support from industry.

(ii) **Climate Change:** Climate change is increasingly becoming a central topic of debate and strategic decision making by Governments and businesses all over the world. The warming of the climate system is unequivocal, as is now evident from observations of increases in global average air and ocean temperature, widespread melting of snow and ice, and rising global mean sea level. It impacts all countries, but is particularly severe for developing countries like India, given their vulnerabilities, inadequate means and limited capacities to adapt to its effects. The present plan of Government of India constitutes one of the strongest responses to global climate change by any developing country. India has already achieved emission intensity reduction by 17.6% between 1990 and 2005. Going forward, given the recent successes of Indian industry in energy efficiency, renewable energy and green buildings and enhanced commitment to address climate change issues, the 20-25% emission intensity reduction goals, set out by the Indian Government, should be achievable. As India reduces emission intensity of its economy by 20-25% by 2020, numerous investment opportunities are likely to emerge in the key sectors. These include (a) Industrial energy efficiency: An investment opportunity of Rs 82575 million exist in industrial energy efficiency leading to annual saving potential of Rs 37510 million (b) Renewable energy: 20,000 MW target of solar energy capacity by 2022 and pipeline of other renewable energy projects such as biomass, wind and small hydro present huge investment opportunity in the sector in coming years (c) Green Buildings: One billion sq. ft. of green buildings is being targeted to be set-up in India by the year 2012, leading to significant investment requirement in the sector and (d) Cleaner Conventional Energy Technologies: Indian Government has set a target of having upto 50% of new thermal power generation capacity based on clean coal technologies. The investment requirement in clean conventional energy technologies is relatively higher, at present.

(iii) **CSR & Community Development:** CII has envisaged a National Movement for Mainstreaming CSR for Sustained Inclusiveness as part of its Social Development Agenda. The CII National Committee on Corporate Social Responsibility & Community Development was constituted in 2001 to make CSR an actionable business agenda. The Committee develops CSR guidelines and promotes the sharing of CSR experiences and best practices. CII also organizes an annual CSR Summit to enable the stakeholders to review and strengthen the CSR Movement. The CII Development Initiatives ensures the continuity of these programmes, particularly with respect to women empowerment, industry-NGO partnership, and persons with disabilities.

(iv) **Disaster Management:** Every year, natural and manmade disasters cause enormous loss of lives and property across the country. CII has sought to involve Indian industry in the implementation of the different schemes under the National Disaster Management Plan. CII also works with various agencies to capacitate different segments of the urban and rural populations to combat and manage major disasters. In line with this, CII conducts training and certification programmes, organizes workshops and conferences, releases publications, resource directories and multimedia kits for mass awareness, and provides relief and rehabilitation support to affected people.

(v) **Education:** CII's Education initiatives are aimed both at School Education and Higher education. The CII Education Council has two Committees – School Education Committee and the Higher Education Committee. CII has

been actively working in the areas of Policy Recommendations on Public-Private-Partnerships in School & Higher Education, Right to Education, Accreditation, Upgradation of School & Higher Education, etc.

(*vi*) **Environment:** India's rapid economic growth in last several years has made us aware of two stark realities: it has lifted millions out of poverty; and that this economic growth has been accompanied by accelerated depletion of natural resources and rapid deterioration in environment quality. Even after six decades of effort to support development and growth, the dimensions of poverty in India is staggering. India is ranked 127th in the Human Development Index. As such poverty and destitution affects the well being of us all. India is not endowed with sufficient natural capital in comparison to the population it supports. Though India is home to 18% of the world's population, it only has 2.4% of the planet's landmass, 4% of the freshwater resources and about a percent of the world's forest. India's ecosystems are already highly degraded. Most Indian rivers have water quality unfit for direct human use. Air quality in Indian cities is degrading despite significant improvements in emissions from vehicles and industries. The country however continues to remain on the threshold of a grave ecological crisis. The current paradigm of rapid economic growth along with the need of conserving the natural and ecological resources, challenges the very foundation of the manner in which business is done today. It challenges the traditional business management theory, which echoes Milton Friedman's famous statement that there is only one responsibility of business: to use its resources and engage in activities designed to increase its profits.' The fact that rapid economic growth is the only realistic means to lift the poor out of extreme poverty and the fact that most economic activities depend on product and services provided by the ecosystems, necessitates the ushering of a new business paradigm which enables rapid economic growth without compromising the capacity of the ecosystem to sustain, nurture and fuel economic development and human well-being. For the business fraternity, this calls for a sustainability approach of doing business, wherein business success is measured not only in terms of its financial bottom line, but also in terms of its performance in social and environmental areas. The integration of triple bottom line in the mainstream business practices is what is often referred as Corporate Sustainability.

(*vii*) **Industry - NGO Partnerships:** CII works to strengthen the relationship between corporates and voluntary organisations. The CII Committee on Industry-NGO Partnerships was constituted in 2007 to identify, document and demonstrate successful partnership models, and to build capacity for sustaining the partnerships. The Committee holds interactive sessions for sharing of knowledge and experiences in building these partnerships. A compendium on successful Industry-NGO partnership models has also been released.

(*viii*) **Public Health:** Health is not only a basic human right, but also a key precondition to economic development. CII has worked to place the issue of public health on every corporate boardroom agenda. The focus of attention is on prevention of communicable diseases, promotion of healthy workplace conditions, raising nutrition levels among women and children, among others. (a) HIV/AIDS Prevention: To prevent the spread of HIV/AIDS and to care for those affected by it, CII has framed an HIV/AIDS code for industry which includes the development of a workplace policy and protocols for care, support and treatment services. This includes training of doctors and paramedics in HIV medicine, setting up of counseling help lines, developing a biometric Health Smart Card, partnerships with international agencies and formation of a Global Business Coalitions for sharing of preventive best practices on HIV/AIDS, TB and Malaria (GFATM). CII has worked to promote public-private partnerships for setting up corporate owned / managed anti-retroviral therapy (ART) centres. The main ones are: ACC at Wadi, Karnataka; Ballarpur Industries at Chandrapur, Maharashtra; Godrej and Boyce Manufacturing at Vikhroli, Mumbai; Bajaj Auto in Pimpri, Pune; Reliance Industries in Patalganga, Maharashtra; and ACC with Christian Medical College (CMC) at Vellore, Tamil Nadu. Further, CII in a joint study with the World Bank Institute has highlighted the capacity of the IT industry to prevent the young and vulnerable populations from contracting HIV/AIDS and in reducing the social stigma attached to the affected people (b) Tuberculosis Control CII in partnership with Revised National TB Control Programme (RNTCP) has facilitated the setting up of DOTS centres in the PPP mode. Companies like Reliance Industries Limited, Jubilant Organosys, L&T, Becton Dickinson, Hindalco, NTPC and others have pro-actively supported this initiative.

(*ix*) **Rural Development:** The CII Development Initiatives has enlisted wide scale industry support to unlock the growth potential of rural India. In creating tangible rural assets for sustainable development, CII has focused attention on improving rural income and employment levels, rural infrastructure development, education and healthcare facilities, and promotion of rural businesses. Rural Business Hubs: CII partners the Ministry of Panchayati Raj, Government of India, in promoting Rural Business Hubs (RBHs) across the country. Within this framework of partnership, initiatives have been taken to link up Indian corporates with different Panchyati Raj Institutions (PRIs) to identify and develop rural business clusters. While this would help the rural businesses to move up the economic value chain, the corporate would discover new markets and sourcing options. Nearly 200 MOUs have already been signed to promote RBHs. Healthy & Educated Villages: CII has sought Indian industry's active engagement for improving rural infrastructure for safe drinking water, sewage and garbage disposal, schools, sanitation, roads, tele-medicine, etc. Major corporates like DSCL, Hero Honda, Bharti Foundation, Sona Group, Luxor, HCL, GHPL, Coca Cola Foundation, and others have come forth to support these initiatives. Seven villages in the states of Rajasthan, Uttar Pradesh, Haryana, and Punjab will receive special attention under this initiative. E-Portal: Knowledge is the true liberator of a developing society. CII is developing an E-Portal that will enable rural businesses to access real time market information for better price realization for their products. The portal will functions like a knowledge bank on rural products and services, build buyer-seller interaction, and facilitate multifold B2B linkages.

(*x*) Skills Development: CII has turned the limelight on skills development across the country to align industry manpower needs with the skilling initiatives underway and improve the employability of the working population including school drop-outs, semi-skilled and un-skilled workers. Due efforts are underway to create a new wave of entrepreneurship in the country that will result in further employment generation. CII has launched its own Skills Development Initiative, which is aligned, to the National Skills Development Agenda to skill 500 million people by 2022. In this endeavour, CII has set up its first skills centre at Chhindwara, MP, to train people in bar bending, grinding, pipe fitting, welding, etc. CII along with HPCL launched the 'Swavalamban' project to train 2,200 youth in multiple trades. The programmes have high local relevancy, in-built flexibility and are modular in form.

(*xi*) Special Abilities: CII takes key initiatives to train and support Persons With Disabilities (PWDs) to help them become productive manpower resources. For this, a National Group on Special Ability was constituted to: Place disability on corporate agenda Explore & promote employment /self-employment opportunities for the target group. Ability Forums/Core Groups have been set up with corporates, NGOs, training institutes, government officials, experts and persons with special abilities. The CII Corporate Code on Disability has been circulated among CII members for adoption. The objective is to ensure 1% of their workforce is drawn from the pool of trained PWDs. CII has recruited people with disabilities as employees. A special job portal called http://www.Employability.co.in has also been launched, and several member companies have registered on the portal as potential recruiters. CII encourages its members to donate financial resources and support infrastructure to NGOs that support the development of PWDs. The team holds sensitization programmes, recruitment drives and skills training programmes, and brings out reports and manuals on the subject.

(*xii*) Women Empowerment: The CII National Committee on Women Empowerment works with industry to strengthen women's role and participation in the economic sphere and community affairs. The focus areas are: Gender equality at workplace; Prevention of sexual harassment at workplace and Women empowerment at the community level. CII has also instituted the annual CII Woman Exemplar Award to honour women who have taken development initiatives against all odds in the fields of education and literacy, health and micro enterprises. The Committee conducts periodic studies and prepares manuals and reports on women empowerment in the workplace, and holds conferences, seminars, workshops and gender sensitization programmes with partner organisations like the United Nations Fund for Women (UNIFEM).

(*xiii*) International Forum: CII international undertakes activities to connect Indian business with global business. Such activities include meeting the Heads of State and Government, decision-makers, networking with counterpart organisations, multilateral and academic institutions and other policy making bodies. The set-up of nine overseas offices helps CII to disseminate vital information related to markets and joint venture possibilities to Indian and foreign companies. International events are organised as a part of its global business networking initiatives. Trade fairs, seminars, overseas missions, and conferences also develop strong contacts. Meetings with visiting Heads of State and Government and high-level ministerial delegations are held for Indian industry regularly. Recently, CII has serviced over 200 business delegations into India, comprising more than 2000 businessmen and has taken 50 Trade Missions out of India. This exchange has resulted in the signing of 71 MoUs. CII's International Department is committed to stepping up its engagement with the world on a wide range of issues that it identifies as being national priorities of corporate India'.

2. Federation of Indian Chamber of Commerce and Industry

The FICCI was established in 1927. It is the largest and oldest apex business organisation in India. Its history is closely interwoven with India's struggle for independence and its subsequent emergence as one of the most rapidly growing economies globally. FICCI plays a leading role in policy debates that are at the forefront of social, economic and political change. Through its 400 professionals, FICCI is active in 39 sectors of the economy. FICCI's stand on policy issues is sought out by think tanks, governments and academia. Its publications are widely read for their in-depth research and policy prescriptions. FICCI has joint business councils with 79 countries around the world.

A non-government, not-for-profit organisation, FICCI is the voice of India's business and industry. FICCI has direct membership from the private as well as public sectors, including SMEs and MNCs, and an indirect membership of over 83,000 companies from regional chambers of commerce. FICCI works closely with the government on policy issues, enhancing efficiency, competitiveness and expanding business opportunities for industry through a range of specialized services and global linkages. It also provides a platform for sector specific consensus building and networking. Partnerships with countries across the world carry forward our initiatives in inclusive development, which encompass health, education, livelihood, governance, skill development, etc. FICCI serves as the first port of call for Indian industry and the international business community.

Global Framework of FICCI

Joint Business Councils (JBCs) are institutional mechanisms between FICCI and counterpart apex Chambers in different countries that facilitate regular business to business interaction on a regular basis. JBC arrangements have been established by FICCI with 79 countries. JBCs also provide a variety of business facilitation services by closely working with Government and business promotion organisations in India and the respective partner countries. JBCs also play host to the high-level Government dignitaries who visit India and help build close working relationships between Governments and business. Major activities of the JBCs include exchange of business delegations and joint task forces that help identify the bilateral business co-operation potential and make suitable policy recommendations to Governments. Joint Business Councils are also often held along with the inter-governmental Joint Commission meetings to facilitate Government and business synergy in promoting business linkages. Specific services rendered by JBCs include assistance for setting up Joint ventures, finding sources of investment and technology and providing a clearing house for business enquiries and information.

Initiatives of the FICCI

The FICCI has taken following major initiatives:

FICCI States Division, headquartered at New Delhi is the nerve centre for initiatives undertaken in various States and has as its agenda, inter-alia, the following activities:

(*i*) Stimulating and strengthening the reform process in the States.

(*ii*) Catalyzing and channelizing investment flows to the State specific thrust sectors.

(*iii*) Facilitating and promoting two - way trade flows in goods and services.

(*iv*) Building and fostering public private partnerships and extending the corporate social responsibility agenda among the corporates.

(*v*) Encourage and help Indian enterprises to globalize.

(*vi*) Providing Value Added Services like energy audit, environment audit, water management, B2B meetings, information services etc to enterprises in various States.

These activities are coordinated through FICCI's Regional and State offices at Jaipur, Kolkata, Hyderabad, Chennai, Bangalore, Mumbai and Ahmedabad and FICCI's specialized divisions based at New Delhi.

Membership

As a member of FICCI, members can access a world of opportunities, form networking with the corporate majors of Indian and global industry to assisting in framing economic and industrial policies, through close linkage with the government. FICCI's proactive approach focuses on helping you increase efficiency and competitiveness.

(*a*) Networking

(*i*) Platform to interact with other members, institutions, state & central governments.

(*ii*) Fora to meet global business and political leaders.

(*iii*) Participation in topical seminars, training programmes, conferences and meeting.

(*b*) Policy Work

(i) Participation in different National Policy Committees & Task Forces.

(ii) Expert advice on government legislations, regulations, etc.

(iii) Representations to central & state governments and other institutions.

(iv) Provides information on export and import.

(v) Provides information for technology collaboration and investment.

(vi) Undertakes research studies.

(c) Business Services

(i) Participation in trade fairs & exhibitions.

(ii) Develop business through buyer – seller Fora.

(d) Information Dissemination

(i) Access to publications and reports on a wide range of subjects.

(ii) Directory of Members with company profile.

(iii) Free distribution of Business Digest, A Monthly update on Business News.

(iv) FICCI Awards for companies and institutions and also Individual Awards for Scientist/Technologist.

(v) Regional/State/Zonal and foreign offices providing assistance at all levels.

(e) **Web Services:** Information on important events organized BY FICCI and other activities, press releases, membership etc.

Allied Organisations

Allied organisations attached with the FICCI are as follows:

1. All India Organisation of Employers (AIOE): All India Organisation of Employers, an allied body of FICCI has been serving the cause of Indian enterprises by promoting orderly development of sound industrial relations and promoting better understanding between employers and workers on the mutuality of interests and AIOE had celebrated its Golden Jubilee in 1983.

2. All India Shippers Council (AISC) : As the principal spokesman of shippers, and the chief negotiator of freight rates and related issues of all India character, the AISC is committed to spearhead the cause of the shippers primarily. Among the specific objectives of the Council, as enshrined in its Constitution like to organise consultations between shippers and ship owners/conference lines, port authorities, and Government on matters of common interest; to bring together representative of various shippers associations, trade and industrial associations/ organizations, for consideration and discussion of the problems affecting shippers in India; to represent the views of shippers in regard to the structure of freight rates, availability and adequacy of shipping space, frequency of sailings, terms of shipment, port charges, port facilities, etc.

3. Confederation of Indian Food Trade and Industry (CIFTI): The Confederation of Indian Food Trade & Industry (CIFTI), is the apex body for the food industry in India. Managed by professionals, CIFTI has in-house R&D facility, a laboratory, strong database with which it provides consultancy services.

4. FICCI Alliance for Consumer Care (FACC): FACC, has been set up with support from Department of Consumer Affairs, Government of India. FACC is a unique body in the Public-Private Partnership (PPP) mode. It's mission: Promoting 'Responsible Businesses for Consumer Satisfaction'.

5. FICCI Arbitration and Conciliation Tribunal (FACT): FACT, is a specialized body which provides arbitration/ conciliation and mediation for settlement of domestic and international commercial disputes.

6. FICCI Institute of Intellectual Property Development: The FICCI Institute of Intellectual Property Development undertakes research in IPR issues and promotes knowledge of Intellectual Property Laws of India as well as Intellectual Property Systems of other countries. The institute regularly collaborates with international organizations like the WIPO to facilitate discussions on topical issues.

7. FICCI Ladies Organisation: The primary objective of FLO is to promote entrepreneurship and professional excellence in women. FLO endeavors to enhance the various skills of women through its educational and vocational training programmes, talks, seminars, panel discussion and workshop on a wide range of subjects like information technology, taxation, insurance, venture capital, stock market operations, accountancy, marketing, mutual funds, investment planning, entrepreneurship development programmes etc. We also focus on women related legal and social issues like uniform civil code, domestic violence, etc.

8. FICCI Quality Forum: For enhancement of value to the customer, continuous quality improvement and cost reduction have become essential for any growth-oriented organization. But quality cannot happen by itself, it has to be planned, implemented and managed in a scientific way through a Quality Management System. To make quality happen every employee of the organization requires appropriate knowledge, right skills and positive attitude to perform his/her function.

9. Food Research & Analysis Centre (FRAC): The Food Research & Analysis Centre (FRAC), is an independent food analytical, research and development centre. FRAC ensures sample integrity and authenticity of analysis. It also assists in advising on improvement in quality and safety of food to meet the requirements of domestic and export markets.

10. Indian Council of Arbitration (ICA) : Indian Council of Arbitration (ICA) was established in 1965 to initiate and popularize arbitration in India. ICA is South Asia's premier arbitral institution and is extremely well respected in the circles of judiciary, executive and legislature within India as well as in the fraternity of Arbitral institutions abroad. ICA not only administers arbitration but has also contributed to the development of law and practice of arbitration both nationally and internationally.

11. International Chambers of Commerce (ICC India) : ICC India is one of the most active chapters of the ICC, the world's apex business organisation. In its fold, it has a large membership of corporates, chambers of commerce, trade & industry associations, consultancy organisations. etc. The International linkages of ICC INDIA are far and wide. The ICC network speaks, directly and indirectly, for thousands of individual corporations and industrial and trade associations in over 140 countries. In line with its objectives of promoting liberlisation in the country, accelerating flow of foreign investment and lowering tariff barriers to promote international trade, ICC has been playing a crucial role of interacting with government & business on economic policies. As the process of economic reforms is gaining ground, it is emerging as a rallying point for Indian business in their effort towards globalisation.

12. Socio - Economic Development Foundation (SEDF): FICCI promotes the spirit of enterprise that will make India a globally competitive and socially responsible economy. With this vision, FICCI set up the Socio Economic Development Foundation (FICCI-SEDF) in 1995 to provide an institutional base to the social sector activities of the corporate sector and to promote Corporate Social Responsibility (CSR) amongst Indian companies. Under the able leadership of Mr P M Sinha, former President, Pepsi Cola International for South Asia, FICCI-SEDF is playing a pivotal role in promoting CSR in India and mobilizing corporate support for critical areas like public health, employment of persons with disabilities, support to disabled soldiers & war widows etc. Website: www.ficci-sedf.org

FICCI Forums

Sector Specific Forums of FICCI are as follows:

(*i*) FICCI Boating Forum
(*ii*) FICCI Forum on Medical Device
(*iii*) FICCI Forum on Medical Electronics
(*iv*) FICCI Lifestyle Forum
(*v*) FICCI Habitat Business Forum
(*vi*) FICCI Skill Development Forum
(*vii*) FICCI Trade Facilitation Forum
(*vii*) FICCI Young Leaders Forum

Forum of Parliamentarians

(*i*) India-U.S.
(*ii*) Indo-British
(*iii*) Indo-German
(*iv*) India-Singapore
(*v*) India-European Union
(*vi*) India-Japan
(*vii*) India-Pakistan
(*viii*) India-China

(ix) India-Italy
(x) India-Russia
(xi) India-CIS
(xii) India-Israel

International

(i) Indo-Arab Economic Forum

3. Assocham

The Associated Chambers of Commerce and Industry of India (ASSOCHAM), India's premier apex chamber covers a membership of over 2 lakh companies and professionals across the country. It is generally called as the knowledge architect of corporate India. It was established in 1920 by promoter chambers, representing all regions of India. "The term Chamber of Commerce is understood to mean a voluntary and cooperative organisation of business community established to promote commercial, industrial and civic interests.

History of ASSOCHAM

Chronicling evolution of the chamber posits the advantage of stating at the outset, the schematic unfolding of the tapestry of events that eventually concluded in contrasting interests federating into a coalition of mercantile consolidation.

Against this backdrop, the birth of the Associated Chambers of Commerce of India and Ceylon in 1920 was more than an event - it marked the culmination of a historical process reflecting an age of tumultuous change, a logical, sequential development of the coming together of associations primarily representative of British commercial interests in different parts of the country. While the seed of such a formalised structure was evidently sown by the Calcutta Trades Association, as British trading interests tried to weave themselves into a body, on the lines of the more sophisticated business chambers back home, the Bengal Chamber of Commerce, duly supported by Madras and Bombay chambers, was the prime moving force in the establishment of first-ever apex chamber in India.

The industrialization pattern then obtaining under the British largely influenced the need for collective protection of local business interests along with the mounting inevitability of restructuring neglected sectors and concurrently promoting entrepreneurship. The Chamber movement mirrors a paradox where British manufacturers saw in India a captive market for their goods but the British Indian manufacturers found such move emaciating their growth. Calcutta being the seat of government from where functioned the Legislative Council conferred on Bengal Chamber legitimate proximity gains for interface and enunciation of its needs. Expansion of the representative character of the Council by the new law, that amended the Indian Councils Act in 1909, prompted the Bombay and Bengal Chambers to seek allotment of representative membership in the Council.

The parallel growth of industries had a direct deportment on the chambers. The indigo, tea, jute, cotton textile industry, coal, thermal power generation and the growth of engineering units with British and Indian interests defined the expansion of converging interests. The partition of Bengal in the year 1905 not only gently catalyzed emergence of a cohesive political opposition but also lent the first impetus to conceiving an all-India entity when the captains of industry from the provinces, Ceylon and Burma discussed the necessity of national bonding. Twelve years later, at another such gathering again in Calcutta, in the wake of post-war scenario, the inspiration for a national business organisation was cemented specifically in response to the integration of economic policy into an all-India pattern, an enlarging corpus of legislation, the rapid growth of Indian business, a sharper spirit of trade rivalry, as well as the mobilization of important Indian industrial financial support for political purposes. The idea of an all-India organisation was certainly prompted by the lessons of the war but the transfer of capital to New Delhi in 1911 circumscribed the possibility to continue to profitably lobby with the Government primarily on the Bengal Chamber's strength.

ASSOCHAM's maiden conference opened at the Royal Exchange, Calcutta, on Thursday, January 8, 1920, at three in the afternoon. Lord Chelmsford inaugurated it with the Governor of Bengal, the Earl of Ronaldshay anon, in the presence of the commercial and official elite. ASSOCHAM was more than a chamber for its members; it served as stimulant to other business groups to close ranks. Primarily, it inspired the "Indian" sector, which looked at ASSOCHAM as an example of British business interests lobbying on a national scale and creating the wherewithal for smooth progress.

Association of Chambers of Commerce of India and Ceylon started with 13 Chambers as its original members. These were Bengal Chamber of Commerce, Bombay Chamber of Commerce, Burma Chamber of Commerce, Ceylon Chamber of Commerce, Chittagong Chamber of Commerce, Cochin Chamber of Commerce, Cocanada Chamber of Commerce, Karachi Chamber of Commerce, Madras Chamber of Commerce, Narayangang Chamber of Commerce, Punjab Chamber of Commerce, Tuticorin Chamber of Commerce and Upper India Chamber of Commerce. PHD Chamber of Commerce Industry (PHDCCI), working since 1905, joined ASSOCHAM as its promoter chamber in the year 1922. The Indian Merchants' Chamber, Bombay, then in its eightieth year, joined ASSOCHAM as one of its promoter chambers in 1987. In the same year, the new articles of the Association for ASSOCHAM were worked out and the membership structure of the Chamber was categorized into Promoter Chambers, Patron Members, Ordinary Members and Corporate Associates. For the first time ASSOCHAM also opened itself up for overseas membership. Besides, the managing committee reconstituted to have a President, Senior Vice President, and Vice President and three deputy Presidents, to be advised by forty-member apex advisory body. Not only large industry and trade but also small and medium industrial enterprises, engaged in agriculture and transport, as well as professional bodies and several new industry associations entered ASSOCHAM's fold.

Promoter Chambers

Promoter Chambers of Association are as follow:

(*i*) Bombay Chamber of Commerce and Industry, Mumbai

(*ii*) Cochin Chamber of Commerce and Industry, Cochin

(*iii*) Indian Merchants Chamber, Mumbai

(*iv*) The Madras Chamber of Commerce and Industry

(*v*) RHD Chamber of Commerce and Industry

As an apex industry body, ASSOCHAM represents the interests of industry and trade, interfaces with Government on policy issues and interacts with counterpart international organizations to promote bilateral economic issues. ASSOCHAM is represented on all national and local bodies and is, thus, able to pro-actively convey industry viewpoints, as also communicate and debate issues relating to public-private partnerships for economic development.

ASSOCHAM represents the interests of more than 3,00,000 direct and indirect members. Through its heterogeneous membership, ASSOCHAM combines the entrepreneurial spirit and business acumen of owners with management skills and expertise of professionals to set itself apart as a Chamber with a difference. Currently, ASSOCHAM has 60 Expert Committees covering the entire gamut of economic activity in India. It has been especially acknowledged as a significant voice of Indian industry in the field of Information Technology, Biotechnology, Telecom, Banking & Finance, Company Law, Corporate Finance, Economic and International Affairs, Tourism, Civil Aviation, Corporate Governance, Infrastructure, Energy & Power, Education, Legal Reforms, Real Estate & Rural Development etc.

ASSOCHAM members represent the following sectors:

(*i*) Trade (National and International)

(*ii*) Industry (Domestic and International)

(*iii*) Professionals (e.g. CAs, lawyers, consultants)

(*iv*) Trade and Industry Associations and other Chambers of Commerce

Evolution of Value Creator

ASSOCHAM initiated its endeavour of value creation for Indian industry in 1920. Having in its fold more than 300 Chambers and Trade Associations, and serving more than 2 lakh members from all over India. It has witnessed upswings as well as upheavals of Indian Economy, and contributed significantly by playing a catalytic role in shaping up the Trade, Commerce and Industrial environment of the country. Today, ASSOCHAM has emerged as the fountainhead of Knowledge for Indian industry, which is all set to redefine the dynamics of growth and development in the technology driven cyber age of 'Knowledge Based Economy'. ASSOCHAM derives its strength from its Promoter Chambers and other Industry/Regional Chambers/Associations spread all over the country.

Vision

Empower Indian enterprise by inculcating knowledge that will be the catalyst of growth in the barrier less technology driven global market and help them upscale, align and emerge as formidable player in respective business segments.

Mission

As a representative organ of Corporate India, ASSOCHAM articulates the genuine, legitimate needs and interests of its members. Its mission is to impact the policy and legislative environment so as to foster balanced economic, industrial and social development. We believe education, IT, BT, Health, Corporate Social responsibility and environment to be the critical success factors.

Structure of ASSOCHAM

Membership Structure

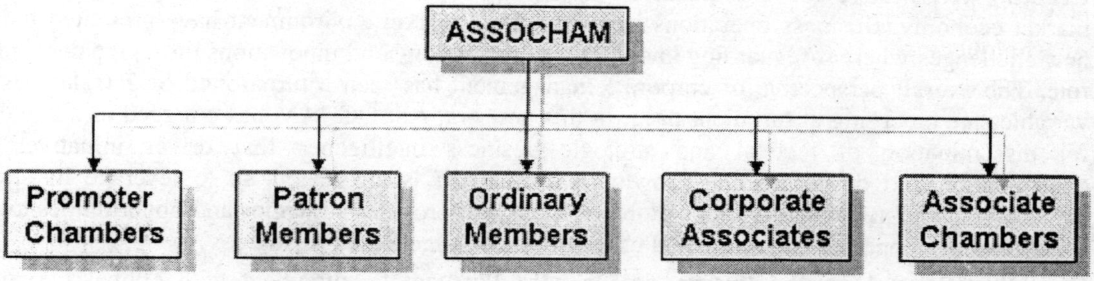

Executive Committee Structure

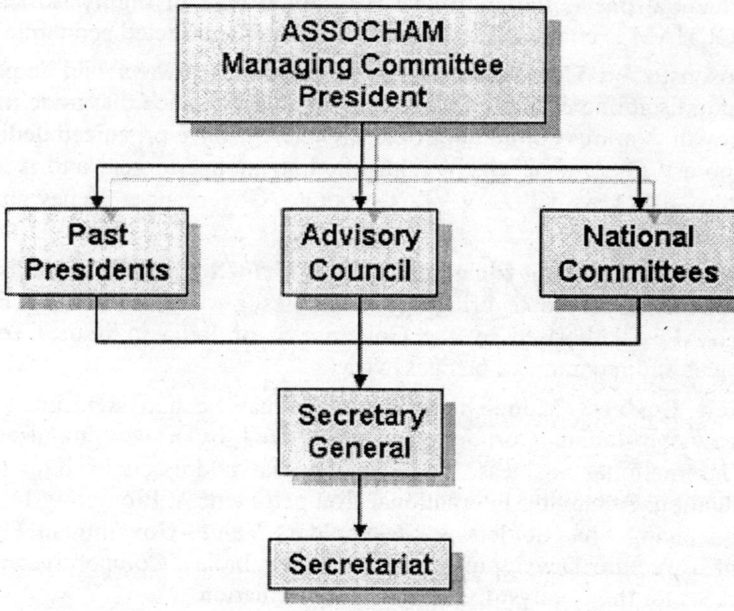

ASSOCHAM provides services in :

(i) BPO Initiatives

(ii) TQM Division

(iii) Biotechnology

Policies of ASSOCHAM

As Stated in ASSOCHAM mission statement, "mission is to impact the policy and legislative environment so as to foster balanced economic, industrial and social development." As such key objectives at ASSOCHAM is to help formulate policy decisions for creating a healthy environment for trade and industry in India.

Towards attaining this objective ASSOCHAM :

(*i*) Have active representation in most Government Advisory Committees

(*ii*) Keep organising Seminars, Workshops, Round Table meetings

(*iii*) Submit representations/memoranda

(*iv*) Bring out publications, periodicals and discussion papers.

Functions of ASSOCHAM

Main functions of ASSOCHAM are as follows:

(*i*) **Creating Knowledge for Competitive Advantage:** 21st century has aligned Indian industry to global market economy. Business operations in international market environment have presented Indian industry new challenges where safeguarding knowledge of technology and innovations through patents play a pivotal role. The overall perspective of corporate management has seen a turnaround of 360 degrees where new variables are emerging at turbulent pace. In this new era, ASSOCHAM has emerged as a key differentiator for dissemination of tactical and strategic business intelligence that drives initiatives for market consolidation and developmental growth. ASSOCHAM is all geared up to leverage its strength of its exhaustive understanding of various global markets and provides strategies and opportunities to its members for overall development and optimized usage of 'Knowledge Based Resources'.

(*ii*) **Providing Road Map for Pragmatic Growth:** Pursuant to alignment with Global Economy, various spheres of Indian economy have attained a visible growth, consistency and have catapulted it to the position of fastest growing economy in the world. A number of geo-political factors are responsible for this growth, but the most influential one is the enormous HR capital base of highly skilled managerial and technical manpower. ASSOCHAM is committed to help accomplish the targeted economic growth.

(*iii*) **Generating Consensus on Core Issues:** ASSOCHAM has always laid impetus on building a "broad consensus on fiscal discipline & prudence" leading to an acceptance that trade in global matrix is beneficial for economy's growth. Various committees of ASSOCHAM have organized dedicated sessions on emerging areas of contemporary importance viz. Wealth Maximization, Mergers and Acquisitions, Nanotechnology and Biotechnology, BPO & KPO, VAT, Corporate Governance, Renewable Energy, Public Private Partnership etc.

(*iv*) **Specialised Services - Nurturing Ideas to Catalyze Growth:** ASSOCHAM is always a front runner and has been very actively involved in bringing out studies, surveys and research papers on current topical issues. ASSOCHAM is authorised by the Government of India to issue Certificates of Origin, Certify commercial invoices and recommend business visa.

(*v*) **Insight into 'New Business Models':** ASSOCHAM has been a significant contributory factor in the emergence of new-age Indian Corporates, characterized by a new mindset and global ambition for dominating the international business. The Chamber has addressed itself to the key areas like India as Investment Destination, Achieving International Competitiveness, Promoting International Trade, Corporate Strategies for Enhancing Shareholders & Stakeholders Value, Government Policies in sustaining India's Development, Infrastructure Development for enhancing India's Competitiveness, Building Indian MNCs, Role of Financial Sector the Catalyst for India's Transformation.

(*vi*) **Looking Ahead:** Over the years, ASSOCHAM has transformed itself from a reactive, representation-forwarding organisation to a forceful, proactive, forward-looking institution equipping itself to meet the aspirations of corporate India in the new world of business. Today, there is need for greater involvement of business and industry with the Government in international fora on issues such as intellectual property rights, environmental safeguards, anti-dumping and quality standards etc. The concept of industry-government partnership has therefore assumed vital importance and has to be carefully fostered to speed up the economic and industrial development of the nation. ASSOCHAM is working towards creating a conducive environment for Indian business to compete globally. The Chamber is being re-engineered to shoulder the responsibility of serving its constituents even more effectively and its expertise of professional to set itself apart as a Chamber with a difference.

(*vii*) **ASSOCHAM International:** It has especially focused on Afro-Arab region to assist Indian SME's to expand share of their global market. Successful Indian Trade Fairs in Sudan, Sharjah and Yemen received wide appreciation, more are being planned. Huge trade delegations to Brazil, US, UK, West Africa, China, Pakistan, opening overseas offices in Sharjah, Moscow, China, MOU partnership with business Chambers in more than 45 countries, bringing out Economic and Trade bulletins on Africa and Arab region are only few of constantly expanding of ASSOCHAM.

4. All India Association of Industries (AIAI)

All India Association of Industries (AIAI) is an apex industry association established in the year 1956 by a team of dedicated business persons with the primary task of fostering sustained industrial development in the country. Since its inception, AIAI's primary goal has been to serve the many needs of India's industrial and business communities. It provides an effective platform to address the issues relating to trade and industry to the Government both at Central and State levels. It also helps the Indian industries in meeting the challenge of liberalisation and globalisation by providing a vital link to explore the world of new opportunities. The opening up of the economy has resulted in the entry of a large number of foreign competitors and an increased global focus of domestic industry resulting into dynamic growth and greater competitiveness of corporate India. Thus, AIAI's chief mission is to foster a free, healthy and competitive business environment in India. The opening up the economy has resulted in the entry of a large number of foreign competitors and an increased global focus of domestic industry, resulting into dynamic growth and greater competitiveness of corporate India. Thus, AIAI's chief mission is to foster a free, healthy and competitive business environment in India.

AIAI has set up specific Councils to understand the impact of globalization & liberalization on respective sector/segment of industry and make valuable suggestions to the concerned authorities. These include:

(*i*) Housing / Constructions Council

(*ii*) Environment & Beautification Council

(*iii*) International Trade Promotion Council

(*iv*) Entertainment Council

(*v*) Women Entrepreneur Council

(*vi*) Banking, Finance & Insurance Council

(*vii*) Capital Market Council

(*viii*) Direct Tax Council

(*ix*) Indirect Tax Council

Information Technology Council AIAI is benefited by its affiliation with UNIDO and UNCTAD.

Activities of AIAI

Major Activities of AIAI are as follows:

(*i*) **Promotion of industries:** AIAI actively promotes and fosters interests of industrial and business houses through seminars and workshops at the state and national levels. These events are aimed at promoting trade, investment, technological advancement, manpower development and business opportunities in India. Through these events, it addresses problems pertaining to industry and trade on specific subjects. It represents & constantly endeavors to promote large, medium and small-scale industries involved in almost all major manufacturing fields including engineering, cotton, textiles, rayon, chemicals, pharmaceuticals, metals, rubber, sugar, plastics, paper and many other sectors.

It successfully organized the XIth International Conference on Small and Medium Enterprises in Mumbai, which was inaugurated by the Maharashtra Governor, Dr. P.C. Alexander. Over 300 delegates from over 36 countries attended the conference, in addition to a 50-member delegation from Pakistan. The Pakistani delegation comprised women entrepreneurs who exhibited their wares, namely textiles, leather, stone work, etc. H.E. Mr. Fiorenzo Stolfi, Minister for Industry, Post and Telecommunication, San Marino and H.E. Mr. Brooke Debebe, Vice Minister for the Ministry of Trade and Industry, Ethiopia participated in the conference in addition to senior government officials.

Other seminars organized by the AIAI include:

(*i*) Capital market reform, inaugurated by Shri Yashwant Sinha, honourable Minister for Finance. The next capital market reforms seminars is scheduled to be held in December.

(*ii*) Economic reforms addressed by Dr. Bimal Jain, Governor of RBI & Dr. D.R. Mehta, Chairman, SEBI.

(*iii*) Power Sector reforms inaugurated by Mr. Rangarajan Kumarmangalam.

***(ii)* Providing Representation:** AIAI further represents the industry's views and influences and sensitizes the government machinery on policies and legislation, which affect industry and trade. This is achieved by representing members on the various high-powered government advisory boards and committees. The association seeks the views of its members on issues that affect industry and trade through its various committees and study groups involving members of different industries. Representatives chosen from its members are invited to sit on various important policy advisory boards and expert committees of the capital market, textile, software, direct taxes, indirect taxes, pharmaceuticals, banking and finance, small - scale industries exports and infrastructure. The AIAI has representation on Reserve Bank of India and several other advisory committees of the State and Central Government. The association has direct membership of over 1200 members and over 60 affiliated industrial associations with indirect membership of over 25,000 members from large, medium and small scale sectors as well as export houses and star export houses. The association organizes Open House Meetings of Commissioners of Sales Tax, Income Tax, Octroi & other officials with its members to amicably settle this problem.

***(iii)* Trade Fairs:** AIAI has organized a number of successful trade fairs, which have been patronized by leading companies. These include industrial exhibitions as well as exhibitions in the field of finance and investment, automobile and three-wheelers, India fair etc. AIAI has hosted its annual "Global India Conference on Trade and Investment" for the fourth year in succession. The annual conference is a major event. It has been addressed by the Prime Minister, Finance Minister and other Union Ministers, Governors and Chief Ministers of various States and other international dignitaries. The main objective of the conference is to focus on economic reforms successfully implemented by India and challenging changes in the international trade arena. This conference provides Indian trading houses, businesspersons and overseas investors a platform for better appreciation and understanding of such changes to operate effectively in international markets and fully share India's growth potential.

***(iv)* Overseas Activities:** AIAI acts as a bridge between its members and overseas business communities to promote bilateral trade by organizing activities to promote trade, investment, technology-transfer and manpower training The association endeavors to promote bilateral trade and in order to facilitate the goal regularly organizes one to one business meetings with various foreign dignitaries and delegations from abroad. It has till date signed over 36 Memorandum of Understanding (MOUs) with various International Chambers of Commerce. Some of the recent delegations have been from USA, Czech Republic, Poland, Russia, Mauritius, Madagascar, Baharain & others. A book, titled 'WTO, Impact on Indian Business' encompassing the entire gamut of the emerging New World trading order has been published by AIAI's. Chapters address key issues like implementation of the WTO agreement, trade-related aspects of intellectual property, WTO and the competition policy and new millennium implications.

***(v)* Members of Government Bodies:** AIAI has its representation on the following:

(i) Central Council of Excise and Customs

(ii) Finance Ministry's Pre Budget Meeting

(iii) All India Export Advisory Committee, RBI

(iv) Small Scale Industry Board, Government of India

(v) Industry Advisory Committee, Government of Maharashtra

(vi) Small Scale Industry Upgradation and Technology Committee, Government of India

(vii) National Advisory Board of Small Scale Industries Development Bank India (SIDBI)

(viii) Standing Committee on Exchange Control, RBI

(ix) Grievance Committee, Jawaharlal Nehru Port Trust

(x) High Power Consultative Committee on Power Reforms, Ministry of Power

(xi) Standing Committee on Small Scale Industry, RBI

(xii) Labour Advisory Committee, Government of Maharashtra

(xiii) All Regional Advisory Committee, Central Excise & Customs-Mumbai

(xiv) National Steel Consumers Council, Government of India

(xv) Export Promotion Committee, Ministry of External Affairs

5. Standing Conference on Public Enterprises (SCOPE)

A Society "New Horizon" was established in New Delhi, India on September 29, 1970 for promoting better understanding among the public about the individual and collective contribution of the public sector in building the industrial base of the country. Within a short span of three years, the founding fathers visualized a greater role for this Society and converted it into an apex body for all Central Public Sector Enterprises. SCOPE thus came into being on April 10, 1973. It was formally recognized by the Government of India on 8th November 1976 by a decision of Union Cabinet.

Vision

The vision of the SCOPE is "To enable its member enterprises to be globally competitive in a market driven environment".

Mission

Role of SCOPE

Role of SCOPE are as follows:

(i) **Enhancing** standards of Corporate Governance and Corporate Social Responsibility in PSEs to the best prevalent practices in the world.

(ii) **Sharing** knowledge with international bodies like OECD, ILO etc. to benchmark standards of governance. Also organizing interaction between international/ government delegations and PSEs.

(iii) **Developing** effective leaders to meet ever increasing requirement of public enterprises.

(iv) **Interfacing** with the government, regulatory bodies and policy makers for creating favourable policies and a regulatory framework to safeguard the interests of public enterprises and improve their competitiveness.

(v) **Networking** with professional institutes of repute to identify and organize programmes of high quality on topical issues.

(vi) **Recognizing** significant achievements of public enterprises in various fields, leading to business excellence and competitive advantage; motivating them to achieve higher goals of excellence; and, rewarding those who have demonstrated extraordinary skills and have made a mark in chosen field.

(vii) **Representing** as the Employers' Organizations of Indian Public Enterprises at National and International fora in order to make them better place to work.

(viii) **Showcasing** performance, contribution and achievements of PSEs in order to improve their image.

(ix) **Empowering** women employees of PSEs and creating gender sensitivity among employees.

Activities of SCOPE

Consultative Management : SCOPE performs a consultative and interactive role between the enterprises and various Ministries/Departments of the government. It encourages and generates the atmosphere of collective endeavour for public enterprises. It works with the member enterprises, governments, international organizations and NGOs to help, enhance efficiency in member enterprises. Its mandate includes promoting debate with top management and key decision-makers to develop strategies for improving performance and developing a competitive edge. SCOPE organizes interactions/discussion meetings with eminent personalities and interest groups to evolve a view and suggest new policy initiatives. It also organizes numerous seminars, workshops, training programmes and conferences to bring under sharp focus economic and management issues and for training the managers of the enterprises to compete in increasingly competitive business environment.

Objectives of SCOPE

The charter of 'SCOPE' formally was drawn up in 1970 and revised in 1980. It stated that among the major objectives are 'to initiate sponsor and undertake research project, promote better understanding of the role and performance of the public sector and stimulate and encourage and provide knowledge on it in India and abroad.'

It has also been stated that the 'SCOPE' looks upon its tasks as both internal and external to the PEs. Internally, it would endeavor to assist the PEs in such ways as would improve its total boundary role in conveying such information and advice to the community and the government as would generally help the public sector in its role.

Functions of SCOPE

The following are the main functions of SCOPE:

1. It functions as a consultative body. It interacts with the government on one hand and with PSEs with the other.
2. It creates an atmosphere of collective endavour for public enterprises to achieve national goals set public sector. It organizes seminars, meetings conferences to bring under sharp focus the problems and issues pertaining to public enterprises.
3. It functions as an employer's organization and is recognized as such by Government of India and ILO. SCOPE is the only public sector employers organization which was admitted as a full member of international organization of Employers, Geneva.
4. It publishes authentic literature on management disciplines and functioning of PSUs. It regularly brings out a monthly Kaleidoscope.
5. It is represented on various government bodies including Ministry, Labour's Tripartite Committees, Central Advisory Council of Trade and Industry and Employers Provident Fund Board.

Membership of SCOPE

All the central government PEs may become the member of the SCOPE. The membership is also open to the nationalized banks and state government enterprises. But the state government enterprises may be admitted to the membership of SCOPE only with the prior approval of its executive board. At present the membership stand at 137 PEs including a few nationalized commercial banks and state government enterprises.

In this regard, it is notable that efforts are being made to organize state government enterprises due to their growing size and numbers into a similar organisation at the state level which could be affiliated to the SCOPE. To encourage this idea, the state government enterprises in Andhra Pradesh have already established the 'State Conference of Public Enterprises – AP' which has since been affiliated to scope.

Financial Resources

The main source of finance for SCOPE is the annual subscription of member companies. The annual subscription for membership is Rs. 5,000 and entrance fees of Rs. 10,000. Besides this, consulting fees have also become the source of revenue of SCOPE in recent years.

Management

As far as the policy decisions are concerned, the governing authority is the supreme authority of the SCOPE. The chief executive of the member enterprises are represented in the governing council. The Governing Council holds its meeting once or twice a year to lay down basic framework of policies of SCOPE. The members of the Governing Council elect the members of the executive board and its Chairman and Vice-chairman for term of two years. In the executive board, there are 25 members including Chairman, Vice-chairman and Director General of the BPE besides three co-opted members, who are experts from the field of administration, management and education.

Operational Areas

The following are main activities of SCOPE:

1. Consultative Management: The SCOPE is responsible to provide consultancy facilities to the Government of India, member companies and other enterprises as the case may be. The Government of India refers to the Executive Board of SCOPE all major policy matters for the purpose of seeking the views of PEs before the formulation of policies, The executive board after the careful deliberations tenders its advice to the government of India. Member companies may also refer their problems to the executive board of SCOPE. In order to have the collective advice on the matters. Similarly, joint sector enterprises , ancillary units and other groups of enterprises may also seek advice for their problems. In this connection, it is notable that SCOPE Executive Board is progressively becoming a lively force and forum for the exchange of experience and other consultative opinion.

The SCOPE has constituted various study groups to examine and access in detail various problems of PEs. It included finance, human resource development, marketing, production accounting, management information system and many other areas of management for the purpose of studying the practices, identifying the problems, evaluating the variables and suggesting the ways and means for the purpose of promotion of effective management techniques in PEs. The inter-corporate study of management practices in efficiently managed companies renders valuable guidance to other PEs and joint sector units.

2. Co-ordination: The SCOPE has also been responsible for the co-ordination of common programmes and activities of PEs if there is need for such co-ordination. In this connection, mention may be made for the co-ordinating role played by the SCOPE in the participation of PEs in "Asia-72". The SCOPE has also taken active part in organizing sports and welfare programmes.

3. Construction Work: The SCOPE is also responsible for the supervision of construction of building complexes for PEs wherever such a supervision is sought for. Recently, SCOPE undertook the construction of a multi-storied building complex at Lodhi Road, New Delhi, with a management committee representing the participating companies with the secretary general, Waris R. Kidwai as an ex-officio member secretary of the committee and R.C. Dutt as Honorary Part-time Chairman. Recently, Rs. 70 crores for Yamuna complex is also assigned to SCOPE.

4. Information and Research Work: With the help of BPE, the scope has started publications to throw light on the role and achievement of PEs. These publications include public enterprises in India-A Perspective View, written by P.J. Fernandes, Industrial Relations in Public Enterprises, the Directory of Key Personnel in Public Enterprises and who is who. It has also stared the publication of 'Public Enterprises Review' for distribution among PEs. The quarterly journal, State Enterprises, has already achieved the distinction for its contents which is also brought out by the SCOPE on quarterly basis.

5. Study Circle: SCOPE occasionally organizes the meetings and conferences in which PEs are participating to a large extent. The main purpose of these meetings and conferences is to educate the public in general and PEs in particular and to share each other's experiences on matters of burning problems.

6. It is member of Indian Employers Association. It is also member of International Employer's Organisation. It represents international employers in the meetings of International Labour Organisations.

7. It has fraternal linkages with nationalized industries Britain, International Centre for Public Enterprises, Yugoslavia, Centre for Public Enterprises, Brussels, Standing Committee for Public Enterprise, Tanzania, British Council and the University of Leeds.

8. It promotes economic researches in the field of economic collaboration, technology transfer, tenure of chief executives, parliamentary control, evaluation of comparative profitability of public and private enterprises etc.

9. The SCOPE participates in international business meetings of Indo-Korea trade council, Confederation of Asian Chamber of Commerce and Industries, Korea, Indo-American Trade Council, Indo Arab Trade Council etc.

10. The government has nominated SCOPE in Central Advisory Council for Trade, Central Advisory Council for Industry Employees, State Insurance Corporation, Employees Provident Fund Corporation, Management Council of National Productivity Council, Executive Board of Administrative Staff College of India etc.

Role of SCOPE in New Environment

"In recent years, the scope has been trying to adjust itself with the changing environment of public enterprises in India. In this context, the SCOPE in considering allowing privatized PEs to remain members even after disinvestment. As part of its restructuring and refocusing plan in the post liberalization and post divestment scenario, the organisation is also pushing for the closure of unviable PEs. Restructuring of viable ones and rationalization of labour laws to allow government owned companies to hire and fire."[2] However, the SCOPE is in the process of restructuring its articles of association to allow privatized companies to remain members. According to D.K. Verma, Chairman of SCOPE, a number of PEs are members of industry organizations like the Confederation of Indian Industry (CII), so there is no reason why privatized companies can't be member of SCOPE.

The SCOPE has new role to play in the changed scenario-post liberalization, the role of PEs will also change while the role of some PEs like the trading companies will decline, enterprises in other areas, like manufacturing, services and infrastructure will have larger role to play in the new environment. Given the way the government is executing the privatization programme, it would be better to think that there will no drastic change in number of PEs in near future. While the government has managed to privatized only two companies within the last two years, the total number of PEs has gone up rather than come down. The SCOPE is also mooting the creation of fund for the revival of PEs which can be restructured. The reason revival packages have failed in the past is that the money was put into companies which unviable. Besides, it would be better to advocate the closure of unavailable units, the decision to close units should be commercial not a political decision.

A number of companies which the government took over, were unviable to start with. These benefits will not benefit by fund infusion and should be closed down in the first phase. On disinvestment, however the SCOPE is of the opinion that the Government needs to take another look at its policies. For instance, as valuation, there is need to develop a consensus and get the approval of the policy makers for the methodologies to be used. The government do not seem serious about disinvestment.

Scope Centre for Development

Scope has set up a Centre for Development to help enterprises develop strategic direction and capabilities to meet rising expectations from diverse stakeholders; to facilitate and provide a range of management services to the enterprises to enable them acquire and sustain a vast portfolio of skills in effectively managing business in a competitive and global environment; and, to act as nodal point for sharing and disseminating learning for enterprises excellence. To meet these objectives, the Centre undertake studies, research, preparation of status papers, survey on selective basis by engaging appropriate institutions/individuals, in order to provide necessary inputs for creating awareness and influencing policy formulation. It identifies the needs and organizes high quality programmes /conferences/seminars/ workshop etc in order to spread the learning and focus attention on relevant issues. The Centre also networks with member organization and professional institutions and work towards assisting the member enterprises in a manner that helps them to achieve their strategic goals. It also provides consultancy services in collaboration with reputed professional institutions.

Critical Evaluation

The SCOPE has done well in the areas of organizing seminars, publications and research work. But there is still scope for better and improved working. There has been a lot of criticism by the media, public and politicians regarding the working of PEs which demoralizes the managers. It is for the SCOPE to counter the baseless charges against the PEs. It should tell the public and media the economic and social objectives for which the PEs are working and what are their constraints and limitations. It would also plead the case of PEs with the government about the growing interference of bureaucracy in their working and also discuss the problem of autonomy. But at the same time, it would also formulate action programmes for the better performance of PEs so that they cannot be criticized by the public or media unnecessarily.

Practice Questions

Objective Type Questions

1. Which one is the oldest Organisation:
   (*a*) Engineering Association of India
   (*b*) Indian Engineering Association
   (*c*) Engineering and Trades Association
   (*d*) Association of Indian Engineering Industry
2. CII was established in:
   (*a*) 1952 (*b*) 1972
   (*c*) 1992 (*d*) 2002
3. Integrity India campaign was launched by the
   (*a*) ASSOCHAM (*b*) CII
   (*c*) FICCI (*d*) SCOPE
4. Indian Economic Summit is being organized in partnership with:
   (*a*) WTO trade fund
   (*b*) IMF Economic Trust
   (*c*) World Bank Economic Development Programme

(*d*) World Economic Forum

5. FICCI was established in:
   (*a*) 1907
   (*b*) 1927
   (*c*) 1947
   (*d*) 1957

Ans: 1.(c), 2. (c), 3. (b), 4. (d), 5. (b)

Short Answer Questions

1. What are the objectives of CII?
2. What are the sectors generally comes under the scope of CII?
3. What are the functions of FICCI?
4. Who are the sectoral members of the ASSOCHAM?
5. What are the vision and mission of the SCOPE?

Long Answer Questions

1. Discuss the different divisions and committees of CII.
2. Examine the perspective of CII activities in India.
3. Discuss the different development initiatives taken up by the CII.
4. Explain the role and objectives of FICCI.
5. Discuss the different functions of ASSOCHAM.
6. Critically examine the activities of All India Association of Industry.
7. Explain the objectives and working of SCOPE in the context of public enterprises in India.

References

1. M.R. Dhekney, Chambers of Commerce and Business Associations in India, Popular Prakashan, 1971,p.2
2. Jagdish Prakash, Nageshwar Rao, Mata Badal Shukla, Administration of Public Enterprises in India, Himalaya Publishing House, 2010, p.509
3. www.ficci.com
4. www.assocham.org
5. www.cii.in
6. www.aiiindia.com
7. www.scopeonline.in

24 CORPORATE ETHICS IN INDIA

Corporates are legal entity and they free to formulate their own vision and mission. They are also supposed to set the tone of their operational behaviour. Operational behavior integrates the practices that are the base for relationships management with different parties. Companies have their own separate identity with their shareholders. Traditional thinking advocates that managers have to maximize the value of the firm and consequently maximizing the wealth of their shareholders as they are the risk bearers of the business. But at practical parlance, it is not fair. Contemporary theory suggests that there are many contributors in the wellbeing of the company. These contributors are called as stakeholders. These stakeholders include managers, employers, customers, suppliers, creditors, government, employees, shareholders and the community. These stakeholders need care and consideration at the hands of companies. Managers take the risk and transfer the risk to the shareholders and employees are also working hard to achieve the goal of the company. Similarly, suppliers ensure timely and steady supply of materials and related services to the company. The society bears the cost of growing pollution and other hazards created by the industries. The customers being a part of the society also create demand for the products and services being produced by the company. Bankers are providing funding facilities to the company. The government facilitates the transition from project idea to selling the products and services. These contributors do not expect any reward or pie from the profits of the company. These stakeholders are just to want to know the answer for their contributions –what they should expect from the company? They expect from the company only implementation of principles of honesty, quality rationality, justifiability, sincerity and societal orientation in its working behaviour. They want integration of morality in their corporate behaviour. Business has to promote its growth with fairness and trust. Stakeholders are always concerned with the level of ethical behaviour of the company as it enable the company to develop a long term brand equity. The business is also expected to share a part of its prosperity with the community in the midst of which it is located by offering amenities and services not otherwise available to the needy in that community. Business decisions and activities affect the expectations of stakeholders. Each enterprise faces unique political, economic, social, and technological pressures. Each and every enterprise has its own organizational culture that influences its stakeholders. However, behaviour model of the company can demonstrate a process through which owners and managers can identify enterprise stakeholders. They are required to foster reasonable stakeholder expectations; and inspire, encourage, and support for remedial actions in the interest of these stakeholders.

Indian Ethos

The terms-ethos, values, ethics and morals can be used interchangeably to explain similar set of ideas. Human concern for values has been a subject matter of deliberation among intellectuals and practioners in India. The concept of values is called as 'dharma'. The word "dharma" is derived from "dhri" which means to sustain. It also means duties and obligations. Dharma is not the same thing as religion. Dharma is seen as performance of one's duties towards ourselves, family, organization, society and the entire world. Dharma is the prerogative of humans, without which they are not worthy of being called humans.

Essential Elements of Indian Ethos

Following are the essential elements of Indian ethos:

1. Entire cosmos is pervaded by the diving power. All are interconnected and there is oneness or unitiveness in all life. All life is one.
2. Each soul is potentially divine and part of the cosmic power.
3. The same supreme truth is revealed through many paths.
4. Whole world is one extended family.
5. Let all be happy, let all be free from disease, let all see well being of each other, and let no one suffer from misery.

Culture

It can be defined as "the persons mental programming, mind software or mind sets. Culture includes a sense and space, communication and language, dress and appearance, food and feeding habits, time and time consciousness relationships, values, norms, beliefs, and attitudes, mental process and learning and work habits and practices."[1]

"Each culture of the world has its own ethical practices. The basic values of the society constitutes the core of its culture. Ethics, thus, has an intimate relationship with the culture of a place. Ethics is a normative science of the conduct of human being living in societies. The study of human conduct leads necessarily to the study of social life of man and consequently to its culture. It is not possible to study the moral values of man without studying the culture from which it originates. Man being the social animal, cannot live alone and hence, his conduct has a direct or indirect reference to the culture he belongs to. His moral standards and value system is constructed by the customs and norms of his culture."[2]

Thus, culture generally means that mock of life of a particular group of people specially with reference to their pattern of life in society, their dress, rituals, beliefs, rules, regulations, conduct, behaviour and ethical practices.

Characteristics of Culture

Important characteristics of culture are as follows:

1. Culture is a collective mental programming, which is acquired from family and society.
2. Culture is transmitted from one generation to another. But culture may die also due to interference from external sources.
3. Cultural is internal to man-culture related to mental programming. Therefore, it is internal to a man. This characteristic becomes clearer.
4. All cultures have all the human values. All cultures the world over share the same set of human values. However, they differ in terms of the preference, which each one of these give to the values.

Nature of Corporate Ethics

Ethics are defined by the concise Oxford Dictionary as "moral principles" or as "rules of conduct". It is a combination of moral principles or manner of actions, which are acceptable or unacceptable in any field of human activity. Corporate ethics is a specialized study of morality in the area of business. It concentrates on moral standards as they apply to business policies, institutions, and behavior. The ethical issues involve judgement about the rightness or wrongness of behaviour. These issues are also guiding force for the behaviour and decision-making process in the company. Various laws strive to advocate ethical standards at the minimum floor level, in actual practice corporate should strive to practice ethical conduct in their various activities at a higher level. Dharma is also equivalent to ethics. The concept of "Dharma" refers to what we ought to hold and to which we ought to fasten ourselves. A code of conduct is not merely a set of regulations of do's and don'ts. It is an endeavour to define the norms of behaviour of corporates which uses the wealth of the society.

Management of Corporate Ethics

Concept of corporate ethics generally applied to the business having separate entity from its owners. However, these separate entities are not involved in the decision making process. Managers at different levels are required to take decision within the business entity. Top level managers take decisions that affect the organisations policies and that determine how lower level managers confront decisions that involve applying organizational policies to their day to day circumstances. Since managers are taking decisions it is their sense of right and wrong that ultimately determines the extent of corporate ethical environment. Corporate ethics is a form of applied ethics or professional ethics that examines ethical principles and moral or ethical problems that arise in a business environment. It applies to all aspects of business conduct and is relevant to the conduct of individuals and business organizations as a whole.

The study of ethics in management addresses individual decisions in the context of certain rules of conduct or moral standards. Ethical behaviour, then refers to individual conduct that is considered "right" or "good" in the context of a governing moral code. "It confirms not only to the law, but also to a broader set of moral principles expected by all or by a segment of society. In contrast, unethical behavior covers any individual conduct that is "wrong" or "bad" within this moral code. It may or may not be illegal, but it falls short of the broader set of moral principles expected by society."[3]

Human beings are the active segment of the Corporate business. The companies cannot and shall not be immune to ethics. The goal of corporate business is to provide goods and services to customers and earn profits. The company has to ensure the supply of goods and services at reasonable price and of a reasonable quality. A society consists of people who have common ends and whose activities are organized by a system of institutions designed to achieve these ends. Family, community, society, schools, religion, temples, government etc are the basic institutions which are the base for formulation of values and moral standards. These institutions helps in designing the sub-systems : (a) production of the goods and services the members of society want and need, and (b) distribution of these goods and services to the various members of society. Thus, economic institutions determine who will carry out the work of production, how that work will be organized, what resources that work will consume, and how its products and benefits will be distributed among society's members. Corporate enterprises are the economic institutions through which people in modern societies carry on the tasks of producing and distributing the goods and services. They provide the fundamental structures within which the members of society combine their scarce resources-land, labour, capital, and technology- into usable goods, and they provide the channels through which these goods are distributed in the form of consumer products, employee salaries, investors' return, and government taxes.

Thus, corporate ethics is a study of moral standards and how these apply to the systems and organizations through which modern societies produce and distribute goods and services, and to the people who work within these organizations. It includes not only the analysis of moral norms and moral values, but also attempts to apply the conclusions of this analysis to that assortment of institutions, technologies, transactions, activities and pursuits that we call business enterprises.

Corporate Values and Image

Corporate value reflect the values of entrepreneurs at the top level. The esteem of a company generally governed by the values that the entrepreneurs/promoters of any organisation cherish. Some organizations emphasis on integrity, independence, etc. while other values hard work, interdependence and cooperation. Consistent values help in formulation of organizational norms. Some values like tolerance, empathy, risk-taking, etc. get embedded in the fabric of an organisation culture.

The values and attitude of people are important for any company as social factors affect its strategic management decisions. This is more important for a growing company as it has to form an image in society. There is growing trend that the real success of an entrepreneur depends on the adherence of social norms valued by the society. It is the public image of the company that carries for a long period amongst its stakeholders. Public interest is to be taken care of by the company as it is the most important value dimension of the public image. "Toothpaste is very personal to people and hence it enjoys a brand loyalty. In a society where herbal ingredients are valued by the users, the presence of turmeric or meswak is advertised by the manufacturer to woo his customers. Any ingredient which is a taboo for users is avoided in the manufacturer of the firm. The soft drink similarly enjoys a brand loyalty and a news item in the paper about traces of lizards eggs in the water used for soft drinks would definitely mar its image and the product may never to take off. A courier service company may built a public image for fast delivery of goods, and any action by the company contrary to this public image may be extremely harmful to the company."

Factors Governing Corporate Ethics: Following factors affecting the level of corporate ethics:

1. Legislative Framework: Ethics is a voluntary phenomenon. It cannot be forced but it should be persuaded. However, if corporates are not giving due weightage to ethics in their behavior it is for the laws to intervene in the process. Laws are generally passed as result of low ethical standards or the failure to recognise social issues. Legal action or government directives are the result of social pressure. A practice can be made illegal if society views it as being unethical. For example, if contributions to political parties by corporates are being viewed as excessive and unethical then the practice can be banned.

2. Regulatory Framework of the Government: From time to time, government regulates the working conditions, product safety, statutory warnings (on cigarettes and other harmful products) etc. These are all supported by laws or guidelines. These guidelines help the entrepreneurs in determining the working behaviour as per the acceptable standards and practices. Similarly, Jago Grahak Jago is another persuading strategy among the potential consumers about the corporate business practices. This has also been launched by the Ministry of Consumer Affairs to improve awareness about corporate defaults in their marketing practices.

3. Corporates Ethical Codes: Many times company provides specific guidelines to their managers and employees about the ethical codes of behaviour. One important question in such instances is whether individuals within organizations are really governed by the code of ethics or give lip services to the guidelines.

4. Societal Obligations: Social forces and pressure have considerable influence on ethics in business. Job reservation to the handicapped in corporates is an important example of societal obligations being fulfilled by them. Society in fact, forces the entrepreneurs to alter their decisions by taking a broader view of the environment and the needs of society.

5. Corporate Vision and Mission: Every day ethical decisions are usually made between the lesser of the two evils rather than obvious right and wrong dimension of the judgement. These judgements generally include different types of values being persued by the industrial house in the vision and mission of the group companies. In this context, we can include the norms of ethical standards formulated by the Tata and Birla group of companies.

Scope of Corporate Ethics

Corporate ethics include three dimensions. These are systemic, corporate, and individual environment.

1. Systemic Issues: These are ethical questions raised about the economic, political, legal, and other social systems within which corporate enterprises are expected to operate. These are set by the society, government and other agencies involved in ethical movements. These include questions about the morality of morality of economic system, laws, regulations, industrial structures, and social practices within which Indian Corporate Enterprises are required to achieve their vision and mission.

2. Corporate issues: These are ethical questions raised about a particular company. These include questions about the morality of the activities, policies, practices, or organizational structure of an individual company taken as a whole. Individual behaviour of the company set the agenda for other companies working in the industry concern and managers and employees are expected to comply with these standards. Generally, individual companies try to formulate their own ethical standards.

3. Individual issues: These are ethical questions raised about a particular individual or particular individuals within a company. These include questions about the morality of the decisions, actions, or character of an individual manager Deepak Parekh (HDFC Bank), H V Kamath (ICICI Bank) have tried to integral their personal values in their organizational values.

Sources of the Ethical Behaviour : Major sources of the ethical behaviour of corporate are as follows:

1. Values and Goals: There is an important relationship between goals and values of an organisation. The goals of the organisation are influenced by leadership, knowledge and skills, amity, influence and power and survival. All these factors change the goals of the organisation and consequently corporates expect values based behaviour from their individual managers.

2. Values forming Institution: The life and development of society produce values. There are so many organizations like family, school, state and religion which are the basic sources of values for individuals. The basic purpose of values formation by these institutions is that they prescribe what is good or bad for an individual. And at a later stage inculcation of these values enable the managers to work for values in their companies.

3. Work and Career: Work consists of the tasks or responsibilities associated with the job or position in an organisation. In organisation, the work is organized and directed for the achievement of desired end. An individual's experience over a period of time constitutes his career work and career creates special values that give unity, cohesion and meaning to persons and groups.

4. Professional's Codes: In recent days more and more professionals are being appointed by the corporates. These professionals are required to go by the values and code of conduct prescribed by the relevant professional institutes and Associations. Professional's codes are the sources of ethical norms for managers in business organizations. These codes are consistent with customs, beliefs, social values, public laws and generally desirable behaviour. The Institute of Chartered Accountant of India, Institution of Engineers, Institute of Company Secretaries of India and All India Management Association etc have prescribed a set of code of conduct for their members.

Rationale of Corporate Ethics: Rationale of corporate ethics are as follows:

1. Survival of business: Any individual business will collapse if all of its managers, employees, and customers come to think that it is morally permissible to steal from, lie to, or break their agreements with the company.

2. Need of a Stable Society: All businesses require a stable society in which they are supposed to carry on their business dealings. Stability of any society requires that its members adhere to some minimal standards of ethics. It will create a conducive environment for the development of economic and social institutions.

3. Consistent with Business Objectives: Ethics should be brought into business by showing that ethical considerations are consistent with business pursuits, in particular with the pursuit of profit. That ethics is consistent with the pursuit of profit can be shown by simply finding examples of companies where a history of good ethics has existed side by side with a history of profitable operations.

4. Growing Clout of Business: The power and influence of business in society is greater than ever before. Evidence suggests that many members of the public are uneasy with such developments. Ethics helps us to understand why this is happening, what will be its implications and how we will address this situation.

5. Safeguarding Public from Business Malpractices: Business malpractices have the potential to inflict enormous harm on individuals, communities, and the environment. Ethics seeks, to improve the human condition by focusing on the causes and consequences of these malpractices being done by the corporates.

6. Effective Decision Making: Ethics help to improve the corporate ethical decision-making with the appropriate knowledge and tools that allow them to correctly identify, diagnose, analyse, and provide solutions to the ethical problem and dilemmas they are confronted with day to day decision making having implications for the stakeholders.

7. Corporate Effectiveness: Ethics develops the ability to assess the benefits and problems associated with different ways of managing ethics in organizations. It also improves the knowledge that transcends the traditional framework of business studies which have focused on the relevance of ethics in business.

Importance of Corporate Ethics

Importance of corporate ethics are as follows:

1. Basic Human Needs: Ethics corresponds to basic human needs. It is human trait that man desires to be ethical: not only in his private life but also in his business affairs where, being a manager, he knows his decisions may affect the lives of thousands of employees or customers.

2. Improve Creditability: Values creates credibility with the public. A company perceived by the public to be ethically and socially responsive would be honoured and respected even by those who have no intimate knowledge of its actual working. There will be an instinctive prejudice in favour of its product, since people believes that the company offers value for their money. Public issues attract an immediate response from the company as it affects its credibility.

3. Improves Coordination: Values gives credibility to the management by coordinating the language of value from the top to the lower level in the organisations. Organisational ethics, when perceived by the employees as genuine and create common goals, improves ethical environment. The entrepreneur has credibility with its employees precisely because it has credibility with the public. Neither sound business strategy, nor a generous compensation policy and fringe benefits can win the employee credibility. Perceived moral and social uprightness about the company by its employees can be the basis for credibility among the employees.

4. Better Decision Making: Values help better decision making. An ethical attitude helps the management to make better decisions, i.e., decisions which are in the interest of the public, their employees, and the company's own long good, even through the decision making is slower. Ethics force a management to take various aspects of economic, social decisions keeping in mind their ethical implications.

5. Trade Off between Ethics and Profits: Ethic and profit can go together. A company, which is inspired by ethical conducts, is also profitable one. Value driven companies are sure to be successful in long run, though in the short run they can loose money. Ethics help the company to develop a long term brand equity in the society which ultimately improves sales and profit.

6. Humanitarian Approach: An ethical oriented management takes measures to prevent pollution and protects workers health. Leading business houses had already initiated social responsibility initiatives to protect the environment, provides social welfare amenities to the workers etc. These business houses are incurring huge expenditures without any mandatory initiative of the government. It is a sharing of wealth by the company in favour of society at large.

Morality

Moral norms can usually be expressed as general rules or statements. These norms describe the objects or features of objects that have worth, such as "Honesty is good" and "Injustice is bad." These norms or standards differ from country to country and from culture to culture.

Typically a person's moral standards are first absorbed as child from family, friends, and various societal influences such as church, school, television, magazines, music, and associations. Person grows up, experience, learning, and intellectual development may lead the maturing person to revise these standards. Some are discarded, and new ones may be adopted to replace them. Moral standards can be contrasted with standards we hold about things that are not moral.

Features of Moral Standards

Important features of moral standards are as follows:

(*i*) Moral standards deal with matters that can seriously injure or seriously benefit human beings. Human being constitutes the society. Society is supposed to formulate moral standards for its member. They are required to follow them in their actual life. If individual member of the society is not following it then members reputation will be affected in the society itself.

(*ii*) Moral standards are not established or changed by the decisions of particular authoritative bodies. Laws and legal standards are established by the authority of a legislature or the decisions of voters. However, Moral standards, however, are not established by authority nor does their validity rest on voting procedures. The validity of moral standards rests on the adequacy of the reasons that are taken to support and justify them; so long as these reasons are adequate, the standards remain valid.

(*iii*) Moral standards are more important to other values including self-interest. If a person has a moral obligation to do something, then he is supposed to do it even if he has conflicts with other non-moral values or self-interest.

(*iv*) Moral standards are based on impartial considerations. Basically, the moral point of view goes beyond personal interests. It is concerned with "universal" standpoint in which everyone's interests are impartially counted as equal. Moral standards are associated with special emotions and have a special vocabulary.

(*v*) Moral standards deal with matters of serious consequences. They are based on good reasons and not on authority, overriding self-interest and ego. These are based on impartial considerations, and whose transgression is associated with feelings of guilt and shame.

(*vi*) Ethics is the discipline that examines the moral standards of a society. It asks how these standards apply to our lives and whether these standards are reasonable or unreasonable- e.g, whether they are supported by good reasons or poor ones. Therefore, a person starts to do ethics when he takes the moral standards absorbed from family, church, and friends. The persons himself is a part of the society.

(*vii*) Ethics is the study of moral standards. The ultimate aim of ethics is to develop a body of moral standards that are reasonable to hold. The standards should be justifiable and must have societal acceptance.

(*viii*) Ethics is a normative study of ethics. A normative study is an investigation that attempts to reach normative conclusions- that is, conclusions about what things are good or bad or about what actions are right or wrong. It aims to discover what should be? Ethics is the study of moral standards whose explicit purpose is to determine as far as possible which standards are correct or supported by the best reasons, and so it attempts to reach conclusions about morally right and wrong and morally good and bad.

(ix) The social sciences are engaged in a descriptive study of ethics. A descriptive study is one that does not try to reach any conclusions about what things are truly good or bad or right or wrong. It attempts to explain the world without reaching any conclusions about whether the world is as it should be.

Moral Reasoning

Moral reasoning refers to the reasoning process by which human behaviour, institutions, or policies are judged to be in accordance with or in violation of moral standards. Moral reasoning always involves two essential components: (a) an understanding of what reasonable moral standards require, prohibit, value, or condemn; and (b) evidence or information that shows that a particular person, policy, institution, or behavior has the kinds of features that these moral standards require, prohibit, value, or condemn. However, moral reasoning should fulfill the following conditions:

(i) **Logical Moral Reasoning.** The analysis of moral reasoning requires that the logic of the arguments used to establish a moral judgement by rigorously examining, all the unspoken moral and factual assumptions. However, both assumptions and premises be displayed and subjected to criticism.

(ii) **Factual Evidence Required:** Factual evidence cited in support of a person's judgment must be accurate, relevant, and complete. Factual evidence lays the foundation for moral reasoning. It provides practice orientation for moral reasoning.

(iii) **Consistent Moral Standards:** They must be consistent with other standards and beliefs the person holds. Inconsistency between a person's moral standards can be uncovered and corrected by examining situations in which these moral standards require incompatible things.

Morality vs. Ethics

In common usage, the terms 'ethics' and 'morality' are often used interchangeably. However, sometime a technical difference is made differences between the two terms. Morality is concerned with the norms, values, and beliefs embedded in social processes which define right and wrong for an individual or a community. Ethics is concerned with the study of morality and the application of reason to elucidate specific rules and principles that determine right and wrong for any given situation. These rules and principles are called ethical theories.

Trusteeship

A trust is normally created when a fund or asset is earmarked for a specific purpose. A wealthy person may set apart some funds for a specific purpose and request a trusted individual or a corporate like a bank, to manage it and make sure that the benefits are made available to the specified beneficiaries.

Gandhian concept is also relevant to corporate enterprises. In his trusteeship concept Gandhiji had made the following observations.

(i) Ownership is a costly and illusory concept to ensure permanency and succession.

(ii) It gives birth to attachment, exploitation, possessiveness and greed, exploitation and revenge.

(iii) All assets must be held in trust and used for the good of all.

(iv) Distribution of assets and the benefits of the operations be equitable, not equal

(v) The owner of wealth has the right to a honourable livelihood the rest is that of the community.

The Gandhian Concept of Trusteeship also said that

"Trusteeship provides a means of transforming the present capitalist order of society into an egalitarian one. It gives no quarter to capitalism but gives the present owning class, a chance of reforming itself. It is based on the faith that human nature is never beyond redemption. It does not recognise any right of private ownership of property, except so far as it may be permitted by society for its own welfare. It does not exclude legislative regulation of the ownership and use of wealth."[4] "Thus, under State regulated ownership, an individual will not be free to hold or use his wealth for selfish satisfaction or in disregard of the interests of Society."[5]

Gandhiji's concept of trusteeship was founded on non-violence. He though that the very idea of ownership was at the root of violence. People really together only when they rise above conflicts of interests, envy and competition.

Trusteeship was seen as a means of bringing people together. He had said, "If one has come by a fair amount of wealth, either by way of legacy or by mean of trade and industry, he must know that all that wealth does not belong to him. What belongs to him is the right to an honourable livelihood." Trusteeship followed the vedic dictum or renounce (rights and pleasures of self) and enjoy (in the pleasures of others). This is also the basis of the commandment in all religions: to share one's strengths and assets with others.

Ethical Code

An ethical code is adopted by an organization is to assist the persons working in its own system. They are generally persuaded to understand the difference between 'right' and 'wrong' and to apply this understanding their decision making process. The ethical code therefore generally implies documents at three levels:

(*i*) **Code of ethics (Corporate ethics):** A code of ethics often focuses on social issues. It may set out general principles about an organization's beliefs on matters such as mission, quality, privacy or the environment. It may delineate proper procedures to determine whether a violation of the code of ethics has occurred and, if so, what remedies are available to correct it. The effectiveness of such codes of ethics depends on the extent to which management supports these corrective measures. These codes of ethics are voluntary in nature.

(*ii*) **Code of conduct (Employee ethics):** A code of conduct is a document designed to influence the behavior of employees. They set out the procedures to be used in specific ethical situations, such as conflicts of interest or the acceptance of gifts, and delineate the procedures to determine whether a violation of the code of ethics occurred and, if so, what remedial actions are in place to make the behaviour of employees more acceptable to the ethical environment. The effectiveness of such codes of ethics depends on the extent to which management supports them with sanctions and rewards. Violations of a code of conduct may subject the violator to the organization's remedies which can under particular circumstances result in the termination of employment.

(*iii*) **Code of practice (Professional ethics):** A code of practice is adopted by a profession or by a governmental or non-governmental organization to regulate that profession. A code of practice may be styled as a code of professional responsibility, which discusses difficult issues, difficult decisions that will often need to be made, and provide a clear account of what behaviour is considered "ethical" or "correct" or "right" in the relevant circumstances. In a membership context, failure to comply with a code of practice can result in expulsion from the professional organization. Professional ethics concerns the moral issues that arise because of the specialist knowledge that professionals attain, and how the use of this knowledge should be governed when providing a service to the public at large.

Prime Minister's 10 Point Social Charter for Indian Corporates[6]

Hon'ble Prime Minister Dr. Manmohan Singh Outlined a 10 point social charter for Indian Industry to make our country's growth process both efficient and inclusive. Dr. Singh invited corporate India to be a partner in making ours a more humane and just society.

The Ten Point Social Charter spelt out by the prime minister are :

(i) healthy respect for workers and their investment in welfare,

(ii) corporate social responsibility,

(iii) employment to the less privileged,

(iv) resist excessive remuneration and discourage conspicuous consumption,

(v) investment in people and in their skills,

(vi) desist from non-competitive behaviour,

(vii) invest in environment-friendly technologies,

(viii) promote enterprise and innovation,

(ix) fight corruption at all levels,

(x) promote socially responsible media and finance socially responsible advertising.

TATA COMPANY

The Tata Group is a multinational conglomerate company headquartered in Mumbai, India. In terms of market capitalization and revenues, Tata Group is the largest private corporate group in India and has been recognized as one of the most respected companies in the world. It has interests in steel, automobiles, information technology, communication, power, tea and hospitality. The Tata Group has operations in more than 85 countries across six continents and its companies export products and services to 80 nations. The Tata Group comprises 114 companies and subsidiaries in seven business sectors, 27 of which are publicly listed. 65.8% of the ownership of Tata Group is held in charitable trusts. Companies which form a major part of the group include Tata Steel, Corus Steel, Tata Motors, Tata Consultancy Services, Tata Technologies, Tata Tea, Titan Industries, Tata Power, Tata Communications, Tata Teleservices and the Taj Hotels.

The group takes the name of its founder, Jamshedji Tata, a member of whose family has almost invariably been the chairman of the group. The chairman of the Tata group is Ratan Tata, who took over from J. R. D. Tata in 1991 and is one of the major international business figures in the age of globality. The company is currently in its fifth generation of family stewardship. The 2009 annual survey by the Reputation Institute ranked Tata Group as the 11th most reputable company in the world. The survey included 600 global companies.

History

The beginnings of the Tata Group can be traced back to 1868, when Jamshedji Nusserwanji Tata established a trading company dealing in cotton in Bombay (now Mumbai), British India. This was followed by the installation of Empress Mills in Nagpur in 1877. Taj Mahal Hotel in Bombay (now Mumbai) was opened for business in 1903. Sir Dorab Tata, the eldest son of Jamshedji became the chairman of the group after his father's death in 1904. Under him, the group ventured into steel production (1905) and hydroelectric power generation (1910). After the death of Dorab Tata in 1934, Nowroji Saklatwala headed the group till 1938. He was succeeded by Jehangir Ratanji Dadabhoy Tata. The group expanded significantly under him with the establishment of Tata Chemicals (1939), Tata Motors and Tata Industries (both 1945), Voltas (1954), Tata Tea (1962), Tata Consultancy Services (1968) and Titan Industries (1984). Ratan Tata, the incumbent chairman of the group succeeded JRD Tata in 1991.

Values and purpose

Purpose : Tata group are committed to improving the quality of life of the communities we serve. We do this by striving for leadership and global competitiveness in the business sectors in which we operate. Our practice of returning to society what we earn evokes trust among consumers, employees, shareholders and the community. We are committed to protecting this heritage of leadership with trust through the manner in which we conduct our business.

Core values : Tata has always been values-driven. These values continue to direct the growth and business of Tata companies. The five core Tata values underpinning the way we do business are:

(i) **Integrity:** We must conduct our business fairly, with honesty and transparency. Everything we do must stand the test of public scrutiny.

(ii) **Understanding:** We must be caring, show respect, compassion and humanity for our colleagues and customers around the world, and always work for the benefit of the communities we serve.

(iii) **Excellence:** We must constantly strive to achieve the highest possible standards in our day-to-day work and in the quality of the goods and services we provide.

(iv) **Unity:** We must work cohesively with our colleagues across the group and with our customers and partners around the world, building strong relationships based on tolerance, understanding and mutual cooperation.

(v) **Responsibility:** We must continue to be responsible, sensitive to the countries, communities and environments in which we work, always ensuring that what comes from the people goes back to the people many times over.

Tata Code of Conduct

This comprehensive document serves as the ethical road map for Tata employees and companies, and provides the guidelines by which the group conducts its businesses.

Clause:1

National interest: The Tata group is committed to benefit the economic development of the countries in which it operates. No Tata company shall undertake any project or activity to the detriment of the wider interests of the communities in which it operates. A Tata company's management practices and business conduct shall benefit the country, localities and communities in which it operates, to the extent possible and affordable, and shall be in accordance with the laws of the land. A Tata company, in the course of its business activities, shall respect the culture, customs and traditions of each country and region in which it operates. It shall conform to trade procedures, including licensing, documentation and other necessary formalities, as applicable.

Clause:2

Financial reporting and records: A Tata company shall prepare and maintain its accounts fairly and accurately and in accordance with the accounting and financial reporting standards which represent the generally accepted guidelines, principles, standards, laws and regulations of the country in which the company conducts its business affairs. Internal accounting and audit procedures shall reflect, fairly and accurately, all of the company's business transactions and disposition of assets, and shall have internal controls to provide assurance to the company's board and shareholders that the transactions are accurate and legitimate. All required information shall be accessible to company auditors and other authorised parties and government agencies. There shall be no willful omissions of any company transactions from the books and records, no advance-income recognition and no hidden bank account and funds.

Any willful, material misrepresentation of and / or misinformation on the financial accounts and reports shall be regarded as a violation of the Code, apart from inviting appropriate civil or criminal action under the relevant laws. No employee shall make, authorise, abet or collude in an improper payment, unlawful commission or bribing.

Clause:3

Competition: A Tata company shall fully support the development and operation of competitive open markets and shall promote the liberalisation of trade and investment in each country and market in which it operates. Specifically, no Tata company or employee shall engage in restrictive trade practices, abuse of market dominance or similar unfair trade activities. A Tata company or employee shall market the company's products and services on their own merits and shall not make unfair and misleading statements about competitors' products and services. Any collection of competitive information shall be made only in the normal course of business and shall be obtained only through legally permitted sources and means.

Clause:4

Equal opportunities employer: A Tata company shall provide equal opportunities to all its employees and all qualified applicants for employment without regard to their race, caste, religion, colour, ancestry, marital status, gender, sexual orientation, age, nationality, ethnic origin or disability. Human resource policies shall promote diversity and equality in the workplace, as well as compliance with all local labour laws, while encouraging the adoption of international best practices.

Employees of a Tata company shall be treated with dignity and in accordance with the Tata policy of maintaining a work environment free of all forms of harassment, whether physical, verbal or psychological. Employee policies and practices shall be administered in a manner consistent with applicable laws and other provisions of this Code, respect for the right to privacy and the right to be heard, and that in all matters equal opportunity is provided to those eligible and decisions are based on merit.

Clause:5

Gifts and donations: A Tata company and its employees shall neither receive nor offer or make, directly or indirectly, any illegal payments, remuneration, gifts, donations or comparable benefits that are intended, or perceived, to obtain uncompetitive favours for the conduct of its business. The company shall cooperate with governmental authorities in efforts to eliminate all forms of bribery, fraud and corruption. However, a Tata company and its employees may, with full disclosure, accept and offer nominal gifts, provided such gifts are customarily given and / or are of a commemorative nature. Each company shall have a policy to clarify its rules and regulations on gifts and entertainment, to be used for the guidance of its employees.

Clause:6

Government agencies: A Tata company and its employees shall not, unless mandated under applicable laws, offer or give any company funds or property as donation to any government agency or its representative, directly or through intermediaries, in order to obtain any favourable performance of official duties. A Tata company shall comply with government procurement regulations and shall be transparent in all its dealings with government agencies.

Clause:7

Political non-alignment: A Tata company shall be committed to and support the constitution and governance systems of the country in which it operates. A Tata company shall not support any specific political party or candidate for political office. The company's conduct shall preclude any activity that could be interpreted as mutual dependence / favour with any political body or person, and shall not offer or give any company funds or property as donations to any political party, candidate or campaign.

Clause:8

Health, safety and environment: A Tata company shall strive to provide a safe, healthy, clean and ergonomic working environment for its people. It shall prevent the wasteful use of natural resources and be committed to improving the environment, particularly with regard to the emission of greenhouse gases, and shall endeavour to offset the effect of climate change in all spheres of its activities. A Tata company, in the process of production and sale of its products and services, shall strive for economic, social and environmental sustainability.

Clause:9

Quality of products and services: A Tata company shall be committed to supply goods and services of world class quality standards, backed by after-sales services consistent with the requirements of its customers, while striving for their total satisfaction. The quality standards of the company's goods and services shall meet applicable national and international standards. A Tata company shall display adequate health and safety labels, caveats and other necessary information on its product packaging.

Clause:10

Corporate citizenship: A Tata company shall be committed to good corporate citizenship, not only in the compliance of all relevant laws and regulations but also by actively assisting in the improvement of quality of life of the people in the communities in which it operates. The company shall encourage volunteering by its employees and collaboration with community groups. Tata companies are also encouraged to develop systematic processes and conduct management reviews, as stated in the Tata 'corporate sustainability protocol', from time to time so as to set strategic direction for social development activity. The company shall not treat these activities as optional, but should strive to incorporate them as an integral part of its business plan.

Clause:11

Cooperation of Tata companies: A Tata company shall cooperate with other Tata companies including applicable joint ventures, by sharing knowledge and physical, human and management resources, and by making efforts to resolve disputes amicably, as long as this does not adversely affect its business interests and shareholder value. In the procurement of products and services, a Tata company shall give preference to other Tata companies, as long as they can provide these on competitive terms relative to third parties.

Clause:12

Public representation of the company and the group: The Tata group honours the information requirements of the public and its stakeholders. In all its public appearances, with respect to disclosing company and business information to public constituencies such as the media, the financial community, employees, shareholders, agents, franchisees, dealers, distributors and importers, a Tata company or the Tata group shall be represented only by specifically authorised directors and employees. It shall be the sole responsibility of these authorised representatives to disclose information about the company or the group.

Clause:13

Third party representation: Parties which have business dealings with the Tata group but are not members of the group, such as consultants, agents, sales representatives, distributors, channel partners, contractors and suppliers, shall not be authorised to represent a Tata company without the written permission of the Tata company, and / or if their business conduct and ethics are known to be inconsistent with the Code.

Third parties and their employees are expected to abide by the Code in their interaction with, and on behalf of, a Tata company. Tata companies are encouraged to sign a non-disclosure agreement with third parties to support confidentiality of information.

Clause:14

Use of the Tata brand: The use of the Tata name and trademark shall be governed by manuals, codes and agreements to be issued by Tata Sons. The use of the Tata brand is defined in and regulated by the Tata Brand Equity and Business Promotion agreement. No third party or joint venture shall use the Tata brand to further its interests without specific authorisation.

Clause:15

Group policies: A Tata company shall recommend to its board of directors the adoption of policies and guidelines periodically formulated by Tata Sons.

Clause:16

Shareholders: A Tata company shall be committed to enhancing shareholder value and complying with all regulations and laws that govern shareholder rights. The board of directors of a Tata company shall duly and fairly inform its shareholders about all relevant aspects of the company's business, and disclose such information in accordance with relevant regulations and agreements.

Clause:17

Ethical conduct: Every employee of a Tata company, including full-time directors and the chief executive, shall exhibit culturally appropriate deportment in the countries they operate in, and deal on behalf of the company with professionalism, honesty and integrity, while conforming to high moral and ethical standards. Such conduct shall be fair and transparent and be perceived to be so by third parties. Every employee of a Tata company shall preserve the human rights of every individual and the community, and shall strive to honour commitments. Every employee shall be responsible for the implementation of and compliance with the Code in his / her environment. Failure to adhere to the Code could attract severe consequences, including termination of employment.

Clause:18

Regulatory compliance: Employees of a Tata company, in their business conduct, shall comply with all applicable laws and regulations, in letter and spirit, in all the territories in which they operate. If the ethical and professional standards of applicable laws and regulations are below that of the Code, then the standards of the Code shall prevail. Directors of a Tata company shall comply with applicable laws and regulations of all the relevant regulatory and other authorities. As good governance practice they shall safeguard the confidentiality of all information received by them by virtue of their position.

Clause:19

Concurrent employment: Consistent with applicable laws, an employee of a Tata company shall not, without the requisite, officially written approval of the company, accept employment or a position of responsibility (such as a consultant or a director) with any other company, nor provide freelance services to anyone, with or without remuneration. In the case of a full-time director or the chief executive, such approval must be obtained from the board of directors of the company.

Clause:20

Conflict of interest: An employee or director of a Tata company shall always act in the interest of the company, and ensure that any business or personal association which he / she may have does not involve a conflict of interest with the operations of the company and his / her role therein. An employee, including the executive director (other than independent director) of a Tata company, shall not accept a position of responsibility in any other non-Tata company or not-for-profit organisation without specific sanction. The above shall not apply to (whether for remuneration or otherwise):

(*a*) Nominations to the boards of Tata companies, joint ventures or associate companies.

(*b*) Memberships / positions of responsibility in educational / professional bodies, wherein such association will benefit the employee / Tata company.

(*c*) Nominations / memberships in government committees / bodies or organisations.

(*d*) Exceptional circumstances, as determined by the competent authority.

Competent authority, in the case of all employees, shall be the chief executive, who in turn shall report such exceptional cases to the board of directors on a quarterly basis. In case of the chief executive and executive directors, the Group Corporate Centre shall be the competent authority. An employee or a director of a Tata company shall not engage in any business, relationship or activity which might conflict with the interest of his / her company or the Tata group. A conflict of interest, actual or potential, may arise where, directly or indirect.

(*a*) An employee of a Tata company engages in a business, relationship or activity with anyone who is party to a transaction with his / her company.

(*b*) An employee is in a position to derive an improper benefit, personally or to any of his / her relatives, by making or influencing decisions relating to any transaction.

(*c*) An independent judgement of the company's or group's best interest cannot be exercised.

The main areas of such actual or potential conflicts of interest shall include the following:

(*a*) An employee or a full-time director of a Tata company conducting business on behalf of his / her company or being in a position to influence a decision with regard to his / her company's business with a supplier or customer where his / her relative is a principal officer or representative, resulting in benefit to him / her or his / her relative.

(b) Award of benefits such as increase in salary or other remuneration, posting, promotion or recruitment of a relative of an employee of a Tata company, where such an individual is in a position to influence decisions with regard to such benefits.

(*c*) The interest of the company or the group can be compromised or defeated.

Clause:21

Securities transactions and confidential information: An employee of a Tata company and his / her immediate family shall not derive any benefit or counsel, or assist others to derive any benefit, from access to and possession of information about the company or group or its clients or suppliers that is not in the public domain and, thus, constitutes unpublished, price-sensitive insider information.

An employee of a Tata company shall not use or proliferate information that is not available to the investing public, and which therefore constitutes insider information, for making or giving advice on investment decisions about the securities of the respective Tata company, group, client or supplier on which such insider information has been obtained.

Such insider information might include (without limitation) the following:

(*i*) Acquisition and divestiture of businesses or business units.

(*ii*) Financial information such as profits, earnings and dividends.

(*iii*) Announcement of new product introductions or developments.

(*iv*) Asset revaluations.

(*v*) Investment decisions / plans.

(*vi*) Restructuring plans.

(*vii*) Major supply and delivery agreements.

(*viii*) Raising of finances.

An employee of a Tata company shall also respect and observe the confidentiality of information pertaining to other companies, their patents, intellectual property rights, trademarks and inventions; and strictly observe a practice of non-disclosure.

Clause:22

Protecting company assets: The assets of a Tata company shall not be misused; they shall be employed primarily and judiciously for the purpose of conducting the business for which they are duly authorised. These include tangible assets such as equipment and machinery, systems, facilities, materials and resources, as well as intangible assets such as information technology and systems, proprietary information, intellectual property, and relationships with customers and suppliers.

Clause:23

Citizenship: The involvement of a Tata employee in civic or public affairs shall be with express approval from the chief executive of his / her company, subject to this involvement having no adverse impact on the business affairs of the company or the Tata group.

Clause:24

Integrity of data furnished: Every employee of a Tata company shall ensure, at all times, the integrity of data or information furnished by him/her to the company. He/she shall be entirely responsible in ensuring that the confidentiality of all data is retained and in no circumstance transferred to any outside person/party in the course of normal operations without express guidelines from or, the approval of the management.

Clause:25

Reporting concerns: Every employee of a Tata company shall promptly report to the management, and / or third-party ethics helpline, when she / he becomes aware of any actual or possible violation of the Code or an event of misconduct, act of misdemeanour or act not in the company's interest. Such reporting shall be made available to suppliers and partners, too. Any Tata employee can choose to make a protected disclosure under the whistleblower policy of the company, providing for reporting to the chairperson of the audit committee or the board of directors or specified authority. Such a protected disclosure shall be forwarded, when there is reasonable evidence to conclude that a violation is possible or has taken place, with a covering letter, which shall bear the identity of the whistleblower. The company shall ensure protection to the whistleblower and any attempts to intimidate him / her would be treated as a violation of the Code.

Company's Commitment

(*i*) **Community initiatives:** The many companies of Tata are involved in a wide variety of community development projects and programmes, principally in India but also, increasingly, in different parts of the world (these initiatives are distinct, and separated, from the social uplift efforts of the Tata trusts). The community development endeavours of Tata companies cover many areas, from health and education to livelihoods, women-children welfare and more.

(*ii*) **Environment:** The Tata ethos places a special emphasis on environmental and ecological issues. Its efforts to preserve and regenerate the environment find expression in the slew of projects and programmes it has undertaken in and around its facilities and operations. A focus area, in this context, is the climate change crisis.

(*iii*) **Tata Trusts:** The Tata founders bequeathed most of their personal wealth to the many trusts they created for the greater good of India and its people. Today, the Tata trusts control 65.8 per cent of the shares of Tata Sons, the holding Tata company. The wealth that accrues from this asset supports an assortment of causes, institutions and individuals in a wide variety of areas.

(*iv*) **Institutions:** Tata's endeavour to strengthen the fabric of India has manifested itself in multiple ways. A crucial component of the Tata idea of nation building was, and remains, the creation and sustaining of exceptional institutions of learning, research, knowledge and intellectual capital. Indian Institute of Science, Bangalore; JRD Tata Eco technology Centre, Chennai; Tata Institute of Fundamental Research, Mumbai, Tata Institute of Social Sciences, Tata Memorial Centre, Tata Medical Center are the examples.

(*v*) **Sports and Arts:** Tata's long-standing support for sports and the arts in India has spawned a wide variety of efforts in both spheres: from creating academies in different sporting disciplines and backing talented sportspeople to helping the cause of culture in the country in many ways.

(*vi*) **Code of Honour:** Code of honour is a special edition of Tata Review, which features the corporate sustainability and community initiatives undertaken by Tata and the Tata Trusts.

(*vii*) **Tata Jagriti Yatra (A journey of discovery) :** The Tata Jagriti Yatra initiative was started in 2008 and involves potential social and business entrepreneurs, aged 20-25 years. This experiential train journey gives participants an opportunity to meet iconic leaders who are developing unique solutions to India's challenges.

Practice Questions

Objective Type Questions

1. A teleological approach to business ethics proposes that the guiding principle should be:
   (*a*) People
   (*b*) Purpose
   (*c*) Power
   (*d*) Practice
2. Ethical behaviour is a matter of:
   (*a*) Obeying the rule
   (*b*) Juggling standards and business needs
   (*c*) Action on a considered judgement
   (*d*) None of these
3. Morality is not concerned with:
   (*a*) norms
   (*b*) believes
   (*c*) values
   (*d*) principles
4. Business ethics helps in solving except:
   (*a*) ethical expectations
   (*b*) ethical problems
   (*c*) ethical code
   (*d*) ethical dilemmas
5. The term 'culture' has its root in:
   (*a*) Sociology
   (*b*) Social anthropology
   (*c*) Vedic studies
   (*d*) Ethnography

Ans: 1. (b), 2. (c) 3. (d), 4. (c), 5. (b)

Short Answer Questions

1. What is culture?
2. What is Dharma?
3. What do you mean by Ethics?
4. What is spirituality?
5. What is trusteeship?

6. What do you mean by business ethics?
7. What do you mean by ethical code?
8. What is morality?

Long Answer Questions

1. What is Business Ethics? Examine its relevance.
2. Explain the nature of spirituality. Also discuss its different types.
3. What do you mean by secularism? Examine its different components.
4. What do you mean by Indian Ethos? Examine the problems we are facing in preserving our ethos.
5. Examine the concept of trusteeship. How does it affect the working of the Indian corporate sector?

References

1. Satpathy. Biswajit, Indian Ethos and Values, Elite Publications, 2002, p1
2. Raj Rituparna, A Study in Business Ethics, Himalaya Publishing House, Mumbai, 2003,p77
3. Courtland. L.Bovee, John V.Thill, Marian Burk Wood, George P.Dovel, Management, McGraw-Hill. Inc., 1993, p.118
4. Mahatma Gandhi- Harijan.14.5.1939
5. Pyarelal Harijan, 25.10.1952
6. Kaleido SCOPE, Vol. 27, No.1, June 2007